VEDIC INDEX
OF
NAMES AND SUBJECTS

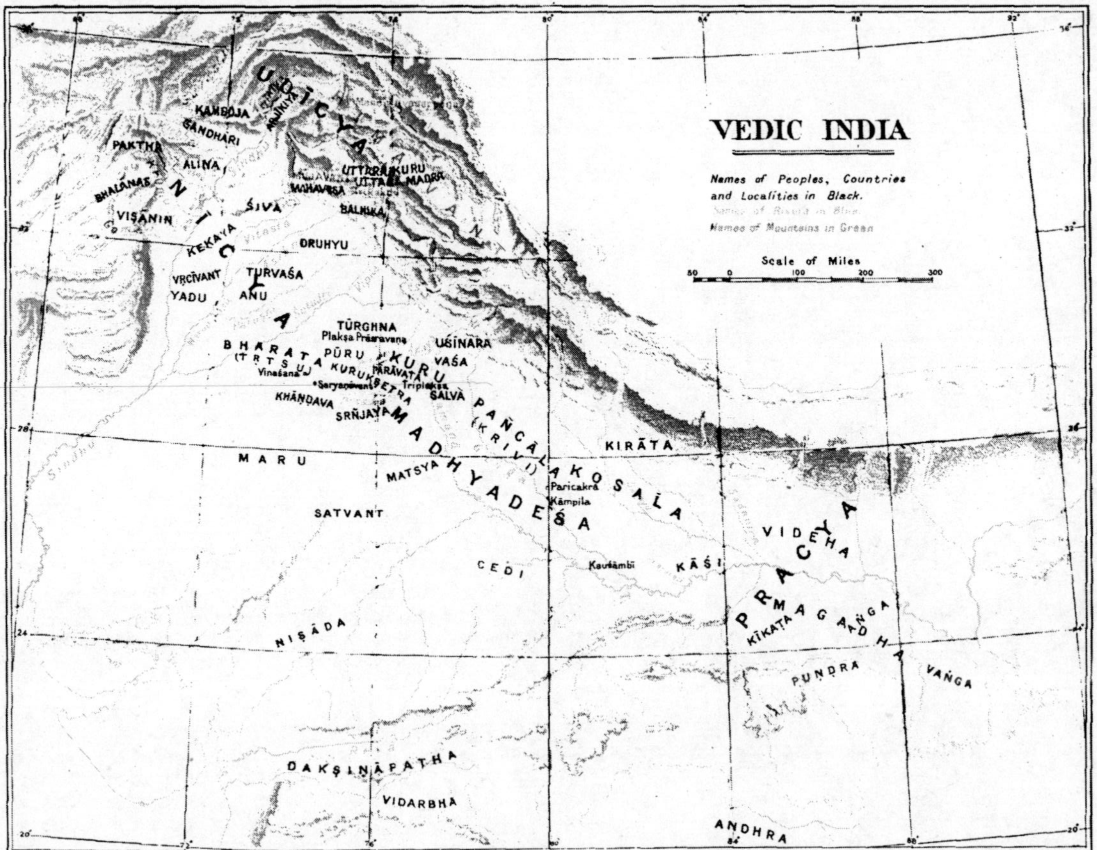
VEDIC INDIA
Names of Peoples, Countries and Localities in Black.
Names of Mountains in Green
Scale of Miles
50 0 100 200 300
KAMBOJA
GANDHĀRI
PAKTHA
ALINA
BHALĀNAS
VIṢĀṆIN
ŚIVA
KEKAYA
DRUHYU
UTTARA KURU
MAHAVṚṢA
BALHIKA
VṚCĪVANT
YADU
TURVAŚA
ANU
TŪRGHNA
Plakṣa Prāsravaṇa
BHARATA
(TṚTSU)
Vinaśana
PŪRU
KURU
KURUKṢETRA
PĀRĀVATA
Triplakṣa
UŚĪNARA
VAŚA
SALVA
KHĀṆḌAVA
SṚÑJAYA
PAÑCĀLA
(KRIVI)
MADHYADEŚA
MARU
MATSYA
SATVANT
KIRĀTA
KOSALA
Paricakrā
Kāmpila
CEDI
Kauśāmbī
KĀŚI
VIDEHA
PRĀCYA
MAGADHA
AṄGA
KĪKAṬA
PUṆḌRA
VAṄGA
NIṢĀDA
DAKṢIṆĀPATHA
VIDARBHA
ANDHRA

VEDIC INDEX
OF
NAMES AND SUBJECTS

ARTHUR ANTHONY MACDONELL

And

ARTHUR BERRIEDALE KEITH

VOL. I

MOTILAL BANARSIDASS PUBLISHERS
PRIVATE LIMITED • DELHI

Reprint: Delhi, 1958, 1967, 1982, 1995, 2007
First Edition: London, 1912

ISBN: 978-81-208-1332-8 (Vol. I)
ISBN: 978-81-208-1331-1 (Set)

MOTILAL BANARSIDASS
41 U.A. Bungalow Road, Jawahar Nagar, Delhi 110 007
8 Mahalaxmi Chamber, 22 Bhulabhai Desai Road, Mumbai 400 026
236, 9th Main III Block, Jayanagar, Bangalore 560 011
203 Royapettah High Road, Mylapore, Chennai 600 004
Sanas Plaza, 1302 Baji Rao Road, Pune 411 002
8 Camac Street, Kolkata 700 017
Ashok Rajpath, Patna 800 004
Chowk, Varanasi 221 001

Printed in India
BY JAINENDRA PRAKASH JAIN AT SHRI JAINENDRA PRESS,
A-45 NARAINA, PHASE-I, NEW DELHI 110 028
AND PUBLISHED BY NARENDRA PRAKASH JAIN FOR
MOTILAL BANARSIDASS PUBLISHERS PRIVATE LIMITED,
BUNGALOW ROAD, DELHI 110 007

PREFACE

Inception and Progress of the Book.—The origination of the present work was due to Professor T. W. Rhys Davids at the time when, several years ago, he was appointed general editor of the Indian Text Series to be published under the auspices of the Secretary of State for India. He then asked me to contribute a work supplying the historical material, as represented by proper names, to be found in the earliest period of Indian literature antecedent to the rise of Buddhism towards the close of the sixth century B.C. Since the subject came within the range of my special studies and moreover appeared to be one of considerable importance, I agreed to the proposal. But I did so with hesitation, because my leisure for a long time to come was already mortgaged by two works which involved much labour and on which I was already engaged. I soon came to the conclusion that till those works—the *Bṛhaddevatā* and the *Vedic Grammar*—were out of my hands, I could spare no time for the third book, the mere preparation, to say nothing of the publication, of which would thus have to be postponed for several years. Another hindrance would be caused by the tour of study and research in India which I contemplated making at the earliest opportunity. With the prospect of these long delays before me, I was tempted to throw up a task that seemed to have been rashly undertaken. At the same time, I was reluctant either to abandon or to put off indefinitely what I had once begun. It also seemed a pity to relinquish an enterprise which, if properly carried out, promised to be very useful.

Under these circumstances, collaboration appeared the only way out of the difficulty. I bethought myself of Mr. A. B. Keith, who, as Boden Sanskrit scholar, had been my pupil for four years, and who had already assisted me since 1899, not only by reading the proofs of, but by suggesting improvements in, my *History of Sanskrit Literature* and my *Sanskrit Grammar for Beginners*, as well as my edition of the *Bṛhaddevatā*, then commencing to be printed. I accordingly asked him if he had the time and inclination to collaborate with me in the proposed work by at once beginning to collect material for it. He consented without hesitation, and the Secretary of State for India readily sanctioned this modification of the arrangements already made. There was no other man to whom I could have entrusted with such complete confidence the task of carrying out this preliminary work accurately and rapidly.

In 1909, about a year after my return from India, Mr. Keith supplied me with a considerable part of his collectanea, while my *Vedic Grammar* was still passing through the press. The regular printing did not begin till early in 1910, about the time when that work was published. The interval was taken up with preparing a sufficient amount of 'copy' for the printer, as well as with settling various questions of arrangement and typography.

Mode of Collaboration.—Our respective shares in the production of the book are, generally stated, as follows: Dr. Keith has collected the material, while I have acted chiefly as an editor, planning the scope of the work, arranging the distribution of text and notes, selecting the type to be used, cutting out, adding to or modifying the matter, weighing the evidence for different interpretations and conclusions, and deciding as to which view, in case of possible alternatives, should be preferred. Having written up in its final form every article contained in the book, I accept the responsibility for every statement and opinion expressed in it. I do not think that Dr. Keith and I have disagreed upon any material point. When we have differed on minor questions, he has deferred to my judgment, though his view may have been right just as often as mine. Where erroneous conclusions have been drawn, the reader will be helped to correct them by the method I have pursued of supplying from the original texts the evidence on which such conclusions are based.

Scope of the Work.—At the outset it was proposed, as I have already stated, that the book should furnish the historical material in Vedic literature as represented by proper names. As soon, however, as I began to examine more carefully the historical material thus available, I became convinced that restriction to proper names would result in a harvest too meagre to deserve being gathered in the form of a book. It seemed essential to collect all the historical matter accessible to us in the earliest literary documents of India, and thus to furnish a conspectus of the most ancient phase of Āryan civilization that can be realized by direct evidence. If properly and thoroughly treated this matter would, I felt sure, yield a book of genuine value, a comprehensive work on Vedic antiquities; for it would include all the information that can be extracted from Vedic literature on such topics as agriculture, astronomy, burial, caste, clothing, crime, diseases, economic conditions, food and drink, gambling, kingship, law and justice, marriage, morality, occupations, polyandry and polygamy, the position of women, usury, village communities, war, wedding ceremonies, widow burning, witchcraft, and many others. The proper names would embrace not only persons, tribes, and peoples, but also mountains, rivers, and countries. The geographical distribution of the Vedic population would thus also be presented.

From the historical data amplified in this way I proposed, however, to exclude matter belonging to the domain of religion, which it seemed better to relegate to a separate work. At the same time it soon became clear that certain aspects of religious activity inseparably connected with the social and political life of the age would have to be admitted, such as the functions of the main priests and some festivals or ritual practices. Again, certain names of perhaps purely mythological figures might have to be mentioned. The evidence is occasionally insufficient to show whether a name represents an actual historical personage: a demon or a mythical hero or priest may be meant. An undoubted demon may even have to be included, such as the one that is supposed to cause eclipses, because he belongs to the domain of primitive astronomy.

Chronological Limits.—The period which the book was intended to embrace had been decided at the outset as that of the Vedas and Brāhmaṇas. The upper limit here is the date of the oldest hymns of the Rigveda. That date is uncertain, but my conviction (set forth in my *History of Sanskrit Literature*, pp. 11-12) that it is not much earlier than 1200 B.C. still remains unshaken. It does not appear to me to be in the slightest degree invalidated by Professor Hugo Winckler's discoveries at Boghaz-köi, in Asia Minor, in the year 1907. That scholar has deciphered, in an inscription of about 1400 B.C. found there, the names of certain deities as *mi-it-ra*, *uru-w-na*, *in-da-ra*, and *na-ša-at-ti-ia*, which correspond to those of the important Vedic gods Mitra, Varuṇa, Indra, and Nāsatya. Three inferences may be drawn from the occurrence of these names. They may have been derived from Vedic India; in that case the Vedic religion must have flourished in India considerably before 1400 B.C., even though the hymns that have come down to us may not have been composed before that date. But that these names should have travelled all the way from India to Asia Minor is a hypothesis so highly improbable that it may be dismissed. Secondly, the names may belong to the early Iranian period after the Iranians had separated from the Indians, but before their language had reached the phonetic stage of the Avesta. This seems the most probable theory, both chronologically and geographically. It implies only that the Indian branch had separated from the Iranian, not that it had already entered

India. Lastly, the names, being common to the Iranian and Indian languages, might be assigned to the Indo-Iranian period when the two branches were still one people living in Iran. This theory would still allow two centuries for separation, migration to India, and the commencement of Vedic literature in the north-west of India.

The lower limit of the Vedic period is the epoch of the rise and spread of Buddhism, or, roughly, 500 B.C. The Brāhmaṇa literature to be exploited was assumed to be undoubtedly anterior to that date. The boundary line would, however, to some extent have to be overstepped by drawing on the Sūtras for evidence where the Vedas and Brāhmaṇas fail. But though the Sūtras are roughly contemporaneous with the first three centuries of Buddhism, they are practically an epitome of the practices of the Brāhmaṇa period, and are thus often of great value in illustration or corroboration of the facts of that period. They are also important as representing the Brahminical evidence for those three centuries, especially as it is somewhat uncertain how far even the earliest Buddhist literary sources go back in an authentic form to the three centuries following the death of Buddha. Names and practices not referred to before the Sūtras were, however, to be mentioned only incidentally if at all: the few cases to the contrary that actually occur are not real exceptions, because they are derived from Vedic verses quoted in Sūtras, or from Brāhmaṇa parts of Sūtras such as Baudhāyana.

Method Pursued.—Such was the scope of the work on which I finally decided before it was begun, and the plan has been adhered to in its execution as regards the contents. The manner in which those contents were to be presented was the next question to be settled and acted upon. Though both Dr. Keith and myself are familiar with the literature of the Vedic period from which the facts collected in these two volumes are drawn, and the mutual check exercised by two workers sifting the same material acts as a safeguard, it is nevertheless not always possible to exclude the risk of error or unconscious bias in estimating evidence often obscure and doubtful. I have, therefore, throughout attached great importance to stating not only the evidence of the texts themselves from a first-hand knowledge, but also to setting forth fully the opinions of other authorities when the interpretation is uncertain. The Sanskrit scholar will thus be enabled to test without difficulty the correctness of the conclusions drawn directly from the original sources, while others will be protected from having to rely exclusively on what may possibly be one-sided views. Articles have often been illustrated by adducing parallels from the institutions of cognate Āryan nations, as that on 'Caste' (treated under **Varṇa**, ii. 427-471). I have further endeavoured to utilize, chiefly in the notes, knowledge gained from a first-hand study of the archæological remains and of the modern conditions of India. Such knowledge, acquired during my tour in 1907-08, I have found to be of great value to me both as a student and as a teacher.

Arrangement.—The matter contained in these volumes is treated not in chapters, but in articles disposed in alphabetical order. That order was practically necessary when proper names only were to be included; when subjects were subsequently added to the plan, it still remained the most convenient method of arrangement. As all articles appear under Sanskrit words, the order which the latter follow is naturally that of the Sanskrit alphabet. This arrangement need, however, occasion no inconvenience to those users of the book who are unfamiliar with Sanskrit, because all the information they want can be found by reference to the full English Index at the end of Vol. ii. The Sanskrit Index, which contains, in addition to the terms representing the subjects treated, all incidental Sanskrit words occurring in the articles, is of course arranged in the Sanskrit order. For the purpose of obviating any possible inconvenience, the sequence of the Sanskrit alphabet is given on the last page of this preface. With the same end in view I have given translations or explanations of all Sanskrit words and expressions, because the latter, though generally clear to Sanskrit scholars, would be unintelligible to others. Compound Sanskrit words have been divided into their component parts by the use of hyphens. In the case of obscure or irregularly formed Sanskrit words, I have sometimes added etymological explanations, which may be useful even to the Sanskrit scholar.

I have long had a rooted objection to crowding the letter-press of a book with parentheses containing a string of references or incidental explanations, because these distract the attention of the reader and interfere with his grasping the argument rapidly. I have accordingly in the present work (as in several previous ones) cleared the text of such obstructive matter, relegating references and minor explanations, illustrations, or discussions, to the notes. The sole exceptions are short references consisting of figures only, and occurring in articles of two or three lines in length. Thus, in the article 'Kauṣārava' (i. 194), the figures (viii. 28) are added in parentheses at the end of the line. To have made a footnote out of these figures alone would have been a pedantic and an absurd application of the general principle.

The **notes** are placed in two columns, because this arrangement enables the reader to find them more rapidly than any other. They come at the end of, and immediately below, each article. It is only when the article is a long one extending beyond the first page that the notes do not all occupy this position. Those referring to each page are then placed at the foot of that page, and only those referring to the last page come at the end of the article (*cf.*, *e.g.*, 1. **Akṣa**).

The **headlines** are so arranged as to help the reader in finding what he wants quickly, as well as to convey the maximum of information. A glance at the inner corners at the top will show the alphabetical range of the articles occurring in any two pages, the one indicating the first word on the left page, the other the last word on the right page. The rest of the headline of each page supplies a summary of the contents of that page. I have never been able to find any rational explanation why the title of the book held in one's hand should be printed at the top of at least half, sometimes of all, the pages it contains. How this practice can possibly assist the reader is hard to understand.

Typographical Details.—Every Sanskrit word used as the title of an article is printed in thick type for the purpose of catching the eye of the reader more readily. Every such word mentioned in another article is on its first occurrence there similarly printed. This is both a simpler and a clearer way of referring to a word used in another place than the employment of parentheses and additional words or abbreviations, like 'see' or '*cf.*,' which tend to distract the attention of the reader (see, *e.g.*, **Agastya**). Both Sanskrit names (including titles of books) and ordinary Sanskrit terms used as English words are printed in Roman type, but then always with a capital (*e.g.*, Purohita). Italic type is employed for Sanskrit words quoted as such, for expressions from other languages such as Latin or French, for the titles of all except Sanskrit books (*e.g.*, Oldenberg, *Buddha*), and even of Sanskrit books when a particular edition is intended (thus Roth, *Nirukta*, but Yāska, Nirukta). English words are italicized only when in long articles the titles of subdivisions are given. All these uses of italics will be found exemplified in the articles 2. **Akṣa** and 3. **Akṣa.**

As regards numerals, Roman figures are employed to indicate the main divisions of a work, the subordinate parts being expressed by Arabic figures. Thus 'Rigveda, ii. 3, 5,' means 'book 2, hymn 3, verse 5.' The volume, on the other hand, is referred to by an Arabic numeral, the following figure indicating the page. Thus 'Max Müller, *Ṛgveda*, 2, 135' means 'volume 2 of Max Müller's edition of the Rigveda, page 135.'

I have avoided abbreviating the titles of books or journals even when they occur often, or are mentioned in the notes only. Contracted titles are as a rule intelligible to the general reader only by reference to an explanatory list appearing at the beginning or the end of a book. When a work is written consecutively, such an abbreviation can be looked up on its first occurrence, and as it is usually met with again at short intervals its explanation will be remembered. But in a book arranged in dictionary form, the occurrence of abridged titles becomes irksome to the reader because he meets them at any part of the book he opens, and often many at the same time; he will probably therefore be continually consulting the explanatory list. Hence I have only admitted the contractions 'Rv.' for Rigveda and 'Av.' for Atharvaveda, as these texts are constantly referred to, often several times in the same article. In some works, such as the *Encyclopædia of Indo-Āryan Research*, excessively contracted titles, frequently assuming the appearance of algebraic symbols, become necessary owing to the great mass of bibliographical references required. In the present work such economy of space was in no way called for. If, however, the book had been intended for the use of Sanskrit scholars only, I should certainly have shortened many titles here given in full, for there are numerous formulaic abbreviations that are familiar to all specialists.

Transliteration.—The system here followed is that which has been adopted by the Royal Asiatic Society of Great Britain and Ireland, and is generally employed elsewhere also. The chief difficulties caused to the non-scholar by this method of reproducing Sanskrit words are due, on the one hand, to the inadequacy of the Roman alphabet, which necessitates the use of diacritical marks, and, on the other, to the conventional use of two consonants in English, in certain cases, to represent a single sound, as *ch*, *sh*, *ph*, and *th*. The letter ṣ here is the equivalent of *sh* in 'shun'; *ś* is somewhat thinner in pronunciation, like the *ss* in 'session'; *ṃ* resembles the *n* in the French 'bon'; and *ḥ* the German *ch* in 'ach.' The palatal *c* is to be sounded like the initial *ch* in Churchill; *ch* has an aspirate sound like that of the *ch* in the middle of the same word; *ph* and *th* are also aspirates, as in the English 'up-hill' and 'ant-hill' respectively. The vowels must all be pronounced as in Italian: short when unmarked (except *e* and *o*, which are always long), long when they have a horizontal stroke above; thus *i* is sounded as in 'pin,' *ī* like *ee* in 'seen.' The vowel *ṛ* may be pronounced like *ri* in 'risk.'

The Map.—In order that the reader may be enabled to visualize in a general way the territory known to and occupied by the Vedic tribes, I have prefixed to the first volume a map of Vedic India. Here the home of the Indo-Aryans of the earliest period—that of the Rigveda—is the territory drained by the Indus river system, lying between the 35th and 28th parallel of northern latitude and between 70° and 78° eastern longitude, and corresponding roughly to the North-West Frontier Province and the Panjab of the present day. The eastern limit was probably the Yamunā, though the Ganges was already known. In the subsequent Vedic period—that of the later Vedas and of the Brāhmaṇas—the Indo-Āryan settlers gradually occupied the whole of the Ganges Valley down to the delta of that river. But the home of the fully developed culture of the Brāhmaṇas lay in the territory extending in a south-easterly direction from longitude 74° to 85°, between the confluence of the Sarasvatī and Dṛṣadvatī in the west and that of the Sadānīrā and Ganges on the east, and embracing roughly the south-eastern portion of the Panjab and the United Provinces of to-day. East of longitude 85° lay, to the north and south of the Ganges, the imperfectly Brahminized country corresponding to the modern Tirhut and Bihār, where Buddhism arose at the end of the Vedic period.

I ought to warn readers against placing too much reliance on the details of this map, because it is largely conjectural owing to the lack of precise geographical statement in the texts. The student, when using it, should always refer to the evidence furnished by the articles under each name that appears on the map. The identification of many of the Vedic rivers with those of modern India is certain; but even here the exact channels in which they flowed in ancient times is doubtful. Thus the Indus, some of the Panjab rivers, and the old Sarasvatī have been shown by Raverty, in an article in the *Journal of the Asiatic Society of Bengal* for 1892, to have changed their courses considerably, even within historical times. It must be remembered that all the rivers of Vedic India traversed the alluvial plains of the north, and were, therefore, unlike the rivers of the Deccan, which flow in rocky beds, liable to constant fluctuations in their channels. Again, the Vedic tribes are nearly always mentioned so vaguely in the texts that they can only be approximately located by the rivers with which they are connected, or by the way in which their names are associated or grouped. Many such names had to be omitted altogether in the map because of the total lack of evidence for their localization. Some help may be obtained from the geographical position in the post-Vedic period of tribes mentioned in Vedic literature. But this evidence is apt to be doubtful, because the Vedic period was largely one of migration, and various tribes may then have occupied localities much farther north or west than those in which they were later permanently settled. The general evidence of the map, however uncertain many of the details may be, leaves no room for doubt as to the route by which the Āryans entered India, or as to the direction of the successive stages of the migration by which they eventually spread their civilization over the whole of the peninsula.

Conclusion.—The first volume was ready for issue more than a year ago, but to publish it without the indexes, which would necessarily have to appear at the end of the second volume, seemed to me to be perfectly useless. I therefore preferred to wait till the whole book could be brought out in a complete form. As both Dr. Keith and myself have each read one proof and nearly always two revises of every sheet before it went to press, all but trivial errors and misprints ought to have been eliminated. I hope, however, that these two volumes will prove to be not only correct in form, but also valuable in matter, after our joint efforts to bring together and present their contents in a convenient and trustworthy manner.

A. A. MACDONELL.

OXFORD,
July 18, 1912.

Order of the Sanskrit Alphabet.

a ā i ī u ū ṛ ṝ ḷ; e ai o au; k kh g gh, ṅ; c ch j jh ñ; ṭ ṭh ḍ ḍh ṇ; t th d dh n; p ph b bh m; y r l v; ś ṣ s h.

VEDIC INDEX OF NAMES AND SUBJECTS.

Aṃśu.—1. Name of a protégé of the Aśvins in the Rigveda.[1] 2. **Dhānaṃjayya**, pupil of **Amāvāsya Śāṇḍilyāyana**, according to the Vaṃśa Brāhmaṇa.[2]

[1] viii. 5, 26. *Cf.* Ludwig, Translation of the Rigveda, 3, 160; Hopkins, *Journal of the American Oriental Society*, 17, 89; Sieg, *Die Sagenstoffe des Ṛgveda*, 129, suggests that he may be identical with **Khela**.

[2] *Indische Studien*, 4, 373.

Aṃhasas-pati.—This is the name of the intercalary month in the Vājasaneyi Saṃhitā (vii. 30; xxii. 31). See **Māsa**.

Akra.—In several passages of the Rigveda[1] this word means, according to Geldner,[2] 'horse.' Roth[3] suggests that 'riding horse' is the precise sense. *Cf.* **Aśva**.

[1] i. 143, 7; 189, 7; iii. 1, 12; iv. 6, 3; x. 77, 2.

[2] *Vedische Studien*, 1, 168, 169.

[3] *Zeitschrift der Deutschen Morgenländischen Gesellschaft*, 48, 118. *Cf.* Max Müller, *Sacred Books of the East*, 32, 414.

1. **Akṣa**, 'axle,' is a part of a chariot often referred to in the Rigveda[1] and later. It was apparently[2] fastened to the body of the chariot (**Kośa**) by straps (*akṣā-nah*, lit. 'tied to the axle,' though this word is also[3] rendered 'horse'). The heating of the axle and the danger of its breaking were known.[4] The part of the axle round which the nave of the wheel revolved was called **Āṇi**, 'pin.'

[1] i. 30, 14; 166, 9; iii. 53, 17; vi. 24, 3; x. 89, 4, etc.

[2] Zimmer, *Altindisches Leben*, 246.

[3] Rv. x. 53, 7. *Cf.* Roth, St. Petersburg Dictionary, *s.v.*

[4] Rv. i. 164, 13.

2. **Akṣa.**—This word occurs frequently, from the Rigveda onwards, both in the singular and plural, meaning 'die' and 'dice.' Dicing, along with horse-racing, was one of the main amusements of the Vedic Indian; but, despite the frequent mention of the game in the literature, there is considerable difficulty in obtaining any clear picture of the mode in which it was played.

(1) *The Material.*—The dice appear normally to have been made of Vibhīdaka nuts. Such dice are alluded to in both the Rigveda[1] and the Atharvaveda,[2] hence being called 'brown' (*babhru*), and 'born on a windy spot.'[3] In the ritual game of dice at the Agnyādheya and the Rājasūya ceremonies the material of the dice is not specified, but it is possible that occasionally gold imitations of Vibhīdaka nuts were used.[4] There is no clear trace in the Vedic literature of the later use of cowries as dice.[5]

(2) *The Number.*—In the Rigveda[6] the dicer is described as 'leader of a great horde' (*senānīr mahato gaṇasya*), and in another passage[7] the number is given as *tri-pañcāśaḥ*, an expression which has been variously interpreted. Ludwig,[8] Weber,[9] and Zimmer[10] render it as fifteen, which is grammatically hardly possible. Roth[11] and Grassmann[12] render it as 'consisting of fifty-three.' Lüders[13] takes it as 'consisting of one hundred and fifty,' but he points out that this may be merely a vague expression for a large number. For a small number Zimmer[14] cites a reference in the Rigveda[15] to one who fears 'him who holds four' (*caturaś cid dadamānāt*), but the sense of that passage is dependent on the view taken of the method of playing the game.

(3) *The Method of Play.*—In several passages of the later

[1] vii. 86, 6; x. 34, 1.

[2] Av. Paipp. xx. 4, 6.

[3] Rv. x. 34, 5; Av. vii. 114, 7; Rv. x. 34, 1.

[4] Sāyaṇa on Taittirīya Saṃhitā, i. 8, 6, 12; Śatapatha Brāhmaṇa, v. 4, 4, 6.

[5] Sāyaṇa, *loc. cit.*, and on Rv. i. 41, 9; Mahīdhara on Vājasaneyi Saṃhitā, x. 28.

[6] x. 34, 12.

[7] x. 34, 8.

[8] See his translation.

[9] *Über das Rājāsūya*, 72.

[10] *Altindisches Leben*, 284.

[11] Following Sāyaṇa on Rv. x. 34, 8.

[12] In his translation.

[13] *Das Würfelspiel im alten Indien*, 25.

[14] *Op. cit.*, 283.

[15] i. 41, 9.

Saṃhitās and Brāhmaṇas lists are given of expressions connected with dicing. The names are Kṛta, Tretā, Dvāpara, Āskanda, and Abhibhū in the Taittirīya Saṃhitā.[16] In the Vājasaneyi Saṃhitā,[17] among the victims at the Puruṣamedha, the *kitava* is offered to the Akṣarāja, the *ādinava-darśa* to the Kṛta, the *kalpin* to the Tretā, the *adhi-kalpin* to the Dvāpara, the *sabhā-sthāṇu* to the Āskanda. The lists in the parallel version of the Taittirīya Brāhmaṇa are *kitava*, *sabhāvin*, *ādinava-darśa*, *bahiḥ-sad*, and *sabhā-sthāṇu*,[18] and Aksarāja, Kṛta, Tretā, Dvāpara, and Kali. From the Śatapatha Brāhmaṇa[19] it appears that another name of Kali was Abhibhū, and the parallel lists in the Taittirīya and Vājasaneyi Saṃhitās suggest that Abhibhū and Akṣarāja are identical, though both appear in the late Taittirīya Brāhmaṇa list. The names of some of these throws go back even to the Rigveda and the Atharvaveda. Kali occurs in the latter,[20] and Lüders[21] shows that in a considerable number of passages in the former Kṛta means a 'throw' (not 'a stake'[22] or 'what is won'[23]), and this sense is clearly found in the Atharvaveda.[24] Moreover, that there were more throws (*ayāḥ*) than one is proved by a passage in the Rigveda,[25] when the gods are compared to throws as giving or destroying wealth.

The nature of the throws is obscure. The St. Petersburg Dictionary conjectures that the names given above were applied either to dice marked 4, 3, 2, or 1, or to the sides of the dice so marked, and the latter interpretation is supported by some late commentators.[26] But there is no evidence for the former interpretation, and, as regards the latter, the shape of the Vibhīdaka nuts,[27] used as dice, forbids any side being properly on the top. Light is thrown on the expressions by the descrip-

16 iv. 3, 3, 1. 2.

17 xxx. 18.

18 iii. 4, 1, 16. These must be persons conversant with dicing, but the exact sense of the names is unknown.

19 v. 4, 4, 6.

20 vii. 114, 1.

21 *Op. cit.*, 43 *et seq.*

22 St. Petersburg Dictionary, *s.v.*

23 Grassmann's Dictionary, *s.v.*

24 vii. 52. See Rv. x. 42, 9 (*kṛtaṃ vicinoti*); 43, 5; x. 102, 2; v. 60, 1; ix. 97, 58: i. 132, 1; x. 34, 6; i. 100, 9; viii. 19, 10.

25 x. 116, 9.

26 Ānandagiri on Chāndogya Upaniṣad, iv. 1. 4; Nīlakaṇṭha on Mahābhārata, iv. 50, 24.

27 Lüders, *op. cit.*, 18.

tion of a ritual game[28] at the Agnyādheya and at the Rājasūya ceremonies. The details are not certain,[29] but it is clear that the game consisted in securing even numbers of dice, usually a number divisible by four, the Kṛta, the other three throws then being the Tretā, when three remained over after division by four; the Dvāpara, when two was the remainder; and the Kali, when one remained. If five were the dividing number, then the throw which showed no remainder was Kali, the Kṛta was that when four was left, and so on. The dice had no numerals marked on them, the only question being what was the total number of the dice themselves.

There is no reason to doubt that the game as played in the Rigveda was based on the same principle, though the details must remain doubtful. The number of dice used was certainly large,[30] and the reference to throwing fours,[31] and losing by one, points to the use of the Kṛta as the winning throw. The Atharvaveda,[32] on the other hand, possibly knew of the Kali as the winning throw. In one respect the ordinary game must have differed from the ritual game. In the latter the players merely pick out the number of dice required—no doubt to avoid ominous errors, such as must have happened if a real game had been played. In the secular game the dice were thrown,[33] perhaps on the principle suggested by Lüders:[34] the one throwing a certain number on the place of playing, and the other then throwing a number to make up with those already thrown a multiple of four or five. This theory, at any rate, accounts for the later stress laid on the power of computation in a player, as in the Nala.

No board appears to have been used, but a depression on which

[28] Baudhāyana Śrauta Sūtra, ii. 8; 9; Āpastamba Śrauta Sūtra, v. 19, 4; 20, 1, with Rudradatta's note, for the Agnyādheya. Āpastamba, xviii. 18, 16 *et seq.*, describes the Rājasūya game, and *cf.* Maitrāyaṇī Saṃhitā, iv. 4, 6; Taittirīya Brāhmaṇa, i. 7, 10, 5; Śatapatha Brāhmaṇa, v. 4, 4, 6; Kātyāyana Śrauta Sūtra, xv. 7, 5 *et seq.* For Kṛta as four, see Śatapatha Brāhmaṇa, xiii. 3, 2, 1; Taittirīya Brāhmaṇa, i. 5, 11, 1.

[29] See Caland, *Zeitschrift der Deutschen Morgenländischen Gesellschaft*, 62, 123 *et seq.*

[30] Rv. x. 34, 8.

[31] Rv. i. 41, 9. In x. 34, 2, the loss is ascribed to *akṣasya ekaparasya*, which confirms the explanation of Dvāpara given in Pāṇini, ii. 1, 10.

[32] vii. 114, 1.

[33] Rv. x. 34, 1. 8. 9; Av. iv. 38, 3.

[34] *Op. cit.* 56.

the dice were thrown (*adhi-devana, devana*,[35] *iriṇa*[36]), was made in the ground. No dice box was used, but reference is made to a case for keeping dice in (*akṣā-vapana*[37]). The throw was called *graha*[38] or earlier *grābha*.[39] The stake is called *vij*.[40] Serious losses could be made at dicing : in the Rigveda a dicer laments the loss of all his property, including his wife.[41] Lüders[42] finds a different form of the game referred to in the Chāndogya Upaniṣad.[43]

[35] *Adhidevana* in Av. v. 31, 6 ; vi. 70, 1 ; Maitrāyaṇī Saṃhitā, i. 6, 11 ; iv. 4, 6, etc. ; *devana* in Rv. x. 43, 5. The falling of the dice on the ground is referred to in Av. vii. 114, 2.

[36] Rv. x. 34, 1.

[37] Śatapatha Brāhmaṇa, v. 3, 1, 11.

[38] Av. iv. 38, 1 *et seq.* ; *cf.* vii. 114, 5.

[39] Rv. viii. 81, 1 ; ix. 106, 3.

[40] Rv. i. 92, 10 ; ii. 12, 5 ; *lakṣa* in ii. 12, 4, and often *dhana*. So Lüders, *op. cit.*, 10, n. 5 ; 62, n. 1. Roth and Zimmer, *op. cit.*, 286, render 'he makes the dice secretly disappear' (i. 92, 10).

[41] Rv. x. 34, 2. For cheating at play *cf.* Rv. v. 85, 8 ; vii. 86, 6 ; 104 14 ; Av. vi. 118.

[42] *Op. cit.*, 61.

[43] iv. 1, 4 ; 6. According to Nīlakaṇṭha on Harivaṃśa, ii. 61, 39, the stake was divided into ten parts, and the Kali then took one, the Dvāpara three, the Tretā six, and the Kṛta all ten. This explanation seems harsh.

Cf. Roth, Gurupūjākaumudī, 1-4 ; Zimmer, *Altindisches Leben*, 283-287 ; Lüders, *Das Würfelspiel im alten Indien* ; Caland, *Zeitschrift der Deutschen Morgenländischen Gesellschaft*, 62, 123 *et seq.* ; Keith, *Journal of the Royal Asiatic Society*, 1908, 823 *et seq.*

3. **Akṣa.**—In the Chāndogya Upaniṣad (vii. 3, 1) this word seems to denote the nut of the Vibhīdaka (*Terminalia bellerica*).

Akṣata or **Akṣita.**—In one passage of the Atharvaveda,[1] dealing with the **Jāyānya**, mention is made of a remedy for sores designated both Akṣita and Sukṣata, or, according to the reading of the Kauṣika Sūtra, Akṣata and Sukṣata, while Sāyaṇa has Akṣita and Sukṣita. Bloomfield[2] renders 'not caused by cutting' and 'caused by cutting.' Formerly[3] he suggested 'tumour' or 'boil.' Whitney[4] thinks that two varieties of Jāyānya are meant. Ludwig[5] reads with Sāyaṇa *akṣita*, which he renders by 'not firmly established' in the invalid. Zimmer[6] finds in it a disease Kṣata.

[1] vii. 76, 4.

[2] *Hymns of the Atharvaveda*, 17, 562.

[3] *Journal of the American Oriental Society*, 13, cxvii. *et seq.*

[4] Translation of the Atharvaveda, 442.

[5] Translation of the Rigveda, 3, 500.

[6] *Altindisches Leben*, 377.

Akṣā-vapana. See **Akṣa.**

Akṣu.—The word occurs in two passages of the Atharvaveda[1] and one of the Rigveda.[2] Roth[3] renders it by 'net,' while Böhtlingk[4] suggests 'axle of a car.' Geldner[5] sees in it a stake or pole used with a fishermen's net (**Jāla**),[6] the pole of a wagon,[7] and the pole of a house, whether vertical or horizontal, he leaves uncertain (see **Vaṃśa**).[8] Bloomfield[9] takes it as a covering of wickerwork stretched across a beam and sloping down to both sides—like a thatched roof, and this best explains the epithet 'thousand-eyed' (*i.e.*, with countless holes) ascribed to it. In the other Atharvaveda passage[10] he accepts the sense 'net,' and doubts if the word in the Rigveda is not an adjective (*a-kṣu*) as it is taken by Sāyaṇa. See also **Gṛha.**

[1] viii. 8, 18 (*akṣujālābhyām*); ix. 3, 18.
[2] i. 180, 5.
[3] St. Petersburg Dictionary, *s.v.*
[4] Dictionary, *s.v.*
[5] *Vedische Studien*, 1, 136.
[6] Av. viii. 8, 18.
[7] Av. i. 180, 5.
[8] ix. 3, 18.
[9] *Hymns of the Atharvaveda*, 598.
[10] Av. viii. 8, 18.

Cf. Zimmer, *Altindisches Leben*, 153, 265; Whitney, Translation of the Atharvaveda, 506, 526; Oldenberg, *Ṛgveda-Noten*, 1, 179.

Agasti.—This form of **Agastya's** name occurs once in the Atharvaveda,[1] where he appears as a favourite of Mitra and Varuṇa.

[1] iv. 9, 3. *Cf.* Sieg, *Die Sagenstoffe des Ṛgveda*, 127, n. 5.

Agastya.—This is the name of a sage, of mythical character, who plays a great part in the later literature. He was a **Māna,**[1] and therefore is called **Mānya**[2] and son of Māna, and only once is there a reference[3] to the legend prevalent in later times that he was a son of Mitra and Varuṇa.

His greatest feat was the reconciliation of Indra and the Maruts after Indra had been annoyed at his proposing to give the Maruts an offering to the exclusion of Indra. This feat is the subject of three hymns of the Rigveda,[4] and is often referred

[1] Rv. vii. 33, 10 (Agastya), 13 (Māna).
[2] Rv. i. 165, 15=166, 15=167, 11=168, 10; 165, 14; 177, 5; 184, 4 (Mānya); i. 189, 8; 117, 11 (*Mānasya sūnu*).
[3] Rv. vii. 33, 13. *Cf.* Geldner, *Vedische Studien*, 2, 138 *et seq.*
[4] Rv. i. 165; 170; 171.

to in the Brāhmaṇas,[5] though the exact details and significance of the legend are variously treated by Oldenberg,[6] Sieg,[7] Hertel,[8] and von Schroeder.[9]

He also appears in a strange dialogue with Lopāmudrā in the Rigveda,[10] which appears to show him as an ascetic who finally yields to temptation. Von Schroeder[11] regards it as a ritual drama of vegetation magic.

In another passage of the Rigveda[12] he appears as helping in the Aśvins' gift of a leg to Viśpalā. Sāyaṇa holds that he was the Purohita of **Khela,** and Sieg[13] accepts this view, while Pischel[14] thinks that Khela is a deity, Vivasvant.

Geldner[15] shows from the Rigveda[16] that Agastya, as brother of Vasiṣṭha—both being miraculous sons of Mitra and Varuṇa—introduces **Vasiṣṭha** to the **Tṛtsus.** There are two other references to Agastya in the Rigveda, the one[17] including him in a long list of persons, the other alluding to his sister's sons (*nadbhyaḥ*),[18] apparently **Bandhu,** etc. In the Atharvaveda[19] he appears as connected with witchcraft, and in a long list of sages.[20] In the Maitrāyaṇī Saṃhitā[21] cows, with a peculiar mark on their ears (*viṣṭya-karṇyaḥ*), are associated with him.

[5] Taittirīya Saṃhitā, vii. 5, 5, 2; Taittirīya Brāhmaṇa, ii. 7, 11, 1; Maitrāyaṇī Saṃhitā, ii. 1, 8; Kāṭhaka Saṃhitā, x. 11; Pañcaviṃśa Brāhmaṇa, xxi. 14, 5; Aitareya Brāhmaṇa, v. 16; Kauṣītaki Brāhmaṇa, xxvi. 9.

[6] *Zeitschrift der Deutschen Morgenländischen Gesellschaft*, 39, 60 *et seq.*

[7] *Die Sagenstoffe des Ṛgveda*, 108-119.

[8] *Vienna Oriental Journal*, 18, 152-154.

[9] *Mysterium und Mimus im Rigveda*, 91 *et seq.*

[10] i. 179. *Cf.* Sieg, *op. cit.*, 120-126; Oldenberg, *op. cit.*, 66-68.

[11] *Op. cit.*, 156-172.

[12] i. 117, 11; *cf.* i. 116, 15.

[13] *Op. cit.*, 128.

[14] *Vedische Studien*, 1, 171-173.

[15] *Vedische Studien*, 2, 138, 143.

[16] Rv. vii. 33, 10. 13.

[17] vii. 5, 26. Sieg, 129, suggests that this refers to the Khela legend.

[18] x. 60, 6.

[19] ii. 32, 3; iv. 37, 1. Perhaps for this reason the Rigveda Anukramaṇī ascribes to him (Rv. i. 191) a magic hymn.

[20] xviii. 3, 15.

[21] iv. 2, 9.

Cf. Ludwig, Translation of the Rigveda, 3, 117; Sieg, *Die Sagenstoffe des Ṛgveda*, 106-129; Macdonell, *Bṛhaddevatā*, 2, 136 *et seq.*; Oldenberg, *Zeitschrift der Deutschen Morgenländischen Gesellschaft*, 42, 221; *Ṛgveda-Noten*, 1, 110.

Agāra.—This rare word is found as 'house' in the Kauṣītaki Upaniṣad.[1]

[1] ii. 15. *Cf. āgara*, 'chamber' (?), in Av. iv. 36, 3; Bloomfield, *Hymns of the Atharvaveda*, 407. Agāra occurs also in Āśvalāyana Gṛhya Sūtra, i. 7, 21.

Agni-dagdha.—This epithet ('burnt with fire')[1] applies to the dead who were burned on the funeral pyre. This is one of the two normal methods of disposing of the dead, the other being burial (*an-agnidagdhāḥ*, 'not burnt with fire').[2] The Atharvaveda[3] adds two further modes of disposal to those—viz., casting out (*paroptāḥ*), and the exposure of the dead (*uddhitāḥ*). The exact sense of these expressions is doubtful. Zimmer[4] considers that the former is a parallel to the Iranian practice of casting out the dead to be devoured by beasts, and that the latter refers to the old who are exposed when helpless.[5] Whitney[6] refers the latter expression to the exposure of the dead body on a raised platform of some sort.

Burial was clearly not rare in the Rigvedic period: a whole hymn[7] describes the ritual attending it. The dead man was buried apparently in full attire, with his bow in his hand, and probably at one time his wife was immolated to accompany him, in accordance with a practice common among savage tribes. But in the Vedic period both customs appear in a modified form: the son takes the bow from the hand of the dead man, and the widow is led away from her dead husband by his brother or other nearest kinsman. A stone is set between the dead and the living to separate them. In the Atharvaveda,[8] but not in the Rigveda, a coffin (*vṛkṣa*) is alluded to. In both Saṃhitās[9] occur other allusions to the 'house of earth' (*bhūmi-gṛha*). To remove the apparent discrepancy between burning and burial, by assuming that the references to burial are to the burial of the burned bones, as does Oldenberg,[10] is unnecessary and improbable, as burning and burial subsisted side by side in Greece for many years.

Burning was, however, equally usual, and it grew steadily in frequency, for in the Chāndogya Upaniṣad[11] the adornment

[1] Rv. x. 15, 14; Taittirīya Brāhmaṇa, iii. 1, 1, 7; *dagdhāḥ*, Av. xviii. 2, 34.

[2] Rv., *loc. cit.*; =*nikhātāḥ*, Av. xviii. 2, 34.

[3] *Loc. cit.*

[4] *Altindisches Leben*, 402.

[5] Rv. viii. 51, 2.

[6] Translation of the Atharvaveda, 841.

[7] x. 18. The interpretation of v. 8 is a famous crux, see **Patnī**.

[8] xviii. 2, 25; 3, 70.

[9] Rv. vii. 89, 1; Av. v. 30, 14; xviii. 2, 52.

[10] *Religion des Veda*, 571.

[11] viii. 8, 5.

of the body of the dead with curd (**Āmikṣā**), clothes, and ornaments, in order to win the next world, is referred to as something erroneous and wrong, and in the funeral Mantras of the Vājasaneyi Saṃhitā[12] only burning seems to be contemplated; the verses which refer to burial here really alluding to the burial of the ashes in the burying-ground (*śmaśāna*).[13] The body was wrapped in fat,[14] as we learn from the funeral hymn in the Rigveda, a goat being apparently burned with it,[15] to act as a guide on the way to the next world. According to the Atharvaveda[16] a draft-ox was burned presumably for the dead to ride with in the next world. It was expected that the dead would revive with his whole body and all his limbs (*sarva-tanūḥ sāṅgaḥ*),[17] although it is also said[18] that the eye goes to the sun, the breath to the wind, and so forth.

Before burial or burning, the corpse was washed,[19] a clog (*kūdī*) being tied to the foot to prevent the deceased returning to earth.[20]

[12] xxxv. *Cf.* also Kauśika Sūtra, 80 *et seq.*, which treats the Atharvaveda hymns, xviii. 1-3, as intended for burning only.

[13] Av. v. 31, 8; x. 1, 18; Taittirīya Saṃhitā, v. 2, 8, 5; 4, 11, 3.

[14] Rv. x. 16, 7.

[15] Rv. x. 16, 4. But *aja* may mean 'the unborn part,' as Weber prefers to take it, Proceedings of the Berlin Academy, 1895, 847.

[16] xii. 2, 48.

[17] Śatapatha Brāhmaṇa, iv. 6, 1, 1; xi. 1, 8, 6; xii. 8, 3, 31. *Cf.* Av. xi. 3, 32. This fact probably explains the use of *śeṣaḥ* in Rv. x. 16, 5. The dead enjoy sexual pleasures in the next world; see Muir, *Sanskrit Texts*, 5, 307, n. 462.

[18] Rv. x. 16, 3.

[19] Av. v. 19, 14.

[20] Av. v. 19, 12; see Roth, *Festgruss an Böhtlingk*, 98; Bloomfield, *American Journal of Philology*, 12, 416.

Cf. Zimmer, *Altindisches Leben*, 401-407; Roth, *Zeitschrift der Deutschen Morgenländischen Gesellschaft*, 8, 468 *et seq.*; *Siebenzig Lieder*, 150 *et seq.*; Oldenberg, *Religion des Veda*, 570 *et seq.*; Caland, *Die altindischen Todten- und Bestattungsgebräuche*; von Schroeder, *Indiens Literatur und Cultur*, 40-42; Hillebrandt, *Vedische Mythology*, 3, 413-423; *Rituallitteratur*, 87 *et seq.*; Macdonell, *Vedic Mythology*, 165, 166; Proceedings of the Berlin Academy, 1895, 815 *et seq.*

Agni-bhū Kāśyapa is mentioned in the Vaṃśa Brāhmaṇa[1] as a pupil of **Indrabhū Kāśyapa.**

[1] *Indische Studien*, 4, 374

Agni-śāla.—This term, which designates part of the sacrificial apparatus,[1] is applied in the Atharvaveda[2] to a part of an ordinary house, presumably the central hall where the fire-place was.

[1] Vājasaneyi Saṃhitā, xix. 18.
[2] ix. 3, 7.
Cf. Bloomfield, *Hymns of the Atharvaveda*, 598; Zimmer, *Altindisches Leben*, 154.

Aghā.—In the wedding hymn of the Rigveda[1] it is said that cows are slain in the Aghās, and the wedding takes place at the **Arjunīs** (dual). The Atharvaveda[2] has the ordinary **Maghās** instead. It is impossible to resist the conclusion that the reading of the Rigveda was deliberately altered because of the connection of the slaughter of kine with sin (*agha*)—possibly, too, with a further desire to emphasize the contrast with *aghnyā*, a name for 'cow.' Moreover, in the Taittirīya Brāhmaṇa[3] occurs the formula 'Svāhā to the Maghās, Svāhā to the Anaghās.' See also **Nakṣatra.**

[1] x. 85, 13.
[2] xiv. 1, 13.
[3] iii. 1, 4, 8.
Cf. Weber, *Naxatra*, 2, 364; Proceedings of the Berlin Academy, 1894, 804; Jacobi, *Festgruss an Roth*, 69; Winternitz, *Das altindische Hochzeitsrituell*, 32; Whitney, Translation of the Atharvaveda, 742; Thibaut, *Indian Antiquary*, 24, 95.

Aghāśva.—The name of a serpent in the Atharvaveda.[1]

[1] x. 4, 10. *Cf.* Zimmer, *Altindisches Leben*, 95.

A-ghnyā.—See **Māṃsa.**

Aṅka.—The Taittirīya Saṃhitā[1] and Brāhmaṇa[2] refer to two Aṅkas and two Nyaṅkas as parts of a chariot. The meaning of these terms is quite obscure. The commentators refer them to the sides or wheels. Zimmer[3] compares the Greek ἄντυγες[4] and thinks that the Aṅkau were the upper border of the body of the chariot (*kośa, vandhura*), and the Nyaṅkau the lower rims for greater security. Oldenberg[5] confesses that the exact sense is impossible to make out, but considers that the terms at once refer to parts of the chariot and to divinities, while Böhtlingk[6] takes the term as referring to divinities alone.

[1] i. 7, 7, 2.
[2] ii. 7, 8, 1. *Cf.* Pañcaviṃśa Brāhmaṇa, i. 7, 5.
[3] *Altindisches Leben*, 251, 252.
[4] *Iliad*, v. 728. *Cf.* Smith's *Dictionary of Antiquities*, 1, 578.
[5] *Sacred Books of the East*, 29, 364, on Pāraskara Gṛhya Sūtra, iii. 14, 6.
[6] Dictionary, *s.v.*

Aṅga.—The name occurs only once in the Atharvaveda[1] in connection with the **Gandhāris, Mūjavants,** and **Magadhas,** as distinct peoples. They appear also in the Gopatha Brāhmaṇa[2] in the compound name *Aṅga-magadhāḥ.* As in later times they were settled on the Sone and Ganges,[3] their earlier seat was presumably there also. See also **Vaṅga.**

[1] v. 22, 14.

[2] ii. 9.

[3] *Cf.* Zimmer, *Altindisches Leben,* 35; Bloomfield, *Hymns of the Atharvaveda,* 446, 449; Pargiter, *Journal of the Royal Asiatic Society,* 1908, 852, inclines to regard them as a non-Aryan people that came over-sea to Eastern India. There is nothing in the Vedic literature to throw light on this hypothesis.

Aṅga Vairocana.—He is included in the list of anointed kings in the Aitareya Brāhmaṇa.[1] His Purohita was **Udamaya,** an Ātreya.

[1] viii. 22. *Cf.* Oldenberg, *Zeitschrift der Deutschen Morgenländischen Gesellschaft,* 42, 214.

Aṅgārāvakṣayaṇa.—A word of doubtful meaning found in the Bṛhadāraṇyaka Upaniṣad.[1] It is rendered 'tongs' by Max Müller and Böhtlingk in their translations. The St. Petersburg Dictionary explains it as 'a vessel in which coals are extinguished,' and Monier-Williams as 'an instrument for extinguishing coals.' The smaller St. Petersburg Dictionary renders the word 'coal-shovel or tongs.' *Cf.* **Ulmukāvakṣayaṇa.**

[1] iii. 9, 18.

Aṅgiras.—The Aṅgirases appear in the Rigveda[1] as semi-mythical beings, and no really historical character can be assigned even to those passages[2] which recognize a father of the race, Aṅgiras. Later, however, there were definite families of Aṅgirases, to whose ritual practices (*ayana, dvirātra*) references are made.[3]

[1] *Cf.* Hillebrandt, *Vedische Mythologie,* ii. 156-169.

[2] Rv. i. 45, 3; 139, 9; iii. 31, 7, etc.; Chāndogya Upaniṣad, i, 2, 10.

[3] Av. xviii. 4, 8, but this may be mythical; Pañcaviṃśa Brāhmaṇa, xx. 11, 1; Taittirīya Saṃhitā, vii. 1, 4, 1. *Cf.* Macdonell, *Vedic Mythology,* 142, 143.

Aṅguṣṭha.—As a measure of size this word appears in the Kāṭhaka Upaniṣad (iv. 12; vi. 17).

A-cyut.—He acted as Pratihartṛ at the Sattra celebrated by the Vibhindukīyas and described in the Jaiminīya Brāhmaṇa.[1]

[1] iii. 233. See *Journal of the American Oriental Society*, 18, 38.

Aja, Ajā.—This is the ordinary name for goat in the Rigveda[1] and the later literature. The goat is also called **Basta, Chāga, Chagala.** Goats and sheep (*ajāvayaḥ*) are very frequently mentioned together.[2] The female goat is spoken of as producing two or three kids,[3] and goat's milk is well known.[4] The goat as representative of Pūṣan plays an important part in the ritual of burial.[5] The occupation of a goatherd (*ajapāla*) was a recognized one, being distinguished from that of a cowherd and of a shepherd.[6]

[1] *Aja* in Rv. x. 16, 4; i. 162, 2. 4; Av. ix. 5, 1; Vājasaneyi Saṃhitā, xxi. 9, etc.; *ajā* in Rv. viii. 70, 15; Av. vi. 71, 1; Vājasaneyi Saṃhitā, xxiii., 56, etc.

[2] Rv. x. 90, 10; Av. viii. 7, 25; Vājasaneyi Saṃhitā, iii. 43, etc.

[3] Taittirīya Saṃhitā, vi. 5, 10, 1.

[4] Taittirīya Saṃhitā, iv. 1, 6, 1; v. 1, 7, 4. *Cf.* Hillebrandt, *Vedische Mythologie*, 3, 364, n. 4.

[5] Rv. x. 16, 4, etc. *Cf.* p. 9.

[6] Vājasaneyi Saṃhitā, xxx. 11; Taittirīya Brāhmaṇa, iii. 4, 9, 1.

Aja.—The Ajas are named in one verse of the Rigveda[1] as having been defeated by the **Tṛtsus** under **Sudās.** They are there mentioned with the **Yakṣus** and **Śigrus**, and Zimmer[2] conjectures that they formed part of a confederacy under Bheda against Sudās. The name has been regarded as a sign of totemism,[3] but this is very uncertain, and it is impossible to say if they were or were not Āryans.

[1] vii. 18, 19.

[2] *Altindisches Leben*, 127. *Cf.* Ludwig, Translation of the Rigveda, 3, 173.

[3] *Cf.* Macdonell, *Vedic Mythology*, 153; Keith, *Journal of the Royal Asiatic Society*, 1907, 929; Aitareya Āraṇyaka, 200, 21; Risley, *Peoples of India*, 83 *et seq.*

Ajakāva.—This name of a poisonous scorpion occurs once in the Rigveda.[1]

[1] vii. 50, 1. *Cf.* Zimmer, *Altindisches Leben*, 99.

Aja-gara ('goat-swallower') occurs in the Atharvaveda[1] and in the list of animals at the Aśvamedha,[2] or horse sacrifice, as the

[1] xi. 2, 25; xx. 129, 17.

[2] Taittirīya Saṃhitā, v. 5, 14, 1; Maitrāyaṇī Saṃhitā, iii. 14, 19; Vājasaneyi Saṃhitā, xxiv. 38.

name of the boa-constrictor. Elsewhere[3] it is called Vāhasa. It denotes a person at the snake feast in the Pañcaviṃśa Brāhmaṇa.[4]

[3] Taittirīya Saṃhitā, v. 5, 13, 1; Vājasaneyi Saṃhitā, xxiv. 34.

[4] xxv. 15, in the form of Ajagāva, with which *cf.* **Ajakāva.**

Aja-mīḍha.—The Ājamīḍhas, or descendants of Ajamīḍha, are referred to in a hymn of the Rigveda.[1] Ludwig[2] and Oldenberg[3] deduce from the use of this patronymic that Ajamīḍha was the seer of that hymn.

[1] iv. 44, 6.

[2] Translation of the Rigveda, 3, 123, 135.

[3] *Zeitschrift der Deutschen Morgenländischen Gesellschaft*, 42, 215.

Aja-śṛṅgī.—This plant ('goat's horn'), equated by the commentator with Viṣāṇin (the *Odina pinnata*), is celebrated as a demon-destroyer in the Atharvaveda.[1] Its other name is **Arāṭakī.**[2] Weber[3] suggests that it is the *Prosopis spicigera* or *Mimosa suma.*

[1] iv. 37.

[2] iv. 37, 6.

[3] *Indische Studien*, 18, 144. *Cf.* Bloomfield, *Hymns of the Atharvaveda*, 408, 409; Zimmer, *Altindisches Leben*, 68; Caland, *Altindisches Zauberritual*, 89.

Ajāta-śatru.—He is mentioned as a King of Kāśī (Kāśya) in the Bṛhadāraṇyaka[1] and Kauṣītaki[2] Upaniṣads, where he instructs the proud Brāhmaṇa Bālāki as to the real nature of the self. He is not to be identified with the Ajātasattu of the Buddhist texts.[3]

[1] ii. 1, 1.

[2] iv. 1.

[3] *Cf.* Weber, *Indische Studien*, 1, 213; Hoernle, *Osteology*, 106; Keith, *Zeitschrift der Deutschen Morgenländischen Gesellschaft*, 62, 138.

Ajñāta-yakṣma, the 'unknown sickness,' is mentioned in the Rigveda,[1] Atharvaveda,[2] and Kāṭhaka Saṃhitā.[3] It is referred to in connection with Rājayakṣma. Grohmann[4] thinks that the two are different forms of disease, hypertrophy and atrophy, the purpose of the spell in the Rigveda being thus the removal of all disease. From the Atharvaveda[5] he deduces its identity with **Balāsa.** Zimmer,[6] however, points out that this

[1] x. 161, 1=Av. iii. 11, 1.

[2] vi. 127, 3.

[3] xiii. 16.

[4] *Indische Studien*, 9, 400.

[5] vi. 127, 3.

[6] *Altindisches Leben*, 377, 378.

Cf. Bloomfield, *Hymns of the Atharvaveda*, 342; Atharvaveda, 60; Jolly, *Medicin* (in Bühler's Encyclopædia), 89.

conclusion is unjustified, leaving the disease unidentified, which seems to accord with its name.

Ajina.—This word denotes generally the skin of an animal —*e.g.*, a gazelle,[1] as well as that of a goat (**Aja**).[2] The use of skins as clothing is shown by the adjective 'clothed in skins' (*ajina-vāsin*) in the Śatapatha Brāhmaṇa,[3] and the furrier's trade is mentioned in the Vājasaneyi Saṃhitā.[4] The Maruts also wear deer-skins,[5] and the wild ascetics (*muni*) of a late Rigveda hymn[6] seem to be clad in skins (**Mala**).

[1] Av. v. 21, 7.
[2] Śatapatha Brāhmaṇa, v. 2, 1, 21. 24
[3] iii. 9, 1, 12.
[4] xxx. 15 (*ajina-saṃdha*); Taittirīya Brāhmaṇa, iii. 2, 13, 1 (*ajina-saṃdhāya*).
[5] Rv. i. 166, 10.
[6] x. 136, 2. *Cf.* Zimmer, *Altindisches Leben*, 262.

Ajira.—He was Subrahmaṇya priest at the snake festival of the Pañcaviṃśa Brāhmaṇa.[1]

[1] xxv. 15. See Weber, *Indische Studien*, 1, 35.

Ajīgarta Sauyavasa.—This is the name given to the father of **Śunaḥśepa** in the famous legend of the Aitareya Brāhmaṇa,[1] perhaps invented for the occasion, as Weber[2] suggests.

[1] vii. 15; 17. *Cf.* Śāṅkhāyana Srauta Sūtra, xv. 19.
[2] *Indische Studien*, 1, 460; Roth, St. Petersburg Dictionary, *s.v.*

A-jyeyatā. See **Brāhmaṇa.**

Aṇīcin Mauna.—He is mentioned as an authority on ritual, and contemporary with **Jābāla** and **Citra Gauśrāyaṇi** or **Gauśra**, in the Kauṣītaki Brāhmaṇa.[1]

[1] xxiii. 5.

Aṇu.—This is the designation in the Vājasaneyi Saṃhitā[1] and the Bṛhadāraṇyaka Upaniṣad[2] of a cultivated grain, apparently the *Panicum miliaceum.*

[1] xviii. 12.
[2] vi. 3, 13 (Kāṇva), where see Dviveda's note.

Atithi ('guest').—A hymn of the Atharvaveda[1] celebrates in detail the merits of hospitality. The guest should be fed before

[1] ix. 6.

the host eats, water should be offered to him, and so forth. The Taittirīya Upaniṣad[2] also lays stress on hospitality, using the expression 'one whose deity is his guest' (*atithi-deva*). In the Aitareya Āraṇyaka[3] it is said that only the good are deemed worthy of receiving hospitality. The guest-offering forms a regular part of the ritual,[4] and cows were regularly slain in honour of guests.[5]

[2] i. 11, 2.
[3] i. 1, 1.
[4] Śatapatha Brāhmaṇa, vii. 3, 2, 1.
[5] *Cf.* Bloomfield, *American Journal of Philology*, 17, 426; Hillebrandt, *Ritual-litteratur*, 79.

Atithi-gva.—This name occurs frequently in the Rigveda, apparently applying, in nearly all cases, to the same king, otherwise called **Divodāsa.** The identity of the two persons has been denied by Bergaigne,[1] but is certainly proved by a number of passages, when the two names occur together,[2] in connection with the defeat of **Śambara.** In other passages[3] Atithigva is said to have assisted Indra in slaying Parṇaya and Karañja. Sometimes he is only vaguely referred to, while once[5] he is mentioned as an enemy of Turvaśa and Yadu. Again[6] Atithigva is coupled with **Āyu** and **Kutsa** as defeated by **Tūrvayāṇa.**

A different Atithigva appears to be referred to in a Dānastuti[7] ('Praise of Gifts'), where his son, **Indrota,** is mentioned.

Roth[8] distinguishes three Atithigvas—the Atithigva Divodāsa, the enemy of Parṇaya and Karañja, and the enemy of Tūrvayāṇa. But the various passages can be reconciled, especially if it is admitted that Atithigva Divodāsa was already an ancient hero in the earliest hymns, and was becoming almost mythical.

[1] *Religion Védique*, 2, 342 *et seq.*
[2] Rv. i. 51, 6; 112, 14; 130, 7; iv. 26, 3; vi. 47, 22.
[3] Rv. i. 53, 8; x. 48, 8.
[4] Rv. vi. 26, 3.
[5] Rv. vii. 19, 8. There is no ground for assuming the reference here to be to a later Atithigva.
[6] Rv. i. 53, 10; ii. 14, 7; vi. 18, 13; viii. 53, 2.
[7] Rv. viii. 68, 16. 17.
[8] St. Petersburg Dictionary, *s.v.*
Cf. Ludwig, Translation of the Rigveda, 3, 123; Bloomfield, *American Journal of Philology*, 17, 426, who renders the name 'presenting cows to guests.'

Ati-dhanvan Śaunaka.—He is mentioned as a teacher in the Chāndogya Upaniṣad[1] and the Vaṃsa Brāhmaṇa.[2]

[1] i. 9, 3.
[2] *Indische Studien*, 4, 384.

A-tṛṇāda.—This term ('not eating grass') was applied, according to the Bṛhadāraṇyaka Upaniṣad, to a newborn calf.[1]

[1] i. 5, 2. *Cf.* Zimmer, *Altindisches Leben*, 268.

1. **Atka.**—This word occurs frequently in the Rigveda, but its sense is doubtful. Roth, Grassmann, Ludwig, Zimmer,[1] and others render it as 'garment' in several passages,[2] when the expressions 'put on' (*vyā* or *prati muñc*) or 'put off' (*muñc*) are used of it, and when it is said to be 'woven' (*vyuta*)[3] or 'well-fitting' (*surabhi*).[4] On the other hand, Pischel[5] denies that this sense occurs, and otherwise explains the passages. He takes the term to mean 'axe' in four places.[6]

[1] *Altindisches Leben*, 262.

[2] i. 95, 7; ii. 35, 14; iv. 18, 5; v. 55, 6; 74, 5; vi. 29, 3; viii. 41, 7; ix. 101, 14; 107, 13; Sāmaveda, ii. 1193.

[3] Rv. i. 122, 2.

[4] Rv. vi. 29, 3; x. 123, 7.

[5] *Vedische Studien*, 2, 193-204.

[6] Rv. v. 55, 6; vi. 33, 3; x. 49, 3; 99, 9. *Cf.* Oldenberg, *Ṛgveda-Noten*, 1, 94, n. 1.

2. **Atka.**—In two passages of the Rigveda[1] this word is regarded as a proper name by Roth, Grassmann, and Ludwig. But Zimmer[2] explains it in these passages as the 'armour of a warrior as a whole,' and Pischel[3] thinks that in both cases an 'axe' is meant.

[1] x. 49, 3; 99, 9.

[2] *Altindisches Leben*, 262, 297.

[3] *Vedische Studien*, 2, 195.

Aty-aṃhas Āruṇi.—According to the Taittirīya Brāhmaṇa (iii. 10, 9, 3-5), this teacher sent a pupil to question **Plakṣa Dayyāṃpati** as to the Sāvitra (a form of Agni). For this impertinence his pupil was severely rebuked.

Aty-arāti Jānaṃ-tapi, though not a prince, was taught the Rājasūya by **Vāsiṣṭha Satyahavya**, and thereupon conquered the earth. When Vāsiṣṭha reminded him of his indebtedness, and claimed a great reward, the warrior replied irascibly that he intended to conquer the **Uttara Kurus**, and that Vāsiṣṭha would then become King of the Earth, Atyarāti himself being his general (*senā-pati*). Vāsiṣṭha replied that as no mortal man could conquer the Uttara Kurus he was cheated of his reward.

He consequently procured Atyarāti's defeat and death at the hands of **Amitratapana Śuṣmiṇa Śaibya.**[1]

[1] Aitareya Brāhmaṇa, viii. 23. *Cf.* Weber, *Indische Studien*, 1, 214.

Atri.—Neither Atri himself nor the Atris can claim any historical reality,[1] beyond the fact that Maṇḍala V. of the Rigveda is attributed, no doubt correctly, to the family of the Atris.[2] The Atris as a family probably stood in close relations with the **Priyamedhas**[3] and **Kaṇvas,**[4] perhaps also with the **Gotamas**[5] and **Kākṣīvatas.**[6] The mention of both the **Paruṣṇī** and the **Yamunā** in one hymn[7] of the fifth Maṇḍala seems to justify the presumption that the family was spread over a wide extent of territory.

[1] For Atri in the Rigveda, see Macdonell, *Vedic Mythology*, 145. *Cf.* also Av. ii. 32, 3; iv. 29, 3; Mantra Brāhmaṇa, ii. 7, 1; Taittirīya Āraṇyaka, iv. 36, etc.; Bṛhadāraṇyaka Upaniṣad, ii. 2, 4.

[2] *Cf.* Rv. v. 39, 5; 67, 5; Kauṣītaki Brāhmaṇa, xxiv. 3; Aitareya Āraṇyaka, ii. 2, 1.

[3] *Cf.* Rv. i. 45, 3; 139, 9; viii. 5, 25; Aitareya Brāhmaṇa, viii. 22.

[4] *Cf.* Rv. i. 118, 7; v. 41, 4; x. 150, 5.

[5] *Cf.* Rv. i. 183, 5.

[6] *Cf.* Rv. x. 143, 1.

[7] Rv. v. 52, 9. 17. *Cf.* Ludwig, Translation of the Rigveda, 3, 128, 142; Bergaigne, *Religion Védique*, 2, 469; Oldenberg, *Zeitschrift der Deutschen Morgenländischen Gesellschaft*, 42, 212-215; Hillebrandt, *Vedische Mythologie*, 3, 310.

Atharī.—This word occurs only in the Rigveda,[1] and the sense is doubtful. Roth,[2] followed by most interpreters, renders it 'point of a lance,' but Pischel[3] thinks that it means 'an elephant.'

[1] iv. 6, 8.

[2] St. Petersburg Dictionary, *s.v.*

[3] *Vedische Studien*, 1, 99.

Atharvan.—The name in the singular denotes the head of a semi-divine family of mythical priests,[1] of whom nothing historical can be said. In the plural the family as a whole is meant. In a few places an actual family seems to be referred to. Thus, for instance, they are mentioned as recipients of gifts in the Dānastuti[2] ('Praise of Gifts'), of **Aśvattha's**

[1] See Macdonell, *Vedic Mythology*, 141. In the Vaṃśa of the Bṛhadāraṇyaka Upaniṣad, ii. 6, 3, Atharvan Daiva is characteristically the pupil of Mṛtyu.

[2] Rv. vi. 47, 24.

generosity; their use of milk mingled with honey in the ritual is referred to;[3] and a cow that miscarries (*ava-tokā*) from accident is dedicated to the Atharvans, according to the Taittirīya Brāhmaṇa.[4]

[3] Rv. ix. 11, 2.

[4] iii. 4, 11, 1. *Cf.* Vājasaneyi Saṃhitā, xxx. 15.

Cf. Bloomfield, *Hymns of the Atharvaveda*, xxxv. *et seq.*, who (p. xxxviii) takes *avatokā* as a woman, and the Atharvans as the hymns; Hillebrandt, *Vedische Mythologie*, 2, 174 *et seq.*

Atharvāṇaḥ.—This expression[1] is used with **Aṅgirasaḥ**, to denote the Atharvaveda. The compound **Atharvāṅgirasaḥ** is employed in the same sense.

[1] Taittirīya Brāhmaṇa, iii. 12, 9, 1; Pañcaviṃśa Brāhmaṇa, xvi. 10, 10; Śatapatha Brāhmaṇa, xiii. 4, 3, 5 *et seq.*

Atharvāṅgirasaḥ.—This is the collective name of the Atharvaveda in several passages[1] of the later Brāhmaṇas. It occurs once in the Atharvaveda itself,[2] while the term Atharvaveda is not found before the Sūtra period.[3] The compound seems, according to Bloomfield,[4] to denote the two elements which make up the Atharvaveda. The former part refers to the auspicious practices of the Veda (*bheṣajāni*);[5] the latter to its hostile witchcraft, the *yātu*[6] or *abhi-cāra*.[7] This theory is supported by the names of the two mythic personages **Ghora Āṅgirasa** and **Bhiṣaj Ātharvaṇa**, as well as by the connection of Atharvāṇaḥ and **Ātharvaṇāni** with healing (*bheṣaja*) in the Pañcaviṃśa Brāhmaṇa.[8] Moreover, the term *bheṣajā* ('remedies') designates in the Atharvaveda[9] that Veda itself, while in the Śatapatha Brāhmaṇa[10] *yātu* ('sorcery') conveys the same meaning. The evidence, however, being by no means convincing, it remains probable that there existed no clear differentiation between the two sages as responsible for the Atharvaveda as a whole.

[1] Taittirīya Brāhmaṇa, iii. 12, 8, 2; Taittirīya Āraṇyaka, ii. 9; 10; Śatapatha Brāhmaṇa, xi. 5, 6, 7; Bṛhadāraṇyaka Upaniṣad, ii. 4, 10; iv. 1, 2; 5, 11; Chāndogya Upaniṣad, iii. 4, 1. 2; Taittirīya Upaniṣad, ii. 3, 1.

[2] x. 7, 20.

[3] Śāṅkhāyana Srauta Sūtra, xvi. 2, 9, etc.

[4] *Journal of the American Oriental Society*, 11, 387 *et seq.*; *Hymns of the Atharvaveda*, xviii. *et seq.*

[5] Av. xi. 6, 14.

[6] Satapatha Brāhmaṇa, x. 5, 2, 20.

[7] Kauśika Sūtra, 3, 19.

[8] xii. 9, 10; xvi. 10, 10.

[9] x. 6, 14.

[10] x. 5. 2, 20.

Cf. Hillebrandt, *Vedische Mythologie*, 2, 177.

A-dṛṣṭa.—'The unseen' is a term used in the Rigveda[1] and the Atharvaveda[2] to designate a species of vermin. The sun is also described as 'the slayer of the unseen' (*adṛṣṭa-han*),[3] and as a counterpart a 'seen' (*dṛṣṭa*) is mentioned.[4] In one passage[5] the epithets 'seen' and 'unseen' are applied to the worm (**Kṛmi**), their use being no doubt due to the widespread theory of diseases being due to worms, whether discernable by examination or not.[6]

1 Rv. i. 191, 4=Av. vi. 52, 2.
2 vi. 52, 3.
3 Rv. i. 191, 9=Av. vi. 52, 1; Av. v. 23, 6.
4 Av. ii. 31, 2; viii. 8, 15.
5 Av. v. 23, 6. 7.
6 Kuhn, *Zeitschrift für vergleichende Sprachforschung*, 13, 135 *et seq.*; Bloomfield, *Hymns of the Atharvaveda*, 313-315; Zimmer, *Altindisches Leben*, 98.

Adma-sad.—This expression (*lit.* 'sitting at the meal'), found several times in the Rigveda,[1] is usually rendered 'guest at the feast,' but Geldner[2] adduces reasons to show that it means 'a fly,' so called because of its settling on food.

1 i. 124, 4; vi. 30, 3; vii. 83, 7; viii. 44, 29; *adma-sadvan*, vi. 4, 4.
2 *Vedische Studien*, 2, 179, 180; but *cf.* Oldenberg, *Vedaforschung*, 90.

Adri.—Zimmer[1] deduces from the use of this word ('rock,' 'stone') in a passage of the Rigveda,[2] that sling-stones were used in Vedic fighting. But the passage is mythical, referring to Indra's aid, and cannot be used with any certainty as evidence for human war. More probably it merely denotes Indra's bolt. See also **Aśani.**

1 *Altindisches Leben*, 301. *Cf.* Roth, St. Petersburg Dictionary, *s.v.*
2 i. 51, 3.

Adhi-devana.—The place where the dice were thrown is thus designated in the Atharvaveda[1] and the Śatapatha Brāhmaṇa,[2] according to Lüders.[3] Roth,[4] followed by Whitney, takes it to mean 'gambling-board.' See **Akṣa.**

1 v. 31, 6; vi. 70, 1.
2 v. 4, 4, 20. 22. 23.
3 *Das Würfelspiel im alten Indien*, 11-13.
4 St. Petersburg Dictionary, *s.v.*

Adhi-rāja.—The word occurs fairly often throughout the early literature,[1] denoting 'overlord' among kings or princes.

1 Rv. x. 128, 9; Av. vi. 98, 1; ix. 10, 24; Taittirīya Saṃhitā, ii. 4, 14, 2; Maitrāyaṇī Saṃhitā, iv. 12, 3; Kāṭhaka Saṃhitā, viii. 17; Taittirīya Brāhmaṇa, iii. 1, 2, 9 (*adhirājan*); Śatapatha Brāhmaṇa, v. 4, 2, 2; Nirukta, viii. 2.

In no passage is it clear that a real over-king is meant, as the word *rājan* may mean king or merely prince, a person of royal blood. On the whole it seems most probable that the word connotes no more than 'king' as opposed to 'prince.'

Adhi-ṣavaṇa.—The two Adhiṣavaṇas[1] are usually understood, as by Roth[2] and Zimmer,[3] to designate the two boards between which the Soma was pressed. Hillebrandt,[4] however, shows from the ritual that the boards were not placed one over the other, but were placed one behind the other, the two serving as a foundation upon which the Soma was pressed by a stone. This theory seems to account best for the etymological sense of the name 'over-press,' as well as for the use of the word as an adjective ('used for pressing *upon*'). But according to the procedure as witnessed by Haug[5] in the Deccan, the shoots of the plant are first placed on the skin, one of the boards being then laid over them and pounded with a stone. The shoots are then taken out and placed upon the board, the second board being then laid over them.

[1] Vājasaneyi Saṃhitā, xviii. 21; Av. v. 20, 10; Śatapatha Brāhmaṇa, iii. 9, 4, 1; 5, 3, 22 (*adhiṣavaṇe phalake*); Aitareya Brāhmaṇa, vii. 32 (*adhiṣavaṇaṃ carma*, 'the skin upon which the pressing takes place'; *adhiṣavaṇe phalake*, 'the boards on which the pressing takes place,' etc.).

[2] St. Petersburg Dictionary, *s.v.*

[3] *Altindisches Leben*, 277.

[4] *Vedische Mythologie*, 1, 148 *et seq.*

[5] See Haug, Aitareya Brāhmaṇa, 2, p. 488, n. 10.

Adhī-vāsa.—This word[1] denotes the 'upper garment' of the Vedic Indian. Its exact nature is not described, but as the king in the ritual set forth in the Śatapatha Brāhmaṇa[2] puts on first an undergarment, then a garment, and finally an upper garment it presumably denotes some sort of cloak or mantle.

[1] Rv. i. 140, 9; 162, 16; x. 5, 4; Śatapatha Brāhmaṇa, v. 3, 5, 22 (*pratimuñc*, 'put on'); 4, 4, 3 (*ā-stṛ*, 'spread out'), etc.

[2] v. 3, 5, 19 *et seq.* *Cf.* Zimmer, *Altindisches Leben*, 268.

Adhyāṇḍā.—This is a plant mentioned with many others in the Śatapatha Brāhmaṇa (xiii. 8, 1, 16).

Adhri-gu.—This is the name of a man twice referred to in the Rigveda[1] as a protégé of the Aśvins and of Indra respectively.

[1] i. 112, 20; viii. 12, 2. *Cf.* Hopkins, *Journal of the American Oriental Society*, 17, 90.

Adhvaryu.—In one passage of the Rigveda[1] Hillebrandt[2] thinks that the five Adhvaryus who are mentioned do not designate actual priests, but refer to the five planets which move about in the heavens like the Adhvaryu priests on the sacrificial ground. See also **Graha.**

[1] iii. 7, 7.

[2] *Vedische Mythologie*, 3, 423.

An-agni-dagdha, 'not burnt with fire.' See **Agni-dagdha,** 'burnt with fire.'

Anaḍ-vāh (lit. 'cart-drawer').—This is the common[1] name of oxen as employed for drawing carts (**Anas**). Such oxen were normally castrated,[2] though not always. Female draft cattle were also used (*anaḍuhī*), but rarely.[3] See also **Gō.**

[1] Rv. x. 59, 10; 85, 10; iii. 53, 18; Av. iii. 11, 5; iv. 11, 1, etc.; Aitareya Brāhmaṇa, i. 14; Śatapatha Brāhmaṇa, ii. 1, 4, 17, etc.

[2] *Cf.* Kātyāyana Śrauta Sūtra, xv. 1, 5 (*anaḍvān sāṇḍaḥ*).

[3] Av. iv. 11; Śatapatha Brāhmaṇa, v. 3, 4, 11. 13.

Cf. Weber, *Indische Studien*, 13, 151, n.; Zimmer, *Altindisches Leben*, 226.

Anas.—This is the term[1] used to designate the draft wagon, as opposed to the chariot (*ratha*) for war or sport, with which it is sometimes expressly contrasted,[2] though Indra is once said to be 'seated in a wagon' (*anar-viś*)[3] instead of on a chariot. Though Uṣas, Goddess of Dawn, sometimes rides on a chariot (*ratha*), the wagon is her characteristic vehicle.[4] Of its construction we know little. The bridal wagon on which Sūryā, the daughter of the Sun, was borne in the marriage hymn in the Rigveda had a covering (**Chadis**).[5] The axle-box (**Kha**) is also

[1] Rv. iv. 30, 10; x. 85, 10; 86, 18, etc.; Śatapatha Brāhmaṇa, i. 1, 2, 5, etc.; Chāndogya Upaniṣad, vii. 15, 1; Kauṣītaki Upaniṣad, iii. 8, etc.

[2] Rv. iii. 33, 9.

[3] Rv. i. 121, 7.

[4] Rv. ii. 15, 6; iv. 30, 11; viii. 91, 7; x. 73, 6; 138, 5.

[5] Rv. x. 85, 10.

mentioned.[6] In the Atharvaveda[7] Vipatha appears to denote a rough vehicle used for bad tracks. The wagon was usually drawn by oxen (**Anaḍvāh**), as in wedding processions.[8] The wagon of Dawn is described as drawn by ruddy cows or bulls.[9]

[6] Rv. viii. 91, 7; Jaiminīya Upaniṣad Brāhmaṇa, i. 3.

[7] xv. 2, 1.

[8] Rv. x. 85, 11.

[9] Macdonell, *Vedic Mythology*, 47. *Cf.* Zimmer, *Altindisches Leben*, 246; Geldner, *Vedische Studien*, 2, 4.

Anās. See **Dasyu.**

Anitabhā in the Rigveda[1] is taken by Max Müller[2] to denote some river.

[1] v. 53, 9.

[2] *Sacred Books of the East*, 32, 323; but *cf.* **Rasā.**

Anu, Ānava.—Grassmann and Roth[1] see in these words designations of people foreign to the Aryans. But it is clear[2] that they denote a special people, the Anus, who are mentioned with the **Yadus, Turvaśas, Druhyus,** and **Pūrus,**[3] with the Druhyus,[4] and with the Turvaśas, Yadus, and Druhyus.[5] It is also a fair conclusion from their mention in a passage of the Rigveda[6] that they dwelt on the Paruṣṇī. The inference that the Bhṛgus were connected with this tribe is much more doubtful,[7] for it rests solely on the fact that in one place[8] the Bhṛgus and Druhyus are mentioned together, and not Anus and Druhyus. Ānava is used as an epithet of Agni,[9] but also in the sense of 'Anu prince,'[10] in one case in conjunction with Turvaśa.[11]

[1] St. Petersburg Dictionary.

[2] Zimmer, *Altindisches Leben*, 125.

[3] Rv. i. 108, 8.

[4] Rv. vii. 18, 14.

[5] viii. 10, 5.

[6] Rv. viii. 74, 15, compared with vii. 18, 14.

[7] Oldenberg, *Zeitschrift der Deutschen Morgenländischen Gesellschaft*, 42, 221, n. 1.

[8] Rv. vii. 18, 4.

[9] Rv. viii. 74, 4. *Cf.* Rv. v. 31, 4, where the Anus prepare the chariot of the Aśvins.

[10] Rv. vii. 18, 13.

[11] viii. 4, 1. Apparently as prince also in vi. 62, 9. *Cf.* **Kuruṅga.**

Cf. Ludwig, Translation of the Rigveda, 3, 205; Hillebrandt, *Vedische Mythologie*, 3, 153; Macdonell, *Sanskrit Literature*, 154.

Anu-kṣattṛ.—This word occurs in the list of victims at the Puruṣamedha,[1] and means, according to Mahīdhara,[2] 'an attendant on the door-keeper,' and, according to Sāyaṇa, 'an attendant on the charioteer' (*sārathi*). See also **Kṣattṛ.**

[1] Vājasaneyi Saṃhitā, xxx. 11; 73; Taittirīya Brāhmaṇa, iii. 4, 9, 1.

[2] On Vājasaneyi Saṃhitā, *loc. cit.*

[3] On Taittirīya Brāhmaṇa, *loc. cit.*

Anu-cara.—This is a general expression[1] for an 'attendant' (the feminine being Anucarī),[2] but it is not often used.

[1] Vājasaneyi Saṃhitā, xxx. 13; Taittirīya Brāhmaṇa, iii. 4, 7, 1.
[2] Satapatha Brāhmaṇa, xiii. 5, 4, 27 (apparently slave girls are meant, 400 being enumerated).

Anu-mati. See **Māsa.**

Anu-rādhā. See **Nakṣatra.**

Anu-vaktṛ Satya Sātya-kīrta is mentioned as a teacher in the Jaiminīya Brāhmaṇa Upaniṣad (i. 5, 4).

Anuvyā-khyāna is a species of writing referred to in the Bṛhadāraṇyaka Upaniṣad.[1] Śaṅkara interprets it as 'explanation of the Mantras.' As the term, in the plural, follows **Sūtras,** this interpretation is reasonable. Sieg,[2] however, equates the word with **Anvākhyāna,** 'supplementary narrative.'

[1] ii. 4, 10; iv. 1, 2; 5, 11.
[2] *Die Sagenstoffe des Ṛgveda*, 34.

Anu-śāsana in the plural denotes in the Śatapatha Brāhmaṇa (xi. 5, 6, 8) some form of literature; according to Sāyaṇa, the Vedāṅgas.

Anu-śikha is the name of the Potṛ at the snake festival in the Pañcaviṃśa Brāhmaṇa.[1]

[1] xxv. 15. *Cf.* Weber, *Indische Studien*, 1, 35.

Ante-vāsin, 'dwelling near,' is the epithet of the **Brahmacārin** who lives in the house of his teacher. The expression does not occur before the late Brāhmaṇa period.[1] Secrecy is often enjoined on others than Antevāsins.[2]

[1] Satapatha Brāhmaṇa, v. 1, 5, 17; Bṛhadāraṇyaka Upaniṣad, vi. 3, 7; Chāndogya Upaniṣad, iii. 11, 5; iv. 10, 1; Taittirīya Upaniṣad, i. 3, 3; 11, 1.
[2] Aitareya Āraṇyaka, iii. 2, 6; Sāṅkhāyana Āraṇyaka, viii. 11.

Andhra is the name of a people, and is mentioned with the **Puṇḍras, Śabaras, Pulindas,** and **Mūtibas,** as being the outcasts resulting from the refusal of the fifty eldest sons of **Viśvāmitra** to accept his adoption of **Śunaḥśepa.**[1] It may fairly be deduced

[1] Aitareya Brāhmaṇa, vii. 18; Śāṅkhāyana Śrauta Sūtra, xv. 26, where instead of *udāntyaḥ* ('beyond the borders') the reading is *udañcaḥ* ('northern'), but the former is obviously correct. The Śāṅkhāyana omits the Pulindas, and has Mūcīpas.

from this statement that these people were recognized as non-Aryan, as the Andhras certainly seem to have been.[2]

[2] Vincent Smith, *Zeitschrift der Deutschen Morgenländischen Gesellschaft*, 56, 657 *et seq.*, who places them originally in Eastern India between the Kṛṣṇā and Godāvarī rivers; *cf.* Rapson, *Catalogue of Indian Coins*, xv., xvi.; Bhandarkar, *Bombay Gazetteer*, I. ii. 138.

Anyataḥ-plakṣā ('with wave-leafed fig-trees on one side only') is the name of a lake in Kurukṣetra according to the Śatapatha Brāhmaṇa,[1] where it occurs in the story of Purūravas and Urvaśī. Pischel[2] places it somewhere in Sirmor.

[1] xi. 5, 1, 4.

[2] *Vedische Studien*, 2, 217.

Anya-vāpa ('sowing for others').—The cuckoo is so called[1] from its habit of depositing its eggs in the nests of other birds.

[1] Vājasaneyi Saṃhitā, xxiv. 37; Maitrāyaṇī Saṃhitā, iii. 14, 18.

Anvā-khyāna.—From the literal translation ('after-story') the meaning of 'supplementary narrative' seems to follow. In two[1] of its three occurrences in the Śatapatha Brāhmaṇa this sense is hardly felt, the expression being used to indicate a subsequent portion of the book itself. But in the third[2] passage it is distinguished from the **Itihāsa** ('story') proper, and there must mean 'supplementary narrative.' *Cf.* **Anuvyākhyāna.**

[1] vi. 5, 2, 22; 6, 4, 7 (the reference is to vi. 6, 4, 8).

[2] xi. 1, 6, 9.
Cf. Sieg, *Die Sagenstoffe des Ṛgveda*, 34.

Apa-cit.—This word occurs several times in the Atharvaveda.[1] It is held by Roth,[2] Zimmer,[3] and others to denote an insect whose sting produced swellings, etc. (*glau*). But Bloomfield[4] shows that the disease, scrofulous swellings, is what is really meant, as is shown by the rendering (*gaṇḍa-mālā*, 'inflammation of the glands of the neck') of Keśava and Sāyaṇa, and by the parallelism of the later disease, *apacī*, the derivation being from *apa* and *ci*, 'to pick off.'

[1] vi. 25, 1; 83, 1; vii. 75, 1; 77, 1.

[2] St. Petersburg Dictionary, *s.v.*

[3] *Altindisches Leben*, 97. So also Ludwig, Translation of the Rigveda, 342, 500.

[4] *American Journal of Philology*, 11, 320 *et seq.*; *Hymns of the Atharvaveda*, 503, 504. *Cf.* Jolly, *Medicin*, 89; Whitney, Translation of the Atharvaveda, 343.

Apa-śraya. See **Upaśraya.**

Apa-skambha.—The word occurs only in one passage of the Atharvaveda, where the tip of it is mentioned as poisoned. Roth[1] suggests that the fastening of the arrow-point to the shaft is meant. Whitney[2] inclines to this version, but suggests corruption of text. Zimmer[3] follows Roth. Ludwig[4] renders the word by 'barb.' Bloomfield[5] thinks it means 'tearing (arrow),' a sense deduced from the etymology.

[1] St. Petersburg Dictionary, *s.v.* The passage is Av. iv. 6, 4.

[2] Translation of the Atharvaveda, 153.

[3] *Altindisches Leben*, 300.

[4] Translation of the Rigveda, 3, 512.

[5] *Hymns of the Atharvaveda*, 375.

Apācyas.—The kings of the 'Westerners' are referred to in the Aitareya Brāhmaṇa (viii. 14) in connection with those of the **Nīcyas.**

Apāna.—The word appears repeatedly in the Atharvaveda,[1] and later as one of the vital breaths (**Prāṇa**), usually with Prāṇa, and often with one or more of the other three. Its original sense[2] appears to have been 'inspiration.' Its connection with the lower part of the body (*nābhi*, 'navel'), which is found already in the Aitareya Upaniṣad,[3] is not unnatural.

[1] Av. ii. 28, 3; v. 30, 12, etc.; Vājasaneyi Saṃhitā, xiii. 19; 24, etc.

[2] See Caland, *Zeitschrift der Deutschen Morgenländischen Gesellschaft*, lv. 261; 56, 556-558, correcting Ewing, *Journal of the American Oriental Society*, 22, 249 *et seq.*

[3] Aitareya Upaniṣad, i. 4, etc. *Cf.* Deussen, *Philosophy of the Upanishads*, 263 *et seq.*

Apā-mārga.—A plant (*Achyranthes aspera*) used frequently[1] in witchcraft practices, and for medical purposes, especially against **Kṣetriya.** It is described in the Atharvaveda[2] as 'revertive' (*punaḥ-sara*), either, as Roth[3] and Zimmer[4] think, because of its having reverted leaves (a view also accepted by Whitney[5]),

[1] Atharvaveda, iv. 17, 6; 18, 7; 19, 4; vii. 65, 2; Vājasaneyi Saṃhitā, xxxv. 11; Taittirīya Brāhmaṇa, i. 7, 1, 8; Śatapatha Brāhmaṇa, v. 2, 4, 14; xiii. 8, 4, 4.

[2] iv. 17, 2.

[3] St. Petersburg Dictionary, *s.v.*

[4] *Altindisches Leben*, 67.

[5] Translation of the Atharvaveda, 180.

or because, as Bloomfield[6] holds, it wards off a spell by causing it to recoil on its user.

[6] *Hymns of the Atharvaveda*, 394. *Cf.* Bloomfield, *Journal of the American Oriental Society*, 15, 160, 161; Weber, *Indische Studien*, 18, 94.

Apā-lamba.—By this word[1] is denoted a brake or drag, let down (from *lamb*, 'hang down') to check the speed of a **wagon.**

[1] Satapatha Brāhmaṇa, iii. 3, 4, 13. *Cf.* Caland and Henry, *L'Agniṣṭoma*, 50; Roth, St. Petersburg Dictionary, *s.v.*; Eggeling, *Sacred Books of the East*, 26, 79.

Apāṣṭha.—This word occurs twice in the Atharvaveda,[1] denoting the barb of an arrow.

[1] iv. 6, 5; v. 18, 7 (*śatāpāṣṭha*, 'hundred-barbed'). *Cf.* Zimmer, *Altindisches Leben*, 300; Bloomfield, *Hymns of the Atharvaveda*, 375.

Api-śarvara. See **Ahan.**

Apī.—Ludwig[1] finds an Apī whose sons are described as not performing sacrifice (*a-yajña-sāc*) and as breakers of the law of Mitra-Varuṇa in the Rigveda.[2] Roth[3] and Grassmann take the expression used (*apyaḥ putrāḥ*) as referring to the sons of the waters.

[1] Translation of the Rigveda, 3, 158, 159.

[2] vi. 67, 9.

[3] St. Petersburg Dictionary, *s.v.*, *apya.*

Apūpa is the general word from the Rigveda[1] onwards for a cake, which might be mixed with ghee (*ghṛtavant*),[2] or be made of rice (*vrīhi*),[3] or of barley (*yava*).[4] In the Chāndogya Upaniṣad[5] there is a difference of interpretation. Max Müller renders it as 'hive,' Böhtlingk as 'honeycomb,' Little[6] as 'cake.'

[1] iii. 52, 7.

[2] Rv. x. 45, 9.

[3] Śatapatha Brāhmaṇa, ii. 2, 3, 12. 13.

[4] Śatapatha Brāhmaṇa, iv. 2, 5, 19.

[5] iii. 1, 1.

[6] *Grammatical Index*, *s.v.*

Apnavāna appears only twice in the Rigveda[1] as an ancient sage, coupled with the Bhṛgus, to whose family Ludwig[2] conjectures him to have belonged.

[1] iv. 7, 1; viii. 91, 4.

[2] Translation of the Rigveda, 3, 128.

A-prati-ratha ('he who has no match in fight') is the name of an obviously invented Ṛṣi, to whom is ascribed by the Aitareya Brāhmaṇa[1] and Śatapatha Brāhmaṇa[2] the composition of a Rigveda hymn[3] celebrating Indra as the invincible warrior.

[1] viii. 10. [2] ix. 2, 3, 1. 5. [3] x. 103.

Apvā.—A disease affecting the stomach,[1] possibly dysentery, as suggested by Zimmer,[2] on the ground that the disease is invoked to confound the enemy.[3] Weber[4] considers that it is diarrhœa induced by fear, as often in the Epic.[5] This view is supported by Bloomfield,[6] and was apparently that of Yāska.[7]

[1] Av. ix. 8, 9.
[2] *Altindisches Leben*, 389.
[3] Rv. x. 103, 12=Av. iii. 2, 5= Sāmaveda, ii. 1211=Vājasaneyi Saṃhitā, xvii. 44.
[4] *Indische Studien*, 9, 482; 17, 184.
[5] *Indische Studien*, 17, 184.
[6] *Hymns of the Atharvaveda*, 327.
[7] Nirukta, ix. 33.
Cf. Whitney, Translation of the Atharvaveda, 86, 87.

Apsas.—This word usually refers to the body, meaning 'front part.'[1] In one passage of the Rigveda,[2] however, the adjective 'with a long front part' (*dīrghāpsas*) is applied to the chariot (**Ratha**).

[1] See Pischel, *Vedische Studien*, 1, 308-313; 2, 245, 246.
[2] i. 122, 15. *Cf.* Roth, St. Petersburg Dictionary, *s.v.*

Abhi-krośaka designates one of the victims in the Puruṣamedha, meaning, perhaps, 'herald.' The commentator Mahīdhara[1] renders it as 'reviler' (*nindaka*).

[1] Vājasaneyi Saṃhitā, xxx. 20. *Cf.* Anukrośaka, Taittirīya Brāhmaṇa, iii. 4, 15, 1.

Abhi-jit. See **Nakṣatra.**

Abhi-pitva. See **Ahan.**

Abhi-pratārin Kākṣa-seni is mentioned in the Jaiminīya Upaniṣad Brāhmaṇa,[1] the Chāndogya Upaniṣad,[2] and the Pañcaviṃśa Brāhmaṇa,[3] as engaged in discussions on philosophy. The Jaiminīya Brāhmaṇa[4] further reports that his sons divided the property amongst themselves while he was yet alive. He was a Kuru and a prince.

[1] i. 59, 1; iii. 1, 21; 2, 2. 13.
[2] iv. 3, 5.
[3] x. 5, 7; xiv. 1, 12. 15.
[4] iii. 156 (*Journal of the American Oriental Society*, 26, 61).

Abhi-praśnin.—This term occurs after **Praśnin**, and followed by **Praśnavivāka** in the list of victims for the Puruṣamedha given in the Taittirīya Brāhmaṇa[1] and the Vājasaneyi Saṃhitā.[2] The commentators, Sāyaṇa and Mahīdhara, see in it merely a reference to an inquisitive man. But there can be little doubt that the term must have had a legal reference of some sort—perhaps indicating the defendant as opposed to plaintiff and judge.

[1] iii. 4, 6, 1.

[2] xxx. 10.

Abhi-śrī ('admixture').—This word[1] designates the milk used to mingle with the Soma juice before it was offered.

[1] Rv. ix. 79, 5; 86. 27. *Cf.* Zimmer, *Altindisches Leben*, 227; Hillebrandt, *Vedische Mythologie*, i. 211.

Abhi-ṣavaṇī. — Zimmer[1] renders the expression in the Atharvaveda[2] as a pressing instrument, but it appears to be merely an adjective, (waters) 'used in pressing.'[3]

[1] *Altindisches Leben*, 277.

[2] ix. 6, 16.

[3] *Cf.* Whitney's Translation of Av. ix. 6, 16.

Abhi-ṣeka ('besprinkling').—The Vedic king was consecrated after his election with an elaborate ritual, which is fully described in the Taittirīya,[1] Pañcaviṃśa,[2] Śatapatha,[3] and Aitareya Brāhmaṇas,[4] and for which the Mantras are given in the Saṃhitās.[5] The consecration took place by sprinkling with water (*abhiṣecanīyā āpaḥ*).[6] Only kings could be consecrated, the people not being worthy of it (*anabhiṣecanīyāḥ*).[7] The sprinkler (*abhiṣektṛ*) is mentioned in the list of victims at the Puruṣamedha.[8] The Abhiṣeka is an essential part of the **Rājasūya**, or sacrifice of royal inauguration, being the second of its component members.

[1] i. 7, 5.

[2] xviii. 8 *et seq.*

[3] v. 3, 3 *et seq.*

[4] viii. 5 *et seq.*

[5] Taittirīya Saṃhitā, i. 8, 11; Kāṭhaka Saṃhitā, xv. 6; Maitrāyaṇī Saṃhitā, ii. 6; Vājasaneyi Saṃhitā, x. 1-4.

[6] Śatapatha Brāhmaṇa, v. 3, 5, 10-15.

[7] Śatapatha Brāhmaṇa, xiii. 4, 2, 17.

[8] Vājasaneyi Saṃhitā, xxx. 12; Taittirīya Brāhmaṇa, iii. 4, 8, 1.

[9] *Cf.* Hillebrandt, *Rituallitteratur*, 143-147; Eggeling, *Sacred Books of the East*, 41, xxvi; Weber, *Über den Rājasūya.*

Abhīśu is a common Vedic word[1] denoting the 'reins' or 'bridle' of the chariot horses. The use of the plural is due to the fact that two or four horses, possibly five (*daśābhīśu* 'ten-bridled'),[2] were yoked to the car.

[1] Rv. i. 38, 12; v. 44, 4; vi. 75, 6; viii. 33, 11; Av. vi. 137, 2; viii. 8, 22; Vājasaneyi Saṃhitā, xxxiv. 6; Śatapatha Brāhmaṇa, v. 4, 3, 14 (where it =*raśmayaḥ*, 'reins'), etc.

[2] Rv. x. 94, 7.

Abhy-agni Aitaśāyana.—This man was, according to the Aitareya Brāhmaṇa,[1] unfortunate enough to quarrel with his father, **Aitaśa.** The result was that he and his progeny were called the worst of the **Aurvas.** In the version of the Kauṣītaki Brāhmaṇa,[2] the **Aitaśāyana Ājāneyas** take the place of the Abhyagnis and the **Bhṛgus** of the **Aurvas,** the latter being probably a branch of the former family.

[1] vi. 33.

[2] xxx. 5. *Cf.* Hillebrandt, *Vedische Mythologie*, 2, 173.

Abhyā-vartin Cāyamāna appears in a Dānastuti (' Praise of Gifts ') in the Rigveda,[1] and as conqueror of the Vṛcīvants under the leader **Varaśikha.** It is probable, though not absolutely certain, that he is identical with the **Sṛñjaya Daivavāta,** mentioned in the same hymn[2] as having the **Turvaśas** and **Vṛcīvants** defeated for him by Indra. In this case he would be prince (*samrāj*) of the Sṛñjayas. Daivavāta is mentioned elsewhere[3] as a worshipper of Agni.

Abhyāvartin is also referred to as a Pārthava. Ludwig[4] and Hillebrandt[5] maintained that he is thus a Parthian, the latter using the evidence of the two places mentioned in the description[6] of Daivavāta's victories, **Hariyūpīyā** and **Yavyāvatī,** as proofs for the western position of Abhyāvartin's people in Arachosia, in Iran. But Zimmer[7] is probably right in holding that the name Pārthava merely means ' a descendant of Pṛthu,' and that its similarity to the Iranian Parthians is only on a par with the numerous other points of identity between the Indian and Iranian cultures.

[1] vi. 27, 8. 5.

[2] vi. 27, 7.

[3] iv. 15, 4.

[4] Translation of the Rigveda, 3, 198 *et seq.*

[5] *Vedische Mythologie*, 1, 105; 3, 268, n. 1. *Cf.* Grierson, *Journal of the Royal Asiatic Society*, 1908, 604 *et seq.*

[6] Rv. vi. 27, 5. 6.

[7] *Altindisches Leben*, 133 *et seq.*, 433; Bergaigne, *Religion Védique*, 2, 362.

A-bhrātaraḥ ('brotherless').—The lot of girls without brothers is referred to in the Rigveda[1] as unsatisfactory—apparently they became prostitutes. The Nirukta[2] expressly forbids marriage with a brotherless maiden, probably because of the risk of her being made a *putrikā* ('adoptive daughter') by her father—that is, any son of hers being counted as belonging to her father's, instead of to her husband's, family. See **Ayogū.**

[1] i. 124, 7; iv. 5, 5. *Cf.* Av. i. 17, 1.
[2] iii. 5 (*abhrātrī*).
Cf. Bloomfield, *Hymns of the Atharvaveda*, 259; Zimmer, *Altindisches Leben*, 328.

Abhri ('spade') is a Vedic word[1] of frequent occurrence. Various possible materials and forms are enumerated in the Śatapatha Brāhmaṇa.[2] It may be made of bamboo or of the wood of Vikaṅkata or Udumbara. It may be a span or a cubit in size. It is hollow, and either one or both edges are sharp. From this it would appear that the handle was made of some wood, but the head of some metal.

[1] Av. iv. 7, 5. 6 (*abhri-khāte* is 'dug out with a spade,' not 'prepared ground' with Roth, St. Petersburg Dictionary, *s.v.*); x. 4, 14; *hiraṇyayībhir abhribhiḥ*, 'with golden spades'); Vājasaneyi Saṃhitā, v. 22; xi. 10; xxxvii. 1; Pañcaviṃśa Brāhmaṇa, xvi. 6; Śatapatha Brāhmaṇa, ii. 3, 2, 15, etc.
[2] vi. 3, 1, 30 *et seq.*

Amatra was a vessel into which the Soma, after being pressed, was poured,[1] and out of which the libation to the god was made.[2]

[1] Rv. ii. 14, 1; v. 51, 4; vi. 42, 2, etc.
[2] Rv. x. 29, 7.
Cf. Zimmer, *Altindisches Leben*, 278; Oldenberg, *Ṛgveda Noten*, 1, 61.

Amalā.—This plant[1] is probably the *Emblica officinalis*, or Myrobalan tree; also called **Āmalaka**, or **Āmalakā.**[2]

[1] Jaiminīya Upaniṣad Brāhmaṇa, i. 38, 6.
[2] The reading in Chāndogya Upaniṣad, vii. 3, 1, is *vāmalake*, which may give *ă*° or *ā*°.

Amā-jur is an epithet[1] denoting maidens 'who grow old at home' without finding husbands, or, as they are elsewhere called, 'who sit with their father' (*pitṛ-ṣad*). A well-known example of such was Ghoṣā.[2]

[1] Rv. ii. 17, 7; viii. 21, 15; x 37, 3.
[2] Rv. i. 117, 7. *Cf.* Zimmer, *Altindisches Leben*, 305.

Amā-vāsya Śāṇḍilyāyana is mentioned in the Vaṃśa Brāhmaṇa[1] as the teacher of **Aṃśu Dhānaṃjayya.**

[1] *Indische Studien*, iv, 373.

Amitra-tapana Śuṣmiṇa Śaibya is the name of him who killed **Atyarāti Jānaṃtapi,** according to the Aitareya Brāhmaṇa (viii. 23).

A-mūlā ('without root') is the name in the Atharvaveda[1] of a plant (*Methonica superba*), which was used for poisoning arrows. Bloomfield,[2] however, renders it as 'movable property.'

[1] v. 31 4. *Cf.* Weber, *Indische Studien*, 18, 286; Whitney, Translation of the Atharvaveda, 279, accepts 'rootless (plant).'

[2] *Hymns of the Atharvaveda*, 457.

Ambarīṣa is mentioned as a Vārṣāgira in the Rigveda[1] along with **Ṛjrāśva, Sahadeva, Surādhas,** and **Bhayamāna.**

[1] i. 100, 17. *Cf.* Ludwig, Translation of the Rigveda, 3, 140.

Ambaṣṭha. See **Āmbaṣṭhya.**

Aya. See **Akṣa.**

Ayas.—The exact metal denoted by this word when used by itself, as always in the Rigveda,[1] is uncertain. As favouring the sense of 'bronze' rather than that of 'iron' may perhaps be cited with Zimmer[2] the fact that Agni is called *ayo-daṃṣṭra*, 'with teeth of Ayas,'[3] with reference to the colour of his flames, and that the car-seat of Mitra and Varuṇa is called *ayaḥ-sthūṇa*,[4] 'with pillars of Ayas' at the setting of the sun.[5] Moreover, in the Vājasaneyi Saṃhitā,[6] Ayas is enumerated in a list of six metals: gold (*hiraṇya*), Ayas, Śyāma, Loha, lead (*sīsa*), tin (*trapu*). Here *śyāma* ('swarthy') and *loha* ('red') must mean 'iron' and 'copper' respectively; *ayas* would therefore seem to mean 'bronze.' In many passages in the Atharvaveda[7] and

[1] Rv. i. 57, 3; 163, 9; iv. 2, 17; vi 3, 5.

[2] *Altindisches Leben*, 52.

[3] Rv. i. 88, 5; x. 87, 2.

[4] Rv. v. 62, 8 (*cf.* 7).

[5] But this is not convincing, as in the same verse it is said to be 'of golden appearance at the flush of dawn.'

[6] xviii. 13.

[7] xi. 3, 1. 7; Maitrāyaṇī Saṃhitā, iv. 2, 9.

other books, the Ayas is divided into two species—the *śyāma* ('iron') and the *lohita* ('copper' or 'bronze'). In the Śatapatha Brāhmaṇa[8] a distinction is drawn between Ayas and *lohāyasa*, which may either be a distinction between iron and copper as understood by Eggeling,[9] or between copper and bronze as held by Schrader.[10] In one passage of the Atharvaveda,[11] the sense of iron seems certain. Possibly, too, the arrow of the Rigveda,[12] which had a tip of Ayas (*yasyā ayo mukham*), was pointed with iron. Copper, however, is conceivable, and bronze quite likely.

Iron is called *śyāma ayas* or *śyāma* alone.[13] See also **Kārṣṇāyasa**. Copper is **Lohāyasa** or **Lohitāyasa**.

The smelting (*dhmā* 'to blow') of the metal is frequently referred to. The Śatapatha Brāhmaṇa[14] states that if 'well smelted' (*bahu-dhmātam*) it is like gold, referring evidently to bronze. A heater of Ayas is mentioned in the Vājasaneyi Saṃhitā,[15] and bowls of Ayas are also spoken of.[16]

[8] v. 4, 1, 2.
[9] *Sacred Books of the East*, 41, 90.
[10] *Prehistoric Antiquities*, 189.
[11] v. 28, 1.
[12] vi. 75, 15.
[13] Av. ix. 5, 4.
[14] vi. 1, 3, 5. *Cf.* vi. 1, 1, 13; v. 1, 2, 14; xii. 7, 1, 7; 2, 10, etc.
[15] xxx. 14; Taittirīya Brāhmaṇa, iii. 4, 10, 1.
[16] Av. viii. 10, 22; Maitrāyaṇī Saṃhitā, iv. 2, 13.

Aya-sthūṇa.—He was Gṛhapati ('householder,' the sacrificer at sacrificial sessions) of those whose Adhvaryu was Śaulvāyana, and taught the latter the proper mode of using certain spoons.[1]

[1] Śatapatha Brāhmaṇa, xi. 4, 2, 17 *et seq.*

Ayāsya Āṅgirasa.—This sage appears to be mentioned in two passages of the Rigveda,[1] and the Anukramaṇī ascribes to him several hymns of the Rigveda (ix. 44-46; x. 67; 68). In the Brāhmaṇa tradition he was Udgātṛ at the Rājasūya or Royal Inauguration Sacrifice, at which Śunaḥśepa was to have been slain, and his Udgītha (Sāmaveda chant) is referred to elsewhere.[3] He is also referred to several times as a ritual

[1] x. 67, 1; 108, 8. Perhaps x. 92, 15 also refers to him, but not i. 62, 7; x. 138, 4.
[2] Aitareya Brāhmaṇa, vii. 16.
[3] Jaiminīya Upaniṣad Brāhmaṇa, ii. 7, 2. 6; 8, 3. *Cf.* Chāndogya Upaniṣad, i. 2, 12.

authority.[4] In the Vaṃśas, or Genealogies of the Bṛhadāraṇyaka Upaniṣad,[5] he is named as the pupil of Ābhūti Tvāṣṭra.

[4] Pañcaviṃśa Brāhmaṇa, xiv. 3, 22; xvi. 12, 4; xi. 8, 10; Bṛhadāraṇyaka Upaniṣad, i. 3, 8. 19. 24; Kauṣitaki Brāhmaṇa, xxx. 6.
[5] ii. 6, 3; iv. 6, 3 (in both recensions).

Cf. Ludwig, Translation of the Rigveda, 3, 136; Hillebrandt, *Vedische Mythologie*, 2, 159; Weber, *Indische Studien*, 1, 255, n.; Pischel, *Vedische Studien*, 3, 204.

Ayogū is a word of quite doubtful meaning, found in the list of victims in the Vājasaneyi Saṃhitā.[1] It may, like the late *āyogava*, denote a member of a mixed caste (theoretically a descendant of a Śūdra by a Vaiśya wife).[2] Weber[3] rendered it as 'unchaste woman.'[4] Zimmer thinks it denotes a brotherless maiden who is exposed to the dangers of prostitution (*cf.* *āyogava*).

[1] xxx. 5; Taittirīya Brāhmaṇa, iii. 4, 1, 1.
[2] St. Petersburg Dictionary, *s.v.*
[3] *Indische Streifen*, 1, 76, n. b. In the *Zeitschrift der Deutschen Morgenländischen Gesellschaft*, 18, 277, he thought it referred to dicing (*ayas*). Risley, *Peoples of India*, 250, regards the Āyogavas as a functional caste of carpenters (*cf.* Manu, x. 48).
[4] *Altindisches Leben*, 328.

Ara. See **Ratha.**

Araṭu.—A plant[1] (*Colosanthes Indica*) from the wood of which the axle of a chariot was sometimes made.[2]

[1] Av. xx. 131, 17.
[2] Rv. viii. 46, 27.

Cf. Zimmer, *Altindisches Leben*, 62, 247.

Araṇya.—This term denotes the uncultivated land—not necessarily forest land—beyond the village. It is contrasted with home (*amā*),[1] and with the plough land (*kṛṣi*),[2] being spoken of as apart (*tiras*) from men.[3] It is also contrasted with the **Grāma**,[4] and it is the place where thieves live.[5] The character of the forest is described in a hymn of the Rigveda[6] to the forest spirit (Araṇyānī). The dead are carried there for burial,[7] and hermits live there.[8] Forest fires were common.[9]

[1] Rv. vi. 24, 10.
[2] Av. ii. 4, 5.
[3] Śatapatha Brāhmaṇa, xiii. 6, 2, 20.
[4] Av. xii. 1, 56; Rv. i. 163, 11; Vājasaneyi Saṃhitā, iii. 45; xx. 17.
[5] Śatapatha Brāhmaṇa, v. 2, 3, 5; xiii. 2, 4, 4.
[6] x. 146.
[7] Bṛhadāraṇyaka Upaniṣad, v. 11.
[8] Chāndogya Upaniṣad, viii. 5, 3.
[9] Rv. i. 65, 4; 94, 10. 11; ii. 14, 2; x. 92, 1; 142, 4; Av. vii. 50, etc.

Cf. Zimmer, *Altindisches Leben*, 48, 142.

Aratni.—This word, which primarily means 'elbow,' occurs frequently from the Rigveda[1] onwards as denoting a measure of length ('ell' or 'cubit'), the distance from the elbow to the tip of the hand. The exact length nowhere appears from the early texts.

[1] Rv. viii. 80, 8; Av. xix. 57, 6; Aitareya Brāhmaṇa, viii. 5; Satapatha Brāhmaṇa, vi. 3, 1, 33, etc. For Rv. viii. 80, 8, see also **Āji**.

A-rājānaḥ, 'not princes,' is a term used to describe persons in two passages of the Śatapatha Brāhmaṇa,[1] and in the Aitareya Brāhmaṇa.[2] Weber[3] also finds them mentioned in the Atharvaveda,[4] and thinks that they—**Sūtas** ('charioteers') and **Grāmaṇīs** ('troop-leaders') there referred to—were called thus because, while not themselves princes, they assisted in the consecration of princes.

[1] iii. 4, 1, 7. 8; xiii. 4, 2, 17.
[2] viii. 23.
[3] *Indische Studien*, 17, 199.
[4] iii. 5, 7, where he emends *rājānaḥ* to *a-rājānaḥ* (see Whitney's note on the passage). *Cf.* Bloomfield, *Hymns of the Atharvaveda*, 333; Weber, *Über den Rājasūya*, 22 *et seq.*

Arāṭakī is a plant mentioned once in the Atharvaveda,[1] and apparently identical with the **Ajaśṛṅgī**. *Cf.* also **Araṭu**.

[1] iv. 37, 6.
Cf. Zimmer, *Altindisches Leben*, 68; Bloomfield, *Hymns of the Atharvaveda*, 408.

Arāḍa Dātreya Śaunaka.—He is mentioned in the Vaṃśa Brāhmaṇa[1] as the pupil of **Dṛti Aindrota Śaunaka.**

[1] *Indische Studien*, 4, 384.

Aritra denotes the 'oar' by which boats were propelled. The Rigveda[1] and the Vājasaneyi Saṃhitā[2] speak of a vessel with a hundred oars, and a boat (*nau*) is said to be 'propelled by oars' (*aritra-paraṇa*).[3] In two passages of the Rigveda[4] the term, according to the St. Petersburg Dictionary, denotes a part of a chariot. The rower of a boat is called *aritṛ*.[5] See **Nau**.

[1] i. 116, 5.
[2] xxi. 7.
[3] Rv. x. 101, 2. *Cf.* Śatapatha Brāhmaṇa, iv. 2, 5, 10.
[4] i. 46, 8; *daśāritra*, ii. 18, 1.
[5] Rv. ii. 42, 1; ix. 95, 2.
Cf. Zimmer, *Altindisches Leben*, 256.

Ariṃ-dama Sana-śruta is mentioned as a Mahārāja in the Aitareya Brāhmaṇa, vii. 34.

Arim-ejaya is mentioned as one who served as Adhvaryu at the snake feast celebrated in the Pañcaviṃśa Brāhmaṇa.[1]

[1] xxv. 15. See Weber, *Indische Studien*, 1, 35.

Aruṇa Āṭa was Achāvāka at the snake feast in the Pañcaviṃśa Brāhmaṇa (xxv. 15).

Aruṇa Aupaveśi Gautama is the full style[1] of a teacher, who is repeatedly referred to in the later Saṃhitās[2] and Brāhmaṇas,[3] and whose son was the famous **Uddālaka Āruṇi.** He was a pupil of Upaveśa,[4] and a contemporary of the prince **Aśvapati,** by whom he was instructed. *Cf.* **Āruṇa.**

[1] Taittirīya Saṃhitā, vi. 1, 9, 2; 4, 5, 1; Maitrāyaṇī Saṃhitā, i. 4, 10; iii. 6, 4. 6; 7, 4; 8, 6; 10, 5; Kāṭhaka Saṃhitā, xxvi. 10.

[2] Taittirīya Brāhmaṇa, ii. 1, 5, 11; Satapatha Brāhmaṇa, ii. 2, 2, 20; xi. 4, 1, 4; 5, 3, 2.

[3] Bṛhadāraṇyaka Upaniṣad, vi. 5, 3 (in both recensions).

[4] Śatapatha Brāhmaṇa, x. 6, 1, 2. *Cf.* Geldner, *Vedische Studien*, 3, 146, n. 4.

1. **Arundhatī** is the name of a plant celebrated in several passages of the Atharvaveda[1] as possessing healing properties in case of wounds, as a febrifuge, and as inducing cows to give milk. The plant was a climber which attached itself to trees like the **Plakṣa, Aśvattha, Nyagrodha,** and **Parṇa.**[2] It was of golden colour (*hiraṇya-varṇā*), and had a hairy stem (*lomaśa-vakṣaṇā*).[3] It was also called Silācī, and the **Lākṣā** appears to have been a product of it.[4]

[1] iv. 12, 1; v. 5, 5. 9; vi. 59, 1. 2; viii. 7, 6; xix. 38, 1.

[2] Av. v. 5, 5.

[3] Av. v. 5, 7; Pischel, *Vedische Studien*, 1, 174; Bloomfield, *Zeitschrift der Deutschen Morgenländischen Gesellschaft*, 48, 574.

[4] *Cf.* Whitney's note on Av. iv. 12; Bloomfield, *Atharvaveda*, 61.

2. **Arundhatī,** as the name of a star, is often referred to in the Sūtra literature, but only once in a late Āraṇyaka.[1]

[1] Taittirīya Āraṇyaka, iii. 9, 2.

Arka, as the name of the tree *Colotropis gigantea*, is perhaps found in one obscure passage of the Atharvaveda.[1]

[1] vi. 72, 1, where see Whitney's note. *Cf.* St. Petersburg Dictionary, *s.v.*

Argala.—The word which is usual later to denote the wooden pin of a door is found in the Śāṅkhāyana Āraṇyaka (ii. 16) in the compound *argaleṣīke* to denote the pin and bar of the door of a cow-pen. *Cf.* **Iṣīkā.**

Argala Kāhoḍi is mentioned in the Kāṭhaka Samhitā (xxv. 7) as a teacher. The name may, however, be Aryala, as suggested in the St. Petersburg Dictionary, *s.v.*, and as read by v. Schroeder in his edition. The Kapiṣṭhala (xxxix. 5) has Ayala. See below.

Arcant is possibly, as Ludwig[1] thinks, the name of the author of a hymn of the Rigveda[2]; but the word may be merely the ordinary participle 'praising.'

[1] Translation of the Rigveda, 3, 133.

[2] x. 149, 5.

Arcanānas.—In one passage of the Rigveda[1] the gods Mitra-Varuṇa are besought to protect Arcanānas. He is also invoked with **Śyāvāśva** and several other ancestors enumerated in the Atharvaveda.[2] He appears as father of Śyāvāśva in the Pañcaviṃśa Brāhmaṇa.[3] The later tradition makes him play a part in the legend of his son's wedding, which Sieg[4] endeavours to show is known to the Rigveda.

[1] v. 64, 7.

[2] xviii. 3, 15.

[3] viii. 5, 9.

[4] *Die Sagenstoffe des Ṛgveda*, 50 *et seq.* *Cf.* Ludwig, Translation of the Rigveda, 3, 127; Oldenberg, *Ṛgveda-Noten*, 1, 354.

Arcā. See **Brāhmaṇa.**

Arjunī is, in the Rigveda,[1] the name of the **Nakṣatra** ('lunar mansion'), elsewhere[2] called Phalgunī. It occurs in the marriage hymn, with **Aghā** for Maghā, and, like that word, is apparently a deliberate modification.

[1] x. 85, 13.

[2] Av. xiv. 1, 13. *Cf.* Śatapatha Brāhmaṇa, ii. 1, 11, 2.

Arbuda is mentioned as Grāvastut priest at the snake festival described in the Pañcaviṃśa Brāhmaṇa.[1] He is obviously the same mythical figure as Arbuda Kādraveya, a seer spoken of in the Aitareya[2] and Kauṣītaki Brāhmaṇas[3] as a maker of Mantras.

[1] xxv. 15.
[2] vi. 1.
[3] xxix. 1. *Cf.* Śatapatha Brāhmaṇa, xiii. 4, 3, 9.

Arya.—This word is not common in the older literature, in places where the quantity of the first vowel is fixed as short, except in a mere adjectival sense. Geldner,[1] indeed, contends that no other sense is anywhere needed; but Roth[2] and Zimmer[3] agree in thinking that in several passages of the Vājasaneyi Saṃhitā[4] the word has the same sense as **Ārya**, and this appears probable. Whether it is necessary to ascribe this sense to the word in the compound *arya-patnī*[5] applied to the waters set free by Indra, is more doubtful. The commentator, Mahīdhara,[6] suggests that the word means a **Vaiśya**, not an Ārya generally. This view is supported by the explanation in the Śatapatha Brāhmaṇa[7] of one of the passages of the Vājasaneyi Saṃhitā.[8] But though the use of Arya to denote a Vaiśya became common later, it is not clear that it was original.

[1] *Vedische Studien*, 3, 96.
[2] St. Petersburg Dictionary, *s.v.*
[3] *Altindisches Leben*, 214, 215.
[4] xiv. 30; xx. 17; xxiii. 21; xxvi. 2. *Cf.* also Kāṭhaka Saṃhitā, xxxviii. 5; Taittirīya Saṃhitā, vii. 4, 19, 3. In Atharvaveda, xix. 32, 8, an analogous form occurs, as contrasted with *brāhmaṇa*, *rājanya*, and *śūdra*; but even there Whitney renders it as 'Āryan.' *Cf.* xix. 62, 1; Rv. viii. 94, 3; Pischel, *Zeitschrift der Deutschen Morgenländischen Gesellschaft*, 40, 125.
[5] Rv. vii. 6, 5; x. 43, 8.
[6] On Vājasaneyi Saṃhitā, xxiii. 30.
[7] xiii. 2, 9, 8. Contrast Śāṅkhāyana Srauta Sūtra, xvi. 4, 4 *et seq.*, where Arya appears to be taken in the wider sense.
[8] xxiii. 30. *Cf.* Ludwig, Translation of the Rigveda, 3, 212; Weber, *Indische Studien*, x. 6; Oldenberg, *Ṛgveda-Noten*, 1, 126, 363.

Aryamṇaḥ Panthā, 'Aryaman's Way,' an expression which occurs in the Brāhmaṇas,[1] denotes, according to Weber,[2] 'the milky way,' but, according to Hillebrandt,[3] 'the ecliptic.'

[1] Taittirīya Brāhmaṇa, i. 7, 6, 6; Pañcaviṃśa Brāhmaṇa, xxv. 12, 3; Śatapatha Brāhmaṇa, v. 3, 1, 2.
[2] *Über den Rājasūya*, 48, 2.
[3] *Vedische Mythologie*, 3, 79, 80.

Aryala.—Those at whose snake feast the Gṛhapati was Aryala, and the Hotṛ was **Āruṇi** are mentioned in the Pañcaviṃśa Brāhmaṇa (xxiii. 1, 5). See also **Argala.**

Arvant. See **Aśva.**

Arśas is the name of a disease mentioned in the Vājasaneyi Saṃhitā[1] with consumption and other ailments. It appears to designate 'hæmorrhoids,' as in the later medical literature.

[1] xii. 98.
Cf. Zimmer, *Altindisches Leben*, 398; Roth, St. Petersburg Dictionary, *s.v.*

Alaja designates some kind of bird—one of the victims in the Aśvamedha,[1] or Horse Sacrifice.

[1] Taittirīya Saṃhitā, v. 4, 11, 1; 5, 20, 1; Maitrāyaṇī Saṃhitā, iii. 14, 18; Kāṭhaka Saṃhitā, xxi. 4; Vājasaneyi Saṃhitā, xxiv. 34.

Alaji is the name of a disease in the Atharvaveda.[1] The later *alajī* denotes an eye-disease—a discharge at the junction of the cornea and the sclerotica.

[1] ix. 8, 20. *Cf.* Zimmer, *Altindisches Leben*, 390; St. Petersburg Dictionary, *s.v.*

Alamma Pārijānata is mentioned in the Pañcaviṃśa Brāhmaṇa (xiii. 4, 11; 10, 8) as a sage.

Alasālā.—This word occurring only in one passage of the Atharvaveda (vi. 16, 4) is said to denote a grain-creeper.

Alāṇḍu.—This is the reading in the text of the Atharvaveda[1] of the name of a species of worm. Bloomfield[2] shows reason to adopt the reading Algaṇḍu as the correct form of the word.

[1] ii. 31, 2.
[2] *Hymns of the Atharvaveda*, 315.

Alābu.—The bottle-gourd (*Lagenaria vulgaris*). Vessels made of it are referred to in the Atharvaveda.[1]

[1] viii. 10, 29. 30; xx. 132, 1. 2. *Cf. alāpu* in Maitrāyaṇī Saṃhitā, iv. 2, 13.

Alāyya is a word occurring in an obscure verse of the Rigveda,[1] and appearing to be a proper name. Hillebrandt,[2] however, amends the text so as to remove the name. The St. Petersburg Dictionary suggests that it refers to Indra. Pischel[3] holds that

[1] ix. 67, 20.
[2] *Zeitschrift der Deutschen Morgenländischen Gesellschaft*, 48, 418.
[3] *Zeitschrift der Deutschen Morgenländischen Gesellschaft*, 48, 701.

it is the name of a person whose axe was stolen, and for whom the hymn was written as a spell for the recovery of the axe.

Aliklava is a kind of carrion bird mentioned in the Atharvaveda.[1]

[1] xi. 2, 2; 9, 9. *Cf.* Zimmer, *Altindisches Leben*, 88.

Alina is the name of a people mentioned once only in the Rigveda.[1] Roth[2] thought that the Alinas were allies—possibly a subdivision—of the **Tṛtsus.** Ludwig[3] more probably thinks that they were defeated by **Sudās,** together with the **Pakthas, Bhalānas, Śivas,** and **Viṣāṇins,** with whom they are mentioned, at the **Paruṣṇī**; and Zimmer[4] suggests that they lived to the north-east of Kafiristan.

[1] vii. 18, 7.

[2] *Zur Litteratur und Geschichte des Weda*, 95; Zimmer, *Altindisches Leben*, 126.

[3] Translation of the Rigveda, 3, 207.

[4] *Op. cit.*, 431. The land is mentioned by Hiouen Thsang.

Alīkayu Vācas-patya is twice mentioned as an authority in the Kauṣītaki Brāhmaṇa (xxvi. 5; xxviii. 4).

Alpa-śayu is a kind of insect mentioned in the Atharvaveda.[1]

[1] iv. 36, 9.
Cf. Bloomfield, *Hymns of the Atharvaveda*, 408; Whitney, Translation of the Atharvaveda, 210.

Avakā is an aquatic plant (*Blyxa octandra*) frequently referred to in the Atharvaveda as well as in the later Saṃhitās[2] and Brāhmaṇas.[3] The Gandharvas are said to eat it.[4] Its later name is *śaivala*, and it is identical with the **Śīpāla.**

[1] viii. 7, 9; 37, 8-10.

[2] Taittirīya Saṃhitā, iv. 6, 1, 1; v. 4, 2, 1; 4, 3; Vājasaneyi Saṃhitā, xvii. 4; xxv. 1; Maitrāyaṇī Saṃhitā, ii. 10, 1.

[3] Śatapatha Brāhmaṇa, vii. 5, 1, 11; viii. 3, 2, 5; ix. 1, 2, 20. 22; xiii. 8, 3, 13.

[4] Av. iv. 37, 8.

[5] With which it is glossed in Āśvalāyana Gṛhya Sūtra, ii. 8; iv. 4. *Cf.* Bloomfield, *Proceedings of the American Oriental Society*, October, 1890, xli.-xliii.; *American Journal of Philology*, 11, 349; Zimmer, *Altindisches Leben*, 71.

Avata, a word occurring several times in the Rigveda,[1] denotes a well, artificially made (*khan* 'to dig') in contrast with a spring

[1] i. 55, 8; 85, 10. 11; 116, 9. 22; 130, 2; iv. 17, 16; 50, 3; viii. 49, 6; 62, 6; 72, 10. 12; x. 25, 4; 101, 5. 7. *Cf.* Nirukta, v. 26.

(*utsa*), though the latter expression is also applied to an artificial well. Such wells were covered by the makers,[2] and are described as unfailing (*a-kṣita*) and full of water.[3] The water was raised by a wheel (*cakra*) of stone, to which was fastened a strap (*varatrā*), with a pail (*kośa*)[4] attached to it. When raised it was poured (*siñc*) into buckets (*āhāva*) of wood.[5] Sometimes those wells appear to have been used for irrigation purposes, the water being led off into broad channels (*sūrmī suṣirā*).[6]

² Rv. i. 55, 8.
³ Rv. x. 101, 6, etc.
⁴ *Aṃsatra-kośam*, Rv. x. 101, 7, is best thus rendered. For the stone wheel (*aśma-cakra*) which was above (*uccā-cakra*), see Rv. x. 101, 7; viii. 72, 10. For the *varatrā*, see Rv. x. 101, 6. Perhaps *kū-cakra* in Rv. x. 102, 11, is another name for the wheel, but *cf.* St. Petersburg Dictionary, *s.v.*
⁵ Rv. x. 101, 6. 7.
⁶ Rv. viii. 69, 12. *Cf.* Zimmer, *Altindisches Leben*, 156, 157; Geldner, *Vedische Studien*, 2, 14.

Avatsāra is mentioned as a seer in the Rigveda,[1] as a priest in the Aitareya Brāhmaṇa,[2] and as Prāsravaṇa (or Prāśravaṇa), son of Prasravaṇa, in the Kauṣītaki Brāhmaṇa.[3] A hymn of the Rigveda[4] is incorrectly ascribed to him in the Anukramaṇī.

¹ v. 44, 10.
² ii. 24.
³ xiii. 3.
⁴ ix. 58. *Cf.* Ludwig, Translation of the Rigveda, 3, 138; Weber, *Indische Studien*, 1, 188; 2, 315; Sieg, *Die Sagenstoffe des Ṛgveda*, 62 *et seq*

A-vadhyatā. See **Brāhmaṇa.**

Avasa in the adjective *an-avasa* in the Rigveda[1] may mean 'drag.'

¹ vi. 66, 7. *Cf.* Max Müller, *Sacred Books of the East*, 32, 372.

Ava-skava.—A kind of worm, mentioned along with others in the Atharvaveda.[1]

¹ ii. 31, 4. *Cf.* Whitney, *ad loc.*; Weber, *Indische Studien*, 13, 201; Zimmer, *Altindisches Leben*, 90; Bloomfield, *Hymns of the Atharvaveda*, 316.

Avāta. See **Vāta.**

Avi.—'Sheep' are repeatedly mentioned in the Rigveda, and later, often in conjunction with goats (*aja*). The wolf (*vṛka*) was their great enemy,[1] and they were tended by shepherds.[2]

¹ Av. v. 8, 4; Rv. viii. 34, 3; 66, 8.
² *Avi-pāla*, Vājasaneyi Saṃhitā, xxx. 11; Śatapatha Brāhmaṇa, iv. 1, 5, 2; *avi-pa*, Taittirīya Brāhmaṇa, iii. 4, 9, 1.

Sheep as well as kine were captured from the enemy.[3] The Soma sieve was made of sheep's wool, and is repeatedly referred to (*avi, meṣī, avya, avyaya*).[4] Considerable herds must have existed, as Ṛjrāśva is said[5] to have slain one hundred rams, and in a Dānastuti ('Praise of Gifts')[6] a hundred sheep are mentioned as a gift. The (*meṣa*,[7] *vṛṣṇi*[8]) ram was sometimes castrated (*petva*).[9] The main use of sheep was their wool; hence the expression 'woolly' (*ūrṇāvatī*)[10] is employed to designate a sheep. In the Vājasaneyi Saṃhitā[11] the ram is described as 'woolly,' and as 'the skin of beasts, quadruped and biped,' with reference to the use of its wool as clothing for men and shelter for animals. Pūṣan is said[12] to weave raiment from the wool of sheep. Normally the sheep stayed out at pasture; in an obscure passage of the Rigveda[13] reference appears to be made to rams in stall. Gandhāra[14] ewes were famous for their wool. Pischel[15] considers that the **Paruṣṇī**[16] was named from its richness in sheep, *parus*[17] denoting the 'flocks' of wool.

3 Rv. viii. 86, 2.

4 Rv. ix. 109, 16; 36, 4, etc. See Hillebrandt, *Vedische Mythologie*, 1, 203.

5 Rv. i. 116, 17.

6 Rv. viii. 67, 3.

7 Rv. i. 43, 6; 116, 16, etc.

8 Taittirīya Saṃhitā, ii. 3, 7, 4, etc.

9 Rv. vii. 18, 17; Av. iv. 4, 8; Taittirīya Saṃhitā, v. 5, 22, 1; Vājasaneyi Saṃhitā, xxix. 58; 59.

10 Rv. viii. 67, 3. *Cf.* x. 75, 8; so *urā*, x. 95, 3.

11 xiii. 50.

12 Rv. x. 26, 6.

13 x. 106, 5.

14 Rv. i. 126, 7.

15 *Vedische Studien*, 2, 210.

16 Rv. iv. 22, 2; v. 52, 9.

17 Rv. ix. 15, 6; *parvan*, iv. 22, 2. *Cf.* Zimmer, *Altindisches Leben*, 229, 230; Oldenberg, *Ṛgveda-Noten*, 1, 348.

Aśani.—Zimmer[1] cites this word from the Rigveda[2] as denoting a sling stone, and compares a similar use of **Adri.**[3] In either case, however, the weapons are mythical, being used in descriptions of Indra's deeds. Schrader[4] also cites *aśan* in this sense, but no Vedic passage requires this sense.

1 *Altindisches Leben*, 301.

2 vi. 6, 5. *Cf.* 1, 121, 9.

3 i. 51, 3.

4 *Prehistoric Antiquities*, 221.

Aśma-gandhā ('rock-smell') is a plant mentioned in the Śatapatha Brāhmaṇa,[1] probably identical with the late *aśva-gandhā*, 'horse-smell' (*Physalis flexuosa*).

1 xiii. 8, 1, 16, with Eggeling's note in the *Sacred Books of the East*, 44, 427.

Aśva is the commonest word for 'horse' in the Vedic literature. The horse is also called 'the runner' (*atya*), 'the swift' (*arvant*), 'the strong,' for pulling (*vājin*), 'the runner' (*sapti*), and 'the speeding' (*haya*). The mare is termed *aśvā, atyā, arvatī, vaḍavā*, etc. Horses of various colour were known, dun (*harita, hari*), ruddy (*aruṇa, aruṣa, piśaṅga, rohita*), dark brown (*śyāva*), white (*śveta*), etc. A white horse with black ears is mentioned in the Atharvaveda as of special value.[1] Horses were highly prized,[2] and were not rare, as Roth[3] thought, for as many as four hundred mares are mentioned in one Dānastuti ('Praise of Gifts').[4] They were on occasion ornamented with pearls and gold.[5]

Mares were preferred for drawing chariots because of their swiftness and sureness.[6] They were also used for drawing carts, but were not ordinarily so employed.[7] No mention is made of riding in battle, but for other purposes it was not unknown.[8]

Horses were often kept in stalls,[9] and fed there.[10] But they were also allowed to go out to grass,[11] and were then hobbled.[12] They were watered to cool them after racing.[13] Their attendants

[1] Av. v. 17, 15.

[2] Rv. i. 83, 1; iv. 32, 17; v. 4, 11; viii. 78, 2, etc.

[3] *Zeitschrift der Deutschen Morgenländischen Gesellschaft*, 35, 686.

[4] Rv. viii. 55, 3. *Cf.* v. 33, 8; vi. 47, 22-24; 63, 10; viii. 6, 47; 46, 22, and Hopkins, *American Journal of Philology*, 15, 157.

[5] Rv. x. 68, 11.

[6] Pischel, *Zeitschrift der Deutschen Morgenländischen Gesellschaft*, 35, 712-714; *Vedische Studien*, 1, 10, 305. *Cf. ratho vadhūmān*, Rv. i. 126, 3; vii. 18, 22, *vājinīvān*, vii. 69, 1.

[7] Śatapatha Brāhmaṇa, v. 5, 4, 35.

[8] The Aśvins ride, Rv. v. 61, 1-3. An *aśva-sāda* is referred to in Vājasaneyi Saṃhitā, xxx. 13; Taittirīya Brāhmaṇa, iii. 4, 7, 1; and riding is meant in Rv. i. 162, 17; 163, 9. Av. xi. 10, 24. is doubtful. *Cf.* Hopkins, *Journal of the American Oriental Society*, 13, 262; Ludwig, Translation of the Rigveda, 3, 221. Zimmer, *Altindisches Leben*, 230, denies the use; but see p. 295, where it is admitted for ordinary purposes.

[9] *Cf.* the epithet of richness, 'filling the stalls with horses' (*aśva-pastya*), in Rv. ix. 86, 41, and see Av. vi. 77, 1; xix. 55, 1.

[10] Av. *loc. cit.*

[11] Zimmer, *op. cit.*, 232, denies this, but it is the natural sense of the Vājasaneyi Saṃhitā, xv. 41.

[12] The expression for this is *paḍbīśa*, Rv. i. 162, 14. 16; Bṛhadāraṇyaka Upaniṣad, vi. 2, 13; Chāndogya Upaniṣad, v. 1, 12; Śāṅkhāyana Āraṇyaka, ix. 7. *Cf.* Pischel, *Vedische Studien*, 1, 234-236.

[13] Rv. ii. 13, 5; 34, 3; Maitrāyaṇī Saṃhitā, i. 11, 6; Pischel, *op. cit.*, 1, 189, 190.

are frequently referred to (*aśva-pāla*,[14] *aśva-pa*,[15] *aśva-pati*).[16] Stallions were frequently castrated (*vadhri*).[17]

Besides reins (*raśmayaḥ*), reference is made to halters (*aśvābhidhānī*),[18] and whips (*aśvājanī*).[19] See also **Ratha.**

Horses from the Indus were of special value,[20] as also horses from the **Sarasvatī.**

[14] Śāṅkhāyana Srauta Sūtra, xvi. 4, 5.

[15] Vājasaneyi Saṃhitā, xxx. 11; Taittirīya Brāhmaṇa, iii. 4, 9, 1.

[16] Vājasaneyi Saṃhitā, xvi. 24; Kāṭhaka Saṃhitā, xvii. 13.

[17] Rv. viii. 46, 30.

[18] Av. iv. 36, 10; v. 14, 6; Aitareya Brāhmaṇa, vi. 35; Śatapatha Brāhmaṇa, vi. 3, 1, 26; xiii. 1, 2, 1.

[19] Rv. v. 62, 7; vi. 75, 13; Vājasaneyi Saṃhitā, xxix. 50.

[20] Bṛhadāraṇyaka Upaniṣad, vi. 2, 13; Śāṅkhāyana Āraṇyaka, ix. 7; *vājinīvatī* as epithet of Sindhu, Rv. x. 75, 8, of Sarasvatī, i. 3, 10; ii. 41, 18; vi. 61, 3. 4; vii. 96, 3; Pischel, *op. cit.*, i. 10. *Cf.* Zimmer, *op. cit.*, 230-232.

Aśva-tara, Aśva-tarī are respectively the masculine and feminine name of 'mule.' These animals are mentioned frequently from the Atharvaveda[1] onwards. They were known not to be fruitful,[2] and were probably considered inferior to horses,[3] but a mule-car was quite common.[4]

[1] iv. 4, 8; viii. 8, 22; Aitareya Brāhmaṇa, iii. 47; iv. 9; Śatapatha Brāhmaṇa, xii. 4, 1, 10, etc.; Jaiminīya Upaniṣad Brāhmaṇa, i. 4, 4.

[2] Taittirīya Saṃhitā, vii. 1, 1, 2. 3. *Cf.* Adbhutá Brāhmaṇa in *Indische Studien*, 1, 40.

[3] As were asses, Taittirīya Saṃhitā, v. 1, 2, 2; Satapatha Brāhmaṇa, vi. 4, 4, 7.

[4] Aitareya Brāhmaṇa, iv. 9; Chāndogya Upaniṣad, iv. 2, 1 (in both passages *aśvatarī-ratha*). *Cf.* Oertel, *Transactions of the Connecticut Academy of Arts and Sciences*, 15, 175.

1. **Aśva-ttha** ('horse-stand') is one of India's greatest trees, the *Ficus religiosa*, later called *pippala*[1] (now Peepal). Vessels made of the wood of the Aśvattha are mentioned in the Rigveda,[2] and the tree itself is constantly referred to later.[3] Its hard wood formed the upper of the two pieces of wood used for kindling fire, the lower being of **Śamī.**[4] It planted its roots in shoots of other trees, especially the **Khadira,** and destroyed them;[5] hence it is called 'the destroyer' (*vaibādha*). Its berries

[1] The word *pippala* as a neuter occurs once in the Rv. (i. 164, 20) designating the berry of the Peepal-tree.

[2] i. 135, 8; x. 97, 5.

[3] Atharvaveda, iii. 6, 1; iv. 37, 4, etc.

[4] Av. vi. 11, 1; Śatapatha Brāhmaṇa, xi. 5, 1, 13.

[5] Av. iii. 6.

are referred to as sweet, and as eaten by birds.[6] The gods are said to sit under it in the third heaven.[7] It and **Nyagrodha** are styled the 'crested ones' (*śikhaṇḍin*).[8]

[6] Rv. i. 164, 20. 22.
[7] Av. v. 4, 3. *Cf.* Chāndogya Upaniṣad, viii. 5, 3; Kauṣītaki Upaniṣad, i. 3.
[8] Av. iv. 37, 4. *Cf.* Zimmer, *Altindisches Leben*, 57, 58.

2. **Aśva-ttha.**—This prince is celebrated in a Dānastuti[1] as having given gifts to Pāyu. He is identified with **Divodāsa** by Griffith,[2] but it is impossible to be certain of this identification.

[1] Rv. vi. 47, 24.
[2] *Hymns of the Rigveda*, 1, 611. The name is spelt Aśvatha in the text, but that is merely the usual shortened spelling of the group *tth*.

Aśva-dāvan.—Ludwig[1] finds a prince of this name in a passage of the Rigveda,[2] where a gift of fifty horses is mentioned, but the word appears to be an epithet of Indra ('bestower of horses').

[1] Translation of the Rigveda, 3, 274.
[2] v. 18, 3.

Aśva-pati ('lord of horses') is a name of a prince of the **Kekayas**, who instructed **Prācīnaśāla** and other Brahmins.[1]

[1] Chāndogya Upaniṣad, v. 11, 4; Satapatha Brāhmaṇa, x. 6, 1, 2.

Aśva-medha ('offering a horse-sacrifice') is a prince mentioned in a hymn of the Rigveda,[1] which contains a Dānastuti ('Praise of Gifts') of **Tryaruṇa**, and to which three verses have been added in praise of Aśvamedha. See also **Āśvamedha.**

[1] v. 27, 4-6. *Cf.* Ludwig, Translation of the Rigveda, 3, 275.

Aśva-yujau. See **Nakṣatra.**

Aśvala, the Hotṛ priest of **Janaka**, King of **Videha**, appears as an authority in the Bṛhadāraṇyaka Upaniṣad (iii. 1, 2. 10).

Aśva-vāra, Aśva-vāla ('hair of a horse's tail').—The former form occurs in the Maitrāyaṇī Saṃhitā,[1] the latter in the

[1] iii. 7, 9.

Kāṭhaka [2] and Kapiṣṭhala Saṃhitās [3] and Śatapatha Brāhmaṇa,[4] denoting a species of reed (*Saccharum spontaneum*).

[2] xxiv. 8.
[3] xxxviii. 1.
[4] iii. 4, 1, 7. *Cf.* Von Schroeder's edition of the Maitrāyaṇī Saṃhitā, i., p. xv.

Aśva-sūkti is the name of a seer to whom the Rigveda Anukramaṇī ascribes two hymns of the Rigveda.[1] The Pañcaviṃśa Brāhmaṇa [2] knows a Sāman of Aśvasūkti.

[1] viii. 14; 15.
[2] xix. 4, 10. *Cf.* Oldenberg, *Zeitschrift der Deutschen Morgenländischen Gesellschaft*, 42, 230, n. 4.

Aśvinī. See **Nakṣatra.**

Aṣāḍha Kaiśin is the name of a man referred to in a corrupt and obscure passage of the Kāṭhaka Saṃhitā [1] as connected with the defeat of the **Pañcālas** by the **Kuntis.**

[1] xxvi. 9; Kapiṣṭhala, xli. 7. See Weber, *Indische Studien*, 3. 471.

Aṣāḍha Uttara Pārāśarya is mentioned as a teacher in a Vaṃśa or Genealogy in the Jaiminīya Upaniṣad Brāhmaṇa (iii. 41, 1).

Aṣāḍhā. See **Nakṣatra.**

Aṣāḍhi Sauśromateya was a man who is stated in the Śatapatha Brāhmaṇa (vi. 2, 1, 37) to have died because the heads for the sacrifice in connection with the laying of the bricks of the fire-altar had been obtained in an improper manner.

Aṣṭaka is mentioned in the Aitareya Brāhmaṇa [1] as one of the sons of **Viśvāmitra.**

[1] vii. 17. Also in the Sāṅkhāyana Srauta Sūtra, xv. 26.

Aṣṭakā. See **Māsa.**

Aṣṭa-karṇī is an expression which occurs in one passage of the Rigveda,[1] and which Roth [2] was at first inclined to interpret

[1] x. 62, 7.
[2] St. Petersburg Dictionary, *s. v.*

as a proper name. There can, however, be no doubt that it means a cow, not a man, as suggested by Grassmann. The exact reason why a cow should be so described is uncertain. Roth[3] was later inclined to see in it the sense 'having pierced ears,' similar epithets being at a later period known to Pāṇini[4] (*bhinna-karṇa*, *chinna-karṇa*). Grassmann's more obvious rendering, 'having the sign for (the number) 8 marked on the ear,' is supported by the similar epithets, 'having the mark of a lute on the ear' (*karkari-karṇyaḥ*), 'having the mark of a sickle on the ear' (*dātra-karṇyaḥ*), 'having the mark of a stake on the ear' (*sthūṇā-karṇyaḥ*), 'having the ears bored' (*chidra-karṇyaḥ*), and *viṣṭya-karṇyaḥ*, given in the Maitrāyaṇī Saṃhitā.[5] The simple meaning, 'with marked ears,' is, however, supported by the same passage of the Maitrāyaṇī, where the verb *akṣ* occurs in the sense 'to mark.' In the Atharvaveda the mark used is the Mithuna, no doubt as a magical device to secure fertility.

The marking of ears was apparently a regular practice. It is twice referred to in the Atharvaveda.[6] The mark is termed *lakṣman*,[7] and was made with a copper-knife[8] (*lohita*). The Maitrayaṇī Saṃhitā[9] forbids the use of an arrow-shaft (*tejana*), or of iron, but permits that of a stem of sugar-cane (*ikṣu-kāṇḍa*) or copper.

[3] *Cf.* Böhtlingk, Dictionary, *s.v.*
[4] vi. 3, 115.
[5] iv. 2, 9.
[6] vi. 141, 1. 2 ; xii. 4, 6.
[7] Av. vi. 141, 2 ; Maitrāyaṇī Saṃhitā, *loc. cit.*
[8] Av., *loc. cit.*
[9] *Loc. cit.*
Cf. Zimmer, *Altindisches Leben*, 234, 348 ; Delbrück, *Gurupūjākaumudī*, 48, 49 ; Weber, *Indische Studien*, 13, 466 ; Whitney, Translation of the Atharvaveda, 387.

Aṣṭā-daṃṣṭra Vairūpa.—To him the Pañcaviṃśa Brāhmaṇa (viii. 9, 21) ascribes two Sāmans.

Aṣṭrā is the plougher's 'goad,' the badge of agriculture. It is mentioned several times in the Rigveda.[1]

[1] iv. 57, 4 ; vi. 53, 9 ; 58, 2 ; *aṣṭrā-vin* occurs in x. 102, 8. See also Kauśika Sūtra, 80. *Cf.* Roscher, *Archiv für Religionswissenschaft*, 1, 63 ; Hillebrandt, *Vedische Mythologie*, 3, 364, n. 8.

Asamāti Rātha-prauṣṭha.—The story of the quarrel between Asamāti, the Ikṣvāku prince of the Rathaproṣṭha family, and his priests, the Gaupāyanas, is found only in the later Brāhmaṇas.[1] It appears to be based on a misreading of the Rigveda,[2] where *asamāti* is merely an adjective. The later story is that the king was induced to abandon his family priests by two Asuras, Kirāta and Ākuli, who by their magic compassed the death of Subandhu, one of the brother priests, and that the others revived him by the use of the hymns (Rigveda, x. 57-60).

[1] Jaiminīya Brāhmaṇa, iii. 167 (*Journal of the American Oriental Society*, 18, 41 *et seq.*); Sāṭyāyanaka, cited in Sāyaṇa on Rv. x. 57, 1; 60, 7; Bṛhaddevatā, vii. 83 *et seq.*, with Macdonell's notes; Pañcaviṃśa Brāhmaṇa, xiii. 12, 5.

[2] x. 60, 2. 5; Av. vi. 79, 1. *Cf.* Bloomfield, *Hymns of the Atharvaveda*, 499; Max Müller, *Journal of the R[oyal] Asiatic Society*, 1866, 426-465; Bö[htl]ingk's Dictionary, *s.v.*; Hopkins, *T[ransa]ctions of the Connecticut Academy [of Arts] and Sciences*, 15, 48, n. 1.

Asi usually denotes the sacrificial knife,[1] but occasio[nally it] appears to mean a knife used in war.[2] Mention is made [o]f a sheath (*vavri*)[3] to which a belt (*vāla*)[4] was attached. Th[e] word *asi-dhārā*[5] also denotes 'sheath.'

[1] Rv. i. 162, 20; x. 79, 6; 86, 18; Av. ix. 3, 9; x. 1, 20, etc.

[2] Av. xi. 9, 1. The use of the 'sword' increases in the Epic period. See Hopkins, *Journal of the American Oriental Society*, 13, 284.

[3] Kāṭhaka Saṃhitā, xv. 4.

[4] *Ibid.*; Maitrāyaṇī Saṃhitā, ii. 6, 5.

[5] Jaiminīya Upaniṣad Brāhmaṇa, iii. 139.

Asiknī ('black') is the name in the Rigveda[1] of the river known later as Candra-bhāgā, and to the Greeks as Akesines, now the Chenab in the Punjab.

[1] viii. 20, 25; x. 75, 5; Nirukta, ix. 26. *Cf.* Zimmer, *Altindisches Leben*, 12.

1. **Asita** is a name of the 'black snake,' referred to in the later Saṃhitās.[1]

[1] Av. iii. 27, 1; v. 13, 5. 6; vi. 56, 2, etc.; Taittirīya Saṃhitā, v. 5, 10, 1; Maitrāyaṇī Saṃhitā, iii. 14, 18; perhaps Vājasaneyi Saṃhitā, xxiv. 37.

2. **Asita.**—(*a*) A mythical sage of this name figures as a magician in the Atharvaveda in conjunction with **Gaya**[1] or with **Jamadagni.**[2] In the Śatapatha Brāhmaṇa[3] he appears as

[1] Av. i. 14, 4.

[2] Av. vi. 137, 1.

[3] xiii. 4, 3, 11.

Asita Dhānva,[4] and as Daivala or Devala in the Pañcaviṃsa Brāhmaṇa[5] and Kāṭhaka Saṃhitā.[6]

[4] Dhānvana in the Śāṅkhāyana Srauta Sūtra, xvi. 2, 19.
[5] xiv. 11, 18. 19, *Cf.* xv. 5, 27.
[6] xxii. 11. *Cf.* Ludwig, Translation of the Rigveda, 3, 132.

(*b*) **Asita Vārṣa-gaṇa** is a pupil of **Harita Kaśyapa** according to the Vaṃśa or Genealogy in the Bṛhadāraṇyaka Upaniṣad.[1]

[1] vi. 5, 3 (Kāṇva=vi. 4, 33, Mādhyandina).

Asita-mṛga is the designation in the Aitareya Brāhmaṇa[1] of a family of the **Kaśyapas** who were excluded from a sacrifice by **Janamejaya,** but who took away the conduct of the offering from the **Bhūtavīras,** whom the king employed. In the Jaiminīya Brāhmaṇa[2] and the Ṣaḍviṃsa Brāhmaṇa[3] the Asita-mṛgas are called 'sons of the Kaśyapas,' and one is mentioned as **Kusurubindu**[4] **Auddālaki.**

[1] vii. 27. *Cf.* Eggeling, *Sacred Books of the East*, 43, 345.
[2] i. 75.
[3] i. 4.
[4] Variously read as Asurbinda, Kusurbinda, Kusurubinda.

Asura-vidyā, 'the science of the Asuras,' the term used in the Śāṅkhāyana and Āśvalāyana[1] Śrauta Sūtras as the equivalent of the term *māyā* employed in the Śatapatha Brāhmaṇa,[2] clearly means 'magic,' as it is rendered by Professor Eggeling.[3]

[1] x. 7.
[2] xiii. 4, 3, 11. *Cf.* Śāṅkhāyana Śrauta Sūtra, x. 61, 2. 21.
[3] *Sacred Books of the East*, 44, 368.

Astṛ, 'shooter,' is a term frequently used in the Rigveda[1] and Atharvaveda[2] for the archer who fought from the chariot.

[1] i. 8, 4; 64, 10; ii. 42, 2, etc.
[2] vi. 93, 1. 2; xi. 2, 7. *Cf.* Zimmer, *Altindisches Leben*, 296.

Ahan, 'day.' Like other peoples, the Indians used night as a general expression of time as well as day, but by no means predominantly.[1] Night is also termed the dark (*kṛṣṇa*), as

[1] Rv. iv. 16, 19; viii. 26, 3; i. 70, 4. *Cf.* Av. x. 7, 42.

opposed to the light (*arjuna*), day.[2] Aho-rātra[3] is a regular term for 'day and night' combined.

The day itself is variously divided. In the Atharvaveda[4] a division into 'the rising sun' (*udyan sūryaḥ*), 'the coming together of the cows' (*saṃ-gava*), 'midday' (*madhyaṃ-dina*), 'afternoon' (*aparāhṇa*), and 'sunset' (*astaṃ-yan*) is found. In the Taittirīya Brāhmaṇa[5] the same series appears with 'early' (*prātar*) and 'evening' (*sāyāhna*) substituted for the first and last members, while a shorter list gives *prātar, saṃgava, sāyam.* In the Maitrāyaṇī Saṃhitā[6] there is the series 'dawn' (*uṣas*), *saṃgava, madhyaṃdina,* and *aparāhṇa.*

The morning is also, according to Zimmer, called *api-śarvara,*[7] as the time when the dark is just past. It is named *svasara,*[8] as the time when the cows are feeding, before the first milking at the *saṃgava,* or when the birds are awakening.[9] It is also called *pra-pitva,*[10] according to Zimmer.[11] But Geldner[12] points out that that term refers to the late midday, which also is called *api-śarvara,* as bordering on the coming night, being the time when day is hastening to its close, as in a race. From another point of view, evening is called *abhi-pitva,*[13] the time when all come to rest. Or again, morning and evening are denoted as the dawning of the sun (*uditā sūryasya*), or its setting (*ni-mruc*). The midday is regularly *madhyam ahnām,*[14] *madhye,*[15] or *madhyaṃdina. Saṃgava*[16] is the forenoon, between the early morning (*prātar*) and midday (*madhyaṃdina*).

The divisions of time less than the day are seldom precisely given. In the Śatapatha Brāhmaṇa,[17] however, a day and

2 Rv. vi. 9, 1.

3 Rv. x. 190, 2; Av. xiii. 3, 8, etc.; Vājasaneyi Saṃhitā, xxiii. 41, etc.

4 ix. 6, 45.

5 i. 5, 3, 1; 4, 9, 2.

6 iv. 2, 11.

7 Rv. iii. 9, 7; *cf.* Oldenberg, *Ṛgveda-Noten*, 1, 230.

8 Rv. ii. 34, 8; ix. 94, 2.

9 Rv. ii. 19, 2; 34, 5.

10 Rv. vii. 41, 4; viii. 1, 29. Sieg, *Die Sagenstoffe des Ṛgveda*, 127 *et seq.*, interprets *paritakmyāyām* (Rv. i. 116, 15) similarly.

11 *Altindisches Leben*, 362.

12 *Vedische Studien*, 2, 155-179.

13 Rv. i. 126, 3; iv. 34, 5.

14 Rv. vii. 41, 4.

15 Rv. viii. 27, 20.

16 *Cf.* Rv. v. 76, 3 (*saṃgave, prātar ahno, madhyaṃdine*); Taittirīya Brāhmaṇa, ii. 1, 1, 3; Jaiminīya Upaniṣad Brāhmaṇa, i. 12, 4; Aitareya Brāhmaṇa, iii. 18, 14; Geldner, *Vedische Studien*, 3, 112, 113. Zimmer, *op. cit.*, 362, places it too early—before the cows are driven out.

17 xii. 3, 2, 5. *Cf.* Taittirīya Brāhmaṇa, iii. 10, 1, 1 *et seq.*

night make up 30 *muhūrtas*; 1 *muhūrta* = 15 *kṣipra*; 1 *kṣipra* = 15 *etarhi*; 1 *etarhi* = 15 *idāni*; 1 *idāni* = 15 breathings; 1 breathing = 1 spiration; 1 spiration = 1 twinkling (*nimeṣa*), etc. In the Śāṅkhāyana Āraṇyaka[18] the series is *dhvaṃsayo, nimeṣāḥ, kāṣṭhāḥ, kalāḥ, kṣanā, muhūrtā, ahorātrāḥ*. A thirtyfold division of day as well as of night is seen in one passage of the Rigveda[19] by Zimmer, who compares the Babylonian sixtyfold division of the day and night. But the expression used—thirty Yojanas—is too vague and obscure—Bergaigne[20] refers it to the firmament—to build any theory upon with safety.

The longer divisions of time are regularly 'half month' (*ardha-māsa*), 'month' (*māsa*), 'season' (*ṛtu*) and 'year' (*saṃvatsara*), which often[21] occur in this sequence after *ahorātrāṇi* ('days and nights').

[18] vii. 20. *Cf.* Śāṅkhāyana Srauta Sūtra, xiv. 78 *et seq.*; Weber, *Indische Streifen*, 1, 92-95.

[19] Rv. i. 123, 8.

[20] *Religion Védique*, 3, 283 *et seq.* *Cf.* Roth, St. Petersburg Dictionary, *s.v. kratu*.

[21] Taittirīya Saṃhitā, vii. 1, 15; Maitrāyaṇī Saṃhitā, iii. 12, 7; Vājasaneyi Saṃhitā, xxii. 28; Śāṅkhāyana Āraṇyaka, vii. 20; Bṛhadāraṇyaka Upaniṣad, iii. 8, 9, etc. *Cf.* Zimmer, *Altindisches Leben*, 361-363.

Ahalyā Maitreyī is practically a mythical name, the existence of the lady whose story is alluded to in several Brāhmaṇas[1] being derived from the epithet of Indra, 'lover of Ahalyā' (*ahalyāyai jāra*).

[1] Satapatha Brāhmaṇa, iii. 3, 4, 18; Jaiminīya Brāhmaṇa, ii. 79; Ṣaḍviṃśa Brāhmaṇa, i. 1.

Ahi.—This word occurs frequently from the Rigveda[1] onwards to denote 'snake.' Reference is several times[2] made to its casting its slough. Mention is also made of the serpent's peculiar movement,[3] which earns for it the designation[4] of 'the toothed rope' (*datvatī rajjuḥ*). The poisonous character

[1] vii. 104, 7, etc. The word *sarpa*, which is usual in the Atharvaveda, occurs only once (x. 16, 6) in the Rv.

[2] Rv. ix. 86, 44; Av. i. 27; Satapatha Brāhmaṇa, xi. 2, 6, 13; Bṛhadāraṇyaka Upaniṣad, iv. 4, 10; Jaiminīya Brāhmaṇa, i. 9; ii. 139; Kāṭhaka Upaniṣad, ii. 6; 17.

[3] Aitareya Āraṇyaka, v. 1, 4.

[4] Av. iv. 3, 2.

of its bite is spoken of,[5] as well as the torpidity of the reptile in winter, when it creeps into the earth.[6] The cast skin is used as an amulet against highwaymen.[7] Mention is made of a mythical horse, Paidva, which the Aśvins gave to Pedu as a protection against snakes,[8] and which is invoked as a destroyer of serpents.[9] The ichneumon (*nakula*) is regarded as their deadly enemy, and as immune against their poison through the use of a healing plant,[10] while men kill them with sticks[11] or strike off their heads.[12]

Many species of snakes are mentioned: see **Aghāśva, Ajagara, Asita, Kaṅkaparvan, Karikrata, Kalmāṣagrīva, Kasarṇīla, Kumbhīnasa, Tiraścarāji, Taimāta, Darvi, Daśonasi, Puṣkarasāda, Pṛdāku, Lohitāhi, Śarkoṭa, Śvitra, Sarpa.**

5 Rv. vii. 104, 7; Av. x. 4, 4 *et seq.*; 6, 56.

6 Av. xii. 1, 46.

7 Av. i. 27.

8 Rv. i. 117-119.

9 Av. x. 4, 6. 10.

10 Av. vi. 139, 5; viii. 7, 23.

11 Av. x. 4, 9.

12 Av. vi. 67, 2. See Zimmer, *Altindisches Leben*, 94, 95.

Ahīnā Āśvatthya was a sage (*muni*) who achieved immortality by knowledge of a certain rite (*sāvitram*).[1]

1 Taittirīya Brāhmaṇa, iii. 10, 9, 10. The form of the first name is remarkable. The second may be compared with **Aśvattha.**

Ā.

Ākuli.—This mythical priest plays, together with **Kirāta**, a part in the later tale of **Asamāti** and the **Gaupāyanas.**

Āktākṣya is mentioned as a teacher who had peculiar views on the fire ritual (*agni-citi*), which are rejected in the Śatapatha Brāhmaṇa.[1]

1 vi. 1, 2, 24. *Cf.* Lévi, *La Doctrine du Sacrifice*, 140.

Ā-kramaṇa.—In the Jaiminīya Upaniṣad Brāhmaṇa[1] (i. 3) this word is used with the specific sense of 'steps to climb trees.'

Ākhu.—The exact sense of this word is uncertain. Zimmer[1] renders it 'mole,' while Roth[2] prefers 'mouse' or 'rat.' It is frequently mentioned in the later Saṃhitās,[3] and is known to the Rigveda,[4] where, however, the word is regarded by Pischel[5] as having acquired the secondary sense of 'thief.' This is denied by Hillebrandt.[6]

[1] *Altindisches Leben*, 84, 85, followed by Bloomfield, *Hymns of the Atharvaveda*, 142.

[2] St. Petersburg Dictionary, *s.v.*, followed by Whitney, Translation of the Atharvaveda, 317, 318.

[3] Taittirīya Saṃhitā, v. 5, 14, 1; Maitrāyaṇī Saṃhitā, iii. 14, 7; Vājasaneyi Saṃhitā, iii. 57; xxiv. 26; 28; Av. vi. 50, 1.

[4] ix. 67, 30.

[5] *Vedische Studien*, 2, 246; *Zeitschrift der Deutschen Morgenländischen Gesellschaft*, 48, 701.

[6] *Zeitschrift*, 48, 418; *Vedainterpretation*, 7.

Ā-khyāna.—In the Aitareya Brāhmaṇa[1] we hear of the Śaunaḥśepa Ākhyāna, 'the story of **Śunaḥśepa**,' which is told by the Hotṛ priest at the Rājasūya ('royal inauguration'). The series of stories[2] used at the Aśvamedha ('horse sacrifice') during the year while the sacrificial horse is allowed to wander at its will is called the 'cyclic' (*pari-plavam*). The Aitareya Brāhmaṇa[3] mentions also Ākhyāna-vids ('men versed in tales'), who tell the Sauparṇa legend, elsewhere[4] known as a **Vyākhyāna.** Yāska, in the Nirukta,[5] frequently uses the term, sometimes in a pregnant sense as denoting the doctrine of the Aitihāsikas or traditional interpreters of the Rigveda.[6]

[1] vii. 18, 10. *Cf.* Śāṅkhāyana Śrauta Sūtra, xv. 27.

[2] Śatapatha Brāhmaṇa, xiii. 4, 3, 2. 15.

[3] iii. 25, 1.

[4] Śatapatha Brāhmaṇa, iii. 6, 2, 7.

[5] v. 21; vii. 7.

[6] xi. 19; 25.

Cf. Sieg, *Die Sagenstoffe des Ṛgveda*, 16 *et seq.*

Ā-khyāyikā.—This word occurs apparently but once in the Vedic literature, in the late Taittirīya Āraṇyaka,[1] where its significance is doubtful.

[1] i. 6, 3. *Cf.* Sieg, *Die Sagenstoffe des Ṛgveda*, 20, n. 1.

Āgastya appears as a teacher in the Aitareya (iii. 1, 1) and Śāṅkhāyana (vii. 2) Āraṇyakas.

Āgni-veśi Śatri.—A prince of this name appears to be referred to in a Dānastuti ('Praise of Gifts') in the Rigveda.[1]

[1] v. 34, 9. *Cf.* Ludwig, Translation of the Rigveda, 3, 155.

Āgni-veśya.—Several teachers of this name are mentioned in the Vaṃśas or Genealogies of the Bṛhadāraṇyaka Upaniṣad. In the Mādhyandina recension[1] Āgniveśya is a pupil of **Saitava.** In the Kāṇva recension he is a pupil of **Śāṇḍilya** and **Ānabhimlāta** in one Vaṃśa,[2] and of **Gārgya** in the second Vaṃśa.[3]

[1] ii. 5, 21, iv. 5, 27.
[2] ii. 6, 2.
[3] iv. 6, 2.

Ā-ghāṭi is a musical instrument, the 'cymbal,' used to accompany dancing. It is known to the Rigveda[1] and Atharvaveda.[2]

[1] x. 146, 2.
[2] iv. 37, 4 (*āghāṭa*). *Cf.* Zimmer, *Altindisches Leben*, 289.

Āṅgirasa is a title denoting a claim to be of the family of **Aṅgiras,** borne by many sages and teachers, like **Kṛṣṇa, Ājīgarti, Cyavana, Ayāsya, Saṃvarta, Sudhanvan,** etc.

Āja-keśin is the name of a family in which, according to the Jaiminīya Upaniṣad Brāhmaṇa (i. 9, 3), **Baka** used violence against Indra.

Ājani.—This word is used to denote a 'goad' in the Atharvaveda (iii. 25, 5).

Ājāta-śatrava. See **Bhadrasena.**

Āji is constantly used in the Rigveda[1] and the later literature to express the sense of 'a race,' and only seldom denotes 'a battle.' Horse-racing was one of the favourite amusements of the Vedic Indian,[2] the other being dicing

[1] v. 37, 7; vi. 24, 6, etc.
[2] Zimmer, *Altindisches Leben*, 291; Geldner, *Vedische Studien*, 1, 120; 2, 1 *et seq.*

(Akṣa). The racecourse, called Kāṣṭhā[3] or Āji[4] itself, appears from the Atharvaveda[5] to have been a quasi-circular one to a mark (*kārṣman*[6]) and back again. In the Rigveda the course is described as broad (*urvī*), and the distance as measured out (*apāvṛktā aratnayaḥ*).[7] Prizes (*dhana*) were offered (*dhā*),[8] and eagerly competed for. Other words for victory and the prize are *kāra*[9] and *bhara*;[10] and to 'run a race' is described by the expressions *ājim aj, i, dhāv, sṛ.*[11] The person who instituted a race is referred to as *āji-sṛt*,[12] and Indra is called *āji-kṛt*[13] ('race-maker'), and *āji-pati*[14] ('lord of the race').

The swift steeds (*vājin, atya*) used for the races were often washed and adorned.[15] According to Pischel[16] the name of one swift mare is preserved—viz., Viśpalā,[17] whose broken leg was replaced by the Aśvins in a race; but the interpretation is very doubtful. Geldner[18] has also found a comic picture of a horse-chariot race in the Mudgala hymn in the Rigveda, but Bloomfield[19] has shown that that interpretation is unsound. Pischel[20] also seeks to show that races were run in honour of gods, but the evidence for the theory is inadequate.[21]

[3] Rv. viii. 80, 8; Av. ii. 14, 6.

[4] Rv. iv. 24, 8; Av. xiii. 2, 4.

[5] ii. 14, 6; xiii. 2 4.

[6] Rv. ix. 36, 1; 74, 8.

[7] The sense is doubtful in Rv. viii. 80, 8. Zimmer suggests that it may mean 'the course is straight,' without twistings, for which idea *cf.* Geldner, *Vedische Studien*, 2, 160, quoting the comparison of the courser's race with a bowstring (Rv. iii. 53, 24). It is also rendered 'the barriers are removed.'

[8] Rv. i. 81, 3; 116, 15; vi. 45, 1 *et seq.*; viii. 80, 8; ix. 53, 2; 109, 10. According to Geldner, *Vedische Studien*, 1, 120, n. 2, *dhana* is from *dhan*, 'start.' *Cf.* Pischel, *ibid.*, 171. *Cf. dhanasā*, Rv. i. 112, 7. 10; ii. 10, 6; viii. 3, 15, etc.

[9] Rv. v. 29, 8; ix. 14, 1.

[10] Rv. v. 29, 8; ix. 16, 5, etc.

[11] Aitareya Brāhmaṇa, ii. 25; iv. 27; Śatapatha Brāhmaṇa, ii. 4, 3, 4; v. 1, 1, 3; 4, 1; vi. 1, 2, 12; vii. 1, 2, 1, etc.

[12] Satapatha Brāhmaṇa, v. 1, 5, 10. 28; xi. 1, 2, 13.

[13] Rv. viii. 53, 6.

[14] *Ibid.*, 14.

[15] Rv. ii. 34, 3; ix. 109, 10; x. 68, 11.

[16] *Vedische Studien*, 1, 171-173. *Cf.* Sieg, *Die Sagenstoffe des Ṛgveda*, 127 *et seq.*

[17] Rv. i. 116, 15. Pischel finds here a race in honour of Vivasvant, but his equation of Khela and Vivasvant is denied even by Sieg, who accepts his theory of Viśpalā.

[18] *Vedische Studien*, 2, 1 *et seq.*

[19] *Zeitschrift der Deutschen Morgenländischen Gesellschaft*, 48, 541 *et seq.* Von Schroeder, *Mysterium und Mimus im Rigveda*, 346 *et seq.*, follows Geldner. *Cf.* Winternitz, *Vienna Oriental Journal*, 23, 137.

[20] *Vedische Studien*, 1, 172.

[21] Sieg, *op. cit.*, 128.

A formal race, however, is a feature of the ritual of the Rājasūya or royal consecration.[22]

[22] Taittirīya Saṃhitā, i. 8, 15; Taittirīya Brāhmaṇa, i. 7, 9; Kāṭhaka Saṃhitā, xv. 8; Vājasaneyi Saṃhitā, x. 19 *et seq.*; Satapatha Brāhmaṇa, v. 4, 2; 3.
Cf. Oldenberg, *Ṛgveda-Noten*, 1, 43.

Ājīgarti.—See **Śunaḥśepa,** who bears this patronymic in the Aitareya Brāhmaṇa.[1] He is called an Āṅgirasa in the Kāṭhaka Saṃhitā.[2]

[1] vii. 17. *Cf.* Śāṅkhāyana Srauta Sūtra, xvi. 11, 2.
[2] xix. 11.

Ājya. See **Ghṛta.**

Āñjana.—A salve frequently referred to in the Atharvaveda,[1] which came from Mount **Trikakubh**[2] in the Himālaya, and was used to anoint the eyes.[3] The region of the **Yamunā**[4] is also given as a possible place of origin, and the ointment is declared as potent to remove jaundice, **Yakṣma, Jāyānya,** and other diseases.[5] A female ointment-maker is mentioned in the list of victims of the Puruṣamedha ('human sacrifice').[6]

[1] iv. 9; vi. 102, 3; ix. 6, 11; xix. 44.
[2] Av. iv. 9, 9. 10; xix. 44, 6.
[3] *Cf.* Av. iv. 9, 1 (*akṣyam*); Aitareya Brāhmaṇa, i. 3. Hence the legend in the Taittirīya Saṃhitā, vi. 1, 1, 5; *cf.* i. 2, 1, 2; Maitrāyaṇī Saṃhitā, iii. 6, 3; Śatapatha Brāhmaṇa, iii. 1, 3, 15; Vājasaneyi Saṃhitā, iv. 3.
[4] Av. iv. 9, 10.
[5] Av. xix. 44, 1 *et seq.*
[6] Vājasaneyi Saṃhitā, xxx. 14 (*āñjanī-kārī*); Taittirīya Brāhmaṇa, iii. 4, 10, 1.

Cf. Zimmer, *Altindisches Leben*, 5, 69; Bloomfield, *Hymns of the Atharvaveda* 381 *et seq.*; *American Journal of Philology*, 17, 405, 406; Whitney, Translation of the Atharvaveda, 159.

Āṭikī is the name of the wife of **Uṣasti** in the Chāndogya Upaniṣad (i. 10, 1).

Āṭṇāra.—Patronymic of **Para.**

Āḍambara was a kind of 'drum.' A 'drummer' (*āḍambarāghāta*) is mentioned in the list of victims at the Puruṣa-medha ('human sacrifice') in the Vājasaneyi Saṃhitā.[1]

[1] xxx. 19. *Cf.* Satapatha Brāhmaṇa, xiv. 4, 8, 1.

Āṇi.—This word, which is found in the Rigveda,[1] but rarely later,[2] appears to be best taken with Roth[3] and Zimmer[4] as denoting the part of the axle of the chariot which is inserted into the nave of the wheel. Sāyaṇa renders it as lynch-pin, and this sense is accepted by Leumann,[5] being apparently also found in the Nirukta.[6] In one place in the Rigveda[7] the word appears by synecdoche to denote the whole chariot, but the passage is, according to Geldner,[8] completely obscure.

[1] i. 35, 6; v. 43, 8.
[2] In a Mantra in the Aitareya Āraṇyaka, ii. 7. See Keith's edition, pp. 266, 267, and **Vāṇī**.
[3] St. Petersburg Dictionary, *s.v.*
[4] *Altindisches Leben*, 247.
[5] *Etymologisches Wörterbuch*, 30.
[6] vi. 32.
[7] i. 63, 8. *Cf.* Pischel, *Vedische Studien*, 1, 96.
[8] Geldner, *ibid.*, 1, 141, n. 3.

Āṇḍīka ('bearing eggs') is a term found in the Atharvaveda[1] denoting an edible plant, apparently with fruit or leaves of egg shape (*āṇḍa*), akin to the lotus.

[1] iv. 34, 5; v. 17, 16. In the first passage the Paippalāda version has *pauṇḍarīka* in its place; Whitney, Translation of the Atharvaveda, 207. *Cf.* Zimmer, *Altindisches Leben*, 70; Weber, *Indische Studien*, 18, 138.

Ātā.—The framework of the door of a house appears to be denoted by the plural of this word in the Rigveda[1] (though in all passages there it is used only by synecdoche of the doors of the sky), and in the Vājasaneyi Saṃhitā.[2] Zimmer[3] compares the Latin *antae*, to which the word etymologically corresponds.[4]

[1] i. 56, 5; 113, 14; iii. 43, 6; ix. 5, 5 (*ātaiḥ*).
[2] xxix. 5 (*ātaiḥ*). *Cf.* *ātābhiḥ* in Durga on Nirukta, iv. 18.
[3] *Altindisches Leben*, 154.
[4] Brugmann, *Grundriss*, 1, 209; 2, 214.

Āti, an aquatic bird. The Apsarases in the legend of Purūravas and Urvaśī appear to him like Ātis, probably swans.[1] The birds appear also in the list of animals in the Aśvamedha ('horse sacrifice'),[2] where Mahīdhara[3] renders them as the

[1] Rv. x. 95, 9. *Cf.* Satapatha Brāhmaṇa, xi. 5, 1, 4.
[2] Taittirīya Saṃhitā, v. 5, 13, 1; Maitrāyaṇī Saṃhitā, iii. 14, 18; Vājasaneyi Saṃhitā, xxiv. 34.
[3] On Vājasaneyi Saṃhitā, *loc. cit.*

later Āḍī (*Turdus ginginianus*), and Sāyaṇa[4] quotes a view, according to which the Āti was the Cāṣa, or blue jay (*Coracias indica*).

[4] On Taittirīya Saṃhitā, *loc. cit.* *Cf.* Zimmer, *Altindisches Leben*, 89.

Ātithi-gva.—Patronymic of **Indrota.**

Ātreya is the patronymic of a pupil of Māṇṭi in the Bṛhadāraṇyaka Upaniṣad.[1] An Ātreya appears as a Purohita of **Aṅga** in the Aitareya Brāhmaṇa.[2] An Ātreya was regularly the priest in certain rites,[3] and an Ātreyī occurs in an obscure passage in the Śatapatha Brāhmaṇa.[4]

[1] ii. 6, 3; iv. 6, 3 (in both versions).
[2] viii. 22.
[3] *Ibid.*, vii. 7; Śatapatha Brāhmaṇa, iv. 3, 4, 21; Kātyāyana Srauta Sūtra, x. 2, 21 (*sadasaḥ purastāt*).
[4] i. 4, 5, 13. *Cf.* Roth, St. Petersburg Dictionary, *s.v.*

Ātreyī-putra is mentioned as a pupil of **Gautamīputra** in a Vaṃśa, or Genealogy, in the Bṛhadāraṇyaka Upaniṣad (vi. 5, 2, in both versions).

Ātharvaṇa, a patronymic formed from the name of the mythic Atharvan, is found normally in the plural neuter as a designation of the hymns of the Atharvans. This use appears in the late nineteenth book of the Atharvaveda,[1] and in the Pañcaviṃśa Brāhmaṇa.[2] In the singular the expression Ātharvaṇa (Veda), though not occurring till the Chāndogya Upaniṣad,[3] is earlier than the term 'Atharvaveda,' which is first found in the Sūtras.[4] In the Nidāna Sūtra[5] Ātharvaṇikas, or 'followers of the Atharvaveda,' appear.

Specific but mainly mythical Ātharvaṇas are **Kabandha, Bṛhaddiva, Bhiṣaj, Dadhyañc,** and **Vicārin.**

[1] xix. 23, 1. [2] xii. 9, 10.
[3] vii. 1, 2. 4; 2, 1; 7, 1.
[4] Śāṅkhāyana Śrauta Sūtra, xvi. 2, 10, etc.
[5] ii. 12.

Cf. Bloomfield, *Hymns of the Atharvaveda*, xxv.; *Atharvaveda*, 8 *et seq.*

Ā-darśa, 'mirror,' is a term found only in the Upaniṣads[1] and Āraṇyakas.[2]

[1] Bṛhadāraṇyaka Upaniṣad, ii. 1, 9; iii. 9, 15; Chāndogya Upaniṣad, viii. 7, 4; Kauṣītaki Upaniṣad, iv. 2; 11.

[2] Aitareya Āraṇyaka, iii. 2, 4; Sāṅkhāyana Āraṇyaka, viii. 7.

Ādāra was a kind of plant which was prescribed as a substitute for **Soma.**[1] It is identified in the Śatapatha Brāhmaṇa[2] with **Pūtīka.**

[1] Satapatha Brāhmaṇa, iv. 5, 10, 4.
[2] xiv. 1, 2, 12. *Cf.* Kāṭhaka Saṃhitā, xxiv. 3; Kātyāyana Śrauta Sūtra, xxv. 12, 19.

Cf. Zimmer, *Altindisches Leben*, 276.

Ānanda-ja Cāndhanāyana is mentioned as a pupil of **Śāmba** in the Vaṃśa Brāhmaṇa.[1]

[1] *Indische Studien*, 4, 372.

Ānabhi-mlāta is mentioned in a Vaṃśa, or Genealogy, in the Bṛhadāraṇyaka Upaniṣad[1] as a pupil of Ānabhimlāta.

[1] ii. 6, 2 (not in the Mādhyandina version).

Ānava. See **Anu.**

Ānūka.—Geldner[1] thinks that in its solitary occurrence in the Rigveda[2] this word means an ornament. Roth[3] takes it adverbially, and so do Ludwig and Oldenberg.

[1] *Vedische Studien*, 3, 94.
[2] v. 33, 9.
[3] St. Petersburg Dictionary, *s.v.*

Āpayā is the name of a river mentioned once only in the Rigveda,[1] when it occurs between the **Dṛṣadvatī** and the **Sarasvatī.** Ludwig[2] was inclined to identify it with the Āpagā as a name for the Ganges, but Zimmer[3] correctly places it near the Sarasvatī, either as the small tributary which flows past Thānesar or the modern Indramatī farther west, while Pischel[4] assigns it to **Kurukṣetra,** of which the Āpayā is mentioned as a famous river in the Mahābhārata.[5]

[1] iii. 23, 4.
[2] Translation of the Rigveda, 3, 200. But *cf. ibid.*, 4, 304.
[3] *Altindisches Leben*, 18.
[4] *Vedische Studien*, 2, 218.
[5] Mahābhārata, iii. 83, 68.

Ābayu is apparently the name of a plant in the Atharvaveda;[1] the mustard plant[2] may have been meant, but the sense is quite uncertain.[3]

[1] vi. 16, 1.

[2] Bloomfield, *Hymns of the Atharvaveda*, 465, following the indication of the use of the hymn in the Kauśika Sūtra.

[3] Whitney, Translation of the Atharvaveda, 292; Zimmer, *Altindisches Leben*, 72.

Ābhi-pratāriṇa.—Patronymic of **Vṛddhadyumna.**

Ā bhūti Tvāṣṭra is mentioned in two Vaṃśas, or Genealogies, of the Bṛhadāraṇyaka Upaniṣad[1] as a pupil of **Viśvarūpa Tvāṣṭra,** both teachers being no doubt equally mythical.

[1] ii. 6, 3; iv. 6, 3 (in both recensions).

Āmalaka (neuter), a common word later, is found in the Chāndogya Upaniṣad (vii. 3, 1), denoting the Myrobalan fruit. *Cf.* **Amalā.**

Āmikṣā designates a mess of clotted curds. It is not known to the Rigveda, but occurs in all the later Saṃhitās,[1] Brāhmaṇas,[2] etc., and is associated with the Vaiśya in the Taittirīya Āraṇyaka.[3]

[1] Av. x. 9, 13; Taittirīya Saṃhitā, ii. 5, 5, 4; iii. 3, 9, 2; vi. 2, 5, 3; Maitrāyaṇī Saṃhitā, ii. 1, 9; Vājasaneyi Saṃhitā, xix. 21; 23, etc.

[2] Satapatha Brāhmaṇa, i. 8, 1, 7. 9; iii. 3, 3, 2, etc.; Taittirīya Āraṇyaka, ii. 8, 8; Jaiminīya Brāhmaṇa, ii. 438 (*Journal of the American Oriental Society*, 19, 99, 101); Chāndogya Upaniṣad, viii. 8, 5, etc.

[3] *Loc. cit.* *Cf.* Mānava Srauta Sūtra, ii. 2, 40.

Āmba denotes in the Taittirīya[1] and Kāṭhaka[2] Saṃhitās a grain, called **Nāmba** in the Śatapatha Brāhmaṇa.[3]

[1] i. 8, 10, 1. [2] xv. 5. [3] v. 3, 3, 8.

Āmbaṣṭhya is mentioned in the Aitareya Brāhmaṇa (viii. 21) as a king, whose priest for the Rājasūya, or royal inauguration, was **Nārada.** Presumably the name is local, meaning 'King of the Ambaṣṭhas,' as interpreted in the St. Petersburg Dictionary. Later the term Ambaṣṭha denotes 'a man of mingled Brāhmaṇa and Vaiśya parentage by father and mother' respectively.

Ā-yatana.—The general sense of 'abode' or 'home' appears to be limited in one passage of the Chāndogya Upaniṣad (vii. 24, 2) to the sense of 'holy place,' 'sanctuary,' which is found in the epic.

Āyavasa is mentioned apparently as a king in a corrupt and unintelligible verse of the Rigveda.[1]

[1] i. 122, 15. *Cf.* Ludwig, Translation of the Rigveda, 3, 206; Roth, St. Petersburg Dictionary, *s.v.*

Āyu appears in the Rigveda[1] with **Kutsa** and **Atithigva** as having been defeated, with Indra's aid, by **Tūrvayāṇa,** who is believed by Pischel[2] to have been King of the **Pakthas.** Possibly he is elsewhere[3] referred to as victorious, by Indra's aid, over **Veśa.** Elsewhere he is quite mythical.[4]

[1] i. 53, 10; ii. 14, 7; vi. 18, 3; viii. 53, 2; Bergaigne, *Religion Védique*, 1, 60.

[2] *Vedische Studien*, 1, 71-75.

[3] Rv. x. 49, 5; but the word is possibly not a proper name.

[4] *Cf.* Macdonell, *Vedic Mythology*, 100, 135, 140.

Āyuta. See **Ghṛta.**

Ā-yudha, 'weapon,' in its widest sense covers the whole of a Kṣatriya's warlike equipment, which in the Aitareya Brāhmaṇa[1] is summed up as horse-chariot (*aśva-ratha*), bow and arrows (*iṣu-dhanva*), and corselet (*kavaca*). As the bow and arrow (*iṣu, dhanvan*) were essential as the main weapons of the Vedic fighter, they are probably meant when Āyudha is used specifically of weapons, as often from the Rigveda[2] onwards. The battle hymn in the Rigveda[3] confirms this view, as it presents to us the warrior armed with bow and arrow on his chariot, and clad in armour (**Varman**), with a guard (**Hastaghna**) on the left arm to avoid the friction of the bow-string. The corselet was not a single solid piece of metal, but consisted of many pieces fitted together (*syūta*);[4] it may

[1] vii. 19, 2.

[2] i. 39, 2; 61, 13; 92, 1; ii. 30, 9, etc.; Av. vi. 133, 2, etc.

[3] vi. 75.

[4] Rv. i. 31, 15.

have been made either of metal plates or, as is more likely, of some stiff material plated with metal. In addition the warrior wore a helmet (**Śiprā**). There is no trace of the use of a shield, nor is there any clear record of the employment of greaves or other guard for the feet.[5] Skill in the use of weapons is referred to in the Rigveda.[6]

It is doubtful whether sling stones (**Adri, Aśani**) were in ordinary use. The hook (*aṅkuśa*)[7] also is merely a divine weapon, and the axe (*svadhiti*,[8] *vāśī, paraśu*) does not occur in mortal combats. For the use of the spear see **Ṛṣṭi, Rambhiṇī, Śakti, Śaru**; of the sword, **Asi, Kṛti.** Neither weapon can be considered ordinary in warfare, nor was the club (**Vajra**) used. For the modes of warfare see **Saṃgrāma.**

[5] Grassmann saw greaves in *vaṭūriṇā padā* in Rv. i. 133, 2, but this is most improbable.

[6] i. 92, 1. *Cf.* Geldner, *Vedische Studien*, 3, 183; Hopkins, *Journal of the American Oriental Society*, 13, 295.

[7] Rv. viii. 17, 10; x. 44, 9; 134, 6; Av. vi. 83, 3. *Cf.* Muir, *Sanskrit Texts*, 5, 87.

[8] Rv. v. 32, 10; ix. 67, 30; x. 43, 9. *Cf.* Zimmer, *Altindisches Leben*, 298-301; Muir, *Sanskrit Texts*, 5, 469-472; Hopkins, *Journal of the American Oriental Society*, 13, 281 *et seq.*

Āyogava.—Marutta Āvi-kṣita, the Āyogava king, is mentioned as a sacrificer in the Śatapatha Brāhmaṇa,[1] where also a Gāthā ('stanza') celebrating his sacrifice is cited. *Cf.* **Ayogū.**

[1] xiii. 5, 4, 6. *Cf.* Śāṅkhāyana Srauta Sūtra, xvi. 9, 14-16.

Āraṅgara is one of the names of the bee found in the Rigveda.[1] Other names are **Sarah** and **Bhṛṅgā.**

[1] x. 106, 10. *Cf.* Zimmer, *Altindisches Leben*, 97.

Ārā, a word later[1] known as an 'awl' or 'gimlet,' occurs in the Rigveda[2] only to designate a weapon of Pūṣan, with whose pastoral character its later use for piercing leather is consistent. *Cf.* **Vāśī.**

[1] Hillebrandt, *Vedische Mythologie*, 3, 365, n. 1.

[2] vi. 53, 8.

Ārāḍhi.—Patronymic of **Saujāta.** *Cf.* **Arāḍa.**

Āruṇa Aupa-veśi.—So the manuscripts let us read the former word in the Maitrāyaṇī Saṃhitā, but this is doubtless an error for **Aruṇa.**

Āruṇi is the patronymic normally referring to **Uddālaka,** son of **Aruṇa Aupaveśi.** Uddālaka is probably also meant by Āruṇi Yaśasvin, who occurs as a teacher of the Subrahmaṇyā (a kind of recitation) in the Jaiminīya Brāhmaṇa.[1] Āruṇis are referred to both in the Jaiminīya Upaniṣad Brāhmaṇa[2] and in the Kāṭhaka Saṃhitā,[3] as well as in the Aitareya Āraṇyaka.[4]

1 ii. 80.
2 ii. 5, 1. *Cf.* Keith, *Aitareya Āraṇyaka*, 204.
3 xiii. 12.
4 ii. 4. 1.

Āruṇeya.—An epithet of **Śvetaketu,** indicating his descent from **Uddālaka Āruṇi** and **Aruṇa Aupaveśi.** It is apparently confined to the Śatapatha Brāhmaṇa[1] and Chāndogya Upaniṣad,[2] in which Śvetaketu plays a great part.

1 x. 3, 4, 1; xi. 2, 7, 12; 5, 4, 18; 6, 2, 1; xii. 2, 1, 9; Bṛhadāraṇyaka Upaniṣad, vi. 2, 1.
2 v. 3, 1; vi. 1, 1.

Ārkṣa.—Patronymic of **Śrutarvan** and of **Aśvamedha.**

Ārjīka[1] and **Ārjīkīya**[2] (masc.), **Ārjīkīyā**[3] (fem.).—The two masculine forms probably denote the people or land, while the feminine word designates the river of the land. Hillebrandt[4] locates the country in or near Kaśmir, as Arrian[5] mentions Arsaces, brother of Abhisares, who presumably took his name from his people, and Abhisāra bordered on Kaśmir. Pischel[6] accepts Ārjīka as designating a country, which he, however, thinks cannot be identified. But neither Roth[7] nor Zimmer[8] recognizes the word as a proper name. On the other hand, all authorities agree in regarding Ārjīkīyā as the name of a

1 Singular: Rv. viii. 7, 29; ix. 113, 2. Plural: ix. 65, 23.
2 Rv. viii. 64, 11.
3 Rv. x. 75, 5.
4 *Vedische Mythologie*, 1, 126-137.
5 Anabasis, v. 29, 4.
6 *Vedische Studien*, 2, 209, 217.
7 St. Petersburg Dictionary.
8 *Altindisches Leben*, 12-14.

river. Roth[9] does so in one passage[10] only, elsewhere seeing references to Soma vessels; but it seems necessary to treat the word alike in all passages containing it. Zimmer does not locate the river, and Pischel denies the possibility of its identification. Hillebrandt thinks it may have been the Upper Indus, or the **Vitastā** (the Jhelum), or some other stream. Grassmann follows Yāska[11] in identifying it with the the **Vipāś** (Beäs), but this is rendered improbable by the position of the name in the hymn in praise of rivers (*nadī-stuti*).[12] Brunnhofer[13] identifies it with the Arghesan, a tributary of the Arghanab.

9 *Op. cit., s.v. suṣomā.*
10 Rv. x.75, 5.
11 Nirukta, ix. 26.
12 Rv. x. 75.
13 *Iran und Turan*, 52. *Cf.* Max Müller, *Sacred Books of the East*, 32, 398; 399.

Ārjuneya.—In the Rigveda[1] this name occurs as the patronymic of **Kautsa.**

1 i. 112, 23; iv. 26, 1; vii. 19, 2; viii. 1, 11.

Ārtabhāgī-putra is mentioned as a pupil of **Śauṅgī-putra** in a Vaṃśa or Genealogy in the Bṛhadāraṇyaka Upaniṣad.[1] Ārtabhāga is a patronymic of Jaratkārava in the same Upaniṣad.[2]

1 vi. 5, 2 (also in the Mādhyandina version).
2 iii. 2, 1. 13.

Ārtava.—This expression denotes a portion of the year consisting of more seasons than one. But it does not bear the exact sense of 'half-year,' as suggested by Zimmer.[1] This is shown by the fact that it occurs regularly in the plural, not in the dual. In the Atharvaveda it occurs between seasons and years (*hāyana*),[2] but also in the combinations, 'seasons, Ārtavas, months, years';[3] 'half-months, months, Ārtavas, seasons';[4]

1 *Altindisches Leben*, 374.
2 iii. 10, 9.
3 iii. 10, 10.
4 xi. 7, 20. *Cf.* xv. 6, 6; 17, 6.

'seasons, Ārtavas, months, half-months, days and nights, day';[5] and in the Vājasaneyi Saṃhitā 'months, seasons, Ārtavas, the year,'[6] or simply with the seasons.[7]

[5] xvi. 8, 18.

[6] xxii. 28.

[7] Av. v. 28, 2. 13; x. 6, 18; 7, 5; xi. 3, 17; 6, 17; Taittirīya Saṃhitā, vii. 2, 6, 1. 3. Kauṣītaki Upaniṣad, i. 3, cited in this sense in the St. Petersburg Dictionary, is not so to be understood, as the word there is merely adjectival.

Ārtnī denotes the end of the bow to which the bow-string (*jyā*) was attached.[1] The string was not normally kept fastened to both ends of the bow, but when an arrow was to be shot it was strung taut.[2] On the other hand, the legend of the death of Viṣṇu, told in the later Saṃhitās[3] and Brāhmaṇas,[4] expressly contemplates his leaning on his strung bow, which cleaves his head by the sudden springing apart of the two ends when the bow-string is gnawed through.

[1] Rv. vi. 75, 4; Av. i. 1, 3; Maitrāyaṇī Saṃhitā, ii. 9, 2; Kāṭhaka Saṃhitā, xvii. 11; Vājasaneyi Saṃhitā, xvi. 9, etc.

[2] Rv. x. 166, 3. *Cf.* Av. vi. 42, 1.

[3] Maitrāyaṇī Saṃhitā, iv. 5, 9.

[4] Pañcaviṃśa Brāhmaṇa, vii. 5, 6; Satapatha Brāhmaṇa, xiv. 1, 1, 7 *et seq.*

Cf. Zimmer, *Altindisches Leben*, 297, 298; Hopkins, *Journal of the American Oriental Society*, 13, 270.

Ārya is the normal designation in the Vedic literature from the Rigveda[1] onwards of an Āryan, a member of the three upper classes, **Brāhmaṇa, Kṣatriya,** or **Vaiśya,** as the formal division is given in the Śatapatha Brāhmaṇa.[2] The Ārya stands in opposition to the **Dāsa,**[3] but also to the **Śūdra.** Sometimes[4] the expression is restricted to the Vaiśya caste,

[1] Rv. i. 51, 8; 130, 8; 156, 5, etc.

[2] iv. 1, 6 (Kāṇva recension).

[3] Rv. i. 51, 8. 9; 103, 3; vi. 20, 10; 25, 2. 3, etc. (opposed to Dāsa); Av. iv. 20, 4. 8; Maitrāyaṇī Saṃhitā, iv. 6, 6; Vājasaneyi Saṃhitā, xiv. 30, etc. (opposed to Śūdra).

[4] Zimmer, *Altindisches Leben*, 205, 215, finds this use—understanding Ārya as meant—in Atharvaveda, xix. 32, 8, and 62, 1, as well as in passages where Śūdrāryau is found. Lanman, in Whitney's Translation of the Atharvaveda, 948, 1003, quotes his view with approval; but Whitney's version leaves no doubt that he read and understood the text as Ārya, the Āryan, not the Vaiśya. For Whitney's view, Av. iv. 20, 4. 8 may be cited; and so Roth, St. Petersburg Dictionary, *s.v.*, takes the passages. In Taittirīya Saṃhitā, iv. 3, 10, 8, Śūdrāryau must mean Śūdra and Vaiśya; but the Padapāṭha takes it as Arya, and so does Zimmer.

the Brāhmaṇa and the Kṣatriya receiving special designations; but this use is not common, and it is often uncertain also whether **Arya** is not meant. The phrase Śūdrāryau[5] is especially ambiguous, but appears to have denoted originally the Śūdra and the Āryan, for in the Mahāvrata ceremony the fight between a Śūdra and an Ārya is represented in the Taittirīya Brāhmaṇa as one between a Brāhmaṇa and a Śūdra, though the Sūtra treats it as a fight between a Vaiśya and a Śūdra.

The word Ārya (fem. Āryā or Ārī) also occurs frequently used as an adjective to describe the Āryan classes (*viśaḥ*),[6] or name (*nāman*),[7] or caste (*varṇa*),[8] or dwellings (*dhāman*);[9] or again reference is made to the Āryan supremacy (*vrata*)[10] being extended over the land. Āryan foes (*vṛtra*)[11] are referred to beside Dāsa foes, and there are many[12] references to war of Āryan versus Āryan, as well as to war of Āryan against Dāsa. From this it can be fairly deduced that even by the time of the Rigveda the Āryan communities had advanced far beyond the stage of simple conquest of the aborigines. In the later Saṃhitās and Brāhmaṇas the wars alluded to seem mainly Āryan wars, no doubt in consequence of the fusion of Ārya and Dāsa into one community.

Weber[13] considers that the five peoples known to the Rigveda were the Āryans and the four peoples of the quarters (*diś*) of the earth, but this is doubtful. Āryan speech (*vāc*)[14] is specially referred to in the Aitareya and Śāṅkhāyana Āraṇyakas.

[5] See Taittirīya Saṃhitā, vii. 5, 9, 3, with Kātyāyana Śrauta Sūtra, xiii. 3, 7. 8; Kāṭhaka Saṃhitā, xxxiv. 5; Pañcaviṃśa Brāhmaṇa, v. 5, 17; Taittirīya Brāhmaṇa, i. 2, 6, 7; Lāṭyāyana Sūtra, iv. 2, 5; Śāṅkhāyana Śrauta Sūtra, xvii. 6, 2; Anupada Sūtra, vii. 10.

[6] Rv. i. 77, 3; 96, 31; x. 11, 4; 43, 4, etc.

[7] Rv. x. 49, 3.

[8] Rv. iii. 34, 9. *Cf.* **Varṇa**.

[9] Rv. ix. 63, 14.

[10] Rv. x. 65, 11. So Agni and Indra are styled Āryan, as supporters of the Āryan people (Rv. vi. 60, 6).

[11] Rv. vi. 33, 3; vii. 83, 1; x. 69, 6.

[12] Rv. i. 102, 5; iii. 32, 14; vi. 22, 10; 25, 2. 3; viii. 2, 4. 27; x. 38, 3; 83, 1; 102, 3, etc.

[13] *Indische Studien*, 17, 288. *Cf.* Roth, St. Petersburg Dictionary, *s.v. kṛṣṭi*, and **Pañca Janāsaḥ**.

[14] Aitareya Āraṇyaka, iii. 2, 5; Śāṅkhāyana Āraṇyaka, viii. 9. *Cf.* Keith, *Aitareya Āraṇyaka*, 196, 255; and **Vāc**.

Cf. Ludwig, Translation of the Rigveda, 3, 207 *et seq.*; Zimmer, *Altindisches Leben*, 214 *et seq.*

Ārya. See **Mālya.**

Arṣṭi-ṣeṇa.—Patronymic of **Devāpi.**[1]

[1] Rv. x. 98, 5. 6. 8; Nirukta, ii. 11; Bṛhaddevatā, vii. 155.

Āla appears to mean 'weed' in the Atharvaveda,[1] and to form part of three other words,[2] denoting, according to Sāyaṇa, grass-creepers (*sasya-vallī*)—viz., Alasālā, Silañjālā,[3] and Nīlāgalasāla. Whitney,[4] however, does not think that the words can be given any determinate sense.

[1] Av. vi. 16, 3. But Whitney takes the word as a verb, comparing v. 22, 6.

[2] Av. vi. 16, 4.

[3] Sāyaṇa reads Salāñjālā, and the manuscripts of the Kauśika Sūtra (vi. 16), have Silāñjālā. But *cf.* **Silācī.**

[4] Translation of the Atharvaveda, 292, 293. *Cf.* Bloomfield, *Hymns of the Atharvaveda*, 466.

Ālambāyanī-putra is mentioned in a Vaṃśa or Genealogy of the Kāṇva recension of the Bṛhadāraṇyaka Upaniṣad (vi. 5, 2) as a pupil of **Ālambī-putra.** In the Mādhyandina recension (vi. 4, 32) the relation is reversed, for there he is teacher of Ālambī-putra and pupil of **Jāyantī-putra.**

Ālambī-putra is a pupil of **Jāyantī-putra** according to a Vaṃśa in the Kāṇva recension of the Bṛhadāraṇyaka Upaniṣad (vi. 5, 2), but of **Ālambāyanī-putra** according to the Mādhyandina (vi. 4, 32).

Āligī is the name of a kind of serpent in the Atharvaveda (v. 13, 7). *Cf.* **Viligī.**

Ā-vasatha ('dwelling').—The precise sense[1] of this term appears to be a place for the reception of guests, especially Brāhmaṇas and others on the occasion of feasts and sacrifices (somewhat like the modern meaning of Dharma-śālā as a rest-house for pilgrims), a use derived from the more general sense of 'abode.'[2]

[1] Av. ix. 6, 5 (a hymn in praise of entertaining Brāhmaṇas); Taittirīya Brāhmaṇa, i. 1, 10, 6; iii. 7, 4, 6; Satapatha Brāhmaṇa, xii. 4, 4, 6 (where Eggeling renders the word as if meaning 'house' merely); Chāndogya Upaniṣad, iv. 1, 1, etc. Details are given in the Sūtras—*e.g.*, Āpastamba Śrauta Sūtra, v. 9, 3; Dharma Sūtra, ii. 9, 25, 4.

[2] *E.g.*, Aitareya Upaniṣad, iii. 12. *Cf.* Hillebrandt *Vedische Mythologie*, 2, 120, n. 1.

Āvika ('coming from the sheep,' *avi*) is a term for 'wool,' which occurs first in the Bṛhadāraṇyaka Upaniṣad (ii. 3, 6). *Cf.* **Avi.**

Āvi-kṣita.—Patronymic of **Marutta,**[1] the **Āyogava.**

[1] Aitareya Brāhmaṇa, viii. 21; Śatapatha Brāhmaṇa, xiii. 5, 4, 6.

Ā-śarīka appears to denote a disease in a hymn of the Atharvaveda[1] celebrating the powers of the **Jaṅgiḍa** plant. Zimmer[2] thinks that it merely denotes the pain in the limbs accompanying fever. Whitney[3] suggests taking the word as merely an epithet.

[1] xix. 34, 10.
[2] *Altindisches Leben*, 65, 391.
[3] Translation of the Atharvaveda, 953. *Cf.* Bloomfield, *Hymns of the Atharvaveda*, 673.

Ā-śir ('admixture') denotes the mixing, and more especially the milk mixed with the juice, of the Soma before it was offered to the gods. In this sense it is not rare from the Rigveda[1] onwards. Not milk alone was employed for this purpose. The epithet 'having three admixtures' applied to Soma[2] is explained by the other epithets, 'mixed with milk' (*gavāśir*), 'mixed with curds' (*dadhy-āśir*), and 'mixed with grain' (*yavāśir*)—all referring to Soma.

[1] i. 134, 6; iii. 53, 14; viii. 2, 10. 11, etc.; Av. ii. 29, 1, etc.; Nirukta, vi. 8; 32.
[2] Rv. v. 27, 5; *cf.* viii. 2, 7. *Cf.* Hillebrandt, *Vedische Mythologie*, 1, 209 *et seq.*

Āśī-viṣa, occurring only in the Aitareya Brāhmaṇa,[1] is understood by Roth[2] as designating a particular kind of snake, and perhaps means 'having poison (*viṣa*) in its fangs' (*āśī*).

[1] vi. 1.
[2] St. Petersburg Dictionary, *s.v.* It is a common word in the Epic and later.

Āśu, the 'swift,' is frequently used without **Aśva** to denote the chariot steed from the Rigveda[1] onwards.

[1] ii. 16, 3; 31, 2; 38, 3, etc.; Av. ii. 14, 6; iv. 27, 1; xiii. 2, 2; Taittirīya Saṃhitā, i. 8, 10; Satapatha Brāhmaṇa, v. 3, 3, 3, etc.

Āśuṃ-ga in the Atharvaveda[1] seems to denote some sort of animal. It is qualified by the word 'young' (*śiśuka*), and Roth[2] suggests that it may mean a bird ('swift-flying'), or that the expression denotes 'a foal going to its dam' (*āśu-ga*). Sāyaṇa, however, reads the accompanying word as *śuśuka*, which he assumes to denote an animal. Bloomfield[3] renders the two words 'a swift (*āśuṃga*) foal (*śiśuka*),' thus agreeing with one of Roth's suggestions in sense, though not in the explanation of Aśuṃga.

[1] vi. 14, 3.
[2] St. Petersburg Dictionary, *s.v.*
[3] *Hymns of the Atharvaveda*, 464. *Cf.* Whitney, Translation of the Atharvaveda, 291.

Ā-śrama ('resting-place') does not occur in any Upaniṣad which can be regarded as pre-Buddhistic. Its earliest use as denoting the stages of a Hindu's life is found in the Śvetāśvatara Upaniṣad.[1] In one passage[2] of the Chāndogya Upaniṣad reference is made only to the **Brahmacārin** and householder, to whom, as a reward for study, the procreation of children, the practice of Yoga, abstention from injury to living creatures, and sacrifices, freedom from transmigration are promised. In another place[3] three states are contemplated, but not as consecutive. The Brahmacārin may either become a householder or become an anchorite, or remain in his teacher's house all his life. Similarly, reference[4] is made to the death of the anchorite in the forest, or the sacrifice in the village. In contrast with all three[5] is the man who stands fast in Brahman (Brahmasaṃstha). In the Bṛhadāraṇyaka Upaniṣad[6] the knower of the Ātman is contrasted with those who (1) study, or (2) sacrifice and give alms, or (3) are anchorites, and in another place[7] with those who sacrifice and make benefactions, and those who practice asceticism. This position of superiority to, and distinction from, the Āśramas became later a fourth[8] Āśrama,

[1] *Atyāśramin*, Śvetāśvatara Upaniṣad, vi. 21; Maitrāyaṇī Upaniṣad, iv. 3, etc.
[2] viii. 5.
[3] ii. 23, 1.
[4] v. 10.
[5] ii. 23, 1.
[6] iv. 2, 22. *Cf.* iii. 5.
[7] iii. 8, 10.
[8] Jābāla Upaniṣad, 4. *Cf.* Muṇḍaka Upaniṣad, ii. 1, 7.

the **Gṛhastha,** or householder, who was in the second stage, being required to pass not only into the stage of **Vānaprastha,** but also that of the Sannyāsin (**Bhikṣu, Parivrājaka**). The first stage, that of the **Brahmacārin,** was still obligatory, but was no longer allowed to remain a permanent one, as was originally possible.

Cf. Deussen, *Philosophy of the Upanishads*, 60, 367 *et seq.*

Ā-śreṣā, Ā-śleṣā. See **Nakṣatra.**

Āśva-ghna.—This name occurs in one passage of the Rigveda,[1] in a very obscure hymn, where it appears to denote a prince who had made offerings to Indra, and who may, as Ludwig[2] thinks, have been called **Vitaraṇa.**

[1] x. 61, 21.

[2] Translation of the Rigveda, 3, 165.

Aśvatara Āśvi, or **Āśvatarāśvi.**—These two expressions are used[1] as patronymics of **Buḍila,** denoting, according to Sāyaṇa,[2] that he was son of Aśva, and descendant of Aśvatara.

[1] The first is found in Aitareya Brāhmaṇa, vi. 30; the second in Śatapatha Brāhmaṇa, iv. 6, 1, 9; x. 6, 1, 1; Bṛhadāraṇyaka Upaniṣad, iv. 15, 8; Chāndogya Upaniṣad, v. 11, 1; 16, 1.

[2] On Aitareya Brāhmaṇa, *loc. cit.*

Āśva-tthya.—Patronymic of Ahīnā.[1]

[1] Taittirīya Brāhmaṇa, iii. 10, 9, 10. Possibly to be read Āśvathya.

Aśva-medha is the patronymic of an unnamed prince, who occurs in a Dānastuti ('Praise of Gifts') in the Rigveda (viii. 68, 15. 16).

Āśva-vāla.—From this adjective ('made of horse-tail grass'), applied to a strew (*prastara*) in the Śatapatha Brāhmaṇa (iii. 4, 1, 17; 6, 3, 10), follows the existence of the Aśvavāla grass (*Saccharum spontaneum*).

Āśva-sūkti is mentioned in Pañcaviṃśa Brāhmaṇa (xix. 4, 2, *et seq.*) as an author of Sāmans (Soma chants) along with **Gausūkti.**

Āśvina, or **Āśvīna,** designates, in the Atharvaveda[1] and two Brāhmaṇas,[2] the length of journey made in a day by a horseman (*aśvin*). The exact distance is not defined. In the Atharva it appears to exceed five leagues, being mentioned immediately after a distance of three or five **Yojanas**; in the Aitareya Brāhmaṇa the heavenly world is placed at a distance of a thousand **Āśvinas.**

[1] vi. 131, 3.

[2] Aitareya Brāhmaṇa, ii. 17; Pañcaviṃśa Brāhmaṇa in *Indische Studien*, 1, 34.

Āṣādhi Sauśromateya.—According to the Śatapatha Brāhmaṇa,[1] he was ruined because the heads were put on at the Agniciti in a certain manner, and not correctly.

[1] vi. 2, 1, 37. Eggeling has Aṣāḍhi, but as it is a patronymic of Aṣāḍha, the form Āṣāḍhi seems correct.

Āṣṭrā seems in the Kāṭhaka Saṃhitā (xxxvii. 1) to denote the ploughman's goad.

Āṣṭrī.—In the Rigveda[1] the word seems to denote a fireplace. The evil bird is entreated not to settle there on the hearth.

[1] x. 165, 3. *Cf.* Schrader, *Prehistoric Antiquities*, 347.

Āsaṅga Plāyogi is a king who appears in a Dānastuti ('Praise of Gifts') in the Rigveda[1] as a generous patron. Owing, however, to the addition of a curious phallic verse to the hymn, and its early misunderstanding,[2] a legend was invented that he lost his manhood and became a woman, but by the intercession of **Medhyātithi** was transformed into a man, much to the delight of his wife, **Śaśvatī,** whose existence is based on a misunderstanding of the phrase 'every woman' (*śaśvatī nārī*) in the added verse.[3] Another misunderstanding

[1] viii. 1, 32. 33.

[2] viii. 1, 34. See Hopkins, *Religions of India*, 150, n. 1; Bṛhaddevatā, ii. 83; vi. 41, with Macdonell's notes. Dyādviveda gives the tale at length in Vedic words taken from the Nighaṇṭu, a curious *jeu d'esprit*. See the extract from the Nītimañjarī given by Sieg, *Die Sagenstoffe des Ṛgveda*, 40, 41.

[3] viii. 1, 34.

of the Dānastuti[4] gives him a son Svanad-ratha, really a mere epithet, and makes him a descendant of Yadu.

[4] viii. 1, 31. 32. *Cf.* Ludwig, Translation of the Rigveda, 3, 159; Hopkins, *Journal of the American Oriental Society*, 17, 89; Griffith, *Hymns of the Rigveda*, 2, 106, 107; Oldenberg, *Ṛgveda-Noten*, 1, 354.

Ā-sandī.—This is a generic term for a seat of some sort, occurring frequently in the later Saṃhitās[1] and Brāhmaṇas,[2] but not in the Rigveda. In the Atharvaveda[3] the settle brought for the **Vrātya** is described at length. It had two feet, lengthwise and cross-pieces, forward and cross-cords, showing that it was made of wood and also cording. It was also covered with a cushion (**Āstaraṇa**) and a pillow (**Upabarhaṇa**), had a seat (**Āsāda**) and a support (**Upaśraya**). Similar seat are described in the Kauṣītaki Upaniṣad[4] and the Jaimir Brāhmaṇa.[5] The seat for the king at the royal consecratic is described in very similar terms in the Aitareya Brāhmaṇa,[6] where the height of the feet is placed at a span, and the lengthwise and cross-pieces are each to be a cubit, while the interwoven part (*vivayana*) is to be of Muñja grass, and the seat of Udumbara wood. In another passage of the Atharvaveda[7] Lanman seems to take the seat meant as a 'long reclining chair.' There also a cushion (**Upadhāna**) and coverlet (**Upavāsana**) are mentioned. The Śatapatha Brāhmaṇa repeatedly describes the Āsandī in terms showing that it was an elaborate seat. In one place[8] it is said to be made of Khadira wood, perforated (*vi-tṛṇṇā*), and joined with straps (*vardhra-yutā*) like that of the Bhāratas. At the Sautrāmaṇī rite[9] (an Indra sacrifice) the seat is of Udumbara wood, is knee-high, and of unlimited width and depth, and is covered with plaited reed-work. The

[1] Av. xiv. 2, 65; xv. 3, 2 *et seq.*; Taittirīya Saṃhitā, vii. 5, 8, 5; Vājasaneyi Saṃhitā, viii. 56; xix. 16; 86, etc.

[2] Aitareya Brāhmaṇa, viii. 5; 6; 12; Śatapatha Brāhmaṇa, iii. 3, 4, 26; v. 2, 1, 22; 4, 4, 1, etc.

[3] xv. 3, 2 *et seq.*

[4] i. 5. *Cf.* Weber, *Indische Studien*, 1, 397; Keith, *Śāṅkhāyana Araṇyaka*, 19.

[5] ii. 24.

[6] viii. 5; 6; 12.

[7] xiv. 2, 65. See his note in Whitney's Translation of the Atharvaveda, 765.

[8] v. 4, 4, 1.

[9] xii. 8, 3, 4 *et seq.*

imperial seat[10] is to be shoulder-high, of Udumbara wood, and wound all over with cords of Balvaja grass (*Eleusina indica*). Elsewhere[11] the seat is a span high, a cubit in width and depth, of Udumbara wood, and covered with reed-grass cords, and daubed with clay.

[10] xiv. 1, 3, 8 *et seq.*

[11] vi. 7, 1, 12 *et seq.*

Cf. Zimmer, *Altindisches Leben*, 155.

Āsandī-vant, 'possessing the throne,' is the title of the royal city of **Janamejaya Pārikṣita,** in which the horse, for his famous Aśvamedha, was bound. The authorities both cite a Gāthā for the fact, but they differ as to the priest who celebrated the rite. In the Śatapatha Brāhmaṇa[1] he is stated to have been Indrota Daivāpa Śaunaka, but in the Aitareya[2] **Tura Kāvaṣeya.**

[1] xiii. 5, 4, 2.

[2] viii. 21. *Cf.* Śāṅkhāyana Śrauta Sūtra, xvi. 9, 1. Pāṇini, viii. 2, 12, knows the name.

Ā-sāda, 'seat,' occurs in the Atharvaveda[1] as a description of part of the settle (**Āsandī**) of the **Vrātya.** It seems best to regard it with Whitney[2] as the seat proper; Aufrecht,[3] Zimmer,[4] and Roth[5] render it as the 'cushion for the seat,' but that is sufficiently described by the word **Āstaraṇa.**

[1] xv. 3, 8.

[2] Translation of the Atharvaveda, 771.

[3] *Indische Studien*, 1, 131.

[4] *Altindisches Leben*, 155.

[5] St. Petersburg Dictionary, *s.v.*

Āsurāyaṇa is mentioned as a pupil of **Traivaṇi** in the first two Vaṃśas[1] (lists of teachers) of the Bṛhadāraṇyaka Upaniṣad in both recensions, but as a pupil of **Āsuri** in the third Vaṃśa.[2]

[1] ii. 6, 3; iv. 6, 3.

[2] vi. 5, 2. *Cf.* Weber, *Indische Studien*, 1, 434, n.

Āsuri occurs in the first two Vaṃśas[1] (lists of teachers) of the Bṛhadāraṇyaka Upaniṣad as a pupil of **Bhāradvāja** and teacher of **Aupajandhani,** but in the third[2] as a pupil of **Yājñavalkya** and teacher of **Āsurāyaṇa.** He appears as a

[1] ii. 6, 3; iv. 6, 3.

[2] vi. 5, 2.

ritual authority in the first four books of the Śatapatha Brāhmaṇa,[3] and as an authority on dogmatic, specially noted for his insistence on truth, in the last book.[4]

[3] i. 6, 3, 26; ii. 1, 4, 27; 3, 1, 9; 4, 1, 2; 6, 1, 25. 33; 3, 17; iv. 5, 8, 14.

[4] xiv. 1, 1, 33, and notes 1, 2. *Cf.* Weber, *Indische Studien*, 1, 430 [illegible], whose suggestion of the identity of this teacher and the founder of the Sāṃkhya system is not, however, acceptable. See Garbe, *Sāṃkhya Philosophie*, 29, 30.

Āsuri-vāsin is a name of **Prāśnī-putra** in a Vaṃśa (list of teachers) of the Bṛhadāraṇyaka Upaniṣad (vi. 5, 2, in both recensions).

Ā-secana designates a vessel to hold liquids, such as meat juice (*yūṣan*)[1] or ghee.[2] Of its shape and make we know nothing.

[1] Rv. i. 162, 13.

[2] Satapatha Brāhmaṇa, ii. 1, 9, 5. *Cf.* Zimmer, *Altindisches Leben*, 271.

Ā-staraṇa denotes the coverlet of the settle (**Āsandī**) of the **Vrātya.**[1] A tiger's skin serves as the coverlet of the king's seat in the royal consecration (Rājasūya).[2] In the Kauṣītaki Upaniṣad[3] the word used is **Upastaraṇa.**

[1] Av. xv. 3, 7.

[2] Aitareya Brāhmaṇa, viii. 5.

[3] i. 5. *Cf.* Zimmer, *Altindisches Leben*, 155.

Āstra-budhna is the name of a man whom Indra is said in the Rigveda[1] to have assisted. It is not clear whether **Venya,** who is mentioned in the same line, was his friend[2] or his enemy,[3] whom Indra saved or defeated for him.

[1] x. 171, 3.

[2] So Grassmann and Griffith in their translations.

[3] So Ludwig, Translation of the Rigveda, 3, 167.

Ā-sthātṛ.—The warrior in the chariot is once thus designated (as 'standing on the car') in the Rigveda.[1] Normally he is named **Rathin** or **Ratheṣṭhā.**

[1] vi. 47, 26. *Cf.* Zimmer, *Altindisches Leben*, 296.

Ā-srāva ('discharge') denotes a disease, thrice referred to in the Atharvaveda,[1] the precise nature of which is uncertain. The Scholiast[2] in one place interprets it as painful urination (*mūtrātisāra*), while Lanman[3] suggests diabetes. Bloomfield[4] takes it to be diarrhœa, and Zimmer[5] argues that as the remedy is called 'wound healer' (*arus-srāṇa*), the sense is 'the flux from unhealed wounds.' Whitney[6] renders it 'flux,' and questions Bloomfield's rendering. Ludwig[7] translates it vaguely by 'sickness' and 'cold.'

[1] i. 2, 4; ii. 3, 2; vi. 44, 2.
[2] On Av. i. 2, 4. *Cf.* on ii. 3, 2.
[3] In Whitney's Translation of the Atharvaveda, 3.
[4] *American Journal of Philology*, 7, 467; *Journal of the American Oriental Society*, 13, cxiii; *Hymns of the Atharvaveda*, 233, 234.
[5] *Altindisches Leben*, 392.
[6] *Op. cit.*, 3, 41.
[7] Translation of the Rigveda, 3, 507, 509.

Āhanasyā ('unchaste').—This word in the plural ('lascivious verses') denotes a section (xx. 136) of the Kuntāpa hymns of the Atharvaveda, which are of an obscene character.[1]

[1] Aitareya Brāhmaṇa, vi. 36; Kauṣītaki Brāhmaṇa, xxx. 7. *Cf.* Bloomfield, *Atharvaveda*, 99.

Ā-hāva denotes a pail or bucket, especially in conjunction with a well (**Avata**).[1]

[1] Rv. i. 34, 8; vi. 7, 2; x. 101, 5; 112, 6; Nirukta, v. 26.

Āhneya.—Patronymic of **Śauca** (Taittirīya Āraṇyaka, ii. 12).

I.

Ikṣu, the generic name for the sugar-cane, is first found in the Atharvaveda[1] and the later Saṃhitās.[2] Whether it grew wild, or was cultivated, does not appear from the references.

[1] i. 34, 5.
[2] Maitrāyaṇī Saṃhitā, iii. 7, 9; iv. 2, 9 (*ikṣu-kāṇḍa*). In Vājasaneyi Saṃhitā, xxv. 1; Taittirīya Saṃhitā, vii. 3, 16, 1; Kāṭhaka Aśvamedha, iii. 8, 'eyelash' is meant. *Cf.* Zimmer, *Altindisches Leben*, 72; Roth, St. Petersburg Dictionary, *s.v.*

Ikṣvāku.—In the Rigveda this name occurs but once,[1] and in a doubtful context. It is clear, however, that it denotes a prince; later interpretations make **Asamāti**, whose name is read into the hymn, an Ikṣvāku prince.[2] In the Atharvaveda[3] also the name is found in only one passage, where it is uncertain whether a descendant of Ikṣvāku, or Ikṣvāku himself, is referred to; in either case he seems to be regarded as an ancient hero. In the Pañcaviṃśa Brāhmaṇa[4] mention is made of **Tryaruṇa Traidhātva** Aikṣvāka, who is identical with the **Tryaruṇa Traivṛṣṇa** of the Bṛhaddevatā,[5] and with **Tryaruṇa Trasadasyu** in the Rigveda.[6] The connection of Trasadasyu with the Ikṣvākus is confirmed by the fact that **Purukutsa** was an Aikṣvāka, according to the Śatapatha Brāhmaṇa.[7] Thus the Ikṣvāku line was originally a line of princes of the Pūrus. Zimmer[8] places them on the upper Indus, but they may well have been somewhat further east.[9] Later Ikṣvāku is connected with Ayodhyā.

[1] x. 60, 4.

[2] *Cf.* Jaiminīya Brāhmaṇa, iii. 167; Sāṭyāyanaka in Max Müller, Rigveda, 4, c-cvii, 167; *Journal of the American Oriental Society*, 18, 42; Bṛhaddevatā, vii. 85 *et seq.*, with Macdonell's notes.

[3] xiv. 39, 9. *Cf.* Bloomfield, *Hymns of the Atharvaveda*, 680; Whitney, Translation of the Atharvaveda, 961.

[4] xiii. 3, 12.

[5] v. 14 *et seq.*

[6] v. 27, 3. *Cf.* Sieg, *Die Sagenstoffe des Ṛgveda*, 68-75; Macdonell, *Bṛhaddevatā*, 2, 170; Oldenberg, *Vedic Hymns*, 366 *et seq.*; Ludwig, Translation of the Rigveda, 3, 133, 138; 4, 324.

[7] xiii. 5, 4, 5.

[8] *Altindisches Leben*, 104, 130.

[9] *Cf.* Pischel, *Vedische Studien*, 2, 218; Geldner, *ibid.*, 3, 152.

1. **Iṭa.**—This word occurs twice in the Atharvaveda. In the first passage[1] it seems to denote a bulrush of the sort that dies in a year; in the second[2] it refers to the reed work of the house.

[1] vi. 14, 3. *Cf.* iv. 19, 1; Bloomfield, *Hymns of the Atharvaveda*, 464.

[2] ix. 3, 18. *Cf.* Pischel, *Zeitschrift der Deutschen Morgenländischen Gesellschaft*, 35, 718.

2. **Iṭa** appears as a Ṛṣi and a protégé of Indra in one hymn of the Rigveda.[1] Roth,[2] however, thinks that the word is really part of a verb (*iṭ*) meaning 'to err, wander' (cp. *aṭ*), and

[1] x. 171, 1.

[2] St. Petersburg Dictionary, *s.v.*

that the name is a mere misunderstanding. It is already so regarded in the Anukramaṇī, but not apparently in the Bṛhaddevatā.[3]

[3] viii. 73. *Cf.* Ludwig, Translation of the Rigveda, 3, 133.

Iṭant Kāvya is the name of a sage, contemporary with **Keśin Dārbhya,** in the Kauṣitaki Brāhmaṇa.[1] He is also mentioned as Iḍhant in the Pañcaviṃśa Brāhmaṇa.[2]

[1] vii. 4. *Cf.* Weber, *Indische Studien*, 1, 293; 2, 308.

[2] xiv. 9, 16.

Itihāsa, as a kind of literature, is repeatedly mentioned along with **Purāṇa** in the later texts of the Vedic period. The earliest reference to both occurs in the late fifteenth book of the Atharvaveda.[1] Itihāsa then appears in the Śatapatha Brāhmaṇa,[2] the Jaiminīya,[3] Bṛhadāraṇyaka,[4] and Chāndogya Upaniṣads.[5] In the latter it is expressly declared with Purāṇa to make up the fifth Veda, while the Śāṅkhāyana Śrauta Sūtra[6] makes the Itihāsa a Veda and the Purāṇa a Veda. The Itihāsa-veda and the Purāṇa-veda appear also in the Gopatha Brāhmaṇa,[7] while the Śatapatha[8] identifies the Itihāsa as well as the Purāṇa with the Veda. In one passage **Anvākhyāna** and Itihāsa are distinguished[9] as different classes of works, but the exact point of distinction is obscure; probably the former was supplementary. The Taittirīya Āraṇyaka[10] mentions Itihāsas and Purāṇas in the plural.

There is nothing to show in the older literature what distinction there was, if any, between Itihāsa and Purāṇa; and the late literature,[11] which has been elaborately examined by Sieg,[12] yields no consistent result. Geldner[13] has conjectured that there existed a single work, the Itihāsa-purāṇa, a collection

[1] xv. 6, 4 *et seq.*

[2] xiii. 4, 3, 12. 13, and as compounded in xi. 5, 6, 8; 7, 9.

[3] i. 53.

[4] ii. 4, 10; iv. 1, 2; v. 11.

[5] iii. 4, 1. 2; vii. 1, 2. 4; 2, 1; 7, 1.

[6] xvi. 2, 21. 27.

[7] i. 10.

[8] xiii. 4, 3, 12. 13.

[9] xi. 1, 6, 9. *Cf.* p. 24.

[10] ii. 9.

[11] See Sāyaṇa's Introduction to the Rigveda, p. 12 (ed. Max Müller), and his commentary on Satapatha Brāhmaṇa, xi. 5, 6, 8; Śaṃkara on Bṛhadāraṇyaka Upaniṣad, ii. 4, 10.

[12] *Die Sagenstoffe des Ṛgveda*, 31 *et seq.*

[13] *Vedische Studien*, 1, 290. *Cf.* Sieg, *op. cit.*, 33.

of the old legends of all sorts, heroic, cosmogonic, genealogical; but though a work called Itihāsa, and another called Purāṇa, were probably known to Patañjali,[14] the inaccuracy of Geldner's view is proved by the fact that Yāska shows no sign of having known any such work. To him the Itihāsa may be a part of the Mantra literature itself,[15] Aitihāsikas being merely people who interpret the Rigveda by seeing in it legends where others see myths.[16] The fact, however, that the use of the compound form is rare, and that Yāska regularly has Itihāsa,[17] not Itihāsa-purāṇa, is against the theory of there ever having been one work.

The relation of Itihāsa to **Ākhyāna** is also uncertain. Sieg[18] considers that the words Itihāsa and Purāṇa referred to the great body of mythology, legendary history, and cosmogonic legend available to the Vedic poets, and roughly classed as a fifth Veda, though not definitely and finally fixed. Thus, Anvākhyānas, **Anuvyākhyānas**, and **Vyākhyānas** could arise, and separate Ākhyānas could still exist outside the cycle, while an Ākhyāna could also be a part of the Itihāsa-purāṇa. He also suggests that the word Ākhyāna has special reference to the form of the narrative. Oldenberg,[19] following Windisch,[20] and followed by Geldner,[21] Sieg, and others, has found in the Ākhyāna form a mixture of prose and verse, alternating as the narrative was concerned with the mere accessory parts of the tale, or with the chief points, at which the poetic form was naturally produced to correspond with the stress of the emotion. This theory has been severely criticized by Hertel[22] and von Schroeder.[23] These scholars, in accordance with older suggestions of Max Müller[24] and Lévi,[25] see in the

[14] Vārttika on Pāṇini, iv. 2, 60, and Mahābhāṣya (ed. Kielhorn), 2, 284.

[15] Nirukta, iv. 6.

[16] *Ibid.*, ii. 16; xii. 1.

[17] *Ibid.*, ii. 10; 24; iv. 6; x. 26; xii. 10.

[18] *Op. cit.*, 31 *et seq.*

[19] *Zeitschrift der Deutschen Morgenländischen Gesellschaft*, 37, 54 *et seq.*; 39, 52 *et seq.* *Cf.* also *Göttingische Gelehrte Anzeigen*, 1908, 67 *et seq.*

[20] *Verhandlungen der dreiunddreissigsten Versammlung deutscher Philologen und Schulmänner in Gera* (1879), 15 *et seq.*

[21] *Vedische Studien*, 1, 284; 2, 1 *et seq.*

[22] *Vienna Oriental Journal*, 18, 59 *et seq.*; 23, 273 *et seq.* *Cf.* Winternitz, *ibid.*, 23, 102 *et seq.*

[23] *Mysterium und Mimus im Rigveda*, 3 *et seq.*

[24] *Sacred Books of the East*, 32, 183.

[25] *Le Théâtre indien*, 303, 307.

so-called Ākhyāna hymns of the Rigveda, in which Oldenberg finds actual specimens of the supposed literary genus, though the prose has been lost, actual remains of ritual dramas. Elsewhere[26] it has been suggested that the hymns in question are merely literary dialogues.

[26] Keith, *Journal of the Royal Asiatic Society*, 1909, 200 *et seq.*

Id-, Idā-, Idu- Vatsara. See **Saṃvatsara.**

Indra-gopa ('protected by Indra'), masc., is a designation of the cochineal insect in the Bṛhadāraṇyaka Upaniṣad (ii. 3, 6).

Indra-dyumna Bhāllaveya Vaiyāghra-padya is mentioned as a teacher who with others was unable to agree as to the nature of Agni Vaiśvānara, and who was instructed by **Aśvapati Kaikeya.**[1] As Bhāllaveya he is cited several times in the Śatapatha Brāhmaṇa[2] on ritual points.

[1] Satapatha Brāhmaṇa, x. 6, 1, 1 *et seq.*; Chāndogya Upaniṣad, v. 11, 1 *et seq.*

[2] i. 6, 1, 19; xiii. 5, 3, 4. *Cf.* ii. 1, 4, 6.

Indra-bhū Kāśyapa is mentioned as a pupil of **Mitrabhū Kāśyapa** in the Vaṃśa Brāhmaṇa.[1]

[1] *Indische Studien*, 4, 374.

1. **Indrota** is twice mentioned in the Rigveda[1] in a Dānastuti ('Praise of Liberality') as a giver of gifts. In the second passage he has the epithet Ātithigva, which shows conclusively that he was a son of Atithigva, as Ludwig[2] holds, and not of Ṛkṣa, as Roth[3] states.

[1] viii. 68, 10 *et seq.*

[2] Translation of the Rigveda, 3, 163.

[3] St. Petersburg Dictionary, *s.v.*

2. **Indrota Daivāpa Śaunaka** is mentioned in the Śatapatha Brāhmaṇa[1] as the priest who officiated at the horse

[1] xiii. 5, 3, 5; 4, 1; Sāṅkhāyana Srauta Sūtra, xvi. 7, 7; 8, 27.

sacrifice of **Janamejaya**, although this honour is attributed in the Aitareya Brāhmaṇa[2] to **Tura Kāvaṣeya.** He also appears in the Jaiminīya Upaniṣad Brāhmaṇa[3] as a pupil of **Śruta**, and is mentioned in the Vaṃśa Brāhmaṇa.[4] He cannot be connected in any way with **Devāpi**, who occurs in the Rigveda.[5]

[2] viii. 21.

[3] iii. 40, 1.

[4] *Indische Studien*, 4, 384, 385.

[5] x. 98. *Cf.* Oldenberg, *Zeitschrift der Deutschen Morgenländischen Gesellschaft*, 42, 240.

1. **Ibha** is a word of somewhat doubtful sense and interpretation. It is found only in the Saṃhitās,[1] and especially in the Rigveda.[2] According to Roth[3] and Ludwig[4] the sense is 'retainer,' and Zimmer[5] thinks that it includes not only dependants and servants, but also the royal family and the youthful cadets of the chief families. In the opinion of Pischel and Geldner[6] it denotes 'elephant.' This view is supported by the authority of the commentators Sāyaṇa[7] and Mahīdhara;[8] the Nirukta,[9] too, gives 'elephant' as one of the senses of the word. Megasthenes[10] and Nearchos[11] tell us that elephants were a royal prerogative, and the derivative word **Ibhya** may thus be naturally explained as denoting merely 'rich' (lit., 'possessor of elephants').[12]

[1] Taittirīya Saṃhitā, i. 2, 14, 1; Vājasaneyi Saṃhitā, xiii. 9.

[2] i. 84, 17; iv. 4, 1; ix. 57, 3, and perhaps vi. 20, 8.

[3] St. Petersburg Dictionary, *s.v.*

[4] Translation of the Rigveda, 3, 246, 247.

[5] *Altindisches Leben*, 167.

[6] *Vedische Studien*, 1, xv, xvi.

[7] On Taittirīya Saṃhitā, *loc. cit.*

[8] On Vājasaneyi Saṃhitā, *loc. cit.*

[9] vi. 12. It gives also the sense 'retainer,' and in Aśoka's Edicts, No. 5, Bühler, *Zeitschrift der Deutschen Morgenländischen Gesellschaft*, 37, 279, finds a Vaiśya denoted by its Pāli form.

[10] *Apud* Strabo, 704.

[11] *Ibid.*, 705.

[12] But it may equally well be explained as 'rich' from the other sense of the primary word: 'possessor of (many) retainers.'

2. **Ibha** in one passage of the Rigveda[1] appears certainly to be intended as an abbreviation of the proper name **Smadibha.**

[1] vi. 20, 8. *Cf.* Pischel and Geldner, *Vedische Studien*, 1, xvi; Roth, St. Petersburg Dictionary, *s.v.*; Oldenberg, *Ṛgveda-Noten*, 1, 380. Zimmer, *Altindisches Leben*, 167, treats it as 'retinue,' as does Ludwig, Translation of the Rigveda, 3, 246, 247.

Ibhya occurs once in the Rigveda[1] in the plural, when a king is said to devour his Ibhyas as the fire the forest; and twice in the Chāndogya Upaniṣad,[2] in one passage as the first member of a compound, and in the other as either a proper name or an adjective. Roth,[3] Ludwig,[4] and Zimmer[5] interpret the word as 'retainers' in the Rigveda, but in the Chāndogya Upaniṣad Roth thinks it means 'rich.' Pischel and Geldner[6] accept the sense in all passages. Böhtlingk in his translation of the Chāndogya treats the word as simply a proper name, 'Ibhya's village' (*ibhya-grāma*) and 'Ibhya.'

[1] i. 65, 4.
[2] i. 10, 1. 2.
[3] St. Petersburg Dictionary, *s.v.*
[4] Translation of the Rigveda, 3, 247.
[5] *Altindisches Leben*, 168.
[6] *Vedische Studien*, 1, xvi. *Cf.* Sāyaṇa on Rigveda, *loc. cit.*, *dhaninaḥ*, and Śaṃkara on Chāndogya Upaniṣad, *loc. cit.*, *īśvaro hastyāroho vā*; Weber, *Indische Studien*, 1. 476. *Cf.* also Little, *Grammatical Index*, 35.

Iriṇa (neut.) occurs not rarely in the later Saṃhitās[1] and Brāhmaṇas[2] in the sense of 'a cleft in the ground,' usually natural (*sva-kṛta*). The same meaning is also, as Pischel[3] shows, to be ascribed to it in three passages of the Rigveda,[4] in one[5] of which the hole is referred to as 'made by water' (*apā kṛtam*). In another passage of the Rigveda[6] the word refers to the place on which the dice are thrown. Hence Pischel[7] concludes that the dicing-board must have been so called because it contained holes into which the dice had to be thrown if possible. Lüders,[8] however, points out that this assumption is not necessary; the dice (**Akṣa**) were merely thrown on a space dug out, which could be called **Iriṇa**, as being a hole in the ground, though not a natural one. This view is supported by the commentary of Sāyaṇa,[9] as well as by Durga in his note on the Nirukta.[10]

[1] Av. iv. 15, 12; Taittirīya Saṃhitā, ii. 5, 1, 3; iii. 4, 8, 5; v. 2, 4, 3; Kāṭhaka Saṃhitā, ix. 16.
[2] Śatapatha Brāhmaṇa, v. 2, 3, 2; vii. 2, 1, 8.
[3] *Vedische Studien*, 2, 222-225.
[4] i. 186, 9; viii. 4, 3; 87, 1. 4.
[5] viii. 4, 3.
[6] x. 34, 1. 9.
[7] *Op. cit.*, 2, 225.
[8] *Das Würfelspiel im alten Indien*, 14.
[9] On Rv., *loc. cit.* (*ā-sphāra*).
[10] ix. 8 (*āsphuraka-sthāna*).

Iṣa Śyāvāśvi is mentioned in a Vaṃśa ('list of teachers') of the Jaiminīya Upaniṣad Brāhmaṇa (iv. 16, 1) as a pupil of Agastya.

Iṣīkā, 'a stalk of reed grass,' occurs frequently from the Atharvaveda[1] onwards, often as an emblem of fragility. In the Śāṅkhāyana Āraṇyaka[2] it seems to denote the pin fixed in the bar of a pen to keep cattle in (*argaleṣīke*, 'bolt and pin'). A basket (*śūrpa*) of Iṣīkā is referred to in the Śatapatha Brāhmaṇa.[3]

1 Av. vii. 56, 4; xii. 2, 54; Śatapatha Brāhmaṇa, iv. 3, 4, 16, etc.; Jaiminīya Brāhmaṇa, i. 9; ii. 134; Chāndogya Upaniṣad, v. 24, 3; Kāṭhaka Upaniṣad, ii. 6, 17, etc.; Nirukta, ix. 8.

2 ii. 16 (*v. l.* °*ike*).

3 i. 1, 4, 19.

Cf. Zimmer, *Altindisches Leben*, 71; Oertel, *Journal of the American Oriental Society*, 19, 122, n. 3.

Iṣu is the usual name for 'arrow' from the Rigveda[1] onwards. Other names are **Śarya, Śārī,** and **Bāṇa.** In the hymn of the Rigveda,[2] which gives a catalogue of armour, two kinds of arrows are distinctly referred to: the one is poisoned (*ālāktā*), and has a head of horn (*ruru-śīrṣṇī*); the other is copper-, bronze-, or iron-headed (*ayo-mukham*). Poisoned (*digdhā*) arrows are also referred to in the Atharvaveda.[3] The arrows were feathered.[4] The parts of an arrow are enumerated in the Atharvaveda[5] as the shaft (*śalya*), the feather-socket (*parṇa-dhi*), the point (*śṛṅga*), the neck of the point in which the shaft is fixed (*kulmala*), and the **Apaskambha** and **Apāṣṭha,** which are of more doubtful significance. In the Aitareya Brāhmaṇa[6] the parts of an arrow are given as the point (*anīka*), the *śalya*, *tejana*, and the feathers (*parṇāni*), where *śalya* and *tejana* must apparently mean the upper and lower parts of the shaft, since it is reasonable to suppose that the arrow is described as a whole consecutively. So in the Atharvaveda[7] the arrow of Kāma is described as having feathers, a shaft

1 ii. 24, 8; viii. 7, 4, etc.; Av. i. 13, 4, etc.; Vājasaneyi Saṃhitā, xvi. 3, etc.; Nirukta, ix. 18.

2 vi. 75, 15.

3 iv. 6, 7; v. 18, 8. 15; 31, 4.

4 Rv. x. 18, 14; vi. 75, 11; Av. v. 25, 1.

5 iv. 6.

6 i. 25.

7 Av. iii. 25, 2.

(*śalya*), and a firm fastening (*kulmala*).[8] The arrow was shot from the ear, and so is described in the Rigveda[9] as 'having the ear for its place of birth.'

As a measure of length, the Iṣu was five spans, say three feet.[10] A regular profession of arrow-making existed (*iṣu-kṛt*,[11] *iṣu-kāra*).[12]

8 See also Maitrāyaṇī Saṃhitā, iii. 8, 1. 2; Kāṭhaka Saṃhitā, xxv. 1.

9 Rv. vi. 75, 3; ii. 24, 8 (*karṇa-yoni*).

10 Satapatha Brāhmaṇa, vi. 5, 2, 10.

11 Vājasaneyi Saṃhitā, xvi. 46. *Cf.* Rv. i. 184, 3.

12 *Ibid.*, xxx. 7; Taittirīya Brāhmaṇa, iii. 4, 3, 1.

Cf. Zimmer, *Altindisches Leben*, 300; Weber, *Indische Studien*, 18, 29, 286; Hopkins, *Journal of the American Oriental Society*, 13, 275 *et seq.*; 25, 337.

Iṣu Tri-kāṇḍā is the name given in the Aitareya Brāhmaṇa[1] to some constellation, perhaps Orion's girdle. It is mentioned with **Mṛga, Mṛgavyādha,** and **Rohiṇī.**

1 iii. 33. *Cf.* Hillebrandt, *Vedische Mythologie*, 2, 205, n.

Iṣu-dhi ('arrow-holder') is the name of the quiver which was carried by every bowman. The word is common from the Rigveda[1] onwards. No trace is to be found in Vedic literature of the later practice of carrying two quivers.[2] According to Pischel,[3] the curious expression *iṣu-kṛt* in the Rigveda[4] means quiver.

1 i. 33, 3; vi. 75, 5; x. 95, 3; Av. ii. 33, 2; iv. 10, 6, etc.; Nirukta, ix. 13.

2 Hopkins, *Journal of the American Oriental Society*, 13, 274. Each quiver held from ten to twenty arrows.

3 *Vedische Studien*, 1, 17. But see Oldenberg, *Ṛgveda-Noten*, 1, 182.

4 i. 184, 3.

Cf. Zimmer, *Altindisches Leben*, 300.

Ī.

Īṣā denotes the 'pole of a chariot.' Normally the chariot had one pole (*ekeṣaḥ*),[1] but sometimes two poles are referred to.[2] The word is often[3] compounded with **Yuga,** 'yoke,' into which it was fastened (see **Kha**), and tied with ropes.[4] Exactly how it was attached to the chariot we do not know.[5] See also **Ratha.**

1 Rv. x. 135, 3; iii. 53, 17; viii. 5, 29; Av. viii. 8, 23.

2 *Cf.* Av. ii. 8, 4; Satapatha Brāhmaṇa, i. 1, 2, 12 (*īṣā-yugāni*, but in iii. 9, 4, 3 dual); Kātyāyana Śrauta Sūtra, vii. 9, 14, etc.

3 Av., *loc. cit.*, etc.

4 Rv. x. 60, 8. *Cf.* iii. 6, 6.

5 *Vāṇī* in Rv. i. 119, 5 is taken by Zimmer, *Altindisches Leben*, 249, to refer to the front part of the chariot, but it seems simply to be 'voice.'

U.

Ukṣan. See **Go.**

Ukṣaṇyāyana is mentioned in a Dānastuti ('Praise of Gifts') in the Rigveda[1] along with **Harayāṇa** and **Suṣāman.** Ludwig[2] thinks that all three are identical. Roth[3] finds a reference to Ukṣan himself in the verb *ukṣaṇyati*[4] and in the adjective *ukṣaṇyu.*[5]

[1] viii. 25, 22.
[2] Translation of the Rigveda, 3, 162, 276.
[3] St. Petersburg Dictionary, *s.v.*
[4] Rv. viii. 26, 9.
[5] Rv. viii. 23, 16.

Ukṣṇo-randhra Kāvya is mentioned as a seer in the Pañcaviṃśa Brāhmaṇa (xiii. 9, 19).[1]

[1] *Cf.* Max Müller, *Sacred Books of the East*, 32, 397.

Ukhā is the regular word for a 'cooking pot,' usually mentioned in connexion with sacrifice, from the Rigveda[1] onwards. It was made of clay (*mṛṇ-mayī*).[2] See also **Sthālī.**

[1] i. 162, 13. 15; iii. 53, 22; Av. xii. 3, 23; Taittirīya Saṃhitā, v. 1, 6, 3, etc.
[2] Vājasaneyi Saṃhitā, xi. 59; Taittirīya Saṃhitā, iv. 1, 5, 4.
Cf. Zimmer, *Altindisches Leben*, 253, 271.

Ugra in one passage of the Bṛhadāraṇyaka Upaniṣad[1] seems to have a technical force, denoting 'man in authority,' or according to Max Müller's rendering, 'policeman.' Roth[2] compares a passage in the Rigveda,[3] where, however, the word has simply the general sense of 'mighty man.' Böhtlingk,[4] in his rendering of the Upaniṣad, treats the word as merely adjectival.

[1] iv. 3, 37. 38.
[2] St. Petersburg Dictionary, *s.v.*
[3] vii. 38, 6.
[4] P. 66 (with *pratyenasaḥ*).

Ugra-deva is mentioned with **Turvaśa** and **Yadu** in the Rigveda[1] apparently as a powerful protector. The name occurs also in the Pañcaviṃśa Brāhmaṇa[2] and the Taittirīya Āraṇyaka,[3] where he is styled **Rājani** and called a leper (*kilāsa*).

[1] i. 36, 18 (Ugrādeva).
[2] xiv. 3, 17; xxiii. 16, 11.
[3] v. 4, 12.
Cf. Ludwig, Translation of the Rigveda, 3, 147; Roth, St. Petersburg Dictionary, *s.v.*, who suggests that in the Rv. passage the word should be taken adjectivally.

Ugra-sena is mentioned in the Śatapatha Brāhmaṇa (xiii. 5, 4, 3), and in a Gāthā there cited as being, with **Bhīmasena** and **Śrutasena,** a Pārikṣitīya and a brother of **Janamejaya.** The brothers were cleansed by the horse sacrifice from sin.

Uccaiḥ-śravas Kaupayeya appears in the Jaiminīya Upaniṣad Brāhmaṇa (iii. 29, 1-3) as a king of the **Kurus** and as maternal uncle of **Keśin.** His connexion with the Kurus is borne out by the fact that **Upamaśravas** was son of **Kuru-śravaṇa,** the names being strikingly similar.

Uc-chīrṣaka.—This word, occurring in the description of the couch (*paryaṅka*) in the Kauṣītaki Upaniṣad[1] (i. 5), apparently denotes a cushion for the head. See also **Āsandī.**

[1] *Cf.* Weber, *Indische Studien*, 1, 403; Zimmer, *Altindisches Leben*, 155.

Uttara Kuru.—The Uttara Kurus, who play a mythical part in the Epic and later literature, are still a historical people in the Aitareya Brāhmaṇa,[1] where they are located beyond the Himālaya (*pareṇa Himavantam*). In another passage,[2] however, the country of the Uttara Kurus is stated by **Vāsiṣṭha Sātyahavya** to be a land of the gods (*deva-kṣetra*), but **Jānaṃtapi Atyarāti** was anxious to conquer it, so that it is still not wholly mythical. It is reasonable to accept Zimmer's view that the northern Kurus were settled in Kaśmīr, especially as **Kurukṣetra** is the region where tribes advancing from Kaśmīr might naturally be found. *Cf.* **Udīcyas.**

[1] viii. 14.
[2] viii. 23.
Cf. Weber, *Indische Studien*, 1, 165; Zimmer, *Altindisches Leben*, 101, 102; Hopkins, *Journal of the American Oriental Society*, 13, 75, n.

Uttara Madra is the name of a tribe mentioned with the **Uttara Kurus** in the Aitareya Brāhmaṇa[1] as living beyond the Himālaya. Zimmer[2] points out that in the Vaṃśa Brāhmaṇa[3] **Kāmboja Aupamanyava** is a pupil of **Madragāra,** and thence

[1] viii. 14. [2] *Altindisches Leben*, 102. [3] *Indische Studien*, 4, 371.

infers that Kambojas and Madras were not far distant in space. This conclusion is perfectly reasonable in view of the probable position of the Kāmbojas.[4]

[4] See map in Pargiter, *Journal of the Royal Asiatic Society*, 1908, p. 332. *Cf.* Weber, *Indische Studien*, 1, 165.

Ut-tāna Āṅgirasa is mentioned in the Taittirīya Brāhmaṇa[1] as a quasi-mythical person who received all good things, and yet was not harmed, as he was really a form of the earth, according to Sāyaṇa's[2] explanation. His name occurs also in the Kāṭhaka Saṃhitā,[3] the Pañcaviṃśa Brāhmaṇa,[4] and the Taittirīya Āraṇyaka.[5]

[1] ii. 3, 2, 5. *Cf.* ii. 2, 5, 3.
[2] On Taittirīya Brāhmaṇa, ii. 3, 2, 5.
[3] ix. 9.
[4] i. 8, 11.
[5] iii. 10, 2, 3.

Udag-ayana. See **Sūrya.**

Ud-aṅka Śaulbāyana.—His views on Brahman, which he identified with the vital airs (*prāṇa*), are mentioned in the Bṛhadāraṇyaka Upaniṣad (iv. 1, 3). He would thus have been a contemporary of **Janaka** of Videha. He is also mentioned in the Taittirīya Saṃhitā (vii. 5, 4, 2) as holding that the Daśarātra ceremony was the prosperity or best part of the Sattra (' sacrificial session ').

Ud-añcana.—This word, occurring only metaphorically in the Rigveda,[1] means a ' pail ' or ' bucket ' in the Brāhmaṇas.[2]

[1] v. 44, 13 (*dhiyām udañcanaḥ*, ' a very well of prayers ').
[2] Aitareya Brāhmaṇa, vii. 32; Śatapatha Brāhmaṇa, iv. 3, 5, 21.

Udamaya Ātreya is mentioned in the Aitareya Brāhmaṇa (viii. 22) as Purohita, or domestic priest, of **Aṅga Vairocana.**

Udara Śāṇḍilya is mentioned as a teacher in the Chāndogya Upaniṣad,[1] and as a pupil of **Atidhanvan Śaunaka** in the Vaṃśa Brāhmaṇa.[2]

[1] i. 9, 3.
[2] *Indische Studien*, 4, 384.

Udala, a Vaiśvāmitra, is mentioned in the Pañcaviṃśa Brāhmaṇa (xiv. 11, 33) as the seer of a Sāman.

Ud-āja is the word used in the Maitrāyaṇī Saṃhitā[1] to denote the share of the booty of war taken by the king after a victory (*saṃgrāmaṃ jitvā*). This interpretation, which is that of Delbrück,[2] is clearly correct, as against the older version, 'march out,' given by von Schroeder[3] and accepted by Böhtlingk.[4] The Udāja thus corresponds precisely with the Homeric γέρας. This sense also suits Nirāja, the variant of both the Kāṭhaka[5] and the Kapiṣṭhala[6] Saṃhitās.

[1] i. 10, 16; iv. 3, 1.
[2] *Festgruss an Böhtlingk*, 25.
[3] Maitrāyaṇī Saṃhitā, 1, xv.
[4] Dictionary, *s.v.*
[5] xxviii. 3.
[6] xliv. 3.

Udāna is usually the fifth of the vital breaths (**Prāṇa**) when five are enumerated.[1] Sometimes[2] it appears as the second, coming after Prāṇa, and followed by Vyāna or Samāna. Again,[3] it is found simply opposed to Prāṇa, or it simply follows Prāṇa and Apāna.[4] In the Śatapatha Brāhmaṇa[5] it is treated as the breath that consumes food, a notion traceable in the later Upaniṣads,[6] while it is also regarded as the wind that rises up by the throat,[7] and leads the spirit forth at death.[8]

[1] *E.g.*, Maitrāyaṇī Saṃhitā, iii. 12, 9; Kāṭhaka Saṃhitā, v. 4; 10; Śatapatha Brāhmaṇa, ix. 2, 2, 5; xi. 8, 3, 6 (in the order Prāṇa, Vyāna, Apāna, Udāna, Samāna); Bṛhadāraṇyaka Upaniṣad, i. 5, 3; iii. 4, 1 (Samāna is omitted); iii. 9, 26; Chāndogya Upaniṣad, iii. 13, 5; v. 23, 1. 2; Aitareya Āraṇyaka, ii. 3, 3, etc.
[2] Vājasaneyi Saṃhitā, i. 20; vii. 27; Śatapatha Brāhmaṇa, ix. 4, 2, 10, etc. (with Vyāna); Aitareya Brāhmaṇa, i. 7, 2 (with Samāna).
[3] Vājasaneyi Saṃhitā, vi. 20; Śatapatha Brāhmaṇa, iv. 1, 2, 2; ix. 2, 4, 5, etc.
[4] Śāṅkhāyana Āraṇyaka, viii. 8; xi. 1.
[5] xi. 2, 4, 5.
[6] Maitrāyaṇī Upaniṣad, ii. 6.
[7] Amṛtabindu Upaniṣad, 34.
[8] Praśna Upaniṣad, iii. 7. *Cf.* Deussen, *Philosophy of the Upaniṣads*, 280.

Ud-īcyas.—The Brāhmaṇas of the northern parts are referred to in the Śatapatha Brāhmaṇa[1] as engaging, with **Svaidāyana Śaunaka** as their spokesman, in a dispute with the Kurupañcāla Brāhmaṇa **Uddālaka Āruṇi,** and as vanquishing him. Their relation to the Kurupañcālas appears also from the fact that in

[1] xi. 4, 1, 1. *Cf.* Gopatha Brāhmaṇa, i. 3, 6.

the same Brāhmaṇa[2] reference is made to the speech of the north being similar to that of the Kurupañcālas. The speech of the Northerners was also celebrated for purity; hence Brāhmaṇas used to go to the north for purposes of study, according to the Kauṣītaki Brāhmaṇa,[3] while in the Buddhist texts the school of Takṣaśilā (in Gandhāra) is famous as a resort of students.[4] Possibly, too, Sanskrit was specially developed in Kaśmīr, as suggested by Franke.[5] See also **Kuru.**

[2] iii. 2, 3, 15. *Cf.* Weber, *Indische Studien*, 1, 191; Lévi, *La Doctrine du Sacrifice*, 35.

[3] vii. 6. *Cf.* Weber, *op. cit.*, 1, 153; 2, 309.

[4] Rhys Davids, *Buddhist India*, 8, 28, 203.

[5] *Cf.* *Pāli und Sanskrit* (1902), 88, 89.

Udumbara.—This name of the *Ficus glomerata* does not occur in the Rigveda, but is often found from the Atharvaveda[1] onwards. For ritual purposes of all kinds its wood was constantly used. The sacrificial post (*yūpa*)[2] and the sacrificial ladle[3] were made of it, and amulets of Udumbara are mentioned.[4] Its wood, like that of other kinds of figtree—**Aśvattha, Nyagrodha,** and **Plakṣa**—was considered suitable for employment at the sacrifice.[5] The sweetness of its fruit is referred to in the Aitareya Brāhmaṇa,[6] where it is put on the same level as **Madhu.** It is there also spoken of as ripening three times a year.[7] A forest of Udumbara trees is mentioned in the Pañcaviṃśa Brāhmaṇa.[8]

[1] xix. 31, 1; Taittirīya Saṃhitā, ii. 1, 1, 6, etc.; Śatapatha Brāhmaṇa, iii. 2, 1, 33; vii. 4, 1, 38, etc.

[2] Taittirīya Saṃhitā, ii. 1, 1, 6.

[3] *Ibid.*, v. 4, 7, 3.

[4] Atharvaveda, xix. 31, 1.

[5] Taittirīya Saṃhitā, iii. 4, 8, 4.

[6] vii. 15.

[7] v. 24.

[8] xvi. 6, 4.

Cf. Zimmer, *Altindisches Leben*, 59.

Uddālaka Āruṇi.—Uddālaka, son of Aruṇa, is one of the most prominent teachers of the Vedic period. He was a Brāhmaṇa of the Kurupañcālas, according to the Śatapatha Brāhmaṇa.[1] This statement is confirmed by the fact that he was teacher of **Proti Kausurubindi** of Kauśāmbī,[2] and that his son

[1] xi. 4, 1, 2. *Cf.* Gopatha Brāhmaṇa, i. 3, 6.

[2] xii. 2, 2, 13.

Śvetaketu is found disputing among the Pañcālas.[3] He was a pupil of Aruṇa, his father,[4] as well as of Patañcala Kāpya,[5] of Madra, while he was the teacher of the famous Yājñavalkya[6] Vājasaneya and of Kauṣītaki,[7] although the former is represented elsewhere[8] as having silenced him. He overcame in argument Prācīnayogya Śauceya,[9] and apparently also Bhadrasena Ājātaśatrava,[10] though the text here seems to read the name as Āraṇi. He was a Gautama,[11] and is often alluded to as such. As an authority on questions of ritual and philosophy, he is repeatedly referred to by his patronymic name Āruṇi in the Śatapatha Brāhmaṇa,[12] the Bṛhadāraṇyaka Upaniṣad,[13] the Chāndogya Upaniṣad,[14] and occasionally in the Aitareya,[15] the Kauṣītaki,[16] and the Ṣaḍviṃśa[17] Brāhmaṇas, as well as the Kauṣītaki Upaniṣad.[18] In the Maitrāyaṇī Saṃhitā he is not mentioned, according to Geldner,[19] but only his father Aruṇa; his name does not occur, according to Weber,[20] in the Pañcaviṃśa Brāhmaṇa, but in the Kāṭhaka Saṃhitā[21] he is, as Āruṇi, known as a contemporary of **Divodāsa Bhaimaseni,** and in the Jaiminīya Upaniṣad Brāhmaṇa[22] he is mentioned as serving **Vāsiṣṭha Caikitāneya.** In the Taittirīya tradition he seldom appears. There is an allusion in the Taittirīya Saṃhitā[23] to Kusurubinda Auddālaki, and according to the Taittirīya Brāhmaṇa,[24] Naciketas was a son of Vājaśravasa Gautama, who

[3] Bṛhadāraṇyaka Upaniṣad, vi. 1, 1; Chāndogya Upaniṣad, v. 3, 1.

[4] Bṛhadāraṇyaka Upaniṣad, vi. 4, 33 (in both recensions).

[5] *Ibid.*, iii. 7, 1.

[6] *Ibid.*, vi. 3, 15; 4, 33.

[7] Śāṅkhāyana Āraṇyaka, xv.

[8] Bṛhadāraṇyaka Upaniṣad, iii. 7, 31.

[9] Satapatha Brāhmaṇa, xi. 5, 3, 1 *et seq.*

[10] v. 5, 5, 14. Eggeling, *Sacred Books of the East*, 41, 141, has Āraṇi. There is a chronological difficulty in taking Āruṇi as meant, since Ājātaśatrava must presumably have been a descendant of Ajātaśatru, a contemporary of Janaka (see Kauṣītaki Upaniṣad, iv. 1), who again was a patron of Yājñavalkya, a pupil of Āruṇi. But this difficulty is not fatal.

[11] Śatapatha Brāhmaṇa, xi. 5, 3, 2; Kauṣītaki Upaniṣad, i. 1.

[12] i. 1, 2, 11; ii. 2, 1, 34; iii. 3, 4, 19; iv. 4, 8, 9; xi. 2, 6, 12.

[13] iii. 5, 1.

[14] iii. 11, 4; v. 11, 2; 17, 1; vi. 8, 1.

[15] viii. 7.

[16] xxvi. 4.

[17] i. 6.

[18] i. 1 *et seq.*

[19] *Vedische Studien*, 3, 146.

[20] *Indian Literature*, 69. But *cf.* xxiii. 1, 5.

[21] vii. 8. *Cf.* viii. 6.

[22] i. 42, 1.

[23] vii. 2, 2, 1 (a late passage).

[24] iii. 11, 8, 1 *et seq.*

is made out to be Uddālaka by Sāyaṇa.[25] But the episode of Naciketas, being somewhat unreal, cannot be regarded as of historical value in proving relationship. Aruṇa is known to the Taittirīya Saṃhitā. A real son of Uddālaka was the famous **Śvetaketu,** who is expressly reported by Āpastamba[26] to have been in his time an Avara or later authority, a statement of importance for the date of Āruṇi.

25 On Taittirīya Brāhmaṇa, *loc. cit.* *Cf.* Kāthaka Upaniṣad, i. 11.

26 See Bühler, *Sacred Books of the East*, 2, xxxviii; Keith, *Aitareya Āraṇyaka*, 39. *Cf.* Weber, *Indische Studien*, 1, 170, n.; 2, 201, 202; Oldenberg, *Buddha*, 396, n.; Eggeling, *Sacred Books of the East*, 12, xl., xli.

Uddālakāyana is mentioned as a pupil of Jābālāyana in the second Vaṃśa (list of teachers) contained in the Kāṇva recension of the Bṛhadāraṇyaka Upaniṣad (iv. 6, 2).

Udra is the name of an animal occurring only in the list of sacrificial victims at the Aśvamedha given in the Saṃhitās of the Yajurveda.[1] According to Mahīdhara[2] it was a crab; but as the commentary on the Taittirīya Saṃhitā[3] calls it a water-cat, there can be no doubt that it was an otter.

1 Taittirīya Saṃhitā, v. 5, 20, 1; Maitrāyaṇī Saṃhitā, iii. 14, 18; Vājasaneyi Saṃhitā, xxiv. 37.

2 On Vājasaneyi Saṃhitā, *loc. cit.*

3 *Loc. cit.* *Cf.* Zimmer, *Altindisches Leben*, 95, 96; Schrader, *Prehistoric Antiquities*, 247. *Udrin* occurs in the Baudhāyana Śrauta Sūtra, ii. 5.

Uddhi[1] denotes some part of a chariot, probably the seat,[2] but, according to Roth,[3] the frame resting on the axle.

1 Av. viii. 8, 22; Śatapatha Brāhmaṇa, xii. 2, 2, 2; Aitareya Āraṇyaka, ii. 3, 8.

2 So Whitney's Translation of the Atharvaveda, 506; Eggeling, *Sacred Books of the East*, 44, 149.

3 St. Petersburg Dictionary, *s.v.*

Upa-ketu is the name of a man mentioned in the Kāṭhaka Saṃhitā (xiii. 1).

Upa-kosala Kāmalāyana is mentioned as a teacher and a pupil of **Satyakāma Jābāla** in the Chāndogya Upaniṣad (iv. 10, 1; 14, 1).

Upa-kvasa is the name in the Atharvaveda (vi. 50, 2) of a noxious insect injurious to seed. Sāyaṇa, however, reads the word as a plural adjective (*a-pakvasaḥ = a-dagdhāḥ*), but the Paippalāda recension supports the form *upakvasaḥ*.

Cf. Zimmer, *Altindisches Leben*, 237; Bloomfield, *Hymns of the Atharvaveda*, 486; Whitney's Translation of the Atharvaveda, 318.

Upa-gu Sauśravasa is mentioned in the Pañcaviṃśa Brāhmaṇa (xiv. 6, 8) as Purohita of **Kutsa Aurava,** by whom he was murdered because of his paying homage to Indra.

Cf. Hillebrandt, *Vedische Mythologie*, 3, 268; Hopkins, *Transactions of the Connecticut Academy of Arts and Sciences*, 15, 57.

Upa-cit occurs in the Vājasaneyi Saṃhitā[1] as the name of a disease, which Roth[2] renders as 'swelling,' and which Bloomfield[3] identifies with **Apacit.**

[1] xii. 97.

[2] St. Petersburg Dictionary, *s.v.*

[3] *Proceedings of the American Oriental Society*, October, 1887, xviii.

Upa-jihvikā, Upa-jīkā, Upa-dīkā are all forms of one word denoting a species of ant.[1] To these ants is attributed in the Atharvaveda[2] the power of penetrating to water which possesses curative properties. They were accordingly used in all sorts of spells against poisoning. The belief in their healing qualities was no doubt due to the well-known properties of the earth of ant-heaps which contains their water.

[1] *Upajihvikā* is the form in Rv. viii. 102, 21; *upajīkā* in Av. ii. 3, 4; vi. 100, 2; but *upacīkā* in both passages in the Paippalāda recension; *upadīkā* in the Taittirīya Brāhmaṇa, i. 1, 3, 4; Taittirīya Āraṇyaka, v. 1, 4; 10, 9; Śatapatha Brāhmaṇa, xiv. 1, 1, 8.

[2] vi. 100, 2.

Cf. Bloomfield, *American Journal of Philology*, 7, 482 *et seq.*; *Hymns of the Atharvaveda*, 511; Whitney's Translation of the Atharvaveda, 41, 354; Bergaigne and Henry, *Manuel Védique*, 153.

Upa-dhāna denotes the 'cushion' of a seat (**Āsandī**) in the Atharvaveda (xiv. 2, 65). It corresponds to the **Upabarhaṇa** of other texts.

Upa-dhi occurs once each in the Rigveda[1] and the Atharvaveda,[2] in conjunction with **Pradhi,** denoting part of the wheel of a chariot. It is impossible to decide exactly what part is meant. Roth,[3] Zimmer[4] and Bloomfield,[5] agree in thinking that the word denotes the spokes collectively. Whitney,[6] considering this improbable, prefers to see in it the designation of a solid wheel, Pradhi being presumably the rim and Upadhi the rest. Other possibilities[7] are that the Upadhi is a rim beneath the felly, or the felly itself as compared with the tire (ordinarily **Pavi**).

[1] ii. 39, 4.
[2] vi. 70, 3.
[3] St. Petersburg Dictionary, *s.v.*
[4] *Altindisches Leben*, 248 (ignoring the Atharvaveda passage).
[5] *Hymns of the Atharvaveda*, 493.
[6] Translation of the Atharvaveda, 334.
[7] Bloomfield, *loc. cit.*

Upa-niṣad in the Brāhmaṇas[1] normally denotes the 'secret sense' of some word or text, sometimes the 'secret rule' of the mendicant. But in the Bṛhadāraṇyaka Upaniṣad[2] it is already used in the plural as the designation of a class of writings, no doubt actually existing and similar to the Upaniṣads in the nature of their subject-matter and its treatment. Similarly the sections of the Taittirīya Upaniṣad end with the words *ity upaniṣad*. The Aitareya Āraṇyaka[3] commences its third part with the title 'The Upaniṣad of the Saṃhitā,' and the title occurs also in the Śāṅkhāyana Āraṇyaka.[4] The exact primary sense of the expression is doubtful. The natural derivation, adopted by Max Müller[5] and usual ever since, makes the word mean firstly a session of pupils, hence secret doctrine, and secondly the title of a work on secret doctrine. Oldenberg,[6] however, traces the use of the word to the earlier

[1] Śatapatha Brāhmaṇa, x. 3, 5, 12; 4, 5, 1; 5, 1, 1; xii. 2, 2, 23, etc.; Chāndogya Upaniṣad, i. 1, 10; 13, 4; viii. 8, 4. 5; Bṛhadāraṇyaka Upaniṣad, ii. 1, 20; iv. 2, 1; v. 5, 3; Aitareya Āraṇyaka, iii. 1, 6; 2, 5; Kauṣītaki Upaniṣad, ii. 1, etc.
[2] ii. 4, 10; iv. 1, 2; 5, 11.
[3] iii. 1, 1.
[4] vii. 2. *Cf.* Taittirīya Upaniṣad, i. 3, 1.
[5] *Sacred Books of the East*, 1, xxxiii *et seq. Cf.* St. Petersburg Dictionary, *s.v.*; Macdonell, *Sanskrit Literature*, 204.
[6] *Zeitschrift der Deutschen Morgenländischen Gesellschaft*, 50, 457; 54, 70; *Die Literatur des alten Indien*, 72.

sense of 'worship' (*cf. upāsana*). Deussen[7] considers the original sense to have been 'secret word,' next 'secret text,' and then 'secret import,' but this order of meaning is improbable. Hopkins[8] suggests that Upaniṣad denotes a subsidiary treatise, but this sense does not account naturally for the common use as 'secret meaning,' which is far more frequent than any other.

7 *Philosophy of the Upaniṣads*, 16 *et seq*.

8 *Religions of India*, 218.

Upa-pati, 'the gallant,' is mentioned with the Jāra, 'lover,' in the Vājasaneyi Saṃhitā[1] as a victim in the human sacrifice (*puruṣamedha*).

1 xxx. 9: Taittirīya Brāhmaṇa, iii. 4, 4, 1.

Upa-barhaṇa denotes a 'pillow' or 'cushion,' especially of a seat (*āsandī*), occurring in the Rigveda,[1] the Atharvaveda,[2] and the Brāhmaṇas.[3] The feminine Upabarhaṇī is found in the Rigveda with the same sense, but used metaphorically of the earth.

1 x. 85, 7.

2 ix. 5, 28; xii. 2, 19. 20; xv. 3, 7.

3 Aitareya Brāhmaṇa, viii. 12; Śatapatha Brāhmaṇa, xiii. 8, 4, 10; Kauṣītaki Upaniṣad, i. 5; Taittirīya Brāhmaṇa, i. 1, 6, 10; 6, 8, 9; Kāṭhaka Saṃhitā, xxviii. 4, etc.

Upa-manthanī is used in the Bṛhadāraṇyaka Upaniṣad[1] to denote 'churning sticks.' In the Vājasaneyi Saṃhitā[2] the 'churner' (*upamanthitṛ*) is included in the list of victims at the human sacrifice (*puruṣamedha*), and the verb *upa-manth* is often used of churning or mixing fluids.[3]

1 vi. 3, 13.

2 xxx. 12; Taittirīya Brāhmaṇa, iii. 4, 8, 1.

3 Taittirīya Brāhmaṇa, i. 6, 8, 4. 5; Śatapatha Brāhmaṇa, ii. 6, 1, 6; Chāndogya Upaniṣad, v. 2, 4.

Upa-manyu is, according to Ludwig,[1] the name of a person in the Rigveda,[2] but is more probably explained by Roth[3] as a mere epithet.

1 Translation of the Rigveda, 3, 113.

2 i. 102. 9.

3 St. Petersburg Dictionary, *s.v.*

Upama-śravas is mentioned in a hymn of the Rigveda[1] as a son of **Kuruśravaṇa,** and grandson of **Medhātithi.** The exact force of the reference to him is, however, uncertain. According to the Bṛhaddevatā,[2] followed by Ludwig,[3] and by Lanman,[4] the poet in the hymn consoles Upamaśravas for the death of his grandfather, Medhātithi. Geldner,[5] on the other hand, thinks that the poet, who was **Kavaṣa Ailūṣa,** was ill-treated by his patron's son, Upamaśravas, and cast into a ditch or well, where he uttered his complaint and appeal for mercy. But of this there is no adequate evidence, and the tradition of the Bṛhaddevatā seems sound.

[1] x. 33, 6. 7.
[2] vii. 35. 36, with Macdonell's notes.
[3] Translation of the Rigveda, 3, 165.
[4] *Sanskrit Reader*, 386, 389.
[5] *Vedische Studien*, 2, 150, n.

Upa-mit occurs twice in the Rigveda,[1] and once in the Atharvaveda,[2] as the designation of some part of a house. The passages in the Rigveda leave little doubt that the word means an upright pillar. As it is, in the Atharvaveda, coupled with **Parimit** and **Pratimit,** the conclusion is natural that the latter word denotes the beams supporting the Upamit, presumably by leaning against it at an angle, while **Parimit** denotes the beams connecting the Upamits horizontally. These interpretations, however, can only be conjectural. See also **Gṛha.**

[1] i. 59, 1; iv. 5, 1.
[2] ix. 3, 1.
Cf. Zimmer, *Altindisches Leben*, 153; Bloomfield, *Hymns of the Atharvaveda*, 596; Whitney, Translation of the Atharvaveda, 525.

Upara, which, according to Pischel,[1] means 'stone' in general, is the technical name of the stone on which the Soma plant was laid in order to be pounded for the extraction of the juice by other stones (*adri, grāvan*). The word is rare, occurring only thrice in the Rigveda,[2] and once in the Atharvaveda.[3]

[1] *Vedische Studien*, 1, 109. This is the sense of the form *upala* (Vājasaneyi Saṃhitā, xxv. 8, etc.).
[2] i. 79, 3; x. 94, 5; 175, 3.
[3] vi. 49, 3.
Cf. Hillebrandt, *Vedische Mythologie*, 1, 154; Whitney, Translation of the Atharvaveda, 317; Von Schroeder, *Mysterium und Mimus*, 414.

Upala-prakṣiṇī occurs once in the Rigveda,[1] where it designates the occupation of a woman, as opposed to that of her son, who is a poet (*kāru*), and to that of his father, who is a physician (*bhiṣaj*). Yāska[2] renders the word by 'maker of groats' (*saktu-kārikā*), and Roth,[3] Grassmann,[4] Zimmer,[5] as well as others, connect it with the operation of grinding corn. Pischel,[6] however, who points out that corn was not ground between two stones, but beaten on a stone with a pestle (*dṛṣad*), considers that Upala-prakṣiṇī denotes a woman that assisted at the crushing of Soma (*cf.* **Upara**). Von Schroeder,[7] who more correctly points out that there is no objection to regarding *upala* as the mortar in which the corn was placed and then beaten with the pestle, renders the word literally as 'one who fills the (lower) stone (with corn).'

[1] ix. 112, 3.

[2] Nirukta, vi. 5.

[3] St. Petersburg Dictionary, *s.v.*

[4] *Ibid.*; *s.v.*, 'fitting the upper (to the lower) millstone.'

[5] *Altindisches Leben*, 269. *Cf.* Hillebrandt, *Vedachrestomathie*, *s.v.*, who, taking *pṛc* in the sense of 'fill,' explains the compound as 'filling the upper millstone,' an interpretation which as it stands is unintelligible.

[6] *Vedische Studien*, 1, 308-310.

[7] *Mysterium und Mimus*, 412 *et seq.* Von Schroeder does not accept the view that the mother of the singer is alluded to; but it seems impossible to draw any other conclusion from the language of the passage, and his own explanation of the word as referring to a corn-mother is very improbable; *cf.* Keith, *Journal of the Royal Asiatic Society*, 1909, 204.

Upalā in the Brāhmaṇas[1] may denote the upper and smaller 'stone,' which was used as a pestle with the **Dṛṣad** as the mortar, whereas **Upara** in the Saṃhitās denotes rather the mortar, and Dṛṣad the pestle. But see **Dṛṣad.**

[1] Śatapatha Brāhmaṇa, i. 1, 1, 22; ii. 1, 14, 17; ii. 2, 2, 1, etc. *Cf.* Von Schroeder, *Mysterium und Mimus*, 413, n. 3.

Upa-vāka occurs in the Vājasaneyi Saṃhitā[1] and the Brāhmaṇas[2] as a description of a species of grain, the *Wrightia antidysenterica*, known later as Indra-yava. The commentator Mahīdhara[3] simply glosses it with the more general term **Yava.**

[1] xix. 22; 90; xxi. 30 (as 'healing').

[2] Śatapatha Brāhmaṇa, xii. 7, 1, 3; 2, 9, etc.

According to the Vājasaneyi Saṃhitā, it formed the essential element of gruel (*karambha*), and Upavāka groats (*saktavaḥ*) are mentioned in the Śatapatha Brāhmaṇa.[4]

[3] On Vājasaneyi Saṃhitā, xix. 22.

[4] xii. 9, 1, 5.

Cf. Zimmer, *Altindisches Leben*, 240, 270.

Upa-veśi is mentioned as a pupil of **Kuśri** in a Vaṃśa (list of teachers) in the Bṛhadāraṇyaka Upaniṣad (vi. 5, 3, in both recensions). See also **Aupaveśi.**

Upa-śrī, Upa-śraya, are two readings of the same term. The former is found in one recension of the Kauṣītaki Upaniṣad,[1] while the latter is probably the reading of the other recension of the Upaniṣad,[2] and certainly the reading in one passage of the Atharvaveda,[3] though the text has *apaśrayaḥ*, which is accepted as possible by Roth.[4] In both cases the term clearly means something connected with a couch (**Āsandī** in the Atharvaveda, **Paryaṅka** in the Kauṣītaki Upaniṣad). Aufrecht,[5] Roth,[6] and Max Müller[7] render it as 'coverlet' or 'cushion,' but Whitney[8] seems evidently right in holding that it must mean a 'support' or something similar.

[1] i. 5.

[2] See Keith, *Śāṅkhāyana Āraṇyaka*, 20, n. 3.

[3] xv. 3, 8. *Cf.* Whitney's note in his Translation.

[4] St. Petersburg Dictionary, *s.v.*, and still followed by Böhtlingk, Dictionary, *s.v.*

[5] *Indische Studien*, 1, 131.

[6] *S.v. apaśraya.*

[7] *Sacred Books af the East*, 1, 278.

[8] Translation of the Atharvaveda, 777.

Cf. Weber, *Indische Studien*, 1, 402; Zimmer, *Altindisches Leben*, 155.

Upa-staraṇa denotes in the description of the couch (**Paryaṅka**) in the Kauṣītaki Upaniṣad[1] a 'coverlet,' and has this sense, used metaphorically, in the Rigveda[2] also. In the Atharvaveda[3] it seems to have the same meaning. Whitney,[4] however, renders it 'couch,' though he translates[5] the parallel word **Āstaraṇa** in another passage[6] by 'cushion.'

[1] i. 5.

[2] ix. 69, 5.

[3] v. 19, 12.

[4] Translation of the Atharvaveda, 254.

[5] *Ibid.*, 776.

[6] xv. 3, 7.

Cf. Weber, *Indische Studien*, 1, 403; Zimmer, *Altindisches Leben*, 155.

Upa-sti denotes both in the Rigveda[1] and the Atharvaveda[2] a 'dependent,' just as later in the Epic[3] the subordination of the Vaiśya to the two superior castes is expressed by the verb *upa-sthā*, 'stand under,' 'support.' The word also appears, with the same sense, in the form of Sti, but only in the Rigveda.[4] The exact nature of the dependence connoted by the term is quite uncertain. Zimmer[5] conjectures that the 'dependents' were the members of defeated Aryan tribes who became clients of the king, as among the Greeks, Romans, and Germans, the term possibly including persons who had lost their freedom through dicing.[6] The evidence of the Atharvaveda[7] shows that among the Upastis were included the chariot-makers (*ratha-kāra*), the smiths (*takṣan*), and the charioteers (*sūta*), and troop-leaders (*grāma-ṇī*), while the Rigveda passages negative the possibility of the 'subjects' (*sti*) being the whole people. It is therefore fair to assume that they were the clients proper of the king, not servile, but attached in a special relation to him as opposed to the ordinary population. They may well have included among them not only the classes suggested by Zimmer, but also higher elements, such as refugees from other clans, as well as ambitious men who sought advancement in the royal service. Indeed, the Sūta and the Grāmaṇī were, as such, officers of the king's household—kingmakers, not themselves kings, as they are described in the Atharvaveda.[8] The use of the word in the Taittirīya Saṃhitā,[9] the Taittirīya Brāhmaṇa,[10] and the Kāṭhaka,[11] is purely metaphorical, as well as in the one passage of the Rigveda in which it occurs. In the Paippalāda recension of the Atharvaveda,[12] Vaiśya, Śūdra, and Ārya are referred to as Upastis, perhaps in the general sense of 'subject.'

1 x. 97, 23 (= Vājasaneyi Saṃhitā, xii. 101; Av. vi. 15, 1).

2 iii. 5, 6.

3 Hopkins, *Journal of the American Oriental Society*, 13, 92.

4 vii. 19, 11; x. 148, 4; *sti-pa*, vii. 66, 3; x. 69, 4.

5 *Altindisches Leben*, 184, 185.

6 Rv. x. 34.

7 Av. iii. 5, 6. 7.

8 iii. 5, 7.

9 vii. 2, 5, 4. *Cf.* vi. 5, 8, 2.

10 iii. 3, 5, 4.

11 xxxi. 9.

12 iii. 5, 7.

Cf. Ludwig, Translation of the Rigveda, 3, 246; Whitney, Translation of the Atharvaveda, 92; Weber, *Indische Studien*, 17, 196 *et seq.*

Upa-stuta is mentioned several times in the Rigveda,[1] always as a sage of old, and usually in connexion with Kaṇva, who was aided or favoured by Agni, the Aśvins, and other gods. The Upastutas, sons of Vṛṣṭihavya,[2] are mentioned as singers.[3]

[1] i. 36, 10. 17; 112, 15; viii. 5, 25; x. 115, 8.
[2] x. 115, 9.
[3] viii. 103, 8; x. 115, 9.

Cf. Ludwig, Translation of the Rigveda, 3, 108; Max Müller, *Sacred Books of the East*, 32, 152, 153.

Upa-hvara denotes, in one passage of the Rigveda,[1] according to Geldner,[2] the body of a chariot (*upa-stha*).

[1] i. 87, 2.
[2] *Vedische Studien*, 3, 46.

Upānasa is in the Atharvaveda[1] opposed to **Akṣa**, and must mean something like 'the body of the wagon,' though Sāyaṇa suggests that it signifies either a 'granary' or a 'wagon full of grain.' In the Rigveda,[2] where the word occurs only once, its sense is doubtful. Pischel[3] explains the form which occurs there not as an adjective, but as an infinitive.

[1] ii. 14, 2.
[2] x. 105, 4.
[3] *Vedische Studien*, 1, 197.

Cf. Bloomfield, *Hymns of the Atharvaveda*, 301; Whitney, Translation of the Atharvaveda, 56.

Upā-nah is the regular word for a 'sandal' or 'shoe' from the later Saṃhitās[1] onwards. Boarskin is mentioned in the Śatapatha Brāhmaṇa[2] as a material of which shoes were made. The combination 'staff and sandals' (*daṇḍopānaha*) occurs as early as the Kauṣītaki Brāhmaṇa.[3]

[1] Taittirīya Saṃhitā, v. 4, 4, 4; 6, 6, 1, etc.
[2] v. 4, 3, 19.
[3] iii. 3.

Upāvi Jāna-śruteya is mentioned in the Aitareya Brāhmaṇa (i. 25, 15) as an authority on the Upasads (a kind of Soma ceremony).

Upoditi Gaupāleya is mentioned in the Pañcaviṃśa Brāhmaṇa (xii. 13, 11) as a seer of Sāmans.

Ubhayā-dant, 'having incisors in both jaws,' is an expression employed to distinguish, among domestic animals, the horse, the ass, etc., from the goat, the sheep, and cattle. The distinction occurs in a late hymn of the Rigveda,[1] and is several times alluded to in the later Saṃhitās[2] and the Brāhmaṇas.[3] In one passage of the Taittirīya Saṃhitā[4] man is classed with the horse as *ubhayā-dant*. The opposite is *anyato-dant*, 'having incisors in one jaw only,' a term regularly applied to cattle,[5] the eight incisors of which are, in fact, limited to the lower jaw. The ass is styled *ubhayā-dant* in the Atharvaveda.[6] In one passage of the Atharvaveda,[7] however, the epithet is applied to a ram; but the sense here is that a marvel occurs, just as in the Rigveda[8] a ram destroys a lioness. Bloomfield[9] suggests in the Atharvaveda passage another reading which would mean 'horse.' A parallel division of animals is that of the Taittirīya[10] and Vājasaneyi Saṃhitās[11] into 'whole-hoofed' (*eka-śapha*) and 'small' (*kṣudra*).

Zimmer[12] seeks to show from the Greek ἀμφώδοντα[13] and the Latin *ambidens*[14] that the Indo-European was familiar with the division of the five sacrificial animals into the two classes of man and horse on the one hand, and cattle, sheep, and goats on the other. But this supposition is not necessary.

1 x. 90, 10.
2 Taittirīya Saṃhitā, ii. 2, 6, 3; v. 1, 2, 6; Maitrāyaṇī Saṃhitā, i. 8, 1.
3 Śatapatha Brāhmaṇa, i. 6, 3, 30 (*ubhayato-dant*).
4 ii. 2, 6, 3.
5 Taittirīya Saṃhitā, ii. 1, 1, 5; v. 1, 2, 6; 5, 1, 3.
6 v. 31, 3.
7 v. 19, 2.
8 viii. 18, 17.
9 *Hymns of the Atharvaveda*, 434.
10 iv. 3, 10, 2.
11 xiv. 30.
12 *Altindisches Leben*, 74-76.
13 Aristotle, *Hist. An.*, ii. 1, 8.
14 Festus *apud* Paulum Diaconum. *Cf.* Weber, *Indische Studien*, 10, 58.

Urā as a name for 'sheep' is confined to the Rigveda.[1] It is curious that in one of its two occurrences the wolf should be referred to as terrifying sheep, and that the epithet of the wolf, *urā-mathi*, 'killing sheep,' should occur once in the Rigveda,[2] both references being in one book of the Saṃhitā, a fact which suggests a dialectical origin of the word *urā*. See also **Avi**.

1 viii. 34, 3.
2 viii. 66, 8. *Cf.* Nirukta, v. 21.

Uru-kakṣa occurs in only one passage of the Rigveda,[1] where the sense of the word is much disputed. The reading of the text is *uruḥ kakṣo na gāṅgyaḥ*, which may refer to a man, Urukakṣa, 'dwelling on the Ganges,'[2] or to a man, son of Gaṅgā, or to a wood so called,[3] or may simply denote the 'broad thicket on the Ganges.'[4]

[1] vi. 45, 31.

[2] Grassmann; St. Petersburg Dictionary. *Cf.* Macdonell, *Vedic Grammar*, 291.

[3] Ludwig's translation (*der wald Urukakṣa*, or *das weite dickicht*).

[4] Weber, *Episches im vedischen Ritual*, 28, n. 5; Oldenberg, *Ṛgveda-Noten*, 1, 396.

Uru-kṣaya.—A family of Urukṣayas, singers and worshippers of Agni, is referred to in one hymn of the Rigveda (x. 118, 8. 9).

Cf. Ludwig, Translation of the Rigveda, 3, 167.

Uruñjirā is given in the Nirukta (ix. 26) as one of the names of the river **Vipāś** (now Beäs).

Urvarā is with **Kṣetra** the regular expression, from the Rigveda[1] onwards, denoting a piece of 'ploughland' (*ἄρουρα*). Fertile (*apnasvatī*) fields[2] are spoken of as well as waste fields (*ārtanā*).[3] Intensive cultivation by means of irrigation is clearly referred to both in the Rigveda[4] and in the Atharvaveda,[5] while allusion is also made to the use of manure.[6] The fields (*kṣetra*) were carefully measured according to the Rigveda.[7] This fact points clearly to individual ownership in land for the plough, a conclusion supported by the reference of Apālā, in a hymn of the Rigveda,[8] to her father's field (*urvarā*), which is put on the same level as his head of hair as a personal possession. Consistent with this are the epithets 'winning fields' (*urvarā-sā, urvarā-jit, kṣetra-sā*),[9] while 'lord of fields' used of a god[10] is presumably a transfer of a human epithet (*urvarā-pati*). Moreover, fields are spoken of in the same

[1] i. 127, 6; iv. 41, 6; v. 33, 4; vi. 25, 4; x. 30, 3; 142, 3, etc.; Av. x. 6, 33; 10, 8; xiv. 2, 14, etc.

[2] Rv. i. 127, 6.

[3] *Ibid.*

[4] vii. 49, 2.

[5] i. 6, 4; xix. 2, 2.

[6] Av. iii. 14, 3, 4; xix. 31, 3.

[7] i. 110, 5.

[8] viii. 91, 5.

[9] Rv. iv. 38, 1, and vi. 20, 1; ii. 21, 1; iv. 38, 1.

[10] viii. 21, 3. *Cf.* **Kṣetra.**

connexion as children,[11] and the conquest of fields (*kṣetrāṇi saṃ-ji*) is often referred to in the Saṃhitās.[12] Very probably, as suggested by Pischel,[13] the ploughland was bounded by grass land (perhaps denoted by **Khila, Khilya**) which in all likelihood would be joint property on the analogy of property elsewhere. There is no trace in Vedic literature of communal property in the sense of ownership by a community of any sort,[14] nor is there mention of communal cultivation. Individual property in land seems also presumed later on. In the Chāndogya Upaniṣad[15] the things given as examples of wealth include fields and houses (*āyatanāni*). The Greek evidence[16] also points to individual ownership. The precise nature of the ownership is of course not determined by the expression 'individual ownership.' The legal relationship of the head of a family and its members is nowhere explained, and can only be conjectured (see **Pitṛ**). Very often a family may have lived together with undivided shares in the land. The rules about the inheritance of landed property do not occur before the Sūtras.[17] In the Śatapatha Brāhmaṇa[18] the giving of land as a fee to priests is mentioned, but with reproof: land was no doubt even then a very special kind of property, not lightly to be given away or parted with.[19]

[11] Rv. iv. 41, 6, etc.

[12] Taittirīya Saṃhitā, iii. 2, 8, 5; Kāṭhaka Saṃhitā, v. 2; Maitrāyaṇī Saṃhitā, iv. 12, 3.

[13] *Vedische Studien*, 2, 204-207.

[14] *Cf.* Baden Powell, *Indian Village Community* (1899); Zimmer, *Altindisches Leben*, 236; Mrs. Rhys Davids, *Journal of the Royal Asiatic Society*, 1901, 860.

[15] vii. 24, 2.

[16] *Cf.* Diodorus, ii. 40; Arrian, *Indica*, 11; Strabo, p. 703; Hopkins, *Journal of the American Oriental Society*, 13, 87 *et seq.* *Cf. ibid.*, 20, 22, 23.

[17] *Cf.* Gautama Dharma Sūtra, xviii. 5 *et seq.*; Baudhāyana Dharma Sūtra, ii. 2, 3; Āpastamba Dharma Sūtra, ii. 6, 14. Of course, the rules probably go back to the earlier period, but how far it is impossible to say. With the settlement of the country, however, inheritance of land and its partition must have become inevitable.

[18] xiii. 6, 2, 18; 7, 1, 13. 15.

[19] It is significant that in the famous episode (Taittirīya Saṃhitā, iii. 1, 9, 4) of Manu's division of his property, from which Nābhānediṣṭha was excluded, this exclusion is made good by the son's obtaining cattle (*paśavaḥ*). It is clear that cattle, not land, was the real foundation of wealth, just as in Ireland, Italy (*cf. pecunia*), Greece, etc. Cattle could be, and were, used individually, but land was not open to a man's free disposal; no doubt, at any rate, the consent of the family or the community might be required, but we are reduced to reliance on analogy in view of the silence of the texts. *Cf.* Schrader, *Prehistoric Antiquities*, 289; Jolly, *Recht und Sitte*, 94-96; Rhys Davids, *Buddhist India*, 48 *et seq.*

On the relation of the owners of land to the king and others see **Grāma**; on its cultivation see **Kṛṣi.**

Urvārū, f., **Urvāruka**, n., 'cucumber.' The former[1] of these words denotes the plant, the latter[2] the fruit, but both are very rare. The passages all seem to refer to the fact that the stem of the plant becomes loosened when the fruit is ripe.[3] The fruit is also called Urvāru in a Brāhmaṇa.[4]

1 Av. vi. 14, 2.

2 Rv. vii. 59, 12 = Av. xiv. 1, 17 = Maitrāyaṇī Saṃhitā, i. 10, 4 = Taittirīya Saṃhitā, i. 8, 6, 2 = Vājasaneyi Saṃhitā, iii. 60.

3 Sāyaṇa on Av. vi. 14, 2.

4 Pañcaviṃśa Brāhmaṇa, ix. 2, 19.

Cf. Zimmer, *Altindisches Leben*, 242.

Ula is the name of some unknown wild animal, perhaps, as Whitney[1] suggests, the 'jackal.' It is mentioned in the Atharvaveda[2] and later Saṃhitās,[3] but not definitely identified by the commentators.

1 Translation of the Atharvaveda, 669.

2 xii. 1, 49.

3 Taittirīya Saṃhitā, v. 5, 12, 1 (as *ūla*); Maitrāyaṇī Saṃhitā, iii. 13, 12; 14, 2; Vājasaneyi Saṃhitā, xxiv. 31. *Cf. ulala* in Baudhāyana Śrauta Sūtra, ii. 5.

Cf. Zimmer, *Altindisches Leben*, 82.

Ula Vārṣṇi-vṛddha is mentioned as a teacher in the Kauṣītaki Brāhmaṇa (vii. 4).

Ulapa[1] is the name of a species of grass referred to in the Rigveda and the later Saṃhitās.[2]

1 x. 142, 3.

2 Av. vii. 66, 1. Adjectives derived from the word are *ulapya* (Vājasaneyi Saṃhitā, xvi. 45, etc.) and *upolapa* (Maitrāyaṇī Saṃhitā, i. 7, 2).

Ulukya Jāna-śruteya is mentioned as a teacher in the Jaiminīya Upaniṣad Brāhmaṇa (i. 6, 3).

Ulūka is the ordinary word for 'owl' from the Rigveda[1] onwards. The bird was noted for its cry,[2] and was deemed the harbinger of ill-fortune (*nairṛta*).[3] Owls were offered at the horse sacrifice to the forest trees,[4] no doubt because they roosted there.

1 x. 165, 4.
2 Rv. *loc. cit.*
3 Av. vi. 19, 2; Taittirīya Saṃhitā, v. 5, 18, 1; Vājasaneyi Saṃhitā, xxiv. 38.
4 Vājasaneyi Saṃhitā, xxiv. 23; Maitrāyaṇī Saṃhitā, iii. 14, 4.

Ulūkhala is the regular expression for 'mortar' from the Rigveda[1] onwards, occurring frequently also in the compound[2] Ulūkala-musala, 'mortar and pestle.' The exact construction of the vessel is quite unknown till we reach the Sūtra period.

1 i. 28, 6, Av. x. 9, 26; xi. 3, 3; xii. 3, 13; Taittirīya Saṃhitā, v. 2, 8, 7; vii. 2, 1, 3; Śatapatha Brāhmaṇa, i. 1, 4, 6, etc.
2 Av. ix. 6, 15; Śatapatha Brāhmaṇa, i. 1, 1, 22.

Ulkā regularly denotes a meteor from the Rigveda[1] onwards. In the Brāhmaṇas[2] it also signifies a 'firebrand.' The much rarer form Ulkuṣī[3] has both senses.

1 iv. 4, 2; x. 68, 4; Av. xix. 9, 8; Ṣaḍviṃśa Brāhmaṇa, vi. 8, etc.
2 Śatapatha Brāhmaṇa, v. 5, 4, 19.
3 As 'meteor,' Av. v. 17, 4; Śatapatha Brāhmaṇa, xi. 2, 7, 21; as 'firebrand,' *ibid.*, iii. 9, 2, 9.

Ulmuka is the common word in the Brāhmaṇas[1] for 'firebrand,' from which a coal (*aṅgāra*)[2] could be taken.

1 Aitareya Brāhmaṇa, ii. 11; Satapatha Brāhmaṇa, i. 8, 2, 1; ii. 1, 4, 28, etc.; Jaiminīya Brāhmaṇa, ii. 76 (*Journal of the American Oriental Society*, 15, 239).
2 Satapatha Brāhmaṇa, xii. 4, 3, 3; Jaiminīya Brāhmaṇa, i. 61, 1 (*Journal of the American Oriental Society*, 23, 342).

Ulmukāvakṣayaṇa is an expression that occurs several times in the Śatapatha Brāhmaṇa,[1] signifying a 'means of extinguishing (*ava-kṣayaṇa*) a firebrand,' or possibly more precisely 'tongs.' Compare **Aṅgārāvakṣayaṇa.**

1 iv. 6, 8, 7; v. 2, 4, 15; xi. 6, 3, 3; Jaiminīya Brāhmaṇa, ii. 76. *Cf.* Böhtlingk, Dictionary, *s.v.*

Uśanas Kāvya is an ancient seer, already a half-mythical figure in the Rigveda,[1] where he is often mentioned, especially as associated with Kutsa and Indra. Later on[2] he becomes the Purohita of the Asuras in their contests with the gods. A variant of his name is Kavi Uśanas.[3] He appears in the Brāhmaṇas as a teacher also.[4]

[1] i. 51, 10; 83, 5; 121, 12; iv. 16, 2; vi. 20, 11; viii. 23, 17; ix. 87, 3; 97, 7; x. 40, 7; probably also i. 130, 9; v. 31, 8; 34, 2; viii. 7, 26; x. 22, 6. Also in Av. iv. 29, 6.

[2] Taittirīya Saṃhitā, ii. 5, 8, 5; Pañcaviṃśa Brāhmaṇa, vii. 5, 20; Śāṅkhāyana Srauta Sūtra, xiv. 27, 1.

[3] Rv. iv. 26, 1.

[4] Pañcaviṃśa Brāhmaṇa, xiv. 12, 5; Jaiminīya Upaniṣad Brāhmaṇa, ii. 7, 2, 6.

Cf. Roth, St. Petersburg Dictionary, *s.v.*; Geldner, *Vedische Studien*, 2, 167 *et seq.*; Bergaigne, *Religion Védique*, 2, 339 *et seq.*; Macdonell, *Vedic Mythology*, p. 147.

Uśanā occurs in the Śatapatha Brāhmaṇa (iii. 4, 3, 13; iv. 2, 5, 15) as the name of a plant from which Soma was prepared.

Uśīnara.—In the Aitareya Brāhmaṇa[1] the Kuru-Pañcālas are mentioned as dwelling together in the 'Middle Country' with the Vaśas and the Uśīnaras. In the Kauṣītaki Upaniṣad[2] also the Uśīnaras are associated with the Kuru-Pañcālas and Vaśas, but in the Gopatha Brāhmaṇa[3] the Uśīnaras and Vaśas are regarded as northerners. In the Rigveda[4] the people is alluded to in one passage by reference to their queen, Uśīnarāṇī. Zimmer[5] thinks that the Uśīnaras earlier lived farther to the north-west, but for this there is no clear evidence. His theory is based merely on the fact that the Anukramaṇī (Index) of the Rigveda ascribes one hymn[6] to Śibi Auśīnara, and that the Śibis were known to Alexander's followers as Σίβοι,[7] living between the Indus and the Akesines (Chenab). But this is in no way conclusive, as the Śibis, at any rate in Epic times,[8] occupied the land to the north of Kurukṣetra, and there is no reason whatever to show that in the Vedic period the Uśīnaras were farther west than the 'Middle Country.'

[1] viii. 14.

[2] iv. 1. See Keith, *Śāṅkhāyana Āraṇyaka*, 36.

[3] ii. 9.

[4] x. 59, 10.

[5] *Altindisches Leben*, 130.

[6] Rv. x. 179.

[7] Diodorus, xvii. 19.

[8] See Pargiter's map, *Journal of the Royal Asiatic Society*, 1908, p. 322.

Cf. Weber, *Indische Studien*, 1, 213, 419; Hultzsch, *Indian Antiquary*, 34, 179.

Uṣa, 'salt ground,' occurs as a variant of Ūṣa in the Maitrāyaṇī Saṃhitā (i. 6, 3).

Uṣasta Cākrāyaṇa is mentioned as a teacher in the Bṛhadāraṇyaka (iii. 5, 1) and Chāndogya (i. 10, 1; 11, 1) Upaniṣads, the name in the latter work appearing as Uṣasti.

Uṣṭi, Uṣṭra.—Both of these words, of which the former is quite rare,[1] must have the same sense. Roth[2] and Aufrecht[3] hold that in the Rigveda[4] and the Brāhmaṇas[5] the sense is 'humped bull' or 'buffalo,' but the former thinks that in the Vājasaneyi Saṃhitā[6] the sense is doubtful, and 'camel' may be meant. Hopkins[7] is decidedly of opinion that the sense in every case is 'camel.' The animal was used as a beast of burden yoked in fours.[8]

1 Perhaps in Rv. x. 106, 2; Taittirīya Saṃhitā, v. 6, 21, 1; Kāṭhaka Saṃhitā, xv. 2.

2 St. Petersburg Dictionary, *s.v.*

3 Cited in Muir, *Sanskrit Texts*, 5, 468. *Cf.* Zimmer, *Altindisches Leben*, 224.

4 i. 138, 2; viii. 5, 37; 6, 48; 46, 22. 31; Av. xx. 127, 2; 132, 13; Vājasaneyi Saṃhitā, xiii. 50.

5 Śatapatha Brāhmaṇa, 1, 2, 3, 9, etc.; Aitareya Brāhmaṇa, ii. 8.

6 xxiv. 28. 39.

7 *Journal of the American Oriental Society*, 17, 83.

8 Av. xx. 127, 2; Rv. viii. 6, 48.

Uṣṇīṣa denotes the 'turban' worn by Vedic Indians, men and women[1] alike. The Vrātya's turban is expressly referred to in the Atharvaveda[2] and the Pañcaviṃśa Brāhmaṇa.[3] A turban was also worn at the Vājapeya[4] and the Rājasūya[5] ceremonies by the king as a token of his position.

1 Aitareya Brāhmaṇa, vi. 1; Śatapatha Brāhmaṇa, iii. 3, 2, 3; iv. 5, 2, 7 (used at the sacrifice to wrap the embryo in): xiv. 2, 1, 8 (Indrāṇī's Uṣṇīṣa), etc.; Kāṭhaka Saṃhitā, xiii. 10.

2 xv. 2, 1.

3 xvii. 1, 14. *Cf.* xvi. 6, 13.

4 Śatapatha Brāhmaṇa, v. 3, 5, 23.

5 Maitrāyaṇī Saṃhitā, iv. 4, 3.

Uṣyala occurs once in the description of the couch or the bridal car in the Atharvaveda,[1] where it seems to mean the four 'frame-pieces.' The form is doubtful: *uṣpala* is possible.[2]

1 xiv. 1, 60.

2 Whitney, Translation of the Atharvaveda, 385. *Cf.* Zimmer, *Altindisches Leben*, 155; Whitney, *op. cit.*, 752.

Usra, m.; **Usrā**, f.; **Usrika**, m.; **Usriya**, m.; **Usriyā**, f. All these words denote a 'bull' or a 'cow,' occurring frequently in the Rigveda,[1] and sometimes later,[2] but usually with some reference to the morning light. In some passages the sense is doubtful. See **Go.**

1 *Usra*, Rv. vi. 12, 4; *usrā*, i. 3, 8; viii. 75, 8; 96, 8; ix. 58, 2, etc.; *usrika*, i. 190, 5; *usriya*, v. 58, 6 (with *vṛṣabhaḥ*); ix. 74, 3; *usriyā*, i. 153, 4; 180, 3; ii. 40, 2, etc. In ix. 70, 6, *usriya* is applied to a calf; and in ix. 68, 1; 93, 2, *usriyā* means 'milk.'

2 *Usrau dhūrṣāhau*, Vājasaneyi Saṃhitā, iv. 33; *usrā*, Av. xii. 3, 37; *usriya*, Av. i. 12, 1; *usriyā*, Av. ix. 4, 1; Vājasaneyi Saṃhitā, xxxv. 2. 3. In Av. v. 20, 1; 28, 3, it means 'cowhide,' or perhaps in v. 28, 3, 'milk.'

Ū.

Ūrjayant Aupamanyava is mentioned in the Vaṃśa Brāhmaṇa[1] as a pupil of **Bhānumant Aupamanyava.**

1 *Indische Studien*, 4, 372.

Ūrjayantī is regarded by Ludwig[1] in one passage of the Rigveda[2] as the name of a fort, the stronghold of **Nārmara.** The verse is, however, quite unintelligible.[3]

1 Translation of the Rigveda, 3, 152.

2 ii. 13, 8.

3 Sāyaṇa makes Urjayantī a Piśācī; Grassmann, the sun; Roth, *s.v. ūrjay*, takes it adjectivally. *Cf.* Oldenberg, *Ṛgveda-Noten*, 1, 199.

Ūrjavya, a word occurring only once in the Rigveda,[1] is taken by Ludwig[2] to be the name of a sacrificer. Roth,[3] however, regards the word as an adjective meaning 'rich in strength,' and this is the more probable interpretation.

1 v. 41, 20.

2 Translation of the Rigveda, 3, 155.

3 St. Petersburg Dictionary, *s.v.*

Ūrṇa-nābhi,[1] **Ūrṇa-vābhi**, **Ūrṇā-vant** are all names of the spider in the later Saṃhitās and the Brāhmaṇas in allusion to the insect's spinning threads of wool, as it were.

1 *Ūrṇa-nābhi* ('having wool in its navel'), Taittirīya Brāhmaṇa, i. 1, 2, 5; Bṛhadāraṇyaka Upaniṣad, ii. 1, 23; *ūrṇa-vābhī* ('wool-spinner'), Kāṭhaka Saṃhitā, viii. 1; Śatapatha Brāhmaṇa, xiv. 5, 1, 23; *ūrṇā-vant* ('possessing wool'), Kauṣītaki Brāhmaṇa, xix. 3 (in a Mantra).

Ūrṇā, 'wool,' is very frequently mentioned from the Rigveda[1] onwards. The Paruṣṇī country was famous for its wool,[2] like Gandhāra[3] for its sheep. The term for the separate tufts was *parvan*[4] or *parus*.[5] 'Soft as wool' (*ūrṇa-mradas*)[6] is not a rare epithet. The sheep is called 'woolly' (*ūrṇāvatī*).[7] 'Woollen thread' (*ūrṇā-sūtra*) is repeatedly referred to in the later Saṃhitās[8] and the Brāhmaṇas.[9] The word *ūrṇā* was not restricted to the sense of sheep's wool,[10] but might denote goat's hair also.[11]

1 iv. 22, 2; v. 52, 9; Śatapatha Brāhmaṇa, xii. 5, 1, 13; 7, 2, 10, etc.; *ūrṇāyu*, 'woolly,' Vājasaneyi Saṃhitā, xiii. 50; Pañcaviṃśa Brāhmaṇa, xii. 11, 10.

2 Rv., *loc. cit.*; Pischel, *Vedische Studien*, 2, 210. But *cf.* Max Müller, *Sacred Books of the East*, 32, 315.

3 Rv. i. 126, 7.

4 Rv. iv. 22, 10.

5 Rv. ix. 15, 6.

6 Rv. v. 5, 4; x. 18, 10; Vājasaneyi Saṃhitā, ii. 2; iv. 10; xxi. 33, etc.

7 Rv. viii. 56, 3.

8 Maitrāyaṇī Saṃhitā, iii. 11, 9; Kāṭhaka Samhitā, xxxviii. 3; Vājasaneyi Saṃhitā, xix. 80, etc. *Cf.* *ūrṇā-stukā*, Aitareya Brāhmaṇa, i. 28; Kāṭhaka Saṃhitā, xxv. 3.

9 Taittirīya Brāhmaṇa, ii. 6, 4; Śatapatha Brāhmaṇa, xii. 7, 2, 11, etc.

10 *Cf.* *anaiḍakīr ūrṇāḥ* ('wool not coming from the *eḍaka*,' a species of sheep) in Śatapatha Brāhmaṇa, ii. 5, 2, 15.

11 *Cf.* Hopkins, *Journal of the American Oriental Society*, 17, 83, n.

Ūrṇā-vatī.—In the hymn of the Rigveda[1] which celebrates the rivers Ludwig[2] finds a reference to an affluent of the Indus called Ūrṇāvatī. This interpretation, however, seems certainly wrong. Roth[3] renders the word merely as 'woolly,' and Zimmer[4] rejects Ludwig's explanation on the ground that it throws the structure of the hymn into confusion. Pischel[5] makes the word an epithet of the Indus, 'rich in sheep.'

1 x. 75, 8.

2 Translation of the Rigveda, 3, 200.

3 St. Petersburg Dictionary, *s.v.*

4 *Altindisches Leben*, 429.

5 *Vedische Studien*, 2, 210.

Ūrdara.—This word occurs once in the Rigveda,[1] when reference is made to filling Indra with Soma as one fills an

1 ii. 14, 11.

Ūrdara with grain (**Yava**). Sāyaṇa renders it 'granary,' but Roth[2] and Zimmer[3] seem more correct in simply making it a measure for holding grain, or 'garner.'

[2] St. Petersburg Dictionary, *s.v.*

[3] *Altindisches Leben*, 238.

Ūla is a variant of **Ula.**

Ūṣa in the later Saṃhitās[1] and Brāhmaṇas[2] denotes salt ground suited for cattle. *Cf.* **Uṣa.**

[1] Taittirīya Saṃhitā, v. 2, 3. 2, etc.

[2] Aitareya Brāhmaṇa, iv. 27; Satapatha Brāhmaṇa, v. 2, 1, 16, etc.

Ṛ.

1. **Ṛkṣa,** 'bear,' is found only once in the Rigveda,[1] and seldom later,[2] the animal having evidently been scarce in the regions occupied by the Vedic Indians. Not more frequent[3] is the use of the word in the plural to denote the 'seven bears,' later called the 'seven Ṛṣis,'[4] the constellation of the 'Great Bear' (*ἄρκτος, ursa*).

[1] v. 56, 3.

[2] Maitrāyaṇī Saṃhitā, iii. 14, 17; Vājasaneyi Saṃhitā, xxiv. 36; Jaiminīya Brāhmaṇa, i. 184. *Cf.* Zimmer, *Altindisches Leben*, 81.

[3] Rv. i. 24, 10; Śatapatha Brāhmaṇa, ii. 1, 2, 4; Taittirīya Āraṇyaka, i. 11, 2. *Cf.* Hillebrandt, *Vedische Mythologie*, 3, 422.

[4] *Cf.* Macdonell, *Vedic Mythology*, p. 144 (D).

2. **Ṛkṣa** is the name of a patron mentioned in one verse of a Dānastuti ('Praise of Gifts') in the Rigveda,[1] his son being referred to in the next verse as **Ārkṣa.**

[1] viii. 68, 15. *Cf.* Ludwig, Translation of the Rigveda, 3, 163.

Ṛkṣākā is a word occurring once in an obscure passage of the Atharvaveda.[1] The sense is quite unknown. Weber[2] thinks it refers to the 'milky way,' but his view rests on no evidence. Whitney[3] despairs of the passage.

[1] xviii. 2, 31.

[2] *Festgruss an Roth*, 138, n. 2; Berlin Catalogue, 2, 59, n.; *Proceedings of the Berlin Academy*, 1895, 856.

[3] Translation of the Atharvaveda, 840.

Ṛkṣīkā, a word found in the Atharvaveda,[1] the Vājasaneyi Saṃhitā,[2] and the Śatapatha Brāhmaṇa,[3] appears to denote a demon. Harisvāmin, however, in his commentary on the Śatapatha Brāhmaṇa, connects the word with **Ṛkṣa**, as meaning 'bear.'

[1] xii. 1, 49.
[2] xxx. 8.
[3] xiii. 2, 4, 2. 4. *Cf.* Eggeling, *Sacred Books of the East*, 44, 307.

Ṛg-veda, the formal name of the collection of Ṛcs, first appears in the Brāhmaṇas,[1] and thereafter frequently in the Āraṇyakas[2] and Upaniṣads.[3]

[1] Aitareya Brāhmaṇa, i. 32, and implied in Taittirīya Brāhmaṇa, iii. 12, 9, 1; Śatapatha Brāhmaṇa, vi. 5, 4, 6; 8, 3; xii. 3, 4, 9.
[2] Aitareya Āraṇyaka, iii. 2, 3. 5; Sāṅkhāyana Āraṇyaka, viii. 3. 8.
[3] Bṛhadāraṇyaka Upaniṣad, i. 5, 12; ii. 4, 10; iv. 1, 6; 5, 11; Chāndogya Upaniṣad, i. 3, 7; iii. 1, 2. 3; 15, 7; vii. 1, 2. 4; 2, 1; 7, 1.

Ṛjiśvan is mentioned several times in the Rigveda,[1] but always in a vague manner, as if very ancient. He assists Indra in fights against demoniac figures like Pipru and the dusky brood (*kṛṣṇa-garbhāḥ*). According to Ludwig,[2] he was called Auśija's son,[3] but this is doubtful. He is twice[4] clearly called Vaidathina, or descendant of Vidathin.

[1] i. 51, 5; 53, 8; 101, 1; vi. 20, 7; viii. 49, 10; x. 99, 11; 138, 3.
[2] Translation of the Rigveda, 3, 143, 149.
[3] Rv. x. 99, 11. *Cf.* **Auśija**.
[4] Rv. iv. 16, 13; v. 29, 11.
Cf. Macdonell, *Vedic Mythology*, p. 161 (C).

Ṛjūnas is mentioned once only in the Rigveda[1] along with six other Soma sacrificers.

[1] viii. 52, 2. *Cf.* Ludwig, Translation of the Rigveda, 3, 163.

Ṛjrāśva appears in the Rigveda[1] as one of the **Vārṣāgiras**, along with **Ambarīṣa**, **Surādhas**, **Sahadeva**, and **Bhayamāna**, and as apparently victorious in a race. Elsewhere[2] in the

[1] i. 100, 16. 17.
[2] i. 116, 17; 117, 16. 17.

Rigveda he is celebrated as having been blinded by his father for slaying one hundred rams for a she-wolf, and as having been restored to sight by the Aśvins, a legend of quite obscure meaning.

Cf. Macdonell, *Vedic Mythology*, p. 52.

Ṛṇa, 'debt,' is repeatedly mentioned from the Rigveda[1] onwards, having apparently been a normal condition among the Vedic Indians. Reference is often made[2] to debts contracted at dicing. To pay off a debt was called *ṛṇaṃ saṃ-nī*.[3] Allusion is made to debt contracted without intention of payment.[4]

The result of non-payment of a debt might be very serious: the dicer might fall into slavery.[5] Debtors, like other malefactors, such as thieves, were frequently bound by their creditors to posts (*dru-pada*),[6] presumably as a means of putting pressure on them or their friends to pay up the debt.

The amount of interest payable is impossible to make out. In one passage of the Rigveda and Atharvaveda[7] an eighth (*śapha*) and a sixteenth (*kalā*) are mentioned as paid, but it is quite uncertain whether interest or an instalment of the principal is meant. Presumably the interest would be paid in kind.

How far a debt was a heritable interest or obligation does not appear. The Kauśika Sūtra[8] regards three hymns of the

1 ii. 27, 4, etc., usually in a metaphorical sense.

2 Rv. x. 34, 10; Av. vi. 119, 1.

3 Rv. viii. 47, 17 = Av. vi. 46, 3.

4 Av. vi. 119, 1.

5 Rv. x. 34. *Cf.* Lüders, *Das Würfelspiel im alten Indien*, 61.

6 Rv. x. 34, 4, seems to refer rather to the binding and taking away as a slave, though Pischel, *Vedische Studien*, 1, 228, explains it as the binding of a debtor for non-payment, interpreting the obscure verse i. 169, 7, in the same way. But Av. vi. 115, 2. 3, may refer to debt, and if this is the meaning the allusion to binding to a post as a punishment is clear. See, however, Bloomfield, *Hymns of the Atharvaveda*, 528, n. 1; Whitney, Translation of the Atharvaveda, 364, who interprets the hymn as referring only to sin. Rv. i. 24, 13. 15; Av. vi. 63, 3=84, 4; 121, 1 *et seq.*, are general; while Rv. vii. 86, 5; Av. xix. 47, 9; 50, 1, refer to the binding of thieves in the stocks. *Cf.* **Taskara.**

7 Rv. viii. 47, 17=Av. vi. 46, 3.

8 xlvi. 36-40. See Caland, *Altindisches Zauberritual*, 154; Bloomfield, *op. cit.*, 528.

Atharvaveda[9] as applicable to the occasion of the payment of a debt after the creditor's decease. For the payment of a debt by a relation of the debtor the evidence is still less clear.[10]

Zimmer[11] thinks that payments of debt were made in the presence of witnesses who could be appealed to in case of dispute. This conclusion is, however, very uncertain, resting solely on a vague verse in the Atharvaveda.[12]

9 vi. 117-119. The name for unpaid debt is in Av. vi. 117, 1, *apamityam apratīttam*. In the Taittirīya Saṃhitā, iii. 3, 8, 1, *kusīdam apratīttam*; in the Maitrāyaṇī Saṃhitā, iv. 14, 17, and Taittirīya Āraṇyaka, ii. 3, 1, 8, *kusīdam apratītam*; in the Mantra Brāhmaṇa, ii. 3, 20, *apradattam*.

10 *Cf.* Rv. iv. 3, 13 (a brother's sin or debt); Jolly, *Recht und Sitte*, 99, 100.

11 *Altindisches Leben*, 181. This suggestion is ignored by Bloomfield, *op. cit.*, 375, and Whitney, *op. cit.*, 304.

12 vi. 32, 3 = viii. 8, 21. *Cf.* Śāṅkhāyana Āraṇyaka, xii. 14, and see **Jñātṛ**.

Cf. Zimmer, *op. cit.*, 181, 182; 259.

Ṛṇaṃ-caya, a prince of the **Ruśamas,** is celebrated in a Dānastuti (' Praise of Gifts ') of the Rigveda (v. 30, 12. 14) for his generosity to a poet named **Babhru.**

Cf. Zimmer, *Altindisches Leben*, 129; Bṛhaddevatā, ed. Macdonell, 2, 169, 174.

Ṛtu, 'season,' is a term repeatedly mentioned from the Rigveda[1] onwards. Three seasons of the year are often alluded to,[2] but the names are not usually specified. In one passage of the Rigveda[3] spring (*vasanta*), summer (*grīṣma*), and autumn (*śarad*) are given. The Rigveda knows also the rainy season (*prā-vṛṣ*) and the winter (*himā, hemanta*). A more usual[4] division (not found in the Rigveda) is into five seasons,

1 i. 49, 3; 84, 18, etc.

2 *Cf.* Rv. i. 164, 2 (*tri-nābhi*), 48 (*trīṇi nabhyāni*); also perhaps the Ṛbhus as the genii of the three seasons and the three dawns. *Cf.* Macdonell, *Vedic Mythology*, p. 133; Hillebrandt, *Vedische Mythologie*, 2, 33 *et seq.*; Śatapatha Brāhmaṇa, xiv. 1, 1, 28, and the *cāturmāsyāni*, or four-monthly sacrifices performed at the beginning of the seasons in the ritual (Weber, *Naxatra*, 2, 329 *et seq.*).

3 x. 90, 6. Hillebrandt, *op. cit.*, 2, 35, finds in Rv. v. 14, 4; ix. 91, 6, reference to three seasons in the triad *gāvaḥ* (? spring), *āpaḥ* (rains), *svar* (=*gharma*), and in the ritual literature (Āpastamba Śrauta Sūtra, viii. 4, 2) in the threefold division into *ṛta*, *gharma*, and *oṣadhi*.

4 Av. viii. 2, 22; 9, 15; xiii. 1, 18; Taittirīya Saṃhitā, i. 6, 2, 3; iv. 3, 3, 1. 2; v. 1, 10, 3; 3, 1, 2; 4. 12, 2; 6. 10, 1; 7, 2, 4; vii. 1, 18, 1. 2; Maitrāyaṇī Saṃhitā, i. 7, 3; iii. 4, 8; 13, 1; Kāṭhaka Saṃhitā, iv. 14; ix. 16; Vājasaneyi Saṃhitā, x. 10-14; Śatapatha Brāhmaṇa, i. 3, 5, 11; vi. 2, 2, 3, etc.; Taittirīya Brāhmaṇa, iii. 10, 4, 1; 11, 10, 4, etc. *Cf.* Rv. i. 164, 13. See also Weber, *op. cit.*, 2, 352.

vasanta, grīṣma, varṣā, śarad, hemanta-śiśira ; but occasionally the five are otherwise divided, *varṣā-śarad* being made one season.[5] Sometimes six[6] seasons are reckoned, *hemanta* and *śiśira* being divided, so that the six seasons can be made parallel to the twelve months of the year. A still more artificial arrangement[7] makes the seasons seven, possibly by reckoning the intercalary month as a season, as Weber and Zimmer[8] hold, or more probably because of the predilection for the number seven, as Roth[9] suggests. Occasionally the word *ṛtu* is applied to the months.[10] The last season, according to the Śatapatha Brāhmaṇa,[11] is *hemanta*.

The growth of the division of the seasons from three to five is rightly explained by Zimmer[12] as indicating the advance of the Vedic Indians towards the east. It is not Rigvedic, but dominates the later Saṃhitās. Traces of an earlier division of the year into winter and summer do not appear clearly in the Rigveda, where the appropriate words *himā* and *samā* are merely general appellations of the year, and where *śarad*[13] is commoner than either as a designation of the year, because it denotes the harvest, a time of overwhelming importance to a young agricultural people. The division of the year in one passage of the Atharvaveda[14] into two periods of six months is merely formal, and in no way an indication of old tradition.

5 Satapatha Brāhmaṇa, xiii. 6, 1, 10. 11.

6 Av. vi. 55, 2; xii. 1, 36; Taittirīya Saṃhitā, v. 1, 5, 2; 7, 3; 2. 6, 1, etc.; Maitrāyaṇī Saṃhitā, i. 7, 3; iii. 11, 12; Kāṭhaka Saṃhitā, viii. 6; Vājasaneyi Saṃhitā, xxi. 23-28; Śatapatha Brāhmaṇa, i. 7, 2, 21; ii. 4, 2, 24; xii. 8, 2, 34; Taittirīya Brāhmaṇa, ii. 6, 19, etc. *Cf.* also Rv. i. 23, 15, as interpreted by Roth, St. Petersburg Dictionary, *s.v. indu*.

7 Av. vi. 61, 2; viii. 9, 18; Śatapatha Brāhmaṇa, viii. 5, 1, 15; ix. 1, 2, 31; 2, 3, 45; 3, 1, 19; 5, 2, 8; perhaps Av. iv. 11, 9, and *cf.* Rv. i. 164, 1.

8 *Indische Studien*, 18, 44; *Altindisches Leben*, 374.

9 St. Petersburg Dictionary, *s.v. ṛtu*. *Cf.* Hopkins, *Religions of India*, 18, 33.

10 Av. xv. 4; Taittirīya Saṃhitā, iv. 4, 11, 1; Vājasaneyi Saṃhitā, xiii. 25; xiv. 6. 15. 26. 27; xv. 57, etc.

11 i. 5, 3, 13.

12 *Op. cit.*, 373.

13 Hopkins, *American Journal of Philology*, 15, 159, 160; Weber, *Indische Studien*, 17, 232; Bühler, *Zeitschrift der Deutschen Morgenländischen Gesellschaft*, 41, 28.

14 viii. 9, 17. *Cf.* Zimmer, 372.

Ṛtu-parṇa appears in a Brāhmaṇa-like passage of the Baudhāyana Śrauta Sūtra[1] as son of Bhaṅgāśvina and king of Śaphāla. In the Āpastamba Śrauta Sūtra[2] are mentioned Ṛtuparṇa-Kayovadhī Bhaṅgyaśvinau.

[1] xx. 12.

[2] xxi. 20, 3.

Cf. Caland, *Zeitschrift der Deutschen Morgenländischen Gesellschaft*, 57, 745.

Ṛtv-ij is the regular term for 'sacrificial priest,' covering all the different kinds of priests employed at the sacrifice. It appears certain that all the priests were Brāhmaṇas.[1] The number of priests officiating at a sacrifice with different functions was almost certainly seven. The oldest list, occurring in one passage of the Rigveda,[2] enumerates their names as Hotṛ, Potṛ, Neṣṭṛ, Agnīdh, Praśāstṛ, Adhvaryu, Brahman, besides the institutor of the sacrifice. The number of seven probably explains the phrase 'seven Hotṛs' occurring so frequently in the Rigveda, and is most likely connected with that of the mythical 'seven Ṛṣis.' It may be compared with the eight of Iran.[3] The chief of the seven priests was the Hotṛ, who was the singer of the hymns, and in the early times their composer also. The Adhvaryu performed the practical work of the sacrifice, and accompanied his performance with muttered formulas of prayer and deprecation of evil. His chief assistance was derived from the Agnīdh, the two performing the smaller sacrifices without other help in practical matters. The Praśāstṛ, Upavaktṛ, or Maitrāvaruṇa, as he was variously called, appeared only in the greater sacrifices as giving instructions to the Hotṛ, and as entrusted with certain litanies. The Potṛ, Neṣṭṛ, and Brahman belonged to the ritual of the Soma sacrifice, the latter being later styled Brāhmaṇācchamsin to distinguish him from the priest who in the later

[1] This is assumed throughout the Vedic texts, and is accompanied by the rule that no Kṣatriya can eat of the sacrificial offering (*cf.* Aitareya Brāhmaṇa, vii. 26): no doubt because only the Brāhmaṇas were sufficiently holy to receive the divine essence of the sacrifice into which, by partaking of it, the deity has entered in part.

[2] ii. 1, 2. *Cf.* Oldenberg, *Religion des Veda*, 383.

[3] Darmesteter, *Le Zend-Avesta*, 1, lxx *et seq.*

ritual acted as supervisor. Other priests referred to in the Rigveda[4] are the singers of Sāmans or chants, the Udgātṛ and his assistant the Prastotṛ, while the Pratihartṛ, another assistant, though not mentioned, may quite well have been known. Their functions undoubtedly represent a later stage of the ritual, the development of the elaborate series of sacrificial calls on the one hand, and on the other the use of long hymns addressed to the Soma plant. Other priests, such as the Achāvāka,[5] the Grāvastut, the Unnetṛ, and the Subrahmaṇya, were known later in the developed ritual of the Brāhmaṇas, making in all sixteen priests, who were technically and artificially classed in four groups[6]: Hotṛ, Maitrāvaruṇa, Achāvāka, and Grāvastut; Udgātṛ, Prastotṛ, Pratihartṛ, and Subrahmaṇya; Adhvaryu, Pratisthātṛ, Neṣṭṛ, and Unnetṛ; Brahman, Brāhmaṇācchaṃsin, Agnīdhra, and Potṛ.

Apart from all these priests was the **Purohita**, who was the spiritual adviser of the king in all his religious duties. Geldner[7] holds that, as a rule, when the Purohita actually took part in one of the great sacrifices he played the part of the Brahman, in the sense of the priest who superintended the whole conduct of the ritual. He sees evidence for this view in a considerable number of passages of the Rigveda[8] and the later literature,[9] where Purohita and Brahman were combined or identified. Oldenberg,[10] however, more correctly points out

[4] Rv. viii. 81, 5.

[5] *Cf.*, for the Achāvāka, Kauṣītaki Brāhmaṇa, xxviii. 4; Aitareya Brāhmaṇa, vi. 14, 8, etc.; Bergaigne, *Recherches sur l'histoire de la liturgie védique*, 47; Oldenberg, *Religion des Veda*, 397, n. 2. The other three occur in the Aitareya and other Brāhmaṇas. See St. Petersburg Dictionary, *s.v.*

[6] Āśvalāyana Śrauta Sūtra, iv. 1, 4-6; Śāṅkhāyana Śrauta Sūtras, xiii. 14, 1, etc. In the Rigveda Sūtra the order of the four sets is Hotṛ, Brahman, Udgātṛ, and Adhvaryu. Sometimes a seventeenth priest is mentioned, but he was not usually approved, though the Kauṣītakins maintained him as the Sadasya. See Satapatha Brāhmaṇa, x. 4, 1, 19; Eggeling, *Sacred Books of the East*, 43, 348, n.; Keith, *Aitareya Āraṇyaka*, 37; Weber, *Indische Studien*, 9, 375.

[7] *Vedische Studien*, 2, 143 *et seq.*

[8] Rv. i. 44, 10; 94, 6; viii. 27, 1, etc.

[9] Bṛhaspati is Purohita of the gods, Rv. ii. 24, 9; Taittirīya Brāhmaṇa, ii. 7, 1, 2; Aitareya Brāhmaṇa, iii. 17, 2; Śatapatha Brāhmaṇa, v. 3, 1, 2; but Brahman in Rv. x. 141, 3; Kauṣītaki Brāhmaṇa, vi. 13; Śatapatha Brāhmaṇa, i. 7, 4, 21. Vasiṣṭha is Purohita, Rv. x. 150, 5, of Sudās Paijavana, Śāṅkhāyana Śrauta Sūtra, xvi. 11, 4; but Brahman of the Sunaḥśepa sacrifice, *ibid.*, xv. 21.

[10] *Op. cit.*, 380 *et seq.*

that in the earlier period this was not the case: the Purohita was then normally the Hotṛ, the singer of the most important of the songs; it was only later that the Brahman, who in the capacity of overseer of the rite is not known to the Rigveda, acquired the function of general supervision hitherto exercised by the Purohita, who was *ex officio* skilled in the use of magic and in guarding the king by spells which could also be applied to guarding the sacrifice from evil demons. With this agrees the fact that Agni, pre-eminently[11] the Purohita of men, is also a Hotṛ, and that the two divine Hotṛs of the Āprī hymns are called[12] the divine Purohitas. On the other hand, the rule is explicitly recognized in the Aitareya Brāhmaṇa[13] that a Kṣatriya should have a Brahman as a Purohita; and in the Taittirīya Saṃhitā[14] the Vasiṣṭha family have a special claim to the office of Brahman-Purohita, perhaps an indication that it was they who first as Purohitas exchanged the function of Hotṛs for that of Brahmans in the sacrificial ritual.

The sacrifices were performed for an individual in the great majority of cases. The Sattra,[15] or prolonged sacrificial session, was, however, performed for the common benefit of the priests taking part in it, though its advantageous results could only be secured if all the members actually engaged were consecrated (*dīkṣita*). Sacrifices for a people as such were unknown. The sacrifice for the king was, it is true, intended to bring about the prosperity of his people also; but it is characteristic that the prayer[16] for welfare includes by name only the priest and the king, referring to the people indirectly in connexion with the prosperity of their cattle and agriculture.

[11] Agni as Hotṛ and Purohita occurs in Rv. i. 1, 1; iii. 3, 2; 11, 1; v. 11, 2. His Purohitaship is described in terms characteristic of the Hotṛ's functions in Rv. viii. 27, 1; x. 1, 6. Devāpi is Purohita and Hotṛ, Rv. x. 98.

[12] Rv. x. 66, 13; in x. 70, 7, *purohitāv ṛtvijā*.

[13] vii. 26.

[14] iii. 5, 2, 1, etc.

[15] Oldenberg, 371.

[16] Vājasaneyi Saṃhitā, xxii. 22; Taittirīya Saṃhitā, vii. 5, 18; Maitrāyaṇī Saṃhitā, iii. 12, 6; Kāṭhaka Saṃhitā, v. 5, 14, etc.

Cf. Weber, *Indische Studien*, 10, 141 *et seq.*; 376 *et seq.*; Hillebrandt, *Rituallitteratur*, 97; Oldenberg, *op. cit.*, 370-397; Ludwig, Translation of the Rigveda, 3, 224.

Ṛśya.—This is the correct[1] spelling of a word that occurs in the Rigveda[2] and the later literature[3] meaning 'stag,' the feminine being **Rohit.**[4] Apparently deer were caught in pits (*ṛśya-da*).[5] The procreative power of the stag (*ārśya vṛṣṇya*) was celebrated.[6]

[1] It appears in Av. iv. 4, 7, as Ṛśa; as Ṛṣya in Maitrāyaṇī Saṃhitā, iii. 14, 9. 18.

[2] viii. 4, 10.

[3] Av. iv. 4, 5. 7; v. 14, 3; i. 18, 4 (*ṛśya-pad*); Vājasaneyi Saṃhitā, xxiv. 27. 37; Aitareya Brāhmaṇa, iii. 33; citation in Śāṅkhāyana Śrauta Sūtra, viii. 25, 8, etc.

[4] Av. iv. 4, 7.

[5] Rv. x. 39, 8.

[6] Av. iv. 4, 5.

Cf. Weber, *Indische Studien*, 18, 18; Zimmer, *Altindisches Leben*, 82; Whitney, Translation of the Atharvaveda, 150, 151.

1. **Ṛṣabha** is the common name of the 'bull' from the Rigveda[1] onwards.[2] See also **Go.**

[1] vi. 16, 47; 28, 8; x. 91, 14, etc.

[2] Av. iii. 6, 4; 23, 4, etc.; Taittirīya Saṃhitā, ii. 1, 3, 2, etc.; Vājasaneyi Saṃhitā, xxi. 22, etc.; Pañcaviṃśa Brāhmaṇa, xiii. 5, 18, etc.

2. **Ṛṣabha,** king of the Śviknas, appears in the Śatapatha Brāhmaṇa[1] with the patronymic Yājñatura, as one of those who performed an Aśvamedha or horse sacrifice. He is also mentioned there[2] as having probably been the source of a saying of **Gaurīviti Śāktya's.**

[1] xiii. 5, 4, 15. *Cf.* Śāṅkhāyana Śrauta Sūtra, xvi. 9, 8-10.

[2] xii. 8, 3, 7.

3. **Ṛṣabha** is mentioned in the Aitareya Brāhmaṇa (vii. 17) as a son of Viśvāmitra.

Ṛṣi, 'seer,' is primarily a composer of hymns to the gods. In the Rigveda[1] reference is often made to previous singers and to contemporary poets. Old poems were inherited and refurbished by members of the composer's family,[2] but the great aim of the singers was to produce new and approved hymns.[3] It is not till the time of the Brāhmaṇas that the

[1] i. 1, 2; 45, 3; viii. 43, 13, etc.

[2] i. 89, 3; 96, 2; iii. 39, 2; viii. 6, 11. 43; 76, 6, etc.

[3] i. 109, 2; ii. 18, 3; iii. 62, 7; vi. 50, 6; vii. 14, 4; 93, 1; viii. 23, 14, etc.

composition of hymns appears to have fallen into disuse,[4] though poetry was still produced, for example, in the form of **Gāthās**, which the priests were required to compose themselves[5] and sing to the accompaniment of the lute at the sacrifice. The Ṛṣi was the most exalted of Brāhmaṇas,[6] and his skill, which is often compared with that of a carpenter,[7] was regarded as heaven-sent.[8] The Purohita, whether as Hotṛ or as Brahman (see **Ṛtvij**), was a singer.[9] No doubt the Ṛṣis were normally[10] attached to the houses of the great, the petty kings of Vedic times, or the nobles of the royal household. Nor need it be doubted that occasionally[11] the princes themselves essayed poetry: a Rājanyarṣi, the prototype of the later Rājarṣi or 'royal seer,' who appears in the Pañcaviṃśa Brāhmaṇa,[12] though he must be mythical as Oldenberg[13] points out, indicates that kings cultivated poetry[14] just as later they engaged in philosophic disputations.[15] Normally, however, the poetical function is Brahminical, Viśāmitra and others not being kings, but merely Brāhmaṇas, in the Rigveda.

In the later literature the Ṛṣis are the poets of the hymns preserved in the Saṃhitās, a Ṛṣi being regularly[16] cited when a Vedic Saṃhitā is quoted. Moreover, the Ṛṣis become the representatives of a sacred past, and are regarded as holy sages,

[4] Geldner, *Vedische Studien*, 2, 151.

[5] Satapatha Brāhmaṇa, xiii. 4, 2, 8; 3, 5.

[6] Rv. ix. 96, 6, etc. *Cf.* Satapatha Brāhmaṇa, xii. 4, 4, 6, where preeminence is assigned to a Brāhmaṇa descended from a Ṛṣi.

[7] Rv. i. 130, 6; v. 2, 11; 29, 15; 73, 10; x. 39, 14. So a poet is a Kāru (if from *kṛ*, 'make,' but usually derived from *kṛ*, 'commemorate'), and makes (*kṛ*, Rv. ii. 39, 8; viii. 62, 4) as well as creates (*jan*, Rv. vii. 15, 4; viii. 88, 4) hymns.

[8] Rv. i. 37, 4; vii. 36, 1. 9; viii. 32, 27; 57, 6, etc.

[9] Rv. i. 151, 7; Geldner, *op. cit.*, 2, 153; Oldenberg, *Religion des Veda*, 380.

[10] Geldner, *op. cit.*, 2, 154, cites the Dānastutis as characteristic of princes in the tradition of the Bṛhaddevatā, etc.

[11] *Ibid.*, 154.

[12] xii. 12, 6, etc.

[13] *Zeitschrift der Deutschen Morgenländischen Gesellschaft*, 45, 235, n. 3.

[14] Later on it was deemed quite normal and natural. See the story of Rathavīti Dārbhya, or Dālbhya, himself a royal seer, and Taranta and Purumīḷha, seers and also kings, in Bṛhaddevata, v. 50 *et seq.*

[15] *Cf.* Garbe, *Philosophy of Ancient India*, 73 *et seq.*; Deussen, *Philosophy of the Upaniṣads*, 16 *et seq.*; Keith, *Aitareya Āraṇyaka*, 50.

[16] Aitareya Brāhmaṇa, ii. 25; viii. 26; Śatapatha Brāhmaṇa, i. 7, 4, 4; ii. 2, 3, 6; 5, 1, 4; vi. 1, 1, 1, etc.; Nirukta, vii. 3, etc.

whose deeds are narrated as if they were the deeds of gods or Asuras.[17] They are typified by a particular group of seven,[18] mentioned four times in the Rigveda,[19] several times in the later Saṃhitās,[20] and enumerated in the Bṛhadāraṇyaka Upaniṣad[21] as Gotama, Bharadvāja, Viśvāmitra, Jamadagni, Vasiṣṭha, Kaśyapa, and Atri. In the Rigveda itself Kutsa,[22] Atri,[23] Rebha,[24] Agastya,[25] the Kuśikas,[26] Vasiṣṭha,[27] Vyaśva,[28] and others appear as Ṛṣis; and the Atharvaveda[29] contains a long list, including Aṅgiras, Agasti, Jamadagni, Atri, Kaśyapa, Vasiṣṭha, Bharadvāja, Gaviṣṭhira, Viśvāmitra, Kutsa, Kakṣīvant, Kaṇva, Medhātithi, Triśoka, Uśanā Kāvya, Gotama, and Mudgala.

Competition among the bards appears to have been known. This is one of the sides of the riddle poetry (**Brahmodya**) that forms a distinctive feature[30] of the Vedic ritual of the Aśvamedha, or horse sacrifice. In the Upaniṣad period such competitions were quite frequent. The most famous was that of Yājñavalkya, which was held at the court of Janaka of Videha, as detailed in the Bṛhadāraṇyaka Upaniṣad,[31] and which was a source of annoyance to **Ajātaśatru** of **Kāśī**.[32] According to an analogous practice, a Brāhmaṇa, like **Uddālaka Aruṇi**, would go about disputing with all he came across, and compete with them for a prize of money.[33]

[17] Aitareya Brāhmaṇa, i. 17; ii. 19; Śatapatha Brāhmaṇa, i. 6, 2, 7, etc.

[18] *Cf. Indische Studien*, 8, 167.

[19] iv. 42, 8; x. 109, 4; 130, 7; Macdonell, *Vedic Mythology*, p. 144.

[20] Vājasaneyi Saṃhitā, xiv. 24; Av. xi. 1, 1. 24; xii. 1, 39, etc.

[21] ii. 2, 6.

[22] i. 106, 6.

[23] i. 117, 3.

[24] i. 117, 4.

[25] i. 179, 6.

[26] iii. 53, 10.

[27] vii. 33, 13.

[28] viii. 23, 16.

[29] iv. 29. *Cf.* xviii. 3, 15. 16.

[30] Zimmer, *Altindisches Leben*, 345, 346; Bloomfield, *Journal of the American Oriental Society*, 15, 172; *Religion des Veda*, 216 *et seq.*

[31] iii. 1, 1 *et seq.*

[32] *Bṛhadāraṇyaka Upaniṣad*, ii. 1, 1 *et seq.*; Kauṣītaki Upaniṣad, iv. 1 *et seq.*

[33] Śatapatha Brāhmaṇa, xi. 4, 1, 1 *et seq.*; Gopatha Brāhmaṇa, i. 3, 8 *et seq.*; Geldner, *Vedische Studien*, 2, 185, 344.

Cf. Zimmer, *Altindisches Leben*, 340-347; Muir, *Sanskrit Texts*, 3, 120 *et seq.*

Ṛṣis.—The term 'Seven Ṛṣis' denotes the 'Great Bear' (see 1. **Ṛkṣa**) in one passage of the Rigveda,[1] and occasionally

[1] x. 82, 2.

later.[2] This is probably a secondary use, instead of the seven Ṛkṣas, brought about by the frequent mention of the seven Ṛṣis.

[2] Av. vi. 40, 1 (where, however, Whitney, Translation of the Atharvaveda, 310, merely renders it as 'seven seers,' and appears not to take it in a technical sense); Śatapatha Brāhmaṇa, ii. 1, 2, 4; xiii. 8, 1, 9; Nirukta, x. 26, etc.

Cf. Hillebrandt, *Vedische Mythologie*, 3, 422; Roth, St. Petersburg Dictionary, *s.v.*; Macdonell, *Vedic Mythology*, p. 144.

Ṛṣṭi is a term frequently employed in the Rigveda[1] to designate a weapon held in the hands of the Maruts, and doubtless meant to indicate lightning. That it denotes a spear in mortal warfare, as Zimmer[2] thinks, is not shown by a single passage.[3]

[1] Rv. i. 37, 1; 64, 4. 8; 166, 4; v. 52, 6; 54, 11; 57, 6; viii. 20, 11. Indra has a Ṛṣṭi in Rv. i. 169, 3 (*cf.* Av. iv. 37, 8). *Cf.* Macdonell, *Vedic Mythology*, p. 79.

[2] *Altindisches Leben*, 301.

[3] Rv. i. 167, 3; vii. 55, 2; viii. 28, 5; x. 87, 7. 24 are all mythological or contain similes.

Cf. Schrader, *Prehistoric Antiquities*, 221.

Ṛṣṭi-ṣeṇa is mentioned in the Nirukta[1] as an explanation of the patronymic **Ārṣṭiṣeṇa,** but nothing else is known of him.

[1] ii. 11. *Cf.* Sieg, *Die Sagenstoffe des Ṛgveda*, 130, 136.

Ṛṣya-śṛṅga appears as a teacher, pupil of Kāśyapa, and as bearing the patronymic Kāśyapa in the Jaiminīya Upaniṣad Brāhmaṇa[1] and in the Vaṃśa Brāhmaṇa.[2] The more correct spelling of the name is Ṛśya-śṛṅga.[3]

[1] iii. 40, 1 (in a Vaṃśa, or list of teachers).

[2] *Indische Studien*, 4, 374, 385.

[3] The later legend connected with the name may contain old elements (see Lüders, *Die Sage von Ṛshyaśṛṅga*, 1897; Von Schroeder, *Mysterium und Mimus*, 292-301), but it is not known to any Vedic text.

E.

Eka-dyū is mentioned as a poet in one hymn of the Rigveda.[1]

[1] viii. 80, 10. *Cf.* Ludwig, Translation of the Rigveda, 3, 112.

Eka-yāvan Gāṃ-dama is a man mentioned in the Pañcaviṃśa Brāhmaṇa[1] and the Taittirīya Brāhmaṇa.[2]

[1] xxi. 14, 20.

[2] ii. 7, 11 (Kāṃdama).

Cf. Weber, *Indische Studien*, i. 32; Hopkins, *Transactions of the Connecticut Academy of Arts and Sciences*, 15, 69.

Eka-rāj, 'sole ruler,' 'monarch,' seems to mean no more than 'king.' In the Rigveda[1] the term is used metaphorically only. But it is found with the literal sense in the Aitareya Brāhmaṇa,[2] as well as in the Atharvaveda.[3]

[1] viii. 37, 3.
[2] viii. 15.
[3] iii. 4, 1.
Cf. Weber, *Rājasūya*, 141.

Ekāyana denotes some object of study in the Chāndogya Upaniṣad.[1] The St. Petersburg Dictionary renders it 'doctrine (*ayana*) of unity' (*eka*), 'monotheism,' while Max Müller prefers 'ethics,' and Monier-Williams in his Dictionary 'worldly wisdom.'[2]

[1] vii. 1, 2. 4; 2, 1; 7, 1.
[2] Max Müller and Monier-Williams thus follow Śaṅkara's interpretation as *nīti-śāstra*, 'moral teaching.' *Cf.* Weber, *Indische Studien*, 1, 267, 484; Little, *Grammatical Index*, 43.

Ekāṣṭakā.—That Aṣṭakā is the eighth day after the full moon appears clearly from the Atharvaveda.[1] Ekāṣṭakā, or 'sole Aṣṭakā,' must denote not merely any Aṣṭakā, but some particular one. Sāyaṇa, in his commentary on the Atharvaveda,[2] in which a whole hymn celebrates the Ekāṣṭakā, fixes the date meant by the term as the eighth day in the dark half of the month of Māgha (January—February). The Ekāṣṭakā is declared in the Taittirīya Saṃhitā[3] to be the time for the consecration (*dīkṣā*) of those who are going to perform a year-long sacrifice. See also **Māsa**.

[1] xv. 16, 2. *Cf.* Śatapatha Brāhmaṇa, vi. 2, 2, 23; 4, 2, 10.
[2] iii. 10.
[3] vii. 4, 8, 1. *Cf.* iii. 3, 8, 4; iv. 3, 11, 1; v. 7, 2, 2; Pañcaviṃśa Brāhmaṇa, v. 9, 4.
Cf. Zimmer, *Altindisches Leben*, 365; Weber, *Naxatra*, 2, 341, 342.

Ejatka is the name of an insect in the Atharvaveda.[1]

[1] v. 23, 7. *Cf.* Zimmer, *Altindisches Leben*, 98; Whitney, Translation of the Atharvaveda, 262.

Eḍaka appears to denote a 'vicious ram' in the Śatapatha[1] and Jaiminīya[2] Brāhmaṇas.

[1] xii. 4, 1, 4; *cf.* ii. 5, 2, 15.
[2] i. 51, 4 (*Journal of the American Oriental Society*, 23, 332). *Cf.* Eggeling, *Sacred Books of the East*, 44, 178.

Eṇī denotes the 'female antelope' in the later Saṃhitās,[1] perhaps as the feminine of **Eta.**

[1] Av. v. 14, 11; Taittirīya Saṃhitā, v. 5, 15, 1; Maitrāyaṇī Saṃhitā, iii. 14, 17; Vājasaneyi Saṃhitā, xxiv. 36; *Cf.* Zimmer, *Altindisches Leben*, 82.

Eta in the plural (*etāḥ*) denotes the steeds of the Maruts, being a swift species of deer, which are mentioned several times in the Rigveda,[1] and the skins of which are also said to be worn by the Maruts on their shoulders.[2] The epithet *pṛthu-budhna*, once applied to them in the Rigveda,[3] and variously interpreted as 'broad-hoofed,'[4] 'broad-chested,'[5] and 'broad in the hinder part,'[6] seems to indicate that they were not gazelles.[7]

[1] i. 165, 2; 169, 6. 7; v. 54, 5; x. 77, 2.
[2] Rv. i. 166, 10. *Cf.* Roth, St. Petersburg Dictionary, *s.v.*
[3] i. 169, 6.
[4] By Grassman and Zimmer.
[5] Griffith, *Hymns of the Rigveda*, 1, 235.
[6] Monier-Williams, Dictionary, *s.v.*
[7] *Cf.* Zimmer, *Altindisches Leben*, 83.

1. **Etaśa** is in several passages of the Rigveda,[1] according to Roth[2] the name of a protégé whom Indra helped against the sun-god Sūrya. But in all these passages Etaśa seems merely to designate the horse of the sun.

[1] i. 62, 15; iv. 30, 6; v. 29, 5.
[2] St. Petersburg Dictionary, *s.v.*
[3] Macdonell, *Vedic Mythology*, pp. 149, 150.

2. **Etaśa** is in the Kauṣītaki Brāhmaṇa[1] the name of a sage who is said to have cursed his children because they interrupted him in the midst of a rite; hence the Aitaśāyanas (descendants of Etaśa) are declared to be the worst of the Bhṛgus. The same story appears in the Aitareya Brāhmaṇa,[2] where, however, the sage's name is Aitaśa, and the Aitaśāyanas are described as the worst of the Aurvas.

[1] xxx. 5.
[2] vi. 33. *Cf.* Hillebrandt, *Vedische Mythologie*, 2, 173.

Edidhiṣuḥ-pati is a term occurring only in the Vājasaneyi Saṃhitā,[1] where the commentator Mahīdhara interprets it as

[1] xxx. 9.

meaning the 'husband of a younger sister married before the elder sister.' Though this sense is probably correct, the form is doubtless, as Delbrück[2] points out, corrupt. See **Didhiṣūpati**.

2 *Die indogermanischen Verwandschaftsnamen*, 569, n. 1.

Eraṇḍa, the castor-oil plant (*Ricinus communis*), is first mentioned in the Śāṅkhāyana Āraṇyaka (xii. 8).

Evāvada is regarded by Ludwig[1] in a very obscure passage of the Rigveda[2] as the name of a singer beside **Kṣatra, Manasa,** and **Yajata**. The commentator Sāyaṇa also interprets the word as a proper name. Roth,[3] however, considers it to be an adjective meaning 'truthful.'

1 Translation of the Rigveda, 3, 138.

2 v. 44, 10.

3 St. Petersburg Dictionary, *s.v.*

AI.

Aikādaśākṣa Mānu-tantavya appears in the Aitareya Brāhmaṇa[1] as a king who observed the rule of sacrificing when the sun had risen (*udita-homin*), and as a contemporary of **Nagarin Jāna-śruteya**.

1 v 30. *Cf.* Weber, *Indische Studien*, 1, 223.

Aikṣvāka, 'descendant of Ikṣvāku,' is the patronymic borne by **Purukutsa** in the Śatapatha Brāhmaṇa.[1] Another Aikṣvāka is Vārṣṇi, a teacher mentioned in the Jaiminīya Upaniṣad Brāhmaṇa.[2] A king **Hariścandra Vaidhasa** Aikṣvāka is known to the Aitareya Brāhmaṇa,[3] and **Tryaruṇa** is an Aikṣvāka in the Pañcaviṃśa Brāhmaṇa.[4]

1 xiii. 5, 4, 5.

2 i. 5, 4.

3 vii. 13, 16.

4 xiii. 3, 12.

Aitareya, perhaps a patronymic from Itara, though the commentator Sāyaṇa[1] regards the word as a metronymic from

1 Cited by Aufrecht, *Aitareya Brāhmaṇa*, 3.

Itarā, is an epithet of **Mahidāsa** in the Aitareya Āraṇyaka[2] and the Chāndogya Upaniṣad.[3]

[2] ii. 1, 8; 3, 7.

[3] iii. 16, 7. *Cf.* Weber, *Indische Studien*, 1, 389. The form Aitareyin occurs in the Anupada Sūtra, viii. 1; Āśvalāyana Srauta Sūtra, i. 3, etc.; and a Mahaitareya in Āśvalāyana Gṛhya Sūtra, iii. 4, 4, etc.

Aitaśa, Aitaśāyana. See **Etaśa, Etaśāyana.** The Aitaśa-pralāpa, or 'Discourse of Aitaśa,' is a part of the Atharvaveda.[1]

[1] xx. 129-132. *Cf.* Bṛhaddevatā, viii. 101, with Macdonell's note.

Aiti-hāsika.—This term was applied to the people who explained the Vedic hymns by treating them as legendary history (**Itihāsa**), as Sieg[1] shows by the passages of the Nirukta,[2] where their views are opposed to those of the **Nairuktas**, who relied rather on etymology. Sieg[3] also seems right in finding them in the Naidānas of the Nirukta:[4] it is possible that their textbook was called the Nidāna.

[1] *Die Sagenstoffe des Ṛgveda*, 13 *et seq.*

[2] ii. 16; xii. 1, etc.

[3] *Op. cit.*, 29.

[4] vi. 9; vii. 6.

Aibhāvata, 'descendant of Ibhāvant,' is the patronymic of **Pratīdarśa.**[1]

[1] Satapatha Brāhmaṇa, xii. 8, 2, 3.

Airāvata, 'son of Irāvant,' is the patronymic of Dhṛtarāṣṭra, as a snake demon,[1] in the Atharvaveda[2] and the Pañcaviṃśa Brāhmaṇa.[3]

[1] In the later literature Airāvata is the elephant of Indra: perhaps connected with this Vedic snake demon, as *nāga* means both 'serpent' and 'elephant.'

[2] viii. 10, 29.

[3] xxv. 15, 3.

Ailūṣa, 'descendant of Ilūṣa,' is the patronymic of **Kavaṣa.**

Aiṣa-kṛta. See **Śitibāhu.**

Aiṣā-vīra.—The Śatapatha Brāhmaṇa once[1] refers to the Aiṣā-vīras as officiating at a sacrifice, with the implication that they were bad sacrificers. Sāyaṇa regards the word as a proper name (' descendants of Eṣavīra '), denoting the members of a despised family. But Roth may be right in explaining the word both in the passage mentioned above and elsewhere as meaning ' weak '[2] or ' insignificant man.'[3]

1 xi. 2, 7, 32.

2 In the St. Petersburg Dictionary, *s.v.*

3 In Böhtlingk's Dictionary, *s.v.* (' one who wishes to be a man, but is not '). *Cf.* Śatapatha Brāhmaṇa, ix. 5, 1, 16; Kauṣītaki Brāhmaṇa, i. 1, where, however, Lindner's edition reads *saiṣā vīra iva.* *Cf.* Weber, *Indische Studien*, 1, 228; Eggeling, *Sacred Books of the East*, 44, 45.

Aiṣumata, ' descendant of Iṣumant,' is the patronymic of **Trāta** in the Vaṃśa Brāhmaṇa.[1]

1 *Indische Studien*, 4, 372.

O.

Ogaṇa is a word occurring only once, as a plural, in the Rigveda,[1] where it appears to indicate persons hostile to the seer of the hymn, and apparently opposed to the Āryan religion. Ludwig[2] regards the term as the proper name of a people, but Pischel[3] thinks that it is merely an adjective meaning ' weak ' (*ogaṇa*=*ava-gaṇa*), as in Pāli.

1 x. 89, 15.

2 Translation of the Rigveda, 5, 209.

3 *Vedische Studien*, 2, 191, 192.

Otu in Vedic literature[1] denotes the ' woof ' in weaving, and corresponds to **Tantu**, ' the warp,' the roots *vā*,[2] ' to weave,' and *tan*,[3] ' to stretch,' from which these two terms are derived, being used in parallel senses. In the process of weaving a shuttle (**Tasara**) was used. The ' weaver ' is termed *vāya*,[4] and the ' loom ' *veman*.[5] A wooden peg (**Mayūkha**) was used to

1 Rv. vi. 9, 2. 3; Av. xiv. 2, 51; Taittirīya Saṃhitā, vi. 1, 1, 4, etc.

2 Rv. vi. 9, 2, etc.

3 Vājasaneyi Saṃhitā, xix. 80; Rv. x. 130, 2; Av. x. 7, 43, etc.

4 Rv. x. 26, 6, etc.

5 Vājasaneyi Saṃhitā, xix. 83.

stretch the web on, while lead was employed as a weight to extend it.[6]

The work of weaving was probably the special care of women.[7] A metaphor in the Atharvaveda[8] personifies Night and Day as two sisters weaving the web of the year, the nights serving as warp, the days as woof.

[6] Vājasaneyi Saṃhitā, xix. 80.
[7] Av. x. 7, 42; xiv. 2, 51. *Cf.* Rv. i. 92, 3.
[8] x. 7, 42; Taittirīya Brāhmaṇa, ii. 5, 5, 3.

Cf. Zimmer, *Altindisches Leben*, 254, 255; Muir, *Sanskrit Texts*, 5, 465.

Odana is a common expression[1] denoting a mess, usually of grain cooked with milk (*kṣīra-pākam odanam*).[2] Special varieties are mentioned, such as the 'milk-mess' (*kṣīraudana*),[3] the 'curd-mess' (*dadhy-odana*),[4] the 'bean-mess' (*mudgaudana*),[5] the 'sesame-mess' (*tilaudana*),[6] the 'water-mess' (*udaudana*),[7] the 'meat-mess' (*māṃsaudana*),[8] the 'ghee-mess' (*ghṛtaudana*),[9] etc.

[1] Rv. viii. 69, 14, etc.; Av. iv. 14, 7, etc.
[2] Rv. viii. 77, 10.
[3] Śatapatha Brāhmaṇa, ii. 5, 3, 4; xi. 5, 7, 5; Bṛhadāraṇyaka Upaniṣad, vi. 4, 13.
[4] Bṛhadāraṇyaka Upaniṣad, vi. 4, 14.
[5] Śāṅkhāyana Āraṇyaka, xii. 8.
[6] *Ibid.*; Bṛhadāraṇyaka Upaniṣad, vi. 4, 15.
[7] *Ibid.*, vi. 4, 15.
[8] *Ibid.*, vi. 4, 16; Satapatha Brāhmaṇa, xi. 5, 7, 5; Śāṅkhāyana Āraṇyaka, xii. 8.
[9] Śāṅkhāyana Āraṇyaka, xii. 8.

Opaśa is a word of somewhat doubtful sense, occurring in the Rigveda,[1] the Atharvaveda,[2] and occasionally later.[3] It probably means a 'plait' as used in dressing the hair, especially of women,[4] but apparently, in earlier times,[5] of men also. The goddess Sinīvālī is called *svaupaśā*,[6] an epithet of doubtful sense, from which Zimmer[7] conjectures that the wearing of

[1] x. 85, 8. *Cf.* i. 173, 6; viii. 14, 5; ix. 71, 1.
[2] vi. 138, 1. 2; ix. 3, 8, where it is applied metaphorically in describing the roof of a house.
[3] Pañcaviṃśa Brāhmaṇa, iv. 1, 1.
[4] Av. vi. 138, 1. 2.
[5] Rv. i. 173, 6; viii. 14, 5.
[6] Taittirīya Saṃhitā, iv. 1, 5, 3; Maitrāyaṇī Saṃhitā, ii. 7, 5; Vājasaneyi Saṃhitā, xi. 56. The reading is uncertain. Bloomfield (see below) assumes *sv-opaśā* to be the correct form ('having a fair *opaśa*').
[7] *Altindisches Leben*, 264.

false plaits of hair was not unknown in Vedic times. What was the difference between the braids referred to in the epithets *pṛthu-ṣṭuka,*[8] 'having broad braids,' and *viṣita-ṣṭuka,*[9] 'having loosened braids,' and the Opaśa cannot be made out from the evidence available. Geldner[10] thinks that the original sense was 'horn,' and that when the word applies to Indra[11] it means 'diadem.'

[8] Rv. x. 86, 8.

[9] Rv. i. 167, 5 (of Rodasī).

[10] *Vedische Studien,* 1, 131, quoting Pañcaviṃśa Brāhmaṇa, xiii. 4, 3, where *dvy-opaśāḥ* is used of cattle; but the sense may be figurative.

[11] Rv. viii. 14, 5.

Cf. Bloomfield, *Hymns of the Atharvaveda,* 538, 539; Whitney, Translation of the Atharvaveda, 348.

Oṣadhi.—Roughly speaking, the vegetable world is divided in Vedic literature[1] between Oṣadhi or **Vīrudh** 'plants' and **Vana** or **Vṛkṣa** 'trees.' Oṣadhi is employed in opposition to Vīrudh to denote plants as possessing a healing power or some other quality useful to men, while Vīrudh is rather a generic term for minor vegetable growths, but sometimes,[2] when occurring beside Oṣadhi, signifies those plants which do not possess medicinal properties.

A list of the minor parts of which a plant is made up is given in the later Saṃhitās.[3] It comprises the root (*mūla*), the panicle (*tūla*), the stem (*kāṇḍa*), the twig (*valśa*), the flower (*puṣpa*), and the fruit (*phala*), while trees[4] have, in addition, a corona (*skandha*), branches (*śākhā*), and leaves (*parṇa*). The Atharvaveda[5] gives an elaborate, though not very intelligible, division of plants into those which expand (*pra-stṛṇatīḥ*), are bushy (*stambinīḥ*), have only one sheath (*eka-śuṅgāḥ*), are creepers (*pra-tanvatīḥ*), have many stalks (*aṃśumatīḥ*), are

[1] Rv. x. 97 and *passim*. *Oṣadhi-vanaspati* is a frequent compound, from the Śatapatha Brāhmaṇa (vi. 1, 1, 12) onwards. The medicinal properties of plants account for the epithet 'of manifold powers' (*nānā-vīryā*) applied to them in Av. xii. 1, 2.

[2] Taittirīya Saṃhitā, ii. 5, 3, 2.

[3] *Ibid.*, vii. 3, 19, 1; Vājasaneyi Saṃhitā, xxii. 28.

[4] Taittirīya Saṃhitā, vii. 3, 20, 1. *Cf.* Rv. i. 32, 5; Av. x. 7, 38.

[5] viii. 7, 4, with Whitney's notes. *Cf.* Bloomfield, *Hymns of the Atharvaveda,* 579; Henry, *Les livres VIII. et IX. de l'Atharvavéda,* 58 *et seq.*

jointed (*kāṇḍinīḥ*), or have spreading branches (*vi-śākhāḥ*). In the Rigveda[6] plants are termed 'fruitful' (*phalinīḥ*), 'blossoming' (*puṣpavatīḥ*), and 'having flowers' (*pra-sūvarīḥ*).

[6] x. 97. 3. 15. *Cf.* Zimmer, *Altindisches Leben*, 57.

AU.

Aukṣa-gandhi ('having the smell of bull's grease') appears in the Atharvaveda[1] as the name of an Apsaras, beside other names, of which **Guggulū** and **Naladī** clearly indicate plants. This name, therefore, presumably also denotes some sort of fragrant plant. Aukṣa in the same Saṃhitā[2] means 'bull's grease' (from *ukṣan*, 'bull').

[1] iv. 37. 3.
[2] ii. 36, 7.
Cf. Zimmer, *Altindisches Leben*, 69; Bloomfield, *Hymns of the Atharvaveda*, 324; Whitney, Translation of the Atharvaveda, 211, 212, and on Aukṣa, *ibid.*, 82, 83.

Augra-sainya, 'descendant of Ugrasena,' is the patronymic of King **Yuddhāṃśrauṣṭi** in the Aitareya Brāhmaṇa (viii. 21).

Audanya, 'descendant of Udanya or Odana,' is the patronymic in the Śatapatha Brāhmaṇa[1] of Muṇḍibha, who is credited with inventing an expiation for the crime of slaying a Brahmin. In the Taittirīya Brāhmaṇa[2] the name appears in the form of Audanyava.

[1] xiii. 3, 5, 4.
[2] iii. 9, 15, 3. *Cf.* St. Petersburg Dictionary, *s.v.* Odana; Eggeling, *Sacred Books of the East*, 44, 341, n. 1.

Audamaya is Weber's[1] reading of the name of the Ātreya, who was Purohita of **Aṅga Vairocana,** according to the Aitareya Brāhmaṇa.[2] Aufrecht, however, in his edition more probably takes the correct form of the name to be **Udamaya.**

[1] *Indische Studien*, 1, 228.
[2] viii. 22. *Cf.* St. Petersburg Dictionary, *s.v.* Udamaya.

Auda-vāhi, 'descendant of Udavāha,' appears in the first two Vaṃśas (lists of teachers) of the Bṛhadāraṇyaka Upaniṣad[1] as a teacher of Bhāradvāja.

[1] ii. 5, 20; iv. 5, 26 (in the Mādhyaṃdina recension).

Aud-umbarāyaṇa, 'descendant of Udumbara,' is the patronymic of a grammarian in the Nirukta (i. 1).

Aud-dālaki, 'descendant of Uddālaka,' is the patronymic of the teacher variously called **Asurbinda**[1] or **Kusurubinda,**[2] and of **Śvetaketu.**[3]

[1] Jaiminīya Brāhmaṇa, i. 75 (*Journal of the American Oriental Society*, 23, 327).

[2] Ṣaḍviṃśa Brāhmaṇa, i. 16; Pañcaviṃśa Brāhmaṇa, xxii. 15, 10.

[3] Śatapatha Brāhmaṇa, iii. 4, 3, 13; iv. 2, 5, 15. He is perhaps also meant in Kaṭha Upaniṣad, i. 11.

Aud-bhāri, 'descendant of Udbhāra,' is the patronymic in the Śatapatha Brāhmaṇa (xi. 8, 4, 6) of **Khaṇḍika**, teacher of **Keśin.**

Aupa-jandhani, 'descendant of Upajandhana,' is the patronymic of a teacher mentioned in the Bṛhadāraṇyaka Upaniṣad[1] as a pupil of **Āsuri,** and also [2] as a pupil of **Sāyakāyana.**

[1] ii. 6, 3; iv. 6, 3 (in Vaṃśas).

[2] iv. 5, 27 (in the Mādhyaṃdina recension).

Aupa-tasvini, 'descendant of Upatasvina,' is the patronymic of **Rāma** in the Śatapatha Brāhmaṇa (iv. 6, 1, 7).

Aupa-manyava, 'descendant of Upamanyu,' is the patronymic of various persons: see **Kāmboja, Prācīnaśāla, Mahāśāla.** The best known bearer of the name is the grammarian who disagreed with the onomatopoetic theory of the derivation of names, and who is mentioned by Yāska.[1] An Aupamanyavīputra occurs in the Baudhāyana Śrauta Sūtra[2] as a teacher.

[1] i. 1; ii. 2. 6. 11, etc.

[2] xxii. 1 *et seq.*

Aupara, 'descendant of Upara,' is the patronymic of **Daṇḍa** in the Taittirīya Saṃhitā (vi. 2, 9, 4).

Aupa-veśi, 'descendant of Upaveśa,' is the patronymic borne by **Aruṇa**, father of Uddālaka.[1]

[1] See Kāṭhaka Saṃhitā, xxvi. 10, and **Aruṇa.**

Aupasvatī-putra, 'son of a female descendant of Upasvant' (?), is mentioned as a pupil of **Pārāśarīputra** in a Vaṃśa (list of teachers) of the Bṛhadāraṇyaka Upaniṣad.[1]

[1] vi. 5, 1 (only in the Kāṇva recension).

Aupāvi ('descendant of Upāva') **Jāna-śruteya** ('descendant of Janaśruti'), appears in the Śatapatha Brāhmaṇa[1] and the Maitrāyaṇī Saṃhitā[2] as a sacrificer who used to offer the Vājapeya sacrifice and ascend to the other world.

[1] v. 1, 1, 5. 7.
[2] i. 4, 5. *Cf.* Weber, *Indische Studien*, 1, 222, 223.

Aupoditi, 'descendant of Upodita,' is the patronymic applied in the Taittirīya Saṃhitā[1] to **Tumiñja,** and in the Baudhāyana Śrauta Sūtra[2] to **Gaupālāyana**, son of **Vyāghrapad,** Sthapati ('general') of the Kurus. In the form of Aupoditeya, a metronymic from Upoditā, the name is found in the Śatapatha Brāhmaṇa,[3] where the Kāṇva text calls him Tumiñja Aupoditeya Vaiyāghrapadya.

[1] i. 7, 2, 1.
[2] xx. 25.
[3] i. 9, 3, 16.

Cf. Eggeling, *Sacred Books of the East*, 12, 271, n. 2.

Aurṇa-vābha, 'descendant of Ūrṇavābhi.' (1) This is the name of a pupil of **Kauṇḍinya** mentioned in a Vaṃśa (list of teachers) of the Bṛhadāraṇyaka Upaniṣad.[1] (2) A teacher of this name is frequently referred to in the Nirukta. His explanations in two passages[2] agree with those of the Nairuktas

[1] iv. 5, 26 (Mādhyaṃdina recension).
[2] vii. 15; xii. 19.

or etymological school of interpreters of the Rigveda. In other passages[3] he appears rather to belong to the school of the **Aitihāsikas,** who relied on traditional legends. He was thus probably, as Sieg[4] suggests, an eclectic.

[3] vi. 13; xii. 1.

[4] *Die Sagenstoffe des Ṛgveda*, 13, n. 1.

Aurva, 'descendant of Uru or Urva,' appears in the Rigveda[1] in close connexion with **Bhṛgu,** being probably a Bhṛgu himself. As in one passage of the Aitareya Brāhmaṇa,[2] the descendants of Aitaśa are called the worst of the Aurvas, while the parallel version of the Kauṣītaki Brāhmaṇa[3] calls them the worst of the Bhṛgus, the Aurvas must have been a branch of the larger family of the Bhṛgus. Aurva himself is said in the Taittirīya Saṃhitā[4] to have received offspring from Atri. In the Pañcaviṃśa Brāhmaṇa[5] two Aurvas are referred to as authorities. See also **Kutsa.**

[1] viii. 102, 4.
[2] vi. 33.
[3] xxx. 5.
[4] vii. 1, 8, 1.
[5] xxi. 10, 6. Hopkins, *Transactions of the Connecticut Academy of Arts and Sciences*, 15, 54, reads *ūrvau*.

Cf. Hillebrandt, *Vedische Mythologie*, 2, 173, n. 1.

Aulāna is a word occurring in a single passage of the Rigveda,[1] where it may possibly be a patronymic of **Śaṃtanu** as a 'descendant of Ula.' Ludwig,[2] however, conjectures that the reading should be 'Kaulāna.' Sieg[3] regards Aulāna as a later descendant[4] of Śaṃtanu, who utilized the story of Devāpi's rain-making as an introduction to his rain hymn.

[1] x. 98, 11.
[2] Translation of the Rigveda, 3, 166.
[3] *Die Sagenstoffe des Ṛgveda*, 141.
[4] *Cf.* Sāyaṇa on Rv. x. 98, 11: *Kuru-kula-jātaḥ Śāṃtanavaḥ*, 'a descendant of Śaṃtanu, born in the family of the Kurus.'

Auluṇḍya, 'descendant of Uluṇḍa,' is the patronymic of **Supratīta** in the Vaṃśa Brāhmaṇa.[1]

[1] *Indische Studien*, 4, 372.

Auśija, 'descendant of Uśij,' is a patronymic clearly applied to **Kakṣīvant** in the Rigveda.[1] It is also applied to **Ṛjiśvan,**[2] but Ludwig[3] thinks that the correct reading of the passage in question is *auśijasyarjiśvā*, 'Ṛjiśvan, son of Auśija.' In one verse[4] Auśija and Kakṣīvant are both mentioned, but in such a way that two different persons must apparently be meant. In other passages where the patronymic occurs alone, it is doubtful who is meant, or whether a proper name at all is intended.[5] Kakṣīvant Auśija appears also in the Pañcaviṃśa Brāhmaṇa[6] and elsewhere.

[1] i. 18, 1.

[2] x. 99, 11.

[3] Translation of the Rigveda, 3, 143, 149.

[4] Rv. i. 112, 11.

[5] Rv. i. 119, 9; 122, 4; iv. 21, 6. 7; v. 41, 5; vi. 4, 6. *Cf.* St. Petersburg Dictionary, *s.v.*

[6] xiv. 11, 16. See Hopkins, *Transactions of the Connecticut Academy of Arts and Sciences*, xv. 56, n., and **Kakṣīvant**, n. 15.

Auṣṭrākṣi, 'descendant of Uṣṭrākṣa,' occurs as the patronymic of **Sāti** in the Vaṃśa Brāhmaṇa.[1]

[1] *Indische Studien*, 4, 372. *Cf.* Weber, *Indian Literature*, 75.

K.

Kaṃsa, a word denoting a 'pot or vessel of metal,' occurs in the Atharvaveda and elsewhere.[1]

[1] Av. x. 10, 5; Aitareya Brāhmaṇa, viii. 10; Bṛhadāraṇyaka Upaniṣad, vi. 3, 1, etc.; Nirukta, vii. 23; Śāṅkhāyana Āraṇyaka, xii. 8.

Kakara occurs in the Yajurveda Saṃhitās[1] as the name of a victim at the horse sacrifice (Aśvamedha). It probably denotes some 'sort of bird,' as rendered by the commentator Mahīdhara.[2]

[1] Maitrāyaṇī Saṃhitā, iii. 14, 1; Vājasaneyi Saṃhitā, xx. 24.

[2] On Vājasaneyi Saṃhitā, *loc. cit.* *Cf.* Zimmer, *Altindisches Leben*, 94.

Kakuṭha, a word occurring in the Maitrāyaṇī Saṃhitā,[1] presumably denotes some kind of animal. According to Böhtlingk,[2] it is identical with **Kakkaṭa.**

[1] iii. 14, 13.

[2] Dictionary, *s.v.*

Kakuha, a word occurring several times in the Rigveda,[1] is understood by Roth[2] to designate part of a chariot, perhaps the seat. Ludwig,[3] again, regards it in one passage[4] as the proper name of a Yādava prince who took spoil from **Tirindira,** the **Parśu,** but this view is hardly probable.[5] It is, on the whole, most likely that the word always means 'chief,' 'pre-eminent,' being applied as an epithet to horses, chariots, princes, etc.[6] This is the only sense given by Grassmann,[7] and later adopted by Roth.[8]

[1] i. 46, 3; 181 5; 184, 3; ii. 34, 11; iii. 54, 14; v. 73, 7; 75, 4; viii. 6, 48.

[2] St. Petersburg Dictionary, *s.v.*

[3] Translation of the Rigveda, 2, 182; 3, 160, 161; 5, 142.

[4] viii. 6, 48.

[5] Weber, *Episches im vedischen Ritual*, 36, 37.

[6] So certainly in Rv. viii. 45, 14; ix. 67, 8; Taittirīya Saṃhitā, iii. 3, 3, 1. 2, and often in the older form *kakubha.*

[7] In his Lexicon, *s.v.*

[8] In Böhtlingk's Dictionary, *s.v.*

Kakkaṭa denotes the 'crab' in the Yajurveda Saṃhitās,[1] being a Prākritized form of Karkaṭa, which is common in the later literature.[2] Roth,[3] however, takes the word to mean a bird, and compares **Kakara.** See also **Kakuṭha.**

[1] Taittirīya Saṃhitā, v. 5, 15, 1 (where Weber has *katkaṭa*); Vājasaneyi Saṃhitā, xxiv. 32.

[2] Zimmer, *Altindisches Leben*, 95.

[3] St. Petersburg Dictionary, *s.v.*

Kakṣa is the name of two men mentioned as teachers in a Vaṃśa (list of teachers) of the Jaiminīya Upaniṣad Brāhmaṇa. One is Kakṣa Vārakya, pupil of **Proṣṭhapada Vārakya,**[1] and the other Kakṣa Vārāki[2] or Vārakya,[3] pupil of **Dakṣa Kātyāyani Ātreya.** See also **Urukakṣa.**

[1] iii. 41, 1. [2] iii. 41, 1. [3] iv. 17, 1.

Kakṣīvant is the name of a Ṛṣi mentioned frequently in the Rigveda,[1] and occasionally elsewhere.[2] He appears to have been a descendant of a female slave named Uśij.[3] He must have been a **Pajra** by family, as he bears the epithet Pajriya,[4]

[1] i. 18, 1; 51, 13; 112, 11; 116, 7; 117, 6; 126, 3; iv. 26, 1; viii. 9, 10; ix. 74, 8; x. 25, 10; 61, 16.

[2] Av. iv. 29, 5, and passages noted below.

[3] Rv. i. 18, 1; perhaps also i. 112, 11, but Auśija may there be a separate name (see **Auśija**). *Cf.* Pañcaviṃśa Brāhmaṇa, xiv. 11, 16.

[4] Rv. i. 116, 7; 117, 6.

and his descendants are called Pajras.[5] In a hymn of the Rigveda[6] he celebrates the prince **Svanaya Bhāvya,** who dwelt on the **Sindhu** (Indus), as having bestowed magnificent gifts on him ; and the list of Nārāśaṃsas (' Praises of Heroes ') in the Śāṅkhāyana Śrauta Sūtra[7] mentions one by Kakṣīvant Auśija in honour of Svanaya Bhāvayavya. In his old age he obtained as a wife the maiden **Vṛcayā.**[8] He appears to have lived to be a hundred,[9] the typical length of life in the Vedas. He seems always to be thought of as belonging to the past, and in a hymn of the fourth book of the Rigveda[10] he is mentioned with the semi-mythical **Kutsa** and **Kavi Uśanas.** Later, also, he is a teacher of bygone days.[11]

In Vedic literature he is not connected with **Dīrghatamas** beyond being once mentioned along with him in a hymn of the Rigveda.[12] But in the Bṛhaddevatā[13] he appears as a son of Dīrghatamas by a slave woman, Uśij.

Weber[14] considers that Kakṣīvant was originally a Kṣatriya, not a Brāhmaṇa, quoting in favour of this view the fact that he is mentioned beside kings like **Para Āṭṇāra, Vītahavya Śrāyasa,** and **Trasadasyu Paurukutsya.**[15] But that these are all kings is an unnecessary assumption : these persons are mentioned in the passages in question undoubtedly only as famous men of old, to whom are ascribed mythical sacrificial performances, and who thus gained numerous sons.

[5] Rv. i. 126, 4.

[6] i. 126.

[7] xvi. 4, 5.

[8] Rv. i. 51, 13.

[9] Rv. ix. 74, 8.

[10] iv. 26, 1.

[11] Av. iv. 29, 5 ; xviii. 3, 15 ; Aitareya Brāhmaṇa, i. 21, 6. 7 ; Jaiminīya Upaniṣad Brāhmaṇa, ii. 6, 11.

[12] viii. 9, 10.

[13] iv. 11 *et seq.*

[14] *Episches im vedischen Ritual*, 22-25.

[15] Taittirīya Saṃhitā, v. 6, 5, 3 ; Kāṭhaka Saṃhitā, xxii. 3 ; Pañcaviṃśa Brāhmaṇa, xxv. 16, 3. *Cf.* xiv. 11, 16.

Cf. Oldenberg, *Zeitschrift der Deutschen Morgenländischen Gesellschaft*, 42, 221, 236, n. 1 ; Ludwig, Translation of the Rigveda, 3, 102 ; Geldner, *Rigveda, Kommentar*, 23, 24.

Kaṅka is the name of a bird, usually taken to mean ' heron,'[1] but, at any rate in some passages, rather denoting some bird of prey.[2] It first appears in the Yajurveda Saṃhitās.[3]

[1] Zimmer, *Altindisches Leben*, 92.

[2] Roth, St. Petersburg Dictionary, *s.v. Cf.* Sāṅkhāyana Āraṇyaka, xii. 13.

[3] Taittirīya Saṃhitā, v. 4, 11, 1 (*kaṅka-cit*, an altar ' piled in the form of a heron ') ; Vājasaneyi Saṃhitā, xxiv. 31 ; Maitrāyaṇī Saṃhitā, iii. 14, 12 ; Sāmaveda, ii. 9, 3, 6, 1.

Kaṅkata is the name of an animal mentioned once in the Rigveda.[1] According to Sāyaṇa it is a destructive beast; perhaps, as Grassmann renders it, a 'scorpion.'

[1] i. 191, 1. *Cf.* Zimmer, *Altindisches Leben*, 98.

Kaṅkatīya is the name of a family said in the Śatapatha Brāhmaṇa[1] to have learned from **Śāṇḍilya** the piling up of the sacrificial fire (*agni-cayana*). In the Āpastamba Śrauta Sūtra[2] a Kaṅkati Brāhmaṇa, no doubt the textbook of the school, is referred to. It may have been identical with the Chāgaleya Brāhmaṇa, cited in the Baudhāyana Śrauta Sūtra.[3]

[1] ix. 4, 4, 17.
[2] xiv. 20, 4.
[3] xxv. 5. *Cf.* Caland, *Über das rituelle Sūtra des Baudhāyana*, 40.

Kaṅka-parvan ('heron-jointed'?), a term occurring once in the Atharvaveda,[1] is applied to a snake, meaning perhaps 'scorpion.' As the Paippalāda recension has a different reading (*aṅga-parvaṇaḥ*), the passage may be corrupt.

[1] vii. 56, 1. *Cf.* Zimmer, *Altindisches Leben*, 94; Whitney, Translation of the Atharvaveda, 426; Bloomfield, *Hymns of the Atharvaveda*, 553; Böhtlingk, Dictionary, *s v.*

Kaṭa denotes a 'mat,' which was 'made of reeds' (*vaitasa*). The maker of mats from reeds (*bidala-kārī*) is mentioned in the Vājasaneyi Saṃhitā,[2] and the process of splitting reeds for the purpose is referred to in the Atharvaveda.[3]

[1] Taittirīya Saṃhitā, v. 3, 12, 2. *Cf.* Śatapatha Brāhmaṇa, xiii. 3, 1, 3.
[2] xxx. 8, with Mahīdhara's Commentary. *Bidala-kāra* is read in the Taittirīya Brāhmaṇa, iii. 4, 5, 1.
[3] vi. 138, 5.
Cf. Zimmer, *Altindisches Leben*, 255.

Kaṇṭakī-kārī, 'worker in thorns,' is one of the victims at the human sacrifice (Puruṣamedha) in the Vājasaneyi Saṃhitā.[1] No doubt the thorns were cut up and used to plait mats (**Kaṭa**) or to stuff cushions.

[1] xxx. 8. The Taittirīya Brāhmaṇa, iii.4, 5, 1, has *kaṇṭaka-kāra*. *Cf.* Zimmer, *Altindisches Leben*, 255.

Kaṇva is the name of an ancient Ṛṣi repeatedly referred to in the Rigveda and later.[1] His sons and descendants,[2] the Kaṇvas, are also often mentioned, especially in the eighth book of the Rigveda, the authorship of that book, as well as of part of the first, being attributed to this family. A descendant of Kaṇva is also denoted by the name in the singular, either alone[3] or accompanied by a patronymic, as Kaṇva Nārṣada[4] and Kaṇva Śrāyasa,[5] besides in the plural the Kaṇvas Sauśravasas.[6] The Kaṇva family appears to have been connected with the Atri family,[7] but not to have been of great importance.[8] In one passage of the Atharvaveda[9] they seem to be definitely regarded with hostility.

1 Rv. i. 36, 8. 10. 11. 17. 19; 39. 7. 9; 47. 5; 112, 5; 117, 18; 118, 7; 139, 9; v. 41, 4; viii. 5. 23. 25; 7. 18; 8, 20; 49. 10; 50, 10; x. 71, 11; 115, 5; 150, 5; Av. iv. 37, 1; vii. 15, 1; xviii. 3, 15; Vājasaneyi Saṃhitā, xvii. 74; Pañcaviṃśa Brāhmaṇa, viii. 2, 2; ix. 2, 6; Kauṣītaki Brāhmaṇa, xxviii. 8. Kaṇvavat occurs in Rv. viii. 6, 11; 52, 8; Av. ii. 32, 3; Kaṇva-mant in Rv. viii. 2, 22.

2 As *Kaṇvāḥ* (in the plural), Rv. i. 14, 2. 5; 37. 1. 14; 44. 8; 46, 9; 47, 2. 4-10; 49. 4; viii. 2, 16; 3, 16; 4, 2. 3; 5. 4; 6, 3. 18. 21. 31. 34. 47; 7, 32; 8, 3; 9. 14; 32, 1; 33. 3; 34. 4; as *Kaṇvasya sūnavaḥ*, Rv. i. 45. 5; as *putrāḥ*, viii. 8, 4. 8; as *Kāṇvāyanāḥ*, viii. 55, 4. *Kāṇva* is found in viii. 1, 8; 2, 40; 4, 20; 7, 19; 9. 3. 9; 10, 2.

3 *E.g.*, Rv. i. 48, 4; viii. 34. 1, and probably elsewhere.

4 Rv. i. 117, 8; Av. iv. 19, 2; Ludwig, Translation of the Rigveda, 3, 150.

5 Taittirīya Saṃhitā, v. 4, 7. 5; Kāṭhaka Saṃhitā, xxi. 8; Maitrāyaṇī Saṃhitā, iii. 3, 9.

6 Kāṭhaka Saṃhitā, xiii. 12. There is also Vatsa Kāṇva in Śāṅkhāyana Śrauta Sūtra, xvi. 11, 20.

7 Oldenberg, *Zeitschrift der Deutschen Morgenländischen Gesellschaft*, 42, 214.

8 Hillebrandt, *Vedische Mythologie*, 3, 285. *Cf.* 1, 207, 438.

9 Av. ii. 25. *Cf.* Vārttika on Pāṇini, iii. 1, 14; Bergaigne, *Religion Védique*, 2, 465; Hillebrandt, *op. cit.*, 1, 207; Oldenberg, *Ṛgveda-Noten*, 1, 110.

Cf. Oldenberg, *op. cit.*, 216 *et seq.*; Ludwig, *op. cit.*, 3, 105.

Kathā.—The later use of this word[1] in the sense of a 'philosophical discussion' appears in the Chāndogya Upaniṣad.[2]

1 Colebrooke, *Miscellaneous Essays*, 1, 293.

2 i. 8, 1: *hantodgīthe kathāṃ vadāma*, 'let us begin a discussion regarding the Udgītha.'

Kadrū, a word occurring only once in the Rigveda,[1] is interpreted by Ludwig[2] as the name of a priest, but it more probably means a Soma vessel.[3]

1 viii. 45, 26.

2 Translation of the Rigveda, 3, 162.

3 St. Petersburg Dictionary, *s.v.*

Kanaknaka, a word occurring once in the Atharvaveda,[1] either denotes a poison or is an adjective qualifying *kāṇḍā-viṣa*, a species of poison.

[1] x. 4, 22. *Cf.* Bloomfield, *Hymns of the Atharvaveda*, 604; Whitney, Translation of the Atharvaveda, 578.

Kanā, Kanyā.—Both these words, of which the former is very rare,[1] while the latter is the normal term from the Rigveda[2] onwards, denote 'maiden' or 'young woman.' It is doubtful whether Kanīnakā (accented on the final syllable) has this meaning,[3] or only denotes the pupil of the eye,[4] which is the sense of *kanīnakā* or *kanīnikā* (both accented on the antepenultimate) in the later Saṃhitās and the Brāhmaṇas. See also **Strī.**

[1] Rv. x. 61, 5, etc.

[2] i. 123, 10; 161, 5; iii. 23, 10, etc.; Av. i. 14, 2; xi. 5, 18; xii. 1, 25, etc.

[3] Roth, St. Petersburg Dictionary, *s.v.*, cites in this sense Rv. iv. 32, 23; x. 40, 9; Nirukta, iv. 15; but neither of the Rv. passages is at all clear.

[4] See Bloomfield, *Hymns of the Atharvaveda*, 401; Keith, *Aitareya Āraṇyaka*, 207. Other rare forms are *kanyanā*, Rv. viii. 35, 5; *kanyalā*, Av. v. 5, 3; xiv. 2, 52.

Kapanā, from its solitary occurrence in the Rigveda,[1] appears to mean a 'worm' that destroys the leaves of trees, and is so interpreted in the Nirukta.[2]

[1] v. 54, 6.

[2] vi. 4. *Cf.* Zimmer, *Altindisches Leben*, 97; Max Müller, *Sacred Books of the East*, 32, 330.

Kaparda, 'braid,' **Kapardin,** 'wearing braids.' These words refer to the Vedic custom of wearing the hair in braids or plaits. Thus a maiden is said to have her hair in four plaits (*catuṣ-kapardā*),[1] and the goddess Sinīvālī is described as 'wearing fair braids' (*su-kapardā*).[2] Men also wore their hair in this style, for both Rudra[3] and Pūṣan[4] are said to have done so, while the **Vasiṣṭhas**[5] were distinguished by wearing their hair in a plait on the right (*dakṣiṇatas-kaparda*). The opposite was to wear one's hair 'plain' (*pulasti*).[6] See also **Opaśa.**

[1] Rv. x. 114, 3.

[2] Vājasaneyi Saṃhitā, xi. 56.

[3] Rv. i. 114, 1. 5; Vājasaneyi Saṃhitā, xvi. 10. 29. 43. 48. 59.

[4] Rv. vi. 55, 2; ix. 67. 11.

[5] Rv. vii. 33, 1. *Cf.* 83, 8.

[6] Vājasaneyi Saṃhitā, xvi. 43.

Cf. Zimmer, *Altindisches Leben*, 264, 265; Muir, *Sanskrit Texts*, v. 462; Max Müller, *Sacred Books of the East*, 32, 424.

1. **Kapi**, 'monkey,' occurs only once in the Rigveda[1] with reference to Vṛṣā-kapi, the 'Man-ape,' in the dialogue of Indra and Indrāṇī in the presence of Vṛṣākapi. There the ape is termed the 'tawny' (*harita*). In the Atharvaveda[2] the monkey is mentioned several times as hairy, and an enemy of dogs. That the ape was tamed appears from its position in the Vṛṣākapi hymn, and from the mention, in the Taittirīya Saṃhitā,[3] of a **Mayu** as belonging to the forest. See also **Mayu**, **Markaṭa**, and **Puruṣa Hastin.**

[1] x. 86, 5. *Cf.* Oldenberg, *Religion des Veda*, 174; Geldner, *Vedische Studien*, 2, 22 *et seq.*; von Schroeder, *Mysterium und Mimus*, 304 *et seq.*; Schirmeisen, *Die Arischen Göttergestalten*, 218 *et seq.*; Tilak, *Orion*, 170-197.

[2] iii. 9, 4; iv. 32, 11; vi. 49, 1. *Cf.* also Chāndogya Upaniṣad, i. 6, 7 (*kapy-āsa*, 'seat of an ape').

[3] iv. 2, 10, 1. *Cf.* Zimmer, *Altindisches Leben*, 85, 86.

2. **Kapi** is, according to the St. Petersburg Dictionary, another name for Luśa Khārgali in the Kāṭhaka Saṃhitā (xxx. 2), but the name appears rather to be **Luśākapi.**

Kapiñjala, the name of the 'francoline partridge' or 'hazel-cock,' is found in all the Yajurveda Saṃhitās,[1] and occasionally later.[2]

[1] Taittirīya Saṃhitā, ii. 5, 1, 1; v. 5, 16, 1; Maitrāyaṇī Saṃhitā, iii. 14, 1; Kāṭhaka Saṃhitā, xii. 10; Vājasaneyi Saṃhitā, xxiv. 20. 38.

[2] Satapatha Brāhmaṇa, i. 6, 3, 3; v. 5, 4, 4; xiii. 5, 1, 13; Jaiminīya Brāhmaṇa, i. 154, 2 (*Transactions of the Connecticut Academy of Arts and Sciences*, 15, 181).

Cf. Zimmer, *Altindisches Leben*, 91.

Kapila appears in the Śvetāśvatara Upaniṣad[1] as a teacher, according to Weber[2] and Garbe,[3] who think that the expression *kapila ṛṣiḥ* there refers to the founder of the Sāṅkhya philosophy. But this is doubtful.[4]

[1] v. 2.

[2] *Indische Studien*, 1, 24 *et seq.*; 5, 412; *Indian Literature*, 236.

[3] *Sāṅkhya Philosophie*, 27 *et seq.*; Translation of the Sāṅkhyatattvakaumudī, 531.

[4] Max Müller, *Sacred Books of the East*, 2, xli, and Deussen, in his translation (*Sechzig Upanishads*, 304), do not take the word as a teacher's name. The latter renders *kapila ṛṣiḥ*, by 'the red sage,' as referring to Hiraṇyagarbha.

Kapi-vana Bhauvāyana is mentioned as a teacher in the Yajurveda Saṃhitās[1] and the Pañcaviṃśa Brāhmaṇa.[2] A rite called Kapivana's Dvyaha ('ceremony lasting two days') is also referred to in the Kātyāyana Śrauta Sūtra.[3]

[1] Maitrāyaṇī Saṃhitā, i. 4, 5; Kāṭhaka Saṃhitā, xxxii. 2.
[2] xx. 13, 4.
[3] xxv. 2, 3. *Cf.* Āśvalāyana Srauta Sūtra, x. 2.
Cf. Weber, *Indische Studien*, 1, 24; 3, 473; Hopkins, *Transactions of the Connecticut Academy of Arts and Sciences*, 15, 55, n. 2; Hillebrandt, *Vedische Mythologie*, 2, 157.

Kapota is the name of a bird, probably the 'pigeon' (its sense in the later language), occurring from the Rigveda onwards.[1] It is associated in some passages[2] with the owl (**Ulūka**) as a messenger of Nirṛti ('dissolution,' 'misfortune'). This aspect of the pigeon as a bird of evil omen is probably based on an ancient belief which is also found beyond the confines of India.[3]

[1] Rv. i. 30, 4; Av. xx. 135, 12; Maitrāyaṇī Saṃhitā, iii. 14, 4; Vājasaneyi Saṃhitā, xxiv. 23. 38.
[2] Rv. x. 165, 1-5; Av. vi. 29, 2.
[3] *Cf.* Schrader, *Prehistoric Antiquities*, 253.
Cf. Zimmer, *Altindisches Leben*, 89; St. Petersburg Dictionary, *s.v.*

Kabandha Ātharvaṇa is mentioned in the Bṛhadāraṇyaka Upaniṣad[1] along with **Sudhanvan Āṅgirasa,** as a teacher, but is semi-mythical. His son was **Vicārin Kābandhi.**

[1] vi. 7, 1. *Cf.* also Gopatha Brāhmaṇa, i. 2, 9. 18; Hillebrandt, *Vedische Mythologie*, 2, 176, n. 4; Weber, *Indian Literature*, 149.

Kama-dyū appears once in the Rigveda[1] as the wife of **Vimada.** She is probably identical with the 'maiden' (*yoṣā*) of **Purumitra,** no doubt his daughter. She is elsewhere[2] referred to in connexion with Vimada, who appears to have taken her for his bride against the will of her father.

[1] x. 65, 12.
[2] i. 117, 20; x. 39, 7.
Cf. Zimmer, *Altindisches Leben*, 310.

Kambala denotes in the Atharvaveda[1] a 'woollen coverlet' or 'blanket.'

[1] xiv. 2, 66. 67. *Cf.* Nirukta, ii. 2.

Kamboja.—Yāska, in the Nirukta,[1] refers to the speech of the Kambojas as differing from that of the other Āryas. The Kambojas were later settled to the north-west of the Indus, and are known as Kambujiya in the old Persian inscriptions. A teacher, **Kāmboja Aupamanyava,** pupil of **Madragāra,** is mentioned in the Vaṃśa Brāhmaṇa.[2] This points to a possible connexion of the Madras, or more probably the **Uttara Madras,** with the Kambojas, who probably had Iranian as well as Indian affinities.

1 ii. 2.

2 *Indische Studien*, 4, 372.

Cf. Zimmer, *Altindisches Leben*, 102; Weber, *Indische Streifen*, 2, 493; 3, 384; *Indische Studien*, 10, 7; *Episches im vedischen Ritual*, 45; Max Müller, *Zeitschrift der Deutschen Morgenländischen Gesellschaft*, 7, 373. On the relation of Indian and Iranian, see also Jacobi, *Journal of the Royal Asiatic Society*, 1909, 721 *et seq.*; 1910, 457 *et seq.*; Oldenberg, *ibid.*, 1095 *et seq.*; Keith, *ibid.*, 1100 *et seq.*; Kennedy, *ibid.*, 1107 *et seq.*; and see **Parśu.**

Karañja, a word which in the Sūtras and later denotes the tree *Pongamia glabra*, occurs only twice in the Rigveda[1] as the name of a foe of Indra, but whether a demon or a man[2] is intended remains uncertain.

1 i. 53, 8; x. 48, 8.

2 Zimmer, *Altindisches Leben*, 63; Ludwig, Translation of the Rigveda, 3, 149; Hillebrandt, *Vedische Mythologie*, 3, 292.

Karambha is the name, from the Rigveda onwards,[1] of a kind of porridge made of grain (**Yava**), which was unhusked, parched slightly, and kneaded.[2] It was the especial sacrificial portion of Pūṣan, no doubt in his capacity of an agricultural deity. Karambha was also made of barley (**Upavāka**)[3] or of sesame (**Tirya**).[4]

1 Rv. i. 187, 16; iii. 52, 7; vi. 56, 1; 57, 2; viii. 102, 2; Av. iv. 7, 2. 3; vi. 16, 1; Taittirīya Saṃhitā, iii. 1, 10, 2; vi. 5, 11, 4, etc.

2 Śatapatha Brāhmaṇa, ii. 5, 2, 14; iv. 2, 4, 18. *Cf.* Schrader, *Prehistoric Antiquities*, 317; Eggeling, *Sacred Books of the East*, 12, 395, n. 1.

3 Vājasaneyi Saṃhitā, xix. 22.

4 Av. iv. 7, 3, but see Bloomfield, *Hymns of the Atharvaveda*, 377; Whitney, Translation of the Atharvaveda, 155.

Cf. Zimmer, *Altindisches Leben*, 270.

Karikrata denotes, according to Zimmer,[1] a snake in the Atharvaveda.[2]

[1] *Altindisches Leben*, 95

[2] x. 4, 13. The Paippalāda version has Kanikrada.

Karīra, the name of a leafless shrub, *Capparis aphylla,* or its fruit, first appears in the Taittirīya Saṃhitā.[1]

[1] ii. 4, 9, 2; Kāṭhaka Saṃhitā, xi. 11; xxxvi. 7; Śatapatha Brāhmaṇa, ii. 5, 2, 11.

Karīṣa denotes 'dry cow dung' in the Śatapatha Brāhmaṇa.[1] The Atharvaveda[2] shows that the value of the natural manure of animals in the fields was appreciated.

[1] ii. 1, 1, 7.

[2] Av. iii. 14, 3. 4; xix. 31, 3.

Cf. Zimmer, *Altindisches Leben*, 236.

1. **Karkandhu** is the ordinary word for 'jujube,' the tree (*Zizyphus jujuba*) and the fruit, from the Yajurveda Saṃhitās onwards.[1] The berry is red (*rohita*).[2] Compare **Kuvala** and **Badara,** which denote the fruit.

[1] Kāṭhaka Saṃhitā, xii. 10; Maitrāyaṇī Saṃhitā, iii. 11, 2; Vājasaneyi Saṃhitā, xix. 23. 91; xxi. 32; xxiv. 2; Śatapatha Brāhmaṇa, v. 5, 4, 10; xii. 7, 2, 9; 9, 1, 5, etc.; Jaiminīya Brāhmaṇa, ii. 156, 5.

[2] Vājasaneyi Saṃhitā, xxiv. 2.

Cf. Zimmer, *Altindisches Leben*, 242.

2. **Karkandhu** is only the name borne by a protégé of the Aśvins in the Rigveda (i. 112, 6). Its identity with the word for jujube indicates that the latter, though not otherwise mentioned there, was known at the time of the Rigveda.

Karkari, a musical instrument, probably the 'lute,' occurs from the Rigveda onwards.[1] The Maitrāyaṇī Saṃhitā[2] mentions cattle branded on the ears with a mark resembling a lute (*karkari-karṇyaḥ*).

[1] Rv. ii. 43, 3; Av. iv. 37, 4. *Cf.* xx. 132, 3. 8.

[2] iv. 2, 9. *Cf.* Delbrück, *Gurupūjākaumudī*, 48, 49.

Cf. Zimmer, *Altindisches Leben*, 289.

Karkī may denote in one passage of the Atharvaveda[1] a 'white cow,' according to the suggestion of Roth.[2]

[1] iv. 38, 6. 7. *Cf.* Bloomfield, *Hymns of the Atharvaveda*, 414.

[2] St. Petersburg Dictionary and Böhtlingk's Dictionary, *s.v.*

Karṇa-śobhana denotes an 'ornament for the ear' in the Rigveda,[1] apparently for the use of men. Some deity is called 'gold-eared' in another passage of the Rigveda.[2] Hopkins[3] considers the use of ear-rings later than that of necklets and wristlets.

[1] viii. 78, 3.

[2] i. 122, 14. See also i. 64, 10.

[3] *Journal of the American Oriental Society*, 17, 35.

Cf. Zimmer, *Altindisches Leben*, 262.

Karṇa-śravas Āṅgirasa is mentioned in the Pañcaviṃśa Brāhmaṇa (xiii. 11, 14) as a seer of Sāmans or chants, the same tale being told of him as of **Dāvasu.**

Karmāra, the 'smith,' is several times mentioned with approval in the Vedic Saṃhitās.[1] In the Atharvaveda[2] smiths appear with fishermen (*dhīvānaḥ*) and chariot-builders (*ratha-kārāḥ*), all being classified as clever workers (*manīṣiṇaḥ*): possibly a quasi-caste of smiths was already developing from the guild organization that probably existed.[3]

Little is known of the smith's methods of work and of his tools. No doubt he smelted (*dhmā*) the ore in the fire; hence he is called *dhmātṛ*, the 'smelter.'[4] Mention is also made of

[1] Rv. x. 72, 2; Av. iii. 5, 6; Kāṭhaka Saṃhitā, xvii. 13; Maitrāyaṇī Saṃhitā, ii. 9, 5; Vājasaneyi Saṃhitā, xvi. 27; xxx. 7. *Cf. karmāra*, Rv. ix. 112, 2; Taittirīya Brāhmaṇa, iii. 4, 3, 1.

[2] iii. 5, 6. The exact sense of the passage is doubtful. Zimmer, *Altindisches Leben*, 252; Bloomfield, *Hymns of the Atharvaveda*, 144; and Whitney, Translation of the Atharvaveda, 92, take the reference to be to 'skilled chariot-makers' (*dhīvāno ratha-kārāḥ*) and 'clever smiths,' but this is perhaps less likely. The commentator interprets *dhīvānaḥ* as 'fishermen' (in the later language *dhīvara* means both a 'clever man' and a 'fisherman').

[3] *Cf.* Fick, *Die sociale Gliederung*, 182.

[4] Rv. v. 9, 5.

his bellows of birds' feathers.[5] He made metal vessels (*gharma ayasmaya*)[6] to be put on the fire: even the Soma cup could occasionally be made of hammered metal (*ayo-hata*).[7]

5 Rv. ix. 112, 2.
6 Rv. v. 30, 15.
7 Rv. ix. 1, 2.
Cf. Zimmer, *op. cit.*, 252, 253; Weber, *Indische Studien*, 17, 196 *et seq.*; *Über den Rājasūya*, 19 *et seq.*

Karvara, a word found in one passage of the Atharvaveda,[1] seems to mean some kind of fish[2] caught by a fisherman (*pauñjiṣṭha*).

1 x. 4, 19.
2 Zimmer, *Altindisches Leben*, 96; Whitney, Translation of the Atharvaveda, 578.

Karṣū, a rare word found in the Śatapatha Brāhmaṇa,[1] denotes a 'furrow' or 'trench.'

1 i. 8, 1, 3; xiii. 8, 3, 10. *Cf.* Schrader, *Prehistoric Antiquities*, 283.

Kalaviṅka, a name of the 'sparrow,' is found in the Yajurveda Saṃhitās,[1] and occasionally later.[2]

1 Taittirīya Saṃhitā, ii. 5, 1, 2; Maitrāyaṇī Saṃhitā, iii. 14, 1; Kāṭhaka Saṃhitā, xii. 10; Vājasaneyi Saṃhitā, xxiv. 20. 31.
2 Satapatha Brāhmaṇa, i. 6, 3, 4; v. 5, 4, 5; Jaiminīya Brāhmaṇa, ii. 154, 3 (*Transactions of the Connecticut Academy of Arts and Sciences*, 15, 181). *Cf.* Zimmer, *Altindisches Leben*, 91.

Kalaśa is, from the Rigveda onwards,[1] a common word for 'pot' or 'jar,' probably either formed of a gourd or made of clay (unburnt or baked), as we know that both kinds of pot were in use.[2] The wooden Soma tub (*droṇa-kalaśa*) is frequently referred to in the ritual. See also **Kośa**.

1 Rv. i. 117, 12; iii. 32, 15; iv. 27, 5; 32, 19, etc.; Av. iii. 12, 7; ix. 1, 6; 4, 15; xviii. 4, 13, etc. In Rv. x. 32, 9, the word, according to the St. Petersburg Dictionary, is used as a proper name, but the passage is very doubtful.
2 Av. iv. 17, 4; Taittirīya Saṃhitā, i. 1, 8, 1; iv. 1, 5, 4; v. 1, 7, 2; Vājasaneyi Saṃhitā, i. 22; xi. 59. *Cf.* Zimmer, *Altindisches Leben*, 253; Eggeling, *Sacred Books of the East*, 26, 257; Oertel, *Transactions of the Connecticut Academy of Arts and Sciences*, 15, 185, n. 3; Hillebrandt, *Vedische Mythologie*, 1, 183 *et seq.*

Kalā denotes a fractional part, normally 'one-sixteenth,' in the Rigveda[1] and later.[2] It is often mentioned in connexion with **Śapha**, 'one-eighth.'

[1] viii. 47, 17.

[2] Av. vi. 96, 3; xix. 57, 1; Taittirīya Saṃhitā, vi. 1, 10, 1; Maitrāyaṇī Saṃhitā, iii. 7, 7; Śatapatha Brāhmaṇa, iii. 3, 3, 1; xii. 8, 3, 13, etc.; Nirukta, xi. 12. *Cf.* Hopkins, *Journal of the American Oriental Society*, 16, 278; Zimmer, *Altindisches Leben*, 259.

1. **Kali.** See **Akṣa.**

2. **Kali** occurs in the Rigveda, twice in the singular[1] as the name of a protégé of the Aśvins, and once in the plural.[2] The persons meant in the latter passage seem to be different from the former one. The Kalis are once mentioned in the Atharvaveda[3] beside the Gandharvas.[4]

[1] i. 112, 15; x. 39, 8.

[2] viii. 66, 15.

[3] x. 10, 13.

[4] These Kalis may be connected with dicing, as in the Atharvaveda the Apsarases, the wives of the Gandharvas, are fond of dice, and bestow luck at play. See Macdonell, *Vedic Mythology*, p. 135.

Cf. Hopkins, *Journal of the American Oriental Society*, 17, 89; Ludwig, Translation of the Rigveda, 3, 163.

Kalpa in the Taittirīya Āraṇyaka (ii. 10) seems to denote Kalpa Sūtra.

Kalmāṣa-grīva ('speckled-neck') is the name of a snake in the Atharvaveda.[1]

[1] iii. 27, 5 (where the Paippalāda recension has *kulmāṣa-*); xii. 3, 59. *Cf.* Taittirīya Saṃhitā, v. 5, 10, 2.

Cf. Zimmer, *Altindisches Leben*, 94, 95.

Kalyāṇa is the name, in the Pañcaviṃśa Brāhmaṇa,[1] of an Āṅgirasa who saw the Aurṇāyava Sāman.

[1] xii. 11, 10. *Cf.* Hopkins, *Transactions of the Connecticut Academy of Arts and Sciences*, 15, 68, n. 2.

Kavaca denotes a 'corselet' or 'breastplate' in the Atharvaveda[1] and later.[2] There is nothing to show whether it was made of metal, but that it was so is quite possible (see **Varman**). The Atharvaveda[3] refers to a 'corselet-strap' (*kavaca-pāśa*), which may point to a linen corselet such as those known to Herodotus.[4]

1 Av. xi. 10, 22 (*kavacin*).

2 Śatapatha Brāhmaṇa, xiii. 2, 2, 7; Aitareya Brāhmaṇa, vii. 19, 2; Nirukta, v. 25 (*kavaca*); Śatapatha Brāhmaṇa, xiii. 1, 6, 3; 4, 1, 5; Aitareya Brāhmaṇa, iii. 48; Vājasaneyi Saṃhitā, xvi. 45 (*kavacin*).

3 xi. 10, 22.

4 Bloomfield, *Hymns of the Atharvaveda*, 129, and Whitney, Translation of the Atharvaveda, 659, seem to recognize coats of mail only.

Kavaṣa is mentioned in a hymn of the Rigveda[1] as one of those whom, together with the **Druhyu** king, Indra overthrew for the **Tṛtsus.** The Anukramaṇī (Index) also attributes to him the authorship of several hymns of the Rigveda, including two (x. 32. 33) that deal with a prince **Kuruśravaṇa** and his descendant **Upamaśravas.** There seems no reason to doubt this attribution, which is accepted by both Zimmer[2] and Geldner.[3] The former holds that Kavaṣa was the Purohita of the joint tribes named **Vaikarṇa,** in whom he sees the Kuru-Krivi (Pañcāla) peoples, and that Kavaṣa in that capacity is mentioned in the Rigveda as representative of those peoples. He also suggests that the language of Rigveda x. 33, 4 is best explained by the reduced position in which the Kuru-Krivis found themselves on their defeat by the Tṛtsus. Ludwig,[4] on the other hand, thinks that Kavaṣa was the priest of the five peoples. Geldner[5] holds that Kavaṣa was the Purohita of Kuruśravaṇa, by whose son, Upamaśravas, he was ill-treated, and that he composed Rigveda x. 33 to deprecate the anger of his royal master. Hopkins[6] thinks that he was a king.

In the Brāhmaṇas of the Rigveda[7] mention is made of

1 vii. 18, 12.

2 *Altindisches Leben*, 127.

3 *Vedische Studien*, 2, 150.

4 Translation of the Rigveda, 3, 139.

5 *Loc. cit.*

6 *Journal of the American Oriental Society*, 15, 261, 263.

7 Aitareya Brāhmaṇa, ii. 19; Kauṣītaki Brāhmaṇa, xii. 1. 3.

Cf. Weber, *Indische Studien*, 3, 459; Lanman, *Sanskrit Reader*, 386, 387; Pargiter, *Journal of the Royal Asiatic Society*, 1910, 50.

Kavaṣa Ailūṣa, who was a Brāhmaṇa born of a female slave, and was reproached on this ground by the other Ṛṣis. He is possibly identical with the Kavaṣa of the Rigveda.

Kaśa is the name of an unknown animal mentioned as a victim at the horse sacrifice in the Yajurveda Saṃhitās.[1]

[1] Taittirīya Saṃhitā, v. 5, 17, 1; 18, 1; Vājasaneyi Saṃhitā, xxiv. 26; 38. *Cf.* Maitrāyaṇī Saṃhitā, iii. 14, 7. *Cf.* Zimmer, *Altindisches Leben*, 84.

Kaśīkā is the name of an animal mentioned once in the Rigveda,[1] and interpreted as 'weasel' by the commentator Sāyaṇa. Fick[2] suggests that the meaning is 'pole-cat.' Geldner[3] takes it as 'female ichneumon.'

[1] i. 126, 5.
[2] Bezzenberger, *Beiträge*, 3, 165; Schrader, *Prehistoric Antiquities*, 247. *Cf.* Zimmer, *Altindisches Leben*, 84; Hopkins, *Journal of the American Oriental Society*, 17, 57.
[3] *Rigveda, Glossar*, 44.

Kaśipu denotes a 'mat' or 'cushion' made, according to the Atharvaveda,[1] by women from reeds (*naḍa*), which they crushed for the purpose by means of stones. On the other hand, the Śatapatha Brāhmaṇa[2] refers to a mat as made of gold.

[1] vi. 138, 5.
[2] xiii. 4, 3, 1.

Kaśu is the name of a prince mentioned in the Rigveda with the patronymic Caidya, or descendant of **Cedi**, as a generous patron of the singer, who praises the liberality of the Cedis. Neither this king nor the Cedis appear again in Vedic literature.

[1] viii. 5, 37. *Cf.* Zimmer, *Altindisches Leben*, 129.

Kaśo-jū occurs once in the Rigveda (i. 112, 14) either as a proper name or as an epithet of **Divodāsa**. The sense of the word is quite uncertain.

Kaśyapa, a word denoting 'tortoise,' occurs in the Atharvaveda[1] and often later.[2]

[1] iv. 20, 7.
[2] Maitrāyaṇī Saṃhitā, iii. 14, 18; Vājasaneyi Saṃhitā, xxiv. 37; Śatapatha Brāhmaṇa, vii. 5, 1, 5; Aitareya Brāhmaṇa, ii. 6. *Cf.* Weber, *Indische Studien*, 18, 86; Bloomfield, *American Journal of Philology*, 17, 403.

Kaśyapa is the name of a sage who is mentioned only once in the Rigveda,[1] but is a common figure in the later Saṃhitās.[2] He is always of a mythical character, as belonging to the distant past. According to the Aitareya Brāhmaṇa,[3] he anointed King **Viśvakarman Bhauvana**, and in the Upaniṣads[4] he is mentioned as a Ṛṣi. The Kaśyapas appear in connexion with **Janamejaya** in the Aitareya Brāhmaṇa.[5]

[1] ix. 114, 2.

[2] Sāmaveda, i. 1, 2, 4, 10; 4, 2, 3, 2 (but in these passages the St. Petersburg Dictionary, *s.v.*, accepts the sense of a divine being, identical with Prajāpati); Av. i. 14, 4; ii. 33, 7; iv. 20, 7; 29, 3; 37, 1; Maitrāyaṇī Saṃhitā, iv. 2, 9; Vājasaneyi Saṃhitā, iii. 62.

[3] viii. 21; Satapatha Brāhmaṇa, xiii. 7, 1, 15.

[4] Bṛhadāraṇyaka Upaniṣad, ii. 2, 6; Jaiminīya Brāhmaṇa, iv. 3, 1 (in a quotation).

[5] vii. 27. *Cf.* Oldenberg, *Zeitschrift der Deutschen Morgenländischen Gesellschaft*, 42, 235, n. 1.

Kaśyapa Naidhruvi is mentioned as a teacher in the last Vaṃśa (list of teachers) of the Śatapatha Brāhmaṇa.[1]

[1] Bṛhadāraṇyaka Upaniṣad, vi. 4, 33 (Mādhyaṃdina=vi. 5, 3, Kāṇva).

Kaṣkaṣa designates a kind of worm in the Atharvaveda.[1]

[1] v. 23, 7. *Cf.* Zimmer, *Altindisches Leben*, 98.

Kasarṇīla is the name of a kind of snake in the Atharvaveda.[1] It occurs also in the form Kasarṇīra, personified as the seer Kasarṇīra Kādraveya in the Taittirīya Sāṃhita.[2]

[1] x. 4, 5, where the Paippalāda recension has *kvaṣarṇīla*.

[2] i. 5, 4, 1. *Cf.* Zimmer, *Altindisches Leben*, 98; Bloomfield, *Hymns of the Atharvaveda*, 607.

Ka-stambhī denotes in the Śatapatha Brāhmaṇa[1] a piece of wood used as a prop for the end of a wagon-pole to rest on.

[1] i. 1, 2, 9. *Cf.* Caland and Henry, *L'Agniṣṭoma*, 49; Eggeling, *Sacred Books of the East*, 12, 14, n. 1.

Kahoḍa Kauṣītaki[1] or **Kauṣītakeya**[2] is mentioned in the Śatapatha Brāhmaṇa,[1] the Bṛhadāraṇyaka Upaniṣad,[2] and the Śāṅkhāyana Āraṇyaka,[1] as a teacher, contemporary with Yājñavalkya. *Cf.* **Kāhoḍi.**

[1] Śatapatha Brāhmaṇa, ii. 4, 3, 1; Sāṅkhāyana Āraṇyaka, xv.

[2] Bṛhadāraṇyaka Upaniṣad, iii. 5, 1.

Kākambīra is the name in the Rigveda[1] of a useful tree of some kind.

[1] vi. 48, 17. *Cf.* Zimmer, *Altindisches Leben*, 62.

Kākṣa-seni is the patronymic ('son of Kakṣasena') of **Abhipratārin** in the Pañcaviṃśa Brāhmaṇa (xiv. 1, 12).

Kākṣīvata. See **Nodhas.**

Kāṭhaka, the name of the recension of the Black Yajurveda belonging to the school of the Kaṭhas, is mentioned in the Nirukta[1] of Yāska and in the Anupada Sūtra.[2] The Saṃhitā which bears the name has been in part edited by L. v. Schroeder.[3]

[1] x. 4.
[2] iii. 11; vii. 11.
[3] Two volumes have so far appeared, the first containing i-xviii, the second xix-xxx. *Cf. Indische Studien*, 1, 44; 3, 451; von Schroeder, Kāṭhaka Saṃhitā, 1900, 1909; *Zeitschrift der Deutschen Morgenländischen Gesellschaft*, 49, 145-171; *Die Tübinger Kaṭha-Handschriften*, Vienna, 1898; *Zwei Handschriften der K.K. Hofbibliothek in Wien mit Fragmenten des Kāṭhaka*, Vienna, 1896.

Kāṇṭhe-viddhi ('descendant of Kaṇṭheviddha') is mentioned as a teacher in the Vaṃśa Brāhmaṇa.[1]

[1] *Indische Studien*, 4, 382.

Kāṇḍa-vīṇā, the name of a musical instrument, a kind of lute made out of joints of reed, which is mentioned as used at the Mahāvrata ceremony in the Kāṭhaka Saṃhitā.[1]

[1] xxxiv. 5 (*Indische Studien*, 3, 477). *Cf.* Lāṭyāyana Srauta Sūtra, iv. 2, 6; Kātyāyana Srauta Sūtra, xiii. 3, 16; Sāṅkhāyana Śrauta Sūtra, xvii. 3, 12.

Kāṇḍviya is mentioned as an Udgātṛ in the Jaiminīya Upaniṣad Brāhmaṇa (iii. 10, 2).

Kāṇva. See **Kaṇva**: among others, **Devātithi, Medhātithi, Vatsa,** were prominent members of the Kaṇva family.

Kāṇvī-putra is mentioned as a pupil of **Kāpīputra** in the last Vaṃśa (list of teachers) of the Bṛhadāraṇyaka Upaniṣad.[1]

[1] vi. 5, 1 (Kāṇva recension).

Kāṇvāyana ('descendant of Kaṇva') and **Kāṇvyāyana** ('descendant of Kāṇvya') are patronymics occurring in the Rigveda[1] and the Ṣaḍviṃśa Brāhmaṇa[2] respectively.

[1] viii. 55, 4.
[2] *Indische Studien*, 1, 38; Sāyaṇa on Rv. i. 51, 1; viii. 2, 40.

Kātyāyani. See **Dakṣa.**

Kātyāyanī is the name of one of the two wives of **Yājña-valkya** in the Bṛhadāraṇyaka Upaniṣad.[1]

[1] ii. 4, 1; iv. 5, 1. 2. A Kātya appears in the Baudhāyana Śrauta Sūtra, ii. 15 *et seq.* See Weber, *Indian Literature*, 138.

Kātyāyanī-putra, 'son of Kātyāyanī,' is mentioned in the last Vaṃśa (list of teachers) of the Bṛhadāraṇyaka Upaniṣad[1] as a pupil of **Gotamīputra** and of **Kauśikīputra.** A Jātū-karṇya Kātyāyanīputra is named as a teacher in the Śāṅkh-āyana Āraṇyaka.[2]

[1] vi. 5, 1, Kāṇva. [2] viii. 10. *Cf.* Weber, *Indian Literature*, 138.

Kānāndha is mentioned in the Baudhāyana Śrauta Sūtra (xxi. 10) as son of **Vadhryaśva.**

Kānīta is the patronymic ('son of Kanīta') in the Rigveda[1] of **Pṛthuśravas.**

[1] viii. 46, 21. 24. *Cf.* Śāṅkhāyana Śrauta Sūtra, xvi. 11, 23.

Kānīna in the Atharvaveda[1] apparently denotes the 'son of a maiden.' See **Pati.**

[1] v. 5, 8. *Cf.* Zimmer, *Altindisches Leben*, 334.

Kāṇḍā-viṣa in the Atharvaveda (x. 4, 22) denotes some kind of poison. *Cf.* **Kanaknaka.**

Kāpaṭava Su-nītha is mentioned in the Vaṃśa Brāhmaṇa[1] as a pupil of **Sutemanas Śāṇḍilyāyana.**

[1] *Indische Studien*, 4, 383.

Kāpileya.—The Kāpileyas and the **Bābhravas** are mentioned in the Aitareya Brāhmaṇa[1] as descendants of **Devarāta Vaiśvāmitra,** the adoptive name of **Śunaḥśepa.**

[1] vii. 17. *Cf.* Weber, *Indische Studien*, 1, 216, n., 433.

Kāpī-putra ('son of Kāpī') is mentioned in the last Vaṃśa (list of teachers) of the Kāṇva recension of the Bṛhadāraṇyaka Upaniṣad (vi. 5, 1) as a pupil of **Ātreyīputra.**

Kāpeya ('descendant of Kapi'). The Kāpeyas are mentioned as priests of **Citraratha** in the Kāṭhaka Saṃhitā[1] and the Pañcaviṃśa Brāhmaṇa.[2] See also **Śaunaka.**

[1] xiii. 12.

[2] xx. 12, 5. *Cf.* Hopkins, *Transactions of the Connecticut Academy of Arts and Sciences*, 15, 52, 53; Hillebrandt, *Vedische Mythologie*, 2, 157.

Kāpya ('descendant of Kapi') is the patronymic of Sanaka and Navaka, two obviously fictitious persons who served at the Sattra ('sacrificial session') of the Vibhindukīyas in the Jaiminīya Brāhmaṇa.[1] It is also the patronymic of Patañcala in the Bṛhadāraṇyaka Upaniṣad.[2] See also **Kaiśorya.**

[1] iii. 233.

[2] iii. 3, 1; 7, 1. *Cf.* Weber, *Indian Literature*, 126, 137.

Kābandhi ('descendant of Kabandha') is the patronymic of **Vicārin** in the Gopatha Brāhmaṇa (i. 2, 9. 18).

Kāma-pri ('descendant of Kāmapra') is the patronymic of **Marutta** in the Aitareya Brāhmaṇa (viii. 21). In the St. Petersburg Dictionary it is suggested that the reading in this passage should be *kāmapre*, 'fulfilling desires,' as an epithet of the sacrifice (*yajñe*).

Kāmalāyana ('descendant of Kamala') is the patronymic of **Upakosala** in the Chāndogya Upaniṣad (iv. 10, 1).

Kāmpīla.—In one passage of the Yajurveda Saṃhitās[1] the epithet Kāmpīla-vāsinī is applied to a woman, perhaps the king's Mahiṣī or chief wife, whose duty it was to sleep beside the slaughtered animal at the horse sacrifice (Aśvamedha). The exact interpretation of the passage is very uncertain, but both Weber[2] and Zimmer[3] agree in regarding Kāmpīla as the name of the town known as Kāmpīlya in the later literature, and the capital of Pañcāla in Madhyadeśa.

1 Taittirīya Saṃhitā, vii. 4, 19, 1; Maitrāyaṇī Saṃhitā, iii. 12, 20; Kāṭhaka Saṃhitā, Aśvamedha, iv. 8; Vājasaneyi Saṃhitā, xxiii. 18; Taittirīya Brāhmaṇa, iii. 9, 6; Satapatha Brāhmaṇa, xiii. 2, 8, 3.

2 *Indische Studien*, 1, 184; *Indian Literature*, 114, 115.

3 *Altindisches Leben*, 36, 37. So also Ludwig, Translation of the Rigveda, 3, 204; von Schroeder, Maitrāyaṇī Saṃhitā, 1, xxi; *Indiens Literatur und Cultur*, 164; Eggeling, *Sacred Books of the East*, 44, 321, 322.

Kāmboja ('native of **Kamboja**') **Aupamanyava** ('descendant of Upamanyu') is mentioned as a teacher in the Vaṃśa Brāhmaṇa.[1]

1 Weber, *Indische Studien*, 4, 372; *Episches im vedischen Ritual*, 45; Zimmer, *Altindisches Leben*, 102.

Kārapacava is the name in the Pañcaviṃśa Brāhmaṇa[1] of a place on the **Yamunā**.

1 xxv. 10, 23. *Cf.* Āśvalāyana Śrauta Sūtra, xii. 6; Śāṅkhāyana Śrauta Sūtra, xiii. 29, 25; Kātyāyana Śrauta Sūtra, xxiv. 6, 10; Weber, *Indische Studien*, 1, 34.

Kāraskara is the name of a people mentioned in the Baudhāyana Śrauta Sūtra[1] and the Āpastamba[2] and Hiraṇyakeśi[3] Sūtras.

1 xx. 13 (14). *Cf.* Baudhāyana Dharma Sūtra, i. 2, 14.

2 xxii. 6, 18.

3 xvii. 6. *Cf.* Bühler, *Sacred Books of the East*, 14, 148; Caland, *Zeitschrift der Deutschen Morgenländischen Gesellschaft*, 56, 553.

Kāri is the name of one of the victims of the human sacrifice (Puruṣamedha) in the Vājasaneyi Saṃhitā,[1] and is there dedicated to 'laughter.' The commentator Mahīdhara[2] interprets the word as 'worker' (*karaṇa-śīla*), but the St. Petersburg Dictionary suggests that it means a 'jubilant' person (as derived from the root *kṛ*, 'to praise').

[1] xxx. 6. 20; Taittirīya Brāhmaṇa, iii. 4, 2, 1.

[2] On Vājasaneyi Saṃhitā, *loc. cit.*

Kārīradi is the name of persons mentioned in the Jaiminīya Upaniṣad Brāhmaṇa (ii. 4, 4) as holding a special view of the Udgītha (Sāmaveda Chant).

Kāru, 'poet,' is a word almost confined to the Rigveda.[1] There is evidence that the poet was regarded as a professional man, just as much as the physician (**Bhiṣaj**).[2] The poets, no doubt, mainly lived at the courts of princes amid their retainers,[3] though they would probably also sing the praises of rich merchants. There was probably no essential connexion between the priest and the poet. Though the priest was often a poet, yet poetry can hardly have been restricted to the priestly caste. Indeed, at the horse sacrifice (Aśvamedha) the Śatapatha Brāhmaṇa[4] expressly requires that one of the singers of panegyrics should be a Rājanya, while the other was a Brāhmaṇa, both singing verses of their own composition. The Anukramaṇī (Index) in several cases[5] attributes hymns of the Rigveda to princes; and even though this may often be merely the same sort of procedure[6] as has made Śūdraka the author of the Mṛcchakaṭikā, or Harṣa of the Ratnāvalī, and has given us royal teachers of the Brahman doctrine,[7] still the Indian tradition evidently saw nothing odd in the idea of non-Brāhmaṇas as poets. Most of the non-sacred poetry has,

[1] i. 148, 2; 165, 12; 177, 5; 178, 3; ii. 43, 1; iii. 33, 8; 39, 7; v. 33, 7; vii. 27; 68, 9; 72, 4, etc.; Maitrāyaṇī Saṃhitā, i. 8, 7; Gopatha Brāhmaṇa, i. 2, 21.

[2] ix. 112, 3.

[3] vii. 73, 1.

[4] xiii. 1, 5, 1, 4, 3, 5.

[5] *E.g.*, x. 92 is attributed to **Śāryāta Mānava**.

[6] See Pischel, *Vedische Studien*, 3, 202.

[7] Weber, *Episches im vedischen Ritual*, 20, n. 4, sees in Av. xx. a recension of Kṣatriya character. He also finds Kṣatriyas in **Viśvāmitra** and **Kakṣīvant**, but hardly with reason. *Cf.* **Varṇa**.

however, disappeared, for the epic is a product, as it stands, of a later period. See also **Ṛṣi.**

Kārotara appears to denote in the Rigveda,[1] and occasionally later,[2] a 'filter' or 'sieve' for purifying the liquor called **Surā.**

[1] i. 116, 7.

[2] Vājasaneyi Saṃhitā, xix. 16. 82; Satapatha Brāhmaṇa, xii. 9, 1, 2; Kauṣītaki Brāhmaṇa, ii. 7. *Cf.* Zimmer, *Altindisches Leben*, 280.

Kārotī is mentioned in the Śatapatha Brāhmaṇa (ix. 5, 2, 15) as a place, or perhaps a river, where **Tura Kāvaṣeya** made a fire-altar—that is, as a seat of the fire-cult *par excellence.*

Kārśakeyī-putra ('son of Kārśakeyī') is the name of a man mentioned in the last Vaṃśa (list of teachers) of the Bṛhadāraṇyaka Upaniṣad. In the Kāṇva (vi. 5, 2) recension he is a pupil of **Prācīnayogīputra**; in the Mādhyaṃdina (vi. 4, 33) recension his teacher's name is **Prāśnīputra Āsurivāsin.**

Kārṣṇāyasa ('black metal'), a word found in the Upaniṣads,[1] must clearly mean 'iron.' See **Ayas.**

[1] Chāndogya Upaniṣad, iv. 17, 7; vi. 1, 5; Jaiminīya Upaniṣad Brāhmaṇa, iii. 17, 3. *Cf.* Zimmer, *Altindisches Leben*, 52.

Kārṣman, a word meaning literally 'furrow,' and found only in the Rigveda,[1] is the designation of the goal in the chariot race. The competitor probably turned round it and came back to the starting-place.[2]

[1] i. 116, 17; ix. 36, 1; 74, 8.

[2] Av. ii. 14, 6. *Cf.* Zimmer, *Altindisches Leben*, 291, 292.

Kārṣmarya is the name of a tree (*Gmelina arborea*) which is often alluded to in the Taittirīya Saṃhitā,[1] the Maitrāyaṇī Saṃhitā,[2] and the Śatapatha Brāhmaṇa.[3]

[1] v. 2, 7, 3. 4; vi. 2, 1, 5.

[2] iii. 2, 6; 7, 9.

[3] iii. 4, 1, 6; 8, 2, 17; iv. 3, 3, 6; vii. 4, 1, 37. *Cf.* Zimmer, *Altindisches Leben*, 62.

Kāla, the generic expression for 'time,' first occurs in the Rigveda,[1] where, however, it is used only once, in the late tenth book. It is known to the Atharvaveda,[2] where Kāla has already developed the sense of time as fate. The word is frequent in the Brāhmaṇas,[3] superseding the earlier use of **Ṛtu.** The more general division of time is into 'past' (*bhūta*), 'present' (*bhavat*), and 'future' (*bhaviṣyat*).[4] For other divisions see **Ahan, Māsa, Saṃvatsara.**

1 x. 42, 9.
2 xix. 53. 54.
3 Śatapatha Brāhmaṇa, i. 7, 3, 3; ii. 4, 2, 4; iii. 8, 3, 36; vii. 2, 2, 21, etc.
4 *E.g.*, Sāṅkhāyana Āraṇyaka, vii. 20.

Kālakā is the name of one of the victims at the horse sacrifice (Aśvamedha) in the Yajurveda Saṃhitās,[1] variously identified with a bird[2] or a chameleon.[3]

1 Taittirīya Saṃhitā, v. 5, 15, 1; Maitrāyaṇī Saṃhitā, iii. 14, 16; Vājasaneyi Saṃhitā, xxiv. 35.
2 Mahīdhara on Vājasaneyi Saṃhitā, *loc. cit.*
3 Sāyaṇa on Taittirīya Saṃhitā, *loc. cit.* *Cf.* Zimmer, *Altindisches Leben*, 99.

Kāla-kāñja.—In the Atharvaveda[1] mention is made of the Kālakāñjas as being in the sky. Both Roth[2] and Zimmer[3] hold that some constellation is meant. But as the defeat of the Kālakāñjas is one of Indra's exploits,[4] it is doubtful whether any stress can be laid on that interpretation of the passage in the Atharvaveda. Whitney[5] suggests that the three stars of Orion are meant, Bloomfield[6] that the galaxy or the stars in general are intended.

1 vi. 80, 2.
2 St. Petersburg Dictionary, *s.v.*
3 *Altindisches Leben*, 353.
4 Kāṭhaka Saṃhitā, viii. 1. *Cf.* also Maitrāyaṇī Saṃhitā, i. 6, 9; Taittirīya Brāhmaṇa, i. 1, 2, 4-6; Kauṣītaki Upaniṣad, iii. 1.
5 Translation of the Atharvaveda, 341.
6 *Hymns of the Atharvaveda*, 500; *Journal of the American Oriental Society*, 15, 163-169.

Cf. Weber, *Indische Studien*, 1, 410, 414 *et seq.*; 3, 465; Oertel, *Journal of the American Oriental Society*, 19, 121.

Kāvaṣeya ('descendant of Kavaṣa') is the constant patronymic of **Tura.** The Kāvaṣeyas are also mentioned as teachers of philosophical points in the Rigveda Āraṇyakas.[1]

[1] Aitareya Āraṇyaka, iii. 2, 6; Sāṅkhāyana Āraṇyaka, viii. 11. *Cf.* Weber, *Indische Studien*, 1, 391, n.; 2, 418; Keith, *Aitareya Āraṇyaka*, 257.

Kāvya ('descendant of Kavi') is the constant[1] patronymic of **Uśanas.** In the Pañcaviṃśa Brāhmaṇa it is also applied to **Iḍhat**[2] and **Ukṣṇorandhra.**[3]

[1] Rv. i. 51, 11; 83, 5; 121, 12; vi. 20, 11; viii. 23, 17; Av. iv. 29, 6; Taittirīya Saṃhitā, ii. 5, 8, 5, etc.

[2] xiv. 9, 16.

[3] xiii. 9, 19.

Cf. Hopkins, *Transactions of the Connecticut Academy of Arts and Sciences*, 15, 48, 49.

Kāśa.—Roth[1] finds this word, which denotes a species of grass (*Saccharum spontaneum*) used for mats, etc., in one passage of the Rigveda,[2] but the reading is uncertain. The word has this sense in the Taittirīya Āraṇyaka.[3]

[1] St. Petersburg Dictionary, *s.v.*

[2] x. 100, 10.

[3] vi. 9, 1.

Kāśi, Kāśya.—The name Kāśi denotes (in the plural[1]) the people of Kāśi (Benares), and Kāśya, the king of Kāśi. The Śatapatha Brāhmaṇa[2] tells of **Dhṛtarāṣṭra,** king of Kāśi, who was defeated by **Śatānīka Sātrājita,** with the result that the Kāśis, down to the time of the Brāhmaṇa, gave up the kindling of the sacred fire. Sātrājita was a **Bharata.** We hear also of **Ajātaśatru** as a king of Kāśi;[3] and no doubt **Bhadrasena Ajātaśatrava,** a contemporary of **Uddālaka,** was also a king of Kāśi.

The Kāśis and **Videhas** were closely connected, as was natural in view of their geographical position. The compound name Kāśi-Videha occurs in the Kauṣītaki Upaniṣad;[4] in the Bṛhadāraṇyaka Upaniṣad[5] **Gārgī** describes Ajātaśatru as either a Kāśi or a Videha king. The Śāṅkhāyana Śrauta Sūtra[6]

[1] Satapatha Brāhmaṇa, xiii. 5, 4, 19. 21. The plural occurs also in the Paippalāda recension of the Atharvaveda, v. 22, 14.

[2] xiii. 5, 4, 19.

[3] Bṛhadāraṇyaka Upaniṣad, ii. 1, 1; iii. 8, 2; Kauṣītaki Upaniṣad, iv. 1.

[4] Kauṣītaki Upaniṣad, *loc. cit.*

[5] iii. 8, 2.

[6] xvi. 29, 5.

mentions one Purohita as acting for the kings of Kāśi, Kosala, and Videha; and the Baudhāyana Śrauta Sūtra[7] mentions Kāśi and Videha in close proximity. Weber,[8] indeed, throws out the suggestion that the Kāśis and the Videhas together constitute the **Uśīnaras**, whose name is very rare in Vedic literature.

As Kosala and Videha were in close connexion, Kāśi and Kosala are found combined in the compound name Kāśi-Kauśalyas of the Gopatha Brāhmaṇa.[9]

Though Kāśi is a late word, it is quite possible that the town is older, as the river **Varaṇāvatī** referred to in the Atharvaveda[10] may be connected with the later Vārāṇasī (Benares).

It is significant that while the Kāśis, Kosalas, and Videhas were united, any relations which the Kuru-Pañcala peoples may have had with them were hostile. It is a fair conclusion that between these two great groups of peoples there did exist some political conflict as well as probably a difference of culture in some degree. The Śatapatha Brāhmaṇa,[11] in the story of the advance of Āryan civilization over Kosala and Videha, preserves a clear tradition of this time, and a piece of evidence that in the Kuru-Pañcāla country lay the real centre of the Brāhmaṇa culture (see also **Kuru-Pañcāla**). That the Kosala-Videhas were originally settlers of older date than the Kuru-Pañcālas is reasonably obvious from their geographical position, but the true Brāhmaṇa culture appears to have been brought to them from the Kuru-Pañcala country. It is very probable that the East was less Āryan than the West, and that it was less completely reduced under Brahmin spiritual supremacy, as the movement of Buddhism was Eastern, and the Buddhist texts[12] reveal a position in which the Kṣatriyas rank above Brāhmaṇas. With this agrees the fact that the later Vedic texts[13] display

[7] xxi. 13.

[8] *Cf.* Weber, *Indische Studien*, 1, 212, 213.

[9] i. 2, 9.

[10] iv. 7. 1. *Cf.* Zimmer, *Altindisches Leben*, 20; Bloomfield, *Hymns of the Atharvaveda*, 376.

[11] i. 4, 1, 10 *et seq.* *Cf.* Weber, *Indische Studien*, 1, 170 *et seq.*; Eggeling, *Sacred Books of the East*, 12, xlii *et seq.*, 104, n. 1.

[12] See Fick, *Die sociale Gliederung*, chap. iv.

[13] Kātyāyana Srauta Sūtra, xxii. 4, 22; Lāṭyāyana Śrauta Sūtra, viii. 6, 28. See Weber, *Indische Studien*, 10, 99; Fick, *op. cit.*, 140, n. 1; and *cf.* **Magadha**.

towards the people of Magadha a marked antipathy, which may be reasonably explained by that people's lack of orthodoxy, and which may perhaps be traced as far back as the Vājasaneyi Saṃhitā.[14] It is, of course, possible that the Kosala-Videhas and Kāśis actually were merely offshoots of the tribes later known as the Kuru-Pañcālas, and that they by reason of distance and less complete subjugation of the aborigines lost their Brahminical culture. This hypothesis, however, appears less likely, though it might be supported by a literal interpretation of the legend of the Aryan migration in the Śatapatha Brāhmaṇa.[15]

[14] xxx. 5. 22. See **Magadha**.

[15] *Cf.* Eggeling, *loc. cit.*, 104, n. 1. *Cf.* Grierson, *Journal of the Royal Asiatic Society*, 1908, 837, 1143; Keith, *ibid.*, 831, 1138; Oldenberg, *Buddha*, 402 *et seq.*

Kāśyapa ('descendant of Kaśyapa') is a common patronymic,[1] and is applied specially to **Ṛśyaśṛṅga, Devataras Śyāvasāyana, Śūṣa Vāhneya.**

[1] Satapatha Brāhmaṇa, vii. 5, 1, 5; Taittirīya Āraṇyaka, ii. 18; x. 1, 8, etc.

Kāśyapī-bālākyā-māṭharī-putra ('son of Kāśyapī, Bālākyā, and Māṭharī'). This curious name is given in the Bṛhadāraṇyaka Upaniṣad[1] to a teacher, pupil of **Kautsīputra.**

[1] vi. 4, 31 (Mādhyaṃdina recension).

Kāṣāyaṇa is mentioned in the second Vaṃśa (list of teachers) of the Bṛhadāraṇyaka Upaniṣad as a teacher, pupil of Sāyakāyana according to the Kāṇva (iv. 6, 2), of Saukarāyaṇa according to the Mādhyaṃdina recension (iv. 5, 27).

Kāṣṭhā seems to have the sense in the Rigveda[1] of 'course' for a chariot race. It also means in the Rigveda[2] and later[3] 'goal,' either like the **Kārṣman** the turning place, or the final goal (*paramā kāṣṭhā*).

[1] i. 37, 10; 65, 3; iv. 58, 7; vi. 46, 1; vii. 93, 3; viii. 80, 8; ix. 21, 7.

[2] x. 102, 9, is perhaps so to be taken.

[3] Av. ii. 14, 6; Taittirīya Saṃhitā, i. 6, 9, 3; Vājasaneyi Saṃhitā, ix. 13; Aitareya Brāhmaṇa, iv. 7; Satapatha Brāhmaṇa, xi. 5, 7, 2, etc.

Cf. Zimmer, *Altindisches Leben*, 291, 292; Max Müller, *Sacred Books of the East*, 32, 77.

Kās, Kāsa, Kāsā, Kāsikā.—All these four forms[1] of the same word denote 'cough,' which is mentioned in the Atharvaveda as accompanying a headache,[2] as a symptom in fever (**Takman**),[3] and as an independent disease.[4]

[1] Kās: Av. i. 12, 3; v. 22, 10; Kāsa: Av. v. 22, 11 (probably); Kāsā: Av. vi. 105, 1 *et seq.*; Kāsikā: Av. v. 22, 12; xi. 2, 22.

[2] Av. i. 12, 3.

[3] v. 22, 10.

[4] vi. 105.

Cf. Zimmer, *Altindisches Leben*, 385; Grohmann, *Indische Studien*, 9, 394; Jolly, *Medicin*, 89.

Kāhoḍi ('descendant of Kahoḍa') is the patronymic of **Argala** in the Kāṭhaka Saṃhitā (xxv. 5).

Kiṃśuka is the name of a tree (*Butea frondosa*) mentioned in the wedding hymn of the Rigveda,[1] the bridal car being described as adorned with its blossoms (*su-kiṃśuka*).

[1] x. 85, 20. *Cf.* Zimmer, *Altindisches Leben*, 62. Sāyaṇa thinks the meaning is that the car is made of the wood of the tree.

Kiki-dīvi denotes some kind of bird, perhaps the blue jay.[1] According to the commentator, it means 'partridge' (*tittiri*) in the Taittirīya Saṃhitā.[2]

[1] Roth, St. Petersburg Dictionary, *s.v.* See Rv. x. 97, 13.

[2] v. 6, 22, 1.

Cf. Zimmer, *Altindisches Leben*, 92; Schrader, *Prehistoric Antiquities*, 251.

Kitava, 'the gambler,' is frequently referred to in the Rigveda[1] and later.[2] A father is represented as chastising his son for gambling.[3] The gambler seems at times to have fallen, along with his family, into servitude, presumably by selling himself to pay his debts.[4] Technical names[5] for different sorts of gamblers given in the Yajurveda Saṃhitās are Ādinava-darśa,

[1] ii. 29, 5; v. 85, 8; x. 34, 3. 7. 10. 11. 13.

[2] Av. vii. 50, 1; 109, 3; Vājasaneyi Saṃhitā, xxx. 8. 18. 22; Aitareya Brāhmaṇa, ii. 19, etc.

[3] Rv. ii. 29, 5. *Cf.* **Pitṛ.**

[4] Rv. x. 34. *Cf.* perhaps the *bhakta-dāsa*, 'slave for hire,' of the Mānava Dharma Sāstra, viii. 415; Fick, *Die sociale Gliederung*, 197.

[5] Taittirīya Saṃhitā, iv. 3, 3, 1 *et seq.*; Vājasaneyi Saṃhitā, xxx. 18.

Kalpin, Adhi-kalpin, and Sabhā-sthāṇu. None of these can be safely[6] explained, though the last has usually[7] been taken as a satirical name derived from the gambler's devotion to the dicing place (**Sabhā**), 'pillar of the dicing hall.' The first literally means 'seeing ill-luck,'[8] and may refer to the quickness of the dicer to note an error on the part of his antagonist, or to his eagerness to see the defeat of his rival.

[6] *Cf.* Weber, *Zeitschrift der Deutschen Morgenländischen Gesellschaft*, 18, 282; Zimmer, *Altindisches Leben*, 284.

[7] So Mahīdhara on Vājasaneyi Saṃhitā, xxx. 18; Sāyaṇa on Taittirīya Brāhmaṇa, iii. 4, 16, 1.

[8] *Cf.* Roth, St. Petersburg Dictionary, *s.v.*; Weber, *loc. cit.*

Kiṃ-puruṣa, lit. 'what sort of man,' appears in the Brāhmaṇas[1] to designate the 'ape,' which is a mimic man. Possibly the same sense should be seen in the passage of the Vājasaneyi Saṃhitā,[2] where it occurs, and where Roth[3] assumes it to refer to a contemptible man. Max Müller[4] renders it 'savage.'

[1] Aitareya Brāhmaṇa, ii. 8; Satapatha Brāhmaṇa, i. 2, 3, 9; vii. 5, 2, 32.

[2] xxx. 16; Taittirīya Brāhmaṇa, iii. 4, 12, 1.

[3] St. Petersburg Dictionary, *s.v.*

[4] *Ancient Sanskrit Literature*, 420.

Cf. Weber, *Indische Studien*, 9, 246; *Omina und Portenta*, 356; Eggeling, *Sacred Books of the East*, 12, 51, n. 3.

Kiyāmbu is the name of one of the water-plants which are to grow, according to a funeral hymn in the Rigveda,[1] on the place where the body of the dead was burned. The word seems to mean 'having some water,' possibly by popular etymology.[2]

[1] x. 16, 13=Av. xviii. 3, 6.

[2] *Cf.* Sāyaṇa on Rv., *loc. cit.*, and on Taittirīya Āraṇyaka, vi. 4, 1, 2, where Kyāmbu is the form.

Cf. Zimmer, *Altindisches Leben*, 62; Bloomfield, *Proceedings of the American Oriental Society*, October, 1890, xl.

1. **Kirāta** is a name applied to a people living in the caves of the mountains, as appears clearly from the dedication of the Kirāta to the caves (*guhā*) in the Vājasaneyi Saṃhitā,[1] and from the reference in the Atharvaveda[2] to a Kirāta girl (*kairātikā*), who digs a remedy on the ridges of the mountains.

[1] xxx. 16; Taittirīya Brāhmaṇa, iii. 4, 12, 1.

[2] x. 4, 14.

Later[3] the people called Kirātas were located in Eastern Nepal, but the name seems to have been applied to any hill folk, no doubt aborigines, though the Mānava Dharma Śāstra[4] regards them as degraded Kṣatriyas.

[3] Lassen, *Indische Alterthumskunde*, 1², 530, 534.

[4] x. 44.

Cf. Zimmer, *Altindisches Leben*, 32; Ludwig, Translation of the Rigveda, 3, 207; V. Smith, *Journal of the Royal Asiatic Society*, 1909, 258, n. 1; Lévi, *Le Népal*, 2, 77.

2. **Kirāta.**—In the story of **Asamāti** there appear, as the two priests who are opposed to the **Gaupāyanas,** Kirāta and **Akuli** according to the Pañcaviṃśa Brāhmaṇa,[1] or Kilāta and Ākuli according to the Śatapatha Brāhmaṇa.[2] No doubt the name is chosen, not as that of a historic person, but as a suitable designation of a hostile priest; for it is probably identical with the name of the mountaineers described in the preceding article.

[1] xiii. 12, 5 (where the text reads *kirāta-kulyau*). Böhtlingk, Dictionary, *s.v.*, takes the word, with Sāyaṇa, as an adjective, *kirāta-kula*, 'of the family of Kirāta.' The reading in the Bṛhaddevatā (vii. 86) is *kirātākulī*.

[2] i. 1, 4, 14 (where the text reads *kilātākulī*). *Cf.* also Sāṭyāyanaka Brāhmaṇa *apud* Sāyaṇa on Rv. x. 57, 1; 60, 1; Jaiminīya Brāhmaṇa, iii. 167; *Journal of the American Oriental Society*, 18, 41 *et seq.*; Hopkins, *Transactions of the Connecticut Academy of Arts and Sciences*, 15, 48, n. 1.

Kilāta is the form of the name 2. **Kirāta** that appears in the Śatapatha, Śāṭyāyanaka, and Jaiminīya Brāhmaṇas.[1]

[1] See note [2] under the preceding article.

Kilāsa is the name of a disease, 'white leprosy,' in the Atharvaveda[1] and the Vājasaneyi Saṃhitā, etc.[2] It resulted in the appearance of grey (*palita*) and white (*śukla*, *śveta*) spots all over the skin. Haug gave the same sense to *alasa* in the Aitareya Brāhmaṇa,[3] but this is doubtful. The fem. Kilāsī is taken by Max Müller to mean a 'spotted deer' in one passage of the Rigveda.[4]

[1] i. 23, 24.

[2] xxx. 21; Pañcaviṃśa Brāhmaṇa, xiv. 3, 17; xxiii. 11, 11; Taittirīya Āraṇyaka, v. 4, 12. *Cf.* Zimmer, *Altindisches Leben*, 391; Bloomfield, *Hymns of the Atharvaveda*, 266; Jolly, *Medicin*, 98; Hopkins, *Transactions of the Connecticut Academy of Arts and Sciences*, 15, 68.

[3] vi. 33, 5.

[4] v. 53, 1.

Kīkaṭa.—The name of this people occurs only in one passage of the Rigveda, where they appear as hostile to the singer and as under the leadership of **Pramaganda.** Yāska[2] declares that Kīkaṭa was the name of a non-Āryan country, and later[3] Kīkaṭa is given as a synonym of Magadha. Hence Zimmer[4] concludes that the Kīkaṭas were a non-Āryan people living in the country later known as Magadha. Weber[5] holds that this people were located in Magadha, but were Āryan, though at variance with other Āryan tribes, perhaps because of heretical tendencies, for Magadha was later a seat of Buddhism. But the identification is uncertain, and is doubted by Oldenberg[6] and Hillebrandt[7]

[1] iii. 53, 14.
[2] Nirukta, vi. 32.
[3] St. Petersburg Dictionary, *s.v.*
[4] *Altindisches Leben*, 31, 118. *Cf.* Geldner, *Rigveda, Kommentar*, 58.
[5] *Indische Studien*, 1, 186; *Indian Literature*, 79, n. *.
[6] *Buddha*, 402, 403; *Ṛgveda-Noten*, 1, 253.
[7] *Vedische Mythologie*, 1, 14-18.

Kīṭa is the name of a species of worm mentioned in the Atharvaveda,[1] and frequently in the Upaniṣads.[2]

[1] ix. 4, 16.
[2] Bṛhadāraṇyaka Upaniṣad, vi. 1, 19; 2, 14; Chāndogya Upaniṣad, vi. 9, 3; 10, 2; vii. 2, 1; 7, 1; Kauṣītaki Upaniṣad, i. 2, etc.
Cf. Zimmer, *Altindisches Leben*, 98.

Kīnāśa, a name of the ploughman or cultivator of the soil, is found in the Rigveda[1] and the later Saṃhitās.[2] See **Kṛṣi.**

[1] iv. 57, 8.
[2] Av. iv. 11, 10; vi. 30, 1; Vājasaneyi Saṃhitā, xxx. 11; Taittirīya Brāhmaṇa, ii. 4, 8, 7.
Cf. Zimmer, *Altindisches Leben*, 237; Weber, *Indische Studien*, 18, 45; Hopkins, *Journal of the American Oriental Society*, 17, 86, n.

Kīri is in the Rigveda[1] a regular designation of the 'poet.' *Cf.* **Ṛṣi.**

[1] i. 31, 13; ii. 12, 6; v. 52, 12 (*kīriṇaḥ*; Max Müller, *Sacred Books of the East*, 32, 317). But see Geldner, *Rigveda, Glossar*, 46; Pischel, *Vedische Studien*, 1, 223.

Kīrśā, the name of some kind of animal, or perhaps bird, is mentioned in the list of victims for the horse sacrifice (Aśvamedha) in the Taittirīya Saṃhitā.[1]

[1] v. 5, 20, 1. *Cf.* Zimmer, *Altindisches Leben*, 99; St. Petersburg Dictionary, *s.v.*

Kīlāla, a word denoting a 'sweet drink,' is found in all the later Saṃhitās,[1] but not in the Rigveda. As the Surā-kāra, 'maker of Surā,' is dedicated in the list of victims in the human sacrifice[2] (Puruṣamedha) to Kīlāla, it must have been a drink of somewhat the same nature as the **Surā** itself, possibly, as Zimmer[3] suggests, a kind of rum.

[1] Av. iv. 11, 10; 26, 6; 27, 5; vi. 69, 1; x. 6, 25; xii. 1, 59; Taittirīya Brāhmaṇa, ii. 6, 12, 13; Maitrāyaṇī Saṃhitā, ii. 7, 12; iii. 11, 3. 4; Vājasaneyi Saṃhitā, ii. 34; iii. 43; xx. 65; xxx. 11, etc.

[2] Vājasaneyi Saṃhitā, xxx. 11; Taittirīya Brāhmaṇa, iii. 4, 9, 1.

[3] *Altindisches Leben*, 281.

Kīśmīla denotes, according to Böhtlingk,[1] a certain disease in the Paippalāda recension of the Atharvaveda.[2]

[1] Dictionary, *s.v.*

[2] xix. 8, 4.

Kīsta in two passages of the Rigveda[1] means 'poet,' like **Kīri**.

[1] i. 127, 7; vi. 67, 10. *Cf.* Yāska, Nirukta, iii. 15.

Kukkuṭa, 'cock,' occurs in the Yajurveda[1] only.[2]

[1] Vājasaneyi Saṃhitā, i. 16. *Cf.* Zimmer, *Altindisches Leben*, 91.

[2] It is common in the later language.

Kuṭaru is, according to the commentator Mahīdhara,[1] synonymous with **Kukkuṭa**, 'cock.' The word is found in the Yajurveda Saṃhitās only.[2]

[1] On Vājasaneyi Saṃhitā, xxiv. 23.

[2] Taittirīya Saṃhitā, v. 5, 17, 1; Maitrāyaṇī Saṃhitā, i. 1, 6; iii. 14, 4. 20; iv. 1, 6; Vājasaneyi Saṃhitā, xxiv. 23, 39.

Cf. Zimmer, *Altindisches Leben*, 93.

Kuṇḍa-pāyin ('drinking from a jug') is the name of a teacher mentioned in the Pañcaviṃśa Brāhmaṇa[1] and in the Sūtras.[2]

[1] xxv. 4, 4.

[2] Āśvalāyana Srauta Sūtra, xii. 4, 6; Kātyāyana Srauta Sūtra, xxiv. 4, 21.

Kuṇḍa-pāyya ('descendant of Kuṇḍapāyin') is a patronymic connected with a man named **Śṛṅgavṛṣ** in one passage of the Rigveda.[1]

[1] viii. 17, 13. *Cf.* Ludwig, Translation of the Rigveda, 3, 161; Hopkins, *Journal of the American Oriental Society*, 17, 90.

Kuṇḍṛṇācī is the name of an animal of unknown character occurring in the lists of victims at the horse sacrifice (Aśvamedha) in the Yajurveda Saṃhitās.[1] The word also occurs in one passage of the Rigveda,[2] in which a bird would seem to be intended, though Sāyaṇa interprets it as meaning 'with crooked flight' (*kuṭila-gatyā*). In his commentary on the Taittirīya Saṃhitā[3] he takes the word to denote the house-lizard (*gṛha-godhikā*).

[1] Taittirīya Saṃhitā, v. 5, 16, 1; Maitrāyaṇī Saṃhitā, iii. 14, 18; Vājasaneyi Saṃhitā, xxiv. 37.

[2] i. 29, 6.

[3] v. 5, 16, 1.

Cf. Zimmer, *Altindisches Leben*, 89.

Kutsa is the name of a hero frequently mentioned in the Rigveda, which, however, gives practically no information about him, for he was no doubt already a figure of the mythic past. He is several times[1] called Ārjuneya, 'descendant of Arjuna,' and is usually[2] associated with Indra in the exploit of defeating the demon Śuṣṇa and winning the sun. He is said[3] to have defeated **Smadibha, Tugra,** and the **Vetasus**, but, on the other hand, he is several times[4] mentioned with **Atithigva** and **Āyu** as being vanquished by Indra, his defeat in one passage[5] being attributed to **Tūrvayāṇa**. Elsewhere[6] he appears with Atithigva as a friend of Indra's. In the later literature he is seldom[7] mentioned except in connexion with the myth of his binding Indra, which is found in the Brāhmaṇas,[8] and which is based on an obscure verse in the Rigveda.[9]

[1] Rv. iv. 26, 1; vii. 19, 2; viii. 1, 11.

[2] Rv. i. 63, 3; 121, 19; 174, 5; 175, 4; iv. 30, 4; v. 29, 4; vi. 20, 5; vii. 19, 2; x. 99, 9.

[3] Rv. x. 49, 4.

[4] Rv. i. 53, 10; ii. 14, 7; viii. 53, 2. *Cf.* iv. 26, 1.

[5] Rv. i. 53, 10.

[6] Rv. i. 51, 6; vi. 26, 3.

[7] *E.g.*, Av. iv. 29, 5; Pañcaviṃśa Brāhmaṇa, xiv. 11, 26.

[8] Pañcaviṃśa Brāhmaṇa, ix. 2, 22; Śāṭyāyanaka in Sāyaṇa on Rv. x. 38, 5; Jaiminīya Brāhmaṇa, i. 228; Oertel, *Journal of the American Oriental Society*, 18, 31.

[9] x. 38, 5.

The Kutsas, or descendants of Kutsa, are mentioned in one hymn of the Rigveda.[10]

[10] vii. 25, 5.
Cf. Ludwig, Translation of the Rigveda, 3, 113, 148; Oldenberg, *Zeitschrift der Deutschen Morgenländischen Gesellschaft*, 42, 210, 211; Hillebrandt, *Vedische Mythologie*, 3, 284 *et seq.*, who suggests that perhaps two Kutsas—one a friend of Indra, and the other a foe —may be distinguished; Geldner, *Vedische Studien*, 3, 171; Hopkins, *Transactions of the Connecticut Academy of Arts and Sciences*, 15, 57, n. 1.

Kutsa Aurava ('son of Uru') is mentioned in the Pañcaviṃśa Brāhmaṇa[1] as having murdered his domestic priest (*purohita*), **Upagu Sauśravasa,** because the father of the latter insisted on paying homage to Indra. This fact may be compared with the hostility to Indra of **Kutsa** according to certain passages of the Rigveda.[2]

[1] xiv. 6, 8.
[2] See **Kutsa**.
Cf. Hillebrandt, *Vedische Mythologie*, 3, 284; Hopkins, *Transactions of the Connecticut Academy of Arts and Sciences*, 15, 57; Weber, *Indische Studien*, 10, 32.

Kunti.—The Kuntis are referred to in an obscure and corrupt passage of the Kāṭhaka Saṃhitā[1] as having defeated the **Pañcālas.**

[1] xxvi. 9. See Weber, *Indische Studien*, 3, 471, and *cf.* perhaps Maitrāyaṇī Saṃhitā, iv. 2, 6.

Kubera Vārakya is mentioned in a list of teachers in the Jaiminīya Upaniṣad Brāhmaṇa (iii. 41, 1) as a pupil of **Jayanta Vārakya.**

Kubhā is the name of a river mentioned twice in the Rigveda,[1] and no doubt identical with the modern Kabul river, the Greek Κωφήν.

[1] v. 53, 9; x. 75, 6. *Cf.* Zimmer, *Altindisches Leben*, 14; Ludwig, Translation of the Rigveda, 3, 200.

Kubhra is the name of some animal in the Maitrāyaṇī Saṃhitā (ii. 5, 3).

Ku-muda is the name of a plant mentioned with other water plants in one passage of the Atharvaveda.[1] It is no doubt the white water-lily (*Nymphæa esculenta*), being the name of that plant in post-Vedic Sanskrit also.

[1] iv. 34, 5. *Cf.* Zimmer, *Altindisches Leben*, 70.

Kumba is mentioned with **Opaśa** and **Kurīra** as an ornament of women's hair in the Atharvaveda.[1] Geldner[2] thinks that, like those two words, it originally meant 'horn,' but this is very doubtful. Indian tradition[3] simply regards the term as denoting a female adornment connected with the dressing of the hair.

[1] vi. 138, 3.
[2] *Vedische Studien*, 1, 131.
[3] Sāyaṇa on Av. vi. 138, 3.
Cf. Zimmer, *Altindisches Leben*, 265; Bloomfield, *Hymns of the Atharvaveda*, 538, 539; Whitney, Translation of the Atharvaveda, 348; Caland, *Über das rituelle Sūtra des Baudhāyana*, 59.

Kumbyā or **Kumvyā** is a word mentioned after Ṛc, Yajus, Sāman, and Gāthā in the Śatapatha Brāhmaṇa[1] to denote a form of speech. In the Aitareya Āraṇyaka[2] it appears as one of the forms of measured speech together with Ṛc and Gāthā. The precise meaning of the term is unknown. Weber[3] suggests the sense 'refrain.'

[1] xi. 5, 7, 10.
[2] ii. 3, 6.
[3] *Indische Studien*, 10, 111, n.
Cf. Keith, *Aitareya Āraṇyaka*, 221; Eggeling, *Sacred Books of the East*, 44, 101.

Kumbha is a word of frequent occurrence in the Rigveda,[1] as well as later,[2] and denotes a 'pot.' Usually no doubt made of clay, it was easily broken.[3] See also **Ukhā**.

[1] i. 116, 7; 117, 6; vii. 33, 13, etc.
[2] Av. i. 6, 4; iii. 12, 7, etc.; Vājasaneyi Saṃhitā, xix. 87, etc.
[3] Rv. x. 89, 7.
Cf. Schrader, *Prehistoric Antiquities*, 367.

Kumbhī-nasa ('pot-nosed') is the name of an animal mentioned in the list of victims at the horse sacrifice (Aśvamedha) in the Taittirīya Saṃhitā.[1] Possibly some sort of snake is meant, as in the later literature.

[1] v. 5, 14, 1. *Cf.* Zimmer, *Altindisches Leben*, 95; St. Petersburg Dictionary, *s.v.*

Kuya-vāc ('evil-speaking') appears in one passage of the Rigveda[1] to denote a demon slain by Indra, probably as a personification of the barbarian opponents of the Āryans. The expression *mṛdhra-vāc* ('speaking insultingly') is similarly used of barbarians in the Rigveda.[2]

[1] i. 174, 7.

[2] v. 29, 10; 32, 8. See **Dasyu**.

Kurīra, like **Opaśa** and **Kumba**, denotes some sort of female head ornament in the description of the bride's adornment in the wedding hymn of the Rigveda[1] and in the Atharvaveda.[2] According to the Yajurveda Saṃhitās,[3] the goddess Sinīvālī is described by the epithets *su-kapardā*, *su-kurīra*, *sv-opaśā*, as wearing a beautiful head-dress.

According to Geldner,[4] the word originally meant 'horn'; but this is uncertain, as this sense is not required in any passage in which the term occurs.[5]

[1] x. 85, 8.

[2] vi. 138, 3.

[3] Taittirīya Saṃhitā, iv. 1, 5, 3; Maitrāyaṇī Saṃhitā, ii. 7, 5; Vājasaneyi Saṃhitā, xi. 56.

[4] *Vedische Studien*, 1, 131, 132.

[5] Gopatha Brāhmaṇa, i. 3, 21 (=Vaitāna Sūtra, xi. 22), cited by Geldner, is quite vague.

Cf. Zimmer, *Altindisches Leben*, 265; Bloomfield, *Hymns of the Atharvaveda*, 539; Whitney, Translation of the Atharvaveda, 348; Caland, *Über das rituelle Sūtra des Baudhāyana*, 59.

Kurīrin ('having a **Kurīra**') is a word occurring in an ambiguous passage of the Atharvaveda,[1] in which it may be taken either as a noun meaning a 'crested animal,' perhaps as Zimmer[2] suggests the 'peacock,' or as an epithet of the word **Aja**, 'goat,' in which case it might mean 'horned.' But even in the latter alternative a metaphorical application of the word seems sufficient, just as in the Pañcaviṃśa Brāhmaṇa[3] **Opaśa** is used of the horns of cattle, and thus renders unnecessary the adoption of Geldner's[4] view that the original meaning of **Kurīra** is 'horn.'

[1] v. 31, 2.

[2] *Altindisches Leben*, 91.

[3] xiii. 4, 3.

[4] *Vedische Studien*, 1, 130.

Cf. Bloomfield, *Hymns of the Atharvaveda*, 457, 539; Weber, *Indische Studien*, 18, 285; Whitney, Translation of the Atharvaveda, 279.

Kuru.—The Kurus appear as by far the most important people in the Brāhmaṇa literature. There is clear evidence that it was in the country of the Kurus, or the allied Kuru-Pañcālas, that the great Brāhmaṇas were composed.[1] The Kurus are comparatively seldom mentioned alone, their name being usually coupled with that of the Pañcālas on account of the intimate connexion of the two peoples. The Kuru-Pañcālas are often expressly referred to as a united nation.[2] In the land of the Kuru-Pañcālas speech is said to have its particular home;[3] the mode of sacrifice among the Kuru-Pañcālas is proclaimed to be the best;[4] the Kuru-Pañcāla kings perform the Rājasūya or royal sacrifice;[5] their princes march forth on raids in the dewy season, and return in the hot season.[6] Later on the Kuru-Pañcāla Brahmins are famous in the Upaniṣads.[7] Weber[8] and Grierson[9] have sought to find traces in Vedic literature of a breach between the two tribes, the latter scholar seeing therein a confirmation of the theory that the Kurus belonged to the later stream of immigrants into India, who were specially Brahminical, as opposed to the Pañcālas, who were anti-Brahminical. In support of this view, Weber refers to the story in the Kāṭhaka Saṃhitā[10] of a dispute between **Vaka Dālbhya** and **Dhṛtarāṣṭra Vaicitravīrya,** the former being held to be by origin a Pañcāla, while the latter is held

[1] For the Pañcaviṃśa Brāhmaṇa, *cf.* Hopkins, *Transactions of the Connecticut Academy of Arts and Sciences*, 15, 49, 50, with Weber, *Indian Literature*, 67, 68; for the Aitareya Brāhmaṇa and the Śāṅkhāyana Brāhmaṇa, Weber, *loc. cit.*, 45; for the Aitareya and Sāṅkhāyana Āraṇyakas, Keith, *Journal of the Royal Asiatic Society*, 1908, 387; for the Śatapatha Brāhmaṇa, Weber, *loc. cit.*, 132, *Transactions of the Berlin Academy*, 1895, 859. The Jaiminīya Brāhmaṇa refers repeatedly to the Kuru-Pañcālas, whose name also occurs in the late and confused Gopatha Brāhmaṇa. For the Taittirīya Brāhmaṇa, see i. 8, 4, 1. 2, and for the Maitrāyaṇī Saṃhitā, iv. 2, 6.

[2] Jaiminīya Upaniṣad Brāhmaṇa, iii. 7, 6; 8, 7; iv. 7, 2; Kauṣītaki Upaniṣad, iv. 1; Gopatha Brāhmaṇa, i. 2, 9; Kāṭhaka Saṃhitā, x. 6; Vājasaneyi Saṃhitā, xi. 3, 3 (Kāṇva recension).

[3] Śatapatha Brāhmaṇa, iii. 2, 3, 15.

[4] *Ibid.*, i. 7, 2, 8; *cf. Kuru-vājapeya* in Sāṅkhāyana Śrauta Sūtra, xv. 3, 15; Lāṭyāyana Śrauta Sūtra, viii. 11, 18.

[5] Śatapatha Brāhmaṇa, v. 5, 2, 3. 5.

[6] Taittirīya Brāhmaṇa, i. 8, 4, 1. 2.

[7] Jaiminīya Brāhmaṇa, ii. 78; Jaiminīya Upaniṣad Brāhmaṇa, iii. 30, 6; iv. 6, 2; Bṛhadāraṇyaka Upaniṣad, iii. 1, 1; 9, 20, etc.

[8] *Indische Studien*, 3, 470; *Indian Literature*, 114.

[9] *Journal of the Royal Asiatic Society*, 1908, 602-607; 837-844.

[10] x. 6. *Cf.* Eggeling, *Sacred Books of the East*, 12, xli.

to be a Kuru. But there is no trace of a quarrel between Kurus and Pañcālas in the passage in question, which merely preserves the record of a dispute on a ritual matter between a priest and a prince: the same passage refers to the Naimiṣīya sacrifice among the Kuru-Pañcālas, and emphasizes the close connexion of the two peoples.[11] Secondly, Weber conjectures in the Vājasaneyi Saṃhitā[12] that **Subhadrikā** of **Kāmpīla** was the chief queen of the king of a tribe living in the neighbourhood of the clan, for whose king the horse sacrifice described in the Saṃhitā was performed. But the interpretation of this passage by Weber is open to grave doubt;[13] and in the Kāṇva recension of the Saṃhitā[14] a passage used at the Rājasūya shows that the Kuru-Pañcālas had actually one king. Moreover, there is the evidence of the Śatapatha Brāhmaṇa[15] that the old name of the Pañcālas was **Krivi**. This word looks very like a variant of Kuru, and Zimmer[16] plausibly conjectures that the Kurus and Krivis formed the **Vaikarṇa**[17] of the Rigveda, especially as both peoples are found about the Sindhu and the Asiknī.[18]

The Kurus alone are chiefly mentioned in connexion with the locality which they occupied, **Kurukṣetra**. We are told, however, of a domestic priest (**Purohita**) in the service of both the Kurus and the **Sṛñjayas**,[19] who must therefore at one time have been closely connected.[20] In the Chāndogya Upaniṣad reference is made to the Kurus being saved by a mare (*aśvā*),[21] and to some disaster which befel them owing to a hailstorm.[22] In the Sūtras, again, a ceremony (Vājapeya) of the Kurus is mentioned.[23] There also a curse, which was pronounced on them and led to their being driven from Kurukṣetra, is alluded to.[24]

[11] See Keith, *Journal of the Royal Asiatic Society*, 1908, 831-836; 1138-1142.

[12] xxiii. 18.

[13] Eggeling, *Sacred Books of the East*, 44, 322.

[14] xi. 3, 3. *Cf.* Weber, *Indian Literature*, 114, note *.

[15] xiii. 5, 4, 7.

[16] *Altindisches Leben*, 103.

[17] vii. 18, 11.

[18] Keith, *loc. cit.*, 835.

[19] Śatapatha Brāhmaṇa, ii. 4, 4, 5.

[20] *Cf.* Weber, *Indian Literature*, 123.

[21] iv. 17, 9: for *aśvā* Böhtlingk in his edition reads *akṣṇā*, followed by Little, *Grammatical Index*, 1.

[22] i. 10, 1.

[23] Śāṅkhāyana Śrauta Sūtra, xv. 3, 15.

[24] *Ibid.*, xv. 16, 11. *Cf.* Weber, *Indian Literature*, 136.

This possibly adumbrates the misfortunes of the Kauravas in the epic tradition.

In the Rigveda the Kurus do not appear under that name as a people. But mention is made of a prince, **Kuruśravaṇa** (' Glory of the Kurus '),[25] and of a **Pākasthāman Kaurayāṇa.**[26] In the Atharvaveda[27] there occurs as a king of the Kurus **Parikṣit,** whose son, **Janamejaya,** is mentioned in the Śatapatha Brāhmaṇa[28] as one of the great performers of the horse sacrifice.

It is a probable conjecture of Oldenberg's[29] that the Kuru people, as known later, included some of the tribes referred to by other names in the Rigveda. Kuruśravaṇa, shown by his name to be connected with the Kurus, is in the Rigveda called Trāsadasyava, ' descendant of **Trasadasyu,**' who is well known as a king of the **Pūrus.** Moreover, it is likely that the **Tṛtsu-Bharatas,** who appear in the Rigveda as enemies of the Pūrus, later coalesced with them to form the Kuru people.[30] Since the Bharatas appear so prominently in the Brāhmaṇa texts as a great people of the past, while the later literature ignores them in its list of nations, it is difficult to avoid the conclusion that they became merged in some other tribe. Moreover, there is evidence that the Bharatas occupied the territory in which the Kurus were later found. Two of them are spoken of in a hymn of the Rigveda[31] as having kindled fire on the **Dṛṣadvatī,** the **Āpayā,** and the **Sarasvatī**—that is to say, in the sacred places of the later Kurukṣetra. Similarly, the goddess Bhāratī (' belonging to the Bharatas ') is constantly mentioned in the Āprī (' propitiatory ') hymns together with Sarasvatī.[32] Again, according to the Śatapatha Brāhmaṇa, one Bharata king was victorious over the Kāśis,[33] and another made offerings to Gaṅgā and Yamunā,[34] while raids of the Bharatas against the **Satvants** are mentioned in the Aitareya Brāhmaṇa.[35] Nor is it

25 Rv. x. 33, 4.
26 Rv. viii. 3, 21.
27 xx. 127, 7 *et seq.*; Khila, v. 10.
28 xiii. 5, 4.
29 *Buddha*, 403, 404.
30 *Ibid.*, 406-409.
31 iii. 23.
32 *Cf.* Scheftelowitz, *Die Apokryphen des Ṛgveda*, 145.
33 xiii. 5, 4, 11.
34 *Ibid.*, 21.
35 Aitareya Brāhmaṇa, ii. 25 (*cf.* Haug's edition, 2, 128, n. 3); Oldenberg, *Buddha*, 407, note *.

without importance that the Bharatas appear as a variant for the Kuru-Pañcālas in a passage of the Vājasaneyi Saṃhitā,[36] and that in the list of the great performers of the horse sacrifice the names of one Kuru and two Bharata princes are given without any mention of the people over which they ruled, while in other cases that information is specifically given.[37]

The territory of the Kuru-Pañcālas is declared in the Aitareya Brāhmaṇa to be the middle country (**Madhyadeśa**).[38] A group of the Kuru people still remained further north—the **Uttara Kurus** beyond the Himālaya. It appears from a passage of the Śatapatha Brāhmaṇa that the speech of the Northerners—that is, presumably, the Northern Kurus—and of the Kuru-Pañcālas was similar, and regarded as specially pure.[39] There seems little doubt that the Brahminical culture was developed in the country of the Kuru-Pañcālas, and that it spread thence east, south, and west. Traces of this are seen in the Vrātya Stomas (sacrifices for the admission of non-Brahminical Āryans) of the Pañcaviṃśa Brāhmaṇa,[40] and in the fact that in the Śāṅkhāyana Āraṇyaka it is unusual for a Brahmin to dwell in the territory of **Magadha.**[41] The repeated mention of Kuru-Pañcāla Brahmins is another indication of their missionary activity.[42]

The geographical position of the Kuru-Pañcālas renders it probable that they were later immigrants into India than the **Kosala-Videha** or the **Kāśis,**[43] who must have been pushed

[36] xi. 3, 3. See note 14; Oldenberg, *Buddha*, 408, 409.

[37] Oldenberg, 409, note *.

[38] viii. 14. *Cf.* Oldenberg, 392, 393.

[39] iii. 2, 3, 15. This is the sense which it appears to bear, as the Kuru-Pañcālas can hardly be reckoned as being northerly (Oldenberg, 395), and the Kauṣītaki Brāhmaṇa, vii. 6 (*Indische Studien*, 2, 309) is independent evidence for the pure speech of the north. *Cf.* Eggeling, *Sacred Books of the East*, 12, xlii., n.; Weber, *Indian Literature*, 45; *Indische Studien*, 1, 191.

[40] xvii. 1, 1. See also Av. xv. with Whitney's and Lanman's notes; Weber, *Indische Studien*, 1, 33 *et seq.*; *Indian Literature*, 67, 78, 80.

[41] vii. 13. *Cf.* Oldenberg, *Buddha*, 400, note *; Weber, *Indian Literature*, 112, n. 126.

[42] See *e.g.* Śatapatha Brāhmaṇa, xi. 4, 1, 2, and note 6.

[43] This is recognized, *e.g.*, by Oldenberg, *Buddha*, 9. 391, 398, 399; Lanman, *Sanskrit Reader*, 297, etc. The narrative of the Śatapatha Brāhmaṇa, i. 4, 1, 10 *et seq.* (Weber, *Indische Studien*, 1, 170), rather implies that the Kosala-Videhas are offshoots of the Kuru-Pañcālas, but Oldenberg and Macdonell (*Sanskrit Literature*, 214 interpret this as referring to the spread of Vedic tradition and culture, not of nationality.

into their more eastward territories by a new wave of Āryan settlers from the west. But there is no evidence in Vedic literature to show in what relation of time the immigration of the latter peoples stood to that of their neighbours on the west. It has, however, been conjectured,[44] mainly on the ground of later linguistic phenomena, which have no cogency for the Vedic period, that the Kurus were later immigrants, who, coming by a new route, thrust themselves between the original Āryan tribes which were already in occupation of the country from east to west. *Cf.* also **Kṛtvan.** For other Kuru princes see **Kauravya.**

[44] *Cf.* Grierson, *Languages of India*, 52 *et seq.*; *Journal of the Royal Asiatic Society*, 1908, 837 *et seq.* On the other hand, it is probably an error to assume that the Bharatas were originally situated far west of Kurukṣetra, and that the main action of the Rigveda was confined to the Panjab. When Vasiṣṭha celebrates the crossing of the Vipāś and Śutudrī (Rv. iii. 33), he probably came from the east, as Pischel, *Vedische Studien*, 2, 218, points out, and not from the west. Adopting the ordinary view, Hopkins, *India, Old and New*, 52, finds it necessary to suggest that Yamunā is only another name in the Rv. for the Paruṣṇī. But the necessity for this suggestion, which is not in itself plausible, disappears when it is realized that the Bharatas held a territory roughly corresponding to Kurukṣetra, and bounded on the east by the Yamunā. On the other hand, Hillebrandt, *Vedische Mythologie*, 1, 142, 143, places the Kurus near the Ārjīkīyā in Kaśmīr, which puts them too far north. So also Zimmer, *Altindisches Leben*, 103, and Eggeling, *Sacred Books of the East*, 12, xlii. It seems probable that the Kurus were at a very early period widely scattered to the north of the Himālaya, in Kurukṣetra, and about the Sindhu and Asiknī.

Cf. Oldenberg, *Buddha*, 400 *et seq.*; Macdonell, *Sanskrit Literature*, 152-157; von Schroeder, *Indiens Literatur und Cultur*, 164 *et seq.*; Weber, *Indische Studien*, 1, 187 *et seq.*; *Indian Literature*, 114, 135, 136; Rhys Davids, *Buddhist India*, 27; Pargiter, *Journal of the Royal Asiatic Society*, 1908, 333 *et seq.*; Hopkins, *Journal of the American Oriental Society*, 13, 205, n.

Kuru-kṣetra ('land of the Kurus') is always regarded in the Brāhmaṇa texts[1] as a particularly sacred country. Within its boundaries flowed the rivers **Dṛṣadvatī** and **Sarasvatī,** as well as the **Āpayā.**[2] Here, too, was situated **Śaryaṇāvant,**[3] which

[1] Pañcaviṃśa Brāhmaṇa, xxv. 10; Śatapatha Brāhmaṇa, iv. 1, 5, 13; xi. 5, 1, 4; xiv. 1, 1, 2; Aitareya Brāhmaṇa, vii. 30; Maitrāyaṇī Saṃhitā, ii. 1, 4; iv. 5, 9; Jaiminīya Brāhmaṇa, iii. 126 (*Journal of the American Oriental Society*, 11, cxlvi); Śāṅkhāyana Śrauta Sūtra, xv. 16, 11, etc.

[2] *Cf.* Rv. iii. 23; Pischel, *Vedische Studien*, 2, 218.

[3] See Pischel, *loc. cit.*, and *cf.* **Ārjīkīyā.**

appears to have been a lake, like that known to the Śatapatha Brāhmaṇa by the name of **Anyataḥ-plakṣā.**[4] According to Pischel, there was also in Kurukṣetra a stream called **Pastyā,**[5] which he sees in certain passages of the Rigveda. The boundaries of Kurukṣetra are given in a passage of the Taittirīya Āraṇyaka[6] as being Khāṇḍava on the south, the Tūrghna on the north, and the Parīṇah on the west. Roughly speaking, it corresponded to the modern Sirhind.

[4] Satapatha Brāhmaṇa, xi. 5, 1, 4.
[5] Pischel, *loc. cit.*, 219.
[6] v. 1, 1. These places cannot be further identified. See also **Maru.**

Cf. von Schroeder, *Indiens Literatur und Cultur*, 164, 165; Max Müller, *Sacred Books of the East*, 32, 398, 399; Weber, *Indische Studien*, 1, 78, 79; Macdonell, *Sanskrit Literature*, 174. Eggeling, *Sacred Books of the East*, 12, xli., seems to place Kurukṣetra, as lying between the Yamunā aud Gaṅgā, too far east.

Kuruṅga is mentioned in the Rigveda[1] as a prince and a patron. Ludwig[2] suggests that he was a king of the **Anus,** but for this theory there seems no good ground. As the **Turvaśas** are mentioned in the same verse, he may possibly have been one of their kings. The name suggests a connexion with the **Kurus,** and it may be noted that in the Śatapatha Brāhmaṇa[3] the Turvaśas are connected with the **Pañcālas** (**Krivis**).

[1] viii. 4, 19; Nirukta, vi. 22.
[2] Translation of the Rigveda, 3, 160.
[3] xi. 5, 4, 16. See Oldenberg, *Buddha*, 404.

Kuru-śravaṇa Trāsadasyava is alluded to as dead in a hymn of the Rigveda,[1] which refers also to his son **Upamaśravas,** and his father **Mitrātithi.** In another hymn[2] he is mentioned as still alive. His name connects him on the one hand with the **Kurus,** and on the other with **Trasadasyu** and the **Pūrus.**

[1] x. 33, 4. *Cf.* Bṛhaddevatā, vii. 35, 36.
[2] x. 32, 9. *Cf.* Ludwig, Translation of the Rigveda, 3, 165; Geldner, *Vedische Studien*, 2, 150, 184; Lanman, *Sanskrit Reader*, 386.

Kurūru, apparently the name of a species of worm, is mentioned twice in the Atharvaveda.[1]

[1] ii. 31, 2; ix. 2, 22. *Cf.* Zimmer, *Altindisches Leben*, 98.

Kurkura is an onomatopoetic name for the dog in the Atharvaveda.[1] See also **Śvan.**

[1] vii. 95, 2. *Cf.* Zimmer, *Altindisches Leben*, 233.

Kula, Kula-pā.—As an uncompounded word, Kula does not occur before the period of the Brāhmaṇas.[1] It denotes the 'home' or 'house of the family,' and by metonymy the family itself, as connected with the home. The Kula-pā (lit. 'house protector'), or chief of the family, is mentioned in the Rigveda[2] as inferior to and attendant on the **Vrājapati** in war, the latter being perhaps the leader of the village contingent of the clan. In the Atharvaveda[3] a girl is ironically called Kulapā, because she is left without a husband in the world, and has only Yama (the god of death) for a spouse.

The use of the term Kula points clearly to a system of individual families, each no doubt consisting of several members under the headship of the father or eldest brother, whose Kula the dwelling is. As distinct from **Gotra,** Kula seems to mean the family in the narrower sense of the members who still live in one house, the undivided family. *Cf.* **Gṛha, Grāma, Jana, Viś.**

[1] Śatapatha Brāhmaṇa, i. 1, 2, 22; ii. 1, 4, 4; 4, 1, 14; xi. 5, 3, 11; 8, 1, 3; xiii. 4, 2, 17; Bṛhadāraṇyaka Upaniṣad, i. 5, 32; Chāndogya Upaniṣad, iii., 13, 6, etc.

[2] x. 179, 2.

[3] i. 14, 3. *Cf.* Whitney, Translation of the Atharvaveda, 15; Bloomfield, *Hymns of the Atharvaveda*, 252, correcting Zimmer, *Altindisches Leben*, 314.

Cf. Zimmer, *op. cit.*, 162.

Kulāla, the word denoting a 'potter,' occurs in the Śatarudriya, or litany to Rudra in the Yajurveda.[1]

[1] Vājasaneyi Saṃhitā, xvi. 27. *Cf. kulāla-kṛta*, 'made by a potter,' Maitrāyaṇi Saṃhitā, i. 8, 3, and **Kaulāla.**

Kuliśa, 'axe,' is mentioned in the Rigveda as used for the making of chariots,[1] and also in warfare,[2] while the Atharvaveda refers to its employment in cutting down trees.[3]

[1] iii. 2, 1.

[2] i. 32, 5.

[3] ii. 12, 3.

Cf. Zimmer, *Altindisches Leben*, 252.

Kulīkaya is the form in the Taittirīya Saṃhitā[1] of the name of an animal, apparently a kind of fish, as explained by Mahīdhara in his commentary, which is called Kulīpaya in the Vājasaneyi Saṃhitā,[2] and Purīkaya in the Atharvaveda,[3] variants probably due to the faulty tradition of an unfamiliar name.

[1] v. 5, 13, 1.
[2] xxiv. 21. 35.
[3] xi. 2, 25. The commentator reads Pulīkaya, as in the Maitrāyaṇī Saṃhitā, iii. 14, 2. See Whitney, Translation of the Atharvaveda, 624.
Cf. Zimmer, *Altindisches Leben*, 96.

Kulīkā is the name of a bird mentioned in the list of victims at the horse sacrifice in the Vājasaneyi Saṃhitā.[1] The Maitrāyaṇī Saṃhitā[2] has Pulīkā instead.

[1] xxiv. 24.
[2] iii. 14, 5.
Cf. Zimmer, *Altindisches Leben*, 94.

Kuluṅga is the name of an animal, perhaps a gazelle, mentioned in the list of victims at the horse sacrifice in the Yajurveda.[1]

[1] Taittirīya Saṃhitā, v. 5, 11, 1; Maitrāyaṇī Saṃhitā, iii. 14, 9. 13 (with the variant Kulaṅga); Vājasaneyi Saṃhitā, xxiv. 27. 32.
Cf. Zimmer, *Altindisches Leben*, 83.

Kulmala seems, in the Atharvaveda,[1] the Maitrāyaṇī Saṃhitā,[2] and the Śatapatha Brāhmaṇa,[3] to denote the neck of an arrow in which the shaft is fixed.

[1] iv. 6, 5; v. 18, 15.
[2] iii. 8, 1. 2.
[3] iii. 4, 4, 14.

Kumala-barhis is mentioned in the Pañcaviṃśa Brāhmaṇa (xv. 3, 21) as the seer of a Sāman or Chant.

Kumāra Hārita is mentioned in the first Vaṃśa (list of teachers) in the Bṛhadāraṇyaka Upaniṣad[1] as a pupil of **Gālava.**

[1] ii. 5, 22 (Mādhyaṃdina = ii. 6, 3, Kāṇva).

Kulmāṣa, a word mentioned by the Chāndogya Upaniṣad[1] in the plural, is interpreted by the commentator as 'bad beans' (*kutsitā māṣāḥ*), a version adopted by Böhtlingk in his

[1] i. 10, 2. 7.

Dictionary.[2] Little[3] renders it 'sour gruel' in accordance with the Nirukta.[4]

[2] *Cf.* Bhāgavata Purāṇa, v. 9, 12, where it is glossed 'worm-eaten beans.'

[3] *Grammatical Index*, 52.

[4] i. 4.

Kulyā in two passages of the Rigveda,[1] according to Muir,[2] possibly refers to artificial watercourses flowing into a reservoir (*hrada*). See **Avata.**

[1] iii. 45, 3; x. 43, 7.

[2] *Sanskrit Texts*, 5, 465, 466.

Kuvaya. See **Kvayi.**

Kuvala is a name of the jujube fruit (*Zizyphus jujuba*) occurring frequently in the Yajurveda Saṃhitās[1] and Brāhmaṇas[2] in connexion with **Karkandhu** and **Badara.** See also **Kola.**

[1] Maitrāyaṇī Saṃhitā, iii. 11, 2; Vājasaneyi Saṃhitā, xix. 22, 89; xxi. 29; Kāṭhaka Saṃhitā, xii. 10.

[2] Śatapatha Brāhmaṇa, v. 5, 4, 10; xii. 7, 1, 2; 2, 9; 9, 1, 5, etc. *Cf.* Zimmer, *Altindisches Leben*, 242.

Kuśa, a word later denoting the 'sacred grass' (*Poa cynosuroides*), is taken by the St. Petersburg Dictionary to mean simply 'grass' in the passages of the Śatapatha Brāhmaṇa in which it occurs.

[1] ii. 5, 2, 15; iii. 1, 2, 16; v. 3, 2, 7, etc. Kuśā and Kuśī occur in Maitrāyaṇī Saṃhitā, iv. 5, 7; Śatapatha Brāhmaṇa, iii. 6, 2, 9; Taittirīya Brāhmaṇa, i. 5, 10, 1. 2. 7, apparently denoting pins of wood or metal, used as a mark in a special mode of recitation.

Ku-śara is mentioned with **Śara** and other grasses in one hymn of the Rigveda[1] as affording lurking places for serpents.

[1] i. 191, 3. *Cf.* Zimmer, *Altindisches Leben*, 72.

Kuśika is the probably mythical forefather[1] of the Kuśikas, and especially the father of the most important member of that family, **Viśvāmitra.**[2] The Kuśikas are repeatedly referred

[1] Nirukta, ii. 25.

[2] Rv. iii. 33, 5.

to in the third Maṇḍala of the Rigveda,[3] and figure in the legend of Śunaḥśepa in the Aitareya Brāhmaṇa.[4] They were clearly a family of priests who attached themselves to the service of the princes of the **Bharatas.** They were especially devoted to the worship of Indra; hence he is styled Kauśika even in the Rigveda.[5]

[3] iii. 26, 1; 29, 15; 30, 20; 33, 5; 42, 9; 50, 4; 53, 9. 10.

[4] vii. 18; Sāṅkhāyana Srauta Sūtra, xv. 27.

[5] i. 10, 11, with Sāyaṇa's note. *Cf.* Maitrāyaṇī Saṃhitā, iv. 5, 7; Śatapatha Brāhmaṇa, iii. 3, 4, 19; Taittirīya Āraṇyaka, i. 12, 4; Macdonell, *Vedic Mythology*, pp. 62, 63. *Cf.* Weber, *Indische Studien*, 1, 38; Muir, *Sanskrit Texts*, 1², 342 *et seq.*; Ludwig, Translation of the Rigveda, 3, 101, 121; Macdonell, *Sanskrit Literature*, 155; Oldenberg, *Zeitschrift der Deutschen Morgenländischen Gesellschaft*, 42, 209.

Kuśri Vāja-śravasa appears as a teacher concerned with the lore of the sacred fire in the Śatapatha Brāhmaṇa,[1] and in the last Vaṃśa (list of teachers) of the Bṛhadāraṇyaka Upaniṣad[2] he is mentioned as a pupil of **Vājaśravas.** It is not clear whether he is identical with the Kuśri of the last Vaṃśa of the Bṛhadāraṇyaka[3] in the Kāṇva recension, and of the Vaṃśa in the tenth book of the Śatapatha,[4] who is mentioned as a pupil of **Yajñavacas Rājastambāyana.**

[1] x. 5, 5, 1.

[2] vi. 4, 33 (Mādhyaṃdina = vi. 5, 3, Kāṇva).

[3] vi. 5, 4 (Kāṇva only).

[4] x. 6, 5, 9. In the Vaṃśas the name is accented Kúśri, but in x. 5, 5, 1, as Kuśrí; no stress can, however, be laid on this. *Cf.* Weber, *Indische Studien*, 1, 70; Eggeling, *Sacred Books of the East*, 12, xxxiii.

Ku-ṣaṇḍa is mentioned with **Ṣaṇḍa** as a priest at the snake festival described in the Pañcaviṃśa Brāhmaṇa.[1]

[1] xxv. 15, 3. *Cf.* Weber, *Indische Studien*, 1, 34; Lāṭyāyana Śrauta Sūtra, x. 20, 10.

1. **Kuṣītaka** denotes, according to the commentary on the one passage of the Taittirīya Saṃhitā[1] in which it is found, the sea crow (*samudra-kāka*).

[1] v. 5, 13, 1. *Cf.* Zimmer, *Altindisches Leben*, 72.

2. **Kuṣītaka Sāma-śravasa** is mentioned in the Pañcaviṃśa Brāhmaṇa[1] as the Gṛhapati, or householder at a sacrificial session, of the Kauṣītakis.

[1] xvii. 4. *Cf.* Weber, *Indische Studien*, 1, 34.

Kuṣumbhaka seems in one passage of the Rigveda[1] to mean a poisonous insect, Kuṣumbha in the Atharvaveda[2] clearly having the sense of a poison bag. Sāyaṇa renders it as 'ichneumon' (*nakula*).

[1] i. 191, 16. The sense of 'poison-bag' is possible in i. 191, 15, and is accepted there by Böhtlingk in his Dictionary.

[2] ii. 32, 6. *Cf.* Zimmer, *Altindisches Leben*, 99; Griffith, *Hymns of the Rigveda*, 1, 257.

1. **Kuṣṭha** is the name of a plant (*Costus speciosus* or *arabicus*)[1] which is prominent in the Atharvaveda.[2] It grew especially on the mountains, along with the Soma, on the high peaks of the Himālaya (*Himavant*) where the eagles nest, and was thence brought east to men.[3] Like Soma, it is said to have grown in the third heaven under the famous **Aśvattha** tree, where the gods were wont to assemble, and thence it was brought in a golden ship.[4] As a remedy, it held the highest place among herbs, being called by the auspicious names Nagha-māra and Naghā-riṣa, and styled the offspring of Jīvala and Jīvalā, the 'lively' ones.[5] It cured headache (*śīrṣāmaya*), diseases of the eyes, bodily affliction,[6] but especially fever—hence called 'fever-destroyer' (*takma-nāśana*)—and consumption (**Yakṣma**). From its general properties it was also named 'all-healing' (*viśva-bheṣaja*).[7] Its aromatic qualities were apparently known, as it is classed with 'salve' (**Āñjana**) and 'nard' (**Nalada**).[8]

[1] Or *Saussurea auriculata*, Hillebrandt, *Vedische Mythologie*, 1, 65.
[2] v. 4; vi. 102; xix. 139.
[3] v. 4, 1. 2. 8; xix. 39, 1.
[4] v. 4, 3-6; vi. 75, 1. 2; xix. 39, 6-8.
[5] v. 4, 1; xix. 39, 4.
[6] v. 4, 10.
[7] xix. 39, 9.
[8] vi. 102, 3.

Cf. Grohmann, *Indische Studien*, 9, 420 *et seq.*; Zimmer, *Altindisches Leben*, 63, 64; Bloomfield, *Hymns of the Atharvaveda*, 415, 680; Whitney, Translation of the Atharvaveda, 227, 228.

2. **Kuṣṭha.**—In one passage of the Maitrāyaṇī Saṃhitā[1] there is a series of fractions, **Kalā, Kuṣṭha, Śapha, Pad,** which appear to denote one-sixteenth, one-twelfth, one-eighth, and one-fourth respectively.

[1] iii. 7, 7. *Cf.* Böhtlingk, Dictionary, *s.v.*

Kusīdin is a designation of the 'usurer' found in the Śatapatha Brāhmaṇa[1] and the Nirukta,[2] and often in the Sūtras. Jolly,[3] referring doubtless to the expression *kusīda apratītta*,[4] 'a loan not yet repaid,' occurring in connexion with *an-ṛṇa*, 'free from debt,' appears to be right in taking Kusīda to have the sense of 'loan' in the Taittirīya Saṃhitā. The rate of interest on loans is not specified before the Sūtra period.[5] *Cf.* **Ṛṇa.**

[1] xiii. 4, 3, 11.
[2] vi. 32.
[3] *Recht und Sitte*, 98, 99.
[4] iii. 3, 8, 1. 2.
[5] *E.g.*, Gautama Sūtra, xii. 29 *et seq.* *Cf.* Zimmer, *Altindisches Leben*, 259.

Kusurubinda Auddālaki appears as an authority on ritual matters in the Pañcaviṃśa Brāhmaṇa,[1] the Taittirīya Saṃhitā,[2] the Jaiminīya Brāhmaṇa,[3] and the Ṣaḍviṃśa Brāhmaṇa.[4] He may have been the brother of **Śvetaketu,** as suggested by Weber.[5]

[1] xxii. 15, 1. 10.
[2] vii. 2, 2, 1.
[3] i. 75 (*Journal of the American Oriental Society*, 23, 327), where the reading seems to be Asurbinda.
[4] i. 16. See Weber, *Indische Studien*, 1, 39. The name is there read as Kusurubindu; in the Śāṅkhāyana Śrauta Sūtra, xvi. 22, 14 it is Kusurabindu.
[5] *Indische Studien*, 5, 61, n.

Kuhū. See **Māsa.**

Kūcakra is a word occurring only once in an obscure verse of the Rigveda,[1] where Zimmer[2] suggests that it has the sense of the wheel by which water is raised from a well. Much more probable is the interpretation of Roth,[3] who understands it to mean the female breast.

[1] x. 102, 11.
[2] *Altindisches Leben*, 157. *Cf.* Geldner, *Vedische Studien*, 2, 14.
[3] St. Petersburg Dictionary, *s.v.*

Kūṭa, a word found in the Rigveda,[1] the Atharvaveda,[2] and the Brāhmaṇas,[3] is of doubtful signification. On the whole,

[1] x. 102, 4.
[2] viii. 8, 16.
[3] Aitareya Brāhmaṇa, vi. 24; Śatapatha Brāhmaṇa, iii. 8, 1, 15; Jaiminīya Brāhmaṇa, i. 49, 9; 50, 2 (*Journal of the American Oriental Society*, 19, 114).

the most probable sense is hammer,[4] which suits every passage adequately. The St. Petersburg Dictionary renders it 'horn,' which is the sense accepted by Whitney[5] for the Atharvaveda passage where it occurs. Geldner[6] thinks that it means 'trap.'

[4] So Bloomfield, *Zeitschrift der Deutschen Morgenländischen Gesellschaft*, 48, 546; *Hymns of the Atharvaveda*, 585.

[5] Translation of the Atharvaveda, 505.

[6] *Vedische Studien*, 1, 138; 2, 7. *Cf.* von Bradke, *Zeitschrift der Deutschen Morgenländischen Gesellschaft*, 46, 458; Kuhn's *Zeitschrift*, 34, 156; Weber, *Indische Studien*, 9, 222.

Kūdī, written also Kūṭī in the manuscripts, occurs in the Atharvaveda[1] and the Kauśika Sūtra[2] denoting a twig—identified by the scholiast with **Badarī**, the jujube—which was tied to the bodies of the dead to efface their traces, presumably in order to render the return of the spirit to the old home difficult.

[1] v. 19, 12.

[2] Bloomfield's edition, xliv. *Cf.* Bloomfield, *American Journal of Philology*, 11, 355; 12, 416; Roth, *Festgruss an Böhtlingk*, 98; Whitney, Translation of the Atharvaveda, 254; Macdonell, *Vedic Mythology*, p. 165.

Kūpa occurs in the Rigveda[1] and later literature[2] denoting an artificial hollow in the earth, or pit. In some cases they must have been deep, as Trita in the myth is said to have fallen into one from which he could not escape unaided.[3]

[1] i. 105, 17.

[2] Av. v. 31, 8; Śatapatha Brāhmaṇa, iii. 5, 4, 1; iv. 4, 5, 3; vi. 3, 3, 26, etc.; Jaiminīya Brāhmaṇa, i. 184, etc. The adjective *kūpya*, 'being in a hole,' occurs frequently in the later Saṃhitās.

[3] Macdonell, *Vedic Mythology*, p. 67.

Kūbara in the Maitrāyaṇī Saṃhitā (ii. 1, 11) and **Kūbarī** in the Śatapatha Brāhmaṇa (iv. 6, 9, 11. 12) and the Kauṣītaki Brāhmaṇa (xxvii. 6) denote the pole of a cart.

Kūrca is found in the Taittirīya Saṃhitā[1] and later[2] denoting a bundle of grass used as a seat. In one passage of the Śatapatha Brāhmaṇa[3] a golden Kūrca is referred to.

[1] vii. 5, 8, 5.

[2] Śatapatha Brāhmaṇa, xi. 5, 3, 4. 7; Bṛhadāraṇyaka Upaniṣad, ii. 11, 1; Aitareya Āraṇyaka, v. 1, 4.

[3] xiii. 4, 3, 1.

Kūrma, the 'tortoise,' is mentioned frequently in the later Saṃhitās[1] and Brāhmaṇas,[2] but nothing is said of its characteristics. See also **Kaśyapa.**

[1] Av. ix. 4, 16; Taittirīya Saṃhitā, ii. 6, 3, 3; v. 2, 8, 4. 5; 7, 13, 1; Maitrāyaṇī Saṃhitā, iii. 15, 3; Vājasaneyi Saṃhitā, xxiv. 34, etc.

[2] Śatapatha Brāhmaṇa, i. 6, 2, 3; vi. 1, 1, 12, etc.

Cf. Zimmer, *Altindisches Leben*, 95; Macdonell, *Vedic Mythology*, p. 153.

Kūśāmba Svāyava Lātavya is mentioned in the Pañcaviṃśa Brāhmaṇa[1] as a priest. His name apparently means[2] Kūśāmba,[3] of the Lātavya clan, son of Svāyu.

[1] viii. 6, 8.

[2] The form is peculiar, as Kuśāmba would be expected.

[3] Hopkins, *Transactions of the Connecticut Academy of Arts and Sciences*, 15, 55, n. 2.

Kṛkalāsa denotes the 'chameleon' mentioned in the list of sacrificial victims at the horse sacrifice in the Yajurveda[1] and later.[2] The female chameleon, Kṛkalāsī, is also referred to in the Brāhmaṇas.[3] See **Godhā** and **Śayaṇḍaka.**

[1] Taittirīya Saṃhitā, v. 5, 19, 1; Maitrāyaṇī Saṃhitā, iii. 14, 21; Vājasaneyi Saṃhitā, xxiv. 40.

[2] Bṛhadāraṇyaka Upaniṣad, i. 5, 22.

[3] Jaiminīya Brāhmaṇa, i. 221 (*Journal of the American Oriental Society*, 18, 29); Sāṭyāyanaka in Sāyaṇa on Rv. viii. 91.

Cf. Zimmer, *Altindisches Leben*, 95.

Kṛka-vāku, the 'cock,' being named in the Atharvaveda[1] with sheep, goats, and other domesticated animals, was presumably tamed.[2] In the list of victims at the horse sacrifice in the Yajurveda,[3] it appears as dedicated to Savitṛ: Yāska[4] explains this by the fact that it declares the time of day (*kālānuvāda*). The commentator Mahīdhara[5] explains the name by *tāmra-cūḍa*, 'red-crested.' It is of course onomatopoetic ('calling kṛka').[6] See also **Kukkuṭa.**

[1] v. 31, 2. *Cf.* x. 136, 10.

[2] *Cf.*, however, Sāyaṇa on Taittirīya Saṃhitā, v. 5, 18, 1, who says that it is a 'forest' Kukkuṭa.

[3] Taittirīya Saṃhitā, *loc. cit.*; Maitrāyaṇī Saṃhitā, iii. 14, 15; Vājasaneyi Saṃhitā, xxiv. 35.

[4] Nirukta, xii. 3.

[5] On Vājasaneyi Saṃhitā, *loc. cit.*

[6] Schrader, *Prehistoric Antiquities*, 251; Weber, *Indische Studien*, 18, 285.

Cf. Zimmer, *Altindisches Leben*, 91.

Kṛta. See 2. **Akṣa** and 2. **Yuga.**

Kṛti.—From one passage in the Rigveda,[1] where the Maruts are described as having Kṛtis, Zimmer[2] concludes that the word means a dagger used in war. But there is no evidence that Kṛti was ever a human weapon. See **Asi.**

[1] i. 168, 3.
[2] *Altindisches Leben*, 301. *Cf.* Schrader, *Prehistoric Antiquities*, 221.

Kṛttikās. See **Nakṣatra.**

Kṛtvan.—In one passage of the Rigveda[1] the word Kṛtvan in the plural is mentioned with the **Ārjīkas** and the five peoples. Pischel[2] thinks that it means a people, and Sāyaṇa expressly says that the Kṛtvans designate a country.[3] The name in that case would point to some connexion with the **Kurus** or **Krivis.** Hillebrandt,[4] however, thinks that the word is an adjective which qualifies Ārjīkas and designates this people as magicians, being applied to them by an opponent. In favour of this view, he quotes Hiouen Thsang's statement[5] that the neighbouring kings held the base Kaśmīrians in such scorn as to refuse all alliance with them, and to give them the name of Ki-li-to, or Kṛtyas. He suggests that the Ārjīkas settled in Kaśmīr in ancient times already had the same evil reputation as their successors in later days.

[1] ix. 65, 23.
[2] *Vedische Studien*, 2, 209.
[3] *Kṛtvāna iti deśābhidhānam.*
[4] *Vedische Mythologie*, 1, 136, 137.
[5] Cunningham, *Ancient Geography of India*, 93.
Cf. Roth, St. Petersburg Dictionary, *s.v.*

Kṛpa is mentioned in the Rigveda,[1] along with **Ruśama** and **Śyāvaka,** as a protégé of Indra.

[1] viii. 3, 12; 4, 2. *Cf.* Ludwig, Translation of the Rigveda, 3, 162.

Kṛmi, 'worm.' In the later Saṃhitās,[1] and especially in the Atharvaveda,[2] worms play a considerable part. They are

[1] Taittirīya Saṃhitā, v. 5, 11, 1; Maitrāyaṇī Saṃhitā, iii. 14, 11; Vājasaneyi Saṃhitā, xxiv. 30; Mantra Brāhmaṇa, ii. 7; Taittirīya Āraṇyaka, iv. 36; Śatapatha Brāhmaṇa, v. 4, 1, 2; and *cf.* Rv. i. 191.
[2] ii. 31. 32; v. 23.

regarded as poisonous, and are spoken of as found in the mountains, in forests, in waters, in plants, and in the human body. In accordance with widespread primitive ideas, they are considered to be the causes of disease in men and animals. The Atharvaveda contains three hymns[2] as charms directed against them. The first of these hymns is of a general character, the second is meant to destroy worms in cattle, and the third is intended to cure children of worms. When found in men, worms are said to have their place in the head and ribs,[3] and to creep into the eyes, nose, and teeth.[4] They are described as dark brown, but white in the fore part of the body, with black ears, and as having three heads.[5] They are given many specific names: **Alāṇḍu, Ejatka, Kaṣkaṣa, Kīṭa, Kurūru, Nīlaṅgu, Yevāṣa, Vaghā, Vṛkṣasarpī, Śaluna, Śavarta, Śipavitnuka, Stega.**

[3] Av. ii. 31, 4.
[4] Av. v. 23, 3.
[5] Av. v. 23, 4 *et seq.*

Cf. Zimmer, *Altindisches Leben*, 98, 393; Kuhn, *Zeitschrift für vergleichende Sprachforschung*, 13, 49 *et seq.*; 113 *et seq.*; Bloomfield, *Hymns of the Atharvaveda*, 313 *et seq.*; Weber, *Indische Studien*, 13, 199; Whitney, Translation of the Atharvaveda, 73.

Kṛmuka is the name in the Kāṭhaka Saṃhitā[1] and the Śatapatha Brāhmaṇa[2] of a species of wood used for fuel.[3]

[1] xix. 10.
[2] vi. 6, 2, 11.
[3] *Ibid.* (*Krāmuka* as applied to *samidh*).

Kṛśa is mentioned with **Saṃvarta** as a pious sacrificer to Indra in one of the Vālakhilya hymns of the Rigveda[1] and in another[2] as a speaker of truth, while a third is traditionally[3] ascribed to his authorship. He seems also to be mentioned with **Śayu** as a protégé of the Aśvins in another hymn of the Rigveda,[4] but here the word may merely denote the 'feeble man.'[5]

[1] viii. 54, 2.
[2] viii. 59, 3.
[3] *Indische Studien*, 1, 293, n.
[4] x. 40, 8.
[5] Roth, St. Petersburg Dictionary, *s.v.*

Cf. Ludwig, Translation of the Rigveda, 3, 132, 164.

Kṛśana, 'pearl.' In the Rigveda pearls are mentioned as adorning the car of Savitṛ[1] as well as being used for the adornment of a horse.[2] Hence the horse is spoken of as the 'pearled one' (*kṛśanāvant*).[3] The Atharvaveda[4] also refers to pearls, and mentions that 'pearl shell' (*śaṅkhaḥ kṛśanaḥ*) won from the sea was used as an amulet.[5] The Nighaṇṭu[6] renders the word as 'gold.'

[1] i. 35, 4.
[2] x. 68, 1.
[3] i. 126, 4. *Cf. kṛśanin*, vii. 18, 23.
[4] x. 1, 7.
[5] iv. 10, 1. 3.
[6] i. 2. *Cf.* Sāma Mantra Brāhmaṇa, 1, 6, 22.

Cf. Zimmer, *Altindisches Leben*, 53, 54; Lanman in Whitney, Translation of the Atharvaveda, 161.

Kṛśānu appears in the Rigveda as a mythological personage.[1] In one verse,[2] however, Roth[3] sees in this word the name of a bowman, but there seems no reason to dissociate this passage from the rest.

[1] Macdonell, *Vedic Mythology*, pp. 74, 112, 137; Hillebrandt, *Vedische Mythologie*, 1, 448.
[2] i. 112, 21.
[3] St. Petersburg Dictionary, *s.v.*, 4.

Kṛṣi, 'ploughing.' The cultivation of the soil was no doubt known to the Indians before they separated from the Iranians, as is indicated by the identity of the expressions *yavaṃ kṛṣ* and *sasya* in the Rigveda with *yao karesh* and *hahya* in the Avesta, referring to the ploughing in of the seed and to the grain which resulted.[1] But it is not without significance that the expressions for ploughing occur mainly in the first[2] and tenth[3] books of the Rigveda, and only rarely in the so-called 'family' books (ii.-vii.).[4] In the Atharvaveda **Pṛthī Vainya** is credited with the origination of ploughing,[5] and even in the Rigveda the Aśvins are spoken of as concerned with the sowing of grain by means of the plough.[6] In the later Saṃhitās and the Brāhmaṇas ploughing is repeatedly referred to.[7]

[1] Zimmer, *Altindisches Leben*, 235; Hopkins, *Journal of the American Oriental Society*, 17, 85.
[2] Forms of the root *kṛṣ*, 'to plough,' occur in Rv. i. 23, 15; 176, 2.
[3] Rv. x. 34, 13; 117, 7. In x. 146, 6, *akṛṣīvala*, 'not agricultural,' occurs. *Cf.* x. 101, 4.
[4] *Kṛṣ* is also found in viii. 20, 19; 22, 6; in the family books only in iv. 57, 4, and as *vi-kṛṣ* in iv. 57, 8.
[5] viii. 10, 24.
[6] i. 117, 21.
[7] *Kṛṣi* is found, *e.g.*, in Av. ii. 4, 5; viii. 2, 19; 10, 24; x. 6, 12; xii. 2, 27, etc.; Taittirīya Saṃhitā, vii. 1, 11, 1, etc.; Maitrāyaṇī Saṃhitā, i. 2, 2; iii. 6, 8; Vājasaneyi Saṃhitā, iv. 10; ix. 22; xiv. 19. 21, etc.; Śatapatha Brāhmaṇa, vii. 2, 2, 7; viii. 6, 2, 2; Taittirīya Brāhmaṇa, iii. 1, 2, 5, etc. In Av. vi. 116, 1, *kārṣīvaṇa* denotes a 'plougher.' See also **Kārṣman**.

Even in the Rigveda[8] there is clear proof of the importance attached to agriculture. In the Pañcaviṃśa Brāhmaṇa[9] the **Vrātyas**, Hindus without the pale of Brahminism, are described as not cultivating the soil.

The plough land was called **Urvarā** or **Kṣetra**; manure (**Śakan, Karīṣa**) was used, and irrigation was practised (**Khanitra**). The plough (**Lāṅgala, Sīra**) was drawn by oxen, teams of six, eight, or even twelve being employed.[10] The operations of agriculture are neatly summed up in the Śatapatha Brāhmaṇa[11] as 'ploughing, sowing, reaping, and threshing' (*kṛṣantaḥ, vapantaḥ, lunantaḥ, mṛṇantaḥ*). The ripe grain was cut with a sickle (**Dātra, Sṛṇi**), bound into bundles[12] (**Parṣa**), and beaten out on the floor of the granary (**Khala**).[13] The grain was then separated from the straw and refuse either by a sieve (**Titau**) or a winnowing fan (**Śūrpa**).[14] The winnower was called **Dhānyākṛt,**[15] and the grain was measured in a vessel called **Ūrdara.**[16]

The Rigveda leaves us in doubt as to the kind of grain grown, for **Yava** is a word of doubtful signification, and **Dhānā** is also vague. In the later Saṃhitās[17] things are different. Rice (**Vrīhi**) appears, Yava means barley, with a species styled **Upavāka.** Beans (**Mudga, Māṣa**), sesamum (**Tila**), and other grains (**Aṇu, Khalva, Godhūma, Nīvāra, Priyaṅgu, Masūra, Śyāmāka**) are mentioned, while cucumbers (**Urvārū, Urvārūka**) were known. It is uncertain whether fruit trees (**Vṛkṣa**) were cultivated, or merely grew wild;[18] but frequent mention is made of the jujube (**Karkandhu, Kuvala, Badara**).

The seasons for agriculture are briefly summed up in a passage of the Taittirīya Saṃhitā:[19] barley ripened in summer, being no doubt sown, as in modern India, in winter; rice

[8] x. 34, 13; 117, 7. *Cf.* Hopkins, *India, Old and New*, 208.

[9] xvii. 1.

[10] Av. vi. 91, 1; Kāṭhaka Saṃhitā, xv. 2. *Cf.* Rv. viii. 6, 48; x. 101, 4.

[11] i. 6, 1, 3.

[12] viii. 78, 10; x. 101, 3; 131, 2.

[13] Rv. x. 48, 7.

[14] Rv. x. 71, 2; Av. xii. 3, 19. The technical terms are *tuṣair vi-vic*, Av. xi. 1, 12; *palāvān apa-vic*, xii. 3, 19.

[15] Rv. x. 94, 13.

[16] Rv. ii. 14, 11. See also **Sthivi.**

[17] See Vājasaneyi Saṃhitā, xviii. 12, for a list.

[18] The pulling of ripe fruit is referred to in Rv. iii. 45, 4. *Cf. pakvā śākhā*, Rv. i. 8, 8; *vṛkṣa pakva*, Rv. iv. 20, 5; Av. xx. 127, 4. But that does not prove arboriculture.

[19] vii. 2, 10, 2.

ripened in autumn, being sown in the beginning of the rains; beans and sesamum, planted at the time of the summer rains, ripened in the winter and the cool season. There were two harvests (**Sasya**) a year according to the Taittirīya Saṃhitā;[20] the winter crop was ripe by the month of Caitra (March-April) according to the Kauṣītaki Brāhmaṇa.[21]

The farmer had plenty of trouble of his own: moles destroyed the seed, birds and various kinds of reptiles (**Upakvasa, Jabhya, Tarda, Pataṅga**) injured the young shoots, excessive rain or drought might damage the crops. The Atharvaveda contains spells to prevent these evils.[22]

[20] v. 1, 7, 3.

[21] xix. 3. *Cf.* Keith, *Śāṅkhāyana Āraṇyaka*, 81, n. 1.

[22] See Av. vi. 50. 142; vii. 11. *Cf.* Zimmer, *Altindisches Leben*, 235-243.

Kṛṣṭi denotes 'people' in general from the Rigveda[1] onwards. Its common and regular use in this sense appears to show that the Āryans, when they invaded India, were already agriculturists, though the employment of the words referring to ploughing mentioned under **Kṛṣi** indicates that not all of the people devoted themselves equally to that occupation. Indra and Agni are *par excellence* the lords of men (Kṛṣṭi).[2] Sometimes the word is further defined by the addition of an adjective meaning 'belonging to mankind,' 'of men' (*mānuṣīḥ*,[3] *mānavīḥ*).[4]

Special mention is frequently[5] made of the 'five peoples' (*pañca kṛṣṭayaḥ*). The exact sense of this expression is doubtful. See **Panca Janāsaḥ**.

[1] i. 52, 11; 100, 10; 160, 5; 189, 3; iii. 49, 1; iv. 21, 2, etc.; Av. xii. 1, 3. 4.

[2] i. 177, 1; iv. 17, 5; vii. 26, 5; viii. 13, 9 (Indra); i. 59, 5; vi. 18, 2; vii. 5, 5 (Agni).

[3] Rv. i. 59, 5; vi. 18, 2.

[4] Av. iii. 24, 3.

[5] Rv. ii. 2, 10; iii. 53, 16; iv. 38, 10; x. 60, 4; 119, 6; 178, 3; Av. iii. 24, 2; xii. 1, 42.

Cf. Zimmer, *Altindisches Leben*, 141.

1. **Kṛṣṇa** ('black') denotes a dark-coloured animal or bird. In some passages,[1] as the context shows, an antelope is certainly

[1] Taittirīya Saṃhitā, v. 2, 6, 5; vi. 1, 3, 1; Śatapatha Brāhmaṇa, i. 1, 4, 1; iii. 2, 1, 28. So *kṛṣṇa-viṣāṇā*, 'horn of the black antelope,' *ibid.*, iii. 2, 1, 18. 28; 2, 20; iv. 4, 5, 2; v. 4, 2, 5; Taittirīya Saṃhitā, vi. 1, 3, 7. See also the Aśvamedha passages, Maitrāyaṇī Saṃhitā, iii. 14, 17; Vājasaneyi Saṃhitā, xxiv. 36 (*cf.* ii. 1).

meant. In a few others[2] a bird of prey seems indicated. See also **Kṛṣṇājina.**

[2] Rv. x. 94, 5; Av. xi. 2, 2; Śāṅkhāyana Āraṇyaka, xii. 27.

2. **Kṛṣṇa** appears as the name of a seer in one hymn of the Rigveda.[1] Tradition assigns to him or to Viśvaka, son of Kṛṣṇa (*Kārṣṇi*), the authorship of the following hymn.[2] The word Kṛṣṇiya may be a patronymic[3] formed from the same name in two other hymns of the Rigveda,[4] where the Aśvins are said to have restored **Viṣṇāpū** to Viśvaka Kṛṣṇiya. In that case Kṛṣṇa would seem to be the grandfather of Viṣṇāpū. This Kṛṣṇa may be identical with Kṛṣṇa Āṅgirasa mentioned in the Kausītaki Brāhmaṇa.[5]

[1] viii. 85, 3. 4.
[2] viii. 86.
[3] i. 116, 23; 117, 7.
[4] As a patronymic, it would be an isolated formation (*cf.* however *Pajriya*), instead of *Kārṣṇya*. *Cf.* Macdonell, *Vedic Grammar*, 228*a* and 200.
[5] xxx. 9.

Cf. Ludwig, Translation of the Rigveda, 3, 108; Macdonell, *Vedic Mythology*, p. 52.

3. **Kṛṣṇa Devakī-putra** is mentioned in the Chāndogya Upaniṣad[1] as a pupil of the mythical **Ghora Āṅgirasa.** Tradition,[2] and several modern writers like Grierson, Garbe, and von Schroeder, recognize in him the hero Kṛṣṇa, who later is deified. In their view he is a Kṣatriya teacher of morals, as opposed to Brahminism.[3] This is extremely doubtful. It appears better either to regard the coincidence of name as accidental, or to suppose that the reference is a piece of Euhemerism. To identify this Kṛṣṇa with the preceding, as does the St. Petersburg Dictionary, seems to be quite groundless.

[1] iii. 17, 6.
[2] *Cf.* Weber, *Indian Literature*, 169.
[3] Von Schroeder, *Vienna Oriental Journal*, 19, 414, 415; Grierson, *Encyclopædia of Religions*, article 'Bhakti'; Garbe, *Bhagavadgītā*.

Cf. Weber, *op. cit.*, 71; 148; Hopkins, *Journal of the Royal Asiatic Society*, 1905, 386.

4. **Kṛṣṇa Hārīta** is mentioned as a teacher in the Aitareya Āraṇyaka.[1] The Śāṅkhāyana Āraṇyaka[2] has Kṛtsna in the parallel passage.

[1] iii. 2, 6.
[2] viii. 10.

Cf. Weber, *Indische Studien*, 1, 391, n.; *Indian Literature*, 50.

Kṛṣṇa-datta Lauhitya ('descendant of Lohita') is mentioned in a Vaṃśa (list of teachers) of the Jaiminīya Upaniṣad Brāhmaṇa (iii. 42, 1) as a pupil of **Śyāmasujayanta Lauhitya.**

Kṛṣṇa-dhṛti Sātyaki ('descendant of Satyaka') is mentioned in a Vaṃśa (list of teachers) of the Jaiminīya Upaniṣad Brāhmaṇa (iii. 42, 1) as a pupil of **Satyaśravas.**

Kṛṣṇa-rāta Lauhitya ('descendant of Lohita') is mentioned in a Vaṃśa (list of teachers) of the Jaiminīya Upaniṣad Brāhmaṇa (iii. 42, 1) as a pupil of **Śyāmaiajayanta Lauhitya.**

Kṛṣṇala denotes the berry of the *Abrus precatorius*, used as a weight according to the later authorities, one Māṣa ('bean') being equated to four Kṛṣṇalas.[1] In the sense of a weight it occurs in the Taittirīya[2] and other Saṃhitās,[3] and later.[4]

1 Manu, viii. 134.
2 ii. 3, 2, 1 *et seq.*
3 Maitrāyaṇī Saṃhitā, ii. 2, 2; Kāṭhaka Saṃhitā, xi. 4 (*hiraṇya kṛṣṇala*).
4 Taittirīya Brāhmaṇa, i. 3, 6, 7; Anupada Sūtra, ix. 6. In the later language it is also called *raktikā* or *guñjā* (being a smooth red berry with a black spot at one end).

Cf. Weber's edition of the Jyotiṣa, 82 *et seq.*; *Indische Streifen*, 1, 102, 103.

Kṛṣṇājina is the skin (*ajina*) of the black antelope (**Kṛṣṇa.**) It is repeatedly referred to in the later Saṃhitās and Brāhmaṇas[1] with regard to its ritual use.

1 Av. ix. 6, 17; Taittirīya Saṃhitā, ii. 4, 9, 2; v. 4, 4, 4; Śatapatha Brāhmaṇa, i. 1, 1, 22; 4, 1; 9, 2, 35, etc.

Kṛṣṇāyasa ('black metal'), 'iron,' is referred to in the Chāndogya Upaniṣad (vi. 1, 6). See also **Ayas** and **Kārṣṇāyasa.**

Kṛsara, a term denoting a mess of rice and sesamum, often mentioned in the Sūtras, occurs in the Ṣaḍviṃśa Brāḥmaṇa.[1]

1 v. 2. *Cf.* Weber, *Omina und Portenta*, 315 *et seq.*

Kekaya is the name of a tribe which in later days, and probably also in Vedic times, was settled in the north-west, between the **Sindhu** (Indus) and **Vitastā.**[1] In the Vedic texts the Kekayas are mentioned indirectly only in the name of their prince **Aśvapati Kaikeya.**[2]

[1] Pargiter, *Journal of the Royal Asiatic Society*, 1908, 317, 332.

[2] Śatapatha Brāhmaṇa, x. 6, 1, 2 *et seq.*; Chāndogya Upaniṣad, v. 11, 4.

Cf. Weber, *Indian Literature*, 120; *Indische Studien*, 1, 126.

1. **Ketu** is a term which Weber[1] understands in the sense of 'meteor' or 'comet' in the late Adbhuta Brāhmaṇa.

[1] *Indische Studien*, 1, 41. The *aruṇāḥ ketavaḥ* (Av. xi. 10, 1. 2. 7), referred to in this sense in the St. Petersburg Dictionary, are not so treated by Böhtlingk in his Dictionary.

2. **Ketu Vājya** ('descendant of Vāja') is mentioned as a teacher in the Vaṃśa Brāhmaṇa.[1]

[1] *Indische Studien*, 4, 372.

Kevarta, Kaivarta are two variant forms denoting 'fisherman' in the Vājasaneyi Saṃhitā[1] and Taittirīya Brāhmaṇa[2] lists of victims at the Puruṣamedha, or human sacrifice.

[1] xxx. 16, with Mahīdhara's note.

[2] iii. 4, 12, 1, with Sāyaṇa's note.

Keśa, 'hair of the head,' is repeatedly mentioned in the later Saṃhitās and Brāhmaṇas.[1] The hair was a matter of great care to the Vedic Indian, and several hymns of the Atharvaveda[2] are directed to securing its plentiful growth. Cutting or shaving (*vap*) the hair is often referred to.[3] For a man to wear long hair was considered effeminate.[4] As to modes of dressing the hair see **Opaśa** and **Kaparda**; as to the beard see **Śmaśru.**

[1] Av. v. 19, 3; vi. 136, 3, etc.; Vājasaneyi Saṃhitā, xix. 22; xx. 5; xxv. 3; Śatapatha Brāhmaṇa, ii. 5, 2, 48, etc.

[2] vi. 136. 137. *Cf.* Zimmer, *Altindisches Leben*, 68; Bloomfield, *Hymns of the Atharvaveda*, 536, 537.

[3] Av. viii. 2, 17; Satapatha Brāhmaṇa, v. 5, 3, 1, etc. *Cf.* Oldenberg, *Religion des Veda*, 425 *et seq.*

[4] Śatapatha Brāhmaṇa, v. 1, 2, 14. But *cf.* Vincent Smith, *Indian Antiquary*, 34, 203.

1. **Keśin** is the name of a people occurring in the Śatapatha Brāhmaṇa,[1] where their king is mentioned as learning from **Khaṇḍika** the atonement for a bad omen at the sacrifice.

[1] xi. 8, 4, 6. *Cf.* Pāṇini, vi. 4, 165; Eggeling, *Sacred Books of the East*, 44, 131, 134.

2. **Keśin Dārbhya**[1] or **Dālbhya**[2] ('descendant of Darbha') is a somewhat enigmatic figure. According to the Śatapatha Brāhmaṇa[3] and the Jaiminīya Upaniṣad Brāhmaṇa[4] he was a king, sister's son of **Uccaiḥśravas**, according to the latter authority. His people were the **Pañcālas**, of whom the Keśins must therefore have been a branch, and who are said to have been threefold (*tryanīka*).[5] A story is told of his having a ritual dispute with **Ṣaṇḍika** in the Maitrāyaṇī Saṃhitā[6]; this appears in another form in the Śatapatha Brāhmaṇa.[3] He was a contemporary of a fellow sage, **Keśin Sātyakāmi**, according to the Maitrāyaṇī[7] and Taittirīya[8] Saṃhitās. The Pañçaviṃśa Brāhmaṇa[9] attributes to him a Sāman or chant, and the Kauṣītaki Brāhmaṇa[10] tells how he was taught by a golden bird.

In view of the fact that the early literature always refers to Dārbhya as a sage, it seems doubtful whether the commentator is right in thinking that the Śatapatha refers to a king and a people, when a sage alone may well be meant, while the Jaiminīya Upaniṣad Brāhmaṇa is of no great authority. The latter work may have assumed that the reference in the Kāṭhaka Saṃhitā[11] to the Keśin people signifies kingship, but this is hardly necessary.

1 This is the form of the name in the Jaiminīya Upaniṣad Brāhmaṇa, the Maitrāyaṇī Saṃhitā, the Taittirīya Saṃhitā, and the Kauṣītaki Brāhmaṇa; also later in the Bṛhaddevatā.

2 This is the form in the Kāṭhaka Saṃhitā and the Pañcaviṃśa Brāhmaṇa. It also appears later in the Rigveda Anukramaṇī.

3 xi. 8, 4, 1 *et seq.*, as explained by Sāyaṇa.

4 iii. 29, 1 *et seq.*

5 Kāṭhaka Saṃhitā, xxx. 2 (Weber, *Indische Studien*, 3, 471); Jaiminīya Upaniṣad Brāhmaṇa, *loc. cit.*; Baudhāyana Śrauta Sūtra, xx. 25.

6 i. 4, 12 (von Schroeder gives no variant reading; but *ṣ* and *kh* are constantly confused in manuscripts).

7 i. 6, 5.

8 ii. 6, 2, 3.

9 xiii. 10, 8.

10 vii. 4.

11 xxx. 2.

Cf. Weber, *Indische Studien*, 1, 193, 209; 2, 308; Hopkins, *Transactions of the Connecticut Academy of Arts and Sciences*, 15, 58, 59; Sieg, *Die Sagenstoffe des Ṛgveda*, 62, n. 2.

3. **Keśin Sātya-kāmi** ('descendant of Satyakāma') is mentioned as a teacher and contemporary of **Keśin Dārbhya** in the Taittirīya (ii. 6, 2, 3) and Maitrāyaṇī (i. 6, 5) Saṃhitās.

Kesara-prābandhā.—In the list of the crimes of the **Vaitahavyas** narrated in the Atharvaveda[1] is the cooking of the last she-goat (*caramājām*) of Kesaraprābandhā, who may presumably be deemed to have been a woman, 'having braided hair.'[2] Ludwig,[3] followed by Whitney,[4] appears to amend the passage (*carama-jām*) as meaning 'the last-born calf' of Kesaraprābandhā, a cow. But this interpretation does not suit the name so well.

[1] v. 18, 11.
[2] Bloomfield, *Hymns of the Atharvaveda*, 432, 433.
[3] Translation of the Rigveda, 2, 447.
[4] Translation of the Atharvaveda, 252.

Kaikeya, 'king of the Kekayas,' is an epithet of **Aśvapati.**[1]

[1] Śatapatha Brāhmaṇa, x. 6, 1, 2; Chāndogya Upaniṣad, v. 11, 4.

Kairāta is the name of a snake in the Atharvaveda[1]—possibly, but not probably, the modern Karait.

[1] v. 13, 5. *Cf.* Whitney, Translation of the Atharvaveda, 243.

Kairātikā, a 'maiden of the **Kirāta** people,' is mentioned in the Atharvaveda (x. 4, 14) as digging up roots for medicinal use.

Kairiśi, 'descendant of Kiriśa,' is the patronymic of **Sutvan** in the Aitareya Brāhmaṇa (viii. 28).

Kaivarta. See **Kevarta.**

Kaiśinī.—The *Kaiśinyaḥ prajāḥ*, 'offspring or people[1] of Keśin,' are mentioned in an obscure passage of the Śatapatha Brāhmaṇa[2] either as still existing at the date of the Brāhmaṇa[3] or as extinct.

[1] So Sāyaṇa.
[2] xi. 8, 4, 6.
[3] *Cf.* Eggeling, *Sacred Books of the East*, 44, 134.

Cf. Weber, *Indische Studien*, 1, 208.

Kaiśorya, 'descendant of Kaiśori,' is the patronymic of **Kāpya** in the first two Vaṃśas (lists of teachers) in the Bṛhadāraṇyaka Upaniṣad.[1]

[1] ii. 5, 22; iv. 5, 28 (Mādhyaṃdina = ii. 6, 3; iv. 6, 3 Kāṇva).

1. **Koka**, a word occurring in the Rigveda[1] and the Atharvaveda,[2] seems to denote the 'cuckoo.' In all the three passages in which it is found, Sāyaṇa explains it as the **Cakravāka**. Roth[3] renders it in the Atharvaveda passages as a certain destructive parasitic animal. *Cf.* **Anyavāpa**.

[1] vii. 104, 22 (*koka-yātu*, a ghost in the shape of a cuckoo).

[2] v. 23, 4; viii. 6, 2.

[3] St. Petersburg Dictionary, *s.v.*, 6. *Cf.* Bloomfield, *Hymns of the Atharvaveda*, 454; Whitney, Translation of the Atharvaveda, 262; Geldner, *Rigveda, Glossar*, 49; Zimmer, *Altindisches Leben*, 92.

2. **Koka** is mentioned in the Śatapatha Brāhmaṇa (xiii. 5, 4, 17) as a son of the Pañcāla king, **Sātrāsāha**.

Kokila, a very frequent word in the Epic and later, denoting the cuckoo, is only inferred for the Vedic period from its being the name of a Rājaputra in the Kāṭhaka Anukramaṇī.[1]

[1] Weber, *Indische Studien*, 3, 460.

Koṇeya, Kauṇeya. See **Rajana**.

Kola, another form of **Kuvala**, the *Zizyphus jujuba*, is mentioned in the Chāndogya Upaniṣad (vii. 3, 1).

1. **Kośa** is the name in the Rigveda[1] for the 'bucket' used in drawing water by means of a rope from a well (**Avata**). In the ritual[2] it denotes a large vessel to hold Soma, as opposed to **Kalaśa**.

[1] i. 130, 2; iii. 32, 15; iv. 17, 6. *Cf.* Zimmer, *Altindisches Leben*, 156.

[2] Rv. ix. 75, 3; Av. xviii. 4, 30, etc. *Cf.* Hillebrandt, *Vedische Mythologie*, 1, 183 *et seq.*

2. **Kośa** denotes the body of a chariot.[1] Presumably it was fastened to the axles, but it was probably not very secure, as the body of Pūṣan's chariot is said not to fall.[2] The ropes[3] used to fasten the Kośa are perhaps referred to in the word *akṣā-nah*.[4] By synecdoche this word also denotes the whole chariot.[5] See also **Vandhura, Ratha.**

[1] Rv. i. 87, 2; x. 85, 7, etc.

[2] Rv. vi. 54, 3.

[3] *Gāvaḥ*, Rv. viii. 48, 5.

[4] See under 1. **Akṣa**.

[5] Rv. viii. 20, 8; 22, 9. *Cf.* Zimmer, *op. cit.*, 246.

3. **Kośa.**—The exact sense of this word in **Kośa-kārī**, the designation of a female victim at the Puruṣamedha, or human sacrifice,[1] is uncertain. It may be 'sheath.'

[1] Vājasaneyi Saṃhitā, xxx. 14; Taittirīya Brāhmaṇa, iii. 4, 10, 1.

Koṣa.—The Koṣas appear as a priestly family in the Śatapatha Brāhmaṇa, where one of them, **Suśravas**, is mentioned by name.[2]

[1] x. 5, 5, 8.

[2] x. 5, 5, 1.

Kosala is the name of a people not occurring in the earliest Vedic literature. In the story of the spread of Āryan culture told in the Śatapatha Brāhmaṇa,[1] the Kosala-Videhas, as the offspring of **Videgha Māthava**, appear as falling later than the Kuru-Pañcālas under the influence of Brahminism. The same passage gives the **Sadānīrā** as the boundary of the two peoples —Kosala and Videha. Elsewhere[2] the Kausalya, or Kosala king, **Para Āṭṇāra Hairaṇyanābha**, is described as having performed the great Aśvamedha, or horse sacrifice. Connexion with **Kāśi** and **Videha** appears also from a passage of the Śāṅkhāyana Śrauta Sūtra.[3] Weber[4] points out that Āśvalāyana, who was very probably a descendant of **Aśvala**, the Hotṛ priest of Videha, is called a Kosala in the Praśna Upaniṣad.[5] The later distinction of North and South Kosala is unknown to both Vedic and Buddhist literature.[6]

Kosala lay to the north-east of the Ganges, and corresponded roughly to the modern Oudh.

[1] i. 4, 1, 1 *et seq.*

[2] Śatapatha Brāhmaṇa, xiii. 5, 4, 4. *Cf.* Hiraṇya-nābha, a Rājaputra, in Praśna Upaniṣad, iii. 2, and Śāṅkhāyana Śrauta Sūtra, xvi. 9, 13, as a Kausalya, while *ibid.*, 11, Para is styled Vaideha.

[3] xvi. 29, 5.

[4] *Indische Studien*, 1, 182, 441.

[5] vi. 1.

[6] Oldenberg, *Buddha*, 393, n.

Cf. von Schroeder, *Indiens Literatur und Cultur*, 167; Eggeling, *Sacred Books of the East*, 12, xlii; Weber, *Indian Literature*, 39, 132 *et seq.*; Macdonell, *Sanskrit Literature*, 213-215; Rhys Davids, *Buddhist India*, 25.

Kaukūsta is mentioned in the Śatapatha Brāhmaṇa[1] as a giver of a Dakṣiṇā, or gift to the priests officiating at a sacrifice. The Kāṇva recension reads the name **Kaükthasta.**[2]

[1] iv. 6, 1, 13.

[2] Eggeling, *Sacred Books of the East*, 26, 426, n. 1. *Cf.* Weber, *Indian Literature*, 134.

Kauṇeya. See **Rajana.**

Kauṇṭha-ravya is mentioned as a teacher in the Aitareya[1] and Śāṅkhāyana Āraṇyakas.[2]

[1] iii. 2, 2.

[2] vii. 14; viii. 2.
Cf. Keith, *Aitareya Āraṇyaka*, 249.

Kauṇḍinī. See **Pārāśarīkauṇḍinīputra.**

Kauṇḍinya is mentioned as a pupil of **Śāṇḍilya** in the first two Vaṃśas (lists of teachers) in the Bṛhadāraṇyaka Upaniṣad.[1] See also **Vidarbhīkauṇḍinya,** and the following.

[1] ii. 5, 20; iv. 5, 26 (Mādhyaṃdina=ii. 6, 1; iv. 6, 1, Kāṇva).

Kauṇḍinyāyana is mentioned in the first Vaṃśa (list of teachers) of the Mādhyaṃdina recension of the Bṛhadāraṇyaka Upaniṣad[1] as a pupil of Kauṇḍinya, pupil of Kauṇḍinya and Āgniveśya; in the second[2] as a pupil of the two Kauṇḍinyas, pupils of Aurṇavābha, pupil of Kauṇḍinya, pupil of Kauṇḍinya, pupil of Kauṇḍinya and Āgniveśya. Neither Vaṃśa is of much value.[3]

[1] ii. 5, 20.
[2] iv. 5, 26.

[3] Eggeling, *Sacred Books of the East*, 12, xxxiv.

Kautasta, a word occurring once in the dual, is apparently a patronymic of **Arimejaya** and **Janamejaya,** two Adhvaryu priests at the snake sacrifice described in the Pañcaviṃśa Brāhmaṇa.[1]

[1] xxv. 15, 3. *Cf.* Weber, *Indische Studien*, 1, 35.

Kautsa ('descendant of Kutsa') is mentioned in the Śatapatha Brāhmaṇa[1] as a pupil of **Māhitthi.** A Kautsa is also attacked in the Nirukta[2] as denying the value of the Vedas, and there is a strong ritual tradition of hostility to the Kautsas.[3]

[1] x. 6, 5, 9; Bṛhadāraṇyaka Upaniṣad, vi. 5, 4 (Kāṇva recension only).
[2] i. 15.
[3] *E.g.*, Āpastamba Śrauta Sūtra, x. 20, 12; Hillebrandt, *Vedische Mythologie*, 3, 285. *Cf.* Weber, *Indian Literature*, 77, 140.

Kautsī-putra ('son of a female descendant of **Kutsa**') is mentioned as a pupil of **Baudhīputra** in the last Vaṃśa (list of teachers) of the Bṛhadāraṇyaka Upaniṣad in the Mādhyaṃdina recension (vi. 4, 31).

Kaupayeya is the patronymic of **Uccaiḥśravas.**

Kaumbhya ('descendant of Kumbhya') is the patronymic of **Babhru.**

Kaurama. See **Kaurava.**

Kaurayāṇa is apparently a patronymic of **Pākasthāman** in the Rigveda.[1] Hopkins[2] suggests that Kaurāyaṇa may be meant.

[1] viii. 3, 21. *Cf.* Nirukta, v. 25.
[2] *Journal of the American Oriental Society*, 17, 90, n. 2.

Kaurava is the reading of the text of the Khilas[1] and of some manuscripts of the Śāṅkhāyana Śrauta Sūtra[2] for the Kaurama of the Atharvaveda,[3] who appears in a Dānastuti ('Praise of Gifts') as a generous donor among the **Ruśamas.**

[1] v. 8, 1 (Scheftelowitz, *Die Apokryphen des Ṛgveda*, 155).
[2] xii. 14, 1.
[3] xx. 127, 1.
Cf. Bloomfield, *Hymns of the Atharvaveda*, 689.

Kauravya ('belonging to the **Kurus**'). A man of the Kuru people, is described in the Atharvaveda as enjoying prosperity with his wife under the rule of King **Parikṣit.**[1] Mention is also made of the Kauravya king **Balhika Prātipīya** in the Śatapatha Brāhmaṇa,[2] and in the later legend **Ārṣṭiṣeṇa** and **Devāpi** are alleged to have been Kauravyas.[3]

[1] xx. 127, 8; Khila, v. 10, 2; Śāṅkhāyana Śrauta Sūtra, xii. 17, 2. *Cf.* a Mantra in the Vaitāna Sūtra, xxxiv. 9.
[2] xii. 9, 3, 3.
[3] Nirukta, ii. 10.

Kauravyāyaṇī-putra ('son of a female descendant of **Kuru**') is mentioned as a teacher in the Bṛhadāraṇyaka Upaniṣad (v. 1, 1).

Kauru-pañcāla, 'belonging to the Kuru-Pañcālas,' is an epithet of **Āruṇi** in the Śatapatha Brāhmana (xi. 4, 1, 2), and a practice of those tribes is designated by this word in the same work (i. 7, 2, 8).

Kaulakāvatī are two persons mentioned in the Maitrāyanī Saṃhitā (ii. 1, 3) as having given advice, in the capacity of priests, to **Rathaprota Dārbhya.**

Kaulāla is a word denoting a hereditary potter ('son of a *kulāla* or potter') according to the commentator Mahīdhara on the Vājasaneyi Saṃhitā.[1] The other Saṃhitās[2] have **Kulāla.**

[1] xxx. 7.

[2] Maitrāyaṇī Saṃhitā, ii. 9, 5; Kāṭhaka Saṃhitā, xvii. 13, and *cf.* Vājasaneyi Saṃhitā, xvi. 27.

Kaulitara is mentioned in the Rigveda[1] as a **Dāsa.** Apparently the name is an epithet of **Śambara,** meaning 'son of Kulitara': this points to Śambara having been a terrestrial foe, and not a mere demon.[2]

[1] iv. 30, 14.

[2] *Cf.* Hillebrandt, *Vedische Mythologie,* 3, 273; Macdonell, *Vedic Mythology,* pp. 64, 161.

Kaulīka, like **Kulīkā,** is the name of some sort of bird in the list of victims at the Aśvamedha, or horse sacrifice, in the Yajurveda.[1]

[1] Vājasaneyi Saṃhitā, xxiv. 24; Maitrāyaṇī Saṃhitā, iii. 14, 5.

Kauśāmbeya is the patronymic ('descendant of Kuśāmba') of a teacher **Proti** in the Śatapatha Brāhmaṇa[1] according to the St. Petersburg Dictionary: a view supported by the fact that **Kūśāmba** actually occurs as the name of a man in the Pañcaviṃśa Brāhmaṇa.[2] It is, however, possible that the word means a 'native of the town Kauśāmbī' as understood by Harisvāmin in his commentary on the Śatapatha Brāhmana.[3]

[1] xii. 2, 2, 13; Gopatha Brāhmaṇa, i. 2, 24.

[2] viii. 6, 8. The name is also found later (in the Epic) in the form of Kuśāmba.

[3] Eggeling, *Sacred Books of the East,* 44, 153, n. 5. *Cf.* Weber, *Indische Studien,* 1, 193; Rhys Davids, *Buddhist India,* 3, 36; Oldenberg, *Buddha,* 397.

Kauśika is an epithet of Indra as 'connected with the Kuśikas,' and also of **Viśvāmitra** as 'son of Kuśika.'[1] A teacher named Kauśika is mentioned as a pupil of **Kauṇḍinya** in the first two Vaṃśas (lists of teachers) of the Bṛhadāraṇyaka Upaniṣad.[2]

[1] In a late Khila, Scheftelowitz, *Die Apokryphen des Ṛgveda*, 104.

[2] ii. 6, 1 ; iv. 6, 1 (Kāṇva recension).

Kauśikāyani ('descendant of Kauśika') is mentioned as a teacher and a pupil of **Ghṛtakauśika** in the first two Vaṃśas (lists of teachers) of the Bṛhadāraṇyaka Upaniṣad.[1]

[1] ii. 5, 21 ; iv. 5, 27 (Mādhyaṃdina = ii. 6, 3 ; iv. 6, 3, Kāṇva).

Kauśikī-putra ('son of a female descendant of Kuśika') is mentioned in a Vaṃśa (list of teachers) in the Kāṇva recension of the Bṛhadāraṇyaka Upaniṣad (vi. 5, 1) as a pupil of **Ālambīputra** and **Vaiyāghrapadīputra.**

Kauśreya ('descendant of Kuśri') is the patronymic of **Somadakṣa** in the Kāṭhaka Saṃhitā (xx. 8 ; xxi. 9).

Kauṣārava ('descendant of Kuṣāru') is the patronymic of **Maitreya** in the Aitareya Brāhmaṇa (viii. 28).

Kauṣītaki ('descendant of Kuṣītaka') is the patronymic of a teacher, or series of teachers, to whom the doctrines set forth in the Kauṣītaki Brāhmaṇa[1] and in the Śāṅkhāyana Āraṇyaka,[2] and the Śrauta and Gṛhya Sūtras,[3] are referred. He is rarely mentioned elsewhere.[4] The doctrine of Kauṣītaki is called the Kauṣītaka.[5] The pupils of Kauṣītaki are known as the Kauṣītakis in the Nidāna Sūtra,[6] and in the Pañcaviṃśa Brāhmaṇa[7]

[1] ii. 9 ; vii. 4. 10 ; viii. 8 ; xi. 5. 7 ; xiv. 3. 4 ; xv. 2 ; xvi. 9 ; xviii. 5 ; xxii. 1. 2 ; xxiii. 1. 4 ; xxiv. 8. 9 ; xxv. 8. 10. 14. 15, etc.

[2] ii. 17 ; xv. 1 ; Kauṣītaki Upaniṣad, ii. 1. 7.

[3] Śāṅkhāyana Śrauta Sūtra, iv. 15, 11 ; vii. 21, 6 ; ix. 20, 33 ; xi. 11, 3. 6, etc.

[4] Śatapatha Brāhmaṇa, ii. 4, 3, 1 ; Chāndogya Upaniṣad, i. 5, 2.

[5] Kauṣītaki Brāhmaṇa, iii. 1 ; xix. 3 ; Sāṅkhāyana Śrauta Sūtra, iv. 2, 13 ; xi. 14, 26 ; Anupada Sūtra, ii. 7 ; vii. 11 ; viii. 5, etc.

[6] vi. 12.

[7] xvii. 4, 3.

they with Kuṣītaka are stated to have been cursed by **Luśākapi.** Elsewhere[8] they are called Kauṣītakins. If the Śāṅkhāyana Āraṇyaka[9] can be trusted, there were among them at least two leading teachers, **Kahoḍa** and **Sarvajit,** the former of whom is mentioned elsewhere.[10]

[8] Āpastamba Śrauta Sūtra, x. 1, 10; Āśvalāyana Gṛhya Sūtra, i. 23.

[9] *Cf.* Keith, *Śāṅkhāyana Āraṇyaka,* 14, 24, 71.

[10] Śatapatha Brāhmaṇa, ii. 4, 3, 1; Bṛhadāraṇyaka Upaniṣad, iii. 4, 1; Āśvalāyana Gṛhya Sūtra, iii. 4. *Cf.* Weber, *Indische Studien,* 1, 259; 2, 289 *et seq.*; *Indian Literature,* 44 *et seq.*; Lindner, *Kauṣītaki Brāhmaṇa,* ix.

Kauṣya, 'descendant of Koṣa,' is the patronymic of **Suśravas.**

Kausalya, 'prince of Kosala,' is the designation of **Para Āṭṇāra** in the Śatapatha Brāhmaṇa,[1] and of **Hiraṇyanābha** in the Śāṅkhāyana Śrauta Sūtra.[2] Āśvalāyana is styled Kausalya, as 'belonging to the Kosala country,' in the Praśna Upaniṣad,[3] and the Kāśi-Kausalyāḥ, or the 'Kāśis and people of Kosala,' are mentioned in the Gopatha Brāhmaṇa.[4]

[1] xiii. 5, 4, 4.

[2] xvi. 9, 13. *Cf.* xvi. 29, 5.

[3] i. 1.

[4] i. 2, 9 (spelt *Kauśalyāḥ*).

Kausita appears in the Maitrāyaṇī Saṃhitā (ii. 1, 11) in connexion with the demon Kusitāyin as the name of a lake. The Kāṭhaka Saṃhitā (x. 5) has Kausida instead.

Kausurubindi, 'descendant of **Kusurubinda,**' is the patronymic of **Proti Kauśāmbeya** in the Śatapatha Brāhmaṇa (xii. 2, 2, 13). In the Gopatha Brāhmaṇa (i. 4, 24) the form is Kausuravindu.

Kauhaḍa, 'descendant of Kohaḍa,' is the patronymic of a teacher, **Mitravinda,** mentioned in the Vaṃśa Brāhmana,[1] as well as of **Śravaṇadatta.**

[1] Weber, *Indische Studien,* 4, 372, 382 *et seq.* A school of Kauhaḍīyas is known in the Gobhila Gṛhya Sūtra, iii. 4, 34.

Kratu-jit Jānaki (' descendant of **Janaka** ') is mentioned in the Yajurveda[1] as the priest of **Rajana Kauṇeya.** See also **Kratuvid.**

[1] Taittirīya Saṃhitā, ii. 3, 8, 1; Kāṭhaka Saṃhitā, xi. 1. *Cf.* Weber, *Indische Studien,* 3, 474.

Kratu-vid Jānaki ('descendant of **Janaka**') is mentioned in the Aitareya Brāhmaṇa (vii. 34) as having learned a certain doctrine regarding Soma from Agni.

Kraya, 'sale,' is a word which does not actually occur in the Rigveda, though the verb *krī,* from which this noun is derived, is found there.[1] Both noun and verb are common in the later Saṃhitās.[2] Sale appears to have regularly consisted in barter in the Rigveda:[3] ten cows are regarded as a possible price for an (image of) Indra to be used as a fetish, while elsewhere not a hundred, nor a thousand, nor a myriad are considered as an adequate price (*śulka*) for the purchase of Indra.[4] The Atharvaveda[5] mentions, as possible objects of commerce, garments (*dūrśa*), coverlets (*pavasta*), and goatskins (*ajina*). The haggling of the market was already familiar in the days of the Rigveda,[6] and a characteristic hymn of the Atharvaveda[7] is directed to procuring success in trade. The 'price' was called **Vasna,** and the 'merchant' **Vaṇij**, his greed being well known.[8]

There is little evidence of a standard of value in currency having been adopted. When no specific mention is made of the standard, the unit was probably the cow.[9] In a considerable number of passages of the Śatapatha Brāhmaṇa[10] and elsewhere,[11] however, the expression *hiraṇyaṃ śata-mānam* suggests that there must have been some standard other than

1 iv. 24, 10.

2 *Kraya:* Taittirīya Saṃhitā, iii. 1, 2, 1; vi. 1, 3, 3; Vājasaneyi Saṃhitā, viii. 55; xix. 13; Śatapatha Brāhmaṇa, iii. 3, 2, 10, etc.; *krī:* Av. iii. 15, 2; Taittirīya Saṃhitā, vi. 1, 10, 3; vii. 1, 6, 2, etc.; *apa-krī:* Av. viii. 7, 11; *pari-krī:* Av. iv. 7, 6, etc.; *vi-krī:* Vājasaneyi Saṃhitā, iii. 49, etc.

3 iv. 24, 10.

4 Rv. viii. 1, 5.

5 iv. 7, 6.

6 iv. 24, 9. See Oldenberg, *Ṛgveda-Noten*, 1, 419, 420, correcting Sieg, *Die Sagenstoffe des Ṛgveda*, 91, and Geldner's *Kommentar* on iv. 24.

7 iii. 15. See Bloomfield, *Hymns of the Atharvaveda*, 352; Whitney, Translation of the Atharvaveda, 111, 112.

8 Rv. i. 33, 3, and see **Paṇi**.

9 *Cf.* Harisvāmin on Satapatha Brāhmaṇa, xiii. 4, 2, 1, where he renders *sahasrārha* as equal to 'worth a thousand cows,' in which Eggeling follows him; Saṃkṣiptasāra on Kātyāyana Śrauta Sūtra, xxii. 10, 33.

10 xii. 7, 2, 13; 9, 1, 4; xiii. 1, 1, 4; 2, 3, 2; 4, 1, 13; xiv. 3, 1, 32. *Cf.* v. 5, 5, 16; xiii. 4, 1, 6.

11 Pañcaviṃśa Brāhmaṇa, xviii. 3, 2, where a long series of compounds of numerals with *-māna* occurs; Kāṭhaka Saṃhitā, viii. 5; xiv. 8; xxii. 8.

cows, though it might in all these passages be rendered as 'gold worth a hundred cows.' But the use of the **Kṛṣṇala** as a measure of weight[12] suggests that the meaning is 'gold weighing a hundred Kṛṣṇalas,' and this seems the more probable explanation. This unit seems not to be known in the Rigveda, where the meaning of the term **Manā**, which occurs once, is mysterious, and where necklets (**Niṣka**) seem to have been one of the more portable forms of wealth, like jewellery in modern India, and may perhaps have served as a means of exchange.

[12] *Cf.* Kāṭhaka Saṃhitā, xi. 4; Taittirīya Brāhmaṇa, i. 3, 6, 7; Anupada Sūtra, ix. 6; Weber, *Indische Streifen*, 1, 99-103.

Cf. Zimmer, *Altindisches Leben*, 255-260. Barter had for the most part passed away by the time of the Jātakas, an illustration of the modern character of the society they represent. See Mrs. Rhys Davids, *Journal of the Royal Asiatic Society*, 1901, 874 *et seq.*

Kravaṇa, a word occurring only once in the Rigveda,[1] is understood by Ludwig[2] as the name of the Hotṛ priest or the sacrificer. Roth considered it an adjective without at first[3] assigning a sense, but afterwards[4] as meaning 'timid.' Sāyaṇa interprets it as 'worshipping.' Oldenberg[5] considers the meaning uncertain, suggesting as possible 'the slayer of the victim.'

[1] v. 44, 9.
[2] Translation of the Rigveda, 3, 138.
[3] St. Petersburg Dictionary, *s.v.*
[4] Böhtlingk's Dictionary, *s.v.*
[5] *Ṛgveda-Noten*, 1, 342.

Kravya, 'raw flesh,' is never mentioned in Vedic literature as eaten by men. Demons alone are spoken of as consuming it,[1] apart from Agni being called *kravyād*, 'eating raw flesh,' as consumer of the bodies of the dead.[2] The man who in the Rigveda is compelled by starvation to eat dog's flesh, nevertheless cooks it.[3]

[1] Rv. vii. 104, 2; x. 87, 2. 19; 162, 2; Av. iii. 28, 2; iv. 36, 3; v. 29 10, etc.
[2] Rv. x. 16, 9. 10. See Macdonell, *Vedic Mythology*, pp. 97, 165.
[3] iv. 18, 13.

Cf. Zimmer, *Altindisches Leben*, 270, 271.

Krātu-jāteya is a patronymic of **Rāma Krātujāteya Vaiyāghrapadya** in the Jaiminīya Upaniṣad Brāhmaṇa (iii. 40, 2; iv. 16, 1).

Krimi. See **Kṛmi**.

Krivi is asserted in the Śatapatha Brāhmaṇa[1] to have been the older name of the **Pañcālas.** This statement is supported by the name of the king there mentioned, **Kraivya Pāñcāla.** The Krivis appear in the Rigveda[2] as settled on the **Sindhu** and the **Asiknī.** It is a plausible conjecture of Zimmer's[3] that with the **Kurus** they made up the **Vaikarṇa** people.[4] The importance of the Pañcālas, and the insignificance of the Krivis, may be explained in part by the fact that the later Kuru-Pañcāla alliance included the **Bharatas.** It is also probable, as Oldenberg[5] suggests, from the Śatapatha Brāhmaṇa,[6] that the **Turvaśas** were included in the Pañcālas, and as the latter name indicates, probably other tribes also. Or, if Hopkins' view[7] is accepted that Turvaśa was king of the Yadus, the latter may in part have been allied with the Krivis to form the Pañcālas.

[1] xiii. 5, 4, 7.

[2] viii. 20, 24; 22, 12. Elsewhere Krivi is doubtful in sense. In several passages (i. 30, 1; viii. 87, 1; ix. 9, 6, and perhaps i. 166, 6, where *krivir-datī* is an epithet of lightning) Oldenberg, *Ṛgveda-Noten*, i. 166, 341, understands the word to mean 'horse.' Elsewhere (ii. 17, 6; 22, 2; viii. 51, 8) he takes it to be a proper name, while in v. 44, 4, he is doubtful. In the passages last cited this view may very well be correct.

[3] *Altindisches Leben*, 103.

[4] *Cf.* **Kavaṣa.**

[5] *Buddha*, 404.

[6] xiii. 5, 4, 16.

[7] *Journal of the American Oriental Society*, 15, 258 *et seq.* This view is hardly convincing, while the disappearance of the Turvaśas is easily to be accounted for by their being merged, along with the Krivis, in the Pañcālas. The name of Krivi is lost in the Epic as completely as that of Turvaśa (Pargiter, *Journal of the Royal Asiatic Society*, 1910, 48, notes 4, 5).

Cf. Macdonell, *Sanskrit Literature*, 155, 157; Grierson, *Journal of the Royal Asiatic Society*, 1908, 602-607; Keith, *ibid.*, 831 *et seq.*; Ludwig, Translation of the Rigveda, 3, 152, 153; Eggeling, *Sacred Books of the East*, 12, xli.; Max Müller, *Sacred Books of the East*, 32, 407.

Krīta Vaitahotra ('descendant of Vītahotra') is mentioned in the Maitrāyaṇī Saṃhitā (iv. 2, 6) in connexion with the **Kurus.**

1. **Kruñc,**[1] **Kruñca,**[2] **Krauñca,**[3] are variant forms denoting the 'curlew' or 'snipe.' To it is attributed in the Yajurveda[1]

[1] Maitrāyaṇī Saṃhitā, iii. 11, 6; Kāṭhaka Saṃhitā, xxxviii. 1; Vājasaneyi Saṃhitā, xix. 73 *et seq.*; Taittirīya Brāhmaṇa, ii, 6, 2, 1-3.

[2] Vājasaneyi Saṃhitā, xxiv. 22. 31 (in xxv. 6 the sense is quite uncertain); Maitrāyaṇī Saṃhitā, iii. 14, 3.

[3] Taittirīya Saṃhitā, v. 5, 12, 1.

the faculty, later assigned to the **Haṃsa,** of extracting milk from water when the two fluids are mixed.[4]

[4] Lanman, *Journal of the American Oriental Society*, 19, 151-158; Macdonell, *Sanskrit Literature*, 150. *Cf.* Zimmer, *Altindisches Leben*, 91, 92.

2. **Kruñc Āṅgirasa** is in the Pañcaviṃśa Brāhmaṇa[1] the name of the seer of a Sāman or Chant called the Krauñca. It is doubtless invented to explain the name of the Chant on the ordinary principle that Sāmans are called after their authors, though this rule has many exceptions.[2]

[1] xiii. 9, 11; 11, 20.

[2] Hopkins, *Transactions of the Connecticut Academy of Arts and Sciences*, 15, 68. *Cf.* Hillebrandt, *Vedische Mythologie*, 2, 160.

Krumu is the name of a stream mentioned twice in the Rigveda—once in the fifth book[1] and once in the last, in the Nadī-stuti, or 'praise of rivers.'[2] There can be little doubt that this river is identical with the modern Kurum, a western tributary of the Indus.[3]

[1] v. 53, 9.

[2] x. 75, 6.

[3] Roth, *Nirukta, Erläuterungen*, 43; Zimmer, *Altindisches Leben*, 14; Ludwig, Translation of the Rigveda, 3, 200.

Krumuka as the name of 'wood' appears to be a variant form of **Kṛmuka.**

[1] Taittirīya Saṃhitā, v. 1, 9, 3; Taittirīya Brāhmaṇa, i. 4, 7, 3.

Kraivya. Pāñcāla, the king of the **Krivis,**[1] is mentioned in the Śatapatha Brāhmaṇa[2] as having performed the Aśvamedha, or horse sacrifice, on the **Parivakrā.** Eggeling,[3] however, takes the word as a proper name, 'Kraivya, the Pāñcāla king.'

[1] So the St. Petersburg Dictionary, *s.v.*; Weber, *Indian Literature*, 125, n.; Oldenberg, *Buddha*, 409, n.

[2] xiii. 5, 4, 7.

[3] *Sacred Books of the East*, 44, 397 (but *cf.* p. 398, top).

Krośa, as a measure of distance (lit. 'a shout,' as expressing the range of the voice), is found in the Pañcaviṃśa Brāhmaṇa.[1]

[1] xvi. 13, 12. *Cf.* Weber, *Indische Studien*, 8, 432 *et seq.* In the later literature it is equivalent to about two miles. The word still survives in the vernacular form of Kos as the most popular measure of distance in India.

Kroṣṭṛ (lit. 'howler'), the 'jackal,' is mentioned in the Rigveda[1] as by nature cowardly compared with the wild boar (**Varāha**). In the Atharvaveda[2] it is spoken of as devouring corpses. The word also occurs in the Vājasaneyi Saṃhitā,[3] where the commentator glosses it with Sṛgāla, another name of the jackal. See also **Lopāśa.**

[1] x. 28, 1.
[2] xi. 2, 2.
[3] xxiv. 32.
Cf. Zimmer, *Altindisches Leben*, 84.

1. **Krauñca.** See **Kruñc.**

2. **Krauñca,** as the name of a mountain, occurs only in the latest Vedic literature.[1]

[1] Taittirīya Āraṇyaka, i. 31, 2. See Weber, *Indian Literature*, 93; *Indische Studien*, 1, 78.

Krauñcikī-putra, 'son of a female descendant of Krauñca,' is mentioned as a pupil of **Vaiṭṭabhatīputra**[1] in the last Vaṃśa (list of teachers) in the Bṛhadāraṇyaka Upaniṣad.[2]

[1] Vaidabhṛtī-putra in the Mādhyaṃdina recension, vi. 4, 32.
[2] vi. 5, 2 (Kāṇva).

Krauṣṭuki, 'descendant of Kroṣṭuka,' is mentioned as a grammarian in the Nirukta,[1] the Bṛhaddevatā,[2] and the Chandas,[3] but as an astrologer in a Pariśiṣṭa of the Atharvaveda.[4]

[1] viii. 2.
[2] iv. 137. *Cf. Indische Studien*, 1, 105.
[3] 5.
[4] Weber, Berlin Catalogue of Sanskrit MSS., 1, 94. See Bolling and von Negelein, *The Pariśiṣṭas of the Atharvaveda*, 2, 438 *et seq.*, where in Pariśiṣṭa lxviii (Svapnādhyāyaḥ), i. 2; ii. 8, the name appears as Kroṣṭuki.
Cf. Weber, *Jyotiṣa*, 12; *Indian Literature*, 61.

Kvayi is the name of some species of bird in the Yajurveda,[1] occurring in the list of victims at the Aśvamedha, or horse sacrifice. The form in the Maitrāyaṇī Saṃhitā[2] is Kuvaya.

[1] Taittirīya Saṃhitā, v. 5, 17, 1; Vājasaneyi Saṃhitā, xxiv. 29.
[2] iii. 14, 18.
Cf. Zimmer, *Altindisches Leben*, 99

Kvala is a substance, perhaps[1] identical with **Kuvala**, the fruit of the jujube, used to coagulate milk according to the Taittirīya Saṃhitā.[2]

[1] St. Petersburg Dictionary, *s.v.*

[2] ii. 5, 3, 5. *Cf.* Zimmer, *Altindisches Leben*, 227.

Kṣata is regarded by *Zimmer*[1] as denoting a special disease (a sort of *Phthisis pulmonalis*) in the Atharvaveda,[2] but the word is probably only an adjective.[3]

[1] *Altindisches Leben*, 377.

[2] vii. 76, 4 (where the reading is doubtful, the text having *akṣita*. See **Akṣata**).

[3] Bloomfield, *Hymns of the Atharvaveda*, 509; Whitney, Translation of the Atharvaveda, 442.

Kṣattṛ is a word of frequent occurrence in the later Saṃhitās and Brāhmaṇas, denoting a member of the royal entourage, but the sense is somewhat uncertain. In the Rigveda[1] it is used of a god as the 'distributor' of good things to his worshippers; the same sense seems to be found in the Atharvaveda[2] and elsewhere.[3] In one passage of the Vājasaneyi Saṃhitā[4] the interpretation 'doorkeeper' is given by the commentator Mahīdhara, a sense which seems possible in other passages,[5] while Sāyaṇa ascribes to it in one passage of the Śatapatha Brāhmaṇa[6] the more dignified meaning of *antaḥpurādhyakṣa*, 'a chamberlain.' In other passages,[7] again, the sense of 'charioteer' is not unlikely. Later the Kṣattṛ was regarded as a man of mixed caste.[8]

[1] vi. 13, 2.

[2] iii. 24, 7; v. 17, 4.

[3] Śatapatha Brāhmaṇa, xiii. 5, 4, 6; Śāṅkhāyana Śrauta Sūtra, xvi. 9, 16.

[4] xxx. 13. *Cf.* Taittirīya Brāhmaṇa, i. 7, 3, 5.

[5] Taittirīya Saṃhitā, iv. 5, 4, 2; Maitrāyaṇī Saṃhitā, ii. 9, 4; Kāṭhaka Saṃhitā, xvii. 13; Chāndogya Upaniṣad, iv. 1, 5; Pañcaviṃśa Brāhmaṇa, xix. 1, 4.

[6] v. 3, 1, 7. *Cf.* on xiii. 4, 2, 5 (*āyavyayādhyakṣa*), and Harisvāmin on xiii. 5, 4, 6 (*kośādhyakṣa*). The scholiast on the Kātyāyana Śrauta Sūtra, xv. 3, 9, has *mantrī dūto vā*; on xx. 1, 16, *pratihāro dūto vā*. Eggeling, *Sacred Books of the East*, 41, 61, etc., renders it 'chamberlain.'

[7] Vājasaneyi Saṃhitā, xvi. 26; Taittirīya Brāhmaṇa, iii. 4, 7, 1, with the scholiast's note, and *ibid.*, *anukṣattṛ*, rendered as *sārather anucara*, 'the attendant of the charioteer'; Śāṅkhāyana Śrauta Sūtra, xvi. 1, 20, with the scholiast's note.

[8] Muir, *Sanskrit Texts*, 1^2, 481.

Cf. Weber, *Indische Studien*, 2, 36; 17, 290: St. Petersburg Dictionary, *s.v.*

1. **Kṣatra,** in the general sense of 'dominion,' 'rule,' 'power,' as exercised by gods and men, occurs frequently from the Rigveda[1] onwards. The word is also found in the concrete sense of 'rulers' in the Rigveda[2] and later;[3] but in no case does it in the Rigveda certainly[4] mean what it regularly denotes in the later Saṃhitās,[5] the ruling class as opposed to the priests (**Brahman**), the subject people (**Viś, Vaiśya**), and the servile class (**Śūdra**). See also **Kṣatriya.** A Kṣatra-pati is several times mentioned[6] as an equivalent of 'king.'

[1] i. 24, 11; 136, 1. 3; iv. 17. 1; v. 62, 6, etc.; Av. iii. 5, 2; v. 18, 4, etc. So *kṣatra-śrī*, Rv. i. 25, 5; vi. 26, 8; *kṣatra-bhṛt*, 'bringers of lordship.' Taittirīya Saṃhitā, ii. 4, 7, 2; Taittirīya Brāhmaṇa, ii. 4, 6, 12; 7, 6, 3; Vājasaneyi Saṃhitā, xxvii. 7, etc.

[2] Singular: i. 157, 2; viii. 35, 17.

[3] Plural: Av. iv. 22, 2; Vājasaneyi Saṃhitā, x. 17; Taittirīya Brāhmaṇa, ii. 7, 6, 3.

[4] See Roth, St. Petersburg Dictionary, *s.v.*, and **Varṇa**.

[5] Av. ii. 15, 4; ix. 7, 9; xii. 5, 8; xv. 10, 5, etc.; Taittirīya Saṃhitā, i. 6, 1, 2; ii. 2, 11, 2, etc.; Vājasaneyi Saṃhitā, v. 27: xiv. 24; xviii. 38, etc. See other citations under **Varṇa**.

[6] Taittirīya Saṃhitā, i. 8, 14, 2; Vājasaneyi Saṃhitā, x. 17; Taittirīya Brāhmaṇa, i. 7, 8, 5; Śatapatha Brāhmaṇa, v. 4, 2, 2.

2. **Kṣatra** seems to be the name of a man mentioned with others, including **Manasa, Yajata,** and **Avatsāra,** in one quite obscure passage of the Rigveda.[1]

[1] v. 44, 10. *Cf.* Ludwig, Translation of the Rigveda, 3, 138.

Kṣatra-vidyā, 'the science of the ruling class,' is mentioned in the Chāndogya Upaniṣad.[1] Śaṅkara glosses the term with *dhanur-veda,* 'the science of the bow,' which is the most probable sense.[2]

[1] vii. 1, 2. 4; 2, 1; 7, 1.

[2] Hopkins, *Journal of the American Oriental Society*, 13, 104.

Kṣatriya.—As the origin of caste, the relation of the castes, intermarriage, and cognate matters may most conveniently be discussed under **Varṇa,** this article will be confined to determining, as far as possible, the real character of the class called Kṣatriyas, or collectively **Kṣatra.**

The evidence of the Jātakas[1] points to the word Khattiya

[1] See Fick, *Die sociale Gliederung im nordöstlichen Indien zu Buddhas Zeit*, 59 *et seq.*; Rhys Davids, *Dialogues of the Buddha*, 1, 95 *et seq.*; *Buddhist India*, 52 *et seq.*

denoting the members of the old Āryan nobility who had led the tribes to conquest, as well as those families of the aborigines who had managed to maintain their princely status in spite of the conquest. In the epic[2] also the term Kṣatriya seems to include these persons, but it has probably a wider signification than Khattiya, and would cover all the royal military vassals and feudal chiefs, expressing, in fact, pretty much the same as the *barones* of early English history. Neither in the Jātakas[3] nor in the epic[4] is the term co-extensive with all warriors; the army contains many besides the Kṣatriyas, who are the leaders or officers, rather than the rank and file.

In the later Saṃhitās[5] and the Brāhmaṇas[6] the Kṣatriya stands as a definite member of the social body, distinct from the priest, the subject people, and the slaves, **Brāhmaṇa, Vaiśya,** and **Śūdra.** It is significant that Rājanya is a variant to Kṣatriya, and an earlier one. Hence it is reasonable to suppose that the Kṣatriya and Rājanya are both of similar origin, being princely or connected with royalty. Moreover, the early use of Kṣatriya in the Rigveda[7] is exclusively connected with royal authority or divine authority.

It is impossible to say exactly what persons would be included in the term Kṣatriya. That it covered the royal house and the various branches of the royal family may be regarded as certain. It, no doubt, also included the nobles and their families: this would explain the occasional opposition of Rājanya and Kṣatriya, as in the Aitareya Brāhmaṇa,[8] where a Rājanya asks a Kṣatriya for a place for sacrifice (*deva-yajana*). Thus, when strictly applied, Kṣatriya would have a wider denotation than Rājanya. As a rule, however, the two expressions are identical, and both are used as evidence in what follows. That Kṣatriya ever included the mere fighting

[2] Hopkins, *Journal of the American Oriental Society*, 13, 73 *et seq.*

[3] Fick, *op. cit.*, 52, n. 2.

[4] Hopkins, *op. cit.*, 184 *et seq.*, 190.

[5] Av. vi. 76, 3. 4; xii. 5, 5. 44. 46, etc.; Vājasaneyi Saṃhitā, xxx. 5, etc. See **Varṇa** and **Rājanya**.

[6] Aitareya Brāhmaṇa, vii. 24, etc.; Śatapatha Brāhmaṇa, i. 3, 2, 15; iv. 1, 4, 5. 6, etc. See **Varṇa**.

[7] iv. 12, 3; 42, 1; v. 69, 1; vii. 64, 2; viii. 25, 8; 56, 1; x. 109, 3. *Cf.* Vājasaneyi Saṃhitā, iv. 19; x. 4; Taittirīya Brāhmaṇa, ii. 4, 7, 7.

[8] vii. 20. *Cf.* Pañcaviṃśa Brāhmaṇa, xxiv. 18, 2; Kāṭhaka Saṃhitā, xx. 1.

man has not been proved: in the Rigveda[9] and later[10] others than Kṣatriyas regularly fought; but possibly if the nobles had retinues as the kings had, Kṣatriya would embrace those retainers who had military functions. The term did not apply to all members of the royal entourage; for example, the **Grāmaṇī** was usually a Vaiśya.

The connexion of the Kṣatriyas with the Brahmins was very close. The prosperity of the two is repeatedly asserted[11] to be indissolubly associated, especially in the relation of king (**Rājan**) and domestic priest (**Purohita**). Sometimes there was feud between Kṣatriya and Brahmin.[12] His management of the sacrifice then gave the Brahmin power to ruin the Kṣatriya by embroiling him with the people[13] or with other Kṣatriyas.[14]

Towards the common people, on the other hand, the Kṣatriya stood in a relation of well-nigh unquestioned superiority.[15] There are, however, references to occasional feuds between

[9] In the following passages there is reference to the people (*viś*) fighting: i. 69, 3; 126, 5 (*cf.*, however, Pischel, *Vedische Studien*, 2, 121); iv. 24, 4; vi. 26, 1; vii. 79, 2; viii. 18, 18; 96, 15; probably also vii. 33, 6, where the *Tṛtsūnāṃ viśaḥ* means 'the subjects of the Tṛtsu princes,' as Geldner, *Vedische Studien*, 2, 136, thinks. In vi. 41, 5, on the other hand, the people and wars (*pṛtanāsu*) are contrasted, the normal rule of the common folk being peace.

[10] In Av. ix. 7, 9, the people are clearly designated as *balam*, or 'force,' a regular term later for an armed force. The later law books (*e.g.*, Gautama, vii. 6; Vasiṣṭha, ii. 22) allow even Brahmins to maintain themselves by the occupation of Kṣatriyas in case of need. For the Epic, *cf.* Hopkins, *op. cit.*, 94, 95; 184 *et seq.*

[11] Taittirīya Saṃhitā, v. 1, 10, 3; Maitrāyaṇī Saṃhitā, ii. 2, 3; iii. 1, 9; 2, 3; iv. 3, 9; Kāṭhaka Saṃhitā, xxix. 10; Vājasaneyi Saṃhitā, v. 27; vii. 21; xviii. 14; xix. 5; xxxviii. 14, etc.; Pañcaviṃśa Brāhmaṇa, xi. 11, 9; Aitareya Brāhmaṇa, vii. 22; Śatapatha Brāhmaṇa, i. 2, 1, 7; iii. 5, 2, 11; 6, 1, 17; vi. 6, 3, 14. The superiority of the Rājanya to all other castes is asserted in Taittirīya Saṃhitā, ii. 5, 10, 1, etc. The superiority of the Brahmin to the Kṣatriya is sometimes asserted—*e.g.*, in the Atharvaveda hymns, v. 18. 19; Maitrāyaṇī Saṃhitā, iv. 3, 8; Vājasaneyi Saṃhitā, xxi. 21; Śatapatha Brāhmaṇa, xiii. 1, 9, 1; 3, 7, 8. So the Rājasūya sacrifice of the king is inferior to the highest sacrifice (the Vājapeya) of the priest (*ibid.*, v. 1, 1, 12), and though the Brahmin goes after the king, he is yet stronger than he (v. 4, 2, 7, and v. 4, 4, 15). *Cf.* Hopkins, *op. cit.*, 76.

[12] Kāṭhaka Saṃhitā, xxviii. 5; Av. v. 18. 19.

[13] *E.g.*, Taittirīya Saṃhitā, ii. 2, 11, 2; Maitrāyaṇī Saṃhitā, i. 6, 5; ii. 1, 9; iii. 3, 10; Kāṭhaka Saṃhitā, xxix. 8, etc.

[14] Maitrāyaṇī Saṃhitā, iii. 3, 10, etc.

[15] Kāṭhaka Saṃhitā, xvi. 4; xxi. 10; xxii. 9; xxix. 9, 10; Aitareya Brāhmaṇa, ii. 33; Śatapatha Brāhmaṇa, xi. 2, 7, 15. 16, etc.; Maitrāyaṇī Saṃhitā, iv. 4, 9. 10; 6, 8, etc.

the people and the nobles,[16] in which no doubt the inferior numbers of the latter were compensated by their superior arms and prowess. In the Aitareya Brāhmaṇa[17] the Vaiśya is described as tributary to another (*anyasya bali-kṛt*), to be devoured by another (*anyasyādya*), and to be oppressed at will (*yathākāma-jyeya*). Probably these epithets apply most strictly to the relation of the king and his people, but the passage shows that the people were greatly at the mercy of the nobles. No doubt the king granted to them the right, which may have been hereditary, to be supported by the common people, whose feudal superiors they thus became. In return for these privileges the Kṣatriyas had probably duties of protection to perform, as well as some judicial functions, to judge from an obscure passage of the Kāṭhaka Saṃhitā.[18]

The main duty of the Kṣatriya in the small states[19] of the Vedic period was readiness for war. The bow is thus his special attribute,[20] just as the goad is that of the agriculturist; for the bow is the main weapon of the Veda. Whether the Kṣatriyas paid much attention to mental occupations is uncertain. In the latest stratum of the Brāhmaṇa literature there are references to learned princes like **Janaka** of **Videha**, who is said to have become a Brahmin (*brahmā*), apparently in the sense that he had the full knowledge which a Brahmin possessed.[21] Other learned Kṣatriyas of this period were

[16] *Cf.* note 13; Taittirīya Saṃhitā, v. 4, 6, 7; Maitrāyaṇī Saṃhitā, iv. 6, 7.

[17] vii. 29. *Cf.* **Rājan.**

[18] xxvii. 4 (*tasmād rājanyenādhyakṣeṇa vaiśyaṃ ghnanti*, 'so with a Rājanya as a supervisor [?] they smite a Vaiśya'). It is not clear whether *han* here means 'kill' or 'beat.'

[19] See Hopkins, *Transactions of the Connecticut Academy of Arts and Sciences*, 15, 30, n. 2.

[20] Av. xviii. 2, 60; Kāṭhaka Saṃhitā, xviii. 9; xxxvii. 1; Śatapatha Brāhmaṇa, v. 3, 5, 30; Taittirīya Āraṇyaka, vi. 1, 3. In the Aitareya Brāhmaṇa, vii. 19, the list is longer—chariot, breastplate (**Kavaca**), bow and arrow (*iṣu-dhanvan*)—and in the prayer for the prosperity of the Kṣatriya (called, as usual in the older texts, Rājanya), at the Aśvamedha, the Rājanya is to be an archer and a good chariot-fighter; Taittirīya Saṃhitā, vii. 5, 18, 1; Maitrāyaṇī Saṃhitā, iii. 12, 6; Kāṭhaka Saṃhitā, Aśvamedha, v. 14; Vājasaneyi Saṃhitā, xxii. 2. So Indra is the god of the Kṣatriyas, Maitrāyaṇī Saṃhitā, ii. 3, 1; iv. 5, 8, etc.

[21] Śatapatha Brāhmaṇa, xi. 6, 2, 1. *Cf.* Kauṣītaki Upaniṣad, iv. 1. See Max Müller, *Ancient Sanskrit Literature*, 421 *et seq.*; Muir, *Sanskrit Texts*, 1², 426 *et seq.* Similarly at the Dīkṣā a Kṣatriya becomes temporarily a Brahmin, Aitareya Brāhmaṇa, vii. 23. *Cf.* Śatapatha Brāhmaṇa, iii. 4, 1, 3.

Pravāhaṇa Jaivali,[22] **Aśvapati Kaikeya,**[23] and **Ajātaśatru.**[24] Garbe,[25] Grierson,[26] and others believe they are justified in holding the view that the Kṣatriyas developed a special philosophy of their own as opposed to Brahminism, which appears later as Bhakti, or Faith. On the other hand, there is clear evidence[27] that the opinion of Kṣatriyas on such topics were held in little respect, and it must be remembered that to attribute wisdom to a king was a delicate and effective piece of flattery. There are earlier references to royal sages (*rājanyarṣi*),[28] but it is very doubtful if much stress can be laid on them, and none can be laid on the later tradition of Sāyaṇa.[29] Again, the Nirukta[30] gives a tradition relating how **Devāpi**, a king's son, became the Purohita of his younger brother **Śaṃtanu**; but it is very doubtful if the story can really be traced with Sieg[31] in the Rigveda[32] itself. In any case, the stories refer only to a few selected Kṣatriyas of high rank, while there is no evidence that the average Kṣatriya was concerned with intellectual pursuits. Nor is there any reference to Kṣatriyas engaging in agriculture or in trade or commerce. It may be assumed that the duties of administration and war were adequate to absorb his attention. On the other hand, we do hear of a Rājanya

[22] Bṛhadāraṇyaka Upaniṣad, vi. 1, 1; Chāndogya Upaniṣad, i. 8, 1; v. 3, 1; Muir, *op. cit.*, 433-435; 515; Weber, *Indische Studien*, 10, 117; Max Müller, *Sacred Books of the East*, 1, lxxv.

[23] Śatapatha Brāhmaṇa, x. 6, 1, 2 *et seq.*

[24] Bṛhadāraṇyaka Upaniṣad, ii. 1, 1; Kauṣītaki Upaniṣad, iv. 1.

[25] *Beiträge zur indischen Kulturgeschichte*, 1 *et seq. Cf.* Deussen, *Philosophy of the Upanishads*, 17 *et seq.*; Winterniz, *Geschichte der indischen Litteratur*, 1, 199.

[26] Article 'Bhakti' in *Encyclopædia of Religion and Ethics*; *Journal of the Royal Asiatic Society*, 1908, 843.

[27] Śatapatha Brāhmaṇa, viii. 1, 4, 10. *Cf.* Oldenberg, *Buddha*, 73, n. 1; Keith, *Aitareya Āraṇyaka*, 50, 257; *Journal of the Royal Asiatic Society*, 1908, 868, 883, 1140-1142. Professor Eggeling concurs in the view that the Kṣatriya share in the religious movement was not substantially real.

[28] *E.g.*, in Pañcaviṃśa Brāhmaṇa, xii. 12, 6; but see on this Oldenberg, *Zeitschrift der Deutschen Morgenländischen Gesellschaft*, 42, 235, n., and **Varṇa**.

[29] Cited in Muir, *op. cit.*, 1², 265 *et seq.*

[30] ii. 10.

[31] *Die Sagenstoffe des Ṛgveda*, 91 *et seq.* See **Devāpi**.

[32] x. 98. The case of **Viśvāmitra** may also be cited; but his royal rank, which is attested by the mention of him as a Rājaputra in the Aitareya Brāhmaṇa, vii. 17, is at most merely a matter of descent, and is of very doubtful authenticity. See under **Varṇa**.

as a lute player and singer at the Aśvamedha or horse sacrifice.[33]

Of the training and education of a Kṣatriya we have no record; presumably, as in fact if not in theory later on, he was mainly instructed in the art of war, the science of the bow, and the rudimentary administrative functions which would devolve on him. At this early state of the development of the nobility which appears to be represented in the Rigveda, it was probably not unusual or impossible for a Vaiśya to become a Kṣatriya; at least, this assumption best explains the phrase[34] 'claiming falsely a Kṣatriya's rank' (*kṣatriyaṃ mithuyā dhārayantam*).

The king and the Kṣatriyas must have stood in a particularly close relation. The former being the Kṣatriya *par excellence*, it is to him rather than to the ordinary Kṣatriya that we must refer passages like that in the Śatapatha Brāhmaṇa,[35] where it is said that the Kṣatriya, with the consent of the clansmen, gives a settlement to a man: clearly a parallel to the rule found among many peoples that the chief, but only with the consent of the people, can make a grant of unoccupied land. In the same Brāhmaṇa[36] it is said that a Kṣatriya consecrates a Kṣatriya, a clear reference, as the commentator explains, to the practice of the old king consecrating the prince (*kumāra*) who is to succeed him; and again,[37] the Kṣatriya and the Purohita are regarded as alone complete in contrast with other people, the parallel with the Purohita here suggesting that the Kṣatriya *par excellence* is meant. On the other hand, the king is sometimes contrasted with the Rājanya.[38]

The Sūtra literature contains elaborate rules[39] for the educa-

[33] Śatapatha Brāhmaṇa, xiii. 4, 3, 5. This mention is proof of the existence of a class of Kṣatriya bards (as opposed to priestly reciters), from whose productions the Epic naturally grew up. *Cf.* Hopkins, *Journal of the American Oriental Society*, 15, 258.

[34] vii. 104, 13. *Cf.* for a similarly false claim to be a Brahmin, x. 71, 8.

[35] vii. 1, 1, 8.

[36] xii. 8, 3, 19; Eggeling, *Sacred Books of the East*, 44, 254, n. 1.

[37] *Cf.* Eggeling, *ibid.*, 41, 259.

[38] Śatapatha Brāhmaṇa, xiii. 4, 2, 17, and see **Rājanya.**

[39] See references in Bühler, *Sacred Books of the East*, 14, 395, 396.

Cf. Zimmer, *Altindisches Leben*, 212 *et seq.*; Ludwig, Translation of the Rigveda, 3, 231 *et seq.*; von Schroeder, *Indiens Literatur und Cultur*, 151 *et seq.*; Weber, *Indische Studien*, 10, 4 *et seq.* (where practically every passage on the subject is cited or referred to); Hopkins, *Journal of the American Oriental Society*, 13, 98 *et seq.* (for the Epic parallels).

tion and occupations of Kṣatriyas, but their contents cannot always be traced in the Brāhmaṇa literature, and their value is questionable.

Kṣa-pāvan, 'protector of the earth,'[1] is an epithet of a king,[2] or denotes a king[3] in the Rigveda. The word is significant, as showing the function of the king as the protector of the tribal territory.

[1] The word occurs only in the nominative singular as *kṣapāvān*, which would be the regular form from a stem *kṣapāvant;* but it is probably an irregularity for *kṣapāvā*. *Cf.* Oldenberg, *Ṛgveda-Noten*, 1, 72.

[2] iii. 55, 17.

[3] i. 70, 5; vii. 10, 5; viii. 71, 2; x. 29, 1.

Cf. *kṣiti-pa*, 'guardian of earth,' 'king,' in later Sanskrit.

Kṣiti is in the Rigveda[1] a regular word for 'dwelling,' and in particular the *kṣitir dhruvā*, 'the secure dwelling,' is mentioned[2] in a context that shows it to be equivalent to the **Vṛjana** or **Grāma** regarded as a stronghold. From this sense is developed that of the peoples occupying the settlements,[3] and in particular the five peoples[4] (for whom see **Pañca Janāsaḥ**).

[1] i. 65, 3; iii. 13, 4; v. 37, 4, etc.

[2] i. 73, 4 (*cf.* 2); vii. 88, 7. See Zimmer, *Altindisches Leben*, 142.

[3] Rv. iii. 38, 1; iv. 24, 4; 38, 5; v. 1, 10, etc.

[4] i. 7, 9; 176, 3; v. 35, 2; vi. 46, 7; vii. 75, 4; 79, 1.

Kṣipta, 'a wound' (caused by shooting), or 'bruise' (caused by throwing), is mentioned in the Atharvaveda,[1] together with a remedy for it, the **Pippalī**.

[1] vi. 109, 1. 3. *Cf.* Zimmer, *Altindisches Leben*, 389.

Kṣipra-śyena, 'swift falcon,' is the name of a bird in the Maitrāyaṇī Saṃhitā (iii. 14, 11) and the Śatapatha Brāhmaṇa x. 5, 2, 10).

Kṣīra, 'milk,' also called **Go** or **Payas**, played a large part in the economy of the Vedic Indians.[1] It was taken warm (*pakva*

[1] The word *kṣīra* does not occur in Rv. ii.-vii. It is found in i. 109, 3; 164, 7; viii. 2, 9; ix. 67, 32; x. 87, 16 (=Av. viii. 3, 15). See Hopkins, *Journal of the American Oriental Society*, 17, 64, 73 *et seq*. See also Av. ii. 26, 4; v. 19, 5; x. 9, 12, etc.; Taittirīya Saṃhitā, iii. 4, 8, 7, etc.

as it came from the cow,[2] or was used with grain to make a 'mess cooked with milk' (*kṣīra-pākam odanam*).[3] It was also used for mixing with Soma (**Abhiśrī, Āśir**). From it butter (**Ghṛta**) was made. Milk was also curdled, the **Pūtīkā** and **Kvala** plants, among others, being used for the purpose.[4] The curdled milk (**Dadhi**) was undoubtedly used for food; and a kind of cheese is perhaps referred to in one passage of the Rigveda.[5] Goat's milk (*aja-kṣīra*) is also mentioned.[6]

[2] i. 62, 9; 180, 3; iii. 30, 4.

[3] Rv. viii. 77, 10; Av. xiii. 2, 20. *Cf. kṣīra-śrī*, 'milk-mixed,' Taittirīya Saṃhitā, iv. 4, 9, 1; Vājasaneyi Saṃhitā, viii. 57, etc.

[4] Taittirīya Saṃhitā, ii. 5, 3, 5.

[5] vi. 48, 18.

[6] Śatapatha Brāhmaṇa, xiv. 1, 2, 13; see **Aja**.

Cf. Zimmer, *Altindisches Leben*, 63, 226, 226, 268.

Kṣīraudana, 'rice cooked with milk,' is mentioned frequently in the Śatapatha Brāhmaṇa (ii. 5, 3, 4; xi. 5, 7, 5, etc.).

Kṣudra-sūktas, 'makers of short hymns,' is the name given in the Aitareya Āraṇyaka[1] to the authors of certain hymns of the Rigveda. *Cf.* **Mahāsūkta.**

[1] ii. 2, 2. *Cf.* Keith, *Aitareya Āraṇyaka*, 212, and Macdonell, *Bṛhaddevatā*, notes on iii. 116.

Kṣumpa is a word occurring only in one passage of the Rigveda,[1] where it seems to mean a 'bush.' The Nirukta[2] identifies it with the Ahichatraka, a 'mushroom.'

[1] i. 84, 8.

[2] v. 16. *Cf.* Benfey, *Sāmaveda, Glossar*, 53.

Kṣura occurs three times in the Rigveda. The word appears to have the general sense of 'blade'[1] in one passage,[2] possibly also in another,[3] where it is said that the hare swallowed a

[1] Hopkins, *Journal of the American Oriental Society*, 17, 61, 69. *Cf.* 13, 292 (as 'knife' in the Epic).

[2] i. 166, 10 (*paviṣu kṣurāḥ* on the fellies of the Maruts' car; possibly 'razors' may be meant, as Max Müller says in his note on this passage, *Sacred Books of the East*, 32, 235, n. 4).

[3] x. 28, 9, where Sāyaṇa renders it as meaning 'having claws.' The later tradition ascribes the swallowing to a goat.

Kṣura, and where the sense 'blade' is adequate. In the third passage[4] there seems to be a reference to the sharpening of a razor on a grindstone[5] (*bhurijos*, the dual denoting precisely, as Pischel[6] points out, the two sides of the apparatus, between which the stone revolved like the modern grindstone). But Muir,[7] following another view of Roth,[8] adopts the sense 'the edge of scissors,' which, however, hardly suits the other passage, one in the Atharvaveda,[9] where a Kṣura is described as moving about on the *bhurijos*,[10] as the tongue on the lip. The meaning 'razor' is perfectly clear in the Atharvaveda,[11] where shaving by means of it is mentioned; in many other passages[12] either sense is adequate. A *kṣuro bhṛjvān* occurs in the Yajurveda:[13] it seems to denote, as Bloomfield[14] suggests, a razor with a strop (in the shape of a small grinding apparatus). Kṣura-dhārā[15] denotes 'the edge of a razor,' like *kṣurasya dhārā*.[16] In the Upaniṣads[17] a razor-case (Kṣura-dhāna) is mentioned. See also **Śmaśru**.

[4] viii. 4, 16 (*saṃ naḥ śiśīhi bhurijor iva kṣuram*, 'sharpen us like a razor on a grindstone or stropping apparatus').

[5] Roth, St. Petersburg Dictionary, *s.v.*

[6] *Vedische Studien*, 1, 243.

[7] *Sanskrit Texts*, 5, 466.

[8] St. Petersburg Dictionary, *s.v. bhurij*.

[9] xx. 127, 4.

[10] Bloomfield, *Hymns of the Atharvaveda*, 197, translates *bhurijos* by 'on a strop.'

[11] vi. 68, 1. 3; viii. 2, 7.

[12] Śatapatha Brāhmaṇa, ii. 6, 4, 5; iii. 1, 2, 7; *kṣura-pavi*, Av. xii. 5, 20. 55; Taittirīya Saṃhitā, ii. 1, 5, 7; 5, 5, 6; v. 6, 6, 1; Śatapatha Brāhmaṇa, iii. 6, 2, 9, etc.; Maitrāyaṇī Saṃhitā, i. 10, 14; Kāṭhaka Saṃhitā, xxxvi. 8; Nirukta, v. 5.

[13] Taittirīya Saṃhitā, iv. 3, 12, 3. *Cf.* Maitrāyaṇī Saṃhitā, ii. 8, 7; Vājasaneyi Saṃhitā, xv. 4; Śatapatha Brāhmaṇa, viii. 5, 2, 4.

[14] *American Journal of Philology*, 17, 418.

[15] Jaiminīya Upaniṣad Brāhmaṇa, iii. 13, 9.

[16] Bṛhadāraṇyaka Upaniṣad, iii. 3, 2.

[17] Kauṣītaki Upaniṣad, iv. 20.

Cf. Zimmer, *Altindisches Leben*, 266; Pischel, *Vedische Studien*, 1, 239-243; Schrader, *Prehistoric Antiquities*, 38 *et seq.*

Kṣetra, 'field.' The use of this word in the Rigveda points clearly to the existence of separate fields[1] carefully measured off,[2] though in some passages the meaning is less definite,

[1] x. 33, 6. *Cf.* iii. 31, 15; v. 62, 7.

[2] i. 110, 5.

indicating cultivated land generally.[3] In the Atharvaveda[4] and later the sense of a separate field is clearly marked, though the more general use is also found.[5] The deity Kṣetrasya Pati,[6] 'Lord of the Field,' should probably be understood as the god presiding over each field, just as Vāstoṣ Pati presides over each dwelling.[7] It is a fair conclusion from the evidence that the system of separate holdings already existed in early Vedic times.[8] See also **Urvarā, Khilya.**

[3] i. 100, 18; ix. 85, 4; 91, 6; *Kṣetra-jeṣa*, i. 33, 15, 'acquisition of land'; *kṣetrā-sā*, iv. 38, 1, 'gaining land'; *kṣetraṃ-jaya*, 'conquering cultivated land,' Maitrāyaṇī Saṃhitā, ii. 2, 11. The wider sense of 'place' also occurs, v. 2, 3; 45, 9; vi. 47, 20, etc., and often later.

[4] iv. 18, 5; v. 31, 4; x. 1, 18; xi. 1, 22; Taittirīya Saṃhitā, ii. 2, 1, 2; Chāndogya Upaniṣad, vii. 24, 2, etc.

[5] Av. ii. 29, 3; xiv. 2, 7; Śatapatha Brāhmaṇa, i. 4, 1, 15. 16, etc.

[6] Rv. iv. 37, 1. 2; vii. 35, 10; x. 66, 13; Av. ii. 8, 5; *kṣetrasya patnī*, 'Mistress of the Field,' 12, 1; *kṣetrāṇāṃ patiḥ*, 'Lord of Fields,' Vājasaneyi Saṃhitā, xvi. 18.

[7] Macdonell, *Vedic Mythology*, p. 138.

Cf. Zimmer, *Altindisches Leben*, 236; Śatapatha Brāhmaṇa, vii. 1, 1, 8, where the Kṣatriya, with the consent of the people, gives a settlement to a man: that is, presumably assigns to him a definite Kṣetra for his own, probably measured out as recorded in Rv. i. 110, 5.

Kṣetriya is a disease which is mentioned several times in the Atharvaveda, and against which three hymns are specially directed.[1] It is also mentioned in the Kāṭhaka Saṃhitā[2] and the Taittirīya Brāhmaṇa.[3] The commentators on the Atharvaveda agree in taking it to be a hereditary disease. The word may mean 'organic,'[4] or possibly 'produced in the field,' as a theory of its origin. What disease is really intended is quite uncertain. Weber[5] considered that the aim of the Atharvan hymns was to drive away injury threatening the fields, but this is improbable. Bloomfield[6] suggests 'scrofula' or 'syphilis.' The remedies mentioned throw no light on the symptoms.

[1] ii. 8. 10; iii. 7. *Cf.* ii. 14, 5; iv. 18, 7.

[2] xv. 1.

[3] ii. 5, 6, 1-3, where the form is Kṣetrī, explained as a demon causing illness, merely an incorrect version of Av. iii. 10.

[4] St. Petersburg Dictionary, *s.v.*

[5] *Indische Studien*, 5, 145; 13, 150 *et seq.*: 17, 208; *Naxatra*, 2, 292.

[6] *Atharvaveda*, 60.

Cf. Bloomfield, *Hymns of the Atharvaveda*, 286 *et seq.*; Whitney, Translation of the Atharvaveda, 48, 49; Zimmer, *Altindisches Leben*, 391, 392; Speijer, *De ceremonia apud Indos quæ jātakarma vocatur*, 76-83; Pāṇini, v. 2, 92, with the Kāśikā Vṛtti.

Kṣema-dhṛtvan Pauṇḍarīka ('descendant of Puṇḍarīka') is mentioned in the Pañcaviṃśa Brāhmaṇa[1] as having sacrificed on the bank of the river **Sudāman**.

[1] xxii. 18, 7. *Cf*. Weber, *Indische Studien*, 1, 32. Later, the name is Kṣema-dhanvan, Harivaṃśa, 824, etc.

Kṣaimi, 'descendant of Kṣema,' is the patronymic of **Sudakṣiṇa** in the Jaiminīya Upaniṣad Brāhmaṇa (iii. 6, 3; 7, 1, etc.; 8, 6).

Kṣoṇī.—This word, when used in the plural, denotes, according to the St. Petersburg Dictionary and Ludwig,[1] in several passages of the Rigveda,[2] the free retainers of the king. Geldner[3] at one time thought it referred to the wives of the king, pointing to polygamy; but later[4] he concluded that it means certain divine wives.

[1] Translation of the Rigveda, 3, 247.

[2] i. 57, 4; 173, 7; viii. 3, 10; 13, 17; x. 95, 19. In ii. 34, 13; x. 22, 9, the sense is doubtful.

[3] Bezzenberger, *Beiträge*, 11, 327.

[4] *Vedische Studien*, 1, 279, 283.

Kṣauma, 'a linen garment,' is mentioned in the Maitrāyaṇī Saṃhitā (iii. 6, 7, etc.) and in the Sūtras.

Kṣviṅkā is mentioned once in the Rigveda[1] as a bird of prey. The word also occurs in the list of victims at the Aśvamedha, or horse sacrifice, in the Taittirīya Saṃhitā,[2] where the commentary absurdly explains it as 'a red-mouthed female ape' (*rakta-mukhī vānarī*).

[1] x. 87, 7.

[2] v. 5, 15, 1.

Cf. Zimmer, *Altindisches Leben*, 93.

KH.

Kha denotes in the Rigveda[1] and later[2] the hole in the nave of the wheel in which the axle is inserted. There was a difference, it seems, in the size of the hole in the wheel of a cart (**Anas**) and of a chariot (**Ratha**).[3] See also 1. **Yuga**.

[1] Rv. viii. 77, 3; 91, 7; x. 156, 3, where only the Kha is referred to. *Cf.* the adjective *su-kha*, 'having a good axle-hole,' 'running easily'; later, 'agreeable.'

[2] Bṛhadāraṇyaka Upaniṣad, v. 12, 1 (Mādhyaṃdina; v. 10, 1 Kāṇva).

[3] Jaiminīya Upaniṣad Brāhmaṇa, 1, 3, 6; Geldner, *Vedische Studien*, 2, 333. *Cf.* Zimmer, *Altindisches Leben*, 247.

Khaṅga. See **Khaḍga.**

Khaḍga is the reading in the Maitrāyaṇī Saṃhitā[1] of the name of an animal which, in the text of the Vājasaneyi Saṃhitā,[2] variously appears as Khaṅga and Khaḍga. The rhinoceros seems clearly to be meant.[3] In the Śāṅkhāyana Śrauta Sūtra[4] a rhinoceros hide is mentioned as the covering of a chariot.

[1] iii. 14, 21.

[2] xxiv. 40.

[3] Zimmer, *Altindisches Leben*, 86.

[4] xiv. 33, 26 (*khāḍga-kavaca aśvaratha*).

Khaṇḍika Audbhāri ('descendant of Udbhāra') is mentioned in the Śatapatha Brāhmaṇa[1] as a teacher of **Keśin**, and in the Maitrāyaṇī Saṃhitā[2] as having been defeated by Keśin as a sacrificer. A Khāṇḍika appears in the Baudhāyana Śrauta Sūtra[3] as an enemy of Keśin.

[1] xi. 8, 4, 1.

[2] i. 4, 12, where Ṣaṇḍika is the reading of the MSS.

[3] Caland, *Über das rituelle Sūtra des Baudhāyana*, 20.

Khadira is mentioned frequently from the Rigveda[1] onwards[2] as a tree with hard wood[3]—the *Acacia catechu*. The **Aśvattha** is referred to as engrafting itself upon it in the Atharvaveda,[4]

[1] iii. 53, 19.

[2] Av. iii. 6, 1; v. 5, 5; viii. 8, 3; x. 6, 6; Maitrāyaṇī Saṃhitā, iii. 9, 3, etc. So *khādira*, 'made of Khadira-wood,' Taittirīya Saṃhitā, iii. 5, 7, 1; Aitareya Brāhmaṇa, ii. 1; Śatapatha Brāhmaṇa, i. 3, 3, 20; iii. 6, 2, 12, etc.

[3] Av. x. 6, 6.

[4] iii. 6, 1. *Cf.* viii. 8, 3.

and from it the climbing plant **Arundhatī** is said to have sprung.[5] The *sruva* or sacrificial ladle is spoken of as having been made from it,[6] no doubt because of its hardness. It is in the same passage also said to have sprung from the sap (*rasa*) of the Gāyatrī. There is no clear reference to Catechu having been prepared from its core,[7] as it was later. The core (*sāra*) was used for making amulets.[8]

5 Av. v. 5, 5.
6 Taittirīya Saṃhitā, iii. 5, 7, 1.
7 It is called *bahu-sāra*, 'of great strength,' in the Śatapatha Brāhmaṇa, xiii. 4, 4, 9.
8 Śāṅkhāyana Āraṇyaka, xii. 8.
Cf. Zimmer, *Altindisches Leben*, 58, 58.

Kha-dyota ('sky-illuminator'), 'the firefly,' is mentioned in the Chāndogya Upaniṣad (vi. 7, 3. 5).

Khanitra, a 'shovel' or 'spade' for digging, is mentioned in the Rigveda[1] and later.[2]

1 i. 179, 6 (possibly metaphorical: see Oldenberg, *Ṛgveda-Noten*, 1, 172; the passage is obscure).
2 Lāṭyāyana Śrauta Sūtra, viii. 2, 4, etc.

Khanitrima, 'produced by digging,' as an epithet of *āpaḥ*, 'waters,' clearly refers to artificial water channels used for irrigation, as practised in the times of the Rigveda[1] and the Atharvaveda.[2]

1 vii. 49, 2.
2 i. 6, 4; xix. 2, 2.
Cf. Zimmer, *Altindisches Leben*, 236; Muir, *Sanskrit Texts*, 5, 466.

Khara, 'ass,' is mentioned in the Aitareya Āraṇyaka,[1] where a team of asses is alluded to. Probably the passages in the Śatapatha Brāhmaṇa,[2] where the word is used to denote an earth mound on which the sacrificial vessels were placed, presuppose the sense of 'ass,' the mound being shaped in this form.[3]

1 iii. 2, 4.
2 v. 1, 2, 15; xiv. 1, 2, 17; 2, 2, 30.
3 *Cf.* St. Petersburg Dictionary, *s.v.*

Khargalā is an 'owl' or other nocturnal bird mentioned in one passage of the Rigveda.[1]

[1] vii. 104, 17. *Cf.* Kauśika Sūtra, 107; Zimmer, *Altindisches Leben*, 93.

Kharjūra is the name of a tree (*Phœnix silvestris*) which is mentioned in the Yajurveda.[1]

[1] Taittirīya Saṃhitā, ii. 4, 9, 2; Kāṭhaka Saṃhitā, xi. 10; xxxvi. 7. *Cf.* Zimmer, *Altindisches Leben*, 63.

Khala, the 'threshing-floor,' is mentioned in the Rigveda[1] and the Atharvaveda.[2] See **Kṛṣi**.

[1] x. 48, 7; Nirukta, iii. 10.
[2] xi. 3, 9; *khala-ja*, 'produced on a threshing-floor,' viii. 6, 15; *khalya*, 'being on a threshing-floor,' Maitrāyaṇī Saṃhitā, ii. 9, 6.
Cf. Zimmer, *Altindisches Leben*, 238.

Khala-kula is a word occurring in the Bṛhadāraṇyaka Upaniṣad,[1] where Sāyaṇa glosses it by Kulattha, a kind of pulse (*Dolichos uniflorus*).

[1] vi. 3, 22 (Mādhyaṃdina = vi. 3, 13 Kāṇva). *Cf.* Weber, *Indische Studien*, 1, 355.

Khalva is some sort of grain or leguminous plant, perhaps, as Weber[1] thinks, the *Phaselus radiatus*. It is mentioned with other grains of all sorts in the Vājasaneyi Saṃhitā,[2] and as being crushed with the **Dṛṣad** in the Atharvaveda.[3] It occurs also in the Bṛhadāraṇyaka Upaniṣad,[4] where Śaṅkara glosses it with *niṣpāva*.

[1] *Indische Studien*, 1, 355.
[2] xviii. 12, where Mahīdhara glosses it by *caṇaka*, 'chick-pea.'
[3] ii. 31, 1; v. 23, 8.
[4] vi. 3, 22 (Mādhyaṃdina = vi. 3, 13 Kāṇva).
Cf. Zimmer, *Altindisches Leben*, 241.

Khāṇḍava is mentioned in the Taittirīya Āraṇyaka[1] as one of the boundaries of **Kurukṣetra**. There seems no reason to doubt its identity with the famous Khāṇḍava forest of the Mahābhārata. The name occurs also in the Pañcaviṃśa Brāhmaṇa[2] and the Śāṭyāyanaka.[3]

[1] v. 1, 1.
[2] xxv. 3, 6.
[3] Max Müller, *Ṛgveda*,[2] iv, ci.
Cf. Weber, *Indische Studien*, 1, 78.

Khādi occurs frequently in the Rigveda denoting either anklets[1] or armlets,[2] or sometimes rings on the hands.[3] Max Müller[4] considers that the word means quoits, the later Cakra.[5] The rings were sometimes of gold.[6]

[1] v. 54, 11, and perhaps 53, 4.

[2] This is what Khādis on the shoulders must mean, i. 166, 9; vii. 56, 13.

[3] i. 168, 3; *khādi-hasta*, 'with rings on the hands,' 5, 58, 2. So Roth takes Khādin in vi. 16, 40; St. Petersburg Dictionary, *s.v.* Khādin occurs also in ii. 34, 2; x. 38, 1.

[4] *Sacred Books of the East*, 32, 120, 230.

[5] *Cf. vṛṣa-khādi*, Rv. i. 64, 10.

[6] *Hiraṇya-khādi*, Śāṅkhāyana Śrauta Sūtra, iii. 5, 12; viii. 23, 6.

Cf. Zimmer, *Altindisches Leben*, 262; Muir, *Sanskrit Texts*, 5, 149.

Khārī designates a measure of Soma in one passage of the Rigveda.[1]

[1] iv. 32, 17. *Cf.* Zimmer, *Altindisches Leben*, 280.

Khārgali, 'descendant of Khargalā or Khṛgala,' is the metronymic or patronymic of Luśākapi.[1]

[1] Kāṭhaka Saṃhitā, xxx. 2; Pañcaviṃśa Brāhmaṇa, xvii. 4, 3.

1. **Khila**,[1] **Khilya**[2] appear to have the same meaning. According to Roth,[3] these terms denote the waste land lying between cultivated fields; but he admits that this sense does not suit the passage of the Rigveda[4] in which it is said that the god places the worshipper on an unbroken Khilya (*abhinne khilye*), and he accordingly conjectures the reading *akhilya-bhinne*, 'land unbroken by barren strips.' Pischel[5] thinks that the meaning intended is broad lands, which were used for the pasturing of the cattle of the community, and were not broken up by cultivated fields. Oldenberg,[6] however, points out that the sense is rather the land which lay between cultivated fields, but which need not be deemed to have been unfertile, as Roth thought. This agrees with the fact that in Vedic times separate fields were already known: see **Kṣetra.**

[1] Av. vii. 115, 4; Śatapatha Brāhmaṇa, viii. 3, 4, 1.

[2] Rv. vi. 28, 2; x. 142, 3.

[3] St. Petersburg Dictionary, *s.v.* So Whitney on Av., *loc. cit.*

[4] vi. 28, 2.

[5] *Vedische Studien*, 2, 205.

[6] *Ṛgveda-Noten*, 1, 385, 386.

Cf. Zimmer, *Altindisches Leben*, 236; Ludwig, Translation of the Rigveda, 3, 499; Keith, *Journal of the Royal Asiatic Society*, 1910, 228.

2. **Khila** as a designation of certain hymns appended to the received text of the Rigveda occurs only in the Sūtra period.[1] The term is a metaphorical application of the preceding word, 'a space not filled up,' 'a supplement.'

[1] See Scheftelowitz, *Die Apokryphen des Ṛgveda*, 16 *et seq.*

Khṛgala, or, as the Paippalāda recension of the Atharvaveda[1] has it, Khugila, is an obscure expression found in two passages only—once in the Rigveda,[2] and once in the Atharvaveda.[1] In the former the meaning 'crutch' seems required; in the latter Sāyaṇa glosses it by 'armour' (*tanu-trāṇa*), but the sense is quite uncertain.

[1] iii. 9, 3.
[2] ii. 39, 4.
Cf. Bloomfield, *Hymns of the Atharvaveda*, 340; Whitney, Translation of the Atharvaveda, 98.

Khela occurs in one passage of the Rigveda,[1] where Pischel[2] considers that a god, Vivasvant, is meant, and that races were run in his honour, explaining thus the phrase *ājā khelasya,* as 'in the race of Khela.' Roth[3] thinks that a man is meant, and Sieg,[4] following Sāyaṇa, sees in him a king whose Purohita was **Agastya.** See also **Aṃśu.**

[1] i. 116, 15.
[2] *Vedische Studien*, 1, 171-173.
[3] St. Petersburg Dictionary, *s.v.*
[4] *Die Sagenstoffe des Ṛgveda*, 127, 128.
Cf. Ludwig, Translation of the Rigveda, 4, 28.

G.

Gaṅgā, the modern Ganges, is mentioned directly in the Rigveda only once, in the Nadī-stuti or 'Praise of Rivers.'[1] But it is also referred to in the derivative form *gāṅgyaḥ* as an epithet of **Urukakṣa.**[3] The name of this river does not occur

[1] x. 75, 5.
[2] vi. 45, 31.
[3] The reference to the Gaṅgā remains, even if with Oldenberg (*Ṛgveda-Noten*, 1, 396) we assume that a thicket is meant, and not a proper name (*cf.* Wackernagel, *Altindische Grammatik*, 2, 288). See also Weber, Proceedings of the Berlin Academy, 1898, 563, n. 1.

in the other Saṃhitās, but appears in the Śatapatha Brāhmaṇa,[4] where victories of **Bharata Dauḥṣanti** on both Gaṅgā and **Yamunā** are referred to, and in the Taittirīya Āraṇyaka[5] especial honour is assigned to those who dwell between the Gaṅgā and the Yamunā, this being, no doubt, the region in which that text originated. The identification of the Gaṅgā with the Apayā[6] made by Ludwig[7] must be rejected: see **Āpayā.**

[4] xiii. 5, 4, 11. The victory on the Gaṅgā represents the farthest extent of Bharata or Kuru rule. *Cf.* Aitareya Brāhmaṇa, viii. 23, and a verse in the Vaitāna Sūtra, xxxiv. 9, where the Sarasvatī is also referred to.

[5] ii. 20.

[6] Rv. iii. 23, 4.

[7] Translation of the Rigveda, 3, 200.

Cf. Zimmer, *Altindisches Leben*, 4, 5.

Gaja, the common name of the elephant in Epic[1] and later Sanskrit, is only found in the late Adbhuta Brāhmaṇa.[2] See **Hastin.**

[1] Hopkins, *Journal of the American Oriental Society*, 13, 265, 269.

[2] *Indische Studien*, 1, 39.

Gaṇaka, 'an astrologer,' occurs in the list of victims at the Puruṣamedha, or human sacrifice, in the Yajurveda.[1] See also **Nakṣatradarśa.**

[1] Vājasaneyi Saṃhitā, xxx. 20; Taittirīya Brāhmaṇa, iii. 4, 15, 1. *Cf.* Weber, *Indische Streifen*, 1, 78.

Gandharvāyaṇa Bāleya ('descendant of Bali') **Āgniveśya** is mentioned as a Pañcāla in the Baudhāyana Śrauta Sūtra (xx. 25).

Gandhāra is a later form of the name of the people called **Gandhāri** in the Rigveda and Atharvaveda. In the Chāndogya Upaniṣad[1] the Gandhāras are referred to as being distant from the writer. See also **Gāndhāra.**

[1] vi. 14, 1. 2. See Oldenberg, *Buddha*, 399, n.; Weber, *Indische Studien*, 1, 219, n. On the other hand, Max Müller, *Sacred Books of the East*, 15, 106, thought the passage meant that the Gandhāras were near the writer.

Gandhāri is the name of a people in the north-west of India. In the Rigveda[1] the good wool of the sheep of the Gandhāris is referred to. The Gandhāris are also mentioned with the **Mūjavants, Angas,** and **Magadhas** in the Atharvaveda.[2] Gandhāris[3] or Gāndhāris[4] are also spoken of in the Śrauta Sūtras.[5] *Zimmer*[6] considers that they were settled in Vedic times on the south bank of the **Kubhā** up to its mouth in the Indus, and for some distance down the east side of the Indus itself. They later formed a portion of the Persian empire, and detachments of Gandarians accompanied Xerxes in his expedition against Greece.[7]

1 i. 126, 7.

2 v. 22, 14. The latter two tribes are apparently the Eastern limit of the poet's knowledge, the two former the Northern.

3 Hiraṇyakeśi Śrauta Sūtra, xvii. 6; Āpastamba Śrauta Sūtra, xxii. 6, 18.

4 Baudhāyana Śrauta Sūtra, xxi. 13.

5 See Caland, *Zeitschrift der Deutschen Morgenländischen Gesellschaft*, 56, 553.

6 *Altindisches Leben*, 30, 31.

7 Keith, *Aitareya Āraṇyaka*, 23. *Cf.* Ludwig, Translation of the Rigveda, 3, 206.

Gabhasti denotes, according to Roth,[1] the pole of a chariot in the epithet *syūma-gabhasti*, 'having reins as a pole,' used of the car of the gods in the Rigveda,[2] and independently in the plural in the Taittirīya Brāhmaṇa.[3] The meaning is, however, doubtful.[4] Roth[5] himself suggests that *syūma-gabhasti* may refer to a sort of double reins.

1 St. Petersburg Dictionary, *s.v.*

2 i. 122, 5; vii. 71, 3.

3 ii. 7, 13, 4.

4 See Oldenberg, *Ṛgveda-Noten*, 1, 55.

5 *Op. cit.*, *s.v.*

1. **Gaya,** 'house,' is a common word in the Rigveda,[1] and sometimes occurs later.[2] As its sense includes the inmates as well as their belongings, it is equivalent to 'household.'

1 i. 74, 2; v. 10, 3; 44, 7; vi. 2, 8, etc.

2 Av. vi. 3, 3; 84, 1; Vājasaneyi Saṃhitā, xxvii. 3.

2. **Gaya Plāta** ('son of Plati') is referred to in the Rigveda,[1] two hymns of which he clearly claims to have composed, and which are attributed to him in the Sarvānukramaṇī and the

1 x. 63, 17; 64, 17 (as son of Plati).

Aitareya Brāhmaṇa.[2] In the Atharvaveda[3] he appears with **Asita** and **Kaśyapa** as a half-mythical magician.[4]

[2] v. 2.

[3] i. 14, 4. *Cf.* also the Khila after Rv. v. 51, 15; *Indische Studien*, 3, 214.

[4] Bloomfield, *American Journal of Philology*, 17, 403.

Cf. Ludwig, Translation of the Rigveda, 3, 133; Weber, *Indische Studien*, 3, 460.

1. **Gara,** 'poison,' is referred to in the Atharvaveda[1] in the compound *gara-gīrṇa*, 'poisoned.' In the Śatapatha Brāhmaṇa[2] it means simply a 'fluid.'

[1] v. 18, 13. *Cf. gara* alone, Pañcaviṃśa Brāhmaṇa, xix. 4, 2 (see *Indische Studien*, 1, 33); Taittirīya Āraṇyaka, i. 9, 10; *gara-gir*, 'poisoned,' Pañcaviṃśa Brāhmaṇa, xvii. 1, 9; xix. 4, 2. 10.

[2] xi. 5, 8, 6.

2. **Gara** is mentioned in the Pañcaviṃśa Brāhmaṇa[1] as the author of a Sāman or Chant, and as a friend of Indra.

[1] ix. 2, 16. *Cf.* Hopkins, *Transactions of the Connecticut Academy of Arts and Sciences*, 15, 52.

Garga is the name of a sage who is not mentioned in any of the Saṃhitās,[1] but his descendants, the *Gargāḥ Prāvareyāḥ*, are referred to in the Kāṭhaka Saṃhitā.[2] Garga himself does not occur till the Sūtra period.[3]

[1] The authorship of Rv. vi. 47 is attributed to Garga Bhāradvāja in the Anukramaṇī.

[2] xiii. 12. *Cf.* Weber, *Indische Studien*, 3, 374

[3] Garga-trirātra, Garga-tryaha, a three-night or three-day feast of Garga. See Āśvalāyana Srauta Sūtra, x. 2; Śāṅkhāyana Śrauta Sūtra, xvi. 22, 2; Kātyāyana Śrauta Sūtra, xxiii. 2, 8.

Gargara, apparently the designation of a musical instrument, is mentioned once in the Rigveda.[1]

[1] viii. 69, 9. *Cf.* Hillebrandt, *Vedische Mythologie*, 1, 144, n. 1; Zimmer, *Altindisches Leben*, 289.

Garta in the Rigveda[1] primarily denotes the seat of the chariot on which the archer sat. It seems to have been of considerable

[1] vi. 20, 9. Zimmer, *Altindisches Leben*, 246, 247. Zimmer wrongly takes this passage to refer to standing in the car. See Hopkins, *Journal of the American Oriental Society*, 13, 238, 239; Geldner, *Vedische Studien*, 3, 48, and *cf. garta-sad*, 'sitting on the car seat,' in Rv. ii. 33, 11.

size, being described as *bṛhant*,[2] 'large.' The word then comes to denote the chariot[3] itself, either really or metaphorically.[4]

[2] v. 62, 8; 68, 5.

[3] So probably in v. 62, 5; *gartā-ruh*, 'mounting the chariot,' in Rv. i. 124, 7; Nirukta, iii. 5, may refer merely to mounting the seat. The passage is obscure; see Geldner, *Rigveda, Kommentar*, 22.

[4] vii. 64, 4 (of the hymn).

Gardabha, 'the ass,' is mentioned in the Rigveda[1] as inferior to the horse. In the Taittirīya Saṃhitā he again appears as inferior to the horse,[2] but at the same time as the best bearer of burdens (*bhāra-bhāritama*) among animals.[3] The same authority styles the ass *dvi-retas*, 'having double seed,'[4] in allusion to his breeding with the mare as well as the she-ass. The smallness of the young of the ass, and his capacity for eating, are both referred to.[5] The disagreeable cry of the animal is mentioned in the Atharvaveda,[6] and in allusion to this the term 'ass' is applied opprobriously to a singer in the Rigveda.[7] A hundred asses are spoken of as a gift to a singer in a Vālakhilya hymn.[8] The mule (*aśvatara*) is the offspring of an ass and a mare, the latter, like the ass, being called *dvi-retas*,[9] 'receiving double seed,' for similar reasons. The male ass is often also termed **Rāsabha.** The female ass, Gardabhī, is mentioned in the Atharvaveda[10] and the Bṛhadāraṇyaka Upaniṣad.[11]

[1] iii. 53, 23. A car drawn by asses is referred to in the Aitareya Brāhmaṇa, iv. 9; see also **Khara.**

[2] v. 1, 2, 1. 2.

[3] v. 1, 5, 5.

[4] v. 1, 5, 5; vii. 1, 1, 2; Jaiminīya Brāhmaṇa, i. 57, 4 (Oertel, *Transactions of the Connecticut Academy of Arts and Sciences*, 15, 177-180): of the Rāsabha, Śatapatha Brāhmaṇa, vi. 3, 1, 23.

[5] Taittirīya Saṃhitā, v. 1, 5, 5.

[6] viii. 6, 10.

[7] i. 29, 5.

[8] viii. 56, 3.

[9] Taittirīya Saṃhitā, vii. 1, 1, 2. 3; Pañcaviṃśa Brāhmaṇa, vi. 1, 6; Jaiminīya Brāhmaṇa, i. 57, 4.

[10] x. 1, 4.

[11] i. 4, 8. For other references to the ass as Gardabha, see Av. v. 31, 3; Aitareya Brāhmaṇa, iii. 34; Śatapatha Brāhmaṇa, iv. 5, 1, 9; xii. 7, 1, 5.

Cf. Zimmer, *Altindisches Leben*, 232, 233.

Gardabhī-mukha is mentioned as a teacher in the Vaṃśa Brāhmaṇa.[1]

[1] *Indische Studien*, 4, 384.

Gardabhī-vipīta, or **Gardabhī-vibhīta,** is the name of a teacher who was a Bhāradvāja and a contemporary of **Janaka,** mentioned in the Bṛhadāraṇyaka Upaniṣad.

[1] iv. 1, 11 (Mādhyaṃdina=iv. 1, 5 Kāṇva).

Garmut is the name of a kind of wild bean mentioned in the Taittirīya Saṃhitā.[1] The Kāṭhaka Saṃhitā[2] has the form Ganmut, which is probably a false reading. The adjective *gārmuta,* 'made from the Garmut bean,' is found in the Maitrāyaṇī Saṃhitā.[3]

[1] ii. 4, 4, 1. 2.
[2] x. 11.
[3] ii. 2, 4.

Cf. St. Petersburg Dictionary, *s.v.;* Zimmer, *Altindisches Leben*, 71.

Galunta is a word occurring only once in the Atharvaveda,[1] apparently in the sense of 'swelling,'[2] but Whitney[3] translates it by 'neck.'

[1] vi. 83, 3.
[2] Bloomfield, *Proceedings of the American Oriental Society*, October, 1887, xvi; *Hymns of the Atharvaveda*, 505.
[3] Translation of the Atharvaveda, 343.

Galūnasa Ārkṣākāyaṇa ('descendant of Ṛkṣāka') is mentioned as a teacher in the Jaiminīya Upaniṣad Brāhmaṇa (i. 38, 4).

Gavaya, the name of a species of ox (*Bos gavaeus*) occurs frequently from the Rigveda[1] onwards.[2] It is mentioned with **Gaura** and **Mahiṣa** in the Vājasaneyi Saṃhitā,[3] where also a wild Gavaya is spoken of.[4]

[1] iv. 21, 8.
[2] Maitrāyaṇī Saṃhitā, iii. 14, 10; Kāṭhaka Saṃhitā, xvi. 17; Vājasaneyi Saṃhitā, xxiv. 28; Aitareya Brāhmaṇa, ii. 8; iii. 34; Śatapatha Brāhmaṇa, i. 2, 3, 9; Śāṅkhāyana Śrauta Sūtra, xvi. 3, 14, etc.
[3] xxiv. 28.
[4] xiii. 49; Taittirīya Saṃhitā, iv. 2, 10, 3; Maitrāyaṇī Saṃhitā, ii. 7, 17; Kāṭhaka Saṃhitā, xvi. 17.

Cf. Zimmer, *Altindisches Leben*, 83, 84.

Gavāśir, 'mixed with milk,' is a frequent epithet of **Soma** in the Rigveda.[1]

[1] i. 137, 1; 187, 9; ii. 41, 3; iii. 32, 2; 42, 1. 7; viii. 52, 10; 101, 10. *Cf.* Zimmer, *Altindisches Leben*, 279.

Gav-iṣṭi (lit. 'desire of cows') in several passages of the Rigveda[1] denotes 'conflict' or 'battle,' evidently with reference to cattle raids. Gavyā[2] is similarly used.

[1] i. 91, 23; iii. 47, 4; v. 63, 5; vi. 31, 3; 47, 20; 59, 7; viii. 24, 2; ix. 76, 2. So Av. iv. 24, 5.
[2] Rv. vii. 18, 7.

Gavi-ṣṭhira Ātreya ('descendant of **Atri**') is mentioned as a **Ṛṣi**, or seer, in the Rigveda[1] and the Atharvaveda.[2]

[1] v. 1, 12; x. 150, 5.
[2] iv. 29, 5. See also Āśvalāyana Srauta Sūtra, xii. 14, ᵛ.

Cf. Ludwig, Translation of the Rigveda, 3, 126.

Gavīdhukā,[1] **Gavedhukā,**[2] is the name of a species of grass (*Coix barbata*). It is also referred to in the adjectival forms *gāvīdhuka*[3] and *gāvedhuka*.[4] It was boiled with rice[5] (*gavīdhukā-yavāgū*) or barley[6] (*gavedhukā-saktavaḥ*) in preparing gruel.

[1] Taittirīya Saṃhitā, v. 4, 3, 2.
[2] Śatapatha Brāhmaṇa, v. 2, 4, 13; 3, 1, 10; xiv. 1, 2, 19.
[3] Taittirīya Saṃhitā, i. 8, 7, 1; 9, 2; Taittirīya Brāhmaṇa, i. 7, 3, 6; Maitrāyaṇī Saṃhitā, ii. 6, 5; iv. 3, 8; Vājasaneyi Saṃhitā, xv. 5.
[4] Śatapatha Brāhmaṇa, v. 2, 4, 11. 13; 3, 1, 10; 3, 7.
[5] Taittirīya Saṃhitā, v. 4, 3, 2.
[6] Śatapatha Brāhmaṇa, ix. 1, 1, 8.

Gavya. See **Gavyūti.**

Gavyā. See **Gaviṣṭi.**

Gavyūti in the Rigveda[1] means, according to Roth,[2] grass land for the pasturing of cattle, in which sense Gavya is also found.[3] Thence it derives the sense of a measure of distance found in the Pañcaviṃśa Brāhmaṇa.[4] Geldner, on the other hand, takes the original meaning to be 'road,' real[6] or metaphorical,[7] thence a measure of distance,[8] and finally 'land.'[9]

[1] i. 25, 16; iii. 62, 16; v. 66, 3; vii. 77, 4, etc.
[2] St. Petersburg Dictionary, *s.v.*
[3] Aitareya Brāhmaṇa, iv. 28; St. Petersburg Dictionary, *s.v.* 3b.
[4] Pañcaviṃśa Brāhmaṇa, xvi. 13, 12.
[5] *Vedische Studien*, 2, 290, 291.
[6] Rv. i. 25, 16.
[7] Rv. vi. 47, 20; x. 14, 2.
[8] Rv. viii. 60, 20, and n. 4.
[9] Rv. iii. 62, 16; vii. 62, 5; 65, 4; viii. 5, 6.

Gāṅgya, 'being on the Ganges,' is the epithet of **Urukakṣa**[1] or of a thicket[2] in the Rigveda.[3]

[1] Roth, St. Petersburg Dictionary, *s.v.* *Cf.* Wackernagel, *Altindische Grammatik*, 2, 288; Weber, *Episches im vedischen Ritual*, 28.

[2] Oldenberg, *Ṛgveda-Noten*, 1, 398.

[3] vi. 45, 31.

Cf. Weber, *Indische Studien*, 2, 291, n.

Gāṅgyāyani, 'descendant of Gāṅgya,' occurs as the patronymic of **Citra** in the Kauṣītaki Upaniṣad.[1]

[1] i. 1. There is a *v.l.* Gārgyāyaṇi. *Cf.* Weber, *Indische Studien*, 1, 395.

Gātu. See **Gāthā**.

Gāthā in the Rigveda[1] usually means only 'song,' 'verse,' like Gātu.[2] In one passage,[3] however, it already has a more special sense, as it is classed with **Nārāśaṃsī** and **Raibhī**, a collocation repeatedly found later.[4] The commentators identify the three terms with certain verses of the Atharvaveda,[5] but Oldenberg[6] has shown that this identification is incorrect for the Rigveda. Gāthās are often mentioned elsewhere,[7] and are referred to as metrical in the Aitareya Āraṇyaka,[8] where the **Ṛc**, **Kumbyā**, and Gāthā are classed as forms of verse. The Aitareya Brāhmaṇa[9] distinguishes between Ṛc and Gāthā as divine and human respectively. According to the usage of the

[1] viii. 32, 1; 71, 14; 98, 9; ix. 99, 4; *gātha*, i. 167, 6; ix. 11, 4; *gātha-pati*, 'lord of song,' i. 43, 4; *gāthā-nī*, 'leading a song,' i. 190, 1; viii. 92, 2; *ṛju-gātha*, 'singing correctly,' v. 44, 5; *gāthin*, 'singer,' i. 7, 1. *Cf.* Hopkins, *Journal of the American Oriental Society*, 17, 65.

[2] i. 151, 2; ii. 20, 5; iii. 4, 4; iv. 4, 6; v. 87, 8; x. 20, 4; 122, 2.

[3] x. 85, 6.

[4] Taittirīya Saṃhitā, vii. 5, 11, 2; Kāṭhaka Saṃhitā, Aśvamedha, v. 2; Aitareya Brāhmaṇa, vi. 32; Kauṣītaki Brāhmaṇa, xxx. 5; Śatapatha Brāhmaṇa, xi. 5, 6, 8, where Raibhī does not occur; Gopatha Brāhmaṇa, ii. 6, 12.

[5] Viz., Gāthā = Av. xx. 127, 12 *et seq.*; Nārāśaṃsī = Av. xx. 127, 1-3; Raibhī = Av. xx. 127, 4-6; while *ibid.*, 7-10, are known as Pārikṣityaḥ (*scil.*, *ṛcaḥ*).

[6] *Zeitschrift der Deutschen Morgenländischen Gesellschaft*, 42, 238. Bloomfield, *Hymns of the Atharvaveda*, 689 *et seq.*, seems to accept the identification even for the Rigveda.

[7] Av. x. 10, 20; xv. 6, 4 (distinct from Nārāśaṃsī); Śatapatha Brāhmaṇa, iii. 2, 4, 16; xi. 5, 7, 10; xiii. 1, 5, 6; 4, 2, 8; 5, 4, 2; Taittirīya Āraṇyaka, ii. 10 (distinct from Nārāśaṃsī); Chāndogya Upaniṣad, iv. 17, 9, etc.

[8] ii. 3, 6, with Keith's note; Śatapatha Brāhmaṇa, xi. 5, 7, 10.

[9] vii. 18. The story of Śunaḥśepa is described as *śata-gātham*, 'told in a hundred Gāthās.'

Brāhmaṇas and the liturgical literature, as stated by the St. Petersburg Dictionary, the Gāthās are, though religious in content, distinguished from Ṛc, Yajus, and Sāman as non-Vedic—that is, are not Mantras. This view is consistent with the fact that the phrase **Yajña-gāthā**, meaning a verse summarizing a sacrificial usage, is not rare. The Śatapatha Brāhmaṇa[10] preserves several Gāthās, which generally accord with this description as epitomizing the sacrifices of famous kings, and the Maitrāyaṇī Saṃhitā[11] states that a Gāthā is sung at a wedding. Sometimes[12] Gāthā is qualified as **Nārāśaṃsī**, where it must be a eulogy of a generous donor.

[10] xiii. 5, 4, etc., and see xiii. 4, 2, 8, where the Gāthās are plainly Dānastutis, or 'praises of gifts,' just as the Nārāśaṃsī verses are declared to be in the Bṛhaddevatā, iii. 154.

[11] iii. 7, 3.

[12] Taittirīya Brāhmaṇa, i. 3, 2, 6. So Eggeling, *Sacred Books of the East*, 44, 98, takes Śatapatha Brāhmaṇa, xi. 5, 6, 8, where Sāyaṇa hesitates between identifying the two and distinguishing them. It seems reasonable to regard Gāthā as the wider term which covers, but is not coextensive with, Nārāśaṃsī. *Cf.* Sāyaṇa's example of a Gāthā in his commentary on Aitareya Āraṇyaka, ii. 3, 6: *prātaḥ prātar anṛtaṃ te vadanti*, 'they every morning tell an untruth,' which is clearly not a Nārāśaṃsī.

Cf. Bloomfield, *Hymns of the Atharvaveda*, 689 *et seq.*; Weber, *Episches im Vedischen Ritual*, 4 *et seq.*; Max Müller, *Ancient Sanskrit Literature*, 493.

Gāthin is mentioned as the son of **Kuśika** and father of **Viśvāmitra** in the Sarvānukramaṇī. It is difficult to say whether this tradition is correct; it derives some support from the Aitareya Brāhmaṇa (vii. 18), where reference is made to the divine lore (*daiva veda*) of the Gāthins, which is said to be shared by **Śunaḥśepa** as a result of his adoption by **Viśvāmitra**. See **Gāthina**.

Gāthina.—The sons of Viśvāmitra are described in the Aitareya Brāhmaṇa[1] as Gāthinas, or descendants of Gāthin, who, according to tradition, was their grandfather;[2] and **Viśvāmitra** himself is styled Gāthina in the Sarvānukramaṇī.

[1] vii. 18. *Cf.* Āśvalāyana Śrauta Sūtra, vii. 18; Weber, *Episches im Vedischen Ritual*, 16, n. 3.

[2] *Cf.* Muir, *Sanskrit Texts*, 1^2, 348 *et seq.*; Pargiter, *Journal of the Royal Asiatic Society*, 1910, 32 *et seq.*

Gāṃ-dama is the form in the Pañcaviṃśa Brāhmaṇa[1] of the name of **Ekayāvan,** which in the Taittirīya Brāhmaṇa[2] is read as Kāṃdama.

[1] xxi. 14, 20.
[2] ii. 7, 11, 2. *Cf.* Hopkins, *Transactions of the Connecticut Academy of Arts and Sciences*, 15, 69.

Gāndhāra, 'a king of Gandhāra' named **Nagnajit,** is mentioned in the Aitareya Brāhmaṇa.[1] In the Śatapatha Brāhmaṇa[2] he or some descendant figures as **Svarjit Nāgnajita** or Nagnajit, and as giving an opinion on the ritual, which is rejected with the observation that the author was merely a princely person (*rājanya-bandhu*).

[1] vii. 34. in the list of teachers who handed down the knowledge of the substitute for Soma.
[2] viii. 1, 4, 10.

Gārgī Vācaknavī is referred to in the Bṛhadāraṇyaka Upaniṣad[1] as a female contemporary and rival of **Yājñavalkya.**

[1] iii. 6, 1; 8, 1. *Cf.* Weber, *Indische Studien*, 10, 118.

Gārgī-putra, 'son of Gargī,' occurs as the name of three teachers in the last Vaṃśa (list of teachers) in the Mādhyaṃdina recension of the Bṛhadāraṇyaka Upaniṣad (vi. 4, 30). The earliest of these three was the pupil of **Bāḍeyīputra** and the teacher of the second Gārgīputra. The latter was the teacher of **Pārāśarīkauṇḍinīputra,** the teacher of the third Gārgīputra.

Gārgya, 'descendant of Garga,' is the patronymic of **Bālāki** in the Bṛhadāraṇyaka[1] and the Kauṣītaki[2] Upaniṣads. Two Gārgyas are mentioned in the second Vaṃśa (list of teachers) in the Bṛhadāraṇyaka Upaniṣad[3]: one of them is the pupil of Gārgya, who again is the pupil of Gautama. Others occur in the Taittirīya Āraṇyaka[4] and in the Nirukta,[5] as well as later in the ritual Sūtras. Thus the family was evidently long connected with the development of liturgy and grammar.

[1] ii. 1, 1.
[2] iv. 1.
[3] iv. 6, 2 (Kāṇva).
[4] i. 7, 3.
[5] i. 3. 12; iii. 13.

Gārgyāyaṇa, 'descendant of Gārgya,' is mentioned as a pupil of **Uddālakāyana** in the second Vaṃśa (list of teachers) in the Bṛhadāraṇyaka Upaniṣad (iv. 6, 2 Kāṇva).

Gārgyāyaṇi, 'descendant of Gārgya,' is a variant reading for **Gāṅgyāyani** as the patronymic of **Citra** in the Kauṣītaki Upaniṣad (i. 1).

Gālava is mentioned as a pupil of **Vidarbhīkauṇḍinya** in the first two Vaṃśas (lists of teachers) in the Bṛhadāraṇyaka Upaniṣad.[1] It is possibly the same man that is referred to regarding a point of ritual in the Aitareya Āraṇyaka.[2] A grammarian of this name is mentioned in the Nirukta.[3]

1 ii. 5, 22; iv. 5, 28 (Mādhyaṃdina = ii. 6, 3; iv. 6, 3 Kāṇva).
2 v. 3, 3.
3 iv. 3. *Cf.* Pāṇini, vi. 3. 61; vii. 1, 74; 3. 99; viii. 4, 67.

Giri, 'mountain' or 'height,' is a word that occurs repeatedly in the Rigveda.[1] Thus reference is made to the trees on the hills, hence called 'tree-haired' (*vṛkṣa-keśāḥ*),[2] and to the streams proceeding from the hills to the sea (*samudra*).[3] The term is frequently coupled with the adjectival *parvata*.[4] The Rigveda mentions the waters from the hills,[5] and the Atharvaveda[6] refers to the snowy mountains. Actual names of mountains, as **Mūjavant, Trikakud, Himavant**, are very rare. References to **Krauñca, Mahāmeru**, and **Maināga**, are confined to the Taittirīya Āraṇyaka, while **Nāvaprabhraṃśana** can no longer be considered a proper name.[7]

1 i. 56, 3; 61, 14; 63, 1; iv. 20, 6; vi. 24, 8, etc.
2 Rv. v. 41, 11.
3 Rv. vii. 95, 2.
4 Rv. i. 56, 4; viii. 64, 5; Av. iv. 7, 8; vi. 12, 3; 17, 3; ix. 1, 18, etc.
5 Rv. vi. 66, 11, on which passage, see Oldenberg, *Ṛgveda-Noten*, 1, 411; viii. 32, 4; x. 68, 1, etc.
6 xii. 1, 11. See **Himavant**.
7 Av. xix. 37, 8, with Whitney's note in his Translation; Macdonell, *Journal of the Royal Asiatic Society* 1909, 1107. *Cf.* Zimmer, *Altindisches Leben*, 47.

Giri-kṣit Auccā-manyava, 'descendant of Uccāmanyu,' is mentioned in the Pañcaviṃśa Brāhmaṇa (x. 5, 7) as a contemporary of **Abhipratārin Kākṣaseni**.

Giri-ja Bābhravya, 'descendant of Babhru,' is mentioned in the Aitareya Brāhmaṇa (vii. 1) as having been taught by **Śrauta** the method of dividing the sacrificial animal (*paśor vibhakti*).

Guggulu, 'bdellium,' is referred to in one passage of the Atharvaveda[1] as produced by the Sindhu[2] and by the sea. The latter source presumably alludes, as Zimmer[3] assumes, to sea-borne trade, bdellium being the gum of a tree, not a product of the sea. It is, however, possible that in this passage some other substance may be meant. The word in this form also occurs elsewhere in the Atharvaveda[4] and later;[5] it is often[6] mentioned in the older form of **Gulgulu**, between which and Guggulu the manuscripts constantly vary.

[1] xix. 38, 2.

[2] Or 'from streams' (*saindhava*), as Roth, St. Petersburg Dictionary, *s.v. guggulu*, suggests.

[3] *Altindisches Leben*, 28.

[4] ii. 36, 7.

[5] Aitareya Brāhmaṇa, i. 28.

[6] Taittirīya Saṃhitā, vi. 2, 8, 6; Maitrāyaṇī Saṃhitā, iii. 8, 5; Pañcaviṃśa Brāhmaṇa, xxiv. 13; Śatapatha Brāhmaṇa, iii. 5, 2, 16.

Cf. Bloomfield, *Hymns of the Atharvaveda*, 675; Lassen, *Indische Alterthumskunde*, 1^2, 339; Whitney, Translation of the Atharvaveda, 957, 958.

Guṅgu.—The descendants of Guṅgu are referred to as Guṅgus in a hymn of the Rigveda,[1] apparently as friends of **Atithigva**. Possibly a people may be meant.

[1] x. 48, 8. *Cf.* Ludwig, Translation of the Rigveda, 3, 165.

Gupta is the name in the Jaiminīya Upaniṣad Brāhmaṇa (iii. 42) of **Vaipaścita Dārḍhajayanti Gupta Lauhitya.** All the three other names being patronymics show that he was descended from the families of Vipaścit, Dṛḍhajayanta, and Lohita.

Gulgulu. See **Guggulu.**

Gṛtsa-mada is the name of a seer to whom the Sarvānukramaṇī attributes the authorship of the second Maṇḍala of the Rigveda. This tradition is supported by the Aitareya Brāhmaṇa[1] and the Aitareya Āraṇyaka.[2] The Kauṣītaki Brāhmaṇa[3] speaks of him as a **Bhārgava**, 'descendant of Bhṛgu,' with a variant **Bābhrava**, 'descendant of Babhru,' but the later tradition keeps to the former patronymic.[4] The Gṛtsamadas are often mentioned in the second Maṇḍala of the Rigveda,[5] and are also called Śunahotras,[6] but never Gārtsamadas or Śaunahotras, and Gṛtsamada himself never occurs there.[7]

[1] v. 2, 4.
[2] ii. 2, 1.
[3] xxii. 4. *Cf.* Gārtsamadī, xxviii. 2.
[4] Muir, *Sanskrit Texts*, 1², 226 *et seq.*
[5] ii. 4, 9; 19, 8; 39, 8; 41, 18.
[6] ii. 18, 6; 41, 14. 17.
[7] Oldenberg, *Zeitschrift der Deutschen Morgenländischen Gesellschaft*, 42, 200, 201.

Cf. Ludwig, Translation of the Rigveda, 3, 118; Hillebrandt, *Vedische Mythologie*, 3, 287.

Gṛdhra, 'the vulture,' is often mentioned from the Rigveda[1] downwards.[2] The swiftness of its flight[3] and its fondness for devouring carrion are especially noticed.[4] More generally the word is used to designate any bird of prey, the eagle (**Śyena**) being classed as the chief of the Gṛdhras.[5]

[1] i. 118, 4; ii. 39, 1; vii. 104, 22; x. 123, 8.
[2] Av. vii. 95, 1; xi. 2, 2; 9, 9; 10. 8. 24; Taittirīya Saṃhitā, iv. 4, 7, 1; v. 5, 20, 1; Maitrāyaṇī Saṃhitā, iv. 9, 19; Taittirīya Āraṇyaka, iv. 29; Adbhuta Brāhmaṇa in *Indische Studien*, 1, 40; etc.
[3] Rv. ii. 39, 1.
[4] Av. xi. 10, 8. 24; Maitrāyaṇī Saṃhitā, *loc. cit.*
[5] Rv. ix. 96, 6.

Cf. Zimmer, *Altindisches Leben*, 88; Hillebrandt, *Vedische Mythologie*, 1, 225.

Gṛṣṭi, 'a young cow,' which has only calved once, occurs in the Rigveda[1] and the Atharvaveda,[2] as well as in the later Sūtra literature.[3]

[1] iv. 18, 10.
[2] ii. 13, 3; viii. 9, 24; xix. 24, 5.
[3] Kauśika Sūtra, 19. 24, etc.

Gṛha is used in the singular,[1] or oftener in the plural,[2] to denote the 'house' of the Vedic Indian. **Dama** or **Dam** has

[1] Rv. iii. 53, 6; iv. 49, 6; viii. 10, 1, etc.; Av. vii. 83, 1; x. 6, 4; Aitareya Brāhmaṇa, viii. 21.
[2] Rv. ii. 42, 3; v. 76, 4; x. 18, 12; 85, 26; 142, 4; 165, 2; Av. i. 27, 4; iii. 10, 11; vi. 137, 1; Aitareya Brāhmaṇa, ii. 31; viii. 26; Vājasaneyi Saṃhitā, ii. 32; iv. 33; xviii. 44; Śatapatha Brāhmaṇa, i. 1, 2, 22; 6, 1, 19, etc.

the same sense, while **Pastyā** and **Harmya** denote more especially the home with its surroundings, the family settlement. The house held not only the family, which might be of considerable size, but also the cattle[3] and the sheep[4] at night. It was composed of several rooms, as the use of the plural indicates, and it could be securely shut up.[5] The door (**Dvār**, **Dvāra**) is often referred to, and from it the house is called **Duroṇa.** In every house the fire was kept burning.[6]

Very little is known of the structure of the house. Presumably stone was not used,[7] and houses were, as in Megasthenes' time,[8] built of wood. The hymns of the Atharvaveda[9] give some information about the construction of a house, but the details are extremely obscure, for most of the expressions used do not recur in any context in which their sense is clear. According to Zimmer,[10] four pillars (**Upamit**) were set up on a good site, and against them beams were leant at an angle as props (**Pratimit**). The upright pillars were connected by cross beams (**Parimit**) resting upon them. The roof was formed of ribs of bamboo cane (*vaṃśa*),[11] a ridge called **Viṣūvant,** and a net (**Akṣu**), which may mean a thatched covering[12] over the bamboo ribs. The walls were filled up with grass in bundles (*palada*), and the whole structure was held together with ties of

[3] Rv. vii. 56, 16; Av. i. 3, 4; ix. 3, 13.

[4] Rv. x. 106, 5; Av. iii. 3.

[5] Rv. vii. 85, 6.

[6] Rv. i. 69, 2. *Cf.* the Gārhapatya Agni, Av. v. 31, 5; vi. 120, 1; 121, 2; viii. 10[2]; ix. 6, 30; xii. 2, 34; xviii. 4, 8; Vājasaneyi Saṃhitā, iii. 39; xix. 18; Aitareya Brāhmaṇa, vii. 6. 12; Kauṣītaki Brāhmaṇa, ii. 1; Śatapatha Brāhmaṇa, iii. 6, 1, 28; vii. 1, 1, 6, etc.

[7] Zimmer, *Altindisches Leben*, 153. Muir's view, *Sanskrit Texts*, 5, 461, that clay was used can only apply to the minor finishing of the walls of a house.

[8] Arrian, *Indica*, x. 2.

[9] iii. 12; ix. 3. See Bloomfield, *Hymns of the Atharvaveda*, 343 *et seq.*; Weber, *Indische Studien*, 17, 234 *et seq.*; Whitney, Translation of the Atharvaveda, 525 *et seq.*

[10] *Op. cit.*, 153. No certainty can attach to the rendering of the words.

[11] It seems likely that, as the ribs were of bamboo and were probably fixed in the ridge, the roof was wagonheaded, like the huts of the Todas at the present day (see illustrations in Rivers, *The Todas*, pp. 25, 27, 28, 51), and the rock-cut Chaityas, or Assembly Halls, of the Buddhists in Western India, in some of the earliest of which the wooden ribs of the arched roof are still preserved. See Fergusson, *History of Indian Architecture*,[2] 2, 135, *cf.* 126.

[12] Av. ix. 3, 8, where Bloomfield, *op. cit.*, 598, thinks of a wickerwork roof; Geldner, *Vedische Studien*, 1, 136, of a pole with countless holes.

various sorts (*nahana, prāṇāha, saṃdaṃśa, pariṣvañjalya*).[13] In connexion with the house, mention is made of four terms which, though primarily sacrificial in meaning, seem to designate parts of the building: Havirdhāna, 'oblation-holder'; Agniśāla,[14] 'fire-place'; Patnīnāṃ Sadana, 'wives' room'; and Sadas, 'sitting room.' Slings or hanging vessels (**Śikya**) are also mentioned.[15] Reedwork (*iṭa*) is spoken of, no doubt as part of the finishing of the walls of the house.[16] The sides are called **Pakṣa**. The door with its framework was named **Ātā**.

[13] Av. ix. 3, 4. 5.

[14] Zimmer conjecturally identifies the Agniśāla with the central room, the Havirdhāna with a place for keeping the grain, etc. (*e.g.*, Av. iii. 3, 4), the Patnīnāṃ Sadana with the women's apartments, and the Sadas with the subsidiary buildings.

[15] Av. ix. 3, 6. See Whitney, *op. cit.*, 526; Bloomfield, *op. cit.*, 597.

[16] Av. ix. 3, 17.

Cf. Zimmer, *Altindisches Leben*, 148-156.

Gṛha-pa[1] or **Gṛha-pati**[2] is the regular name, from the Rigveda onwards, of the householder as master of the house. Similarly the mistress is called Gṛha-patnī.[3] For the powers and position of the Gṛhapati see **Pitṛ**.

[1] Vājasaneyi Saṃhitā, xxx. 11.

[2] Rv. vi. 53, 2; Av. xiv. 1, 51; xix. 31, 13; Śatapatha Brāhmaṇa, iv. 6, 8, 5; viii. 6, 1, 11, and repeatedly as an epithet of Agni, Rv. i. 12, 6; 36, 5; 60, 4; vi. 48, 8; Vājasaneyi Saṃhitā, ii. 27; iii. 39; ix. 39; xxiv. 24, etc.

[3] Rv. x. 85, 26; Av. iii. 24, 6. *Cf.* Gārhapatya, Rv. i. 15, 12; vi. 15, 19; x. 85, 27. 36.

Gṛhya denotes the members of the house or family in the Śatapatha Brāhmaṇa.

[1] ii. 5, 2, 14; 3, 16; 6, 2, 4; iii. 4, 1, 6; xii. 4, 1, 4. *Cf. gṛhāḥ*, i. 7, 4, 12.

Gairi-kṣita, 'descendant of **Girikṣit**,' is the patronymic of **Trasadasyu** in the Rigveda,[1] and of the **Yaskas** in the Kāṭhaka Saṃhitā.[2]

[1] v. 33, 8; Ludwig, Translation of the Rigveda, 3, 155, 174.

[2] xiii. 12; Weber, *Indische Studien*, 3, 474, 475.

1. **Go** (*a*), 'ox' or 'cow.'[1] These were among the chief sources of wealth to the Vedic Indian, and are repeatedly

[1] i. 83, 1; 135, 8; ii. 23, 18, etc.; *gāva ukṣaṇaḥ*, i. 168, 2; Av. iii. 11, 8; Vājasaneyi Saṃhitā, xxi. 20; *gāvo dhenavaḥ*, Rv. i. 173, 1; vi. 45, 28; x. 95, 6; Vājasaneyi Saṃhitā, xxi. 19, etc.

referred to from the Rigveda onwards.[2] The milk (**Kṣīra**) was either drunk fresh or made into butter (**Ghṛta**) or curds (**Dadhi**), or was mixed with **Soma** or used for cooking with grain (**Kṣīraudana**). The cows were milked thrice a day, early (*prātar-doha*), in the forenoon (**Saṃgava**), and in the evening (*sāyaṃ-doha*).[3] Thrice a day they were driven out to graze, according to the Taittirīya Brāhmaṇa[4] (*prātaḥ, saṃgave, sāyam*). The first milking was productive, the last two scanty.[3] According to the Aitareya Brāhmaṇa,[5] among the Bharatas the herds in the evening are in the **Goṣṭha**, at midday in the **Saṃgavinī**. This passage Sāyaṇa expands by saying that the herds go home to the Śālā, or house for animals, at night so far as they consist of animals giving milk, while the others stayed out in the Goṣṭha, or open pasturage; but both were together in the cattle-shed during the heat of the day. The time before the Saṃgava, when the cows were grazing freely on the pastureland, was called **Svasara**.[6] When the cows were out feeding they were separated from the calves, which were, however, allowed to join them at the Saṃgava,[7] and sometimes in the evening.[8]

While grazing the cattle were under the care of a herdsman (**Gopā, Gopāla**) armed with a goad,[9] but they were liable to all sorts of dangers, such as being lost, falling into pits, breaking limbs,[10]

[2] The five sacrificial animals are man, goat, sheep, ox, horse, Sāṅkhāyana Śrauta Sūtra, ix. 23, 4; Śatapatha Brāhmaṇa, ii. 4, 3, 13; iii. 1, 2, 13; iv. 5, 5, 10; xiv. 1, 1, 32.

[3] Taittirīya Saṃhitā, vii. 5, 3, 1.

[4] i. 4, 9, 2. The exact sense of this notice is obscure. Strictly speaking, the cows were driven out from the cattle-shed in the morning, spent the heat of the day in the Saṃgavinī, were then driven out during the evening to graze, and finally came or were driven home, as is often mentioned: Rv. i. 66, 5; 149, 4; Vājasaneyi Saṃhitā, xv. 41.

[5] iii. 18, 14.

[6] Rv. ii. 2, 2; 34, 8; v. 62, 2; viii. 88, 1; ix. 94, 2. The going of the cows to their pasture in the morning is often referred to—*e.g.*, Rv. i. 25, 16; x. 97, 8.

[7] Rv. ii. 2, 2; viii. 88, 1; Taittirīya Brāhmaṇa, ii. 1, 1, 3; Śaṅkara on Chāndogya Upaniṣad, ii. 9, 4; Jaiminīya Upaniṣad Brāhmaṇa, i. 12, 4; Nārāyaṇa on Āśvalāyana Śrauta Sūtra, iii. 12, 2.

[8] Gobhila Gṛhya Sūtra, iii. 8, 7; Rv. ii. 2, 2. See Geldner, *Vedische Studien*, 2, 111-114.

[9] *Pavīravān*, Rv. x. 60, 3, is probably so meant. The usual name was **Aṣṭrā**, the significant mark of a **Vaiśya**. *Cf.* Rv. vii. 33, 6.

[10] Rv. i. 120, 8; vi. 54, 5-7. Also Pūṣan was the special deity expected to guard cattle, and hence is called *anaṣṭa-paśu*, 'losing no kine.' See Rv. x. 17, 2, and Macdonell, *Vedic Mythology*, p. 36.

and being stolen. The marking of the ears of cattle was repeatedly adopted, no doubt, to indicate ownership.[11]

Large herds of cattle were well-known, as is shown by the Dānastutis, or 'praises of gifts,' in the Rigveda,[12] even when allowances are made for the exaggeration of priestly gratitude. The importance attached to the possession of cattle is shown[13] by the numerous passages in which the gods are asked to prosper them, and by the repeated prayers[14] for wealth in kine. Hence, too, forays for cattle (**Gaviṣṭi**) were well known; the Bharata host is called the 'horde desiring cows' (*gavyan grāmaḥ*) in the Rigveda;[15] and a verbal root *gup*,[16] 'to protect,' was evolved as early as the Rigveda from the denominative *go-pāya*, 'to guard cows.' The Vedic poets[17] do not hesitate to compare their songs with the lowing of cows, or to liken the choir of the singing Apsarases to cows.[18]

The cattle of the Vedic period were of many colours: red (*rohita*), light (*śukra*), dappled (*pṛśni*), even black (*kṛṣṇa*).[19] Zimmer[20] sees a reference to cows with blazes on the face in one passage of the Rigveda,[21] but this is uncertain.

Oxen were regularly used for ploughing or for drawing wagons (*anaḍvāh*), in which case they were, it seems, usually castrated.[22] Cows were not properly used for drawing carts, though they at times did so.[23] The flesh of both cows and bulls was sometimes eaten (**Māṃsa**). Cattle were certainly the

[11] Rv. vi. 28, 3; Maitrāyaṇī Saṃhitā, iv. 2, 9, and *cf.* **Aṣṭakarṇī** and **Svadhiti**.

[12] Rv. viii. 5, 37, etc. *Cf.* Pañcaviṃśa Brāhmaṇa, xvii. 14, 2; Aitareya Brāhmaṇa, viii. 21. 23; Śatapatha Brāhmaṇa, xiii. 5, 4, 8 *et seq.*

[13] Rv. i. 43, 2; 162, 22; v. 4, 11; ix. 9, 9, etc.; Av. i. 31, 4; ii. 26, 4; v. 29, 2; vi. 68, 3; viii. 7, 11, x. 1, 17. 29; xi. 2, 9. 21, etc.; Taittirīya Saṃhitā, iii. 2, 3, 1; v. 5, 5, 1; vi. 5, 10, 1; Vājasaneyi Saṃhitā, iii. 59.

[14] Rv. i. 83, 1; iv. 32, 17; v. 4, 11; viii. 89, 2, etc.

[15] iii. 33, 11.

[16] Rv. vii. 103, 9; Av. x. 9, 7, 8; xix. 27, 9. 10. *Cf.* Macdonell, *Vedic Grammar*, p. 358, n. 13.

[17] Rv. vii. 32, 22; viii. 95, 1; 106, 1; ix. 12, 2, etc.

[18] Rv. x. 95, 6. It is, however, uncertain whether the names of Apsarases are meant in this passage. *Cf.* Ludwig, Translation of the Rigveda, 5, 517.

[19] Rv. i. 62, 9. Various other colours are mentioned in the lists of animals at the Aśvamedha, or human sacrifice, in the Yajurveda, but apparently as exceptional.

[20] *Altindisches Leben*, 226.

[21] i. 87, 1. It is also rendered as 'the heavens with stars.'

[22] Av. iii. 9, 2; vi. 138, 2; Taittirīya Saṃhitā, i. 8. 9, 1; Weber, *Indische Studien*, 13, 151, n. See **Mahānirāṣṭa**.

[23] Śatapatha Brāhmaṇa, v. 2, 4, 13.

objects of individual ownership, and they formed one of the standards of exchange and valuation (see **Kraya**).

(*b*) The term **Go** is often applied to express the products of the cow. It frequently means the milk,[1] but rarely the flesh[2] of the animal. In many passages it designates leather used as the material of various objects, as a bowstring,[3] or a sling,[4] or thongs to fasten part of the chariot,[5] or reins,[6] or the lash of a whip.[7] See also **Carman**, with which Go is sometimes synonymous.[8]

[1] Rv. i. 33, 10; 151, 8; 181, 8; ii. 30, 7; iv. 27, 5; ix. 46, 4; 71, 5.
[2] Rv. x. 16, 7 (in the funeral ritual).
[3] Rv. vi. 75, 11; x. 27, 22; Av. i. 2, 3.
[4] Rv. i. 121, 9.
[5] Rv. vi. 47, 26; viii. 59, 5.
[6] Rv. vi. 46, 14.
[7] Rv. vi. 53, 9.
[8] Rv. x. 94, 9.
Cf. Zimmer, *Altindisches Leben*, 228.

(*c*) **Gāvaḥ** means the stars of heaven in two passages of the Rigveda,[1] according to Roth.[2]

[1] i. 154, 6; vii. 36, 1.
[2] St. Petersburg Dictionary, *s.v.* 5.

2. **Go Āṅgirasa** ('descendant of **Aṅgiras**') is the reputed author of a Sāman or Chant in the Pañcaviṃśa Brāhmaṇa.[1] There is little doubt that he is mythical.[2]

[1] xvi. 7, 7. *Cf.* Lāṭyāyana Śrauta Sūtra, vi. 11, 3.
[2] Hillebrandt, *Vedische Mythologie*, 2, 160; Hopkins, *Transactions of the Connecticut Academy of Arts and Sciences*, 15, 68.

Go-ghāta, 'a cow-killer,' is enumerated in the list of victims at the Puruṣamedha, or human sacrifice, in the Yajurveda.[1] See **Māṃsa**.

[1] Vājasaneyi Saṃhitā, xxx. 18; Taittirīya Brāhmaṇa, iii. 4, 16, 1.

Gotama is mentioned several times in the Rigveda,[1] but never in such a way as to denote personal authorship of any hymn.[2] It seems clear that he was closely connected with the

[1] Rv. i. 62, 13; 78, 2; 84, 5; 85, 11; iv. 4, 11.
[2] Oldenberg, *Zeitschrift der Deutschen Morgenländischen Gesellschaft*, 42, 215.

Aṅgirases, for the Gotamas frequently refer to **Aṅgiras.**[3] That he bore the patronymic Rāhūgaṇa is rendered probable by one hymn of the Rigveda,[4] and is assumed in the Śatapatha Brāhmaṇa,[5] where he appears as the Purohita, or domestic priest, of **Māthava Videgha,** and as a bearer of Vedic civilization. He is also mentioned in the same Brāhmaṇa[6] as a contemporary of **Janaka** of **Videha,** and **Yājñavalkya,** and as the author of a Stoma.[7] He occurs, moreover, in two passages of the Atharvaveda.[8]

The Gotamas are mentioned in several passages of the Rigveda,[9] **Vāmadeva** and **Nodhas** being specified as sons of Gotama. They include the **Vājaśravases.** See also **Gautama.**

3 *Cf.* Rv. i. 62, 1; 71, 2; 74, 5; 75, 2; 78, 3; iv. 2, 5; 16, 8, etc.

4 Rv. i. 78, 5. *Cf.* Oldenberg, *loc. cit.*, 236, n. 1.

5 i. 4, 1, 10 *et seq.*; xi. 4, 3, 20. The former passage is wrongly cited by Sāyaṇa on Rv. i. 81, 3. See Weber, *Indische Studien*, 2, 9, n.

6 xi. 4, 3, 20.

7 xiii. 5, 1, 1; Āśvalāyana Śrauta Sūtra, ix. 5, 6; 10, 8, etc.

8 iv. 29, 6; xviii. 3, 16. See also Ṣaḍviṃśa Brāhmaṇa in *Indische Studien*, 1, 38; Bṛhadāraṇyaka Upaniṣad, ii. 2, 6.

9 i. 60, 5; 61, 16; 63, 9; 77, 5; 78, 1; 88, 4; 92, 7; iv. 32, 9. 12; viii. 88, 4. *Cf.* Āśvalāyana Śrauta Sūtra, xii. 10.

Cf. Ludwig, Translation of the Rigveda, 3, 110, 123; Weber, *Indische Studien*, 1, 170, 180; Geldner, *Vedische Studien*, 3, 151, 152.

Gotamī-putra, 'son of Gotamī,' is mentioned as a pupil of **Bhāradvājī-putra** in the Kāṇva recension of the Bṛhadāraṇyaka Upaniṣad (vi. 5, 1). See also **Gautamī-putra.**

Gotra occurs several times in the Rigveda[1] in the account of the mythic exploits of Indra. Roth[2] interprets the word as 'cowstall,' while Geldner[3] thinks 'herd' is meant. The latter sense seems to explain best the employment which the term shows in the later literature as denoting the 'family' or 'clan,' and which is found in the Chāndogya Upaniṣad.[4]

In the Gṛhya Sūtras[5] stress is laid on the prohibition of

1 i. 51, 3; ii. 17, 1; 23, 18; iii. 39, 4; 43, 7; viii. 74, 5; x. 48, 2; 103, 7.

2 St. Petersburg Dictionary, *s.v.*

3 *Vedische Studien*, 2, 275, 276, where he divides the passages according as real or mythical herds are meant.

4 iv. 4, 1. So Śāṅkhāyana Śrauta Sūtra, i. 4, 16, etc.; Āśvalāyana Gṛhya Sūtra, iv. 4, etc.; Kauṣītaki Brāhmaṇa, xxv. 15.

5 Gobhila Gṛhya Sūtra, iii. 4, 4; Āpastamba Dharma Sūtra, ii. 5, 11, 15. 16, in Max Müller, *Ancient Sanskrit Literature*, 387. For *sapiṇḍa*, see Gautama Dharma Sūtra, xiv. 13; Vasiṣṭha Dharma Sūtra, iv. 17-19.

marriage within a Gotra, or with a Sapiṇḍa of the mother of the bridegroom—that is to say, roughly, with agnates and cognates. Senart[6] has emphasized this fact as a basis of caste, on the ground that marriage within a *curia*, *phratria*, or caste (**Varṇa**) was Indo-European, as was marriage outside the circle of agnates and cognates. But there is no evidence at all[7] to prove that this practice was Indo-European, while in India the Śatapatha[8] expressly recognizes marriage within the third or fourth degree on either side. According to Sāyaṇa, the Kāṇvas accepted marriage in the third degree, the Saurāṣṭras only in the fourth, while the scholiast on the Vajrasūcī[9] adds to the Kāṇvas the Andhras and the Dākṣiṇātyas, and remarks that the Vājasaneyins forbade marriage with the daughter of the mother's brother. All apparently allowed marriage with the daughter of a paternal uncle, which later was quite excluded. Change of Gotra was quite possible, as in the case of **Śunaḥśepa** and **Gṛtsamada,** who, once an Aṅgirasa, became a Bhārgava.[10]

[6] *Les Castes dans l'Inde*, 210 *et seq.* *Cf.* De la Vallée Poussin, *Le Védisme*, 15.

[7] Keith, *Journal of the Royal Asiatic Society*, 1909, 471, 472.

[8] i. 8, 3, 6.

[9] See Weber, *Indische Studien*, 10, 73-76.

[10] Hillebrandt, *Vedische Mythologie*, 2, 157; *Festgruss an Roth*, 108.

Cf. Jolly, *Recht und Sitte*, 61 *et seq.*; Zimmer, *Altindisches Leben*, 323.

Go-dāna appears to mean 'the whiskers' in the Śatapatha Brāhmaṇa,[1] where the person, being consecrated, first shaves off the right and then the left 'whisker.' Later on the Godānavidhi, or ceremony of shaving the head, is a regular part of the initiation of a youth on the attainment of manhood and on marriage;[2] but though the ceremony is recognized in the Atharvaveda,[3] the name[4] does not occur there.

[1] iii. 1, 2, 5. 6.

[2] Āśvalāyana Gṛhya Sūtra, i. 19; Śāṅkhāyana Gṛhya Sūtra, i. 28, etc.

[3] vi. 68. See Kauśika Sūtra, liii. 17-20. But Av. ii. 13 is not to be classed here as in the Kauśika; it refers to the giving of a new garment to a child, and the removal of its first wrap. See Whitney, Translation of the Atharvaveda, 56, 57, correcting Weber, *Indische Studien*, 13, 173, and Zimmer, *Altindisches Leben*, 322, 323. *Cf.* Bloomfield, *Hymns of the Atharvaveda*, 306, 574, 665.

[4] The meaning 'whisker' is a secondary one, derived, doubtless, from the 'gift of a cow' (*go-dāna*), accompanying the ceremony of shaving the whiskers or hair.

Godhā.—(*a*) The sense of 'bowstring' seems certain in one passage of the Rigveda,[1] and possible in another.[2] Roth[3] also adopts this meaning in the only passage of the Atharvaveda[4] where the word occurs.

[1] x. 28, 10. 11.

[2] viii. 69, 9. See Hopkins, *Journal of the American Oriental Society*, 17, 53.

[3] St. Petersburg Dictionary, *s.v.* 1.

[4] iv. 3, 6.

(*b*) In one passage of the Rigveda[1] the sense of 'musical instrument' is recognized by Roth and by Hillebrandt[2] for this word.

[1] viii. 69, 9.

[2] *Vedische Mythologie*, 1, 144, n. 1.

(*c*) Elsewhere[1] an animal seems to be meant, perhaps the 'crocodile,' as Ludwig[2] and Weber[3] think; perhaps a large 'lizard,' as Roth and Zimmer[4] assume. An animal is probably also meant in the Atharvaveda.[5]

[1] Taittirīya Saṃhitā, v. 5, 15, 1; Vājasaneyi Saṃhitā, xxiv. 35; Pañcaviṃśa Brāhmaṇa, ix. 2, 14; Baudhāyana Śrauta Sūtra, ii. 5; Jaiminīya Brāhmaṇa, i. 221; Śāṭyāyanaka in Sāyaṇa on Rv. viii. 91; *Journal of the American Oriental Society*, 18, 29.

[2] Translation of the Rigveda, 3, 499.

[3] *Indische Studien*, 18, 15, 16. Bloomfield, *Hymns of the Atharvaveda*, 368, renders the word vaguely by 'dragon.'

[4] *Altindisches Leben*, 95.

[5] iv. 3, 6, where Whitney offers no rendering at all.

Go-dhūma, 'wheat,' is frequently referred to in the plural in the Yajurveda Saṃhitās[1] and Brāhmaṇas,[2] and is expressly distinguished from 'rice' (**Vrīhi**) or 'barley' (**Yava**).[3] 'Groats' (*saktavaḥ*) made of this grain are also mentioned.[4] The word occurs in the singular in the Śatapatha Brāhmaṇa.[5]

[1] Maitrāyaṇī Saṃhitā, i. 2, 8; Vājasaneyi Saṃhitā, xviii. 12; xix. 22. 89; xxi. 29, etc.

[2] Śatapatha Brāhmaṇa, xii. 7, 1, 2; 2, 9; Bṛhadāraṇyaka Upaniṣad, vi. 3, 22 (Mādhyaṃdina = vi. 3, 13 Kāṇva), etc.

[3] Taittirīya Brāhmaṇa, i. 3, 7, 2.

[4] Śatapatha Brāhmaṇa, xii. 9, 1, 5.

[5] v. 2, 1, 6.

Cf. Zimmer, *Altindisches Leben*, 241.

Go-pati, 'lord of cows,' is freely used in the Rigveda[1] to denote any lord or master, a natural usage considering that cattle formed the main species of wealth.

[1] i. 101, 4; iv. 24, 1; vi. 45, 21; vii. 18, 4, etc. Av. iii. 14, 6, etc.

Gopa-vana is the name of a poet of the race of Atri in the Rigveda.[1] See **Gaupavana.**

[1] viii. 74, 11. *Cf.* Weber, *Indische Studien*, 1, 215; Ludwig, Translation of the Rigveda, 3, 107.

Go-pā and **Go-pāla**, 'protector of cows,' occur in the Rigveda[1] and later, but the former is usually metaphorical in sense, applying to any protector, while the latter has the literal force of 'cow-herd.'

[1] *Gopā:* Rv. i. 164, 21; ii. 23, 6; iii. 10, 2; v. 12, 4, etc.; *Gopāla:* Vājasaneyi Saṃhitā, xxx. 11; Śatapatha Brāhmaṇa, iv. 1, 5, 4. *Gopā*, in the sense of 'guardian,' occurs in the Pañcaviṃśa Brāhmaṇa, xxiv. 18, in a compound. *Gopītha*, in the sense of 'protection,' occurs in Rv. v. 65, 6; x. 35, 14, etc. *Goptṛ*, 'protector,' first occurs in Av. x. 10, 5, and is thereafter common.

Go-bala ('ox-strength') **Vārṣṇa** ('descendant of Vṛṣṇi') is mentioned as a teacher in the Taittirīya Saṃhitā (iii. 11, 9, 3) and the Jaiminīya Upaniṣad Brāhmaṇa (i. 6, 1).

Go-matī, 'possessing cows,' is mentioned as a river in the Nadī-stuti, or 'Praise of Rivers,' in the tenth Maṇḍala of the Rigveda.[1] In that hymn a river flowing into the Indus must be meant, and its identification[2] with the Gomal, a western tributary of the Indus, cannot be doubted. In one other passage of the Rigveda[3] the accentuation of Gomatī shows that a river is meant. It is possible that in a third passage[4] the reading should be changed to *gomatīr* from *gómatīr*. Geldner[5] suggests that in the two last passages the Gumti, or rather its four upper arms (hence the use of the plural) is meant: this accords well with the later use of the name and with the general probability of the river here intended being in **Kurukṣetra**, as the centre of Vedic civilization.[6]

[1] x. 75, 6.

[2] Zimmer, *Altindisches Leben*, 14; Ludwig, Translation of the Rigveda, 3, 200.

[3] viii. 24, 30.

[4] v. 61, 19. See Oldenberg, *Rgveda-Noten*, 1, 355, 356.

[5] *Vedische Studien*, 3, 152, n. 2.

[6] Pischel, *Vedische Studien*, 2, 218; Hopkins, *Journal of the American Oriental Society*, 19, 19 *et seq.*; Macdonell, *Sanskrit Literature*, 174; Keith, *Journal of the Royal Asiatic Society*, 1908, 1141.

Go-māyu, 'lowing like a cow,' does not occur as the name of the 'jackal' till the late Adbhuta Brāhmaṇa.[1]

[1] *Indische Studien*, 1, 40.

Go-mṛga, a species of ox, now called Gayal (*Bos gavaeus*), is mentioned in the list of victims at the Aśvamedha, or horse sacrifice, in the Yajurveda Saṃhitās[1] and Brāhmaṇas.[2] In the Taittirīya Saṃhitā[3] it is declared to be neither a wild nor a tame animal; this presumably means that it was semi-domesticated, or perhaps that it was both tamed and found wild. With the name of this animal may be compared the Mṛga Mahiṣa, which is clearly mentioned as wild in the Rigveda.[4] See also **Gayava.**

[1] Maitrāyaṇī Saṃhitā, iii. 14, 11; Vājasaneyi Saṃhitā, xxiv. 1. 30.

[2] Śatapatha Brāhmaṇa, xiii. 3, 4, 3; 5, 2, 10; Taittirīya Brāhmaṇa, iii. 8, 20, 5.

[3] ii. 1, 10, 2.

[4] ix. 92, 6.

Cf. Zimmer, *Altindisches Leben*, 83, 84; Eggeling, *Sacred Books of the East*, 44, 338, n. 1.

Golattikā is the name of some unknown animal in the list of victims at the Aśvamedha, or horse sacrifice, in the Yajurveda.[1]

[1] Taittirīya Saṃhitā, v. 5, 16, 1; Maitrāyaṇī Saṃhitā, iii. 14, 18; Vājasaneyi Saṃhitā, xxiv. 37. *Cf.* Zimmer, *Altindisches Leben*, 99.

Go-vikartana ('cow-butcher') designates the 'huntsman' in the Śatapatha Brāhmaṇa (v. 3, 1, 10).[1] See **Goghāta.**

[1] *Cf.* Taittirīya Brāhmaṇa, iii. 4, 16, 1; Vājasaneyi Saṃhitā, xxx. 18; Weber, *Indische Streifen*, 1, 82.

Go-vyaca. See **Vyaca.**

Gośarya is the name of a protégé of the Aśvins in the Rigveda (viii. 8, 20; 49, 1; 50, 10).

Go-śru Jābāla is mentioned as a sage in the Jaiminīya Upaniṣad Brāhmaṇa (iii. 7, 7).

Go-śruti Vaiyāghra-padya ('descendant of Vyāghrapad') is mentioned as a pupil of **Satyakāma** in the Chāndogya Upaniṣad (v. 2, 3). In the Śāṅkhāyana Āraṇyaka (ix. 7) the name appears as Gośruta.

Go-ṣādī ('sitting on a cow') is the name of a bird in the list of victims at the Aśvamedha, or horse sacrifice, in the Yajurveda.[1]

[1] Maitrāyaṇī Saṃhitā, iii. 14, 5; Vājasaneyi Saṃhitā, xxiv. 24. *Cf.* Zimmer, *Altindisches Leben*, 94.

Go-ṣūktin is mentioned in the Sarvānukramaṇī as the author of Rigveda viii. 14 and 15, and a Sāman or Chant of his seems to be referred to in the Pañcaviṃśa Brāhmaṇa (xix. 4, 9), under the title of Gauṣūkta. But see **Gauṣūkti**.

Go-ṣṭha, 'standing-place for cows,' denotes not so much a 'cowstall' as the 'grazing ground of cows,' as Geldner[1] shows from a passage of the Aitareya Brāhmaṇa[2] and from a note of Mahīdhara on the Vājasaneyi Saṃhitā.[3] This sense suits adequately all the passages of the Rigveda[4] where it occurs, and it greatly improves the interpretation of a hymn of the Atharvaveda,[5] besides being acceptable elsewhere.[6] See also **Go**.

[1] *Vedische Studien*, 3, 112, 113.
[2] iii. 18, 14.
[3] iii. 21.
[4] i. 191, 4; vi. 28, 1; viii. 43, 17.
[5] iii. 14, 1. 5. 6, where Whitney's rendering 'stall' is very unsatisfactory, and Bloomfield's 'stable' is no better.
[6] Av. ii. 26, 2; Vājasaneyi Saṃhitā, iii. 21; v. 17; Śatapatha Brāhmaṇa, xi. 8, 3, 2, etc.; Kāṭhaka Saṃhitā, vii. 7; Maitrāyaṇī Saṃhitā, iv. 2, 11.

Gautama, 'descendant of Gotama,' is a common patronymic, being applied to **Aruṇa**,[1] **Uddālaka Āruṇi**,[2] **Kuśri**,[3] **Sāti**,[4] **Hāridrumata**.[5]

Several Gautamas are mentioned in the Vaṃśas (lists of teachers) in the Bṛhadāraṇyaka Upaniṣad as pupils of **Āgniveśya**,[6] of **Saitava** and **Prācīnayogya**,[7] of **Saitava**,[8] of **Bhārad-**

[1] Śatapatha Brāhmaṇa, x. 6, 1, 4.
[2] *Ibid.*, xi. 4, 1, 3; 5, 1, 2; Bṛhadāraṇyaka Upaniṣad, vi. 1, 7; Chāndogya Upaniṣad, v. 3, 6 *et seq.*; Kauṣītaki Upaniṣad, i. 1; Jaiminīya Upaniṣad Brāhmaṇa, i. 42, 1.
[3] Śatapatha Brāhmaṇa, x. 5, 5, 1.
[4] Vaṃśa Brāhmaṇa in *Indische Studien*, 4, 373.
[5] Chāndogya Upaniṣad, iv. 4, 3.
[6] Bṛhadāraṇyaka Upaniṣad, ii. 6, 1 (Kāṇva).
[7] *Ibid.*, ii. 6, 2.
[8] *Ibid.*, iv. 6, 2.

vāja,[9] of **Gautama**,[10] and of **Vātsya**.[11] A Gautama is also referred to elsewhere.

[9] *Ibid.*, ii. 6, 2 (Kāṇva = ii. 5, 22; iv. 5, 27 Mādhyaṃdina).

[10] *Ibid.*, ii. 6, 3; iv. 6, 3 (Kāṇva = ii. 5, 22; iv. 5, 28 Mādhyaṃdina).

[11] *Ibid.*, ii. 6, 3; iv. 6, 3 (Kāṇva = ii. 5, 20. 22; iv. 5, 26 Mādhyaṃdina). The Mādhyaṃdina, ii. 5, 20; iv. 5, 26, knows a Gautama, pupil of **Vaijavāpāyana** and **Vaiṣṭhapureya**.

Gautamī-putra ('son of a female descendant of Gotama') is mentioned in the Kāṇva recension of the Bṛhadāraṇyaka Upaniṣad (vi. 5, 2) as a pupil of **Bhāradvājīputra**. In the Mādhyaṃdina (vi. 4, 31) a Gautamīputra is a pupil of **Ātreyīputra**, pupil of a Gautamīputra, pupil of **Vātsīputra**. See also **Gotamīputra**.

Gaupa-vana ('descendant of **Gopavana**') is mentioned as a pupil of **Pautimāṣya** in the first two Vaṃśas (lists of teachers) in the Kāṇva recension of the Bṛhadāraṇyaka Upaniṣad (ii. 6, 1; iv. 6, 1).

Gaupāyana ('descendant of Gopa'). The Gaupāyanas appear in the legend of **Asamāti**, **Kirāta**, and **Ākuli**, which is first met with in the Brāhmaṇas.[1]

[1] Pañcaviṃśa Brāhmaṇa, xiii. 12, 5; Jaiminīya Brāhmaṇa, iii. 167 (*Journal of the American Oriental Society*, 18, 41); Śāṭyāyanaka in Sāyaṇa on Rv. x. 57 (Max Müller's edition, 4^2,c *et seq.*); Bṛhaddevatā, vii. 83 *et seq.*, with Macdonell's notes.

Gaupālāyana ('descendant of Gopāla') is the patronymic of **Śucivṛkṣa** in the Maitrāyaṇī Saṃhitā.[1] It is also the patronymic of **Aupoḍiti**, Sthapati of the **Kurus**, in the Baudhāyana Śrauta Sūtra,[2] and, as Gaupāleya, of Upoditi or Aupoditi in the Pañcaviṃśa Brāhmaṇa.[3]

[1] iii. 10, 4 (p. 135, line 9). *Cf.* Aitareya Brāhmaṇa, iii. 48, 9, where Aufrecht reads *Gaupalāyana*.

[2] xx. 25.

[3] xii. 13, 11, where the edition has *Upoditi*.

Gaura, a species of ox (*Bos gaurus*), is frequently mentioned with the **Gavaya** from the Rigveda[1] onwards.[2] As the Vājasaneyi Saṃhitā[3] expressly mentions wild (*āraṇya*) Gauras, they

[1] i. 16, 5; iv. 21, 8; 58, 2; v. 78, 2; vii. 69, 6; 98, 1, etc.

[2] Maitrāyaṇī Saṃhitā, iii. 14, 10, Vājasaneyi Saṃhitā, xxiv. 28; Aitareya Brāhmaṇa, iii. 34, etc.

[3] xiii. 48.

must usually have been tame. The female, Gaurī, is also often referred to.[4] The compound term Gaura-mṛga ('the Gaura wild beast') is sometimes met with.[5]

[4] Rv. i. 84, 10; iv. 12, 6; ix. 12, 3; and in the obscure verse i. 164, 11.

[5] Vājasaneyi Saṃhitā, xxiv. 32; Aitareya Brāhmaṇa, ii. 8.

Cf. Zimmer, *Altindisches Leben*, 83, 224.

Gauri-vīti Śāktya ('descendant of **Śakti**') or **Gaurīviti**, as the name is also spelt,[1] is the Ṛṣi, or Seer, of a hymn of the Rigveda,[2] and is frequently mentioned in the Brāhmaṇas.[3] According to the Jaiminīya Brāhmaṇa,[4] he was Prastotṛ at the Sattra, or sacrificial session, celebrated by the **Vibhindukīyas** and mentioned in that Brāhmaṇa.

[1] Satapatha Brāhmaṇa, xii. 8, 3, 7; Pañcaviṃśa Brāhmaṇa, xi. 5; xii. 13; xxv. 7.

[2] v. 29, 11.

[3] Aitareya Brāhmaṇa, iii. 19; viii. 2; and see n. 1.

[4] ii. 233 (*Journal of the American Oriental Society*, 18, 38).

Cf. Ludwig, Translation of the Rigveda, 3, 126; Oldenberg, *Zeitschrift der Deutschen Morgenländischen Gesellschaft*, 42, 215.

Gauśra ('descendant of Guśri') is the name of a teacher mentioned in the Kauṣītaki Brāhmaṇa (xvi. 9; xxiii. 5). See **Gauśla.**

Gauśrāyaṇi ('descendant of Gauśra') is the patronymic of a teacher, **Citra,** in the Kauṣītaki Brāhmaṇa (xxiii. 5).

Gauśla, a variant of **Gauśra,** is the name of a teacher represented as in disagreement with **Buḍila Āśvatara Āśvi** in the Aitareya Brāhmaṇa.[1]

[1] vi. 30. *Cf.* Gopatha Brāhmaṇa, ii. 6, 9 (Gośla).

Gau-ṣūkti is the name of a pupil of **Iṣa Śyāvāśvi** according to the Jaiminīya Upaniṣad Brāhmaṇa[1] in a Vaṃśa (list of teachers). It is also the name, in the Pañcaviṃśa Brāhmaṇa,[2]

[1] iv. 16, 1.

[2] xix. 4, 9. *Cf.* St. Petersburg Dictionary, *s.v.*; Hopkins, *Transactions of the Connecticut Academy of Arts and Sciences*, 15, 30.

of a teacher who appears to have been needlessly invented to explain the Gauṣūkta Sāman (chant), which is really the Sāman of **Goṣūktin.**

Graha ('seizing') is a term applied to the sun in the Satapatha Brāhmaṇa,[1] most probably not in the later sense of 'planet,' but to denote a power exercising magical influence.[2] The sense of 'planet' seems first to occur in the later literature, as in the Maitrāyaṇī Upaniṣad.[3] The question whether the planets were known to the Vedic Indians is involved in obscurity. Oldenberg[4] recognizes them in the Ādityas, whose number is, he believes, seven: sun, moon, and the five planets. But this view, though it cannot be said to be impossible or even unlikely, is not susceptible of proof, and has been rejected by Hillebrandt,[5] Pischel,[6] von Schroeder,[7] Macdonell,[8] and Bloomfield,[9] among others. Hillebrandt[10] sees the planets in the five Adhvaryus mentioned in the Rigveda,[11] but this is a mere conjecture. The five bulls (*ukṣāṇaḥ*) in another passage of the Rigveda[12] have received a similar interpretation with equal uncertainty,[13] and Durga, in his commentary on the Nirukta,[14] even explains the term *bhūmija*, 'earth-born,' which is only mentioned by Yāska, as meaning the planet Mars.[15] Thibaut,[16] who is generally sceptical as to the mention of planets in the Veda, thinks that Bṛhaspati there refers to Jupiter; but this is extremely improbable, though in the Taittirīya Saṃhitā[17] Bṛhaspati is made the regent of Tiṣya. A reference to the

[1] iv. 6, 5, 1.

[2] St. Petersburg Dictionary, *s.v.*; Eggeling, *Sacred Books of the East*, 26, 432, n. 2.

[3] vi. 16. See Weber, *Indian Literature*, 98, n.

[4] *Religion des Veda*, 185 *et seq.*; *Zeitschrift der Deutschen Morgenländischen Gesellschaft*, 50, 56 *et seq.*

[5] *Vedische Mythologie*, 3, 102 *et seq.*

[6] *Göttingische Gelehrte Anzeigen*, 1895, 447.

[7] *Vienna Oriental Journal*, 9, 109.

[8] *Vedic Mythology*, p. 44.

[9] *Religion of the Veda*, 133 *et seq.*

[10] *Vedische Mythologie*, 3, 423.

[11] iii. 7, 7.

[12] i. 105, 10. *Cf.* also i. 105, 16, with Oldenberg's note.

[13] Hopkins, *Journal of the American Oriental Society*, 24, 36.

[14] i. 14.

[15] See Weber, *Jyotiṣa*, 10, n. 2.

[16] *Astronomie, Astrologie, und Mathematik*, 6.

[17] iv. 4 10, 1. *Cf.* Macdonell, *Vedic Mythology*, pp. 102-104.

planets is much more probable in the seven suns (*sapta sūryāḥ*) of the late Taittirīya Āraṇyaka.[18] On the other hand, Ludwig's efforts to find the five planets with the sun, the moon, and the twenty-seven Nakṣatras (lunar mansions) in the Rigveda, as corresponding to the number thirty-four used in connexion with light[19] (*jyotis*) and the ribs of the sacrificial horse,[20] is far-fetched. See also **Śukra, Manthin, Vena.**

[18] i. 7. See on them Weber, *Omina und Portenta*, 339; *Indische Studien*, 2, 238; 9, 363; 10, 240, 271; *Jyotiṣa*, 10; *Rāmāyaṇa*, 28, n. 2.

[19] x. 55, 3. [20] i. 162, 18.

Cf. Ludwig, Translation of the Rigveda, 3, 183 *et seq.*; Zimmer, *Altindisches Leben*, 354 *et seq.*; Max Müller, *Ṛgveda*, iv.[2], xxx. *et seq.*; Whitney, *Oriental and Linguistic Essays*, 2, 412, n. *Journal of the American Oriental Society* 16, lxxxviii.

Grābha (lit. 'grasping') designates the 'throw' of dice in the Rigveda.[1] See also **Glaha.**

[1] viii. 81, 1; ix. 106, 3. *Cf.* Lüders, *Das Würfelspiel im alten Indien*, 49, 50.

Grāma.—The primitive sense of this word, which occurs frequently from the Rigveda[1] onwards, appears to have been 'village.' The Vedic Indians must have dwelt in villages which were scattered over the country, some close together,[2] some far apart, and were connected by roads.[3] The village is regularly contrasted with the forest (*araṇya*), and its animals and plants with those that lived or grew wild in the woods.[4] The villages contained cattle, horses, and other domestic animals, as well as men.[5] Grain was also stored in them.[6] In the evening the cattle regularly returned thither from the forest.[7] The villages were probably open, though perhaps a fort (**Pur**) might on

[1] i. 44, 10; 114, 1; ii. 12, 7 (perhaps to be taken as in n. 10); x. 146, 1; 149, 4, etc.; Av. iv. 36, 7. 8; v. 17, 4; vi. 40, 2, etc.; Vājasaneyi Saṃhitā, iii. 45; xx. 17, etc.

[2] Śatapatha Brāhmaṇa, xiii. 2, 4, 2; Aitareya Brāhmaṇa, iii. 44.

[3] Chāndogya Upaniṣad, viii. 6, 2.

[4] Animals: Rv. x. 90, 8; Av. ii. 34, 4; iii. 10, 6; 31, 3; Taittirīya Saṃhitā, vii. 2, 2, 1; Kāṭhaka Saṃhitā, vii. 7; xiii. 1; Vājasaneyi Saṃhitā, ix. 32; Pañcaviṃśa Brāhmaṇa, xvi. 1, 9; Śatapatha Brāhmaṇa, iii. 8. 4, 16, etc. Plants: Taittirīya Saṃhitā, v. 2, 5, 5; vii. 3, 4, 1, etc.

[5] Av. iv. 22, 2; viii. 7, 11, etc.

[6] Bṛhadāraṇyaka Upaniṣad, vi. 3, 13 (Kāṇva = 22, Mādhyaṃdina).

[7] Rv. x. 149, 4; Maitrāyaṇī Saṃhitā, iv. 1, 1.

occasion be built inside.[8] Presumably they consisted of detached houses with enclosures, but no details are to be found in Vedic literature. Large villages (*mahāgrāmāḥ*) were known.[9]

The relation of the villagers is difficult to ascertain with precision. In several passages[10] the word occurs with what appears to be the derivative sense of 'body of men.' This sense presumably started from the use of the word to denote the 'village folk,' as when **Śaryāta Mānava** is said in the Śatapatha Brāhmaṇa[11] to have wandered about with his 'village' (*grāmeṇa*); but, as Zimmer[12] observes, this restricted sense nowhere appears clearly in the Rigveda,[13] where indeed the 'folk' (*janà*)[14] of the Bharatas is in one passage[15] called the 'horde seeking cows' (*gavyan grāmaḥ*). Zimmer[16] tends to regard the Grāma as a clan, and as standing midway between the family and the tribe (**Viś**). The Grāma may, however, perhaps be regarded more correctly[17] as an aggregate of several families, not necessarily forming a clan, but only part of a clan (**Viś**), as is often the case at the present day.[18]

Vedic literature tells us very little about the social economy of the village. There is nothing to show that the community as such held land. What little evidence there is indicates that individual tenure of land was known (see **Urvarā, Kṣetra**), but this, in effect though not in law, presumably meant tenure by a family rather than by an individual person. The expression

[8] As nowadays. See Zimmer, *Altindisches Leben*, 144, citing Hügel, Kashmir, 2, 45.

[9] Jaiminīya Upaniṣad Brāhmaṇa, iii. 13, 4.

[10] Rv. i. 100, 10; iii. 33, 11; x. 27, 1; 127, 5; Av. iv. 7, 5; v. 20, 3 (where, however, 'villages' is quite probable); Śatapatha Brāhmaṇa, iv. 1, 5, 2; vi. 7, 4, 9; xii. 4, 1, 3. *Cf.* n. 1.

[11] iv. 1, 5, 2. 7.

[12] *Altindisches Leben*, 161.

[13] See passages cited in n. 10.

[14] Rv. iii. 53, 12.

[15] Rv. iii. 33, 11.

[16] *Op. cit.*, 159, 160, where, however, his language is not very clear. *Cf.* Hopkins, *Religions of India*, 27, who points out that Zimmer is inaccurate in identifying the tribe with Viś. It is the clan, a division below that of the tribe (**Jana**).

[17] A village might contain a whole clan, but probably it contained at most a section of a clan. By family is meant a Hindu joint family; but the extent to which such families existed, and the number of persons included, cannot even be conjectured from the available evidence. *Cf.* Schrader, *Prehistoric Antiquities*, 393; Leist, *Altarisches Jus Gentium*, 34.

[18] *Cf.* Baden Powell, *Village Communities in India*, 85 *et seq.*

'desirous of a village' (*grāma-kāma*), which occurs frequently in the later Saṃhitās,[19] points, however, to the practice of the king's granting to his favourites his royal prerogatives over villages so far as fiscal matters were concerned. Later[20] the idea developed that the king was owner of all the land, and parallel with that idea the view that the holders of such grants were landlords. But of either idea there is no vestige in Vedic literature beyond the word *grāma-kāma*, which much more probably refers to the grant of regalia than to the grant of land, as Teutonic parallels show.[21] Such grants probably tended to depress the position of the actual cultivators, and to turn them into tenants, but they can hardly have had this effect to any appreciable extent in early times.

The village does not appear to have been a unit for legal purposes in early days,[22] and it can hardly be said to have been a political unit. The village no doubt, as later, included in its members various menials, besides the cultivating owners, and also the Brāhmaṇas and Kṣatriyas who might hold interest in it by royal grant or usage without actually cultivating land, such as chariot-makers (**Ratha-kāra**), carpenters (**Takṣan**), smiths (**Karmāra**), and others, but they did not presumably, in any sense, form part of the brotherhood.[23] All alike were politically subject to the king, and bound to render him food or service or other tribute, unless he had transferred his rights to

[19] Taittirīya Saṃhitā, ii. 1, 1, 2; 3, 2; 3, 9, 2; Maitrāyaṇī Saṃhitā, ii. 1, 9; 2, 3; iv. 2, 7, etc.; Hopkins, *Transactions of the Connecticut Academy of Arts and Sciences*, 15, 32, thinks that *grāma* here means 'herd' (of cattle).

[20] *Cf.* Baden Powell, *Indian Village Community*, 207 *et seq.* Whether or not the idea is already found in Manu, ix. 34, is disputed and uncertain. See **Rājan.** The germ of it lies in a different sphere—the right of the **Kṣatriya**, with the consent of the clan, to apportion land (Śatapatha Brāhmaṇa, vii. 1, 1, 8).

[21] *Cf.* Pollock and Maitland, *History of English Law*, 2, 237 *et seq.*; Baden Powell, *Village Communities in India*, 83; Rhys Davids, *Buddhist India*, 48. It may be mentioned that we have no Vedic evidence as to the non-sale of land by the members of a family, except the indications mentioned under **Urvarā.** The later evidence is overwhelming for *grāma*, meaning 'village.' *Cf.* Chāndogya Upaniṣad, iv. 2, 4; Śāṅkhāyana Gṛhya Sūtra, i. 14; Kauśika Sūtra, 94.

[22] *Cf.* Foy, *Die königliche Gewalt*, 20, n.; Jolly, *Recht und Sitte*, 93; Hopkins, *Journal of the American Oriental Society*, 13, 78, 128.

[23] *Cf.* Baden Powell, *Indian Village Community*, 17, 18.

others of the royal family or household, as was no doubt often the case, either in whole or part. The king's share in a village is referred to as early as the Atharvaveda.[24]

At the head of the village was the Grāma-ṇī, or 'leader of the village,' who is referred to in the Rigveda,[25] and often in the later Saṃhitās and in the Brāhmaṇas.[26] The exact meaning of the title is not certain. By *Zimmer*[27] the Grāmaṇī is regarded as having had military functions only, and he is certainly often connected with the **Senānī**, or 'leader of an army.' But there is no reason so to restrict the sense: presumably the Grāmaṇī was the head of the village both for civil purposes and for military operations. He is ranked in the Śatapatha Brāhmaṇa[28] as inferior to the **Sūta**, or 'charioteer,' with whom, however, he is associated[29] as one of the **Ratnins**, the 'jewels' of the royal establishment. The post was especially valuable to a Vaiśya, who, if he attained it, was at the summit of prosperity (*gataśrī*).[30] The Grāmaṇī's connexion with the royal person seems to point to his having been a nominee of the king rather than a popularly elected officer. But the post may have been sometimes hereditary, and sometimes nominated or elective: there is no decisive evidence available. The use of the singular presents difficulties: possibly the Grāmaṇī of the village or city where the royal residence was situated was specially honoured and influential.[31]

[24] iv. 22, 2. *Cf.* n. 20.

[25] x. 62, 11; 107, 5.

[26] Av. iii. 5, 7; xix. 31, 12; Taittirīya Saṃhitā, ii. 5, 4, 4; Maitrāyaṇī Saṃhitā, i. 6, 5 (*grāma-ṇīthya*, 'the rank of Grāmaṇī': *cf.* Taittirīya Saṃhitā, vii. 4, 5, 2); Kāṭhaka Saṃhitā, viii. 4; x. 3; Vājasaneyi Saṃhitā, xv. 15; xxx. 20; Taittirīya Brāhmaṇa, i. 1, 4, 8; 7, 3, 4; ii. 7, 18, 4; Śatapatha Brāhmaṇa, iii. 4, 1, 7; v. 4, 4, 8; viii. 6, 2, 1 (*grāma-ṇīthya*); Bṛhadāraṇyaka Upaniṣad, iv. 3, 37. 38, etc.

[27] *Altindisches Leben*, 171.

[28] v. 4, 4, 18.

[29] Śatapatha Brāhmaṇa, v. 3, 1, 5.

[30] Taittirīya Saṃhitā, ii. 5, 4, 4; Maitrāyaṇī Saṃhitā, i. 6, 5. *Cf.* Weber, *Indische Studien*, 10, 20, n. 2.

[31] Presumably, there must have been many Grāmaṇīs in a kingdom, but the texts seem to contemplate only one as in the royal entourage. *Cf.* also Eggeling, *Sacred Books of the East*, 41, 60, n.; Hopkins, *Journal of the American Oriental Society*, 13, 96; Rhys Davids, *op. cit.*, 48, thinks that he was elected by the village council or a hereditary officer, because the appointment is only claimed for the king in late authorities like Manu, vii. 115. But there is not even so much authority for election or heredity, and we really cannot say how far the power of the early princes extended: it probably varied very much. *Cf.* **Rājan** and **Citraratha**.

Grāmya-vādin apparently means a 'village judge' in the Yajurveda.[1] His **Sabhā**, 'court,' is mentioned in the Maitrāyaṇī Saṃhitā.

[1] Taittirīya Saṃhitā, ii. 3, 1, 3; Kāṭhaka Saṃhitā, xi. 4; Maitrāyaṇī Saṃhitā, ii. 2, 1.

Grāha, 'the seizer,' is the name of a disease in the Śatapatha Brāhmaṇa.[1] In the Atharvaveda[2] it perhaps means 'paralysis' of the thigh.[3]

[1] iii. 5, 3, 25; 6, 1, 25.
[2] xi. 9, 12.
[3] If the reading of the commentary *ūru-grāhaiḥ* be adopted; but Whitney, Translation of the Atharvaveda, 653, retaining the reading of the text *uru-grāhaiḥ*, renders the compound as an adjective, 'wide-gripping.' *Cf.* Bloomfield, *Hymns of the Atharvaveda*, 635.

Grāhi, 'the seizer,' appears in the Rigveda[1] and the Atharvaveda[2] as a female demon of disease. Her son is sleep (*svapna*).[3]

[1] x. 161, 1.
[2] ii. 9, 1; 10, 6. 8; vi. 112, 1; 113, 1; viii. 2, 12; 3, 18; xvi. 7, 1; 8, 1; xix. 45, 5.
[3] xvi. 5, 1; or perhaps 'dream' is meant.

Cf. Weber, *Indische Studien*, 13, 154.

Grīṣma. See **Ṛtu.**

Graivya, in the Atharvaveda,[1] appears to denote 'tumours on the neck' (*grīvāḥ*).

[1] vi. 25, 2; vii. 76, 2. *Cf.* Bloomfield, *Proceedings of the American Oriental Society*, October, 1887, xix.; *Hymns of the Atharvaveda*, 472

Glaha denotes the 'throw' at dice, like **Grābha**, of which it is a later form, occurring in the Atharvaveda.[1]

[1] iv. 28, 1 *et seq.* *Cf.* Lüders, *Das Würfelspiel im alten Indien*, 49.

Glāva Maitreya ('descendant of Maitrī') is mentioned in the Chāndogya Upaniṣad,[1] where he is said to be the same as **Vaka Dālbhya.** He appears as Pratistotṛ at the snake festival of the Pañcaviṃśa Brāhmaṇa,[2] and is referred to in the Ṣaḍviṃśa Brāhmaṇa.[3]

[1] i. 12, 1. 3. *Cf.* Gopatha Brāhmaṇa, i. 1, 31.
[2] xxv. 15, 3.
[3] i. 4.

Cf. Weber, *Indische Studien*, 1, 35. 38.

Glau occurs in the Atharvaveda[1] and in the Aitareya Brāhmaṇa[2] as the name of some symptom of a disease, probably, as Bloomfield[3] thinks, 'boils.' In the one passage of the Vājasaneyi Saṃhita,[4] where it is found the sense is obscure, some part of the sacrificial victim being perhaps meant.[5] *Cf.* **Galunta.**

[1] vi. 83, 3.
[2] i. 25.
[3] *Proceedings of the American Oriental Society*, October, 1887, xv. ; *Hymns of the Atharvaveda*, 17, 503 ; Whitney, Translation of the Atharvaveda, 343.
[4] xxv. 8 ; Maitrāyaṇī Saṃhitā, iii. 15, 7.
[5] St. Petersburg Dictionary, *s.v.* ; Ludwig, Translation of the Rigveda, 3, 500, takes *glau* as 'owl.'

GH.

Gharma denotes in the Rigveda[1] and later[2] the pot used for heating milk, especially for the offering to the Aśvins. It hence often[3] denotes the hot milk itself, or some other hot drink.

[1] iii. 53. 14 ; v. 30, 15 ; 43, 7 ; 76, 1, etc.
[2] Av. vii. 73, 6 ; Vājasaneyi Saṃhitā, viii. 61 ; Aitareya Brāhmaṇa, i. 18. 22, etc.
[3] Rv. i. 119, 2 ; 180, 4 ; vii. 70, 2 ; viii. 9, 4, etc. ; Av. iv. 1, 2 ; Vājasaneyi Saṃhitā, xxxviii. 6, etc.
Cf. Nirukta, vi. 32 ; xi. 42 ; Zimmer, *Altindisches Leben*, 271 ; St. Petersburg Dictionary, *s.v.*

Ghāsa means 'fodder' in the Atharvaveda[1] and later.[2] In the Rigveda[3] Ghāsi is used of the fodder of the horse victim at the Aśvamedha.

[1] Av. iv. 38, 7 ; viii. 7, 8 ; xi. 5, 18, etc.
[2] Vājasaneyi Saṃhitā, xi. 75 ; xxi. 43 ; Taittirīya Saṃhitā, vi. 5, 9, 3 ; Taittirīya Brāhmaṇa, i. 6, 3, 10, etc.
[3] i. 162, 14.

Ghṛṇīvant is the name of some animal in the list of victims at the Aśvamedha, or horse sacrifice, in the Vājasaneyi Saṃhitā.[1] In the parallel passage of the Maitrāyaṇī Saṃhitā[2] Ghṛṇāvant is the reading. Elsewhere the word is adjectival.[3]

[1] xxiv. 39.
[2] iii. 14, 20.
[3] Rv. x. 176, 3.
Cf. Zimmer, *Altindisches Leben*, 99.

Ghṛta, the modern Ghee or 'clarified butter,' is repeatedly mentioned in the Rigveda[1] and later[2] both as in ordinary use and as a customary form of sacrifice. According to a citation in Sāyaṇa's commentary on the Aitareya Brāhmaṇa,[3] the distinction between Ghṛta and **Sarpis** consisted in the latter being butter fully melted, while the former was butter melted and hardened (*ghanī-bhūta*), but this distinction cannot be pressed. Because the butter was thrown into the fire, Agni is styled 'butter-faced' (*ghṛta-pratīka*),[4] 'butter-backed' (*ghṛta-pṛṣṭha*),[5] and 'propitiated with butter' (*ghṛta-prasatta*),[6] and 'fond of butter' (*ghṛta-prī*[7]). Water was used to purify the butter: the waters were therefore called 'butter-cleansing' (*ghṛta-pū*).[8] In the Aitareya Brāhmaṇa[9] it is said that Ājya, Ghṛta, Āyuta, and Navanīta pertain to gods, men, Pitṛs, and embryos respectively.

[1] i. 134, 6; ii. 10, 4; iv. 10, 6; 58, 5. 7. 9; v. 12, 1, etc.

[2] Vājasaneyi Saṃhitā, ii. 22, etc.; Av. iii. 13, 5, etc.; Śatapatha Brāhmaṇa, i. 8, 1, 7 (with **Dadhi, Mastu, Amikṣā**); ix. 2, 1, 1 (**Dadhi, Madhu, Ghṛta**), etc.

[3] i. 3 (p. 240, edition Aufrecht).

[4] Rv. i. 143, 7; iii. 1, 18; v. 11, 1; x. 21, 7, etc.

[5] Rv. i. 164, 1; v. 4, 3; 37, 1; vii. 2, 4, etc.

[6] Rv. v. 15, 1.

[7] Av. xii. 1, 20; xviii. 4, 41.

[8] i. 3.

Cf. Zimmer, *Altindisches Leben*, 227.

Ghṛta-kauśika is mentioned in the first two Vaṃśas (lists of teachers) of the Mādhyaṃdina recension of the Bṛhadāraṇyaka Upaniṣad[1] as a pupil of **Pārāśaryāyaṇa.**

[1] ii. 5, 21; iv. 5, 27. *Cf.* Weber, *Indische Studien*, 4, 384.

Ghora Āṅgirasa is the name of a mythical teacher in the Kauṣītaki Brāhmaṇa[1] and the Chāndogya Upaniṣad,[2] where he is teacher of the strange **Kṛṣṇa Devakīputra.** That the name is certainly a mere figment is shown by the fact that this 'dread descendant of the Aṅgirases' has a counterpart in **Bhiṣaj Ātharvaṇa,**[3] 'the healing descendant of the Atharvans,' while in the Rigveda Sūtras[4] the *Atharvāṇo vedaḥ* is connected

[1] xxx. 6. *Cf.* Āśvalāyana Śrauta Sūtra, xii. 10.

[2] iii. 17, 6.

[3] Weber, *Indische Studien*, 3, 459.

[4] Āśvalāyana Śrauta Sūtra, x. 7; Śāṅkhāyana Śrauta Sūtra, xvi. 2; *Journal of the American Oriental Society*, 17, 181.

with *bheṣajam* and the *Āṅgiraso vedaḥ* with *ghoram*. He is accordingly a personification of the dark side of the practice of the Atharvaveda.[5] He is also mentioned in the Aśvamedha section of the Kāṭhaka Saṃhitā.[6]

[5] Bloomfield, *Hymns of the Atharvaveda*, xx, xxi, xxxviii; *Atharvaveda*, 8, 23; Macdonell, *Sanskrit Literature*, 189, 190; Hillebrandt, *Vedische Mythologie*, 2, 160, n. 4.

[6] i. 1.

Ghoṣa. See **Ghoṣā.**

Ghoṣavant. See **Svara.**

Ghoṣā is mentioned as a protégée of the Aśvins in two passages of the Rigveda,[1] probably as the recipient of a husband, who is perhaps referred to in another passage[2] as Arjuna, though this is not likely. Sāyaṇa finds a reference there to a skin disease, which is considered in the later tradition of the Bṛhaddevatā[3] to have been the cause of her remaining unwed, but this view is not tenable. According to Sāyaṇa, her son, Suhastya, is alluded to in an obscure verse of the Rigveda[4]; Oldenberg,[5] however, here sees a reference to Ghoṣā herself, while Pischel[6] thinks that the form (*ghoṣe*) is not a noun at all, but verbal.

[1] i. 117, 7; x. 40, 5. *Cf.* x. 39, 3. 6.

[2] i. 122, 5. See Oldenberg, *Ṛgveda-Noten*, 1, 123.

[3] vii. 41-48, with Macdonell's notes.

[4] i. 120, 5.

[5] *Op. cit.*, 119. Suhastya is apparently invented from x. 41, 3, probably assisted by the fact that Vadhrimatī was given a son, **Hiraṇyahasta**, by the Aśvins (Rv. i. 117, 24).

[6] *Vedische Studien*, 1, 4; 2, 92.

Cf. Ludwig, Translation of the Rigveda, 3, 143; *Über Methode bei Interpretation des Rigveda*, 43; Muir, *Sanskrit Texts*, 5, 247; Macdonell, *Vedic Mythology*, p. 52.

C.

Caka is mentioned with Piśaṅga as one of the two Unnetṛ priests at the snake festival in the Pañcaviṃśa Brāhmaṇa.[1]

[1] xxv. 15, 3. *Cf.* Weber, *Indische Studien*, 1, 35, who reads *Cakka*; 10, 142, n. 3, 144

Cakra, the 'wheel' of a chariot or wagon, is repeatedly mentioned from the Rigveda[1] onwards, often in a metaphorical sense. The wheel was fixed on the axle (**Akṣa**) when the chariot was required for use; this required considerable strength, as is shown by a reference in the Rigveda.[2] The wheel consisted normally of spokes (**Ara**), and a nave (**Nābhi**),[3] in the opening (**Kha**) of which the end of the axle (**Āṇi**) was inserted. An indication of the importance attached to the strength of the wheel is the celebration of the car of the god Pūṣan as having a wheel that suffers no damage.[4] The usual number of wheels was two,[5] but in seven passages of the Rigveda[6] a chariot is called 'three-wheeled,' in a few others 'seven-wheeled,'[7] while in one of the Atharvaveda[8] it is styled 'eight-wheeled.' Zimmer[9] argues that these epithets do not refer to real chariots, pointing out that in all the passages where *tri-cakra*, 'three-wheeled,' occurs there is a mythical reference. On the other hand, Weber[10] thinks that there might have been chariots with three wheels, one being in the centre between the two occupants. This is not very conclusive; at any rate, the seven-wheeled and the eight-wheeled chariots can hardly be regarded as indicating the existence of real vehicles with that number of wheels.

In the Śatapatha Brāhmaṇa[11] the potter's wheel (*kaulāla-cakra*) is referred to.

[1] i. 130, 9; 155, 6; 164, 2. 11. 14; 174, 5; iv. 1, 3, etc.

[2] Av. xi. 7, 4; xix. 53, 1. 2, etc.

[3] Rv. viii. 41, 6.

[4] Rv. vi. 54, 3.

[5] Rv. viii. 5, 29; Chāndogya Upaniṣad, iv. 16, 5; Kauṣītaki Upaniṣad, i. 4.

[6] i. 118, 2; 157, 3; 183, 1; viii. 58, 3; x. 41, 1; 85, 14 (all of the Aśvins' chariot); iv. 36, 1 (of a chariot made by the Ṛbhus, who are three in number).

[7] Rv. i. 164, 3. 12; ii. 40, 3.

[8] xi. 4, 22.

[9] *Altindisches Leben*, viii., ix.

[10] *Proceedings of the Berlin Academy*, 1898, 564, quoting Virchow, *Zeitschrift für Ethnologie*, 5, 200.

[11] xi. 8, 1, 1.

Cf. Zimmer, *op. cit.*, 247.

Cakra-vāka is the name, apparently derived from the nature of its cry, of a species of gander (*Anas casarca*), the modern Chakwā, as it is called in Hindī, or Brahmany duck in English.[1] It is mentioned in the Rigveda[2] and in the list of victims at the

[1] Griffith, *Hymns of the Rigveda*, 1, 309, n. 4.

[2] ii. 39, 3.

Aśvamedha, or horse sacrifice, in the Yajurveda,[3] while in the Atharvaveda[4] it already appears as the type of conjugal fidelity, its characteristic in the classical literature.

[3] Maitrāyaṇī Saṃhitā, iii. 14, 3. 13; Vājasaneyi Saṃhitā, xxiv. 22. 32; xxv. 8.

[4] xiv. 2, 64.

Cf. Zimmer, *Altindisches Leben*, 89.

Cakṣus, 'eye.' The 'evil eye' (*ghoraṃ cakṣus*) was well known in the Atharvaveda, which contains spells to counteract its influence.[1] As remedies against it are mentioned salve from Mount **Trikakubh**[2] and the **Jaṅgiḍa** plant.[3] In the wedding ceremony the wife is entreated not to have the evil eye (*aghora-cakṣus*).[4] The structure of the eye, and its division into white (*śukla*), dark (*kṛṣṇa*), and the pupil (*kanīnakā*) are repeatedly referred to in the later Brāhmaṇas.[5] The disease **Alaji** appears to have been an affection of the eyes.

[1] ii. 7; xix. 45, are so employed in the ritual.

[2] Av. iv. 9, 6.

[3] Av. xix. 35, 3.

[4] Pāraskara Gṛhya Sūtra, i. 4; Śāṅkhāyana Gṛhya Sūtra, i. 16.

[5] Śatapatha Brāhmaṇa, xii. 8, 2, 26; Jaiminīya Brāhmaṇa, i. 254. 324; Jaiminīya Upaniṣad Brāhmaṇa, i. 26, 1; 34, 1; Bṛhadāraṇyaka Upaniṣad, ii. 2, 2; Aitareya Āraṇyaka, ii. 1, 5, etc. So the man (*puruṣa*) in the eye is repeatedly mentioned: Chāndogya Upaniṣad, i. 7, 5; iv. 15, 1; Bṛhadāraṇyaka Upaniṣad, ii. 3, 5; iv. 2, 2; v. 5, 2. 4, etc.; Jaiminīya Upaniṣad Brāhmaṇa, i. 27, 2 The Bṛhadāraṇyaka Upaniṣad, ii. 2, 3, adds the water (*āpaḥ*) in the eye, the upper and the lower lids (*vartanī*), and seven red lines (*lohinyo rājayaḥ*).

Cf. Weber, *Indische Studien*, 13, 149.

Caṇḍāla,[1] **Cāṇḍāla,**[2] are the variant forms of the name of a despised caste, which in origin was probably a tribal body,[3] but which in the Brahminical theory was the offspring of Śūdra fathers and Brahmin mothers.[4] The references to the caste in the Yajurveda Saṃhitās and in the Upaniṣads show clearly that it was a degraded one, but they yield no particulars.

[1] Chāndogya Upaniṣad, v. 10, 7, 24, 4; Āśvalāyana Gṛhya Sūtra, iv. 9; Śāṅkhāyana Gṛhya Sūtra, ii. 12; vi. 1, etc.

[2] Vājasaneyi Saṃhitā, xxx. 21; Taittirīya Brāhmaṇa, iii. 4, 17, 1; Bṛhadāraṇyaka Upaniṣad, iv. 1, 22.

[3] Fick, *Die sociale Gliederung*, 204 *et seq*.

[4] Apparently accepted for the Vedic period by Zimmer, *Altindisches Leben*, 217.

Cf. von Schroeder, *Indiens Literatur und Cultur*, 433.

Catuṣ-pad, 'quadruped,' is a regular name for animals from the Rigveda[1] onwards, being frequently contrasted with **Dvipad,** 'biped.'[2] Catuṣ-pāda, as an adjective applying to *paśavaḥ*, 'animals,' is also found.[3]

[1] Rv. i. 49, 3; 94, 5; 119, 1; iii. 62, 14, etc.; Av. iv. 11, 5; x. 8, 21; Vājasaneyi Saṃhitā, viii. 30; ix. 31; xiv. 8. 25, etc.; Aitareya Brāhmaṇa, vi. 2; viii. 20, etc.

[2] Rv. x. 117, 8; Av. vi. 107, 1, etc.

[3] Aitareya Brāhmaṇa, ii. 18; vi. 2; Śatapatha Brāhmaṇa, iii. 7, 3, 2; vi. 8, 2, 17, etc.

1. **Candra,**[1] **Candra-mas,**[2] are the names of the 'moon,' the latter occurring from the Rigveda onwards, but the former being first used in this sense by the Atharvaveda. Very little is said about the moon in Vedic literature, except as identified with **Soma,**[3] both alike being described as waxing and waning. Reference is, however, made to the regular changes of the moon, and to its alternation with the sun,[5] to which it, as Soma, is declared in the Rigveda to be married.[6] Mention is also made of its disappearance at the time of new moon,[7] and of its birth from the light of the sun.[8] In the Atharvaveda[9] reference is made to demons eclipsing the moon (*grahāś cāndramāsāḥ*).

For the phases of the moon, and the month as a measure of time, see **Māsa.** For the moon and its mansions, see **Nakṣatra.**

[1] Av. ii. 15, 2; 22, 1; iii. 31, 6, etc.; Vājasaneyi Saṃhitā, xxii. 28; xxxix. 2; Śatapatha Brāhmaṇa, vi. 2, 2, 16, etc.

[2] Rv. i. 105, 1; viii. 82, 8; x. 64, 3; 85, 19; Av. xi. 6, 7; Vājasaneyi Saṃhitā, i. 28; xxiii. 10. 59, etc.

[3] See Macdonell, *Vedic Mythology*, pp. 112, 113 The identification is clearly found in the later parts of the Rigveda.

[4] Rv. x. 55, 5. *Cf.* Av. x. 8, 32.

[5] Rv. x. 68, 10. *Cf.* i. 62, 8; 72, 10.

[6] x. 85, 18. 19.

[7] Śatapatha Brāhmaṇa, i. 6, 4, 18; iv. 6, 7, 12; xi. 1, 6, 19; xiv. 4, 2, 13; Aitareya Brāhmaṇa, viii. 28, 8; perhaps Rv. x. 138, 4.

[8] Rv. ix. 71, 9; 76, 4; 86, 32; Sāmaveda, ii. 9, 2, 12, 1; Hillebrandt, *Vedische Mythologie*, 1, 463 *et seq*. *Cf.* **Sūrya.**

[9] xix. 9, 10. Av. vi. 128 is also regarded by the Kauśika Sūtra, c. 3, as referring to an eclipse of the moon. See Bloomfield, *Hymns of the Atharvaveda*, 533.

Cf. Zimmer, *Altindisches Leben*, 349, 350, 352.

2. **Candra** appears to denote 'gold' in a certain number of passages from the Rigveda onwards.[1]

[1] Rv. ii. 2, 4; iii. 31, 5; Av. xii. 2, 53; Taittirīya Saṃhitā, i. 2, 7, 1; Kāṭhaka Saṃhitā, ii. 6; Vājasaneyi Saṃhitā, iv. 26; xix. 93; Pañcaviṃśa Brāhmaṇa, vi. 6; Śatapatha Brāhmaṇa, iii. 3, 3, 4, etc. *Cf.* the adjective *candrin* in Vājasaneyi Saṃhitā, xx. 37; xxxi. 31.

Capya is found in the Vājasaneyi Saṃhitā[1] and the Śatapatha Brāhmaṇa[2] as the name of a sacrificial vessel.

[1] xix. 88; Maitrāyaṇī Saṃhitā, iii. 2, 9; Kāṭhaka Saṃhitā, xxxviii. 3.

[2] xii. 7, 2, 13; 9, 1, 3.

Camasa denotes a 'drinking vessel,' usually as employed for holding **Soma** at the sacrifice. It is frequently mentioned from the Rigveda onwards.[1] It was made of wood (*vṛkṣa*),[2] and is hence called *dru*.[3] According to the Śatapatha Brāhmaṇa,[4] it was made of **Udumbara** wood.

[1] Rv. i. 20, 6; 110, 3; viii. 82, 7; x. 16, 8; 68, 8; 96, 9, etc.; Av. vii. 73, 3; xviii. 3, 54; Vājasaneyi Saṃhitā, xxiii. 13, etc.; Nirukta, xi. 2; xii. 38.

[2] Rv. x. 68, 8.

[3] Rv. i. 161, 1.

[4] vii. 2, 11, 2.

Cf. Zimmer, *Altindisches Leben*, 280; Hillebrandt, *Vedische Mythologie*, 1, 167, 168.

Camū is a term of somewhat doubtful sense occurring repeatedly in the Rigveda, and connected with the preparation of Soma. Zimmer[1] considers that in the dual it denotes the two boards between which, in his opinion, the Soma was crushed (*cf.* **Adhiṣavaṇa**). Roth,[2] however, appears to be right in taking the normal sense to designate a vessel into which the Soma was poured from the press, and Hillebrandt[3] shows clearly that when it occurs in the plural[4] it always has this sense, corresponding to the Graha-pātras of the later ritual, and that sometimes it is so used in the singular[5] or dual[6] also. In some cases,[7] however, he recognizes its use as denoting the mortar in which the Soma was pressed: he may be right here, as this mode of preparation was probably Indo-Iranian.[8]

In a derivative sense Camū appears in the Śatapatha Brāhmaṇa[9] to denote a trough, either of solid stone or consisting of

[1] *Altindisches Leben*, 277, 278.

[2] St. Petersburg Dictionary, *s.v.* *Cf.* Grassmann, *Rigveda*, 1, 15.

[3] *Vedische Mythologie*, 1, 164-175.

[4] Rv. iii. 48, 5; viii. 2, 8; 82, 7. 8; ix. 20, 6; 62, 16; 63, 2; 92, 2; 93, 3; 97, 21. 37. 46; 99, 6. 8.

[5] Rv. ix. 107, 18; x. 91, 15.

[6] Rv. ix. 69, 5; 71, 1; 72, 5; 86, 47; 96, 20. 21; 97. 2. 48; 103, 4; 107, 10; 108, 10.

[7] Singular: Rv. v. 51, 4; viii. 4, 4; 76, 10; ix. 46, 3; x. 24, 1. Dual: i. 28, 9; iv. 18, 3; vi. 57, 2; ix. 36, 1.

[8] Hillebrandt, *op. cit.*, 1, 158-164.

[9] xiii. 8, 2, 1; Eggeling, *Sacred Books of the East*, 44, 430, n. 1. In Śāṅkhāyana Śrauta Sūtra, xiv. 22, 19, the sense is doubtful.

Cf. Macdonell, *Vedic Mythology*, pp. 105 *et seq.*

bricks, used by the Eastern people to protect the body of the dead from contact with the earth, like modern stone-lined graves or vaults.

Caraka primarily denotes a 'wandering student,' a sense actually found in the Bṛhadāraṇyaka Upaniṣad.[1] More especially it denotes the members of a school of the Black Yajurveda, the practices of which are several times referred to with disapproval in the Śatapatha Brāhmaṇa.[2] In the Vājasaneyi Saṃhitā[3] the Caraka teacher (*Carakācārya*) is enumerated among the sacrificial victims at the Puruṣamedha, or human sacrifice. His dedication there to ill-doing is a clear hint of a ritual feud.

[1] iii. 3, 1.

[2] iii. 8, 2, 24 (where the reference is to Taittirīya Saṃhitā vi. 3, 9, 6; 10, 2, or some parallel passage); iv. 1, 2, 19; 2, 3, 15; 4, 1. 10; vi. 2, 2, 1. 10; viii. 1, 3, 7; 7, 1, 14. 24.

[3] xxx. 18; Taittirīya Brāhmaṇa, iii. 4, 16, 1. Its occurrence in the latter text renders improbable von Schroeder's view, *Indiens Literatur und Cultur*, 188, that Caraka included all the Black Yajurveda schools.

Cf. Weber, *Indische Studien*, 2, 287, n. 2; 3, 256, 257, 454; *Indian Literature*, 87; Zimmer, *Altindisches Leben*, 212.

Caraka-brāhmaṇa is the name of a work from which Sāyaṇa quotes in his commentary on the Rigveda.[1]

[1] viii. 66, 10; Macdonell, *Vedic Mythology*, p. 41.

Carācara ('running about'), a term found classed with **Sarīsṛpa** in the Yajurveda Saṃhitās,[1] must apparently denote some kind of animal.

[1] Taittirīya Saṃhitā, i. 8, 13, 3; Kāṭhaka Saṃhitā, xv. 3; Maitrāyaṇī Saṃhitā, iii. 12, 10; Vājasaneyi Saṃhitā, xxii. 29.

Caru designates a 'kettle' or 'pot' from the Rigveda onwards.[1] It had a lid (*apidhāna*) and hooks (*aṅka*) by which it could be hung over a fire.[2] It was made of iron or bronze[3]

[1] Rv. i. 7, 6; vii. 104, 2; ix. 52, 3; x. 86, 18; 167, 4; Av. iv. 7, 4; ix. 5, 6; xi. 1, 16; 3, 18; xviii. 4, 16 *et seq.*, etc. It is called *pañca-bila*, 'with five openings,' in the Taittirīya Saṃhitā, i. 6, 1, 2; Kāṭhaka Saṃhitā, v. 6; xxxii. 6; Maitrāyaṇī Saṃhitā, i. 4, 4. 9, etc.

[2] Rv. i. 162, 13; Av. xviii. 4, 53.

[3] Satapatha Brāhmaṇa, xiii. 3, 4, 5 *Cf.* Zimmer, *Altindisches Leben*, 271.

(*ayasmaya*). The word is also secondarily used[4] to denote the contents of the pot, the mess of grain which was cooked in it.

[4] Taittirīya Saṃhitā, i. 8, 10, 1; Aitareya Brāhmaṇa, i. 1; Śatapatha Brāhmaṇa, i. 7, 4, 7; ii. 5, 3, 4; iii. 2, 3, 1, etc. *Cf.* Weber, *Indische Studien*, 9, 216.

Carman, denoting 'hide' in general, is a common expression from the Rigveda onwards.[1] The oxhide was turned to many uses, such as the manufacture of bowstrings, slings, and reins (see **Go**). It was especially often employed to place above the boards[2] on which the Soma was pressed with the stones.[3] It was possibly also used for making skin bags.[4] Carmaṇya denotes leather-work generally in the Aitareya Brāhmaṇa.[5]

The art of tanning hides (*mlā*) was known as early as the Rigveda,[6] where also the word for 'tanner' (*carmamna*) occurs.[7] Details of the process are lacking, but the Śatapatha Brāhmaṇa[8] refers to stretching out a hide with pegs (*śaṅkubhiḥ*), and the Rigveda[9] mentions the wetting of the hide.

[1] Rv. i. 85, 5; 110, 8; 161, 7; iii. 60, 2; iv. 13, 4, etc.; Av. v. 8, 13; x. 9, 2; xi. 1, 9, etc.; Taittirīya Saṃhitā, iii. 1, 7, 1; vi. 1, 9, 2, etc. The stem *carma*, neuter (loc., *carme*), is found in the Taittirīya Brāhmaṇa, ii. 7, 2, 2.

[2] Hillebrandt, *Vedische Mythologie*, 1, 148-150; 181-183.

[3] Rv. x. 94, 9; 116, 4.

[4] Rv. x. 106, 10, is so taken by Zimmer, *Altindisches Leben*, 228, who compares *Odyssey*, x. 19.

[5] v. 32. *Cf. paricarmaṇya*, Sāṅkhāyana Āraṇyaka, ii. 1.

[6] viii. 55, 3 (a late hymn).

[7] viii. 5, 38; Vājasaneyi Saṃhitā, xxx. 15; Taittirīya Brāhmaṇa, iii. 4, 13, 1. For the form, *cf.* Macdonell, *Vedic Grammar*, p. 38, n. 1; p. 249, n. 4.

[8] ii. 1, 1, 9.

[9] i. 85, 5.

Cf. Zimmer, *Altindisches Leben*, 228, 253.

Carṣaṇi, used in the plural, denotes in the Rigveda[1] 'men' in general or 'people,' conceived either as active beings[2] or as cultivators[3] in opposition to nomads. The expression 'king of men' (*rājā carṣaṇīnām*) is frequently found.[4] The 'people' are

[1] Rv. i. 86, 5; 184, 4; iii. 43, 2; iv. 7, 4; v. 23, 1; vi. 2, 2; x. 180, 3, etc.

[2] If derived from *car*, 'move,' which is probable.

[3] If derived from *kṛṣ*, 'plough' or 'till.'

[4] Rv. iii. 10, 1; v. 39, 4; vi. 30, 5; viii. 70, 1; x. 139, 1, etc.

also mentioned in connexion with war.[5] In the Atharvaveda[6] 'animals' (*paśu*) and 'men' (*carṣaṇi*) are spoken of together.

For the five *carṣaṇayaḥ*,[7] see **Pañca Janāsaḥ.**

[5] Rv. i. 55, 1; 109, 6; iv. 31, 4; 37, 8; vi. 31, 1, etc.

[6] xiii. 1, 38.

[7] Rv. v. 86, 2; vii. 15, 2; ix. 101, 9. For the derivation, see Macdonell, *Vedic Grammar*, 185, and especially 122, 2*a* (from *car*, 'move'); Monier Williams, Dictionary, *s.v.* (from *kṛṣ*, 'plough').

Caṣāla, the mortar-shaped top-piece of the sacrificial post (**Yūpa**), is mentioned from the Rigveda onwards.[1] In one passage of the Śatapatha Brāhmaṇa[2] it is directed to be made of wheaten dough (*gaudhūma*).

[1] Rv. i. 162, 6; Taittirīya Saṃhitā, vi. 3, 4, 2. 7; Kāṭhaka Saṃhitā, xxvi. 4, etc.; Maitrāyaṇī Saṃhitā, i. 11, 8, etc.

[2] v. 2, 1, 6.

Cf. Eggeling, *Sacred Books of the East*, 26, 168, n. 1; 41, 31, n. 1.

Cākra is the name of a man, variously styled Revottaras Sthapati Pāṭava Cākra[1] and Revottaras Pāṭava Cākra Sthapati,[2] who is mentioned in the Śatapatha Brāhmaṇa only. He is there said to have been expelled by the **Sṛñjayas**, but to have restored to them their prince **Duṣṭarītu** despite the opposition of the Kauravya king **Balhika Prātipīya.**[2] He must have been a sage rather than a warrior, as the first passage of the Śatapatha Brāhmaṇa[1] shows him in the capacity of a teacher only. *Cf.* **Sthapati.**

[1] Śatapatha Brāhmaṇa, xii. 8, 1, 17.

[2] *Ibid.*, xii. 9, 3, 1 *et seq.*

Cf. Weber, *Indische Studien*, 1, 205-207; 10, 85, n. 1; *Indian Literature*, 123; Eggeling, *Sacred Books of the East*, 44, 269 *et seq.*, whose version is followed above.

Cākrāyaṇa, 'descendant of Cakra,' is the patronymic of **Uṣasta** or **Uṣasti.**[1]

[1] Bṛhadāraṇyaka Upaniṣad, iii. 5, 1; Chāndogya Upaniṣad, i. 10, 1; 11, 1.

Cāṇḍāla. See **Caṇḍāla.**

Cākṣuṣa, a word occurring once only in the Atharvaveda,[1] is, according to the St. Petersburg Dictionary, a patronymic (of Suyāman, a personification). Whitney[2] treats it as probably a simple adjective ('of sight').

[1] xvi. 7, 7.

[2] Translation of the Atharvaveda, 800.

Cātur-māsya, 'four-monthly,' denotes the festival of the Vedic ritual held at the beginning of the three seasons of four months each, into which the Vedic year was artificially divided.[1] It is clear that the sacrifices commenced with the beginning of each season,[2] and it is certain that the first of them, the Vaiśvadeva, coincided with the Phālgunī full moon,[3] the second, the Varuṇa-praghāsas, with the Āṣāḍhī full moon,[4] and the third, the Sāka-medha, with the Kārttikī full moon.[5] There were, however, two alternative datings: the festivals could also be held in the Caitrī, the Śrāvaṇī, and Āgrahāyaṇī (Mārgaśīrṣī) full moons,[6] or in the Vaiśākhī, Bhādrapadī, and Pauṣī full moons.[7] Neither of the later datings is found in a Brāhmaṇa text, but each may well have been known early, since the Taittirīya Saṃhitā[8] and the Pañcaviṃśa Brāhmaṇa[9] both recognize the full moon in the month Caitra as an alternative to the full moon in the month Phālguna, for the beginning of the year.

Jacobi considers that the commencement of the year with the full moon in the asterism Phalgunī, which is supported by other evidence,[10] indicates that the year at one time began with the winter solstice with the moon in Phalgunī, corresponding to the summer solstice when the sun was in Phalgunī. These astronomical conditions, he believes, existed in the time of the Rigveda,[11] and prevailed in the fourth millennium B.C. The alternative

[1] Taittirīya Saṃhitā, i. 6, 10, 3; Taittirīya Brāhmaṇa, i. 4, 9, 5; ii. 2, 2, 2; Śatapatha Brāhmaṇa, i. 6, 3, 36; ii. 5, 2, 48; 6, 4, 1; v. 2, 3, 10; xiii. 2, 5, 2; Kauṣītaki Brāhmaṇa, v. 1, etc.

[2] Śatapatha Brāhmaṇa, i. 6 3, 36 (*cf.* xiv. 1, 1, 28); Kauṣītaki Brāhmaṇa, v. 1.

[3] In the month Phālguna, or February-March.

[4] In the month Āṣāḍha, or June-July.

[5] That is, in the month Kārttika, when the moon is in the asterism Kṛttikā: Śatapatha Brāhmaṇa, ii. 6, 3, 13; Kauṣītaki Brāhmaṇa, v. 1, etc.

[6] Śāṅkhāyana Śrauta Sūtra, iii. 13, 1; 14, 1. 2; 15, 1. These are the full-moon days in the months Caitra (March-April), Śrāvaṇa (July-August), and Mārgaśīrṣa (November-December) respectively.

[7] Deva's Paddhati on Kātyāyana Srauta Sūtra, pp. 430, 450, 497. These are the full-moon days in the months Vaiśākha (April-May), Bhādrapada (August-September), and Pauṣa (December-January) respectively.

[8] vii. 4, 8, 1. 2.

[9] v. 9, 8. 11.

[10] *Indian Antiquary*, 23, 156 *et seq.*; *Zeitschrift der Deutschen Morgenländischen Gesellschaft*, 49, 223 *et seq.*; 50, 72-81.

[11] vii. 103, 9; x. 85, 13. *Cf. Festgruss an Rudolf von Roth*, 68 *et seq.*

dates would then indicate periods when the winter solstice coincided with the Caitrī or the Vaiśākhī full moon. But Oldenberg[12] and Thibaut[13] seem clearly right in holding that the coincidence of Phālgunī with the beginning of spring,[14] which is certain, is fatal to this view, and that there is no difficulty in regarding this date as consistent with the date of the winter solstice in the new moon of Māgha, which is given by the Kauṣītaki Brāhmaṇa,[15] and which forms the basis of the calculations of the Jyotiṣa.[16] The full moon in Phālguna would be placed about one month and a half after the winter solstice, or, say, in the first week of February, which date, according to Thibaut, may reasonably be deemed to mark the beginning of a new season in India about 800 B.C. At the same time it must be remembered that the date was necessarily artificial, inasmuch as the year was divided into three seasons, each of four months, and the Indian year does not in fact consist of three equal seasons. The variations of the other datings would then not be unnatural if any school wished to defer its spring festival, the Vaiśvadeva, to the time when spring had really manifested itself. See also **Saṃvatsara.**

12 *Zeitschrift der Deutschen Morgenländischen Gesellschaft*, 48, 630 *et seq.*; 49, 475, 476; 50, 453-457.

13 *Indian Antiquary*, 24, 86 *et seq.*

14 See Taittirīya Brāhmaṇa, i. 1, 2, 6. 8; Śatapatha Brāhmaṇa, xiii. 4, 1, 2-4. So the Phālgunī full moon is called 'the mouth of the seasons (*ṛtūnāṃ mukham*) — *e.g.*, Pañcaviṃśa Brāhmaṇa, xxi. 15, 2; Kāṭhaka Saṃhitā, viii. 1; Maitrāyaṇī Saṃhitā, i. 6, 9; and the first season is always spring: Śatapatha Brāhmaṇa, i. 5, 3, 8-14; ii. 1, 3, 1; vii. 2, 4, 26; xi. 2, 7, 32; xii. 8, 2, 34; xiii. 5, 4, 28; Taittirīya Saṃhitā, ii. 1, 2, 5; Kāṭhaka Saṃhitā, xiii. 1. 7, etc. See Weber, *Naxatra*, 2, 352.

15 xix. 3.

16 Thibaut, *Astronomie, Astrologie, und Mathematik*, 17, 18.

Cf. Weber, *Naxatra*, 2, 329 *et seq.*; Whitney, *Journal of the American Oriental Society*, 16, lxxxvi., lxxxvii.; Keith, *Journal of the Royal Asiatic Society*, 1909, 1101-1104.

Cāndhanāyana is the patronymic of **Ānandaja** in the Vaṃśa Brāhmaṇa.[1]

1 *Indische Studien*, 4, 372, 383.

Cāyamāna is the patronymic in the Rigveda (vi. 27, 5. 8) of **Abhyāvartin.**

Cāṣa, the 'blue woodpecker' (*Coracias indica*), is mentioned in the Rigveda,[1] as well as in the list of victims at the Aśvamedha, or horse sacrifice, in the Yajurveda.[2]

[1] x. 97, 13.
[2] Maitrāyaṇī Saṃhitā, iii. 14, 4; 15, 9; Vājasaneyi Saṃhitā, xxiv. 23; xxv. 7. *Cf*. Zimmer, *Altindisches Leben*, 92.

Ciccika is a bird mentioned with the equally unknown **Vṛṣārava** in one hymn of the Rigveda.[1] It may perhaps be compared with the Ciṭaka mentioned by Dārila in his commentary on the Kauśika Sūtra.[2]

[1] x. 146, 2.
[2] xxvi. 20; Bloomfield, *Hymns of the Atharvaveda*, 266.
Cf. Zimmer, *Altindisches Leben*, 90; Griffith, *Hymns of the Rigveda*, 2, 589.

Citra is the name of several persons. (*a*) The Rigveda[1] contains a Dānastuti ('Praise of Gifts') of a prince Citra. The later legend[2] attributes this panegyric to Sobhari, and describes Citra as king of the rats.

[1] viii. 21, 18.
[2] Bṛhaddevatā, vii. 58 *et seq.*, with Macdonell's notes.

(*b*) Citra Gāṅgyāyani or Gārgyāyaṇi is mentioned in the Kauṣītaki Upaniṣad[1] as a contemporary of **Āruṇi** and **Śvetaketu.**

[1] i. 1. *Cf*. Weber, *Indische Studien*, 1, 395; Keith, *Śāṅkhāyana Āraṇyaka*, 16, n. 1.

(*c*) Citra Gauśrāyaṇi is mentioned as a teacher in the Kauṣītaki Brāhmaṇa.[1]

[1] xxiii. 5. *Cf*. Weber, *loc. cit.*

Citra-ratha ('having a brilliant car') is the name of two persons.

(*a*) It designates an Āryan prince, who, with Arṇa, was defeated by Indra for the Turvaśa-Yadus on the **Sarayu** (perhaps the modern Sarju in Oudh), according to the Rigveda (iv. 30, 18). The locality would accord with the close connexion of Turvaśa and **Krivi** or **Pañcāla.**

(*b*) Citraratha is also the name of a king for whom the **Kāpeyas** performed a special kind of sacrifice (*dvirātra*), with the result, according to the Pañcaviṃśa Brāhmaṇa,[1] that in the Caitrarathi family only one member was a Kṣatra-pati, the rest dependents. Apparently this must mean that the Caitrarathis were distinguished from other families of princes by the fact that the chief of the clan received a markedly higher position than in most cases, in which probably the heads of the family were rather an oligarchy than a monarch and his dependents. See **Rājan.**

[1] xx. 12, 5. *Cf.* Hopkins, *Transactions of the Connecticut Academy of Arts and Sciences*, 15, 52, 53; Weber, *Indische Studien*, 1, 32; *Indian Literature*, 68, n.

Citrā. See **Nakṣatra.**

Cilvaṭi is the name of an unknown animal in the Gopatha Brāhmaṇa (i. 2, 7).

Cīpudru designates some substance mentioned in a hymn of the Atharvaveda[1] as of use in healing. The commentator Sāyaṇa reads Cīpadru, and explains the word as a kind of tree. This interpretation is supported by the fact that the Kauśika Sūtra[2] refers to the employment of splinters of Palāśa wood in the ritual application of this hymn.[3] Whitney[4] suggests that the form of the word should be Cīpuḍu.

[1] vi. 127, 2.

[2] xxvi. 34.

[3] Av. vi. 127.

[4] Translation of the Atharvaveda, 376.

Cf. Bloomfield, *Hymns of the Atharvaveda*, 350-352; *Atharvaveda*, 62; Zimmer, *Altindisches Leben*, 386. The text of Roth and Whitney reads by error *Śīpudru*.

Cumuri is the name of an enemy of **Dabhīti**, for whom he, along with his friend **Dhuni**, is mentioned in the Rigveda[1] as having been defeated by Indra. Elsewhere[2] the two are spoken of, along with **Śambara**, **Pipru**, and Śuṣṇa, as having been crushed by Indra, who destroyed their castles. It is impossible to say whether real men or demons are meant, but in favour of

[1] vi. 20, 13; x. 113, 9. In vi. 26, 6, Cumuri alone is mentioned, and Dāsas or Dasyus generally are stated to have been subdued for Dabhīti in iv. 30, 21; ii. 13, 9. See also ii. 15, 9; vii. 19, 4.

[2] Rv. vi. 18, 8.

a man being denoted by Cumuri is the form of the name, which seems not to be Āryan.[3]

[3] Wackernagel, *Altindische Grammatik*, 1, xxii.
Cf. Hillebrandt, *Vedische Mythologie*, 3, 275; Macdonell, *Vedic Mythology*, p. 162.

Cūḍa Bhāgavitti ('descendant of Bhagavitta') is mentioned in the Bṛhadāraṇyaka Upaniṣad[1] as a pupil of **Madhuka Paiṅgya.**

[1] vi. 3, 9 (Kāṇva = vi. 3, 17. 18 Mādhyaṃdina). The text of the Kāṇva has, as usual, Cūla.

Cūrṇa appears to denote an aromatic powder in the phrase *cūrṇa-hasta,* used of the Apsarases in the Kauṣītaki Upaniṣad (i. 4).

Cedi is the name of a people who, with their king **Kaśu,** the Caidya, are mentioned only in a Dānastuti ('Praise of Gifts'), occurring at the end of one hymn of the Rigveda,[1] where their generosity is celebrated as unsurpassed. They occur later in the Epic with the **Matsyas,** and lived in Bandela Khaṇḍa (Bundelkhand).[2] In Vedic times they were probably situated in much the same locality.

[1] viii. 5, 37-39.
[2] Lassen, *Indische Alterthumskunde*, 1², 688, n. 3; Zimmer, *Altindisches Leben*, 129; Pargiter, *Journal of the Royal Asiatic Society*, 1908, 332; Oldenberg, *Buddha*, 402.

Celaka Śāṇḍilyāyana ('descendant of **Śāṇḍilya** ') is mentioned as a teacher in the Śatapatha Brāhmaṇa (x. 4, 5, 3).

Caikitāneya ('descendant of Cekitāna') is mentioned as a teacher in the Jaiminīya Upaniṣad Brāhmaṇa.[1] The Caikitāneyas are also referred to there[2] in connexion with the Sāman which they worshipped. **Brahmadatta** Caikitāneya is brought into connexion with the Sāman in the Bṛhadāraṇyaka Upaniṣad,[3] and **Vāsiṣṭha** Caikitāneya is known to the Ṣaḍviṃśa[4] and Vaṃśa Brāhmaṇas.[5] The word is a patronymic, formed from

[1] i. 37, 7; ii. 5, 2.
[2] i. 42, 1.
[3] i. 3, 24.
[4] iv. 1.
[5] *Indische Studien*, 4, 373, 384.

Caikitāna, according to Śaṅkara,[6] but more probably from Cekitāna,[7] a name found in the Epic.

[6] On Bṛhadāraṇyaka Upaniṣad, *loc. cit.*

[7] St. Petersburg Dictionary, *s.v.*

Caikitāyana, 'descendant of Cikitāyana[1] or Cekita,'[2] is the patronymic of **Dālbhya** in the Chāndogya Upaniṣad.[3]

[1] Śaṅkara on Chāndogya Upaniṣad, i. 8, 1.

[2] St. Petersburg Dictionary, *s.v.*

[3] i. 8, 1.

Caitra is the patronymic of **Yajñasena** in the Kāṭhaka Saṃhitā (xxi. 4).

Caitra-rathi. See **Citraratha** and **Satyādhivāka.**

Caitriyāyaṇa is the patronymic or metronymic of the teacher **Yajñasena** in the Taittirīya Saṃhitā (v. 3, 8, 1).

Caidya. See **Cedi.**

Cailaki, 'descendant of **Celaka**,' is the patronymic of Jīvala in the Śatapatha Brāhmaṇa (ii. 3, 1, 34).

Cora, 'thief,' is only found in the Taittirīya Āraṇyaka, a late work, in its last book (x. 65). The Vedic terms are **Taskara Tāyu, Stena,** and **Paripanthin.**

Cyavatāna Mārutāśva ('descendant of Marutāśva') is apparently the name of a prince in a Dānastuti ('Praise of Gifts'), in the Rigveda.[1] Two distinct persons may, however, be meant.

[1] v. 33, 9. *Cf.* Ludwig, Translation of the Rigveda, 3. 155.

Cyavana,[1] **Cyavāna,**[2] are variant forms of the name of an ancient Ṛṣi, or seer. The Rigveda[3] represents him as an old decrepit man, to whom the Aśvins restored youth and strength, making him acceptable to his wife, and a husband of maidens.

[1] This form is found even in the Nirukta (iv. 19), regularly in all the Vedic texts other than the Rigveda, and in the Epic.

[2] The Rv. has this form throughout.

[3] i. 116, 10; 117, 13; 118, 6; v. 74, 5; vii. 68, 6; 71, 5; x. 39, 4.

The legend is given in another form in the Śatapatha Brāhmaṇa,[4] where Cyavana is described as wedding Sukanyā, the daughter of **Śaryāta.** He is there called a Bhṛgu or Āṅgirasa, and is represented as having been rejuvenated by immersion in a pond—the first occurrence of a motive, later very common in Oriental literature. Another legend about Cyavāna is apparently alluded to in an obscure hymn of the Rigveda,[5] where he seems to be opposed to the **Paktha** prince **Tūrvayāṇa,** an Indra worshipper, while Cyavāna seems to have been specially connected with the Aśvins. This explanation of the hymn, suggested by Pischel,[6] is corroborated by the Jaiminīya Brāhmaṇa,[7] which relates that **Vidanvant,** another son of Bhṛgu, supported Cyavana against Indra, who was angry with him for sacrificing to the Aśvins; it is also noteworthy that the Aśvins appear in the Śatapatha Brāhmaṇa[8] as obtaining a share in the sacrifice on the suggestion of Sukanyā. But a reconciliation of Indra and Cyavana must have taken place, because the Aitareya Brāhmaṇa[9] relates the inauguration of **Śāryāta** by Cyavana with the great Indra consecration (*aindreṇa mahābhiṣekeṇa*). In the Pañcaviṃśa Brāhmaṇa[10] Cyavana is mentioned as a seer of Sāmans or Chants.

[4] iv. 1, 5, 1 *et seq.*

[5] x. 61, 1-3.

[6] *Vedische Studien*, 1, 71-77; accepted by Griffith, *Hymns of the Rigveda*, 2, 465.

[7] iii. 121-128; *Journal of the American Oriental Society*, 11, cxlvi; 26, 43 *et seq.*

[8] iv. 1, 5, 13 *et seq.*

[9] viii. 21, 4; Pischel, *op. cit.*, 1, 75.

[10] xiii. 5, 12; xix. 3, 6; xiv. 6, 10; xi. 8, 11.

Cf. Muir, *Sanskrit Texts*, 5, 243. 250-254; Ludwig, Translation of the Rigveda, 3, 156; Macdonell, *Vedic Mythology*, pp. 51, 52; Hopkins, *Journal of the American Oriental Society*, 26, 43 *et seq.*; *Transactions of the Connecticut Academy of Arts and Sciences*, 15, 56, 57.

CH.

Chaga is the name of the 'goat' in the Taittirīya Saṃhitā (v. 6, 22, 1). *Cf.* **Aja** and **Chāga.**

Chadis is used once in the Rigveda,[1] and not rarely later,[2] to denote the covering of a wagon or the thatch of a house, or

[1] x. 85, 10 (of Sūryā's bridal car).

[2] Taittirīya Saṃhitā, vi. 2, 9, 4; 10, 5. 7; Vājasaneyi Saṃhitā, v. 28; Aitareya Brāhmaṇa, i. 29; Śatapatha Brāhmaṇa, iii. 5, 3, 9, etc.

something analogous to these. Weber[3] thinks that in one passage of the Atharvaveda[4] the word designates a constellation, and Whitney,[5] who does not decide whether that interpretation is necessary, suggests that the constellation γ, ξ, η, π Aquarii may be meant, since the next verse mentions **Vicṛtau,** which is the constellation λ and ν Scorpionis, and is not far from Aquarius. See also **Chardis.**

[3] *Indische Studien*, 17, 208.
[4] iii. 7, 3.
[5] Translation of the Atharvaveda, 95. *Cf.* Bloomfield, *Hymns of the Atharvaveda*, 336.

1. **Chandas** in the Rigveda usually denotes a 'song of praise' or 'hymn.'[1] The original sense of the word, as derived from the verb *chand*, 'to please,' was probably 'attractive spell,' 'magic hymn,'[2] which prevailed on the gods. In a very late hymn of the Rigveda,[3] as well as in one of the Atharvaveda,[4] the word is mentioned in the plural (*chandāṃsi*), beside Ṛc (*ṛcaḥ*), Sāman (*sāmāni*), and Yajus, and seems to retain its original meaning, not improbably with reference to the magical subject-matter of the Atharvaveda. From denoting a (metrical) hymn it comes to mean 'metre' in a very late verse of the Rigveda,[5] in which the 'Gāyatrī, the Triṣṭubh, and all (*sarvā*) the metres (*chandāṃsi*) are mentioned. In the later Saṃhitās three[6] or seven[7] metres are enumerated, and in the Śatapatha Brāhmaṇa[8] eight. By the time of the Rigveda Prātiśākhya[9] the metres were subjected to a detailed examination, though much earlier references are found to the number of syllables in the several metres.[10] Later the word definitely denotes a Vedic text generally, as in the Śatapatha Brāhmaṇa.[11]

[1] Rv. x. 85, 8 (an obscure verse); 114, 5; Av. iv. 34, 1; v. 26, 5; vi. 124, 1; xi. 7, 8, etc.
[2] *Cf.* Roth in St. Petersburg Dictionary, *s.v.*
[3] Rv. x. 90, 9.
[4] Av. xi. 7, 24.
[5] x. 14, 16.
[6] Av. xviii. 1, 17; Vājasaneyi Saṃhitā, i. 27, etc.
[7] Av. viii. 9, 17. 19, etc.
[8] viii. 3, 3, 6, etc.
[9] xvi. 1 *et seq.* *Cf.* Max Müller, *Sacred Books of the East*, 32, xcv. *et seq.*
[10] Kāṭhaka Saṃhitā, xiv. 4; Jaittirīya Saṃhitā, vi. 1, 2, 7.
[11] xi. 5, 7, 3. So Gobhila Gṛhya Sūtra, iii. 3, 4. 15, etc.

2. **Chandas** occurs in one passage of the Atharvaveda[1] in the adjectival compound *bṛhac-chandas*, which is used of a house, and must mean 'having a large roof.' Bloomfield[2] accepts the reading as correct, but Whitney[3] considers emendation to **Chadis** necessary.

1 iii. 12, 3.
2 *Hymns of the Atharvaveda*, 345; Zimmer, *Altindisches Leben*, 150.
3 Translation of the Atharvaveda, 105.

Chando-ga, 'metre-singing,' is the term applied to reciters of the Sāmans, no doubt because these chants were sung according to their order in the Chandaārcika of the Sāmaveda. It is only found in the Śatapatha Brāhmaṇa,[1] and often in the Sūtras.[2]

1 x. 5, 2, 10.
2 Baudhāyana Śrauta Sūtra, ii. 2; xxii. 4; Śāṅkhāyana Srauta Sūtra, x. 8, 33; xiii. 1, etc.

Cf. Oldenberg, *Göttingische Gelehrte Anzeigen*, 1908, 720.

Chardis occurs often in the Rigveda,[1] and occasionally later,[2] denoting a secure dwelling-place. The word appears to be incorrectly written, because the metre shows that the first syllable is always short. Roth[3] accordingly suggested that **Chadis** should be read instead. But Chadis means 'roof,' while Chardis never has that sense. Bartholomae[4] is therefore probably right in suggesting some other form, such as Chaḍis.

1 i. 48, 15; 114, 5; vi. 15, 3; 46, 9. 12, etc.
2 Taittirīya Saṃhitā, iv. 2, 9, 2; 3, 6, 1; Vājasaneyi Saṃhitā, xiii. 19; xiv. 12.
3 St. Petersburg Dictionary, *s.v.*; Oldenberg, *Prolegomena*, 477.
4 *Studien*, 1, 47; 2, 58. *Cf.* Wackernagel, *Altindische Grammatik*, 1, xii., n. 2; Oldenberg, *Zeitschrift der Deutschen Morgenländischen Gesellschaft*, 55, 312.

Chāga, 'goat,' is found in the Rigveda,[1] and not rarely later.[2] See **Aja** and **Chaga**.

1 i. 162, 3.
2 Vājasaneyi Saṃhitā, xix. 89; xxi. 40. 41; Satapatha Brāhmaṇa, iii. 3, 3, 4; v. 1, 3, 14; Maitrāyaṇī Saṃhitā, iii. 11, 2.

J.

Jagat, 'moving,' is applied sometimes in the Atharvaveda, and later to the domestic animals in particular, as opposed to wild animals (*śvapad*).[1] Occasionally the cow is mentioned separately, when the word *jagat* covers the rest of the domesticated animals.[2]

[1] Av. viii. 5, 11, etc.

[2] Av. i. 31, 4; x. 1, 29; xix. 47, 10; Vājasaneyi Saṃhitā, iii. 59. In the Rv. the sense of animal in general is usually sufficient; but *cf. jagatī* in i. 157, 5; vi. 72, 4.

Cf. Zimmer, *Altindisches Leben*, 150, n.

Jaṅgiḍa is the name of a healing plant mentioned in the hymns of the Atharvaveda.[1] It was used as an amulet against the diseases, or symptoms of disease, **Takman, Balāsa, Āśarīka, Viśarīka, Pṛṣṭyāmaya,**[2] fevers and rheumatic pains, **Viṣkandha** and **Saṃskandha,**[3] **Jambha**, and so on. But it is also regarded as a specific against all diseases, and as the best of healing powers.[4] It is said to be produced from the juices (*rasa*) of ploughing (*kṛṣi*),[5] but this need only mean that it grew in cultivated land, not that it was itself cultivated. What plant the name designates is quite uncertain, for it disappears in the later literature. Caland[6] takes it in the Kauśika Sūtra to be the *Terminalia arjuneya.*

[1] ii. 4; xix. 34. 35.

[2] Av. xix. 34, 10.

[3] Av. ii. 4, 1; xix. 34, 1. 5.

[4] Av. xix. 34, 9. 7.

[5] Av. ii. 4, 5.

[6] *Altindisches Zauberritual*, 15, rendering Kauśika Sūtra, viii. 15.

Cf. Bloomfield, *Hymns of the Atharvaveda*, 433; Whitney, Translation of the Atharvaveda, 42; Weber, *Indische Studien*, 13, 141; Grohmann, *ibid.*, 9, 417; Zimmer, *Altindisches Leben*, 65, 66, 390.

Jatū, the 'bat,' occurs in the Atharvaveda,[1] and is mentioned as one of the victims at the Aśvamedha, or horse sacrifice, in the Yajurveda.[2]

[1] ix. 2, 22.

[2] Maitrāyaṇī Saṃhitā, iii. 14, 6; Vājasaneyi Saṃhitā, xxiv. 25. 26.

Cf. Zimmer, *Altindisches Leben*, 86.

Jana, besides meaning 'man' as an individual, with a tendency to the collective sense, commonly denotes a 'people' or 'tribe' in the Rigveda and later. Thus, the 'five tribes' (**Panca Janāḥ** or **Janāsaḥ**) are frequently referred to, and in one hymn of the Rigveda[1] the 'people of Yadu' (*yādva jana*) and the **Yadus** (*yādvāḥ*) are synonymous. Again, the king (*rājan*) is described as 'protector (*gopā*) of the people (*janasya*),'[2] and there are other references to king and Jana.[3] The people of the **Bharatas** (*bhārata jana*) is also mentioned;[4] there is no ground to assume with Hopkins[5] that Jana in this case means a clan or horde (**Grāma**), as distinguished from a people.

It is difficult to say exactly how a people was divided. Zimmer[6] argues from a passage in the Rigveda[7] that a people was divided into cantons (**Viś**), cantons into joint families or clans, or village communities (**Grāma, Vṛjana**), and these again into single families. He thinks that the four divisions are reflected in the passage in question by Jana, Viś, Janman, and Putrāḥ, or sons, and argues that each village community was originally founded on relationship. But it is very doubtful whether this precise division of the people can be pressed. The division of the Jana into several Viś may be regarded as probable, for it is supported by the evidence of another passage of the Rigveda,[8] which mentions the Viś as a unit of the fighting men, and thus shows that, as in Homeric times and in ancient Germany, relationship was deemed a good principle of military arrangement. But the subdivision of the Viś into several Grāmas is very doubtful. Zimmer[9] admits that neither Grāma[10]

[1] viii. 6, 46. 48.

[2] Rv. iii. 43, 5. So Soma is called *gopati janasya*, 'protector of the people,' Rv. ix. 35, 5.

[3] Rv. v. 58, 4.

[4] Rv. iii. 53, 12. See also **Bharata**. *Cf.* also x. 174, 5=Av. i. 29, 6.

[5] *Religions of India*, 26, 27. It is true that the Bharatas are called a *gavyan grāmaḥ*, 'a horde eager for booty,' in Rv. iii. 33, 11; but Grāma has there merely a general application. See n. 10.

[6] *Altindisches Leben*, 159, 160.

[7] ii. 26, 3.

[8] x. 84, 4. *Viśaḥ* may have the same sense in several other passages—iv. 24, 4; v. 61, 1; vi. 26, 1; vii. 79, 2; viii. 12, 29—but it need not necessarily bear this sense. But in x. 91, 2, there is a clear contrast between Viś and Jana.

[9] *Op. cit.*, 161. He also relies on Rv. v. 53, 11, where the Maruts are divided into *śardha*, *vrāta*, and *gaṇa*; but these words are vague.

[10] Rv. iii. 33. 11. See n. 5.

nor **Vṛjana**[11] has the special sense of a subdivision of the Viś when used for war, for both words only denote generally an armed host. He finds other designations of the village host in **Vrā**[12] and in **Vrāja,**[13] but it is sufficient to say that the former passage is of extremely doubtful import,[14] and that the latter has no reference to war at all. It is therefore impossible to state in what exact relation the Grāma in Vedic times stood to the Viś or to the family (Kula or Gotra). The confusion is increased by the vagueness of the sense of both Grāma and Viś. If the latter be regarded as a local division, then no doubt the Grāma must have been a part of a district; but if a Viś was a unit of relationship, then a Grāma may have contained families of different Viśes, or may have sometimes coincided with a Viś, or have contained only a part of a Viś. But in any case the original state of affairs must have been greatly modified by the rise of the system of caste, and the substitution of a hierarchical for a political point of view. The elements of the people were represented by the family—either as an individual family inhabiting one home (**Kula**), and consisting often, no doubt, of a joint family of brothers, or as a patriarchal family of sons who still lived with their father—and by the clan, the later **Gotra,** which included all those who claimed a common ancestor. The Gotra may be regarded as roughly corresponding to the Latin *gens* and the Greek γένος, and possibly the Viś may be the equivalent of the *curia* and φρήτρη, and the Jana of the *tribus* and φῦλον or φύλη.[15] These three divisions may also be seen in the Viś, Zantu, and Daqyu of the Iranian world, where the use of Viś suggests that in the Indian Viś a relationship based on blood rather than locality is meant—and perhaps even in the *vicus*, *pagus*, and *civitas* of the old German polity described in the Germania[16] of Tacitus. The family in some form appears as the third element of the Jana in a passage of the Rigveda,[17] where the house (*gṛha*) is

[11] Rv. vii. 32, 27; x. 42, 10.

[12] Rv. i. 126, 5 (*viśyā iva vrāḥ*).

[13] Rv. x. 179, 2 = Av. vii. 72, 2.

[14] *Cf.* Pischel, *Vedische Studien*, 2, 121, 319.

[15] *Cf. Iliad*, 2, 362.

[16] Chap. vii. Zimmer gives other equations, for which *cf.* Schrader, *Prehistoric Antiquities*, 393 *et seq.* The exact parallelism cannot in any case be pressed.

[17] x. 91, 2, where *janaṃ janam* and *viśaṃ viśam* occur, and where a contrast must be meant.

contrasted with the Jana and the Viś. Possibly, too, another passage[18] contrasts the *adhvara*, or family sacrifice, with that of the Jana or Viś, rather than, as Zimmer[19] thinks, the village with the two larger units. But it is significant of the particularism of the Vedic Indians that while the king maintained a fire which might be regarded as the sacred fire of the tribe, there is no sure trace[20] of any intermediate cult between that of the king and that of the individual householder. The real elements in the state are the Gotra and the Jana, just as ultimately the *gens* and *tribus*, the γένος and φῦλον, are alone important. It may be that Viś sometimes represents in the older texts what later was known as the Gotra. See **Viś**.

This appears clearly when the constitution of society in the Brāhmaṇa period is considered. The tribe or people still exists, and is presupposed, but the division into Viś disappears. The real division is now the separate castes (**Varṇa**), but the numerous sections into which each of them is divided appear to be based in part on the ancient Gotra.

[18] Rv. vii. 82, 1.

[19] *Altindisches Leben*, 435.

[20] Hillebrandt, *Vedische Mythologie*, 2, 126.

Cf. Macdonell, *Sanskrit Literature*, 158; von Schroeder, *Indiens Literatur und Cultur*, 32, 33; Jolly, *Zeitschrift der Deutschen Morgenländischen Gesellschaft*, 50, 512 *et seq.*

2. **Jana Śārkarākṣya** ('descendant of **Śarkarākṣa**') is mentioned as a teacher in the Śatapatha Brāhmaṇa (x. 6, 1, 1 *et seq.*) and the Chāndogya Upaniṣad (v. 11, 1; 15, 1). He was a contemporary of **Aśvapati Kaikeya**, and of **Aruṇa Aupaveśi** and his son **Uddālaka Āruṇi**.

Janaka, king of Videha, plays a considerable part in the Śatapatha Brāhmaṇa[1] and the Bṛhadāraṇyaka Upaniṣad,[2] as well as in the Jaiminīya Brāhmaṇa[3] and the Kauṣītaki Upaniṣad.[4] He was a contemporary of **Yājñavalkya Vāja-**

[1] xi. 3, 1, 2; 4, 3, 20; 6, 2, 1 *et seq.*

[2] iii. 1, 1; iv. 1, 1; 2, 1; 4, 7; v. 14, 8.

[3] i. 19, 2 (*Journal of the American Oriental Society*, 23, 329); ii. 76 (*ibid.*, 15, 238).

[4] iv. 1.

saneya,[5] of **Śvetaketu Āruṇeya**, and of other sages.[6] He had become famous for his generosity and his interest in the discussion of the nature of Brahman, as ultimate basis of reality, in the life-time of **Ajātaśatru** of Kāśi.[7] It is significant that he maintained a close intercourse with the Brahmins of the Kuru-Pañcālas, such as Yājñavalkya and Śvetaketu; for this indicates that the home of the philosophy of the Upaniṣads was in the Kuru-Pañcāla country rather than in the east. There is a statement in the Śatapatha Brāhmaṇa[8] that he became a Brahmin (*brahmā*). This does not, however, signify a change of caste, but merely that in knowledge he became a Brahmin (see **Kṣatriya**). Janaka is occasionally mentioned in later texts: in the Taittirīya Brāhmaṇa[9] he has already become quite mythical; in the Śāṅkhāyana Śrauta Sūtra[10] a *sapta-rātra* or seven nights' rite is ascribed to him.

It is natural to attempt to date Janaka by his being a contemporary of Ajātaśatru, and by identifying the latter with the Ajātasattu of the Pāli texts[11]: this would make the end of the sixth century B.C. the approximate date of Janaka.[12] But it is very doubtful whether this identification can be supported: Ajātaśatru was king of Kāśi, whereas Ajātasattu was king of Magadha, and his only connexion with Kāśi was through his marriage with the daughter of Pasenadi of Kosala.[13] Moreover, the acceptance of this chronology would be difficult to reconcile with the history of the development of thought; for it would make the rise of Buddhism contemporaneous with the Upaniṣads, whereas it is reasonably certain that the older Upaniṣads preceded Buddhism.[14] Nor do the Vedic texts know anything of Bimbisāra or Pasenadi, or any of the other princes famed in Buddhist records.

[5] Śatapatha Brāhmaṇa, xi. 3, 1, 2; 4, 3, 20; Bṛhadāraṇyaka Upaniṣad, *loc. cit.*; Jaiminīya Brāhmaṇa, *loc. cit.*

[6] Śatapatha Brāhmaṇa, xi. 6, 2, 1 *et seq.*

[7] Kauṣītaki Upaniṣad, *loc. cit.*; Bṛhadāraṇyaka Upaniṣad, ii. 1, 1.

[8] xi. 6, 2, 10.

[9] iii. 10, 9, 9.

[10] xvi. 26, 7.

[11] Vincent Smith, *Early History of India*, 26 *et seq.*

[12] Hoernle, *Osteology*, 106.

[13] Rhys Davids, *Buddhist India*, 3 *et seq.*

[14] See *e.g.*, von Schroeder, *Indiens Literatur and Cultur*, 243; Macdonell, *Sanskrit Literature*, 224; Deussen, *Philosophy of the Upaniṣads*, 23 *et seq.*; Keith, *Aitareya Āraṇyaka*, 25, 29.

The identification[15] of Janaka of Videha and the father of Sītā is less open to objection, but it cannot be proved, and is somewhat doubtful. In the Sūtras Janaka appears as an ancient king who knew of a time when wifely honour was less respected than later.[16]

[15] *Cf.* Weber, *Indian Literature*, 135; Von Schroeder, *op. cit.*, 189; Macdonell, *op. cit.*, 214.

[16] Jolly, *Recht und Sitte*, 48.

Cf. Muir, *Sanskrit Texts*, 5, 426 *et seq.*; Max Müller, *Ancient Sanskrit Literature*, 421 *et seq.*; Von Schroeder, *op. cit.*, 187-189; Weber, *Indische Studien*, 1, 175, 231; Oldenberg, *Buddha*, 31, n., who properly emphasizes the difficulty of attaching much importance to the names of the leaders of the thought of the Upaniṣads.

Janatā, a word frequently found in the later Saṃhitās[1] and the Brāhmaṇas,[2] denotes the people as a community (*cf.* **Sabhā**) or as a religious unit.

[1] Taittirīya Saṃhitā, ii. 2, 1, 4; 6, 4; 3, 4, 2; Kāṭhaka Saṃhitā, ix. 17; Av. v. 18, 12, etc.

[2] Taittirīya Brāhmaṇa, i. 4, 6, 1; ii. 3, 1, 3; Aitareya Brāhmaṇa, i. 7. 9: iii. 31; v. 9, etc.

Cf. Weber, *Indische Studien*, 13, 153, n.

Jana-pada in the Brāhmaṇas denotes both the 'people,' as opposed to the king,[1] and the 'land' or 'realm.'[2] The 'subjects' are also denoted by the adjectival *jānapada*.[3]

[1] Aitareya Brāhmaṇa, viii. 14 (plural); Śatapatha Brāhmaṇa, xiii. 4, 2, 17.

[2] Taittirīya Brāhmaṇa, ii. 3, 9, 9; Bṛhadāraṇyaka Upaniṣad, ii. 1, 20; Chāndogya Upaniṣad, v. 11, 5; viii. 1, 5.

[3] Śatapatha Brāhmaṇa, xiv. 5, 1, 20.

1. **Janam-ejaya** ('man-impelling') is the name of a king, a **Pārikṣita**,[1] famous towards the end of the Brāhmaṇa period. He is mentioned in the Śatapatha Brāhmaṇa[2] as owning horses which when wearied were refreshed with sweet drinks, and as a performer of the Aśvamedha, or horse sacrifice.[3] His capital, according to a Gāthā quoted in the Śatapatha[4] and the Aitareya Brāhmaṇas,[5] was **Āsandīvant.** His brothers **Ugrasena, Bhīmasena,** and **Śrutasena** are mentioned as having

[1] Satapatha Brāhmaṇa, xiii. 5, 4, 1 *et seq.*; Aitareya Brāhmaṇa, vii. 34; viii. 11. 21; Śāṅkhāyana Śrauta Sūtra, xvi. 8, 27, etc.

[2] xi. 5, 5, 13.

[3] xiii. 5, 4, 1-3.

[4] xiii. 5, 4, 2.

[5] viii. 21.

by the horse sacrifice purified themselves from sin. The priest who performed the sacrifice for him was **Indrota Daivāpi Śaunaka.**[6] On the other hand the Aitareya Brāhmaṇa,[7] which also mentions his Aśvamedha, names **Tura Kāvaṣeya** as his priest. It also contains an obscure tale stating that at one sacrifice of his he did not employ the **Kaśyapas**, but the **Bhūtavīras**, being, however, induced by the **Asitamṛgas** to have recourse to the Kaśyapas again.[8] He was a **Kuru** prince; see **Parikṣit.** The Gopatha Brāhmaṇa[9] tells an absurd tale about him, evidently as of an ancient hero.

[6] Satapatha Brāhmaṇa, xiii. 5, 4, 1; Śāṅkhāyana Śrauta Sūtra, *loc. cit.*
[7] viii. 21. *Cf.* iv. 27; vii. 34.
[8] vii. 27. *Cf.* Weber, *Indische Studien*, 1, 204; Muir, *Sanskrit Texts*, 1[2], 438, n. 229; Eggeling, *Sacred Books of the East*, 43, 345, n.
[9] i. 2, 5.
Cf. Weber, *Indian Literature*, 123-125; 134-136; Oldenberg, *Zeitschrift der Deutschen Morgenländischen Gesellschaft*, 37, 65 *et seq.*; 42, 239; Pargiter, *Journal of the Royal Asiatic Society*, 1910, 28 *et seq.*

2. **Janam-ejaya** is in the Pañcaviṃśa Brāhmaṇa[1] the name of a priest who officiated at the snake sacrifice.

[1] xxv. 15, 3. *Cf.* Weber, *Indische Studien*, 1, 35.

Jana-śruta ('famed among men') **Kāṇḍviya** is the name of a pupil of **Hṛtsvāśaya,** mentioned in a Vaṃśa (list of teachers) in the Jaiminīya Upaniṣad Brāhmaṇa (iii. 40, 2), and of Vārakya, a pupil of **Jayanta,** referred to in the same Brāhmaṇa (iii. 41, 1; iv. 17, 1). *Cf.* **Jānaśruti.**

Jani, Janī.—These words appear to denote 'wife,' usually applying to her in relation to her husband (**Pati**). The more general sense of 'woman' is doubtful; for when Uṣas is called a fair Janī,[1] 'wife' may be meant, and the other passage[2] cited for this sense by Delbrück,[3] which refers to the begetting of children, seems to demand the sense of 'wives.' Since the words usually appear in the plural,[4] it is possible they may

[1] Rv. iv. 52, 1.
[2] v. 61, 3.
[3] *Die indogermanischen Verwandschaftsnamen*, 413.
[4] i. 85, 1; iv. 5, 5; 19, 5; vii. 18, 2; 26, 3; ix. 86, 32; Vājasaneyi Saṃhitā, xii. 35; xx. 40. 43, etc. *Cf.* Rv. x. 43, 1. In x. 110, 5, the phrase is *patibhyo na janayaḥ*, where both plurals may be generic.

refer not to 'wives' proper, but to Hetairai. This is, however, rendered unlikely because the Rigveda[5] uses the phrase *patyur janitvam*, denoting 'wifehood to a husband,' as well as the expression *janayo na patnīḥ*,[6] 'like wives (who are) mistresses,'[7] besides containing passages in which the word has reference to marriage.[8] The singular occurs in the dialogue of Yama and Yamī.[9]

[5] x. 18, 8. *Cf. janitvana* in viii. 2, 42.

[6] i. 62, 10; 186, 7.

[7] The distinction of sense was probably this: *jani* meant 'wife,' as bearing children (from *jan*, 'beget'), while *patnī* was 'wife,' as being 'mistress' of the house (feminine of *pati*, 'lord,' 'husband').

[8] v. 61, 3. So in x. 40, 10, the word seems certainly to refer to marriage.

[9] x. 10, 3.

Janitṛ[1] and **Janitrī**[2] are frequent words, in the Rigveda and later, for 'father' and 'mother' regarded as the 'begetter' and the 'bearer' respectively of the child. See **Pitṛ, Mātṛ.**

[1] Rv. i. 129, 11; 164, 33; iii. 1, 10; 54, 9, etc.; Av. iv. 1, 7; Vājasaneyi Saṃhitā, xix. 87, etc.

[2] Rv. iii. 48, 2; 54, 14; Av. vi. 110, 13; ix. 5, 30, etc.

Jantu, besides the general sense of 'man,' has also in a few passages[1] the more restricted sense of 'follower' or 'subject.' The 'followers of **Śvaitreya**'[2] may be compared with the 'subjects (*viśaḥ*) of **Tṛṇaskanda**.'[3]

[1] Rv. I. 94, 5; x. 140, 4.

[2] Rv. v. 19, 3.

[3] Rv. i. 172, 3.

Janman appears to have the sense of 'relations' in two passages of the Rigveda,[1] being used collectively in the second of them.

[1] iii. 15, 2; ii. 26, 3 (where *janena, viśā, janmanā, putraiḥ*, is the series). *Cf.* Zimmer, *Altindisches Leben*, 160, and see **Jana** and **Viś**.

Janya has in the Rigveda (iv. 38, 6) and the Atharvaveda (xi. 8, 1) the special sense of 'bridesman.'

Jabālā is the name of the mother of an illegitimate son, **Satyakāma**, in the Chāndogya Upaniṣad (iv. 4, 1. 2. 4).

Jabhya, 'snapper,' denotes in the Atharvaveda[1] an insect destructive to grain.

[1] vi. 50, 2. *Cf.* Zimmer, *Altindisches Leben*, 237.

Jamad-agni is one of the somewhat mythical sages of the Rigveda, where he is frequently mentioned. In some passages[1] his name occurs in such a way as to indicate that he is the author of the hymn; once[2] he is thus associated with **Viśvāmitra.** In other passages[3] he is merely referred to, and the Jamadagnis are mentioned once.[4] In the Atharvaveda,[5] as well as the Yajurveda Saṃhitās[6] and the Brāhmaṇas,[7] he is quite a frequent figure. Here he appears as a friend of Viśvāmitra[8] and a rival of **Vasiṣṭha.**[9] He owed his prosperity to his *catūrātra*, or 'four-night' ritual, with which his family were also very successful.[10] In the Atharvaveda[11] Jamadagni is connected with **Atri** and **Kaṇva,** as well as **Asita** and **Vītahavya.** He was Adhvaryu priest at the proposed sacrifice of **Śunaḥśepa.**[12]

[1] Rv. iii. 62, 18; viii. 101, 8; ix. 62, 24; 65, 25.

[2] Rv. x. 167, 4.

[3] Rv. vii. 96, 3; ix. 97, 51.

[4] Rv. iii. 53, 15. 16.

[5] ii. 32, 3 (*cf.* Taittirīya Āraṇyaka, iv. 36; Mantra Brāhmaṇa, ii. 7, 1); iv. 29, 3; v. 28, 7; vi. 137, 1; xviii. 3, 15. 16.

[6] Taittirīya Saṃhitā, ii. 2, 12, 4; iii. 1, 7, 3; 3, 5, 2; v. 2, 10, 5; 4, 11, 3; Maitrāyaṇī Saṃhitā, ii. 7, 19; iv. 2, 9; Kāṭhaka Saṃhitā, xvi. 19; xx. 9; Vājasaneyi Saṃhitā, iii. 62; xiii. 56.

[7] Pañcaviṃśa Brāhmaṇa, ix. 4, 14; xiii. 5, 15; xxi. 10, 5-7; xxii. 7, 2; Aitareya Brāhmaṇa, vii. 16; Śatapatha Brāhmaṇa, xiii. 2, 2, 14; Taittirīya Āraṇyaka, i. 9, 7; Bṛhadāraṇyaka Upaniṣad, ii. 2, 4; Jaiminīya Upaniṣad Brāhmaṇa, iii. 3, 11; iv. 3, 1, etc.

[8] Taittirīya Saṃhitā, iii. 1, 7, 3; v. 4, 11, 3; Pañcaviṃśa Brāhmaṇa, xiii. 5, 15.

[9] Taittirīya Saṃhitā, *loc. cit.*

[10] Pañcaviṃśa Brāhmaṇa, xxi. 10, 5-7.

[11] ii. 32, 3; vi. 137, 1.

[12] Aitareya Brāhmaṇa, vii. 16.

Cf. Hopkins, *Transactions of the Connecticut Academy of Arts and Sciences*, 15, 53, 54; Bloomfield, *Hymns of the Atharvaveda*, 319; Weber, *Indische Studien*, 10, 95.

Jambha occurs twice in the Atharvaveda as the name of a disease or a demon of disease. In one passage[1] it is said to be cured by the **Jaṅgiḍa** plant; in the other[2] it is described as *saṃhanuḥ*, 'bringing the jaws together.' Weber[3] argued from

[1] ii. 4, 2. [2] viii. 1, 16. [3] *Indische Studien*, 13, 142.

the Kauśika Sūtra[4] that it was a child's ailment, especially 'teething.' Bloomfield[5] considers it to mean 'convulsions,' while Caland[6] thinks it denotes 'tetanus.' Whitney[7] decides for 'lockjaw' or 'convulsions.'

[4] xxxii. 1.
[5] *Hymns of the Atharvaveda*, 283.
[6] *Zeitschrift der Deutschen Morgenländischen Gesellschaft*, 53, 224; *Altindisches Zauberritual*, 103.
[7] Translation of the Atharvaveda, 42.
Cf. Zimmer, *Altindisches Leben*, 392.

Jambhaka, as the name of a demon, presumably identical with the demon causing **Jambha**, is mentioned in the Vājasaneyi Saṃhitā[1] and the Śāṅkhāyana Āraṇyaka.[2]

[1] xxx. 16.
[2] xii. 25. *Cf.* Keith, *Śāṅkhāyana Āraṇyaka*, 67, n. 7.

Jayaka Lauhitya ('descendant of Lohita') is mentioned in a Vaṃśa (list of teachers) of the Jaiminīya Upaniṣad Brāhmaṇa (iii. 42, 1) as a pupil of **Yaśasvin Jayanta Lauhitya.**

Jayanta is the name of several teachers in the Jaiminīya Upaniṣad Brāhmaṇa:

(*a*) Jayanta Pārāśarya ('descendant of **Parāśara**') is mentioned as a pupil of **Vipaścit** in a Vaṃśa (list of teachers).[1]

(*b*) Jayanta Vārakya ('descendant of Varaka') appears in the same Vaṃśa[1] as a pupil of **Kubera Vārakya.** His grandfather is also mentioned there as a pupil of **Kaṃsa Vārakya.**

(*c*) A Jayanta Vārakya, pupil of **Suyajña Śāṇḍilya,** perhaps identical with the preceding, is found in another Vaṃśa.[2]

(*d*) Jayanta is a name of **Yaśasvin Lauhitya.**[3]

See also **Dakṣa Jayanta Lauhitya.**

[1] iii. 41, 1.
[2] iv. 17, 1.
[3] iii. 42, 1. Not only is the formation of the name a late one (*cf.* Whitney, *Sanskrit Grammar*, 1209*d*, and Macdonell, *Vedic Grammar*, 191*a*), but the Upaniṣad in which it occurs is also a late one.

Jarā-bodha, a word occurring only once in the Rigveda,[1] is of doubtful meaning. It is held by Ludwig[2] to be the name of

[1] i. 27, 10.
[2] Translation of the Rigveda, 3, 103.

a seer. Roth[3] regards it as a mere adjective meaning 'attending to the invocation,' which is perhaps the most probable interpretation. Oldenburg,[4] however, thinks that the word is a proper name, the literal sense being 'alert in old age.'

[3] St. Petersburg Dictionary, *s.v.* *Cf.* Nirukta, x. 8.

[4] *Ṛgveda-Noten*, 1, 23. He compares the *ṛṣī bodha-pratībodhau* of Av. v. 30, 10.

Jarāyu is found once in the Atharvaveda[1] in the sense of a 'serpent's skin.' Usually[2] it denotes the outer covering (chorion) of the embryo, as opposed to the *ulva*, the inner covering (amnion).

Living things are occasionally classified according to their mode of origin. In the Chāndogya Upaniṣad[3] they are divided into (*a*) *āṇḍa-ja*, 'egg-born'; (*b*) *jīva-ja*, 'born alive,' or born from the womb; (*c*) *udbhij-ja*, 'propagated by sprouts.' In the Aitareya Āraṇyaka[4] the division is fourfold: (*a*) *āṇḍa-ja*; (*b*) *jāru-ja*, that is, *jarāyu-ja* (found in the Atharvaveda,[5] and needlessly read here by Böhtlingk[6]); (*c*) *udbhij-ja*; and (*d*) *sveda-ja*, 'sweat-born,' explained as 'insects.'

[1] i. 27, 1.

[2] Rv. v. 78, 8; Av. i. 11, 4; vi. 49, 1; ix. 4, 4; Taittirīya Saṃhitā, vi. 5, 6, 3; Vājasaneyi Saṃhitā, x. 8; xix. 76; Aitareya Brāhmaṇa, i. 3; Śatapatha Brāhmaṇa, iii. 2, 1, 11, etc; Chāndogya Upaniṣad, iii. 19, 2, etc.

[3] vi. 3, 1.

[4] ii. 6.

[5] i. 12, 1.

[6] See *jāru* in Jaiminīya Brāhmaṇa, ii. 430, 6.

Cf. Deussen, *Philosophy of the Upanishads*, 196, 292; Keith, *Aitareya Āraṇyaka*, 235.

1. **Jaritṛ** is the regular term in the Rigveda,[1] and occasionally later,[2] for a singer of hymns of praise or worshipper.

[1] i. 2, 2; 165, 14; ii. 33, 11; iii. 60, 7, etc.

[2] Av. v. 11, 8; xx. 135, 1, etc.

2. **Jaritṛ.**—According to Sieg,[1] mention is made in one hymn of the Rigveda[2] of Jaritṛ, one of the Śārṅgas. That hymn he seeks to bring into connexion with the epic[3] tradition

[1] *Die Sagenstoffe des Ṛgveda*, 44 *et seq.*

[2] x. 142.

[3] Mahābhārata, i. 222, 1 *et seq.*

of the Ṛṣi Mandapāla, who wedded Jaritā, a female Śārṅga bird—apparently a hen sparrow (*caṭakā*)—and had four sons. These being abandoned by him and exposed to the danger of being consumed by a forest fire, prayed to Agni with the hymn Rigveda x. 142. This interpretation is very doubtful, though Sāyaṇa[4] appears to have adopted it.

[4] On Rv. x. 142, 7. 8.

Jarūtha, mentioned in three passages of the Rigveda,[1] appears to denote a demon defeated by Agni.[2] Ludwig, however, followed by Griffith,[3] sees in him a foe slain in a battle in which **Vasiṣṭha,** the traditional author of the seventh Maṇḍala of the Rigveda, was Purohita, or domestic priest.

[1] vii. 1, 7; 9, 6; x. 80, 3.
[2] Roth, St. Petersburg Dictionary, *s.v.*; Nirukta, vi. 17.
[3] *Hymns of the Rigveda*, 2, 11, n.

Jartila, 'wild sesamum,' is mentioned in the Taittirīya Saṃhitā (v. 4, 3, 2) as an unsuitable sacrificial offering. In the Śatapatha Brāhmaṇa (ix. 1, 1, 3) sesamum seeds are regarded as combining the qualities of cultivation (viz., edibility) with those of wild growth (because they are produced on unploughed land).

Jarvara was Gṛhapati or 'householder' at the snake festival described in the Pañcaviṃśa Brāhmaṇa.[1]

[1] xxv. 15, 3. *Cf.* Weber, *Indische Studien*, 1, 35.

Jala Jātūkarṇya ('descendant of Jātūkarṇa'), is mentioned in the Śāṅkhāyana Śrauta Sūtra (xvi. 29, 6) as having obtained the position of Purohita, or domestic priest, of the three peoples or kings of **Kāśi, Videha,** and **Kosala.**

Jalāṣa-bheṣaja, 'whose remedy is Jalāṣa,' is an epithet of Rudra in the Rigveda[1] and the Atharvaveda.[2] The word

[1] i. 43, 4; viii. 29, 5.
[2] ii. 27, 6. It also occurs in the Nīlarudra Upaniṣad (a very late work), 3, and *jalāṣa* as an adjective is found in Rv. ii. 33, 7; viii. 35, 6.

Jālāṣa occurs in a hymn of the Atharvaveda,[3] where it denotes a remedy, perhaps, for a tumour or boil.[4] The commentator on this passage and the Kauśika Sūtra[5] regard Jālāṣa as meaning 'urine,' which seems a probable interpretation.[6] But Geldner[7] thinks that rain-water, conceived as urine, is meant; and the Naighaṇṭuka[8] identifies *jalāṣa* and *udaka* 'water.'

[3] vi. 57.

[4] Bloomfield, *American Journal of Philology*, 11, 321 *et seq.*; *Hymns of the Atharvaveda*, 489.

[5] xxxi. 11.

[6] Bloomfield, *American Journal of Philology*, 12, 425 *et seq.*

[7] *Vedische Studien*, 3, 139, n. 2.

[8] i. 12.

Cf. Whitney, Translation of the Atharvaveda, 323, 324; Macdonell, *Vedic Mythology*, pp. 76, 77; Hopkins, *Proceedings of the American Oriental Society*, 1894, cl.

Jaṣa is the name of some aquatic animal or fish in the Atharvaveda[1] and the Taittirīya Saṃhitā.[2] The commentary on the latter text explains it by *makara*, probably meaning 'dolphin.' The word also occurs in the Gopatha Brāhmaṇa.[3] *Cf.* **Jhaṣa.**

[1] xi. 2, 25. There are various readings: *jhaṣa*, *jakha*, *jagha*.

[2] v. 5, 13, 1.

[3] ii. 2, 5.

Cf. Zimmer, *Altindisches Leben*, 96; Whitney, Translation of the Atharvaveda, 624.

Jahakā, the 'polecat,' is mentioned as a victim at the Aśvamedha, or horse sacrifice, in the Yajurveda.[1] Sāyaṇa[2] thinks it means a jackal living in holes (*vila-vāsī kroṣṭā*).

[1] Taittirīya Saṃhitā, v. 5, 18, 1; Maitrāyaṇī Saṃhitā, iii. 14, 17; Vājasaneyi Saṃhitā, xxiv. 36. *Cf.* Zimmer, *Altindisches Leben*, 86.

[2] On Taittirīya Saṃhitā, *loc. cit.*

Jahnu occurs only in the plural in the legend of **Śunaḥśepa,** who is said to have obtained, as Devarāta, both the lordship of the Jahnus and the divine lore of the Gāthins.[1] A **Jāhnava,** or descendant of Jahnu, was, according to the Pañcaviṃśa

[1] Aitareya Brāhmaṇa, vii. 18 (*Jahnūnāṃ cādhipatye daive vede ca Gāthinām*); Āśvalāyana Śrauta Sūtra, xii. 14; Śāṅkhāyana Srauta Sūtra, xv. 27 (p. 195, l. 21, ed. Hillebrandt, where the reading is different and the sense altered: *Jahnūnāṃ cādhitasthire daive vede ca Gāthinaḥ*. The two *ca*'s cannot be justified, and the text must be incorrect).

Brāhmaṇa,[2] **Viśvāmitra,** who is said, by means of a certain *catū-rātra* or 'four-night' ritual, to have secured the kingdom for the Jahnus in their conflict with the **Vṛcīvants.** He is here described as a king. Again, in the Aitareya Brāhmaṇa,[3] Viśvāmitra is addressed as a *rāja-putra*, 'prince,' and *Bharata-rṣabha*, 'bull of the Bharatas.' It is therefore clear that the Brāhmaṇas, though not the Saṃhitās, saw in him at once a priest and a prince by origin, though there is no trace whatever of their seeing in him a prince who won Brahmanhood as in the version of the later texts.[4]

A Jahnāvī is mentioned twice in the Rigveda,[5] being either the wife of Jahnu, or, as Sāyaṇa thinks, the race of Jahnu. The family must clearly once have been a great one, later merged in the Bharatas.

[2] xxi. 12. *Cf.* Hopkins, *Transactions of the Connecticut Academy of Arts and Sciences*, 15, 54, who correctly explains the passage which Sāyaṇa misunderstands.

[3] vii. 17, 6. 7.

[4] Muir, *Sanskrit Texts*, 1,[2] 337 *et seq.*

[5] i. 116, 19; iii. 58, 6. *Cf.* Ludwig, Translation of the Rigveda, 3, 153.

Jāta Śākāyanya ('descendant of Śāka') is mentioned as a ritual authority and contemporary of **Śaṅkha** in the Kāṭhaka Saṃhitā (xxii. 7).

Jāta-rūpa, 'possessing native beauty,' is the name of 'gold' in the later Brāhmaṇas[1] and the Sūtras.[2]

[1] Aitareya Brāhmaṇa, viii. 13 (*jāta-rūpa-maya*, 'composed of gold'); Bṛhadāraṇyaka Upaniṣad, vi. 4, 25; Naighaṇṭuka, i. 2.

[2] *Rajata-jātarūpe*, 'silver and gold,' Lāṭyāyana Srauta Sūtra, i. 6, 24. *Cf.* viii. 1, 3; Kauśika Sūtra, x. 16; xiii. 3, etc.; Sāṅkhāyana Śrauta Sūtra, iii. 19, 9.

Jāti, which in the Pāli[1] texts is the word denoting 'caste,' does not occur at all in the early Vedic literature; when it is found, as in the Kātyāyana Śrauta Sūtra,[2] it has only the sense of 'family' (for which *cf.* **Kula, Gotra,** and **Viś**). For the influence of the family system on the growth of caste, see **Varṇa.** To assume that it was the basis of caste, as does

[1] Fick, *Die sociale Gliederung*, 22, n. 4.

[2] xv. 4, 14. So *jātīya*, xx. 2, 11, etc.

Senart,[3] is difficult in face of the late appearance of words for family and of stress on family.[4]

[3] *Les Castes dans l'Inde* (1896).

[4] Fick, *op. cit.*, 3; Oldenberg, *Zeitschrift der Deutschen Morgenländischen Gesellschaft*, 51, 267 *et seq.*

Jātū-karṇya, 'descendant of **Jātūkarṇa,**' is the patronymic of several persons.

(*a*) A pupil of **Āsurāyaṇa** and **Yāska** bears this name in a Vaṃśa (list of teachers) of the Bṛhadāraṇyaka Upaniṣad in the Kāṇva recension.[1] In the Mādhyaṃdina[2] he is a pupil of **Bhāradvāja.**

(*b*) A Kātyāyanī-putra, 'son of Kātyāyanī,' bears this name in the Śāṅkhāyana Āraṇyaka.[3]

(*c*) A Jātūkarṇya is mentioned in the Kauṣītaki Brāhmaṇa[4] as a contemporary of **Alīkayu Vācaspatya** and other sages.

(*d*) Jātūkarṇya is in the Sūtras[5] frequently a patronymic of teachers whose identity cannot be determined. The same person or different persons may here be meant.

[1] ii. 6, 3; iv. 6, 3.

[2] ii. 5, 21; iv. 5, 27.

[3] viii. 10.

[4] xxvi. 5 (Jātukarṇya in Lindner's index, 159, is a misprint).

[5] Aitareya Āraṇyaka, v. 3, 3; Śāṅkhāyana Srauta Sūtra, i. 2, 17; iii. 16, 14; 20, 19; xvi. 29, 6 (**Jala**); Kātyāyana Srauta Sūtra, iv. 1, 27; xx. 3, 17; xxv. 7, 34, etc.

Cf. Weber, *Indian Literature*, 138-140.

Jātū-ṣṭhira occurs in one verse of the Rigveda[1] where Sāyaṇa and Ludwig[2] interpret the word as a proper name. Roth[3] renders it as an adjective meaning 'naturally powerful.'[4]

[1] ii. 13, 11.

[2] Translation of the Rigveda, 3, 152.

[3] St. Petersburg Dictionary, *s.v.* (with a wrong reference, ii. 23, 11).

[4] *Urkräftig*. Grassmann, *Wörterbuch*, similarly explains the word as 'powerful by nature or birth' (*jātū*).

Jāna, 'descendant of Jana,' is the patronymic of **Vṛśa** in the Pañcaviṃśa Brāhmaṇa[1] and apparently in the Śāṭyāyanaka.[2]

[1] xiii. 3, 12.

[2] In Sāyaṇa on Rv. v. 5. *Cf.* Bṛhaddevatā, v. 14 *et seq.*, with Macdonell's notes; Sieg, *Die Sagenstoffe des Ṛgveda*, 64 *et seq.*

Jānaka, 'descendant of Janaka,' is the patronymic of **Kratuvid** in some MSS. of the Aitareya Brāhmaṇa.[1] In the Taittirīya Saṃhitā[2] the name appears instead as **Kratujit Jānaki.** Jānaka is also, according to some manuscripts of the Bṛhadāraṇyaka Upaniṣad,[3] the patronymic of **Āyasthūṇa,** but is here no doubt a misreading of **Jānaki.**

1 vii. 34. 2 ii. 3, 8, 1; Kāṭhaka Saṃhitā, xi. 1. 3 vi. 3, 10 (Kāṇva).

Jānaki, 'descendant of Janaka,' is the patronymic of **Kratujit** in the Taittirīya Saṃhitā,[1] of **Kratuvid** in the Aitareya Brāhmaṇa,[2] and of **Āyasthūṇa** in the Bṛhadāraṇyaka Upaniṣad,[3] where he is mentioned as a pupil of **Cūḍa Bhāgavitti,** and as teacher of **Satyakāma Jābāla.**

1 ii. 3, 8, 1; Kāṭhaka Saṃhitā, xi. 1. 2 vii. 34.
3 vi. 3, 10 (Kāṇva = vi. 3, 18. 19, Mādhyaṃdina).

Jānaṃ-tapi, 'descendant of Janaṃtapa,' is the patronymic of **Atyarāti** in the Aitareya Brāhmaṇa (viii. 23).

Jāna-pada. See **Janapada.**

Jāna-śruti, 'descendant of Jānaśruta,' is the patronymic of **Pautrāyaṇa** in the Chāndogya Upaniṣad (iv. 1, 1; 2, 1).

Jāna-śruteya, 'descendant of Jānaśruti' or of 'Janaśrutā,' is the patronymic or metronymic of several persons—**Upāvi**[1] or **Aupāvi,**[2] **Ulukya,**[3] **Nagarin,**[4] and **Sāyaka.**[5]

1 Aitareya Brāhmaṇa, i. 25, 115.
2 Śatapatha Brāhmaṇa, v. 1, 1, 5. 7; Maitrāyaṇī Saṃhitā, i. 4, 5.
3 Jaiminīya Upaniṣad Brāhmaṇa, i. 6, 3.
4 *Ibid.*, iii. 40, 2.
5 *Ibid.*

Jābāla, 'descendant of **Jabālā,**' is the metronymic of **Mahāśāla**[1] and **Satyakāma.**[2] Jābāla is also mentioned as a teacher in the Jaiminīya Upaniṣad Brāhmaṇa,[3] which refers to the

1 Śatapatha Brāhmaṇa, x. 3, 3, 1; 6, 1, 1.
2 *Ibid.*, xiii. 5, 3, 1; Bṛhadāraṇyaka Upaniṣad, iv. 1, 14; vi. 3, 19; Chāndogya Upaniṣad, iv. 4, 1, etc.; Aitareya Brāhmaṇa, viii. 7.
3 iii. 9, 9.

Jābālas[4] as well. The Jābāla Gṛhapatis are spoken of in the Kauṣītaki Brāhmaṇa.[5]

[4] iii. 7, 2.

[5] xxiii. 5.

Cf. Weber, *Indische Studien*, 1, 395.

Jābālāyana, 'descendant of Jābāla,' is the patronymic of a teacher, a pupil of **Mādhyaṃdināyana**, who is mentioned in the second Vaṃśa (list of teachers) of the Kāṇva recension of the Bṛhadāraṇyaka Upaniṣad (iv. 6, 2).

Jāmadagniya is the patronymic of two 'descendants of Jamadagni' in the Taittirīya Saṃhitā.[1] It appears from the Pañcaviṃśa Brāhmaṇa[2] that the **Aurvas** are meant, and that Jamadagni's descendants were ever prosperous.

[1] vii. 1, 9, 1.

[2] xxi. 10, 6.

Cf. Weber, *Indische Studien*, 12, 251, n.; Hopkins, *Transactions of the Connecticut Academy of Arts and Sciences*, 15, 54.

Jāmātṛ is a rare word denoting 'son-in-law' in the Rigveda,[1] where also occurs the word **Vijāmātṛ**, denoting an 'unsatisfactory son-in-law,' as one who does not pay a sufficient price, or one who, having other defects, must purchase a bride. Friendly relations between son-in-law and father-in-law are referred to in the Rigveda.[2]

[1] viii. 2, 20. Vāyu is called the *jāmātṛ* of Tvaṣṭṛ in viii. 26, 21. 22. *Cf.* Delbrück, *Die indogermanischen Verwandtschaftsnamen*, 517; Pischel, *Vedische Studien*, 2, 78, 79.

[2] x. 28, 1. *Cf.* Bloomfield, *Journal of the American Oriental Society*, 15, 255.

Jāmi, a word which appears originally to have meant 'related in blood,' is not rarely used as an epithet of 'sister' (**Svasṛ**), and sometimes even denotes 'sister' itself, the emphasis being on the blood-relationship.[1] So it appears in a passage of the Atharvaveda,[2] where 'brotherless sisters'

[1] *Cf.* Delbrück, *Die indogermanischen Verwandtschaftsnamen*, 463, 464. As 'relation,' it occurs, *e.g.*, Rv. i. 31, 10; 75. 3. 4; 100, 11; 124, 6, etc.; as 'sister,' Rv. i. 65, 7; x. 10, 10, etc.; with *svasā*, i. 123, 5; 185, 5; iii. 1, 11; ix. 65, 1; 89, 4, etc.

[2] i. 17, 1.

(*abhrātara iva jāmayaḥ*) are referred to. The word is similarly used in the dispute occurring in the Aitareya Brāhmaṇa[3] as to the precedence of Rākā, or of the wives of the gods, in a certain rite. One party is there described as holding that the sister should be preferred (*jāmyai vai pūrva-peyam*)—apparently at a ceremonial family meal—to the wife, presumably as being of one blood with the husband, while the wife is not (being *anyo-daryā*, 'of another womb').[4] In the neuter[5] the word means 'relationship,' like *jāmi-tva*, which also occurs in the Rigveda.[6]

[3] iii. 37.
[4] Delbrück, *loc. cit.*
[5] Rv. iii. 54, 9; x. 10, 4; *jāmi-kṛt*, 'making relationship,' Av. iv. 19, 1. *Cf.* Aitareya Brāhmaṇa, *loc. cit.*
[6] i. 105, 9; 166, 13; x, 55, 4; 64, 13.

Jāmi-śaṃsa, the 'imprecation by a sister' or 'relation,' is mentioned in the Atharvaveda,[1] showing that family disputes were not rare. This is also indicated by the word **Bhrātṛvya**, which, while properly meaning 'father's brother's son,' regularly denotes simply 'enemy.'

[1] ii. 10, 1 (=Taittirīya Brāhmaṇa, ii. 5, 6, 3), and personified in ix. 4, 15. *Cf. jāmyāḥ śapathaḥ*, Av. ii. 7, 2; Bloomfield, *Hymns of the Atharvaveda*, 362.

Jāmbila, 'hollow of the knee,'[1] occurs once in the Maitrāyaṇī Saṃhitā.[2] The word also occurs in the form of Jāmbīla in the Kāṭhaka Saṃhitā[3] and the Vājasaneyi Saṃhitā.[4] Mahīdhara, in his commentary on the latter text, interprets the word as 'knee-pan,' which he says is so named because of its resemblance to the citron, *jāmbīra*.

[1] Perhaps for *jānu-bila*. *Cf.* Macdonell, *Vedic Grammar*, p. 11, n. 4.
[2] iii. 15, 3.
[3] v. 13, 1.
[4] xxv. 3.

Jāyantī-putra, 'son of Jāyantī,' is mentioned in the last Vaṃśa (list of teachers) in the Bṛhadāraṇyaka Upaniṣad[1] as a pupil of **Māṇḍūkāyanīputra.**

[1] vi. 5, 2 (Kāṇva=vi. 4, 32 Mādhyaṃdina).

Jāyā regularly denotes 'wife,' and, as opposed to **Patnī**, wife as an object of marital affection, the source of the continuance of the race.[1] So it is used of the wife of the gambler, and of the wife of the Brāhmaṇa in the Rigveda;[2] it is also frequently combined with **Pati**, 'husband,'[3] both there and in the later literature.[4] Patnī, on the other hand, is used to denote the wife as partner in the sacrifice;[5] when no share in it is assigned to her, she is called Jāyā.[6] The distinction is, of course, merely relative; hence one text[7] calls Manu's wife Jāyā, another[8] Patnī. Later on Jāyā is superseded by Dāra.

[1] Delbrück, *Die indogermanischen Verwandtschaftsnamen*, 411, 412. *Cf.* Rv. i. 105, 2; 124, 7; iii. 53. 4; iv. 3, 2; 18, 3; ix. 82, 4; x. 10, 7; 17, 1; 71, 4, etc.; Av. iii. 30, 2; vi. 60, 1, etc.

[2] x. 34, 2. 3. 13, and x. 109.

[3] Rv. iv. 3, 2; x. 149, 4.

[4] Aitareya Brāhmaṇa, iii. 23, 1. *Cf.* vii. 13, 10; Śatapatha Brāhmaṇa, iv. 6, 7, 9. *Cf.* Maitrāyaṇī Saṃhitā, i. 6, 12.

[5] Śatapatha Brāhmaṇa, i. 9, 2, 14.

[6] i. 1, 4, 13.

[7] *Ibid.*, i. 1, 4, 16.

[8] Maitrāyaṇī Saṃhitā, iv. 8, 1.

Jāyānya,[1] **Jāyenya,**[2] are variant forms of the name of a disease mentioned in the Atharvaveda and the Taittirīya Saṃhitā. In one passage of the former text[3] it is mentioned with jaundice (*harimā*) and pains in the limbs (*aṅga-bhedo visalpakaḥ*). Zimmer[4] thinks these are its symptoms, and identifies it with a kind of Yakṣma, or disease of the lungs. Bloomfield[5] prefers to identify it with syphilis, in accordance with certain indications in the ritual of the Kauśika Sūtra.[6] Roth conjectures 'gout,' but Whitney[7] leaves the nature of the disease doubtful.

[1] Av. vii. 76, 3-5; xix. 44, 2.

[2] ii. 3, 5, 2; 5, 6, 5.

[3] xix. 44, 2.

[4] *Altindisches Leben*, 377, following Wise, *Hindu System of Medicine*, 321, describing Akṣata.

[5] *American Journal of Philology*, 11, 320 *et seq.*; *Hymns of the Atharvaveda*, 559-561.

[6] xxxii. 11. *Cf.* also the commentary on Av. vii. 76, and Taittirīya Saṃhitā, *loc. cit.*

[7] Translation of the Atharvaveda, 442. *Cf.* Henry, *Le livre vii de l'Atharvavéda*, 98.

Jāra, 'lover,' has no sinister sense in the early texts[1] generally, where the word applies to any lover. But it seems probable that the Jāra at the Puruṣamedha, or human sacrifice,[2]

[1] Rv. i. 66, 8; 117, 18; 134, 3; 152, 4; ix. 32, 5, etc. The word is often used mythologically, as, *e.g.*, *jāra uṣasām*, 'lover of the dawns,' vii. 9, 1. *Cf.* Zimmer, *Altindisches Leben*, 308.

[2] Vājasaneyi Saṃhitā, xxx. 9; Taittirīya Brāhmaṇa, iii. 4, 4, 1.

must be regarded as an illegitimate lover; this sense also appears in the Bṛhadāraṇyaka Upaniṣad,[3] and Indra is styled the lover of **Ahalyā,** wife of **Gautama.**[4]

[3] vi. 4, 11.

[4] Macdonell, *Vedic Mythology*, p. 65.

Jārat-kārava ('descendant of Jaratkāru') **Ārtabhāga** ('descendant of Ṛtabhāga') is the name of a teacher mentioned in the Śāṅkhāyana Āraṇyaka (vii. 20) and the Bṛhadāraṇyaka Upaniṣad (iii. 2, 1, in both recensions).

Jāru. See **Jarāyu.**

Jāla occurs in the Atharvaveda[1] and the Sūtras[2] in the sense of 'net.' Jālaka is used in the Bṛhadāraṇyaka Upaniṣad[3] of a reticulated membrane resembling a woven covering.

[1] viii. 8, 5. 8 (as used against foes); x. 1, 30.

[2] Kātyāyana Srauta Sūtra, vii. 4, 7, etc.

[3] iv. 2, 3.

Jālāṣa. See **Jalāṣa,** which is read by Sāyaṇa in the Atharvaveda (vi. 57, 2) for Jālāṣa.[1]

[1] *Cf.* Bloomfield, *American Journal of Philology*, 11, 320.

Jāṣkamada is the name of an unknown animal in the Atharvaveda.[1]

[1] xi. 9, 9. *Cf.* Zimmer, *Altindisches Leben*, 88.

Jās-pati occurs once in the Rigveda[1] in the sense of the 'head of the family.' The abstract formed from this word, Jās-patya, apparently denoting 'lordship of children,' is also found there.[2]

[1] i. 185, 8.

[2] Rv. v. 28, 3; x. 85, 23.

Jāhuṣa is the name in the Rigveda[1] of a protégé of the Aśvins.

[1] i. 116, 10; vii. 71, 5. *Cf.* Ludwig, Translation of the Rigveda, 3, 159.

Jāhnava, 'descendant of **Jahnu,**' is the patronymic of **Viśvāmitra** in the Pañcaviṃśa Brāhmaṇa.[1] This fact is of some importance as disproving Aufrecht's theory[2] that the Jahnus were the clan of **Ajīgarta,** the father of **Śunaḥśepa.**

[1] xxi. 12. *Cf.* Weber, *Indische Studien*, 1, 32; Hopkins, *Transactions of the Connecticut Academy of Arts and Sciences*, 15, 54.

[2] Aitareya Brāhmaṇa, 424.

Jitvan Śailini is the name of a teacher in the Bṛhadāraṇyaka Upaniṣad,[1] a contemporary of **Janaka** and **Yājñavalkya.** He held that speech (*vāc*) was Brahman.

[1] iv. 1, 2 (Kāṇva = iv. 1, 5 Mādhyaṃdina, which has Śailina as the patronymic).

Jihvāvant Bādhyoga is the name, in the last Vaṃśa (list of teachers) of the Bṛhadāraṇyaka Upaniṣad,[1] of a teacher, pupil of **Asita Vārṣagaṇa.**

[1] vi. 5, 3 (Kāṇva = vi. 4, 33 Mādhyaṃdina).

Jīva-gṛbh, 'seizing alive,' is, according to Roth,[1] the term for a police official in the Rigveda.[2] But although this sense is rendered possible by the mention of **Madhyamaśī,** perhaps 'arbitrator,' in the same passage,[3] it is neither necessary nor probable.[4]

[1] St Petersburg Dictionary, *s.v.*; *Siebenzig Lieder*, 174.

[2] x. 97, 11.

[3] Rv. x. 97, 12.

[4] Zimmer, *Altindisches Leben*, 180.

Jīva-ja. See **Jarāyu.**

Jīvant appears to denote a certain plant in one passage of the Atharvaveda,[1] where the edition of Roth and Whitney has the unjustified emendation **Jīvala.**[2]

[1] xix. 39, 3. *Cf.* Whitney, Translation of the Atharvaveda, 960.

[2] With this conjectural form, *cf.* Jīvalā, an epithet of a plant in Av. vi. 59, 3; viii. 2, 6; 7, 6; xix. 39, 3.

Jīvala Cailaki, 'descendant of Celaka,' is mentioned in the Śatapatha Brāhmaṇa[1] as reproving **Takṣan.**

[1] ii. 3, 1, 31-35. *Cf.* Lévi, *La Doctrine du Sacrifice*, 140.

Juhū is the regular name in the Rigveda and later for the tongue-shaped ladle in which butter was offered to the gods.

[1] Rv. viii. 44, 5; x. 21, 3; Av. xviii. 4, 5. 6, etc.

Jūrṇi, 'firebrand,' is regarded by *Zimmer*[1] as one of the weapons of the Vedic Indians. But since it is only mentioned in the Rigveda[2] as a weapon used by demons, its employment in normal war cannot be safely assumed.

[1] *Altindisches Leben*, 301.

[2] i. 129, 8. *Cf.* Nirukta, vi. 4.

Jūrṇī is one of the names given to serpents in a hymn of the Atharvaveda (ii. 24, 5), perhaps from their habit of casting their slough. See **Ahi.**

Jetṛ. See **Sṛṇi.**

Jaitrāyaṇa Saho-jit is apparently in the Kāṭhaka Saṃhitā[1] the name of a prince who celebrated the Rājasūya, or 'royal consecration.' Von Schroeder[2] quotes in support of Jaitrāyaṇa as a proper name the derivative Jaitrāyaṇi, 'descendant of Jaitra,' formed according to the Gaṇa *karṇādi*, which is referred to by Pāṇini;[3] but it should be noted that in the parallel passage of the Kapiṣṭhala Saṃhitā[4] the reading is different, and no proper personal name appears, the subject being Indra, the god. This reading seems much more probable, for the verse should be general, and suit every king performing the rite.

[1] xviii. 5.

[2] *Zeitschrift der Deutschen Morgenländischen Gesellschaft*, 49, 168.

[3] iv. 2, 80.

[4] xxviii. 5, cited by von Schroeder *Kāṭhaka*, 1, p. 269.

Jaimini does not appear till the Sūtra period.[1] But a Jaiminīya Saṃhitā of the Sāmaveda is extant, and has been edited and discussed by Caland;[2] and a Jaiminīya Brāhmaṇa, of which a special section is the Jaiminīya Upaniṣad Brāhmaṇa,[3] is known and has formed the subject of several articles by Oertel.[4]

1 Āśvalāyana Gṛhya Sūtra, iii. 4; Śāṅkhāyana Gṛhya Sūtra, iv. 10; vi. 6, etc. He appears also as a pupil of Vyāsa, Sāmavidhāna Brāhmaṇa, *ad fin.*; Weber, *Indische Studien*, 4, 377. *Cf.* his *Indian Literature*, 56.

2 As part ii. of Hillebrandt's *Indische Forschungen*, *Breslau*, 1907. See Oldenberg, *Göttingische Gelehrte Anzeigen*, 1908, 712 *et seq.*

3 Edited by Oertel, *Journal of the American Oriental Society*, 16, 79-260.

4 *Journal of the American Oriental Society*, 18, 15 *et seq.*; 19, 97; 23, 325; 26, 176, 306; 28, 81; *Actes du onzième Congrès International des Orientalistes*, 1, 225; *Transactions of the Connecticut Academy of Arts and Sciences*, 15, 155 *et seq.*

Jaivantāyana, 'descendant of Jīvanta,' is mentioned in the Bṛhadāraṇyaka Upaniṣad[1] as a teacher, with **Śaunaka** and **Raibhya**, of **Rauhiṇāyana.**

1 iv. 5, 26 (Mādhyaṃdina). The name is recognised by Pāṇini, iv. 1, 103.

Jaivala or **Jaivali,** 'descendant of Jīvala,' is the patronymic of **Pravāhaṇa** in the Bṛhadāraṇyaka[1] and Chāndogya Upaniṣads.[2] Jaivali, the king, in the Jaiminīya Upaniṣad Brāhmaṇa[3] is the same person.

1 vi. 2, 1 (Kāṇva = vi. 1, 1 Mādhyaṃdina), where the form is Jaivala.

2 i. 8, 1. 2. 8; v. 3, 1.

3 i. 38, 4.

Jñātṛ occurs in two passages of the Atharvaveda[1] and one of the Śāṅkhāyana Āraṇyaka[2] with a somewhat obscure sense. Zimmer[3] conjectures not unnaturally that the word is a technical term taken from law, meaning 'witness.' The reference is, perhaps, to a custom of carrying on transactions of business before witnesses as practised in other primitive societies.[4] Roth[5] suggests that the word has the sense of

1 vi. 32, 3; viii. 8, 21.

2 xii. 14. *Cf.* Keith, *Śāṅkhāyana Āraṇyaka*, 66, n. 4.

3 *Altindisches Leben*, 181.

4 In Manu, viii. 57, the word is a various reading for *sākṣin*, 'witness.' *Cf.* Jolly, *Recht und Sitte*, 140.

5 St. Petersburg Dictionary, *s.v.*

'surety.' But Bloomfield[6] and Whitney[7] ignore these interpretations.

[6] *Hymns of the Atharvaveda*, 475.

[7] Translation of the Atharvaveda, 306.

Jñāti (masc.), a word which originally seems to have meant 'acquaintance,'[1] denotes in the Rigveda[2] and later[3] a 'relation,' apparently one who was connected by blood on the father's side, though the passages do not necessarily require the limitation. But this sense follows naturally enough from the patriarchal basis of Vedic society.[4]

[1] Being in all probability derived from *jñā*, 'know,' not from *jan*, 'beget,' as would at first sight seem more likely on account of the sense. *Cf.* the St. Petersburg Dictionary, *s.v.*

[2] vii. 55, 5, seems to refer to the members of the joint family sleeping in the paternal house; x. 66, 14; 85, 28 (the kinsmen of the bride are meant); 117, 9 (perhaps 'brother and sister' are meant by *jñāti* here, but 'kinsfolk' will do; *cf.* Muir, *Sanskrit Texts*, 5, 432).

[3] Av. xii. 5, 44 (where Whitney in his Translation renders the word by 'acquaintances,' which seems too vague and feeble); Taittirīya Brāhmaṇa, i. 6, 5, 2; Satapatha Brāhmaṇa, i. 6, 4, 3 (*jñātibhyāṃ vā sakhibhyāṃ vā*, where 'relations' are contrasted with 'friends' or 'companions'); ii. 2, 2, 20; 5, 2, 20; xi. 3, 3, 7, etc.

[4] For the transition from the etymological meaning, *cf.* γνωτός, γνωτή, which in Homer designate 'brother' and 'sister'; St. Petersburg Dictionary, *s.v.*

Jyā is the regular word for 'bowstring' in the Rigveda[1] and later.[2] The making of bowstrings was a special craft, as is shown by the occurrence of the Jyā-kāra, or 'maker of bowstrings,' among the victims at the Puruṣamedha, or human sacrifice, in the Yajurveda.[3] The bowstring consisted of a thong of ox-hide.[4] It was not usually kept taut,[5] but was specially tightened when the bow was to be used.[6] The sound of the bowstring (*jyā-ghoṣa*) is referred to in the Atharvaveda.[7] *Cf.* **Ārtnī.**

[1] iv. 27, 3; vi. 75, 3; x. 51, 6, etc.

[2] Av. i. 1, 3; v. 13, 6; vi. 42, 1; Vājasaneyi Saṃhitā, xvi. 9; xxix. 51, etc.

[3] Vājasaneyi Saṃhitā, xxx. 7; Taittirīya Brāhmaṇa, iii. 4, 3, 1.

[4] Rv. vi. 75, 3; Av. i. 1, 3. In the Epic the bowstring is made of hemp (*maurvī*); Hopkins, *Journal of the American Oriental Society*, 13, 271.

[5] Av. vi. 42, 1.

[6] Rv. x. 166, 3.

[7] v. 21, 9.

Cf. Zimmer, *Altindisches Leben*, 298 299.

Jyākā means 'bowstring,' with a contemptuous sense, in the Rigveda,[1] and in the simple sense in the Atharvaveda.[2]

[1] x. 133, 1, where *anyakeṣāṃ jyākāḥ* is unmistakably contemptuous. *Cf.* Macdonell, *Vedic Grammar*, p. 137.
[2] i. 2, 2.

Jyā-pāśa means 'bowstring' in the Atharvaveda (xi. 10, 22).

Jyā-hroḍa occurs in the description of the arms of the **Vrātya** in the Pañcaviṃśa Brāhmaṇa,[1] and is also mentioned in the Sūtras.[2] The sense is somewhat obscure, for one Sūtra describes it as a 'bow not meant for use' (*ayogyaṃ dhanus*),[3] while the other speaks of it as a 'bow without an arrow' (*dhanuṣka aniṣu*).[4] Some sort of a bow, therefore, seems to be meant.

[1] xvii. 1, 14 (spelt *-hṇoḍa* in text, *-hnoḍa* in comm.).
[2] Kātyāyana Śrauta Sūtra, xxii. 4, 11 (spelt *-hroḍa*); Lāṭyāyana Śrauta Sūtra, viii. 6, 8 (spelt *-hnoḍa*: the editor notes that the Drāhyāyaṇa Sūtra has the same reading).
[3] Kātyāyana, *loc. cit.*
[4] Lāṭyāyana, *loc. cit.*
Cf. Zimmer, *Altindisches Leben*, 38; Hopkins, *Transactions of the Connecticut Academy of Arts and Sciences*, 15, 32; Weber, *Indische Studien*, 1, 33, 52.

Jyeṣṭha, ordinarily meaning 'greatest,' has further the specific sense of 'eldest'[1] brother in the Rigveda.[2] It also means the eldest among sons, which is another side of the same sense.[3]

[1] With changed accent, *jyeṣṭhá*. *Cf.* Macdonell, *Vedic Grammar*, p. 83, 14.
[2] iv. 33, 5; x. 11, 2.
[3] Av. xii. 2, 35; Aitareya Brāhmaṇa, vii. 17; Śatapatha Brāhmaṇa, xi. 5, 3, 8, *and cf.* **Jyaiṣṭhineya**.

Jyeṣṭha-ghnī, 'slaying the eldest,' is the name of a **Nakṣatra**, or lunar mansion, usually called **Jyeṣṭhā**, in the Atharvaveda[1] and the Taittirīya Brāhmaṇa.[2] It is Antares or *Cor Scipionis*.

[1] vi. 110, 2. *Cf.* vi. 112, 1.
[2] i. 5, 2, 8. *Cf.* Whitney, Translation of the Atharvaveda, 361.

Jyeṣṭhā. See **Nakṣatra**.

Jyaiṣṭhineya denotes, in combination with **Jyeṣṭha**, the eldest,' a 'son of the father's first wife' (*jyeṣṭhā*), in the Brāhmaṇas.[1]

[1] Taittirīya Brāhmaṇa, ii. 1, 8, 1 (opposed to *kaniṣṭha* and *kāniṣṭhineya*); Pañcaviṃśa Brāhmaṇa, ii. 1, 2; xx. 5, 2.

Jyotiṣa, 'astronomy.' It is important to note that no reference to any work on astronomy occurs in the Saṃhitās or Brāhmaṇas. The text which claims to represent the astronomical science of the Veda has been edited by Weber,[1] and has frequently been discussed since.[2] Its date is unknown, but is undoubtedly late, as is shown alike by the contents and form of the work.

[1] *Ueber den Vedakalender namens Jyotiṣam* (1862).

[2] See references in Thibaut, *Astronomie, Astrologie und Mathematik*, 20, 29.

Jvālāyana, 'descendant of Jvāla,' is the name of a man, a pupil of **Gauṣūkti**, mentioned in the Jaiminīya Upaniṣad Brāhmaṇa (iv. 16, 1), in a list of teachers.

JH.

Jhaṣa is mentioned in the story of Manu told in the Śatapatha Brāhmaṇa,[1] where it means a 'great fish' (*mahā-matsya*) according to the commentator. Eggeling[2] suggests that a horned fish is meant, because in the Taittirīya Saṃhitā[3] the Iḍā, or personified libation, is represented as a cow, and this may have brought in the idea of a horned fish in the later form of an old legend. But *cf.* **Jaṣa.**

[1] i. 8, 1, 4.

[2] *Sacred Books of the East*, 12, 217, n. 3; 26, xxxi.

[3] i. 7, 1; ii. 6, 7.

T.

Takavāna appears to be a patronymic from Taku,[1] and to be the name of a seer in the Rigveda,[2] presumably a descendant of Taku Kakṣīvant, for his name occurs in a group of hymns composed by the Kākṣīvatas.[3]

[1] *Cf.* Bhṛgavāṇa, from Bhṛgu; Roth, St. Petersburg Dictionary, *s.v. Taku*, as an adjective (?), occurs in Rigveda, ix. 97, 52.

[2] i. 120, 6.

[3] Oldenberg, *Zeitschrift der Deutschen Morgenländischen Gesellschaft*, 42, 221. *Cf.* Pischel, *Vedische Studien*, 2, 92; Ludwig, *Über Methode bei Interpretation des Ṛgveda*, 47.

Takman is a disease repeatedly mentioned in the Atharvaveda, but later not known under this name. It is the subject of five hymns[1] of the Atharvaveda, and is often mentioned elsewhere.[2] Weber[3] first identified it with 'fever,' and Grohmann[4] showed that all the symptoms pointed to that ailment.[5] Reference is made to the alternate hot and shivering fits of the patient,[6] to the yellow colour of the jaundice which accompanies the fever,[7] and to its peculiar periodicity. The words used to describe its varieties are *anye-dyuḥ*,[8] *ubhaya-dyuḥ*,[9] *tṛtīyaka*,[10] *vi-tṛtīya*,[11] and *sadaṃ-di*,[12] the exact sense of most of which terms is somewhat uncertain. It is agreed[13] that the first epithet designates the fever known as *quotidianus*, which recurs each day at the same hour, though the word is curious (lit.

[1] i. 25; v. 22; vi. 20; vii. 116; xix. 39 (*cf.* v. 4).

[2] Av. iv. 9, 8; v. 4, 1. 9; 30, 16; ix. 8, 6; xi. 2, 22. 26, etc.

[3] *Indische Studien*, 4, 119; Roth, *Zur Litteratur und Geschichte des Weda*, 39, had, from the use of Kuṣṭha as a remedy, regarded it as denoting 'leprosy,' and was followed by Pictet, Kuhn's *Zeitschrift*, 5, 337. Muir, *Sanskrit Texts*, 4, 280, thought 'consumption' was meant.

[4] *Indische Studien*, 9, 381 *et seq.*

[5] See also Bloomfield, *Hymns of the Atharvaveda*, 451 *et seq.*; Zimmer, *Altindisches Leben*, 379-385, and compare the *jvara* (a non-Vedic word) of the classical medicine, Wise, *Hindu System of Medicine*, 219 *et seq.*; Jolly, *Medicin*, 70-72. Dārila and Keśava, the commentators on the Kauśika Sūtra, everywhere equate *takman* and *jvara*.

[6] Av. i. 25, 2-4; v. 22, 2. 7. 10; vi. 20, 3; vii. 116, 1.

[7] Av. i. 25, 2; v. 22, 2; vi. 20, 3.

[8] Av. i. 25, 4; vii. 116, 2.

[9] *Ibid.*

[10] Av. i. 25, 4; v. 22, 13; xix. 39, 10.

[11] Av. v. 22, 13.

[12] Av. v. 22, 13; xix. 39, 10.

[13] Grohmann, *op. cit.*, 387; Zimmer, *op. cit.*, 382; Bloomfield, *op. cit.*, 274.

'on the other—*i.e.*, next, day'). The *ubhaya-dyuḥ* ('on both days') variety appears to mean a disease recurring for two successive days, the third being free; this corresponds to the *rhythmus quartanus complicatus.*[14] But Sāyaṇa considers that it means a fever recurring on the third day, the 'tertian.' The *tṛtīyaka*, however, must be the 'tertian' fever,[15] though Zimmer[16] suggests that it may mean a fever which is fatal at the third paroxysm. Grohmann[17] regards the *vi-tṛtīyaka* as equivalent to the *tertiana duplicata*, a common form in southern countries, in which the fever occurs daily, but with a correspondence in point of time or severity of attack on alternate days. Bloomfield[18] suggests that it is identical with the *ubhaya-dyuḥ* variety. The *sadaṃ-di*[19] type appears to be the kind later known as *saṃtata-jvara* ('continuous fever'), in which there are attacks of several days' duration, with an interval followed by a fresh period of attack. Fever occurred at different seasons, in the autumn (*śārada*), in the hot weather (*graiṣma*), in the rains (*vārṣika*),[20] but was especially prevalent in the first, as is indicated by the epithet *viśva-śārada*, 'occurring every autumn.'[21]

The disease is said to arise when Agni enters the waters.[22] From this Weber[23] deduced that it was considered to be the result of a chill supervening on heat, or the influence of heat on marshy land. Grohmann[24] preferred to see in this connexion of the origin of the disease with Agni's entering the waters[25] an allusion to the fact that fever arises in the rainy season, the time when Agni, as lightning, descends to earth with the rain. Zimmer,[26] who accepts this view, further refers to the prevalence

[14] Grohmann, 388; Zimmer, 382; Bloomfield, 274. It may conceivably be the form styled Cāturthaka Viparyaya (Wise, *op. cit.*, 232), in which the paroxysm occurs every fourth day, and lasts for two days.

[15] Sāyaṇa on Av. i. 25, 4; Bloomfield, 451. It is the *jvara tṛtīyaka* of Suśruta (2, 404, 7).

[16] *Op. cit.*, 383, quoting Hügel, Kashmir, 1, 133.

[17] *Op. cit.*, 388.

[18] *Op. cit.*, 451.

[19] Of doubtful derivation: either 'always cutting' (*cf.* Sāyaṇa on Av. xix. 39, 10), or 'always fastening upon' (Roth, St. Petersburg Dictionary, *s.v.*), or 'belonging to every day' = *sadaṃ-dina* (Zimmer, 383, n.; Bloomfield, 452).

[20] Av. v. 22, 13.

[21] Av. ix. 8, 6; xix. 34, 10.

[22] Av. i. 25, 1.

[23] *Indische Studien*, 4, 119.

[24] *Ibid.*, 9, 493.

[25] Macdonell, *Vedic Mythology*, p. 92.

[26] *Op. cit.*, 384.

of fever in the Terai, and interprets *vanya*, an epithet of fever found in the Atharvaveda,[27] as meaning 'sprung from the forest,' pointing out that fever is mentioned as prevalent among the **Mūjavants** and **Mahāvṛṣas**, two mountain tribes of the western Himālaya.[28] There is no trace of fever having been observed to be caused by the bite of the *anopheles* mosquito, which breeds in stagnant water: this theory has without reason been held to be known to classical Indian medicine.[29]

Among the symptoms of Takman, or among complications accompanying it, are mentioned 'itch' (**Pāman**), 'headache' (*śīrṣa-śoka*),[30] 'cough' (**Kāsikā**), and 'consumption,' or perhaps some form of itch (**Balāsa**).

It is perhaps significant that the Takman does not appear until the Atharvaveda. It is quite possible that the Vedic Āryans, when first settled in India, did not know the disease, which would take some generations to become endemic and recognized as dangerous. What remedies they used against it is quite uncertain, for the Atharvaveda mentions only spells and the **Kuṣṭha**, which can hardly have been an effective remedy, though still used in later times. Fever must, even in the Atharvan period, have claimed many victims, or it would not be mentioned so prominently.

27 Av. vi. 20, 4.

28 Av. v. 22, 5.

29 Jolly, *Journal of the Royal Asiatic Society*, 1906, 222.

30 Av. xix. 39, 10.

For the present position of the disease in India, *cf.* the Report of the Simla Conference of 1909.

Takvan,[1] **Takvarī,**[2] seem in the Rigveda to denote a 'swift-flying bird.' Sāyaṇa[3] explains Takvan as a swift steed.

1 Rv. i. 66, 2. *Cf.* i. 134, 5, and **Tsārin**.

2 *Ibid.*, i. 151, 5; x. 91, 2. But in both places the word may be adjectival.

3 On Rv. i. 66, 2.

Takṣaka Vaiśāleya ('descendant of Viśālā') is a mythical figure, mentioned as the son of Virāj in the Atharvaveda,[1] and as Brāhmaṇācchaṃsin priest at the snake sacrifice in the Pañcaviṃśa Brāhmaṇa.[2]

1 vii. 10, 29.

2 xxv. 15, 3. *Cf.* Weber, *Indische Studien*, 1, 35.

1. **Takṣan,** 'carpenter,' is mentioned in the Rigveda[1] and often later.[2] He was employed to do all sorts of work in wood, such as the making of chariots (**Ratha**) and wagons (**Anas**). Carved work of a finer type seems also to have fallen to his lot.[3] The axe (*kuliśa*,[4] *paraśu*[5]) is mentioned as one of his tools, and perhaps the **Bhurij**, a word which is, however, uncertain in sense. In one passage of the Rigveda[6] reference seems to be made to the pains of the carpenter in bending over his work. That the carpenters were a low caste, or formed a separate class of the people, is certainly not true of Vedic times.[7]

[1] ix. 112, 1.
[2] Av. x. 6, 3; Kāṭhaka Saṃhitā, xii. 10; xviii. 13; Maitrāyaṇī Saṃhitā, ii. 9, 5; Vājasaneyi Saṃhitā, xvi. 27; xxx. 6; Taittirīya Brāhmaṇa, iii. 4, 2, 1; Satapatha Brāhmaṇa, i. 1, 3, 12; iii. 6, 4, 4, etc.
[3] Rv. x. 86, 5; Av. xix. 49, 8. *Cf.* Rv. i. 161, 9; iii. 60, 2.
[4] Rv. iii. 2, 1.
[5] Kāṭhaka Saṃhitā, xii. 10.
[6] Rv. i. 105, 18. *Cf.* Roth, *Nirukta, Erläuterungen*, 67; Oldenberg, *Ṛgveda-Noten*, 1, 100.
[7] Fick, *Die sociale Gliederung*, 210, n. 1.
Cf. Zimmer, *Altindisches Leben*, 245, 253.

2. **Takṣan** is mentioned in the Śatapatha Brāhmaṇa[1] as a teacher whose view of a certain formula was not accepted by **Jīvala Cailaki.**

[1] ii. 3, 1, 31-35. *Cf.* Lévi, *La Doctrine du Sacrifice*, 140.

3. **Takṣan.** See **Bṛbu.**

Taṇḍula, 'grain,' especially 'rice grain,' is mentioned very often in the Atharvaveda[1] and later,[2] but not in the Rigveda. This accords with the fact that rice cultivation seems hardly known in the Rigveda.[3] Husked (*karṇa*) and unhusked (*akarṇa*) rice is referred to in the Taittirīya Saṃhitā.[4]

[1] x. 9, 26; xi. 1, 18; xii. 3, 18. 29. 30.
[2] Maitrāyaṇī Saṃhitā, ii. 6, 6; Kāṭhaka Saṃhitā, x. 1, etc.; Aitareya Brāhmaṇa, i. 1; Śatapatha Brāhmaṇa, i. 1, 4, 3; ii. 5, 3, 4; v. 2, 3, 2; vi. 6, 1, 8, etc.; *śyāmāka-taṇḍula*, 'millet grain,' *ibid.*, x. 6, 3, 2; Chāndogya Upaniṣad, iii. 14, 3; *apāmārga-taṇḍula*, 'grain of the *Achyranthes aspera*,' v. 2, 4, 15, etc.
[3] Zimmer, *Altindisches Leben*, 239. See **Vrīhi.**
[4] i. 8, 9, 3. See Pischel, *Vedische Studien*, 1, 190.

Tata, 'dada,' is the pet name for 'father' in the Rigveda[1] and later.[2] *Cf.* **Tāta** and **Pitṛ.**

[1] viii. 91, 6; ix. 112, 3.

[2] Av. v. 24, 16; Taittirīya Saṃhitā, iii. 2, 5, 5; Taittirīya Brāhmaṇa, i. 6, 9, 7; in the vocative as a form of address, Av. viii. 4, 77; Aitareya Brāhmaṇa, v. 14; vii. 15; Aitareya Āraṇyaka, i. 3, 3.

Cf. Delbrück, *Die indogermanischen Verwandtschaftsnamen*, 449.

Tatāmaha, 'grandfather,' is found in the Atharvaveda.[1]

[1] v. 24, 17; viii. 4, 76. It seems to mean literally 'great father,' and to be an analogical formation following *pitāmaha*; Delbrück, *op. cit.*, 473, 474.

Tanaya, n., denotes 'offspring,' 'descendants' in the Rigveda,[1] where also it is often used adjectivally with **Toka.**[2] There seems no ground for the view[3] that *toka* means 'sons,' 'children,' and *tanaya* 'grandchildren.'

[1] i. 96, 4; 183, 3; 184, 5; ii. 23, 19; vii. 1, 21, etc.; *tokaṃ ca tanayaṃ ca*, i. 92, 13; ix. 74, 5. *Cf.* vi. 25, 4; 31, 1; 66, 8; and i. 31, 12, as explained by Pischel, *Vedische Studien*, 3, 193.

[2] Rv. i. 64, 14; 114, 6; 147, 1; 189, 2; ii. 30, 5, etc.; Aitareya Brāhmaṇa, ii. 7.

[3] Nirukta, x. 7; xii. 6.

Cf. St. Petersburg Dictionary, *s.v.* *Tan*, *tana*, and *tanas*, have the same sense as Tanaya. See Rv. vi. 46, 12; 49, 13; vii. 104, 10; viii. 68, 12, etc. (*tan*); viii. 25, 2 (*tana*); v. 70, 4 (*tanas*).

Tanti occurs in one passage of the Rigveda,[1] where Roth[2] renders the plural of the word by 'files' of calves. But it seems rather to have the sense which it has in the later literature, of 'cords,' here used to fasten the calves.

[1] vi. 24, 4.

[2] St. Petersburg Dictionary, *s.v.*

Tantu appears properly to mean 'thread,' and in particular the 'warp' of a piece of weaving, as opposed to **Otu**, the 'woof.' Both senses are found in the Atharvaveda.[1] In the Śatapatha Brāhmaṇa[2] the 'warp' is called *anuchāda*, the 'woof' *paryāsa*, the *tantavaḥ* being the 'threads.' In the Taittirīya Saṃhitā,[3]

[1] xiv. 2, 51 (opposed to *otu*); xv. 3, 6 (the *prāñcaḥ* and *tiryañcaḥ* threads or cords of the throne of the Vrātya [**Āsandī**]).

[2] iii. 1, 2, 18; Eggeling, *Sacred Books of the East*, 26, 8, 9.

[3] vi. 1, 1, 4.

on the other hand, the 'warp' is *prācīna-tāna*, the 'woof' *otu*. The threads or cords of the throne (**Paryaṅka**) are referred to in the Kauṣītaki Upaniṣad.[4]

In the Rigveda the word is used only metaphorically, and this is its most frequent use even in the Brāhmaṇas.[5] See also **Vāṇa.**

[4] i. 5; Keith, *Śāṅkhāyana Āraṇyaka*, 20, n. 2.

[5] St. Petersburg Dictionary, *s.v.* It is applied to the filaments of plants in Rv. x. 134, 5; to the spider's web in Bṛhadāraṇyaka Upaniṣad, ii. 1, 23.

Tantra means, like **Tantu**, the 'warp' of a piece of weaving, or more generally the 'web' itself. It is found in the Rigveda[1] and later.[2]

[1] x. 71, 9.

[2] Av. x. 7, 42; Taittirīya Brāhmaṇa, ii. 5, 5, 3; Pañcaviṃśa Brāhmaṇa, x. 5; Śatapatha Brāhmaṇa, xiv. 2, 2, 22.

Cf. Zimmer, *Altindisches Leben*, 254.

Tapas, Tapasya. See **Māsa.**

Tapo-nitya ('constant in penance') **Pauru-śiṣṭi** ('descendant of Puruśiṣṭa') is the name of a teacher in the Taittirīya Upaniṣad (i. 9, 1) who believed in the value of penance (*tapas*).

Tayādara is the name of an animal only mentioned in the adjectival form *tāyādara* along with **Parasvant,** 'wild ass' (?) in the Atharvaveda.[1]

[1] vi. 72, 2. *Cf.* Whitney, Translation of the Atharvaveda, 335.

Tarakṣu, the 'hyæna,' is mentioned in the list of victims at the Aśvamedha, or horse sacrifice. in the Yajurveda.[1]

[1] Taittirīya Saṃhitā, v. 5, 19, 1, where Sāyaṇa explains the animal to be 'a kind of tiger with an ass's appearance' (*vyāghra-viśeṣo gardabhākāraḥ*); Maitrāyaṇī Saṃhitā, iii. 14, 21; Vājasaneyi Saṃhitā, xxiv. 40.

Cf. Zimmer, *Altindisches Leben*, 81.

Taranta appears, along with **Purumīḍha**, as a patron of **Śyāvāśva** in the Rigveda.[1] In the Pañcaviṃśa Brāhmaṇa[2] and other Brāhmaṇas[3] he, together with Purumīḍha, is described as receiving gifts from **Dhvasra**[4] and **Puruṣanti**; but since the receipt of gifts was forbidden to Kṣatriyas, they for the nonce became Ṛṣis, and composed a passage in honour of the donors.[4] He, like Purumīḍha, was a Vaidadaśvi, or son of Vidadaśva.[5]

1 v. 61, 10.
2 xiii. 7, 12.
3 Jaiminīya Brāhmaṇa, iii. 139; Śāṭyāyanaka *apud* Sāyaṇa on Rv. ix. 58, 3 = Sāmaveda, ii. 410.
4 Rv. ix. 58, 3.
5 *Cf.* Rv. v. 61, 10; notes 2 and 3. This is merely a misunderstanding of the Rv. *Cf.* Oertel, *Journal of the American Oriental Society*, 18, 39; Sieg, *Die Sagenstoffe des Ṛgveda*, 50 *et seq.*; 62, 63; Oldenberg, *Zeitschrift der Deutschen Morgenländischen Gesellschaft*, 42, 232, n. 1; *Ṛgveda-Noten*, 1, 353, 354, where he points out that the Brāhmaṇa tradition, and that of the Bṛhaddevatā (v. 50-81, with Macdonell's notes), are not to be accepted as real explanations of the Rigveda.

Taru, the usual term for 'tree' in classical Sanskrit, never occurs in Vedic literature, except perhaps in one passage of the Rigveda,[1] where Sāyaṇa finds it, and where it can be so translated. But the form (*tarubhiḥ*) is probably to be interpreted otherwise.[2]

1 v. 44, 5.
2 Roth, St. Petersburg Dictionary, *s.v.*, cites *tarobhiḥ* in Rv. ii. 39, 3, as a parallel, and so Oldenberg, *Ṛgveda-Noten*, 1, 341.

Tarukṣa is the name of a man in the Rigveda[1] who is mentioned along with **Balbūtha**, the **Dāsa**, in a Dāna-stuti, or 'Praise of Gifts.'

1 viii. 46, 32. *Cf.* Weber, *Indische Studien*, 1, 391; Zimmer, *Altindisches Leben*, 117.

Tarku, 'spindle,' is known only in Vedic literature from the mention of it in Yāska's Nirukta (ii. 1) as an example of the transposition of letters, the word being derived, according to him, from the root *kart*, 'to spin.'

Tarda, 'borer,' occurs in a hymn of the Atharvaveda[1] enumerating insects that injure grain. Whitney[2] suggests that a kind of mouse or rat may be meant. Roth[3] thought a bird was denoted.

[1] vi. 50, 1. 2.

[2] Translation of the Atharvaveda, 318.

[3] St. Petersburg Dictionary, *s.v.* *Cf.* Bloomfield, *Hymns of the Atharvaveda*, 485.

Tardman in the Atharvaveda[1] applies to the hole in the yoke (**Yuga**). In the Śatapatha Brāhmaṇa[2] it designates a hole in a skin.

[1] xiv. 1, 40.

[2] iii. 2, 1, 2; Eggeling, *Sacred Books of the East*, 26, 26, n. 1.

Tarya is, according to Sāyaṇa, the name of a man in one passage of the Rigveda.[1] But the verse is hopelessly obscure.[2]

[1] v, 44, 12. *Cf.* Ludwig, Translation of the Rigveda, 3, 158, 159.

[2] Oldenberg, *Ṛgveda-Noten*, 1, 342.

Talāśa is the name of a tree in the Atharvaveda.[1] Whitney[2] suggests that it may be the same as *tālīśa* (*Flacourtia cataphracta*).

[1] vi. 15, 3.

[2] Translation of the Atharvaveda, 291. *Cf.* Zimmer, *Altindisches Leben*, 62.

Talpa is the regular term for 'bed' or 'couch' from the Rigveda and the Atharvaveda[1] onwards.[2] One made of **Udumbara** wood is mentioned in the Taittirīya Brāhmaṇa.[3] The violation of the bed of a Guru, or teacher, is already mentioned in the Chāndogya Upaniṣad,[4] while the adjective *talpya*, 'born in the nuptial couch,' denotes 'legitimate' in the Śatapatha Brāhmaṇa.[5]

[1] Rv. vii. 55, 8; Av. v. 17, 12; xiv. 2, 31. 41.

[2] Taittirīya Saṃhitā, vi. 2, 6, 4; Taittirīya Brāhmaṇa, ii. 2, 5, 3; Pañcaviṃśa Brāhmaṇa, xxiii. 4, 2; xxv. 1, 10.

[3] i. 2, 6, 5.

[4] v. 10, 9.

[5] xiii. 1, 6, 2. *Cf.* Zimmer, *Altindisches Leben*, 154.

Talava in the list of victims at the Puruṣamedha, or human sacrifice, in the Yajurveda,[1] denotes a 'musician' of some kind.

[1] Vājasaneyi Saṃhitā, xxx. 20; Taittirīya Brāhmaṇa, iii. 4, 15, 1. *Cf.* Weber, *Indische Streifen*, 1, 83, n. 15.

Taṣṭṛ is found in the Rigveda[1] in the sense of 'carpenter,' like **Takṣan,** which is from the same root *takṣ*, 'to fashion.'

[1] i. 61, 4; 105, 18; 130, 4; iii. 38, 1; vii. 32, 20; x. 93, 12; 119, 5. *Cf.* Nirukta, v. 21.

Tasara denotes the weaver's 'shuttle' in the Rigveda[1] and the Yajurveda Saṃhitās.[2]

[1] x. 130, 2.

[2] Vājasaneyi Saṃhitā, xix. 83; Maitrāyaṇī Saṃhitā, iii. 11, 9; Kāṭhaka Saṃhitā, xxxviii. 3; Taittirīya Brāhmaṇa, ii. 6, 4, 2.

Cf. Zimmer, *Altindisches Leben*, 254.

Taskara occurs in the Rigveda[1] and frequently later,[2] denoting 'thief' or 'robber.' It appears to be practically synonymous with **Stena,** in connexion with which it is often mentioned.[3] The Stena and the Taskara are contrasted in the Vājasaneyi Saṃhitā[4] with the **Malimlu,** who is a burglar or house-breaker, while they are highwaymen, or, as the Rigveda[5] puts it, 'men who haunt the woods and risk their lives' (*tanū-tyajā vanar-gū*). In another passage of the Rigveda,[6] however, the dog is told to bark at the Taskara or the Stena, which clearly points to an attempt at house-breaking. The thief goes about at night,[7] and knows the paths[8] on which he attacks his victim. In one passage of the Rigveda[9] the use of cords is mentioned, but whether to bind the thieves when captured, or to bind the

[1] i. 191, 5; vi. 27, 3; vii. 55, 3; viii. 29, 6.

[2] Av. iv. 3, 2; xix. 47, 7; 50, 5; Vājasaneyi Saṃhitā, xi. 77. 78; xii. 62; xvi. 21, etc; Nirukta, iii. 14.

[3] Rv. vii. 55, 3; Av. xix. 47, 7; 50, 5; Vājasaneyi Saṃhitā, xi. 79; xvi. 21, etc.

[4] xi. 79 (the Malimlu is *janeṣu*, 'among men'; the others *vane*, 'in the forest'). *Cf.* for the Malimlu, Taittirīya Saṃhitā, vi. 3, 2, 6; Atharvaveda, xix. 49, 10.

[5] x. 4, 6.

[6] vii. 55, 3.

[7] Rv. i. 191, 5.

[8] Rv. viii. 29, 6.

[9] x. 4, 6.

victim, is not clear.[10] The Atharvaveda[11] refers to the Stena and the Taskara as cattle and horse thieves.[12]

Tāyu was another name for thief, perhaps of a less distinguished and more domestic character than the highwayman, for though he is referred to as a cattle-thief,[13] he is also alluded to as a stealer of clothes (*vastra-mathi*)[14] and as a debtor.[15] In one passage the Tāyus are said to disappear at the coming of dawn (which is elsewhere called *yāvayad-dveṣas*, 'driving away hostile beings,' and *ṛta-pā*, 'guardian of order'), like the stars of heaven (*nakṣatra*).[16]

In the Śatarudriya litany of the Vājasaneyi Saṃhitā[17] Rudra is called lord of assailers (*ā-vyādhin*), thieves (*stena*), robbers (*taskara*), pickpockets (*stāyu*), stealers (*muṣṇant*), and cutters (*vi-kṛnta*); and designations of sharpers (*gṛtsa*) and bands (*gaṇa, vrāta*), apparently of robbers, are mentioned.[18] It is therefore not surprising that the Rigveda[19] should contain many prayers for safety at home or on the way, or that the Atharvaveda should devote several hymns to night[20] chiefly for protection against the evil doings of thieves and robbers.

Pischel[21] suggests that in one passage of the Rigveda[22] **Vasiṣṭha** is represented as a burglar, but he admits that, since Vasiṣṭha was attacking the house of his father Varuṇa, he was only seeking to obtain what he may have regarded as his own. But the interpretation of the hymn is not certain.[23]

Sāyaṇa's explanation of one passage of the Rigveda,[24] as

[10] Zimmer, *Altindisches Leben*, 178, n.

[11] xix. 50, 5. *Cf.* Rv. x. 97, 10 (*stena*).

[12] Whitney, Translation of the Atharvaveda, 984.

[13] Rv. i. 65, 1; vii. 86, 5.

[14] Rv. iv. 38, 5.

[15] Rv. vi. 12, 5. No doubt this theft is the result of despair at being in debt, which might lead to loss of liberty (Ṛṇa).

[16] Rv. i. 50, 2. *Cf.* Macdonell, *Vedic Mythology*, p. 47.

[17] xvi. 20. 21. *Cf.* Taittirīya Saṃhitā, iv. 5, 4, 1; Kāṭhaka Saṃhitā, xvii. 13; Maitrāyaṇī Saṃhitā, ii. 9, 4.

[18] xvi. 25.

[19] i. 129, 9; ii. 23, 16; vi. 24, 10, 41, 5; 51, 15; x. 63, 16.

[20] Av. xix. 47-50.

[21] *Vedische Studien*, 2, 55, 56. Contrast 1, 106.

[22] Rv. vii. 55.

[23] *Cf.* Aufrecht, *Indische Studien*, 4, 337 *et seq.*; Lanman, *Sanskrit Reader*, 370; Zimmer, *Altindisches Leben*, 308; Bṛhaddevatā, vii. 11 *et seq.*, with Macdonell's notes.

[24] vi. 54, 1.

referring to professional cattle-trackers, like the Khojis of the Panjab, seems quite probable.[25]

The punishment of thieves appears primarily to have been left to the action of the robbed. The practice of binding them in stocks[26] seems clearly referred to. But later, at any rate—and in all probability earlier also, as in other countries—a more severe penalty could be exacted, and death inflicted by the king.[27] There is no hint in Vedic literature of the mode of conviction; a fire ordeal is not known to the Atharvaveda,[28] and the ordeal known to the Chāndogya Upaniṣad[29] is not said to be used in the case of theft. No doubt the stolen property was recovered by the person robbed if he could obtain it. Nothing is known as to what happened if the property had passed from the actual thief into the possession of another person.

[25] Zimmer, *op. cit.*, 182, 183, citing Elliot, *Memoirs*, 1, 276; Jolly, *Recht und Sitte*, 123.

[26] *Cf.* Rv. i. 24, 13. 15; vii. 86, 5; Av. vi. 63, 3=84, 4; 115, 2. 3; 121; xix. 47, 9; 50, 1, all of which passages are cited by Zimmer, 181, 182, to prove this practice. But it must be noted that Rv. vii. 86, 5, alone is not at all conclusive evidence, though Av. xix. 47, 9; 50, 1 (*drupade āhan*), probably mean the same thing. Whitney, Translation of the Atharvaveda, 976, 983, renders the passages as referring to casting a thief into a snare, and Pischel, *Vedische Studien*, 1, 106, makes Rv. vii. 86, 5, refer to the cattle-thief (*paśu-tṛp*) taking away the rope from the calf he means to steal. For Rv. x. 4, 6, see above, n. 10. The German and Slavonic parallels cited by Zimmer, 182, n., support his view. See also for a similar punishment in case of debt, **Ṛṇa.**

[27] Gautama Dharma Sūtra, xii. 43-45; Āpastamba Dharma Sūtra, i. 9, 25, 4. 5; Jolly, *op. cit.*, 124.

[28] Av. ii. 12 was so interpreted by Schlagintweit, *Die Gottesurtheile der Inder*, 9 *et seq.* (1866); Weber, *Indische Studien*, 13, 164 *et seq.*; Ludwig, Translation of the Rigveda, 3, 445; Zimmer, 183 *et seq.*; but see Bloomfield, *American Journal of Philology*, 11, 330 *et seq.*; *Hymns of the Atharvaveda*, 294-296; Whitney, Translation of the Atharvaveda, 54; Grill, *Hundert Lieder*,[2] 47, 85; Jolly, *op. cit.*, 146.

[29] vi. 16; Jolly, *loc. cit.*

Tastuva, or **Tasruva,** as the Paippalāda recension has it, is the name of a remedy against snake poison, and is mentioned along with **Tābuva** in the Atharvaveda.[1]

[1] v. 13, 10. 11. *Cf.* Bloomfield, *Hymns of the Atharvaveda*, 428; Whitney, Translation of the Atharvaveda, 244.

Tājad-bhaṅga ('easily broken') is apparently the name of a tree or plant in the Atharvaveda.[1] The Kauśika Sūtra[2] treats it as a compound word, and its commentator makes it out to be the castor-oil plant (*eraṇḍa*). Whitney,[3] however, treats the expression as two separate words, and thinks that the passage means 'may they be broken suddenly (*tājat*) like hemp (*bhaṅga*).'

1 viii. 8, 3 (a battle hymn).

2 xvi 14. *Cf.* Bloomfield's edition, xliv; *Hymns of the Atharvaveda*, 583, 584; Caland, *Altindisches Zauberritual*, 35; Lanman in Whitney, Translation of the Atharvaveda, 502; Zimmer, *Altindisches Leben*, 72.

3 *Op. cit.*, 504.

Tāṇḍa seems to be the name of a sage to whose school belonged the Tāṇḍa Brāhmaṇa mentioned in the Lāṭyāyana Śrauta Sūtra.[1]

1 vii. 10, 17. *Cf.* Weber, *Indische Studien*, 1, 49.

Tāṇḍa-vinda, or **Tāṇḍa-vindava,** is the name of a teacher mentioned in the Śāṅkhāyana Āraṇyaka.[1]

1 viii. 10. The manuscripts differ as to the form of the name.

Tāṇḍi occurs as the name of a pupil of **Bādarāyaṇa** in the Vaṃśa (list of teachers) at the end of the Sāmavidhāna Brāhmaṇa.[1]

1 See Konow's Translation, 80, n. 2.

Tāṇḍya is the name of a teacher in the Śatapatha Brāhmaṇa,[1] quoted on a point bearing on the Agniciti, or piling of the sacred fire. He is also mentioned in the Vaṃśa Brāhmaṇa.[2] The Tāṇḍya Mahābrāhmaṇa or Pañcaviṃśa Brāhmaṇa[3] of the Sāmaveda represents the school of the Tāṇḍins.

1 vi. 1, 2, 25. *Cf.* Lévi, *La Doctrine du Sacrifice*, 140.

2 Weber, *Indische Studien*, 4, 373, 384.

3 Edited in the *Bibliotheca Indica* Series, 1869-74. See Weber, *Indian Literature*, 66 *et seq.*, 74, 133; Macdonell, *Sanskrit Literature*, 203, 210; Hopkins, *Transactions of the Connecticut Academy of Arts and Sciences*, 15, 23 *et seq.*

Tāta, apparently 'dada's boy,' an affectionate term of address by a father (*cf.* **Tata**) to a son, is found in the Brāhmaṇas,[1] occurring in the vocative only. But in the sense of 'father,' through confusion with Tata, it occurs also as early as the Aitareya Āraṇyaka.[2]

[1] Aitareya Brāhmaṇa, vii. 14, 4; Bṛhadāraṇyaka Upaniṣad, vi. 1, 6; Chāndogya Upaniṣad, iv. 4, 2.

[2] i. 3, 3, where Tata and Tāta are given as variant forms of the address of the child to the father. Little, *Grammatical Index*, 75, takes Tāta to mean 'father' primarily, but this seems unlikely.

Cf. Delbrück, *Die indogermanischen Verwandtschaftsnamen*, 449, 454.

Tādurī is mentioned in a verse of the Atharvaveda[1] together with the female frog (**Maṇḍūkī**). Some similar animal must be meant,[2] but Roth,[3] with the commentator Durga on the Nirukta,[4] regards the word as an adjective describing the frog.

[1] iv. 15, 14.

[2] Whitney, Translation of the Atharvaveda, 175.

[3] St. Petersburg Dictionary, *s.v.*, where he suggests *tāḍurī*, from the root *taḍ*, 'beat,' with the sense of 'splashing.'

[4] ix. 7.

1. **Tānva** in an obscure passage of the Rigveda[1] seems to mean a 'legitimate son,' who is said not to leave the heritage (*riktha*) of his father to his sister (*jāmi*). The exact meaning is probably unascertainable,[2] but the passage may convey a statement of what was no doubt the fact, that the daughter had no share in the paternal inheritance; her brother had to provide for her during her life if she remained unmarried, but she had no independent portion.[3] (See **Dāya**.)

[1] iii. 31, 2.

[2] *Cf.* Griffith, *Hymns of the Rigveda*, 1, 348; Oldenberg, *Ṛgveda Noten*, 1, 240; Geldner, *Vedische Studien*, 3, 34.

[3] *Cf.* Jolly, *Recht und Sitte*, 87, for the modern law of the Panjab.

2. **Tānva** appears to be a patronymic, 'descendant of Tanva,' in a verse of the Rigveda.[1] Ludwig[2] thinks that it is the patronymic of **Duḥśīma**, who is mentioned in the preceding verse, but this is uncertain.

[1] x. 93, 15.

[2] Translation of the Rigveda, 3, 166.

1. **Tāpasa**, 'ascetic,' is not found in Vedic literature till the Upaniṣads.[1]

[1] Bṛhadāraṇyaka Upaniṣad, iv. 3, 22. *Cf.* Fick, *Die sociale Gliederung*, 40.

2. **Tāpasa** is a name of **Datta** who was Hotṛ priest at the snake festival described in the Pañcaviṃśa Brāhmaṇa (xxv. 15).

Tābuva is the name in the Atharvaveda[1] of a remedy against snake poison. The Paippalāda recension has Tāvuca instead. Weber[2] thinks that the original form was Tāthuva, from the root *sthā*, 'stand,' and that it meant 'stopping'; but this is hardly probable.[3]

[1] v. 13, 10.
[2] Proceedings of the Berlin Academy, 1896, 681.
[3] Barth, *Revue de l'Histoire des Religions*, 39, 26. *Cf.* Whitney, Translation of the Atharvaveda, 244; Bloomfield, *Hymns of the Atharvaveda*, 428.

Tāyādara, 'belonging to the **Tayādara**' (Av. vi. 72, 2).

Tāyu, 'thief,' is mentioned several times in the Rigveda.[1] See **Taskara**.

[1] i. 50, 2; 65, 1; iv. 38, 5; v. 15, 5; 52, 12; vi. 12, 5; vii. 86, 5 (*paśu-tṛp*, 'cattle-thief,' see Pischel, *Vedische Studien*, 1, 106).

Tārakā is found several times in the Atharvaveda[1] denoting a star. The masculine form Tāraka occurs in the Taittirīya Brāhmaṇa.[2]

[1] ii. 8, 1; iii. 7, 4; vi. 121, 3; xix. 49, 8.
[2] i. 5, 2, 5.

Tārukṣya is the name of a teacher in the Aitareya[1] and Śāṅkhāyana Āraṇyakas.[2] In the former passage Tārkṣya is a variant reading, and in the latter Tārkṣya is read, but this is probably only due to confusion with Tārkṣya, the reputed author of a Rigvedic hymn.[3]

[1] iii. 1, 6.
[2] vii. 19.
[3] Aitareya Āraṇyaka, i. 5, 2, with Keith's note; Sāṅkhāyana Srauta Sūtra xi. 14, 28; xii. 11, 12; Āśvalāyana Śrauta Sūtra, ix. 1.

Tārkṣya is mentioned in the Rigveda[1] as a divine steed, apparently the sun conceived as a horse.[2] But Foy,[3] judging by the name, apparently a patronymic of **Tṛkṣi**, who is known from the Rigveda[4] onwards as a descendant of **Trasadasyu**, thinks that a real steed, the property of Tṛkṣi, is meant; but this is not very probable.[5] See also **Tārukṣya**.

[1] i. 89, 6; x. 178.
[2] Macdonell, *Vedic Mythology*, p. 149.
[3] Kuhn's *Zeitschrift*, 11, 366, 367.
[4] viii. 22, 7.
[5] In Khila, ii. 4, 1, Tārkṣya is represented as a bird (*vāyasa*), also a symbol of the sun. In the Vājasaneyi Saṃhitā, xv. 18, he is mentioned with Ariṣṭanemi, originally an epithet of his (Rv. i. 89, 6; x. 178, 1), as a person, and in the Śatapatha Brāhmaṇa, xiii. 4, 3, 13, he appears as Vaipaśyata (Vaipaścita in Āśvalāyana Śrauta Sūtra, x. 7), king of the birds (*cf.* Eggeling, *Sacred Books of the East*, 44, 369).

Tārpya denotes in the Atharvaveda[1] and later,[2] a garment made of some material, the nature of which is uncertain. The commentators on the Kātyāyana Śrauta Sūtra and the Śatapatha Brāhmaṇa[3] suggest that a linen garment, or one thrice soaked in ghee, or one made of the *tṛpā* or of the *triparṇa* plant, is meant: it is doubtful whether the sense was known even to the author of the Brāhmaṇa himself. Goldstücker's[4] rendering of the word is 'silken garment,' which Eggeling[5] is inclined to accept.[6]

[1] xviii. 4, 31.
[2] Taittirīya Saṃhitā, ii. 4, 11, 6; Taittirīya Brāhmaṇa, i. 3, 7, 1; 7, 6, 4; Pañcaviṃśa Brāhmaṇa, xxi. 1; Śatapatha Brāhmaṇa, v. 3, 5, 20; Kātyāyana Śrauta Sūtra, xv. 5, 7 *et seq.*; Śāṅkhāyana Śrauta Sūtra, xvi. 12, 19.
[3] v. 3, 5, 20. *Cf.* Kātyāyana, *loc. cit.*; Sāyaṇa on Av., *loc. cit.*; Whitney, Translation of the Atharvaveda, 879.
[4] Dictionary, *s.v. abhiṣecanīya.*
[5] *Sacred Books of the East*, 41, 85, n. 1.

Tārṣṭāgha, a species of tree, is mentioned in the Kauśika Sūtra,[1] while the adjective formed from it, *tārṣṭāghī*, 'derived from the Tārṣṭāgha tree,' is found in the Atharvaveda[2] Weber[3] thinks that the *sarṣapa*, or mustard plant, is meant.

[1] xxv. 23.
[2] v. 29, 15. *Cf.* Whitney's note in his Translation of the Atharvaveda.
[3] *Indische Studien*, 18, 280. *Cf.* Zimmer, *Altindisches Leben*, 62.

Titaü[1] is found once in the Rigveda[2] denoting a 'sieve,' or perhaps 'winnowing fan,' which was used for purifying corn (*saktu*).

[1] On the peculiar form of this word, *cf.* Macdonell, *Vedic Grammar*, 20, 3.

[2] x. 71, 2.
Cf. Zimmer, *Altindisches Leben*, 238.

Tittira, Tittiri, is the name of the partridge in the later Saṃhitās[1] and the Brāhmaṇas,[2] being presumably an onomatopoetic formation. The bird is described as having variegated plumage (*bahu-rūpa*). It is usually associated with the **Kapiñjala** and **Kalaviṅka.**

[1] Taittirīya Saṃhitā, ii. 5, 1, 2; v. 5, 16, 1; Maitrāyaṇī Saṃhitā, ii. 4, 1; Kāṭhaka Saṃhitā, xii. 10; Vājasaneyi Saṃhitā, xxiv. 30. 36. The form Tittira occurs in the Maitrāyaṇī Samhitā, iii. 14, 1.

[2] Śatapatha Brāhmaṇa, i. 6, 3, 5; v. 5, 4, 6; Jaiminīya Brāhmaṇa, ii. 154, 6 (Oertel, *Transactions of the Connecticut Academy of Arts and Sciences*, 15, 181).
Cf. Zimmer, *Altindisches Leben*, 91; Schrader, *Prehistoric Antiquities*, 251.

Tithi, as the name of a lunar day, the thirtieth part of a lunar month of rather over twenty-seven days, is only found in the later Sūtras,[1] being completely unknown to the Brāhmaṇas, in which the only day is the natural one.[2] See **Māsa.**

[1] Gobhila Gṛhya Sūtra, i. 1, 13; ii. 8, 12. 20; Śāṅkhāyana Gṛhya Sūtra, i. 25; v. 2, etc.

[2] Thibaut, *Astronomie, Astrologie und Mathematik*, 7, 8.

Timirgha Daure-śruta ('descendant of Dūreśruta') is mentioned as Agnīdh ('fire-kindling') priest at the snake sacrifice described in the Pañcaviṃśa Brāhmaṇa.[1]

[1] xxv. 15. *Cf.* Weber, *Indische Studien*, 1, 35.

Tiraśca is read in some manuscripts of the Atharvaveda[1] in the description of the Vrātya's throne (**Āsandī**), meaning 'the cross-pieces.' But the reading should be *tiraścye*, which is adjectival, and is used in the same sense.

[1] xv. 3, 5. *Cf.* Whitney, Translation of the Atharvaveda, 776; Keith, *Śāṅkhāyana Āraṇyaka*, 19, n. 3.

Tiraśca-rāji,[1] **Tiraści-rāji,**[2] **Tiraścīna-rāji,**[3] are variant forms of a name for 'snake' (lit., 'striped across'), found in the later Saṃhitās.

[1] Taittirīya Saṃhitā, v. 5, 10, 2; Zimmer, *Altindisches Leben*, 94, 95, reports this form from the Av., but the text and Roth (St. Petersburg Dictionary, *s.v.*) read *tiraści-rāji* there.

[2] Av. iii. 27, 2; vi. 56, 2; vii. 56, 1; x. 4, 13; xii. 3, 56.

[3] Maitrāyaṇī Saṃhitā, ii. 13, 21; Śāṅkhāyana Āraṇyaka, xii. 27.

Cf. Bloomfield, *Hymns of the Atharvaveda*, 488, 553; Keith, *Śāṅkhāyana Āraṇyaka*, 68, n. 2; Weber, *Indische Studien*, 17, 295-297.

Tiraścī is, according to the Anukramaṇī, the author of a Rigvedic hymn[1] in which he appeals to Indra to hear his call. The Pañcaviṃśa Brāhmaṇa[2] adopts this view of the name, and mentions a Tiraścī Āṅgirasa. But Roth[3] thinks that the word is not a proper name at all.

[1] viii. 95, 4.

[2] xii. 6, 12.

[3] *Zeitschrift der Deutschen Morgenländischen Gesellschaft*, 48, 115. *Cf.* Ludwig, Translation of the Rigveda, 5, 187; Hopkins, *Journal of the American Oriental Society*, 17, 90; Macdonell, *Vedic Grammar*, p. 273.

Tiraścīna-vaṃśa, 'cross-beam,' is used to denote a 'beehive' in the Chāndogya Upaniṣad.[1] See also **Vaṃśa.**

[1] iii. 1, 1. *Cf.* Little, *Grammatical Index*, 75.

Tirindira is mentioned in a Dānastuti, or 'Praise of Gifts,' in the Rigveda[1] as having, along with **Parśu,** bestowed gifts on the singer. In the Śāṅkhāyana Śrauta Sūtra[2] this statement is represented by a tale that the Kaṇva Vatsa obtained a gift from Tirindira Pāraśavya, Tirindira and Parśu being in this version thus treated as one and the same man. Ludwig[3] sees in the Rigvedic passage a proof that the Yadus had gained a victory over Tirindira, and gave a part of the booty to the singers; but there is no proof whatever of the correctness of this interpretation, which Zimmer[4] shows to be most unlikely. Yadu princes must be meant by Tirindira and

[1] viii. 6, 46-48.

[2] xvi. 11. 20.

[3] Translation of the Rigveda, 3, 160, 161; 5, 142.

[4] *Altindisches Leben*, 136, 137.

Parśu, though Weber[5] thinks that the singers were Yadus, not the princes. The latter he holds to have been Iranian (*cf.* Τιρίβαζος, and see **Parśu**), and he thinks that in this there is evidence of continual close relations between India and Iran. This is perfectly possible, but the evidence for it is rather slight.

[5] *Indische Studien*, 4, 356, n.; *Indian Literature*, 3, 4; *Episches im vedischen Ritual*, 37, 38.

[6] For the recent controversy as to Iranian names found at Boghaz-kiöi, *cf.* Jacobi, *Journal of the Royal Asiatic Society*, 1909, 721 *et seq.*; Oldenberg, *ibid.*, 1095-1100; Keith, *ibid.*, 1100-1106; Sayce, *ibid.*, 1106, 1107; Kennedy, *ibid.*, 1107-1119. Hillebrandt, *Vedische Mythologie*, 1, 94 *et seq.*, argues in favour of an early connexion of Iranians and Indians in Arachosia, where he places part of the action of the Rigveda. Hopkins, *Journal of the American Oriental Society*, 17, 16, 277, holds that traces of Iranian connexion are signs of late date; Arnold, *ibid.*, 18, 205 *et seq.*, opposes this view.

Tirīṭa[1] is found in the Atharvaveda[2] in the adjectival derivative *tirīṭin* used of a demon, and presumably meaning 'adorned with a tiara.'

[1] Meaning, according to later native lexicographers, 'head-dress' or 'diadem.'

[2] viii. 6, 7. *Cf.* Zimmer, *Altindisches Leben*, 265; Whitney, Translation of the Atharvaveda, 495.

Tirya occurs in the Atharvaveda[1] as an epithet of **Karambha**, 'gruel.' It is probably equivalent to *tilya*, 'made of sesamum,' as rendered by Roth[2] and Whitney,[3] but *tiriya* is read by Roth[4] in the Rāja-nighaṇṭu as a kind of rice.

[1] iv. 7, 3.

[2] St. Petersburg Dictionary, *s.v.*

[3] Translation of the Atharvaveda, 155.

[4] See Whitney, *loc. cit.*, with Lanman's additional note. Bloomfield, *Hymns of the Atharvaveda*, 377, construes the adjective with *viṣam*, and renders 'the poison which comes in a horizontal direction' (*cf. tiryañc*). Grill, *Hundert Lieder*,[2] 121, amends to *atiriya*, 'overflowing.'

Cf. Zimmer, *Altindisches Leben*, 270; Ludwig, Translation of the Rigveda, 3, 201.

Tiryañc Āṅgirasa is mentioned as a seer of Sāmans, or Chants, in the Pañcaviṃśa Brāhmaṇa.[1] The name is doubtless feigned.

[1] xii. 6, 12. *Cf.* Hillebrandt, *Vedische Mythologie*, 2, 160.

Tila denotes in the Atharvaveda[1] and later[2] the sesamum plant, and particularly its grains, from which a rich oil (**Taila**) was extracted. It is often[3] mentioned in connexion with **Māṣa,** 'kidney bean.' The Taittirīya Saṃhitā[4] attributes the bean and the sesamum to the winter (*hemanta*) and the cool (*śiśira*) seasons. The stalk of the sesamum plant (*tila-piñjī*,[5] *til-piñja*[6]) was used for fuel, and the seed was boiled in the form of porridge (*tilaudana*[7]) for food.

[1] ii. 8, 3; vi. 140, 2; xviii. 3, 69; 4, 32.
[2] Taittirīya Saṃhitā, vii. 2, 10, 2; Maitrāyaṇī Saṃhitā, iv. 3, 2; Vājasaneyi Saṃhitā, xviii. 12; Śatapatha Brāhmaṇa, ix. 1, 1, 3, etc.
[3] Av. vi. 140, 2; Vājasaneyi Saṃhitā, *loc. cit.*; Bṛhadāraṇyaka Upaniṣad, vi. 3, 22; Chāndogya Upaniṣad, v. 10, 6, etc.
[4] *Loc. cit.*
[5] Av. ii. 8, 3.
[6] Av. xii. 2, 54.
[7] Bṛhadāraṇyaka Upaniṣad, vi. 4, 16; Śāṅkhāyana Āraṇyaka, xii. 8. *Cf.* Zimmer, *Altindisches Leben*, 240.

Tilvaka is mentioned in the Śatapatha Brāhmaṇa[1] as a tree (*Symplocos racemosa*), near which it is inauspicious to construct a grave. The adjectival derivative *tailvaka*, 'made of the wood of the Tilvaka,' is found in the Maitrāyaṇī Saṃhitā,[2] and is employed to describe the *yūpa*, or sacrificial post, in the Ṣaḍviṃśa Brāhmaṇa.[3]

[1] xiii. 8, 1, 16. [2] iii. 1, 9. [3] iii. 8.

Tiṣya occurs twice in the Rigveda,[1] apparently as the name of a star,[2] though Sāyaṇa takes it to mean the sun. It is doubtless identical with the Avestan Tistrya. Later it is the name of a lunar mansion: see **Nakṣatra.**

[1] v. 54, 13; x. 64, 8 (with Kṛśānu as an archer).
[2] Weber, *Naxatra*, 2, 290; Zimmer, *Altindisches Leben*, 355; Max Müller, *Sacred Books of the East*, 32, 331; Keith, *Śāṅkhāyana Āraṇyaka*, 77, n. 1.

Tisṛ-dhanva, 'a bow with three (arrows),' is mentioned as a gift to the priest at the sacrifice in the Taittirīya Saṃhitā[1] and in the Brāhmaṇas.[2]

[1] i. 8, 19, 1.
[2] Taittirīya Brāhmaṇa, i. 8, 3, 4; ii. 7, 9, 2; Satapatha Brāhmaṇa, xi. 1, 5, 10; xiv. 1, 1, 7.

Tugra appears in the Rigveda[1] as the name of the father of **Bhujyu**, a protégé of the Aśvins, who is accordingly called Tugrya[2] or Taugrya.[3] A different Tugra seems to be referred to in other passages of the Rigveda[4] as an enemy of Indra.

[1] i. 116, 3; 117, 14; vi. 62, 6.
[2] Rv. viii. 3, 23; 74, 14.
[3] Rv. i. 117, 15; 118, 6; 182, 5. 6; viii. 5, 22; x. 39, 4.
[4] vi. 20, 8; 26, 4; x. 49, 4. *Cf.* Oldenberg, *Zeitschrift der Deutschen Morgenländischen Gesellschaft*, 55, 328, 329; Ludwig, Translation of the Rigveda, 3, 157.

Tugrya occurs in the Rigveda as a patronymic of **Bhujyu**,[1] but also in a passage[2] in which no reference to Bhujyu appears to be meant, and in which it may mean 'a man of the house of Tugra.' A similar sense seems to occur in the locative plural feminine in the Rigveda,[3] where (supplying *vikṣu*) the meaning must be 'among the Tugrians.' This explanation may also apply to the epithet of Indra[4] or Soma,[5] *tugryā-vṛdh*, 'rejoicing among the Tugrians.'

[1] Who is also called *Tugrasya sūnu*, Rv. vi. 62, 6. *Cf.* the use of *Pajriya* and perhaps *Kṛṣṇiya* in the patronymic sense without Vṛddhi.
[2] viii. 32, 20.
[3] i. 33, 15. *Cf.* Griffith, *Hymns of the Rigveda*, 1, 47.
[4] viii. 45, 29; 99, 7.
[5] viii. 1, 15, where, however, Roth, St. Petersburg Dictionary, *s.v.*, suggests an alteration to make it refer to Indra.

Cf. Zimmer, *Altindisches Leben*, 128.

Tuc in the Rigveda[1] occasionally occurs denoting 'children.' Tuj occurs rather more often in the same sense.[2] *Cf.* **Tanaya** and **Toka.**

[1] viii. 18, 18; 27, 14; vi. 48, 9.
[2] iii. 45, 4; iv. 1, 3; v. 41, 9; viii. 4, 15.

Tuji is the name in the Rigveda[1] of a protégé of Indra, who in another hymn[2] appears to be called Tūtuji.

[1] vi. 26, 4; x. 49, 4.
[2] vi. 20, 8. *Cf.* Ludwig, Translation of the Rigveda, 3, 156; Oldenberg, *Zeitschrift der Deutschen Morgenländischen Gesellschaft*, 55, 328.

Tumiñja Aupoditi is mentioned in the Taittirīya Saṃhitā (i. 7, 2, 1) as a Hotṛ priest at a Sattra, or 'sacrificial session,' and as having been engaged in a discussion with **Suśravas.**

Tura Kāvaṣeya is mentioned in the Vaṃśa (list of teachers) at the end of the tenth book of the Śatapatha Brāhmaṇa[1] as the source of the doctrine set forth in that book, and as separated, in the succession of teachers, from **Śāṇḍilya** by **Yajñavacas** and **Kuśri.** In the same Brāhmaṇa[2] he is quoted by Śāṇḍilya as having erected a fire-altar on the **Kārotī.** In the Aitareya Brāhmaṇa[3] he appears as a Purohita, or 'domestic priest,' of **Janamejaya Pārikṣita,** whom he consecrated king. In the Bṛhadāraṇyaka Upaniṣad[4] and a Khila[5] he appears as an ancient sage. Oldenberg,[6] no doubt rightly, assigns him to the end of the Vedic period. He is probably[7] identical with Tura, the *deva-muni,* 'saint of the gods,' who is mentioned in the Pañcaviṃśa Brāhmaṇa.[8]

[1] x. 6, 5, 9.
[2] ix. 5, 2, 15.
[3] iv. 27; vii. 34; viii. 21.
[4] vi. 5, 4 (Kāṇva, not in Mādhyaṃdina).
[5] i. 9, 6; Scheftelowitz, *Die Apokryphen des Ṛgveda,* 65, 190.
[6] *Zeitschrift der Deutschen Morgenländischen Gesellschaft,* 42, 239.
[7] So the St. Petersburg Dictionary, *s.v.*
[8] xxv. 14, 5. See Hopkins, *Transactions of the Connecticut Academy of Arts and Sciences,* 15, 68.

Cf. Weber, *Indische Studien,* 1, 203, n.; *Indian Literature,* 120, 131; Eggeling, *Sacred Books of the East,* 43, xviii.

Tura-śravas is the name of a seer mentioned in the Pañcaviṃśa Brāhmaṇa[1] as having pleased Indra by two Sāmans (Chants) of his composition. Indra in return appears to have given him the oblation of the **Pārāvatas** on the **Yamunā.**

[1] ix. 4, 10. *Cf.* Hopkins, *Transactions of the Connecticut Academy of Arts and Sciences,* 15, 53; Max Müller, *Sacred Books of the East,* 32, 316.

Turya-vāh, masc.; **Turyauhī,** fem., 'a four-year-old ox or cow,' is mentioned in the later Saṃhitās.[1]

[1] Taittirīya Saṃhitā, iv. 3, 3, 2; Maitrāyaṇī Saṃhitā, iii. 11, 11; 13, 17; Vājasaneyi Saṃhitā, xiv. 10; xviii. 26, etc.

Turva occurs only once in the Rigveda (x. 62, 10), doubtless as a name of the **Turvaśa** people or king.

Turvaśa occurs frequently in the Rigveda as the name of a man or of a people, usually in connexion with **Yadu.** The two words usually occur in the singular without any connecting particle, *Turvaśa Yadu* or *Yadu Turvaśa.*[2] In a plural form the name Turvaśa occurs once with the Yadus,[3] and once alone[4] in a hymn in which the singular has already been used. In one passage[5] the dual *Turvaśā-Yadū* actually occurs, and in another[6] *Yadus Turvaś ca,* 'Yadu and Turva.' In other passages[7] Turvaśa appears alone, while in one[8] Turvaśa and Yādva occur.

From these facts Hopkins[9] deduces the erroneousness of the ordinary view,[10] according to which Turvaśa is the name of a tribe, the singular denoting the king, and regards Turvaśa as the name of the Yadu king. But the evidence for this is not conclusive. Without laying any stress on the argument based on the theory[11] that the 'five peoples' of the Rigveda are the **Anus, Druhyus,** Turvaśas, Yadus, and **Pūrus,** it is perfectly reasonable to hold that the Turvaśas and Yadus were two distinct though closely allied tribes. Such they evidently were to the seers of the hymns which mention in the dual the *Turvaśā-Yadū* and speak of *Yadus Turvaś ca.* This explanation also suits best the use of the plural of Turvaśa in two Rigvedic hymns.

In the Rigveda the chief exploit of Turvaśa was his participation in the war against **Sudās,** by whom he was defeated.[12] Hopkins[13] suggests that he may have been named Turvaśa because of his fleet (*tura*) escape from the battle. His escape

[1] i. 36, 18; 54, 6; 174, 9; vi. 20, 12; 45, 1; viii. 4, 7; 7, 18; 9, 14; 45, 27; x. 49, 8. In vii. 18, 6, Turvaśa is joined with Yakṣu, apparently a contemptuous variant of Yadu (Hopkins, *Journal of the American Oriental Society*, 15, 261). *Cf.* **Tṛtsu.**

[2] v. 31, 8.

[3] i. 108, 8.

[4] viii. 4, 18; singular with Ānava in viii. 4, 1.

[5] iv. 30, 17.

[6] x. 62, 10. *Cf.* Ludwig, Translation of the Rigveda, 3, 166; Oldenberg, *Zeitschrift der Deutschen Morgenländischen Gesellschaft*, 42, 220, n. 1.

[7] i. 4, 77; vi. 27, 7. *Cf.* viii. 4, 1.

[8] vii. 19, 8.

[9] *Op. cit.*, 258 *et seq.*

[10] Zimmer, *Altindisches Leben*, 122, 124; Oldenberg, *Buddha*, 404; Ludwig, *op. cit.*, 153; Macdonell, *Vedic Mythology*, p. 64; *Sanskrit Literature*, 153 *et seq.*, etc.

[11] Zimmer, 122, 124; Macdonell, 153, 154.

[12] vii. 18, 6.

[13] *Op. cit.*, 264.

may have been assisted by Indra, for in some passages[14] Indra's aid to Turvaśa (and) Yadu is referred to; it is also significant that the Anu, and apparently the Druhyu, kings are mentioned as having been drowned in the defeat, but not the Turvaśa and Yadu kings, and that Turvaśa appears in the eighth book of the Rigveda as a worshipper of Indra with the Anu prince, the successor, presumably, of the one who was drowned.[15] Griffith,[16] however, proposes to refer these passages to a defeat by Turvaśa and Yadu of Arṇa and Citraratha on the **Sarayu**;[17] but the evidence for this is quite inadequate.

Two passages of the Rigveda[18] seem to refer to an attack by Turvaśa and Yadu on **Divodāsa**, the father of Sudās. It is reasonable to suppose that this was an attack of the two peoples on Divodāsa, for there is some improbability of the references being to the Turvaśa, who was concerned in the attack on Sudās, the son.

Zimmer[19] considers that the Turvaśas were also called **Vṛcīvants.** This view is based on a hymn[20] in which reference is made to the defeat of the Vṛcīvants on the **Yavyāvatī** and **Hariyūpīyā** in aid of Daivarāta, and of Turvaśa in aid of **Sṛñjaya**, the latter being elsewhere[21] clearly the son of Devarāta. But as this evidence for the identification of the Turvaśas with the Vṛcīvants is not clear, it seems sufficient[22] to assume that they were allies.

Later, in the Śatapatha Brāhmaṇa,[23] the Turvaśas appear as allies of the Pañcālas, Taurvaśa horses, thirty-three in number, and armed men, to the number of 6,000, being mentioned.[24] But otherwise the name disappears: this lends

[14] Rv. i. 174, 9; iv. 30, 17; v. 31, 8; viii. 4, 7.

[15] Hopkins, 265.

[16] *Hymns of the Rigveda* 1, 433, n.

[17] The hymn is a late one, and the connexion of verse 18, where Arṇa and Citraratha are mentioned, is obscure. *Cf.* Hopkins, 259.

[18] vi. 45, 1; ix. 61, 2 (where Divodāsa is mentioned); vii. 19, 8 (where he appears as Atithigva).

[19] *Op. cit.*, 124.

[20] vi. 27, 5-7.

[21] iv. 15, 4.

[22] Oldenberg, *Buddha*, 404, n. *Cf.* Hillebrandt, *Vedische Mythologie*, 1, 105.

[23] xiii. 5, 4, 16.

[24] The sense is obscure. The St. Petersburg Dictionary takes it apparently as 6,033 horses (of armed warriors); Eggeling, *Sacred Books of the East*, 44, 400, prefers to understand it as 33 horses and 6,000 men; Oldenberg, *loc. cit.*, takes it as 6,033 warriors. Harisvāmin's Commentary, cited by Eggeling, is obscure.

probability to Oldenberg's conjecture[25] that the Turvaśas became merged in the **Pañcāla** people. Hopkins[26] considers that in the Śatapatha passage the horses were merely named from the family of Turvaśa; but this view is less likely, since it ignores the difficulty involved in the reference to the men.

It is impossible to be certain regarding the home of the Turvaśas at the time of their conflict with Sudās. They apparently crossed the **Paruṣṇī**,[27] but from which side is disputed. The view of Pischel[28] and Geldner,[29] that they advanced from the west towards the east, where the **Bharatas** were (see **Kuru**), is the more probable.

25 *Buddha*, 404.

26 *Op. cit.*, 258, n. *Cf.* Weber, *Indische Studien*, 1, 220.

27 Rv. vii. 18.

28 *Vedische Studien*, 2, 218. *Cf.* Zimmer, *Altindisches Leben*, 126.

29 *Vedische Studien*, 3, 152. If in Rv. viii. 20, 24, *turvaśa* is read with Ludwig for *tūrvatha*, they are connected with the **Sindhu**.

Cf. Oldenberg, *Religion des Veda*, 167; Muir, *Sanskrit Texts*, 5, 286; Bergaigne, *Religion Védique*, 2, 354 *et seq*.

Turvīti is mentioned several times in the Rigveda, both in association with Vayya[1] and alone.[2] In three passages[3] reference is made to Indra aiding him over a flood. Ludwig[4] has conjectured that he was king of the Turvaśas and Yadus. But there is no sufficient evidence for this view, though presumably he was of the Turvaśa tribe.

1 i. 54, 6; ii. 13, 12; iv. 19, 6.

2 Rv. i. 36, 18; 61, 11; 112, 23.

3 i. 61, 11; ii. 13, 12; iv. 19, 6.

4 Translation of the Rigveda, 3, 147; 4, 254. *Cf.* **Turvaśa**, and Bergaigne, *Religion Védique*, 2, 358; Oldenberg, *Sacred Books of the East*, 42, 36.

Tulā, 'scales,' is mentioned in the Vājasaneyi Saṃhitā.[1] The Śatapatha Brāhmaṇa[2] also speaks of the balance in connexion with the weighing of a man's good and evil deeds in the next and in this world. This differs very considerably from the later balance[3] ordeal, in which a man was weighed twice, and was pronounced guilty or innocent according as, on the second occasion, he was more or less heavy than on the

1 xxx. 17.

2 xi. 2, 7, 33.

3 Jolly, *Recht und Sitte*, 145.

first. It is not possible to read the later practice into the earlier.[4]

[4] Weber, *Indische Streifen*, 1, 21; 2, 363, quotes Schlagintweit as giving this passage as an example of the balance ordeal. *Cf.* Eggeling, *Sacred Books of the East*, 44, 45, n. 4.

Tuṣa, in the Atharvaveda[1] and later,[2] regularly denotes the 'husk' of grain, often used for a fire.[3]

[1] ix. 6, 16; xi. 1, 12. 29; 3, 5; xii. 3, 19.

[2] Taittirīya Brāhmaṇa, i. 6, 5, 5; Aitareya Brāhmaṇa, ii. 7, 9, etc.

[3] *Tuṣa-pakva*, Taittirīya Saṃhitā, v. 2. 4, 2; Maitrāyaṇī Saṃhitā, iii. 2, 4; Śatapatha Brāhmaṇa, vii. 2, 1, 7.

Tūṇava denotes in the later Saṃhitās[1] and the Brāhmaṇas[2] a musical instrument of wood, probably the 'flute.' A 'flute-blower' is enumerated among the victims of the Puruṣamedha, or 'human sacrifice.'[3]

[1] Taittirīya Samhitā, vi. 1, 4, 1; Maitrāyaṇī Saṃhitā, iii. 6, 8; Kāṭhaka Saṃhitā, xxiii. 4; xxxiv. 5 (*Indische Studien*, 3, 477).

[2] Pañcaviṃśa Brāhmaṇa, vi. 5, 13; Taittirīya Brāhmana, iii. 4, 13, 1; 15, 1; Nirukta, xiii. 9.

[3] Vājasaneyi Saṃhitā, xxx. 19. 20; Taittirīya Brāhmaṇa, *loc. cit.*

Cf. Zimmer, *Altindisches Leben*, 289.

Tūtuji. See **Tuji.**

Tūpara, 'hornless,' is a frequent description of animals intended for the sacrifice, especially of the goat, in the Atharvaveda and later.[1]

[1] Av. xi. 9, 22; Taittirīya Saṃhitā, ii. 1, 1, 4, etc.; Vājasaneyi Saṃhitā, xxiv. 1. 15; xxix. 59, etc.; Satapatha Brāhmaṇa, v. 1, 3, 7, etc.

Tūrghna is mentioned in the Taittirīya Āraṇyaka (v. 1) as the northern part of Kurukṣetra.[1] Its exact position, however, cannot be ascertained.

[1] *Cf.* Weber, *Indische Studien*, 1, 78.

Tūrṇāśa, in the Rigveda,[1] seems to denote a 'mountain torrent.'

[1] viii. 32, 4. *Cf.* Nirukta, v. 16.

Tūrvayāṇa is the name of a prince mentioned in the Rigveda. He appears by name in two passages,[1] and is clearly alluded to in a third,[2] as an enemy of **Atithigva, Āyu,** and **Kutsa.** With this accords the fact that the **Pakthas** were opposed in the battle of the ten kings to the Tṛtsus,[3] and that Tūrvayāṇa is shown by another passage of the Rigveda[4] to have been a prince of the Pakthas. He is there represented as having been a protégé of Indra, who aided him against **Cyavāna** and his guardians, the Maruts. It is not probable that he is identical with **Suśravas.**[5]

[1] i. 53, 10; vi. 18, 13.

[2] ii. 14, 7 (as a comparison of the two preceding passages shows); perhaps also viii. 53, 2. In i. 174, 3, Tūrvayāṇa seems also to be a proper name, though Roth, St. Petersburg Dictionary, *s.v.*, here regards the word as an adjective.

[3] vii. 18.

[4] x. 61, 1 *et seq.*; Pischel, *Vedische Studien*, 1, 71-77.

[5] Mentioned in i. 53, 9. 10. *Cf.* Griffith, *Hymns of the Rigveda*, 1, 75, n.

Tūṣa is found in the later Saṃhitās and the Brāhmaṇas[1] denoting the 'fringe' or 'trimming' of a garment.

[1] Taittirīya Saṃhitā, i. 8, 1, 1; ii. 4, 9, 1; vi. 1, 1, 3; Kāṭhaka Saṃhitā, xxiii. 1; Taittirīya Brāhmaṇa, i. 6, 1, 8; Pañcaviṃśa Brāhmaṇa, xvii. 1, etc.

Cf. Zimmer, *Altindisches Leben*, 262.

Tṛkṣi is, in the Rigveda,[1] the name of a prince who was a Trāsadasyava, 'descendant of **Trasadasyu.**' He also appears with the Druhyu and the Pūru peoples in another hymn.[2] It has been conjectured, but it is not probable, that the steed **Tārkṣya** (as 'belonging to Tṛkṣi') was his.[3]

[1] viii. 22, 7.

[2] vi. 46, 8. It is not certain that the two persons are identical (*cf.* Hillebrandt, *Vedische Mythologie*, 1, 113, notes 3, 4), but it is probable.

[3] Macdonell, *Vedic Mythology*, p. 149.

Tṛṇa, 'grass,' is often mentioned in the Rigveda[1] and later.[2] It was used as straw to roof in a house or hut.[3]

[1] i. 161, 1; 162, 8. 11; x. 102, 10, etc.

[2] Av. ii. 30, 1; vi. 54, 1, etc.; Aitareya Brāhmaṇa, iii. 22; viii. 24, etc.

[3] Av. iii. 12, 5; ix. 3, 4. 7.

Tṛṇa-jalāyuka, 'caterpillar,' is mentioned in the Bṛhadāraṇyaka Upaniṣad (iv. 2, 4).

Tṛṇa-skanda occurs once in the Rigveda[1] as the name of a prince, his subjects (*viśaḥ*) being referred to.[2] The word may originally have meant 'grasshopper.'[3]

[1] i. 172, 3.

[2] Zimmer, *Altindisches Leben*, 159, takes *viśaḥ* as 'cantons,' but see **Viś.**

[3] St. Petersburg Dictionary, *s.v.*

Tṛtīyaka, 'the tertian (fever),' is mentioned in the Atharvaveda (i. 25, 4; v. 22, 13; xix. 39, 10). See **Takman.**

Tṛtsu occurs in the Rigveda, once in the singular[1] and several times in the plural,[2] as a proper name. The Tṛtsus were clearly helpers of **Sudās** in the great battle against the ten kings, **Śimyu,** the **Turvaśa,** the **Druhyu, Kavaṣa,** the **Pūru,** the **Anu, Bheda, Śambara,** the two **Vaikarṇas,** and perhaps the **Yadu,** who led with them as allies[3] the **Matsyas, Pakthas, Bhalānas, Alinas, Viṣāṇins, Śivas, Ajas, Śigrus,** and perhaps Yakṣus.[4] The defeat of the ten kings is celebrated in one

[1] vii. 18, 13.

[2] vii. 18, 7. 15. 19; 33, 5. 6; 83, 4. 6. 8.

[3] They were regarded as enemies of the kings by Roth, *Zur Litteratur und Geschichte des Weda*, 95, and by Zimmer, *op. cit.*, 126. The latter, however, altered his view (see pp. 430, 431, which Hopkins, *op. cit.*, 260, has overlooked), and there is no doubt that the later opinion is correct. *Cf.* also Ludwig, Translation of the Rigveda, 3, 173; Hopkins, 260, 261. Of these tribes the Pakthas, Alinas, Bhalānas, Viṣāṇins, and Śivas, were probably settled in the north-west, to the west of the Indus, and around the Kabul River. The Anus, Pūrus, Turvaśas, Yadus, and Druhyus, were probably tribes of the Panjab; the Ajas, Śigrus, and Yakṣus, tribes of the east, under Bheda; Śambara may also have been a native of the east; Śiṁyu and Kavaṣa are doubtful; and the Vaikarṇau probably belonged to the north-west.

[4] This is uncertain; the text of the Rigveda, vii. 18, 6, has Yakṣu, and the same word recurs in verse 19. On the other hand, the word Yadu would naturally be expected in verse 6, as Turvaśa is mentioned. Zimmer, *Altindisches Leben*, 122, says that Yadu occurs in vii. 18, but on p. 126 he cites Yakṣu in both places, evidently by oversight. Hopkins, *Journal of the American Oriental Society*, 15, 261, n., considers that Turvaśa, the Yakṣu, is a sarcastic expression, instead of Turvaśa, the Yadu, making Turvaśa, whom he regards as king of the Yadus, ridiculous as a member of an insignificant people, and alluding to him also as a sacrificial victim (as it were, *yaṣṭavya*, 'to be offered': *cf. puroḍāś*, 'cake of sacrifice,' in verse 6, as a pun on *purogās*, 'leader'). Whether Yakṣu is used contemptuously for Yadu or not, it seems hard not to believe that the Yadus are referred to.

hymn of the Rigveda,[5] and is evidently alluded to in two others.[6] The great battle took place on the **Paruṣṇī**, but there was also a fight on the **Yamunā** with Bheda, the Ajas, Śigrus, and Yakṣus. As the Yamunā and the Paruṣṇī represent opposite ends of the territory of the Tṛtsus (for we cannot with Hopkins[7] safely identify the streams), it is difficult to see exactly how the ten kings could be confederated, but it should be noted that the references to the ten kings occur in the two later hymns,[6] and not in the hymn[5] describing the battle itself; besides, absolute numerical accuracy cannot be insisted upon.

It is difficult exactly to determine the character of the Tṛtsus, especially in their relation to the Bharatas, who under Viśvāmitra's guidance are represented as prospering and as advancing to the **Vipāś** and **Śutudrī**.[8] Roth ingeniously brought this into connexion with the defeat of his enemies by Sudās, which is celebrated in the seventh book of the Rigveda—a book attributed to the Vasiṣṭha family—and thought that there was a reference in one verse[9] to the defeat of the Bharatas by Sudās. But it seems certain that the verse is mistranslated, and that the Bharatas are really represented as victors with Sudās.[10] Ludwig[11] accordingly identifies the Tṛtsus and the Bharatas. Oldenberg,[12] after accepting this view at first,[13] later expressed the opinion that the Tṛtsus were the priests of the Bharata people, and therefore identical with the Vasiṣṭhas. This view is supported by the fact that in one passage[14] the Tṛtsus are clearly described as wearing their hair in the peculiar manner affected by the Vasiṣṭhas,[15] and would in that passage thus seem to represent the Vasiṣṭhas.

5 vii. 18.

6 vii. 33 and 83.

7 *India, Old and New*, 52. No such conjecture was made by him in the *Journal of the American Oriental Society*, 15, 259 *et seq.*

8 Rv. iii. 33; 53, 9-12.

9 vii. 33, 6. See Roth, *op. cit.*, 90, 121; Muir, *Sanskrit Texts*, 1², 320; Macdonell, *Sanskrit Literature*, 154, 155; von Schroeder, *Indiens Literatur und Cultur*, 35, 36; Hillebrandt, *Vedische Mythologie*, 1, 110, 111; Bloomfield, *Journal of the American Oriental Society*, 16, 41.

10 Oldenberg, *Buddha*, 406; Weber, *Episches im vedischen Ritual*, 34.

11 Translation of the Rigveda, 3, 175.

12 *Zeitschrift der Deutschen Morgenländischen Gesellschaft*, 42, 207. *Cf.* Bergaigne, *Religion Védique*, 2, 362.

13 *Buddha*, 405, 406,

14 Rv. vii. 33, 1 (*śvityañco dakṣiṇataskapardāḥ*).

15 Rv. vii. 83, 8 (*śvityañco . . . kapardinaḥ*).

But Geldner[16] has suggested with great probability that Tṛtsu, who is once mentioned in the singular,[17] means the Tṛtsu king—that is, Sudās.[18] This explanation alone justifies the description[19] of the Bharatas as *Tṛtsūnāṃ viśaḥ*,[20] 'subjects of the Tṛtsus,' meaning the Tṛtsu Gotra or family, for the people could not be said to be subjects of a body of priests. The Vasiṣṭhas might be called Tṛtsus because of their close connexion with the royal house of that people. The reverse process is also quite possible, but is rendered improbable by the fact that the **Pratṛdaḥ** are referred to as receiving Vasiṣṭha.[21] This name of the Tṛtsu dynasty is probably older than its connexion with Vasiṣṭha in the time of Sudās, a conclusion supported by the name of **Pratardana**, who is mentioned later as a descendant of Divodāsa,[22] an ancestor of Sudās. The Tṛtsu dynasty could therefore hardly have been referred to as Vasiṣṭhas. For the further history of the dynasty and its relation with Vasiṣṭha and Viśvāmitra, see **Sudās.**

If the Tṛtsus and their subjects, the Bharatas, were in the Rigvedic period at war with the tribes on either side of the territory between the Paruṣṇī and the Yamunā, it is clear[23] that later on they coalesced with the Pūrus and probably others of those tribes to form the **Kuru** people. Already in the Rigveda[24] the Tṛtsus are allied with the **Sṛñjayas,** and in the Śatapatha Brāhmaṇa[25] one Purohita serves both Kurus and Sṛñjayas.

16 *Vedische Studien*, 2, 136; *Ṛgveda-Glossar*, 74.

17 Rv. vii. 18, 13.

18 *Cf.* Rv. vii. 18, 24. The parallelism of verses 13 and 24 is quite beyond question. Moreover, the praise of Sudās and of the Bharatas is found coupled in Rv. iii. 53, 9. 12. 24, and in Rv. vi. 16, 4. 5, Divodāsa is coupled with the Bharatas in such a way as to suggest irresistibly that Divodāsa was a Bharata.

19 Rv. vii. 33, 6.

20 That this is the sense of *viśaḥ* is almost certain. See Geldner, *Vedische Studien*, *loc. cit.* Zimmer, *Altindisches Leben*, 159, and Hillebrandt, *Vedische Mythologie*, 1, 111, render it 'cantons,' but see **Viś.**

21 Rv. vii. 33, 14. Geldner (*op. cit.*, 138, 139) ingeniously suggests that Vasiṣṭha, being miraculously born, needed a Gotra, and so became a Tṛtsu.

22 Pratardana is mentioned in the Kauṣītaki Brāhmaṇa, xxvi. 5, as Daivodāsi, 'descendant of Divodāsa.'

23 *Cf.* Oldenberg, *Buddha*, 406 *et seq.*, and see **Kuru.**

24 See Rv. vi. 47, where Divodāsa and Sāñjaya are both praised. In vi. 27, 5, the Turvaśas are opposed to the Sṛñjayas, and in vii. 18, 6; 19, 8, the Tṛtsus are opposed to the Turvaśas.

25 ii. 4, 4, 5.

Hillebrandt[26] considers that the Tṛtsus cannot be identified with the Bharatas, but that Sudās and the Bharatas represent an invading body, which, however, became allied with the Tṛtsus and the Vasiṣṭha priests. He also thinks that the Rigveda reveals a time when **Divodāsa**, the grandfather or ancestor of Sudās, was living in Arachosia, on the **Sarasvatī**, and warring against the **Paṇis**, whom he identifies with the Parnians. But this conjecture[27] cannot be regarded as probable. In the Sarasvatī[28] it is not necessary to see any other river than the later Sarasvatī, in the middle country, which flowed within the boundaries of the Tṛtsus: it is also significant that there are references[29] to contests between **Turvaśa Yadu** and Atithigva or Divodāsa. Thus there is no reason to doubt that Divodāsa and the Bharatas were in the middle country, and not in Iran.

26 *Vedische Mythologie*, 1, 98 *et seq.*

27 *Cf.* also Grierson, *Journal of the Royal Asiatic Society*, 1908, 837 *et seq.*

28 Rv. vi. 61, 3. Brunnhofer, *Iran und Turan*, 127, identifies this river with the Oxus, but Hillebrandt identifies it with the Haraqaiti.

29 Rv. ix. 61, 2. *Cf.* vi. 45, 1; Zimmer, *op. cit.*, 124.

Cf. Max Müller, *Sacred Books of the East*, 32, 424.

Tṛṣṭa is mentioned in the Maitrāyaṇī[1] and Kāṭhaka Saṃhitās[2] as being along with **Varutri** the priest of the Asuras.

1 iv. 8, 1. The reading is uncertain; it may be *Tṛṣṭhā-varutrī*. See von Schroeder's edition, p. 106, n.

2 xxx. 1, where again the reading is uncertain. The Kapiṣṭhala Saṃhitā, xlvi. 4, has *Tvaṣṭā - varutrī* (von Schroeder's edition of the Kāthaka, 2, 181, n.).

Cf. Muir, *Sanskrit Texts*, 1[2], 190, 191; Lévi, *La Doctrine du Sacrifice*, 119.

Tṛṣṭāmā is mentioned as a stream in the Nadī-stuti, or 'praise of rivers,' in the Rigveda.[1] There seems to be no means of identifying it.

1 x. 75, 6. *Cf.* Zimmer, *Altindisches Leben*, 14.

Tejana denotes in the Rigveda[1] a rod or staff of reed used for measuring a field. In the Atharvaveda the sense of 'bamboo' is found twice,[2] the bamboo being specified in the

1 i. 110, 5.

2 i. 2, 4; xx. 136, 3 (= Khila, v. 22, 3). *Cf. taijana* as an adjective in Kāṭhaka Saṃhitā, xxi. 10.

second passage as 'of the spring' (*vāsantika*); more particularly it denotes the shaft of an arrow,[3] a sense often found in later Vedic texts.[4]

[3] Av. vi. 49, 1 (Whitney, Translation of the Atharvaveda, 317); *iṣu eka-tejanā*, 'an arrow with one shaft,' vi. 57, 1.

[4] Aitareya Brāhmaṇa, i. 25; iii. 26; Kāṭhaka Saṃhitā, xxv. 1 (with *śṛṅga* and *śalya* as the three parts of an arrow; in Maitrāyaṇī Saṃhitā, iii. 8, 1, *kulmala* takes the place of *tejana*; *cf. ibid.*, 2). The Taittirīya Saṃhitā, vi. 3, 3, 1, has *anīka*, *śalya*, and *tejana*. *Cf.* **Iṣu.**

Tejanī denotes in the later Saṃhitās and Brāhmaṇas a bundle of reeds,[1] and in some cases such a bundle twisted into a rope,[2] for the two ends of the Tejanī are mentioned.

[1] Śatapatha Brāhmaṇa, xiii. 8, 3, 12; perhaps Kāṭhaka Saṃhitā, xxiii. 9.

[2] Kāṭhaka Saṃhitā, xxii. 13; Aitareya Brāhmaṇa, i. 11, as rendered by Sāyaṇa.

Tejas is regarded by Schrader[1] as having in the Rigveda[2] the specific sense of 'axe.' But in all the passages the sense of the 'bolt' of the god is adequate.

[1] *Prehistoric Antiquities*, 221.

[2] *Cf.* vi. 3, 5; 8, 5; 15, 19.

Taittirīya is the name of one of the divisions of the Black Yajurveda, which is, however, not found thus described until the Sūtra period.[1] The school is represented by a Saṃhitā,[2] a Brāhmaṇa,[3] and an Āraṇyaka,[4] besides an Upaniṣad,[5] which forms a part of the Āraṇyaka.

[1] Anupada Sūtra, ii. 6; vii. 7. 10, etc. See Weber *Indian Literature*, 87 *et seq.*; Macdonell, *Sanskrit Literature*, 175 *et seq.*; von Schroeder, Maitrāyaṇī Saṃhitā, 1, x *et seq.*

[2] Edited by Weber, *Indische Studien*, xi, xii, and in the *Bibliotheca Indica*, 1854-1899.

[3] Edited in the *Bibliotheca Indica*, 1855-1870, and in the Ānandāśrama Series, 1898.

[4] Edited in the *Bibliotheca Indica*, 1864-1872, and in the Ānandāśrama Series, 1898.

[5] Edited by Roer, 1850, and in the Ānandāśrama Series, 1889.

Taimāta is twice mentioned as a species of snake in the Atharvaveda.[1]

[1] v. 13, 6; 18, 4. *Cf.* Whitney, Translation of the Atharvaveda, 243; Bloomfield, *Hymns of the Atharvaveda*, 425; Zimmer, *Altindisches Leben*, 95.

Taila, 'sesamum oil,' is mentioned in the Atharvaveda,[1] where[2] reference is made to keeping such oil in jars. In the Śāṅkhāyana Āraṇyaka,[3] reference is made to anointing with sesamum oil.

[1] i. 7, 2 (all the manuscripts have *taula*, which must be wrong; the Paippalāda MS. has *tūla*: see Whitney, Translation of the Atharvaveda, 7).

[2] xx. 136, 16.

[3] xi. 4.

Cf. Zimmer, *Altindisches Leben*, 240, 241.

Toka denotes 'children' or 'descendants' generally in the Rigveda[1] and later.[2] The word is often joined with **Tanaya.**[3]

[1] i. 43, 2; ii. 2, 11; 9, 2; vii. 62, 6; viii. 5, 20; 67, 11, etc.

[2] Av. i. 13, 2; 28, 3; v. 19, 2; Kāṭhaka Saṃhitā, xxxvi. 7 (*Indische Studien*, 3, 466); Śatapatha Brāhmaṇa, vii. 5, 2, 39, etc.

[3] Rv. i. 31, 12; 64, 14; 114, 6; 147, 1; ii. 33, 14; v. 53, 13; vi. 1, 12, etc.; Aitareya Brāhmaṇa, ii. 7.

Tokman, neut., denotes in the Rigveda[1] and later[2] the green shoots of any kind of grain. In the Aitareya Brāhmaṇa[3] reference is made to the shoots of rice (*vrīhi*), large rice (*mahā-vrīhi*), panic seed (*priyaṅgu*), and barley (*yava*).

[1] x. 62, 8.

[2] Vājasaneyi Saṃhitā, xix. 13. 81; xxi. 30. 42; Kāṭhaka Saṃhitā, xii. 11; Maitrāyaṇī Saṃhitā, iii. 11, 9; Taittirīya Brāhmaṇa, ii. 6, 4; Aitareya Brāhmaṇa, viii. 5, etc.

[3] viii. 16. *Cf.* for its use at the Sautrāmaṇī, Hillebrandt, *Rituallitteratur*, 160.

Tottra, a 'goad' for driving cattle, is mentioned in the Śatapatha Brāhmaṇa (xii. 4, 1, 10).

Toda appears once to denote a 'goad' in the Rigveda,[1] but more often[2] it is an agent noun meaning 'impeller.' Geldner[3] considers that in one passage[4] the sense is 'wielder of the rod of punishment' (later *daṇḍa-dhara*)—that is, 'prince.'

[1] iv. 16, 11; Mantra in Kauśika Sūtra, 107.

[2] Rv. vi. 6, 6; 12, 1. 3, are probably so to be understood.

[3] *Vedische Studien*, 3, 74.

[4] Rv. i. 150, 1.

Taugrya, 'descendant of **Tugra**,' is the patronymic of **Bhujyu** in the Rigveda.[1]

[1] i. 117, 16; 118, 6; 182, 5. 6; viii. 5, 22; x. 39, 4.

Taudī in one passage of the Atharvaveda[1] appears to denote a plant.

[1] x. 4, 24. *Cf.* St. Petersburg Dictionary, *s.v.* Whitney, Translation of the Atharvaveda, 578, leaves the word untranslated. Bloomfield, *Hymns of the Atharvaveda*, 608, suggests that it is a fanciful name, 'the piercer,' since it is associated with *ghṛtācī*, 'dripping with ghee,' which is clearly such a word.

Taurvaśa. See **Turvaśa.**

Taula, the reading of the text of the Atharvaveda (i. 7, 2), and a form which is otherwise unknown and cannot be satisfactorily explained, must doubtless be meant for **Taila.**

Tauvilikā, occurring once in a hymn of the Atharvaveda,[1] is a word of quite uncertain sense. Roth[2] thinks it means some kind of beast; Zimmer[3] and Whitney[4] regard it as a sort of plant; Sāyaṇa explains it as a disease-causing demon, while Bloomfield[5] leaves the sense doubtful.

[1] vi. 16, 3.
[2] St. Petersburg Dictionary, *s.v.*
[3] *Altindisches Leben*, 72.
[4] Translation of the Atharvaveda, 292.
[5] *Hymns of the Atharvaveda*, 30, 466.

Trapu denotes 'tin' in the Atharvaveda[1] and later.[2] Its quality of being easily smelted, which Roth[3] thinks is indicated by the name (as derived from the root *trap*, 'be ashamed'), is clearly alluded to in the Atharvaveda passage.

[1] xi. 3, 8.
[2] Kāṭhaka Saṃhitā, xviii. 10; Maitrāyaṇī Saṃhitā, ii. 11, 5; Vājasaneyi Saṃhitā, xviii. 13 (all in enumerations of metals); Taittirīya Brāhmaṇa, iii. 12, 6, 5; Jaiminīya Upaniṣad Brāhmaṇa, iii. 17, 3; Chāndogya Upaniṣad, iv. 17, 7. In Taittirīya Saṃhitā, iv. 7, 5, 1, the form is *trapus*.
[3] St. Petersburg Dictionary, *s.v.* *Cf.* Zimmer, *Altindisches Leben*, 53.

Trasa-dasyu, son of **Purukutsa,**[1] is mentioned in the Rigveda as king of the Pūrus.[2] He was born to Purukutsa by his wife, **Purukutsānī,** at a time of great distress;[3] this, according to Sāyaṇa, refers to Purukutsa's captivity: possibly his death is really meant. Trasadasyu was also a descendant of Giriksit,[4] and Purukutsa was a descendant of Durgaha. The genealogy, therefore, appears to be: Durgaha, Girikṣit, Purukutsa, Trasadasyu. Trasadasyu was the ancestor of **Tṛkṣi,**[5] and, according to Ludwig,[6] had a son Hiraṇin. Trasadasyu's chronological position is determined by the fact that his father, Purukutsa, was a contemporary of Sudās, either as an opponent[7] or as a friend.[8] That Purukutsa was an enemy of Sudās is more probable, because the latter's predecessor, Divodāsa, was apparently[9] at enmity with the Pūrus, and in the battle of the ten kings Pūrus were ranged against Sudās and the Tṛtsus. Trasadasyu himself seems to have been an energetic king. His people, the Pūrus, were settled on the **Sarasvatī,**[10] which was, no doubt, the stream in the middle country, that locality according well with the later union of the Pūrus with the **Kuru** people, who inhabited that country. This union is exemplified in the person of **Kuruśravaṇa,** who is called Trāsadasyava, 'descendant of Trasadasyu,' in the Rigveda,[11] whose father was **Mitrātithi,** and whose son was **Upamaśravas.** The relation of Mitrātithi to Tṛkṣi does not appear.

Another descendant of Trasadasyu was **Tryaruṇa Traivṛṣṇa,** who is simply called Trasadasyu in a hymn of the Rigveda.[12]

1 Rv. v. 33, 8; vii. 19, 3; viii. 19, 36; iv. 42, 8 *et seq.*

2 Rv. iv. 38, 1 *et seq.*; vii. 19, 3. He is merely alluded to in i. 63, 7; 112, 4; viii. 8, 21; 36, 7; 37, 7; 49, 10.

3 Rv. iv. 42, 8 *et seq.*

4 Rv. v. 33, 8.

5 Rv. viii. 22, 7. He was a Pūru king. See vi. 46, 8.

6 Translation of the Rigveda, 3, 155, with reference to Rv. v. 33, 7 *et seq.*

7 So Ludwig, 3, 174, who alters *Sudāsam* to *Sudāse*, in support of this view, in Rv. i. 63, 7. *Cf.* Oldenberg, *Zeitschrift der Deutschen Morgenländischen Gesellschaft*, 42, 204, 205, 219; *Ṛgveda-Noten*, 1, 63; Geldner, *Vedische Studien*, 1, 153; Hillebrandt, *Vedische Mythologie*, 1, 112, n. 1. Foy, Kuhn's *Zeitschrift*, 34, 242, denies that the word in this passage is a proper name at all.

8 *Cf.* Hillebrandt, *loc. cit.*

9 Rv. i. 130, 7; Ludwig, 3, 114; but see Hillebrandt, 1, 113, 114.

10 Rv. vii. 95, 96; Ludwig, 3, 175; Hillebrandt, 1, 115.

11 x. 33, 4. *Cf.* Lanman, *Sanskrit Reader*, 386 *et seq.*; Geldner, *Vedische Studien*, 2, 150, 184.

12 v. 27.

He was not only a 'descendant of Trivṛṣan,' but, according to the Pañcaviṃśa Brāhmaṇa,[13] he was also Traidhātva, 'descendant of Tridhātu.' The order of these two predecessors of Tryaruṇa cannot be determined in any way from Vedic literature. According to the later tradition,[14] a prince named Tridhanvan preceded Tryaruṇa in the succession. Vedic tradition further fails to show in what precise relation Trasadasyu stood to Trivṛṣan or Tryaruṇa.

Trasdasyu Paurukutsa appears in several Brāhmaṇas[15] as a famous sacrificer of ancient times, together with **Para Āṭṇāra, Vītahavya Śrāyasa,** and **Kakṣīvant Auśija,** who in the Jaiminīya Upaniṣad Brāhmaṇa[16] are called 'ancient great kings' (*pūrve mahārājāḥ*).

[13] xiii. 3, 12. The Tāṇḍaka, cited by Sāyaṇa (Sieg, *Die Sagenstoffe des Ṛgveda*, 67), has Trasadasyu, like the Rv.

[14] Harivaṃśa, 714 *et seq.*, where the name (716) is also misread as Tridharman. Traidhātva cannot reasonably be taken as representing a patronymic from Tridhanvan, as Sieg, *op. cit.*, 74-76, seems to do. Trivṛṣan has entirely disappeared from the Epic tradition; there is thus no way of assigning a relative priority to either Trivṛṣan or Tridhanvan.

[15] Pañcaviṃśa Brāhmaṇa, xxv. 16; Kāṭhaka Saṃhitā, xxii. 3 (*Indische Studien*, 3, 473); Taittirīya Saṃhitā, v. 6, 5, 3.

[16] ii. 6, 11.

Cf. Oldenberg, *Zeitschrift der Deutschen Morgenländischen Gesellschaft*, 42, 217 *et seq.*; Hillebrandt, *Vedische Mythologie*, 1, 111-116; 2, 165, n. 4; Weber, *Indische Studien*, 10, 25; Lanman, *Sanskrit Reader*, 386.

Trāta Aiṣumata ('descendant of Iṣumant') is mentioned in the Vaṃśa Brāhmaṇa[1] as a pupil of **Nigaḍa Pārṇavalki.**

[1] i. 3. *Cf.* Weber, *Indische Studien*, 4, 372.

Trāyamāṇa denotes in the Atharvaveda[1] a plant of an unknown species. The word is possibly only an epithet, retaining its participial sense of 'preserving,' though this interpretation is not favoured by the accent.[2]

[1] viii. 2, 6.

[2] *Trāyamāṇā́.* *Cf.* Whitney, Translation of the Atharvaveda, 477.

Trāsadasyava, 'descendant of **Trasadasyu,**' is the patronymic in the Rigveda of **Tṛkṣi**[1] and of **Kuruśravaṇa.**[2] The

[1] viii. 22, 7.

[2] x. 33, 4.

word is also applied to Agni as 'protector of, or worshipped by, Trasadasyu' and his line.[3]

[3] viii. 19, 32; Macdonell, *Vedic Mythology*, p. 96.

Tri-kakud[1] or **Tri-kakubh**,[2] 'having three peaks,' occurs in the Atharvaveda and later as the name of a mountain in the Himālaya, the modern Trikota. From it came the salve (**Āñjana**),[3] which tradition made out to be derived from Vṛtra's eye.[4]

[1] Av. iv. 9, 8; Śatapatha Brāhmaṇa, iii. 1, 3, 12.

[2] Maitrāyaṇī Saṃhitā, iii. 6, 3; Kāṭhaka Saṃhitā, xxiii. 1; Vājasaneyi Saṃhitā, xv. 4; Pañcaviṃśa Brāhmaṇa, xxii. 14.

[3] Hence called *Traikakuda*, Av. iv. 9, 9. 10; xix. 44, 6, etc.

[4] Śatapatha Brāhmaṇa, *loc. cit.*; Maitrāyaṇī and Kāṭhaka Saṃhitās, *loc. cit.*

Cf. Ludwig, Translation of the Rigveda, 3, 198; Zimmer, *Altindisches Leben*, 5, 29, 30; Hillebrandt, *Vedische Mythologie*, 3, 239, n. 4; Bloomfield, *Hymns of the Atharvaveda*, 381.

Tri-kadruka, a term used in the plural only, appears to denote three vessels of some kind for holding Soma.

[1] i. 32, 3; ii. 11, 17; 15, 1; 22, 1; x. 14, 16.

Tri-kharva is the name of a school of priests mentioned in the Pañcaviṃśa Brāhmaṇa (ii. 8, 3) as practising a special rite with success.

Trita is clearly a god[1] in Vedic literature, but Yāska in one passage of the Nirukta[2] already explains the name as that of a Ṛṣi or seer.

[1] Macdonell, *Vedic Mythology*, pp. 67-69.

[2] iv. 6.

Tri-pura, 'a threefold stronghold,' is alluded to in the Brāhmaṇas[1] as a secure protection. But as the passages are mythical no stress can be laid on them as evidence for the existence of forts with three concentric walls.

[1] Śatapatha Brāhmaṇa, vi. 3, 3, 25; Aitareya Brāhmaṇa, ii. 11; Kauṣītaki Brāhmaṇa in *Indische Studien*, 2, 310. See also Taittirīya Saṃhitā, vi. 2, 3; Kāṭhaka Saṃhitā, xxiv. 10, etc., and Lévi, *La Doctrine du Sacrifice*, 46, n 1.

Tri-plakṣa, masc. plur., 'the three fig-trees,' is the name of the place where the **Dṛṣadvatī** disappeared, near the **Yamunā**, according to the Pañcaviṃśa Brāhmaṇa.[1]

[1] xxv. 13, 4. *Cf.* Śāṅkhāyana Śrauta Sūtra, xiii. 29, 33; Lāṭyāyana Śrauta Sūtra, x. 19, 9; Kātyāyana Srauta Sūtra, xxiv. 6, 39.

Triy-avi. See **Tryavi.**

Tri-yuga, neut., is an expression occurring in the Rigveda[1] where it is said that the plants (*oṣadhi*) were born 'three ages' before the gods (*devebhyas triyugaṃ purā*). The commentator on the Nirukta[2] thinks that the ages here meant are the Yugas of the later Indian chronology, the sense of the passage being that the plants were born in the first Yuga. The author of the Śatapatha Brāhmaṇa[3] understands three seasons—spring, the rains, and autumn—to be meant in the verse, taking the two words *triyugaṃ purā* separately as 'formerly, in the three seasons.' The vague sense 'three ages' is quite adequate: the use of 'three' in such cases is a favourite feature in folklore. *Cf.* **Yuga.**

[1] x. 97, 1 = Taittirīya Saṃhitā, iv. 2, 6, 1, and Vājasaneyi Saṃhitā; xii. 75.

[2] ix. 28.

[3] vii. 2, 4, 26.

Cf. Eggeling, *Sacred Books of the East*, 41, 340.

Tri-vatsa, 'three years old,'[1] is an expression applied to cattle in the later Saṃhitās and the Brāhmaṇas.[2]

[1] As regards the form and meaning of this compound, *cf.* **Tryavi**.

[2] Vājasaneyi Saṃhitā, xiv. 10; xviii. 26; xxviii. 27; Pañcaviṃśa Brāhmaṇa, xvi. 13; xviii. 9; xxi. 14, etc. *Cf.* Lāṭyāyana Śrauta Sūtra, viii. 3, 9 *et seq.*, where one explanation of the word is *tri-varṣa*.

Tri-vṛt, 'threefold,' is the designation of an amulet in the Atharvaveda (v. 28, 2. 4).

Tri-veda Kṛṣṇa-rāta Lauhitya ('descendant of Lohita') is the name of a teacher, a pupil of **Śyāmajayanta Lauhitya**, according to a Vaṃśa (list of teachers) in the Jaiminīya Upaniṣad Brāhmaṇa (iii. 42, 1).

Tri-śaṅku is in Vedic literature the name of a sage mentioned as a teacher in the Taittirīya Upaniṣad.[1] There is no trace of the later legend by which he becomes the victim of **Vasiṣṭha**'s curse and the object of **Viśvāmitra**'s solicitude, being eventually fixed in the sky as a constellation.[2] The confusion of the chronology in the tales of Triśaṅku is a good example of the worthlessness of the supposed epic tradition.

[1] i. 10, 1.

[2] See Muir, *Sanskrit Texts*, 1[2], 362, 375 *et seq.*

Tri-śoka is the name of an ancient mythical seer who is mentioned both in the Rigveda[1] and the Atharvaveda.[2] A Sāman, or chant, named after him is referred to in the Pañcaviṃśa Brāhmaṇa.[3]

[1] i. 112, 13; viii. 45, 30. In x. 29, 2, the word seems merely to be an adjective, meaning 'with triple splendour.'

[2] iv. 29, 6.

[3] viii. 1.

Cf. Ludwig, Translation of the Rigveda, 3, 107, 162; Hopkins, *Transactions of the Connecticut Academy of Arts and Sciences*, 15, 33.

Trai-kakuda. See **Trikakud.**

Traitana appears in the Rigveda[1] as a **Dāsa,** an enemy of **Dīrghatamas,** who seems to have engaged him in single combat and defeated him. The St. Petersburg Dictionary suggests that he is rather a supernatural being allied to Trita (*cf.* the Avestan Thrita and Thraetaona).[2]

[1] i. 158, 5.

[2] Macdonell, *Vedic Mythology*, p. 68. *Cf.* Ludwig, Translation of the Rigveda, 3, 151; Oldenberg, *Religion des Veda*, 144.

Trai-dhātva ('descendant of Tridhātu,') is the patronymic of **Tryaruṇa** in the Pañcaviṃśa Brāhmaṇa (xiii. 3, 12).

Trai-pada, neut., occurs as a measure of distance, 'three-quarters' of a **Yojana,** in the Pañcāviṃśa Brāhmaṇa, where half a Yojana is termed **Gavyūti** and a quarter **Krośa.**[1]

[1] xvi. 13. *Cf.* Śāṅkhāyana Śrauta Sūtra, xiv. 41, 12.

Traivaṇi is mentioned as a pupil of **Aupacandhani** or **Aupajandhani** in the first two Vaṃśas (lists of teachers) in the Bṛhadāraṇyaka Upaniṣad.[1] In the Mādhyaṃdina recension[2] his name occurs twice in the second Vaṃśa, in both cases as a pupil of Aupajandhani.

[1] ii. 6, 3 (Kāṇva=ii. 5, 21 Mādhyaṃdina); iv. 6, 3 (=iv. 5, 27).

[2] iv. 5, 27.

Trai-vṛṣṇa, 'descendant of Trivṛṣan,' is the patronymic of **Trayaruṇa** in the Rigveda (v. 27, 1).

Try-aruṇa Trai-vṛṣṇa Trasadasyu is the name of a prince whose generosity to a singer is celebrated in a hymn of the Rigveda.[1] In the Pañcaviṃśa Brāhmaṇa[2] he appears as **Tryaruṇa Traidhātva Aikṣvāka,** and is the hero of the following story. He was out in his chariot with his Purohita, or domestic priest, **Vṛśa Jāna,** and by excessive speed in driving killed a Brahmin boy. This sin was atoned for by the Purohita's using his Vārśa Sāman (chant). The Śāṭyāyana Brāhmaṇa, cited by Sāyaṇa,[3] elaborates the tale. As Vṛśa had held the reins, king and priest accused each other of the murder. The Ikṣvākus being consulted threw the responsibility for the crime on Vṛśa, who thereupon revived the boy by the Vārśa Sāman. In consequence of this unfairness of theirs—being Kṣatriyas they were partial to a Kṣatriya—Agni's glow ceased to burn in their houses. In response to their appeal to restore it, Vṛśa came to them, saw the Piśācī (demoness), who, in the form of Trasadasyu's wife, had stolen the glow, and succeeded in restoring it to Agni. This version with some variations occurs also in the Bṛhaddevatā,[4] which connects the story with a hymn of the Rigveda.[5] Sieg's attempt[6] to show that the hymn really refers to this tale is not at all successful.[7]

[1] v. 27, 1-3.

[2] xiii. 3, 12. *Cf.* the Tāṇḍaka recension, cited in Sāyaṇa, on Rv. v. 2, where Trasadasyu is given as the king's name.

[3] On Rv., *loc. cit.* See also the Jaiminīya Brāhmaṇa version in Oertel, *Journal of the American Oriental Society*, 18, 20.

[4] v. 14 *et seq.*, with Macdonell's notes.

[5] v. 2.

[6] *Die Sagenstoffe des Ṛgveda*, 64-76. *Cf.* Geldner, *Festgruss an Roth*, 192.

[7] See Oldenberg, *Sacred Books of the East*, 46, 366 *et seq.*; *Ṛgveda-Noten*, 1, 312; Hillebrandt, *Göttingische Gelehrte Anzeigen*, 1903, 240 *et seq.*

It is clear that Trasadasyu must here mean 'descendant of Trasadasyu,' and not King Trasadasyu himself. The difference of the patronymics, Traivṛṣṇa and Traidhātva, by which he is referred to can best be explained by assuming that there were two kings, Trivṛṣan and Tridhātu (or possibly Tridhanvan), from whom Tryaruṇa was descended.[8] The connexion with the Ikṣvākus is important (see **Ikṣvāku**).

8 See Sieg, *op. cit.*, 74-76, and **Trasadasyu**.

Try-avi designates a calf eighteen months old[1] in the Rigveda[2] and later Saṃhitās.[3]

1 The etymological meaning is apparently 'having three sheep (periods)'—that is, 'having periods of thrice six months,' just as the adjective *pañcāvi* means 'having five periods of six months,' or 'thirty months old.'

2 iii. 55, 14.

3 Kāṭhaka Saṃhitā, xvii. 2; xviii. 12, etc. (in the form *triyavi*); Vājasaneyi Saṃhitā, xiv. 10; xviii. 26, etc.

Try-āśir, 'with three admixtures,' is an epithet of Soma in the Rigveda.[1] According to Sāyaṇa this means mixed with curds (**Dadhi**), meal (**Saktu**), and milk (**Payas**). More accurately it would seem[2] to denote the milk (*gavāśir*), the barley (*yavāśir*), and the curds (*dadhyāśir*), which were used to mix with the Soma.

1 v. 27, 5. *Cf.* perhaps viii. 2, 7 (*traya Indrasya somāḥ sutāsaḥ*, 'three kinds of Soma pressed for Indra').

2 Hillebrandt, *Vedische Mythologie*, 1, 209; Oldenberg, *Sacred Books of the East*, 46, 422.

Tvac, 'skin,' 'hide,' (*a*) denotes specially in the Rigveda[1] the hide used in the process of extracting the **Soma** juice from the plant. The Soma was pounded with stones (*adri*) upon the skin laid on the pressing boards (*adhiṣavaṇe phalake*),[2] which, however, are not mentioned in the Rigveda. Or if a pestle and mortar were used, the skin was still placed underneath them to catch the drops of juice, not above, as Pischel[3] thought.

1 i. 79, 3; iii. 21, 5; ix. 65, 25; 66, 29; 70, 7; 79, 4; 101, 11, 16, etc.

2 Hillebrandt, *Vedische Mythologie*, 1, 181-183, and **Adhiṣavaṇa**.

3 *Vedische Studien*, 1, 110.

(*b*) Tvac also denotes the rind of the Soma plant that remains after the juice has been extracted.[4]

(*c*) Metaphorically the term *kṛṣṇā tvac*, 'the black skins,' is applied to the aboriginal enemies of the invading Āryans.[5]

4 Rv. ix. 86, 44; Taittirīya Brāhmaṇa, iii. 7, 13, 1; Hillebrandt, *op. cit.*, 52.

5 Rv. i. 130, 8, and probably ix. 41, 1, for which, however, *cf.* Hillebrandt, *op. cit.*, 51, n. 2, and see **Dāsa.**

Tvaṣṭṛ is employed once in the Atharvaveda[1] to denote a 'carpenter,' with a deliberate play on the name of the god Tvaṣṭṛ. He is there mentioned as using an axe (*svadhiti*) to fashion (from wood) 'a well-made form' (*rūpaṃ sukṛtam*). See **Taṣṭṛ.**

1 xii. 3, 33. *Cf.* Whitney, Translation of the Atharvaveda, 688; Bloomfield, *Hymns of the Atharvaveda*, 651.

Tvāṣṭra, 'descendant of Tvaṣṭṛ,' is the patronymic, in the Bṛhadāraṇyaka Upaniṣad,[1] of the mythical teacher **Ābhūti.**

1 ii. 6, 3 (Kāṇva = ii. 5, 22 Mādhyaṃdina); iv. 6, 3 (= iv. 5, 28).

Tsaru.—(*a*) This word seems to denote some sort of crawling animal in one passage of the Rigveda.[1]

1 vii. 50, 1. *Cf.* Zimmer, *Altindisches Leben*, 99.

(*b*) In the later literature the word means a 'handle,' as of a beaker (**Camasa**).[1] In this sense also it seems to occur in the description of the plough (**Lāṅgala**) in the Atharvaveda[2] and the later Saṃhitās.[3]

1 Pañcaviṃśa Brāhmaṇa, xxv. 4. *Cf.* Lāṭyāyana Srauta Sūtra, x. 12, 12, etc.

2 iii. 17, 3, where the ordinary text has *soma-satsaru* (so the Pada text), and the Paippalāda recension has *soma-pitsalam.*

3 Taittirīya Saṃhitā, iv. 2, 5, 6, has *sumati-tsaru*; Maitrāyaṇī Saṃhitā, ii. 7, 12; Kāṭhaka Saṃhitā, xvi. 12; Vājasaneyi Saṃhitā, xii. 71; Vasiṣṭha Dharma Sūtra, ii. 34, have *somapitsaru*, which Vasiṣṭha renders as 'provided with a handle for the drinker of Soma' (*i.e.*, *somapi-tsaru*). Weber, *Indische Studien*, 17, 255, suggests *soma-sa-tsaru*, 'with (*sa-*) strap (*uman*, a conjectural word) and handle' (*tsaru*). Whitney, Translation of the Atharvaveda, 116, prefers to read throughout *sumati-tsaru*, 'with well-smoothed handle,' from the root seen in *matī-kṛ*, etc. *Cf.* Zimmer, *Altindisches Leben*, 236; Bühler, *Sacred Books of the East*, 14, 13.

Tsārin denotes, in one passage of the Rigveda,[1] a 'hunter' engaged in the chase of the *takva* (an unknown beast), according to Ludwig and Max Müller.[2] But this explanation is quite conjectural.

[1] i. 134, 5.

[2] *Sacred Books of the East*, 32, 448.

D.

Daṃśa (lit., 'biter'), 'gad-fly,' is mentioned in the Chāndogya Upaniṣad (vi. 9, 3; 10, 2).

Daṃṣṭra, denoting a prominent tooth, 'tusk,' or 'fang' of an animal, occurs often from the Rigveda onwards.[1]

[1] Rv. ii. 13, 4; x. 87, 3; Av. iv. 36, 2; x. 5, 43; xvi. 7, 3, etc.

Dakṣa Kātyāyani Ātreya ('descendant of Atri') is mentioned in the Vaṃśas (lists of teachers) of the Jaiminīya Upaniṣad Brāhmaṇa (iii. 41, 1; iv. 17, 1) as a pupil of **Śaṅkha Bābhravya.**

Dakṣa Jayanta Lauhitya ('descendant of Lohita') is mentioned in a Vaṃśa (list of teachers) of the Jaiminīya Upaniṣad Brāhmaṇa (iii. 42, 1) as a pupil of **Kṛṣṇarāta Lauhitya.**

Dakṣa Pārvati ('descendant of **Parvata**') is mentioned in the Śatapatha Brāhmaṇa[1] as having performed a certain rite which his descendants, the Dākṣāyaṇas, still maintained, thus enjoying royal dignity down to the time of the Brāhmaṇa itself. He appears in the Kauṣītaki Brāhmaṇa[2] also.

[1] ii. 4, 4, 6.

[2] iv. 4.

Cf. Weber, *Indische Studien*, 1, 223; 4, 358; Eggeling, *Sacred Books of the East*, 12, 374 *et seq.*; Lévi, *La Doctrine du Sacrifice*, 138.

Dakṣiṇatas-kaparda is an epithet of the **Vasiṣṭhas** in the Rigveda (vii. 33, 1) referring to their mode of 'wearing the hair in a braid on the right side.' See **Kaparda.**

Dakṣiṇā appears repeatedly in the Rigveda[1] and later[2] as the designation of the gift presented to priests at the sacrifice, apparently because a cow—a prolific (*dakṣiṇā*) one—was the usual 'fee'[3] on such an occasion.[4] The later Dāna-stutis, or 'Praises of Gifts,' in the Rigveda immensely exaggerate these donations, and the exaggeration grows in the Brāhmaṇas. It is important to notice that these enumerations of gifts in the main include nothing but articles of personal property, such as kine, horses, buffaloes, or camels (*uṣṭra*), ornaments, and so forth, but not land.[5] Reference is, however, made in the Śatapatha Brāhmaṇa[6] to land as a Dakṣiṇā, but with disapproval, probably because the land came to be regarded as inalienable without the consent of the clansmen.[7]

[1] A whole hymn, Rv. x. 107, is devoted to its praise. *Cf.* i. 168, 7; vi. 27, 8; viii. 24, 29; 39, 5; x. 62, 1, etc.

[2] Av. iv. 11, 4; v. 7, 11; xi. 7, 9; 8, 22; xiii. 1, 52; xviii. 4, 8, etc.; Taittirīya Saṃhitā, i. 7, 3, 1; 8, 1, 1; Vājasaneyi Saṃhitā, iv. 19. 23; xix. 30; Taittirīya Brāhmaṇa, i. 7, 3, 3 *et seq.*; Śatapatha Brāhmaṇa, i. 9, 3, 1 *et seq.* The verses (*gāthā nārāśaṃsī*, either as a single expression or as two separate terms) used to win these Dakṣiṇās were notoriously false. See Kāṭhaka Saṃhitā, xiv. 5; Taittirīya Brāhmaṇa, i. 3, 2, 6. 7; Nirukta, i. 7; xi. 2.

[3] The transition of meaning is similar in the use of the English word 'fee': 'cattle,' 'money,' 'payment for service' (see Murray's English Dictionary, *s.v.* 'fee'). *Cf.* also **Go-dāna,** n. 4.

[4] *Cf.* the rule that when nothing is specified a cow is the Dakṣiṇā, Kātyāyana Śrauta Sūtra, xv. 2, 13; Lāṭyāyana Śrauta Sūtra, viii. 1, 2.

[5] So, *e.g.*, Rv. i. 126, 1-4; v. 30, 12-15; viii. 1, 32. 33; 3, 21 *et seq.*; 4, 19-21; 5, 37-39; 6, 46-48; 55; 56; vii. 18, 21-24, and the full list in Ludwig, Translation of the Rigveda, 3, 273-277. *Cf.* Weber, *Indische Studien*, 10, 49 *et seq.* Clothes (*vāsas*) and gold are mentioned as a Dakṣiṇā in Av. ix. 5, 14. The four Dakṣiṇās, according to the Śatapatha Brāhmaṇa, iv. 3, 4, 7, are gold, a cow, clothes, and a horse. This is practically exhaustive if the trappings of the horse and ornaments are included.

[6] xiii. 7, 1, 13, with which compare xiii. 6, 2, 18, where the Brahmin's land is excluded; and see xiii. 7, 1, 15, where the gift of land is disapproved.

[7] Śatapatha Brāhmaṇa, vii. 1, 1, 4. *Cf.* above, pp. 100, n. 19, 246; below, pp. 351, 352.

Cf. Zimmer, *Altindisches Leben*, 169-171; Jolly, *Recht und Sitte*, 104, 105; Weber, *Indische Streifen*, 1, 96-98; Bloomfield, *Religion of the Veda*, 69-74; *Atharvaveda*, 76 *et seq.*, 100, 121.

Dakṣiṇā-patha (lit., 'the road to the south'), 'the south country,' is found, probably as a designation of the Deccan, as early as the Baudhāyana Dharma Sūtra,[1] coupled with

[1] i. 1, 2, 13. *Cf.* Oldenberg, *Buddha*, 394, n., and Baudhāyana Gṛhya Sūtra, v. 13.

Surāṣṭra. A similar expression is *dakṣiṇā padā*, 'with southward foot,' in the Rigveda,[2] referring to the place where the exile (*parā-vṛj*) goes on being expelled. This no doubt simply means 'the south' beyond the limits of the recognized Āryan world, which even as late as the Kauṣītaki Upaniṣad[3] appears as bounded by the Vindhyas on the south.

[2] x. 61, 8. [3] ii. 13.
Cf. Zimmer, *Altindisches Leben*, 185; Weber, *Indische Studien*, 1, 408; Rhys Davids, *Buddhist India*, 30; Keith, *Śāṅkhāyana Āraṇyaka*, 28, n. 1; *Aitareya Āraṇyaka*, 200.

Dakṣiṇā-praṣṭi denotes 'the side horse on the right.' It appears from two passages of the Śatapatha Brāhmaṇa[1] that there were at times four horses yoked to the chariot, the right and the left yoke horse (*dakṣiṇā-yugya, savyā-yugya*) in the middle, flanked by one on each side, the two latter of course not being fastened to the yoke at all, but presumably by traces alongside of the yoke horses. See **Ratha.**

[1] v. 1, 4, 9; ix. 4, 2, 11 (this passage appears to speak of three horses only, but *cf.* v. 4, 3, 17). *Cf.* also Pañcaviṃśa Brāhmaṇa, xvi. 13, 12.

Dakṣiṇāyana. See **Sūrya.**

Dakṣiṇā-yugya, 'the yoke horse on the right,' is mentioned in the Śatapatha Brāhmaṇa (v. 1, 4, 6; 4, 3, 8; ix. 4, 2, 11). See **Ratha.**

Daṇḍa, 'staff.' (*a*) This word is often mentioned in the ordinary sense; for example, when used for driving cattle[1] (*go-ajanāsaḥ*), or as a weapon.[2] A staff was given to a man on consecration for driving away demons, according to the Śatapatha Brāhmaṇa.[3] The staff also played a part in the initiation (*upanayana*) of a youth on attaining manhood.[4] In a modified sense the word is used to denote the handle of a ladle or similar implement.[5]

[1] Rv. vii. 33, 6.
[2] Av. v. 5, 4. *Cf.* Aitareya Brāhmaṇa, ii. 35; Śatapatha Brāhmaṇa, i. 5, 4, 6, etc.
[3] iii. 2, 1, 32.
[4] Āśvalāyana Gṛhya Sūtra, i. 19; 22; Sāṅkhāyana Gṛhya Sūtra, ii. 1. 6. 11, etc.
[5] Aitareya Brāhmaṇa, vii. 5; Śatapatha Brāhmaṇa, vii. 4, 1, 36. Of a musical instrument, Sāṅkhāyana Āraṇyaka, viii. 9; Śrauta Sūtra, xvii. 3, 1 *et seq.*

(*b*) The 'staff' as the symbol of temporal power, implying punishment, is applied by the king (*rāja-preṣito daṇḍaḥ*).[1] The king, in modern phraseology, was the source of criminal law; and he clearly retained this branch of law in his own hands even in later times.[2] The punishment of the non-guilty (*a-daṇḍya*) is given as one of the characteristics of the non-Brahminical **Vrātyas** in the Pañcaviṃśa Brāhmaṇa.[3] See also **Dharma.**

[1] Pāraskara Gṛhya Sūtra, iii. 15. *Cf.* Śatapatha Brāhmaṇa, v. 4, 4, 7, where the king, being himself 'exempt from punishment' (*a-daṇḍya*), inflicts judicial punishment (*daṇḍa-vadha*).

[2] Foy, *Die königliche Gewalt*, 21 *et seq.*

[3] xvii. 1, 9; Weber, *Indische Studien*, 1, 33.

Daṇḍa Aupara ('descendant of Upara') is mentioned in the Taittirīya Saṃhitā (vi. 2, 9, 4) and the Maitrāyaṇī Saṃhitā (iii. 8, 7) as having performed a certain rite.

Daṇḍana occurs in the Atharvaveda[1] among other names of 'reed' or 'cane.'

[1] xii. 2, 54. *Cf.* Whitney, Translation of the Atharvaveda, 682.

Datta Tāpasa was Hotṛ priest at the snake festival described in the Pañcaviṃśa Brāhmaṇa.[1]

[1] xxv. 15, 3. *Cf.* Weber, *Indische Studien*, 1, 35.

Dadhi, 'sour milk,' is repeatedly mentioned in the Rigveda[1] and later.[2] The Śatapatha Brāhmaṇa[3] mentions in order **Ghṛta** ('clarified butter'), Dadhi, **Mastu,** which Eggeling[4] renders 'whey,' and **Āmikṣā,** 'curds.' Dadhi often has the meaning of 'curds' also. It was used for mixing with **Soma.**[5]

[1] viii. 2, 9; ix. 87, 1, etc.

[2] Av. iii. 12, 7; iv. 34, 6; Taittirīya Saṃhitā, ii. 5, 3, 4, etc.; Pañcaviṃśa Brāhmaṇa, xviii. 5, 12, etc.

[3] i. 8, 1, 7. *Cf.* Jaiminīya Brāhmaṇa, ii. 348.

[4] *Sacred Books of the East*, 12, 218.

[5] *Dadhyāśir*, 'mixed with sour milk,' is an epithet of Soma in Rv. i. 5, 5; 137, 2; v. 51, 7; vii. 32, 4. *Cf.* Hillebrandt, *Vedische Mythologie*, 1, 219 *et seq.* *Cf.* Zimmer, *Altindisches Leben*, 227.

Dadhyañc Ātharvaṇa is a purely mythical sage. In the Rigveda[1] he is clearly a divinity of some kind, but in the later

[1] i. 80, 16; 84, 13. 14; 116, 12; 117, 22; 119, 9, etc. See Macdonell, *Vedic Mythology*, pp. 141, 142; Hillebrandt, *Vedische Mythologie*, 1, 176.

Saṃhitās[2] and the Brāhmaṇas[3] he is metamorphosed into a teacher. In the Pañcaviṃśa Brāhmaṇa[4] he is by oversight called an Āṅgirasa.

[2] Taittirīya Saṃhitā, v. 1, 4, 4; 6, 6, 3; Kāṭhaka Saṃhitā, xix. 4.

[3] Śatapatha Brāhmaṇa, iv. 1, 5, 18; vi. 4, 2, 3; xiv. 1, 1, 18. 20. 25; 4, 13; Bṛhadāraṇyaka Upaniṣad, ii. 5, 22; iv. 5, 28, etc.

[4] xii. 8, 6. So also Gopatha Brāhmaṇa, i. 5, 21.

Cf. Bloomfield, *Hymns of the Atharvaveda*, xxxv; *Atharvaveda*, 23, 116, 118, St. Petersburg Dictionary, *s.v.*

Dadhy-āśir. See **Dadhi** and **Soma.**

Dant, Danta, 'tooth,' is frequently mentioned from the Rigveda onwards.[1] Cleansing (*dhāv*) the teeth was an ordinary act, especially in preparation for a sacrifice, and accompanied bathing, shaving of the hair and beard (*keśa-śmaśru*), and the cutting of the nails.[2] A hymn of the Atharvaveda[3] celebrates the appearance of the first two teeth of a child, though its exact interpretation is doubtful.[4] In the Aitareya Brāhmaṇa[5] there is a reference to a child's first teeth falling out. The word seems in the Rigveda[6] once to denote an elephant's tusk. Whether dentistry was practised is doubtful. The occurrence in the Aitareya Āraṇyaka[7] of **Hiraṇya-dant,** 'gold-toothed,' as the name of a man, is perhaps significant, especially as it is certain that the stopping of teeth with gold was known at Rome as early as the legislation of the Twelve Tables.[8]

[1] Rv. vii. 55, 2; x. 68, 6; Av. v. 23, 3; 29, 4; vi. 56, 3, etc. The more usual form is Danta, Rv. iv. 6, 8; vi. 75, 11; Av. iv. 3, 6, etc.

[2] Maitrāyaṇī Saṃhitā, iii. 6, 2 (not exactly paralleled in Taittirīya Saṃhitā, vi. 1, 1, 2 *et seq.*).

[3] vi. 140.

[4] Zimmer, *Altindisches Leben*, 321; Weber, *Indische Studien*, 5, 224; Grill, *Hundert Lieder*,[2] 176; Bloomfield, *Hymns of the Atharvaveda*, 540, 541; *Atharvaveda*, 71; Whitney, Translation of the Atharvaveda, 386.

[5] vii. 14; Śāṅkhāyana Śrauta Sūtra, xv. 18.

[6] iv. 6, 8; Pischel, *Vedische Studien*, 1, 99; Oldenberg, *Sacred Books of the East*, 46, 341, 342.

[7] ii. 1, 5.

[8] Keith, *Aitareya Āraṇyaka*, 206. See Wordsworth, *Fragments and Specimens of Early Latin*, 537.

Dabhīti appears several times in the Rigveda as a hero or sage. Indra overcomes on his behalf **Cumuri** and **Dhuni**;[1]

[1] x. 113, 9; ii. 15, 9; vii. 19, 4.

he pressed Soma for Indra,[2] who rewarded him.[3] For him 30,000 **Dāsas** were sent to sleep,[4] and for him the **Dasyus** were bound without cords.[5] Dabhīti also appears, with **Turvīti,** as a protégé of the Aśvins.[6] There seems no reason to deny that he was a real person.[7]

[2] vi. 20, 13.
[3] vi. 26, 6.
[4] iv. 30, 21.
[5] ii. 13, 9.
[6] i. 112, 23.
[7] Oldenberg, *Religion des Veda*, 155, 157, 158.
Cf. Macdonell, *Vedic Mythology*, p. 162.

Dama, 'house,' is a word that occurs several times in the Rigveda.[1] It denotes, according to Roth,[2] the place in which a man wields uncontrolled power (from the root *dam*, 'control').

[1] i. 1, 8; 61, 9; 75, 5; 143, 4; ii. 1, 2, etc.; Vājasaneyi Saṃhitā, viii. 24.
[2] St. Petersburg Dictionary, *s.v.* But this seems very doubtful in view of the apparent connexion of δόμος and δέμω, 'build,' in Greek.

Dam-pati denotes 'the master of the house'[1] in the Rigveda,[2] but is more often used in the dual to designate 'the master and the mistress,'[3] an expression that may legitimately be deemed to show the high status of women at the time of the Rigveda. See **Strī.**

[1] For the form, *cf.* Macdonell, *Vedic Grammar*, p. 37, n. 9. Pischel, *Vedische Studien*, 2, 307 *et seq.*, argues in favour of the spelling *daṃpati* (adopted by Geldner in his *Ṛgveda, Glossar*). *Cf. patir dan*, Rv. i. 149, 2; Oldenberg, *Sacred Books of the East*, 46, 176, 177.
[2] i. 127, 8; ii. 39, 2; v. 22, 4; viii. 69, 16; 84, 7.
[3] Rv. v. 3, 2; viii. 31, 5; x. 10, 5; 68, 2; 85, 32; 95, 12, etc.; Av. vi. 123, 3; xii. 3, 14; xiv. 2, 9, etc.
Cf. Delbrück, *Die indogermanischen Verwandtschaftsnamen*, 418, 420.

Darbha is the name of a grass in the Rigveda[1] and later.[2] In the Atharvaveda it is used for the calming of anger (*manyu-śamana*),[3] and as an amulet for protection against the scattering of one's hair or the striking of one's breast.[4] It is also said to be 'rich in roots' (*bhūri-mūla*),[5] to possess a thousand leaves (*sahasra-parṇa*) and a hundred stalks (*śata-kāṇḍa*).[6]

[1] i. 191, 3 (with **Śara** and **Kuśara,** varieties of grass).
[2] Av. vi. 43, 2; viii. 7, 20; x. 4, 13; xi. 6, 15; xix. 28, 1, etc.; Taittirīya Saṃhitā, i. 5, 1, 4, etc.
[3] Av. vi. 43.
[4] xix. 32, 2. *Cf.* xix. 30.
[5] Av. vi. 43, 2.
[6] Av. xix. 32, 1.
Cf. Zimmer, *Altindisches Leben*, 70.

Darvi, or **Darvī**, properly denotes a 'ladle,' in which sense it is found in the Rigveda[1] and later.[2] But the word also means a serpent's 'hood' in the Atharvaveda,[3] though Zimmer regards it as the name of a serpent.

[1] v. 6, 9; x. 105, 10.

[2] Av. iii. 10, 7; iv. 14, 7; ix. 6, 17, etc.

[3] x. 1, 13. See Whitney, Translation of the Atharvaveda, 577; Bloomfield, *Hymns of the Atharvaveda*, 153.

[4] *Altindisches Leben*, 95, where he takes **Karikrata** also as the name of a snake.

Darvidā, the 'woodpecker,' is mentioned as a victim at the Aśvamedha, or horse sacrifice, in the Yajurveda.[1] *Cf.* **Dārvāghāta.**

[1] Taittirīya Saṃhitā, v. 5, 13, 1; Maitrāyaṇī Saṃhitā, iii. 14, 15; Vājasaneyi Saṃhitā, xxiv. 3. *Cf.* Zimmer, *Altindisches Leben*, 93. The St. Petersburg Dictionary, *s.v.*, suggests 'wood-piercer' (*dāru-vidha*) as the literal sense. On the etymology, *cf.* F. W. Thomas's article, 'The D-Suffix,' p. 121, in *Transactions of the Cambridge Philological Society*, 5, part ii.

Darśa ('appearance') denotes the new moon day,[1] usually in opposition to the day of full moon (*pūrṇa-māsa*).[2] Most frequently the word occurs in the compound[3] *darśa-pūrṇa-māsau*, 'new and full moon,' the days of special ritual importance.[4] The order of the first two words here is worthy of note, for it distinctly suggests, though it does not conclusively prove, that the month was reckoned from new moon to new moon, not from full moon to full moon. See **Māsa.**

[1] Av. vii. 81, 3. 4; Taittirīya Brāhmaṇa, i. 2, 1, 14; Śatapatha Brāhmaṇa, xi. 2, 2, 1.

[2] Taittirīya Saṃhitā, iii. 4, 4, 1, etc.

[3] *Ibid.*, i. 6, 7, 1; 9, 3; ii. 5, 6, 1; Taittirīya Brāhmaṇa, ii. 2, 2, 1; Aitareya Brāhmaṇa, i. 1; Śatapatha Brāhmaṇa, i. 3, 5, 11, etc.

[4] Hillebrandt, *Das altindische Neu- und Vollmondsopfer*, Jena, 1880; *Ritual-litteratur*, 111-114; Oldenberg, *Religion des Veda*, 439.

Daśa-gva appears in one hymn of the Rigveda[1] as the name of a person who was assisted by Indra. The other references in that work,[2] however, clearly show the mythical character of the Daśagvas, and of any individual among them.

[1] viii. 12, 2.

[2] They are mentioned with the **Navagvas** in i. 62, 4; iii. 39, 5; iv. 51, 4; v. 29, 12; x. 62, 6, and alone in ii. 34 12. See Macdonell, *Vedic Mythology*, p. 144 (C).

Daśatayī in the Nirukta[1] frequently denotes the text of the Rigveda as divided into ten Maṇḍalas.

[1] vii. 8. 20; xi. 16; xii. 40.

Daśa-dyu appears twice in the Rigveda[1] as the name of a hero, but nothing can be made out regarding him or his relation to **Vetasu**, who is mentioned in one passage along with him.

[1] i. 33, 14; vi. 26, 4. *Cf.* Oldenberg, *Zeitschrift der Deutschen Morgenländischen Gesellschaft*, 55, 328.

Daśan, 'ten,' forms the basis of the numerical system of the Vedic Indians, as it does of the Āryan people generally. But it is characteristic of India[1] that there should be found at a very early period long series of names for very high numerals, whereas the Āryan knowledge did not go beyond 1,000. In the Vājasaneyi Saṃhitā[2] the list is 1; 10; 100; 1,000; 10,000 (*ayuta*); 100,000 (*niyuta*); 1,000,000 (*prayuta*); 10,000,000 (*arbuda*); 100,000,000 (*nyarbuda*); 1,000,000,000 (*samudra*); 10,000,000,000 (*madhya*); 100,000,000,000 (*anta*); 1,000,000,000,000 (*parārdha*). In the Kāṭhaka Saṃhitā[3] the list is the same, but *niyuta* and *prayuta* exchange places, and after *nyarbuda* a new figure (*badva*) intervenes, thus increasing *samudra* to 10,000,000,000, and so on. The Taittirīya Saṃhitā has in two places[4] exactly the same list as the Vājasaneyi Saṃhitā. The Maitrāyaṇī Saṃhitā[5] has the list *ayuta*, *prayuta*, then *ayuta* again, *arbuda*, *nyarbuda*, *samudra*, *madhya*, *anta*, *parārdha*. The Pañcaviṃśa Brāhmaṇa[6] has the Vājasaneyi list up to *nyarbuda* inclusive, then follow *nikharvaka*, *badva*, *akṣita*, and apparently *go*= 1,000,000,000,000. The Jaiminīya Upaniṣad Brāhmaṇa[7] list

[1] Thibaut, *Astronomie, Astrologie und Mathematik*, 70

[2] xvii. 2 *et seq.* *Cf.* xxii. 34; Śatapatha Brāhmaṇa, ix. 1, 2, 16.

[3] xxxix. 6. In xvii. 10 the number *badva* disappears, and the list corresponds with that of the Vājasaneyi Saṃhitā, except for the fact that *niyuta* and *prayuta* change places.

[4] iv. 4, 11, 4; vii. 2, 20, 1.

[5] ii. 8, 14.

[6] xvii. 14, 2.

[7] i. 10, 28. 29. *Cf.* Aitareya Āraṇyaka, v. 3, 2; Hopkins, *Transactions of the Connecticut Academy of Arts and Sciences*, 15, 30, n. 2; Keith, *Aitareya Āraṇyaka*, 293, 294.

replaces *nikharvaka* by *nikharva*, *badva* by *padma*, and ends with *akṣitir vyomāntaḥ*. The Śāṅkhāyana Śrauta Sūtra[8] continues the series after *nyarbuda* with *nikharvāda*, *samudra*, *salila*, *antya*, *ananta* (= 10 billions).

But beyond *ayuta*[9] none of these numbers has any vitality. *Badva*, indeed, occurs in the Aitareya Brāhmaṇa,[10] but it cannot there have any precise numerical sense;[11] and later on the names of these high numerals are very much confused.

An arithmetical progression of some interest is found in the Pañcaviṃśa Brāhmaṇa,[12] where occurs a list of sacrificial gifts in which each successive figure doubles the amount of the preceding one. It begins with *dvādaśa-mānaṃ hiraṇyam*, 'gold to the value of 12' (the unit being uncertain, but probably the **Kṛṣṇala**[13]), followed by 'to the value of 24, 48, 96, 192, 384, 768, 1,536, 3072,' then *dve aṣṭāviṃśati-śata-māne*, which must mean $2 \times 128 \times 24$ (the last unit being not a single *māna*, but a number of 24 *mānas*) = 6,144, then 12,288, 24,576, 49,152, 98,304, 196,608, 393,216. With these large numbers may be compared the minute theoretical subdivision of time found in the Śatapatha Brāhmaṇa,[14] where a day is divided into 15 *muhūrtas*—1 *muhūrta* = 15 *kṣipras*, 1 *kṣipra* = 15 *etarhis*, 1 *etarhi* = 15 *idānis*, 1 *idāni* = 15 *prāṇas*. The Śāṅkhāyana Śrauta Sūtra[15] has a decimal division of the day into 15 *muhūrtas*—1 *muhūrta* = 10 *nimeṣas*, 1 *nimeṣa* = 10 *dhvaṃsis*.

Few fractions are mentioned in Vedic literature. *Ardha*, *pāda*, *śapha*, and *kalā* denote $\frac{1}{2}$, $\frac{1}{4}$, $\frac{1}{8}$, $\frac{1}{16}$ respectively, but only

[8] xv. 11, 7.

[9] *Cf.* Rv. iii. 6, 15; viii. 1, 5; 2, 41; 21, 18; 34, 15; 46, 22; Av. viii. 2, 21; 8, 7; x. 8, 24; Pañcaviṃśa Brāhmaṇa, xix. 13, 6; xxi. 18, 3, etc. Zimmer, *Altindisches Leben*, 348, considers that it has not any definite sense in the Rigveda; this cannot be either proved or disproved. The Rv. has the phrase *śatā sahasrāṇi* several times (iv. 32, 18; viii. 32, 18, etc.) = 100,000; and *ayuta* may easily have been already specialized, though it may also have retained a vague sense.

[10] vii. 21. 23.

[11] Weber, *Indische Streifen*, 1, 96.

[12] xviii. 3. *Cf.* Lāṭyāyana Śrauta Sūtra, viii. 10, 1 *et seq.*; Kātyāyana Śrauta Sūtra, xxii. 9, 1-6.

[13] *Cf.* Kātyāyana Śrauta Sūtra, xxii. 9, 1; Weber, *op. cit.*, 102, 103.

[14] xii. 3, 2, 1 *et seq.* *Cf.* also Taittirīya Brāhmaṇa, iii. 10, 1, 1, where a series of names of the divisions of the *muhūrta* is given, apparently as alternatives, not as successive stages (*idānīm*, *tadānīm*, *etarhi*, *kṣipram*, *ajiram*, *āśuḥ* (? *āśu*), *nimeṣaḥ*, *phaṇaḥ*, *dravan*, *atidravan*, *tvaran*, *tvaramāṇaḥ*, *āśuḥ*, *āśīyān*, *javaḥ*). See Weber, *op. cit.*, 92-94.

[15] xiv. 75 *et seq.* *Cf.* Śāṅkhāyana Āraṇyaka, vii. 20.

the first two are common. *Tṛtīya* denotes the third part.[16] In the Rigveda[17] Indra and Viṣṇu are said to have divided 1,000 by 3, though how they did so is uncertain. *Tri-pād* denotes 'three-fourths.'[18]

There is no clear evidence that the Indians of the Vedic period had any knowledge of numerical figures, though it is perfectly possible.[19]

[16] Taittirīya Saṃhitā, ii. 5, 1, 4; v. 2, 6, 2; Taittirīya Brāhmaṇa, i. 1, 6, 1; 7, 1, 2; Śatapatha Brāhmaṇa, iii. 8, 4, 4, etc.

[17] vi. 69, 8 = Av. vii. 44, 1 = Taittirīya Saṃhitā, iii. 2, 11, 2; Aitareya Brāhmaṇa, vi. 15; Śatapatha Brāhmaṇa, iii. 3, 1, 13.

[18] Rv. x. 90, 4.

[19] If *aṣṭa-karṇī* means in Rv. x. 62, 7, having the figure 8 marked on the ears' of cattle, then the mention of numerical signs would be certain. *Cf.* Zimmer, *Altindisches Leben*, 234, 235, 348. But this is doubtful. See Macdonell, *Vedic Grammar*, p. 309, n. 10.

Cf. Macdonell, *Vedic Grammar*, p. 308; Weber, *Indische Streifen*, 1, 90-103; Schrader, *Prehistoric Antiquities*, 349; Kaegi, *Rigveda*, n. 65; Hopkins, *Journal of the American Oriental Society*, 16, 275 *et seq*.

Daśa-puruṣaṃ-rājya, occurring in the Śatapatha Brāhmaṇa,[1] doubtless[2] means 'sovereignty inherited through ten ancestors,' a striking case of hereditary rule. Weber[3] once rendered the word as the 'kingdom[4] of Daśapuru,' comparing the Daśapura of Kālidāsa's Meghadūta[5] and the Daśārṇa of the 'middle country.'

[1] xii. 9, 3, 1. 3.

[2] *Cf.* Āśvalāyana Śrauta Sūtra, ix. 3; Śāṅkhāyana Śrauta Sūtra, xv. 14, 18. So *tri-puruṣa*, 'three generations,' Aitareya Brāhmaṇa, viii. 7. The St. Petersburg Dictionary, *s.v.*, and Eggeling, *Sacred Books of the East*, 44, 269, have the correct rendering.

[3] *Indische Studien*, 1, 209. But see 10, 75, n. 1.

[4] This would be *sāmrājya*, which is always spelt with *m*, not *ṃ*; *cf.* Macdonell, *Vedic Grammar*, 75, 3.

[5] i. 48.

Daśa-māsya, 'ten months old,' describes in the Rigveda[1] and later[2] the embryo immediately before birth. See **Māsa**.

[1] v. 78, 7. 8.

[2] Av. i. 11, 6; iii. 23, 2. There are several references in Vedic literature to birth in the tenth month, as Rv. x. 184, 3, etc.

Cf. Zimmer, *Altindisches Leben*, 366; Weber, *Naxatra*, 2, 313, n. 1.

Daśamī denotes in the Atharvaveda[1] and the Pañcaviṃśa Brāhmaṇa[2] the period of life between 90 and 100 years.

[1] iii. 4, 7.

[2] xxii. 14.

which the Rigveda[3] calls the *daśama yuga*, 'the tenth stage of life.' Longevity seems not to have been rare among the Vedic Indians, for the desire to live a 'hundred autumns' (*śaradaḥ śatam*) is constantly expressed.[4] **Dīrghatamas** is said to have lived 100 years,[5] and **Mahidāsa Aitareya** is credited with 116.[6] Onesikritos[7] reported that they sometimes lived 130 years, a statement with which corresponds the wish expressed in the Jātaka[8] for a life of 120 years. Probably the number was always rather imaginary than real, but the comparative brevity of modern life in India[9] may be accounted for by the cumulative effect of fever, which is hardly known to the Rigveda. See **Takman.**

[3] i. 158, 6.

[4] Rv. i. 89, 9; x. 18, 10, and *passim*. See Lanman, *Sanskrit Reader*, 384; Bloomfield, *Atharvaveda*, 62, 63.

[5] Śāṅkhāyana Āraṇyaka, ii. 17.

[6] Chāndogya Upaniṣad, iii. 16, 7; Jaiminīya Upaniṣad Brāhmaṇa, iv. 2, 11; Keith, *Aitareya Āraṇyaka*, 17.

[7] In Strabo, p. 701.

[8] Ed. Fausböll, ii. 16.

[9] *Indian Empire*, 1, 513 *et seq.*

Daśa-vṛkṣa is the name of a tree, according to Roth,[1] in the Atharvaveda.[2] But Whitney[3] treats the word as a mere adjective meaning 'of ten trees.'

[1] St. Petersburg Dictionary, *s.v.*

[2] ii. 9, 1.

[3] Translation of the Atharvaveda, 50.

Daśa-vraja is the name of a protégé of the Aśvins in the Rigveda (viii. 8, 20; 49, 1; 50, 9).

Daśa-śipra is the name of a sacrificer mentioned in the Rigveda.[1]

[1] viii. 52, 2. *Cf.* Ludwig, Translation of the Rigveda, 3, 163.

Daśā denotes the 'fringe' or 'border' of a garment (*vāsaḥ*) in the Śatapatha Brāhmaṇa.[1] The word also occurs in the compound *daśā-pavitra*,[2] which means 'a filtering cloth with a fringe.'

[1] iii. 3, 2, 9, and often in the Sūtras.

[2] Aitareya Brāhmaṇa, vii. 32; Śatapatha Brāhmaṇa, iv. 2, 2, 11. *Cf.* iv. 1, 1, 28.

Daśoṇi appears in one passage of the Rigveda[1] apparently as a favourite of Indra and as opposed to the **Paṇis,** who fell in hundreds for his benefit. The view of Ludwig[2] that he is here the priest of the Paṇis is very improbable. Elsewhere his name is simply mentioned.[3] See also **Daśoṇya.**

[1] vi. 20, 4. 8.

[2] Translation of the Rigveda, 3, 156; 5, 107.

[3] x. 96, 12, where, however, the word may be merely an epithet of Soma.

Cf. Hillebrandt, *Vedische Mythologie*, 1, 92, n. 1; Oldenberg, *Zeitschrift der Deutschen Morgenländischen Gesellschaft*, 55, 328.

Daśoṇya is the name of a sacrificer mentioned in the Rigveda[1] along with **Daśaśipra** and others. Whether he is identical with **Daśoṇi** cannot be decided.

[1] viii. 52, 2. *Cf.* Ludwig, Translation of the Rigveda, 3, 163.

Daśonasi is the name of a kind of snake in the Atharvaveda.[1] The reading of the Paippalāda recension is Naśonaśī.

[1] x. 4, 17. *Cf.* Zimmer, *Altindisches Leben*, 95; Whitney, Translation of the Atharvaveda, 577.

Dasyave vṛka, 'wolf to the **Dasyu,**' is the name of a man mentioned four times in the Rigveda.[1] In one hymn[2] he is called a Ṛṣi, but in two others[3] he is clearly a prince victorious over the Dasyus, and a generous patron of the singer. It is hardly necessary to assume different persons,[4] for the term Ṛṣi is not altogether inconsistent with royalty. He was son of **Pūtakratu**[5] and **Pūtakratā,**[6] his wife.

[1] viii. 51, 2; 55, 1; 56, 1. 2.

[2] viii. 51.

[3] viii. 55. 56.

[4] Especially as the name occurs only in the small collection of Kāṇva hymns forming the Vālakhilya group in the eighth Maṇḍala.

[5] viii. 56, 2, *Pautakrata.* *Cf.* viii. 68, 17.

[6] viii. 56, 4.

Cf. Ludwig, Translation of the Rigveda, 3, 139, 164; 5, 552.

Dasyave saha is, according to Roth,[1] the name of a man or a clan in the Rigveda.[2] But he admits that the words may

[1] St. Petersburg Dictionary, *s.v.*

[2] i. 36, 18.

be an epithet of Agni. This is the interpretation given to them by Oldenberg.[3]

[3] *Sacred Books of the East*, 46, 33.

Dasyu, a word of somewhat doubtful origin, is in many passages of the Rigveda[1] clearly applied to superhuman enemies. On the other hand, there are several passages in which human foes, probably the aborigines, are thus designated. This may be regarded as certain in those passages where the Dasyu is opposed to the Āryan, who defeats him with the aid of the gods.[2] The great difference between the Dasyus and the Āryans was their religion: the former are styled 'not sacrificing,' 'devoid of rites,' 'addicted to strange vows,' 'god-hating,' and so forth.[3] As compared with the **Dāsa**, they are less distinctively a people: no clans (*viśaḥ*) of the Dasyus are mentioned, and while Indra's *dasyu-hatya*, 'slaughter of the Dasyus,' is often spoken of, there is no corresponding use of *dāsa-hatya*. That the Dasyus were real people is, however, shown by the epitdet *anās* applied to them in one passage of the Rigveda.[5] The sense of this word is not absolutely certain: the Pada text and Sāyaṇa both take it to mean 'without face' (*an-ās*),[6] but the other rendering, 'noseless' (*a-nās*), is quite possible,[7]

[1] i. 34, 7; 100, 18; ii. 13, 9, etc. See Macdonell, *Vedic Mythology*, pp. 157, 158.

[2] Rv. i. 51, 8; 103, 3; 117, 21; ii. 11, 18. 19; iii. 34, 9; vi. 18, 3; vii. 5, 6; x. 49, 3. Probably also in v. 70, 3; x. 83, 6, people are meant.

[3] The Dasyu is called *a-karman*, 'riteless,' x. 22, 8; *a-devayu*, 'indifferent to the gods,' viii. 70, 11; *a-brahman*, 'without devotion,' iv. 16, 9; *a-yajvan*, 'not sacrificing,' viii. 70, 11; *a-yajyu*, *id.*, vii. 6, 3; *a-vrata*, 'lawless,' i. 51, 8; 175, 3; vi. 14, 3; ix. 41, 2; *anya-vrata*, 'following strange ordinances,' viii. 70, 11; *deva-pīyu*, 'reviling the gods,' Av. xii. 1, 37. It is impossible in all cases to be certain that people are meant.

[4] Rv. i. 51, 5. 6; 103, 4; x. 95, 7; 99, 7; 105, 11. *Cf. dasyu-han*, 'Dasyu-slaying,' i. 100, 12; vi. 45, 24; viii. 76, 11; 77, 3; x. 47, 4 (all of Indra); vi. 16, 15; viii. 39, 8 (of Agni), etc.

[5] Rv. v. 29, 10.

[6] This sense allows of two interpretations: 'misfeatured,' which seems that of Roth, St. Petersburg Dictionary, *s.v.*, and Grassmann, *Wörterbuch*; or 'speechless' (that is, unable to speak the language of the Āryans), which is that of Bollensen, *Zeitschrift der Deutschen Morgenländischen Gesellschaft*, 41, 496.

[7] This view is supported by Megasthenes' report as to natives who were ἄστομοι: see Strabo, p. 711; Pliny, *Nat. Hist.*, vii. 2, 18, cited by Zimmer, *Altindisches Leben*, 430. See also Ludwig, Translation of the Rigveda, 2, 109; 5, 95; Hillebrandt, *Vedische Mythologie*, 3, 277; Knauer, Kuhn's *Zeitschrift*, 29, 52; Wackernagel, *Altindische Grammatik*, 2, 293 (accent).

and would accord well with the flat-nosed aborigines of the Dravidian[8] type, whose language still persists among the Brahuis, who are found in the north-west. This interpretation would receive some support from Vṛtra's being called 'broken-nosed' if this were a correct explanation of the obscure word *rujānās*.[9]

The other epithet of the Dasyus is *mṛdhra-vāc*, which occurs with *anās*,[10] and which has been rendered[11] 'of stammering, or unintelligible speech.' This version is by no means certain, and since the epithet is elsewhere[12] applied to Āryans, its correct meaning is more probably 'of hostile speech.'

Dasyu corresponds with the Iranian *daṅhu, daqyu*, which denotes a 'province.' Zimmer[13] thinks that the original meaning was 'enemy,' whence the Iranians developed the sense of 'hostile country,' 'conquered country,' 'province,' while the Indians, retaining the signification of 'enemy,' extended it to include demon foes. Roth[14] considers that the meaning of human enemy is a transfer from the strife of gods

[8] The suggestion in the *Indian Empire*, 1, 390, that the modern Brahui type is the true Dravidian, while the modern Dravidian is the result of fusion with Muṇḍā-speaking tribes, would render this theory improbable. But it seems more probable that the Brahuis in speech preserve the tradition of Dravidian settlements in North India.

[9] See Bloomfield, *American Journal of Philology*, 17, 415 (who takes *rujānāḥ* of Rv. i. 32, 8, as = *rujāna-nāḥ*); Oldenberg, *Ṛgveda-Noten*, 1, 31, 32 (who suggests as possible the analysis of the word as *rujā-anāḥ*). But *cf.* Lanman, *Sanskrit Reader*, 361, who suggests the emendation *rujānaḥ* as nominative singular of the simple participle 'broken'; Macdonell, *Vedic Grammar*, p. 59, n. 1.

[10] Rv. v. 29, 10.

[11] *Cf.* Muir, *Sanskrit Texts*, 2[2], 393 *et seq.*

[12] The expression is used of the Āryan Pūrus in vii. 18, 13; of the Paṇis in vii. 6, 3; and of hostile persons in i. 174, 2; v. 32, 8; x. 23. 5. Roth, *Erläuterungen zum Nirukta*, 97, thinks the sense is 'of insulting speech,' and Zimmer, *op. cit.*, 114, 115, strongly supports this view. But Hillebrandt, *op. cit.*, 1, 89, 90, 114, prefers to see in it 'speaking an enemy's speech,' and thinks that the Pūrus were dialectically different from the Bharatas—a view which can be supported from the Śatapatha Brāhmaṇa, iii. 2, 1, 23. 24, where the Asuras say *he 'lavo* (= *he 'rayo*, 'ho, enemies,' in Sanskrit). See Muir, *op. cit.*, 2[2], 114; Davidson, *Zeitschrift der Deutschen Morgenländischen Gesellschaft*, 37, 23 (the Mahābhāṣya version); Eggeling, *Sacred Books of the East*, 26, 31, n. 3. The word could thus apply to the Dasyus also, as the strange speech of the enemy could be either Āryan or aboriginal.

[13] *Op. cit.*, 110 *et seq.* So Macdonell, *Vedic Mythology*, p. 158.

[14] St. Petersburg Dictionary, *s.v.*

and demons. Lassen[15] attempted to connect the contrast *daqyu : dasyu* with that of *daeva : deva*, and to see in it a result of the religious differences which, according to Haug's theory, had separated the Iranians and the Indians. The word may have originally meant 'ravaged land'[16] as a result of invasion; hence 'enemies' country,' then 'hostile people,' who as human foes were more usually called by the cognate name of **Dāsa.**

Individual Dasyus are **Cumuri, Śambara, Śuṣṇa,** etc.

In the Aitareya Brāhmaṇa[17] the word has, as later,[18] the sense of uncivilized peoples generally.

[15] *Indische Alterthumskunde*, 1², 633 *et seq*. This theory is now generally discredited. *Cf.* Justi, *Göttingische Gelehrte Anzeigen*, 1866, 1446 *et seq.*; Geldner, *Vedische Studien*, 1, 142; Oldenberg, *Religion des Veda*, 162 *et seq.*; Macdonell, *Vedic Mythology*, p. 156.

[16] Both this word and Dāsa appear to be derived from the root *das*, which, according to Whitney, *Roots*, means 'lay waste'; but, according to Roth, 'suffer want,' 'waste away.'

[17] vii. 18, where the descendants of Viśvāmitra are called *dasyūnāṃ bhūyiṣṭhāḥ*; Śāṅkhāyana Śrauta Sūtra, xv. 26, 7.

[18] Manu, v. 131; x. 32. 45; Zimmer, *op. cit.*, 118.

Cf. Hillebrandt, *op. cit.*, 3, 276 *et seq.*; Zimmer, *op. cit.*, 101 *et seq.*

Dākṣāyaṇa, 'descendant of Dakṣa.' The Dākṣāyaṇas are mentioned in the Atharvaveda and the Yajurveda Saṃhitās[1] as having given gold to **Śatānīka.** In the Śatapatha Brāhmaṇa[2] the word is actually used to denote 'gold.' The Dākṣāyaṇas appear there[3] as a race of princes who, because of performing a certain rite, prospered down to the time of the Brāhmaṇa itself.

[1] Av. i. 35, 1. 2; Vājasaneyi Saṃhitā, xxxiv. 51. 52; Kaṭha, cited by von Schroeder, *Tübinger Kaṭha-Handschriften*, 36; Khila, iv. 7, 7. 8.

[2] vi. 7, 4, 2: *dākṣāyaṇa-hasta*, 'golden-handed.' Eggeling, *Sacred Books of the East*, 41, 283, n. 2, seems unnecessarily doubtful as to this.

[3] ii. 4, 4, 6. *Cf.* Aitareya Brāhmaṇa, iii. 40.

Cf. Weber, *Indische Studien*, 1, 224; 4, 358; Ludwig, Translation of the Rigveda, 3, 195; Whitney, Translation of the Atharvaveda, 35; Lévi, *La Doctrine du Sacrifice*, 138.

Dātyauha, a 'gallinule,' is mentioned in the list of victims at the Aśvamedha, or horse sacrifice, in the Yajurveda.[1] The

[1] Taittirīya Saṃhitā, v. 5, 17, 1; Maitrāyaṇī Saṃhitā, iii. 14, 6; Vājasaneyi Saṃhitā, xxiv. 25. 39. Pāṇini, vii. 3, 1, derives the word from *ditya-vah*. *Cf.* Zimmer, *Altindisches Leben*, 91.

word is clearly a variant of *dātyūha*, which occurs in the epics and law books.

Dātra ('cutter'), denoting a 'sickle,' is mentioned in the Rigveda.[1] Cows 'with sickle-shaped marks on their ears' (*dātra-karṇyaḥ*) are referred to in the Maitrāyaṇī Saṃhitā.[2] Otherwise the expression is only found later, occurring in the Sūtra and epic literature.[3] See also **Sṛṇi.**

[1] viii. 78, 10; Nirukta, ii. 1.
[2] iv. 2, 9.
[3] Hopkins, *Journal of the American Oriental Society*, 17, 86.

Cf. Zimmer, *Altindisches Leben*, 238.

Dātreya is the patronymic of **Arāḍa Śaunaka** in the Vaṃśa Brāhmaṇa.[1] Possibly Dārteya, 'descendant of Dṛti,' should be read,[2] but the word may have the same derivation as the latter form with metathesis.

[1] *Indische Studien*, 4, 373.
[2] *Cf.* St. Petersburg Dictionary, *s.v.*

Dādhīca, 'descendant of **Dadhyanc**,' is the patronymic of **Cyavana** in the Pañcaviṃśa Brāhmaṇa (xiv. 6).

1. **Dāna,** 'giving,' 'gift,' is a word of frequent occurrence in the Rigveda, especially in the Dāna-stutis[1] ('Praises of Gifts') of generous patrons (see **Dakṣiṇā**). One of the characteristics of the **Brāhmaṇa** is his right to receive gifts, which it is obligatory on the other castes to present.[2] The gift of a daughter (*kanyāyā dānam*) was a form of marriage[3] (see **Vivāha**), because in it the girl was 'given' away by her father or brother.

[1] The term seems first to occur in the Bṛhaddevatā, vi. 45. 92, and in similar works.
[2] Satapatha Brāhmaṇa, xi. 5, 7, 1; Weber, *Indische Studien*, 10, 47-61.
[3] Nirukta, iii. 4.

2. **Dāna** ('distribution')[1] seems in several passages of the Rigveda[2] to be a designation of the sacrificial feast to which

[1] From *dā*, 'divide.'
[2] i. 55, 7; 48, 4; 180, 5; viii. 46, 26; 60, 8; 99, 4, etc. *Cf.*, however, Pischel *Vedische Studien*, 1, 100.

the god is invited (*cf.* δαίς, δαίτη). In one passage[3] Sāyaṇa thinks that it denotes the *mada-jalāni*, 'drops of water falling from the temples of a rutting elephant,'[4] but this is doubtful. In another passage[5] Roth thinks that 'pasture land' is meant.

[3] Rv. viii. 33, 8; Ludwig, Translation of the Rigveda, 5, 157.

[4] Dāna in this sense, so common in the post-Vedic language, is probably derived from *dā*, 'divide,' meaning originally 'secretion.'

[5] ii. 13, 7.

3. **Dāna** is in three passages of the Rigveda[1] held by Roth to designate a chariot horse.

[1] v. 27, 5; vii. 18, 23; viii. 46, 24. But in all these cases 'gifts' seems an adequate version, 'horses' being understood.

Dāman, a 'rope' or 'girdle,'[1] is often mentioned in the Rigveda and later.[2] Reference is made to the rope of the sacrificial horse,[3] as well as to the practice of tying calves with ropes.[4] The word occurs in the sense of a 'band' of horse hair in the Śatapatha Brāhmaṇa.[5]

[1] Originally 'bond,' from *dā*, 'bind.'

[2] Rv. i. 56, 3, etc.; Av. vi. 63, 1; 103, 2; vii. 103, 1. 2; Taittirīya Saṃhitā, ii. 4, 13, 1, etc.

[3] Rv. i. 162, 8.

[4] Rv. ii. 28, 7.

[5] v. 3, 1, 10. *Cf.* Eggeling, *Sacred Books of the East*, 41, 62, n. 2.

Dāya occurs in the Rigveda[1] only in the sense of 'reward' of exertion (*śrama*), but later it means 'inheritance'—that is, a father's property which is to be divided among his sons either during his lifetime or after his death. The passages all negative the idea that the property of the family was legally family property: it is clear that it was the property of the head of the house, usually the father, and that the other members of the family only had moral claims upon it which the father could ignore, though he might be coerced by his sons if they were physically stronger.

Thus **Manu** is said in the Taittirīya Saṃhitā[2] to have divided his property among his sons. He omitted **Nābhānediṣṭha**,

[1] x. 114, 10.

[2] iii. 1, 9, 4 *et seq.* *Cf.* Muir, *Sanskrit Texts*, 1^2, 191-194; Lévi, *La Doctrine du Sacrifice*, 67, 68.

whom he afterwards taught how to appease the Aṅgirases, and to procure cows. This is a significant indication that the property he divided was movable property, rather than land (**Urvarā**). In the Aitareya Brāhmaṇa[3] the division is said to have been made during Manu's lifetime by his sons, who left only their aged father to Nābhānediṣṭha. According to the Jaiminīya Brāhmaṇa,[4] again, four sons divided the inheritance while their old father, Abhipratārin, was still alive. It is, of course, possible to regard Dāya as denoting the heritable property of the family, but the developed *patria potestas* of the father, which was early very marked, as shown by the legend of **Śunaḥśepa**, is inconsistent with the view that the sons were legally owners with their father, unless and until they actually insisted on a division of the property.[5] Probably—there is no evidence of any decisive character—land was not divided at first, but no doubt its disposal began to follow the analogy of cattle and other movable property as soon as the available supply of arable land became limited.

As for the method of division, it is clear from the Taittirīya Saṃhitā[6] that the elder son was usually preferred; perhaps

[3] v. 14.

[4] iii. 156 (*Journal of the American Oriental Society*, 26, 61, 62).

[5] The same question has been raised as to the origin of English or Teutonic property in land generally. Against any idea even of family ownership in a strict sense of the word, see Fustel de Coulanges, *Recherches sur quelques Problèmes d'Histoire*, 322 *et seq.*; Ashley, in Fustel de Coulanges, *Origin of Property in Land*, xvi xxi; Pollock and Maitland, *History of English Law*, 2, 237 *et seq.* The older view, which accepted family and communal ownership, represented in different forms by Maine (*Village Communities in the East and West*), Stubbs, Green, and others, is defended in a new form by Vinogradoff, *Villanage in England*. See also Keith, *Journal of the African Society*, 6, 201 *et seq.* Jolly, *Recht und Sitte*, 93-96, does not accept the communal ownership of land, but, *ibid.*, 80, is inclined to believe in the joint ownership of a family. He admits that this is inconsistent with the strict rule of *patria potestas*, which still exists in Bengal; Baden Powell, *Village Communities in India*, 133 *et seq.*, doubts the existence in early India of such a *patria potestas*. But the facts seem clearly to show that there was such a power, and that the father owned the property. His sons, as they grew up, came to claim the property, and he might have to divide it; hence the idea naturally developed that every child on birth had a legal share in the property. No doubt also from the first the right to part with land was one which grown-up sons and the rest of the community could object to, once the village had acquired a fixed existence. This would account adequately for the later system. *Cf.* also pp. 100, n. 19; 336, n. 7, and **Rājanya.**

[6] ii. 5, 2, 7.

this was always the case after death. During the father's lifetime another might be preferred, as appears from a passage of the Pañcaviṃśa Brāhmaṇa.[7] Women were excluded from partition or inheritance, according to the Śatapatha Brāhmaṇa[8] and the Nirukta.[9] They were, no doubt, supported by their brothers; but if they had none they might be reduced to prostitution.[10] Detailed rules of inheritance appear in the Sūtras.[11] The heir is called Dāyāda,[12] 'receiver (*ā-da*) of inheritance.'

[7] xvi. 4, 4.

[8] iv. 4, 2, 13.

[9] iii. 4.

[10] *Cf.* **Strī.**

[11] Inheritance is also alluded to in the Aitareya Brāhmaṇa, vii. 17; Śāṅkhāyana Śrauta Sūtra, xv. 27, 3; Śatapatha Brāhmaṇa, i. 7, 2, 22; iii. 2, 1, 18. For the Sūtra rules, see Jolly, *Recht und Sitte*, 80 *et seq.*

[12] Śatapatha Brāhmaṇa, xii. 4, 3, 9; Nirukta, iii. 4; metaphorically, Av. v. 18, 6. 14.

Dāra, 'wife,' is found in the Sūtras (usually as a plural masculine), and once (as a singular) in the Bṛhadāraṇyaka Upaniṣad.[1]

[1] vi. 4, 12 (where *dvāreṇa* is a *varia lectio*; see St. Petersburg Dictionary, *s.v.*). *Cf.* Delbrück, *Die indogermanischen Verwandtschaftsnamen*, 415, 416, who ignores the Bṛhadāraṇyaka passage.

Dāru, 'wood,' is frequently mentioned in the Rigveda and later,[1] denoting amongst other things the pole of a chariot,[2] logs as fuel,[3] the wooden parts of a car,[4] possibly wooden stocks,[5] and so forth.

[1] Rv. vi. 3, 4; x. 145, 4, etc.; Av. x. 4, 3; Taittirīya Saṃhitā, ii. 5, 8, 3, etc.

[2] Rv. x. 102, 8.

[3] Rv. viii. 102, 20.

[4] Śatapatha Brāhmaṇa, vi. 6, 2, 14.

[5] Av. vi. 121, 2. But this is doubtful. *Cf.* **Tāyu** and **Drupada.**

Dārḍha-jayanti, 'descendant of **Dṛḍhajayanta**,' is the patronymic of **Vaipaścita Gupta Lauhitya** and of **Vaipaścita Dṛḍhajayanta Lauhitya** in the Jaiminīya Upaniṣad Brāhmaṇa (iii. 42, 1).

Dārteya, 'descendant of **Dṛti**.' The Dārteyas are mentioned as authorities on sacrificial matters in the Kāṭhaka Saṃhitā[1] and the Pañcaviṃśa Brāhmaṇa.[2]

[1] xxxi. 2 (*Indische Studien*, 3, 473).

[2] xxv. 3, 6.

Dārbhya, 'descendant of Darbha,' is mentioned in a verse of the Rigveda.[1] Roth[2] identifies him with **Śyāvāśva,** but the Bṛhaddevatā[3] with **Rathavīti.** The same patronymic is frequently[4] connected with **Keśin,** and is also applied to **Rathaprota.**[5] See also **Dālbhya.**

[1] v. 61, 17.
[2] St. Petersburg Dictionary, *s.v.*
[3] v. 50. 77.
[4] Taittirīya Saṃhitā, ii. 6, 2, 3; Maitrāyaṇī Saṃhitā, i. 4, 12; 6, 5; Kauṣītaki Brāhmaṇa, vii. 4. *Cf.* Sieg, *Die Sagenstoffe des Ṛgveda*, 62, n. 2.
[5] Maitrāyaṇī Saṃhitā, ii. 1, 3.

Dārv-āghāta, the 'woodpecker,' is included in the list of sacrificial victims at the Aśvamedha, or 'horse sacrifice,' in the Yajurveda.[1]

[1] Taittirīya Saṃhitā, v. 5, 15, 1; Maitrāyaṇī Saṃhitā, iii. 14, 16; Vājasaneyi Saṃhitā, xxiv. 35. *Cf.* Zimmer, *Altindisches Leben*, 92.

Dārv-āhāra, a 'gatherer of wood,' is included in the list of victims at the Puruṣamedha, or 'human sacrifice,' in the Yajurveda.[1]

[1] Vājasaneyī Saṃhitā, xxx. 12; Taittirīya Brāhmaṇa, iii. 4, 8, 1.

Dālbhi, 'descendant of Dalbha,' is the patronymic of **Vaka** in the Kāṭhaka Saṃhitā (x. 6).

Dālbhya, 'descendant of Dalbha,' is a variant of **Dārbhya.** It is the patronymic of (*a*) **Keśin** in the Pañcaviṃśa Brāhmaṇa;[1] (*b*) **Caikitāyana** in the Chāndogya Upaniṣad[2] and the Jaiminīya Upaniṣad Brāhmaṇa;[3] (*c*) **Vaka** in the Chāndogya Upaniṣad[4] and the Kāṭhaka Saṃhitā.[5]

[1] xiii. 10, 8. *Cf.* the Itihāsa, reported by Ṣaḍguruśiṣya (Sarvānukramaṇī, ed. Macdonell, 118). The St. Petersburg Dictionary quotes the Kauṣītaki Brāhmaṇa, vii. 4, for Dālbhya (but also for Dārbhya, which is the reading of Lindner's edition).
[2] i. 8, 1.
[3] i. 38, 1; 56, 3.
[4] i. 2, 13; 12, 1. 3.
[5] xxx. 2, where Dālbhya is read, not Dālbhi, as stated in the St. Petersburg Dictionary, *s.v.* The Kapiṣṭhala Saṃhitā, xlvi. 5, has *Darbhasya*. Dālbhi is found, however, in Kāṭhaka Saṃhitā, x. 6.

Dāva, 'forest fire,' is mentioned in the Atharvaveda[1] and the Śatapatha Brāhmaṇa.[2] In the latter work such fires are referred to as occurring in spring. According to Sieg,[3] a hymn of the Rigveda[4] describes a forest fire. Watchers were employed to guard against surprise from such conflagrations (*dāva-pa*).[5]

1 vii. 45, 2.
2 xi. 2, 7, 32.
3 *Die Sagenstoffe des Ṛgveda*, 44 *et seq*.
4 x. 142. Sieg's interpretation of this hymn is not at all probable.
5 Vājasaneyi Saṃhitā, xxx. 16; Taittirīya Brāhmaṇa, iii. 4, 11, 1.

Dāva-su Āṅgirasa, a seer of Sāmans, or chants, is mentioned in the Pañcaviṃśa Brāhmaṇa.[1]

1 xxv. 5, 12. 14. *Cf.* Hillebrandt, *Vedische Mythologie*, 2, 160.

Dāśa, 'fisherman,' is mentioned in the list of victims at the Puruṣamedha, or 'human sacrifice,' in the Yajurveda.[1] *Cf.* **Dhaivara.**

1 Vājasaneyi Saṃhitā, xxx. 16; Taittirīya Brāhmaṇa, iii. 4, 12, 1. Weber, *Indische Streifen*, 1, 81, renders the word by *Fischerknecht*, perhaps regarding it as equivalent to *dāsa*, 'servant.' *Cf.* Manu, x. 34; St. Petersburg Dictionary, *s.v.* Dāśa, 2. 3.

Dāśataya, 'belonging to the (Rigveda text) divided into ten (books),' is an epithet of Adhyāya, 'section,' in the Nidāna Sūtra.[1] The feminine form of the word is also found in the Kauṣītaki Brāhmaṇa[2] and later.[3]

1 ii. 11 (*Indische Studien*, 1, 45).
2 viii. 7.
3 Ṛgveda Prātiśākhya, xvi. 54; xvii. 30; Śāṅkhāyana Śrauta Sūtra, xii. 2, 16. 22, etc.; Baudhāyana Śrauta Sūtra, xxvi. 13; xxvii. 4, etc.

Dāśa-rājña is the name in the Rigveda[1] and the Atharvaveda[2] of **Sudās'** famous 'battle with the ten kings.' It is somewhat difficult to make out exactly who the kings were (see **Turvaśa**), but the number is probably a round one, and cannot be pressed. The actual battle hymn[3] does not contain

1 vii. 33, 2. 5; 83. 8.
2 x. 128, 12.
3 vii. 18.

the word, and the passages in which it is found may reasonably be considered late.[4]

[4] *Cf.* for the late date of vii. 33, Bergaigne, *L'histoire de la Saṃhita*, 38, 72; Oldenberg, *Prolegomena*, 198, 260, 265, n. 1; Arnold, *Vedic Metre*, 309; Geldner, *Vedische Studien*, 2, 130, opposes this view, but not convincingly.

Dāśarma appears in the Kāṭhaka Saṃhitā[1] as a teacher and a contemporary of **Āruṇi.**

[1] vii. 6. *Cf.* Weber, *Indische Studien*, 3, 472.

Dāsa, like **Dasyu,** sometimes denotes enemies of a demoniac character in the Rigveda,[1] but in many passages[2] the word refers to human foes of the Āryans. The Dāsas are described as having forts (*puraḥ*),[3] and their clans (*viśaḥ*) are mentioned.[4] It is possible that the forts, which are called 'autumnal' (*śāradīḥ*),[5] may be mythical, but it is not essential, for the epithet may allude to their being resorted to in the autumn season. The Dāsa colour (**Varṇa**)[6] is probably an allusion to the black skin of the aborigines, which is also directly mentioned.[7] The aborigines (as Dasyus) are called *anās*, 'noseless' (?),[8] and *mṛdhra-vāc*, 'of hostile speech,'[9] and are probably meant by the phallus-worshippers (*śiśna-devāḥ*, 'whose deity is a phallus') of the Rigveda.[10] It is significant that constant

[1] *Cf.* Macdonell, *Vedic Mythology*, p. 157.

[2] *Cf.* Rv. v. 34, 6; vi. 22, 10; 33, 3; 60, 6; vii. 83, 1; x. 38, 3; 69, 6; 83, 1; Av. v. 11, 3.

[3] ii. 20, 8 (called *āyasīḥ*, 'made of iron'); i. 103, 3; iii. 12, 6; iv. 32, 10. They are called *śāradīḥ*, 'autumnal,' in i. 131, 4; 174, 2; vi. 20, 10. *Cf.* also *dehyaḥ*, 'ramparts,' in vi. 47, 2.

[4] ii. 11, 4; iv. 28, 4; vi. 25, 2.

[5] *Cf.* Macdonell, *Vedic Mythology*, p. 60.

[6] ii. 12, 4; Śāṅkhāyana Śrauta Sūtra, viii. 25, 6. *Cf.* Rv. i. 101, 1; 130, 8; ii. 20, 7; iv. 16, 13; vi. 47, 21; vii. 5, 3. The Ārya colour is mentioned in iii. 34, 9, and the Dāsa is contrasted with the Varṇa (of the singers) in i. 104, 2. The 'white-hued (*śvitnya*) friends' who, in i. 100, 18, aid in the conquest of the Dasyu and Simyu are doubtless Āryans. In the Vājasaneyi Saṃhitā, xxiv. 30, the day and night (*ahorātre*) are paralleled with the Śūdrāryau—that is, probably with the Āryan and Śūdra (the compound is not to be taken as giving the words in the correct order; *cf.* Macdonell, *Vedic Grammar*, 268). See also Muir, *Sanskrit Texts*, 1^2, 140; Weber, *Indische Studien*, 10, 10, 11.

[7] *kṛṣṇā tvac*, 'black skin,' i. 130, 8; ix. 41, 1.

[8] *Cf.* **Dasyu**, notes 6, 7.

[9] v. 29, 10. See **Dasyu**; Geldner, *Rigveda, Glossar*, 138.

[10] vii. 21, 5; x. 99, 3. *Cf.* Macdonell, *op. cit.*, p. 155.

reference is made to the differences in religion between Ārya and Dāsa or Dasyu.[11]

Since the Dāsas were in many cases reduced to slavery, the word Dāsa has the sense of 'slave' in several passages of the Rigveda.[12] Dāsī, the feminine, always has this sense from the Atharvaveda[13] onwards. Aboriginal women were, no doubt, the usual slaves, for on their husbands being slain in battle they would naturally have been taken as servants. They would sometimes also become concubines; thus **Kavaṣa** was taunted with being the son of a female slave (*dāsyāḥ putraḥ*) in the Aitareya Brāhmaṇa.[14]

Ludwig[15] considers that in some passages[16] Dāsa is applied, in the sense of 'enemy,' to Āryan foes, but this is uncertain. Zimmer[17] and Meyer[18] think that Dāsa[19] originally meant 'enemy' in general, later developing in Iran into the name of the Dahae[20] of the Caspian steppes, and in India into a designation of the aborigines. On the other hand, Hillebrandt[21] argues that, as the Dāsas and the Paṇis are mentioned together,[22] they must be deemed to be closely related tribes, identifying

[11] Rv. i. 33, 4. 5; iv. 16, 9; v. 7, 10; 42, 9; vi. 14, 3; viii. 70, 10; x. 22, 7. 8, etc.

[12] vii. 86, 7; viii. 56, 3; x. 62, 10. Roth, St. Petersburg Dictionary, *s.v.*, 2, suggests that in viii. 46, 32, the word *dāsān*, 'slaves,' should be read in place of *dāse*, qualifying **Balbūtha**. Zimmer, *Altindisches Leben*, 117, quotes the passage to indicate the admixture of Āryan and Dāsa blood. See also Av. iv. 9, 8; Chāndogya Upaniṣad, vii. 24, 2. It is uncertain whether *dāsa-pravarga*, as an epithet of *rayi*, 'wealth,' in Rv. i. 92, 8, means 'consisting of troops of slaves.' Geldner, *Rigveda*, *Glossar*, 82, so takes the expression in i. 158, 5.

[13] Av. v. 22, 6; xii. 3, 13; 4, 9; Chāndogya Upaniṣad, v. 13, 2; Bṛhadāraṇyaka Upaniṣad, vi. 1, 10 (Mādhyaṃdina = 2, 7 Kāṇva). Zimmer, 107, sees this sense in *vadhū* in Rv. viii. 19, 36. See also **Vadhūmant**.

[14] ii. 19; Kauṣītaki Brāhmaṇa, xii. 3.

[15] Translation of the Rigveda, 3, 209.

[16] See i. 158, 5; ii. 13, 8; iv. 30, 14. 15; vi. 20, 10; vii. 99, 5; x. 49, 6. 7. None of these passages need certainly be so taken.

[17] *Altindisches Leben*, 110 *et seq.*

[18] *Geschichte des Altertums*, 1, 515.

[19] If derived from *das* in the sense of 'lay waste' (Whitney, *Roots*), the original meaning would have been 'devastator,' 'ravager.'

[20] The Dahae may have been closely allied in race and language with the Iranians, but this is not very clearly proved. *Cf.* E. Kuhn in Kuhn's *Zeitschrift*, 28, 214; Hillebrandt, *Vedische Mythologie*, 1, 95. The possibility or probability of mixture with Mongolian blood is always present. So Zimmer, *op. cit.*, 112, calls the Daoi or Daai of Herodotus, i. 126, a Turanian tribe.

[21] *Op. cit.*, 1, 94.

[22] Rv. v. 34, 6. 7; vii. 6, 3 (Dasyu and Paṇi together); Av. v. 11, 6.

the Paṇis with the Parnians and the Dāsas of the Rigveda with the Dahae. This view, of course, necessitates a transfer of the scenes of the Rigveda, where Dāsas are prominent, and especially those in which Divodāsa—'the heavenly Dāsa'—plays an important part,[23] to the far west. Hillebrandt justifies this by regarding the scene of the sixth book of the Rigveda as quite different from that of the seventh and third, in which Sudās, the Bharatas, Vasiṣṭha, and Viśvāmitra appear. The Sarasvatī of the sixth book he locates in Arachosia, that of the seventh in the 'Middle Country.' It is, however, extremely doubtful whether this theory can be upheld. That Divodāsa should have been a Dāsa, and yet have fought against other Dāsas, is not in itself likely, especially when his son Sudās appears as a protagonist of Āryan civilization. It also seems unreasonable to seek in Arachosia for the river **Sarasvatī**, which it is natural to locate in the 'Middle Country.'

The wealth of the Dāsas was no doubt considerable,[24] but in civilization there is no reason to suppose that they were ever equal to the invaders.[25] Leading Dāsas were **Ilībiśa**, **Cumuri** and **Dhuni**, **Pipru**, **Varcin**, **Śambara**. For names of aboriginal tribes, see **Kirāta**, **Kīkaṭa**, **Caṇḍāla**, **Parṇaka**, **Śiṃyu**.

[23] *Op. cit.*, 1, 96 *et seq.* He argues that Dāsa occurs only four times in Maṇḍala vii., but eight times in vi., and that similarly Śambara, the Dāsa, is mentioned six times in vi., but only twice in vii. But Divodāsa much more probably means, as Oldenberg interprets the name, 'the servant of heaven.' See his *Religion des Veda*, 155, n. 1; Bergaigne, *Religion Védique*, 2, 209; below, p. 363, n. 11.

[24] *Cf.* Rv. i. 176, 4; iv. 30, 13; viii. 40, 6; x. 69, 5; Av. vii. 90, 2.

[25] *Cf.* Rv. ii. 12, 11; iv. 30, 14; vi. 26, 5, whence it appears that the Dāsas were often dwellers in mountains, a natural refuge for beaten tribes.

Cf. Hillebrandt, *Vedische Mythologie*, 3, 269-275, 368; Ludwig, Translation of the Rigveda, 3, 207-213; Zimmer, *Altindisches Leben*, 101-118; Weber, *Indische Studien*, 18, 35 (who derives *dāsa* from *dā*, 'bind'), 254; Muir, *Sanskrit Texts*, 2, 359 *et seq.*; Geldner, *Vedische Studien*, 3, 96.

Dāsa-veśa, occurring only once in the Rigveda,[1] probably designates a Dāsa named **Veśa**. Sāyaṇa's interpretation of the word as 'destruction of foes' can hardly be correct.

[1] ii. 13, 8. *Cf.* Ludwig, Translation of the Rigveda, 3, 209.

Dāsya occurs once in the Bṛhadāraṇyaka Upaniṣad (iv. 2, 30 Mādhyaṃdina = 23 Kāṇva) in the sense of 'slavery.'

Ditya-vāh, m.; **Dityauhī**, f., 'a two-year-old bull or cow,' is mentioned in the later Saṃhitās and the Brāhmaṇas.[1]

1 Taittirīya Saṃhitā, iv. 3, 3, 1; v. 6, 15, 1; Vājasaneyi Saṃhitā, xiv. 10; xviii. 26; xxviii. 25; Pañcaviṃśa Brāhmaṇa, xxi. 1, etc.

Didyu, Didyut, both[1] denote in the Rigveda 'missile,' 'arrow,' whether divine or human.

1 Didyu: i. 71, 5; iv. 41, 4; vii. 56, 9; 85, 2, etc.; Av. i. 2, 3; Vājasaneyi Saṃhitā, ii. 20; x. 17, etc. Didyut: Rv. i. 66, 7; v. 86, 3; vii. 25, 1, etc.; certainly divine in ii. 13, 7.

Didhiṣu in the Rigveda denotes a 'wooer.' It is applied[1] to the relative, probably brother-in-law,[2] who takes the place of the husband at the funeral rite, and who, as in the Hebraic levirate, is to beget a child by the brother's wife if there is no son.[3] Hillebrandt[4] and Lanman[5] consider that the word originally meant only 'wooer,' and applied to the king who, after the chief queen had lain beside the dead victim in the Puruṣamedha or 'human sacrifice,' claimed her again; but this view is hardly plausible.[6] The term is also applied to the god Pūṣan[7] as the wooer of his mother, apparently Sūryā.[8]

1 x. 18, 18 = Av. xviii. 3, 2 (where *didhiṣos* is merely a bad reading) = Taittirīya Āraṇyaka, vi. 1, 3.

2 Āśvalāyana Śrauta Sūtra, iv. 2, 18, where are mentioned the brother-in-law (*devṛ*), a representative of the husband (there is nothing to show whether he is identical with the preceding or not), a pupil, or an aged servant (*jarad-dāsa*).

3 *Cf.* Rv. x. 40, 2; Kaegi, *Der Rigveda*, n. 51.

4 *Zeitschrift der Deutschen Morgenländischen Gesellschaft*, 40, 708 *et seq.*

5 *Sanskrit Reader*, 385.

6 See Whitney, Translation of the Atharvaveda, 848, 849; Keith, *Journal of the Royal Asiatic Society*, 1907, 946.

7 vi. 55, 5.

8 *Cf.* Pischel, *Vedische Studien*, 1, 21; Macdonell, *Vedic Mythology*, p. 35. *Cf.* Geldner, *Rigveda, Kommentar*, 154.

Didhiṣū-pati occurs in the Kāṭhaka[1] and Kapiṣṭhala Saṃhitās,[2] as well as in the Āpastamba,[3] Gautama,[4] and Vasiṣṭha

1 xxxi. 7, quoted in Delbrück, *Die indogermanischen Verwandtschaftsnamen*, 579.

2 xlvii. 7, quoted *ibid.*, 579, 580.

3 ii. 5, 12, 22.

4 xv. 16.

Dharma Sūtras,[5] in lists of people who have committed sin (*enas*). The traditional rendering[6] is 'husband of a woman married a second time'; Manu[7] seems to apply the term to the brother-in-law who is 'married' to his sister-in-law after his brother's death for the purpose of begetting a child, if he displays conjugal affection to her (*anurajyate kāmataḥ*).[8] This sense would be possible, since **Didhiṣu** denotes a 'wooer,' and a widow could be regarded as a 'wooer' when able to control her own choice of a spouse. But another tradition[9] holds that Didhiṣū means the elder sister whose younger sister has married before her. This view is supported by a passage in the Vasiṣṭha Dharma Sūtra,[10] and by the use of the word *agre-didhiṣū-pati*,[11] which must mean the 'husband of a younger sister married before the elder.' In this case also Didhiṣū would mean 'wooer,' the elder sister being so called because, if her parents do not arrange a marriage for her, she is, according to Viṣṇu,[12] to make her own choice of a husband (*kuryāt svayaṃvaram*). See also **Edidhiṣuḥpati** and **Daidhiṣavya.**

[5] i. 18; xx. 7 *et seq.*

[6] St. Petersburg Dictionary, *s.v.* *didhiṣu*, 3.

[7] iii. 173.

[8] *Cf.* Leist, *Altarisches Jus Gentium*, 106.

[9] Laugākṣi, quoted by Kullūka on Manu, iii. 160; Commentary on Āpastamba, *loc. cit.*

[10] xx. 7 *et seq.*

[11] *Cf. agre-didhiṣu*, 'one who woos (a younger sister) before (her elder sister is married),' in Āpastamba, *loc. cit.*; Gautama, xv. 16; Vasiṣṭha, i. 18; Kāṭhaka, *loc. cit.*; *agre-dadhus*, Maitrāyaṇī Saṃhitā, iv. 1, 9; *agre-dadhiṣu*, Kapiṣṭhala, *loc. cit.*; *agra-didhiṣu*, Taittirīya Brāhmaṇa, iii. 2, 8, 11.

[12] Viṣṇu Dharma Sūtra, xxiv. 40. *Cf.* Delbrück, *op. cit.*, 579-586.

Div, 'sky.' The world as a whole is regarded as divided into the three domains of 'earth,' 'air' or 'atmosphere,' and 'heaven' or 'sky' (*div*),[1] or alternatively into 'heaven and earth' (*dyāvā-pṛthivī*),[2] which two are then considered as comprising the universe, the atmosphere being included in the sky. Lightning, wind, and rain belong to the atmosphere, solar and

[1] Rv. ii. 40; viii. 6, 15; 10, 6; 90, 6, etc.

[2] Rv. i. 143, 2; 159, 1; 160, 1; iv. 14, 2, etc.; Bṛhadāraṇyaka Upaniṣad, iii. 8, 3. 9; Chāndogya Upaniṣad, vii. 4, 2; viii. 1, 3. In the Aitareya Āraṇyaka, iii. 1, 2, and the Śāṅkhāyana Āraṇyaka, vii. 3, it is said that when heavy and constant rain falls people say, 'Heaven and earth have united.'

similar phenomena to the sky. In some passages[3] the vault (*nāka*) of the sky is added after the usual triad, and before the celestial light (*svar, jyotis*).

The threefold division of the universe is reflected in a threefold division of the three elements—earth, air, and sky. Thus a highest (*uttama*,[4] *uttara*,[5] *pārya*[6]), a middle, and a lowest heaven are specified.[4] In the Atharvaveda[7] the three heavens are distinguished as 'rich in water' (*udanvatī*), as *pīlumatī* (of uncertain meaning), and as the *pradyaus*, where the Fathers sit. Heaven is frequently called *vyoman* as well as *rocana*[8] (properly the 'luminous space' of heaven), and the dividing firmament which separates the visible upper world from the highest heaven is called, besides *nāka*, 'vault,' *sānu*, 'summit,' *viṣṭap*, 'surface,' and *pṛṣṭha*, 'ridge,' and even 'ridge of the vault,'[9] or 'summit of the vault.'[10]

Similarly three atmospheres (*rajas*), or oftener two, are alluded to,[11] but the division here is merely artificial. In one passage[12] six *rajāṃsi*, 'regions,' are referred to, the heavens and the earths no doubt being meant. The usual name for the atmosphere is *antarikṣa*.

The three earths are equally artificial, the origin of the triad being probably the use of *pṛthivī* in the plural[13] to denote the three divisions of the universe (just as *pitarau*, 'two fathers,' denotes 'father and mother').[14] The earth is called *kṣam*, *kṣā*, *gmā*, or designated by the epithets *mahī*, 'the great,' *pṛthivī* or *urvī*, 'the broad,' *uttānā*, 'the extended,' and is regularly contrasted as *idam*, 'this world here,' with the upper sphere.[15]

3 Av. iv. 14, 3 = Vājasaneyi Saṃhitā, xvii. 67.

4 Rv. v. 60, 6.

5 Rv. iv. 26, 6.

6 Rv. vi. 40, 5. In Rv. v. 4, 3, it is called *tṛtīya*.

7 xviii. 2, 48.

8 *Trīṇi* or *tri rocanā*, Rv. i. 102, 8; 149, 4; v. 69, 1, etc.

9 Rv. i. 125, 5. *Cf.* iii. 2, 12.

10 Rv. viii. 103, 2. *Cf.* also ix. 86, 27.

11 Rv. iv. 53, 5; v. 69, 1. *Cf.* also the references to the 'highest' atmosphere, *uttama*, ix. 22, 5; *parama*, iii. 30, 2; *tṛtīya*, ix. 74, 6; x. 45, 3; 123, 8. The 'lower' (*upara*) or 'terrestrial' (*pārthiva*) is contrasted with the 'heavenly' (*divya*) space. See i. 62, 5; iv. 53, 3.

12 Rv. i. 164, 6. *Cf.* vii. 87, 5.

13 Rv. i. 188, 9. 10; vii. 104, 11.

14 *Cf.* Delbrück, *Altindische Syntax*, p. 98; Macdonell, *Sanskrit Grammar*, 183*c* (p. 158).

15 Rv. i. 22, 17; 154, 1. 3; and regularly in the later Saṃhitās and the Brāhmaṇas.

The shape of the earth is compared with a wheel in the Rigveda,[16] and is expressly called 'circular' (*pari-maṇḍala*) in the Śatapatha Brāhmaṇa.[17] When earth is conjoined with heaven, the two are conceived as great bowls (*camvā*) turned towards each other.[18] In the Aitareya Āraṇyaka[19] the two are regarded as halves of an egg. The distance of heaven from the earth is given by the Atharvaveda[20] as a thousand days' journey for the sun-bird, by the Aitareya Brāhmaṇa[21] as a thousand days' journey for a horse, while the Pañcaviṃśa Brāhmaṇa[22] whimsically estimates the distance as equivalent to a thousand cows standing one on the top of the other.

According to Zimmer,[23] the Vedic poets conceived the atmosphere to be above the earth in its upper division only, but below it in its lower stratum. The evidence,[24] however, for the latter assumption is quite insufficient.[25] The theory of the Aitareya Brāhmaṇa[26] is that the sun merely reverses its bright side at night, turning its light on the stars and the moon while it retraverses its course to the east; and it has been shown[25] that this is probably the doctrine of the Rigveda also.[27] See also **Sūrya** and **Candramās.** For the Vedic knowledge of the planets, see **Graha.**

There is no geographical division of the earth in Vedic literature. The Jaiminīya Upaniṣad Brāhmaṇa[28] states that the centre of the earth is a span north of the **Plakṣa Prāsravaṇā,** and that the centre of the sky is the constellation of the seven Ṛṣis, the Great Bear. For the quarters, see **Diś.**

16 x. 89, 4. On the other hand, the earth is regarded as *catur-bhṛṣṭi*, 'four-cornered,' in Rv. x. 58, 3.

17 Macdonell, *Vedic Mythology*, p. 9.

18 Rv. iii. 55, 20.

19 iii. 1, 2; Śāṅkhāyana Āraṇyaka, vii. 3.

20 x. 8, 18 = xiii. 2, 38; 3, 14.

21 ii. 17. *Cf.* **Āśvina.**

22 xvi. 8, 6; in xxi. 1, 9, with the alternatives of 1,000 days of the journey of a horse, or of the sun, or 1,000 leagues.

23 *Altindisches Leben*, 357, 358.

24 Rv. v. 81, 4; vi. 9, 1; vii. 80, 1.

25 Macdonell, *Vedic Mythology*, p. 10.

26 iii. 44, 4. Speyer's interpretation of this passage, *Journal of the Royal Asiatic Society*, 1906, 723-727, is anticipated and supplemented by Macdonell, *loc. cit.*

27 i. 115, 5; x. 37, 3.

28 iv. 26, 12. *Cf.* Pañcaviṃśa Brāhmaṇa, xxv. 10, 16; Hopkins, *Transactions of the Connecticut Academy of Arts and Sciences*, 15, 31, n. 2. *Cf.* Bergaigne, *Religion Védique*, 1, 1-3; Wallis, *Cosmology of the Rigveda*, 111-117; Zimmer, *op. cit.*, 357-359; Macdonell, *op. cit.*, pp. 8-11; Thibaut, *Astronomie, Astrologie und Mathematik*, 5, 6; Weber, *Indische Studien*, 9, 358-364.

Divodāsa Atithigva is one of the leading princes of the early Vedic age. He was a son of Vadhryaśva,[1] and father, or more probably grandfather, of **Sudās**, the famous king of the **Tṛtsu** family, among the **Bharatas.** Probably Pijavana was the son and Sudās the grandson. Divodāsa was naturally a **Bharata,**[2] and, like Sudās, was an opponent of the **Turvaśas** and **Yadus.**[3] His great enemy was **Śambara**, the **Dāsa**, who was apparently chief of a mountain people,[4] and whom he repeatedly defeated.[5] He was also, it seems, like his father Vadhryaśva,[6] an energetic supporter of the fire ritual, for Agni is once called by his name in the Rigveda.[7] On the other hand, he was defeated, with **Āyu** and **Kutsa**, by Indra's aid. In several passages he seems closely connected with the singer family, the **Bharadvājas.**[8]

From one passage,[9] where Divodāsa is said to have fought against the **Paṇis,** the **Pārāvatas,** and **Bṛsaya,** Hillebrandt[10] has inferred that he was engaged in conflicts with the tribes of Arachosia, and interpreting the name as the 'heavenly Dāsa'[11] conjectures that he was himself a Dāsa. This conclusion is not probable, for the **Sarasvatī** on which the battle in question took place, and which can hardly be the Haraqaiti of Arachosia, would naturally designate the later Sarasvatī, while the Pārāvatas are mentioned in the Pañcaviṃśa Brāhmaṇa,[12] as in the east, about the **Yamunā.** Bergaigne's

[1] Rv. vi. 61, 1.

[2] Rv. vi. 16, 4. 5. 19. For Sudās as his descendant, see vii. 18, 25, with verse 23, where Paijavana is an epithet of Sudās.

[3] As Atithigva, Rv. vii. 19, 8; as Divodāsa, ix. 61, 2.

[4] Rv. i. 130, 7; ii. 12, 11; vi. 26, 5; vii. 18, 20. *Cf.* Macdonell, *Vedic Mythology*, p. 161.

[5] See Rv. i. 112, 14; 116, 18; 119, 4; 130, 7-10; ii. 19, 6; iv. 26, 3; 30, 20; vi. 26, 3. 5; 43, 1; 47, 21. 22; ix. 61, 2.

[6] Rv. x. 69, 1 *et seq. Cf.* Ludwig, Translation of the Rigveda, 3, 176; Hillebrandt, *Vedische Mythologie*, 1, 96, n. 2.

[7] Daivodāsa, 'worshipped by Divodāsa': viii. 103, 2. *Cf.* vi. 16, 5. 19; 31, 1. For the defeat by Indra, *cf.* Rv. i. 53, 10; ii. 14, 7; vi. 18, 13; viii. 64, 2; Bergaigne, *Religion Védique*, 2, 337, 344.

[8] *Cf.* Rv. i. 112, 13. 14; 116, 18; vi. 16, 5; 31, 4; 47, 22 *et seq.*; Pañcaviṃśa Brāhmaṇa, xv. 3, 7; Hillebrandt, *op. cit.*, 1, 104.

[9] vi. 61, 1 *et seq.*

[10] *Op. cit.*, 1, 97 *et seq.*

[11] This is very improbable. See Bergaigne, *op. cit.*, 2, 209; Oldenberg, *Religion des Veda*, 155; *Zeitschrift der Deutschen Morgenländischen Gesellschaft*, 49, 175; 51, 272.

[12] ix. 4, 11. See **Pārāvata**.

opinion[13] that Divodāsa and Atithigva were different people cannot be supported in view of the complete parallelism in the acts of the two persons.[14] See also **Pratardana.**

The people of Divodāsa are referred to in a hymn of the Rigveda.[15]

[13] *Op. cit.*, 2, 342 *et seq.*

[14] Compare, *e.g.*, vii. 19, 8, with ix. 61, 2 (opposed to Turvaśa and Yadu); i. 51, 6; vi. 26, 3, with ii. 19, 6; vi. 31, 4 (defeat of Śambara); and see Hillebrandt, *op. cit.*, 3, 268; Oldenberg, *Zeitschrift der Deutschen Morgenländischen Gesellschaft*, 42, 210 *et seq.*; Macdonell, *op. cit.*, p. 161.

[15] i. 130, 10 (one of the series attributed to Parucchepa).

Cf. Zimmer, *Altindisches Leben*, 126. Oldenberg, *Buddha*, 406; Ludwig, *op. cit.*, 3, 114, 176; Grierson, *Journal of the Royal Asiatic Society*, 1908, 604, 837; Keith, *ibid.*, 831 *et seq.*; 1138 *et seq.* Roth, St. Petersburg Dictionary, *s.v.*, distinguishes two Divodāsas, one being the ancestor or father of Sudās, the other the enemy of Śambara. Divodāsa is not mentioned in Maṇḍalas, iii, v, viii, x.

Divo-dāsa Bhaima-seni ('descendant of Bhīmasena') is mentioned in the Kāṭhaka Saṃhitā[1] as a contemporary of **Āruṇi.**

[1] vii. 1, 8. *Cf.* Weber, *Indische Studien*, 3, 472.

Divya, 'ordeal,' is a term not found until the later literature, but several references to the practice of ordeals have been seen in Vedic literature. The fire ordeal seen in the Atharvaveda[1] by Schlagintweit,[2] Weber,[3] Ludwig,[4] Zimmer,[5] and others, has been disproved by Grill,[6] Bloomfield,[7] and Whitney.[8] But such an ordeal appears in the Pañcaviṃśa Brāhmaṇa,[9] and an ordeal with a glowing axe[10] occurs in the Chāndogya Upaniṣad as applied in an accusation of theft. Geldner[11] suggests that this usage is referred to even in the Rigveda,[12] but this is most improbable.[13] Ludwig[14] and Griffith[15] discover in another

[1] ii. 12.

[2] *Die Gottesurtheile der Indier*, 13 *et seq.*

[3] *Indische Studien*, 13, 168.

[4] Translation of the Rigveda, 3, 445.

[5] *Altindisches Leben*, 184.

[6] *Hundert Lieder*,[2] 45, 87.

[7] *Journal of the American Oriental Society*, 13, ccxxi; *American Journal of Philology*, 11, 334, 335; *Hymns of the Atharvaveda*, 294.

[8] Translation of the Atharvaveda, 54.

[9] xiv. 6, 6.

[10] Chāndogya Upaniṣad, vi. 16.

[11] *Vedische Studien*, 2, 159.

[12] iii. 53, 22.

[13] Oldenberg, *Ṛgveda-Noten*, 1, 254.

[14] *Op. cit.*, 4, 44.

[15] *Hymns of the Rigveda*, 1, 210.

passage of the Rigveda[16] references to **Dīrghatamas'** having been subjected to the fire and water ordeals, but this view cannot be supported. According to Weber,[17] the 'balance' ordeal is referred to in the Śatapatha Brāhmaṇa,[18] but see **Tulā.**

16 i. 158, 4 *et seq.*
17 *Indische Streifen*, 1, 21; 2, 363.
18 xi. 2, 7, 33.
Cf. Jolly, *Recht und Sitte*, 145; *Zeitschrift der Deutschen Morgenländischen Gesellschaft*, 44, 347, 348; Stenzler, *ibid.*, 9, 669 *et seq.*

Divya Śvan, the 'divine dog,' in one passage of the Atharvaveda[1] appears to denote Canis major or Sirius. But Bloomfield[2] thinks that the two divine dogs referred to in the Maitrāyaṇī Saṃhitā[3] and the Taittirīya Brāhmaṇa[4] are the sun and moon, and that the sun is meant in the Atharvaveda.

1 vi. 80, 1.
2 *Journal of the American Oriental Society*, 15, 163; *Hymns of the Atharvaveda*, 500, 501.
3 i. 6, 9.
4 i. 1, 2, 4-6.
Cf. Zimmer, *Altindisches Leben*, 353; Whitney, Translation of the Atharva veda, 341.

Diś, 'direction,' is a word very frequently used in the Rigveda and later[1] to denote a quarter of the sky. As a general rule, four quarters are mentioned—east, south, west, north.[2] But the number of the 'directions' is sometimes increased up to ten by the addition to these four of various others. The five points include the zenith (*ūrdhvā*);[3] the six, the zenith and the nadir (*ūrdhvā* and *avācī*);[4] the seven, the zenith, the ground on which one stands (*dhruvā*), and the air (*antarikṣa*) between these two (*vyadhvā*);[5] the eight include the intermediate quarters (S.E., S.W., N.E., N.W.);[6] the nine add to these the zenith;[7] the ten, zenith and nadir.[8] The number

1 Rv. i. 124, 3; 183, 5; iii. 30, 12; Av. iii. 31, 4; xi. 2, 12, etc.
2 Rv. vii. 72, 5; x. 36, 14; 42, 11; Av. xv. 2, 1 *et seq.*, etc.
3 Taittirīya Saṃhitā, vii. 1, 15; Maitrāyaṇī Saṃhitā, ii. 8, 9.
4 Maitrāyaṇī Saṃhitā, iii. 12, 8; Vājasaneyi Saṃhitā, xxii. 24; Bṛhadāraṇyaka Upaniṣad, iv. 2, 4.
5 Rv. ix. 114, 3; Av. iv. 40, 1; Śatapatha Brāhmaṇa, vii. 4, 1, 20; ix. 5, 2, 8; Taittirīya Āraṇyaka, i. 7.
6 Taittirīya Saṃhitā, vii, 1, 15; Satapatha Brāhmaṇa, i. 8, 1, 40, etc.
7 Śāṅkhāyana Śrauta Sūtra, xvi. 28, 2.
8 Rv. i. 164, 14; viii. 101, 13; Śatapatha Brāhmaṇa, vi. 2, 2, 34; viii. 4, 2, 13, etc.

five is sometimes made up by the ground beneath the observer's feet (*dhruvā*),[9] and the number six by that point (*dhruvā*) and the zenith (*ūrdhvā*);[10] the 'lofty' (*bṛhatī*)[11] sometimes taking the place of the 'vertical' (*ūrdhvā*).

[9] Av. viii. 9, 15; xiii. 3, 6; xv. 14, 1-5; Vājasaneyi Saṃhitā, ix. 32; Śatapatha Brāhmaṇa, ix. 4, 3, 10, and *cf.* **Dhruvā.**

[10] Av. iii. 27, 1; iv. 14, 8; xii. 3, 55; xv. 4, 1 *et seq.*; xviii. 3, 34; Aitareya Brāhmaṇa, viii. 14, etc. *Cf.* Rv. x. 14, 16.

[11] Vājasaneyi Saṃhitā, xiv. 13; Kāṭhaka Saṃhitā, xvii. 8.

Cf. Zimmer, *Altindisches Leben*, 359; Weber, *Proceedings of the Berlin Academy*, 1895, 846; *Indische Studien*, 17, 293, 294; 18, 153; St. Petersburg Dictionary, *s.v.*

Dīrgha-tamas ('long darkness') **Māmateya** ('son of Mamatā') **Aucathya** ('son of Ucatha') is mentioned as a singer in one hymn of the Rigveda,[1] and is referred to in several passages[2] by his metronymic, Māmateya, alone. He is said, both in the Rigveda[1] and in the Śāṅkhāyana Āraṇyaka,[3] to have attained the tenth decade of life. In the Aitareya Brāhmaṇa[4] he appears as the priest of **Bharata.** The Bṛhaddevatā[5] contains a preposterous legend made up of fragments of the Rigveda,[6] according to which Dīrghatamas was born blind, but recovered his sight; in old age he was thrown into a river by his servants, one of whom, **Traitana**, attacked him, but killed himself instead. Carried down by the stream, he was cast up in the Aṅga country, where he married Uśij, a slave girl, and begot **Kakṣīvant.** The two legends here combined are not even consistent, for the second ignores Dīrghatamas' recovery of sight. To attach any historical importance to them, as does Pargiter,[7] would seem to be unwise.

[1] i. 158, 1. 6.

[2] i. 147, 3; 152, 6; iv. 4, 13. In viii. 9, 10, Dīrghatamas is mentioned with Kakṣīvant, but not as a relative.

[3] ii. 17; Keith, *Śāṅkhāyana Āraṇyaka*, 14.

[4] viii. 23.

[5] iv. 11-15; 21-25, with Macdonell's notes.

[6] From i. 140-164, which hymns are traditionally attributed to Dīrghatamas. But see Oldenberg, *Zeitschrift der Deutschen Morgenländischen Gesellschaft*, 42, 221.

[7] *Journal of the Royal Asiatic Society*, 1910, 44.

Cf. Ludwig, Translation of the Rigveda, 3, 164, 165; Muir, *Sanskrit Texts*, 1², 226, 232, 247, 268, 279.

Dīrgha-nītha appears to be the proper name of a sacrificer in one hymn of the Rigveda.[1]

[1] viii. 50, 10. *Cf.* Roth, St. Petersburg Dictionary, *s.v.* Ludwig understands the word as an adjective, meaning 'of long duration.'

Dīrgha-śravas ('far-famed') is the name of a royal seer who, according to the Pañcaviṃśa Brāhmaṇa,[1] having been banished from his kingdom, and suffering from actual hunger, 'saw' a certain Sāman (chant), and thus obtained food. In one passage of the Rigveda[2] an Auśija,[3] a merchant (*vaṇij*), is mentioned as *dīrgha-śravas*, which may be a proper name, as Sāyaṇa holds, or an adjective, as it is understood by Roth.[4]

[1] xv. 3, 25.

[2] i. 112, 11.

[3] A metronymic, 'descendant of Uśij,' according to Sāyaṇa; but an adjective, meaning 'desirous,' according to Roth, St. Petersburg Dictionary, *s.v.*

[4] St. Petersburg Dictionary, *s.v.*

Cf. Ludwig, Translation of the Rigveda, 3, 114.

Dīrghāpsas, used in the Rigveda[1] as an epithet of a chariot, means, according to Roth,[2] 'having a long front part.'

[1] i. 122, 15.

[2] St. Petersburg Dictionary, *s.v.*

Cf. Pischel, *Vedische Studien*, 1, 312.

Dīrghāyutva, 'longevity,' is a constant object of the prayers of the Vedic Indians,[1] and length of life is never deprecated in the Saṃhitās and Brāhmaṇas, while the Atharvaveda[2] is full of spells intended to prolong existence (*āyuṣyāṇi*).

[1] Rv. x. 62, 2; Av. i. 22, 2, etc.; Vājasaneyi Saṃhitā, xviii. 6; Śatapatha Brāhmaṇa, i. 9, 1, 13, etc. So the adjective *dīrghāyus*, Rv. iv. 15, 9. 10; x. 85, 39; Vājasaneyi Saṃhitā, xii. 100, etc. The Brāhmaṇas regularly express the reward for ritual actions by the phrase *sarvam āyur eti*, 'he lives all his days.' The ideal of life is 100 years. See Weber, *Indische Studien*, 17, 193; *Festgruss an Roth*, 137; Lanman, *Sanskrit Reader*, 384.

[2] ii. 13; 28; 29; vii. 32, and many other hymns. See Bloomfield, *Hymns of the Atharvaveda*, 49 *et seq.*; *Atharvaveda*, 63-65.

Dīrghāraṇya, 'wide tract of forest,' in the Aitareya[1] and Śatapatha[2] Brāhmaṇas refers to the extensive jungles which

[1] iii. 44; vi. 23.

[2] xiii. 3, 7, 10.

must clearly then have covered Northern India. In one of the Aitareya passages[3] it is said that in the east the villages are close together and frequent, while in the west there are forests.

[3] iii. 44.

Dīv (fem.) in the Rigveda[1] and the Atharvaveda[2] denotes the 'game of dice.' See **Akṣa.**

[1] x. 27, 17.

[2] vii. 50 9; 109, 5.

Dughā, 'yielding milk,' denotes 'cow' in a few passages in the Saṃhitās.[1]

[1] Rv. viii. 50, 3; x. 67, 1; Vājasaneyi Saṃhitā, xxviii. 16. 39, etc.

Dundubhi, apparently an onomatopoetic word, means 'drum,' as used in both war and peace. It is often mentioned from the Rigveda[1] onwards.[2] A special sort of drum was the 'earth drum,' made by digging a hole in the ground and covering it with a hide. This was employed in the Mahāvrata, a rite performed at the winter solstice, for the purpose of driving away influences hostile to the return of the sun.[3] A 'drum-beater' is included in the list of sacrificial victims at the Puruṣamedha or 'human sacrifice.'[4]

[1] i. 28, 5; vi. 47, 29. 31.

[2] Av. v. 20, 1 *et seq.*; 21, 7; 31, 7; vi. 38, 4; xii. 1, 41; Taittirīya Brāhmaṇa, i. 3, 6, 2; Śatapatha Brāhmaṇa, v. 1, 5, 6; *dundubhya*, 'connected with the drum,' Vājasaneyi Saṃhitā, xvi. 35.

[3] Kāṭhaka Saṃhitā, xxxiv. 5 (*Indische Studien*, 3, 477); Śāṅkhāyana Śrauta Sūtra, xvii. 14, 11; Aitareya Āraṇyaka, v. 1, 5, with Keith's notes; Hillebrandt, *Vedische Mythologie*, 1, 148, n. 2; Friedlaender, *Śāṅkhāyana Āraṇyaka*, 29, 45.

[4] Taittirīya Brāhmaṇa, iii. 4, 13, 1 (not in the Vājasaneyi Saṃhitā). *Cf.* Bṛhadāraṇyaka Upaniṣad, ii. 4, 6.

Cf. Zimmer, *Altindisches Leben*, 289; and for the epic drum in battle, Hopkins, *Journal of the American Oriental Society*, 13, 318.

Dur is used several times in the Rigveda[1] to denote 'door,' both literally and metaphorically.

[1] i. 68, 10; 113, 4; 121, 4; 188, 5; ii. 2, 7, etc.

Duroṇa is used in the Rigveda,[1] and sometimes later,[2] to denote 'home,' both literally and metaphorically. See **Gṛha.**

[1] iii. 1, 18; 25, 5; iv. 13, 1; v. 76, 4, etc.

[2] Av. vii. 17, 3; Vājasaneyi Saṃhitā, xxxiii. 72, etc.

Dur-ga, 'hard to approach,' occurs in the Rigveda as a neuter substantive only, sometimes in the sense of 'fort,' 'stronghold.'[1] *Cf.* **Pur.**

[1] v. 34, 7; vii. 25, 2.

Dur-gaha is mentioned in a hymn of the Rigveda,[1] where his grandsons are lauded for their generosity, though Sāyaṇa renders the word adjectivally.[2] In another passage of the Rigveda,[3] however, Sāyaṇa sees in the epithet Daurgaha a description of **Purukutsa** as Durgaha's son, who was either captured by the enemy or slain, and whose wife, **Purukutsānī**, then obtained a son, **Trasadasyu**, to restore the line; he also quotes a story, not found in the Bṛhaddevatā,[4] to support this interpretation. On the other hand, the Śatapatha Brāhmaṇa[5] seems to take Daurgaha as meaning a horse. Sieg[6] thinks that the same sense should be adopted in the Rigveda passage, which he interprets as referring to the sacrifice of a horse, Daurgaha, by King Purukutsa to gain a son; he also sees in Dadhikrāvan, with Pischel[7] and Ludwig,[8] a real horse, the charger of Trasadasyu. The Śatapatha Brāhmaṇa's interpretation of Daurgaha is, however, doubtful, and cannot be regarded as receiving support from the case of Dadhikrāvan, who was probably a divinity, and not a real horse at all.[9]

[1] viii. 65, 12.

[2] 'Plunged in distress' (*duḥkhaṃ gāhamāna*).

[3] iv. 42, 8.

[4] As Roth, St. Petersburg Dictionary, *s.v.*, says it is.

[5] xiii. 5, 4, 5. According to the Naighaṇṭuka (i. 14), Daurgaha is a synonym of 'horse.'

[6] *Die Sagenstoffe des Ṛgveda*, 96-102.

[7] *Vedische Studien*, 1, 124.

[8] Translation of the Rigveda, 4, 79. *Cf.* Oldenberg, *Religion des Veda*, 71.

[9] Macdonell, *Vedic Mythology*, pp. 148, 149.

Cf. Ludwig, *op. cit.*, 3, 163, 174; Oldenberg, *Ṛgveda-Noten*, 1, 301, 302.

Dur-ṇāman, 'of evil name,' is the designation in the Rigveda[1] and the Atharvaveda[2] of a demon causing disease, or the disease itself. The Nirukta[3] explains the words as meaning a 'worm,' an interpretation which accords with the wide-spread belief in disease-causing worms.[4] Later Durnāman denotes 'hæmorrhoids.'[5]

[1] x. 162, 2.

[2] ii. 25, 2; viii. 6, 1 *et seq.*; xvi. 6, 7; xix. 36, 1 *et seq.* So also the feminine Durṇāmnī, iv. 17, 5; xix. 36, 6.

[3] vi. 12.

[4] Bloomfield, *Atharvaveda*, 61; *Hymns of the Atharvaveda*, 314 *et seq.*, 351.

[5] Suśruta, 1, 177, 10, etc.

Dur-mukha, 'ugly-faced,' is the name, in the Aitareya Brāhmaṇa,[1] of a Pāñcāla, that is, Pañcāla king, who conquered the world, and whose priest was **Bṛhaduktha.**

[1] viii. 23. The reading may be *a-rājā*, 'not a king,' but this is not necessary.

Durya, 'belonging to the door or house,' appears in several passages of the Saṃhitās[1] as a plural substantive denoting the 'door-posts,' or more generally 'dwelling.'

[1] Masculine plural, Rv. i. 91, 19; x. 40, 12; Taittirīya Saṃhitā, i. 6, 3, 1; Vājasaneyi Saṃhitā, i. 11; feminine plural, Rv. iv. 1, 9. 18; 2, 12; vii. 1, 11.

Duryoṇa occurs a few times in the Rigveda[1] in the sense of 'house.'

[1] i. 174, 7; v. 29, 10; 32, 8.

Dur-varāha probably denotes a 'wild boar.' It is mentioned in the Śatapatha Brāhmaṇa[1] and the Jaiminīya Upaniṣad Brāhmaṇa.[2]

[1] xii. 4, 1, 4.

[2] i. 51, 4 (*Journal of the American Oriental Society*, 23, 332).

Dulā. See **Nakṣatra (Kṛttikās).**

Duś-carman, 'afflicted with a skin disease,' occurs in the Taittirīya Saṃhitā[1] and Brāhmaṇa.[2] The disease meant is probably leprosy, the usual name of which is **Kilāsa.**[3]

[1] ii. 1, 4, 3; 5. 1, 7.

[2] i. 7, 8, 3.

[3] Pañcaviṃśa Brāhmaṇa, xiv. 3, 17; xxiii. 16, 11; Taittirīya Āraṇyaka, v. 4, 12.

Duḥ-śāsu is possibly a proper name in the Rigveda,[1] and would then denote an enemy of **Kuruśravaṇa**. Ludwig[2] thinks that he was a **Parśu** or Persian, but this is most improbable, and the word may simply be an adjective meaning 'malignant.'

1 x. 33, 1.

2 Translation of the Rigveda, 3, 165.

Duḥ-śīma is mentioned in the Rigveda[1] as a generous donor, his patronymic perhaps being **Tānva.**[2]

1 x. 93, 14.

2 x. 93, 15. *Cf.* Ludwig, Translation of the Rigveda, 3, 166.

Duṣ-ṭarītu, 'hard to defeat,' is the name of a king of the **Sṛñjayas**, who was deposed from a principality that had existed for ten generations, but was re-instated by **Cākra Sthapati** in spite of the resistance of **Balhika Prātipīya**, according to the Śatapatha Brāhmana.[1]

1 xii. 9, 3, 1 *et seq.* *Cf.* Weber, *Indische Studien*, 1, 205-207.

Duḥ-ṣanta. See **Dauḥṣanti.**

Duhitṛ is the regular designation of 'daughter' from the Rigveda onwards.[1] The word appears to be derived from *duh*, 'milk,' in the sense of one who nourishes a child, rather than as the 'milker' of the primitive family or the suckling.[2] See also **Strī, Pati, Pitṛ, Bhrātṛ.**

1 Rv. viii. 101, 15; x. 17, 1; 40, 5; 61, 5. 7; Av. ii. 14, 2; vi. 100, 3; vii. 12, 1; x. 1, 25; Śatapatha Brāhmaṇa, i. 7, 4, 1; 8, 1, 8, etc.

2 Delbrück, *Die indogermanischen Verwandtschaftsnamen*, 454.

Dūta, 'messenger' or 'envoy,' is found several times in the Rigveda[1] and later,[2] used metaphorically. The **Sūta** seems to have performed the duties later assigned to the Dūta.

1 iii. 3, 2; vi. 8, 4; vii. 3, 3; x. 14, 12.

2 Av. viii. 8, 10, etc.; Satapatha Brāhmaṇa, iii. 5, 1, 6; Kauṣītaki Upaniṣad, ii. 1, etc. The feminine form Dūtī is found in Rv. x. 108, 2. 3, in the story of Saramā's mission to the Paṇis. Dūtya, 'mission,' occurs in Rv. i. 12, 4; 161, 1; iv. 7, 8; 8, 4, etc.

Dūrvā, a species of grass (*Panicum dactylon*), is mentioned frequently from the Rigveda[1] onwards.[2] It grew in damp ground.[3] A simile occurring in the Rigveda[4] seems to indicate that the ears lay horizontal with the stem. *Cf.* **Pākadūrvā.**

[1] x. 16, 13; 134, 5; 142, 8.
[2] Taittirīya Saṃhitā, iv. 2, 9, 2; v. 2, 8, 3; Vājasaneyi Saṃhitā, xiii. 20; Aitareya Brāhmaṇa, viii. 5. 8; Śatapatha Brāhmaṇa, iv. 5, 10, 5; vii. 4, 2, 10. 12, etc.
[3] Rv. x. 16, 13; 142, 8.
[4] x. 134, 5.

Cf. Zimmer, *Altindisches Leben*, 70.

Dūrśa, denoting some kind of garment, is mentioned twice in the Atharvaveda.[1] Weber[2] thinks that it was worn by the aborigines.

[1] iv. 7, 6; viii. 6, 11.
[2] *Indische Studien*, 18, 29.

Dūṣīkā, 'rheum of the eyes,' is mentioned as a disease in the Atharvaveda[1] and later.[2]

[1] xvi. 6, 8.
[2] Kāṭhaka Saṃhitā, xxxiv. 12; Vājasaneyi Saṃhitā, xxv. 9; Śatapatha Brāhmaṇa, iii. 1, 3, 10.

Dṛḍha-cyut Āgasti ('descendant of Agastya') is mentioned in the Jaiminīya Brāhmaṇa[1] as having been Udgātṛ priest at the Sattra ('sacrificial session') of the Vibhindukīyas.

[1] iii. 233 (*Journal of the American Oriental Society*, 18, 38). He is given in the Anukramaṇī (where the form of the patronymic is Āgastya) as the author of Rv. ix. 25. *Cf. Indische Studien*, 3, 219.

Dṛḍha-jayanta. See **Vipaścit** and **Vaipaścita.**

1. **Dṛti**, a 'leather bag to hold fluids,' is frequently mentioned in the Rigveda[1] and later.[2] In one passage[3] it is called *dhmāta*, 'inflated,' the man afflicted with dropsy being compared with such a bag. Milk (**Kṣīra**) and intoxicating liquor (**Surā**) are mentioned as kept in bags.[4]

[1] i. 191, 10; iv. 51, 1. 3; v. 83, 7; vi. 48, 18; 103, 2; viii. 5, 19; 9, 18.
[2] Av. vii. 18, 1; Taittirīya Saṃhitā, i. 8, 19, 1; Vājasaneyi Saṃhitā, xxvi. 18. 19; Taittirīya Brāhmaṇa, i. 8, 3, 4; Pañcaviṃśa Brāhmaṇa, v. 10, 2, etc.
[3] Rv. vii. 89, 2. *Cf.* Hopkins, *Journal of the American Oriental Society*, 20, 30.
[4] Pañcaviṃśa Brāhmaṇa, xiv. 11, 26; xvi. 13, 13.

2. **Dṛti Aindrota** ('descendant of **Indrota**') is mentioned in the Pañcaviṃśa Brāhmaṇā[1] as a contemporary of **Abhipratārin Kākṣaseni** and as a pupil of **Indrota Daivāpa** in a Vaṃśa (list of teachers) in the Jaiminīya Upaniṣad Brāhmaṇa.[2] Possibly the same Dṛti is meant in the compound Dṛti-Vātavantau, which is found in the Pañcaviṃśa Brāhmaṇa.[3] The former is here said to have continued, after the Mahāvrata was over, the sacrificial session in which both had been engaged, with the result that his descendants prospered more than the Vātavatas.

1 xiv. 1, 12. 15.

2 iii. 40, 2.

3 xxv. 3, 6. So a Sattra of a year's duration is later called *Dṛti-vātavator ayana*, Kātyāyana Śrauta Sūtra, xxiv. 4, 16; 6, 25; Āśvalāyana Śrauta Sūtra, xii. 3; Śāṅkhāyana Srauta Sūtra, xiii. 23, 1; Lāṭyāyana Śrauta Sūtra, x. 10, 7.

Cf. Hopkins, *Transactions of the Connecticut Academy of Arts and Sciences*, 15, 52, 53.

Dṛpta-bālāki Gārgya ('descendant of **Garga**') is the name of a teacher who is mentioned in the Bṛhadāraṇyaka Upaniṣad (ii. 1, 1) as a contemporary of **Ajātaśatru** of **Kāśi**.

Dṛbhīka is the name of a man[1] or a demon,[2] who, according to the Rigveda,[3] was slain by Indra.

1 Ludwig, Translation of the Rigveda, 3, 152, 207, who compares the Derbikes; Macdonell, *Vedic Mythology*, p. 162.

2 Grassmann, *Wörterbuch*, *s.v.*; Roth, St. Petersburg Dictionary, *s.v.*; Geldner, *Rigveda, Glossar*, 85.

3 ii. 14, 3.

Dṛśāna Bhārgava ('descendant of **Bhṛgu**') is mentioned as a seer in the Kāṭhaka Saṃhitā.[1]

1 xvi. 8. *Cf.* Weber, *Indische Studien*, 3, 459.

Dṛṣad appears in the Rigveda[1] and Atharvaveda[2] to denote not a millstone,[3] but merely a stone used to pound grain, which was placed on another stone as a support. When used later[4]

1 vii. 104, 22; viii. 72, 4.

2 ii. 31, 1; v. 23, 8.

3 Roth, St. Petersburg Dictionary, *s.v.*; Zimmer, *Altindisches Leben*, 269.

4 Taittirīya Saṃhitā, i. 6, 8, 3; 9, 3; Śatapatha Brāhmaṇa, i. 1, 1, 22; ii. 6 1, 9, etc.

in connexion with **Upalā**, the lower and the upper millstone, or mortar and pestle may be meant; but this is not certain. Eggeling[5] renders them as the large and small millstones. See also **Upara** and **Upalā**.

[5] *Sacred Books of the East*, 12, 11 (*dṛṣad-upale*, which are here distinguished from 'mortar and pestle,' *ulūkhala-musale*).

Cf. Pischel, *Vedische Studien*, 1, 108, 109.

Dṛṣadvatī, 'stony,' is the name of a river which flows into the **Sarasvatī** after running for a time parallel to it. It is mentioned in the Rigveda,[1] along with the Sarasvatī and the **Āpayā**, as the scene of action of the Bharata princes. In the Pañcaviṃśa Brāhmaṇa[2] and later[3] the Dṛṣadvatī and the Sarasvatī are the scene of special sacrifices. In Manu[4] these two rivers form the western boundary of the Middle Country.

[1] iii. 23, 4.
[2] xxv. 10. 13.
[3] Kātyāyana Srauta Sūtra, xxiv. 6, 6. 38; Lāṭyāyana Śrauta Sūtra, x. 19, 4.
[4] ii. 17.

Cf. Zimmer, *Altindisches Leben*, 18; Weber, *Indische Studien*, 1, 34; *Indian Literature*, 67, 102; Macdonell, *Vedic Mythology*, p. 87.

Dṛṣṭa. See **Adṛṣṭa.**

Devaka Mānyamāna ('descendant of Manyamāna') appears in the Rigveda[1] as an opponent of the Tṛtsus, and as connected with Śambara. Possibly, however, as Grassmann suggests, the words should be understood as denoting Śambara, 'who deemed himself a god,' *devaka* being used contemptuously.[2]

[1] vii. 18, 20 (*devakaṃ cin mānyamānam*).

[2] *Cf.* Rv. ii. 11, 2 (*amartyaṃ cid dāsam manyamānam*).

Cf. Ludwig, Translation of the Rigveda, 3, 173.

Devakī-putra, 'son of Devakī,' is the metronymic of **Kṛṣṇa** in the Chāndogya Upaniṣad.[1] According to the Epic,[2] a Devaka was father of Devakī, Kṛṣṇa's mother; the St. Petersburg Dictionary suggests that he was the 'king of the Gandharvas', also referred to in the Epic.[3]

[1] iii. 17, 6.
[2] Mahābhārata, i. 4480; v. 80, etc.
[3] *Ibid.*, i. 2704.

Deva-jana-vidyā, 'knowledge of divine beings,' is one of the sciences enumerated in the Śatapatha Brāhmaṇa[1] and the Chāndogya Upaniṣad.[2]

[1] xiii. 4, 3, 10. *Cf.* x. 5, 2, 20.

[2] vii. 1, 2. 4; 2, 1; 7, 1.

Deva-taras Śyāvasāyana Kāśyapa ('descendant of Kaśyapa') is mentioned in the Jaiminīya Upaniṣad Brāhmaṇa[1] as a pupil of **Ṛśyaśṛṅga**. In the Vaṃśa Brāhmaṇa,[2] as Śāvasāyana, he is a pupil of his father Śavas, who again was a pupil of Kāśyapa.

[1] iii. 40, 2.

[2] *Indische Studien*, 4, 373.

Devatyā occurs in the text of the Atharvaveda,[1] where it must, if the reading is correct, denote some animal.[2] But the reading should no doubt be *rohiṇī-devatyās*, 'having the red one as deity.'[3]

[1] i. 22, 3.

[2] Roth, St. Petersburg Dictionary, *s.v.*

[3] Whitney, Translation of the Atharvaveda, 23.

Devana is mentioned once in the Rigveda[1] in connexion with dicing. The word must designate the place on which the dice are thrown (elsewhere called **Adhidevana**), and it is so explained by Durga in his commentary on the Nirukta.[2]

[1] x. 43, 5.

[2] v. 22.

Cf. Lüders, *Das Würfelspiel im alten Indien*, 14.

Deva-nakṣatra, 'asterism of the gods,' is the name applied in the Taittirīya Brāhmaṇa[1] to the first fourteen lunar mansions, which are said to be south, while the others are called Yama-nakṣatra, 'asterisms of Yama,' and are said to be north. See **Nakṣatra**.

[1] i. 5, 2, 6. 7. *Cf.* Weber, *Naxatra*, 2, 309, 310.

Deva-bhāga Śrautarṣa is mentioned in the Śatapatha Brāhmaṇa[1] as the Purohita, or 'domestic priest,' of both the

[1] ii. 4, 4, 5. This passage is misquoted by Sāyaṇa on Rv. i. 81, 3. See Weber, *Indische Studien*, 2, 9, n.; Geldner, *Vedische Studien*, 3, 152.

Sṛñjayas and the **Kurus.** In the Aitareya Brāhmaṇa[2] he is said to have taught **Girija Bābhravya** the science of the dissection of the sacrificial animal (*paśor vibhakti*). In the Taittirīya Brāhmaṇa[3] he is an authority on the Sāvitra Agni.

[2] vii. 1.

[3] iii. 10, 9, 11.

Deva-malimluc, 'robber of the gods,' is the epithet of Rahasya,[1] who is said in the Pañcaviṃśa Brāhmaṇa[2] to have slain the pious **Vaikhānasas** at **Munimaraṇa** (' saint's death '). He was apparently an Asura, but may have been a real person.

[1] Or Rahasyu.

[2] xiv. 4, 7. *Cf.* Hopkins, *Transactions of the Connecticut Academy of Arts and Sciences*, 15, 51, 52.

Deva-muni, 'divine saint,' is the epithet of **Tura** in the Pañcaviṃśa Brāhmaṇa (xxv. 14, 5). The name is given in the Anukramaṇī to the author of a hymn of the Rigveda (x. 146).

Deva-rājan apparently denotes a king of Brahminical descent in the phrase 'Sāmans of Devarājans' in the Pancaviṃśa Brāhmaṇa (xviii. 10, 5). *Cf.* **Rājanyarṣi** and **Varṇa.**

Deva-rāta (' god-given ') **Vaiśvāmitra** (' descendant of **Viśvāmitra** ') is the name given to Śunaḥśepa after his adoption by Viśvāmitra in the Aitareya Brāhmaṇa.[1]

[1] vii. 17. *Cf.* Śāṅkhāyana Śrauta Sūtra, xv. 27.

Devala is mentioned as a Ṛṣi in the Kāṭhaka Saṃhitā (xxii. 11). See also **Daivala.**

Devavant is mentioned in a Dānastuti (' Praise of Gifts ') in the Rigveda[1] as the ancestor of **Sudās,** apparently his grandfather; or if **Pijavana** be accepted as Sudās' father, and **Divodāsa** as his grandfather, then his great-great-grandfather, and father of **Vadhryaśva.** The succession in the latter case would then be Devavant, Vadhryaśva, Divodāsa, Pijavana, Sudās.

[1] vii. 18, 22. *Cf.* Ludwig, Translation of the Rigveda, 3, 171; Geldner, *Vedische Studien*, 2, 138.

Deva-vāta ('desired of the gods') is the name of a **Bharata** prince in the Rigveda,[1] where he is mentioned as sacrificing on the **Dṛṣadvatī, Sarasvatī,** and **Āpayā.**

[1] iii. 23, 2. *Cf.* Oldenberg, *Buddha*, 409; Pischel, *Vedische Studien*, 2, 218.

Deva-vidyā, 'knowledge of the gods,' is one of the sciences enumerated in the Chāndogya Upaniṣad (vii. 1, 2, 4; 2, 1; 7, 1).

Deva-śravas is the name of a **Bharata** prince who with **Devavāta** appears as a sacrificer on the **Dṛṣadvatī, Sarasvatī,** and **Āpayā** in the Rigveda.[1]

[1] iii. 23, 2. 3. In the Anukramaṇī he is called a son of Yama, and has a hymn, x. 17, ascribed to him.

Devātithi Kāṇva ('descendant of **Kaṇva**') is mentioned in the Pañcaviṃśa Brāhmaṇa[1] as the seer of a Sāman (chant) by which he turned pumpkins into cows for himself and his son when they were starving in the desert, whither they had been driven by rivals. He is also the reputed author of a hymn of the Rigveda.[2]

[1] ix. 2, 19.
[2] viii. 4.
Cf. Hopkins, *Transactions of the Connecticut Academy of Arts and Sciences*, 15, 61.

Devāpi Ārṣṭiṣeṇa ('descendant of Ṛṣṭiṣeṇa') is mentioned in a hymn of the Rigveda[1] and in the Nirukta.[2] According to the latter source there were two brothers, **Devāpi** and **Śantanu,** princes of the Kurus. The elder was Devāpi, but Śantanu got himself anointed king, whereupon no rain fell for twelve years. The drought being attributed by the Brahmins to his having superseded his elder brother, Śantanu offered the kingdom to Devāpi. The latter, however, refused, but acting as Purohita, or domestic priest, for his brother, obtained rain. The Bṛhaddevatā[3] tells much the same tale, but adds that the reason for Devāpi's exclusion from the throne was the fact that he suffered from a skin disease. The Epic and later legends further

[1] x. 98.
[2] ii. 10.
[3] vii. 148 *et seq.*, with Macdonell's notes.

develop the story, presenting two somewhat discrepant accounts. According to the one version,[4] the ground of Devāpi's being passed over was leprosy, while in the other his devoting himself to asceticism in his youth was the cause of his brother's taking his place. The Epic,[5] moreover, treats him as a son of Pratīpa, and names as his brothers Bāhlīka[6] and Ārṣṭiṣeṇa,[7] who is a new figure developed from the patronymic of Devāpi. Possibly Sieg[8] is right in holding that two stories, those of Devāpi, Pratīpa's son, and of Devāpi, Ṛṣṭiṣeṇa's son, have been confused; but in any case it is impossible to extract history from them.[9]

The Rigvedic hymn certainly appears to represent Devāpi as sacrificing for Śantanu, who seems to be called **Aulāna.**[10] But there is no trace in it of the brotherhood of the two men, nor is there anything to show that Devāpi was not a Brahmin, but a Kṣatriya. Sieg,[11] who interprets the hymn by the Nirukta, thinks that he was a Kṣatriya, but on this occasion was enabled by the favour of Bṛhaspati to officiate as priest, and that the hymn shows clear recognition of the unusual character of his action; but this view seems very improbable.

[4] Mahābhārata, v. 5054 *et seq.* (=149, 15 *et seq.*), where Śāntanu is (as also in the Agni, cclxxvii. 34, the Brahma, xiii. 114, 118, and the Viṣṇu Purāṇas) the form of the name; Matsya Purāṇa, l. 39 *et seq.*, in which, as well as in the Bhāgavata, ix. 22, 12. 13, and the Vāyu Purāṇa, xcix. 234, 237, the form is Śantanu.

[5] Mahābhārata, i. 3751 (=94, 62); ix. 2285 (=40, 1); Vāyu Purāṇa, ii. 37, 230, etc.

[6] Mahābhārata, cited in n. 4; Harivaṃśa, 1819.

[7] *Ibid.*, cited in n. 5.

[8] *Die Sagenstoffe des Ṛgveda*, 136.

[9] As does Pargiter, *Journal of the Royal Asiatic Society*, 1910, 52, 53.

[10] Rv. x. 98, 11.

[11] *Op. cit.*, 129-142.

Cf. Muir, *Sanskrit Texts*, 1², 272 *et seq.*; Weber, *Indische Studien*, 1, 203; Ludwig, Translation of the Rigveda, 3, 192 *et seq.*; Macdonell, *Bṛhaddevatā*, 1, xxix; Zimmer, *Altindisches Leben*, 131, 132.

Devṛ is a rare word denoting the wife's 'brother-in-law' (that is, the husband's brother). He is included with the sisters of the husband among those over whom the wife of the husband—his elder brother—rules;[1] at the same time the wife is to be devoted to him,[2] and friendly to him.[3] After the death

[1] Rv. x. 85, 46. *Cf.* **Pati.**

[2] Rv. x. 85, 44.

[3] Av. xiv. 2, 18. *Cf.* xiv. 1, 39.

of the husband the Devṛ could perform the duty of begetting a son for him.[4] No word occurs for the wife's brother corresponding to Devṛ.

[4] Rv. x. 40, 2. *Cf.* x. 18, 8; Kaegi, *Der Rigveda*, n. 51; Lanman, *Sanskrit Reader*, 385; Whitney, Translation of the Atharvaveda, 948. *Cf.* Delbrück, *Die indogermanischen Verwandtschaftsnamen*, 516.

Deśa, 'land,' is a word that does not come into use till the time of the Upaniṣads and Sūtras,[1] excepting one occurrence in the latest period of the Brāhmaṇa[2] literature, and one in a much-discussed passage of the Vājasaneyi Saṃhitā,[3] where the **Sarasvatī** is mentioned as having five tributaries. This passage militates against the view that Sarasvatī was a name of the Indus, because the use of Deśa here seems to indicate[4] that the seer of the verse placed the Sarasvatī in the Madhyadeśa or 'Middle Country,' to which all the geographical data of the Yajurvedas point.[5]

[1] Where its use becomes common: Bṛhadāraṇyaka Upaniṣad, iv. 1, 16; 2, 3; Śāṅkhāyana Śrauta Sūtra, iv. 14, 6; Kātyāyana Srauta Sūtra. xv. 4, 17, etc. So the adjective *deśīya*, 'belonging to a land,' Kātyāyana, xxii. 4, 22; Lāṭyāyana Srauta Sūtra, viii. 6, 28.

[2] Aitareya Brāhmaṇa, viii. 10 (a late passage).

[3] xxxiv. 11.

[4] *Cf.* Zimmer, *Altindisches Leben*, 10, who thinks that the word crept into the text, where the Sarasvatī originally meant the Indus, with the five tributaries of the Panjab.

[5] Macdonell, *Sanskrit Literature*, 174.

Dehī in two passages of the Rigveda[1] refers to defences thrown up against an enemy, apparently earthworks or dikes. *Cf.* **Pur.**

[1] vi. 47, 2; vii. 6, 5. *Cf.* Schrader, *Prehistoric Antiquities*, 344; Zimmer, *Altindisches Leben*, 143.

Daidhiṣavya is mentioned in a Mantra of the Taittirīya Saṃhitā.[1] Apparently the word (as derived from **Didhiṣū**) denotes the son of a younger sister married before the elder sister,[2] rather than the son of a woman twice married, the explanation of the St. Petersburg Dictionary.

[1] iii. 2, 4, 4; Kātyāyana Śrauta Sūtra, ii. 1, 22; Kauśika Sūtra, 3, 5; 137, 37.

[2] *American Journal of Philology*, 17, 431, n.

Daiyāmpāti, 'descendant of Dayāmpāta,' is the name of a teacher of the east, who was instructed by **Śāṇḍilyāyana,** according to the Śatapatha Brāhmaṇa (ix. 5, 1, 14), in the lore of the construction of the fire-altar. The same patronymic is given, in the form of Dayyāmpāti, to **Plakṣa,** the contemporary of **Atyaṃhas** in the Taittirīya Brāhmaṇa (iii. 10, 9, 3-5).

1. **Daiva** (masc.) appears in the list of sciences in the Chāndogya Upaniṣad,[1] where Śaṅkara explains it as *utpāta-jñāna,* apparently the 'knowledge of portents.' The St. Petersburg Dictionary suggests that the word is here used adjectivally, and this view is followed by Little[2] and by Böhtlingk in his translation.[3]

[1] vii. 1, 2. 4; 2, 1; 7, 1.
[2] *Grammatical Index,* 83.
[3] Though he does not render it (*Daiva Nidhi*).

2. **Daiva** is the patronymic of the mythical Atharvan in the first two Vaṃśas (lists of teachers) of the Bṛhadāraṇyaka Upaniṣad.[1]

[1] ii. 5, 22; iv. 5, 28 (Mādhyaṃdina).

Daivala, 'descendant of Devala,' is the patronymic of **Asita** in the Pañcaviṃśa Brāhmaṇa (xiv. 11, 18).

Daiva-vāta, 'descendant of **Devavāta,**' is the patronymic of **Sṛñjaya,** probably the Sṛñjaya king, in the Rigveda. He is mentioned[1] as a devotee of the fire cult, and as victorious over the **Turvaśa** king and the **Vṛcīvants.**[2] According to Zimmer,[3] his name was **Abhyāvartin Cāyamāna Pārthava** ('descendant of Pṛthu'), but Hillebrandt[4] recognizes this as doubtful, though he none the less places the Sṛñjayas to the west of the Indus with **Divodāsa.** What is more important is to note that the name suggests connexion with the Bharata **Devavāta,** and as **Kurus** and Sṛñjayas were closely connected[5] this is not immaterial.

[1] Rv. iv. 15, 4.
[2] Rv. vi. 27, 7.
[3] *Altindisches Leben,* 133, 134.
[4] *Vedische Mythologie,* 1, 105, 106.
[5] Śatapatha Brāhmaṇa, ii. 4, 4, 5. *Cf.* Oldenberg, *Buddha,* 402, 405; Ludwig, Translation of the Rigveda, 3, 153.

Daivāpa, 'descendant of **Devāpi**,' is the patronymic of **Indrota** in the Śatapatha Brāhmaṇa[1] and the Jaiminīya Upaniṣad Brāhmaṇa.[2] No connexion can be traced with the Devāpi of the Rigveda.[3]

[1] xiii. 5, 4, 1.
[2] iii. 40, 1.
[3] x. 98. See Oldenberg, *Zeitschrift der Deutschen Morgenländischen Gesellschaft*, 42, 240.

Daivāvṛdha, 'descendant of Devāvṛdha,' is the patronymic of **Babhru** in the Aitareya Brāhmaṇa (vii. 34).

Daivo-dāsi, 'descendant of **Divodāsa**,' is the patronymic of **Pratardana** in the Kauṣītaki Brāhmaṇa[1] and the Kauṣītaki Upaniṣad.[2] It is impossible to ascertain whether the famous Divodāsa is meant.

[1] xxvi. 5.
[2] iii. 1. *Cf.* Weber, *Indische Studien*, 1, 214.

Doṣā, 'evening,' is frequently referred to from the Rigveda[1] onwards,[2] usually as contrasted with *uṣas*, 'dawn.' In the Chāndogya Upaniṣad[3] the word is contrasted with *prātar*, 'early.' See also **Ahan**.

[1] i. 34, 3; 179, 1; ii. 8, 3; iv. 2, 8; v. 5, 6; 32, 11; vi. 5, 2, etc.
[2] Av. vi. 1, 1; Nirukta, iv. 17.
[3] vi. 13, 1.

Doha, 'milking,' is a common word in the Atharvaveda[1] and later.[2] Reference is made in the Sūtras[3] to the *sāyaṃ-doha*, 'evening milking,' and the *prātar-doha*, 'morning milking.' Dohana has the same sense.[4] See also **Go**.

[1] iv. 11, 4. 9. 12; v. 17, 17; viii. 9, 15 (where five milkings are referred to metaphorically). In Rv. x. 42, 2, the literal sense is found.
[2] Vājasaneyi Saṃhitā, viii. 62; Taittirīya Brāhmaṇa, i. 1, 10, 2; ii. 2, 9, 9, etc.
[3] Kātyāyana Śrauta Sūtra, iv. 2, 38, etc.
[4] Rv. viii. 12, 32; Satapatha Brāhmaṇa, ix. 2, 3, 30; Kātyāyana Śrauta Sūtra, iv. 2, 37, etc.

Daure-śravas, 'descendant of Dūreśravas,' is the patronymic of the priest **Pṛthuśravas**, who officiated at the snake sacrifice described in the Pañcaviṃśa Brāhmaṇa (xxv. 15, 3).

Daure-śruta, 'descendant of Dūreśruta,' is the patronymic of the priest **Timirgha**, who officiated at the snake sacrifice described in the Pañcaviṃśa Brāhmaṇa (xxv. 15, 3).

Daur-gaha. See **Durgaha.**

Dauḥ-ṣanti ('descendant of Duḥṣanta') is the patronymic of Bharata in the Aitareya (viii. 23) and Śatapatha (xiii. 5, 4, 11) Brāhmaṇas.

Dyutāna Māruta ('descendant of the Maruts') is the name of a divine being invoked in the Vājasaneyi Saṃhitā[1] and the Taittirīya Saṃhitā,[2] and also mentioned in the Kāṭhaka Saṃhitā.[3] In the Śatapatha[4] Brāhmaṇa the name is explained to mean Vāyu, while in the Pañcaviṃśa Brāhmaṇa[5] he seems to be regarded as the author of a Sāman (chant). He is treated as a Ṛṣi by the Anukramaṇī, which credits him with the authorship of a hymn of the Rigveda (viii. 96).

[1] v. 27.
[2] v. 5, 9, 4. *Cf.* vi. 2, 10, 4.
[3] xv. 7.
[4] iii. 6, 1, 16.
[5] xvii. 1, 7. *Cf.* vi. 4, 2.
Cf. Hillebrandt, *Vedische Mythologie*, 3, 311; *Indische Studien*, 3, 220.

Dyumna, according to Pischel,[1] denotes 'raft' in one passage of the Rigveda.[2]

[1] *Zeitschrift der Deutschen Morgenländischen Gesellschaft*, 35, 720 *et seq.*
[2] viii. 19, 14.

Dyūta, 'dicing,' is mentioned in the Atharvaveda[1] and the Sūtras.[2] See **Akṣa.**

[1] xii. 3, 46.
[2] Kātyāyana Śrauta Sūtra, xv. 6, 2; Lāṭyāyana Śrauta Sūtra, iv. 10, 23, etc.

Dyotana is, according to Sāyaṇa, the name of a prince in the Rigveda.[1] This is probably correct, though the word may also[2] be interpreted as denoting 'glorification'; but it is not clear what relation existed between Dyotana and the other persons mentioned in the same passage, **Vetasu, Daśoṇi, Tūtuji,** and **Tugra.**

[1] vi. 20, 8.
[2] As by Griffith, *Hymns of the Rigveda*, 1, 380. *Cf.* Oldenberg, *Zeitschrift der Deutschen Morgenländischen Gesellschaft*, 55, 328.

Drapsa is a common word from the Rigveda onwards[1] for a 'drop': according to Sāyaṇa,[2] a 'thick drop' as opposed to *stoka*, a 'small drop.' Hence there frequently occurs the expression *dadhi-drapsa*,' drop of curds.'[3] In the Rigveda[4] the word normally denotes the thick drops of Soma or the Soma itself.

In two passages[5] Roth[6] sees the sense of 'banner,' which is adopted by Oldenberg.[7] Geldner,[8] on the other hand, considers that 'dust' is meant, but this interpretation is not very probable. Max Müller[9] renders the word 'rain-drop' in one of the passages.

1 Rv. i. 94, 11 (perhaps a 'drop' of fire); v. 63, 4 ('rain-drop'); vii. 33, 11 (=*retas*); Śatapatha Brāhmaṇa, vi. 1, 2, 6; *drapsin* ('thick-flowing'), xi. 4, 1, 15.

2 Taittirīya Saṃhitā, 1, p. 70, 7. *Cf.* the epithet *uru-drapsa*, Taittirīya Saṃhitā, iii. 3, 10, 2; Sāyaṇa, on Av. xviii. 4, 18, takes *drapsa* to mean 'drops of curd'; so Agnisvāmin on Lāṭyāyana Śrauta Sūtra, iii. 2, 4.

3 Śatapatha Brāhmaṇa, ix. 2, 3, 40.

4 ix. 78, 4; 85, 10; 89, 2; 97, 56; 106, 8; x. 11, 4; 17, 11. 12. *Cf.* Taittirīya Saṃhitā, iii. 3, 9. 1.

5 iv. 13, 2, and *drapsin* in i. 64, 2.

6 St. Petersburg Dictionary, *s.v.* *satvan*; Böhtlingk, Dictionary, *s.v.* *drapsa*, *drapsin*.

7 *Sacred Books of the East*, 46, 357; *Ṛgveda-Noten*, 1, 64, 65.

8 *Vedische Studien*, 3, 57, 58; *Rigveda, Glossar*, 88.

9 *Sacred Books of the East*, 32, 104. *Cf.* Macdonell, *Vedic Mythology*, p. 80, with reference to Rv. i. 64, 2.

Cf. Macdonell, *op. cit.*, pp. 105, 113.

Drāpi occurs several times in the Rigveda[1] in the sense of 'mantle' or 'cloak.'[2] Sāyaṇa, however, renders the word by 'coat of mail'[3] (*kavaca*). This seems needless, but none of the passages are very decisive one way or the other.

1 i. 25, 13; 116, 10; iv. 53, 2; ix. 86, 14; 100, 9; Av. iii. 13, 1.

2 Roth, St. Petersburg Dictionary, *s.v.*; Muir, *Sanskrit Texts*, 5, 472; Schrader, *Prehistoric Antiquities*, 333.

3 *Cf.* Max Müller, *Ancient Sanskrit Literature*, 536; Pischel, *Vedische Studien*, 2, 201, 202.

Dru denotes a vessel made of wood,[1] and in particular the vessel used at the Soma sacrifice,[2] perhaps, as Hillebrandt[3] suggests, to catch the Soma juice when running through the sieve. In the Taittirīya Brāhmaṇa[4] the word simply means 'wood.'

1 Rv. i. 161, 1; v. 86, 3; viii. 66, 11; in x. 101, 10, the mortar seems meant. In v. 86, 3, Böhtlingk takes it to denote a 'wooden handle.'

2 ix. 1, 2; 65, 6; 98, 2.

3 *Vedische Mythologie*, 1, 191, 192.

4 i. 3, 9, 1. So often in compounds, *e.g.*, Rv. ii. 7, 6; vi. 12, 4, etc.

Dru-ghaṇa is found in the Mudgala hymn of the Rigveda[1] and in the Atharvaveda.[2] The sense is uncertain. Yāska[3] renders it as a '*ghana* made of wood,' probably, as Roth[4] takes it, meaning a 'club of wood.' Geldner[5] thinks that it was a wooden bull used by Mudgala as a substitute for a second bull when he wanted to join in a race. But this interpretation of the legend is very improbable.[6] Whitney[7] translates the word as 'tree-smiter' in the Atharvaveda, quoting Sāyaṇa, who explains it as a 'cutting instrument,' so called because trees are struck with it.

1 x. 102, 9.
2 vii. 28, 1.
3 Nirukta, ix. 23.
4 St. Petersburg Dictionary, *s.v.*
5 *Vedische Studien*, 2, 3, 4.
6 *Cf.* von Bradke, *Zeitschrift der Deutschen Morgenländischen Gesellschaft*, 46, 462; Bloomfield, *ibid.*, 48, 456; Franke, *Vienna Oriental Journal*, 8, 342.
7 Translation of the Atharvaveda, 407.

Dru-pada, a 'wooden pillar' or 'post,' is several times referred to in the Rigveda[1] and later.[2] Śunaḥśepa was bound to three posts for sacrifice.[3] Thieves, there is some evidence to show, were tied to posts as a penalty for stealing.[4]

1 i. 24, 13; iv. 32, 23.
2 Av. vi. 63, 3; 115, 2; xix. 47, 9; Vājasaneyi Saṃhitā, xx. 20.
3 Rv. i. 24, 13.
4 Av. xix. 47, 9; 50, 1. *Cf.* vi. 63, 3 =84, 4. See Zimmer, *Altindisches Leben*, 181, 182, and **Taskara**, n. 26.

Druma, 'tree,' is not found until the later period in the Ṣaḍviṃśa Brāhmaṇa (v. 11) and the Nirukta (iv. 19; v. 26; ix. 23).

Druvaya, 'wooden,' is used in the Atharvaveda[1] as an epithet of the drum.

1 v. 20, 2. *Cf.* xi. 1, 12, where it is an epithet of *upaśvasa*, 'blower,' possibly 'bellows'; but the manuscripts in part read *dhruvaye*, and the Paippalāda has *druye*.

Dru-han, 'wood-cutter,' seems to be meant by the word *druhantara* in the Rigveda,[1] where it is usually taken as *druhaṃtara*, 'fiend-overpowering.' But as an epithet of *paraśu*, 'axe,' the other sense ('mighty wood-cutter')[2] is more probable.[3]

1 i. 127, 2.
2 But if this explanation is correct, the word should have the accentuation of the comparative. See Oldenberg, *Sacred Books of the East*, 46, 132.
3 *Cf.* Oldenberg, *Ṛgveda-Noten*, 1, 130.

Druhyu is the name of a people mentioned several times in the Rigveda. In one passage[1] it occurs, in the plural, with the **Yadus, Turvaśas, Anus**, and **Pūrus**, suggesting that these are the famous five peoples of the Rigveda.[2] Again, the Druhyu king shared in the defeat of his allies by **Sudās**, and appears to have perished in the waters.[3] In a second passage Druhyu, Anu, Turvaśa, and Yadu are all mentioned in the singular,[4] while in another Pūru and Druhyu occur.[5] From the tribal grouping it is probable that the Druhyus were a north-western people,[6] and the later tradition of the Epic connects Gāndhāra and Druhyu.[7]

[1] i. 108, 8.

[2] *Cf.* Zimmer, *Altindisches Leben*, 122, 125; Hopkins, *Journal of the American Oriental Society*, 15, 258 *et seq.*

[3] vii. 18.

[4] viii. 10, 5.

[5] vi. 46, 8.

[6] Roth, *Zur Litteratur und Geschichte des Weda*, 131-133.

[7] Pargiter, *Journal of the Royal Asiatic Society*, 1910, 49.

Cf. Ludwig, Translation of the Rigveda, 3, 205; Macdonell, *Vedic Mythology*, p. 140.

Droṇa denotes in the Rigveda[1] a 'wooden trough,' and more specifically it designates in the plural vessels used for holding Soma.[2] The great wooden reservoir for Soma is called a Droṇa-kalaśa.[3] The altar was sometimes made in the form of a Droṇa.[4]

[1] vi. 2, 8; 37, 2; 44, 20; ix. 93, 1; Nirukta, v. 26.

[2] ix. 3, 1; 15, 7; 28, 4; 30, 4; 67, 14, etc. *Cf.* Zimmer, *Altindisches Leben*, 280.

[3] Taittirīya Saṃhitā, iii. 2, 1, 2; Vājasaneyi Saṃhitā, xviii. 21; xix. 27; Aitareya Brāhmaṇa, vii. 17. 32. Śatapatha Brāhmaṇa, i. 6, 3, 17, etc.

[4] Maitrāyaṇī Saṃhitā, iii. 4, 7; Kāṭhaka Saṃhitā, xxi. 4; Śatapatha Brāhmaṇa, vi. 7, 2, 8.

Droṇāhāva is used as an epithet of **Avata**, 'well,' in the Rigveda,[1] apparently in the sense of 'having wooden buckets' with reference to the drawing up of water.

[1] x. 101, 7. *Cf.* Zimmer, *Altindisches Leben*, 157.

Dvādaśa, 'consisting of twelve,'[1] is used of the year in the Rigveda (vii. 103, 9). See **Nakṣatra.**

[1] *Cf.* Oldenberg, *Zeitschrift der Deutschen Morgenländischen Gesellschaft*, 48, 645 *et seq.*

Dvāpara. See **Akṣa** and **Yuga.**

Dvār is frequently used from the Rigveda[1] onwards[2] to denote the 'door' of a house. The later form, Dvāra, has the same sense.[3] *Cf.* **Gṛha.** The 'door-fastener' is called Dvāra-pidhāna in the Śatapatha Brāhmaṇa.[4]

[1] i. 13, 6.

[2] Av. viii. 3, 22; xiv. 1, 63; Vājasaneyi Saṃhitā, xxx. 10; Śatapatha Brāhmaṇa, xi. 1, 1, 2; xiv. 3, 1, 13, etc.

[3] Śatapatha Brāhmaṇa, i. 6, 1, 19; iv. 3, 5, 9; 6, 7, 9; xi. 4, 4, 2, etc. Av. x. 8, 43, has *nava-dvāra*, 'having nine openings,' of the body.

[4] xi. 1, 1, 1. *Cf. dvāra-bāhū*, 'doorposts,' in Lāṭyāyana Śrauta Sūtra, i. 3, 1; ii. 3, 9.

Dvāra-pa, 'door-keeper,' is only found in a metaphorical sense in the Aitareya Brāhmaṇa (i. 30), where Viṣṇu is called the 'doorkeeper' of the gods, and in the Chāndogya Upaniṣad (iii. 13, 6).

Dvi-gat Bhārgava ('descendant of **Bhṛgu**') is mentioned in the Pañcaviṃśa Brāhmaṇa (xiv. 9) as the seer of a Sāman or Chant, by means of which he twice went to the heavenly world.

Dvi-ja, 'twice-born,' as an epithet of the Āryans generally, or of the Brahmins in particular, is not found in Vedic literature except in a quite obscure verse of the Atharvaveda.[1]

[1] xix. 71, 1. *Cf.* Whitney, Translation of the Atharvaveda, 1008; Zimmer, *Altindisches Leben*, 204. Neither *dvi-janman* nor *dvi-jāti* occurs early, and the idea is not in this form an early one.

Dvi-pād, 'two-footed,' 'biped,' denotes man, as opposed to quadrupeds, from the Rigveda[1] onwards.[2]

[1] i. 49, 3; iii. 62, 14; viii. 27, 12; x. 97, 20; 117, 8.

[2] Av. ii. 34, 1; x. 1, 24; Vājasaneyi Saṃhitā, viii. 30; ix. 31; xiii. 17; xiv. 8, etc.

Dvi-bandhu is in an obscure hymn of the Rigveda,[1] according to Roth[2] and Grassmann,[3] the name of a man, while Ludwig[4] renders it as a simple adjective meaning 'of double kinship.'

[1] x. 61, 17.

[2] St. Petersburg Dictionary.

[3] *Wörterbuch, s.v.*, and Translation of the Rigveda, 2, 475.

[4] Translation of the Rigveda, 2, 643, and 5, 526.

Dvi-rāja (neut.), 'conflict between two kings,' or 'battle,' is mentioned in the Atharvaveda (v. 20, 9). *Cf.* **Dāśarājña.**

Dvi-retas, 'having double seed,' is an epithet of both the ass[1] and the mare.[2]

1 Aitareya Brāhmaṇa, iv. 9; Śatapatha Brāhmaṇa, vi. 3, 1, 23. *Cf.* **Gardabha.**
2 Pañcaviṃśa Brāhmaṇa, vi. 1, 4.

Dvīpa, 'island,' is mentioned in the Rigveda[1] and later.[2] But there is no reason to imagine that the islands referred to were other than sandbanks in the great rivers, Indus or Ganges.[3] Vedic literature knows nothing of the system of geography according to which the earth consists of four, seven, or thirteen Dvīpas grouped round Mount Meru.

1 i. 169, 3.
2 Kāṭhaka Saṃhitā, xiii. 2; Śatapatha Brāhmaṇa, xii. 2, 1, 3; Lāṭyāyana Śrauta Sūtra, i. 6, 10.
3 Zimmer, *Altindisches Leben*, 256.

Dvīpin,[1] 'panther' or 'leopard,' is mentioned in the Atharvaveda[2] and the Maitrāyaṇī Saṃhitā.[3]

1 Lit., 'insulated'—*i.e.*, 'spotted.'
2 iv. 8, 7; vi. 38, 2; xix. 49, 4, in every case associated with the tiger.
3 ii. 1, 9.
Cf. Zimmer, *Altindisches Leben*, 80.

Dvaita-vana, 'descendant of Dvitavana,' is the patronymic of **Dhvasan,** the king of the **Matsyas,** whose Aśvamedha, or 'horse sacrifice,' is mentioned in the Śatapatha Brāhmaṇa (xiii. 5, 4, 9).

Dvy-opaśa. See **Opaśa.**

DH.

Dhana, 'prize,' is often found in the Rigveda,[1] probably the prize in racing rather than the 'booty' in battle. It also denotes[2] the 'stake' at dicing. In some passages it possibly means the 'contest' itself.[3] More generally it denotes 'wealth' or 'gift.'[4] But it sometimes expresses 'booty,'[5] probably from the notion of 'wealth' rather than of 'prize.'

1 Rv. i. 81, 3; vi. 45, 2; viii. 80, 8; ix. 53, 2; 109, 10. *Cf.* Geldner, *Vedische Studien*, 1, 120; Pischel, *ibid.*, 1, 171.

2 Rv. x. 34, 10; Av. iv. 38, 3.

3 Rv. i. 31, 6; v. 35, 7; vii. 38, 8; viii. 5, 26; 8, 21; 49, 9; 50, 9; x. 48, 5, etc.

4 Rv. i. 42, 6; x. 18, 2; 84, 7; Av. i. 15, 3; ii. 7, 4; iii. 15, 2; v. 19, 9; vi. 81, 1; vii. 81, 4; viii. 5, 16, etc.

5 Rv. i. 74, 3; 157, 2, etc.

Dhana-dhānī, a 'treasure house,' is mentioned in the Taittirīya Āraṇyaka (x. 67).

Dhaniṣṭhā ('very rich'), used in the plural, is the later name[1] of the lunar mansion (**Nakṣatra**) **Śraviṣṭhā.**

1 Sāntikalpa, 13; Śāṅkhāyana Gṛhya Sūtra, i. 26.

Dhanu (fem.), 'sandbank,' occurs several times in the Rigveda,[1] but only metaphorically of the clouds in the atmosphere. Dhanū is found in the Atharvaveda,[2] where it seems to denote a sandbag used to prevent bleeding.[3] *Cf.* **Dhanvan.**

1 i. 33, 4; 144, 5; viii. 3, 19; x. 4, 3; 27, 17.

2 i. 17, 4.

3 Weber, *Indische Studien*, 4, 411; Whitney, Translation of the Atharvaveda, 18; Bloomfield, *Hymns of the Atharvaveda*, 259, 260.

Dhanus, the 'bow,' frequently mentioned in the Rigveda[1] and later,[2] was the chief weapon of the Vedic Indian.[3] The last act of the funeral rite included the removal of the bow from

1 viii. 72, 4; 77, 11; ix. 99, 1; x. 18, 9; 125, 6.

2 Av. iv. 4, 6; 6, 6; v. 18, 8; vii. 50, 9; Vājasaneyi Saṃhitā, xvi. 10; Pañcaviṃśa Brāhmaṇa, vii. 5, 6; Aitareya Brāhmaṇa, vii. 14; Śatapatha Brāhmaṇa, i. 5, 4, 6; v. 3, 1, 11, etc.

3 Rv. vi. 75, 2. Practically no other weapon plays any substantial part in Vedic warfare.

the right hand of the dead man.[4] The weapon was composed of a stout staff bent into a curved shape (*vakra*),[5] and of a bow-string (**Jyā**) made of a strip of cowhide[6] which joined the ends. The tips of the bow, when the string was fastened, were called **Ārtnī**. Relaxed when not in actual use, the bow was specially strung up when needed for shooting.[7] The stages of the process are given in detail in the Vājasaneyi Saṃhitā:[8] the stringing (*ā-tan*) of the bow, the placing (*prati-dhā*) of the arrow, the bending (*ā-yam*) of the bow, and the shooting (*as*). The arrow was discharged from the ear,[9] and is hence called *karṇa-yoni*,[10] 'having the ear as its point of origin.'[10] The making of bows was a regular profession (*dhanuṣ-kāra*,[11] *dhanuṣ-kṛt*).[12] For the arrow see **Iṣu**, and for the handguard **Hastaghna**.

[4] Rv. x. 18, 9.

[5] Av. iv. 6, 4.

[6] Rv. vi. 75, 11; Av. i. 2, 3.

[7] Rv. x. 166, 3; Av. vi. 42, 1.

[8] xvi. 22.

[9] Rv. vi. 75, 2 *et seq.* So also in the Epic, Hopkins, *Journal of the American Oriental Society*, 13, 271. The Homeric method is to draw to the breast—*e.g.*, *Iliad*, iv. 123.

[10] Rv. ii. 24, 8.

[11] xxx. 7.

[12] xvi. 46.

Cf. Zimmer, *Altindisches Leben*, 298, 299; Hopkins, *op. cit.*, 13, 270 *et seq.* The Epic bow is about 5½ feet, and the arrow 3 feet in length.

1. **Dhanvan**, 'bow,' is found frequently in the Rigveda[1] and later.[2] It also occurs in the compounds *iṣu-dhanva*, 'bow and arrow,'[3] *ājya-dhanva*,[4] 'having clarified butter for its bow,'[5] *adhijya-dhanva*, 'bow with string fixed,' etc. *Cf.* **Dhanus.**

[1] ii. 24, 8; 33, 10; vi. 59, 7; 75, 2; viii. 20, 2; ix. 69, 1; Nirukta, ix. 17.

[2] Av. i. 3, 9; iv. 4, 7; xi. 9, 1, etc.; Vājasaneyi Saṃhitā, xvi. 9, etc.

[3] Aitareya Brāhmaṇa, vii. 19; *iṣu-dhanvin*, Taittirīya Saṃhitā, v. 1, 2.

[4] Aitareya Brāhmaṇa, i. 25.

[5] Śatapatha Brāhmaṇa, ix. 1, 1, 6.

2. **Dhanvan**, 'desert,' is repeatedly mentioned in the Rigveda[1] and later.[2] Death from thirst in the desert was not rare,[3] and

[1] ii. 38, 7; iii. 45, 1; iv. 17, 2; 19, 7; 33, 7; v. 53, 6; 83, 10, etc. In i. 116, 4, the strand of the ocean (**Samudra**) is mentioned.

[2] Av. v. 13, 1; vi. 100, 1; vii. 41, 1, etc.

[3] Aitareya Brāhmaṇa, ii. 19.

the value of a spring in the desert was fully appreciated.[4] The great desert east of the **Sindhu** (Indus) and the **Śutudrī** (Sutlej) is possibly referred to in one hymn of the Rigveda.[5]

[4] Rv. x. 4, 1. *Cf.* vi. 34, 4, etc.; Av. i. 6, 4; xix. 2, 2.
[5] x. 86, 20.
Cf. Zimmer, *Altindisches Leben*, 47, 48.

Dhamani, 'reed,' appears to denote 'pipe' in a passage of the Rigveda[1] and in a citation appearing in the Nirukta.[2] In the Atharvaveda[3] it denotes, perhaps, 'artery' or 'vein,' or more generally 'intestinal channel,' being coupled in some passages[4] with **Hirā.**

[1] ii. 11, 8. [2] vi. 24.
[3] i. 17, 23; ii. 33, 6; vi. 90, 2; vii. 35, 2. *Cf.* Chāndogya Upaniṣad, iii. 19, 2.
[4] i. 17, 3; vii. 35, 2.
Cf. Bloomfield, *Hymns of the Atharvaveda*, 259, 546.

Dharuṇa in one passage of the Vājasaneyi Saṃhitā (viii. 51) denotes a 'sucking calf.'

Dharma,[1] **Dharman,**[2] are the regular words, the latter in the Rigveda,[1] and both later,[2] for 'law' or 'custom.' But there is very little evidence in the early literature as to the administration of justice or the code of law followed. On the other hand, the Dharma Sūtras[3] contain full particulars.

(1) *Criminal Law.*—The crimes recognized in Vedic literature vary greatly in importance, while there is no distinction adopted in principle between real crimes and what now are regarded as fanciful bodily defects or infringements of merely

[1] i. 22, 18; 164. 43. 50; iii. 3, 1; 17, 1; 60, 6; v. 26, 6; 63, 7; 72, 2, etc.; Av. xiv. 1, 51; Vājasaneyi Saṃhitā, x. 29, etc. *Cf.* Geldner, *Rigveda, Glossar*, 90.
[2] Dharma is found in Av. xi. 7, 17; xii. 5, 7; xviii. 3, 1; Taittirīya Saṃhitā, iii. 5, 2, 2; Vājasaneyi Saṃhitā, xv. 6; xx. 9; xxx. 6, etc.
[3] See Jolly, *Recht und Sitte*; Foy, *Die königliche Gewalt nach den altindischen Rechtsbüchern*; Bühler, *Sacred Books of the East*, 2 and 14.

conventional practices.[4] The crimes enumerated include the slaying of an embryo (*bhrūṇa*),[5] the slaying of a man (*vīra*),[6] and the slaying of a Brahmin,[7] a much more serious crime. Treachery is mentioned in the Pañcaviṃśa Brāhmaṇa[8] as being punishable by death, as it was punished later.[9] But there is no trace of an organized criminal justice vested either in the king or in the people. There still seems to have prevailed the system of wergeld (**Vaira**), which indicates that criminal justice remained in the hands of those who were wronged. In the Sūtras,[10] on the other hand, the king's peace is recognized as infringed by crimes, a penalty being paid to him, or, according to the Brahminical textbooks, to the Brahmins. It may there-

[4] Compare the list in Maitrāyaṇī Saṃhitā, iv. 1, 9; Kāṭhaka Saṃhitā, xxxi. 7; Kapiṣṭhala Saṃhitā, xlvii. 7; and Taittirīya Brāhmaṇa, iii. 2, 8, 11 (see Delbrück, *Die indogermanischen Verwandtschaftsnamen*, 579 *et seq.*), where bodily defects (bad nails and discoloured teeth), marrying a younger daughter when her elder sister was unmarried, are coupled with murder, though not equated with it. See also Chāndogya Upaniṣad, v. 11, 5, where Aśvapati's list of sinners includes a drinker of intoxicating liquor, a thief, and one who does not maintain a sacrificial fire.

[5] Taittirīya Saṃhitā, vi. 5, 10, 2; Kāṭhaka Saṃhitā, xxvii. 9; xxxi. 7; Kapiṣṭhala Saṃhitā, xli. 7; Maitrāyaṇī Saṃhitā, iv. 1, 9; Taittirīya Brāhmaṇa, iii. 2, 8, 12; Taittirīya Āraṇyaka, ii. 7, 8; 8, 3; Bṛhadāraṇyaka Upaniṣad, iv. 1, 22; Nirukta, vi. 27; Kauṣītaki Upaniṣad, iii. 1. *Cf.* Av. vi. 112, 3; 113, 2; Weber, *Indische Studien*, 9, 481; 10, 66; Bloomfield, *Hymns of the Atharvaveda*, 522; *American Journal of Philology*, 17, 430.

[6] Kāṭhaka, xxxi. 7; Kapiṣṭhala, *loc. cit.*; Maitrāyaṇī, *loc. cit.*; Taittirīya Brāhmaṇa, *loc. cit.*; Vājasaneyi Saṃhitā, xxx. 5, and *cf.* **Vaira**. For cases of justifiable homicide, see, *e.g.*, Vasiṣṭha Dharma Sūtra, iii. 15-18. *Cf.* also the story of **Vṛśa Jāna** in Pañcaviṃśa Brāhmaṇa, xiii. 3, 12, where the death of a boy by careless driving is mentioned, and the king is reproached for it by his Purohita. They dispute as to the guilt, and, according to one version (see Sieg, *Die Sagenstoffe des Ṛgveda*, 66, 67), the **Ikṣvākus** decide that the action was sinful, and required expiation.

[7] Taittirīya Saṃhitā, ii. 5, 1, 2; v. 3, 12, 1; vi. 5, 10, 2; Kāṭhaka Saṃhitā, xxxi. 7 (where the Kapiṣṭhala has *brahma-jya*, 'oppressor of a Brahmin'); Taittirīya Brāhmaṇa, iii. 2, 8, 12. The Taittirīya Āraṇyaka, x. 38, declares that the slaying of a Brahmin alone is truly murder, and the Śatapatha Brāhmaṇa, xiii. 3, 1, 1 *et seq.*, states that the sin of murdering a Brahmin can be expiated only by the performance of an Aśvamedha, or 'horse sacrifice'—the *ne plus ultra* of human generosity to Brahmins. See also Nirukta, vi. 27. The later tradition also interprets *bhrūṇa* as Brahmin (see Śaṅkara, cited in Weber, *Indische Studien*, 1, 410, n.; Keith, *Śāṅkhāyana Āraṇyaka*, 30, n. 5; Konow, *Sāmavidhāna Brāhmaṇa*, 46, n. 1, and *cf.* Vasiṣṭha Dharma Sūtra, xx. 23).

[8] xiv. 6, 8, the story of **Kutsa**.

[9] Jolly, *op. cit.*, 127.

[10] See references in Bühler, *Sacred Books of the East*, 14, 345.

fore reasonably be conjectured that the royal power of jurisdiction steadily increased; the references in the Śatapatha Brāhmaṇa to the king as wielding punishment (**Daṇḍa**) confirm this supposition. Whether, as the analogy of other systems suggests, the king was assisted in his judicial duties, as he undoubtedly was later, by assessors, presumably of the Brahmin caste, cannot be made out clearly.[11]

The procedure adopted in deciding cases is quite uncertain. In the Chāndogya Upaniṣad[12] the ordeal of the red-hot axe is mentioned as applied in an accusation of theft. It must apparently be understood to have been inflicted by the direction of the king. But no other judicial ordeal is known to Vedic literature (see **Divya**). The punishment of theft was in some cases at least death, probably when the thief was taken red-handed;[13] in other cases binding to posts was the penalty,[14] presumably accompanied by the return of the stolen goods. In the Chāndogya Upaniṣad[15] the list of sins given as apparently equal in wickedness is stealing gold, drinking spirits, defiling a Guru's bed, and the murder of a Brahmin.

(2) *Civil Law.*—There is little recorded as to civil law in Vedic literature. The relations of the family and the question of family property are dealt with under **Urvarā, Kṣetra, Pati**; succession and partition of property are treated under **Dāya.** As regards the transfer of chattels—for land as transferable *inter vivos* is hardly yet recognized, save exceptionally as a sacrificial fee (**Dakṣiṇā**), and then disapproved[16]—the recognized modes are gift (**Dāna**) and barter or sale (**Kraya**), which includes exchange. Original acquisition of land was no doubt brought

[11] Compare the story of the death of the child killed by Tryaruṇa, and the decision of the Ikṣvākus referred to in n. 6 above, and the notice in Kāṭhaka Saṃhitā, xxvii. 4, that a Rājanya is *adhyakṣa*, when a Sūdra is punished (*han*).

[12] vi. 16. *Cf.* Weber, *Indian Literature*, 72, 73.

[13] Gautama Dharma Sūtra, xii. 43; Āpastamba Dharma Sūtra, i. 9, 25, 4.

[14] See Av. xix. 47, 9; 50, 1, and **Taskara.**

[15] v. 10, 9. Another list is given in Taittirīya Āraṇyaka, x. 65, which includes slaying a Brahmin, defiling a Guru's bed, stealing a cow, drinking Surā, and killing an embryo, along with irregularities in offering a Śrāddha, 'water offering to the dead.' *Cf.* also Nirukta, vi. 27, for a list of seven. Many more appear in the Sāmavidhāna Brāhmaṇa, but that work cannot claim to be a Brāhmaṇa proper.

[16] Śatapatha Brāhmaṇa, xiii. 7, 1, 13.

about by occupation and apportionment among the tribesmen,[17] while chattels were acquired by taking possession of them, provided that they were found on one's own land or on unoccupied land, and did not belong to any other person originally. The Sūtras[18] contain rules for the disposal of lost property, which tend to give it to the king, with the deduction of a percentage for the finder, unless the latter is a Brahmin, who keeps it all. As for contract, save in regard to money-lending (for which see **Ṛṇa**), practically nothing is to be gathered from Vedic literature, doubtless because of the primitive conditions prevailing in that early period. Much of the labour, which would in a more developed society have been done by workers for hire, would be performed by slaves (*cf.* **Dāsa, Śūdra**), while the technical workers of the village—of whom long lists are given in the Vājasaneyi Saṃhitā[19] and the Taittirīya Brāhmaṇa[20]—may have been recompensed not by any sum based on each piece of work done, but by fixed allowances, much as the village servants are in modern times.[21] But this must remain a matter of conjecture, and it is uncertain what exact status the carpenter or smith held in the village. Similarly it is impossible to trace in the early literature any legal theory or practice as to torts, but rules as to penalties for insults appear in the Sūtras.[22]

Very little is recorded as to procedure. The list[23] of victims at the Puruṣamedha, or 'horse sacrifice,' includes a *praśnin*, an *abhi-praśnin*, and a *praśna-vivāka*, in whom it is not unreasonable to see the plaintiff, the defendant, and the arbitrator or judge: the terms may refer to what is probably an early

[17] *Cf.* Cæsar, *Bellum Gallicum*, iv. 1; vi. 22; Tacitus, *Germania*, 26, for Germany; Mommsen, *Römisches Staatsrecht*, 3, 1, 21, for the Roman *hortus;* and the Greek κλῆρος, Lang, *Homer and the Epic*, 236-241; Ridgeway, *Journal of Hellenic Studies*, 6, 319 *et seq.*; Grote, *History of Greece*, 2, 36, 37. See also Pollock and Maitland, *History of English Law*, 2, 337 *et seq.*; Baden Powell, *Village Communities in India*, 6 *et seq.*; 131.

[18] Gautama Dharma Sūtra, x. 36 *et seq.*

[19] xxx.

[20] iii. 4. See Zimmer, *Altindisches Leben*, 426 *et seq.*; Weber, *Indische Streifen*, 1, 75 *et seq.*

[21] *Cf.* Maine, *Village Communities*, 127, 175; Baden Powell, *op. cit.*, 124 *et seq.*; Grote, *History of Greece*, 2, 36, n. 2.

[22] *Cf.* Jolly, *op. cit.*, 126-128.

[23] Vājasaneyi Saṃhitā, xxx. 10; Taittirīya Brāhmaṇa, iii. 4, 6, 1.

form of judicial procedure, a voluntary arbitration. The same idea may be conveyed by the word *madhyama-śī*, 'lying in the midst,' which occurs in the Rigveda,[24] and which Roth,[25] followed by Zimmer,[26] understood to mean an arbitrator or judge, the expression being derived from the judge acting with other judicial persons,[27] and being surrounded by the assembly of the people. But this interpretation is uncertain; Whitney[28] thinks that the word merely alludes to a chief round whom his men encamp. The king is later the chief civil judge, and may presumably have been so earlier, no doubt in conjunction with the elders of the tribe, but for this we are reduced to conjecture.[29]

The use of witnesses as evidence is uncertain (see **Jñātṛ**), and the ordeal is not recorded as deciding any civil matter except the dispute between **Vatsa** and his rival as to the true Brahminical descent of the former, which was settled by his walking unharmed through the flame of a fire.[30] But it is probable on analogy that the ordeal may have been used for the purpose of deciding disputes. Whether the oath was so used cannot be certainly shown. It appears, however, that a Brahmin was preferred in legal matters to a non-Brahmin.[31]

There are very few references to police officials: no doubt the king employed some of his dependents to execute sentences and arrest offenders (see **Ugra, Jīvagṛbh**).

(3) *Morality.*—It is convenient to notice under this head

[24] x. 97, 12 = Av. iv. 9, 4 = Vājasaneyi Saṃhitā, xii. 86. *Madhyamaśīvan*, in the Jaiminīya Brāhmaṇa, ii. 408, is of quite doubtful sense.

[25] *Siebenzig Lieder*, 174. This fact renders doubtful Lanman's view (Whitney, Translation of the Atharvaveda, 159) that the St. Petersburg Dictionary, in giving *intercessor* as the interpretation, did not mean 'mediator,' but 'adversary.'

[26] *Altindisches Leben*, 180.

[27] As, apparently, in early Germany. See Cæsar, *Bellum Gallicum*, vi. 23; Tacitus, *Germania*, 11. 12; Coulanges, *Recherches sur quelques problèmes d'histoire*, 361 *et seq.*

[28] See n. 25.

[29] *Cf.* the later Pariṣad, Gautama Dharma Sūtra, xxviii. 48. 49; Baudhāyana Dharma Sūtra, i. 1, 7-16; Vasiṣṭha Dharma Sūtra, xi. 5-7, 20; Jolly, *op. cit.*, 132 *et seq.* The parallels from other Āryan peoples suggest the use of assessors, as in the Anglo-Saxon courts of the shire and hundred. *Cf.* Sohm, *Altdeutsches Reichs- und Gerichtsverfassung*, 6 *et seq.*

[30] Pañcaviṃśa Brāhmaṇa, xiv. 6, 6.

[31] Taittirīya Saṃhitā, ii. 5, 11, 9, which seems to refer either to giving evidence for or passing judgment on a case when both a Brahmin and a non-Brahmin are engaged.

several points bearing on the moral condition of the people: (*a*) the exposure of children; (*b*) the exposure of the aged; (*c*) prostitution; (*d*) adultery; (*e*) incest.

(*a*) The exposure of girl infants is asserted by Zimmer[32] on the strength of a passage in the Kāṭhaka Saṃhitā,[33] but it seems clear that the passage has been misunderstood,[34] and that it refers merely to laying the child aside, not exposing it, while a boy was lifted up. It is, however, true that the birth of a girl was not at all popular, not an unnatural sentiment in an early society, and paralleled among other Āryan peoples.[35]

(*b*) The exposure of the aged is also inferred by Zimmer[36] from a passage of the Rigveda,[37] and from the mention of persons exposed (*ud-hitāḥ*) in the Atharvaveda.[38] The latter passage may well refer merely to the bodies being exposed after death to the elements (as is done by the Parsīs). The former passage merely refers to the individual case of some person who may have been cast out, and proves absolutely nothing as to a habitual or recognized custom, nor can such a custom be inferred from, *e.g.*, the legend of **Cyavāna.**

(*c*) That prostitution existed in Rigvedic times is certain, but its extent is disputed. Brotherless girls were frequently reduced to becoming prostitutes;[39] the putting away of an illegitimate child is referred to in the Rigveda;[40] besides the

[32] *Altindisches Leben*, 319, 320. *Cf.* also Weber, *Indische Studien*, 5, 54, 260; Kaegi, *Der Rigveda*, n. 49; Schrader, *Prehistoric Antiquities*, 389, 390; Ludwig, Translation of the Rigveda, 6, 142; Pischel, *Vedische Studien*, 2, 48.

[33] xxvii. 9. *Cf.* Taittirīya Saṃhitā, vi. 5, 10, 3; Śāṅkhāyana Śrauta Sūtra, xv. 17, 12; Nirukta iii. 4.

[34] Böhtlingk, *Zeitschrift der Deutschen Morgenländischen Gesellschaft*, 44, 494-496. The traditional rendering of the passages is not that it refers to exposure, but to getting rid of a daughter on her marriage.

[35] Av. viii. 6, 25; Aitareya Brāhmaṇa, vii. 15; Max Müller, *Ancient Sanskrit Literature*, 409; Zimmer, *op. cit.*, 320; Schrader, *op. cit.*, 390.

[36] *Op. cit.*, 327, 328. Strabo, pp. 513, 517, 520, reports the practice as prevailing in Iran, Bactria, and the Massagetae; it prevailed among the Norsemen, Weinhold, *Altnordisches Leben*, 473, and conceivably among the early Romans (*depontani senes*, Cicero, *Pro Roscio*, 100; but this and other cases may be really instances of the ritual casting into water of the worn-out vegetation spirit for the purpose of reviving it). See Kaegi, *op. cit.*, n. 50; Schrader, *op. cit.*, 379, n.

[37] viii. 51, 2.

[38] xviii. 2, 34. See **Anagnidagdha.**

[39] Rv. i. 124, 7; iv. 5, 5; Av. i. 17, 1; and *cf.* **Ayogū.**

[40] ii. 29, 1. *Cf.* Max Müller, *op. cit.*, 26.

terms *puṃścalī*[41] and *mahānagnī*,[42] which undoubtedly mean 'harlot,' there are other clear references to prostitution;[43] and expressions like *kumārī-putra*, 'son of a maiden,'[44] and the 'son of an unmarried girl' (*agrū*), spoken of in the Rigveda[45] as exposed and attacked by animals, point in the same direction. The Vājasaneyi Saṃhitā[46] seems to recognize prostitution as a profession. Pischel[47] sees many references to Hetairai in the Rigveda, which as Geldner[48] insists reflects in its imagery the court life of Indian princes. But the correctness of the view of these two scholars on this point is not by any means certain.[49]

(*d*) Adultery was generally regarded among Āryan peoples as a serious offence against the husband of the woman affected. We accordingly find in the legal literature of India traces of the rule that an adulterer can be slain with impunity if taken in the act.[50] Weber,[51] however, has adduced some material indicating an indifference to these matters in Vedic times, and Ludwig[52] has adopted the same view. But, as Delbrück[53] has clearly shown, the evidence is not convincing; the cited prescriptions[54] forbidding connexion with another man's wife during a certain rite do not imply that such connexion would otherwise be allowed: the ritual of the Varuṇa-praghāsas,[55] when a wife names her lover or lovers, seems originally to have been a solemn means of banishing the evil brought on a family by a wife's fall; **Yājñavalkya's** famous saying[56] that no one

[41] Av. xv. 2, etc.

[42] Av. xiv. 1, 36; xx. 136, 5 *et seq.*; Aitareya Brāhmaṇa, i. 27. *Cf. nagnā* in Av. v. 7, 8.

[43] Rv. i. 167, 4 (Wilson, Translation of the Rigveda, 2, xvii), can hardly be so interpreted; see Zimmer, *op. cit.*, 332, n. Max Müller, *Sacred Books of the East*, 32, 277, interprets it as a reference to polyandry, but this is still more doubtful; but see Rv. viii. 17, 7.

[44] Vājasaneyi Saṃhitā, xxx. 6; Taittirīya Brāhmaṇa, iii. 4, 2, 1.

[45] iv. 19, 9; 30, 16. 19; ii. 13, 12; 15, 17; Zimmer, *op. cit.*, 334, 335.

[46] Apparently this is meant by the epithets *atiṣkadvarī* (*apaskadvarī* in the Taittirīya Brāhmaṇa, iii. 4, 11, 1), *atītvarī*, *vijarjarā*, in the Vājasaneyi Saṃhitā, xxx. 15.

[47] *Vedische Studien*, 1, xxv; 196, 275, 299, 309, etc.; 2, 120.

[48] *Ibid.*, 2, 154.

[49] *Cf.* Winternitz, *Geschichte der indischen Litteratur*, 1, 60; Jolly, *op. cit.*, 48.

[50] Leist, *Altarisches Jus Gentium*, 276 *et seq.*, 309.

[51] *Indische Studien*, 10, 83 *et seq.*

[52] *Op. cit.*, 5, 573.

[53] *Die indogermanischen Verwandtschaftsnamen*, 545 *et seq.*

[54] Taittirīya Saṃhitā, v. 6, 8, 3; Maitrāyaṇī Saṃhitā, iii. 4, 7.

[55] Maitrāyaṇī Saṃhitā, i. 10, 11; Śatapatha Brāhmaṇa, ii. 5, 2, 20.

[56] Śatapatha Brāhmaṇa, i. 3, 1, 21.

cares whether a wife is 'unchaste' (*paraḥ-puṃsā*) or not is a mere mistranslation,[57] the expression *paraḥ-puṃsā* really meaning 'removed from the male persons.' And the uncertainty asserted in some passages[58] as to origin from a Ṛṣi is not a sign of doubtful descent, but is due to the fact that Ṛṣihood was a difficult matter to ascertain. None the less woman's position was lowered by the prevalence of polygamy, and such stories as that of Ahalyā and Indra[59] are not compatible with a very high standard of morality. A similar conclusion is pointed to by references in the Yajurveda[60] to relations between the Ārya man and the Śūdrā woman, and by a spell given in the Bṛhadāraṇyaka Upaniṣad[61] to expiate relations with the wife of a Śrotriya (Brahmin theologian).

(*e*) Incest was recognized in the marriage of brother and sister as appears from the legend of Yama and Yamī in the Rigveda,[62] which clearly shows that such a marriage was not approved by the feeling of the Vedic age. There is also another hymn[63] in which reference to such intercourse appears to be made. Mention is further made in the Rigveda[64] to the wedlock of Prajāpati and his daughter, which is, however, interpreted mythologically in the Brāhmaṇas,[65] an interpretation which may be correct. That incest, however, actually did take place is clear from the Atharvaveda;[66] but even though the mythological interpretation of the passage were not justified, no conclusion could be drawn from the hymn as to the normal occurrence of such relations.

57 So Böhtlingk, Dictionary, *s.v.*; Delbrück, *op. cit.*, 548.

58 Maitrāyaṇī Saṃhitā, i. 4, 11; Gopatha Brāhmaṇa, cited in Ludwig, *loc. cit.*

59 *Cf.* Macdonell, *Vedic Mythology*, p. 65.

60 Taittirīya Saṃhitā, vii. 4, 19, 2. 3; Vājasaneyi Saṃhitā, xxiii. 30. 31.

61 vi. 4, 11.

62 x. 10.

63 x. 162, 5.

64 x. 61, 5-7.

65 Aitareya Brāhmaṇa, iii. 33; Satapatha Brāhmaṇa, i. 7, 4, 1; Muir, *Sanskrit Texts*, 4, 46, 47; Max Müller, *op. cit.*, 529, 530.

66 viii. 6, 7.

1. **Dhava** is the name of a tree (*Grislea tormentosa*) mentioned, together with the **Plakṣa, Aśvattha,** and **Khādira,** in the Atharvaveda.[1]

1 v. 5, 5; xx. 137, 11. *Cf.* Zimmer, *Altindisches Leben*, 62.

2. **Dhava**, 'man,' is not found before the Nirukta.[1] The word clearly owes its existence merely to *vidhavā*, 'widow,' wrongly interpreted as *vi-dhavā*, 'without a husband.'

[1] iii. 15. *Cf.* Naighaṇṭuka, ii. 3.

Dhavitra, occurring in the Śatapatha Brāhmaṇa[1] and the Taittirīya Āraṇyaka,[2] denotes a 'fan' of hide or leather for blowing the sacrificial fire.

[1] xiv. 1, 3, 30; 3, 1, 21.

[2] v. 4, 33.

Dhānaṃ-jayya, 'descendant of **Dhanaṃ-jaya**,' is the patronymic of **Aṃśu** in the Vaṃśa Brāhmaṇa.[1]

[1] *Indische Studien*, 4, 373. Under this patronymic he is frequently named by Lāṭyāyana Srauta Sūtra, i. 1, 25; ii. 1, 2; 9, 10, etc. (misread Dhānaṃjapya in many manuscripts). *Cf.* Weber, *Indian Literature*, 76, 77, 82.

Dhānā, always used in the plural, and frequently referred to in the Rigveda[1] and later,[2] means 'grains of corn.' They were sometimes parched (*bhṛjj*),[3] and were regularly mixed with Soma.[4]

[1] i. 16, 2; iii. 35, 3; 52, 5; vi. 29, 4, etc.

[2] Av. xviii. 3, 69; 4, 32. 34; Vājasaneyi Saṃhitā, xix. 21. 22; Taittirīya Brāhmaṇa, i. 5, 11, 2, etc.

[3] Rv. iv. 24, 7.

[4] Rv. iii. 43, 4; 52, 1; viii. 91, 2; Taittirīya Saṃhitā, iii. 1, 10, 2; Satapatha Brāhmaṇa, iv. 4, 3, 9.

Cf. Schrader, *Prehistoric Antiquities*, 283.

Dhānya (neut.), a derivative from the preceding word,[1] denotes 'grain' in general. It is found in the Rigveda[2] and later.[3] According to the Bṛhadāraṇyaka Upaniṣad,[4] there are ten cultivated (*grāmyāṇi*) kinds of grain: rice and barley (*vrīhi-yavāḥ*), sesamum and beans (*tila-māṣāḥ*), Panicum Miliaceum and Italicum (*aṇu-priyaṅgavaḥ*), maize (*godhūmāḥ*), lentils (*masūrāḥ*), Khalvāḥ and Dolichos uniflorus (*khala-kulāḥ*). The

[1] Primarily as an adjective, 'consisting of grain.'

[2] vi. 13, 4.

[3] Av. iii. 24, 2. 4; v. 29, 7; vi. 50, 1; Kauṣītaki Brāhmaṇa, xi. 8; Ṣaḍviṃśa Brāhmaṇa, v. 5, etc.

[4] vi. 3, 22 (Mādhyaṃdina = 13 Kāṇva).

horse is called 'corn-eating' (*dhānyāda*) in the Aitareya[5] and Śatapatha[6] Brāhmaṇas, and men are mentioned as 'purifying corn' (*dhānyā-kṛt*) in the Rigveda.[8]

[5] viii. 21.
[6] xiii. 5, 4, 2.
[7] Lit., 'preparing corn.'
[8] x. 94, 13.

Dhānva is the patronymic of **Asita** in the Śatapatha Brāhmaṇa.[1] In the Śāṅkhāyana Śrauta Sūtra[2] the form of the name is Dhānvana.

[1] xiii. 4, 3, 11; Āśvalāyana Śrauta Sūtra, x. 7.
[2] xvi. 2, 20.

Dhāman denotes in the Rigveda[1] and later[2] 'dwelling' and 'house,' or sometimes[3] its inmates. The word is also[4] found in the sense of 'ordinance,' 'law,' expressing much the same as **Dharman**, especially in conjunction[5] with Ṛta, 'eternal order.' Hillebrandt[6] sees in one passage[7] the sense of **Nakṣatra.**

[1] i. 144, 1; ii. 3, 2; iii. 55, 10; vii. 61, 4; 87, 2; x. 13, 1, etc.
[2] Av. iv. 25, 7; vii. 68, 1; xii. 1, 52; Vājasaneyi Saṃhitā, iv. 34; Taittirīya Āraṇyaka, ii. 7, 2.
[3] Rv. viii. 101, 6; ix. 63, 14; x. 82, 3; Av. ii. 14, 6. Many of the examples given in the St. Petersburg Dictionary, *s.v.*, *C*, are doubtful.
[4] Rv. iv. 55, 2; vi. 21, 3; vii. 63, 3; viii. 41, 10; x. 48, 11.
[5] Rv. i. 123, 9; iv. 7, 7; vii. 36, 5; x. 124, 3.
[6] *Vedische Mythologie*, 1, 446.
[7] Rv. ix. 66, 2.
Cf. Geldner, *Rigveda*, *Glossar*, 92, 93.

Dhārā denotes the 'edge' of a weapon,[1] as of an axe (*svadhiti*),[2] or of a razor (*kṣura*).[3] See also **Asi**.

[1] Rv. vi. 3, 5; 47, 10. *Cf.* viii. 73, 9; Taittirīya Āraṇyaka, iv. 38, 1, for metaphorical applications.
[2] Kauśika Sūtra, 44.
[3] Bṛhadāraṇyaka Upaniṣad, iii. 3, 2.

Dhiṣaṇā, according to the St. Petersburg Dictionary, denotes[1] an implement used in preparing the Soma, 'bowl' or 'vat,' and by metonymy also the Soma draught itself.[2] The dual, by

[1] Rv. i. 96, 1; 102, 1; 109, 3. 4; iii. 49, 1; iv. 34, 1; 36, 8; viii. 61, 9; ix. 59, 2; x. 17, 12; 30, 6; Vājasaneyi Saṃhitā, i. 19; vi. 26. 35, etc.
[2] Rv. i. 102, 7; iii. 32, 14; 49, 4; vi. 19, 2; vii. 90, 3; viii. 15, 7; x. 96, 10, etc.

a metaphor,[3] also expresses the 'two worlds,' heaven and earth.[4] Hillebrandt,[5] however, thinks that the word properly means earth,[6] in the dual heaven and earth,[7] in the plural the triad, earth, atmosphere, and heaven,[8] while in some passages[9] Dhiṣaṇā denotes the Vedi, the excavated ground used as an altar. This is not, however, certain, while it seems clear that the Vājasaneyi[10] and Taittirīya[11] Saṃhitās understand the Dhiṣaṇās (dual) to be the planks over which the pressing of the Soma took place (*adhiṣavaṇa-phalake*).[12] Pischel[13] sees in Dhiṣaṇā a goddess of wealth akin to Aditi and the earth.

[3] Like **Camū**.

[4] Rv. i. 160, 1; vi. 8, 3; 50, 3; 70, 3; x. 44, 8; in the plural, 'the three worlds,' Rv. v. 69, 2. In other passages, Rv. i. 22, 10; iii. 56, 6; v. 41, 8; vi. 11, 3; x. 35, 7, the sense of 'a genius of prosperity' was assigned to Dhiṣaṇā by Roth.

[5] *Vedische Mythologie*, 1, 175-181.

[6] Rv. i. 22, 10; 96, 1; 102, 1; iii. 31, 13; 56, 6; vi. 19, 2; vii. 90, 3; viii. 15, 7; x. 30, 6; 35, 7; 96, 10.

[7] See n. 3; also Rv. viii. 61, 2; *nivid* in Sāṅkhāyana Śrauta Sūtra, viii. 19, 4.

[8] Rv. iv. 36, 8; v. 69, 2; ix. 59, 2.

[9] Rv. i. 109, 3-4; iii. 2, 1; 49, 4 (or perhaps 'earth'); iv. 34, 1; v. 41, 8; vi. 11, 3; x. 17, 12.

[10] vii. 26.

[11] iii. 1, 10, 1.

[12] Mahīdhara on Vājasaneyi Saṃhitā, vii. 26; Sāyaṇa on Taittirīya Saṃhitā, *loc. cit.*

[13] *Vedische Studien*, 2, 82-87. *Cf.* Macdonell, *Vedic Mythology*, p. 124; Oldenberg, *Sacred Books of the East*, 46, 120-122.

Dhī, 'thought,' is used several times in the Rigveda[1] to denote the 'prayer' or 'hymn of praise' of the singer. One poet speaks of himself as 'weaving' such a prayer,[2] while another refers to his 'ancient ancestral hymn,' which he refurbishes presumably for use.[3]

[1] i. 3, 5; 135, 5; 151, 6; 185, 8; ii. 3, 8 (where it is connected with **Sarasvatī**); 40, 5, etc.

[2] Rv. ii. 28, 5.

[3] Rv. iii. 39, 2.

Cf. Zimmer, *Altindisches Leben*, 338.

Dhīti has in several passages of the Rigveda[1] practically the same sense as **Dhī**, 'prayer,' or 'hymn of praise.'

[1] i. 110, 1; iii. 12, 7; 52, 6; v. 25, 3; 53, 11; vi. 15, 9, etc.; Nirukta, ii. 24.

Dhīra Śāta-parṇeya ('descendant of Śataparṇa') is mentioned in the Śatapatha Brāhmaṇa (x. 3, 3, 1) as a pupil of **Mahāśāla**.

Dhīvan occurs in the Atharvaveda,[1] where it may either be taken with Roth,[2] Bloomfield,[3] and Whitney[4] as an epithet of 'chariot-builders' (*ratha-kārāḥ*), meaning 'clever,' or be construed with the scholiast as denoting 'fishermen' (*dhīvara*). The Paippalāda recension has *takṣāṇaḥ*, 'carpenters.'

[1] iii. 5, 6.
[2] St. Petersburg Dictionary, *s.v.*
[3] *Hymns of the Atharvaveda*, 114.
[4] Translation of the Atharvaveda, 114. *Cf.* Weber, *Indische Studien*, 17, 194 *et seq.*; Zimmer, *Altindisches Leben*, 252.

Dhuṅkṣā is the name of some sort of bird in the list of victims at the Aśvamedha, or 'horse sacrifice,' in the Yajurveda Saṃhitās.[1] See also **Dhūṅkṣṇā** and **Dhvāṅkṣa**.

[1] Maitrāyaṇī Saṃhitā, iii. 14, 12; Vājasaneyi Saṃhitā, xxiv. 31. *Cf.* Zimmer, *Altindisches Leben*, 93.

Dhuni is the name of a foe of Indra, normally mentioned along with **Cumuri** in the Rigveda.[1] He and Cumuri seem to have been opposed to **Dabhīti**.[2] His name is probably that of an aboriginal chief.[3]

[1] ii. 15, 9; vi. 18, 8; 20, 13; vii. 19, 4.
[2] Rv. x. 113, 9.
[3] Wackernagel, *Altindische Grammatik*, 1, xxii; Macdonell, *Vedic Mythology*, p. 162. *Cf.* Oldenberg, *Religion des Veda*, 157, 158.

Dhur in the Rigveda[1] and later[2] denotes, according to the St. Petersburg Dictionary, that part of the yoke which is placed on the shoulders of the animals drawing the chariot or cart, whence they are called *dhūr-ṣāh*, 'yoke-bearing,' in the Vājasaneyi Saṃhitā.[3] In one passage of the Rigveda[4] the sense is uncertain: Roth[5] takes it to mean the pin at either end of the axle (**Akṣa**) which goes through the nave of the wheel, and would thus be equivalent to **Āṇi**, and Oldenberg[6]

[1] i. 84, 16; 100, 16; 134, 3; 164, 19; ii. 18, 7; iii. 35, 2; v. 55, 6; vii. 34, 4, etc.
[2] Av. v. 17, 18; Aitareya Brāhmaṇa vi. 18; Satapatha Brāhmaṇa, i. 1, 2 10; 4, 4, 13, etc.; Aitareya Āraṇyaka i. 5, 2 (the Dhur is the end), etc.
[3] iv. 33. *Cf.* **Usra**.
[4] v. 43, 8.
[5] St. Petersburg Dictionary, *s.v.*, 2.
[6] *Ṛgveda - Noten*, 1, 339; Griffith, *Hymns of the Rigveda*, 1, 508. The *akṣa-dhurau* are mentioned in the Āpastamba Srauta Sūtra, xi. 6, 5; Kātyāyana Srauta Sūtra, viii. 3, 22. *Cf.* Caland and Henry, *L'Agniṣṭoma*, 81.

seems to adopt the same view. Monier Williams[7] seems to think that 'load' is meant, but this is not probable. It is possible that Dhur has the sense of 'pole,'[8] and then more generally still the pole and the axle together regarded as the drawing part of the chariot: this might explain the use in the doubtful passage of the Rigveda.

[7] Dictionary, *s.v.*

[8] Zimmer, *Altindisches Leben*, 246. Later, the word means the 'end of the pole,' a sense already found in the Aitareya Āraṇyaka (n. 2). This modification of meaning seems to be due to the fact that the yoke is at the end of the pole. See also **Dhūrṣad**.

Dhūṅkṣṇā is the form in the Taittirīya Saṃhitā[1] of the name of the bird elsewhere found as **Dhuṅkṣā.** It is glossed as 'white crow' (*śveta-kākī*).

[1] v. 5, 19, 1. Zimmer, *Altindisches Leben*, 93, gives the form as Dhūṅkṣṇa, perhaps in error. *Cf.* also **Dhvāṅkṣa**.

Dhūma-ketu, 'smoke-bannered,' is an epithet of Mṛtyu, 'death,' in the Atharvaveda.[1] Zimmer[2] thinks that a comet is meant, but Whitney[3] considers this extremely improbable. Lanman[4] plausibly suggests that the smoke of the funeral pile is referred to.

[1] xix. 9, 10.

[2] *Altindisches Leben*, 358.

[3] Translation of the Atharvaveda, 914.

[4] *Ibid.*

Dhūmra in the Taittirīya Saṃhitā (i. 8, 21, 1) denotes 'camel' according to Böhtlingk's Dictionary.

Dhūr-ṣad means, according to Roth,[1] 'standing under the yoke' and so 'burden-bearing,' and thus metaphorically 'promoting,' in the passages of the Rigveda[2] where it occurs. More probable, however, is the view[3] that it means 'sitting on the pole,' that is, 'charioteer,' with reference to the fact that

[1] St. Petersburg Dictionary, *s.v.*

[2] i. 143, 7; ii. 2, 1; 34, 4 (but *cf.* Pischel, *Vedische Studien*, 1, 301). In x. 132, 7, Roth renders 'resting on the yoke.'

[3] *Cf.* Hopkins, *Journal of the American Oriental Society*, 13, 237 *et seq.*; Keith, *Aitareya Āraṇyaka*, 195.

to get near his horses the charioteer might well go forward and sit on the pole or even on the yoke.[4]

[4] *Cf.* Mahābhārata, viii. 617 : *dhuryān dhuryagatān sūtān.*

1. **Dhṛta-rāṣṭra** (' having his kingdom firmly established ') is the name of a snake demon with the patronymic **Airāvata**, ' descendant of **Irāvant**,' in the Atharvaveda[1] and the Pañcaviṃśa Brāhmaṇa.[2]

[1] viii. 10, 29.
[2] xxv. 15, 3. *Cf.* Jaiminīya Upaniṣad Brāhmaṇa, iv. 26, 15 ; Weber, *Indische Studien*, 17, 257.

2. **Dhṛtarāṣṭra Vaicitra-vīrya** (' descendant of Vicitravīrya ') is mentioned in a passage of the Kāṭhaka Saṃhitā,[1] which is, unhappily, far from intelligible. But there is no ground for supposing that he was a Kuru-Pañcāla king ; he seems rather to have lived at some distance from the Kuru-Pañcālas. There is no good reason to deny his identity[2] with the Dhṛtarāṣṭra of the Śatapatha Brāhmaṇa,[3] king of **Kāśi**, who was defeated, when he attempted to offer a horse sacrifice, by **Sātrājita Śatānīka**. The fact that the latter was a **Bharata** also points to Dhṛtarāṣṭra's not having been a Kuru-Pañcāla at all. In the Kāṭhaka Saṃhitā he appears as having a dispute with **Vaka Dālbhi** ; but even assuming that the latter was a Pañcāla, there is nothing to hint that the former was a Kuru or that this dispute is a sign of an early hostility of Kuru and Pañcāla.[4] It is true that in the Epic **Śantanu** and Vicitravīrya and Dhṛtarāṣṭra himself are all connected, but this connexion seems to be due, as so often in the Epic, to a confused derangement of great figures of the past.

[1] x. 6. *Cf.* Weber, *Indische Studien*, 3, 469 *et seq.*
[2] As does Weber, *Indian Literature*, 90, 114, 125 ; *Episches im vedischen Ritual*, 7, 8. Roth, St. Petersburg Dictionary, *s.v.*, treats them as identical.
[3] xiii. 5, 4, 22.
[4] Keith, *Journal of the Royal Asiatic Society*, 1908, 831 *et seq.* This argument is independent of the identification of the two Dhṛtarāṣṭras, but is confirmed by it.

Dhṛṣṭi, found in the dual in the Taittirīya Āraṇyaka,[1] the Śatapatha Brāhmaṇa,[2] and the Sūtras,[3] seems to denote ' fire-tongs.'

[1] v. 9, 8.
[2] xiv. 3, 1, 22.
[3] Kātyāyana Śrauta Sūtra, xxvi. 2, 10, etc.

Dhenā denotes a 'milch cow,'[1] or in the plural, 'draughts of milk.'[2] In two passages[3] Roth[4] takes the word to mean 'mare,' and in another the 'team' of Vāyu's chariot. Benfey,[6] on the other hand, renders it 'lips' in one passage,[7] with Sāyaṇa and with Durga's commentary on the Nirukta.[8] Geldner[9] assigns to the word the senses of 'lips,'[10] 'speech,'[11] 'cow,'[12] 'beloved,'[13] and 'streams.'[14]

1 Rv. iii. 34, 3 (Macdonell, *Vedic Mythology*, p. 61); v. 62, 2. *Cf.* Geldner, *Vedische Studien*, 3, 114.

2 Rv. iii. 1, 9; iv. 58, 6, etc.

3 i. 101, 10; v. 30, 9.

4 St. Petersburg Dictionary, *s.v.*

5 Rv. i. 2, 3.

6 *Orient und Occident*, 3, 130.

7 Rv. i. 101, 10.

8 vi. 17. *Cf.* Zimmer, *Altindisches Leben*, 249.

9 *Vedische Studien*, 3, 35-43; 166; *Rigveda, Glossar*, 95.

10 Rv. i. 101, 10; iii. 1, 9.

11 Rv. iv. 58, 6; i. 55, 4; 141, 1; viii. 32, 22; x. 104, 3. 10.

12 Rv. v. 62, 2, and Vāyu's cow of plenty, i. 2, 3.

13 Rv. v. 30, 9.

14 Rv. vii. 21, 3; iii. 34, 3.

Cf. Max Müller, *Sacred Books of the East*, 32, 441, 442.

Dhenu in the Rigveda[1] and later[2] means 'milch cow,' which is often mentioned with special reference to the production of milk,[3] and is contrasted with the 'bull' (*vṛṣabha*,[4] *pumāṃs*,[5] *anaḍvāh*).[6] In the plural[7] the word denotes 'draughts of milk.' The derivative, *dhenukā*, means merely 'female.'[8]

1 i. 32, 9 (*saha-vatsā*, 'with her calf'); 134, 4; ii. 2, 2; 34, 8; vi. 135, 8, etc.

2 Av. v. 17, 18; vii. 104, 1; Taittirīya Saṃhitā, ii. 6, 2, 3; Maitrāyaṇī Saṃhitā, iv. 4, 8; Vājasaneyi Saṃhitā, xviii. 27; Śatapatha Brāhmaṇa, ii. 2, 1, 21, etc.

3 Rv. vii. 33, 22; viii. 14, 3; Av. iv. 34, 8 (*kāma-dughā*, 'milking desires,' the later 'cow of plenty' of the Epic); Satapatha Brāhmaṇa, xii. 8, 2, 2.

4 Rv. x. 5, 7.

5 Av. xi. 1, 34.

6 Vājasaneyi Saṃhitā, xviii. 27; Satapatha Brāhmaṇa, iii. 1, 2, 21.

7 Rv. iv. 22, 6; viii. 2, 6; 4, 8; ix. 61, 21; 72, 1, etc.

8 Av. iii. 23, 4; Pañcaviṃśa Brāhmaṇa, xxv. 10, 23; Āśvalāyana Śrauta Sūtra, xii. 6, etc.

Dhenu-ṣṭarī in the Kāṭhaka (xiii. 6) and Maitrāyaṇī Saṃhitā (ii. 5, 4) denotes a cow which has ceased to give milk.

Dhaivara means a 'fisherman,' as a member of a caste,[1] in the list of victims at the Puruṣamedha, or 'human sacrifice,' in the Yajurveda.[2] *Cf.* **Dhīvara.**

1 This seems to be shown by the patronymic form, 'descendant of a *dhīvara*.'

2 Vājasaneyi Saṃhitā, xxx. 16; Taittirīya Brāhmaṇa, iii. 4, 15, 1.

Dhmātṛ (lit. 'blower') occurs twice in one passage of the Rigveda[1] in the two forms, *dhmātā*, nom. 'smelter,' and *dhmātarī*, which, according to the Padapāṭha, stands for *dhmātari*, a locative probably meaning 'in the smelting furnace.'[2] Geldner,[3] Bartholomae,[4] and Oldenburg[5] regard the latter form as a locative infinitive, 'in the smelting.' Ludwig[6] and Neisser[7] think *dhmātarī* is a nom. sing. masc. used in the same sense as *dhmātā*. Smelting is also clearly referred to,[8] and the smelter is described as using the wings of birds (*parṇa śakunānām*) to fan the flame.[9] That the art was widely applied is shown by the fact that reference is made to arrows with points of **Ayas**,[10] to kettles which were fashioned of the same metal and could be placed upon a fire,[11] and to Soma cups of beaten Ayas.[12]

1 v. 9, 5.

2 Macdonell, *Journal of the Royal Asiatic Society*, 1893, 446.

3 *Vedische Studien*, 1, 146, n. 1.

4 *Indogermanische Forschungen*, 1, 496, n. 2.

5 *Sacred Books of the East*, 46, 388.

6 *Infinitiv im Veda*, 9; Translation of the Rigveda, 4, 334.

7 Bezzenberger's *Beiträge*, 20, 40.

8 Rv. iv. 2, 17. In the Śatapatha Brāhmaṇa, vi. 1, 3, 5, **Ayas** is smelted from the ore (*aśman*), and gold from the Ayas.

9 Rv. ix. 112, 2.

10 *Cf.* **Iṣu.**

11 Rv. v. 30, 15.

12 Rv. ix. 1, 2.

Cf. Zimmer, *Altindisches Leben*, 252; Schrader, *Prehistoric Antiquities*, 159.

Dhrāji in the Rigveda[1] and later[2] denotes the 'sweep' of the wind, referring no doubt to the violent gales which often blow in India devastating the forests, and which figure in the descriptions of the Maruts, or storm gods.[3]

1 i. 164, 44; x. 97,.13; 136, 2.

2 Av. iii. 1, 5; Maitrāyaṇī Saṃhitā, i. 2, 17; iv. 9, 5; Taittirīya Āraṇyaka, i 11, 19, etc.

3 *Cf.* Max Müller, *Sacred Books of the East*, xxxii, xxiii *et seq.*; Macdonell, *Vedic Mythology*, p. 79.

Dhruva in the Sūtras[1] denotes the pole star, being mentioned in connexion with the marriage ritual, in which the star is pointed out to the bride as an emblem of constancy. In the

1 Āśvalāyana Gṛhya Sūtra, i. 7, 22; Śāṅkhāyana Gṛhya Sūtra, i. 17, 2 *et seq*; Lāṭyāyana Śrauta Sūtra, iii. 3, 6, etc. It is to be noted that the marriage Mantras, of which we have a great many, do not include any reference to the Dhruva; but it is not possible to say definitely whether the practice is really an old one or not.

Maitrāyaṇī Upaniṣad,[2] a late work, the movement of the Dhruva (*dhruvasya pracalanam*) is mentioned, but this can hardly be interpreted as referring to an actual observed motion of the nominal pole star,[3] but rather to an extraordinary event, such as a destruction of the world, as Cowell understood the expression.[4] Jacobi[5] sees in the motion of the Dhruva the possibility of fixing a date, on the ground that the only star which could have been deemed a pole star, as 'immovable,' was one (*a* Draconis) of the third millenium B.C. But this attempt to extract chronology from the name of the star is of very doubtful validity.[6]

[2] See Max Müller, *Sacred Books of the East*, 15, 289; Weber, *Indische Studien*, 2, 396.

[3] As understood by Weber, *Indian Literature*, 98, n. 103; Bühler, *Indian Antiquary*, 23, 245, n. 21; Jacobi, *Zeitschrift der Deutschen Morgenländischen Gesellschaft*, 49, 228, n. 2.

[4] In his edition of the Upaniṣad, p. 244.

[5] *Indian Antiquary*, 23, 157; *Zeitschrift*, *loc. cit.*, 50, 69 *et seq.*; *Journal of the Royal Asiatic Society*, 1909, 721 *et seq.*; 1910, 461 *et seq.*

[6] Whitney, *Journal of the American Oriental Society*, 16, xc; Keith, *Journal of the Royal Asiatic Society*, 1909, 1102; 1910, 465 *et seq.*

Dhruvā, 'fixed,' as an epithet of **Diś**, 'cardinal point,' denotes the ground under one's feet.

[1] Av. iii. 27, 5; xii. 3, 59; xv. 6, 1; Aitareya Brāhmaṇa, viii. 14 (*cf.* **Madhyadeśa**); Bṛhadāraṇyaka Upaniṣad, iii. 9, 25, etc.

Dhvaja occurs twice in the Rigveda[1] in the sense of 'banner' used in battle. It is characteristic of Vedic fighting that in both passages reference is made to arrows being discharged and falling on the banners.

[1] vii. 85, 2; x. 103, 11. In Epic warfare banners are of vast importance —*e.g.*, Rāmāyaṇa, ii. 67, 26; they were attached to a pole on the chariot, Mahābhārata, vii. 3332, etc. The army was called *dhvajinī*, 'bannered host,' *ibid.*, i. 2875, etc.

Dhvanya is apparently the name of a patron, son of **Lakṣmaṇa**, in a hymn of the Rigveda.[1]

[1] v. 33, 10. *Cf.* Ludwig, Translation of the Rigveda, 3, 155.

Dhvasan Dvaita-vana ('descendant of Dvitavana') is the name in the Śatapatha Brāhmaṇa[1] of the king of the **Matsyas** who celebrated an Aśvamedha, or 'horse sacrifice,' near the **Sarasvatī**.

[1] xiii. 5, 4, 9. *Cf.* Weber, *Indische Studien*, 1, 211; *Episches im vedischen Ritual*, 6.

Dhvasanti is in one passage of the Rigveda[1] mentioned together with **Puruṣanti** as having been aided by the Aśvins. There can be no doubt that this is the longer form of the name **Dhvasra**, which is found with Puruṣanti both in the Rigveda[2] and in the Pañcaviṃśa Brāhmaṇa.[3]

[1] i. 112, 23.

[2] ix. 58. 3 = Sv. ii. 409.

[3] xiii. 7, 12 (where the dual of Dhvasra appears as a feminine *Dhvasre*). *Cf.* Sieg, *Die Sagenstoffe des Ṛgveda*, 62, 63; Benfey, *Sāmaveda*, 105, 126, who is inclined to think that Dhvasanti and Puruṣanti are names of women.

Dhvasra is named with **Puruṣanti** in the Pañcaviṃśa Brāhmaṇa[1] as giving gifts to **Taranta** and **Purumīḍha**. These two, being kings, could not[2] properly accept gifts which Brāhmaṇas alone could accept, but by becoming authors of a verse of the Rigveda[3] they qualified themselves to accept them. The verse mentions the names in the dual as *Dhvasrayoḥ Puruṣantyoḥ*, 'from the two, Dhvasra and Puruṣanti.'[4] In the Pañcaviṃśa Brāhmaṇa[5] the names occur in the dual as *Dhvasre Puruṣantī*, a reading which is confirmed by the Nidāna Sūtra.[6] The former is necessarily a feminine form, though Sāyaṇa, in his comment on the passage, explains it as really an irregular masculine. According to Roth,[7] the feminine is a corruption based on the dual form in the verse of the Rigveda mentioned above; but the names may be those of women,[8] as Benfey[9]

[1] xiii. 7, 12. *Cf.* Jaiminīya Brāhmaṇa, iii. 139; Sāṭyāyanaka, *apud* Sāyaṇa, on Rv. ix. 58, 3.

[2] Mānava Dharma Śāstra, x. 75-77.

[3] ix. 58, 3.

[4] Both words are in the dual, as if they were members of a Dvandva compound. *Cf.* Macdonell, *Vedic Grammar*, 261.

[5] *Loc. cit.*

[6] ix. 9.

[7] St. Petersburg Dictionary, *s.v.* *dhvasra*.

[8] The first would in that case be Dhvasrā.

[9] *Sāmaveda*, 105, 126, under Dhvasanti and Puruṣanti.

inclines to believe. Weber[10] suggests that the two were demons, but this is, as Sieg[11] shows, quite unnecessary. Dhvasra is no doubt identical with **Dhvasanti**.

[10] *Episches im vedischen Ritual*, 27, n. 1.

[11] *Die Sagenstoffe des Ṛgveda*, 62, 63.

Cf. Ludwig, Translation of the Rigveda, 3, 139; Oertel, *Journal of the American Oriental Society*, 18, 39; Max Müller, *Sacred Books of the East*, 32, 360, points out that the sense of the Rigveda passage is quite uncertain, and that the two, Taranta and Purumīḷha, as they appear in Rv. v. 61, are rather donors than receivers (see, however, verse 9, *Purumīḷhāya viprāya*). See also Oldenberg, *Zeitschrift der Deutschen Morgenländischen Gesellschaft*, 42, 232; *Ṛgveda-Noten*, 1, 354.

Dhvāṅkṣa, 'crow,' is mentioned twice in the Atharvaveda,[1] and in the Sūtras.[2] Possibly the same bird is meant by the words **Dhuṅkṣā** and **Dhūṅkṣṇā.**

[1] xi. 9, 9; xii. 4, 8.

[2] Kātyāyana Śrauta Sūtra xxv. 6, 9.

Cf. Zimmer, *Altindisches Leben*, 88.

Dhvānta is the name of some wind in the Yajurveda Saṃhitās[1] and later.[2]

[1] Taittirīya Saṃhitā, i. 7, 7, 2; Vājasaneyi Saṃhitā, xxxix. 7.

[2] Taittirīya Brāhmaṇa, ii. 7, 16, 1; Taittirīya Āraṇyaka, iv. 24, 1; 25, 1.

N.

Nakula, 'ichneumon,' is mentioned in the Atharvaveda[1] as being able to cut a snake in two and then join it up again. Its knowledge[2] of a remedy against snake poison is also mentioned. The animal figures in the list of sacrificial victims at the Aśvamedha, or 'horse sacrifice,' in the Yajurveda Saṃhitās.[3]

[1] vi. 139, 5.

[2] Av. viii. 7, 23.

[3] Taittirīya Saṃhitā, v. 5, 12, 1; 21, 1; Vājasaneyi Saṃhitā, xxiv. 26. 2; Maitrāyaṇī Saṃhitā, iii. 14, 7. In the Taittirīya Saṃhitā, vii. 3, 18, 1; Ṛgveda Prātiśākhya, xvii. 9, *nakula* denotes a colour—no doubt that of the ichneumon.

Nakta, 'night,' is found frequently in the Rigveda,[1] and sometimes later,[2] usually in the adverbial form *naktam*, 'by night.'

[1] i. 13, 7; 73, 7; 96, 5; vii. 2, 6; x. 70, 6; adverbially, i. 24, 10; 90, 7; v. 76, 3; vii. 15, 15; 104, 17; viii. 96, 1.

[2] Chāndogya Upaniṣad, viii. 4, 2; adverbially, Av. vi. 128, 4; Śatapatha Brāhmaṇa, ii. 1, 4, 2; xiii. 1, 5, 5, etc.

Nakṣatra is a word of obscure origin and derivation. The Indian interpreters already show a great divergence of opinion as to its primary meaning. The Śatapatha Brāhmaṇa[1] resolves it into *na-ksatra* ('no power'), explaining it by a legend. The Nirukta[2] refers it to the root *nakṣ*, 'obtain,' following the Taittirīya Brāhmaṇa.[3] Aufrecht[4] and Weber[5] derived it from *nakta-tra*, 'guardian of night,' and more recently[6] the derivation from *nak-kṣatra*, 'having rule over night,' seems to be gaining acceptance. The generic meaning of the word therefore seems to be 'star.'

The Nakṣatras as Stars in the Rigveda and Later.—The sense of 'star' appears to be adequate for all or nearly all the passages in which Nakṣatra occurs in the Rigveda.[7] The same sense occurs in the later Saṃhitās also: the sun and the Nakṣatras are mentioned together,[8] or the sun, the moon, and the Nakṣatras,[9] or the moon and the Nakṣatras,[10] or the Nakṣatras alone;[11]

[1] ii. 1, 2, 18. 19. *Cf.* a citation in Nirukta, iii. 20.

[2] *Loc. cit.*, and *cf.* St. Petersburg Dictionary, *s.v.*

[3] i. 5, 2, 5.

[4] Kuhn's *Zeitschrift*, 8, 71, 72. So Eggeling, *Sacred Books of the East*, 12, 288, n. 2.

[5] *Naxatra*, 2, 268.

[6] Macdonell, *Vedic Grammar*, p. 74, line 8.

[7] See i. 50, 2; vii. 86, 1; x. 68, 11; 111, 7; used of the sun itself, vi. 67, 6 (as masculine); vii. 81, 2; x. 88, 13. The sun is allied with them, iii. 54, 19. *Nakṣatra-śavas*, 'equalling the multitude of the stars,' is used as an epithet in x. 21, 10. Even in x. 85, 2, where Soma, on the lap of the Nakṣatras, is mentioned, 'stars' would do; but, as this hymn refers to two of the later Nakṣatras, 'lunar mansions' may well be meant.

[8] Av. vi. 10, 3; Vājasaneyi Saṃhitā, xxiii. 43; Pañcaviṃśa Brāhmaṇa, x. 1, 1; Taittirīya Āraṇyaka, iv. 10, 12.

[9] Av. vi. 128, 3; xv. 6, 2; Taittirīya Saṃhitā, i. 8, 13, 3; Vājasaneyi Saṃhitā, xxii. 29, etc.

[10] Av. v. 24, 10; vi. 86, 2; Taittirīya Saṃhitā, iii. 4, 5, 1; Kāṭhaka Saṃhitā, xxxv. 15; xxxvii. 12; Vājasaneyi Saṃhitā, xxx. 21; xxxix. 2, etc.

[11] Taittirīya Saṃhitā, i. 2, 2, 2; ii 6, 2, 6, etc; Vājasaneyi Saṃhitā, xxx. 21 etc.; Kāṭhaka Saṃhitā, Aśvamedha, v. 5, and very often elsewhere.

but there is no necessity to attribute to the word the sense of 'lunar mansion' in these passages.

On the other hand, the names of at least three of the Nakṣatras in the later sense occur in the Rigveda. Tiṣya,[12] however, does not seem to be mentioned as a lunar mansion. With **Aghās** (plur.) and **Arjunī** (dual)[13] the case is different: it seems probable that they are the later lunar mansions called Maghās (plur.) and Phalgunī (dual). The names appear to have been deliberately changed in the Rigveda, and it must be remembered that the hymn in which they occur, the wedding hymn of Sūryā, has no claim to great age.[14] Ludwig[15] and Zimmer[16] have seen other references to the Nakṣatras as 27 in the Rigveda,[17] but these seem most improbable. Nor do the adjectives *revatī* ('rich') and *punarvasū* ('bringing wealth again') in another hymn[18] appear to refer to the Nakṣatras.

The Nakṣatras as Lunar Mansions.—In several passages of the later Saṃhitās the connexion of the moon and the Nakṣatras is conceived of as a marriage union. Thus in the Kāṭhaka[19] and Taittirīya Saṃhitās[20] it is expressly stated that Soma was wedded to the mansions, but dwelt only with Rohiṇī; the others being angry, he had ultimately to undertake to live with them all equally. Weber[21] hence deduced that the Nakṣatras were regarded as of equal extent, but this is to press the texts unduly, except in the sense of approximate equality. The number of the mansions is not stated as 27 in the story told in the two Saṃhitās: the Taittirīya has 33, and the Kāṭhaka no

12 Rv. v. 59, 13; x. 64, 8; Weber, 2, 290.

13 x. 85, 13; Weber, 364-367, and see references under **Aghā** and **Arjunī**.

14 *Cf.* Arnold, *Vedic Metre*, 322.

15 Translation of the Rigveda, 3, 184 *et seq.*

16 *Altindisches Leben*, 354. *Cf.* Tilak, *Orion*, 158.

17 i. 162, 18 (the 34 ribs of the horse = moon, sun, 5 planets, 27 Nakṣatras); x. 55, 3 (34 lights).

18 x. 19, 1.

19 xi. 3 (*Indische Studien*, 3, 467).

20 ii. 3, 5, 1-3. *Cf.* also iii. 4, 7, 1; Kāṭhaka Saṃhitā, xviii. 14; Vājasaneyi Saṃhitā, xviii. 40; Śatapatha Brāhmaṇa, ix. 4, 1, 9; Ṣaḍviṃśa Brāhmaṇa, iii. 12. The dwelling of the moon in a Nakṣatra is mentioned, Śatapatha Brāhmaṇa, x. 5, 4, 17; Nirukta, v. 21; a Mantra in Kauśika Sūtra, 135; Taittirīya Āraṇyaka, i. 11, 6; v. 12, 1, etc.

21 *Op. cit.*, 277. *Cf.* the later system of the Siddhāntas, Whitney, *Oriental and Linguistic Studies*, 2, 372, and see Tilak, *Orion*, 33 *et seq.*

number; but 27 appears as their number in the list which is found in the Taittirīya Saṃhitā[22] and elsewhere.[23] The number 28 is much less well attested: in one passage of the Taittirīya Brāhmaṇa[24] Abhijit is practically marked as a new comer, though in a later book,[25] in the Maitrāyaṇī Saṃhitā,[26] and in the Atharvaveda list,[27] it has found acceptance. It is perfectly possible that 28 is the earlier number, and that Abhijit dropped out because it was faint, or too far north, or because 27 was a more mystic (3×3×3) number: it is significant that the Chinese Sieou and the Arabic Manāzil are 28 in number.[28] Weber,[29] however, believes that 27 is the older number in India.

The meaning of the number is easily explained when it is remembered that a periodic month occupies something between 27 and 28 days, more nearly the former number. Such a month is in fact recognized in the Lāṭyāyana[30] and Nidāna Sūtras[31] as consisting of 27 days, 12 months making a year of 324 days, a Nakṣatra year, or with an intercalary month, a year of 351 days. The Nidāna Sūtra[32] makes an attempt to introduce the Nakṣatra reckoning into the civil or solar (*sāvana*) year of 360 days, for it holds that the sun spends $13\frac{1}{3}$ days in each Nakṣatra ($13\frac{1}{3} \times 27 = 360$). But the month of 27 or 28 days plays no part in the chronological calculations of the Veda.[33]

The Names of the Nakṣatras.—In addition to the two mentioned in the Rigveda, the earlier Atharvaveda[34] gives the

22 iv. 4, 10, 1-3.

23 Kāṭhaka Saṃhitā, xxxix. 13, but Maitrāyaṇī Saṃhitā, ii. 13, 20, has 28; Taittirīya Brāhmaṇa, i. 5, 1, 1-5, in lists of Nakṣatras. See also Vājasaneyi Saṃhitā, ix. 7; Śatapatha Brāhmaṇa, x. 5, 4, 5; Pañcaviṃśa Brāhmaṇa, xxiii. 23; Kauṣītaki Brāhmaṇa, v. 1; Sāṅkhāyana Āraṇyaka, ii. 16; Taittirīya Saṃhitā, vii. 1, 2, 2; Jyotiṣa, 18. 20 (verse 34 has 28, but it is interpolated); Śāṅkhāyana Śrauta Sūtra, xiv. 78, etc.

24 i. 5, 2, 3. *Cf.* Weber, 1, 360, n.

25 iii. 1, 2, 6.

26 ii. 13, 20.

27 xix. 7, 1; 8, 1 = Nakṣatrakalpa, 10. 26. So in Śāṅkhāyana Gṛhya Sūtra, i. 26.

28 Whitney, *op. cit.*, 409-411; *Journal of the American Oriental Society*, 8, 390.

29 *Op. cit.*, 2, 280; *Indische Studien*, 9, 446; 10, 223, 224, 226, 227.

30 iv. 8, 1 *et seq.*

31 v. 11. 12. See Weber, 2, 281-288.

32 Thibaut, *Astronomie, Astrologie und Mathematik*, 7.

33 See **Māsa**.

34 *I.e.*, books i-xvi.

names of Jyeṣṭhaghnī[35] (the later Jyeṣṭhā) and Vicṛtau,[36] which are mentioned as in close connexion, and of Revatīs (plural) and Kṛttikās.[37] With reference to possible times for the ceremony of the Agnyādhāna, or 'laying of the sacred fires,' the Kāṭhaka Saṃhitā,[38] the Maitrāyaṇī Saṃhitā,[39] and the Taittirīya Brāhmaṇa[40] mention the Nakṣatras called Kṛttikās, Rohiṇī, Phalgunyas, Hasta; the latter Brāhmaṇa adds Punarvasū, and in an additional remark[41] excludes Pūrve Phalgunī in favour of Uttare Phalgunī. The Śatapatha Brāhmaṇa[42] adds Mṛgaśīrṣa and Citrā as possibilities. On the other hand, Punarvasū is recommended by all authorities[43] as suitable for the Punarādheya, 'relaying of the sacred fires,' which takes place if the first fire has failed to effect the aim of its existence, the prosperity of the sacrificer.[44] The Kāṭhaka Saṃhitā,[45] however, allows Anurādhās also.

In the ceremony of the Agnicayana, or 'piling of the fire-altar,' the bricks are assumed to be equal in number to the Nakṣatras. The bricks number 756, and they are equated to 27 Nakṣatras multiplied by 27 secondary Nakṣatras, reckoned as 720 (instead of 729), with the addition of 36 days, the length of an intercalary month. Nothing can be usefully derived from this piece of priestly nonsense.[46] But in connexion with this ceremony the Yajurveda Saṃhitās[47] enumerate the 27

[35] vi. 110, 2. This constellation, 'the slayer of the oldest,' was apparently of evil omen. *Cf.* Taittirīya Brāhmaṇa, i. 5, 2, 8. Whitney, Translation of the Atharvaveda, 361, equates it with Antares or Cor Scorpionis, with or without σ, τ Scorpionis (Jyaiṣṭhaghnī is a misreading in the edition of Whitney and Roth).

[36] vi. 110, 2. It is also mentioned in ii. 8, 1; iii. 7, 4; vi. 121, 3. It is identified by the commentators with Mūla, 'the root,' the two stars, λ and υ Scorpionis, which form the sting of the Scorpion's tail; Whitney, *op. cit.*, 48.

[37] ix. 7, 3.

[38] viii. 1.

[39] i. 6, 9.

[40] i. 1, 2, 1-6.

[41] i. 1, 2, 8.

[42] ii. 1, 2, 1.

[43] Taittirīya Saṃhitā, i. 5, 1, 4; Maitrāyaṇī Saṃhitā, i. 7, 2; Kāṭhaka Saṃhitā, viii. 15; Satapatha Brāhmaṇa, ii. 1, 2, 10; Kauṣītaki Brāhmaṇa, i. 3.

[44] Hillebrandt, *Rituallitteratur*, 109.

[45] viii. 15; Maitrāyaṇī Saṃhitā, i. 7, 2.

[46] Śatapatha Brāhmaṇa, x. 5, 4, 5. See Weber, 2, 298, with whom Eggeling, *Sacred Books of the East*, 43, 383, n. 1, concurs. For a wild speculation, see Shamasastry, *Gavām ayana*, 122 *et seq.*

[47] Taittirīya Saṃhitā, iv. 4, 10, 1-3; Maitrāyaṇī Saṃhitā, ii. 13, 20; Kāṭhaka Saṃhitā, xxxix. 13.

Nakṣatras, and these lists[48] may be given *in extenso* as follows:

	Taittirīya Saṃhitā.	*Maitrāyaṇī Saṃhita.*	*Kāṭhaka Saṃhitā.*
1.	Kṛttikās (fem. plur.) ...	Kṛttikās	Kṛttikās
2.	Rohiṇī	Rohiṇī	Rohiṇī
3.	Mṛgaśīrṣa (neut.) ...	Invagā	Invakā
4.	Ārdrā	Bāhu	Bāhu
5.	Punarvasū (dual) ...	Punarvasu (sing.)	Punarvasu
6.	Tiṣya	Tiṣya	Tiṣya
7.	Āśreṣās (fem. plur.) ...	Āśleṣās (plur.; Pada Aśleṣā)	Āśleṣās (or Aśleṣās)
8.	Maghās (fem. plur.) ...	Maghās	Maghās
9.	Phalgunī (fem. dual) ...	Phalgunīs (plur.)	Phalgunīs
10.	Phalgunī (fem. dual) ...	Phalgunīs (plur.)	Uttarāḥ Phalgunīs
11.	Hasta	Hasta	Hastau (dual)
12.	Citrā	Citrā	Citrā
13.	Svātī	Niṣṭya (neut.)	Niṣṭyā
14.	Viśākhe (fem. dual) ...	Viśākha (neut. sing.) ...	Viśākhā (fem. sing.)
15.	Anūrādhās (plur.) ...	Anūrādhā (Pada Anurādhā)	Anūrādhās (masc. plur.)
16.	Rohiṇī	Jyeṣṭhā	Jyeṣṭhā
17.	Vicṛtau	Mūla (neut.)	Mūla
18.	Aṣāḍhās (fem. plur.) ...	Aṣāḍhās	Aṣāḍhās
19.	Aṣāḍhās (fem. plur.) ...	Aṣāḍhās	Uttarā Aṣāḍhās
20.		Abhijit	
21.	Śroṇā	Śroṇā	Aśvattha
22.	Śraviṣṭhās (plur.) ...	Śraviṣṭhās	Śraviṣṭhās
23.	Śatabhiṣaj	Śatabhiṣaj	Śatabhiṣaj
24.	Proṣṭhapadās (masc. plur.)	Proṣṭhapadās	Proṣṭhapadās
25.	Proṣṭhapadās (masc. plur.)	Proṣṭhapadās	Uttare Proṣṭhapadās
26.	Revatī	Revatī	Revatī
27.	Aśvayujau (dual) ...	Aśvayujau	Aśvayujau
28.	Apabharaṇīs (fem. plur.)	Bharaṇīs	Apabharaṇīs

The Taittirīya Brāhmaṇa[49] has a list of the Nakṣatras which agrees generally with the list of the Saṃhitās. It runs as follows: Kṛttikās, Rohiṇī, Invakās, Bāhū (dual), Tiṣya, Āśleṣās, Maghās, Pūrve Phalgunī, Uttare Phalgunī, Hasta, Citrā, Niṣṭyā, Viśākhe, Anūrādhās, Rohiṇī, Mūlabarhaṇī, Pūrvā Aṣāḍhās, Uttarā Aṣāḍhās, Śroṇā, Śraviṣṭhās, Śatabhiṣaj, Pūrve Proṣṭhapadās, Uttare Proṣṭhapadās, Revatī, Aśvayujau, Apabharaṇīs. In a later book,[50] however, the list grows to 28,

[48] The forms and genders are given as accepted by Weber, 2, 300. The latter depend on references to the names of the Nakṣatras in other passages in some cases—*e.g.*, *Anūrādheṣu*, in Kāṭhaka, viii. 15, shows that the name is a masculine in that Saṃhitā.

[49] i. 5, 1.

[50] iii. 1, 4, 1 *et seq.* *Cf.* iii. 1, 1-2.

and the full moon is inserted after number 14, and the new moon after number 28, as an attempt to bring the Nākṣatra (lunar) month into accordance with the Sāvana (solar) month of 30 days. The names in this second list are as in the Saṃhitās with the following exceptions. The seven stars of the Kṛttikās are named as Ambā, Dulā, Nitatnī, Abhrayantī, Meghayantī, Varṣayantī, Cupuṇīkā, names found also in the Taittirīya[51] and Kāṭhaka Saṃhitās.[52] Beside Mṛgaśīrṣa, Invakās are also mentioned.[53] Then come Ārdrā, Punarvasū, Tiṣya, Āśreṣās, Maghās (beside which Anaghās, Agadās, and Arundhatīs are also mentioned), Phalgunyas (but elsewhere in the dual, Phalgunyau),[54] Phalgunyas, Hasta, Citrā, Niṣṭyā, Viśākhe, Anūrādhās, Jyeṣṭhā, Mūla, Aṣāḍhās, Aṣāḍhās, Abhijit, Śroṇā, Śraviṣṭhās, Śatabhiṣaj, Proṣṭhapadās, Proṣṭhapadās, Revatī, Aśvayujau, Bharaṇyas, but also Apabharaṇīs.[55] Abhijit, which occurs also in an earlier part of the Brāhmaṇa,[56] is perhaps interpolated. But Weber's[57] argument that Abhijit is out of place in this list because Brāhmaṇa is here mentioned as the 28th Nakṣatra, loses some force from the fact (of course unknown to him) that the list in the Maitrāyaṇī Saṃhitā[58] contains 28 Nakṣatras, including Abhijit, and adds Brāhmaṇa at the end as another.

In another passage[59] the Taittirīya Brāhmaṇa divides the Nakṣatras into two sets, the Deva Nakṣatras and the Yama Nakṣatras, being 1–14 and 15–27 (with the omission of Abhijit) respectively. This division corresponds with one in the third book of the Brāhmaṇa[60] where the days of the light half of the month and those of the dark half are equated with the Nakṣatras. The Brāhmaṇa treats the former series as south, the latter as north; but this has no relation to facts, and can only be regarded as a ritual absurdity.

The late nineteenth book of the Atharvaveda contains a list[61] of the Nakṣatras, including Abhijit. The names here

51 iv. 4, 5, 1.

52 xl. 4.

53 iii. 1, 4, 3.

54 iii. 1, 4, 9.

55 iii. 1, 5, 14.

56 i. 5, 2, 3.

57 *Op. cit.*, 305, 306.

58 ii. 13, 20.

59 i. 5, 2, 7. *Cf.* Tilak, *Orion*, 41 *et seq.*

60 iii. 1, 2. *Cf.* Kauṣītaki Brāhmaṇa, iv. 12, with Vināyaka's note.

61 xix. 7, 1 *et seq.* The number is given as 28 in xix. 7, 1 (as emended) and 8, 2. *Cf.* Lanman's introductory note to the former hymn in Whitney's Translation, 906, 907.

given are : Kṛttikās, Rohiṇī, Mṛgaśiras, Ārdrā, Punarvasū, Puṣya, Āśleṣās, Maghās, Pūrvā Phalgunyau (*sic*),[62] Hasta, Citrā, Svāti (masc.),[63] Viśākhe, Anurādhā,[64] Jyeṣṭhā, Mūla, Pūrvā Aṣāḍhās,[65] Uttarā Aṣāḍhās, Abhijit, Śravaṇa, Śraviṣṭhās, Śatabhiṣaj, Dvayā Proṣṭhapadā, Revatī, Aśvayujau, Bharaṇyas.

The Position of the Nakṣatras.—There is nothing definite in Vedic literature regarding the position of most of the Nakṣatras, but the later astronomy precisely locates all of them, and its statements agree on the whole satisfactorily with what is said in the earlier texts, though Weber[66] was inclined to doubt this. The determinations adopted below are due to Whitney[67] in his notes on the Sūrya Siddhānta.

1. **Kṛttikās** are unquestionably η Tauri, etc., the Pleiades. The names of the seven stars forming this constellation, and given above from Yajurveda texts,[68] include three—*abhrayantī*, 'forming clouds'; *meghayantī*, 'making cloudy'; *varṣayantī*, 'causing rain'—which clearly refer to the rainy Pleiades. The word *kṛttikā* possibly means 'web,' from the root *kṛt*, 'spin.'

2. **Rohiṇī**, 'ruddy,' is the name of the conspicuously reddish star, α Tauri or Aldebaran, and denotes the group of the Hyades, $\alpha\ \theta\ \gamma\ \delta\ \epsilon$ Tauri. Its identification seems absolutely assured by the legend of Prajāpati in the Aitareya Brāhmaṇa.[69] He is there represented as pursuing his daughter with incestuous intention, and as having been shot with an arrow (**Iṣu Trikāṇḍā**, 'the belt of Orion') by the 'huntsman' (**Mṛgavyādha**, 'Sirius'). Prajāpati is clearly Orion (Mṛgaśiras being the name of the little group of stars in Orion's head).

3. **Mṛgaśīrṣa** or **Mṛgaśiras**, also called Invakā or Invagā,

[62] The reading Pūrvā Phalgunyau must be wrong ; perhaps Dvaye (*cf.* verse 5) or Pūrve should be read. See Lanman in Whitney, Translation of the Atharvaveda, 908. The Uttare Phalgunyau are omitted.

[63] Svātī should, no doubt, be read ; but for the Svāti (*sic*) of all the manuscripts (Saṃhitā and Pada), *cf.* the *navasrakti* of the Aitareya Āraṇyaka, ii. 3, 6, with Keith's note.

[64] See Lanman in Whitney, 908.

[65] Lanman, *ibid.*, 909, reads Pūrvā Aṣāḍhā and Uttarā Aṣāḍhā ; Whitney reads Pūrvā and Uttarā Aṣāḍhās. The manuscripts have Pūrvā and Uttarc, which cannot stand.

[66] *Op. cit.*, 2, 367 *et seq.*

[67] *Oriental and Linguistic Essays*, 2, 350 *et seq.*

[68] Taittirīya Saṃhitā, iv. 4, 5, 1 ; Kāṭhaka Saṃhitā, xl. 4 ; Taittirīya Brāhmaṇa, iii. 1, 4, 1.

[69] iii. 33. *Cf.* Śatapatha Brāhmaṇa, ii. 1, 2, 8 ; Tilak, *Orion*, 98 *et seq.*

seems to be the faint stars λ, φ,[1] φ[2] Orionis. They are called Andhakā, 'blind,' in the Śāntikalpa of the Atharvaveda, probably because of their dimness.[70]

4. **Ārdrā**, 'moist,' is the name of the brilliant star, α Orionis. But the names by which it is styled, in the plural as Ārdrās in the Śāṅkhāyana Gṛhya Sūtra[71] and the Nakṣatrakalpa,[72] and in the dual as Bāhū, in the Taittirīya Brāhmaṇa,[73] point to a constellation of two or more stars, and it may be noted[74] that the corresponding Chinese Sieou includes the seven brilliant stars composing the shoulders, the belt, and the knees of Orion.

5. **Punarvasū**, 'the two that give wealth again,' denotes the two stars, α and β Geminorum, on the heads of Castor and Pollux. The name is no doubt connected with the beneficent character of the Aśvins, who correspond to the Dioscuri.[75]

6. **Tiṣya** or **Puṣya** includes the somewhat faint group in the body of the Crab, γ, δ, and θ Cancri. The singular is rather curious, as primarily one star would seem to have been meant, and none of the group is at all prominent.[76]

7. **Āśreṣās** or **Āśleṣās**, which in some texts[77] is certainly to be read Aśreṣās or Aśleṣas, denotes δ, ε, η, ρ, σ, and perhaps also ζ, Hydræ. The word means 'embracer,' a name which admirably fits the constellation.

8. **Maghās**, the 'bounties,' are the Sickle, or α, η, γ, ζ, μ, ε Leonis. The variants **Anaghā**, the 'sinless one,' etc., clearly refer to the auspicious influence of the constellation.

9, 10. **Phalgunī, Phalgunyau, Phalgū,**[78] **Phalgunīs, Phalgunyas,** is really a double constellation, divided into Pūrve, 'former,' and Uttare, 'latter.' The former is δ and θ Leonis, the latter β and 93 Leonis. According to Weber, the word denotes, like **Arjunī**, the variant of the Rigveda,[79] a 'bright-coloured' constellation.

70 Whitney, *op. cit.*, 401. *Cf.* Tilak, 102 *et seq.*

71 i. 26.

72 10.

73 i. 5, 1.

74 Whitney, *op. cit.*, 352, 401, n. 1.

75 Oldenberg, *Religion des Veda*, 212; Macdonell, *Vedic Mythology*, p. 53.

76 Whitney, *op. cit.*, 403, n. 1

77 Aśreṣās, Śāṅkhāyana Gṛhya Sūtra, i. 26; Śāntikalpa; Nakṣatrakalpa; Aśleṣās, Śāntikalpa, 2; Nakṣatrakalpa, 4. 48.

78 Kauṣītaki Brāhmaṇa, v. 1.

79 x. 85, 13.

11. **Hasta**, 'hand,' is made up of the five conspicuous stars (δ, γ, ϵ, α, β) in Corvus, a number which the word itself suggests. According to Geldner,[80] the 'five bulls' of the Rigveda are this constellation.

12. **Citrā**, 'bright,' is the beautiful star, α Virginis. It is mentioned in a legend of Indra in the Taittirīya Brāhmaṇa,[81] and in that of the 'two divine dogs' (*divyau śvānau*) in the Śatapatha Brāhmaṇa.[82]

13. **Svātī** or **Niṣṭyā** is later clearly the brilliant star Arcturus or α Bootis, its place in the north being assured by the notice in the Śāntikalpa,[83] where it is said to be 'ever traversing the northern way' (*nityam uttara-mārgagam*). The Taittirīya Brāhmaṇa,[84] however, constructs an asterismal Prajāpati, giving him Citrā (α Virginis) for head, Hasta (Corvus) for hand, the Viśākhe (α and β Libræ) for thighs, and the Anurādhās (β, δ, and π Scorpionis) for standing place, with Niṣṭyā for heart. But Arcturus, being 30° out, spoils this figure, while, on the other hand, the Arabic and Chinese systems have respectively, instead of Arcturus, ι, κ, and λ Virginis and κ Virginis, which would well fit into the Prajāpati figure. But in spite of the force of this argument of Weber's,[85] Whitney[86] is not certain that Niṣṭyā here must mean a star in Virgo, pointing out that the name Niṣṭyā, 'outcast,' suggests the separation of this Nakṣatra from the others in question.

14. **Viśākhe** is the couple of stars α and β Libræ. This mansion is later called Rādhā according to the Amarakośa, and it is curious that in the Atharvaveda[87] the expression *rādho Viśākhe*, 'the Viśākhe are prosperity,' should occur. But probably Rādhā is merely an invention due to the name of the next Nakṣatra, Anurādhā, wrongly conceived as meaning 'that which is after or follows Rādhā.'[88]

15. **Anūrādhās** or **Anurādhā**, 'propitious,' is β, δ, and π (perhaps also ρ) Scorpionis.

80 *Vedische Studien*, 3, 77; Rv. i. 105, 10. *Cf.* below, p. 427, n. 156.

81 Taittirīya Brāhmaṇa, i. 1, 2, 4-6.

82 ii. 1, 2, 13-17. 83 3.

84 i. 5, 2. *Cf.* Tilak, *Orion*, 204.

85 *Op. cit.*, 2, 307, 308.

86 *Op. cit.*, 409.

87 xix. 7.

88 Lanman in Whitney's Translation of the Atharvaveda, 908. *Cf.* Thibaut, *Journal of the Asiatic Society of Bengal*, 63, 156.

16. **Rohiṇī**, 'ruddy'; **Jyeṣṭhaghnī**, 'slaying the eldest'; or **Jyeṣṭhā**, 'eldest,' is the name of the constellation σ, α, and τ Scorpionis, of which the central star, α, is the brilliant reddish Antares (or Cor Scorpionis).

17. **Vicṛtau**, 'the two releasers'; **Mūla**, 'root'; or **Mūla-barhaṇī**, 'uprooting,' denote primarily λ and ν at the extremity of the tail of the Scorpion, but including also the nine or eleven stars from ε to ν.

18, 19. **Aṣāḍhās** ('unconquered'), distinguished as **Pūrvās**, 'former,' and **Uttarās**, 'latter,' are really two constellations, of which the former is composed of γ, δ, ε, and η Sagittarii, or of δ and ε only, and the latter of θ, σ, τ, and ζ Sagittarii, or of two, σ and ζ, only. It is probable that originally only four stars forming a square were meant as included in the whole constellation[89]—viz., σ and ζ, with δ and ε.

20. **Abhijit** is the brilliant star α Lyræ with its two companions ε and ζ. Its location in 60° north latitude is completely discordant with the position of the corresponding Arabian and Chinese asterisms. This fact is considered by Oldenberg[90] to support the view that it was a later addition to the system; its occurrence, however, as early as the Maitrāyaṇī Saṃhitā,[91] which he does not note, somewhat invalidates[92] that view. In the Taittirīya Brāhmaṇa[93] Abhijit is said to be 'over Aṣāḍhās, under Śroṇā,' which Weber[94] held to refer to its position in space, inferring thence that its Vedic position corresponded to that of the Arab Manāzil and the Chinese Sieou—viz., α, β Capricorni. But Whitney[95] argues effectively that the words 'over' and 'under' really refer to the place of Abhijit in the list, 'after' Aṣāḍhās and 'before' Śroṇā.

21. **Śroṇā**, 'lame,' or **Śravaṇa**, 'ear,' denotes the bright star α Aquilæ with β below and γ above it. Weber[96] very need-

[89] *Cf.* Thibaut, *Journal of the Asiatic Society of Bengal*, 63, 156.

[90] *Nachrichten der königl. Gesellschaft der Wissenschaften zu Göttingen*, 1909, 551, 552.

[91] ii. 13, 20.

[92] It is at the same time to be noted that Abhijit is wanting both in the Taittirīya Saṃhitā and in the Kāṭhaka Saṃhitā lists.

[93] i. 5, 2, 3.

[94] *Op. cit.*, 1, 320, 321; 2, 307; *Indische Studien*, 10, 224 *et seq.*

[95] *Journal of the American Oriental Society*, 8, 393.

[96] *Op. cit.*, 2, 382; but see Whitney, 404.

lessly thinks that the name Śravaṇa suggested two ears and the head between. It is quite out of correspondence with the Manāzil and the Sieou, and is clearly an Indian invention.[97]

22. **Śraviṣṭhās**, 'most famous,' or later **Dhaniṣṭhās**,[98] 'most wealthy,' is the diamond-shaped group, α, β, δ, and γ, in the Dolphin, perhaps also ζ in the same constellation. Like the preceding Nakṣatra, it is out of harmony with the Manāzil and Sieou.

23. **Śatabhiṣaj** or **Śatabhiṣa**,[99] 'having a hundred physicians,' seems to be λ Aquarii with the others around it vaguely conceived as numbering a hundred.

24, 25. **Proṣṭha-padās** (fem. plur.), 'feet of a stool,' or later **Bhadra-padās**,[100] 'auspicious feet,' a double asterism forming a square, the former (*pūrva*) consisting of α and β Pegasi, the latter (*uttara*) of γ Pegasi and α Andromedæ.

26. **Revatī**, 'wealthy,' denotes a large number of stars (later 32), of which ζ Piscium, close upon the ecliptic where it was crossed by the equator of about 570 A.D., is given as the southernmost.

27. **Aśva-yujau**, 'the two horse-harnessers,' denotes the stars β and ζ Arietis. Aśvinyau[101] and Aśvinī[102] are later names.

28. **Apabharaṇīs, Bharaṇīs**, or **Bharaṇyas**, 'the bearers,' is the name of the small triangle in the northern part of the Ram known as Musca or 35, 39, and 41 Arietis.

The Nakṣatras and the Months.—In the Brāhmaṇas the Nakṣatra names are regularly used to denote dates. This is done in two ways. The name, if not already a feminine, may be turned into a feminine and compounded with *pūrṇa-māsa*, 'the full moon,' as in *Tiṣyā-pūrṇamāsa*, 'the full moon in the Nakṣatra Tiṣya.'[103] Much more often, however, it is turned into a derivative adjective, used with *paurṇamāsī*, 'the full

97 Oldenberg, *loc. cit.*

98 Śāṅkhāyana Gṛhya Sūtra, i. 26; Śāntikalpa, 13; Dhaniṣṭhā, *ibid.*, 5.

99 So probably in Maitrāyaṇī Saṃhitā, ii. 13, 20, where see von Schroeder's critical note. The Śāntikalpa, 5, and Nakṣatrakalpa, 2, have Śatabhiṣā, and the latter, 1, has Śatabhiṣa (masculine).

100 Śāntikalpa, 5, etc.

101 Śāṅkhāyana Gṛhya Sūtra, i. 26; Nakṣatrakalpa, 9. 30.

102 Nakṣatrakalpa, 4. 45; Śāntikalpa, 5. 11.

103 Taittirīya Saṃhitā, ii. 2, 10, 1. *Cf.* vii. 4, 8, 1. 2; Pañcaviṃśa Brāhmaṇa, v. 9, 1.

moon (night),' or with *amāvāsyā*, 'the new moon (night),' as in *Phālgunī paurṇamāsī*, 'the full-moon night in the Nakṣatra Phalgunī';[104] or, as is usual in the Sūtras, the Nakṣatra adjective alone is used to denote the full-moon night. The month itself is called by a name derived[105] from that of a Nakṣatra, but only Phālguna,[106] Caitra,[107] Vaiśākha,[108] Taiṣya,[109] Māgha[110] occur in the Brāhmaṇas, the complete list later being Phālguna, Caitra, Vaiśākha, Jyaiṣṭha, Āṣāḍha, Śrāvaṇa, Prauṣṭhapada, Āśvayuja, Kārttika, Mārgaśīrṣa, Taiṣya, Māgha. Strictly speaking, these should be lunar months, but the use of a lunar year was clearly very restricted: we have seen that as early as the Taittirīya Brāhmaṇa there was a tendency to equate lunar months with the twelve months of thirty days which made up the solar year (see **Māsa**).

The Nakṣatras and Chronology.—(1) An endeavour has been made to ascertain from the names of the months the period at which the systematic employment of those names was introduced. Sir William Jones[111] refers to this possibility, and Bentley, by the gratuitous assumption that Śrāvaṇa always marked the summer solstice, concluded that the names of the months did not date before B.C. 1181. Weber[112] considered that there was a possibility of fixing a date by this means, but Whitney[113] has convincingly shown that it is an impossible feat, and Thibaut[114] concurs in this view. Twelve became fixed as the number of the months because of the desire, evident in the Brāhmaṇas, somehow or other to harmonize lunar with solar time; but the selection of twelve Nakṣatras out of twenty-seven as connected with the night of full moon can have no chronological significance, because full moon at

[104] Śatapatha Brāhmaṇa, ii. 6, 3, 11 *et seq.*; vi. 2, 2, 18; xiii. 4, 1, 4; Kauṣītaki Brāhmaṇa, i. 3; iv. 4; v. 1. See also Caland, *Über das rituelle Sūtra des Baudhāyana*, 36, 37, and **Māsa**.

[105] Primarily an adjective, with *māsa* to be supplied—*e.g.*, Phālguna, '(the month) connected with the Nakṣatra Phalgunī.'

[106] Pañcaviṃśa Brāhmaṇa, v. 9, 8.

[107] Kauṣītaki Brāhmaṇa, xix. 3.

[108] Śatapatha Brāhmaṇa, xi. 1, 1, 7.

[109] Kauṣītaki Brāhmaṇa, xix. 2. 3.

[110] *Ibid.*; Śatapatha Brāhmaṇa, xiii. 8, 1, 4. For the later list, see Weber, *Naxatra*, 2, 327, 328.

[111] *Asiatic Researches*, 2, 296.

[112] *Op. cit.*, 2, 347, 348; *Indische Studien*, 9, 455; 10, 230, 231.

[113] *Journal of the American Oriental Society*, 6, 413; 8, 85 *et seq.*

[114] *Astronomie, Astrologie und Mathematik*, 16.

no period occurred in those twelve only, but has at all periods occurred in every one of the twenty-seven at regularly recurrent intervals.

(2) All the lists of the Nakṣatras begin with Kṛttīkās. It is only fair to suppose that there was some special reason for this fact. Now the later list of the Nakṣatras begins with Aśvinī, and it was unquestionably rearranged because at the time of its adoption the vernal equinox coincided with the star ζ Piscium on the border of Revatī and Aśvinī,[115] say in the course of the sixth century A.D. Weber[116] has therefore accepted the view that the Kṛttikās were chosen for a similar reason, and the date at which that Nakṣatra coincided with the vernal equinox has been estimated at some period in the third millennium B.C.[117] A very grave objection to this view is its assumption that the sun, and not the moon, was then regarded as connected with the Nakṣatras; and both Thibaut[118] and Oldenberg[119] have pronounced decidedly against the idea of connecting the equinox with the Kṛttikās. Jacobi[120] has contended that in the Rigveda[121] the commencement of the rains and the summer solstice mark the beginning of the new year and the end of the old, and that further the new year began with the summer solstice in Phalgunī.[121] He has also referred to the distinction of the two sets of Deva and Yama Nakṣatras in the Taittirīya Brāhmaṇa[122] as supporting his view of the connexion of the sun and the Nakṣatras. But this view is far from satisfactory: the Rigveda passages cannot yield the sense required except by translating the word *dvādaśa*[123] as 'the twelfth (month)' instead of 'consisting of twelve parts,' that is, 'year,' the accepted

115 *Cf.* Colebrooke, *Essays*, 2, 264; Weber, *Indische Studien*, 10, 234.

116 *Naxatra*, 2, 362-364; *Indische Studien*, 10, 234; *Indian Literature*, 2, n. 2, etc.

117 See Weber, *loc. cit.*; Bühler, *Indian Antiquary*, 23, 245, n. 20; Tilak, *Orion*, 40 *et seq.*

118 *Indian Antiquary*, 24, 96.

119 *Zeitschrift der Deutschen Morgenländischen Gesellschaft*, 48, 631; 49, 473; 50, 451, 452; *Nachrichten der königl. Gesellschaft der Wissenschaften zu Göttingen*, 1909, 564; Keith, *Journal of the Royal Asiatic Society*, 1909, 1103.

120 *Festgruss an Roth*, 68 *et seq.* = *Indian Antiquary*, 23, 154 *et seq.*; *Zeitschrift der Deutschen Morgenländischen Gesellschaft*, 49, 218 *et seq.*; 50, 83; *Journal of the Royal Asiatic Society*, 1910, 463.

121 vii. 103 (the 'frog' hymn); x. 85 (the 'marriage' hymn).

122 i. 5, 2, 8.

123 Rv. vii. 103, 9.

interpretation; and the division of the Nakṣatras is not at all satisfactorily explained by a supposed connexion with the sun. It may further be mentioned that even if the Nakṣatra of Kṛttikās be deemed to have been chosen because of its coincidence with the vernal equinox, both Whitney[124] and Thibaut[125] are prepared to regard it as no more than a careless variant of the date given by the Jyotiṣa, which puts the winter solstice in Māgha.

(3) The winter solstice in Māgha is assured by a Brāhmaṇa text, for the Kauṣītaki Brāhmaṇa[126] expressly places it in the new moon of Māgha (*māghasyāmāvāsyāyām*). It is not very important whether we take this with the commentators[127] as the new moon in the middle of a month commencing with the day after full moon in Taiṣa, or, which is much more likely, as the new moon beginning the month and preceding full moon in Māgha. The datum gives a certain possibility of fixing an epoch in the following way. If the end of Revatī marked the vernal equinox at one period, then the precession of the equinoxes would enable us to calculate at what point of time the vernal equinox was in a position corresponding to the winter solstice in Māgha, when the solstitial colure cut the ecliptic at the beginning of Śraviṣṭhās. This would be, on the strict theory, in the third quarter of Bharaṇī, $6\frac{3}{4}$ asterisms removed from Śraviṣṭhās, and the difference between that and the beginning of Aśvinī =

[124] *Oriental and Linguistic Essays*, 2, 383.

[125] *Indian Antiquary*, 24, 97. *Cf.* Keith, *Journal of the Royal Asiatic Society*, 1910, 464, n. 4.

[126] xix. 3. This was first noticed by Weber, *Naxatra*, 2, 345 *et seq.*, who pointed out its relation to the datum of the Jyotiṣa. The same date as that of the Jyotiṣa is found in a passage of the Baudhāyana Śrauta Sūtra cited by Shamasastry, *Gavām Ayana*, 137 (*māghe māse dhaniṣṭhābhir uttareṇaiti bhānumān, ardhāśleṣasya śrāvaṇasya dakṣiṇenopanivartate*, 'in the month of Māgha the sun goes north with the asterism Dhaniṣṭhās, in the month of Śrāvaṇa he returns south in the middle of the asterism Āśleṣa'; the sense is clear, though the text is corrupt). The passage is apparently not in Caland's manuscripts, or he would have mentioned it in his paper, *Über das rituelle Sūtra des Baudhāyana*, 36, 37. Its date and value are therefore not quite certain.

[127] Vināyaka on Kauṣītaki Brāhmaṇa, *loc. cit.*; Ānartīya on Śāṅkhāyana Śrauta Sūtra, xiii. 19, 1; Weber, *Naxatra*, 2, 345. The assumption of the scholiasts seems to be due to the fact that to their minds a month must end with a new moon (*amānta*) or with full moon (*pūrṇimānta*). But there is no reason to say that in Vedic times the month may not have commenced with the new moon; the Kauṣītaki passage would thus be quite satisfactorily explained.

$1\frac{3}{4}$ asterisms $= 23\frac{1}{3}°$ (27 asterisms being $= 360°$). Taking the starting-point at 499 A.D., the assured period of Varāha Mihira, Jones[128] arrived at the date B.C. 1181 for the vernal equinox corresponding to the winter solstice in Māgha—that is, on the basis of $1° = 72$ years as the precession. Pratt[129] arrived at precisely the same date, taking the same rate of precession and adopting as his basis the ascertained position in the Siddhāntas of the junction star[130] of Maghā, *a* Leonis or Regulus. Davis[131] and Colebrooke[132] arrived at a different date, B.C. 1391, by taking as the basis of their calculation the junction star of Citrā, which happens to be of uncertain position, varying as much as 3° in the different textbooks. But though the twelfth century has received a certain currency as the epoch of the observation in the Jyotiṣa,[133] it is of very doubtful value. As Whitney points out, it is impossible to say that the earlier asterisms coincided in position with the later asterisms of $13\frac{1}{3}°$ extent each. They were not chosen as equal divisions, but as groups of stars which stood in conjunction with the moon; and the result of subsequently making them strictly equal divisions was to throw the principal stars of the later groups altogether out of their asterisms.[134] Nor can we say that the star ζ Piscium early formed the eastern boundary of Revatī; it may possibly not even have been in that asterism at all, for it is far remote from the Chinese and Arabic asterisms corresponding to Revatī. Added to all this, and to the uncertainty of the starting-point—582 A.D., 560 A.D., or 491 A.D. being variants[135]—is the fact that the place of the equinox is not a matter accurately determinable by mere observation, and that the Hindu astronomers of the Vedic period cannot be deemed to have been very accurate observers, since they made no precise determination of the

128 *Asiatic Researches*, 2, 393.

129 *Journal of the Asiatic Society of Bengal*, 31. 49.

130 *Cf.* Whitney, *Oriental and Linguistic Essays*, 2, 373.

131 *Asiatic Researches*, 2, 268; 5, 288.

132 *Essays*, 1, 109, 110. See Sir T. Colebrooke, *Journal of the Royal Asiatic Society*, 1, 335 *et seq.*; Whitney, *op. cit.*, 2, 381, 382.

133 *E.g.*, Lassen, *Indische Alterthumskunde*, 1², 606, 607, 976, and *cf.* Thibaut, *Astronomie, Astrologie und Mathematik*, 17, 18; Tilak, *Orion*, 38, 39.

134 Whitney, *op. cit.*, 2, 375.

135 *Cf.* Whitney, *op. cit.*, 377, 379; Weber, *op. cit.*, 2, 363, 364, where he prefers A.D. 582.

number of days of the year, which even in the Jyotiṣa they do not determine more precisely than as 366 days, and even the Sūrya Siddhānta[136] does not know the precession of the equinoxes. It is therefore only fair to allow a thousand years for possible errors,[137] and the only probable conclusion to be drawn from the datum of the Kauṣītaki Brāhmaṇa is that it was recording an observation which must have been made some centuries B.C., in itself a result quite in harmony with the probable date of the Brāhmaṇa literature,[138] say B.C. 800-600.

(4) Another chronological argument has been derived from the fact that there is a considerable amount of evidence for Phālguna having been regarded as the beginning of the year, since the full moon in Phalgunī is often described as the 'mouth (*mukham*) of the year.'[139] Jacobi[140] considers that this

[136] See Whitney's note on Sūrya Siddhānta, iii. 12; *op. cit.*, 2, 369, n. 1; 374, n. 1. *Cf.* Tilak, *Orion*, 18.

[137] Whitney, 384, followed by Thibaut, *Indian Antiquary*, 24, 98; *Astronomie, Astrologie und Mathematik*, 18. See also Weber, *Indische Studien*, 10, 236; *Indian Literature*, 2, n. 2; Whitney, *Journal of the Royal Asiatic Society*, 1, 313 *et seq.*; in Colebrooke's *Essays*, 1², 120 *et seq.*; Max Müller, in his edition of the Rigveda, iv², xxx *et seq.*, was also inclined to regard the date as very uncertain; only in his popular works (*Chips*, 1, 113, etc.) did he accept 1181 B.C., or rather 1186 B.C., as recalculated by Main from Pratt's calculation. Shamasastry's defence, *Gavām Ayana*, 122 *et seq.*, of the Jyotiṣa shows a misunderstanding the criticisms made. See Keith, *ournal of the Royal Asiatic Society*, 1910, 66, n. 5.

[138] *Cf.* Macdonell, *Sanskrit Literature*, 12, 202; Keith, *Aitareya Āraṇyaka*, 20 *et seq.* It has been put earlier: see Thibaut, *Astronomie*, etc., 18; Bühler, *Zeitschrift der Deutschen Morgenländischen Gesellschaft*, 55, 544, and *cf.* Bühler, *Sacred Books of the East*, 2, xl *et seq.*; *Indian Antiquary*, 23, 247; von Schroeder, *Indiens Literatur und Cultur*, 45 *et seq.* See also Jolly, *Recht und Sitte*, 3; Hillebrandt, *Rituallitteratur*, 31, who are inclined to accept an early date, fourth or fifth century B.C., for the Āpastamba Sūtras, from which a still earlier date for the Brāhmaṇas must be conceded. But Eggeling is more probably correct when he assigns the Āpastamba Sūtras to the third century, B.C. See *Sacred Books of the East*, 12, xl, and it seems unwise unduly to press back the date of Vedic literature. It is noteworthy that in the Epic the solstice is still in Māgha (Mahābhārata, xiii. 168, 6. 28). Reference is, however, made (*ibid.*, i. 71, 34) to the Nakṣatras commencing with Śravaṇa, and the first month is Mārgaśīrṣa (see Hopkins, *Journal of the American Oriental Society*, 24, 21 *et seq.*). *Cf.* also Tilak, *Orion*, 37, 216.

[139] Taittirīya Saṃhitā, vii. 4, 8, 1. 2; Pañcaviṃśa Brāhmaṇa, v. 9, 9. *Cf.* Kauṣītaki Brāhmaṇa, iv. 4; v. 1; Taittirīya Brāhmaṇa, i. 1, 2, 8; Śatapatha Brāhmaṇa, vi. 2, 2, 18; Āśvalāyana Śrauta Sūtra, v. 3. 16. According to the Taittirīya and the Kauṣītaki Brāhmaṇas, the beginning falls at the middle of the joint asterism.

[140] *Indian Antiquary*, 23, 156 *et seq.*; *Zeitschrift der Deutschen Morgenländischen Gesellschaft*, 49, 223 *et seq.*; 50, 72-81. See Tilak, *Orion*, 53 *et seq.*; 198 *et seq.*

was due to the fact that the year was reckoned from the winter solstice, which would coincide with the month of Phālguna about B.C. 4000. Oldenberg[141] and Thibaut,[142] on the other hand, maintain that the choice of Phālguna as the 'mouth' of the year was due to its being the first month of spring. This view is favoured by the fact that there is distinct evidence[143] of the correspondence of Phālguna and the beginning of spring: as we have seen above in the Kauṣītaki Brāhmaṇa, the new moon in Māgha is placed at the winter solstice,[144] which puts the full moon of Phalgunī at a month and a half after the winter solstice, or in the first week of February, a date not in itself improbable, for about B.C. 800, and corresponding with the February 7 of the *veris initium* in the Roman Calendar. This fact accords with the only natural division of the year into three periods of four months, as the rainy season lasts from June 7-10 to October 7-10, and it is certain that the second set of four months dates from the beginning of the rains (see **Cāturmāsya**). Tilak,[145] on the other hand, holds that the winter solstice coincided with Māghī full moon at the time of the Taittirīya Saṃhitā (B.C. 2350), and had coincided with Phālgunī and Caitrī in early periods—viz., B.C. 4000-2500, and B.C. 6000-4000.

(5) The passages of the Taittirīya Saṃhitā[146] and the Pañcaviṃśa Brāhmaṇa,[147] which treat the full moon in Phālguna as the beginning of the year, give as an alternative the full moon in Caitra. Probably the latter month was chosen so as to secure that the initial day should fall well within the season of spring,[148] and was not, as Jacobi believes, a relic of a period

141 *Zeitschrift der Deutschen Morgenländischen Gesellschaft*, 48, 630 *et seq.*; 49, 475, 476; 50, 453-457. *Cf.* Whitney, *Journal of the American Oriental Society*, 16, lxxxvii.

142 *Indian Antiquary*, 24, 86 *et seq.*

143 See Weber, *Naxatra*, 2, 329 *et seq.*, and *cf.* Śatapatha Brāhmaṇa, i. 6, 3, 36; Kauṣītaki Brāhmaṇa, v. 1; a Śruti passage in the commentary on Kātyāyana Śrauta Sūtra, i. 2, 13; Baudhāyana Dharma Sūtra, ii. 2, 4, 23, and especially Śatapatha Brāhmaṇa, xiii. 4, 1, 2. 4. So the Phālguna full moon is called the 'month of the seasons' (*ṛtūnām mukham*) in Kāṭhaka Saṃhitā, viii. 1; Maitrāyaṇī Saṃhitā, i. 6, 9.

144 xix. 2. 3.

145 *Orion*, 53 *et seq.*; 198 *et seq.*

146 vii. 4, 8, 1.

147 v. 9. See Weber, *op. cit.*, 2, 341-344; Thibaut, *Indian Antiquary*, 24, 85 *et seq.*, for a full discussion of the points raised by Tilak, *Orion*, 43 *et seq.*

148 Thibaut, *Indian Antiquary*, 24, 93. On the other side, Tilak, 198 *et seq.*

when the winter solstice corresponded with Caitra. Another alternative is the Ekāṣṭakā, interpreted by the commentators as the eighth day after the full moon in Maghās, a time which might, as being the last quarter of the waning half of the old year, well be considered as representing the end of the year. A fourth alternative is the fourth day before full moon; the full moon meant must be that of Caitra, as Ālekhana quoted by Āpastamba held, not of Māgha, as Āśmarathya, Laugākṣi and the Mīmāṃsists believed, and as Tilak believes.[149]

(6) Others, again, according to the Gṛhya ritual, began the year with the month Mārgaśīrṣa, as is shown by its other name Āgrahāyaṇa[150] (' belonging to the commencement of the year '). Jacobi and Tilak[151] think that this one denoted the autumn equinox in Mṛgaśiras, corresponding to the winter solstice in Phalgunī. But, as Thibaut[152] shows clearly, it was selected as the beginning of a year that was taken to commence with autumn, just as some took the spring to commence with Caitra instead of Phālguna.[153]

(7) Jacobi has also argued, with the support of Bühler,[154] from the terms given for the beginning of Vedic study in the Gṛhya Sūtras, on the principle that study commenced with the rains (as in the Buddhist *vassā*) which mark the summer solstice. He concludes that if Bhādrapada appears as the date of commencing study in some texts, it was fixed thus because at one time Proṣṭhapadās (the early name of Bhadrapadās) coincided with the summer solstice, this having been the case when the winter solstice was in Phālguna. But Whitney[155] has pointed out that this argument is utterly illegitimate; we cannot say that there was any necessary connexion between the rains and learning—a month like Śrāvaṇa might be preferred

[149] Thibaut, *op. cit.*, 94; Tilak, 51 *et seq. Cf.* also Kātyāyana Śrauta Sūtra, xiii. 1. 8-10; Weber, 2, 343, n. 2, 344.

[150] Thibaut, *op. cit.*, 94, 95. *Cf.* Weber, 2, 332-334.

[151] Tilak's view is given in *Orion*, 62 *et seq.* It is based mainly on Amara's (i. 2, 23) *āgra-hāyaṇī* as a synonym of Mṛgaśiras, and on certain myths (chaps. v.-vii.); he equates (221 *et seq.*) Āgrayaṇa and Orion (!).

[152] *Op. cit.*, 94, 95.

[153] A corresponding Kārttika year is not early, Thibaut, *op. cit.*, 96. *Cf.* Weber, *op. cit.*, 2, 334.

[154] *Indian Antiquary*, 23, 242 *et seq.*

[155] *Journal of the American Oriental Society*, 16, lxxxiv *et seq.*

because of its connexion with the word Śravaṇa, 'ear'—and in view of the precession of the equinoxes, we must assume that Bhādrapada was kept because of its traditional coincidence with the beginning of the rains after it had ceased actually so to coincide.[156]

The Origin of the Nakṣatras.—As we have seen, there is no evidence showing the process by which the Nakṣatras may

[156] Mention should here be made of the following points: (1) Jacobi's argument from the word Dhruva, the name of the star pointed out to the bride in the marriage ritual. The word does not occur in the literature anterior to the Gṛhya Sūtras, and it must remain an undecided question whether the practice was or was not old. Jacobi urges that Dhruva means 'fixed,' and that it must originally have referred to a real fixed pole star, and he thinks that such a star could only be found in the third millennium B.C. Whitney and Oldenberg definitely reject this view on the ground that too much must not be made out of a piece of folk-lore, and that the marriage ritual requirements would be satisfied by any star of some magnitude which was approximately polar. This conclusion seems convincing. *Cf.* Keith, *Journal of the Royal Asiatic Society*, 1909, 1102; 1910, 465; *contra*, Jacobi, *ibid.*, 1909, 726 *et seq.*; 1910, 464. (2) The Śatapatha Brāhmaṇa, ii. 1, 2, 3, asserts that the Kṛttikās do not move from the eastern quarter, which the others do; and stress has been laid (by Jacobi, *Journal of the Royal Asiatic Society*, 1910, 463, 464) upon this assertion as giving a date of the third millennium B.C. for the Śatapatha observation. But this notice is quite inadequate to support any such result, and its lack of trustworthiness as a chronological guide is increased by the fact that the Baudhāyana Śrauta Sūtra, xviii 5, has a similar notice, coupled with another notice, which, according to Barth, would only be true somewhere in or after the sixth century A.D., the equatorial point being placed between Citrā and Svātī, which in the early period were both very much north of the equator (see Caland, *Über das rituelle Sūtra des Baudhāyana*, 37-39). The same passage of the Śatapatha Brāhmaṇa, ii. 1, 2, 2, in the Mādhyaṃdina recension, states that the number of the Kṛttikās is greater than that of the stars in any of the other Nakṣatras, which consist of one, two, three, or four stars, or which, according to the Kāṇva recension (see Eggeling, *Sacred Books of the East*, 12, 282, n. 2), have four stars. It is not possible to put much faith in this assertion, for Hasta later has five stars, and its name (with reference to the fingers) suggests five (*cf.* Weber, *Naxatra*, 2, 368, 381), and that number is possibly referred to in the Rigveda (i. 105, 10). See Geldner, *Vedische Studien*, 3, 177. (3) Attempts have been made to regard the names of the Nakṣatras as significant of their position in the list. Thus Bentley, *Historical View*, 2, thought Viśākhā was so called because the equinoctial colure divided the equator about 1426 B.C.; this is refuted by Tilak, *Orion*, 57 *et seq.* Jyeṣṭhaghnī has been interpreted as 'slaying the eldest'—*i.e.*, as marking the new year by putting an end to the old year. Tilak, 90, suggests that Mūla was so called because its acronycal rising marked the beginning of the year when the vernal equinox was near Mṛgaśiras. More probable is Whitney's view, *Sūrya Siddhānta*, 194, that it was the most southern, and so, as it were, the basis of the asterisms.

have originated in India. They are mentioned only as stars in the earlier parts of the Rigveda, then the names of three of them are found in the latest parts of that Saṃhitā, and finally in the later Atharvaveda and in the Yajurveda Saṃhitās the full list appears. It may also be noted that the Vedic Indians show (see **Graha**) a remarkably small knowledge of the other astronomical phenomena; the discovery of a series of 27 lunar mansions by them would therefore be rather surprising. On the other hand, the nature of such an operation is not very complicated; it consists merely in selecting a star or a star group with which the moon is in conjunction. It is thus impossible *a priori* to deny that the Vedic Indians could have invented for themselves a lunar Zodiac.[157]

But the question is complicated by the fact that there exist two similar sets of 28 stars or star groups in Arabia and in China, the Manāzil and the Sieou. The use of the Manāzil in Arabia is consistent and effective; the calendar is regulated by them, and the position of the asterisms corresponds best with the positions required for a lunar Zodiac. The Indians might therefore have borrowed the system from Arabia, but that is a mere possibility, because the evidence for the existence of the Manāzil is long posterior to that for the existence of the Nakṣatras, while again the Mazzaroth or Mazzaloth of the Old Testament[158] may really be the lunar mansions.[159] That the Arabian system is borrowed from India, as Burgess[160] held, is, on the other hand, not at all probable.

Biot, the eminent Chinese scholar, in a series of papers published by him between 1839 and 1861,[161] attempted to prove

157 Max Müller, *Rigveda*, 4^2, xliv *et seq.*, maintains the Indian origin of the system. Thibaut, *Astronomie, Astrologie und Mathematik*, 14, 15, admits it to be possible, as does Whitney, *Oriental and Linguistic Essays*, 2, 418.

158 2 Kings xxiii. 5; Job xxxviii. 32.

159 Weber, *Naxatra*, 1, 317, 318; Whitney, *op. cit.*, 359.

160 *Journal of the American Oriental Society*, 8, 309-334. This was Weber's view also, according to Whitney, 413 *et seq.*; but Weber himself disclaimed it (see *Indische Studien*, 9, 425, 426; 10, 246, 247). On the other hand, Sédillot, *Matériaux pour servir à l'histoire comparée des Sciences Mathématiques par les Grecs et les Orientaux* (Paris, 1845-1849), favoured influence from Arabia on India.

161 Summed up in his two works, *Recherches sur l'ancienne astronomie Chinoise*, and *Études sur l'astronomie Indienne et l'astronomie Chinoise*.

the derivation of the Nakṣatra from the Chinese Sieou. The latter he did not regard as being in origin lunar mansions at all. He thought that they were equatorial stars used, as in modern astronomy, as a standard to which planets or other stars observed in the neighbourhood can be referred; they were, as regards twenty-four of them, selected about B.C. 2357 on account of their proximity to the equator, and of their having the same right ascension as certain circumpolar stars which had attracted the attention of Chinese observers. Four more were added in B.C. 1100 in order to mark the equinoxes and solstices of the period. He held that the list of stars commenced with Mao (=Kṛttikās), which was at the vernal equinox in B.C. 2357. Weber,[162] in an elaborate essay of 1860, disputed this theory, and endeavoured to show that the Chinese literary evidence for the Sieou was late, dating not even from before the third century B.C. The last point does not appear[163] to be correct, but his objections against the basis of Biot's theory were reinforced by Whitney,[164] who insisted that Biot's supposition of the Sieou's not having been ultimately derived from a system of lunar mansions, was untenable. This is admitted by the latest defender of the hypothesis of borrowing from China, Léopold de Saussure,[165], but his arguments in favour of a Chinese origin for the Indian lunar mansions have been refuted by Oldenberg,[166] who has also pointed out[167] that the series does not begin with Mao (=Kṛttikās).

There remains only the possibility that a common source for all the three sets—Nakṣatra, Manāzil, and Sieou—may be found in Babylonia. Hommel[168] has endeavoured to show that recent research has established in Babylonia the existence of a lunar zodiac of twenty-four members headed by the

162 *Naxatra*, 1, 284 *et seq.* (1860).

163 See Chavannes, cited by Oldenberg, *Nachrichten der königl. Gesellschaft der Wissenschaften zu Göttingen*, 1909, 566, 567.

164 *Journal of the American Oriental Society*, 8, 1 *et seq.*; *Oriental and Linguistic Essays*, 2, 385 *et seq.* For his controversy with Weber, see Weber, *Indische Studien*, 9, 424 *et seq.*; 10, 213 *et seq.*; Whitney, *Journal of the American Oriental Society*, 8, 384 *et seq.*

165 T'oung Pao, 1909, 121 *et seq.*; 255 *et seq.*

166 *Nachrichten*, 1909, 544-572.

167 *Ibid.*, 548, n. 9.

168 *Zeitschrift der Deutschen Morgenländischen Gesellschaft*, 45, 592 *et seq.*

Pleiades (=Kṛttikās); but Thibaut's researches[169] are not favourable to this claim. On the other hand, Weber,[170] Whitney,[171] Zimmer,[172] and Oldenberg[173] all incline to the view that in Babylonia is to be found the origin of the system, and this must for the present be regarded as the most probable view, for there are other traces of Babylonian influence in Vedic literature, such as the legend of the flood, perhaps the Ādityas,[174] and possibly the word **Manā.**

[169] *Journal of the Asiatic Society of Bengal*, 63, 144-163. *Cf. Astronomie*, etc., 15; Oldenberg, *op. cit.*, 572.

[170] *Naxatra*, 1, 316 *et seq.*; *Indische Studien*, 10, 246, and elsewhere. Weber, *Nakṣatra*, 2, 362, 400, laid great stress on the fact that the Jyotiṣa, 8, referred to the difference of the longest and shortest day as being six *muhūrtas*, which makes the longest day fourteen hours twenty-four minutes; and he compared the Babylonian day of fourteen hours twenty-five minutes, and a Chinese day of fourteen hours twenty-four minutes. But Whitney, *Oriental and Linguistic Essays*, 2, 417, 418, shows that no stress can be laid on this argument, since the correspondence is only approximate, and the latitudes of the Babylonian and Chinese observations are approximately the same.

[171] See *op. cit.*, 2, 418-420.

[172] *Altindisches Leben*, 356, 357, where he is quite confident of the Semitic origin of the Nakṣatras.

[173] *Op. cit.*, 572.

[174] For the flood, see Zimmer, *op. cit.*, 101, 357, who is opposed to Weber's view (*Indische Studien*, 1, 160; *Indische Streifen*, 1, 11) that the story preserves an old Āryan tradition, and a reminiscence of the home of the Indians beyond the Himālaya (*cf.* Muir, *Sanskrit Texts*, 1², 190; 2², 323, n. 96; Lassen, *Indische Alterthumskunde*, 1², 638, and *cf.* Oldenberg, *Religion des Veda*, 276, n. 3). For the Ādityas, see Oldenberg, *Religion des Veda*, 185 *et seq.*; *Zeitschrift der Deutschen Morgenländischen Gesellschaft*, 50, 43 *et seq.* His view is not accepted by Macdonell, *Vedic Mythology*, p. 44; Bloomfield, *Religion of the Veda*, 133. Still more doubtful is Zimmer's view (*Altindisches Leben*, 363, 364) of the division of day and night into thirty parts, which he sees in Rv. i. 123, 8, and which he thinks is based on the Babylonian division of the same period of time into sixtieths. *Cf.* also V. Smith, *Indian Antiquary*, 34, 230, who argues, but inconclusively, that the use of iron was introduced from Babylonia.

The facts about the Nakṣatras are (with the exception of the data from the Maitrāyaṇī Saṃhitā and the Baudhāyana Śrauta Sūtra) collected in Weber's second essay, *Die vedischen Nachrichten von den Naxatra*, 1861. The first essay, 1860, deals with the problem of origins. See also his discussions in *Indische Studien*, 9, 424 *et seq.*; 10, 213 *et seq.* Whitney's work lies partly in his scientific determination (in many places correcting Colebrooke's discoveries) of the later Naxatras in his edition and version of the Sūrya Siddhānta (*Journal of the American Oriental Society*, 6), and partly in his discussions of the question of origin (*Journal of the American Oriental Society*, 8), *Oriental and Linguistic Essays*, 2, 341-421 (with a stellar chart), and of the question of date as against Jacobi and Tilak's *Orion* (*Journal of the American Oriental Society*, 16, lxxxii *et seq.*). The views of Max Müller are found in his *Rigveda*, 4², xxxiv *et seq.* The modern discussion of the dates inferable from the Nakṣatra was inaugurated by Jacobi (1893) in the *Festgruss an Roth*, 68-74 (translated in the *Indian Antiquary*, 23). See also his articles in the *Nachrichten der königl. Gesellschaft der Wissenschaften zu Göttingen*, 1894, 110 *et seq.*; *Zeitschrift der Deutschen Morgenländischen Gesellschaft*, 49, 218 *et seq.*; 50, 70 *et seq.*; *Journal of the Royal Asiatic Society*, 1909, 721-727. Independently Tilak, in his *Orion*, developed similar views; but most of his special points are disposed of by Whitney in his review cited above. Oldenberg has discussed and refuted Jacobi's arguments in the *Zeitschrift*, 48, 629 *et seq.*; 49, 470 *et seq.*; 50, 450 *et seq.*; *Journal of the Royal Asiatic Society*, 1909, 1090 *et seq.* Thibaut has also rejected Jacobi's views in an article in the *Indian Antiquary*, 24, 85 *et seq.* See also his *Astronomie, Astrologie und Mathematik*, 17-19. The recent literature on the origin of the Nakṣatras consists of articles by Thibaut, *Journal of the Asiatic Society of Bengal*, 63, 144 *et seq.*; Saussure, *T'oung Pao*, 1909, 121 *et seq.*; 255 *et seq.*; Oldenberg, *Nachrichten der königl. Gesellschaft der Wissenschaften zu Göttingen*, 1909, 544 *et seq.* The Nakṣatras in the Epic are dealt with by Hopkins, *Journal of the American Oriental Society*, 24, 29-36. Ludwig's views are given in his Translation of the Rigveda, 3, 183 *et seq.*

Nakṣatra-darśa ('gazer at the lunar mansions'), an 'astrologer,' is mentioned in the list of victims at the Puruṣamedha, or 'human sacrifice,' in the Yajurveda.[1] A notice in the Śatapatha Brāhmaṇa[2] indicates that that work regarded the practice of choosing a particular Nakṣatra under which to set up the sacrificial fires as an idle one, because it decides in favour of choosing the sun as one's Nakṣatra.

1 Vājasaneyi Saṃhitā, xxx. 10; Taittirīya Brāhmaṇa, iii. 4, 4, 1.

2 ii. 1, 2, 19, and *cf.* the Kāṇva text in Eggeling, *Sacred Books of the East*, xii, 288, n. 3.

Nakṣatra-vidyā, the 'science of the lunar mansions,' 'astronomy,' is mentioned with other sciences in the Chāndogya Upaniṣad (vii. 1, 2. 4; 2, 1; 7, 1).

Nakha denotes either the 'nail' of a man,[1] or the 'claw' of a wild beast, such as a tiger.[2] The trimming (*nikṛntana*)[3] of the nails was a regular part of the toilet of the Vedic Indian, especially on occasions of special sanctity, when it accompanied the cleansing of the teeth.[4]

1 Rv. i. 162, 9; x. 163, 5; Av. ii. 33, 6, etc.

2 Rv. iv. 3, 3. *Cf.* x. 28, 10, of the eagle's talon.

3 Chāndogya Upaniṣad, vi. 1, 6.

4 Taittirīya Saṃhitā, ii. 5, 1, 7; Maitrāyaṇī Saṃhitā, iii. 6, 2, etc.; Śatapatha Brāhmaṇa, ii. 1, 3, 4.

Na-ga ('not moving'), 'mountain,' is a word occurring only in a late book of the Atharvaveda (xix. 8, 1), and then in the Sūtras.

Nagara is in early Vedic literature found only in the derivative adjective, used as a proper name, **Nagarin,** but it appears in the sense of 'town' in the Taittirīya Āraṇyaka (i. 11, 18; 31, 4), and frequently in the later language.

Nagarin Jāna-śruteya ('descendant of Janaśruti') is mentioned as a priest in the Aitareya Brāhmaṇa (v. 30), and as Nagarin Jānaśruteya Kāṇḍviya in the Jaiminīya Upaniṣad Brāhmaṇa (iii. 40, 2).

Nagna-jit, King of **Gandhāra,** is mentioned in the Aitareya Brāhmaṇa[1] as having been consecrated by **Parvata** and **Nārada.** The same king is mentioned with his son **Svarjit** in the Śatapatha Brāhmaṇa,[2] where a remark attributed to one of them on a ritual topic is treated with contempt.

[1] vii. 34.
[2] viii. 1, 4, 10. *Cf.* Weber, *Indian Literature,* 132, 134; Muir, *Sanskrit Texts,* 1², 515.

Nagnā. See **Dharma.**

Nagha-māra and **Naghā-riṣa.** See 1. **Kuṣṭha.**

Na-ciketas occurs in the well-known legend of the Taittirīya Brāhmaṇa[1] (where he is a Gotama, the son of **Vāja-śravasa**), and in the Kaṭha Upaniṣad.[2] His historical reality is extremely doubtful: in the Upaniṣad he is called son of Āruṇi Auddālaki or Vājaśravasa, an impossible attribution, and one due only to a desire to give Naciketas a connexion with the famous Āruṇi.

[1] iii. 11, 8.
[2] i. 1, etc. *Cf.* Geldner, *Vedische Studien,* 3, 154, n. 1; Weber, *Indian Literature,* 157; Macdonell, *Vedic Mythology,* p. 168.

1. **Naḍa**, 'reed,' is mentioned in the Rigveda[1] as growing in lakes, and in the Atharvaveda[2] is described as *vārṣika*, 'produced in the rains.' Reeds were used, after being split, for making mats, a work carried out by women.[3] They are frequently mentioned elsewhere.[4] See also **Nada.**

1 viii. 1, 33.
2 iv. 19, 1.
3 Av. vi. 138, 5.
4 Av. vi. 137, 2; xii. 2, 1. 19. 50. 54; Kāṭhaka Saṃhitā, xxv. 7; Śatapatha Brāhmaṇa, i. 1, 4, 19; Taittirīya Āraṇyaka, vi. 7, 10.
Cf. Zimmer, *Altindisches Leben*, 71.

2. **Naḍa Naiṣadha** is mentioned in the Śatapatha Brāhmaṇa,[1] where he seems to be[2] a human king who is compared with Yama, the god of death, because of his conquests. Being there identified with the southern sacrificial fire, he was presumably a king of the south, just as Yama is connected with the south.

1 ii. 2, 2, 1. 2.
2 Weber, *Indische Studien*, 1, 225-227, followed by Eggeling, *Sacred Books of the East*, 12, 338, notes 4 and 5. The printed text has Naiṣidha by error.

Naḍvalā, a 'reed bed,' is mentioned in the Vājasaneyi Saṃhitā (xxx. 16) and the Taittirīya Brāhmaṇa (iii. 4, 12, 1).

Nada is found in several passages of the Ṛigveda,[1] but its sense is still obscure. It is identified by Pischel[2] with **Naḍa**, being explained by him in one passage[3] as a reed boat, which is split, and over which the waters go; in another[4] as a reed whip, of which the sharp points (*karṇa*) are used to urge horses on; and in others[5] again as figuratively designating the penis. Roth[6] takes the sense to be 'bull' (either literally or meta-

1 i. 32, 8; 179, 4; ii. 34, 3; viii. 69, 2; x. 11, 2; 105, 4. *Cf.* Nirukta, v. 2.
2 *Zeitschrift der Deutschen Morgenländischen Gesellschaft*, 35, 717 *et seq.*; *Vedische Studien*, 1, 183 *et seq.*
3 i. 32, 8. Here Caland and Henry, *L'Agniṣṭoma*, 312, n., would read *naḷam.* See also Wackernagel, *Altindische Grammatik*, 1, 173.
4 ii. 34, 3, followed by Max Müller, *Sacred Books of the East*, 32, 301 (who, however, does not construe *āśubhiḥ*, 'sharp,' with *karṇaiḥ* as Pischel does in *Vedische Studien*, 1, 190). He sees 'reed' also in x. 11, 2, but 'horse' in x. 105, 4.
5 i. 179, 4; viii. 69, 2.
6 St. Petersburg Dictionary, *s.v.* The sense of 'bull' seems imperative in viii. 89, 2; it is admissible in i. 179, 4, where 'bull' may denote a man, and in x. 11, 2, and possibly in i. 32, 8, but 'reed' there seems far more likely.

phorically) in all passages. Once at least[7] the 'neigher' (from the root *nad*, 'sound') seems to be meant with reference to Indra's horse. In the phrase *nadasya karṇaiḥ*[8] the sense is, perhaps, 'through the ears of the (side) horse' (that is, by their being ready to hear the word of command) of their chariot, the Maruts 'hasten on with their swift steeds' (*turayanta āśubhiḥ*).

[7] x. 105, 4, and in x. 11, 2. The latter passage suggests that 'river' may, after all, be the sense there.

Cf. Oldenberg, *Ṛgveda-Noten*, 1, 32, 178, 215.

Nadī, 'stream,' is mentioned in the Rigvēda[1] and later.[2] Reference is made to shallows (*gādha*)[3] in the river's bed, to the opposite bank (*pāra*),[4] and to the bathing of horses in streams.[5] Rivers are also mentioned in close connexion with mountains.[6] The title Nadī-pati, 'lord of rivers,'[7] is once used to express 'ocean' or 'sea-water.'

[1] i. 158, 5; ii. 35, 3; iii. 33, 4; v. 46, 6, etc.

[2] Av. iii. 13, 1; xiv. 1, 43.

[3] Rv. vii. 60, 7.

[4] Śatapatha Brāhmaṇa, xi. 1, 6, 6.

[5] Rv. viii. 2, 2.

[6] Rv. v. 55, 7; x. 64, 8.

[7] Śatapatha Brāhmaṇa, v. 3, 4, 10.

Nanā is a familiar name for mother, parallel with **Tata,** for father, with which it is found in a verse of the Rigveda[1] describing the occupations of the parents of the poet.

[1] ix. 112, 3. *Cf.* Nirukta, vi. 6, and see **Upala-prakṣiṇī.**

Nanāndṛ is a word occurring only once in the Rigveda,[1] where it denotes, according to Sāyaṇa, the 'husband's sister,' over whom the wife is to rule. This interpretation is confirmed by the fact that the same position is ascribed to the husband's sister—no doubt while unmarried and living in her brother's care—by the Aitareya Brāhmaṇa.[2]

[1] x. 85, 46.

[2] iii. 22.

Cf. Delbrück, *Die indogermanischen Verwandtschaftsnamen*, 516. The native lexicographers recognize the word, though its occurrence in the later literature is very rare (it has been noted in the Uttararāmacarita). See the St. Petersburg Dictionary, *s.v.*

Napāt in Vedic literature apparently has both the wider sense of 'descendant,'[1] and the narrower one of 'grandson' in the Saṃhitās.[2] In the Brāhmaṇas the word seems hardly to have the sense of 'descendant' at all, while it denotes not only 'grandson,'[3] but also 'great-grandson' in the sequence 'sons, grandsons, great-grandsons' (*putrān, pautrān, naptṝn*).[4] 'Grandson' is also expressed by Pautra ('son's son') in the Atharvaveda and later,[5] while the sense of 'great-grandson' is accurately conveyed as early as the Rigveda[6] by Pra-ṇapāt, used beside Napāt, 'grandson.' Naptī, the feminine, is practically limited to the Saṃhitās,[7] and denotes 'daughter.' The use in the Veda throws no light on the original use of the word.[8]

1 It is equivalent to 'son' in a number of mythological epithets such as *apāṃ napāt*, 'son of waters.'

2 Rv. x. 10, 1, clearly 'son'; vi. 20, 11, may be 'grandson.' Most passages, vi. 50, 15; vii. 18, 22; viii. 65, 12; 102, 7; Vājasaneyi Saṃhitā, xxi. 61; Kāṭhaka Saṃhitā, xxii. 2, require 'descendant.'

3 As in Aitareya Brāhmaṇa, iii. 48: *putra-naptāraḥ*, 'sons and grandsons.' *Cf.* Nirukta, viii. 5.

4 Aitareya Brāhmaṇa, vii. 10, 3; Āpastamba Śrauta Sūtra, x. 11, 5.

5 Av. ix. 5, 30; xi. 7, 16; Aitarey Brāhmaṇa, vii. 10, 3; Taittirīya Brāhmaṇa, ii. 1, 8, 3.

6 Rv. viii. 17, 13, with *napāt*.

7 Rv. iii. 31, 1 (Nirukta, iii. 4); viii. 2, 42. *Cf.* i. 50, 9; ix. 9, 1; 14, 5; 69, 3; Av. i. 28, 4; ii. 14, 1; vii. 82, 6.

8 Delbrück, *Die indogermanischen Verwandtschaftsnamen*, 403-405; Lanmann, *Festgruss an Böhtlingk*, 77.

Naptrī, as feminine of **Napāt**, is found in the Sāmaveda, Āraṇya (v. 13).

Nabha(s), Nabhasya. See **Māsa.**

Nabhāka is the name of a Ṛṣi who is referred to in the Rigveda[1] and the Aitareya Brāhmaṇa.[2] The Anukramaṇī (Index) attributes to **Nābhāka** the composition of several hymns of the Rigveda (viii. 39-42).

1 viii. 40, 4. 5.

2 vi. 24.

Cf. Ludwig, Translation of the Rigveda, 3, 107.

Nabhya, the 'nave' of the wheel, is mentioned in the Atharvaveda[1] and later.[2] See also **Nābhi.**

[1] vi. 70, 3; xii. 1, 12.

[2] Aitareya Brāhmaṇa, iv. 15; Śatapatha Brāhmaṇa, iii. 5, 3, 20; Kauṣītaki Brāhmaṇa, ix. 4; Bṛhadāraṇyaka Upaniṣad, i. 3, 23, etc.

Namī Sāpya is the name of a man in the Rigveda.[1] Weber[2] thinks that he is mentioned as a priest, but the passages suit a king better, and in the Pañcaviṃśa Brāhmaṇa[3] he appears as Namī Sāpya, *Vaideho rājā*, 'King of Videha.' In one passage[4] he is represented as engaged in the contest against Namuci.

[1] vi. 20, 6; x. 48, 9. Simply Namī in i. 53, 7.

[2] *Indische Studien*, 1, 231, 232.

[3] xxv. 10, 17.

[4] Rv. i. 53, 7.

Cf. Ludwig, Translation of the Rigveda, 3, 149; Macdonell, *Vedic Mythology*, p. 161; Hopkins, *Transactions of the Connecticut Academy of Arts and Sciences*, 15, 49. Sāpya may be read Sāyya, but Sāyaṇa recognizes the *p*; Oldenberg, *Zeitschrift der Deutschen Morgenländischen Gesellschaft*, 55, 328.

Nara, Nṛ.—The general name for 'man' in the Rigveda[1] and later[2] is Nṛ, while Nara[3] is found occasionally in the later Saṃhitās and the Brāhmaṇas.[4]

[1] i. 25, 5; 167, 20; 178, 3; ii. 34, 6; iii. 16, 4, etc.

[2] Av. ii. 9, 2; ix. 1, 3; xiv. 2, 9; Aitareya Brāhmaṇa, iii. 34; vi. 27. 32, etc.

[3] This form of the word, common in the post-Vedic language, is secondary, having originated from cases like *naram*, understood as *nara-m*; but its origin goes back to the Indo-Iranian period. See Brugmann, *Grundriss*, 2, 106. *Cf.* Macdonell, *Vedic Grammar*, 318, *a* 5.

[4] Taittirīya Saṃhitā, vii. 1, 12, 1; Satapatha Brāhmaṇa, ix. 3, 1, 3; Nirukta, v. 1, etc.

Narācī occurs once in the Atharvaveda,[1] perhaps meaning a poisonous plant.

[1] v. 31, 4. *Cf.* Weber, *Indische Studien*, 18, 286.

Narya ('manly') is in two passages of the Rigveda (i. 54, 6; 112, 9) understood by the commentator Sāyaṇa as the proper name of a man. See also **Nārya.**

Nalada, nard' (*Nardastachys Jatamansi*) is a plant mentioned in the Atharvaveda,[1] in the Aitareya[2] and the Śāṅkhāyana[3] Āraṇyakas (where it is mentioned as used for a garland), as well as in the Sūtras. In the Atharvaveda[4] the feminine form of the word, Naladī, occurs as the name of an Apsaras, or celestial nymph.

[1] vi. 102, 3.
[2] iii. 2, 4.
[3] xi. 4.
[4] iv. 37, 3.

Cf. Zimmer, *Altindisches Leben*, 68, 69; Grohmann, *Indische Studien*, 9, 420; Caland, *Altindisches Zauberritual*, 177, n. 4.

Navaka is mentioned as having wished for a wife at the Sattra of the **Vibhindukīyas** in the Jaiminīya Brāhmaṇa.[1]

[1] ii. 233 (*Journal of the American Oriental Society*, 18, 38).

Nava-gva occurs in several passages of the Rigveda[1] as a man, an Aṅgiras in the highest degree (*Aṅgirastama*),[2] apparently being the type of the Navagvas,[3] who appear as a mystic race of olden times, coupled with, and conceived probably as related to, the Aṅgirases. They are often associated with the **Daśagvas.**[4]

[1] iv. 51, 4; ix. 108, 4; x. 62, 6.
[2] x. 62, 6.
[3] Rv. i. 62, 4; iii. 39, 5; v. 29, 12; 45, 7. 11; vi. 22, 2; x. 14, 6; 61, 10; 108, 8; Av. xiv. 1, 56; xviii. 3, 20, etc.
[4] Rv. i. 62, 4; iv. 51, 4; v. 29, 12; x. 62, 6, etc.

Cf. Ludwig, Translation of the Rigveda, 3, 165; Macdonell, *Vedic Mythology*, pp. 144 (B), 170.

Nava-nīta, 'fresh butter,' is mentioned frequently in the later Saṃhitās[1] and the Brāhmaṇas.[2] According to the Aitareya Brāhmaṇa[3] this is the kind of butter which is fitted for anointing an embryo (*garbha*), while the gods receive **Ājya,** men fragrant ghee (**Ghṛta**), and the fathers **Āyuta.** Elsewhere[4] it is contrasted with Ghṛta and **Sarpis.**

[1] Taittirīya Saṃhitā, ii. 3, 10, 1; vi. 1, 1, 5; Kāṭhaka Saṃhitā, xi. 7; Maitrāyaṇī Saṃhitā, ii. 3, 4, etc.
[2] Śatapatha Brāhmaṇa, iii. 1, 3, 7. 8; v. 3, 2, 6; Jaiminīya Upaniṣad Brāhmaṇa, iii. 5, 3.
[3] i. 3.
[4] Taittirīya Saṃhitā, ii. 3, 10, 1, etc

Nava-vāstva appears in three passages of the Rigveda. In one[1] he seems to be a protégé of Agni; in another[2] as perhaps a son of **Uśanas** and favourite of Indra, but in the last he seems to be defeated, or even slain, by Indra.[3] But he may be a mythic figure altogether. *Cf.* also **Bṛhadratha.**

[1] i. 36, 18.
[2] vi. 20, 11.
[3] x. 49, 6.
Cf. Bergaigne, *Religion Védique*, 2, 223; Griffith, *Hymns of the Rigveda*, 1, 581; Pischel, *Vedische Studien*, 2, 128, 129; Ludwig, Translation of the Rigveda, 3, 147; *Über die neuesten Arbeiten auf dem Gebiete der Ṛgvedaforschung*, 160; Perry, *Journal of the American Oriental Society*, 11, 202; Macdonell, *Vedic Mythology*, p. 158.

Nah has been taken by Roth[1] and Grassmann[2] to be the stem, meaning 'bond,' of the dative form *nadbhyas*, which occurs once in the Rigveda,[3] and which Sieg[4] thinks means 'sister's sons.' But the sense of this dative is probably rather 'to the grandsons.'[5]

[1] St. Petersburg Dictionary, *s.v.*
[2] *Wörterbuch*, *s.v.*
[3] x. 60, 6.
[4] *Die Sagenstoffe des Ṛgveda*, 129.
[5] Macdonell, *Vedic Grammar*, p. 56, 3*b*.

Nahus occurs several times in the Rigveda, but the exact sense is not certain. Ludwig[1] sees in the Nahus a tribe on the **Sindhu** (Indus)[2] or **Sarasvatī**,[3] rich in horses,[4] allied with the **Bharatas** and **Śimyus**,[5] connected with **Kakṣīvant** and the **Vārṣāgiras**,[6] and having as kings **Maśarśāra** and **Āyavasa**.[7] Roth,[8] on the other hand, sees in Nahus the general sense of 'neighbour' as opposed to a member of one's own people (**Viś**); this interpretation is supported by the occurrence of the phrase *nahuṣo nahuṣṭara*,[9] 'closer than a neighbour.' Nahuṣa has the same sense as Nahus in two passages of the Rigveda,[10] but in

[1] Translation of the Rigveda, 3, 206.
[2] Rv. i. 31, 11; vi. 22, 10; 46, 7; x. 80, 6.
[3] Rv. vii. 95, 2. *Cf.* ix. 88, 2; 91, 2.
[4] Rv. viii. 6, 24.
[5] Rv. i. 100, 18; vii. 18, 5.
[6] Rv. i. 100, 16. 17.
[7] Rv. i. 122, 15. *Cf.* also *nahuṣo viśaḥ*, Rv. vii. 6, 5; x. 49, 8; 99, 7, etc.
[8] St. Petersburg Dictionary, *s.v.*
[9] Rv. x. 49, 8. *Cf.* also viii. 8, 3.
[10] i. 31, 11; v. 12, 6.

one it seems to be intended for the proper name of a man.[11] Possibly Nahus was originally a man like Manu.[12]

[11] Rv. viii. 46, 27.

[12] Oldenberg, *Sacred Books of the East*, 46, 28; Bergaigne, *Religion Védique*, 2, 324. But Nahus, if it was originally the name of a mythic forefather, cannot have been that of a forefather recognized by all the tribes, for there is no passage in which it applies to all men. Geldner, *Ṛgveda*, *Glossar*, 92, regards Nahus as a tribe, Nahuṣa as a king. Zimmer, *Altindisches Leben*, 128, leaves the question open. *Cf.* Muir, *Sanskrit Texts*, 1², 165, n. 7; 179 *et seq.*; 307 *et seq.*

1. **Nāka** denotes the 'firmament' in the Rigveda[1] and later.[2] It is often used with the epithet 'highest' (*uttama*)[3] or 'third' (*tṛtīya*)[4] referring to the threefold division of heaven, parallel to the threefold division of earth, atmosphere, and sky (**Div**). The Nāka is said to be on the third ridge (*pṛṣṭha*), above the luminous space (*rocana*) of the sky.[5] Elsewhere[6] the series earth, atmosphere, sky, and the firmament (*nāka*), heaven (*svar*), the celestial light (*jyotis*), occurs. The word *nāka* is explained in the Brāhmaṇas[7] as derived from *na*, 'not,' and *aka*, 'pain,' because those who go there are free from sorrow.

[1] i 60, 10; 125, 5; iii. 2, 12; iv. 13, 5; vii. 86, 1; 99, 2; viii. 103, 2; ix. 73, 4, etc.

[2] Av. vii. 18, 1; xviii. 2, 47; xiii. 1, 7; Vājasaneyi Saṃhitā, xv. 10; Pañcaviṃśa Brāhmaṇa, xviii. 7, 10; Śatapatha Brāhmaṇa, viii. 5, 3, 4, etc.

[3] Av. iv. 14, 6; xi. 1, 4; Vājasaneyi Saṃhitā, ix. 10; xii. 63.

[4] Av. vi. 122, 4; ix. 5, 1. 4; xviii. 4, 3.

[5] Vājasaneyi Saṃhitā, xv. 50.

[6] Av. iv. 14, 3; Vājasaneyi Saṃhitā, xvii. 67. In Rv. x. 121, 5, the earth and sky (*dyauḥ*), and heaven (*svar*), and the firmament (*nāka*), are all mentioned.

[7] Pañcaviṃśa Brāhmaṇa, x. 1, 18; Satapatha Brāhmaṇa, viii. 4, 1, 24; Nirukta, ii. 14; and *cf.* Chāndogya Upaniṣad, ii. 10, 5.

Cf. Macdonell, *Vedic Mythology*, p. 9; Max Müller, *Sacred Books of the East*, 32, 50, 56, 57.

2. **Nāka** is the name of a teacher in the Jaiminīya Upaniṣad Brāhmaṇa.[1] Presumably he is identical with Nāka Maudgalya ('descendant of Mudgala'), who is mentioned in the Śatapatha Brāhmaṇa,[2] the Bṛhadāraṇyaka Upaniṣad,[3] and the Taittirīya Upaniṣad.[4]

[1] iii. 13, 5.

[2] xii. 5, 2, 1.

[3] vi. 4, 4.

[4] i. 9, 1.

Nākra is the name of an aquatic animal included among the victims at the Aśvamedha, or 'horse sacrifice,' in the Yajurveda Saṃhitās.[1] Perhaps the animal meant is the crocodile, which later is called Nakra.[2]

[1] Taittirīya Saṃhitā, v. 5, 13, 1; Maitrāyaṇī Saṃhitā, iii. 14, 2; Vājasaneyi Saṃhitā, xxiv. 35.

[2] Zimmer, *Altindisches Leben*, 96, following one version given by Mahīdhara on Vājasaneyi Saṃhitā, *loc. cit.*: Hillebrandt, *Vedische Mythologie*, 3, 21, n. 4.

Nāga appears once in the Śatapatha Brāhmaṇa[1] in the form *mahānāga*, where 'great snake' or 'great elephant' may be meant. In the Bṛhadāraṇyaka Upaniṣad,[2] and in a citation found in the Aitareya Brāhmaṇa[3] the sense of 'elephant' is clearly intended. In the Sūtras[4] the mythic Nāga already occurs.

[1] xi. 2, 7, 12.

[2] i. 3, 24.

[3] viii. 22.

[4] Āśvalāyana Gṛhya Sūtra, iii. 4, 1. *Cf.* Winternitz, *Sarpabali*, 43; Macdonell, *Vedic Mythology*, p. 153.

Nāgna-jita, 'descendant of **Nagnajit**,' is the patronymic of **Svarjit** in the Śatapatha Brāhmaṇa (viii. 1, 4, 10).

Nāciketa, 'connected with **Naciketas**,' is the title of a narrative (*upākhyāna*) in the Kāṭhaka Upaniṣad.[1] The word is also applied as an epithet to a special fire in that Upaniṣad[2] and in the Taittirīya Upaniṣad.[3]

[1] iii. 16.

[2] i. 18; ii. 10.

[3] i. 22, 11; 26, 3. *Cf.* Weber, *Indische Studien*, 3, 386. The native lexicographers give Nāchiketa and Nāciketu as synonyms of fire generally.

Nāḍa-pit occurs in the Śatapatha Brāhmaṇa[1] as the birthplace of **Bharata**. The word may, however, be read as Nāḍa-pitī, the name of Bharata's mother,[2] but this is less probable.

[1] xiii. 5, 4, 13.

[2] Weber, *Episches im vedischen Ritual*, 6, n. 3. *Cf.* Leumann, *Zeitschrift der Deutschen Morgenländischen Gesellschaft*, 48, 81.

1. **Nāḍī** denotes a 'vein' or 'artery' in the human body in the Atharvaveda[1] and later,[2] a natural extension of the literal sense of 'reed.'

[1] vi. 138, 4; x. 7, 15. 16.
[2] Kāṭhaka Saṃhitā, xii. 10; Śatapatha Brāhmaṇa, x. 4, 5, 2; Bṛhadāraṇyaka Upaniṣad, ii. 1, 21; iv. 2, 3, etc.; Chāndogya Upaniṣad, viii. 6, 1; Kauṣītaki Upaniṣad, iv. 19.

2. **Nāḍī** means a musical instrument, a 'reed flute,' in the Rigveda[1] as well as the Kāṭhaka Saṃhitā,[2] where in one passage it is mentioned along with the **Tūṇava.**[3]

[1] x. 135, 7.
[2] xxiii. 4; xxxiv. 5.
[3] xxxiv. 5.

Cf. Hopkins, *Journal of the American Oriental Society*, 13, 329.

3. **Nāḍī** in the Yajurveda Saṃhitās[1] seems to mean the box of the chariot wheel.

[1] Taittirīya Saṃhitā, iii. 4, 8, 3; Kāṭhaka Saṃhitā, xxxvii. 12.

Nāḍīkā occurs once in the Atharvaveda,[1] where the sense seems clearly to be 'wind-pipe,' with a reference also to the 'shaft of an arrow' made of reed.

[1] v. 18, 8. *Cf.* Weber, *Indische Studien*, 18, 229; Whitney, Translation of the Atharvaveda, 251; Bloomfield, *Hymns of the Atharvaveda*, 432.

Nātha in Vedic literature[1] appears only as a neuter meaning 'protection,' and is of rare occurrence.[2] Generally, too, very little appears in Vedic literature of practices such as those which produced Anglo-Saxon society or the Roman *patronatus*.

[1] Av. iv. 20, 9; ix. 2, 17; xviii. 1, 13; Taittirīya Brāhmaṇa, i. 6, 4, 1. Also in Av. xiii. 2, 37, *nātha-kāma*, 'seeking help'; xi. 1, 15, *nātha-vid*, 'finding help'; Pañcaviṃśa Brāhmaṇa, xiv. 11, 23, *nātha-vindu*, 'procuring protection,' as the name of a Sāman, or chant.
[2] In the post-Vedic literature, on the other hand, the word is a masculine, meaning 'protector,' and is very common.

Nāpita, 'barber,' is mentioned in the Śatapatha Brāhmaṇa[1] and later.[2] But the older word is Vaptṛ,[3] a derivative of

[1] iii. 1, 2, 2.
[2] Kātyāyana Śrauta Sūtra, vii. 2, 8. 13; Āśvalāyana Gṛhya Sūtra, i. 17, etc.
[3] Rv. x. 142, 4.

vap, 'shave,' with forms of which verb shaving is referred to as early as the Rigveda.[4] The dead were shaved before burial.[5]

[4] x. 142, 4. *Cf.* i. 65, 4; Av. vi. 68; v 2, 17, etc.

[5] Av. v. 19, 4.

Cf. Zimmer, *Altindisches Leben*, 266; Max Müller, *Sacred Books of the East*, 32, 265.

Nābhāka, 'descendant of Nabhāka,' is the name of a Ṛṣi, or seer, in the Rigveda.[1] The Anukramaṇī (Index) ascribes three or four hymns of the Rigveda[2] to him. According to Ludwig,[3] the man was an Āṅgirasa,[4] not a Kaṇva.

[1] viii. 41, 2; Nirukta, x. 5.

[2] viii. 39-41, and doubtfully 42.

[3] Translation of the Rigveda, 3, 107.

[4] viii. 40, 12.

Nābhā-nediṣṭha ('nearest in descent') **Mānava** ('descendant of Manu') is famous in the later Saṃhitās and the Brāhmaṇas[1] for the way in which he was treated when his father **Manu** divided his property among his sons, or they divided it: Nābhānediṣṭha was left out, but was solaced by obtaining, through his father's advice, cows from the Aṅgirases, a feat which is regarded in the Śāṅkhāyana Śrauta Sūtra[2] as on a level with the exploits of other seers who celebrated their patrons in hymns, and as giving rise to the hymn, Rigveda x. 62. Nābhānediṣṭha's hymn is repeatedly mentioned in the Brāhmaṇas,[3] but beyond its authorship nothing is recorded of him. In the Saṃhitā[4] itself he seems to be spoken of as a poet in one passage, which is, however, of quite uncertain meaning.

Nābhānediṣṭha is etymologically connected in all probability with Nabānazdiṣta in the Avesta, which refers to the Fravaṣi of the paoiryō ṭkaēsha and the Fravaṣi of the Nabānazdiṣta. Lassen[5] saw in the legend a reminiscence of an Indo-Iranian split; but Roth[6] showed conclusively that this was impossible, and that Nābhānediṣṭha meant simply 'nearest in birth,' and

[1] Taittirīya Saṃhitā, iii. 1. 9. 4-6; Aitareya Brāhmaṇa, v. 14. *Cf.* Muir, *Sanskrit Texts*, 1², 191 *et seq.*

[2] xvi. 11. 28-30.

[3] Kauṣītaki Brāhmaṇa, xxviii. 4, merely refers to him as connected with the Aṅgirases. See also *ibid.*, xxx. 4; Aitareya Brāhmaṇa, vi. 30. 31; Pañcaviṃśa Brāhmaṇa, xx. 9, 4.

[4] x. 61, 18.

[5] *Indische Alterthumskunde*, 1, 520, and *Addenda*, p. lxxvii.

[6] *Zeitschrift der Deutschen Morgenländischen Gesellschaft*, 6, 243 *et seq.*

Weber[7] admits that the connexion of the words is not one of borrowing on either side, but that in the Avesta it has kept its original sense of 'nearest relation,' while in the Rigveda it has become a proper name.

[7] *Episches im vedischen Ritual*, 40-50. *Cf.* also **Dāya**.

1. **Nābhi** develops from the literal sense of 'navel' the figurative meaning of 'relationship,'[1] or, concretely, 'relation.'[2]

[1] i. 105, 9; 164, 33; ii. 3, 9; 40, 4, etc.; Av. xii. 1, 40; Vājasaneyi Saṃhitā, x. 8; xi. 12; xx. 1, etc.

[2] Rv. i. 163, 12; vi. 47, 28; Vājasaneyi Saṃhitā, xiii. 42. 44. 50, etc.

2. **Nābhi**, 'nave' of a chariot wheel, is mentioned in the Rigveda[1] and later.[2] See also **Ratha**, and *cf.* **Nabhya.**

[1] v. 43, 8; vi. 39, 4; viii. 41, 6.

[2] Av. iii. 30, 6; x. 8, 34; xi. 7, 4; Kāṭhaka Saṃhitā, xi. 4; Bṛhadāraṇyaka Upaniṣad, ii. 5, 11; Chāndogya Upaniṣad, vii. 15, 1; Aitareya Āraṇyaka, iii. 2, 4; Kauṣītaki Upaniṣad, iii. 8.

Nāma-dheya, 'name,' is found in the Rigveda,[1] and often in the later language.[2] See **Nāman.**

[1] x. 71, 1.

[2] Av. vii. 109, 6; Taittirīya Saṃhitā, ii. 4, 9, 3; iii. 3, 4, 1; Śatapatha Brāhmaṇa, xiii. 1, 6, 1; Bṛhadāraṇyaka Upaniṣad, ii. 3, 11; vi. 4, 25; Chāndogya Upaniṣad, vi. 1, 4; Aitareya Upaniṣad, v. 2, etc.

Nāman, 'name,' is a common word from the Rigveda onwards. The Gṛhya Sūtras[1] give elaborate rules for the formation of the names of children, but more important is the distinction between the secret (*guhya*) and the ordinary name, though the rules as to the secret name are not at all consistent. The secret name is already recognized in the Rigveda,[2] and is referred to in the Brāhmaṇas,[3] one secret name, that of Arjuna for Indra, being given in the Śatapatha Brāhmaṇa.[4] It is to be noted that the rule as to giving the

[1] Weber, *Naxatra*, 2, 316 *et seq.*; Hillebrandt, *Rituallitteratur*, 46, 47; Jolly, *Recht und Sitte*, 152.

[2] *Cf.* x. 55, 2; 71, 1, as explained in Aitareya Āraṇyaka, i. 3, 3.

[3] Śatapatha Brāhmaṇa, vi. 1, 3, 9 (the name is given to a child at birth); Bṛhadāraṇyaka Upaniṣad, vi. 4, 25.

[4] ii. 1, 2, 11; v. 4, 3, 7; Weber, 2, 317, n. 3.

designation of a Nakṣatra (lunar asterism) as the secret name or otherwise is not illustrated by a single recorded name of a teacher in the Brāhmaṇas.[5]

The Śatapatha Brāhmaṇa[6] several times mentions the adoption of a second name with a view to securing success, and also refers to the adoption of another name for purposes of distinction.[7]

In actual practice two names are usually found in the Brāhmaṇas, the second being a patronymic or a metronymic, as in **Kakṣīvant Auśija**[8] (if the story of the slave woman Uśij as his mother is correct), or **Bṛhaduktha Vāmneya**,[9] 'son of Vāmnī,' though the relationship may, of course, be not direct parentage, but more remote descent.[10] Three names are less common—for example, **Kūśāmba Svāyava Lātavya**,[11] 'son of Svāyu, of the Lātavya (son of Latu) family,' or **Devataras Śyāvasāyana Kāśyapa**,[12] where the patronymic and the Gotra name are both found. In other cases the names probably have a local reference—*e.g.*, **Kauśāmbeya** and **Gāṅgya**. Frequently the patronymic only is given, as **Bhārgava, Maudgalya,** etc., or two patronymics are used. The simple name is often used for the patronymic—*e.g.*, **Trasadasyu**.[13] In a few cases the name of the wife is formed from the husband's name,[14] as **Uśīnarāṇī, Purukutsānī, Mudgalānī**.

[5] Weber, 2, 318, 319. See **Aṣāḍha, Rauhiṇa, Rauhiṇāyana.**

[6] iii. 6, 2, 24; v. 3, 3, 14; ix. 4, 3, 3, which directs that the name should be derived from a feast performed by the person in question. See also Kāṭhaka Saṃhitā, xxvi. 4; Taittirīya Brāhmaṇa, ii. 7, 17.

[7] Śatapatha Brāhmaṇa, ii. 4, 4, 4. *Cf.* vi. 1, 3, 9.

[8] Pañcaviṃśa Brāhmaṇa, xiv. 11, 17.

[9] *Ibid.*, xiv. 9, 38.

[10] Pargiter, *Journal of the Royal Asiatic Society*, 1910, 14; Hopkins, *Transactions of the Connecticut Academy of Arts and Sciences*, 15, 55, n. 2.

[11] Pañcaviṃśa Brāhmaṇa, viii. 6, 8.

[12] Jaiminīya Upaniṣad Brāhmaṇa, iii. 40, 2.

[13] Śatapatha Brāhmaṇa, vi. 1, 2, 13; Hopkins, *Religions of India*, 201, n. 2.

[14] *Cf.* Macdonell, *Vedic Grammar*, p. 135.

Cf. Weber, *op. cit.*, 2, 316-320; Hopkins, *loc. cit.*

Nāmba is the name of a kind of grain mentioned in the Śatapatha Brāhmaṇa.[1] Āmba is the form of the word in the Taittirīya Saṃhitā[2] and the Kāṭhaka Saṃhitā.[3]

[1] v. 3, 3, 8. [2] i. 8, 10, 1. [3] xv. 15.

Nāya in two passages of the Rigveda[1] is, according to the St. Petersburg Dictionary, probably a proper name. Sāyaṇa takes the word to mean 'leader,' while Pischel[2] considers it a gerund with passive sense.

[1] vi. 24, 10; 46, 11.

[2] *Vedische Studien*, 1, 41. For other explanations, see Oldenberg, *Ṛgveda-Noten*, 1, 123, 370.

Nārada is the name of a mythical seer mentioned several times in the Atharvaveda.[1] In the Aitareya Brāhmaṇa he appears in conjunction with **Parvata** as priest of **Hariścandra**,[2] as teaching **Somaka Sāhadevya**,[3] and as anointing **Āmbāṣṭhya** and **Yudhāṃśrauṣṭi**.[4] In the Maitrāyaṇī Saṃhitā[5] he is mentioned as a teacher, and in the Sāmavidhāna Brāhmaṇa[6] as a pupil of Bṛhaspati. In the Chāndogya Upaniṣad[7] he is coupled with Sanatkumāra.

[1] v. 19, 9; xii. 4, 16. 24. 41.

[2] vii. 13. *Cf.* Śāṅkhāyana Śrauta Sūtra, xv. 17.

[3] vii. 34.

[4] viii. 21.

[5] i. 5, 8.

[6] iii. 9 (the Vaṃśa, or 'list of teachers,' at the end).

[7] vii. 1, 1.

Cf. Weber, *Indische Studien*, 1, 204, n.

Nārāśaṃsī (scil. Ṛc), '(verse) celebrating men,' is mentioned as early as the Rigveda,[1] and is distinguished from **Gāthā** in a number of passages in the later literature.[2] The Kāṭhaka Saṃhitā,[3] while distinguishing the two, asserts that both are false (*anṛtam*). It is hardly probable that the two were absolutely distinct, for the Taittirīya Brāhmaṇa[4] has the phrase 'a Gāthā celebrating men' (*nārāśaṃsī*). What such verses were may be seen from the Śāṅkhāyana Śrauta Sūtra,[5] which enumerates the *Nārāśaṃsāni* at the Puruṣamedha, or 'human

[1] x. 85, 6.

[2] Av. xv. 6, 4; Taittirīya Saṃhitā, vii. 5, 11, 2; Aitareya Brāhmaṇa, vi. 32; Kauṣītaki Brāhmaṇa, xxx. 5; Kāṭhaka Saṃhitā, v. 5, 2; Taittirīya Āraṇyaka, ii. 10, etc.; Weber, *Indische Studien*, 5, 78. The passage, Śatapatha Brāhmaṇa, xi. 5, 6, 8, is uncertain. See Eggeling, *Sacred Books of the East*, 44, 98, n. 5.

[3] xiv. 5; Weber, *Indische Streifen*, 1, 98.

[4] i. 3, 2, 6.

[5] xvi. 11, 1 *et seq.*; Weber, *Episches im vedischen Ritual*, 10 *et seq.*

sacrifice.' They may legitimately be reckoned a^ a source of the epic.[6]

The term Nārāśaṃsī is restricted in some passages[7] to a particular group of three verses of the Atharvaveda,[8] but Oldenberg[9] must be right in holding that the restricted sense is not to be read into the Rigveda.[10] Not even in the Taittirīya Saṃhitā[11] is the technical sense certain, and the Bṛhaddevatā[12] gives the word a general application.

[6] Hopkins, *Journal of the American Oriental Society*, 15, 264, n. Bloomfield, *Atharvaveda*, 100 (*cf. Hymns of the Atharvaveda*, 688, 689), lays stress rather on their character as mere eulogies of donors, and that, no doubt, was one of their sides; but the other elements may have been more prominent in reality than the priestly tradition shows.

[7] Aitareya Brāhmaṇa, vi. 32; Kauṣītaki Brāhmaṇa, xxx. 5. Possibly, in the other passages mentioned in note 2, the reference may be to the Atharvaveda verses, but this is not at all likely.

[8] xx. 127, 1-3 = Śāṅkhāyana Śrauta Sūtra, xii. 14, 1-3. *Cf.* Scheftelowitz, *Die Apokryphen des Ṛgveda*, 155.

[9] *Zeitschrift der Deutschen Morgenländischen Gesellschaft*, 42, 238.

[10] x. 85, 6.

[11] vii. 5, 11, 2.

[12] iii. 154.

Cf. Weber, *Episches im Vedischen Ritual*, 4 *et seq*.

Nārī, 'woman,' occurs in the Rigveda[1] and later.[2] The word seems in the Rigveda[3] to have a distinct reference to a woman as a wife, because it occurs in several passages with distinct reference to matrimonial relations,[3] and in the later Vedic literature, where it is not common, it sometimes[4] has that sense. Delbrück,[5] however, thinks that it does not indicate marital relations, but merely the woman as the sexual complement of the man.

[1] vii. 20, 5; 55, 8; viii. 77, 8; x. 18, 7; 86, 10. 11.

[2] Av. xiv. 2, 13; Vājasaneyi Saṃhitā, xxiii. 36; Aitareya Brāhmaṇa, iii. 34.

[3] i. 73, 3 (*pati-juṣṭā*, 'dear to her husband'); vii. 20. 5; x. 18, 7 (*avidhavāḥ supatnīḥ*, 'not widowed, with noble husbands'), etc.

[4] Gautama Dharma Sūtra, ix. 28.

[5] *Die indogermanischen Verwandtschaftsnamen*, 417, 439.

Nārmara occurs once in a corrupt verse of the Rigveda.[1] Ludwig[2] regards the word as the proper name of the prince of a fort, **Ūrjayantī**, but Roth[3] as that of a demon.

[1] ii. 13, 8.

[2] Translation of the Rigveda, 3, 152.

[3] St. Petersburg Dictionary, *s.v.*

Nārmiṇī is found in the Rigveda[1] as an epithet of **Pur**, 'fort': it must apparently either be a proper name of the fort,[2] or mean 'belonging to Narmin or Narmiṇa,' some prince.[3]

[1] i. 149, 3.

[2] Ludwig, Translation of the Rigveda, 3, 204.

[3] Roth, St. Petersburg Dictionary, *s.v.* Possibly the expression may consist of two words—*na*, 'not' or 'like,' and *armiṇī*, whatever that may mean. See Oldenberg, *Ṛgveda-Noten*, 1, 148; *Sacred Books of the East*, 46, 177.

Nārya, 'descendant of **Narya**,' is the name of a generous donor in the Rigveda.[1]

[1] viii. 24, 29. *Cf.* Ludwig, Translation of the Rigveda, 3, 161, 162.

Nārṣada, 'descendant of Nṛṣad,' is the patronymic of Kaṇva (*i.e.*, a descendant of Kaṇva) in the Atharvaveda,[1] and in one passage of the Rigveda,[2] where probably the same man is referred to in another passage[3] as a protégé of the Aśvins, and perhaps as the husband of **Ruśatī**. But in a third passage of the Rigveda[4] the name seems applied to a demon, though this is not certain.

[1] iv. 19, 2.

[2] x. 31, 11.

[3] i. 117, 8.

[4] x. 61, 13.

Cf. Ludwig, Translation of the Rigveda, 3, 108, 150; Bloomfield, *Hymns of the Atharvaveda*, 397.

Nāva-prabhraṃśana, the 'sliding down of the ship,' is read in Whitney and Roth's text of the Atharvaveda,[1] and has been connected by Weber[2] and others[3] with Manor Avasarpaṇa, the name in the Śatapatha Brāhmaṇa[4] of the northern mountain on which Manu's ship settled on the subsidence of the deluge. But both Bloomfield[5] and Whitney[6] point out that this interpretation is highly improbable, and this view is accepted by

[1] xix. 39, 8, where the reading *nāvaprabhráṃśana* is a conjectural emendation, the manuscripts of the Saṃhitā text all having two accents, *nā́vaprabhráṃśana* (one of them reading *nā́vaḥ-*).

[2] *Indische Streifen*, 1, 11.

[3] *Cf.* Ludwig, Translation of the Rigveda, 3, 198; Eggeling, *Sacred Books of the East*, 12, 218, n.; Zimmer, *Altindisches Leben*, 30.

[4] i. 8, 1, 6.

[5] *Hymns of the Atharvaveda*, 679.

[6] Translation of the Atharvaveda, 961.

Macdonell.[7] The expression is analyzed as *na ava-prabhraṃśana* by the Pada text and the commentator alike, and is never found elsewhere with reference to the descent of a boat or ship.[8]

[7] *Journal of the Royal Asiatic Society*, 1907, 1107, where his acceptance of Weber's interpretation in his *Sanskrit Literature*, 144, is withdrawn.

[8] The word *nau*, ship, never occurs as the first member of a compound in the form of *nāva*, while *pra-bhraṃś*, 'fall down,' is never used of the gliding down of a boat, and would be inappropriately applied in that sense.

Nāvā, 'ship,' occurs once in the Rigveda (i. 97, 8). See **Nau.**

Nāvāja ('ship-propeller'), a 'boatman,' is mentioned in the Śatapatha Brāhmaṇa (ii. 3, 3, 5).

Nāvyā is found several times in the Rigveda[1] and the later literature[2] in the sense of a 'navigable stream.'

[1] i. 33, 11; 80, 8; 121, 13.

[2] Av. viii. 5, 9; Kāṭhaka Saṃhitā, xxiii. 6; Śatapatha Brāhmaṇa, x. 5, 4, 14, etc.

Nāhuṣa, like **Nahus**, means, according to the St. Petersburg Dictionary, in some passages of the Rigveda[1] 'neighbouring' as an adjective, and once[2] as a substantive 'neighbour.' If, on the other hand, Nahus is taken as a proper name, then Nāhuṣa no doubt denotes 'belonging to the Nahus people,' and, as a substantive, 'King of the Nahus.'

[1] i. 100, 16; v. 73, 3; vi. 22, 10; viii. 6, 24.

[2] viii. 95, 2.

Nikothaka Bhāya-jātya ('descendant of Bhayajāta') is mentioned in the Vaṃśa Brāhmaṇa[1] as a pupil of **Pratithi.**

[1] *Indische Studien*, 4, 373. *Cf.* Max Müller, *Ancient Sanskrit Literature*, 444.

Nigada Pārṇa-valki ('descendant of Parṇavalka') is mentioned in the Vaṃśa Brāhmaṇa[1] as a pupil of Giriśarman.

[1] *Indische Studien*, 4, 372. *Cf.* Max Müller, *Ancient Sanskrit Literature*, 443.

Ni-gut occurs in two passages of the Rigveda,[1] where Sāyaṇa takes it to mean 'enemy,' a possible interpretation. Ludwig[2] suggests that non-Āryan foes are meant.

[1] ix. 97, 53, 54; x. 128, 6.

[2] Translation of the Rigveda, 3, 164.

Nigustha is a term of unknown meaning applied in the Śāṅkhāyana Śrauta Sūtra (xvi. 29, 6) to the peoples of Kāśi, Videha, and Kosala.

1. **Ni-tatnī**, 'striking downwards,' occurs in the Atharvaveda[1] as the name of an unknown plant which was used as a means of restoring the hair.

[1] vi. 136; probably 137 also refers to this plant. *Cf.* Kauṣītaki Sūtra, xxxi. 28, with Caland's note in his translation; Bloomfield, *Atharvaveda*, 61; *Hymns of the Atharvaveda*, 536, 537; Whitney, Translation of the Atharvaveda, 383.

2. **Ni-tatnī** is the name of one of the seven **Kṛttikās** in the Taittirīya Brāhmaṇa (iii. 1, 4, 1). See **Nakṣatra.**

Ni-tāna Māruta is the name of a man in the Kāṭhaka Saṃhitā (xxv. 10).

Ni-dāgha ('burning down'), 'summer,' is the name of one of the seasons in the Śatapatha Brāhmaṇa (xiii. 8, 1, 4). See **Naidāgha.**

Ni-dāna is the name of a Sūtra, which is referred to in the Bṛhaddevatā[1] apparently as containing a quotation from the Bhāllavi Brāhmaṇa. The quotation cannot be verified in the existing text of the Sūtra.[2]

[1] v. 23, with Macdonell's note.

[2] Sieg, *Die Sagenstoffe des Ṛgveda*, 65. *Cf.* Weber, *Indische Studien*, 1, 44; Max Müller, *Ancient Sanskrit Literature*, 111, etc.

Ni-dhā, 'net,' is mentioned in the Rigveda[1] and later.[2]

[1] ix. 83, 4; x. 73, 11; Nirukta, iv. 2.

[2] Aitareya Brāhmaṇa, iii. 19.

Ni-dhi means primarily '(place of) deposit,' 'store,'[1] and then 'treasure' generally.[2] In the Chāndogya Upaniṣad[3] Nidhi denotes some sort of science.

[1] Rv. i. 183, 4; v. 43, 8; vii. 67, 7; 69, 3, etc.

[2] Rv. ii. 24, 6; viii. 29, 6; x. 68, 6; Av. x. 7, 23, etc.

[3] vii. 1, 2. 4; 2, 1; 7, 1. The St. Petersburg Dictionary, *s.v.*, and Böhtlingk in his edition, take *daivo nidhiḥ* as one expression. See **Daiva**. Sāyaṇa takes each as a separate entity, and renders Nidhi as *mahākālādinidhiśāstram*, presumably meaning some sort of chronology.

Cf. for Nidhi as 'treasure,' Jolly, *Recht und Sitte*, 103, 104.

Ni-nāhya denotes in the Śatapatha Brāhmaṇa (iii. 9, 2, 8) a 'water jar,' so called, according to the commentator, because it was buried in the ground.[1] Eggeling[2] explains it as 'a vessel or cistern dug into the ground for keeping water cool.'

[1] As meaning etymologically 'to be fastened or fixed down.'

[2] *Sacred Books of the East*, 26, 223, n. 4.

Ninditāśva ('possessing contemptible steeds') is the name of a patron in the Rigveda.[1] The name may suggest connexion with Iran, but such a reference is not at all necessary.[2] Sāyaṇa ingeniously turns the name—probably a nickname—into a compliment by rendering it 'one who puts to shame the horses of his rivals.'

[1] viii. 1, 30.

[2] Hopkins, *Journal of the American Oriental Society*, 17, 90. *Cf.* Ludwig, Translation of the Rigveda, 3, 159.

Ni-pāda in the Rigveda (v. 83, 7) denotes 'low ground,' 'valley,' as opposed to 'hill' (*udvat*). *Cf.* **Nivat**.

Ni-mruc, 'sunset,' is repeatedly mentioned in the Rigveda[1] and later[2] as a division of time.

[1] i. 151, 5; 161, 10; viii. 27, 19; x. 151, 5.

[2] Av. xiii. 3, 21; Taittirīya Saṃhitā, i. 5, 10, 2; Kāṭhaka Saṃhitā, xxxvii. 10; Taittirīya Āraṇyaka, ii. 5, 2, etc.

Nir-aṣṭa, 'castrated,' is found in some of the later Saṃhitās[1] as applied to oxen, and in the Śatapatha Brāhmaṇa[2] to horses.

[1] Taittirīya Saṃhitā, i. 8, 9, 1; 17, 1; Kāṭhaka Saṃhitā, xv. 4. 9.
[2] xiii. 4, 2, 5.

Nir-āla occurs once in the Atharvaveda,[1] where Sāyaṇa regards it as the name of a disease. Bloomfield,[2] with the Padapāṭha, explains it as two words, understanding *nir* as an elliptical imperative, '(go) out,' with the vocative *āla*, a kind of weed. Whitney[3] at first took *āla* to be a verbal form, but finally came to the conclusion that the expression is one word, *nirāla*, of unknown sense.

[1] vi. 16, 3.
[2] *Hymns of the Atharvaveda*, 466.
[3] Translation of the Atharvaveda, 292.

Nirukta, 'explanation' of a word or passage, is found in the Chāndogya Upaniṣad (viii. 3, 3), but does not appear as the name of a work before the later Upaniṣads. It is, however, probable that Yāska's Nirukta is not later than the rise of Buddhism. *Cf.* **Nirvacana.**

Cf. Weber, *Indische Studien*, 1, 13, 17; 3, 260 *et seq.*; *Indian Literature*, 25, 26, 41, 42, etc.; Macdonell, *Sanskrit Literature*, 269, 270; Keith, *Aitareya Āraṇyaka*, 24, 25; Roth, *Nirukta*, xv. *et seq.*

Nir-yāsa denotes the 'exudation' of trees. In the Taittirīya Saṃhitā (ii. 1, 5, 4) it is tabooed as food because of its red colour.

Nir-vacana in the Taittirīya Āraṇyaka[1] and the Nirukta[2] means 'explanation,' especially etymological. *Cf.* **Nirukta.**

[1] i. 6, 3.
[2] ii. 1. *Cf.* *a-nirvacanam*, 'not serving as an explanation,' *ibid.*, vii. 24.

Ni-vat denotes 'valley' in the Rigveda[1] and later.[2]

[1] i. 161, 11; iii. 2, 10; vii. 50, 4; x. 127, 2; 142, 4.
[2] Av. vi. 22, 3; Taittirīya Saṃhitā, iii. 2, 4, 4, etc.

Nivānya-vatsā and **Nivānyā** in the Śatapatha Brāhmaṇa[1] denotes a 'cow with a calf to which she has to be won over,' that is, with a calf substituted for one of her own which has died. Nivānyā[2] is a contracted form of the compound term. Similar expressions are *abhivānya-vatsā*,[3] *abhivānyā*,[4] *vānyā*,[5] and *api-vānya-vatsā*.[6]

[1] xii. 5, 1, 4.
[2] ii. 6, 1, 6.
[3] Aitareya Brāhmaṇa, vii. 2.
[4] Taittirīya Brāhmaṇa, i. 6, 8, 4.
[5] *Ibid.*, ii. 6, 16, 2.
[6] Kauśika Sūtra, lxxxii. 22.
Cf. Lanman in Whitney's Translation of the Atharvaveda, 880.

Ni-vid denotes a brief invocation of the deity that is invited in a liturgy in honour of the god. The Brāhmaṇas[1] repeatedly mention Nivids as inserted in the Śastras (recitations), and the **Khilas** of the Rigveda[2] preserve among them a set of Nivids. But it is doubtful[3] whether the habit of using such brief formulas—the Nivid is usually not more than a Pada or quarter-verse in length—is known to the Rigveda, though it has been seen even there,[4] and the word Nivid is several times found in that Saṃhitā,[5] but hardly in the technical sense of the Brāhmaṇas. In the later Saṃhitās[6] the technical sense is common.

[1] Aitareya Brāhmaṇa, ii. 33. 34; iii. 10. 11; vi. 33. 35; Kauṣītaki Brāhmaṇa, xiv. 1; Śatapatha Brāhmaṇa, iii. 9, 3, 28; xiii. 5, 1. 9, etc.; Aitareya Āraṇyaka, i. 5, 2; Śāṅkhāyana Āraṇyaka, i. 3, etc.
[2] See Scheftelowitz, *Die Apokryphen des Ṛgveda*, 137-143.
[3] The antiquity of the Nivids was asserted by Haug, *Aitareya Brāhmaṇa*, 1, 26 *et seq.*, and often since, *e.g.*, by Tilak, *Orion*, 206; Scheftelowitz, *op. cit.*, 3. It is shown to be most improbable by Weber, *Indische Studien*, 9, 265, 355, and Oldenberg, *Zeitschrift der Deutschen Morgenländischen Gesellschaft*, 42, 242 *et seq.*; *Göttingische Gelehrte Anzeigen*, 1907, 232, 233.
[4] i. 86, 4; Bezzenberger's *Beiträge*, 9, 192. So Oldenberg, *Sacred Books of the East*, 46, 119, 122, takes Rv. i. 96, 2, to refer to the Nivids in the technical sense, but not to the Nivids as preserved.
[5] i. 89, 3; 96, 2; 175, 6; ii. 36, 6; iv. 18, 7; vi. 67, 10.
[6] Av. v. 26, 4; xi. 7, 19; Vājasaneyi Saṃhitā, xix. 25, etc.
Cf. Hillebrandt, *Rituallitteratur*, 102; Oldenberg, *Religion des Veda*, 387, n. 2; Muir, *Sanskrit Texts*, 1², 241.

Nivid-dhāna, 'containing a Nivid,' is found several times as an epithet of a hymn or verse in the Brāhmaṇas.[1]

[1] Aitareya Brāhmaṇa, iii. 17; Kauṣītaki Brāhmaṇa, xxi. 6; xxiv. 4; Śatapatha Brāhmaṇa, xiii. 5, 1, 12; Aitareya Āraṇyaka, i. 2, 2; 5, 3.

Ni-veśana, 'dwelling,' occurs in the Rigveda[1] and the Sūtras. In the latter[2] the word is sometimes contrasted with **Gṛha** as the resting-place of animals.

[1] iv. 19, 9; vii. 19, 5.

[2] Āśvalāyana Gṛhya Sūtra, iv. 6, etc.

Ni-ṣaṅgathi[1] or **Niṣaṅga-dhi**[2] is found in the Yajurveda Saṃhitās. If the second form of the word is correct, the sense may be 'sheath of a sword' (*niṣaṅga*), as it is taken by the St. Petersburg Dictionary, but probably the first form is the correct one, the word then having the same meaning as **Niṣaṅgin.**

[1] Kāṭhaka Saṃhitā, xvii. 11; Maitrāyaṇī Saṃhitā, ii. 9, 2.

[2] Vājasaneyi Saṃhitā, xvi. 10.

Ni-ṣaṅgin is found three times in the Rigveda,[1] where, owing to its following in one passage[2] the words *sudhanvāna iṣumanto*, 'having good bows and arrows,' the sense of *niṣaṅginaḥ* as 'having quivers' seems quite certain. In the Vājasaneyi Saṃhitā[3] it is taken by the commentator Mahīdhara to mean 'having a sword,' a sense which is quite possible both there and in the other passages[4] where it occurs. But the word far more probably means 'having a quiver,' for the bow was the Vedic weapon, not the sword (**Asi**).

[1] iii. 30, 15; v. 57, 2; x. 103, 3.

[2] v. 57, 2.

[3] xvi. 20. *Cf.* Kātyāyana Śrauta Sūtra, xx. 2, 11, with the commentator.

[4] Sāmaveda, ii. 1199; Kāṭhaka Saṃhitā, xvii. 12; xxxvii. 11; Maitrāyaṇī Saṃhitā, ii. 9, 3; Taittirīya Saṃhitā, iv. 5, 3, 1; Śatapatha Brāhmaṇa, xiii. 4, 2, 5.

Cf. Hopkins, *Journal of the American Oriental Society*, 13, 274.

Ni-ṣāda is found in the later Saṃhitās and the Brāhmaṇas.[1] The word seems to denote not so much a particular tribe, but to be the general term for the non-Āryan tribes who were not under Āryan control, as the Śūdras were, for Aupamanyava[2] took the five peoples (*pañca janāḥ*) to be the four castes (*catvāro*

[1] Taittirīya Saṃhitā, iv. 5, 4, 2; Kāṭhaka Saṃhitā, xvii. 13; Maitrāyaṇī Saṃhitā, ii. 9, 5; Vājasaneyi Saṃhitā, xvi. 27; Aitareya Brāhmaṇa, viii. 11; Pañcaviṃśa Brāhmaṇa, xvi. 6, 8, etc.

[2] In Yāska, Nirukta, iii. 8.

varṇāḥ) and the Niṣādas, and the commentator Mahīdhara explains the word where it occurs in the Vājasaneyi Saṃhitā[3] as meaning a Bhilla, or Bhīl. A village of Niṣādas is mentioned in the Lāṭyāyana Śrauta Sūtra,[4] and a Niṣāda **Sthapati**, a leader of some kind, is referred to in the Kātyāyana Śrauta Sūtra[5] and in a Brāhmaṇa cited by the scholiast on that passage. Weber[6] thinks that the Niṣādas were the settled aborigines (from *ni*, 'down,' and *sad*, 'settle'), a view supported by the fact that the ritual of the Viśvajit sacrifice[7] requires a temporary residence with Niṣādas; for the Niṣādas who would permit an Āryan to reside temporarily amongst them must have been partially amenable to Āryan influence. But the name might easily be applied to the whole body of aborigines outside the Āryan organization. Von Schroeder[8] thinks that the Niṣādas were most probably identical with the Nysæans, who, according to the Greek account, sent an embassy to Alexander when he was in the territory of the Aśvakas, but this identification is doubtful.

[3] xvi. 27. *Cf.* xxx. 8.

[4] viii. 2, 8.

[5] i. 1, 12; Weber, *Indische Studien*, 10, 13.

[6] *Indische Studien*, 9, 340. *Cf.* 10, 13, 16.

[7] See Kauṣītaki Brāhmaṇa, xxv. 15; Lāṭyāyana, *loc. cit.*; Pañcaviṃśa Brāhmaṇa, *loc. cit.*

[8] *Indiens Literatur und Cultur*, 366.

Cf. Zimmer, *Altindisches Leben*, 39, 119. In the later system (Manu, x. 8) the Niṣāda is the offspring of a Brāhmaṇa and of a Śūdra woman, while the Bṛhatsaṃhitā of Varāhamihira (xiv. 10) recognizes a kingdom (*rāṣṭra*) of Niṣādas in the south-east of Madhyadeśa. In the Pāli texts (Fick, *Die sociale Gliederung*, 12, 160, 206 *et seq.*) they are wild hunters and fishers. *Cf.* also Muir, *Sanskrit Texts*, 1[2], 301, 303, 366, n. 164, 403, 481.

Niṣka is frequently found in the Rigveda[1] and later[2] denoting a gold ornament worn on the neck, as is shown by the two epithets *niṣka-kaṇṭha*[3] and *niṣka-grīva*,[4] 'having a gold ornament on the neck.' A Niṣka of silver is mentioned in the Pañcaviṃśa Brāhmaṇa.[5] As early as the Rigveda[6] traces are seen of the

[1] ii. 33, 10; viii. 47, 15, etc.

[2] Av. v. 14, 3; vii. 99, 1; xx. 131, 8; Chāndogya Upaniṣad, iv. 2, 1. 2; v. 13, 2; Jaiminīya Upaniṣad Brāhmaṇa, i. 36, 7. 8; Śatapatha Brāhmaṇa, xiii. 4, 1, 7. 11, etc.

[3] Aitareya Brāhmaṇa, viii. 22.

[4] Rv. v. 19, 3; Av. v. 17, 14.

[5] xvii. 1, 14, as worn by the Vrātya. *Cf.* Av. xv. 3.

[6] i. 126, 2.

use of Niṣkas as a sort of currency, for a singer celebrates the receipt of a hundred Niṣkas and a hundred steeds: he could hardly require the Niṣkas merely for purposes of personal adornment. Later the use of Niṣkas as currency is quite clear.[7] *Cf.* also **Kṛṣṇala.**

[7] Av. xx. 127, 3; Lāṭyāyana Śrauta Sūtra, ix. 9, 20, etc. In the Śatapatha Brāhmaṇa, xi. 4, 1, 1. 8; Gopatha Brāhmaṇa, i. 3, 6; the sense of 'coin' is seen by Eggeling, *Sacred Books of the East*, 44, 50, 51, and by Geldner, *Vedische Studien*, 2, 185. *Cf.* Zimmer, *Altindisches Leben*, 51, 259, 263; Geldner, *op. cit.*, 1, 268, n. 2; *Zeitschrift der Deutschen Morgenländischen Gesellschaft*, 40, 127.

Niṣkirīya is the name of a school of priests who are mentioned in the Pañcaviṃśa Brāhmaṇa[1] as holding a Sattra, or 'sacrificial session.'

[1] xii. 5, 14. *Cf.* Hopkins, *Transactions of the Connecticut Academy of Arts and Sciences*, 15, 58.

Niṣṭya means in the Rigveda[1] and later[2] an outsider or stranger. Hence the constellation usually known as Svāti (see **Nakṣatra**) is named Niṣṭyā in the Taittirīya Brāhmaṇa,[3] because it occupies a position markedly away from the ecliptic.

[1] vi. 75, 19; viii. 1, 13; x. 133, 5.

[2] Av. iii. 3, 6; Vājasaneyi, v. 23; Satapatha Brāhmaṇa, i. 6, 4, 17, etc.

[3] i. 5, 2, 2. 3; iii. 1, 1, 13. *Cf.* Max Müller, *Sacred Books of the East*, 32, 215.

Nihākā in the Rigveda[1] and the Taittirīya Saṃhitā[2] appears to denote some phenomenon of a storm, perhaps the 'whirlwind.'

[1] x. 97, 13.

[2] vii. 5, 11, 1 (following *nīhāra*).

Nīkṣaṇa. See **Nekṣaṇa.**

Nīcya ('living below') is a designation of certain nations of the west. The Nīcyas are mentioned in the Aitareya Brāhmaṇa (viii. 14) as distinguished from the people of **Madhyadeśa,** and no doubt mean the inhabitants of the Indus and Panjab regions.

Nītha ('leading'), neut., means musical 'mode' and then 'hymn of praise.'[1] The feminine form Nīthā occurs once in the Rigveda[2] meaning 'artifice.'

[1] Rv. iv. 3, 16; vii. 26, 2; x. 92, 3; Aitareya Brāhmaṇa, ii. 38. *Cf. nīthāvid* of singers (*jaritṛ*) in Rv. iii. 12, 5.

[2] i. 104, 5. *Cf.* the epithet *śata-nītha*, i. 100, 12; 179, 3; x. 69, 7; *sahasra-nītha*, iii. 60, 7; ix. 85, 4; 96, 18 (used of the poet's art, *padavīḥ kavīnām*).

Cf. Muir, *Sanskrit Texts*, 1², 241.

Nīnāha, a word occurring once in the Atharvaveda (xix. 57, 4), seems to denote a 'girdle' or something similar, as derived from the verb *nah*, 'fasten.'

Nīpātithi occurs in the Rigveda[1] as the name of a man to whom a hymn[2] is ascribed by the Anukramaṇī (Index). A Sāman, or Chant, of his is mentioned in the Pañcaviṃśa Brāhmaṇa.[3]

[1] viii. 49, 9, where he appears as engaged in battle; viii. 51, 1, where he seems to be a sacrificer. Either a king or a seer may be meant.

[2] viii. 34. *Cf.* Ludwig, Translation of the Rigveda, 3, 140; Hopkins, *Journal of the American Oriental Society*, 17, 90.

[3] xiv. 10, 4.

Nīlaṅgu is the name of a species of 'worm' in the Yajurveda Saṃhitās[1] in the list of victims at the Aśvamedha, or 'horse sacrifice.'

[1] Taittirīya Saṃhitā, v. 5, 11, 1; Maitrāyaṇī Saṃhitā, iii. 14, 11 (*v.l. nīlāṅgu*); Vājasaneyi Saṃhitā, xxiv. 30. *Cf.* Zimmer, *Altindisches Leben*, 98.

Nīla-śīrṣṇī, 'black-headed,' is the name of an unknown animal in the list of victims at the Aśvamedha, or 'horse sacrifice,' in the Taittirīya Saṃhitā.[1]

[1] v. 5, 15, 1. *Cf.* Zimmer, *Altindisches Leben*, 99.

Nīlāgalasāla, or, as the Paippalāda version reads, **Nīlākala-sālā**, is the name, according to the commentator, of a grain-creeper in the Atharvaveda.[1]

[1] vi. 16, 4. *Cf.* Whitney, Translation of the Atharvaveda, 292, 293; Bloomfield, *Hymns of the Atharvaveda*, 466.

Nīvāra, 'wild rice,' is mentioned in the Yajurveda Saṃhitās[1] and the Brāhmaṇas.[2]

[1] Kāṭhaka Saṃhitā, xii. 4; Maitrāyaṇī Saṃhitā, iii. 4, 10; Vājasaneyi Saṃhitā, xviii. 12.

[2] Śatapatha Brāhmaṇa, v. 1, 4, 14; 3, 3, 5; Taittirīya Brāhmaṇa, i. 3, 6, 7, etc.

Cf. Zimmer, *Altindisches Leben*, 240.

Nīvi is the name of the 'undergarment,' probably a simple apron of cloth, worn by both men and women, but especially by the latter. It is mentioned in the Atharvaveda[1] and later.[2]

[1] viii. 2, 16; xiv. 2, 50. *Cf. nīvi-bhārya*, 'to be borne in the apron,' viii. 6, 20.

[2] Taittirīya Saṃhitā, vi. 1, 1, 3; Vājasaneyi Saṃhitā, iv. 10; Satapatha Brāhmaṇa, i. 3, 3, 6; iii. 2, 1, 15, etc.

Cf. Zimmer, *Altindisches Leben*, 262; Schrader, *Prehistoric Antiquities*, 331.

Nīhāra, 'mist,' occurs in the Rigveda[1] and later.[2]

[1] x. 82, 7.

[2] Taittirīya Saṃhitā, vii. 5, 11, 1; Kāṭhaka Saṃhitā, xxviii. 4; Vājasaneyi Saṃhitā, xxii. 26; xxv. 9; Av. vi. 113, 2; xviii. 3, 60; Taittirīya Āraṇyaka, i. 10, 7; vi. 4, 1; Chāndogya Upaniṣad, iii. 19, 2, etc.

Nṛ. See **Nara.**

Nṛti in one passage of the Atharvaveda[1] seems to mean a bag of skin. But though the Paippalāda recension has the same text, it is clear that we must read **Dṛti** with Roth[2] and Whitney.[3] Ludwig[4] renders the word 'dancer,' which makes no sense in the context.

[1] vi. 18, 3.

[2] St. Petersburg Dictionary, *s.v.*

[3] Translation of the Atharvaveda, 294. *Cf.* Weber, *Indische Studien*, 5, 235; Bloomfield, *Hymns of the Atharvaveda*, 468.

[4] Translation of the Rigveda, 3, 514.

Nṛtū occurs once in the Rigveda[1] denoting a female 'dancer.' In another passage[2] Nṛti is found coupled with *hāsa*, 'laughter,' in the description of the funeral ritual; but though it is clear that a joyful celebration is meant (like the Irish 'wake' or the

[1] i. 92, 4 (where Uṣas, Goddess of Dawn, is compared to a dancer).

[2] x. 18, 3. *Cf.* 29, 2.

old-fashioned feasting in Scotland after a funeral), it is difficult to be certain that actual dancing is here meant. Dancing is, however, often referred to in the Rigveda[3] and later. Nṛtta-gīta, 'dance and song,' are mentioned in the Jaiminīya Brāhmaṇa[4] as found in the sixth world. See also **Śailūṣa.**

[3] i. 10, 1; 92, 4, etc. See Weber, *Indian Literature*, 196 *et seq.*

[4] i. 42 (*Journal of the American Oriental Society*, 15, 235).

Nṛ-pati, 'lord of men,' in the Rigveda[1] and later[2] denotes a 'king' or a man of the ruling class (**Kṣatriya**).

[1] ii. 1, 1. 7; iv. 20, 1; vii. 69, 1; x. 44, 2. 3.

[2] Av. v. 18, 1. 15; Taittirīya Āraṇyaka, vi. 3, 3; x. 77, etc.

Nṛ-medha,[1] **Nṛ-medhas,**[2] is the name of a protégé of Agni in the Rigveda,[3] where he also appears with **Sumedhas** in a hymn that Griffith[4] with justice declares to be unintelligible. In the Taittirīya Saṃhitā[1] he is an unsuccessful rival of **Parucchepa,** and in the Pañcaviṃśa Brāhmaṇa[2] he is an Āṅgirasa and a seer of Sāmans (Chants).

[1] Rv. x. 80, 3; 132, 7; Taittirīya Saṃhitā, ii. 5, 8, 3.

[2] Pañcaviṃśa Brāhmaṇa, viii. 8, 21 *et seq.*

[3] x. 80, 3.

[4] x. 132; Griffith, *Hymns of the Rigveda*, 2, 578, n.

Cf. Hillebrandt, *Vedische Mythologie*, 2, 160; Hopkins, *Transactions of the Connecticut Academy of Arts and Sciences*, 15, 61.

Nṛ-ṣad, 'sitting among men,' is the name of the father of **Kaṇva** in the Rigveda (x. 31, 11). *Cf.* **Nārṣada.**

Nekṣaṇa occurs once in the Atharvaveda,[1] where a 'spit' seems to be meant. In the Rigveda[2] Nīkṣaṇa occurs, and must have the same sense; Oldenberg[3] inclines to think that this word refers to the 'inspection' of food, to see if it is ready (as from *ni-īkṣ*, 'look into').

[1] ix. 6, 17. *Cf.* Kauśika Sūtra, ii. 11; lxxxvii. 12; Whitney, Translation of the Atharvaveda, 540.

[2] i. 162, 13.

[3] *Ṛgveda-Noten*, 1, 155.

Nemi denotes in the Rigveda[1] and later[2] the 'felly' of a chariot wheel. It was required to be of good wood (*su-drū*),[3] and was bent into shape.[4] *Cf.* **Ratha.**

1 i. 32, 15; 141, 9; ii. 5, 3; v. 13, 6; vii. 32, 20; viii. 46, 23; 75, 5, etc.
2 Śatapatha Brāhmaṇa, i. 4, 2, 15; Bṛhadāraṇyaka Upaniṣad, ii. 5, 15, etc.
3 Rv. vii. 32, 20.
4 Rv. viii. 75, 5.
Cf. Zimmer, *Altindisches Leben*, 248.

Neṣṭṛ, the name of one of the chief priests at the Soma sacrifice, occurs in the Rigveda[1] and later.[2] See **Ṛtvij.**

1 i. 15, 3; ii. 5, 5, etc.
2 Taittirīya Saṃhitā, i. 8, 18, 1; vi. 5, 8, 5. 6; Aitareya Brāhmaṇa, vi. 3, 10, etc.; Śatapatha Brāhmaṇa, iii. 8, 2, 1, etc.; Pañcaviṃśa Brāhmaṇa, xxv. 15, etc.
Cf. Hillebrandt, *Vedische Mythologie*, 1, 250, 261, 527.

Naicā-śākha is found in one passage of the Rigveda,[1] where Sāyaṇa renders it as 'of low origin,' but elsewhere[2] he explains it as the name of a place. The former sense is accepted by Grassmann and Ludwig in their versions, and by Zimmer,[3] but Hillebrandt[4] points out that the reference is rather to the 'low-branched' Soma plant. *Cf.* **Kīkaṭa** and **Pramaganda.**

1 vii. 53, 4.
2 See St. Petersburg Dictionary, *s.v.*
3 *Altindisches Leben*, 31.
4 *Vedische Mythologie*, 1, 14-18; 2, 241-245, where he opposes Böhtlingk's view that it is a proper name.

Naicu-dāra occurs in the Pañcaviṃśa Brāhmaṇa,[1] meaning 'composed of the wood of the Nicudāra.' What tree is meant by the latter name is unknown.

1 xxi. 4, 13. *Cf.* Anupada Sūtra, vi. 4.

Naitandhava is mentioned as a place on the **Sarasvatī** in the Pañcaviṃśa Brāhmaṇa[1] and the Sūtras.[2]

1 xxv. 13, 1.
2 Lāṭyāyana Śrauta Sūtra, x. 19, 13; Śāṅkhāyana Śrauta Sūtra, xiii. 29, 31; Kātyāyana Śrauta Sūtra, xxiv. 6, 23.

Nai-dāgha is the name of the 'summer' season in the later Saṃhitās and Brāhmaṇas.[1] *Cf.* **Ṛtu** and **Nidāgha.**

1 Av. ix. 5, 31; Taittirīya Brāhmaṇa, i. 8, 4, 2; Śatapatha Brāhmaṇa, i. 4, 1, 16, etc.; *naidāghīya*, 'belonging to the summer,' Pañcaviṃśa Brāhmaṇa, xxiii. 16, 8, etc.

Nai-dāna is a term applied in the Nirukta[1] to a class of Vedic interpreters. Roth[2] takes the Naidānas to be 'etymologists,' but Sieg[3] thinks they are the same as the **Aitihāsikas** or 'legendarists.'[4]

[1] vi. 9; vii. 12.

[2] St. Petersburg Dictionary, *s.v.* But *cf.* Nirukta, *Erläuterungen*, 220, 221; Muir, *Sanskrit Texts*, 2[2], 176.

[3] *Die Sagenstoffe des Ṛgveda*, 29.

[4] The word seems to mean 'one concerned with the original form' (*nidāna*).

Nai-dhruvi, 'descendant of Nidhruva,' is the patronymic of **Kaśyapa** in the Bṛhadāraṇyaka Upaniṣad.[1]

[1] vi. 4, 33 (Mādhyandina = vi. 5, 3 Kāṇva).

Naimiśi is the epithet of **Śitibāhu Aiṣakṛta** in the Jaiminīya Brāhmaṇa.[1] It is probably to be taken as an indication that Śitibāhu came from the Naimiśa forest.

[1] i. 363 (*Journal of the American Oriental Society*, 26, 192).

Naimiśīya,[1] **Naimiṣīya**[2] denotes the dwellers in the Naimiśa forest. They are mentioned in the Kāṭhaka Saṃhitā[2] and the Brāhmaṇas,[2] being clearly of special sanctity. Hence in the Epic the Mahābhārata is said to have been recited to the Ṛṣis dwelling in the Naimiṣa forest.[3]

[1] Pañcaviṃśa Brāhmaṇa, xxv. 6, 4; Jaiminīya Brāhmaṇa, i. 363 (*Journal of the American Oriental Society*, 26, 192).

[2] Kauṣītaki Brāhmaṇa, xxvi. 5; xxviii. 4; Chāndogya Upaniṣad, i. 2, 13; Naimiṣya, Kāṭhaka Saṃhitā, x. 6 (*Indische Studien*, 3, 469). The cerebral *s* seems to be universal later.

[3] Weber, *Indian Literature*, 34, 45, 54, 68, 70, 185.

Nair-ukta[1] in the Nirukta[2] denotes a man who knows the true etymology of words, and explains their meaning accordingly. Yāska's Nirukta is the classic work of this school, and forms a commentary on an earlier Nirukta, the so-called Naighaṇṭuka, a glossary consisting of five collections of Vedic words.

[1] 'One concerned with etymological explanation' (*nir-ukta*).

[2] i. 12; vi. 11; xi. 19. 29. 31; xii. 10; xiii. 9.

Cf. Weber, *Indian Literature*, 26, 85; *Indische Studien*, 2, 39, n.; Sieg, *Die Sagenstoffe des Ṛgveda*, 10-13; Muir, *Sanskrit Texts*, 2[2], 165 *et seq*

Nai-ṣāda, a 'man of Niṣāda,' is mentioned in the Kauṣītaki Brāhmaṇa (xxv. 15) and the Vājasaneyi Saṃhitā (xxx. 8).

Naiṣidha is the reading in the Śatapatha Brāhmaṇa (ii. 3, 2, 1. 2) of the epithet of **Naḍa**, a king of the south. The later form of the name is Naiṣadha; the St. Petersburg Dictionary suggests that its original form was Naiḥṣidha.

Nodhas is the name of a poet who is mentioned in the Rigveda,[1] and to whom certain of its hymns are ascribed.[2] In the Pañcaviṃśa Brāhmaṇa[3] he is called **Kākṣīvata**, a 'descendant of **Kakṣīvant**.' Ludwig[4] regards him as contemporary with the defeat of **Purukutsa**. He was a **Gotama**.[5]

[1] i. 61, 14; 62, 13; 64, 1, and 124, 4, according to Nirukta, iv. 16.

[2] Aitareya Brāhmaṇa, vi. 18; Rv. i. 58-64 are ascribed to him in the Anukramaṇī (Index).

[3] vii. 10, 10; xxi. 9, 12. *Cf.* Aitareya Brāhmaṇa, iv. 27; viii. 12. 17; Av. xv. 2, 4; 4, 4.

[4] Translation of the Rigveda, 3, 110.

[5] Rv. i. 62, 13; Max Müller, *Sacred Books of the East*, 32, 125. For the controversy as to the meaning of Rv. i. 124, 4, see Oldenberg, *Ṛgveda-Noten*, 1, 137. *Cf.* Hopkins, *Transactions of the Connecticut Academy of Arts and Sciences*, 15, 33.

Nau is the regular word in the Rigveda[1] and later[2] for a 'boat' or 'ship.' In the great majority of cases the ship was merely a boat for crossing rivers, though no doubt a large boat was needed for crossing many of the broad rivers of the Panjab as well as the **Yamunā** and **Gaṅgā**. Often no doubt the Nau was a mere dug-out canoe (*dāru*).[3] It is certainly against the theory[4] of the existence in Vedic times of an extensive sea trade that there is no mention of any of the parts of a ship, such as masts and sails, except the oar (**Aritra**). Yet there are some allusions indicating a trade more extensive than that implied by boats used for crossing rivers. The Atharvaveda[5] compares the ruin of a kingdom where Brahmins are oppressed to the

[1] i. 131, 2; ii. 39, 4; viii. 42, 3; 83, 3, etc.

[2] Av. ii. 36, 5; v. 19, 8; Taittirīya Saṃhitā, v. 3, 10, 1; Vājasaneyi Saṃhitā, x. 19; Aitareya Brāhmaṇa, iv. 13; vi. 6. 21; Śatapatha Brāhmaṇa, i. 8, 1, 4; iv. 2, 5, 10, etc.

[3] Rv. x. 155, 3.

[4] Wilson, *Rigveda*, 1, xli.

[5] v. 19, 8. *Cf.* Hopkins, *American Journal of Philology*, 19, 139. So perhaps the passage, Rv. i. 32, 8, *nadaṃ na bhinnam*, refers to a ship. See **Naḍa**.

sinking of a ship which is leaking (*bhinnā*); though the language here employed can be made to fit the theory that the ship was only a canoe, it cannot naturally be so interpreted. Moreover, there is mention made in the Rigveda[6] of men who go to the ocean (**Samudra**) eager for gain (*saniṣyavaḥ*). It is not altogether satisfactory to restrict such references with Zimmer[7] to the broad stream of the Indus after the union of that river with the tributaries of the Panjab. In the Rigveda[8] too it is said that the Aśvins rescued **Bhujyu** in the ocean with a ship of a hundred oars (*śatāritra*). It is not easy to refuse to recognize here the existence of larger vessels with many oars used for sea voyages. The Baudhāyana Dharma Sūtra,[9] at any rate, clearly refers to maritime navigation. See also **Samudra.**

[6] Rv. i. 56, 2; iv. 55, 6.
[7] *Altindisches Leben*, 22, 23.
[8] i. 116, 3 *et seq.*
[9] i. 2, 4; ii. 2, 2. But it is not of very early date.
Cf. Zimmer, *op. cit.*, 255-257.

Nyag-rodha, 'growing downwards,' is the name of the *Ficus indica*, a tree remarkable for sending down from its branches fibres which take root and form new stems. Though the tree is not mentioned by name in the Rigveda, it appears to have been known, as Pischel[1] has shown from a hymn[2] in which its characteristics may be recognized. It is frequently mentioned in the Atharvaveda[3] and the later literature.[4] The sacrificial bowls (**Camasa**) were made of its wood.[5] It was doubtless of the greatest importance, as in modern times, to the Vedic village. The sister tree, the **Aśvattha** (*Ficus religiosa*), already occurs in the Rigveda.

[1] *Vedische Studien*, 1, 113, 114.
[2] i. 24, 7, where *stūpa* seems to denote the crest or crown of the tree above the main trunk.
[3] iv. 37, 4; v. 5, 5.
[4] Aitareya Brāhmaṇa, vii. 30. 31; Śatapatha Brāhmaṇa, v. 3, 5, 13; xiii. 2, 7, 3; Chāndogya Upaniṣad, vi. 12, 1, etc.
[5] Taittirīya Samhitā, vii. 4, 12, 1; Vājasaneyi Saṃhitā, xxiii. 13.
Cf. Zimmer, *Altindisches Leben*, 58.

Ny-aṅka in the dual denotes in the Taittirīya Saṃhitā[1] and Brāhmaṇa[2] some part of the chariot, parallel with **Aṅka.** The Pañcaviṃśa Brāhmaṇa[3] has Nyaṅkū, the dual of Nyaṅku.

[1] i. 7, 7, 2.
[2] i. 3, 5, 4; ii. 7, 8, 1.
[3] i. 7, 5; Lāṭyāyana Srauta Sūtra, ii. 8, 9.

Nyaṅku is the name of an animal in the list of victims at the Aśvamedha, or 'horse sacrifice,' in the Yajurveda Saṃhitās.[1] It seems clear that a kind a 'gazelle' is meant, but the commentary on the Taittirīya Saṃhitā[1] suggests 'bear' (*ṛkṣa*) as a variant rendering.

[1] Taittirīya Saṃhitā, v. 5, 17, 1; Maitrāyaṇī Saṃhitā, iii. 14, 9; Vājasaneyi Saṃhitā, xxiv. 27. 32. *Cf.* Zimmer, *Altindisches Leben*, 83. The metre *nyaṅku-sāriṇī*, 'with a gazelle's gait,' is already mentioned in the Ṛgveda Prātiśākhya, xvi. 31; Chandas, 5; Nidāna Sūtra, i. 2.

Ny-astikā seems in the Atharvaveda[1] to denote a plant of some kind, identified by the scholiast with the Śaṅkhapuṣpikā (*Andropogon aciculatus*).

[1] vi. 139, 1. *Cf.* Whitney, Translation of the Atharvaveda, 385; Bloomfield, *Hymns of the Atharvaveda*, 539, 540.

Ny-ocanī is found in the marriage hymn of the Rigveda (x. 85, 6), where some kind of ornament worn by women seems to be meant. The commentator Sāyaṇa interprets it as 'female slave.'

P.

Pakti denotes a cooked object, probably a kind of 'cake,' in the Saṃhitās.[1] One who cooks food is called **Paktṛ**.[2]

[1] Rv. iv. 24, 5. 7; 25, 6. 7; vi. 29, 4; Vājasaneyi Saṃhitā, xxi. 59, etc.

[2] Av. x. 9, 7. 11. 25; xi. 1, 17; xii. 3, 17; Satapatha Brāhmaṇa, iii. 3, 4, 17; x. 4, 2, 19.

Paktha is the name of a people in the Rigveda,[1] where they appear as one of the tribes that opposed[2] the **Tṛtsu-Bharatas** in the **Dāśarājña**, or 'battle of the ten kings.' Zimmer[3] compares

[1] vii. 18. 7.

[2] Roth, *Zur Litteratur und Geschichte des Weda*, 95, thought that the Pakthas were allies of the Tṛtsus, but this view is certainly incorrect. *Cf.* Hopkins, *Journal of the American Oriental Society*, 15, 260.

[3] *Altindisches Leben*, 430, 431.

them with the tribe of Πάκτυες and their country Πακτυική, mentioned as in the north-west of India by Herodotus,[4] and with the modern Pakhthūn in Eastern Afghanistan, holding that they were a northern tribe; this is probable, since the Bharatas seem to have occupied the Madhyadeśa, or 'Middle Land.' In three passages of the Rigveda[5] a Paktha is referred to as a protégé of the Aśvins. The second connects him with **Trasadasyu,** whose tribe, the **Pūrus,** were aided by the Pakthas in their unsuccessful onslaught on **Sudās.** In the third passage he seems specified as **Tūrvāyaṇa,** and appears as an opponent of **Cyavāna.**[6] Probably, therefore, Paktha in all cases denotes the king of the Paktha people.

4 vii. 65 (Πάκτυες); iii. 102 and iv. 44 (Πακτυική).

5 viii. 22, 10; 49, 10; x. 61, 1.

6 Pischel, *Vedische Studien*, 1, 71-77.

Pakva, 'cooked,' is used substantively as meaning 'cooked food'[1] or 'cooked milk.'[2] The word is also used of 'baked' bricks.[3]

1 Rv. vi. 63, 9; Av. vi. 119, 2; xii. 3, 55; Śatapatha Brāhmaṇa, i. 5, 1, 26; ii. 6, 1, 7, etc.

2 Rv. i. 62, 9; 180, 3; ii. 40, 2; iii. 30, 14; vi. 44, 24, etc.

3 Śatapatha Brāhmaṇa, vi. 1, 2, 22; vii. 2, 1, 7.

Pakṣa is, in the Atharvaveda,[1] applied to some part of a house, either the 'side posts,' according to Roth,[2] *Zimmer*,[3] and Grill,[4] or 'sides,' as understood by Whitney[5] and Bloomfield.[6] The description of the roof (**Chadis**) in the Atharvaveda[7] as *catuṣ-pakṣa*, 'four-sided,' tells in favour of the second explanation. In the Taittirīya Brāhmaṇa[8] Pakṣa is used of the sides of a chariot. For Pakṣa as the 'half' of a month, see **Māsa.**

1 ix. 3, 4.

2 St. Petersburg Dictionary, *s.v.*

3 *Altindisches Leben*, 153.

4 *Hundert Lieder*², 188.

5 Translation of the Atharvaveda, 526.

6 *Hymns of the Atharvaveda*, 597.

7 iii. 7, 3.

8 i. 5, 12, 5.

Cf. Weber, *Indische Studien*, 17, 210.

Pakṣas is found in the Atharvaveda[1] and the Kauṣītaki Brāhmaṇa[2] meaning the 'sides'[3] of a chariot. In the Kāṭhaka Saṃhitā[4] and the Taittirīya Brāhmaṇa[5] it is used of the sides of a hut or chamber (**Śālā**). In the Vājasaneyi Saṃhitā[6] it means the 'wing' of a door. In the Kauṣītaki Brāhmaṇa[7] the 'half' of an army is so named, and in the Pañcaviṃśa Brāhmaṇa[8] it means the 'half' of a month, or 'fortnight.' *Cf.* **Pakṣa.**

1 viii. 8, 22.
2 vii. 7.
3 Whitney, Translation of the Atharvaveda, 506; Bloomfield, *Hymns of the Atharvaveda*, 117.
4 xxx. 5.
5 i. 2, 3, 1.
6 xxix. 5.
7 ii. 9.
8 xxiii. 6, 6.

Pakṣin in the Rigveda[1] and later[2] denotes a 'winged' creature, more particularly a 'bird.'

1 i. 48, 5; 182, 5; x. 127, 5, etc.
2 Av. iv. 34, 4; xi. 5, 21; xii. 1, 51; xiii. 2, 33; Kāṭhaka Saṃhitā, xxxiv. 8; Aitareya Brāhmaṇa, iv. 23; Bṛhadāraṇyaka Upaniṣad, ii. 5, 18, etc.

Paṅkti, originally a 'set of five,' denotes as early as the Rigveda[1] a 'series' generally. In the Taittirīya Āraṇyaka[2] the word is used of the series of a man's ancestors whom he purifies by certain conduct.

1 x. 117, 8, as taken by the St. Petersburg Dictionary.
2 x. 38, 39.

Pacata, like **Pakti**, denotes 'cooked food' in the Rigveda[1] and later.[2]

1 i. 61, 7; x. 116, 8.
2 Vājasaneyi Saṃhitā, xxi. 60; xxiii. 13; Kauṣītaki Brāhmaṇa, viii. 21, etc.

Pacana in the Rigveda[1] and the Śatapatha Brāhmaṇa[2] denotes a 'vessel for cooking' food.

1 i. 162, 6.
2 vi. 5, 43, 3. 4; xiv. 1, 2, 21.

Pajra is the name of the family from which **Kakṣīvant** sprang (**Pajriya**). It is mentioned several times in the Rigveda.[1] According to Pischel,[2] the epithet *pṛkṣa-yāma*[3] applied to them means 'carrying out brilliant sacrificial performances,' which won for them **Śrutaratha's** generosity. In two passages[4] Roth[5] sees a Pajra called Sāman. This is uncertain, but in any case a Pajra seems clearly alluded to. Elsewhere[6] it is very doubtful whether the word is a proper name at all. In the Śāṭyāyana[7] the Pajras are declared to be Aṅgirases.

[1] i. 117, 10; 122, 7. 8; 126, 4. 5.
[2] *Vedische Studien*, 1, 97, 98.
[3] Rv. i. 127, 8, where Roth (St. Petersburg Dictionary, *s.v.*) thinks this compound is probably a proper name.
[4] Rv. viii. 4, 17; 6, 47.
[5] St. Petersburg Dictionary, *s.v. pajra.*
[6] Rv. i. 190, 5, where the reference is clearly hostile and contemptuous.
[7] Cited by Sāyaṇa on Rv. i. 51, 4.

Pajrā occurs once in the Rigveda,[1] where Ludwig[2] sees in the word the name of the wife of the sacrificer, **Pajra,** while Roth[3] takes it to be an epithet ('stout') of the Soma plant. The sense is thus uncertain.

[1] ix. 82, 14.
[2] Translation of the Rigveda, 3, 110.
[3] St. Petersburg Dictionary, *s.v. pajra.*

Pajriya 'descendant of Pajra,' is the patronymic[1] of **Kakṣīvant** in the Rigveda.[2]

[1] *Cf.* **Tugrya**, n. 1.
[2] i. 116, 7; 117, 6; 120, 5.

Pañca-janāḥ, the 'five peoples,' are mentioned under various names in Vedic literature.[1] Who are meant by the five is very uncertain. The Aitareya Brāhmaṇa[2] explains the five to be gods, men, Gandharvas and Apsarases, snakes, and the Fathers.

[1] Aitareya Brāhmaṇa, iii. 31; iv. 27; Taittirīya Saṃhitā, i. 6, 1, 2; Kāṭhaka Saṃhitā, v. 6; xxxii. 6; Bṛhadāraṇyaka Upaniṣad, iv. 2, 9 (*pañca-janāḥ* as a compound). See also *pañca mānuṣāḥ*, Rv. viii. 9, 2; *mānavāḥ*, Av. iii. 21, 5; 24, 3; xii. 1, 15; *janāḥ*, Rv. iii. 37, 9; 59, 8; vi. 14, 4; viii. 32, 22; ix. 65, 23; 92, 3; x. 45, 6; *kṛṣṭayaḥ*, ii. 2, 10; iii. 53, 16; iv. 38, 10; x. 60, 4; 119, 6; Av. iii. 24, 3; *kṣitayaḥ*, Rv. i. 7, 9; 176, 3; v. 35, 2; vi. 46, 7; vii. 75, 4; 79, 1; *carṣaṇyaḥ*, Rv. v. 86, 2; vii. 15, 2; ix. 101, 9. See Ludwig, Translation of the Rigveda, 3, 204. Every book of the Rigveda has a mention of the five peoples: one such in ii. and iv.; two in i., v., vi., vii., viii.; three in iii. and ix.; four in x.
[2] iii. 31.

Aupamanyava[3] held that the four castes (**Varṇa**) and the **Niṣādas** made up the five, and Sāyaṇa[4] is of the same opinion. Yāska[5] thinks that the five are the Gandharvas, fathers, gods, Asuras, and Rakṣases. No one of these explanations can be regarded as probable. Roth[6] and Geldner[7] think that all the peoples of the earth are meant: just as there are four quarters (**Diś**), there are peoples at the four quarters (N. E. S. W.), with the Āryan folk in the middle. Zimmer[8] opposes this view on the ground that the inclusion of all peoples in one expression is not in harmony with the distinction so often made between Āryan and Dāsa; that neither *janāsaḥ*, 'men,'[9] nor *mānuṣāḥ*, 'people,'[10] could be used of non-Āryans; that the Soma is referred to as being among the five tribes;[11] that the five tribes are mentioned as on the **Sarasvatī**,[12] and that Indra is *pāñca-janya*,[13] 'belonging to the five peoples.' He concludes that Āryans alone are meant, and in particular the five tribes of the **Anus, Druhyus, Yadus, Turvaśas,** and **Pūrus,** who are all mentioned together in one or perhaps two hymns of the Rigveda,[14] and four of whom occur in another hymn.[15] But he admits that the expression might easily be used more generally later. Hopkins[16] has combated Zimmer's view, but his own opinion rests mainly on his theory that there was no people named Turvaśa, but only a king of the Yadus called Turvaśa, and that theory is not very probable.

3 In Yāska, Nirukta, iii. 8.

4 On Rv. i. 7, 9, etc.

5 Nirukta, *loc. cit.*

6 St. Petersburg Dictionary, *s.v. kṛṣṭi*; *Nirukta, Erläuterungen*, 28. For his view, Av. iii. 24, 3, can be cited: *pañca pradiśo mānavīḥ pañca kṛṣṭayaḥ*, 'the five directions, the five races of men.'

7 *Siebenzig Lieder*, 18. See, however, *Ṛgveda, Glossar*, 103, where he recognizes the use of the phrase to denote five tribes, as well as all mankind.

8 *Altindisches Leben*, 119-123. His view is accepted by Macdonell, *Sanskrit Literature*, 153; Muir, *Sanskrit Texts*, 1^2, 179, is doubtful.

9 *Cf.* its use in Rv. ii. 12, *sa janāsa Indraḥ*, where the address must be to Āryan men.

10 *Cf.* Rv. viii. 9, 2, and i. 52, 9, with viii. 70, 11; x. 28, 8.

11 Rv. ix. 65, 23.

12 Rv. vi. 61, 12 (*pañca jātā*). *Cf.* x. 53, 4.

13 v. 32, 11. Agni is 'of the five tribes,' Rv. ix. 66, 20. Atri also is so described, Rv. i. 117, 3.

14 Rv. i. 108, 8. In vii. 18, cited by Zimmer, 122, the five tribes do not occur *eo nomine*, for **Yakṣu** replaces Yadu. But it is probable that Yadu is meant by Yakṣu.

15 Rv. viii. 10, 5.

16 *Journal of the American Oriental Society*, 15, 260.

In the Śatapatha Brāhmaṇa[17] and the Aitareya Brāhmaṇa[18] the five peoples are opposed to the Bharatas, and in the former work[19] seven peoples are alluded to.

17 xiii. 5, 4, 14.
18 viii. 23.
19 It is a conjecture of Weber's, *Indische Studien*, 1, 202, that the five peoples are identical with the **Pañcālas**, and the seven mentioned in Satapatha Brāhmaṇa, xiii. 5, 4, 23, with the Kuru-Pañcālas.

Pañca-daśī, 'the fifteenth day of the month,' is already mentioned in the Taittirīya Brāhmaṇa (i. 5, 10, 5).

Pañca-nada, 'having five streams,' is not found until the epic period as the name of the Panjāb, which has no designation in the earlier literature. The importance of the Panjāb as the home[1] of the Rigveda has been greatly diminished by recent research, Hopkins,[2] Pischel,[3] and Geldner[4] having on different grounds shown reason for believing that the Rigveda, at least in great part, was composed farther east, in the **Madhyadeśa**, which admittedly was the home of the later Vedic culture. Hillebrandt[5] considers that the Rigveda belongs in part to the Panjāb, or rather to Arachosia, and in part to the Middle Country. See also **Kuru, Tṛtsu.**

1 See, *e.g.*, Zimmer, *Altindisches Leben*, 32 *et seq.*
2 *Journal of the American Oriental Society*, 19, 19-28. *Cf.* Macdonell, *Sanskrit Literature*, 145, 441.
3 *Vedische Studien*, 2, 218.
4 *Ibid.*, 3, 152.
5 *Vedische Mythologie*, 1, 98 *et seq.* But see **Divodāsa**. *Cf.* also Weber, *Indische Studien*, 1, 189.

Pañcaviṃśa Brāhmaṇa. See **Tāṇḍya.**

Pañcāla is the later name[1] of the people called **Krivi** in the Rigveda. The Pañcālas are rarely referred to except in connexion with the **Kurus**, and the kings of the Kuru-Pañcālas are mentioned in the Aitareya Brāhmaṇa.[2] In the Kāṭhaka Saṃhitā[3] the Pañcālas appear as the people of **Keśin Dālbhya.**

1 Śatapatha Brāhmaṇa, xiii. 5, 4, 7.
2 viii. 14.
3 xxx. 2 (*Indische Studien*, 3, 471).

In the Upaniṣads and later[4] the Brahmins of the Pañcālas figure as taking part in philosophical and philological discussions. The Saṃhitopaniṣad Brāhmaṇa[5] makes mention of the Prācya-Pāñcālas.

The Pañcālas, no doubt, included other tribes besides the Krivis. The name seems to refer to five tribes, and it has been suggested[6] that the Pañcālas represent the five tribes of the Rigveda, but the suggestion is not very probable. There is no trace in Vedic literature of the Epic division of the Pañcālas into northern (*uttara*) and southern (*dakṣiṇa*). The Śatapatha Brāhmaṇa[7] mentions their town **Paricakrā**; other towns to which allusion seems to be made were **Kāmpīla** and Kauśāmbī.[8] Of their kings and chiefs, as distinguished from kings of the Kuru-Pañcālas, we hear of **Kraivya**, **Durmukha**, **Pravāhaṇa Jaivali**, and **Śona**.

[4] Bṛhadāraṇyaka Upaniṣad, vi. 1, 1 (Mādhyaṃdina = vi. 2, 1 Kāṇva); Chāndogya Upaniṣad, v. 3, 1; Ṛgveda Prātiśākhya, ii. 12, 44; Nidāna Sūtra, i. 6; Sāṅkhāyana Śrauta Sūtra, xii. 13, 6, etc.

[5] 2. *Cf. Indische Studien*, 4, 375, n.; 8, 92, n. 1.

[6] Weber, *Indische Studien*, 1, 202; Geldner, *Vedische Studien*, 3, 108, n. 1. *Cf.* Weber, *op. cit.*, 1, 191 *et seq.*; *Indian Literature*, 10, 90, 114, 115, 125, 135, 136.

[7] xiii. 5, 4, 7.

[8] See **Kauśāmbeya**.

Pañcāla-caṇḍa is the name of a teacher in the Aitareya[1] and the Śāṅkhāyana[2] Āraṇyakas.

[1] iii. 1, 6.

[2] vii. 18.

Cf. Weber, *Indische Studien*, 1, 391; *Indian Literature*, 50, 315, 326.

Pañcāvi occurs several times in the Vājasaneyi Saṃhitā[1] in the sense of 'aged five lamb-periods' (of six months), that is, 'thirty months old.'[2]

[1] xviii. 26; xxi. 14; xxiv. 12; xxviii. 26.

[2] *Cf.* **Tryavi**.

Pañcaudana is an adjective in the Atharvaveda[1] meaning 'prepared with five rice-messes.' The cooking of five rice dishes is referred to in the same Saṃhitā.[2]

[1] iv. 14, 7; ix. 5, 8 *et seq.*

[2] ix. 5, 37.

Paṭala as early as the Aitareya Brāhmaṇa[1] denotes 'section' of a work, a sense occurring in the Sūtras[2] and later.

[1] i. 21. 22.

[2] Śāṅkhāyana Srauta Sūtra, xi. 9, 20; xiii. 21, 2; Āśvalāyana Śrauta Sūtra, iv. 6. 7.

Paṭharvan appears to be the name of a man in the Rigveda.[1] According to Ludwig,[2] however, the word is Paṭharu, and is the name of a fort which was saved by a rain-storm from being set on fire.

[1] i. 112, 17, with Sāyaṇa's note.

[2] Translation of the Rigveda, 3, 204. *Cf.* Griffith, *Hymns of the Rigveda*, 1, 147, 148.

Paḍgṛbhi, 'seizing by the foot,'[1] is the name in the Rigveda[2] of either a man[3] or a demon. See also **Paḍbīśa.**

[1] But it may mean 'seizing with a cord.' *Cf.* Macdonell, *Vedic Grammar*, p. 34 (top); Pischel, *Vedische Studien*, 1, 236.

[2] x. 49, 5.

[3] Ludwig, Translation of the Rigveda, 3, 165.

Paḍ-bīśa, the 'foot-fetter' of a horse in five passages, two in the Rigveda,[1] and one each in the Bṛhadāraṇyaka Upaniṣad,[2] the Chāndogya Upaniṣad,[3] and the Śāṅkhāyana Āraṇyaka.[4] Elsewhere[5] its uses are metaphorical. According to Roth,[6] the literal sense is 'foot-fastening' (*paḍ* being = *pad*, 'foot,' and *bīśa*, written *vīśa* in the Vājasaneyi Saṃhitā, being connected with the Latin *vincire*, 'bind'). Pischel[7] objects that the sense of 'foot-fastening' involves the absurdity, in the Upaniṣad passages, of a fine horse from the **Sindhu** (Indus) being spoken of as tearing up the peg to which it is fastened. He suggests instead the meaning of 'hobble,' which must be right.[8]

[1] i. 162, 14. 16 = Taittirīya Saṃhitā, iv. 6, 9, 1. 2; Vājasaneyi Saṃhitā, xxv. 38. 39.

[2] vi. 2, 13 (Mādhyaṃdina).

[3] v. 1, 12.

[4] ix. 7; Keith, *Śāṅkhāyana Āraṇyaka*, 57, n. 3.

[5] Rv. x. 97, 16; Av. viii. 1, 4; xii. 5, 15; xvi. 8, 27; Taittirīya Brāhmaṇa, i. 6, 10, 3; Mantra Brāhmaṇa, i. 3, 10.

[6] St. Petersburg Dictionary, *s.v.*

[7] *Vedische Studien*, 1, 233-236.

[8] He explains the first part of the word as derived from *paś*, 'tie.' *Cf.* Macdonell, *Vedic Grammar*, p. 34 (top). But the form *paḍ* may be due to a false analogy, and the sense of 'foot-fastener' may express 'hobble' quite satisfactorily; it is not confined to a rope tied to a peg in the ground.

Paṇa, with **Pratipaṇa**, is found in a hymn of the Atharvaveda[1] denoting the process of bargaining and selling. The root *paṇ*, from which the word is derived, is employed in the later Saṃhitās and the Brāhmaṇas,[2] while Paṇana in the Śatapatha Brāhmaṇa[3] denotes 'trafficking.' *Cf.* **Vaṇij**.

[1] iii. 15, 4. 6 (in the Paippalāda recension; Whitney, Translation of the Atharvaveda, 112).

[2] Vājasaneyi Saṃhitā, viii. 55; Śatapatha Brāhmaṇa, iii. 3, 3, 1 *et seq.*; Aitareya Brāhmaṇa, i. 27. *Cf.* Taittirīya Saṃhitā, vi. 1, 10, 1.

[3] iii. 3, 2, 19. The root does not occur in the Rigveda, but its etymology is vouched for by the Greek πέρνημι. *Cf.* Hillebrandt, *Vedische Mythologie*, 1, 84, n. 3.

Paṇi in the Rigveda appears to denote a person who is rich, but who does not give offerings to the gods, or bestow **Dakṣiṇās** on the priests, and who is therefore an object of intense dislike to the composers of the Saṃhitā.[1] Hence the gods are asked to attack the Paṇis, who are also referred to as being defeated with slaughter.[2] The Paṇi is opposed to the pious sacrificer as a niggard,[3] and is spoken of as a wolf,[4] the symbol of enmity. In some passages[5] the Paṇis definitely appear as mythological figures, demons who withhold the cows or waters of heaven, and to whom Saramā goes on a mission from Indra.[6] Among the Paṇis **Bṛbu** was apparently important. In one passage of the Rigveda[7] they are described as **Bekanāṭas**, or 'usurers' (?). In another[8] they are called **Dasyus**, and styled *mṛdhra-vāc*, probably 'of hostile speech,' and *grathin*, a word of uncertain meaning. Hillebrandt[9] thinks that the latter epithet refers to the continuous flow of a speech which

[1] Rv. i. 33, 3; 83, 2; 151, 9; 180, 7; iv. 28, 7; v. 34, 5-7; 61, 8; vi. 13, 3; 53, 3; viii. 64, 2; 97, 2; x. 60, 6; Av. v. 11, 7; xx. 128, 4; Vājasaneyi Saṃhitā, xxxv. 1.

[2] Rv. 1, 83, 4; 184, 2; iii. 58, 2; v. 34, 7; 61, 8; vi. 13, 3; 20, 4; 33, 2; viii. 64, 11.

[3] Rv. i. 124, 10; iv. 51, 3; viii. 45, 14 (where the sense is doubtful). *Cf.* i. 93, 4; v. 61, 1.

[4] Rv. vi. 51, 14.

[5] Rv. i. 32, 11; ii. 24, 6; iv. 58, 4; vi. 44, 22; vii. 9, 2; x. 67, 6; 92, 3; Av. iv. 23, 5; xix. 46, 2; Śatapatha Brāhmaṇa, xiii. 8, 2, 3. It is impossible definitely to decide in which passages the mythical sense is meant. *Cf.* Macdonell, *Vedic Mythology*, p. 157.

[6] Rv. x. 108.

[7] Rv. viii. 66, 10.

[8] Rv. vii. 6, 3.

[9] *Vedische Mythologie*, 1, 89.

is not understood, and that *mṛdhra-vāc* means 'speaking an enemy's speech,' though not necessarily with reference to non-Āryans.[10] In two passages[11] the Paṇis appear as **Dāsas**, and in one[12] a Paṇi is mentioned in connexion with wergeld (**Vaira**), being apparently regarded as equal to a man merely in the price put on his life, but in other respects as inferior.

It is difficult to be certain exactly who a Paṇi was. Roth[13] thinks that the word is derived from *paṇ*, 'barter,' and that the Paṇi is properly the man who will give nothing without return, hence the niggard, who neither worships the gods nor rewards their priests. This view is accepted by Zimmer[14] and by Ludwig.[15] The latter scholar thinks the apparent references to fights with Paṇis are to be explained by their having been aboriginal traders who went in caravans—as in Arabia and Northern Africa—prepared to fight, if need be, to protect their goods against attacks which the Āryans would naturally deem quite justified. He supports this explanation by the references to the Paṇis as Dasyus and Dāsas. It is, however, hardly necessary to do more than regard the Paṇis generally as non-worshippers of the gods favoured by the singers; the term is wide enough to cover either the aborigines or hostile Āryan tribes, as well as demons. Hillebrandt,[16] however, thinks that a real tribe is meant, the Parnians of Strabo, and that they were associated with the Dahae (**Dāsa**). Moreover, he finds them associated in one passage[17] with the **Pārāvatas**, whom

[10] See Satapatha Brāhmaṇa, iii. 2, 1, 23; Muir, *Sanskrit Texts*, 2², 114; Davidson, *Zeitschrift der Deutschen Morgenländischen Gesellschaft*, 37, 23; Eggeling, *Sacred Books of the East*, 26, 31, n. 3.

[11] Rv. v. 34, 5-7; Av. v. 11, 6.

[12] Rv. v. 61, 8. *Cf.* Roth, *Zeitschrift der Deutschen Morgenländischen Gesellschaft*, 41, 673; Max Müller, *Sacred Books of the East*, 32, 361, who thinks that the Paṇi is compared unfavourably with a generous woman, but this is unlikely; Hillebrandt, 1, 92, n. 3; Sieg, *Die Sagenstoffe des Ṛgveda*, 58, 59 Oldenberg, *Ṛgveda-Noten*, 1, 364.

[13] St. Petersburg Dictionary, *s.v.* *Cf.* Yāska, Nirukta, ii. 17; vi. 26.

[14] *Altindisches Leben*, 257. *Cf.* Macdonell, *loc. cit.*; Geldner, *Ṛgveda, Glossar*, 103.

[15] Translation of the Rigveda, 3, 213-215. *Cf.* Bergaigne, *Religion Védique*, 2, 319.

[16] *Vedische Mythologie*, 1, 83 *et seq.*; 3, 268; *Göttingische Gelehrte Anzeigen*, 1894, 648.

[17] Rv. vi. 61, 1-3.

he identifies with the Παρουῆται of Ptolemy,[18] and with **Bṛṣaya**, whom he connects with Βαρσαέντης of Arrian;[19] he also considers that the frequent[20] mention of the Paṇis as opponents of **Divodāsa** shows that the latter was on the Arachosian Haraqaiti (**Sarasvatī**) fighting against the Parnians and Dahae, as well as other Iranian tribes. But the identification of Paṇi and the Parnians is needless, especially as the root *paṇ*, which is found also in the Greek πέρνημι, shows a satisfactory derivation, while the transfer of Dívodāsa to the Haraqaiti is improbable. See also **Divodāsa** and **Bekanāṭa.**

18 vi. 20, 3.
19 iii. 8, 4.
20 The Paṇis occur twelve times in Maṇḍala vi.; once each in ii. and viii.; twice in v. and ix.; thrice in iv. and vii.; six times in viii.; nine times in i.; and four times in x., besides the references in the Saramā hymn, x. 108.

Paṇḍita, a 'learned man,' is not found until the Upaniṣad period.[1]

1 Bṛhadāraṇyaka Upaniṣad, iii. 4, 1; vi. 4, 16. 17; Chāndogya Upaniṣad, vi. 14, 2; Muṇḍaka Upaniṣad, i. 2, 8, etc.

1. **Pataṅga,** 'flying,' denotes a 'winged insect' in the Atharvaveda[1] and the Upaniṣads.[2]

1 vi. 50, 1.
2 Bṛhadāraṇyaka Upaniṣad, vi. 1, 19 (Mādhyaṃdina = vi. 2, 14 Kāṇva); 2, 14 (= 1, 14); Chāndogya Upaniṣad, vi. 9, 3; 10, 2; vii. 2, 1; 7, 1; 8, 1; 10, 1; Adbhuta Brāhmaṇa, vi. 5 (*Indische Studien*, 1, 40).

2. **Pataṅga Prājāpatya** ('descendant of Prajāpati') is credited by the Anukramaṇī (Index) with the authorship of a hymn of the Rigveda[1] in which Pataṅga means the 'sun-bird.' He is also mentioned in the Jaiminīya Upaniṣad Brāhmaṇa.[2]

1 x. 177, 1.
2 iii. 30, 1. *Cf.* Kauṣītaki Brāhmaṇa, xxv. 8; Śāṅkhāyana Śrauta Sūtra, xi. 14, 28.

Patañcala Kāpya is the name of a sage mentioned twice in the Bṛhadāraṇyaka Upaniṣad.[1] According to Weber,[2] his

1 iii. 3, 1; 7, 1.
2 *Indische Studien*, 1, 434. 435; *Indian Literature*, 126, 137, 223, 236, 237.

name is reminiscent of **Kapila** and Patañjali of the Śāṅkhya-Yoga system, but this suggestion may be regarded as quite improbable.[3]

[3] *Cf.* Garbe, *Sāṅkhya Philosophie*, 25, 26.

Patatrin denotes a 'flying creature' generally in the Aitareya Upaniṣad,[1] or more particularly a 'bird' in the Atharvaveda.[2]

[1] iii. 3, 3.

[2] viii. 7, 24; x. 10, 14; xiv. 2, 44.

Patākā, 'banner,' is not found until the Adbhuta Brāhmaṇa.[1] Its Vedic equivalent is **Dhvaja**.

[1] *Indische Studien*, 1, 39, 41 (here erroneously mentioned as *patāka*, masculine).

Pati, Patnī.—Under these words denoting primarily, as the evidence collected in the St. Petersburg Dictionary shows, 'lord' and 'lady,' and so 'husband' and 'wife,' it is convenient to consider the marital relations of the Vedic community.

Child Marriage.—Marriage in the early Vedic texts appears essentially as a union of two persons of full development. This is shown by the numerous references[1] to unmarried girls who grow old in the house of their fathers (*amā-jur*), and who adorn themselves in desire of marriage, as well as to the paraphernalia of spells and potions used in the Atharvavedic tradition[2] to compel the love of man or woman respectively, while even the Rigveda[3] itself seems to present us with a spell by which a

[1] *Cf.* Rv. i. 117, 7; ii. 17, 7; x. 39, 3; 40, 5. **Ghoṣā** is the chief example of this condition. The Atharvaveda (i. 14) also refers to such a case (see Bloomfield, *Hymns of the Atharvaveda*, 253). The ornaments of maidens, especially at seasons of festival, are referred to in Rv. i. 123, 11; vii. 2, 5; Av. ii. 36, 1; xiv. 2, 59 *et seq.*

[2] *Cf.* Av. iii. 18 (= Rv. x. 145); vi. 89; 102; 130; 131; vii. 36; 37; 38. Similarly there are many references to the love of the youth for the maiden, and his seeking her—*e.g.*, Rv. i. 115, 2; Av. ii. 30; iii. 25; vi. 8; 9; 82; to their mutual affection—*e.g.*, Rv. i. 167, 3; ix. 32, 5; 56, 3; x. 34, 5; and to jealousy and love philtres for the purpose of recalling wandering affections—*e.g.*, Av. vi. 18; 42; 43; 94; 139; vii. 45. The gifts of the lover are referred to in Rv. i. 117, 18. Some of these passages may, of course, refer to Hetairai, but not all.

[3] vii. 55, 5. 8. *Cf.* Rv. i. 134, 3; Aufrecht, *Indische Studien*, 4, 337 *et seq.* A different view of the passage is taken by Pischel, *Vedische Studien*, 2, 57 *et seq.* The Atharvaveda (iv. 5) shows that the view of Aufrecht was that early adopted in India.

lover seeks to send all the household to sleep when he visits his beloved. Child wives first occur regularly in the Sūtra period, though it is still uncertain to what extent the rule of marriage before puberty there obtained.[4] The marriage ritual also quite clearly presumes that the marriage is a real and not a nominal one: an essential feature is the taking of the bride to her husband's home, and the ensuing cohabitation.[5]

Limitations on Marriage.—It is difficult to say with certainty within what limits marriage was allowed. The dialogue of Yama and Yamī in the Rigveda[6] seems clearly to point to a prohibition of the marriage of brother and sister. It can hardly be said, as Weber[7] thinks, to point to a practice that was once in use and later became antiquated. In the Gobhila Gṛhya Sūtra[8] and the Dharma Sūtras[9] are found prohibitions against marriage in the **Gotra** ('family') or within six degrees on the mother's or father's side, but in the Śatapatha Brāhmaṇa[10] marriage is allowed in the third or fourth generation, the former being allowed, according to Harisvamin,[11] by the Kāṇvas, and the second by the Saurāṣṭras, while the Dākṣiṇātyas allowed marriage with the daughter of the mother's brother or the son of the father's sister, but presumably not with the daughter of the mother's sister or the son of the father's brother. The prohibition of marriage within the Gotra cannot then have existed,[12] though naturally marriages

[4] *Cf.* Jolly, *Recht und Sitte*, 59; Hopkins, *Journal of the American Oriental Society*, 13, 340 *et seq.*; 23, 356; Risley, *People of India*, 179 *et seq.* There is a possible reference to a child-wife in the Chāndogya Upaniṣad, i. 10, 1. For the Sūtra evidence, see Bhandarkar, *Zeitschrift der Deutschen Morgenländischen Gesellschaft*, 47, 143-156; Jolly, *ibid.*, 46, 413-426; 47, 610-615.

[5] Rv. x. 85, especially verse 29 *et seq.*

[6] x. 10.

[7] *Proceedings of the Berlin Academy*, 1895, 822. *Cf.* also *Indische Studien*, 5, 427; 10, 76, n.; Pischel, *Hermes*, 18, 465-468; Max Müller, *Science of Language*, 2, 507; Herodotus, iii. 19. Crawley's *Mystic Rose* gives strong reasons against the early prevalence of such marriages.

[8] iii. 4, 5.

[9] Āpastamba Dharma Sūtra, ii. 5, 15, 16, etc. *Cf.* Mānava Dharma Śāstra, iii. 5; Yājñavalkya Dharma Śāstra, i. 52, 53.

[10] i. 8, 3, 6.

[11] On Śatapatha Brāhmaṇa, *loc. cit.*

[12] *Cf.* Weber, *Indische Studien*, 10, 75, 76; Max Müller, *Ancient Sanskrit Literature*, 387; Schrader, *Prehistoric Antiquities*, 392; Geiger, *Ostiranische Kultur*, 246; *Zeitschrift der Deutschen Morgenländischen Gesellschaft*, 43, 308-312; Jolly, *Recht und Sitte*, 62, 63; Hopkins, *Journal of the American Oriental Society*, 13, 345 *et seq.*

outside the Gotra were frequent.[13] Similarity of caste was also not an essential to marriage, as hypergamy was permitted even by the Dharma Sūtras,[14] so that a Brāhmaṇa could marry wives of any lower caste, a Kṣatriya wives of the two lowest castes as well as of his own caste, a Vaiśya a Śūdrā as well as a Vaiśyā, although the Śūdrā marriages were later disapproved *in toto*. Instances of such intermarriage are common in the Epic, and are viewed as normal in the Bṛhaddevatā.[15]

It was considered proper that the younger brothers and sisters should not anticipate their elders by marrying before them. The later Saṃhitās and Brāhmaṇas[16] present a series of names expressive of such anticipation, censuring as sinful those who bear them. These terms are the *pari-vividāna*,[17] or perhaps *agre-dadhus*,[18] the man who, though a younger brother, marries before his elder brother, the latter being then called the *parivitta*;[19] the *agre-didhiṣu*,[20] the man who weds a younger daughter while her elder sister is still unmarried; and the **Didhiṣū-pati**,[21] who is the husband of the latter. The passages do not explicitly say that the exact order of birth must always be followed, but the mention of the terms shows that the order was often broken.

Widow Remarriage.—The remarriage of a widow was

[13] *Cf*. Oldenberg, *Zeitschrift der Deutschen Morgenländischen Gesellschaft*, 51, 279.

[14] Gautama Dharma Sūtra, iv. 16; Baudhāyana Dharma Sūtra, i. 16, 2-5; Vasiṣṭha Dharma Sūtra, i. 24; 25; Pāraskara Gṛhya Sūtra, i. 4, etc.; Risley, *People of India*, 156 *et seq*. *Cf*. **Varṇa.**

[15] See Hopkins, cited in note 12; Bṛhaddevatā, v. 79; and **Varṇa.**

[16] See Delbrück, *Die indogermanischen Verwandtschaftsnamen*, 578 *et seq*.

[17] Maitrāyaṇī Saṃhitā, iv. 1, 9, and Kāṭhaka and Kapiṣṭhala Saṃhitās, cited by Delbrück, 579, 580; Vājasaneyi Saṃhitā, xxx. 9. In Āpastamba Dharma Sūtra, ii. 5, 12, 22, the expression is *paryāhita*.

[18] Maitrāyaṇī Saṃhitā, iv. 1, 9, according to Delbrück, 581. But, as *pari-vividāna* follows, it seems very doubtful; the reading is probably wrong, especially in view of the Kāṭhaka and Kapiṣṭhala parallels, which have *agre-didhiṣau* and *agre-ḍadhiṣau*.

[19] See passages cited in note 17; also Av. vi. 112, 3; Taittirīya Brāhmaṇa, iii. 2, 8, 11. Āpastamba Śrauta Sūtra, ix. 12, 11, and Dharma Sūtra, ii. 5, 12, 22, add *parivinna* to *parivitta*, but probably the two words should be identical in sense.

[20] Kāṭhaka Saṃhitā (see note 17) has *agre-didhiṣu*; Kapiṣṭhala, *agre-dadhiṣu*; Taittirīya Brāhmaṇa, iii. 2, 8, 11, *agra-didhiṣu*. The Dharma Sūtras adopt *agre-didhiṣu*.

[21] Kāṭhaka Saṃhitā has *didhiṣū-pati*; Kapiṣṭhala, *dadhiṣū-pati*; and so the Dharma Sūtras. Vājasaneyi Saṃhitā, xxx. 9, has the corrupt *edidhiṣuḥ-pati*.

apparently permitted. This seems originally to have taken the form of the marriage of the widow to the brother or other nearest kinsman of the dead man in order to produce children. At any rate, the ceremony is apparently alluded to in a funeral hymn of the Rigveda;[22] for the alternative explanation, which sees in the verse a reference to the ritual of the Puruṣamedha ('human sacrifice'), although accepted by Hillebrandt[23] and Delbrück,[24] is not at all probable, while the ordinary view is supported by the Sūtra evidence.[25] Moreover, another passage of the Rigveda[26] clearly refers to the marriage of the widow and the husband's brother (*devṛ*), which constitutes what the Indians later knew as Niyoga.[27] This custom was probably not followed except in cases where no son was already born. This custom was hardly remarriage in the strict sense, since the brother might—so far as appears—be already married himself. In the Atharvaveda,[28] a verse refers to a charm which would secure the reunion, in the next world, of a wife and her second husband. Though, as Delbrück[29] thinks, this very possibly refers to a case in which the first husband was still alive,[30] but was impotent or had lost caste (*patita*),[31] still it is certain that the later Dharma Sūtras[32] began to recognize ordinary remarriage in case of the death of the first husband.

22 x. 18, 8.

23 *Zeitschrift der Deutschen Morgenländischen Gesellschaft*, 40, 708.

24 *Die indogermanischen Verwandtschaftsnamen*, 553. *Cf.* also Lanman, *Sanskrit Reader*, 385; for the other view, see Whitney, Translation of the Atharvaveda, 848; Roth, *Siebenzig Lieder*, 151, n.; Zimmer, *Altindisches Leben*, 329.

25 Āśvalāyana Gṛhya Sūtra, iv. 2, 18. *Cf.* Lanman in Whitney, *op. cit.*, 849.

26 x. 40, 2.

27 *Cf.* Yāska, Nirukta, iii. 15, with Roth's note; Geldner, *Ṛgveda, Kommentar*, 160; Weber, *Indische Studien*, v. 343, n.; Hopkins, *Journal of the American Oriental Society*, 13, 355, n., 367; Jolly, *Recht und Sitte*, 71; Muir, *Sanskrit Texts*, 5, 459; von Schroeder, *Indiens Literatur und Cultur*, 429. The custom died out in later times, it seems.

28 ix. 5, 27. 28.

29 *Die indogermanischen Verwandtschaftsnamen*, 553-555. *Cf.* Jolly, *Recht und Sitte*, 59; Hopkins, *Journal of the American Oriental Society*, 13, 371, n.

30 This is certainly the case in Av. v. 17, 8, which, however, merely exalts the sanctity of the Brāhmaṇa, and does not necessarily imply remarriage at all.

31 *E.g.*, Baudhāyana Dharma Sūtra, ii. 2, 3, 27.

32 Vasiṣṭha Dharma Sūtra, xvii. 19. 20. 72-74; Baudhāyana Dharma Sūtra, iv. 1, 16; Mānava Dharma Śāstra, ix. 175. *Cf.* also Muir, *Sanskrit Texts*, 1², 281; 5, 306.

Pischel[33] finds some evidence in the Rigveda[34] to the effect that a woman could remarry if her husband disappeared and could not be found or heard of.

Polygamy.—A Vedic Indian could have more than one wife. This is proved clearly by many passages in the Rigveda;[35] Manu, according to the Maitrāyaṇī Saṃhitā,[36] had ten wives; and the Śatapatha Brāhmaṇa[37] explains polygamy by a characteristic legend. Moreover, the king regularly has four wives attributed to him, the Mahiṣī,[38] the Parivṛktī,[39] the Vāvātā,[40] and the Pālāgalī.[41] The Mahiṣī appears to be the chief wife, being the first one married according to the Śatapatha Brāhmaṇa.[42] The Parivṛktī, 'the neglected,' is explained by Weber[43] and Pischel[44] as one that has had no son. The Vāvātā is 'the favourite,' while the Pālāgalī is, according to Weber, the daughter of the last of the court officials. The names are curious, and not very intelligible, but the evidence points to the wife first wedded alone being a wife in the fullest sense. This view is supported by the fact emphasized by

[33] *Vedische Studien*, 1, 27.

[34] vi. 49, 8. *Cf.* Mahābhārata, iii. 70, 26.

[35] Rv. i. 62, 11; 71, 1; 104, 3; 105, 8; 112, 19; 186, 7; vi. 53, 4; vii. 18, 2; 26, 3; x. 43, 1; 101, 11. *Cf.* Av. iii. 4; Taittirīya Saṃhitā, vi. 5, 1, 4, etc. See Muir, *Sanskrit Texts*, 5, 455 *et seq.*; Schrader, *Prehistoric Antiquities*, 387; Jolly, *Recht und Sitte*, 64; von Schroeder, *Indiens Literatur und Cultur*, 430, 431; Delbrück, *Die indogermanischen Verwandtschaftsnamen*, 539, 540; Hopkins, *Journal of the American Oriental Society*, 13, 353; Bloomfield, *Zeitschrift der Deutschen Morgenländischen Gesellschaft*, 48, 561.

[36] i. 5, 8.

[37] ix. 1, 4, 6.

[38] Taittirīya Brāhmaṇa, iii. 9, 4, 4; Śatapatha Brāhmaṇa, v. 3, 1, 4; vi. 5, 3, 1; vii. 5, 1, 1; xiii. 2, 6, 4; 4, 1, 8; 5, 2, 2. 5. 9; Pañcaviṃśa Brāhmaṇa, xix. 1, 4. *Cf.* Rv. v. 2, 2; 37, 3; Av. ii. 36, 3; Taittirīya Saṃhitā, i. 8, 9, 1; Weber, *Indische Studien*, 5, 220.

[39] *Pari-vṛktā* occurs in Rv. x. 102, 11; Av. vii. 113, 2; xx. 128, 10. 11; Śatapatha Brāhmaṇa, xiii. 2, 6, 6; 4, 1, 8; 5, 2, 7; *parivṛktī* in Taittirīya Saṃhitā, i. 8, 9, 1; Taittirīya Brāhmaṇa, i. 7, 3, 4; iii. 9, 4, 4; Kāṭhaka Saṃhitā, x. 10; xv. 4; Śatapatha Brāhmaṇa, v. 3, 1, 13.

[40] Aitareya Brāhmaṇa, iii. 22; Taittirīya Brāhmaṇa, i. 7, 3, 3; iii. 9, 4, 4; Av. xx. 128, 10. 11; Śatapatha Brāhmaṇa, xiii. 2, 6, 5; 4, 1, 8; 5, 2, 6. *Cf.* Weber, *Indische Studien*, 5, 308, n.; Bloomfield, *Zeitschrift der Deutschen Morgenländischen Gesellschaft*, 48, 553, 554.

[41] Taittirīya Brāhmaṇa, i. 7, 3, 3 *et seq.*; iii. 9, 4, 5; Śatapatha Brāhmaṇa, xiii. 4, 1, 8; Śāṅkhāyana Śrauta Sūtra, xvi. 4, 4.

[42] vi. 5, 3, 1.

[43] *Indische Studien*, 10, 6.

[44] *Vedische Studien*, 2, 199. *Cf.* Geldner, *ibid.*, 2, 38.

Delbrück,[45] that in the sacrifice the Patnī is usually mentioned in the singular, apparent exceptions being due to some mythological reason.[46] Zimmer[47] is of opinion that polygamy is dying out in the Rigvedic period, monogamy being developed from pologamy; Weber,[48] however, thinks that polygamy is secondary, a view that is supported by more recent anthropology.[49]

Polyandry.—On the other hand, polyandry is not Vedic.[50] There is no passage containing any clear reference to such a custom. The most that can be said is that in the Rigveda[51] and the Atharvaveda[52] verses are occasionally found in which husbands are mentioned in relation to a single wife. It is difficult to be certain of the correct explanation of each separate instance of this mode of expression; but even if Weber's[53] view, that the plural is here used *majestatis causā*, is not accepted, Delbrück's[54] explanation by mythology is probably right. In other passages[55] the plural is simply generic.

Marital Relations.—Despite polygamy, however, there is ample evidence that the marriage tie was not, as Weber[56] has suggested, lightly regarded as far as the fidelity of the wife was concerned. There is, however, little trace of the husband's being expected to be faithful as a matter of morality. Several

45 *Indogermanische Verwandtschaftsnamen*, 539. *Cf.* Zimmer, *Altindisches Leben*, 325. Yājñavalkya had, however, two apparently equal wives (Bṛhadāraṇyaka Upaniṣad, iii. 1, and *cf.* Taittirīya Brāhmaṇa, i. 3, 10, 3).

46 *E.g.*, Taittirīya Saṃhitā, ii. 5, 6, 4; Maitrāyaṇī Saṃhitā, iii. 3, 1.

47 *Altindisches Leben*, 323.

48 *Indische Studien*, 5, 222. Weber's theory that *sapatna* cannot be derived from *sapatnī* is, however, quite untenable.

49 See, *e.g.*, Westermaarck, *Origin and Development of Marriage*; Crawley, *Mystic Rose*.

50 Mayr, *Indisches Erbrecht*, Wien, 1873, contends in favour of its existence. But see Weber, *Indische Studien*, 5, 191, 207; 10, 83, 84; Jolly, *Recht und Sitte*, 48; Hopkins, *Journal of the American Oriental Society*, 13, 354 *et seq.*; von Schroeder, *Indiens Literatur und Cultur*, 431, n. 2; *Zeitschrift der Deutschen Morgenländischen Gesellschaft*, 44, 340-342; Delbrück, *Die indogermanischen Verwandtschaftsnamen*, 541-545.

51 x. 85, 37. 38.

52 Av. xiv. 1, 44. 52. 61; 2, 14. 27.

53 *Indische Studien*, 5, 191. So Zimmer, *Altindisches Leben*, 326, who, however, suggests that the plural is generic.

54 *Op. cit.*, 543.

55 Śatapatha Brāhmaṇa, ii. 6, 2, 14. *Cf.* the plural *śvaśurāḥ*, 'fathers-in-law,' in Kāṭhaka Saṃhitā, xii. 12. The Niyoga has, of course, nothing to do with polyandry.

56 *Indische Studien*, 10, 83. *Cf.* Ludwig, Translation of the Rigveda, 5, 573. and *cf.* **Dharma**.

passages,[57] indeed, forbid, with reference to ritual abstinence, intercourse with the *strī* of another. This may imply that adultery on the husband's part was otherwise regarded as venial. But as the word *strī* includes all the 'womenfolk,' daughters and slaves, as well as wife, the conclusion can hardly be drawn that intercourse with another man's 'wife' was normally regarded with indifference.[58] The curious ritual of the Varuṇapraghāsās,[59] in which the wife of the sacrificer is questioned as to her lovers, is shown by Delbrück[60] to be a part of a rite meant to expiate unchastity on the part of a wife, not as a normal question for a sacrificer to put to his own wife. Again, Yājñavalkya's doctrine in the Śatapatha Brāhmaṇa,[61] which seems to assert that no one cares if a wife is unchaste (*paraḥ-puṃsā*) or not, really means that no one cares if the wife is away from the men who are sacrificing, as the wives of the gods are apart from them during the particular rite in question. Monogamy is also evidently approved,[62] so that some higher idea of morality was in course of formation. On the other hand, no Vedic text gives us the rule well known to other Indo Germanic[63] peoples that the adulterer taken in the act can be killed with impunity, though the later legal literature has traces of this rule.[64] There is also abundant evidence that the standard of ordinary sexual morality was not high.

Hetairai.—In the Rigveda[65] there are many references to illegitimate love and to the abandonment of the offspring of

[57] Taittirīya Saṃhitā, v. 6, 8, 3; Maitrāyaṇī Saṃhitā, iii. 4, 7.

[58] *Cf.* above, p. 396.

[59] Maitrāyaṇī Saṃhitā, i. 10, 11; Śatapatha Brāhmaṇa, ii. 5, 2, 20; Taittirīya Brāhmaṇa, i. 6, 5, 2.

[60] *Op. cit.*, 550.

[61] i. 3, 1, 21. *Cf.* Eggeling, *Sacred Books of the East*, 12, 76, n. 2; Böhtlingk, Dictionary, *s.v. paraḥpuṃsā* (*cf.* above, p. 397). Delbrück, *op. cit.*, 551, shows also that neither the Dīkṣā ('consecration') nor the Pravara ('invitation' to Agni, as described by the names of the mythical ancestors of the invoker) gives any countenance to the theory of doubt as to the parentage of the Vedic Indians.

[62] Rv. i. 124, 7; iv. 3, 2; x. 71, 4, etc.

[63] Leist, *Altarisches Jus Gentium*, 276 *et seq*. *Cf.* Schrader, *Prehistoric Antiquities*, 388, 389; Hopkins, *Journal of the American Oriental Society*, 13, 366, 367.

[64] *Cf.* above, p. 396.

[65] Rv. i. 134, 3; iii. 53, 8; viii. 17, 7. *Mahānagnī*, Av. xiv. 1, 36; xx. 136, 5; Aitareya Brāhmaṇa, i. 27, denotes a courtesan. *Cf.* Av. v. 7, 8. So also *puṃścalī*, Av. xv. 2; Vājasaneyi Saṃhitā, xxx. 22; *puṃścalū*, Taittirīya Brāhmaṇa, iii. 4, 15, 1.

such unions,[66] especially in the case of a protégé of Indra, often mentioned as the *parāvṛkta* or *parāvṛj*.[67] The 'son of a maiden' (*kumārī-putra*) is already spoken of in the Vājasaneyi Saṃhitā.[68] Such a person appears with a metronymic in the Upaniṣad period:[69] this custom may be the origin of metronymics such as those which make up a great part of the lists of teachers (Vaṃśas) of the Bṛhadāraṇyaka Upaniṣad.[70] The Vājasaneyi Saṃhitā[71] refers to illicit unions of Śūdra and Ārya, both male and female, besides giving in its list of victims at the Puruṣamedha, or 'human sacrifice,' several whose designations apparently mean 'courtesan' (*atītvarī*)[72] and 'procuress of abortion' (*atiṣkadvarī*),[73] while the 'dyeing woman' (*rajayitrī*) is dedicated to sensuality.[74] Pischel and Geldner also see many references to Hetairai in other passages of the Rigveda,[75] especially where mention is made of Uṣas, the goddess of Dawn, who in their view is the characteristic Hetaira. At any rate, there is little doubt that the 'dancer' (*nṛtū*) referred to in one passage of the Rigveda[76] was a Hetaira. When women are referred to as going to the **Samana**, or 'place of meeting,' Hetairai are probably also meant.[77] Grave cases of immorality are alluded to in the Rigveda.[78] The love of father and daughter, as shown in the myth of Prajāpati,[79] is evidently censured, but the actual existence of this form of incest is recognized in the Atharvaveda.[80] Girls who had lost their

[66] Rv. ii. 29, 1 (*raha-sūḥ*, 'one who bears in secret.' *Cf.* Max Müller, *Ancient Sanskrit Literature*, 26; Zimmer, *Altindisches Leben*, 333, 334).

[67] Rv. ii. 13, 12; 15, 7; iv. 19, 9; 30, 16; Zimmer, *op. cit.*, 335. The child, when exposed, was in danger of being consumed by ants (*vamrī*). *Cf.* below, p. 493.

[68] xxx. 6.

[69] *Cf.* **Jābāla Satyakāma**.

[70] *Cf.* Pāṇini, iv. 1, 116. But the custom may be due simply to polygamy (Keith, *Aitareya Āraṇyaka*, p. 244, n. 2).

[71] xxiii. 30. 31; Taittirīya Saṃhitā, vii. 4, 19, 2. 3.

[72] xxx. 15.

[73] xxx. 15; Taittirīya Brāhmaṇa, iii. 4, 11, 1, has *apaskadvarī*.

[74] xxx. 12; Taittirīya Brāhmaṇa, iii. 4, 7, 1.

[75] *Cf. Vedische Studien*, 1, xxv, 196, 275, 299, 309; 2, 120, 154, 179, etc.; Jolly, *Recht und Sitte*, 48.

[76] i. 92, 4.

[77] Rv. iv. 58, 8; vi. 75, 4; x. 168, 2. Perhaps also *vrā* in i. 124, 8; 126, 5.

[78] x. 162, 5 (brother and sister: *cf.* above, p. 397).

[79] Rv. x. 61, 5-7; Pañcaviṃśa Brāhmaṇa, viii. 2, 10; Aitareya Brāhmaṇa, iii. 33; Śatapatha Brāhmaṇa, i. 7, 4, 1.

[80] viii. 6, 7.

natural protectors—father or brother[81]—were apt to be reduced to live by immorality.

Forms of Marriage.—The state of society revealed in the Vedic age seems to point to considerable freedom on the part of both man and woman in selecting a wife or a husband. At any rate, it is not clear that either the father or the mother controlled the marriage of son or daughter of mature age,[82] though no doubt the parents or parent often arranged a suitable match.[83] The marriage was frequently arranged through an intermediary, the 'wooer' (*vara*),[84] presumably after those concerned had in effect come to an agreement. The sale of a daughter was not unknown,[85] but a certain amount of discredit would seem to have attached to it,[86] and sons-in-law in such cases were sometimes stingy. On the other hand, dowries were not infrequently given, especially no doubt when damsels suffered from bodily defects.[87] Occasionally marriages by

81 Rv. i. 124, 7. *Cf.* **Putrikā**.

82 *Cf.* Delbrück, *op. cit.*, 574. Zimmer, *Altindisches Leben*, 309, asserts that the consent of parent or brother was needed, but no clear evidence of this can be adduced. The later custom is not conclusive, since it is bound up with the usage of child marriage, which deprived both son and daughter of any free choice. *Cf. ibid.*, 315; Kaegi, *Der Rigveda*, 15.

83 This is so natural as not to need express evidence. *Cf.*, *e.g.*, the marriage proposals of Śyāvāśva Ātreya, as detailed in the Bṛhaddevatā, v. 49 *et seq.*; Sieg, *Die Sagenstoffe des Ṛgveda*, 51 *et seq.*

84 Rv. x. 78, 4; 85, 15. 23. Zimmer, *op. cit.*, 310, exalts this into a universal practice, and compares the use of *aryaman*, 'friend,' as 'bride-wooer.' In Śyāvāśva's case, his father acted for him.

85 *Cf.* Maitrāyaṇī Saṃhitā, i. 10, 11; Taittirīya Saṃhitā, ii. 3, 4, 1; Taittirīya Brāhmaṇa, i. 1, 2, 4; Kāṭhaka Saṃhitā, xxxvi. 5. See also Mānava Dharma Śāstra, iii. 53; viii. 204; ix. 98; Megasthenes in McCrindle's translation, p. 70; Weber, *Indische Studien*, 5, 407; Hopkins, *Journal of the American Oriental Society*, 13, 345 *et seq.*; Schrader, *Prehistoric Antiquities*, 381; Pischel, *Vedische Studien*, 2, 78 *et seq.*; Hillebrandt, *Vedische Mythologie*, 3, 86, n.; Jolly, *Recht und Sitte*, 52.

86 Rv. i. 109, 2, refers to the gods Indra and Agni as more generous than a *vijāmātṛ*, 'son-in-law,' or a *syāla*, 'brother-in-law.' The force of *vi* in the former word must be unfavourable, and the sense, as indicated by Pischel, is, no doubt, that a son-in-law who was not in other respects altogether suitable might have to buy his bride at a heavy cost. The *vijāmātṛ* is, in fact, the *aśrīro jāmātā*, the 'ignoble son-in-law,' of Rv. viii. 2, 20. *Cf.* Yāska, Nirukta, vi. 9; Bloomfield, *Journal of the American Oriental Society*, 15, 255.

87 *Cf.* Rv. vi. 28, 5; x. 27, 12; Av. v. 17, 12. Possibly in Rv. i. 109, 2, there is a reference to a generous brother giving his sister a dowry in order to get her a husband. *Cf.* Hopkins, *Journal of the American Oriental Society*, 13, 345; Muir, *Sanskrit Texts*, 5, 459; Kaegi, *Der Rigveda*, n. 352; Zimmer, *op. cit.*, 310, n. It is doubtful whether *anudeyī* in Rv. x. 85, 6, means 'dowry' or not. See Whitney, Translation of the Atharvaveda, 741.

capture may have taken place, but only as knightly feats, as when **Vimada** carried off **Purumitra's** daughter against her father's wish, but very possibly with her own consent.[88] The later law-books and the Epic describe in much detail various forms of marriage, but they all seem reducible to three types: (*a*) that which is based on mutual consent, the *prājāpatya* ('connected with Prajāpati'); (*b*) that in which a price is paid for the bride, the *āsura* ('Asura-like'), *ārṣa* ('connected with the Ṛṣis'), *brāhma* ('relating to Brahman'), or *daiva* ('divine'); (*c*) those which consist in stealing the bride, the *kṣātra* ('warrior-like') or the *rākṣasa* ('demon-like') mode, of all of which traces are found in Vedic literature.[89] For instance, the gift of a maiden for services rendered or other object is exemplified in the story of **Cyavana** in the Jaiminīya Brāhmaṇa,[90] and in that of **Śyāvāśva** in the Bṛhaddevatā.[91]

Wedding Ceremony.—In normal marriages the bridal was celebrated by an elaborate ceremony which bears in essentials and details the strongest resemblance to the form observed by other Indo-Germanic as well as non-Indo-Germanic peoples,[92] and which was destined to secure the stability and fruitfulness of the union. The ceremony commenced at the bride's house,[93] to which the bridegroom with his friends and relations repaired, and in which he met the friends and relations of the bride.[94] A cow or cows were slain for the entertainment of the guests.[95] The bridegroom having caused the bride to mount a stone, formally grasped her hand, and led her round the household

88 *Cf.* Rv. i. 112, 19; 116, 1; 117, 20; x. 39, 7; 65, 12. Sāyaṇa's view that **Kamadyū** was daughter of **Purumitra** seems certain, though Zimmer, *loc. cit.*, is doubtful.

89 Hopkins, *Journal of the American Oriental Society*, 13, 361, 362; Jolly, *Recht und Sitte*, 50 *et seq.*; Pischel, *Vedische Studien*, 1, 29; Schrader, *Prehistoric Antiquities*, 383.

90 iii. 122.

91 v. 49 *et seq.*

92 The older ritual is described with considerable detail in Rv. x. 85 and Av. xiv. 1 and 2. The later ritual, as elaborately traced in the Gṛhya Sūtras, is set out by Weber and Haas, *Indische Studien*, 5, 177-411. See also Leist, *Altarisches Jus Gentium*, 144 *et seq.*; von Schroeder, *Die Hochzeitsgebräuche der Esten*, Berlin, 1888; Schrader, *Prehistoric Antiquities*, 384 *et seq.*; Hopkins, *op. cit.*, 13, 355 *et seq.*; Winternitz, *Das altindische Hochzeitsrituell*, 1892; Whitney, Translation of the Atharvaveda, 739 *et seq.*; Lanman, *Sanskrit Reader*, 389 *et seq.*

93 x. 17, 1.

94 Rv. iv. 58, 9; Av. vi. 60; xiv. 2, 59.

95 Rv. x. 85, 13.

fire.[96] This act constituted the marriage, the husband hence being called 'he who takes by the hand' (*hasta-grābha*).[97] The festivities being over,[98] the bridegroom took the bride to his home on a car in a marriage procession,[99] all to the accompaniment of suitable stanzas. Then followed cohabitation.[100]

Wife's Property and Status.—We have very little information as to the legal relations of wife and husband after marriage. It may be assumed that the husband appropriated the wife's dowry, if any, as well as her earnings, if any: even in the Epic[101] the rise of the recognition of women's property as their own (*strī-dhana*) is only slow. That the husband was absolute master of a wife as of a slave is not probable, though he doubtless exercised the same power of correction as was expressly allowed in the eighteenth century by English law. The poetical ideal[102] of the family was decidedly high, and we have no reason to doubt that it was often actually fulfilled. Moreover, the wife on her marriage was at once given an honoured position in the house: she is emphatically mistress in her husband's home, exercising authority over her father-in-law, her husband's brothers, and her unmarried sisters.[103] No doubt the case contemplated is one in which the eldest son

[96] *Cf.* Rv. x. 85, 36. 38; Av. xiv. 1, 47. 48. Before the bride mounted the stone, the groom repeated, according to the Gṛhya Sūtras (Āśvalāyana, i. 7, 3; Śāṅkhāyana, i. 13, 4; Pāraskara, i. 6, 3, etc.), the words, 'I am he, thou art she; I the Sāman, thou the Ṛc; I the heaven, thou the earth; here will we unite ourselves and produce offspring,' for which see Av. xiv. 2, 71; Kāṭhaka Saṃhitā, xxxv. 18; Aitareya Brāhmaṇa, viii. 27; Bṛhadāraṇyaka Upaniṣad, vi. 4, 19 (Mādhyaṃdina).

[97] x. 18, 8. *Cf.* Av. xiv. 1, 51.

[98] Av. xiv. 2, 59 *et seq.*

[99] Rv. x. 85, 7. 8. 10. 24. 25. 26. 27. 42 *et seq.*; Av. xiv. 1, 60.

[100] See for the purification of the bride's garment, Rv. x. 85, 28-30. 35.

[101] 'They own neither themselves nor an inheritance' (*nātmanaś caneśate na dāyasya*), says the Śatapatha Brāhmaṇa, iv. 4, 2, 13. *Cf.* Maitrāyaṇī Saṃhitā, iv. 6, 4; Taittirīya Saṃhitā, vi. 5, 8, 2; Nirukta, iii. 4. *Cf.* for the Epic, Hopkins, *Journal of the American Oriental Society*, 13, 368. For compulsory obedience of the wife, *cf.* Bṛhadāraṇyaka Upaniṣad, vi. 4, 7. In the same Upaniṣad Yājñavalkya, on retiring from the ordinary life, divides his goods between his two wives.

[102] Rv. viii. 31, 5-9; x. 34, 11; 85, 18. 19. 42 *et seq.*; Av. iii. 30; xiv. 2, 32.

[103] Rv. x. 85, 46. *Cf.* as regards the bridegroom's sisters, Aitareya Brāhmaṇa, iii. 37. In Av. xiv. 2, 26, the daughter-in-law is to be 'wealful' (*śambhūḥ*) to her father-in-law, and 'pleasant' (*syonā*) to her mother-in-law, which is correct on either theory of her position as a daughter or a mistress.

of a family has become its head owing to the decrepitude[104] of the parents, his wife then taking the place of the mistress of the joint family while the brothers and sisters are still unmarried. It is not inconsistent with the great stress elsewhere[105] laid on the respect due to a father-in-law, who then is probably regarded as still in full possession of his faculties, and controls the house while his son continues to live with him. The respect would no doubt equally apply if the son had set up a separate family of his own.[106]

Moreover, the wife was a regular participator in the offerings of the husband. In this connexion the term **Patnī** regularly applies to her in the Brāhmaṇas,[107] where **Jāyā** designates her in her conjugal capacity, not in that of sharer in the sacrifice. In this respect her position gradually deteriorated: thus the Śatapatha Brāhmaṇa[108] describes a certain ceremony in which the wife (*jāyā*) alone offered the oblation in former times, while later a priest might do so instead. The same Brāhmaṇa shows other traces of a lowering in the position of women, probably due to the growing sense of the importance of ceremonial priority.[109] So in the Maitrāyaṇī Saṃhitā[110] women generally are classed with dice and drink as three chief evils, and woman is declared to be 'untruth,'[111] and connected with Nirṛti, 'calamity.'[112] A woman too, according to the Taittirīya Saṃhitā,[113] is inferior even to a bad man, and a sarcastic reference is made in the Kāṭhaka Saṃhitā[114] to her power of

[104] *Cf.* Rv. i. 70, 5, where an old father's goods are divided by his sons, and Zimmer, *Altindisches Leben*, 327. *Cf.* also the possible case of a father who recovers after giving over all his goods to his son, Kauṣītaki Upaniṣad, iv. 15.

[105] Av. viii. 6, 24; Maitrāyaṇī Saṃhitā, ii. 4, 2; Kāṭhaka Saṃhitā, xii. 12 (*Indische Studien*, 5, 260); Taittirīya Brāhmaṇa, ii. 4, 6, 12; Aitareya Brāhmaṇa, iii. 22; Delbrück, *Die indogermanischen Verwandtschaftsnamen*, 514, 515.

[106] No doubt it might also apply even if the father-in-law were decrepit; but it is hardly likely that, in these circumstances, the strong sense of respect evident in Av. viii. 6, 24, which implies fear, would have developed.

[107] Śatapatha Brāhmaṇa, i. 9, 2, 14; Pāṇini, iv. 1, 33; Delbrück, *op. cit.*, 510, 512.

[108] i. 1, 4, 13. For the older practice, *cf.* Rv. i. 122, 2; iii. 53, 4-6; viii. 31, 5 *et seq.*; x. 86, 10, etc.

[109] *E.g.*, i. 3, 1. 9. 12. 13. *Cf.* Lévi, *La doctrine du sacrifice*, 157, 158.

[110] iii. 6, 3.

[111] i. 10, 11.

[112] *Ibid.*

[113] vi. 5, 8, 2. *Cf.* Śatapatha Brāhmaṇa, i. 3, 1, 9.

[114] xxxi. 1. *Cf.* Aitareya Brāhmaṇa, iii. 22.

getting things from her husband by cajolery at nigh . On the other hand must be set the encomia on woman: a woman is half her husband,[115] and completes him;[116] and in the Rigveda[117] attacks on women mingle with the general assumption of their good qualities. None the less, the Brāhmaṇas clearly indicate a gradual decline in their position, which is evident from the rule that requires the wife to eat after her husband.[118] Scolds were also known: the Aitareya Brāhmaṇa[119] praises the wife 'who does not answer back' (*aprativādinī*). Women bore no part in political life: men go to the assembly, not women, the Maitrāyaṇī Saṃhitā[120] expressly says. On the other hand, with the advance of education, women shared in the intellectual interests of the day, as is exemplified by Yājñavalkya's[121] two wives, of whom one was interested in his philosophical discussions, the other not. Other women are also referred to in the Upaniṣads as teachers, but whether they were married is not certain.[122]

But the main object of a woman's marriage was the production of children, this being repeatedly asserted in the Rigveda and later.[123] The desire for offspring, as was natural in a society which mainly counted relationship through the father, took the form of a wish for a son to perform the necessary funeral rites for the father, and to continue his line. It was no doubt possible to adopt a son, but in the Rigveda[124] this custom is plainly viewed as unsatisfactory. The practice

[115] Śatapatha Brāhmaṇa, v. 2, 1, 10.

[116] Bṛhadāraṇyaka Upaniṣad, i. 4, 17.

[117] In viii. 33, 17, Indra is credited with a poor opinion of woman's intelligence, and Purūravas in x. 95, 15, frankly calls them hyenas. They are defended in v. 61, 6-8, but only against mean men (**Paṇi**). *Cf.* Kaegi, *Der Rigveda*, n. 351.

[118] Śatapatha Brāhmaṇa, i. 9, 2, 12; x. 5, 2, 9. *Cf.* Vāsiṣṭha Dharma Sūtra, xii. 13; Baudhāyana Dharma Sūtra, i. 1, 2, 2; Weber, *Indische Studien*, 5, 330, n.; Hopkins, *Journal of the American Oriental Society*, 13, 365, n.

[119] iii. 24, 7. *Cf.* Gopatha Brāhmaṇa, ii. 3, 22; Bloomfield, *Journal of the American Oriental Society*, 19, 14, n. 2.

[120] iv. 7, 4. *Cf.* Av. vii. 38, 4.

[121] Bṛhadāraṇyaka Upaniṣad, iii. 4, 1; iv. 5, 1.

[122] *Cf.* the epithet *gandharva-gṛhītā*, Aitareya Brāhmaṇa, v. 29; Kauṣītaki Brāhmaṇa, ii. 9; Bṛhadāraṇyaka Upaniṣad, iii. 3, 1; 7, 1; and see Āśvalāyana Gṛhya Sūtra. iii. 4, 4; Śāṅkhāyana Gṛhya Sūtra, iv. 10.

[123] Rv. i. 91, 20; 92, 13; iii. 1, 23; x. 85, 25. 41. 42. 45; Av. iii. 23, 2; v. 25, 11; vi. 11, 2, etc.

[124] vii. 4, 7. 8. *Cf.* Nirukta, iii. 2.

is recognized,[125] as we have seen above of Niyoga, in the appointment of a brother to beget children with the wife of a dead man, or perhaps of a man who is childless. 'Sonlessness' (*avīratā*) is placed on the same level as lack of property (*amati*), and Agni is besought to protect from it.[126] The birth of a daughter was certainly not specially welcome: the Atharvaveda[127] in one hymn distinctly invokes the birth of a son, and deprecates that of a daughter, while the Aitareya Brāhmaṇa[128] contains an old verse which says that a daughter is a misery (*kṛpaṇam*), while a son is a light in the highest heaven (*jyotir ha putraḥ parame vyoman*). But there is no proof that the Vedic Indians practised the exposure of female children. This conclusion, deduced from certain passages in the later Saṃhitās[129] by Zimmer[130] and Delbrück,[131] has been disproved by Böhtlingk.

Child Life.—No doubt the care of a child was left to the mother, but we learn little from the earlier literature[132] of the life of the young. The length of the period of pregnancy is frequently placed at ten (doubtless lunar) months.[133] On birth the child was first fed with milk or ghee, and then given the breast.[134] On the eighth day after birth

125 x. 18, 8; 40, 2.

126 Rv. iii. 16, 5.

127 vi. 11, 3. *Cf.* viii. 6, 25.

128 vii. 15. *Cf.* Max Müller, *Ancient Sanskrit Literature*, 409.

129 Taittirīya Saṃhitā, vi. 5, 10, 3; Maitrāyaṇī Saṃhitā, iv. 6, 4; 7, 9; Kāṭhaka Saṃhitā, xxvii. 9; Nirukta, iii. 4; Śāṅkhāyana Śrauta Sūtra, xv. 17, 12.

130 *Altindisches Leben*, 319. *Cf.* Weber, *Naxatra*, 2, 314, n., who cites Pañcaviṃśa Brāhmaṇa, xi. 8, 8, as evidence of the exposure of two boys, but the sense is doubtful.

131 *Die indogermanischen Verwandtschaftsnamen*, 575. See also Weber, *Indische Studien*, 5, 54, 210; Ludwig, Translation of the Rigveda, 6, 142; Kaegi, *Der Rigveda*, n. 49; Schrader, *Prehistoric Antiquities*, 389, 390. Böhtlingk's view is given in *Zeitschrift der Deutschen Morgenländischen Gesellschaft*, 44, 494-496, and *cf.* Pischel, *Vedische Studien*, 2, 48, who compares iv. 18, 5.

132 The later literature is full of details of the ceremonies before and after birth (see Delbrück, *op. cit.*, 573 *et seq.*). Weber, *Naxatra*, 2, 314, n., gives the Vedic embryology; twins were disliked, Aitareya Brāhmaṇa, vii. 9, etc.

133 Rv. v. 78, 9; x. 184, 3; Av. i. 11, 6; iii. 23, 2; Aitareya Brāhmaṇa, vii. 13, 9; Śatapatha Brāhmaṇa, iv. 5, 2, 4; Chāndogya Upaniṣad, v. 9, 1; Weber, *Naxatra*, 2, 314, n. There are in the Av. many spells concerned with birth (i. 11, etc.), and miscarriages are mentioned (*avatokā*, *avasū*, Vājasaneyi Saṃhitā, xxx. 15; Av. viii. 6, 9, etc.).

134 Bṛhadāraṇyaka Upaniṣad, i. 3, 4 (Mādhyaṃdina = i. 5, 2 Kāṇva). *Cf.* also vi. 4, 24 *et seq.*; Satapatha Brāhmaṇa, ii. 5, 1, 6. After being weaned the child is *ati-stana* (Kauṣītaki Brāhmaṇa, xiii. 2).

the infant was washed.[135] The cutting of the teeth was also a solemn occasion,[136] and is the subject of a hymn in the Atharvaveda. Reference is also made to children's learning to speak, which the Taittirīya Saṃhitā[137] ascribes to the end of the first year of life. The Aitareya Āraṇyaka[138] asserts that the words **Tata** and **Tāta**, onomatopoetic words like 'dada,'[139] are the first words of a child's speech, giving therein perhaps an unfair prominence to the father. The Atharvaveda[140] further contains at least one hymn for the ceremony of the first shaving of the young man's beard. The giving of a name was also an occasion of importance, a second one being often added.[141]

Satī.—On the death of her husband, in some cases the widow burned herself or was burned by his relations.[142] This is clearly implied in the reference to this ancient custom in the Atharvaveda.[143] On the other hand, the Rigveda does not contemplate the custom anywhere, but on the contrary considers the widow as married apparently to the brother of the dead man.[144] The custom of Suttee would therefore appear during the Vedic age to have been in abeyance, at least as a general rule. At all times the practice seems to have been mainly usual among families of the warrior class, to judge from the other Indo-Germanic parallels.[145] In other classes

[135] Pañcaviṃśa Brāhmaṇa, xiv. 7, 2 (on Sāmaveda, ii. 525 = Rv. ix. 96, 17). The first ten days were the dangerous period (Aitareya Brāhmaṇa, vii. 14; Pañcaviṃśa Brāhmaṇa, xxii. 14, 3).

[136] Av. vi. 140.

[137] vi. 1, 6, 7. *Cf.* Śatapatha Brāhmaṇa, vii. 4, 2, 38; xi. 1, 6, 3-5.

[138] i. 3, 3.

[139] *Cf.* Delbrück, *op. cit.*, 449, 596.

[140] vi. 68. *Cf.* ii. 13, according to Kauśika Sūtra, 53. 54, and *cf.* Śatapatha Brāhmaṇa, xi. 4, 1, 6.

[141] *Cf.* Aitareya Āraṇyaka, i. 3, 3, with Keith's note; Śatapatha Brāhmaṇa, vi. 1, 3, 9, and **Nāman**.

[142] *Cf.* Schrader, *Prehistoric Antiquities*, 391; von Schroeder, *Indiens Literatur und Cultur*, 41; Jolly, *Recht und Sitte*, 67-69; Weber, *Proceedings of the Berlin Academy*, 1896, 254 *et seq.*; Roth, *Zeitschrift der Deutschen Morgenländischen Gesellschaft*, 8, 468; Wilson, *Journal of the Royal Asiatic Society*, 16, 202; Zimmer, *Altindisches Leben*, 329; Geldner, *Rigveda, Kommentar*, 154.

[143] Av. xviii. 3, 1.

[144] x. 18, 7. 8.

[145] *Cf.* Herodotos, v. 5 (of the Thracians); iv. 71 (of the Scythians); Procopius, *De Bello Gothico*, ii. 14 (of the Heruli). So in Germany Brynhild and Nanna are instances (*cf.* Weinhold, *Altnordisches Leben*, 476 *et seq.*). The universality of the custom must not be exaggerated, as Zimmer, 331, is inclined to do. To burn all the wives of a king would, in primitive ages, have been a

the survival of wives was more necessary, and the remarriage of widows, whether prohibited or allowed in the texts, is proof that there were widows who could be remarried.[146]

wasteful action; even the chief wife would often have had to be spared on one ground or another. The Rigveda already reveals a state of society in which the actual burning of the wife was avoided by a semblance of it in the funeral ritual of (*cf.* Macdonell, *Sanskrit Literature*, 126). The reward of a good wife was to go to the world of her husband (*pati-loka*) after death (*cf.* Av. xiv. 1, 64; xviii. 3, 1; Rv. x. 85, 43). A Vedic citation in the scholiast on Pāṇini, iii. 2, 8, Vārttika, 2, says that a Brahmin woman who drinks **Surā**, an intoxicating liquor, does not go to the world of her husband after death.

[146] *Cf.* perhaps the *gartāruh* of Rv. i. 124, 7, as explained by Yāska, Nirukta, iii. 5; Geldner, *Rigveda, Kommentar*, 22.

Patti is used in the Atharvaveda (vii. 62, 1) to designate the 'foot soldier' in war as opposed to the **Rathin**, 'charioteer,' the latter defeating (*ji*) the former. One of the epithets of Rudra in the Śatarudriya liturgy of the Vājasaneyi Saṃhitā (xvi. 19) is 'lord of footmen' (*pattīnāṃ pati*).

Patnī. See **Pati.** A part of the house is the *Patnīnāṃ Sadana*, mentioned in the Atharvaveda,[1] presumably the women's quarters. The phrase is borrowed from the *Patnī-śāla*, 'hut for the wife,' of the Brāhmaṇa[2] ritual.

[1] ix. 3, 7.

[2] Vājasaneyi Saṃhitā, xix. 18; Śatapatha Brāhmaṇa, iv. 6, 9, 8; x. 2, 3, 1; Aitareya Brāhmaṇa, v. 22 (-*śālā*); Kauṣītaki Brāhmaṇa, xix. 6, etc.

Pathin Saubhara ('descendant of **Sobhari**') is mentioned in the first two Vaṃśas (lists of teachers) in the Bṛhadāraṇyaka Upaniṣad[1] as the pupil of **Ayāsya Āṅgirasa.**

[1] ii. 5, 22 (Mādhyaṃdina = ii. 6, 3 Kāṇva); iv. 5, 28 (Mādhyaṃdina = iv. 6, 3 Kāṇva).

Pathi-kṛt, 'path-maker,' is not a rare epithet in the Rigveda[1] and later,[2] showing clearly the importance naturally attached in primitive times to the finding of roads. The frequency

[1] ii. 23, 6; vi. 21, 12; ix. 106, 5; x. 14, 15; 111, 3, etc.

[2] Av. xviii. 2, 53; 3, 25, etc.

with which the epithet is applied to Agni[3] suggests that there is here an allusion to fire burning the primæval forest and rendering advance possible. The god Pūṣan is *pathi-kṛt*, as guarding the flocks.[4] The Ṛṣis,[5] or seers, as 'path-makers,' may be compared with the Roman Pontifices.

[3] Taittirīya Saṃhitā, ii. 2, 1, 1; Śatapatha Brāhmaṇa, xi. 1, 5, 5; xii. 4, 4, 1; Kauṣītaki Brāhmaṇa, iv. 3, etc.

[4] Sāṅkhāyana Srauta Sūtra, iii. 4, 9; xvi. 1, 17. The Sūtra, xvi. 1, 18, explains *pathi-kṛt* merely as *adhipati*, 'lord'; but the sense must be more pregnant than that.

[5] Rv. x. 14, 15, where the expression refers to their finding the way to the heavenly world; but it is probably a transfer of an epithet of terrestrial application.

Pad in the Atharvaveda (xix. 6, 2) and the Śatapatha Brāhmaṇa (xi. 3, 2, 3) denotes a 'quarter.' This sense is derived from the primary meaning of 'foot,' which as applied to quadrupeds would represent 'one-fourth.' *Cf.* **Pāda.**

Pada in the sense of 'quarter of a stanza' is found as early as the Rigveda[1] and often later.[2] In the Brāhmaṇas it also denotes a 'word' as opposed to a 'letter' (**Varṇa**).[3]

[1] i. 164, 24. 45.

[2] Av. ix. 10, 19; Vājasaneyi Saṃhitā, xix. 25; Aitareya Brāhmaṇa, i. 6. 10. 17, etc.; Kauṣītaki Brāhmaṇa, xxii. 1, 5.

[3] Kauṣītaki Brāhmaṇa, xxvi. 5, where the sequence is half-stanza (*ardharca*), quarter-stanza (*pāda*), word (*pada*), and letter (*varṇa*). *Cf.* Śatapatha Brāhmaṇa, x. 2, 6, 13; xi. 5, 6, 9, etc.

Padi is found once in the Rigveda,[1] where, according to the St. Petersburg Dictionary, the word probably designates some kind of animal. Yāska[2] explains it as equivalent to *gantu*, 'a moving creature,' but Durga[3] as meaning 'bird.' The passage may refer to catching the Padi in a net (? *mukṣījā*).[4]

[1] i. 125, 2.

[2] Nirukta, v. 18.

[3] In his commentary on Nirukta, *loc. cit.*

[4] Oldenberg, *Ṛgveda-Noten*, 1, 129; Zimmer, *Altindisches Leben*, 244.

Payas denotes the 'milk' of the cow in the Rigveda[1] and later.[2] More generally it has also the sense of 'sap' or 'fluid'

[1] i. 164, 28; ii. 14, 10; iv. 3, 9; v. 85, 2; x. 30, 13; 63, 3, etc.

[2] Av. iv. 11, 4; xii. 1, 10; Vājasaneyi Saṃhitā, iv. 3. *Cf.* **Go** and **Kṣīra.**

found in plants,[3] and giving them life and strength. In other passages it denotes the 'water' of heaven.[4] A vow to live for a time on milk alone occurs in the Śatapatha Brāhmaṇa.[5]

[3] Av. iii. 5, 1; x. 1, 12; xiii. 1, 9; Vājasaneyi Saṃhitā, xvii. 1; xviii. 36, etc. So of Soma, Rv. ix. 97, 14.

[4] Rv. i. 64, 5; 166, 3; iii. 33, 1. 4; iv. 57, 8, etc.

[5] *Payo-vrata*, 'one who undergoes a vow (to subsist) on (nothing but) milk,' ix. 5, 1, 1 *et seq.*; Kauṣītaki Brāhmaṇa, viii. 9. The Dīkṣita subsists on it alone.

Payasyā in the later Saṃhitās and Brāhmaṇas[1] denotes curds, said to consist of a mixture of sour milk and hot or cold fresh milk.[2]

[1] Taittirīya Saṃhitā, ii. 3, 13, 2; Taittirīya Brāhmaṇa, i. 5, 11, 2; Aitareya Brāhmaṇa, ii. 22. 24; Śatapatha Brāhmaṇa, ii. 4, 4, 10. 21; 5, 1, 12; 2, 9, etc.

[2] See Eggeling, *Sacred Books of the East*, 12, 381, n. 2.

Para Āṭṇāra ('descendant of Aṭṇāra') appears in the later Saṃhitās[1] and the Brāhmaṇas[2] as one of the ancient great kings who won sons by performing a particular sacrifice. In the Śatapatha Brāhmaṇa[3] he is styled Hairaṇyanābha, 'descendant of Hiraṇyanābha,' and in the Śāṅkhāyana Śrauta Sūtra[4] he is called Para Āhlāra Vaideha, a fact testifying to the close connexion of **Kosala** and **Videha.** A **Yajña-gāthā,** or 'sacrificial verse,' there[5] cited mentions **Hiraṇyanābha Kausalya** in connexion with Para.

[1] Taittirīya Saṃhitā, v. 6, 5, 3; Kāṭhaka Saṃhitā, xxii. 3 (*Indische Studien*, 3, 473).

[2] Pañcaviṃśa Brāhmaṇa, xxv. 16, 3; Jaiminīya Upaniṣad Brāhmaṇa, ii. 6, 11.

[3] xiii. 5, 4, 4.

[4] xvi. 9, 11.

[5] *Ibid.*, 13. *Cf.* Weber, *Indische Studien*, 10, 7; *Episches im vedischen Ritual*, 7; Hillebrandt, *Vedische Mythologie*, 2, 165, n. 4.

Parama-jyā, 'of supreme power,' is understood by Ludwig[1] in one passage of the Rigveda[2] as the proper name of a great man among the **Yadus.** But it is doubtful whether the word is more than an epithet.[3]

[1] Translation of the Rigveda, 3, 159.

[2] viii. 1, 30.

[3] Hopkins, *Journal of the American Oriental Society*, 17, 39.

Paraśu in the Rigveda[1] and later[2] denotes the axe of the woodcutter. Of its form we know nothing. A red-hot axe was used in a form of ordeal (**Divya**) applied in accusations of theft.[3] See also **Parśu.**

[1] i. 127, 3; vii. 104, 21; x. 28, 8; 53, 9, etc.

[2] Av. iii. 19, 4; vii. 28, 1; xi. 9, 1; Kāṭhaka Saṃhitā, xii. 10; Satapatha Brāhmaṇa, iii. 6, 4, 10; Aitareya Brāhmaṇa, ii. 35; Kauṣītaki Brāhmaṇa, x. 1; Kauṣītaki Upaniṣad, ii. 11, etc.

[3] Chāndogya Upaniṣad, vi. 16, 1.

Paraśvan. See **Parasvant.**

Parasvant denotes a large wild animal which Roth[1] conjectures to be the wild ass. It is mentioned in the Vṛṣākapi hymn[2] of the Rigveda, twice in the Atharvaveda,[3] and in the list of victims at the Aśvamedha ('horse sacrifice') in the Yajurveda Saṃhitās,[4] in all of which passages the sense of 'wild ass' is satisfactory. More doubtful is the meaning of the word *paraśvā(n)* in the Kauṣītaki Upaniṣad,[5] where the commentary explains it as 'serpent.' It is, of course, quite possible that the word has nothing to do with *parasvant.* Bühler[6] suggests connexion with the Pāli *palāsāda,* 'rhinoceros.'

[1] St. Petersburg Dictionary, *s.v.*

[2] x. 86, 18.

[3] vi. 72, 2; xx. 131, 22.

[4] Maitrāyaṇī Saṃhitā, iii. 14, 10; Vājasaneyi Saṃhitā, xxiv. 8; Taittirīya Saṃhitā, v. 5, 21, 1, where the commentator takes it to be the wild buffalo.

[5] i. 2.

[6] *Zeitschrift der Deutschen Morgenländischen Gesellschaft,* 48, 63; Keith, *Śāṅkhāyana Āraṇyaka,* 17, n. 1; *Aitareya Āraṇyaka,* 377, n. 1.

Cf. Ludwig, Translation of the Rigveda, 2, 633; Zimmer, *Altindisches Leben,* 86, 87; Whitney, Translation of the Atharvaveda, 335; Geldner, *Rigveda, Glossar,* 105.

Parā-vṛj is a term found in four passages of the Rigveda,[1] in all of which it refers to a person in a forlorn condition, while one[2] of them also speaks of him as going south. Sāyaṇa's[3] view that the word is a proper name is most unlikely, while Grassmann's[4] explanation of it as 'cripple' is still less probable.

[1] i. 112, 8; ii. 13, 12; 15, 7; x. 61, 8.

[2] x. 61, 8.

[3] On i. 112, 8, etc., *cf.* Macdonell, *Vedic Mythology,* 152.

[4] Translation of the Rigveda, 1, 23, and *cf. Wörterbuch, s.v.*

Roth's[5] interpretation of it as 'exile' seems clearly right in the passage which refers to the Parāvṛj as going south. Zimmer[6] accepts Roth's view for this passage, but in the others sees a reference to the child of a maiden exposed by her and in danger of being eaten by insects (*vamrī*). This view is supported by the fact that *parāvṛkta* seems to have the same sense,[7] and is accepted by Oldenberg.[8]

[5] St. Petersburg Dictionary, *s.v.*

[6] *Altindisches Leben*, 185, 334, 335.

[7] Rv. iv. 30, 19. *Cf.* iv. 30, 16; 19, 9.

[8] *Ṛgveda-Noten*, 1, 200. *Cf.* above, p. 481, n. 67.

Cf. Muir, *Sanskrit Texts*, 5, 248; Schrader, *Prehistoric Antiquities*, 402.

Parāśara is mentioned with **Śatayātu** and **Vasiṣṭha** in the Rigvedic hymn celebrating **Sudās'**[1] victory over the ten kings. According to the Nirukta[2] he was a son of Vasiṣṭha, but the Epic version makes him a son of **Śakti** and grandson of Vasiṣṭha. Geldner[3] thinks that he is mentioned in the Rigveda along with Śatayātu, perhaps his uncle, and his grandfather Vasiṣṭha, as the three sages who approached Indra and won his favour for Sudās. He is erroneously credited with the authorship of certain hymns of the Rigveda[4] by the Anukramaṇī (Index).

[1] vii. 18, 21.

[2] vi. 30.

[3] *Vedische Studien*, 2, 132.

[4] i. 65-73.

Cf. Ludwig, Translation of the Rigveda, 3, 110, 111; Weber, *Indische Studien*, 9, 324. The Parāśaras as a school appear in the Kāṭhaka Anukramaṇī (*Indische Studien*, 3, 460).

Pari-kṣit appears in the Atharvaveda[1] as a king in whose realm, that of the Kurus, prosperity and peace abound. The verses in which he is celebrated are later[2] called *Pārikṣityaḥ*, and the Brāhmaṇas explain that Agni is *pari-kṣit* because he dwells among men. Hence Roth[3] and Bloomfield[4] regard Parikṣit in the Atharvaveda not as a human king at all. This may be correct, but it is not certain. Both Zimmer[5] and

[1] xx. 127, 7-10. See also Scheftelowitz, *Die Apokryphen des Veda*, 156, 157, and the verses in the Vaitāna Sūtra, xxxiv. 9. The Vedic spelling is Parikṣit, not Parīkṣit.

[2] Aitareya Brāhmaṇa, vi. 32, 10; Kauṣītaki Brāhmaṇa, xxx. 5; Gopatha Brāhmaṇa, ii. 6, 12; Śāṅkhāyana Śrauta Sūtra, xii. 17.

[3] St. Petersburg Dictionary, *s.v.*

[4] *Hymns of the Atharvaveda*, 690, 691, but see *Atharvaveda*, 101, n. 9.

[5] *Altindisches Leben*, 131.

Oldenberg[6] recognize Parikṣit as a real king, a view supported by the fact that in the later Vedic literature King **Janamejaya** bears the patronymic **Pārikṣita.** If this be so, Parikṣit belonged to the later period, since the Atharvan passage in which his name occurs is certainly late, and none of the other Saṃhitās know Parikṣit at all. The Epic[7] makes him grandfather of Pratiśravas and great-grandfather of Pratīpa, and Zimmer,[5] probably with justice, compares the Prātisutvana and Pratīpa found in another late Atharvan passage.[8] But **Devāpi** and **Śantanu** cannot be brought into connexion with Pratīpa.[9]

6 *Zeitschrift der Deutschen Morgenländischen Gesellschaft*, 42, 237; *Buddha*, 396.

7 See Zimmer, *loc. cit.*

8 xx. 129.

9 Devāpi is really a Brahmin, son of Ṛṣṭiṣeṇa, and not connected directly with Śantanu. Yāska, Nirukta, ii. 10, identifies them as brothers and Kurus; but the former part of the identification is, no doubt, wrong.

Pari-gha denotes an iron bolt or bar in the Chāndogya Upaniṣad (ii. 24, 6. 10. 15) as often later.

Pari-cakrā is according to one reading the name of a **Pañcāla** town mentioned in the Śatapatha Brāhmaṇa[1] and identified by Weber[2] with the later Ekacakrā, which was near **Kāmpīla.**[3] There is a various reading Parivakrā.[4]

1 xiii. 5. 4, 7.

2 *Indische Studien*, 1, 192.

3 Mahābhārata, i. 6094.

4 Accepted by the scholiast and Eggeling, *Sacred Books of the East*, 44, 397.

Pari-cara is found in the Śatapatha Brāhmaṇa[1] in the sense of 'attendant.' In the Kauṣītaki Brāhmaṇa[2] *pari-caraṇa* has the same sense metaphorically, the other two Vedas (Sāma and Yajur) being said to be subsidiary to the Rigveda.

1 iv. 3, 5. 9. *Cf. pari-caritṛ*, Chāndogya Upaniṣad, vii. 8, 1.

2 vi. 11; Max Müller, *Ancient Sanskrit Literature*, 457.

Pari-carmaṇya denotes a thong of leather in the Kauṣītaki Brāhmaṇa (vi. 12) and the Śāṅkhāyana Āraṇyaka (ii. 1).

Pari-takmyā in a number of passages of the Rigveda[1] denotes 'night' according to the St. Petersburg Dictionary.

1 i. 116, 15; iv. 41, 6; 43, 3; v. 30, 13; 31, 11; vi. 24, 9; vii. 69, 4.

Sieg[2] thinks that in one place[3] at least the word signifies the decisive point of the race, something like the sense of **Prapitva.** But this is very doubtful.

[2] *Die Sagenstoffe des Ṛgveda*, 128. *Cf.* Geldner, *Vedische Studien*, 2, 36; *Rigveda, Glossar*, 106.
[3] i. 116, 15.

Pari-dā in a few passages of the Śatapatha Brāhmaṇa[1] has the sense of 'giving oneself up to the mercy or protection of another.'

[1] ii. 4, 1, 11; ix. 2, 1, 17; 4, 2, 17; 4, 5; 5, 1, 53.

Pari-dhāna denotes 'garment,' probably 'under garment,' in the Atharvaveda (viii. 2, 16) and the Bṛhadāraṇyaka Upaniṣad (vi. 1, 10). A garment of saffron is mentioned in the Śāṅkhāyana Āraṇyaka (xi. 4).

Pari-pad seems in the Rigveda[1] to denote a pitfall used to capture lions.

[1] x. 28, 10; metaphorically, viii. 24, 24.

Pari-panthin, 'besetting the path,' denotes 'robber' in the Rigveda[1] and later.[2] *Cf.* **Taskara, Tāyu, Stena.**

[1] i. 42, 3; 103, 6; x. 85, 32.
[2] Av. i. 27, 1; iii. 15, 1; xii. 1, 32; Vājasaneyi Saṃhitā, iv. 34, etc.

Pari-pavana signifies in the Nirukta (iv. 9. 10) an instrument for winnowing grain.

Pari-mit occurs once in the Atharvaveda[1] in the description of a house, meaning perhaps the 'crossbeams' connecting the vertical posts.[2] *Cf.* **Gṛha.**

[1] ix. 3, 1.
[2] Bloomfield, *Hymns of the Atharvaveda*, 596; Zimmer, *Altindisches Leben*, 158; Whitney, Translation of the Atharvaveda, 525.

Pari-moṣa in the Taittirīya Saṃhitā[1] signifies 'theft,' and *parimoṣin* in the Śatapatha Brāhmaṇa[2] 'thief.'

[1] ii. 5, 5, 1; vi. 1, 11, 5.
[2] xi. 6, 3, 11; xiii. 2, 4, 2, etc.

Pari-rathya occurs once in the Atharvaveda[1] meaning either 'road'[2] or a part of the chariot, perhaps as Ludwig[3] and Whitney[4] render it, the 'rim.'

[1] viii. 8, 22.

[2] Bloomfield, *Hymns of the Atharvaveda*, 587, following Nīlakaṇṭha's explanation of *parirathya*, Mahābhārata, viii. 1487.

[3] Translation of the Rigveda, 3, 528.

[4] Translation of the Atharvaveda, 506.

Pari-vakrā is the reading accepted in the Śatapatha Brāhmaṇa (xiii. 5, 4, 7) by the scholiast instead of the variant **Paricakrā**, which is supported by the Epic Ekacakrā.

Pari-vatsara denotes in the Rigveda[1] and later[2] a 'full year.' It is often mentioned with other names of year (see **Saṃvatsara**), and in the later five year cycle counts as the second year.

[1] x. 62, 2.

[2] Taittirīya Brāhmaṇa i. 5, 5, 6; Mahābhārata, i. 3202, etc. So *parivatsarīṇa*, as an adjective, 'relating to a full year,' Rv. vii. 103, 8; Av. iii. 10, 3.

Pari-vāpa in the later Saṃhitās[1] and Brāhmaṇas[2] denotes 'fried grains of rice.'

[1] Taittirīya Saṃhitā, iii. 1, 10, 1; vi. 5, 11, 4; vii. 2, 10, 4; Kāṭhaka Saṃhitā, xxxiv. 11; Vājasaneyi Saṃhitā, xix. 21. 22.

[2] Aitareya Brāhmaṇa, ii. 24; Taittirīya Brāhmaṇa, i. 5, 11, 2, etc.

Pari-vitta denotes an 'elder brother who is not married when his younger brother is.' The term occurs in the list of sinful persons in the Yajurveda Saṃhitās[1] as well as in the Atharvaveda,[2] where Ludwig[3] needlessly proposes to read *parivettā*, the 'younger brother who marries before his eldest brother.' The name for the younger brother in the older texts is Parividāna.[4]

[1] Kāṭhaka Saṃhitā, xxxi. 7; Kapiṣṭhala Saṃhitā, xlvii. 7; Maitrāyaṇī Saṃhitā, iv. 1, 9; Taittirīya Brāhmaṇa, iii. 2, 8, 11; Vājasaneyi Saṃhitā, xxx. 9.

[2] vi. 112, 3.

[3] Translation of the Rigveda, 3, 470.

[4] So in the Kāṭhaka, Kapiṣṭhala, Maitrāyaṇī, and Vājasaneyi Saṃhitās, *loc. cit.*

Cf. Delbrück, *Die indogermanischen Verwandtschaftsnamen*, 580 *et seq.*; Bloomfield, *American Journal of Philology*, 17, 430 *et seq.*; *Hymns of the Atharvaveda*, 522 *et seq.*; Zimmer, *Altindisches Leben*, 315; Whitney, Translation of the Atharvaveda, 362.

Pari-vṛl tā, Pari-vṛktī, Pari-vṛttī, are variant forms of the name of the rejected one among the royal wives. See **Pati.**

Pari-veṣṭṛ in the Atharvaveda[1] and later[2] denotes an 'attendant,' more especially one who serves up food, a 'waiter.' The feminine form Pariveṣṭrī signifies a 'female attendant' or 'handmaid.'[3]

[1] ix. 6, 51.
[2] Taittirīya Saṃhitā, vi. 3, 1, 3; Maitrāyaṇī Saṃhitā, i. 2, 16; Vājasaneyi Saṃhitā, vi. 13; xxx. 12. 13; Taittirīya Brāhmaṇa, iii. 4, 8, 1; Aitareya Brāhmaṇa, viii. 21; Śatapatha Brāhmaṇa, xiii. 5, 4, 6; iii. 8, 2, 3; vi. 2, 13, 3, etc.
[3] Satapatha Brāhmaṇa, xi. 2, 7, 4; Kauṣītaki Upaniṣad, ii. 1; Keith, *Śāṅkhāyana Āraṇyaka*, 21, n. 2.

Pari-vrājaka (lit., 'wandering about') denotes in the Nirukta (i. 14; ii. 8) a 'mendicant monk.'

Pari-ṣad (lit., 'sitting around') denotes in the Upaniṣads[1] an 'assemblage' of advisers in questions of philosophy, and the Gobhila Gṛhya Sūtra[2] refers to a teacher with his Pariṣad or 'council.' In the later literature the word denotes a body of advisers on religious topics, but also the assessors of a judge, or the council of ministers of a prince.[3] But in none of these senses is the word found in the early literature, though the institutions indicated by it must have existed at least in embryo.

[1] Bṛhadāraṇyaka Upaniṣad, vi. 1, 1 (Mādhyaṃdina = vi. 2, 1 Kāṇva); *daivī pariṣad*, Jaiminīya Upaniṣad Brāhmaṇa, ii. 11, 13. 14.
[2] iii. 2, 40.
[3] *Cf.* Jolly, *Recht und Sitte*, 136, 137; Foy, *Die königliche Gewalt*, 16-19, 33-37; 66; Bühler, *Zeitschrift der Deutschen Morgenländischen Gesellschaft*, 48, 55, 56; Hillebrandt, *Vedische Mythologie*, 2, 124.

Pari-ṣkanda (lit., 'leaping around') occurs in the **Vrātya** hymn of the Atharvaveda (xv. 2, 1 *et seq.*) denoting, in the dual, the two footmen running beside a chariot.

Pari-ṣyanda (with water 'flowing around') in two passages of the Śatapatha Brāhmaṇa (ix. 2, 1, 19; xiv. 3, 1, 14) denotes a sandbank or island in a river.

Pari-sāraka is the name of a place, an island formed by the **Sarasvatī** 'flowing around' it, according to a story in the Aitareya Brāhmaṇa (ii. 19).

Pari-srut is the name of a drink which is mentioned first in the Atharvaveda,[1] and which was distinct from both **Surā** and **Soma**,[2] but was intoxicating. According to Mahīdhara,[3] the liquor was made from flowers (**Puṣpa**). Zimmer[4] thinks that it was the family drink, and this is supported by the fact that in the Atharvaveda it twice occurs as a household beverage.[5] Hillebrandt[6] is of opinion that it was very much the same as Surā.

[1] iii. 12, 7; xx. 127, 9. *Cf.* Hopkins, *Journal of the American Oriental Society*, 17, 68.

[2] Śatapatha Brāhmaṇa, v. 1, 2, 14. *Cf.* v. 5, 4, 10; xi. 5, 5, 13; xii. 7, 1, 7; 8, 2, 15; 9, 1, 1.

[3] On Vājasaneyi Saṃhitā, ii. 34.

[4] *Altindisches Leben*, 281, 282.

[5] See also Vājasaneyi Saṃhitā, xix. 15; xx. 59; xxi. 29; Maitrāyaṇī Saṃhitā, iii. 11, 2. Its nature is more elaborately explained in the Kātyāyana Śrauta Sūtra, xiv. 1, 14; xv. 10, 11; Weber, *Indische Studien*, 10, 349, 350.

[6] *Vedische Mythologie*, 1, 24, 8.

1. **Parī-ṇah** appears to denote a 'box' or something similar in the Atharvaveda (xix. 48, 1).

2. **Parī-ṇah** is the name of a place in **Kurukṣetra** mentioned in the Pañcaviṃśa Brāhmaṇa,[1] the Taittirīya Āraṇyaka,[2] and the Sūtras.[3]

[1] xxv. 13, 1.

[2] v. 1, 1.

[3] Lāṭyāyana Śrauta Sūtra, x. 19, 1; Kātyāyana Śrauta Sūtra, xxiv. 6, 34; Śāṅkhāyana Śrauta Sūtra, xiii. 29, 32.

Parī-śāsa is the name of an instrument of the nature of tongs, used to lift the sacrificial kettle off the fire.[1]

[1] Śatapatha Brāhmaṇa, xiv. 1, 3, 1; 2, 1, 16; 2, 54; 3, 1, 20, etc.

Paruc-chepa is the name of a Ṛṣi to whom the Anukramaṇī (Index) attributes a series of hymns[1] in the Rigveda, and whose

[1] Rv. i. 127-139.

authorship is asserted in the Aitareya[2] and the Kauṣītaki[3] Brāhmaṇas, as well as in the Nirukta.[4] In the Taittirīya Saṃhitā[5] he appears as a rival of **Nṛmedhas.**

[2] v. 12. 13 (where hymns Rv. i. 128, 129, 130, 133, 135, 137, 139, are attributed to him).

[3] xxiii. 4. 5.

[4] x. 42.

[5] ii. 5, 8, 3.

Cf. Ludwig, Translation of the Rigveda, 3, 116. Parucchepa's claim to authorship is very doubtful.

Paruṣa seems to mean 'reed' in the Atharvaveda (viii. 8, 4) and 'arrow' in the Śāṅkhāyana Śrauta Sūtra (xiv. 22, 20).

Paruṣṇī is the name of a river which is mentioned in the Nadī-stuti ('Praise of Rivers'),[1] and in the song of Sudās' victory over the ten kings,[2] which seems to have been made decisive by the rise of the river drowning the fugitives.[3] In these passages and one of the eighth book of the Rigveda,[4] where it is called a 'great stream' (*mahenadi*), the name is certainly that of the river later called Ravi (Irāvatī), as recognized by Yāska.[5] Pischel[6] sees a reference to it in two other passages of the Rigveda,[7] where 'wool' (*ūrṇā*) is connected with the word *paruṣṇī*, and the allusion to the river is accepted by Max Müller[8] and Oldenberg,[9] though they are not fully agreed as to the exact sense of the passages in question. Pischel suggests that the name is derived from the 'flocks' (*parus*) of wool, not from the bends of the river, as understood by the Nirukta,[5] or from its reeds, as Roth[10] suggests.

[1] x. 75, 5.

[2] vii. 18, 8. 9.

[3] It is impossible to decide precisely what part the river played in the battle. It is usually held that the enemies of Sudās tried to divert the stream, but failed, and were drowned in its current. So Zimmer, *Altindisches Leben*, 11; Macdonell, *Sanskrit Literature*, 154; Geldner, *Rigveda, Kommentar*, 103, holds that Sudās was caught between two opposing armies, and had to escape over the Paruṣṇī, that his enemies tried to divert it to render him more accessible to their attack, but failed, and were overwhelmed in the river. Hopkins, *India, Old and New*, 52 *et seq.*, may be right in rejecting *in toto* the theory of the attempted diversion of the waters, though in the *Journal of the American Oriental Society*, 15, 261 *et seq.*, he accepted the traditional view.

[4] viii. 74, 15.

[5] Nirukta, ix. 26.

[6] *Vedische Studien*, 2, 208-210.

[7] iv. 22, 2; v. 52, 9.

[8] *Sacred Books of the East*, 32, 315, 323.

[9] *Ṛgveda-Noten*, 1, 348.

[10] St. Petersburg Dictionary, *s.v.* 4*a*.

The mention of the Paruṣṇī and the Yamunā in the hymn celebrating the victory of Sudās has given rise to the conjectures of Hopkins,[11] that the Yamunā in that hymn is merely another name for the Paruṣṇī, and of Geldner,[12] that the Paruṣṇī there is merely a tributary of the Yamunā (Jumna). But neither interpretation is either essential or even probable. The hymn is a condensed one, and may well be taken as celebrating two great victories of Sudās. There is a doubtful reference to the Paruṣṇī in the Atharvaveda.[13]

[11] *Op. cit.*, 52.
[12] *Ṛgveda, Glossar*, 106.
[13] vi. 12, 3. *Cf.* Bloomfield, *Hymns of the Atharvaveda*, 462; Whitney, Translation of the Atharvaveda, 289.

Parus means first a 'limb' or 'member' of the body,[1] and is then applied metaphorically to the divisions of the sacrifice[2] or of the year[3] (*cf.* **Parvan**).

[1] Rv. i. 162, 18; x. 97, 12; 100, 5; Av. i. 12, 3; iv. 12, 2. 3, etc.
[2] Rv. x. 53, 1; Taittirīya Brāhmaṇa, i. 6, 9, 1.
[3] Taittirīya Saṃhitā, ii. 5, 6, 1.

1. **Parṇa** denotes the 'wing' of a bird in the Rigveda[1] and later.[2] It also means the 'feather' of an arrow in a late passage of the Rigveda,[3] and more often later;[4] and the 'leaf' of a tree from the Rigveda onwards.[5]

[1] i. 116, 15; 182, 7; 183, 1; iv. 27, 4, etc.
[2] Av. x. 1, 29; Satapatha Brāhmaṇa, i. 6, 3, 5, etc.
[3] x. 18, 14. *Cf.* Lanman, *Sanskrit Reader*, 386.
[4] Av. v. 25, 1; Kāṭhaka Saṃhitā, xxv. 1; Aitareya Brāhmaṇa, i. 25; iii. 26, etc.
[5] Rv. x. 68, 10; Av. viii. 7, 12; Taittirīya Saṃhitā, ii. 5, 1, 7; Vājasaneyi Saṃhitā, xvi. 46, etc.

2. **Parṇa** denotes the tree *Butea frondosa*, later usually called **Palāśa.** It occurs in the Rigveda[1] in connexion with the **Aśvattha,** and with that tree as well as the **Nyagrodha** in the Atharvaveda,[2] which mentions both amulets[3] and the cover of sacrificial dishes[4] as made from its wood. Its use for the

[1] x. 97, 5.
[2] v. 5, 5.
[3] iii. 5, 4. 8.
[4] xviii. 4, 53.

making of sacrificial implements like the ladle (*juhū*),[5] or sacrificial posts,[6] or the small ladle called *sruva*,[7] is mentioned. The Taittirīya Saṃhitā[8] ascribes its origin to the loss of a feather by the Gāyatrī when winning the Soma. The tree is also often mentioned elsewhere.[9] Reference too is sometimes made to its bark (*parṇa-valka*).[10]

[5] Taittirīya Saṃhitā, iii. 5, 7, 2. *Cf.* Maitrāyaṇī Saṃhitā, iv. 1, 1.

[6] Pañcaviṃśa Brāhmaṇa, xxi. 4, 13.

[7] Kāṭhaka Saṃhitā, xv. 2. *Cf.* viii. 2; Taittirīya Brāhmaṇa, i. 1, 3, 11; 7, 1, 9; 8, 7.

[8] Taittirīya Saṃhitā, *loc. cit.*, and *cf.* Kuhn, *Die Herabkunft des Feuers und des Göttertranks*, 148, 192; Bloomfield, *Journal of the American Oriental Society*, 16, 20. 24; *Hymns of the Atharvaveda*, 331, 332; Whitney, Translation of the Atharvaveda, 91.

[9] Śatapatha Brāhmaṇa, iii. 3, 4, 10; vi. 5, 1, 1; xi. 1, 4, 2; 7, 28; Pañcaviṃśa Brāhmaṇa, ix. 5, 4.

[10] Taittirīya Saṃhitā, ii. 5, 3, 5; Taittirīya Brāhmaṇa, iii. 7, 4, 2. 18, etc.

Cf. Zimmer, *Altindisches Leben*, 59; Weber, *Indische Studien*, 17, 194, 195.

Parṇaka is the name of a man included in the list of victims at the Puruṣamedha ('human sacrifice') in the Vājasaneyi Saṃhitā[1] and the Taittirīya Brāhmaṇa.[2] According to Mahīdhara,[3] a Bhilla is meant—*i.e.*, presumably a wild hillman, for he glosses **Niṣāda** in the same way.[4] Sāyaṇa[5] explains the word as meaning 'one who catches fish by putting over the water a *parṇa* with poison,' but this is apparently a mere etymological guess. Weber's[6] rendering of the term as referring to a savage 'wearing feathers' is ingenious, but uncertain.

[1] xxx. 16.

[2] iii. 4, 12, 1.

[3] On Vājasaneyi Saṃhitā, *loc. cit.*

[4] On Vājasaneyi Saṃhitā, xvi. 27.

[5] On Taittirīya Brāhmaṇa, *loc. cit.*

[6] *Zeitschrift der Deutschen Morgenländischen Gesellschaft*, 18, 281.

Cf. Zimmer, *Altindisches Leben*, 119.

Parṇa-dhi in the Atharvaveda[1] denotes the part of the shaft in which the feather of the arrow is fastened.

[1] iv. 6, 5. *Cf.* Zimmer, *Altindisches Leben*, 300; Bloomfield, *Hymns of the Atharvaveda*, 375; Whitney, Translation of the Atharvaveda, 154.

Parṇaya is the name in two passages of the Rigveda[1] either of a hero, as Ludwig[2] thinks, or of a demon[3] overcome by Indra.

[1] i. 53, 8; x. 48, 2.

[2] Translation of the Rigveda, 3, 149.

[3] St. Petersburg Dictionary, *s.v.*

Pary-aṅka is the name of the seat of the Brahman in the Kauṣītaki Upaniṣad.[1] It seems to correspond to what is elsewhere called **Āsandi**;[2] as used in the Upaniṣad, it can, however, hardly mean a long seat for reclining on, but rather a throne.[3]

[1] i. 5.

[2] Av. xv. 3, 3. *Cf.* xiv. 2, 65; Aitareya Brāhmaṇa, viii. 5. 6. 12.

[3] *Cf.* Weber, *Indische Studien*, 1, 397, 401; Zimmer, *Altindisches Leben*, 155; Lanman in Whitney, Translation of the Atharvaveda, 765, 776.

Pary-āsa is used in the Śatapatha Brāhmaṇa (iii. 1, 2, 18) to denote the woof of cloth, the warp being called *anuchāda*.

1. **Parvata** in the Rigveda[1] and the Atharvaveda[2] is conjoined with *giri* in the sense of 'hill' or 'mountain.' From the Rigveda[3] onwards[4] it is common in this sense as connected with the waters of rivers which flow in the hills.[5] The legend of the mountains having wings is already found in the Saṃhitās.[6] In the Kauṣītaki Upaniṣad[7] are mentioned the southern (*dakṣiṇa*) and the northern (*uttara*) mountains, evidently in allusion to the Himālaya and the Vindhya ranges. The plants (*oṣadhi*) and aromatic products (*añjana*) of the mountains are referred to in the Atharvaveda,[8] and their mineral treasures in the Rigveda.[9]

[1] i. 37, 7; v. 56, 4.

[2] Av. iv. 6, 8; vi. 12, 3; 17, 3; ix. 1, 18; xii. 1, 11.

[3] i. 39, 5; 52, 2; 155, 1; 191, 9; ii. 12, 2. 3; 17, 5, etc.

[4] Av. i. 14, 1; iii. 21, 10; iv. 9, 8; viii. 7, 17; Taittirīya Saṃhitā, iii. 4, 5, 1; Vājasaneyi Saṃhitā, xvii. 1; xviii. 13, etc.

[5] Rv. vii. 34, 23; 35, 8; viii. 18, 16; 31, 10; x. 35, 2; 36, 1, etc.; Pischel, *Vedische Studien*, i. 80; 2, 66.

[6] Kāṭhaka Saṃhitā, xxxvi. 9; Maitrāyaṇī Saṃhitā, i. 10, 13; and Rv. iv. 54, 5, as explained by Pischel, *Vedische Studien*, 1, 174.

[7] ii. 13; Weber, *Indische Studien*, 1, 407; Keith, *Śāṅkhāyana Āraṇyaka*, 28, n. 1.

[8] xix. 44, 6; 45, 7.

[9] x. 69, 6.

2. **Parvata** in one passage of the Rigveda[1] denotes, according to Ludwig,[2] a sacrificer whose generosity is praised. But it is probable that the god Parvata, the spirit of the mountain, is meant.[3]

[1] vii. 87, 8.

[2] Translation of the Rigveda, 3, 159.

[3] St. Petersburg Dictionary, *s.v.*

3. **Parvata** is mentioned several times in the Aitareya Brāhmaṇa[1] along with **Nārada.** The Anukramaṇī (Index) attributes to him the authorship of several hymns of the Rigveda.[2]

[1] vii. 13, 34; viii. 21; Śāṅkhāyana Śrauta Sūtra, xv. 17, 4.

[2] viii. 12; ix. 104; 105.

Parvan denotes the knots of the reed or the joints of a plant,[1] and more generally a part or limb of the body.[2] It also designates a period of time, probably with reference to the breaks in the month at new and full moon.[3] In one passage[4] Geldner[5] thinks the word indicates a song section of the Sāmaveda.

[1] Av. xii. 3, 31; Taittirīya Saṃhitā, i. 1, 2, 1; Śatapatha Brāhmaṇa, vi. 3, 1, 31, and *cf.* Rv. x. 68, 9.

[2] Rv. i. 61, 12; iv. 19, 9; viii. 48, 5; x. 89, 8; Av. i. 11, 1; 12, 2; ii. 9, 1; vi. 14, 1; xi. 8, 12; xii. 5, 71; Aitareya Brāhmaṇa, iii. 31; Śatapatha Brāhmaṇa, i. 6, 3, 35 *et seq.*; iii. 4, 4, 2; vi. 1, 2, 31; x. 4, 5, 2, etc.

[3] Rv. i. 94, 4; Vājasaneyi Saṃhitā, xiii. 43; Śatapatha Brāhmaṇa, i. 6, 3, 35; vi. 2, 2, 34, etc. *Cf.* **Māsa**. In the Sūtras the days of the four-monthly festivals (*cāturmāsya*) are so called: Kātyāyana Srauta Sūtra, v. 2, 13; xxii. 7, 1. 16. 17; xxiv. 4, 30; Śāṅkhāyana Śrauta Sūtra, xiv. 5, 6; 10, 4. 18; Āśvalāyana Śrauta Sūtra, ix. 2, 3; and more often the periods of the change of moon: Kātyāyana Śrauta Sūtra, xxiv. 6, 4. 25. 30; Śāṅkhāyana Śrauta Sūtra, iii. 2, 1; 3, 1; Lāṭyāyana Srauta Sūtra, viii. 8, 46, etc.

[4] vii. 103, 5.

[5] *Ṛgveda, Glossar*, 107.

Cf. Zimmer, *Altindisches Leben*, 364, who quotes Tacitus, *Germania*, 11.

Parśāna, 'hollow,' is mentioned several times in the Rigveda (vii. 104, 5; viii. 7, 34; 45, 41).

1. **Parśu** denotes 'rib' in the Atharvaveda[1] and later.[2] *Cf.* **Śarīra.**

[1] ix. 7, 6; x. 9, 20; xi. 3, 12.

[2] Taittirīya Saṃhitā, vii. 5, 25, 1; Kāṭhaka Saṃhitā, xxxi. 1; Śatapatha Brāhmaṇa, viii. 6, 2, 10; x. 6, 4, 1; xii. 3, 1, 6; Ṣaḍviṃśa Brāhmaṇa, i. 3, etc

2. **Parśu** seems in some passages[1] to denote a 'sickle,' being apparently a variant of **Paraśu.**

[1] Av. xii. 3, 31 (Kauśika Sūtra, i. 24. 25; viii. 11; lxi. 38. 39); perhaps vii. 28, 1 = Taittirīya Saṃhitā, iii. 2, 4, 1. See Whitney, Translation of the Atharvaveda, 407, 408; Bṛhadāraṇyaka Upaniṣad, vi. 4, 26 (where *parśu* is metrically needed), etc. *Cf.* Böhtlingk, Dictionary, *s.v.*

3. **Parśu** in the Nirukta[1] is explained in one passage of the Rigveda[2] as meaning the sides of a cistern (*kūpa*).[3] But the sense of 'ribs' is quite adequate there.

[1] iv. 6.

[2] i. 105, 8; x. 33, 2.

[3] Oldenberg, *Ṛgveda-Noten*, 1, 100; Geldner, *Rigveda, Glossar*, 107.

4. **Parśu** occurs in one passage in a Dānastuti ('praise of gifts') in the Rigveda[1] as the name of a man. It is not certain that he is identical with **Tirindira**, but the Śāṅkhāyana Śrauta Sūtra[2] mentions Tirindira Pāraśavya as the patron of **Vatsa Kāṇva**. In another passage occurring in the Vṛṣākapi hymn,[3] Parśu Mānavī occurs, apparently as a woman, daughter of Manu, but who is meant it is quite impossible to say. Excepting these two, there are no other occurrences in which the word has with any probability the value of a proper name in the Rigveda.

Ludwig,[4] however, sees in several other places an allusion to the Parśus. Thus in one passage of the Rigveda[5] he finds a reference to the defeat of **Kuruśravaṇa** by the Parśus; in another[6] he finds a reference to the Pṛthus and Parśus—*i.e.*, the Parthians and the Persians. He also sees the Parthians in **Pārthava**, a name found in one hymn.[7] The same view is taken by Weber,[8] who holds that historical connexions with the

[1] viii. 6, 46.

[2] xvi. 11, 20.

[3] x. 86, 23. Apparently Vārttika 2, on Pāṇini, iv. 1, 177, where Parśu is explained as a feminine, Princess of the Parśus, refers to this passage. On the sense, *cf.* Geldner, *Vedische Studien*, 2, 42; *Rigveda, Glossar*, 107; and Taittirīya Brāhmaṇa, iii. 2, 2, 2, where the expression occurs, but where the sense is very dubious.

[4] Translation of the Rigveda, 3, 196 *et seq.*

[5] x. 33, 2. The sense here is, no doubt, 'ribs.' See Geldner, *op. cit.*, 2, 184, n. 3; Bergaigne, *Religion Védique*, 2, 362, n.

[6] vii. 83, 1, *pṛthu-parśavaḥ*, which really means either 'with large ribs'—*i.e.*, 'strong,' as Roth, with Sāyaṇa, inclines to take it—or 'with broad axes,' according to Zimmer.

[7] vi. 27, 8.

[8] *Indische Studien*, 4, 379; *Indian Literature*, 4; *Episches im vedischen Ritual*, 36 *et seq.* He confines his view to the equation of Parśu in Rigveda, viii. 6, 46, and the Persians. Hillebrandt, who is inclined to see relations with Iran in early times (see **Paṇi, Pārāvata, Sṛñjaya**), does not in this connexion quote Parśu at all, and, though he mentions Pārthava, does not regard it as probably referring to a Parthian (*Vedische Mythologie*, 1, 105). Brunnhofer, in his various works (*Iran und Turan*, 1889; *vom Pontus bis zum Indus*, 1890, etc.), finds constant references in the Veda to events in Iran, but his theories must be regarded as definitely unscientific. See also Hopkins, *Journal of the American Oriental Society*, 15, 264, n.

Persians are referred to. But Zimmer[9] points out that this conclusion is not justified; the Parśus were known to Pāṇini[10] as a warrior tribe; the Pāraśavas were a tribe in south-west **Madhyadeśa**; and the *Periplus*[11] knows a tribe of Parthoi in north India. At most the only conclusion to be drawn is that the Indians and Iranians were early connected, as was of course the case. Actual historical contact cannot be asserted with any degree of probability.

9 *Altindisches Leben*, 134 *et seq.*; 433. *Ibid.*, 434, 435, he refutes conclusively Ludwig's extraordinary view that Pṛthu and Parśu are dialectical forms of the same word.

10 v. 3, 117.

11 c. 38.

Parṣa occurs in the Rigveda,[1] denoting in the plural 'sheaves' strewn over the threshing floor. *Cf.* **Khala.**

1 x. 48, 7; Nirukta, iii. 10. *Cf.* Zimmer, *Altindisches Leben*, 238. Perhaps *parṣin*, in the compound *iṣu-parṣin* in the Śatapatha Brāhmaṇa, xiii. 4, 2, 5, means 'having a bundle (of arrows).'

Palada occurs twice in one hymn of the Atharvaveda[1] in the description of a house. It seems to mean bundles of straw or reeds used to thatch the house and render the sides wind and weather proof.

1 ix. 3, 5, 17. *Cf.* Zimmer, *Altindisches Leben*, 153; Bloomfield, *Hymns of the Atharvaveda*, 194, 195.

Palasti. See **Palita.**

Palāla is found with Anu-palāla in the Atharvaveda (viii. 6, 2) as the name of a demon. The meaning of the word is 'straw,' in which sense it occurs in the Kauśika Sūtra (lxxx. 27), while the feminine form, Palalī, is found in the Atharvaveda itself (ii. 8, 3) as the straw of barley (**Yava**).

Palāva is found in the Atharvaveda[1] and the Jaiminīya Upaniṣad Brāhmaṇa[2] in the sense of 'chaff.'

1 xii. 3, 19, where some manuscripts read *palāvā*.

2 i 54, 1

Palāśa, like **Parṇa,** denotes 'leaf' in the Brāhmaṇas.[1] It also[2] designates the tree *Butea frondosa*, of which Parṇa is the early name.

[1] Kauṣītaki Brāhmaṇa, x. 2; Śatapatha Brāhmaṇa, i. 5, 4, 5; v. 2, 1, 17 etc.; Chāndogya Upaniṣad, iv. 14, 3.

[2] Aitareya Brāhmaṇa, ii. 1; Śatapatha Brāhmaṇa, i. 3, 3, 19; ii. 6, 2, 8, etc.

Cf. Zimmer, *Altindisches Leben*, 59.

Palita, 'grey-haired,' occurs frequently from the Rigveda[1] onwards.[2] It is the distinctive sign of old age. Those who, like certain descendants of **Jamadagni,** do not grow old,[3] are said not to become grey-haired, while **Bharadvāja** is described as having in his old age become thin and grey-haired.[4] The Śatapatha Brāhmaṇa[5] in one passage observes that grey hairs appear first on the head, and elsewhere[6] alludes to the hair on the arms having become grey.

[1] i. 144, 4; 164, 1; iii. 55, 9; x. 4, 5, etc.

[2] Vājasaneyi Saṃhitā, xxx. 15, etc.

[3] Taittirīya Saṃhitā, vii. 1, 9, 1; Pañcaviṃśa Brāhmaṇa, xxi. 10, 6. *Cf.* Hopkins, *Transactions of the Connecticut Academy of Arts and Sciences*, 15, 54, and Rv. iii. 53, 16, where *palasti* seems to mean *palita*.

[4] Aitareya Brāhmaṇa, iii. 49.

[5] xi. 4, 1, 6. 14.

[6] iii. 8, 2, 25.

Palpūlana is found in the Atharvaveda[1] and the Taittirīya Saṃhitā[2] apparently meaning, properly, 'lye,' or water impregnated with some biting substance for washing clothes. In the Atharvan passage urine seems to be meant.[3] The verb *palpūlaya*, 'to wash with alkaline water,' occurs in the Taittirīya Saṃhitā[2] and the Taittirīya Brāhmaṇa;[4] and the Sūtras refer to hides (*carman*)[5] and garments[6] so washed. *Cf.* also **Vāsaḥ-palpūlī.**

[1] xii. 4, 9. *Cf.* Kauśika Sūtra, xi. 16.

[2] ii. 5, 5, 6.

[3] Whitney, Translation of the Atharvaveda, 695. *Cf.* Bloomfield, *Hymns of the Atharvaveda*, 74, 175.

[4] i. 3, 5, 2. 3.

[5] Kauśika Sūtra, 67.

[6] Śāṅkhāyana Śrauta Sūtra, iii. 8, 12. *Cf.* Baudhāyana Dharma Sūtra, i. 6, 13, 15; Böhtlingk, Dictionary, *s.v.*

Palli-gupta Lauhitya ('descendant of Lohita') is mentioned in a Vaṃśa ('list of teachers') in the Jaiminīya Upaniṣad Brāhmaṇa (iii. 42, 1) as a pupil of **Śyāmajayanta Lauhitya.**

The name is obviously a late one, for Palli is not found in the early literature, and the name of the Lauhitya family is otherwise known in post-Vedic works only.

Pavana ('purifier') in the Atharvaveda[1] denotes an instrument for purifying grain from husks, etc.; either a 'sieve' or a 'winnowing basket' may be meant. In the Sūtras[2] it is mentioned as used for cleaning the bones of the dead after cremation.

[1] iv. 34, 2; xviii. 3, 11. *Cf.* Nirukta, vi. 9.

[2] Āśvalāyana Gṛhya Sūtra, iv. 5. 7.

Pavamāna is a term very frequently applied in the Rigveda to the Soma 'purifying itself' by running through the sieve. Later it appears in a few passages[1] in the sense of 'wind' (as a purifier).

[1] Taittirīya Saṃhitā, vii. 5, 20, 1; Vājasaneyi Saṃhitā, vi. 17; Aitareya Brāhmaṇa, i. 7.

Pavasta in one passage of the Atharvaveda[1] apparently denotes 'covers.'

[1] iv. 5, 6. *Cf.* Whitney, Translation of the Atharvaveda, 156.

Pavi denotes the 'tire' of the wheel of a chariot in the Rigveda[1] and later.[2] Reference is made[3] to the necessity for fastening it on firmly, and the epithet *su-pavi*, 'having a good tire,' is found in the Atharvaveda[4] with *su-nābhi*, 'having a good nave,' and *su-cakra*, 'having a good wheel.' The tires were, of course, of metal,[5] and being sharp,[6] could serve on occasion as weapons.[7] The St. Petersburg Dictionary in one passage of

[1] i. 34, 2; 88, 2; 139, 3; 166, 10, etc.; Nirukta, v. 5.

[2] Sāmaveda, ii. 7, 1, 15, 3, etc.

[3] Rv. vi. 54, 3.

[4] Av. iv. 12, 6.

[5] Of gold in the case of the Aśvins and the Maruts, Rv. i. 64, 11; 180, 1.

[6] Rv. i. 166, 10.

[7] Rv. v. 52, 9. *Cf.* vi. 8, 5, and x 180, 2.

the Vājasaneyi Saṃhitā[8] takes Pavi to mean a metal rim on the stone for pounding Soma, but this seems improbable, because no such metal attachment is elsewhere alluded to. Hillebrandt[9] seems clearly right in accepting the sense of 'sharp edge' in this passage, especially as the stones in the Rigveda[10] are, in allusion to their rolling action, styled 'rims without horses and without chariots' (*anaśvāsaḥ pavayo 'rathāḥ*).

The Nirukta[11] ascribes to Pavi the sense of arrow (*śalya*), but this is very uncertain. The St. Petersburg Dictionary cites for this use two passages of the Rigveda,[12] but in one the secondary sense of sharp-edged weapon with reference to the bolt of Indra is quite likely, and in the other, where the expression *vāṇasya pavi* occurs, the sharp-edged pounding-stone of the 'reed,'[13] meaning the stalk of the Soma plant, may be meant. Hillebrandt[14] thinks a reference to the shape of the Soma plant is intended. Pavī-nasa, the name of a demon mentioned in the Atharvaveda,[15] seems to throw no light on this point, for while the St. Petersburg Dictionary takes it to mean 'whose nose is like a spearhead,' it is translated as 'rim-nosed' (presumably in allusion to the curved shape of the nose) by Whitney.[16]

[8] vi. 30. *Cf.* Śatapatha Brāhmaṇa, iii. 9, 4, 5. Mahīdhara, on the Vājasaneyi Saṃhitā, takes *pavinā* as *vajrasadṛśena*, 'like a thunderbolt,' and Eggeling, *Sacred Books of the East*, 26, 239, 240, renders *pavi* by 'bolt.'

[9] *Vedische Mythologie*, 1, 44.

[10] v. 31, 5.

[11] xii. 30.

[12] ix. 50, 1; x. 180, 2.

[13] *Cf.* Rv. iv. 24, 9, where the expression *vāṇaṃ duhanti*, 'they milk out the reed,' occurs.

[14] *Op. cit.*, 1, 43, 44.

[15] viii. 6, 21.

[16] Translation of the Atharvaveda, 497.

Cf. Zimmer, *Altindisches Leben*, 248; Geldner, *Vedische Studien*, 2, 12, n. 1.

Pavitra denotes in the Rigveda,[1] and later,[2] the sieve used for purifying the Soma, the only mode of purifying it certainly[3] known to the Rigveda. It seems clearly[4] to have been made of

[1] i. 28, 9; iii. 36, 7; viii. 33, 1; 101, 9, etc.

[2] Av. vi. 124, 3; ix. 6, 16; xii. 1, 30; 3, 3. 14. 25, etc.

[3] *Cf.* Hillebrandt, *Vedische Mythologie*, 1, 239, 240.

[4] *Cf.* the names of it: *aṇva*, Rv. ix. 16, 2; *aṇvāni meṣyaḥ*, 86, 47; 107, 11; *avayaḥ*, ii. 36, 1; ix. 86, 11; 91, 2; *tvac* with *avya* or *avyaya*, ix. 69, 3; 70, 7; *meṣyaḥ*, ix. 8, 5; *rūpa avyaya*, ix. 16, 6; *roman*, alone or with *avyaya*; *vāra*, alone or with *avyaya*, etc.

sheep's wool, whether woven or plaited is not certain, for the expressions used are too vague to be decisive, though Zimmer[5] thinks *hvarāṃsi*[6] points to plaiting.

[5] *Altindisches Leben*, 278, n.

[6] ix. 3, 2; 63, 4.

Pavīra, according to the Nirukta,[1] denotes a 'lance.' The epithet derived from this word, *pavīravant* or *pavīrava*, which is found in the Atharvaveda[2] and the Yajurveda Saṃhitās,[3] is used of the plough, apparently in the sense of 'having a metal share.' The same epithet occurs in the Rigveda[4] applied to a man, in the sense of 'having a goad' or 'having a spear.'

[1] xii. 30. In Rv. i. 174, 4, *pavīrava* seems to mean 'thunderbolt.'

[2] iii. 17, 3.

[3] *Pavīravant*, Vājasaneyi Saṃhitā, xii. 71; *pavīrava*, Taittirīya Saṃhitā, iv. 2, 5, 6; Maitrāyaṇī Saṃhitā, ii. 7, 12; Kāṭhaka Saṃhitā, xvi. 11.

[4] x. 60, 3.

Cf. Whitney, Translation of the Atharvaveda, 116.

Pavīru appears in a hymn of the Rigveda[1] as a **Ruśama**, being a prince or at least a wealthy noble.

[1] viii. 51, 9 = Vājasaneyi Saṃhitā, xxxiii. 82.

Paśu means 'animal' generally, including man. There is frequent mention[1] of the five sacrificial animals—the horse, the cow, the sheep, the goat, and man. Seven such domestic animals are spoken of in the Atharvaveda[2] and later;[3] probably, as Whitney[4] observes, merely as a sacred mystic number, not, as the commentator[5] explains, the usual five with the ass and the camel added. Animals are also referred to as *ubhayadant*

[1] Taittirīya Saṃhitā, iv. 2, 10, 1-4; Kāṭhaka Saṃhitā, xvi. 17; Maitrāyaṇī Saṃhitā, ii. 7, 17; Vājasaneyi Saṃhitā, xiii. 47-51. *Cf.* Av. xi. 2, 9; Taittirīya Saṃhitā, iv. 3, 10, 1-3; v. 5, 1, 1. 2; vi. 5, 10, 1; Vājasaneyi Saṃhitā, xiv. 28-31, etc.

[2] Av. iii. 10, 6.

[3] Śatapatha Brāhmaṇa, ii. 8, 4, 16; ix. 3, 1, 20; xii. 8, 3, 13 (where they are called *jāgatāḥ*, perhaps as numbering 12); Pañcaviṃśa Brāhmaṇa, x 2, 7.

[4] Translation of the Atharvaveda, 103.

[5] On Av. iii. 10, 6. The St. Petersburg Dictionary suggests 'mule' and 'ass' as the two making up seven (*cf.* Mahābhārata, vi. 165 *et seq.*). Zimmer's view (*Altindisches Leben*, 76) is that 'goat,' 'sheep,' 'ox,' 'horse,' 'dog,' 'ass,' and 'camel' or 'mule,' are meant.

and *anyatodant*. They are further[6] classified as those which take hold with the hand (*hastādānāḥ*), man (*puruṣa*), elephant (*hastin*), and ape (*markaṭa*), and those which grasp by the mouth (*mukhādānāḥ*). Another division is that of biped (*dvipād*) and quadruped (*catuṣpād*).[7] Man is a biped;[8] he is the first (*prathama*) of the beasts;[9] he alone of animals lives a hundred years (*śatāyus*),[10] and he is king of the animals.[11] He possesses speech (*vāc*) in conjunction with the other animals.[12] In the Aitareya Āraṇyaka[13] an elaborate distinction is drawn between vegetables, animals, and man in point of intellect.

Of animals apart from man a threefold division is offered in the Rigveda[14]—into those of the air (*vāyavyà*), those of the jungle (*āraṇya*), and those of the village (*grāmya*), or tame animals. The division into *āraṇya* and *grāmya* animals is quite common.[15] In the Yajurveda Saṃhitās[16] is found a division into *eka-śapha*, 'whole-hoofed'; *kṣudra*, 'small'; and *āraṇya*, 'wild,' the two former classes denoting the tame animals.[16] The horse and the ass are *eka-śapha*;[17] the *kṣudra* are the sheep, the goat, and the ox: this distinction being parallel to that of *ubhayadant* and *anyatodant*.[18] Zimmer[19] sees in a passage of the Atharvaveda[20] a division of wild animals (*āraṇya*) into five classes: (1) those of the jungle described as the 'dread beasts

[6] Taittirīya Saṃhitā, vi. 4, 5, 7; Maitrāyaṇī Saṃhitā, iv. 5. 7 (where *puruṣa* must be read for *paruṣa*).

[7] Rv. iii. 62, 14; Av. iii. 34, 1, etc. Zimmer, 73, n., suggests that the division is Indo-European, as the Inguvenic tables make a distinction between *dupursus* and *peturpursus*.

[8] Taittirīya Saṃhitā, iv. 2, 10, 1. 2; Vājasaneyi Saṃhitā, xvii. 47. 48.

[9] Śatapatha Brāhmaṇa, vi. 2, 1, 18; vii. 5, 2, 6.

[10] Taittirīya Saṃhitā, iii. 2, 6, 3; Śatapatha Brāhmaṇa, vii. 2, 5, 17.

[11] Kāṭhaka Saṃhitā, xx. 10; Śatapatha Brāhmaṇa, iv. 5, 5, 7. *Cf.* Weber, *Zeitschrift der Deutschen Morgenländischen Gesellschaft*, 18, 274.

[12] Rv. viii. 100, 11.

[13] ii. 3, 2, with Keith's note.

[14] x. 90, 8.

[15] Av. iii. 31, 3. *Cf.* ii. 34, 1, with Whitney's note, Translation of the Atharvaveda, 78; xi. 2, 24; Maitrāyaṇī Saṃhitā, iii. 2, 3; 9, 7; Kāṭhaka Saṃhitā, xiii. 12; Taittirīya Āraṇyaka, iii. 2, 29. 32; Śatapatha Brāhmaṇa, ii. 7, 1, 8; 2, 8. *Cf.* xi. 8, 3, 2, where there is reference to animals being tied up at night in their stalls.

[16] Taittirīya Saṃhitā, iv. 3, 10, 2; Vājasaneyi Saṃhitā, xiv. 30.

[17] Zimmer, 74.

[18] *Cf.* Av. v. 31, 3; Taittirīya Saṃhitā, ii. 2, 6, 3, with Taittirīya Saṃhitā, ii. 1, 1, 5; v. 1, 1, 3; 2, 6.

[19] *Op. cit.*, 77, 78.

[20] xi. 2, 24. 25, compared with xii. 1, 49. 51.

which are in the wood' (*mṛgā bhīmā vane hitāḥ*); (2) winged creatures, represented by the **Haṃsa**, 'gander,' **Suparṇa**, 'eagle,' **Śakuna**, 'bird'; (3) amphibia—**Śiṃśumāra**, 'alligator,' and **Ajagara**, 'crocodile' (?); (4) 'fish,' **Purīkaya**, **Jaṣa**, and **Matsya**; (5) insects and worms (described as *rajasāḥ*). But this division is more ingenious than probable, and it is ignored by both Bloomfield[21] and Whitney.[22]

21 *Hymns of the Atharvaveda*, 631.
22 Translation of the Atharvaveda, 633, 634. *Cf.* Zimmer, *Altindisches Leben*, 72-77.

Paśu-pa denotes 'herdsman' in the Rigveda.[1] Metaphorically the term is applied to Pūṣan.[2]

1 i. 114, 9; 144, 6; iv. 6, 4; x. 142, 2.
2 vi. 58, 2. *Cf.* of Pūṣan and Revatī, Taittirīya Brāhmaṇa, iii. 1, 2, 12.

1. **Paṣṭha-vāh** occurs in the Yajurveda Saṃhitās[1] meaning an ox, four years old, according to the commentators. This qualification is, however, very doubtful, for Paṣṭhauhī, 'cow,' a word occurring quite frequently,[2] is in one passage[3] accompanied by the adjective *prathama-garbhāḥ*, 'having a first calf,' which disproves the theory of the age adopted by the commentators.

1 Taittirīya Saṃhitā, iv. 3, 5, 2; Vājasaneyi Saṃhitā, xiv. 9; xviii. 27; xxi. 17; xxiv. 13. 28. 29, etc.
2 Taittirīya Saṃhitā, vii. 1, 6, 3; Kāṭhaka Saṃhitā, xi. 2; xii. 8; Vājasaneyi Saṃhitā, xviii. 27; Taittirīya Brāhmaṇa, i. 7, 3, 3; 8, 3, 2; ii. 7, 2, 2, etc.
3 Śatapatha Brāhmaṇa, iv. 6, 1, 11.

2. **Paṣṭha-vāh** is mentioned as a seer of Sāmans in the Pañcaviṃśa Brāhmaṇa.[1]

1 xii. 5, 11. *Cf.* Hillebrandt, *Vedische Mythologie*, 2, 160.

Pastya-sad ('sitting in the house') occurs in one passage of the Rigveda,[1] where the sense seems to be 'inmate,' 'companion.'

1 vi. 51, 9. *Cf.* Roth, St. Petersburg Dictionary, *s.v.*; Pischel, *Vedische Studien*, 2, 211.

Pastyā (fem. pl.) is a word occurring in several passages of the Rigveda.[1] Roth[2] ascribes to it the meaning of 'house' or 'dwelling,' in the wide sense of the term, as well as that of the 'family' living in the house; and this view is accepted by Zimmer.[3] On the other hand, Pischel[4] finds in two of the passages[5] usually referred to Pastyā the neuter Pastya, which appears in **Pastya-sad** and in **Pastyā-vant** (where the length of the second syllable is not primitive), and which is certainly found in the Rigveda[6] in the metaphorical sense of 'dwelling,' ascribed to it in the Naighaṇṭuka.[7] In the other passages[8] he thinks the word means 'rivers' or 'waters': in particular, where Soma in the middle of the Pastyās[9] is spoken of, he sees a reference to **Kurukṣetra**, with its several rivers,[10] **Āpayā**, **Dṛṣadvatī**, and **Sarasvatī** (*cf.* 2. **Pastyāvant**). In some passages[11] he sees in Pastyā the proper name of a stream, just as Sindhu primarily means 'river,' then the 'Indus.'

[1] Rv. i. 25, 10; 40, 7; 164, 30; iv. 1, 11; vi. 49, 9; vii. 97, 5; ix. 65, 23; x. 46, 6. See also iv. 55, 3; viii. 27, 5, where Pastyā appears as a goddess.

[2] St. Petersburg Dictionary, *s.v.*

[3] *Altindisches Leben*, 149. *Cf.* Weber, *Über den Rājasūya*, 43, n. 4; 63.

[4] *Vedische Studien*, 2, 211-222. So Geldner, *Rigveda, Glossar*, 107.

[5] vi. 49, 9; vii. 97, 5, where the sense is 'householder' (*gṛha-stha* or *gṛhin*, as Sāyaṇa renders it).

[6] x. 96, 10. 11. In x. 96, 10, Roth takes *pastyoḥ* to denote the two parts of the Soma press, but Pischel, 2, 211, accepts Sāyaṇa's rendering 'heaven and earth.' In the compounds *tri-pastya* of Agni, Rv. viii. 39, 8; *vāja-pastya* of Pūṣan, vi. 58, 2, of Soma, ix. 98, 12; and *vīra-pastya*, v. 50, 4, the primitive word may very well be *pastya*, not *pastyā*.

[7] iii. 4, misquoted by Sāyaṇa on Rv. i. 151, 2, as applying to *pastyā*, whereas it really refers to *pastya*.

[8] Rv. i. 25, 10 = Taittirīya Saṃhitā, i. 8, 16, 1 = Maitrāyaṇī Saṃhitā, i. 6, 2; ii. 6, 12; 7, 16; iv. 4, 6 = Vājasaneyi Saṃhitā, x. 27; Rv. i. 40, 7; 164, 30 (used of Agni's home); iv. 1, 11; ix. 65, 23; x. 46, 6; Taittirīya Saṃhitā, i. 8, 12, 1 = Maitrāyaṇī Saṃhitā, ii. 6, 8 = Vājasaneyi Saṃhitā, x. 7.

[9] Rv. ix. 65, 23.

[10] Rv. iii. 23, 4.

[11] Rv. iv. 55, 3; viii. 27, 5; and in *pastyāvant* in ix. 97, 18.

1. **Pastyā-vant**, explained in the Pada text as Pastya-vant, occurs in several passages of the Rigveda. In two of them[1]

[1] i. 151, 2; ix. 97, 18; but the latter passage is explained by Pischel as referring to **Pastyā**, the river, and by Böhtlingk, Dictionary, *s.v.*, as 'kept in the stall.'

a rich householder seems meant, and in the two others reference to a 'house' is clear.[2]

[2] *Barhis*, Rv. ii. 11, 16, 'of the house'; *kṣayān pastyāvataḥ*, iv. 54, 5, 'abodes having (fixed) habitations.'
Cf. Pischel, *Vedische Studien*, 2, 212.

2. **Pastyā-vant** occurs in one passage of the Rigveda[1] in the locative parallel with **Suṣoma, Śaryaṇāvant,** and **Ārjīka.** It must apparently denote a place, as Pischel[2] argues, probably corresponding to the locality 'in the middle of the streams' (*madhye pastyānāṃ*), elsewhere[3] referred to as the home of Soma. Pischel[4] suggests that Patiāla is meant, though he does not lay any stress on the similarity of name. In the north of Patiāla there are hills where the Soma might have grown. Roth[5] thought that something connected with the Soma press was meant.

[1] viii. 7, 29.
[2] *Vedische Studien*, 2, 209.
[3] Rv. ix. 65, 23.
[4] *Op. cit.*, 2, 219.
[5] St. Petersburg Dictionary, *s.v.* 2. Max Müller, *Sacred Books of the East*, 32, 260, 398, 399, takes Pastyāvant as a place-name, but thinks that *pastyā* denotes 'hamlet,' or, as an epithet of Aditi, refers to her as a 'housewife' (Rv. iv. 55, 3; viii. 27, 5).

Pāṃsu in the Atharvaveda[1] and later[2] denotes 'dust' or 'sand,' usually in the plural. Among the portents enumerated in the Adbhuta Brāhmaṇa[3] is a rain of dust or sand (*pāṃsu-varṣa*), a phenomenon not rare in India.[4]

[1] vii. 109, 2; xii. 1, 26.
[2] Taittirīya Brāhmaṇa, ii. 6, 10, 2; Nirukta, xii. 19, etc.
[3] vi. 8 (*Indische Studien*, 1, 40). *Cf.* Varāhamihira, Bṛhatsaṃhitā, xxii. 6.
[4] The adjective *pāṃsura* is found in Rv. i. 22, 17, with a variant, *pāṃsula*, Sāmaveda, i. 3, 1, 3, 9. *Cf.* Śatapatha Brāhmaṇa, iv. 5, 1, 9.

Pāka-dūrvā is, in a verse of the Rigveda,[1] included with **Kiyāmbu** and **Vyalkaśā** among the plants used for growing on the spot where the corpse of the dead man has been consumed with fire.[2] The verse is repeated in the Taittirīya Āraṇyaka[3]

[1] x. 16, 13.
[2] See Bloomfield, *American Journal of Philology*, 11, 342-350; *Journal of the American Oriental Society*, 15, xxxix.
[3] vi. 4, 1, 2.

with the variant Kyāmbu. In the Atharvaveda[4] he word is read Śāṇḍadūrvā. Pākadūrvā is probably, as Sāyaṇa understands it, *paripakva-dūrvā*, 'ripe or edible millet.' Śāṇḍadūrvā is explained by the commentator[5] in various ways, as millet 'having egg-shaped roots' (*i.e.*, *sāṇḍa*, not *śāṇḍa*), or as 'having long joints,' with the additional remark that it was called *bṛhad-dūrvā*, 'large millet.' In the Taittirīya Āraṇyaka, on the other hand, the commentary explains Pākadūrvā as small millet.

[4] xviii. 3, 6.

[5] Whitney, Translation of the Atharvaveda, 850. *Cf.* Zimmer, *Altindisches Leben*, 70.

Pāka-sthāman Kaurayāṇa is celebrated as a generous donor in a hymn of the Rigveda.[1] Ludwig[2] suggests, without much reason, that he may have been a king of the **Anus.**

[1] viii. 3, 21. 24.

[2] Translation of the Rigveda, 3, 160.

Pākāru is mentioned as a disease, together with **Viṣūcikā** and **Arśas**, 'hæmorrhoids,' in the Vājasaneyi Saṃhitā.[1] Its nature is unknown; the etymology[2] points to the sense of 'developed sores,' 'ulcers.'

[1] xii. 97. *Cf.* Zimmer, *Altindisches Leben*, 393.

[2] From *pāka*, 'maturity,' and *aru*= *arus*, 'sore.'

Pāṅktra is the name of an animal mentioned in the list of victims at the Aśvamedha, or 'horse-sacrifice,' in the Yajurveda Saṃhitās.[1] The 'field-rat' seems to be meant.

[1] Maitrāyaṇī Saṃhitā, iii. 14, 7; Vājasaneyi Saṃhitā, xxiv. 26. *Cf.* Zimmer, *Altindisches Leben*, 85.

Pāñca-janya, 'relating to the five peoples.' See **Pañcajanāḥ.**

Pāñcāla means a 'king of the Pañcāla people,' and is applied to **Durmukha** in the Aitareya Brāhmaṇa[1] and to **Śoṇa** in the Śatapatha Brāhmaṇa.[2] The term is also found in the Jaiminīya Upaniṣad Brāhmaṇa.[3] See also **Pañcāla.**

[1] viii. 23.

[2] xiii. 5, 4, 7.

[3] iii. 29, 1. *Cf.* Kāṭhaka Anukramaṇī in *Indische Studien*, 3 460.

Pāñci, 'descendant of Pañcan,' is the name of a teacher mentioned with disapproval in the Śatapatha Brāhmaṇa.[1]

[1] i. 2, 5, 9; ii. 1, 4, 27. *Cf.* Weber, *Indische Studien*, 1, 434.

Pāṭava, 'descendant of Paṭu,' is a patronymic of **Cākra** in the Śatapatha Brāhmaṇa (xii. 8, 1, 17; 9, 3, 1).

Pāṭā is mentioned in the Atharvaveda[1] and in the Kauśika Sūtra.[2] It is assumed by the commentator to be identical with the later Pāṭhā, the plant *Clypea hernandifolia*, which was much used medicinally, and is still so used at the present day according to Roth.[3] Very possibly the word should be read as Pāṭhā.

[1] ii. 27, 4.

[2] xxxvii. 1; xxxviii. 18. *Cf.* Ṛgvidhāna, iv. 12, 1.

[3] Quoted in Whitney, Translation of the Atharvaveda, 68. *Cf.* Weber, *Indische Studien*, 13, 190; 17, 266; Bloomfield, *Hymns of the Atharvaveda*, 305, n. 1; *Proceedings of the American Oriental Society*, May, 1885, xlii-xliv.

Pāṇi-ghna, 'hand-clapper,' is enumerated among the list of victims at the Puruṣamedha ('human sacrifice') in the Yajurveda.[1] Presumably a man who drives away birds from the fields by making a noise is intended.

[1] Vājasaneyi Saṃhitā, xxx. 20; Taittirīya Brāhmaṇa, iii. 4, 15, 1.

Pāṇḍva in the Śatapatha Brāhmaṇa (v. 3, 5, 21) denotes an uncoloured woollen garment.

Pātalya is found in one passage of the Rigveda[1] meaning some part of the chariot. What it was is quite uncertain. Hopkins[2] suggests that, as in the Epic, it was possibly a piece of wood on the axle to hold the pole of the car.

[1] iii. 53, 17.

[2] *Journal of the American Oriental Society*, 13, 242, 243; 20, 224. *Cf.* Zimmer, *Altindisches Leben*, 251; Geldner, *Rigveda, Glossar*. 108.

Pātra, primarily a 'drinking vessel' (from *pā*, 'to drink') denotes a vessel generally both in the Rigveda[1] and later.[2] It was made either of wood[3] or clay.[4] In some passages[5] the word is, according to Roth, used to indicate a measure. The feminine Pātrī occasionally occurs[6] in the sense of 'vessel.'

[1] i. 82, 4; 110, 5; 162, 13 (to hold the broth from the flesh of the horse); 175, 1; ii. 37, 4; vi. 27, 6, etc.

[2] Av. iv. 17, 4; vi. 142, 1; ix. 6, 17; xii. 3, 25. 36; Taittirīya Saṃhitā, v. 1, 6, 2; vi. 3, 4, 1; Vājasaneyi Saṃhitā, xvi. 62; xix. 86, etc.

[3] Rv. i. 175, 3.

[4] Av. iv. 17, 4.

[5] Av. x. 10, 9; xii. 3, 30; Śatapatha Brāhmaṇa, xiii. 4, 1, 5; Śāṅkhāyana Śrauta Sūtra, xvi. 1, 7, etc.

[6] Aitareya Brāhmaṇa, viii. 17; Śatapatha Brāhmaṇa, i. 1, 2, 8; ii. 5, 3, 6; 6, 2, 7; Śāṅkhāyana Śrauta Sūtra, v. 8, 2.

Cf. Zimmer, *Altindisches Leben*, 271.

Pāthya, a word occurring only once in the Rigveda,[1] is either an epithet meaning 'being in heaven' (*pāthas*), or a patronymic, as Sāyaṇa interprets it, of **Vṛṣan**.

[1] vi. 16, 15. *Cf.* Satapatha Brāhmaṇa, vi. 4, 2, 4; Max Müller, *Sacred Books of the East*, 32, 153.

1. **Pāda** in the Atharvaveda[1] and later[2] denotes the 'foot' of an animal, a bird, and other creatures.

[1] xiv. 1, 60.

[2] Aitareya Brāhmaṇa, viii. 5. 12; Satapatha Brāhmaṇa, xii. 8, 3, 6, etc.; Kauṣītaki Upaniṣad, i. 5.

2. **Pāda**, as a measure of length, denotes 'foot' in the Śatapatha Brāhmaṇa.[1] The term is occasionally[2] used to express a measure of weight. As a fraction it means a 'quarter,' a sense derived from that of 'foot' of a quadruped (just as *śapha*, the divided hoof, comes to mean an 'eighth').

[1] vi. 5, 3, 2; vii. 2, 1, 7; viii. 7, 2, 17; Āśvalāyana Śrauta Sūtra, vi. 10, etc.

[2] Nirukta, ii. 7; Bṛhadāraṇyaka Upaniṣad, iii. 1, 2.

[3] Rv. x. 90, 3. 4.

3. **Pāda** is the regular expression for a 'quarter verse' in the Brāhmaṇas.[1] This sense is merely a limitation of 'quarter' = the 'foot' of a quadruped.

[1] Aitareya Brāhmaṇa, iv. 4; Kauṣītaki Brāhmaṇa, xxvi. 5; Nirukta, vii. 9; xi. 6; Lāṭyāyana Srauta Sūtra, i. 2, 1; x. 6, 9, etc.

Pāna, 'drink,' occurs in the Śatapatha Brāhmaṇa[1] and the Upaniṣads.[2]

[1] xiii. 4, 2, 17.
[2] Bṛhadāraṇyaka Upaniṣad, iv. 1, 43; Chāndogya Upaniṣad, viii. 2, 7, etc.

Pānta occurs several times in the Rigveda,[1] apparently[2] meaning 'drink,' 'beverage' (*cf.* **Pāna**). Geldner,[3] however, thinks that in one passage[4] Pānta is the name of a prince.

[1] i. 122, 1; 155, 1; viii. 92, 1; ix. 65, 28 (a very doubtful passage); x. 88, 1.
[2] So Nirukta, vii. 25; Roth, St. Petersburg Dictionary, *s.v.*; Oldenberg, *Ṛgveda-Noten*, 1, 122, 123.
[3] *Vedische Studien*, 2, 139; *Rigveda, Glossar*, 108.

Pān-nejana in the Śatapatha Brāhmaṇa[1] denotes a 'vessel for washing the feet.'

[1] iii. 8, 2, 1; 9, 3, 27; xiii. 5, 2, 1.

Pāpa-yakṣma. See **Yakṣma.**

Pāpa-sama, a 'bad season,' is in the Taittirīya Saṃhitā[1] opposed to Puṇya-sama, a 'good season.'

[1] iii. 3, 8, 4. *Cf.* Weber, *Naxatra*, 2, 342.

Pāman occurs in the Atharvaveda[1] as the name of a skin disease. The derivative adjective, Pāmana, 'suffering from skin disease,' is found in the later Saṃhitās and the Brāhmaṇas.[2] Since it is mentioned as an accompaniment of fever, probably a cutaneous eruption or scab consequent on fever is meant.

[1] v. 22, 12. *Cf.* for the reading, Whitney, Translation of the Atharvaveda, 261. See also Chāndogya Upaniṣad, iv. 1, 8.
[2] Taittirīya Saṃhitā, vi. 1, 3, 8; Kāṭhaka Saṃhitā, xxiii. 4; Śatapatha Brāhmaṇa, iii. 2, 1, 31.

Cf. Grohmann, *Indische Studien*, 9, 401 *et seq.*; Zimmer, *Altindisches Leben*, 388; Schrader, *Prehistoric Antiquities*, 421, n.; Bloomfield, *Hymns of the Atharvaveda*, 450, 451; *Atharvaveda*, 63.

1. **Pāyu**, meaning 'guard,' 'protector,' occurs several times in the Rigveda.[1]

[1] i. 147, 3; ii. 1, 7; iv. 2, 6; 4, 3. 12; vi. 15, 8; viii. 18, 2; 60, 19; x. 100, 9.

2. **Pāyu** is found in the Rigveda[1] as the name of a poet, a Bhāradvāja. In the Bṛhaddevatā[2] he is credited with assisting **Abhyāvartin Cāyamāna** and **Prastoka Sārñjaya** by consecrating their weapons with a hymn.[3]

[1] vi. 47, 24. *Cf.* Ludwig, Translation of the Rigveda, 3, 128.

[2] v. 124 *et seq.*, with Macdonell's notes.

[3] vi. 75 (the 'battle' hymn).

Pāra, in accordance with its derivation (*pṛ*, 'bring across'), denotes the 'farther bank' of a river or stream, in which sense[1] it occurs in the Rigveda[2] and later.[3]

[1] It also often has the generalized sense of 'extreme limit' or 'end,' as in i. 92, 6 (*tamasas*, 'of darkness'); v. 54, 10 (*adhvanaḥ*, 'of a road').

[2] i. 121, 13 (*nāvyānām*, 'of streams'); viii. 96, 11 (*nadīnām*); i. 167, 2 (*samudrasya*); x. 155, 3 (*sindhoḥ*), etc.

[3] Taittirīya Saṃhitā, vii. 5, 1, 2. 3; Kāṭhaka Saṃhitā, xxxiii. 5; Śatapatha Brāhmaṇa, iii. 6, 2, 4 (*salilasya*); Aitareya Brāhmaṇa, viii. 21 (*pāra-kāma*, 'desiring the farther bank'), etc.

Pārāśavya, 'descendant of Paraśu,' is the patronymic of **Tirindira** in the Śāṅkhāyana Śrauta Sūtra (xvi. 11, 20). *Cf.* **Parśu.**

1. **Pārāvata** occurs in the list of victims at the Aśvamedha ('horse sacrifice'), in the Yajurveda,[1] meaning 'turtle-dove.'

[1] Maitrāyaṇī Saṃhitā, iii. 14, 6; Vājasaneyi Saṃhitā, xxiv. 25.

2. **Pārāvata** occurs in several passages of the Rigveda. Roth[1] thinks that in most places[2] it means 'coming from a distance,' but in two passages[3] he regards it as the proper name of a people on the **Yamunā** (Jumna). It is certain that in the Pañcaviṃśa Brāhmaṇa the Pārāvatas are a people on that river (*cf.* **Turaśravas**). Hillebrandt[4] sees in all the passages[5] the name of a people, comparing the Παρυῆται of

[1] St. Petersburg Dictionary, *s.v.*

[2] Rv. v. 52, 11; viii. 100, 6; Av. xx. 135, 14; *pārāvata-ghnī* of the Sarasvatī, Rv. vi. 61, 2.

[3] Rv. viii. 34, 18; Pañcaviṃśa Brāhmaṇa, ix. 4, 11. *Cf.* Hopkins, *Transactions of the Connecticut Academy of Arts and Sciences*, 15, 53.

[4] *Vedische Mythologie*, 1, 97 *et seq.*; 3, 310, following Brunnhofer, *Iran und Turan*, 99.

[5] See notes 2 and 3.

Ptolemy,[6] who apparently were settled on the northern border of Gedrosia, or the Παροῦται, who were found in Αρεία.[7] He suggests that they were originally 'mountaineers' (*cf.* **Parvata**). Ludwig[8] holds a similar view, and Geldner[9] recognizes a people as meant. The mention of the **Sarasvatī** in connexion with the Pārāvatas[2] in the Rigveda accords generally with their position on the Yamunā in the Pañcaviṃśa Brāhmaṇa.[3]

[6] vi. 20, 3. It is suggested by Hillebrandt that the Ἀπαρύται of Herodotus, iii. 91, may be the same.

[7] Ptolemy, vi. 17.

[8] Translation of the Rigveda, 3, 162, 197.

[9] *Rigveda, Glossar*, 109.

Cf. Hopkins, *Journal of the American Oriental Society*, 17, 91; Max Müller, *Sacred Books of the East*, 32, 316.

Pārāśarī-kauṇḍinī-putra is mentioned in the last Vaṃśa (list of teachers) of the Bṛhadāranyaka Upaniṣad (vi. 4, 30), in the Mādhyaṃdina recension, as a pupil of **Gārgīputra.**

Pārāśarī-putra, 'son of a female descendant of **Parāśara,**' is mentioned in the last Vaṃśa (list of teachers) in the Bṛhadāraṇyaka Upaniṣad as a pupil of **Kātyāyanīputra,**[1] of **Aupasvatīputra,**[1] of **Vātsīputra,**[2] of **Vārkāruṇīputra,**[3] and of **Gārgīputra.**[4] Different men are no doubt meant.

[1] vi. 5, 1, Kāṇva.

[2] vi. 5, 2, Kāṇva.

[3] vi. 4, 31, Mādhyaṃdina.

[4] vi. 4, 30, Mādhyaṃdina.

Pārāśarya, 'descendant of **Parāśara,**' is mentioned in the first two Vaṃśas (lists of teachers) of the Bṛhadāraṇyaka Upaniṣad as a pupil of **Jātūkarṇya**[1] or of **Bhāradvāja.**[2] A Pārāśarya is also mentioned as a pupil of **Baijavāpāyana,**[3] and **Vyāsa Pārāśarya** is the pupil of **Viṣvaksena** according to the Vaṃśa at the end of the Sāmavidhāna Brāhmaṇa.[4] See also **Aṣāḍha, Jayanta, Vipaścit, Sudatta.**

[1] ii. 6, 3; iv. 6, 3, Kāṇva; ii. 5, 21; iv. 5, 27, Mādhyaṃdina.

[2] ii. 5, 20; iv. 5, 26, Mādhyaṃdina; ii. 6, 2; iv. 6, 2. 3, Kāṇva.

[3] ii. 6, 2, Kāṇva.

Cf. Taittirīya Āraṇyaka, i. 9, 2.

[4] Jaiminīya Upaniṣad Brāhmaṇa, iii. 41 1.

Pārāśaryāyaṇa is mentioned in the first two Vaṃśas (lists of teachers) in the Bṛhadāraṇyaka Upaniṣad[1] as a pupil of Pārāśarya.

[1] ii. 5, 21; iv. 5, 27 (Mādhyaṃdina = ii. 6, 3; iv. 6, 3, Kāṇva).

Pārikuṭa is an obscure word—probably corrupt—occurring in a verse cited in the Aitareya Brāhmaṇa (viii. 22, 7), and apparently meaning 'attendant.'

Pārikṣita, 'descendant of **Parikṣit,**' is the patronymic of **Janamejaya** in the Aitareya Brāhmaṇa[1] and the Śatapatha Brāhmaṇa.[2] The Pārikṣitīyas appear in the Śatapatha Brāhmaṇa[3] and the Śāṅkhāyana Śrauta Sūtra[4] as performers of the horse sacrifice. In a Gāthā there cited they are called Pārikṣitas. Apparently they were the brothers of Janamejaya, named **Ugrasena, Bhīmasena,** and **Śrutasena.** In the Bṛhadāraṇyaka Upaniṣad[5] the question whither they have gone is made the subject of a philosophical discussion. It is clear that the family had passed away before the time of the Upaniṣad, and it is also clear that there had been some serious scandal mingled with their greatness which they had, in the opinion of the Brahmins, atoned for by their horse sacrifice with its boundless gifts to the priests. Weber[6] sees in this the germ of the Epic stories which are recorded in the Mahābhārata.

The verses relating to Parikṣit in the Atharvaveda[7] are called Pārikṣityaḥ in the Brāhmaṇas.[8]

[1] vii. 27 and 34; viii. 11.

[2] xiii. 5, 4, 1. *Cf.* Gopatha Brāhmaṇa, i. 2, 6; ii. 6, 12.

[3] xiii. 5, 4, 3.

[4] xvi. 9, 7.

[5] iii. 3, 1.

[6] *Indian Literature,* 125, 126; 135, 136. The later legend of the Pārikṣitas and Vāmadeva's mares is dealt with by Weber in *Vedische Beiträge* (1894).

[7] xx. 127, 7-10; Śāṅkhāyana Srauta Sūtra, xii. 17; Scheftelowitz, *Die Apokryphen des Ṛgveda,* 156, 157.

[8] Aitareya Brāhmaṇa, vi. 32, 10; Kauṣītaki Brāhmaṇa, xxx. 5; Gopatha Brāhmaṇa, ii. 6, 12; Weber, *op. cit.,* 136, n. 144.

Pāri-plava, 'cyclic,' is a term applied to the **Ākhyāna,** or 'tale,' which is to be recited at the Aśvamedha ('horse sacrifice'), and to be repeated at intervals throughout the year. It is mentioned in the Śatapatha Brāhmaṇa[1] and in the Sūtras.[2]

[1] xiii. 4, 3, 2. 15.

[2] Āśvalāyana Srauta Sūtra, x. 6; Śāṅkhāyana Srauta Sūtra, xvi. 1, 26; 2, 36; Lāṭyāyana Śrauta Sūtra, ix. 9, 11.

Pārī-ṇahya denotes 'household utensils' in the Taittirīya Saṃhitā,[1] where it is said that the wife (*patnī*), as mistress of the house, has charge of all these.[2]

[1] vi. 2, 1, 1.

[2] The word occurs later in the variant form of *pāri-ṇāhya* in Manu, ix. 11.

Pārūṣṇa, occurring in the list of victims at the Aśvamedha ('horse sacrifice') in the Yajurveda Saṃhitās,[1] appears to mean some kind of bird.

[1] Maitrāyaṇī Saṃhitā, iii. 14, 4; Vājasaneyi Saṃhitā, xxiv. 24.

Pārovarya-vid in the Nirukta (xiii. 12) denotes 'knowers of tradition.'

Pārṇa-valki, 'descendant of Parṇavalka,' is the patronymic of **Nigada** in the Vaṃśa Brāhmaṇa.[1]

[1] *Indische Studien*, 4, 372; Max Müller, *Ancient Sanskrit Literature*, 443.

Pārthava, 'descendant of **Pṛthu**,' occurs once in the Rigveda,[1] where the Pārthavas are mentioned as generous donors. The passage is somewhat obscure, as there is a reference[2] to a defeat of the **Turvaśas** and the **Vṛcīvants** by **Sṛñjaya Daivavāta**, followed in the next verse by the praise of the bounty to the singer of **Abhyāvartin Cāyamāna**, who was clearly a **Pārthava**, and who, in the earlier part of the hymn, has been referred to as victorious over **Varaśikha**. It is uncertain whether, as Zimmer[3] suggests, the two princes, Abhyāvartin

[1] vi. 27, 8.

[2] vi. 27, 7.

[3] *Altindisches Leben*, 133, 134.

Cāyamāna and Sṛñjaya Daivavāta, are identical or not.[4] That Pārthava has any direct connexion with the Parthians, as held by Brunnhofer, is most improbable.[5] *Cf.* **Parśu.**

[4] *Cf.* Hillebrandt, *Vedische Mythologie*, 1, 105.

[5] *Cf.* Ludwig, Translation of the Rigveda, 3, 196 *et seq.* Herodotos, iii. 93, mentions the Πάρθοι.

Pārtha-śravasa, 'descendant of Pṛthu-śravas,' is found as the name of a demon in the Jaiminīya Upaniṣad Brāhmaṇa.[1]

[1] iv. 26, 15. This form of the name is supported by its occurrence in the Kauśika Sūtra, ix. 10; xvii. 27. But Pārthu- is also possible.

Pārthya, 'descendant of Pṛthi,' is the patronymic of some donor in a hymn of the Rigveda.[1] The form of the name in the Aśvalāyana Śrauta Sūtra[2] is Pārtha.

[1] x. 93, 15.

[2] xii. 10. *Cf.* the Anukramaṇī on Rv. x. 93.

Pārvati, 'descendant of Parvata,' is the patronymic of **Dakṣa** in the Śatapatha (ii. 4, 4, 6) and the Kauṣītaki (iv. 4) Brāhmaṇas.

Pārṣada, which first appears in the Nirukta,[1] denotes a text-book recognized by a school of grammarians.

[1] i. 17. *Cf.* Max Müller, *Ancient Sanskrit Literature*, 128 *et seq.*; Weber, *Studien*, 3, 269; 4, 217.

Pārṣad-vāṇa, 'descendant of Pṛṣadvāṇa,' is mentioned as a wonder-worker in the Rigveda.[1]

[1] viii. 51, 2. *Cf.* Ludwig, Translation of the Rigveda, 3, 139.

Pārṣṇa Śailana is mentioned as a teacher in the Jaiminīya Upaniṣad Brāhmaṇa (ii. 4, 8).

Pālāgala occurs in the Śatapatha Brāhmaṇa[1] apparently in the sense of 'messenger,' or 'bearer of false news.'

[1] v. 3, 1, 11. Eggeling, *Sacred Books of the East*, 26, 64, renders it 'courier.'

Pālāgalī is the name of the fourth and least respected wife of the king.[1] See **Pati.**

[1] Śatapatha Brāhmaṇa, xiii. 4, 1, 8; 5, 2, 8, etc.

Pāvamānī means the verses (*ṛcas*) in the ninth Maṇḍala of the Rigveda 'relating to Soma Pavamāna' ('purifying itself'). The name is found in the Atharvaveda[1] and later,[2] possibly even in one hymn of the Rigveda itself.[3]

[1] xix. 71, 1.
[2] Aitareya Brāhmaṇa, i. 20; ii. 37; Kauṣītaki Brāhmaṇa, xv. 1; Satapatha Brāhmaṇa, xii. 8, 1, 10; Nirukta, xi. 2; xii. 31; Aitareya Āraṇyaka, ii. 2, 2, etc.; Maitrāyaṇī Gṛhya Sūtra, ii. 14.
[3] ix. 67, 31. 32; Geldner, *Vedische Studien*, 3, 99, n. 3.

Pāśa denotes in the Rigveda[1] and later[2] a 'rope' used for fastening or tying up. Rope and knot (*granthi*) are mentioned together in the Atharvaveda.[3] Pāśa is in the Śatapatha Brāhmaṇa[4] used of the rope by which Manu's ship was fastened to the mountain. It is often employed metaphorically of the 'fetter' of Varuṇa.[5]

[1] i. 24, 13. 15; ii. 27, 16; 29, 5, etc.
[2] Av. ii. 12, 2; ix. 3, 2; Vājasaneyi Saṃhitā, vi. 8. 45, etc.
[3] ix. 3, 2.
[4] i. 8, 1, 5.
[5] Rv. vi. 74, 4; vii. 88, 7; x. 85, 24; Av. iv. 16, 6; Taittirīya Saṃhitā, ii. 2, 5, 1, etc.

Pāśin, 'having a noose,' denotes a 'hunter' in the Rigveda[1] and in the Atharvaveda.[2]

[1] iii. 45, 1; ix. 73, 4. So of Nirṛti in Aitareya Brāhmaṇa, iv. 10.
[2] xvii. 1, 8.

Pāśa-dyumna Vāyata is the name of a king to whom the **Vasiṣṭhas** claim to have been preferred by Indra in one hymn of the Rigveda.[1] Apparently he was, as Sāyaṇa says, son of Vayat, who may be compared with the **Vyat** of another passage of the Rigveda.[2] Ludwig[3] sees in him a priest of the **Pṛthus** and **Parśus,** but this is most improbable.[4]

[1] vii. 33, 2.
[2] i. 122, 4.
[3] Translation of the Rigveda, 3, 173.
[4] Geldner, *Vedische Studien*, 2, 130, 139.

Pāṣya occurs in one passage of the Rigveda[1] with reference to the defeat of Vṛtra, and apparently denotes 'stone bulwarks.'

[1] i. 56, 6.

In another passage[2] the word may mean the stones used for pressing Soma.

[2] ix. 102, 2. *Cf.* Macdonell, *Journal of the Royal Asiatic Society*, 1893, 457, 458.

Pika, the Indian 'cuckoo,' is mentioned in the list of victims at the Aśvamedha ('horse sacrifice') in the Yajurveda Saṃhitās.[1] *Cf.* **Anyavāpa, Koka.**

[1] Taittirīya Saṃhitā, v. 5, 15, 1; Maitrāyaṇī Saṃhitā, iii. 14, 20; Vājasaneyi Saṃhitā, xxiv. 39. *Cf.* Zimmer, *Altindisches Leben*, 92.

Piṅgā is found in one passage of the Rigveda,[1] where it is explained by the St. Petersburg Dictionary with Sāyaṇa as 'bowstring,' but where Hillebrandt[2] thinks that a musical instrument of some kind is meant.

[1] viii. 69, 9.

[2] *Vedische Mythologie*, 1, 144, n.

Pijavana is the name of the father of **Sudās** according to the Nirukta.[1] Probably this statement is based on a mere conjecture from the epithet Paijavana used of Sudās in a verse of the Rigveda,[2] but may very well be correct.

[1] ii. 24.

[2] vii. 18, 19. So Aitareya Brāhmaṇa, viii. 21.

Piñjūla denotes a 'bundle' of grass or stalks, especially of **Darbha.** The word is only found in the Brāhmaṇa style.[1]

[1] Kāṭhaka Saṃhitā, xxiii. 1; Aitareya Brāhmaṇa, i. 3; Kauṣītaki Brāhmaṇa, xviii. 8. It appears in the form of *piñjula* in Maitrāyaṇī Saṃhitā, iv. 8, 7; Pāraskara Gṛhya Sūtra, i. 15; of Puñjīla in Taittirīya Saṃhitā, vi. 1, 1, 7; 2, 4, 3; Taittirīya Brāhmaṇa, i. 7, 6, 4; ii. 7, 9, 5.

Piṭhīnas is the name of a man, a friend of Indra, in the Rigveda.[1]

[1] vi. 26, 6. *Cf.* Ludwig, Translation of the Rigveda, 3, 156.

Piṇḍa, denoting specifically a ball of flour offered to the Manes, especially on the evening of new moon, occurs in the Nirukta,[1] and repeatedly in the Sūtras.[2]

[1] iii. 4.

[2] Lāṭyāyana Śrauta Sūtra, ii. 10, 4, etc.

Pitā-putra, 'father and son,' is a compound of rare occurrence.[1]

[1] Av. vi. 112, 2; Śatapatha Brāhmaṇa, xiii. 2, 4, 4.

Pitā-putrīya ('relating to father and son'), used with Sampradāna ('handing over') means the ceremony by which a father, when about to die, bequeathes his bodily and mental powers to his son. It is described in the Kauṣītaki Upaniṣad.[1]

[1] ii. 15. *Cf.* Weber, *Indische Studien*, 1, 408.

Pitā-maha, beside **Tatāmaha**, denotes from the Atharvaveda onwards[1] the 'paternal grandfather,' apparently as a 'father in a higher sense.'[2] The great-grandfather is **Prapitāmaha** and **Pratatāmaha.**[3] It is significant that there are no corresponding Vedic words for maternal grandparents, and that the words used in the latter language, such as Mātāmaha, are imitations of the terms for paternal relations.

In one passage of the Rigveda[4] Delbrück[5] suggests that *mahe pitre* means 'grandfather,' a sense which would well suit the *napātam*, 'grandson,' following, but the sense of the whole passage is uncertain.[6]

We learn very little from the texts of the position of grandparents. No doubt they were entitled to marks of respect similar to those shown to parents,[7] as the epic expressly testifies. A grandfather might easily be the head of the family, or be living with his eldest son, after he ceased to be able to control the family.

The grandmother (Pitāmahī) is not mentioned in the extant Vedic literature.

[1] Av. v. 5, 1; ix. 5, 30; xi. 1, 19; xviii. 4, 35; Taittirīya Saṃhitā, i. 8, 5, 1; vii. 2, 7, 3; Vājasaneyi Saṃhitā, xix. 36; Śatapatha Brāhmaṇa, v. 5, 5, 4.

[2] Delbrück, *Die indogermanischen Verwandtschaftsnamen*, 474.

[3] Av. xviii. 4, 75.

[4] vi. 20, 11.

[5] *Ibid.*, 473.

[6] See Pischel, *Vedische Studien*, 2, 128, n. 1. Roth, St. Petersburg Dictionary, *s.v.*, also doubts the view which is accepted by Delbrück, and denies that in Rv. i. 71, 5, the sense of 'grandfather' can be found.

[7] Delbrück, *op. cit.*, 480, citing Mahābhārata, ii. 1634.

Pitu in the Rigveda[1] and later[2] has the general sense of 'nutriment,' whether food or drink.

[1] i. 61, 7; 132, 6; 187, 1; vi. 20, 4, etc.

[2] Av. iv. 6, 3; Taittirīya Saṃhitā, v. 7, 2, 4; Vājasaneyi Saṃhitā, ii. 20; xii. 65; Aitareya Brāhmaṇa, i. 13.

Pitṛ, common from the Rigveda onwards, denotes 'father,' not so much as the 'begetter' (*janitṛ*),[1] but rather as the protector of the child, this being probably also the etymological sense of the word.[2] The father in the Rigveda[3] stands for all that is good and kind. Hence Agni is compared with a father,[4] while Indra is even dearer than a father.[5] The father carries his son in his arms,[6] and places him on his lap,[7] while the child pulls his garment to attract attention.[8] In later years the son depends on his father for help in trouble,[9] and greets him with joy.[10]

It is difficult to ascertain precisely how far the son was subject to parental control, and how long such control continued. Reference is made in the Rigveda[11] to a father's chastising his son for gambling, and **Ṛjrāśva** is said to have been blinded by his father.[12] From the latter statement Zimmer[13] infers the existence of a developed *patria potestas*, but to lay stress on this isolated and semi-mythical incident would be unwise. It is, however, quite likely that the *patria potestas* was originally strong, for we have other support for the thesis in the Roman *patria potestas*. If there is no proof that a father

[1] *Pitā janitā* is used of gods in the Rigveda—*e.g.*, iv. 17, 12.

[2] As derived from *pā*, 'protect.' But, as Böhtlingk and Roth, St. Petersburg Dictionary, *s.v. Mātar*, footnote, suggest, *pa* and *mā* were probably the much older original onomatopoetic names for 'father' and 'mother,' which in a later reflective age influenced the formation of *pitṛ* and *mātṛ* (which themselves go back to the Indo-European period).

[3] See, *e.g.*, iv. 17, 17; viii. 86, 4.

[4] Rv. x. 7, 3.

[5] Rv. vii. 32, 19; viii. 1, 6.

[6] Rv. i. 38, 1.

[7] Rv. v. 43, 7.

[8] Rv. iii. 53, 2.

[9] In Rv. x. 48, 1, the *jantavaḥ* possibly are the sons.

[10] Rv. vii. 103, 3. *Cf.* i. 24, 1.

[11] Rv. ii. 29, 5.

[12] Rv. i. 116, 16; 117, 17. There is also the case of the sale of Sunaḥśepa, Aitareya Brāhmaṇa, vii. 12-18; and *cf.* Śatapatha Brāhmaṇa, v. 3, 3, 3.

[13] *Altindisches Leben*, 316.

legally controlled his son's wedding,[14] and not much that he controlled his daughter's,[15] the fact is in itself not improbable.

There is again no evidence to show whether a son, when grown up, normally continued to stay with his father, his wife becoming a member of the father's household, or whether he set up a house of his own: probably the custom varied. Nor do we know whether the son was granted a special plot of land on marriage or otherwise, or whether he only came into such property after his father's death. But any excessive estimate of the father's powers over a son who was no longer a minor and naturally under his control, must be qualified by the fact that in his old age the sons might divide their father's property,[16] or he might divide it amongst them,[17] and that when the father-in-law became aged he fell under the control of his son's wife.[18] There are also obscure traces that in old age a father might be exposed, though there is no reason to suppose that this was usual in Vedic India.[19]

Normally the son was bound to give his father full obedience.[20] The later Sūtras show in detail the acts of courtesy which he owed his father, and they allow him to eat the remnants of his father's food.[21] On the other hand, the father was expected to be kind. The story of **Śunaḥśepa** in the Aitareya Brāh-

[14] *Cf.* Delbrück, *Die indogermanischen Verwandtschaftsnamen*, 576. *Ibid.*, 582, he quotes Mahābhārata, xii. 6108 *et seq.*, which refers in one line to the control of the marriage of the son by the father, and in the next to a case of free marriage. The fact is, no doubt, that the son could marry freely, unless his father had arranged matters for him when he was too young to object.

[15] Zimmer, *op. cit.*, 309, assumes this as certain, but it is far from proved. See, however, Jaiminīya Upaniṣad Brāhmaṇa, iii. 12, 2, which is in favour of Zimmer's view. *Cf.* Kaegi, *Der Rigveda*, 15, and **Pati**.

[16] Rv. i. 70, 10; Aitareya Brāhmaṇa, v. 14; Jaiminīya Brāhmaṇa, iii. 156 (*Journal of the American Oriental Society*, 26, 61, 62).

[17] Taittirīya Saṃhitā, iii. 1, 9, 4-6. *Cf.* the handing over from father to son in the Kauṣītaki Upaniṣad, ii. 15. If the father recovered, he lived subject to his son.

[18] Rv. x. 85, 46.

[19] *Cf.* Rv. viii. 51, 2; Av. xviii. 2, 34. The first passage need not refer to exposure, and the second merely refers to the exposure of a dead body; but Zimmer, *Altindisches Leben*, 326-328, thinks that they prove exposure. *Cf.* **Dharma**.

[20] Rv. i. 68, 5.

[21] Āpastamba Dharma Sūtra, i. 1, 4, 11.

maṇa[22] emphasizes the horror with which the father's heartless treatment of his son was viewed. The Upaniṣads[23] insist on the spiritual succession from father to son. The kissing of a son[24] was a frequent and usual token of affection, even in mature years.

On the failure of natural children, adoption was possible.[25] It was even resorted to when natural children existed, but when it was desired to secure the presence in the family of a person of specially high qualifications, as in Viśvāmitra's adoption of Śunaḥśepa.[26] It is not clear that adoption from one caste into another was possible, for there is no good evidence that Viśvāmitra was, as Weber[27] holds, a Kṣatriya who adopted a Brāhmaṇa. Adoption was also not always in high favour: it may be accidental or not that a hymn of the Vasiṣṭha book of the Rigveda[28] condemns the usage. It was also possible for the father who had a daughter, but no sons, to appoint her to bear a son for him. At any rate the practice appears to be referred to in an obscure verse of the Rigveda[29] as interpreted by Yāska.[30] Moreover, it is possible that the difficulty of a brotherless maiden finding a husband[31] may have been due in part to the possibility of her father desiring to make her a Putrikā, the later technical name for a daughter whose son is to belong to her father's family.

There can be no doubt that in a family the father took precedence of the mother.[32] Delbrück[33] explains away the apparent cases to the contrary.[34] There is no trace of the

22 vii. 12 *et seq.*; Śāṅkhāyana Śrauta Sūtra, xv. 17 *et seq.*

23 *E.g.*, Kauṣītaki Upaniṣad, ii. 15; Bṛhadāraṇyaka Upaniṣad, i. 5, 25 (Mādhyaṃdina = i. 5, 17, Kāṇva).

24 See Hopkins, *Journal of the American Oriental Society*, 28, 120-134; Keith, *Śāṅkhāyana Āraṇyaka*, 26, n. 3.

25 *Cf.* Zimmer, *Altindisches Leben*, 318; Mayr, *Indisches Erbrecht*, 73; Jolly, *Die Adoption in Indien* (Würzburg, 1910), 7 *et seq.*

26 Aitareya Brāhmaṇa, vii. 17 *et seq.*; Śāṅkhāyana Śrauta Sūtra, xv. 17. *Cf.* Hillebrandt, *Vedische Mythologie*, 2, 157.

27 *Episches im vedischen Ritual*, 33, 34.

28 vii. 4, 7. 8.

29 iii. 31, 1.

30 iii. 5 *ad fin.* *Cf.* Weber, *Indische Studien*, 5, 343; Geldner, *Vedische Studien*, 3, 34; Oldenberg, *Ṛgveda-Noten*, 1, 239-241.

31 *Cf.* Bhrātṛ.

32 Śatapatha Brāhmaṇa, ii. 5, 1, 18; a citation in Śāṅkhāyana Gṛhya Sūtra, i. 9; Chāndogya Upaniṣad vii. 15, 2.

33 *Die indogermanischen Verwandtschaftsnamen*, 577.

34 Bṛhadāraṇyaka Upaniṣad, iv. 7, 5. Some passages in the Sūtras present difficulties, but they are of no importance for Vedic times proper.

family as a land-owning corporation.[35] The dual form Pitarau regularly means 'father and mother,' 'parents.'[36]

[35] Baden Powell, whose various works (*Indian Village Community*, 1896; *Village Communities in India*, 1899, etc.) have done most to combat the view of the village community in India as a land-holding institution, is prepared to recognize the family as a land-owning unit, considering that the *patria potestas* is a later growth, and not Indian (see, *e.g.*, *Village Communities in India*, 128 *et seq.*). Hopkins *India, Old and New*, 210 *et seq.*, adopts a theory which allows of individual and joint family ownership side by side, the latter being apparently the earlier but the decadent stage. He expressly considers (p. 222) that the son had an indefeasible right to prevent the father from alienating the hereditary land, which could only be parted with by the consent of the village if it were a case of joint ownership (*cf.* the verse cited by Jolly, *Recht und Sitte*, 94). But it must be remembered that, as is very clearly shown in the case of English law by Pollock and Maitland (*History of English Law*, 2, 337-352), the recognition of the rights of sons may well be, not a sign of original joint or family ownership, but a development from the existence of intestate succession, and as in England, so in India, there is no trace of a corporate joint family in the early books. And, as Jolly (*op. cit.*, 76, 80) shows, there are clear traces, both in old and modern times, of a despotic control of the family by the father even after his sons grew up, provided only that he was physically able to control them. The same state of affairs seems proved for early English law, as it is beyond question for Roman law (see Smith's *Dictionary of Antiquities*, 2, 351 *et seq.*). In Greece also, which is sometimes contrasted with Rome, there is the clearest trace of both a real *patria potestas*, and of the absolute ownership of the land by the father as against the son, especially in the archaic laws of Gortyn (see Gardner and Jevons, *Greek Antiquities*, 404, 405, 563, 566).

[36] Rv. i. 20, 4; 160, 3; ii. 17, 7; vii. 67, 1; Kāṭhaka Saṃhitā, xxiii 10; Vājasaneyi Saṃhitā, xix. 11, etc.

Pitṛ-yāṇa, the 'way of the fathers,' mentioned in the Rigveda[1] and later,[2] is opposed to the Deva-yāna, or 'way of the gods.' Tilak[3] considers that the Devayāna corresponds with the Uttarāyaṇa, 'northern journey' of the sun, and the Pitṛyāṇa with the Dakṣiṇāyana, its 'southern journey.' He concludes from a passage of the Śatapatha Brāhmaṇa,[4] where three of the seasons—spring, summer, and the rains—are ascribed to the gods, but the others to the Pitṛs, or Fathers, that the Devayāna began with the vernal equinox, and the Pitṛyāṇa with the autumnal equinox. With this he connects the curious

[1] x. 2, 7. *Cf.* the allusion to it in x. 18, 1, as other than the Devayāna, which appears in x. 98, 11.

[2] Av. viii. 10, 19; xii. 2, 10, etc.; Vājasaneyi Saṃhitā, xix. 45; Chāndogya Upaniṣad, v. 3, 2, etc.

[3] *Orion*, 22 *et seq.*

[4] ii. 1, 3, 1-3.

distinction of Deva- and Yama-Nakṣatras in the Taittirīya Brāhmaṇa.[5] These conclusions are, however, very improbable. *Cf.* **Nakṣatra** and **Sūrya.**

[5] i. 5, 2, 6.

Pitṛ-han, 'parricide,' is found in the Atharvaveda,[1] Paippalāda recension.

[1] ix. 4, 3. *Cf.* Böhtlingk, Dictionary, *s.v.*

Pitrya occurs in the list of sciences given in the Chāndogya Upaniṣad.[1] Apparently it is to be taken as the science relating to the cult of the Manes, as explained by Śaṅkara in his commentary. As it is in that list followed by **Rāśi,** the St. Petersburg Dictionary is inclined to take Pitrya Rāśi as one expression, but in what exact sense does not appear.

[1] vii. 1, 2. 4; 2, 1; 7, 1. *Cf.* Weber, *Indische Studien*, 1, 267; Little, *Grammatical Index*, 98.

Pitva[1] or **Pidva**[2] is the name of an animal included in the list of victims at the Aśvamedha ('horse sacrifice') in the Yajurveda Saṃhitās. According to the commentator on the Taittirīya Saṃhitā[1] it means 'lion.' But it may be identical with **Petva.**

[1] Taittirīya Saṃhitā, v. 5, 17, 1.
[2] Maitrāyaṇī Saṃhitā, iii. 14, 13; Vājasaneyi Saṃhitā, xxiv. 32. *Cf.* Zimmer, *Altindisches Leben*, 79; Bloomfield, *Journal of the American Oriental Society*, 29, 290.

Pināka, 'club,' is found in the Atharvaveda.[1] Later[2] it is used to denote the club of Rudra-Śiva.

[1] i. 27, 2.
[2] Taittirīya Saṃhitā, i. 8, 6, 2; Vājasaneyi Saṃhitā, iii. 61; xvi. 51, etc.

Pinvana occurs in the Śatapatha Brāhmaṇa (xiv. 1, 2, 17; 2, 1, 11; 3, 1, 22) as the name of a vessel used in the ritual.

Pipīla, 'ant,' is mentioned in the Rigveda (x. 16, 6) as eating the flesh of the dead.

Pipīlikā in the Atharvaveda[1] and later[2] denotes an 'ant,' the form of the word referring doubtless not so much to the small species of ant, as it is taken in the later lexicons,[3] but rather to the insect's tiny size, which would naturally be expressed by a diminutive formation of the name. The form Pipīlaka[4] is found in the Chāndogya Upaniṣad.[5]

1 vii. 56, 7. *Cf.* xx. 134, 6.

2 Maitrāyaṇī Saṃhitā, iii. 6, 7; Pañcaviṃśa Brāhmaṇa, v. 6, 10; xv. 17, 8; Bṛhadāraṇyaka Upaniṣad, i. 4, 9. 29 (Mādhyaṃdina=i. 4, 4, 16 Kāṇva); Nirukta, vii. 13; Aitareya Araṇyaka, i. 3, 8; ii. 1, 6.

3 St. Petersburg Dictionary, *s.v.*

4 *Cf. kanīnaka* beside *kanīnikā*, 'pupil of the eye.'

5 vii. 2, 1; 7, 1; 8, 1; 10, 1.

Cf. Zimmer, *Altindisches Leben*, 97; Edgerton, *Journal of the American Oriental Society*, 31, 128.

Pippakā is mentioned in the list of victims at the Aśvamedha ('horse sacrifice') in the Yajurveda Saṃhitās.[1] Some bird seems to be meant.

1 Taittirīya Saṃhitā, v. 5, 19, 1; Maitrāyaṇī Saṃhitā, iii. 14, 21; Vājasaneyi Saṃhitā, xxiv. 40. *Cf.* Zimmer, *Altindisches Leben*, 93.

Pippala, n., is found in two passages of the Rigveda[1] meaning 'berry,' used with a mystic signification, and in neither case with any certain reference to the berry of the fig-tree.[2] In the Bṛhadāraṇyaka Upaniṣad[3] the general sense of 'berry' is not necessary, and the special sense of 'berry' of the Peepal is quite possible: the latter meaning is perhaps intended in the Śatapatha Brāhmaṇa.[4] In the Atharvaveda[5] the feminine form of the word, Pippalī, appears denoting berries used as a remedy for wounds, like **Arundhatī**.[6]

1 i. 164, 20 = Muṇḍaka Upaniṣad, iii. 1, 1; Śvetāśvatara Upaniṣad, iv. 6, 22; v. 54, 12 (the 'berry' of heaven, *nāka*).

2 The word Pippala appears in the later literature as a masculine, denoting the *Ficus religiosa* (**Aśvattha** in Vedic literature).

3 iv. 1, 41.

4 iii. 7, 1, 12.

5 vi. 109, 1. 2.

6 Bloomfield, *Atharvaveda*, 61; *Hymns of the Atharvaveda*, 516; Whitney, Translation of the Atharvaveda, 359, 360; Zimmer, *Altindisches Leben*, 389; Max Müller, *Sacred Books of the East*, 32, 331.

Pippalāda ('eater of berries') is the name of a teacher mentioned in the Praśna Upaniṣad.[1] In the plural the name denotes a school of the Atharvaveda.[2] Their (Paippalāda) recension of the text of the Saṃhitā has been reproduced in facsimile by Garbe and Bloomfield,[3] and in part published.[4]

[1] i. 1.
[2] Weber, *Indische Studien*, 3, 277; *Indian Literature*, 153, 159, 160, 164.
[3] Baltimore, 1901.
[4] The variants of the Paippalāda are given in part in Whitney's Translation of the Atharvaveda, and the text of books i. and ii. has been edited by Barret in the *Journal of the American Oriental Society*, 26, 197-295; 30, 187 *et seq*. *Cf*. also Lanman in Whitney's Translation, lxxix *et seq*

Pipru is the name of a foe of Indra in the Rigveda. He was repeatedly defeated by Indra for **Ṛjiśvan.**[1] Mentioned as possessing forts,[2] he is called a Dāsa[3] as well as an Asura.[4] He is described as having a black brood,[5] and as being allied with blacks.[6] It is uncertain whether he was a demon, according to Roth's[7] view, which is favoured by the use of the word Asura, or a human foe, as Ludwig,[8] Oldenberg,[9] and Hillebrandt[10] believe. The name may mean 'resister,' from the root *pṛ*.

[1] i. 101, 1. 2; iv. 16, 13; v. 29, 11; vi. 20, 7; viii. 49, 10; x. 99, 11; 138, 3. In i. 103, 8; ii. 14, 5; vi. 18, 8, the reference is general to a defeat of Pipru by Indra.
[2] Rv. i. 51, 5; vi. 20, 7.
[3] Rv. viii. 32, 2.
[4] Rv. x. 138, 3.
[5] Rv. i. 101, 1.
[6] iv. 16, 13.
[7] St. Petersburg Dictionary, *s.v.*
[8] Translation of the Rigveda, 3, 149.
[9] *Religion des Veda*, 155.
[10] *Vedische Mythologie*, 3, 273.
Cf. Macdonell, *Vedic Mythology*, p. 161 (C).

Piśa is found in one passage of the Rigveda,[1] where Sāyaṇa takes it to mean a deer (*ruru*).

[1] i. 64, 8. *Cf*. Av. xix. 49, 4; Zimmer, *Altindisches Leben*, 83; Max Müller, *Sacred Books of the East*, 32, 118; Geldner, *Rigveda, Glossar*, 110.

Piśaṅga is the name of one of the two Unnetṛ priests officiating at the snake festival mentioned in the Pañcaviṃśa Brāhmaṇa.[1] *Cf*. **Caka.**

[1] xxv. 15, 3. *Cf*. Weber, *Indische Studien*, 1, 35.

Piśāca is the name of a class of demon mentioned in the Atharvaveda[1] and later.[2] In the Taittirīya Saṃhitā[3] they are associated with Rakṣases and Asuras, while opposed to gods, men, and fathers. In the Atharvaveda[4] they are described as *kravyād*, 'eaters of raw flesh,' which may be the etymological sense of the word Piśāca itself.[5] It is possible that the Piśācas were, as suggested by Grierson,[6] really human foes, like the north-western tribes, who even in later times were reputed eaters of raw flesh (not necessarily as cannibals, but rather as eaters of human flesh in ritual). This is, however, not at all likely, the Piśācas having in all probability only meant 'ghouls' originally: when they appear as human tribes, they were presumably thus designated in scorn. A science called Piśāca-veda[7] or Piśāca-vidyā[8] is known in the later Vedic period.

[1] ii. 18, 4; iv. 20, 6. 9; 36, 4; 37, 10; v. 29, 4. 5. 14; vi. 32, 2; viii. 2, 12; xii. 1, 50. The word occurs once in the Rv. (i. 133, 5) in the form of Piśāci.

[2] See St. Petersburg Dictionary, *s.v.*

[3] ii. 4, 1, 1; Kāṭhaka Saṃhitā, xxxvii. 14.

[4] v. 25, 9.

[5] *Cf.* Oldenberg, *Religion des Veda*, 264, n.

[6] *Cf.* Grierson, *Journal of the Royal Asiatic Society*, 1905, 285-288. *Cf.* Macdonell, *Vedic Mythology*, p. 164 (B).

[7] Gopatha Brāhmaṇa, i. 1, 10.

[8] Āśvalāyana Śrauta Sūtra, x. 7, 6.

Piśita in the Atharvaveda[1] and later[2] denotes raw flesh (*cf.* **Piśāca**). In one passage of the Atharvaveda[3] the sense seems to be 'small piece,' 'bit,' but the St. Petersburg Dictionary suggests that Piśita here stands for *piṣita*, equivalent to *piṣṭa* (what is 'pounded,' then 'particle').

[1] v. 19, 5.

[2] Aitareya Brāhmaṇa, ii. 11; Kauśika Sūtra, xii. 8; xxxv. 18; xxxix. 14, etc.

[3] vi. 127, 1. *Cf.* Bloomfield, *Hymns of the Atharvaveda*, 531; Whitney, Translation of the Atharvaveda, 376.

Piśīla is found in the Śatapatha Brāhmaṇa (ii. 5, 3, 6) as the name of a wooden vessel or dish. In the Lāṭyāyana Śrauta Sūtra (iv. 2, 4. 5) a Piśīla-vīṇā is mentioned, which seems to have been a kind of guitar, with strings stretched over a body of wood.

Piśuna, 'traitor,' is mentioned in the Rigveda[1] and occasionally later.[2]

[1] vii. 104, 20.

[2] Vājasaneyi Saṃhitā, xxx. 13; Chāndogya Upaniṣad, vii. 6, 1; Taittirīya Brāhmaṇa, iii. 4, 7, 1.

Piṣṭa ('pounded'), n., 'meal,' 'flour,' is mentioned in the Brāhmaṇas.[1] In the Atharvaveda[2] reference is made to pounded beans (*māṣāḥ*).

[1] Aitareya Brāhmaṇa, ii. 9; Śatapatha Brāhmaṇa, i. 1, 4, 3; 2, 1, 2; vi 5, 1, 6, etc.

[2] xii. 2, 53.

Pīṭha, 'stool,' does not occur as an uncompounded word before the Sūtras, but the compound *pīṭha-sarpin* ('moving about in a little cart') is found as the designation of a 'cripple' in the Vājasaneyi Saṃhitā (xxx. 21) and the Taittirīya Brāhmaṇa (iii. 4, 17, 1) in the list of victims at the Puruṣamedha ('human sacrifice').

Pītu-dāru is found in the Kāṭhaka Saṃhitā[1] and later[2] denoting the Deodar (*deva-dāru*) tree, or, according to others, the **Khadira** or **Udumbara** tree.[3] *Cf.* **Pūtadru.**

[1] Kāṭhaka Saṃhitā, xxv. 6.

[2] Śatapatha Brāhmaṇa, iii. 5, 2, 15; xiii. 4, 4, 5. 17; Pañcaviṃśa Brāhmaṇa, xxiv. 13, 5.

[3] Mahīdhara on Vājasaneyi Saṃhitā, v. 14; Sāyaṇa on Aitareya Brāhmaṇa, i. 28.

Pīyūṣa is found in the Rigveda[1] and later[2] in the sense of the first milk of the cow after calving, 'biestings.' Usually the term is applied metaphorically to the sap of the Soma plant.[3]

[1] *Cf.* ii. 35, 5, where it is applied figuratively to the mothers of Agni.

[2] Kauśika Sūtra, xix. 15. *Cf.* Av. viii. 9, 24.

[3] Rv. ii. 13, 1; iii. 48, 2; vi. 47, 4; x. 94, 8, etc.

Cf. Geldner, *Rigveda, Glossar*, 110.

Pīlā occurs once in the Atharvaveda[1] as the name of an Apsaras, being no doubt originally a name of some fragrant

[1] iv. 37, 3. *Cf.* Zimmer, *Altindisches Leben*, 69; Whitney, Translation of the Atharvaveda, 211.

plant, like **Naladī** and **Guggulū**, two other names of Apsarases given in the same verse.

Pīlu is the name in the Atharvaveda[1] of a tree (*Careya arborea* or *Salvadora persica*) on the fruit of which doves fed.

[1] xx. 135, 12. *Cf.* Zimmer, *Altindisches Leben*, 62; Weber, *Transactions of the Berlin Academy*, 1895, 861.

Pīlumatī is in the Atharvaveda (xviii. 2, 48) the name of the intermediate heaven lying between the *udanvatī*, 'watery,' and the *pra-dyauḥ*, 'farthest heaven.' It presumably means 'rich in Pīlu.' *Cf.* **Div.**

Puṃś-calī ('running after men') is found in the Vājasaneyi Saṃhitā,[1] the Atharvaveda,[2] and later,[3] to denote a 'wanton woman.' In the Vājasaneyi Saṃhitā[4] also occurs the form Puṃścalū. See also **Dharma** and **Pati.**

[1] xxx. 22.

[2] xv. 2, 1 *et seq.*

[3] Pañcaviṃśa Brāhmaṇa, viii. 1, 10; Kauṣītaki Brāhmaṇa, xxvii. 1; Lāṭyāyana Srauta Sūtra, iv. 3, 9, 11.

[4] xxx. 5. 20; Taittirīya Brāhmaṇa, iii. 4, 1, 1; 15, 1; Kātyāyana Śrauta Sūtra, xiii. 3, 6.

Puṃ-savana ('male-production' ceremony) is found in the Atharvaveda[1] in a hymn which is obviously intended to accompany a rite aiming at securing the birth of a male child, and which is so applied in the ritual.[2]

[1] vi. 11, 1.

[2] Kauśika Sūtra, xxxv. 8. *Cf.* Bloomfield, *Hymns of the Atharvaveda*, 460; Whitney, Translation of the Atharvaveda, 288. The later Gṛhya ritual knows a special rite called Puṃsavana. See Āśvalāyana Gṛhya Sūtra, i. 13; Sāṅkhāyana Gṛhya Sūtra, i. 20; Gobhila Gṛhya Sūtra, ii. 6, 1 *et seq.*; Hillebrandt, *Rituallitteratur*, 41.

Puklaka. See **Paulkasa.**

Puñji-ṣṭha is found in the Yajurveda Saṃhitās[1] and later,[2] apparently meaning 'fisherman,' though Mahīdhara[3] explains it as 'bird-catcher.' *Cf.* **Pauñjiṣṭha.**

[1] Vājasaneyi Saṃhitā, xvi. 27; Taittirīya Saṃhitā, iv. 5, 4, 2; Maitrāyaṇī Saṃhitā, ii. 9, 5; Kāṭhaka Saṃhitā, xvii. 13.

[2] Āśvalāyana Śrauta Sūtra, x. 7; Pāṇini, viii. 3, 97.

[3] On Vājasaneyi Saṃhitā, xvi. 27.

Puñjīla is found in the Taittirīya Saṃhitā[1] and the Taittirīya Brāhmaṇa[2] in the sense of a 'bundle' of grass, being a variant of **Piñjūla.**

[1] vi. 1, 1, 7; 2, 4, 3.

[2] i. 7, 6, 4; ii. 7, 9, 5.

Puṇḍarīka denotes the blossom of the lotus in the Rigveda[1] and later.[2] The Pañcaviṃśa Brāhmaṇa[3] states that the lotus flower is born of the light of the Nakṣatras, and the Atharvaveda[4] compares the human heart to the lotus.[5]

[1] x. 142, 8.

[2] Taittirīya Brāhmaṇa, i. 8, 2, 1; Śatapatha Brāhmaṇa, v. 5, 5, 6; Bṛhadāraṇyaka Upaniṣad, ii. 3, 10; vi. 3, 14; Chāndogya Upaniṣad, i. 6, 7; Aitareya Āraṇyaka, iii. 2, 4.

[3] xviii. 9, 6.

[4] x. 8, 43; Chāndogya Upaniṣad, viii. 1, 1.

[5] In the Taittirīya Saṃhitā, i. 8, 18, 1; Taittirīya Brāhmaṇa, i. 8, 2, 1, *puṇḍari-srajā* denotes a 'wreath of lotus leaves.'

Cf. Zimmer, *Altindisches Leben*, 71.

Puṇḍra is the name of a people regarded as outcasts in the Aitareya Brāhmaṇa.[1] Their name occurs in the Sūtras also.[2] In the Epic their country corresponds with Bengal and Bihar.

[1] vii. 18; Śāṅkhāyana Śrauta Sūtra, xv. 26.

[2] Baudhāyana Dharma Sūtra, i. 2, 14. *Cf.* Caland, *Zeitschrift der Deutschen Morgenländischen Gesellschaft*, 56, 553; Bühler, *Sacred Books of the East*, 14, 148; Oldenberg, *Buddha*, 394, n. For the later geographical position of the Puṇḍras, *cf.* the map in Pargiter, *Journal of the Royal Asiatic Society*, 1908, 333.

Putra is, with **Sūnu,** the usual name for 'son' from the Rigveda onwards.[1] The original sense of the word was apparently 'small,' or something analogous.[2] The form Putraka[3] is often used with the distinct intention of an affectionate address to a younger man, not merely a son proper. Reference is frequently made to the desire for a son.[4] *Cf.* **Pati.**

[1] Rv. ii. 29, 5; v. 47, 6; vi. 9, 2, etc.; Av. iii. 30, 2, etc.

[2] Delbrück, *Die indogermanischen Verwandtschaftsnamen*, 454.

[3] Rv. viii. 69, 8; Aitareya Brāhmaṇa, v. 14; vi. 33 (here the narrative uses Putra; the reported words have Putraka); Satapatha Brāhmaṇa, xi. 6, 1, 2; Pañcaviṃśa Brāhmaṇa, xiii. 3, 21, etc.

[4] Rv. x. 183, 1; Av. vi. 81, 3; xi. 1, 1; Taittirīya Saṃhitā, vi. 5, 6, 1; vii. 1, 8, 1; Taittirīya Brāhmaṇa, i. 1, 9, 1.

Putra-sena is the name of a man in the Maitrāyaṇī Saṃhitā (iv. 6, 6).

Putrikā in the later literature[1] has the technical sense of the daughter of a man without sons, whom he gives in marriage on the express terms that her son shall perform the funeral rites for him, and be counted as his. The thing as well as the name is recognized by Yāska in the Nirukta,[2] and traced to the Rigveda.[3] But the passages in the Rigveda are of very uncertain meaning,[4] and in all probability do not refer to this custom at all.

[1] Mānava Dharma Śāstra, ix. 127 *et seq.*; Gautama Dharma Sūtra, xxviii. 20; Vasiṣṭha Dharma Sūtra, xvii. 17.

[2] iii. 5 *ad fin.*

[3] i. 124, 7. *Cf.* iii. 31, 1.

[4] *Cf.* Geldner, *Vedische Studien*, 3, 34; *Rigveda, Kommentar*, 48, 49; Oldenberg, *Ṛgveda-Noten*, 1, 239 *et seq.*; Roth, *Nirukta, Erläuterungen*, 27; Jolly, *Recht und Sitte*, 72, 73; Bṛhaddevatā, iv. 110. 111, with Macdonell's note; Keith, *Journal of the Royal Asiatic Society*, 1910, 924, 925; Jolly, *Die Adoption in Indien*, 32.

Punar-datta ('given again') is the name of a teacher in the Śāṅkhāyana Āraṇyaka (viii. 8).

Punar-bhū is found in the Atharvaveda[1] meaning a wife who marries again, a rite being mentioned by which she can ensure reunion with her second (not her first) husband in the next world.

[1] ix. 5, 28. *Cf.* Whitney, Translation of the Atharvaveda, 537.

Punar-vasu ('bringing goods again'), used in the dual, denotes the fifth in the series of the Vedic **Nakṣatras**, or 'Lunar Mansions.' Roth[1] takes the word to have this sense in its only occurrence in the Rigveda,[2] but this must be regarded as decidedly doubtful. The term is, however, found in the ordinary lists of the Nakṣatras in the later Saṃhitās and the Brāhmaṇas.[3]

[1] St. Petersburg Dictionary, *s.v.*

[2] x. 19, 1.

[3] Av. xix. 7, 1; Taittirīya Saṃhitā, i. 5, 1, 4; iv. 4, 10, 1; Taittirīya Brāhmaṇa, i. 1, 2, 3; Kauṣītaki Brāhmaṇa, i. 3; Kāṭhaka Saṃhitā, viii. 15; xxxix. 13; Śatapatha Brāhmaṇa, ii. 1, 2, 10, etc.

Cf. Weber, *Naxatra*, 2, 289, 290; Zimmer, *Altindisches Leben*, 355.

Punaḥ-sara, 'recurrent,' is the epithet of the barking dog in the Rigveda,[1] which is told to bark at the thief. It refers, no doubt, to the dog's practice of running to and fro when it barks. It is also applied to a plant, **Apāmārga** (*Achyranthes aspera*), in the Atharvaveda,[2] with the sense of 'having revertent leaves.'

[1] vii. 55, 3; Pischel, *Vedische Studien*, 2, 56, n. 1.

[2] iv. 17, 2; vi. 129, 3; x. 1, 9. *Cf.* Whitney, Translation of the Atharvaveda, 179. Bloomfield, *Hymns of the Atharvaveda*, 394, prefers the sense of 'attacking,' which is the meaning of *prati-sara*, Av. viii. 5, 5. *Cf.* Śatapatha Brāhmaṇa, v. 2, 4, 20.

Pumāṃs denotes in the Rigveda[1] and later[2] man as the 'male.' It has no special reference to marriage like **Pati**, or to heroism like **Nṛ** or **Nara**. In grammar it denotes the masculine gender.[3]

[1] i. 124, 7; 162, 22; iii. 29, 13; iv. 3, 10, etc.

[2] Av. iii. 6, 1; 23, 3; iv. 4, 4; vi. 11, 2; Vājasaneyi Saṃhitā, viii. 5, etc.

[3] Nirukta, iii. 8; Śatapatha Brāhmaṇa, x. 1, 1, 8; 5, 1, 3. *Cf.* iv. 5, 2, 10, and *puṃsā nakṣatreṇa*, 'a Nakṣatra with a masculine name,' in the Bṛhadāraṇyaka Upaniṣad, vi. 3, 1.

Pur is a word of frequent occurrence in the Rigveda[1] and later,[2] meaning 'rampart,' 'fort,' or 'stronghold.' Such fortifications must have been occasionally of considerable size, as one is called 'broad' (*pṛthvī*) and 'wide' (*urvī*).[3] Elsewhere[4] a fort 'made of stone' (*aśmamayī*) is mentioned. Sometimes strongholds 'of iron' (*āyasī*) are referred to,[5] but these are probably only metaphorical. A fort 'full of kine' (*gomatī*) is mentioned,[6] showing that strongholds were used to hold cattle. 'Autumnal' (*śāradī*) forts are named, apparently as belonging to the **Dāsas**: this may refer to the forts in that season being

[1] i. 53, 7; 58, 8; 131, 4; 166, 8; iii. 15, 4; iv. 27, 1, etc.

[2] Taittirīya Brāhmaṇa, i. 7, 7, 5; Aitareya Brāhmaṇa, i. 23; ii. 11; Śatapatha Brāhmaṇa, iii. 4, 4, 3; vi. 3, 3, 25; xi. 1, 1, 2. 3; Chāndogya Upaniṣad, viii. 5, 3, etc.

[3] i. 189, 2.

[4] Rv. iv. 30, 20. Perhaps sun-dried bricks are alluded to by *āmā* (lit. 'raw,' 'unbaked') in Rv. ii. 35, 6.

[5] Rv. i. 58, 8; ii. 20, 8; iv. 27, 1; vii. 3, 7; 15, 4; 95, 1; x. 101, 8. See Muir, *Sanskrit Texts*, 2[2], 378 *et seq.*

[6] Av. viii. 6, 23.

occupied against Āryan attacks or against inundations caused by overflowing rivers. Forts 'with a hundred walls' (*śata-bhuji*) are spoken of.[7]

It would probably be a mistake to regard these forts as permanently occupied fortified places like the fortresses of the mediæval barony. They were probably merely places of refuge against attack, ramparts of hardened earth with palisades and a ditch (*cf.* **Dehī**). Pischel and Geldner,[8] however, think that there were towns with wooden walls and ditches (περίβολος and τάφρος) like the Indian town of Pāṭaliputra known to Megasthenes[9] and the Pāli texts.[10] This is possible, but hardly susceptible of proof, and it is not without significance that the word **Nagara** is of late occurrence. On the whole it is hardly likely that in early Vedic times city life was much developed. In the Epic, according to Hopkins,[11] there are found the Nagara, 'city'; **Grāma,** 'village'; and Ghoṣa, 'ranch.' Vedic literature hardly seems to go beyond the village, no doubt with modifications in its later period.

The siege of forts is mentioned in the Saṃhitās and Brāhmaṇas.[12] According to the Rigveda,[13] fire was used.

[7] Rv. i. 166, 8; vii. 15, 14.

[8] *Vedische Studien*, 1, xxii, xxiii, where *kṣiti dhruvā*, i. 73, 4, is compared.

[9] Strabo, p. 702; Arrian, *Indica*, 10.

[10] Mahāparinibbānasutta, p. 12. *Cf.* Rhys Davids, *Buddhist India*, 262.

[11] *Journal of the American Oriental Society*, 13, 77; 174 *et seq.*

[12] Taittirīya Saṃhitā, vi. 2, 3, 1; Aitareya Brāhmaṇa, i. 23; Śatapatha Brāhmaṇa, iii. 4, 4, 3-5; Gopatha Brāhmaṇa, ii. 2, 7, etc.

[13] vii. 5, 3. Possibly, in some cases, the palisade was no more than a hedge of thorn or a row of stakes (*cf.* Rv. x. 101, 8), as suggested by Zimmer, *Altindisches Leben*, 143, 145; and *cf.* Rv. viii. 53, 5, as corrected by Roth, *Zeitschrift der Deutschen Morgenländischen Gesellschaft*, 48, 109.

Cf. Zimmer, *Altindisches Leben*, 142-148, who compares the fact that neither the Germans (Tacitus, *Germania*, 16) nor the Slavs (Procopius, *De bello Gotico*, iii. 14) lived in towns, but, like the ancient Indians, were scattered in villages, each consisting of the houses and steadings of the several families living in the village. The evidence seems pretty convincing. It is true that the Greeks, when we first find them, evidently knew castles and fortresses of the mediæval type; but the Greeks were clearly an invading race, superimposed on an older and in civilization more advanced people (see, *e.g.*, Burrows, *Discoveries in Crete*). But the Pur may, as Zimmer allows, have sometimes been built within the limits of the village. Whether, as he urges (144), the *śāradī pur* was a protection against the floods of autumn is uncertain. *Cf.* Rv. i. 131, 4; 174, 2; vi. 20, 10. In particular, it is not legitimate to connect the mention of those forts with the fact that the Pūrus lived on either side of the Sindhu (Indus), and to assume that Purukutsa's attack on the aborigines was directed against the forts in which they normally protected themselves on the rising of the river. No argument for the large size of cities can be drawn from the mention in the Kāṭhaka Upaniṣad, v. 1, of *ekādaśa-dvāra* as an epithet of Pura (*cf.* Śvetāśvatara Upaniśad, iii. 18: *nava-dvāra pura,* 'the citadel of nine doors'), because it is used metaphorically of the body, and the number of doors depends on the nature of the body (Keith, *Aitareya Āraṇyaka,* 185). The evidence of the Śatapatha Brāhmaṇa, xi. 1, 1, 2. 3, seems rather to point to only one gate in a city.

Cf. Schrader, *Prehistoric Antiquities,* 412; Muir, *Sanskrit Texts,* 5, 451; Weber, *Indische Studien,* 1, 229; Ludwig, Translation of the Rigveda, 3, 207, and Mahāpur.

Puraṃ-dhi occurs in the Rigveda,[1] possibly as the name of a woman, a protégée of the Aśvins, who gave her a son, **Hiraṇya hasta.**

[1] i. 116, 13. *Cf.* Zimmer, *Altindisches Leben,* 398.

Puraya is the name of a patron celebrated in a Dānastuti ('Praise of Gifts') in the Rigveda.[1]

[1] vi. 63, 9. *Cf.* Ludwig, Translation of the Rigveda, 3, 158.

1. **Purāṇa,** denoting a tale 'of olden times,' is often found[1] in the combination Itihāsa-Purāṇa, which is probably a Dvandva compound meaning '**Itihāsa** and Purāṇa.' It sometimes[2] occurs as a separate word, but beside Itihāsa, no doubt with the same sense as in the Dvandva. Sāyaṇa[3] defines a Purāṇa as a tale which deals with the primitive condition of the universe and the creation of the world, but there is no ground for supposing that this view is correct, or for clearly distinguishing Itihāsa and Purāṇa. See **Itihāsa.**

[1] Satapatha Brāhmaṇa, xi. 5, 6, 8; Chāndogya Upaniṣad, iii. 4, 1. 2; vii. 1, 2. 4; 2, 1; 7, 1.

[2] Av. xv. 6, 4; Śatapatha Brāhmaṇa, xiii. 4, 3, 13; Bṛhadāraṇyaka Upaniṣad, ii 4, 10; iv. 1, 2; 5, 11; Taittirīya Āraṇyaka, ii. 9; Jaiminīya Upaniṣad Brāhmaṇa, i. 53; Purāṇa-veda: Śāṅkhāyana Śrauta Sūtra, xvi. 2, 27; Purāṇa-vidyā: Āśvalāyana Srauta Sūtra, x. 7, etc.

[3] Introduction to Aitareya Brāhmaṇa, cited by St. Petersburg Dictionary, *s.v.*

2. **Purāṇa** is the name of a Ṛṣi in the Kāṭhaka Saṃhitā (xxxix. 7).

Purīkaya is the name of a water animal in the Atharvaveda,[1] being clearly a variant of the name that appears as Pulīkaya in the Maitrāyaṇī Saṃhitā,[2] and as Kulīpaya in the Vājasaneyi Saṃhitā,[3] and as Kulīkaya in the Taittirīya Brāhmaṇa.[4] What animal is meant is quite unknown.

[1] xi. 2, 25.
[2] iii. 14, 2. Pulikā, *ibid.*, 5, is a variant of **Kulīkā**.
[3] xxiv. 21. 35.
[4] v. 5, 13, 1.

Cf. Zimmer, *Altindisches Leben*, 96; Bloomfield, *Zeitschrift der Deutschen Morgenländischen Gesellschaft*, 48, 557; *Hymns of the Atharvaveda*, 621.

Purīṣiṇī is found in a hymn of the Rigveda[1] apparently either as the name of a river,[2] or much more probably as an epithet of the **Sarayu**,[3] meaning, perhaps, 'abounding in water,' 'swollen,'[4] or 'carrying rubble.'[5]

[1] v. 53, 9.
[2] An alternative suggested by Roth, St. Petersburg Dictionary, *s.v.*
[3] Zimmer, *Altindisches Leben*, 17; Geldner, *Rigveda, Glossar*, 111.
[4] Geldner, *loc. cit.*
[5] Roth, *loc. cit.*

Puru-kutsa is the name of a king who is mentioned several times in the Rigveda. In one passage[1] he is mentioned as a contemporary of **Sudās**, but whether as a foe, according to Ludwig,[2] or merely as a contemporary, according to Hillebrandt,[3] is uncertain. In two other passages[4] he is mentioned as victorious by divine favour, and in another[5] he appears as a king of the **Pūrus** and a conqueror of the **Dāsas**. His son was **Trasadasyu**,[6] who is accordingly called **Paurukutsya**[7] or **Paurukutsi**.[8] Different conclusions have been drawn from one hymn of the Rigveda[9] in which the birth of Purukutsa's son,

[1] i. 63, 7.
[2] Translation of the Rigveda, 3, 174, emending *sudāse* in the text to *sudāsam*, plausibly, but not, of course, convincingly.
[3] *Vedische Mythologie*, 1, 115. *Cf.* Oldenberg, *Zeitschrift der Deutschen Morgenländischen Gesellschaft*, 42, 204, 205, 219.
[4] i. 112, 7. 14; 174, 2.
[5] vi. 20, 10. *Cf.* i. 63, 7, where Pūru also is mentioned. Ludwig suggests reading in vi. 20, 10, *saudāsīḥ* for *dāsīḥ*, referring to the forts of Sudās; but this must be regarded as illegitimate. *Cf.* Oldenberg, *Zeitschrift*, 55, 330.
[6] Rv. iv. 42, 8. 9.
[7] Rv. v. 33, 8; viii. 19, 36.
[8] Rv. vii. 19, 3.
[9] Rv. iv. 42, 8. 9, with Sāyaṇa's note; Muir, *Sanskrit Texts*, 1[2], 266, 267.

Trasadasyu, is mentioned. The usual interpretation is that Purukutsa was killed in battle or captured, whereupon his wife secured a son to restore the fortunes of the Pūrus. But Sieg[10] offers a completely different interpretation. According to him the word **daurgahe**, which occurs in the hymn, and which in the ordinary view is rendered 'descendant of Durgaha,' an ancestor of Purukutsa, is the name of a horse, the hymn recording the success of an Aśvamedha ('horse sacrifice') undertaken by Purukutsa for his wife, as by kings in late times, to secure a son. This interpretation is supported by the version of *daurgahe* given in the Śatapatha,[11] but is by no means certain. Moreover, if Purukutsa was a contemporary of Sudās, the defeat of the Pūrus by Sudās in the **Dāśarājña**[12] might well have been the cause of the troubles from which **Purukutsānī**, by the birth of Trasadasyu, rescued the family. In the Śatapatha Brāhmaṇa[13] Purukutsa is called an Aikṣvāka.

[10] *Die Sagenstoffe des Ṛgveda*, 96-102.
[11] xiii. 5, 4, 5.
[12] vii. 18. *Cf.* also the reference to a Pūru defeat in vii. 8, 4.
[13] xiii. 5, 4, 5. *Cf.* **Ikṣvāku, Tryaruṇa**, and Oldenberg, *Buddha*, 403.

Purukutsānī, 'wife of **Purukutsa**,' is mentioned as the mother of **Trasadasyu** in one hymn of the Rigveda (iv. 42, 9).

Puru-ṇītha Śāta-vaneya ('descendant of Śatavani') is the name of a sacrificer, or perhaps a priest, a Bhāradvāja, in the Rigveda.[1] It is doubtful whether he is also mentioned as a singer in another passage of the Rigveda.[2] In both places Roth[3] sees in Puru-ṇītha merely a word meaning 'choral song.'

[1] i. 59, 7.
[2] vii. 9, 6. *Cf.* Ludwig, Translation of the Rigveda, 3, 160; Oldenberg, *Ṛgveda-Noten*, 1, 60.
[3] St. Petersburg Dictionary, *s.v.*

Puru-dama occurs in the plural in the Atharvaveda,[1] where, according to Ludwig,[2] it is probably the proper name of the singers, but by Roth[3] and Whitney[4] is understood as merely an adjective meaning 'possessed of many houses.'

[1] vii. 73, 1.
[2] Translation of the Rigveda, 3, xxv.
[3] St. Petersburg Dictionary, *s.v.*
[4] Translation of the Atharvaveda, 437.

Puru-panthā is mentioned as a generous donor to a **Bharadvāja** in one hymn of the Rigveda (vi. 63, 10).

Puru-māyya occurs in one hymn of the Rigveda[1] as a protégé of Indra. It is quite possible that he was the father of, or at least connected with, **Atithigva, Ṛkṣa**, and **Aśvamedha**, who are celebrated in the hymn.

1 viii. 68, 10. *Cf.* Ludwig, Translation of the Rigveda, 3, 163.

Puru-mitra is mentioned twice in the Rigveda (i. 117, 20; x. 39, 7) as the father of a maiden who wedded **Vimada**, apparently against her father's will.

Puru-mīḷha is mentioned twice in the Rigveda[1] as an ancient sage, in which capacity he appears in the Atharvaveda[2] also. Perhaps the same[3] Purumīḷha is intended in an obscure hymn in the Rigveda,[4] where, according to the legends reported in the Bṛhaddevatā[5] and by Ṣaḍguruśiṣya in his commentary on the Sarvānukramaṇī,[6] and by Sāyaṇa in his commentary on the Rigveda,[4] he as well as **Taranta** was a son of Vidadaśva, and a patron of the singer **Śyāvāśva.** The correctness of the legend has been shown to be most improbable by Oldenberg,[7] who points out[8] that the legend misinterprets the Rigveda by making Purumīḷha a Vaidadaśvi, for he is there only compared in generosity to one.

In another legend found in the Pañcaviṃśa Brāhmaṇa,[9] and based on a hymn of the Rigveda,[10] Purumīḷha and Taranta appear as persons who received gifts from **Dhvasra** and **Puruṣanti,** and as sons of Vidadaśva. The legend, which also occurs in the Śāṭyāyanaka,[11] is apparently best explained by

1 i. 151, 2; 183, 5.

2 iv. 29, 4; xviii. 3, 15.

3 See, however, Weber, *Episches im vedischen Ritual*, 27, n. 3; Sieg, *Die Sagenstoffe des Ṛgveda*, 62, n. 3.

4 v. 61, 9.

5 v. 49 *et seq.*, with Macdonell's notes.

6 Edition Macdonell, pp. 118 *et seq.*

7 *Ṛgveda-Noten*, 1, 353, 354. *Cf.* Max Müller, *Sacred Books of the East*, 32, 359.

8 *Op. cit.*, 354, n. 1.

9 xiii. 7, 12.

10 ix. 58, 3.

11 Cited by Sāyaṇa on Rv., *loc. cit.*

Sieg;[12] who says that as the two were kings they could not under the rules of caste accept gifts, unless for the nonce they became singers. The legend has no claim at all, as Oldenberg[13] shows, to validity.

[12] *Op. cit.*, 63.

[13] *Zeitschrift der Deutschen Morgenländischen Gesellschaft*, 42, 232, n. 1. He points out, *Ṛgveda-Noten*, 1, 354, that the legend is not accepted by the Anukramaṇī (Index), since its list of authors gives Avatsāra as the Ṛṣi, not the two Taranta and Purumīḷha.

END OF VOL. I.

VEDIC INDEX
OF
NAMES AND SUBJECTS

VEDIC INDEX
OF
NAMES AND SUBJECTS

Arthur Anthony Macdonell

And

Arthur Berriedale Keith

VOL. II

MOTILAL BANARSIDASS PUBLISHERS
PRIVATE LIMITED • DELHI

Reprint: Delhi, 1958, 1967, 1982, 1995, 2007
First Edition: London, 1912

ISBN: 978-81-208-1333-5 (Vol. II)
ISBN: 978-81-208-1331-1 (Set)

MOTILAL BANARSIDASS
41 U.A. Bungalow Road, Jawahar Nagar, Delhi 110 007
8 Mahalaxmi Chamber, 22 Bhulabhai Desai Road, Mumbai 400 026
236, 9th Main III Block, Jayanagar, Bangalore 560 011
203 Royapettah High Road, Mylapore, Chennai 600 004
Sanas Plaza, 1302 Baji Rao Road, Pune 411 002
8 Camac Street, Kolkata 700 017
Ashok Rajpath, Patna 800 004
Chowk, Varanasi 221 001

Printed in India
BY JAINENDRA PRAKASH JAIN AT SHRI JAINENDRA PRESS,
A-45 NARAINA, PHASE-I, NEW DELHI 110 028
AND PUBLISHED BY NARENDRA PRAKASH JAIN FOR
MOTILAL BANARSIDASS PUBLISHERS PRIVATE LIMITED,
BUNGALOW ROAD, DELHI 110 007

VEDIC INDEX OF NAMES AND SUBJECTS

Puruṣa, or **Pūruṣa,** is the generic term for 'man' in the Rigveda[1] and later.[2] Man is composed of five parts according to the Atharvaveda,[3] or of six according to the Aitareya Brāhmaṇa,[4] or of sixteen,[5] or of twenty,[6] or of twenty-one,[7] or of twenty-four,[8] or of twenty-five,[9] all more or less fanciful enumerations. Man is the first of animals,[10] but also essentially an animal (see **Paśu**). The height of a man is given in the Kātyāyana Śrauta Sūtra[11] as four Aratnis ('cubits'), each of two Padas ('feet'), each of twelve Aṅgulis ('finger's breadths'); and the term Puruṣa itself is found earlier[12] as a measure of length.

Puruṣa is also applied to denote the length of a man's life, a 'generation';[13] the 'pupil' in the eye;[14] and in the grammatical literature the 'person' of the verb.[15]

1 vii. 104, 15; x. 97, 4. 5. 8; 165, 3.

2 Av. iii. 21, 1; v. 21, 4; viii. 2, 25; 7, 2; xii. 3, 51; 4, 25; xiii. 4, 42, etc.; Taittirīya Saṃhitā, ii. 1, 1, 5; 2, 2, 8; v. 2, 5, 1, etc.

3 xii. 3, 10; Pañcaviṃśa Brāhmaṇa, xiv. 5, 26; Aitareya Brāhmaṇa, ii. 14; vi. 29.

4 ii. 39.

5 Śāṅkhāyana Srauta Sūtra, xvi. 4, 16.

6 Pañcaviṃśa Brāhmaṇa, xxiii. 14, 5.

7 Taittirīya Saṃhitā. v. 1, 8, 1; Śatapatha Brāhmaṇa, xiii. 5, 1, 6; Aitareya Brāhmaṇa, i. 18; Aitareya Āraṇyaka, i. 2, 4, etc.

8 Śatapatha Brāhmaṇa, vi. 2, 1, 23.

9 Śāṅkhāyana Śrauta Sūtra, xvi. 12, 10; Śāṅkhāyana Āraṇyaka, i. 1; Aitareya Āraṇyaka, i. 2, 4.

10 Śatapatha Brāhmaṇa, vi. 2, 1, 18; vii. 5, 2, 17. He is the master of animals, Kāṭhaka Saṃhitā, xx. 10.

11 xvi. 8, 21. 25.

12 Śatapatha Brāhmaṇa, i. 2, 5, 14; xiii. 8, 1, 19; Taittirīya Saṃhitā, v. 2, 5, 1.

13 Taittirīya Saṃhitā, ii. 1, 5, 5; v. 4, 10, 4; Śatapatha Brāhmaṇa, i. 8, 3, 6; *dvi-puruṣa* ('two generations'), Aitareya Brāhmaṇa, viii. 7, etc.

14 Śatapatha Brāhmaṇa, x. 5, 2, 7. 8; xii. 9, 1, 12; Bṛhadāraṇyaka Upaniṣad, ii. 3, 9.

15 Nirukta, vii. 1. 2.

Puruṣa Mṛga, the 'man wild beast,' occurs in the list of victims at the Aśvamedha ('horse sacrifice') in the Yajurveda.[1] Zimmer's[2] view that the ape is meant seems probable. According to him also, the word Puruṣa alone, in two passages of the Atharvaveda,[3] refers to the ape and its cry (*māyu*); but this sense is not necessary, and it is not adopted by Bloomfield,[4] though Whitney[5] does not think the rendering 'cry of a man' satisfactory, the term *māyu* not being properly applicable to the noise made by human beings.

[1] Taittirīya Saṃhitā, v. 5, 15, 1; Maitrāyaṇī Saṃhitā, iii. 14, 16; Vājasaneyi Saṃhitā, xxiv. 35.
[2] *Altindisches Leben*, 85.
[3] vi. 38, 4; xix. 39, 4.
[4] *Hymns of the Atharvaveda*, 117.
[5] Translation of the Atharvaveda, 309.

Puruṣa Hastin ('the man with a hand') is found in the list of victims at the Aśvamedha ('horse sacrifice') in the Yajurveda.[1] It must be the 'ape.'

[1] Vājasaneyi Saṃhitā, xxiv. 29; Maitrāyaṇī Saṃhitā, iii. 14, 8.

Puruṣanti is a name that occurs twice in the Rigveda,[1] in the first passage denoting a protégé of the Aśvins, in the second a patron who gave presents to one of the Vedic singers. In both cases the name is joined with that of **Dhvasanti** or **Dhvasra.** The presumption from the manner in which these three names are mentioned is that they designate men, but the grammatical form of the words might equally well be feminine. Females must be meant, if the evidence of the Pañcaviṃśa Brāhmaṇa[2] is to be taken as decisive, for the form of the first of the two names there occurring, *Dhvasre Puruṣantī*, 'Dhvasrā and Puruṣanti,' is exclusively feminine, though here as well as elsewhere Sāyaṇa[3] interprets the names as masculines. See also **Taranta** and **Purumīḷha.**

[1] i. 112, 23; ix. 58, 3.
[2] xiii. 7, 12. Roth thinks the feminine form *Dhvasre* here is a corruption, based on the dual form occurring in the Rigveda, *Dhvasrayoḥ*, which might be feminine as well as masculine.
[3] Also on the Śāṭyāyanaka, cited on Rv. ix. 58, 3, and on Rv. i. 112, 23.

Cf. Weber, *Episches im vedischen Ritual*, 27, n. 1; Sieg, *Die Sagenstoffe des Ṛgveda*, 62, 63; Oldenberg, *Zeitschrift der Deutschen Morgenländischen Gesellschaft*, 42, 232, n. 1.

Puru-hanman is the name of a Ṛṣi in a hymn of the Rigveda,[1] an **Āṅgirasa,** according to the Rigvedic Anukramaṇī (Index), but according to the Pañcaviṃśa Brāhmaṇa[2] a **Vaikhānasa.**

[1] viii. 70, 2.
[2] xiv. 9, 29. *Cf.* Ludwig, Translation of the Rigveda, 3, 107.

Purū-Ravas is the name of a hero in a hymn of the Rigveda[1] containing a curious dialogue between him and a nymph, Urvaśī, an Apsaras. He is also mentioned in the Śatapatha Brāhmaṇa,[2] where several verses of the Rigvedic dialogue find a setting in a continuous story. In the later literature he is recognized as a king.[3] His name is perhaps intended in one other passage of the Rigveda.[4] It is impossible to say whether he is a mythical figure pure and simple, or really an ancient king. His epithet, Aiḷa,[5] 'descendant of Iḍā' (a sacrificial goddess), is certainly in favour of the former alternative.

[1] x. 95.
[2] xi. 5, 1, 1. *Cf.* iii. 4, 1, 22; Kāṭhaka Saṃhitā, viii. 10; Nirukta, x. 46.
[3] See Geldner, *Vedische Studien*, 1, 283 *et seq.*
[4] i. 31, 4.
[5] Śatapatha Brāhmaṇa, xi. 5, 1, 1.

Cf. Weber, *Indische Studien*, 1, 196; Max Müller, *Chips*, 4[2], 109 *et seq.*; Kuhn, *Die Herabkunft des Feuers*, 85 *et seq.*; Roth, *Nirukta*, *Erläuterungen*, 153; Macdonell, *Vedic Mythology*, 124, 135; Oldenberg, *Sacred Books of the East*, 46, 28, 323.

Purūru is the name of a poet, an **Ātreya,** in the Rigveda,[1] according to Ludwig.[2] But the only form of the word found, *purūruṇā*, seems merely an adverb meaning 'far and wide.'

[1] v. 70, 1.
[2] Translation of the Rigveda, 3, 126. *Cf.* Oldenberg, *Zeitschrift der Deutschen Morgenländischen Gesellschaft*, 42, 215, n. 1; *Ṛgveda-Noten*, 1, 360.

Purū-vasu ('abounding in wealth') is the name of a poet, an **Ātreya,** according to Ludwig,[1] in one passage of the Rigveda.[2] But this is very doubtful.

[1] Translation of the Rigveda, 3, 126.
[2] v. 36, 3. *Cf.* Oldenberg, *Zeitschrift der Deutschen Morgenländischen Gesellschaft*, 42, 215, n. 1; *Ṛgveda-Noten*, 1, 333.

Puro-ḍāś is the name of the sacrificial cake in the Rigveda[1] and later.[2]

[1] iii. 28, -; 41, 3; 52, 2; iv. 24, 5; vi. 23, 7; viii. 31, 2, etc.

[2] Av. ix. 6, 12; x. 9, 25; xii. 4, 35; xviii. 4, 2; Taittirīya Saṃhitā, ii. 3, 2, 8; vii. 1, 9, 1; Vājasaneyi Saṃhitā, xix. 85; xxviii. 23, etc.

Cf. Zimmer, *Altindisches Leben*, 270.

Puro-dhā denotes the office of **Purohita**, 'domestic priest.' Its mention as early as the Atharvaveda,[1] and often later,[2] shows that the post was a fully recognized and usual one.

[1] v. 24, 1.

[2] Taittirīya Saṃhitā, ii. 1, 2, 9; vii. 4, 1, 1; Taittirīya Brāhmaṇa, ii. 7, 1, 2; Pañcaviṃśa Brāhmaṇa, xiii. 3, 12; 9, 27; xv. 4, 7; Aitareya Brāhmaṇa, vii. 31; viii. 24. 27; Śatapatha Brāhmaṇa, iv. 1, 4, 5.

Puro-'nuvākyā ('introductory verse to be recited') is the technical term for the address to a god inviting him to partake of the offering; it was followed by the **Yājyā**, which accompanied the actual oblation.[1] Such addresses are not unknown, but are rare, according to Oldenberg,[2] in the Rigveda; subsequently they are regular, the word itself occurring in the later Saṃhitās[3] and the Brāhmaṇas.[4]

[1] Oldenberg, *Religion des Veda*, 387, 388.

[2] *Zeitschrift der Deutschen Morgenländischen Gesellschaft*, 42, 243 *et seq.*, against Bergaigne, *Recherches sur l'histoire de la liturgie védique*, 13 *et seq.*

[3] Taittirīya Saṃhitā, i. 6, 10, 4; ii. 2, 9, 2; Vājasaneyi Saṃhitā, xx. 12, etc.

[4] Aitareya Brāhmaṇa, i. 4, 17; ii. 13, 26; Taittirīya Brāhmaṇa, i. 3, 1, 3; Śatapatha Brāhmaṇa, ii. 5, 2, 21, etc.

Puro-ruc is the technical description of certain **Nivid** verses which were recited at the morning libation in the Ājya and Praüga ceremonies before the hymn (*sūkta*) of the litany or its parts. It occurs in the later Saṃhitās and the Brāhmaṇas.[1]

[1] Taittirīya Saṃhitā, vi. 5, 10, 13; vii. 2, 7, 4; Aitareya Brāhmaṇa, ii. 39; iii. 9; iv. 5; Kauṣītaki Brāhmaṇa, xiv. 1. 4. 5; Śatapatha Brāhmaṇa, iv. 1, 3, 15; 2, 1, 8; v. 4, 4, 20, etc.

Cf. Hillebrandt, *Rituallitteratur*, 102.

Puro-vāta, the 'east wind,' is mentioned in the later Saṃhitās and the Brāhmaṇas.[1] Geldner[2] thinks it merely means the wind preceding the rains.

[1] Taittirīya Saṃhitā, i. 6, 11, 3; ii. 4, 7, 1; iv. 3, 3, 1; 4, 6, 1; Maitrāyaṇī Saṃhitā, iii. 1, 5; Śatapatha Brāhmaṇa, i. 5, 2, 18; Chāndogya Upaniṣad, ii. 3, 1, etc.

[2] *Vedische Studien*, 3, 120, n. 2.

Puro-hita ('placed in front,' 'appointed') is the name of a priest in the Rigveda[1] and later.[2] The office of Purohita is called Purohiti[3] and **Purodhā.** It is clear that the primary function of the Purohita was that of 'domestic priest' of a king, or perhaps a great noble; his quite exceptional position is shown by the fact that only one Purohita seems ever to be mentioned in Vedic literature.[4] Examples of Purohitas in the Rigveda are **Viśvāmitra**[5] or **Vasiṣṭha**[6] in the service of the Bharata king, **Sudās**, of the **Tṛtsu** family; the Purohita of **Kuruśravaṇa**;[7] and **Devāpi**, the Purohita of **Śantanu.**[8] The Purohita was in all religious matters the *alter ego* of the king. In the ritual[9] it is laid down that a king must have a Purohita, else the gods will not accept his offerings. He ensures the king's safety and victory in battle by his prayers;[10] he procures

[1] i. 1, 1; 44, 10. 12; ii. 24, 9; iii. 2, 8; 3, 2; v. 11, 2; vi. 70, 4, etc.

[2] Av. viii. 5, 5; Vājasaneyi Saṃhitā, ix. 23; xi. 81; xxxi. 20; Aitareya Brāhmaṇa, viii. 24, etc.; Nirukta, ii. 12; vii. 15.

[3] Rv. vii. 60, 12; 83, 4.

[4] Geldner, *Vedische Studien*, 2, 144, thinks that several Purohitas were possible, quoting Sāyaṇa, on Rv. x. 57, 1, who gives the tale of the Gaupāyanas and King Asamāti from the Śāṭyāyanaka, and comparing the case of Vasiṣṭha and Viśvāmitra as Purohitas, probably contemporaneously, of Sudās. But that the two were contemporaneous is most unlikely, especially if we adopt the very probable view of Hopkins (*Journal of the American Oriental Society*, 15, 260 *et seq.*) that Viśvāmitra was with the ten kings (Rv. vii. 18) when they unsuccessfully attacked Sudās. The other narrative has, as Oldenberg, *Religion des Veda*, 375, n. 3, observes, a markedly fictitious character; while every other passage that mentions a Purohita speaks of him in the singular, and as there was only one Brahman priest at the sacrifice, so the Purohita acted as Brahman.

[5] iii. 33. 53. *Cf.* vii. 18.

[6] Rv. vii. 18. 83.

[7] Rv. x. 33. See Geldner, *Vedische Studien*, 2, 150, 184.

[8] Rv. x. 98.

[9] Aitareya Brāhmaṇa, viii. 24.

[10] See Av. iii. 19; Rv. vii. 18, 13, from which Geldner, *op. cit.*, 2, 135, n. 3, concludes that the priest prayed in the **Sabhā**, 'house of assembly,' while the king fought on the field of battle. See Āśvalāyana Gṛhya Sūtra, iii. 12. 19. 20. *Cf.* **Pūru**, n. 2.

the fall of rain for the crops;[11] he is the flaming fire that guards the kingdom.[12] Divodāsa in trouble is rescued by Bharadvāja;[13] and King **Tryaruṇa Traidhātva Aikṣvāka** reproaches his Purohita, **Vṛśa Jāna**, when his car runs over a Brahmin boy and kills him.[14] The close relation of king and Purohita is illustrated by the case of **Kutsa Aurava**, who slew his Purohita, **Upagu Sauśravasa**, for disloyalty in serving Indra, to whom Kutsa was hostile.[15] Other disputes between kings and priests who officiated for them are those of **Janamejaya** and the **Kaśyapas**, and of **Viśvantara** and the **Śyāparṇas**;[16] and between **Asamāti** and the **Gaupāyanas.**[17] In some cases one Purohita served more than one king; for example, **Devabhāga Śrautarṣa** was the Purohita of the **Kurus** and the **Sṛñjayas** at the same time,[18] and **Jala Jātūkarṇya** was the Purohita of the kings of **Kāśi, Videha,** and **Kosala.**[19]

There is no certain proof that the office of Purohita was hereditary in a family, though it probably was so.[20] At any rate, it seems clear from the relations of the Purohita with King **Kuruśravaṇa**, and with his son **Upamaśravas**,[21] that a king would keep on the Purohita of his father.

Zimmer[22] thinks that the king might act as his own Purohita, as shown by the case of King Viśvantara, who sacrificed without the help of the Śyāparṇas,[23] and that a Purohita need not be a priest, as shown by the case of Devāpi and Śantanu.[24] But neither opinion seems to be justified. It is not said that

11 Rv. x. 98.

12 Aitareya Brāhmaṇa, viii. 24. 25.

13 Pañcaviṃśa Brāhmaṇa, xv. 3, 7.

14 *Ibid.*, xiii. 3, 12. See Sieg, *Die Sagenstoffe des Ṛgveda*, 64 *et seq.*

15 *Ibid.*, xiv. 6, 8.

16 Aitareya Brāhmaṇa, vii. 27. 35.

17 See Śāṭyāyanaka, cited by Sāyaṇa, on Rv. x. 57, 1; and *cf.* Jaiminīya Brāhmaṇa, iii. 167 (*Journal of the American Oriental Society*, 18, 41).

18 Śatapatha Brāhmaṇa, ii. 4, 4, 5. According to Sāyaṇa, on Rv. i. 81, 3, it was **Rāhūgaṇa Gotama** who was Purohita: but this is hardly more than a mere blunder. See Geldner, *Vedische Studien*, 3, 152; Weber, *Indische Studien*, 2, 9, n.

19 Śāṅkhāyana Śrauta Sūtra, xvi. 29, 5.

20 See Oldenberg, *Religion des Veda*, 375, who compares the permanent character of the relation of the king and the Purohita with that of husband and wife, as shown in the ritual laid down in the Aitareya Brāhmaṇa, viii. 27.

21 See Rv. x. 33, and n. 7.

22 *Altindisches Leben*, 195, 196.

23 Aitareya Brāhmaṇa, vii. 27; Muir, *Sanskrit Texts*, 5, 436-440.

24 Rv. x. 98.

Viśvantara sacrificed without priests, while Devāpi is not regarded as a king until the Nirukta,[25] and there is no reason to suppose that Yāska's view expressed in that work is correct.

According to Geldner,[26] the Purohita from the beginning acted as the Brahman priest in the sacrificial ritual, being there the general superintendent of the sacrifice. In favour of this view, he cites the fact that Vasiṣṭha is mentioned both as Purohita[27] and as Brahman:[28] at the sacrifice of **Śunaḥśepa** he served as Brahman,[29] but he was the Purohita of Sudās;[30] Bṛhaspati is called the Purohita[31] and the Brahman[32] of the gods; and the Vasiṣṭhas who are Purohitas are also the Brahmans at the sacrifice.[33] It is thus clear that the Brahman was often the Purohita; and it was natural that this should be the case when once the Brahman's place became, as it did in the later ritual, the most important position at the sacrifice.[34] But the Brahman can hardly be said to have held this place in the earlier ritual; Oldenberg[35] seems to be right in holding that the Purohita was originally the Hotṛ priest, the singer *par excellence*, when he took any part at all in the ritual of the great sacrifices with the **Ṛtvijs**. So Devāpi seems clearly to have

25 ii. 10.

26 *Op. cit.*, 2, 144; 3, 155. *Cf.* Pischel, *Göttingische Gelehrte Anzeigen*, 1894, 420; Hillebrandt, *Rituallitteratur*, 13. Rv. i. 94, 6, does not prove that the Purohita was a Ṛtvij; it merely shows that he could be one when he wished.

27 Rv. x. 150, 5.

28 Rv. vii. 33, 11. But this need mean no more than Brahmin.

29 Aitareya Brāhmaṇa, vii. 16, 1; Sāṅkhāyana Srauta Sūtra, xv. 21, 4.

30 Śāṅkhāyana Śrauta Sūtra, xvi. 11 14.

31 Rv. ii. 24, 9; Aitareya Brāhmaṇa, iii. 17, 2; Taittirīya Brāhmaṇa, ii. 7, 1, 2; Śatapatha Brāhmaṇa, v. 3, 1, 2; Śāṅkhāyana Śrauta Sūtra, xiv. 23, 1.

32 Rv. x. 141, 3; Kauṣītaki Brāhmaṇa, vi. 13; Śatapatha Brāhmaṇa, i. 7, 4, 21; Śāṅkhāyana Śrauta Sūtra, iv. 6, 9.

33 Taittirīya Saṃhitā, iii. 5, 2, 1. This point is not in the parallel versions, Kāṭhaka Saṃhitā, xxxvii. 17 (but *cf.* xxvii. 4: *brahma-purohitaṃ kṣatram*, unless this means 'the Kṣatra is inferior to the Brahma'); Pañcaviṃśa Brāhmaṇa, xv. 5, 24, and *cf.* Gopatha Brāhmaṇa, ii. 2, 13. The Atharvan literature (Bloomfield, *Hymns of the Atharvaveda*, lx, lxi) requires a follower of that Veda to act as Brahman, and the spells of the Atharvan are, in fact, closely allied to the spells of the Purohita as represented in the Aitareya Brāhmaṇa, viii. 24-28. *Cf.* Macdonell, *Sanskrit Literature*, 193, 195.

34 See Bloomfield, *op. cit.*, lviii, lxii, lxv, lxviii *et seq.*

35 *Religion des Veda*, 380, 381.

been a Hotṛ;[36] Agni is at once Purohita[37] and Hotṛ;[38] and the 'two divine Hotṛs' referred to in the Āprī litanies are also called the 'two Purohitas.'[39] Later, no doubt, when the priestly activity ceased to centre in the song, the Purohita, with his skill in magic, became the Brahman, who also required magic to undo the errors of the sacrifice.[40]

There is little doubt that in the original growth of the priesthood the Purohita played a considerable part. In historical times he represented the real power of the kingship, and may safely be deemed to have exercised great influence in all public affairs, such as the administration of justice and the king's conduct of business. But it is not at all probable that the Purohita represents, as Roth[41] and Zimmer[42] thought, the source which gave rise to caste. The priestly class is already in existence in the Rigveda (see **Varṇa**).

[36] Rv. x. 98; and *cf.* Pañcaviṃśa Brāhmaṇa, xiv. 6, 8; Āśvalāyana Gṛhya Sūtra, i. 12, 7.

[37] Rv. i. 1, 1; iii. 3, 2; 11, 1; v. 11, 2. In viii. 27, 1; x. 1, 6, he is called Purohita, and credited with the characteristic activities of the Hotṛ priest.

[38] Rv. i. 1, 1; iii. 3, 2; 11, 1; v. 11, 2 etc.

[39] Rv. x. 66, 13; 70, 7.

[40] *Cf.* Aitareya Brāhmaṇa, vii. 26.

[41] *Zur Litteratur und Geschichte des Weda*, 117 *et seq.*

[42] *Altindisches Leben*, 195.

Cf. Zimmer, *Altindisches Leben*, 168, 169; 195 *et seq.*; Max Müller, *Ancient Sanskrit Literature*, 485; Weber, *Indische Studien*, 10, 31-35; 138; Haug, *Brahma und die Brahmanen*, 9 *et seq.*; Geldner, *Vedische Studien*, 2, 144; Oldenberg, *Religion des Veda*, 374-383; Bloomfield, *Hymns of the Atharvaveda*, lxx *et seq.*

Pulasti[1] or **Pulastin**[2] in the Yajurveda Saṃhitās denotes 'wearing the hair plain,' as opposed to *kapardin*, 'wearing the hair in braids.'

[1] Taittirīya Saṃhitā, iv. 5, 9, 1; Vājasaneyi Saṃhitā, xvi. 43.

[2] Kāṭhaka Saṃhitā, xvii. 15. *Cf.* Zimmer, *Altindisches Leben*, 265.

Pulinda is the name of an outcast tribe mentioned with the **Andhras** in the Aitareya Brāhmaṇa,[1] but not in the Śāṅkhāyana Śrauta Sūtra,[2] in connexion with the story of **Śunaḥśepa.** The Pulindas again appear associated with the Andhras in the time of Aśoka.[3]

[1] vii. 18.

[2] xv. 26.

[3] Vincent Smith, *Zeitschrift der Deutschen Morgenländischen Gesellschaft*, 56, 652.

Pulīkaya. See **Purīkaya.**

Pulīkā seems to designate some kind of bird in the Maitrāyaṇī Saṃhitā (iii. 14, 5). The name appears in the form of Kulīkā in the Vājasaneyi Saṃhitā (xxiv. 24).

Puluṣa Prācīna-yogya ('descendant of Prācīnayoga') is the name of a teacher, a pupil of **Dṛti Aindroti Śaunaka**, in a Vaṃśa (list of teachers) of the Jaiminīya Upaniṣad Brāhmaṇa (iii. 40, 2). He taught **Pauluṣi Satyayajña.**

Puṣkara is the name in the Rigveda[1] and later[2] of the blue lotus flower. The Atharvaveda[3] mentions its sweet perfume. The lotus grew in lakes, which were thence called *puṣkariṇī*, 'lotus-bearing.'[4] That the flower was early used for personal adornment is shown by an epithet of the Aśvins, 'lotus-crowned' (*puṣkara-sraj*).[5]

Presumably because of its likeness in shape to the flower of the lotus, the bowl of the ladle is called Puṣkara, perhaps already in the Rigveda,[6] and certainly in the Aitareya Brāhmaṇa.[7] Moreover, according to the Nirukta,[8] Puṣkara means 'water.' a sense actually found in the Śatapatha Brāhmaṇa.[9]

1 vi. 16, 13; vii. 33, 11, may be so taken, though Roth, St. Petersburg Dictionary, *s.v.* 3, and Geldner, *Rigveda, Glossar*, 112, prefer to see in these passages a reference to the bowl of the sacrificial ladle.

2 Av. xi. 3, 8; xii. 1, 24; Taittirīya Saṃhitā, v. 1, 4, 1; 2, 6, 5; 6, 4, 2; Vājasaneyi Saṃhitā, xi. 29; Taittirīya Brāhmaṇa, i. 2, 1, 4; Śatapatha Brāhmaṇa, iv. 5, 1, 16; Maitrāyaṇī Saṃhitā, iii. 1, 5.

3 Av. xii. 1, 24.

4 Rv. v. 78, 7; x. 107, 10; Av. iv. 34, 5; v. 16, 17; Bṛhadāraṇyaka Upaniṣad, iv. 3, 11, etc.

5 Rv. x. 184, 2; Av. iii. 22, 4; Śatapatha Brāhmaṇa, iv. 1, 5, 16, etc.

6 Rv. viii 72, 11, where the sense is doubtful, and the bowl of the ladle is not particularly appropriate. See also note 1.

7 vii. 5.

8 v. 14.

9 vi. 4, 2, 2.

Cf. Zimmer, *Altindisches Leben*, 71.

Puṣkara-sāda, 'sitting on the lotus,' is the name of an animal in the list of victims at the Aśvamedha ('horse sacrifice') in the Yajurveda Saṃhitās.[1] It can hardly be a 'snake,'[2] but rather either, as Roth[3] thinks, a 'bird,' or perhaps, according to the commentator on the Taittirīya Saṃhitā,[1] a 'bee.'

[1] Taittirīya Saṃhitā, v. 5, 14, 1; Maitrāyaṇī Saṃhitā, iii. 14, 12; Vājasaneyi Saṃhitā, xxiv. 31.

[2] Zimmer, *Altindisches Leben*, 95, so takes it.

[3] St. Petersburg Dictionary, *s.v.*

Puṣṭi-gu is the name of a Ṛṣi mentioned in a Vālakhilya hymn of the Rigveda.[1]

[1] viii. 51, 1. *Cf.* Ludwig, Translation of the Rigveda, 3, 140, 141.

Puṣpa in the Atharvaveda[1] and later[2] denotes a 'flower' generally.

[1] viii. 7, 12. *Cf.* x. 8, 34.

[2] Vājasaneyi Saṃhitā, xxii. 28; Pañcaviṃśa Brāhmaṇa, viii. 4, 1; xv. 3, 23; Taittirīya Saṃhitā, v. 4, 4, 2; Chāndogya Upaniṣad, iii. 1, 2; Bṛhadāraṇyaka Upaniṣad, vi. 4, 1, etc.

Puṣya is the name in the Atharvaveda (xix. 7, 2) for the **Nakṣatra** called **Tiṣya** elsewhere.

Cf. Weber, *Naxatra*, 2, 371. On Tiṣya, see also *Journal of the Royal Asiatic Society*, 1911, 514-518; 794-800.

Pūta-kratā is the name of a woman in a Vālakhilya hymn of the Rigveda,[1] perhaps the wife of **Pūtakratu**, but this is doubtful, since the more regular form would be Pūtakratāyī,[2] which Scheftelowitz[3] reads in the hymn.

[1] viii. 64, 4.

[2] Pāṇini, iv. 1, 36.

[3] *Die Apokryphen des Ṛgveda*, 41, 42.

Pūta-kratu ('of clear insight') is the name of a patron in the Rigveda,[1] apparently the son of **Aśvamedha**.

[1] viii. 68, 17. *Cf.* Ludwig, Translation of the Rigveda, 3, 163. Scheftelowitz, *Die Apokryphen des Ṛgveda*, 41, reads Pūtakratu for Pautakrata in Rv. viii. 56, 2, but this is improbable. See Oldenberg, *Göttingische Gelehrte Anzeigen*, 1907, 237, 238; Weber, *Episches im vedischen Ritual*, 39, n. 4.

Pūti-rajju is the name of a certain plant of unknown kind in the Atharvaveda[1] according to Roth.[2] The Kauśika Sūtra[3] treats it as a 'putrid rope,' but Ludwig[4] suggests that a snake is meant.

1 viii. 8, 2.
2 St. Petersburg Dictionary, *s.v.*
3 xvi. 10.
4 Translation of the Rigveda, 3, 527. *Cf.* Whitney's Translation of the Rigveda, 503; Bloomfield, *Hymns of the Atharvaveda*, 583.

Pūtīka is the name of a plant often mentioned[1] as a substitute for the Soma plant. It is also given in the Taittirīya Saṃhitā[2] as a means of making milk curdle, being an alternative to the bark of the *Butea frondosa* (*parṇa-valka*). It is usually identified with the *Guilandina Bonduc*, but Hillebrandt[3] makes it out to be the *Basella Cordifolia*.

1 Kāṭhaka Saṃhitā, xxxiv. 3 (*pūtika*, as quoted in the St. Petersburg Dictionary, *s.v.*); Śatapatha Brāhmaṇa, xiv. 1, 2, 12. *Cf.* iv. 5, 10; 4; Pañcaviṃśa Brāhmaṇa, viii. 4, 1; ix. 5, 3, etc.
2 ii. 5, 3, 5.
3 *Vedische Mythologie*, 1, 24, n. 3. *Cf.* Roth, *Zeitschrift der Deutschen Morgenländischen Gesellschaft*, 35, 689; Zimmer, *Altindisches Leben*, 63, 276.

Pūtu-dru is another name for the Deodar (*deva-dāru*) in the Atharvaveda[1] and the Yajurveda Saṃhitās.[2] The longer form, Pūtu-dāru, is found in the Kauśika Sūtra.[3]

1 viii. 2, 28.
2 Taittirīya Saṃhitā, vi. 2, 8, 4 (in 6 the fruit is meant); Maitrāyaṇī Saṃhitā, iii. 8, 5.
3 viii. 15; lviii. 15.
Cf. Zimmer, *Altindisches Leben*, 59.

Pūru is the name of a people and their king in the Rigveda. They are mentioned with the **Anus, Druhyus, Turvaśas,** and **Yadus** in one passage.[1] They also occur as enemies of the **Tṛtsus** in the hymn of **Sudās'** victory.[2] In another

1 i. 108, 8.
2 vii. 18, 13. *Cf.* **Turvaśa.** Apparently, as Hopkins, *Journal of the American Oriental Society*, 15, 263, n., and Geldner, *Vedische Studien*, 2, 135, think, in this verse the words *jeṣma Pūruṃ vidathe mṛdhravācam* refer to the Pūru king and to the priest **Viśvāmitra,** who prayed for the defeat of Sudās, though in vain. Hopkins seems to take the words *vidathe mṛdhravācam* generally as 'the false speaker in the assembly'; but, according to Geldner, the meaning intended is that, while the king fought, the Purohita prayed in the Sabhā, or meeting house of the people.

hymn[3] Agni of the **Bharatas** is celebrated as victorious over the Pūrus, probably a reference to the same decisive overthrow. On the other hand, victories of the Pūrus over the aborigines seem to be referred to in several passages.[4]

The great kings of the Pūrus were **Purukutsa** and his son **Trasadasyu,** whose name bears testimony to his prowess against aboriginal foes, while a later prince was **Tṛkṣi Trāsadasyava.**

In the Rigveda the Pūrus are expressly[5] mentioned as on the **Sarasvatī.** Zimmer[6] thinks that the **Sindhu** (Indus) is meant in this passage. But Ludwig[7] and Hillebrandt[8] with much greater probability think that the eastern Sarasvatī in Kurukṣetra is meant. This view accords well with the sudden disappearance of the name of the Pūrus from Vedic tradition, a disappearance accounted for by Oldenberg's[9] conjecture that the Pūrus became part of the great Kuru people, just as **Turvaśa** and **Krivi** disappear from the tradition on their being merged in the **Pañcāla** nation. Trāsadasyava, the patronymic of **Kuruśravaṇa** in the Rigveda,[10] shows that the royal families of the Kurus and the Pūrus were allied by intermarriage.

Hillebrandt,[11] admitting that the Pūrus in later times lived in the eastern country round the Sarasvatī, thinks that in earlier days they were to be found to the west of the Indus with **Divodāsa.** This theory must fall with the theory that Divodāsa was in the far west. It might, however, be held to be supported by the fact that Alexander found a Πῶρος—that is, a Paurava prince on the Hydaspes,[12] a sort of half-way locality between the Sarasvatī and the West. But it is quite simple to suppose either that the Hydaspes was the earlier home of the Pūrus, where some remained after the others had

[3] Rv. vii. 8, 4.

[4] i. 59, 6; 131, 4; 174, 2; iv. 21, 10; 38, 1; vi. 20, 10; vii. 5, 3; 19, 3. *Cf.* note 13.

[5] vii. 96, 2. Perhaps they are also meant as living on the **Śaryaṇāvant** in Rv. viii. 64, 10. 11.

[6] *Altindisches Leben*, 124.

[7] Translation of the Rigveda, 3, 175.

[8] *Vedische Mythologie*, 1, 50, 115; 3, 374.

[9] *Buddha*, 404. *Cf.* Ludwig, 3, 205.

[10] x. 33, 4.

[11] *Op. cit.*, 1, 114 *et seq.*

[12] Arrian, *Indica*, viii. 4; ix. 1; xix. 3, etc. See Hillebrandt, *Vedische Mythologie*, 1, 132, 133.

wandered east, or that the later Paurava represents a successful onslaught upon the west from the east.

In several other passages of the Rigveda[13] the Pūrus as a people seem to be meant. The Nirukta[14] recognizes the general sense of 'man,' but in no passage is this really necessary or even probable. So utterly, however, is the tradition lost that the Śatapatha Brāhmaṇa[15] explains Pūru in the Rigveda[16] as an Asura Rakṣas; it is only in the Epic that Pūru revives as the name of a son of Yayāti and Śarmiṣṭhā.[17]

[13] In Rv. i. 36, 1, *Pūrūṇām* might be read for *purūṇām*, with improvement in the sense. In i. 63, 7, there is a reference to the Pūru king, Purukutsa, and Sudās, but in what relation is uncertain (see **Purukutsa**). In i. 130, 7, the Pūru king and Divodāsa Atithigva are both mentioned, apparently as victorious over aboriginal foes. See also i. 129, 5; iv. 39, 2; v. 17, 1; vi. 46, 8; x. 4, 1; 48, 5.

[14] vii. 23; Naighaṇṭuka, ii. 3.

[15] vi. 8, 1, 14.

[16] vii. 8, 4.

[17] Pargiter, *Journal of the Royal Asiatic Society*, 1910, 26, etc. *Cf.* Hillebrandt, *op. cit.*, 1, 110 *et seq.*; Max Müller, *Sacred Books of the East*, 32, 398.

Pūruṣa has in several passages[1] the sense of 'menial' or 'dependent,' like the English 'man.'

[1] Rv. vi. 39, 5 (*cf.*, however, Pischel, *Vedische Studien*, 1, 43); x. 97, 4; Av. iv. 9, 7; x. 1, 17; Śatapatha Brāhmaṇa, vi. 3, 1, 22, etc. *Cf.* Bloomfield, *Hymns of the Atharvaveda*, 383.

Pūrṇa-māsa denotes the full moon and the festival of that day, occurring frequently in the later Saṃhitās.[1] *Cf.* **Māsa.**

[1] Taittirīya Saṃhitā, i. 6, 7, 2; ii. 2, 10, 2; 5, 4, 1; iii. 4, 4, 1; vii. 4, 8, 1; Taittirīya Brāhmaṇa, i. 2, 1, 14; iii. 5, 7, 13; Śatapatha Brāhmaṇa, xi. 2, 4, 8, etc.

Pūrta,[1] or **Pūrti,**[2] occurs in the Rigveda and later denoting the reward to the priest for his services. *Cf.* **Dakṣiṇā.**

[1] Rv. vi. 16, 18; viii. 46, 21; Av. vi. 123, 5; ix. 5, 13; 6, 31; Vājasaneyi Saṃhitā, xviii. 64; Aitareya Brāhmaṇa, vii. 21. 24, etc.

[2] Rv. vi. 13, 6; x. 107, 3; Taittirīya Saṃhitā, i. 2, 3, 2; ii. 4, 7, 1, etc.

Pūr-pati, 'lord of the fort,' occurring only once in the Rigveda,[1] is of somewhat doubtful interpretation. The term

[1] i. 173, 10.

may denote a regular office,[2] similar to that of the **Grāmaṇī**: the **Pur** would then be a permanently occupied settlement. The expression may, however, merely mean the chief over a fort when it was actually occupied against hostile attack. The rarity of the word seems to favour the latter sense.

[2] *Cf.* Sāyaṇa's note on Rv. i. 173, 10; Muir, *Sanskrit Texts*, 5, 456. *Cf.* Ludwig, Translation of the Rigveda, 3, 204.

Pūrva-pakṣa denotes the first half of the month. See **Māsa.**

Pūrva-vayasa, the 'first period of life,' is a term used in the Brāhmaṇas[1] to denote 'youth.'

[1] Pañcaviṃśa Brāhmaṇa, xix. 4, 3; Satapatha Brāhmaṇa, xii. 2, 3, 4; 9, 1, 8; *pūrva-vayasin*, Taittirīya Brāhmaṇa, iii. 8, 13, 3. *Cf.* Aitareya Āraṇyaka, v. 3, 3, where *vatsa* and *tṛtīya*, 'the third (stage),' are used to cover 'youth' and 'old age,' as opposed to manhood, when the knowledge of the doctrines of the Āraṇyaka is to be imparted.

Pūrva-vah is a term applied to the horse (**Aśva**) in the Taittirīya Brāhmaṇa[1] and elsewhere.[2] It may either refer to a horse fastened in front as a 'leader,' or merely mean 'drawing (a chariot) for the first time,' as understood by the commentator on the Taittirīya Brāhmaṇa.

[1] i. 1, 5, 6

[2] Satapatha Brāhmaṇa, ii. 1, 4, 17; Kāṭhaka Saṃhitā, xiii. 3. *Cf.* St. Petersburg Dictionary, *s.v.*

Pūrvāhṇa, 'the earlier (part of the) day,' 'forenoon,' is a common designation of time from the Rigveda[1] onwards.[2] *Cf.* **Ahan.**

[1] x. 34, 11.

[2] Aitareya Brāhmaṇa, vii. 20; Satapatha Brāhmaṇa, i. 6, 3, 12; iii. 4, 4, 2; Chāndogya Upaniṣad, v. 11, 7; Nirukta, viii. 9, etc.

Pūlya, or **Pūlpa**, in the Atharvaveda[1] seems to mean 'shrivelled grain' (*cf.* **Lājā**).

[1] xiv. 2, 63. *Cf.* Whitney, Translation of the Atharvaveda, 765.

Pṛkṣa (literally, perhaps 'swift') is the proper name of a man in an obscure verse of the Rigveda.[1]

[1] ii. 13, 8. *Cf.* Pischel, *Vedische Studien*, 1, 97.

Pṛkṣa-yāma occurs once in the plural in the Rigveda.[1] Roth[2] suggests the sense of 'faring with swift steeds,' and thinks a proper name is meant. Pischel[3] holds that the word is an epithet of the **Pajras**, and that it means 'performing splendid sacrifices.'

[1] i. 122, 7.

[2] St. Petersburg Dictionary, *s.v.*

[3] *Vedische Studien*, 1, 97, 98.

Pṛda. See **Mṛda.**

Pṛt[1] and **Pṛtanā**[2] denote, in the Rigveda and later, 'contest,' whether in arms or in the chariot race. Pṛtanā has also the concrete sense of 'army' in some passages;[3] in the Epic system[4] it denotes a definite body of men, elephants, chariots, and horses. Pṛtanājya[5] has only the sense of 'combat.'

[1] Only in the locative, Rv. ii. 27, 15; 26, 1; iii. 49. 3; vi. 20, 1, etc.; *pṛtsuṣu*, i. 129, 4 (with double case-ending).

[2] Rv. i. 85, 8; 91, 21; 119, 10; 152, 7; ii. 40, 5; iii. 24, 1; vi. 41, 5; x. 29, 8; Vājasaneyi Saṃhitā, xi. 76; Kauṣītaki Brāhmaṇa, xv. 3; Taittirīya Brāhmaṇa, iii. 1, 1, 6; 2, 6, etc.

[3] Rv. vii. 20, 3; viii. 36, 1; 37, 2; Av. vi. 97, 1; viii. 5, 8; Nirukta, ix. 24; perhaps also as neuter in Taittirīya Brāhmaṇa, ii. 4, 7, 5.

[4] Mahābhārata, i. 291.

[5] Rv. iii. 8, 10; 37, 7; vii. 99, 4; viii. 12, 25; ix. 102, 9; Taittirīya Saṃhitā, iii. 4, 4, 1.

Pṛtha, the 'palm' of the hand in the sense of its breath, is used as a measure of length in the Taittirīya Brāhmaṇa.[1]

[1] i. 6, 4, 2. 3; *cf.* Kātyāyana Śrauta Sūtra, vi. 1, 28; Āpastamba Śrauta Sūtra, ii. 2, 7; viii. 5, 10.

Pṛthavāna is in the Rigveda[1] the name of a man, perhaps also called **Duḥśīma**, but this is uncertain. *Cf.* **Pṛthi.**

[1] x. 93, 14. *Cf.* Zimmer, *Altindisches Leben*, 433.

Pṛthi,[1] **Pṛthī**,[2] or **Pṛthu**[3] is the name of a semi-mythical personage who is mentioned in the Rigveda and later as a Ṛṣi, and more specially as the inventor of agriculture[4] and the lord of both worlds, of men and of animals.[5] He bears in several passages[6] the epithet Vainya, 'descendant of Vena,' and must probably be regarded as a culture hero rather than as a real man. According to other accounts,[7] he was the first of consecrated kings. *Cf.* **Pārthiva.**

1 Rv. i. 112, 15, as a seer; as Vainya, Taittirīya Brāhmaṇa, i. 7, 7 4, and perhaps ii. 7, 5, 1 (*Pṛthaye*).

2 As Vainya, Rv. viii. 9, 10; Av. viii. 10, 24; Pañcaviṃśa Brāhmaṇa, xiii. 5, 19; as Pṛthi or Pṛthī, Taittirīya Brāhmaṇa, ii. 7, 5, 1; as Vainya, Śatapatha Brāhmaṇa, v. 3, 5, 4; Kāṭhaka Saṃhitā, xxxvii. 4 (*Indische Studien*, 3, 463). Venya mentioned with Pṛthī in Rv. x. 148, 5, may be meant for his patronymic (= Vainya): *cf.* **Tugrya**, n. 1.

3 Jaiminīya Brāhmaṇa, i. 186 (*Journal of the American Oriental Society*, 19, 125); Jaiminīya Upaniṣad Brāhmaṇa, i. 10, 9; 34, 6; 45, 1.

4 Av., *loc. cit.*

5 Pañcaviṃśa Brāhmaṇa, *loc. cit. Cf.* Taittirīya Brāhmaṇa, ii. 7, 5, 1.

6 See notes 1-3.

7 Śatapatha Brāhmaṇa, *loc. cit.*; Kāṭhaka Saṃhitā, *loc. cit.*; Taittirīya Brāhmaṇa, i. 7, 7, 4.

Cf. Ludwig, Translation of the Rigveda, 3, 166; Weber, *Indische Studien*, 1, 221, 222; Hopkins, *Transactions of the Connecticut Academy of Arts and Sciences*, 15, 50 n. 2; Zimmer, *Altindisches Leben*, 134. Eggeling, *Sacred Books of the East*, 26, 81, gives the name as Pṛthin Vainya; but the oblique cases, when found, are all in favour of Pṛthi or Pṛthī as the stem.

Pṛthivī denotes the 'earth' as the 'broad' one in the Rigveda[1] and later,[2] being often personified as a deity[3] both alone and with **Div**, 'heaven,' as Dyāvā-Pṛthivī.[4] Mention is often made of three earths,[5] of which the world on which we live is the highest.[6] The earth is girdled by the ocean, according to the Aitareya Brāhmaṇa.[7] The Nirukta[8] places one of the three earths in each of the worlds into which the universe is divided

1 Rv. vii. 7, 2. 5; 99, 3; v. 85, 1. 5; viii. 89, 5, etc.

2 Av. xii. 1, 1 *et seq.*; Vājasaneyi Saṃhitā, xi. 53, etc.

3 Rv. iv. 3, 5; 51, 11; v. 49, 5; 84, 1 *et seq.*; vi. 50, 13. 14; vii. 34, 23, etc.; Vājasaneyi Saṃhitā, xii. 103, etc.

4 Rv. iv. 56, 1; vii. 53, 1, etc. See Macdonell, *Vedic Mythology*, pp. 20, 21, 123, 126.

5 Rv. i. 34, 8; iv. 53, 5; vii. 104, 11; Av. iv. 20, 2; Vājasaneyi Saṃhitā, v. 9, etc.

6 Av. vi. 21, 1; xix. 27, 3; 32, 4; 53, 5; Śatapatha Brāhmaṇa, iii. 5, 1, 31; v. 1, 5, 21.

7 viii. 20. This idea is not found in the Saṃhitās, Macdonell, *op. cit.*, p. 9.

8 ix. 31; xi. 36; xii. 30; Naighaṇṭuka, v. 3. 5. 6. *Cf.* Bruce, *Journal of the Royal Asiatic Society*, 19, 321 *et seq.*

(see **Div**). In the Śatapatha Brāhmaṇa[9] the earth is called the 'firstborn of being,' and its riches (*vitta*) are referred to;[10] hence in a late passage of the Śāṅkhāyana Āraṇyaka[11] the earth is styled *vasu-matī*, 'full of wealth.' The word also occurs in the Rigveda,[12] though rarely, in the form of Pṛthvī.[13]

[9] xiv. 1, 2, 10.
[10] Śatapatha Brāhmaṇa, xi. 5, 6, 3.
[11] xiii. 1.
[12] vi. 12, 5; x. 187, 2. *Cf.* Macdonell, *op. cit.*, 34.
[13] The regular adjectival feminine form of *pṛthu*, 'broad.'

Pṛthu. See **Pṛthi.** Ludwig[1] also finds a mention of the Pṛthus as a tribe, allied with the **Parśus**, in one passage of the Rigveda[2] as opponents of the **Tṛtsu Bharatas**. But this interpretation is certainly incorrect.[3] See **Parśu.**

[1] Translation of the Rigveda, 3, 196 *et seq.*
[2] vii. 83, 1.
[3] Zimmer, *Altindisches Leben*, 134 *et seq.*; 433, 434; Geldner, *Vedische Studien*, 2, 184, n. 3; Bergaigne, *Religion Védique*, 2, 362, n.

1. **Pṛthu-śravas** ('far-famed') is mentioned in connexion with **Vaśa** in two hymns[1] of the Rigveda. In the second passage the generosity of Pṛthuśravas Kānīta to Vaśa Aśvya is celebrated, and the Śāṅkhāyana Śrauta Sūtra[2] refers to the episode.

[1] i. 116, 21; viii. 46, 21. *Cf.* Ludwig, Translation of the Rigveda, 3, 162.
[2] xvi. 11, 13.

2. **Pṛthu-śravas Daure-śravasa** ('descendant of Dūreśravas') is the name of the Udgātṛ priest at the snake festival mentioned in the Pañcaviṃśa Brāhmaṇa.[1]

[1] xxv. 15, 3. *Cf.* Weber, *Indische Studien*, 1, 35.

Pṛdāku, the name of a 'snake' in the Atharvaveda,[1] is mentioned in the list of victims at the Aśvamedha ('horse sacrifice'), in the Yajurveda Saṃhitās,[2] and occasionally else-

[1] i. 27, 1; iii. 27, 3; vi. 38, 1; vii. 56, 1; x. 4, 11 *et seq.*; xii. 3, 57.
[2] Taittirīya Saṃhitā, v. 5, 10, 1; Maitrāyaṇī Saṃhitā, iii. 14, 14; Vājasaneyi Saṃhitā, xxiv. 33.

where.[3] Its skin was specially valuable, according to the Atharvaveda.[4]

[3] Vājasaneyi Saṃhitā, vi. 12; Sāṅkhāyana Āraṇyaka, xii. 27.

[4] i. 27, 1.
Cf. Zimmer, *Altindisches Leben*, 94.

Pṛdāku-sānu, 'having the surface of a snake' is taken by Ludwig[1] and Griffith[2] as the name of the institutor of a sacrifice in one hymn of the Rigveda.[3]

[1] Translation of the Rigveda, 3, 161.

[2] *Hymns of the Rigveda*, 2, 141.

[3] viii. 17, 15.

Pṛśana in one passage of the Rigveda[1] is considered by Ludwig[2] to denote a place where a battle was fought.

[1] ix. 97, 54.

[2] Translation of the Rigveda, 3, 164.

1. **Pṛśni-gu** is the name of a man who is mentioned with **Purukutsa** and **Śucanti** as a protégé of the Aśvins in one hymn of the Rigveda (i. 112, 7). Possibly the word is only an epithet of Purukutsa.

Cf. Geldner, *Rigveda, Glossar*, 114.

2. **Pṛśni-gu**, pl., is taken in one passage of the Rigveda[1] by Geldner[2] as denoting the name of a people. But this is not probable.

[1] vii. 18, 10.

[2] *Rigveda, Glossar*, 114.

Pṛśni-parṇī ('having a speckled leaf') is the name of a plant mentioned in a hymn of the Atharvaveda[1] as a protection against evil beings procuring abortion, called Kaṇvas (presumably a sign of hostility to the **Kaṇva** family).[2] It also appears in the Śatapatha Brāhmaṇa,[3] being identified with *Hermionitis cordifolia* by the St. Petersburg Dictionary, but

[1] ii. 25, 1 *et seq.*

[2] *Cf.* Lanman in Whitney's Translation of the Atharvaveda, 65; Bergaigne, *Religion Védique*, 2, 465; Hillebrandt, *Vedische Mythologie*, 1, 207.

[3] xiii. 8, 1, 16.

Roth[4] in a subsequent contribution suggests that it is the same as a plant later called *lakṣmaṇā*, and regarded as curing barrenness. The scholiast on the Kātyāyana Śrauta Sūtra[5] thinks that the *Glycine debilis* is meant.

[4] Cited by Whitney, *loc. cit.*

[5] xxv. 7, 17.

Cf. Weber, *Indische Studien*, 13, 187; Zimmer, *Altindisches Leben*, 69; Bloomfield, *Hymns of the Atharvaveda*, 302.

Pṛṣata is the name of an animal mentioned in the list of victims at the Aśvamedha ('horse sacrifice') in the Yajurveda Saṃhitās.[1] The dappled antelope or gazelle seems to be meant.[2]

[1] Taittirīya Saṃhitā, v. 5, 17, 1; Maitrāyaṇī Saṃhitā, iii. 14, 9. 21; Vājasaneyi Saṃhitā, xxiv. 27. 40.

[2] Nirukta, ii. 2.

Cf. Zimmer, *Altindisches Leben*, 83.

Pṛṣatī in some passages[1] clearly means a 'speckled' cow. The term is, however, generally[2] applied to the team of the Maruts, when its sense is doubtful. The commentators usually explain it as 'speckled antelope.' But Mahīdhara,[3] followed by Roth,[4] prefers to see in it a 'dappled mare': it is true that the Maruts are often called[5] *pṛṣad-aśva*, which is more naturally interpreted as 'having dappled steeds,' than as 'having Pṛṣatīs as steeds.'[6] In the later literature, which Grassmann[7] prefers to follow, the word means the female of the dappled gazelle.

[1] Rv. viii. 64, 10. 11, where 'deer' is nonsense, and 'mares' is improbable. The regular donation is 'cows'; Kāṭhaka Saṃhitā, xii. 2; Śatapatha Brāhmaṇa, v. 5, 2, 9 (see Eggeling, *Sacred Books of the East*, 41, 125); Vājasaneyi Saṃhitā, xxiv. 2 (though this is not certain); Śāṅkhāyana Śrauta Sūtra, xv. 14, 23, etc.

[2] Rv. i. 37, 2; 39, 6; 64, 8; 85, 4. 5; ii. 34, 3; 36, 2; iii. 26, 4; v. 55, 6; 58, 6; 60, 2; i. 162, 21.

[3] On Vājasaneyi Saṃhitā, ii. 16.

[4] St. Petersburg Dictionary, *s.v.* He had earlier (*ibid.*, 1, 1091) been inclined to follow the usual interpretation given by Sāyaṇa on Rv. i. 37, 2, etc., which Benfey, *Orient und Occident*, 2, 250, accepted.

[5] Rv. i. 87, 4; 89, 7; 186, 8; ii. 34, 4; iii. 26, 6; v. 42, 15; vii. 40, 3.

[6] So Sāyaṇa on Rv. i. 87, 4. This view is far-fetched, but is supported, in so far as the interpretation of Pṛṣatī and Aśva is concerned, by such passages as v. 55, 6, where the Maruts are said to yoke the Pṛṣatīs as *aśvān* to their chariots; but the sense may be 'horses (and) dappled (mares).' See, however, Pischel, *Vedische Studien*, 1, 226.

[7] *Wörterbuch*, *s.v.*

Aufrecht[8] concurs in the view of Roth, but Max Müller[9] is inclined to accept the traditional interpretation, while Muir[10] leaves the matter open.

[8] See Muir, *Sanskrit Texts*, 5, 152.
[9] *Sacred Books of the East*, 32, 70; 184.
[10] *Op. cit.*, 5, 151, 152.
Cf. Zimmer, *Altindisches Leben*, 83.

Pṛṣad-ājya denotes 'sprinkled butter'—that is, butter (**Ājya**) mixed with sour milk, in the Rigveda[1] and later.[2]

[1] x. 90, 8.
[2] Taittirīya Saṃhitā, iii. 2, 6, 2; vi. 3, 9, 6; 11, 4; Śatapatha Brāhmaṇa, ii. 5, 2, 41; 4, 2; iii. 8, 4, 8, etc.
Cf. Eggeling, *Sacred Books of the East*, 12, 404, n. 1.

Pṛṣadhra occurs in a Vālakhilya hymn of the Rigveda[1] as the name of a man. He is also mentioned in the Śāṅkhāyana Śrauta Sūtra[2] as a patron of **Praskaṇva**, and called Pṛṣadhra Medhya Mātariśvan (or Mātariśva); but for once there is a discrepancy between the statement of the Sūtra and the text of the Rigveda, for the hymns[3] there attributed to Praskaṇva as in praise of Pṛṣadhra have nothing in them connected with Pṛṣadhra, while the Anukramaṇī (Index) ascribes to Pṛṣadhra himself the authorship of one of them.[4] On the other hand, **Medhya** and **Mātariśvan** appear as separate persons in the Rigveda[1] along with Pṛṣadhra.

[1] viii. 52, 2.
[2] xvi. 11, 25-27.
[3] viii. 55. 56.
[4] viii. 56.
Cf. Weber, *Episches im vedischen Ritual*, 39.

Pṛṣātaka is the name of a mixture like **Pṛṣadājya**, and consisting, according to the late Gṛhyasaṃgraha,[1] of curds (**Dadhi**), honey (**Madhu**), and **Ajya**. It is mentioned in a late passage of the Atharvaveda[2] and in the Sūtras.[3]

[1] ii. 59.
[2] xx. 134, 2.
[3] Mānava Gṛhya Sūtra, ii. 3, etc.
Cf. Bloomfield, *Zeitschrift der Deutschen Morgenländischen Gesellschaft*, 35, 580.

Pṛṣṭyā[1] denotes in the Atharvaveda (vi. 102, 2) the side horse (mare).

[1] So Böhtlingk, Dictionary, *s.v.* Pṛṣṭhyā is read in the St. Petersburg Dictionary. See, however, Grill, *Hundert Lieder*,[2] 169; Bloomfield, *Hymns of the Atharvaveda*, 513.

Pṛṣṭy-āmaya denotes in the Atharvaveda[1] a pain in the sides or ribs.[2] It appears to be mentioned there merely as an accompaniment of fever (**Takman**).

[1] xix. 34, 10. *Cf.* Zimmer, *Altindisches Leben*, 65, 391.

[2] The derivative adjective *pṛṣṭy-āmayin*, 'suffering from a pain in the side,' occurs in Rv. i. 105, 18.

Petva is found twice in the Atharvaveda.[1] In the first passage reference is made to its *vāja*, which Zimmer[2] argues can only mean 'strength,' 'swiftness,' though naturally the sense of 'male power' would seem more appropriate in a spell intended to remove lack of virility. In the second passage the Petva is mentioned as overcoming the horse (see **Ubhayādant**), a miracle which has a parallel in the Rigveda,[3] where the Petva overcomes the female[4] lion. The animal also occurs in the list of victims at the Aśvamedha ('horse sacrifice') in the Yajurveda Saṃhitās,[5] and occasionally elsewhere.[6] It appears to be the 'ram' or the 'wether,' the latter[7] being the sense given to it by the commentator on the Taittirīya Saṃhitā. But there is no conclusive evidence in favour of this meaning, while on the whole the passage of the Atharvaveda, in which *vāja* is found, accords best with the sense of 'ram.' Hopkins,[8] however, renders the word as 'goat,' though for what reason is not clear. Whether it is connected in any way with **Pitva** or **Pidva** is quite uncertain.

[1] iv. 4, 8 ; v. 19, 2.

[2] *Altindisches Leben*, 229, 230.

[3] vii. 18, 17.

[4] *Siṃhyam* in the text. Hopkins, *Journal of the American Oriental Society*, 15, 264, takes it as masculine, and as a play on *śiṃyum*, the name of one of the kings or peoples defeated in the battle of the ten kings. But, admitting the play, *siṃhī* as fem. seems to be still more pointed than *siṃha*, contrasting with the masculine *petva*.

[5] Taittirīya Saṃhitā, v. 5, 22, 1. Though not in the parallel passage of the Vājasaneyi Saṃhitā, it appears to be found in the Kāṭhaka, according to Weber's note in his edition of the Taittirīya Saṃhitā.

[6] Taittirīya Saṃhitā, vi. 2, 8, 4 ; Vājasaneyi Saṃhitā, xxix. 58. 59 ; Taittirīya Brāhmaṇa, i. 2, 5, 3, etc.

[7] *Galita-retasko meṣaḥ.*

[8] *Loc. cit.* ; *India, Old and New*, 58. He thinks the horn of the goat pierced the lion. Curiously enough, Whitney, Translation of the Atharvaveda, 253, renders the word as 'goat' in Av. v. 19, 2, but (p. 151) as 'ram' in iv. 4, 8 ; and Bloomfield, *Hymns of the Atharva-veda*, 434, speaks both of a 'ram' and a 'goat' in connexion with v. 19, 2.

Pedu is the name in the Rigveda[1] of a protégé of the Aśvins, who gave him, in order, as it seems, to replace a bad steed, a mythical horse, hence called Paidva,[2] which probably represents the horse of the sun.[3]

1 Rv. i. 117, 9; 118, 9; 119, 10; vii. 71, 5; x. 39, 10.

2 Rv. ix. 88, 4; Av. x. 4, 5 *et seq.*

3 Macdonell, *Vedic Mythology*, pp. 52, 149.

Peruka occurs in an obscure verse of the Rigveda[1] as the name of a patron of the poet.

1 vi. 63, 9. *Cf.* Ludwig, Translation of the Rigveda, 3, 158.

Peśas denotes in the Rigveda[1] and later[2] an embroidered garment such as a female dancer would wear.[3] The fondness of the Indians for such raiment is noted by Megasthenes[4] and by Arrian,[5] who refer to their ἐσθὴς κατάστικτος. So in one passage[6] a garment (*vastra*) is called *peśana*, with which Roth[7] happily compares the Roman *vestis coloribus intexta*. The making of such garments was a regular occupation of women, as is indicated by the Peśas-kārī, the 'female embroiderer,' figuring in the list of victims at the Puruṣamedha ('human sacrifice') in the Yajurveda,[8] though the commentator on the Taittirīya Brāhmaṇa interprets the word as 'wife of a maker of gold.'[9] Pischel,[10] however, thinks that Peśas never means anything but colour or form.

1 ii. 3, 6; iv. 36, 7; vii. 34, 11; 42, 1.

2 Vājasaneyi Saṃhitā, xix. 82. 89; xx. 40; Aitareya Brāhmaṇa, iii. 10, etc.

3 Rv. i. 92, 4. 5.

4 See Strabo, p. 509, where he refers to a σινδὼν εὐανθής.

5 *Indica*, 5, 9.

6 Rv. x. 1, 6.

7 St. Petersburg Dictionary, *s.v.*

8 Vājasaneyi Saṃhitā, xxx. 9; Taittirīya Brāhmaṇa, iii. 4, 5, 1.

9 *Cf.* perhaps *suvarṇaṃ hiraṇyaṃ peśalam* in the Taittirīya Brāhmaṇa, iii. 3, 4, 5, where *peśala* probably refers to cunningly-worked gold. But this does not suit the compound *peśas-kārī*, which must denote a 'maker of *peśas*,' and *peśas* has not the sense of wrought gold in any passage. *Cf.* also Bṛhadāraṇyaka Upaniṣad, iv. 4, 5; Zimmer, *Altindisches Leben*, 261.

10 *Vedische Studien*, 2, 113-125.

Peśitṛ is the name of one of the victims at the Puruṣamedha ('human sacrifice') in the Yajurveda.[1] The sense is quite

1 Vājasaneyi Saṃhitā, xxx. 12; Taittirīya Brāhmaṇa, iii. 4, 8, 1.

uncertain. The word is rendered by the St. Petersburg Dictionary and by Weber[2] as 'one who cuts in pieces,' a 'carver,' but Sāyaṇa[3] thinks that it means one who causes an enmity which has been lulled to rest to break out again.

[2] *Indische Streifen*, 1, 75, n. 5.

[3] On Taittirīya Brāhmaṇa, *loc. cit.*

Paiṅga-rāja is the name of one of the victims at the Aśvamedha ('horse sacrifice') in the Yajurveda Saṃhitās.[1] That a bird is meant is certain, but what particular kind is quite unknown.

[1] Taittirīya Saṃhitā, v. 5, 13, 1; Maitrāyaṇī Saṃhitā, iii. 14, 16; Vājasaneyi Saṃhitā, xxiv. 34. *Cf.* Zimmer, *Altindisches Leben*, 99.

Paiṅgī-putra ('son of a female descendant of Piṅga') is the name of a teacher, pupil of **Śaunakīputra**, in the last Vaṃśa (list of teachers) of the Bṛhadāraṇyaka Upaniṣad (vi. 4, 30 Mādhyaṃdina).

Paiṅgya, 'descendant of Piṅga,' is the name of a teacher who is repeatedly mentioned as an authority in the Kauṣītaki Brāhmaṇa,[1] where[2] also his doctrine is called the Paiṅgya. This teacher is further referred to in the Śatapatha Brāhmaṇa,[3] which also speaks of **Madhuka** Paiṅgya.[4] It is, of course, impossible to say whether there was only one Paiṅgya or several Paiṅgyas. The followers of Paiṅgya are called Paiṅgins in the Nidāna[5] and Anupada[6] Sūtras. His text-book is called Paiṅga in the Anupada Sūtra,[7] while the Āpastamba Śrauta Sūtra[8] mentions a Paiṅgāyani Brāhmaṇa. It is clear that Paiṅgya was a teacher of a Rigveda school allied to the Kauṣītakis. Paiṅgi is a patronymic of **Yāska** in the Anukramaṇī of the Ātreyī Śākhā.[9]

[1] viii. 9; xvi. 9; xxvi. 3. 4. 14; xxviii. 7. 9; Kauṣītaki Upaniṣad, ii. 2.

[2] iii. 1; xix. 9; xxiv. 4. *Cf. Paiṅgī saṃpad*, xxv. 7. Paiṅgya is found also in the Sāṅkhāyana Srauta Sūtra, iv. 2, 11; xi. 11, 5; 14, 9; xv. 3, 1; xvii. 7, 1. 3; 10, 3; Aitareya Brāhmaṇa, vii. 11.

[3] xii. 2, 2, 4; 4, 8. (Bṛhadāraṇyaka Upaniṣad, vi. 3, 17.)

[4] xi. 7, 2, 8; 16.

[5] iv. 7.

[6] i. 8; ii. 2. 4. 10; vi. 7; xi. 8.

[7] ii. 4; iii. 12; iv. 5.

[8] v. 15, 8; 29, 4.

[9] Weber, *Indische Studien*, 1, 71, n.; 3, 396.

Cf. Weber, *Indische Studien*, 1, 44, 45, 404 *et seq.*; 2, 295; *Indian Literature*, 41, 46, 47, 56, 81, 90, 130, etc.

Paijavana, 'descendant of **Pijavana**,' is the patronymic of **Sudās**.[1] It seems most probable that Pijavana intervened in the line of succession between **Divodāsa** and Sudās, because the two kings have, according to tradition, quite different Purohitas, the former being served by the **Bharadvājas** as his priests, the latter by **Vasiṣṭha** and **Viśvāmitra**;[2] this is more natural if they were divided by a period of time than if they had been, as is usually supposed, father and son. Geldner,[3] however, identifies Divodāsa and Pijavana.

[1] Rv. vii. 18, 22. 25; Nirukta, ii. 24. 25; Aitareya Brāhmaṇa, vii. 34; Śāṅkhāyana Śrauta Sūtra, xvi. 11, 14.

[2] See Hillebrandt, *Vedische Mythologie*, 1, 104 *et seq*.

[3] *Rigveda, Glossar*, 115.

Paidva. See **Pedu.**

Potṛ is the name of one of the priests (**Ṛtvij**) of the sacrificial ritual. Already known to the Rigveda,[1] he is frequently mentioned later in the Brāhmaṇas.[2] But as Oldenberg[3] observes, the Potṛ is not in the later literature a priest of any importance, but is practically a mere name. Judging by the derivation of the name from the root *pū*, 'purify,' it would seem that he was properly engaged in the purification of the *Soma pavamāna*, 'Soma purifying itself,' and was perhaps employed to sing hymns to this Soma. Potra[4] denotes both the office and the Soma vessel of the Potṛ.[5]

[1] i. 94, 6; ii. 5, 2; iv. 9, 3; vii. 16, 5; ix. 67, 22.

[2] Aitareya Brāhmaṇa, vi. 10 *et seq.*; Satapatha Brāhmaṇa, iv. 3, 4, 22; v. 4, 5, 22; xii. 1, 1, 8, etc.

[3] *Religion des Veda*, 383, 391, 395.

[4] Rv. ii. 1, 2, and probably i. 76, 4, though the St. Petersburg Dictionary, *s.v.*, gives this as an example of the second use.

[5] Rv. i. 15, 2; ii. 36, 2; 37, 2. 4.

Pauṃścaleya in the Taittirīya Brāhmaṇa (iii. 8, 4, 2) denotes the son of a courtesan (**Puṃścalī**).

Pauṃsāyana is the patronymic of **Duṣṭarītu** in the Śatapatha Brāhmaṇa (xii. 9, 3, 1).

Pauñji-ṣṭha is the form in the Atharvaveda,[1] the Vājasaneyi Saṃhitā,[2] and the Taittirīya Brāhmaṇa,[3] of the word **Puñjiṣṭha,** denoting 'fisherman.' It is probably a caste name, 'son of a Puñjiṣṭha,' as the designation of a functional caste.

[1] x. 4, 9.

[2] xxx. 8.

[3] iii. 4, 5, 1, where Sāyaṇa glosses it with the word *kaivarta*, also probably the name of a functional caste.

Pauṇḍarīka is the patronymic of **Kṣemadhṛtvan** in the Pañcaviṃśa Brāhmaṇa (xxii. 18, 7).

Pauta-krata, 'descendant of **Pūtakratā,**' is the metronymic of a man, apparently **Dasyave Vṛka**, in the Rigveda.[1] Scheftelowitz[2] proposes to read Pūtakratu with the Kashmir MS. of the Rigveda, arguing that in the same hymn Pūtakratāyī, the wife of Pūtakratu, is referred to, and that therefore Pūtakratu is appropriate, Pūtakratāyī[3] being the feminine, like Manāyī,[4] for Manāvī. But the ordinary reading in the sense of descendant is perfectly legitimate, as Oldenberg[5] has pointed out.

[1] viii. 56, 2.

[2] *Die Apokryphen des Ṛgveda*, 41, 42.

[3] See Pāṇini, iv. 1, 36.

[4] Maitrāyaṇī Saṃhitā, i. 8, 6; Pāṇini, iv. 1, 38. Perhaps also Vasāvī, Rv. x. 73, 4.

[5] *Göttingische Gelehrte Anzeigen*, 1907, 237.

Pautimāṣī-putra, 'son of a female descendant of Pūtimāṣa,' is the metronymic of a teacher in the last Vaṃśa (list of teachers) of the Kāṇva recension of the Bṛhadāraṇyaka Upaniṣad (vi. 5, 1).

Pauti-māṣya, 'descendant of Pūtimāṣa,' is the patronymic of a teacher, a pupil of **Gaupavana**, in the first two Vaṃśas (lists of teachers) of the Kāṇva recension of the Bṛhadāraṇyaka Upaniṣad (ii. 6, 1; iv. 6, 1).

Pautimāṣyāyaṇa, 'descendant of **Pautimāṣya,**' is the patronymic of a teacher, who, with **Kauṇḍinyāyana**, taught **Raibhya,** in the first two Vaṃśas (lists of teachers) of the Mādhyaṃdina recension of the Bṛhadāraṇyaka Upaniṣad (ii. 5, 20; iv. 5, 26).

Pautra ('descended from a son') is the regular term for a 'grandson' from the Atharvaveda[1] onwards.[2] When it is used beside **Naptṛ**,[3] the latter word must denote 'great-grandson.'

[1] ix. 5, 30; xi. 7, 16; xviii. 43, 9.
[2] Aitareya Brāhmaṇa, vii. 10; Taittirīya Brāhmaṇa, ii. 1, 8, 3, etc.
[3] Lāṭyāyana Śrauta Sūtra, i. 3, 18; Āpastamba Śrauta Sūtra, x. 11, 5; Aitareya Brāhmaṇa, vii. 10, 3.
Cf. Delbrück, *Die indogermanischen Verwandtschaftsnamen*, 478.

Paura, 'descendant of Pūru,' is the name of a man, presumably a Pūru prince helped by Indra, in a hymn of the Rigveda.[1] The Greek Πῶρος, the name of Alexander's rival, is probably the representative of this word. Oldenberg[2] sees the same name in another passage also.[3]

[1] viii. 3, 12.
[2] *Ṛgveda-Noten*, 1, 362; as also Grassmann, *Wörterbuch*, *s.v.*
[3] v. 74, 4.

Pauru-kutsa,[1] **Pauru-kutsi**,[2] **Pauru-kutsya**,[3] are variant forms of the patronymic of **Trasadasyu**, the descendant of **Purukutsa**.

[1] Kāṭhaka Saṃhitā, xxii. 3; Pañcaviṃśa Brāhmaṇa, xxv. 16, 3.
[2] Rv. vii. 19, 3.
[3] Rv. v. 33, 8; viii. 19, 36; Taittirīya Saṃhitā, v. 6, 5, 3.

Pauru-śiṣṭi, 'descendant of Puruśiṣṭa,' is the patronymic of **Taponitya** in the Taittirīya Upaniṣad (i. 9, 1 = Taittirīya Āraṇyaka, vii. 8, 1).

Paurṇa-māsī, denoting the 'night of the full moon,' is celebrated in the Atharvaveda[1] as sacred, while it is repeatedly mentioned later.[2] Gobhila[3] defines it as the greatest separation (*vikarṣa*) of the sun and the moon. *Cf.* **Māsa.**

[1] vii. 80.
[2] Taittirīya Saṃhitā, i. 6, 9, 1; ii. 2, 2, 1; iii. 4, 9, 6; Aitareya Brāhmaṇa, vii. 11; Śatapatha Brāhmaṇa, i. 2, 2, 4, etc.
[3] i. 5, 7. Three sorts of full moon are distinguished by Gobhila — that which occurs when the full moon rises at the meeting of day and night (*sandhyā*), when it rises shortly after sunset, or when it stands high in the sky. The two former alternatives are apparently those described in the passage (Aitareya Brāhmaṇa, vii. 11 = Kauṣītaki Brāhmaṇa, iii. 1) as *pūrvā* and *uttarā*. See Weber, Jyotiṣa, 51; Oldenberg, *Sacred Books of the East*, 30, 26, n.

Paulusi, 'descendant of Puluṣa,' is the patronymic of **Satyayajña** in the Śatapatha Brāhmaṇa (x. 6, 1, 1) and the Chāndogya Upaniṣad (v. 11, 1). In the Jaiminīya Upaniṣad Brāhmaṇa (i. 39, 1) the form is Pauluṣita, which is perhaps merely an error.

Paulkasa is the name of one of the victims at the Puruṣamedha ('human sacrifice') in the Yajurveda.[1] The name also occurs in the Bṛhadāraṇyaka Upaniṣad[2] as that of a despised race of men, together with the **Cāṇḍāla**. The Maitrāyaṇī Saṃhitā[3] has the variant Puklaka or Pulkaka, clearly the same as Pulkasa, of which Paulkasa is a derivative form, showing that a caste is meant (*cf.* **Kaulāla, Pauñjiṣṭha**). In the accepted theory[4] the Pulkasa is the son of a Niṣāda or Śūdra by a Kṣatriya woman, but this is merely speculative; the Paulkasa may either have been a functional caste, or, as Fick[5] believes, an aboriginal clan living by catching wild beasts, and only occasionally reduced to menial tasks.

[1] Vājasaneyi Saṃhitā, xxx. 17; Taittirīya Brāhmaṇa, iii. 4, 14, 1.
[2] iv. 3, 22.
[3] i. 6, 11.
[4] *Cf.* St. Petersburg Dictionary, *s.v.*, *Pukkaśa*. Zimmer, *Altindisches Leben*, 217, takes Paulkasa as a mixed caste.
[5] *Die sociale Gliederung*, 206. *Cf.* Eggeling, *Sacred Books of the East*, 44, 416, n. 6.

Pauṣkara-sādi ('descendant of Puṣkarasādi') is the name of a teacher mentioned in the Śāṅkhāyana Āraṇyaka,[1] as well as the Taittirīya Prātiśākhya.[2] A Puṣkarasādi is mentioned in the Dharma Sūtra[3] of Āpastamba and elsewhere.

[1] vii. 17. *Cf.* Keith, *Journal of the Royal Asiatic Society*, 1908, 371.
[2] i. 5; ii. 1. 2. 5; Pāṇini, viii. 4, 48; Vārttika, 3; Kielhorn, *Indian Antiquary*, 16, 103; Pischel, *ibid.*, 34, 26.
[3] i. 6, 19, 7; 10, 28, 1.

Pauṣpiṇḍya is the name of a teacher, a pupil of **Jaimini**, in the Vaṃśa (list of teachers) at the end of the Sāmavidhāna Brāhmaṇa.[1]

[1] *Cf.* Weber, *Indische Studien*, 4, 377.

Pyukṣṇa is found in the Śatapatha Brāhmaṇa (v. 3, 1, 11) denoting the 'covering' for a bow (**Dhanus**), presumably made of skin.

Praüga is apparently equivalent to *pra-yuga*, denoting the fore part of the pole of the cart, the part in front of the yoke. It is mentioned in the Yajurveda Saṃhitās[1] and the Śatapatha Brāhmaṇa,[2] where it is said to be the part of the pole behind the **Kastambhī**, or prop on which the pole rests.

[1] Taittirīya Saṃhitā, v. 4, 11, 1. 2; Kāṭhaka Saṃhitā, xxi. 4.

[2] Śatapatha Brāhmaṇa, i. 1, 2, 9; iii. 5, 3, 4, etc. *Cf.* Zimmer, *Altindisches Leben*, 248; Eggeling, *Sacred Books of the East*, 12, 14, n. 1.

Pra-kaṅkata is the name of some noxious insect in the Rigveda.[1]

[1] i. 191, 7. *Cf.* Zimmer, *Altindisches Leben*, 98.

Pra-karitṛ is the name of one of the victims at the Puruṣamedha ('human sacrifice') in the Yajurveda.[1] The exact sense is uncertain; the commentator Sāyaṇa on the Taittirīya Brāhmaṇa explains it to mean the 'divider of dear ones by producing enmity,' but the sense of 'sprinkler'—that is, 'seasoner'—is more likely.

[1] Vājasaneyi Saṃhitā, xxx. 12; Taittirīya Brāhmaṇa, iii. 4, 8, 1. *Cf.* Eggeling, *Sacred Books of the East*, 44, 315, n. 1; Weber, *Indische Streifen*, 1, 79, n. 6.

Pra-kaśa in the Atharvaveda (ix. 1, 21) seems to mean either the 'thong' or the 'lash' of a whip.

Pra-krama, 'stride,' is mentioned as a measure of distance in the Śatapatha Brāhmaṇa (x. 2, 3, 1 *et seq.*), but its exact length in unknown.

Prakṣa is the form in the Taittirīya Saṃhitā[1] of the usual name, **Plakṣa**, of a tree, being merely a phonetic alteration for the sake of the etymology. According to Aufrecht,[2] the same word is found in two passages of the Sāmaveda,[3] the same reading occurring in the Aitareya Āraṇyaka.[4] Oldenberg,[5] however, questions the correctness of the reading Prakṣa, both in the latter passage and in the Sāmaveda.

[1] vi. 3, 10, 2.

[2] *Rigveda*, 2, xlvi, n.

[3] i. 444; ii. 465.

[4] v. 2, 2, with Keith's notes.

[5] *Ṛgveda-Noten*, 1, 344.

Cf. Zimmer, *Altindisches Leben*, 59.

Pragātha is the name given in the Aitareya Āraṇyaka (ii. 2, 2) to the poets of the eighth Maṇḍala of the Rigveda, so called because they composed Pragātha strophes (that is, verses consisting of a Bṛhatī or Kakubh followed by a Satobṛhatı).

Pra-ghāta is found in the Yajurveda Saṃhitās[1] and the Śatapatha Brāhmaṇa[2] in the sense of the closely woven ends of a cloth from which depend the loose threads of the **Nīvi,** or unwoven fringe.

[1] Taittirīya Saṃhitā, vi. 1, 1, 3; Kāṭhaka Saṃhitā, xxiii. 1. The word does not occur in Maitrāyaṇī Saṃhitā, iii. 6, 2. 3.

[2] iii. 1, 2, 18. *Cf.* Eggeling, *Sacred Books of the East,* 26, 10, n. 1.

Pra-calākā in the Taittirīya Saṃhitā (vii. 5, 11, 1) and the Kāṭhaka Saṃhitā (Aśvamedha, v. 2) seems to mean a 'cloudburst.'

Prajāvant Prājāpatya, 'descendant of Prajāpati,' is, according to the Aitareya Brāhmaṇa (i. 21), the author of a hymn of the Rigveda (x. 183).

Pra-ṇapāt in the Rigveda (viii. 17, 13) denotes 'great-grandson.'

Pra-ṇejana is the word used in the Śatapatha Brāhmaṇa (i. 2, 2, 18) to denote the 'water used for washing.'

Pra-tatāmaha, 'great-grandfather,' is found in the Atharvaveda (xviii. 4, 75).

Pra-tardana is the name in the Kāṭhaka Saṃhitā[1] of a king who had a **Bharadvāja** for his Purohita. In the Kauṣītaki Brāhmaṇa he appears as arriving at the sacrifice of the Ṛṣis in the Naimiṣa forest, and asking them how errors in the sacrifice could be remedied; and as finding **Alīkayu Vācaspata,** the Brahman priest at the sacrifice, unable to say what was to be

[1] xxi. 10.

[2] xxvi. 5.

done. In the Kauṣītaki Upaniṣad[3] it is said that Pratardana Daivodāsi went to Indra's world through his death in battle. The patronymic connects him with **Divodāsa**, the ancestor or father of **Sudās**, and the mention of Bharadvāja (probably 'a Bharadvāja' is meant) as his priest supports the patronymic, for Divodāsa is a special favourite of the singers of the Bharadvāja family. The name, moreover, is reminiscent of the Tṛtsus (the root *tard* appears in both) and of the *Pratṛdaḥ* (see **Pratṛd**). But he is not in Vedic literature a king of Kāśi.[4] Geldner[5] regards him as Divodāsa's son, but this is not likely. *Cf.* **Prātardani.**

[3] iii. 1.
[4] As in the Epic; Pargiter, *Journal of the Royal Asiatic Society*, 1910, 38.
[5] *Vedische Studien*, 2, 138.

Pra-tithi Deva-taratha is the name of a teacher, pupil of **Devataras Śāvasāyana** in the Vaṃśa Brāhmaṇa.[1]

[1] *Indische Studien*, 4, 373, 385; Max Müller, *Ancient Sanskrit Literature*, 444.

Prati-dīvan denotes in the Rigveda (x. 38, 6) and the Atharvaveda (vii. 109, 4) 'opponent in the game of dice.'

Prati-duh has the specific sense of 'fresh milk,' warm from the cow, in the later Saṃhitās[1] and the Brāhmaṇas.[2]

[1] Av. ix. 4, 4; Taittirīya Saṃhitā, ii. 5, 3, 3; Kāṭhaka Saṃhitā, xxxvii. 6, etc.
[2] Pañcaviṃśa Brāhmaṇa, ix. 5, 5; xviii. 4, 2; Śatapatha Brāhmaṇa, iii. 3, 3, 2; Taittirīya Brāhmaṇa, ii. 7, 6, 2, etc.

Prati-dhā apparently means 'draught' or 'pull' in one passage of the Rigveda,[1] where Indra is said to have drunk thirty streams (*sarāṃsi*) with one Pratidhā.

[1] viii. 77, 4; Nirukta, v. 11.

Prati-dhi is mentioned in the Sūryā hymn of the Rigveda[1] as part of the chariot on which the bride is taken home. It is

[1] x. 85, 8.

impossible to determine with certainty exactly what is meant; Roth[2] understands it to mean a cross-piece of wood fastened to the pole.

[2] St. Petersburg Dictionary, *s.v.*

Prati-paṇa is found in the Atharvaveda (iii. 15, 4) denoting 'barter' or 'exchange.' *Cf.* **Paṇa.**

Prati-praśna occurs in the Śatapatha Brāhmaṇa[1] applied to Prajāpati as the decider of doubts; it may have been a technical term for an 'arbitrator' (*cf.* **Madhyamasī** and **Dharma**).

[1] i. 4, 5, 11; iv. 1, 3, 14; Eggeling, *Sacred Books of the East*, 12, 131, and 26, 267, renders *pratipraśnam* by '(went to Prajāpati) for his decision,' which leaves it ambiguous how he took the passages.

Prati-pra-sthātṛ is the name of a priest (**Ṛtvij**), one of the assistants of the Adhvaryu, in the later Saṃhitās and the Brāhmaṇas.[1] He is not mentioned in the Rigveda,[2] but mention is once made in that Saṃhitā[3] of the two Adhvaryus. These may have meant, as later, the Adhvaryu and the Pratiprasthātṛ. Oldenberg,[4] however, thinks that the Adhvaryu and the Agnīdh are intended, a conjecture for which there is some authority.[5]

[1] Taittirīya Saṃhitā, vi. 5, 3, 4; Aitareya Brāhmaṇa, i. 29; vii. 1; Śatapatha Brāhmaṇa, iii. 5, 2, 2; 3, 13, 22, etc.

[2] Oldenberg, *Religion des Veda*, 384, n. 2.

[3] ii. 16, 5.

[4] *Op. cit.*, 390, n. 2.

[5] *Cf.* Rv. x. 41, 3; Mantra in Śāṅkhāyana Śrauta Sūtra, i. 6, 3. *Cf.* Hillebrandt, *Rituallitteratur*, 97.

Prati-prāś. See **Prāś.**

Pratibodhī-putra is a wrong reading for **Prātībodhī-putra.**[1]

[1] *Indische Studien*, 1, 391; Keith, *Aitareya Āraṇyaka*, 244, 310.

Prati-mit is found in the description of a house in the Atharvaveda.[1] The sense must be 'support' of some sort, probably beams leaning up at an angle against the **Upamits.**

[1] ix. 3, 1. *Cf.* Zimmer, *Altindisches Leben*, 153; Bloomfield, *Hymns of the Atharvaveda*, 596.

Prati-veśa, 'neighbour,' occurs, often metaphorically, from the Rigveda[1] onwards.[2]

[1] x. 66, 13.
[2] Taittirīya Saṃhitā, ii. 6, 97; Vājasaneyi Saṃhitā, xi. 75; Kāṭhaka Saṃhitā, xxxvi. 9; Śatapatha Brāhmaṇa, iv. 1, 5, 2; Taittirīya Upaniṣad, i. 4, 3.

Prati-veśya is mentioned in the Vaṃśa (list of teachers) at the end of the Śāṅkhāyana Āraṇyaka (xv. 1) as the pupil of **Bṛhaddiva**. *Cf.* **Prātiveśya**.

Prati-śrutkā, 'echo,' shows that this phenomenon had already received a name as early as the Yajurveda Saṃhitās[1] and the Kauṣītaki Upaniṣad (iv. 13).

[1] Taittirīya Saṃhitā, v. 5, 14, 1; Maitrāyaṇī Saṃhitā, iii. 14, 13; Kāṭhaka Saṃhitā, Aśvamedha, vii. 4; Vājasaneyi Saṃhitā, xxiv. 32; xxx. 19.

Prati-ṣṭhā is found in one passage of the Atharvaveda,[1] where Zimmer[2] thinks the word is used as a technical term of law; possibly a 'sanctuary' may be meant, but it is more than doubtful whether the sense of 'home' or 'abode,' as given by Roth,[3] is not quite adequate. *Cf.* **Jñātṛ**.

[1] vi. 32, 3 = viii. 8, 21 = Śāṅkhāyana Āraṇyaka, xii. 14.
[2] *Altindisches Leben*, 181.
[3] St. Petersburg Dictionary, *s.v.*, 3. So a *pratiṣṭhā-kāma*, 'one desirous of a fixed abode,' Taittirīya Saṃhitā, ii. 1, 3, 4; Pañcaviṃśa Brāhmaṇa, xxiii. 18, 1, etc.

Prati-sara is used in several passages of the Atharvaveda[1] and later[2] to denote an amulet, according to Roth,[3] because it was a band, and so returned on itself (*prati-sṛ*, 'go back'). The sense is doubtful; perhaps 'attacking' may really be the root idea.[4] *Cf.* **Punaḥsara**.

[1] ii. 11, 2; iv. 40, 1; viii. 5, 1. 4.
[2] Satapatha Brāhmaṇa, v. 2, 4, 20; Śāṅkhāyana Āraṇyaka, xii. 30, etc.
[3] St. Petersburg Dictionary, *s.v.*, followed by Eggeling, *Sacred Books of the East*, 41, 53, n. 2.
[4] *Cf.* Bloomfield, *Journal of the American Oriental Society*, 13, cxxxiii; *Hymns of the Atharvaveda*, 576.

Cf. Zimmer, *Altindisches Leben*, 263; Ludwig, Translation of the Rigveda, 3, 345; Weber, *Indische Studien*, 13, 164.

Prati-hartṛ is the name of the assistant of the Udgātṛ in the list of the sixteen priests (**Ṛtvij**). It is found in the later Saṃhitās[1] and the Brāhmaṇas,[2] but not in the Rigveda.[3]

[1] Taittirīya Saṃhitā, iii. 3, 2, 1.
[2] Taittirīya Brāhmaṇa, i. 8, 2, 3; Aitareya Brāhmaṇa, vii. 1; Śatapatha Brāhmaṇa, iv. 3, 4, 22; xii. 1, 1, 8; Pañcaviṃśa Brāhmaṇa, xxv. 15, 3; Chāndogya Upaniṣad, i. 10, 11; 11, 8.
[3] *Cf.* Ludwig, Translation of the Rigveda, 3, 227.

Pratī-darśa Śvaikna is mentioned in the Śatapatha Brāhmaṇa[1] as sacrificing with the Dākṣāyaṇa offering, and as teaching **Suplan Sārñjaya,** who thence became **Sahadeva Sārñjaya.** In a second passage[2] he is called Pratīdarśa Aibhāvata, and again brought into connexion with Suplan Sārñjaya According to Eggeling,[3] he is to be deemed a king of the Śviknas; apparentlv, too, he was a descendant of Ibhāvant. A Pratīdarśa is also mentioned in the Jaiminīya Upaniṣad Brāhmaṇa.[4]

[1] ii. 4, 4, 3.
[2] xii. 8, 2, 3.
[3] *Sacred Books of the East*, 44, 239, n. 2.
[4] iv. 8, 7.

Pratīpa Prātisatvana,[1] or **Prātisutvana,**[2] is the name of a man mentioned in a hymn of the Atharvaveda.[2] Zimmer,[3] with great ingenuity, compares the fact that **Parikṣit** is mentioned as a **Kuru** king in the Atharvaveda,[4] and that, according to the Epic genealogies, his grandson was Pratiśravas, with which name Prātisutvana, as very possibly a Prākritized version of Prātiśrutvana may be compared, and his great-grandson was Pratīpa. The identification cannot, however, be regarded as at all certain, and while the Epic may have derived its genealogy from the Atharvaveda, it may have preserved an independent tradition. Böhtlingk[5] renders *prātisatvanam* as 'in the direction opposed to the Satvans', and this may be right.

[1] So Khila, v. 15, 1; Aitareya Brāhmaṇa, vi. 33, 2.
[2] So Av. xx. 129, 2. *Cf.* Scheftelowitz, *Die Apokryphen des Ṛgveda*, 161; Śāṅkhāyana Śrauta Sūtra, xii. 18, 1.
[3] *Altindisches Leben*, 131.
[4] xx. 127.
[5] Dictionary, *s.v.*

Pratī-bodha is mentioned with **Bodha** in two passages of the Atharvaveda,[1] apparently as the name of a very mythic Ṛṣi, 'Intelligence.'

[1] v. 30, 10; viii. 1, 13. *Cf.* Mānava Gṛhya Sūtra, ii. 15, 1.

Pratṛd occurs once in the plural in a hymn of the Rgveda,[1] where it is clearly a variant of the word **Tṛtsu.** Moreover, the name of King **Pratardana,** a descendant of the Tṛtsu king, **Divodāsa,** confirms the identification of Tṛtsu and Pratṛd.[2]

[1] vii. 33, 14.

[2] See Ludwig, Translation of the Rigveda, 3, 159; Geldner, *Vedische Studien*, 2, 138.

Pra-toda denotes in the Atharvaveda[1] and the Pañcaviṃśa Brāhmaṇa[2] the 'goad' of the **Vrātya,** the non-Brahminical Āryan or aborigine. Later the word is regularly used for 'goad' in general.

[1] xv. 2, 1.

[2] xvii. 1, 14. See Śāṅkhāyana Āraṇyaka, xii. 8; Kātyāyana Śrauta Sūtra, xxii. 4, 10; Lāṭyāyana Śrauta Sūtra, viii. 6, 7; Sāṅkhāyana Srauta Sūtra, xiv. 72, 3. The rendering 'lance' seems to have no authority. But see Weber, *Indian Literature*, 67.

Pratyakṣa-darśana, n., means 'seeing with one's own eyes,' as opposed to seeing in a vision (*svapna*). A section on such visions appears in the Rigveda Āraṇyakas.[1]

[1] Aitareya Āraṇyaka, iii. 2, 4; Śāṅkhāyana Āraṇyaka, viii. 7.

Praty-enas is found with **Ugra** and **Sūta-grāmaṇī** in the Bṛhadāraṇyaka Upaniṣad,[1] clearly denoting an officer of police. The sense must be that of the humbler 'servants' of the king[2] rather than 'magistrates,' as Max Müller, in his translation, takes it. In the Kāṭhaka Saṃhitā[3] and the Śāṅkhāyana Śrauta Sūtra[4] the word means, according to the St. Petersburg Dictionary, the next heir, who is responsible for the debts of a dead man.

[1] iv. 3, 43. 44 (Mādhyaṃdina = iv. 3, 37. 38 Kāṇva).

[2] Böhtlingk's Translation, p. 66, where he takes *ugra* as an adjective.

[3] viii. 4 (*Indische Studien*, 3, 463).

[4] iv. 16, 16. 17.

Pra-dara in the later Saṃhitās[1] and the Brāhmaṇas[2] denotes a 'cleft' in the ground.

[1] Taittirīya Saṃhitā, iii. 4, 8, 5; v. 2, 4, 3; Vājasaneyi Saṃhitā, xxv. 7.
[2] Aitareya Brāhmaṇa, vi. 35, 1; Taittirīya Brāhmaṇa, i. 5, 0, 7; Satapatha Brāhmaṇa, xi. 2, 3, 8; xiii. 8, 3, 10, etc.

Pra-div in the Atharvaveda (xviii. 2, 48) is the third and highest heaven, in which the Fathers dwell. In the Kauṣītaki Brāhmaṇa (xx. 1) it is the fifth of a series of seven heavens.

Pra-diś, like **Diś**, normally designates only a 'quarter' of the sky, or 'point' of the compass. Four,[1] five,[2] six,[3] and seven[4] such points are enumerated, or more generally 'all' are mentioned.[5] In some passages,[6] on the other hand, the word has the definite sense of an 'intermediate quarter,' which is more precisely denoted by *avāntara-diś.*

[1] Rv. i. 164, 42; vii. 35, 8; x. 19, 8; Av. i. 11, 2; iii. 10, 3.
[2] Rv. ix. 86, 29; Av. i. 30, 4; iii. 4, 2; 20, 9.
[3] Av. iv. 11, 1; 20, 2; x. 7, 35.
[4] Vājasaneyi Saṃhitā, xviii. 32.
[5] Rv. vi. 75, 2; x. 121, 4.
[6] Av. v. 28, 2; ix. 2, 21; xix. 20, 2, etc.

Pra-dhana denotes 'contest,' whether the real conflict of war or the competition of the chariot race, in the Rigveda.[1]

[1] i. 116, 2; 154, 3; 169, 2; x. 102, 5, etc.

Pra-dhi is the name of some part of the wheel of a chariot, probably the 'felly.' In one passage of the Rigveda,[1] and in one of the Atharvaveda,[2] the 'nave' (**Nabhya**) and the 'felly' (*pradhi*) are mentioned along with the **Upadhi**, which must then be either a collective name for the spokes or an inner rim within the felly and binding the spokes. In the riddle hymn of the Rigveda[3] twelve Pradhis are mentioned with three naves, one wheel, and three hundred and sixty spokes; what exactly is here meant by this particular term it would be useless to conjecture, though it is clear that the passage as a whole symbolizes

[1] ii. 39, 4.
[2] vi. 70, 3.
[3] i. 164, 48.

the year with three seasons, twelve months, and three hundred and sixty days. Elsewhere[4] the nave and the Pradhi alone are mentioned, or the Pradhi occurs by itself.[5]

[4] Taittirīya Saṃhitā. vii. 4, 11, 2; Aitareya Brāhmaṇa, iv. 15; Bṛhadāraṇyaka Upaniṣad, i. 5, 23.

[5] Rv. iv. 30, 15; x. 102, 7, etc. In Av. xviii. 2, 14, *pradhāv adhi* is merely an incorrect variant of the *pradhāvati* of Rv. x. 154, 1. The same corruption is seen by Lanman (in Whitney's Translation of the Atharvaveda, xcii) in Av. vi. 70, 3 (n. 2).

Cf. Whitney, *op. cit.*, 33; Zimmer, *Altindisches Leben*, 248.

Pra-dhvaṃsana. See **Prādhvaṃsana.**

Pra-paṇa in the Atharvaveda (xii. 15, 4. 5) denotes 'barter' or 'exchange,' balanced by **Pratipaṇa.**

Pra-patha in the Rigveda[1] and the Aitareya Brāhmaṇa[2] denotes a 'long journey.' Wilson[3] has seen in one passage[4] the sense of 'resting-place,' where travellers can obtain food (*khādi*). Zimmer[5] shows that this is impossible, and the reading (*prapatheṣu*) in the passage in question is not improbably[6] an error for *prapadeṣu.* In the Kāṭhaka Saṃhitā[7] the word means a 'broad road.'

[1] x. 17, 4. 6; 63, 16.

[2] vii. 15.

[3] Translation of the Rigveda, 2, 151.

[4] Rv. i. 166, 9.

[5] *Altindisches Leben*, 231.

[6] Roth, St. Petersburg Dictionary, *s.v.*; *Zeitschrift der Deutschen Morgenländischen Gesellschaft*, 48, 108; Oldenberg, *Ṛgveda-Noten*, 1, 166. Böhtlingk, Dictionary, *s.v.*, does not follow Roth.

[7] xxxvii. 14 (*Indische Studien*, 3, 466).

Pra-pathin[1] is the name of a patron, perhaps a Yādava, in one hymn of the Rigveda.[2]

[1] *Prapathī* might be the stem, the word occurring as a proper name in the nominative singular only (*cf.* Macdonell, *Vedic Grammar*, 377, 3); but this is not probable, the stem *prapathin* being otherwise found as an adjective.

[2] viii. 1, 30. *Cf.* Ludwig, Translation of the Rigveda, 3, 159; Hopkins, *Journal of the American Oriental Society*, 17, 90.

Pra-pā seems to denote a 'spring' in the desert in the only Rigveda passage where it occurs.[1] In the Atharvaveda[2] it has merely the sense of 'drinking,' or a 'drink.'

[1] x. 4, 1.

[2] iii. 30, 6. *Cf.* Taittirīya Brāhmaṇa, iii. 10, 1, 2.

Pra-pitāmaha, 'great-grandfather,' is found in the later Saṃhitās[1] and the Brāhmaṇas.[2]

[1] Taittirīya Saṃhitā, i. 8, 5, 1; Vājasaneyi Saṃhitā, xix. 36; Av. xviii. 4, 35.

[2] Śatapatha Brāhmaṇ , ii. 4, 2, 16; xii. 8, 1, 7.

Pra-pitva is found in several passages of the Rigveda as a designation of time. In one passage[1] the sense is made clear by the context: 'at the rising of the sun' (*sūra udite*), 'at mid-day' (*madhyaṃdine divaḥ*), and 'at the Prapitva, bordering on the night' (*apiśarvare*). In another passage[2] the sense of 'late in the day' also seems adequate, while the phrase[3] *abhipitve ahnaḥ*, 'at the close of day,' also denotes the evening. According to Geldner[4] the sense of the word is the 'decisive moment' in a race or a battle, and so the 'end of the day.'[5] *Cf.* **Ahan.**

[1] viii. 1, 29.

[2] vii. 41, 4.

[3] iv. 16, 12.

[4] *Vedische Studien*, 2, 174 *et seq.*

[5] Roth, St. Petersburg Dictionary, *s.v.*, took it to mean 'daybreak'; so also Zimmer, *Altindisches Leben*, 362. Böhtlingk, Dictionary, *s.v.*, on the other hand, gives the meaning as 'decline of day,' 'evening.' See also Bloomfield, *Journal of the American Oriental Society*, 16, 24 *et seq.*; Oldenberg, *Sacred Books of the East*, 46, 183 *et seq.*

Pra-protha is the name in the Pañcaviṃśa Brāhmaṇa (viii. 4, 1) of a plant used as a substitute for Soma.

Pra-pharvī denotes a 'wanton woman' in the Rigveda (x. 85, 22), the Atharvaveda (v. 22, 7), and the Yajurveda Saṃhitās.[1]

[1] Taittirīya Saṃhitā, iv. 2, 5, 6; Maitrāyaṇī Saṃhitā, ii. 7, 12; Kāṭhaka Saṃhitā, xvi. 12; Vājasaneyi Saṃhitā, xii. 71.

Pra-budh, occurring in one passage of the Rigveda (viii. 27, 19), is used in the locative parallel with *nimruci*, 'at the setting (of the sun),' and clearly means 'at the rising (of the sun).'

Pra-maganda is the name of a prince in the Rigveda,[1] where he is mentioned as the king of the **Kīkaṭas**, and where he seems to be designated by the epithet *naicāśākha*, 'belonging to a low branch or race.' On the other hand, Yāska[2] takes Pramaganda to mean the 'son of a usurer,' an explanation that is hardly probable. Hillebrandt[3] thinks that *naicāśākha* refers not to Pramaganda, but to the Soma plant, the plant being called *nīcāśākha*, 'having shoots turned downwards,' and that the passage refers to a raid against the Kīkaṭas, who were not observers of the milk cult or the Soma cult, with the intention of winning their lands where the Soma grew and where there were cows. Böhtlingk,[4] however, questions this view, which is not very probable. A place name is possibly meant by Naicāśākha.[5] The name Pramaganda seems un-Āryan.

[1] iii. 53, 14.
[2] Nirukta, vi. 32.
[3] *Vedische Mythologie*, 1, 14-16; 2, 241-245.
[4] *Proceedings of the Saxon Academy*, December 12, 1891.
[5] Sāyaṇa, in his introduction to his commentary on the Rigveda, p. 4.
Cf. Zimmer, *Altindisches Leben*, 31; Ludwig, Translation of the Rigveda, 3, 153; Geldner, *Rigveda, Kommentar*, 58.

Pra-mandanī is the name of an Apsaras in the Atharvaveda.[1] Probably the word primarily denoted a certain sweet-scented plant, which seems to be the sense of *pra-manda* in the Kauśika Sūtra.[2]

[1] iv. 37, 3.
[2] viii. 17; xxv. 11; xxxii. 29; *niṣpramanda*, xxxvi. 15. *Cf.* Zimmer, *Altindisches Leben*, 69; Caland, *Altindisches Zauberritual*, 15, n. 11.

Pra-mara in one passage of the Rigveda[1] is taken by Ludwig[2] to be a proper name.

[1] x. 27, 20.
[2] Translation of the Rigveda, 3, 165.

Pra-mota is the name of some sort of disease in the Atharvaveda,[1] according to the St. Petersburg Dictionary. Zimmer,[2] however, thinks that the word must be an adjective meaning 'dumb.' This view is accepted, though with doubt, by Whitney[3] and by Bloomfield.[4]

[1] ix. 8, 4.
[2] *Altindisches Leben*, 378, n.
[3] Translation of the Atharvaveda, 550.
[4] *Hymns of the Atharvaveda*, 601.

Pra-yoga is the name of a seer in the Yajurveda Saṃhitās.[1]

[1] Taittirīya Saṃhitā, v. 1, 10, 1; Kāṭhaka Saṃhitā, xix. 10 (*Indische Studien*, 3, 478).

Pra-yogya denotes in the Chāndogya Upaniṣad (viii. 12, 3) an animal yoked to a carriage, 'draught animal.'

Pra-lāpa, 'prattle,' is found with other words of similar import in the Atharvaveda,[1] and in the Brāhmaṇas[2] of the Ṛgveda. The phrase **Aitaśa-pralāpa,** 'Discourse of Aitaśa,' occurs as a designation of certain passages of the Atharvaveda.[3] The name has no justification in the text itself.

[1] xi. 8, 25.

[2] Aitareya Brāhmaṇa, vi. 33; Kauṣītaki Brāhmaṇa, xxx. 5; Śāṅkhāyana Śrauta Sūtra, xii. 17, 6, etc.

[3] See Bloomfield, *Atharvaveda*, pp. 98, 101, n. 12; Scheftelowitz, *Die Apokryphen des Ṛgveda*, 159 *et seq.*; Macdonell, *Bṛhaddevatā*, 2, 323.

Pra-vacana means 'oral instruction,' 'teaching,' in the Śatapatha Brāhmaṇa[1] and later.[2]

[1] xi. 5, 7, 1.

[2] Taittirīya Upaniṣad, i. 1, 3, 9; Kāṭhaka Upaniṣad, ii. 23; Muṇḍaka Upaniṣad, iii. 2, 3, etc.

Pra-vat, 'height,' is contrasted with **Nivat,** 'valley,' in the Rigveda,[1] where it occurs several times.[2] The word is also found later.[3]

[1] vii. 50, 4.

[2] Rv. ii. 13, 2; iv. 17, 7; 22, 4; vi. 17, 12; vii. 32, 27; x. 14, 1; 57, 12; 75, 4.

[3] Av. i. 13, 2; 26, 3; vi. 28, 3; x. 10, 2; xii. 1, 2; xviii. 4, 7.

1. **Pra-vara** denotes properly the 'summons' addressed to Agni at the beginning of the sacrifice to perform his functions. But as Agni was then invoked by the names of the ancestors of the Purohita,[1] the term Pravara denotes the series of ancestors invoked.[2]

[1] Aitareya Brāhmaṇa, vii. 25. See Weber, *Indische Studien*, 10, 78.

[2] Taittirīya Saṃhitā, ii. 5, 1, 9; Śatapatha Brāhmaṇa, i. 5, 1, 1. 20; iii. 7, 4, 9; Aitareya Brāhmaṇa, vii. 31, etc.

2. **Pra-vara,**[1] or **Pra-vāra,**[2] denotes a 'covering' or 'woollen cloth' in the Bṛhadāraṇyaka Upaniṣad.

[1] Bṛhadāraṇyaka Upaniṣad, vi. 1, 10, in the Mādhyaṃdina recension.
[2] Sāyaṇa on Bṛhadāraṇyaka Upaniṣad, *loc. cit.*; and Kāṇva recension, vi. 2, 7.

Pra-varta, occurring in the description of the **Vrātya** in the Atharvaveda (xv. 2, 1, *et seq.*), is explained by the St. Petersburg Dictionary as a 'round ornament.' According to the commentator on the Taittirīya Saṃhitā (2,453 *Bibl. Ind.*), it means an 'ear-ring.'

Pra-valhikā, a 'riddle,' is the name given in the Brāhmaṇas of the Rigveda[1] to certain verses of the Atharvaveda.[2]

[1] Aitareya Brāhmaṇa, vi. 33; Kauṣītaki Brāhmaṇa, xxx. 7.
[2] xx. 133; Śāṅkhāyana Śrauta Sūtra, xii. 22; Khila, v. 10.

Cf. Bloomfield, *Atharvaveda*, 98-100.

Pra-vāta, 'a windy spot,' is mentioned in the Rigveda[1] as the place where the **Vibhītaka** nuts, used as dice (**Akṣa**) grow. In the Taittirīya Saṃhitā[2] reference is made to the exposure of decaying matter in such a place.

[1] x. 34, 1; Nirukta, ix. 8. Geldner, *Rigveda, Glossar*, 119, thinks the reference here is to nuts being blown down in a storm of wind.
[2] vi. 4, 7, 2.

Pra-vāra. See 2. **Pravara.**

Pra-vāsa, 'dwelling abroad,' is mentioned in the Rigveda.[1] Ceremonies applicable to one who has returned from foreign residence are given in the Sūtras.[2]

[1] viii. 29, 8.
[2] Āśvalāyana Gṛhya Sūtra, i. 15; Śāṅkhāyana Gṛhya Sūtra, ii. 17, etc.

Pra-vāhaṇa Jaivali or **Jaivala** ('descendant of **Jīvala**') is the name of a prince, contemporary with **Uddālaka,** who appears in the Upaniṣads[1] as engaged in philosophical discussions. He is probably identical with the Jaivali of the Jaiminīya Upaniṣad Brāhmaṇa.[2]

[1] Bṛhadāraṇyaka Upaniṣad, vi. 1, 1. 7 (Mādhyaṃdina = vi. 2, 1. 4 Kāṇva); Chāndogya Upaniṣad, i. 8, 1; v. 3, 1.

[2] i. 38, 4.

Pra-śas in a Mantra in the Aitareya Brāhmaṇa[1] denotes, according to the St. Petersburg Dictionary, an 'axe,' or some similar instrument for cutting.[2]

[1] ii. 6, 5. *Cf.* Durga on Nirukta, v. 11.

[2] From *śas*, 'to cut.'

Pra-śāstṛ is the name of one of the priests (**Ṛtvij**) at the Vedic sacrifice. In the lesser sacrifices he plays no part at all, but he appears in the animal (*paśu*) and Soma sacrifices, in the former as the only, in the latter as the main, assistant of the **Hotṛ** priest in the singing of the litanies. He is mentioned by name in the Rigveda,[1] and often later.[2] He is also in the Rigveda[3] called **Upavaktṛ**, this name, like Praśāstṛ, being derived from the fact that one of his chief functions was to issue directions (*praiṣa*) to the other priests. Another name for him was Maitrāvaruṇa, because his litanies were mainly addressed to Mitra and Varuṇa, a connexion already visible in the Rigveda.[4] The 'two divine Hotṛs' of the Āprī litanies denote, according to Oldenberg,[5] the heavenly counterparts of the Hotṛ and the Praśāstṛ.

[1] i. 94, 6; ii. 5, 4; *praśāstra*, 'the Soma bowl of the Praśāstṛ,' 36, 6; *praśāstra*, 'the office of the Praśāstṛ,' ii. 1, 2 = x. 91, 10.

[2] Vājasaneyi Saṃhitā, x. 21; Aitareya Brāhmaṇa, v. 34; Śatapatha Brāhmaṇa, iv. 6, 6, 6; xi. 5, 5, 9. etc.

[3] iv. 9, 5; vi. 71, 5; ix. 95, 5. According to Ludwig, Translation of the Rigveda, 3, 226, the Upavaktṛ is the earliest equivalent of the Achāvāka.

[4] ii. 36, 6.

[5] *Religion des Veda*, 391. Ludwig, *op. cit.*, 3, 227, identifies the Praśāstṛ with the **Prastotṛ**, but this is most improbable.

Cf. Oldenberg, *op. cit.*, 383, 390, 391; Weber, *Indische Studien*, 10, 141 *et seq.*

Praśna denotes generally enquiry' or 'disputed question,' the phrase *praśnam eti* having the sense 'he asks a person for the decision of a disputed point' in the Taittirīya Saṃhitā[1] and elsewhere.[2] Thus Praśna comes to have the definite meaning of 'decision' in the Aitareya Brāhmaṇa.[3] In the list of victims at the Puruṣamedha ('human sacrifice') in the Yajurveda[4] are included the Praśnin, the Abhi-praśnin, and the Praśna-vivāka; it is quite likely that here the three parties to a civil case are meant—the plaintiff, the defendant, and the arbitrator or judge (**Madhyamaśī**).

[1] ii. 5, 8, 5; 11, 9.

[2] Taittirīya Brāhmaṇa, ii. 1, 6, 2; Aitareya Brāhmaṇa, iii. 28.

[3] v. 14.

[4] Vājasaneyi Saṃhitā, xxx. 10; Taittirīya Brāhmaṇa, iii. 4, 6, 1.

Praṣṭi, like **Pṛṣṭyā,** denotes a 'side horse,' which, however, possibly[1] did not necessarily mean a horse running beside the yoke-horses, but may also have meant a third horse yoked in front as a leader. This seems to be indicated by the reference in the Rigveda[2] to the Praṣṭi—here applied to the Maruts' team—leading (*vahati*) the team (*rohitaḥ*). In an obscure passage of the Atharvaveda[3] there is a reference to the Praṣṭis in connexion with a *pañca-vāhī*, 'drawn by five,' but it is impossible to gain any clear idea of what is meant. The Praṣṭi is not rarely referred to elsewhere.[4] In one passage[5] the *dhuryau* and the *praṣṭyau* are mentioned together; this probably means the two horses yoked to the pole, with two others fastened in some way one on each side. The adjectives *praṣṭi-mant*,[6] *praṣṭi-vāhana*,[7] *praṣṭi-vāhin*,[8] are all used of **Ratha,** 'chariot,' meaning 'drawn by a side horse (or horses)' in addition to the yoke-horses. *Cf.* **Ratha.**

[1] St. Petersburg Dictionary, *s.v.*

[2] i. 39, 6; viii. 27, 8. In i. 100, 17, *praṣṭibhiḥ* seems to refer to the assistants or comrades of **Ṛjrāśva** (*cf.* Lāṭyāyana Śrauta Sūtra, iii. 12, 14); but Ludwig thinks that the word refers to the steeds by which a victory was won.

[3] x. 8, 8. *Cf.* Whitney, Translation of the Atharvaveda, 597.

[4] Aitareya Brāhmaṇa, viii. 22; Taittirīya Brāhmaṇa, iii. 8, 21, 3; Śatapatha Brāhmaṇa, xiii. 3, 3, 9, etc.

[5] Taittirīya Brāhmaṇa, i. 5, 12, 5.

[6] Rv. vi. 27, 24.

[7] Śatapatha Brāhmaṇa, v. 2, 4, 9.

[8] Taittirīya Brāhmaṇa, i. 3, 6, 4; 7, 1, 5; 9, 1; Pañcaviṃśa Brāhmaṇa, xvi. 13, 12 (where *praṣṭhi-vāhin* and *praṣṭi-vāhin* are confused).

Geldner's conjecture, *Rigveda, Glossar*, 119, that Praṣṭi denotes a horse yoked in the middle, is withdrawn by himself, *Kommentar*, 97.

Cf. Zimmer, *Altindisches Leben*, 250; Max Müller, *Sacred Books of the East*, 32, 102.

Pra-siti in the Vājasaneyi Saṃhitā (ii. 19) and the Taittirīya Brāhmaṇa (iii. 7. 13, 4) denotes a divine 'missile,' but does not seem to be used of human combatants.

Pra-sū in the Rigveda[1] and later[2] denotes the young shoots of grass or herbs used at the sacrifice.

[1] i. 95, 10; iii. 5, 8; vii. 9, 3; 35, 7; viii. 6, 20.

[2] Kāṭhaka Saṃhitā, xxxvi. 2; Taittirīya Brāhmaṇa, i. 6, 3, 2; Śatapatha Brāhmaṇa, ii. 5, 1, 18.

Pra-sṛta is found in the Śatapatha Brāhmaṇa[1] as a measure of capacity, meaning a 'handful.'[2]

[1] iv. 5, 10, 7; xiii. 4, 1, 5; Śāṅkhāyana Śrauta Sūtra, xvi. 1, 7.

[2] Primarily, the word designates the hollowed hand 'stretched out' to receive what is offered.

Pra-skaṇva is the name of a Ṛṣi who is credited by the Anukramaṇī (Index) with the authorship of certain hymns of the Rigveda,[1] where[2] he is mentioned several times. The statement in the Śāṅkhāyana Śrauta Sūtra[3] that he obtained bounty from **Pṛṣadhra Medhya Mātariśvan** is apparently a blunder.[4]

[1] i. 44-50; viii. 49; ix. 95.

[2] i. 44, 6; 45, 3; viii. 3, 9; 51, 2; 54, 8. *Cf.* Nirukta, iii. 17.

[3] xvi. 11, 26.

[4] Weber, *Episches im vedischen Ritual*, 39.

Cf. Ludwig, Translation of the Rigveda, 3, 104 *et seq.*

Pra-stara in the Rigveda[1] and later[2] denotes the grass strewn as a sacrificial seat.

[1] x. 14, 4.

[2] Av. xvi. 2, 6; Taittirīya Saṃhitā, i. 7, 7, 4; Vājasaneyi Saṃhitā, ii. 18; xviii. 63; Aitareya Brāhmaṇa, i. 26; ii. 3; Śatapatha Brāhmaṇa, i. 3, 3, 5, etc.

Pra-stoka is the name of a generous donor in the Rigveda,[1] where Ludwig[2] identifies him with **Divodāsa Atithigva** and

[1] vi. 47, 22.

[2] Translation of the Rigveda, 3, 158.

Aśvattha or Aśvatha. According to the Śāṅkhayana Śrauta Sūtra,[3] **Bharadvāja** obtained gifts from Prastoka **Sārñjaya**, 'descendant of Sṛñjaya.'

[3] xvi. 11, 11.
Cf. Weber, *Episches im vedischen Ritual*, 30, 31; Macdonell, *Bṛhaddevatā*, 2, 198 *et seq*.

Pra-stotṛ is the name of an assistant of the Udgātṛ priest who sings the Prastāva,[1] or prelude of the Sāman chant. His not being mentioned by name in the Rigveda is merely an accident, for he is clearly referred to in one passage,[2] and in the later literature[3] he is a frequent figure. Ludwig[4] erroneously thinks that **Praśāstṛ** is the earlier name of the Prastotṛ.

[1] Pañcaviṃśa Brāhmaṇa, xii. 10, 7; Aitareya Brāhmaṇa, iii. 23; Śatapatha Brāhmaṇa, viii. 7, 4, 6; Chāndogya Upaniṣad, i. 10, 9; ii. 2, 1, etc.
[2] viii. 81, 5 (*pra stoṣat*). See Oldenberg, *Religion des Veda*, 393, n. 3.
[3] Taittirīya Saṃhitā, iii. 3, 2, 1; vi. 6, 3, 1; Taittirīya Brāhmaṇa, i. 8, 2, 3; Aitareya Brāhmaṇa, v. 34; vii. 1; Śatapatha Brāhmaṇa, iv. 2, 5, 3; v. 4, 5, 22; xii. 1, 1, 6, etc.; Chāndogya Upaniṣad, i. 10, 8, etc.
[4] Translation of the Rigveda, 3, 227.

Prasravaṇa. See **Plakṣa.**

Pra-hā in the Rigveda,[1] the Atharvaveda,[2] and the Pañcaviṃśa Brāhmaṇa,[3] denotes a 'winning throw' at dice, or, generally, any 'gain' or 'advantage.'[3]

[1] x. 42, 9.
[2] iv. 38, 3.
[3] xvi. 14, 2; xx. 11, 4.
Cf. Zimmer, *Altindisches Leben*, 241, and *prahāvant*, Rv. iv. 20, 8, meaning 'acquiring gain,' according to the St. Petersburg Dictionary, *s.v.*

Prā-kāra in the Śaṅkhāyana Śrauta Sūtra (xvi. 18, 14) denotes a walled mound supporting a raised platform (*prāsāda*) for spectators.

Prā-kāśa is found several times in the Brāhmaṇas[1] denoting an ornament of metal or a metal mirror. According to Geldner,[2] Prāvepa has the same sense in the Maitrāyaṇī Saṃhitā.[3]

[1] Taittirīya Brāhmaṇa, i. 8, 2, 3; Pañcaviṃśa Brāhmaṇa, xviii. 9, 10; Satapatha Brāhmaṇa, v. 4, 5, 22, etc.
[2] *Rigveda, Glossar*, 120.
[3] iv. 4, 8.

Prā-gahi is the name of a teacher in the Kauṣītaki Brāhmaṇa (xxvi. 4) according to Lindner's edition. *Cf.* **Prāvahi.**

Prācīna-tāna denotes the 'warp' of a piece of cloth in the Taittirīya Saṃhitā (vi. 1, 1, 4). *Cf.* **Prācīnātāna.**

Prācīna-yogī-putra, 'son of a female descendant of Prācīnayoga,' is the name of a teacher, a pupil of **Sāṃjīvīputra** in the last Vaṃśa (list of teachers) in the Mādhyaṃdina recension of the Bṛhadāraṇyaka Upaniṣad (vi. 4, 32).

Prācīna-yogya, 'descendant of Prācīnayoga,' is the name of a teacher, a pupil of **Pārāśarya,** in the first Vaṃśa (list of teachers) in the Bṛhadāraṇyaka Upaniṣad.[1] A Prācīnayogya is mentioned also in the Chāndogya[2] and the Taittirīya[3] Upaniṣads, and the same patronymic is found in the Śatapatha Brāhmaṇa[4] and in the Jaiminīya Upaniṣad Brāhmaṇa (see **Puluṣa, Satyayajña,**[5] **Somaśuṣma**).

[1] ii. 6, 2 (Kāṇva).
[2] v. 13, 1.
[3] i. 6, 2.
[4] (Of **Satyayajña Pauluṣi**) x. 6, 1, 5; (of **Śauceya**) xi. 5, 3, 1. 8 (*cf.* Gopatha Brāhmaṇa, i. 3, 11). *Cf.* Weber, *Indische Studien*, 1, 61; 2, 213; 3, 274.
[5] Called Prācīnayoga in i. 39, 1, but this is probably merely a blunder of the manuscript.

Prācīna-vaṃśa as an adjective denotes 'having the supporting beam of the roof facing the east' in the Śatapatha Brāhmaṇa[1] and the Yajurveda Saṃhitās.[2] The reference is to the central beam running from the middle of the western end of a hall to the middle of the eastern end. This beam was possibly higher than those at the side.

[1] iii. 1, 1, 6. 7; 6, 1, 23; iv. 6, 8, 20.
[2] Kāṭhaka Saṃhitā, xxii. 13; Taittirīya Saṃhitā, vi. 1, 1, 3. *Cf.* Eggeling, *Sacred Books of the East*, 26, 3, n. 2.

Prācīna-śāla Aupamanyava ('descendant of **Upamanyu**') is the name of a householder and theologian in the Chāndogya

Upaniṣad.[1] A Prācīnaśāli appears as an Udgātṛ priest in the Jaiminīya Upaniṣad Brāhmaṇa,[2] and the Prācīnaśālas are mentioned in the same Upaniṣad.[3]

[1] v. 11, 1. See **Mahāśāla**. [2] iii. 7, 2; 10, 2. [3] iii. 10, 1.

Prācīnātāna, denoting the 'warp' of a piece of cloth, is found in the Brāhmaṇas.[1] *Cf.* **Prācīnatāna.**

[1] Aitareya Brāhmaṇa, viii. 12, 3; 17, 2; Kauṣītaki Upaniṣad, i. 5 (*cf.* Keith, *Śāṅkhāyana Āraṇyaka*, 20, n. 2).

Prācīnāvīta[1] denotes the wearing of the sacred thread of the Āryan over the right shoulder and under the left arm, Prācīnāvītin[2] being the name for the man so wearing the thread. Tilak,[3] however, thinks that these terms do not imply the wearing of a thread, but of a garment.

[1] Taittirīya Saṃhitā, ii. 5, 11, 1.
[2] Taittirīya Brāhmaṇa, i. 4, 6, 6; Śatapatha Brāhmaṇa, ii. 4, 2, 2. 9; 6, 1, 8; xii. 5, 1, 6; *prācīnopavīta* has the same sense in Av. ix. 1, 24.
[3] *Orion*, 146, citing Taittirīya Āraṇyaka, ii. 1.

Prācya denotes in the plural 'dwellers in the east.' They are mentioned in the list of peoples in the Aitareya Brāhmaṇa.[1] It is very probable that the **Kāśis, Kosalas, Videhas,** and perhaps **Magadhas,** are meant, as Oldenberg[2] supposes. In the Śatapatha Brāhmaṇa[3] the Easterns are said to call Agni by the name of Śarva, and their mode of making **tombs** is there[4] referred to with disapproval. The Lāṭyāyana Śrauta Sūtra[5] explains the **Vipatha,** 'rough car,' of the Pañcaviṃśa Brāhmaṇa[6] as a car of the Easterns (*prācya-ratha*). In the Saṃhitopaniṣad Brāhmaṇa[7] reference is made to the Prācya-Pāñcālas.

[1] viii. 14.
[2] *Buddha*, 393, n.
[3] i. 7, 3, 8.
[4] xiii. 8, 1, 5; 2, 1. *Cf.* also ix. 5, 1, 64. These passages render improbable the earlier view of Weber (*Indian Literature*, 132, 133) that this Brāhmaṇa is a product of the Eastern peoples, and support his later view that the Śatapatha Brāhmaṇa, like the other great Brāhmaṇas, belongs to the **Madhyadeśa** (see **Kuru**, n. 1).
[5] viii. 6, 9.
[6] xvii. 1.
[7] 2; Weber, *Indian Literature*, 34, n. 25.

Prājāpatya, 'descendant of Prajāpati,' is only a patronymic of mythical persons like Āruṇi Suparṇeya ('descendant of Suparṇā') in the Taittirīya Āraṇyaka (x. 79), or of **Prajāvant** in the Aitareya Brāhmaṇa (i. 21).

Prāṇa, properly denoting 'breath,' is a term of wide and vague significance in Vedic literature. It is frequently mentioned from the Rigveda[1] onwards; in the Āraṇyakas and Upaniṣads it is one of the commonest symbols of the unity of the universe[2] In the narrow sense Prāṇa denotes one of the vital airs, of which five are usually[3] enumerated—Prāṇa, **Apāna, Vyāna, Udāna**, and **Samāna**; but often only two, Prāṇa and Apāna,[4] or Prāṇa and Vyāna,[5] or Prāṇa and Udāna;[6] or three, Prāṇa, Apāna, and Vyāna,[7] or Prāṇa, Udāna, and Vyāna,[8] or Prāṇa, Udāna, and Samāna;[9] or four, Prāṇa, Apāna, Vyāna, and Samāna,[10] or Prāṇa, Apāna, Udāna, Vyāna.[11] The exact sense of each of these breaths when all are mentioned cannot be determined.[12]

Prāṇa is also used in a wider sense to denote the organs of sense,[13] or as Sāyaṇa[14] puts it, the 'orifices of the head,' etc. These are given as six in one passage of the Śatapatha Brāhmaṇa,[15] presumably the eyes, ears, and nostrils. More frequently there are stated to be seven in the head, the mouth being then included.[16] Sometimes again they are mentioned

[1] i. 66, 1; x. 59, 6; 90, 13, etc.

[2] Deussen, *Philosophy of the Upanishads*, 89 *et seq*.

[3] See **Udāna**, n. 1.

[4] Av. ii. 28, 3; v. 4, 7 (Paipp.); vii. 53, 4 (in vii. 53, 3, Apāna, Prāṇa); Taittirīya Saṃhitā, iii. 4, 1, 4, etc.

[5] Av. v, 4, 7; vi. 41, 2, etc.

[6] See **Udāna**, n. 3.

[7] Av. xiii. 2, 46; Maitrāyaṇī Saṃhitā, iv. 5, 6, 9; Vājasaneyi Saṃhitā, xxii. 23; Aitareya Brāhmaṇa, ii. 29; Kauṣītaki Brāhmaṇa, vi. 10; Śāṅkhāyana Āraṇyaka, viii. 8; Taittirīya Upaniṣad, ii. 2, etc.

[8] See **Udāna**, n. 2.

[9] *Ibid*.

[10] Av. x. 2, 13.

[11] Bṛhadāraṇyaka Upaniṣad, iii. 4, 1.

[12] *Cf*. Deussen, *Philosophy of the Upanishads*, 273 *et seq*.

[13] Colebrooke, *Miscellaneous Essays*, 1, 339, 355; St. Petersburg Dictionary, *s.v*. 1.

[14] On Aitareya Āraṇyaka, i. 3, 7.

[15] xiv. 1. 3, 32; 4, 1.

[16] Av. ii. 12, 7; Aitareya Brāhmaṇa, i. 17; iii. 3; Śatapatha Brāhmaṇa, iii. 1, 3, 21; vi. 4 2, 5; xiii. 1, 7, 2; Jaiminīya Upaniṣad Brāhmaṇa, ii. 5, 9, 10; 6, 8, etc.

as nine,[17] or as seven in the head and two below.[18] Ten are counted in the Śatapatha Brāhmaṇa[19] and the Jaiminīya Brāhmaṇa,[20] while even eleven are mentioned in the Kāṭhaka Upaniṣad,[21] and twelve in the Kāṭhaka Saṃhitā,[22] where the two breasts are added. Exactly what organs are taken to make up the numbers beyond seven is not certain.[23] The tenth is the navel (*nābhi*) in the Maitrāyaṇī Saṃhitā;[24] when eleven are named the Brahma-randhra[25] (suture in the crown) may be included; in the Atharvaveda,[26] as interpreted by the Bṛhad āraṇyaka Upaniṣad,[27] the seventh and eighth are the organs of taste and speech respectively. But usually these make one only, and the eighth and ninth are either in the breast[28] or below (the organs of evacuation).[29]

The word Prāṇa has sometimes merely the general sense of breath, even when opposed to Apāna.[30] But its proper sense is beyond question 'breathing forth,' 'expiration,' and not as the St. Petersburg Dictionary explains it, 'the breath inspired;' a version due to the desire to interpret Apāna as 'expiration,' a meaning suggested by the preposition *apa*, 'away.' This being clearly shown both by the native scholiasts[31] and by other evidence,[32] Böhtlingk[33] later accepted the new view.

17 Taittirīya Saṃhitā, iii. 5, 10, 2; Taittirīya Brāhmaṇa, iii. 1, 7, 4; Śatapatha Brāhmaṇa, i. 5, 2, 5: Pañcaviṃśa Brāhmaṇa, xxii. 12, 5; Aitareya Āraṇyaka, i. 4, 1; Śāṅkhāyana Āraṇyaka, ii. 2; Av. v. 28, 1; x. 8, 43 (*navadvāram*), etc.

18 Jaiminīya Upaniṣad Brāhmaṇa, ii. 5, 9, 10; 6, 8.

19 xi. 6, 3, 17, where the eleventh is given as the Ātman.

20 ii. 77 (*Journal of the American Oriental Society*, 15, 240).

21 v. 1.

22 xxxiii. 3.

23 *Cf.* Deussen, *op. cit.*, 269; Keith, *Aitareya Āraṇyaka*, 185, 187.

24 iv. 6, 1; Kāṭhaka Saṃhitā, ix. 16.

25 Aitareya Upaniṣad, i. 3.

26 x. 8, 9.

27 ii. 2, 3, 4.

28 Kāṭhaka Saṃhitā, xxxiii. 3.

29 Jaiminīya Upaniṣad Brāhmaṇa, ii. 5, 9, 10; 6, 8.

30 Av. v. 4, 7 (Paippalāda). See Bloomfield, *Hymns of the Atharvaveda*, 552.

31 Rudradatta on Āpastamba Śrauta Sūtra, xii. 8, 8; xiv. 11, 1; Sāyaṇa on Śatapatha Brāhmaṇa, i. 1, 3, 2; Taittirīya Brāhmaṇa, ii. 5, 6, 4; Śaṅkara on Chāndogya Upaniṣad, i. 3, 2; Ānartīya on Śāṅkhāyana Śrauta Sūtra, vi. 8, 1. 2, etc.

32 Śatapatha Brāhmaṇa, ii. 2, 2, 15, as compared with Kātyāyana Śrauta Sūtra, iv. 8, 29; Bṛhadāraṇyaka Upaniṣad, iii. 2, 2; Jaiminīya Upaniṣad Brāhmaṇa, i. 60, 5; ii. 1, 16. 19; Aitareya Āraṇyaka, v. 1, 4. See Caland, *Zeitschrift der Deutschen Morgenländischen Gesellschaft*, 55, 261-265; 56, 556-558; and **Apāna**.

33 *Zeitschrift*, 55, 518.

Prāṇa-bhṛt denotes a 'living being' or 'man' in the Bṛhadāraṇyaka Upaniṣad[1] and the Śatapatha Brāhmaṇa.[2] Prāṇin has the same sense.[3]

[1] i. 5, 22; iii. 1, 12.
[2] xi. 2, 6, 2.
[3] Aitareya Brāhmaṇa, vii. 13; Śatapatha Brāhmaṇa, vii. 4, 2, 2; x. 4, 2, 2; Chāndogya Upaniṣad, ii. 11, 2; Aitareya Upaniṣad, iii. 3, 3; Nirukta, vi. 36.

Prātar as a denotation of time signifies the 'early morning' in the Rigveda[1] and later.[2] *Cf.* **Ahan.**

[1] i. 125, 1; ii. 18, 1; iii. 41, 2; 52, 1; iv. 35, 7; v. 76, 3, etc.
[2] Av. iv. 11, 12; vi. 128, 2; vii. 101, 1; xi 2, 16; Kāṭhaka Saṃhitā, xxxii. 7; Aitareya Brāhmaṇa, ii. 31; iii. 22. 44; iv. 20; Śatapatha Brāhmaṇa, xi. 5, 1, 12; Chāndogya Upaniṣad, v. 11, 7, etc.

Prātar-anuvāka occurs in the Brāhmaṇas[1] as the name of the litany which begins the morning Soma libation.

[1] Taittirīya Brāhmaṇa, i. 5, 9, 7; ii. 2, 3, 6; Aitareya Brāhmaṇa, ii. 15. 17. 18; iv. 19; v. 33; Śatapatha Brāhmaṇa, iii. 9, 3, 7; iv. 3, 4, 21; xi. 5, 5, 9; Chāndogya Upaniṣad, ii. 24, 3; iv. 16, 2, etc.

Prātar-ahna Kauhala is the name of a teacher, a pupil of **Ketu Vājya**, in the Vaṃśa Brāhmaṇa.[1] *Cf.* **Kauhaḍa.**

[1] *Indische Studien*, 4, 372; Max Müller, *Ancient Sanskrit Literature*, 443.

Prā-tardani, 'descendant of **Pratardana**,' is the name of a prince in one passage of the Rigveda.[1]

[1] vi. 27, 8. *Cf.* Ludwig, Translation of the Rigveda, 3, 157, 159.

Prāti-pīya is the patronymic of **Balhika** in the Śatapatha Brāhmaṇa (xii. 9, 3, 3).

Prāti-veśya is mentioned in the Vaṃśa (list of teachers) in the Śāṅkhāyana Āraṇyaka (xv. 1) as a pupil of **Prativeśya.**

Prāti-sutvana. See **Pratīpa.**

Prātī-bodhī-putra, 'son of a female descendant of Pratī-bodha,' is the name of a teacher in the Aitareya (iii. 1, 5) and the Śāṅkhāyana (vii. 13) Āraṇyakas.

Cf. Keith, *Aitareya Āraṇyaka*, 244, 310.

Pra-tṛda, 'descendant of **Pratṛd**,' is the patronymic of a teacher called **Bhālla** in the Jaiminīya Upaniṣad Brāhmaṇa (iii. 31, 4), and of another teacher in the Bṛhadāraṇyaka Upaniṣad (v. 13, 2).

Prā-deśa[1] frequently occurs in the Brāhmaṇas[2] as a measure of length, a 'span.'[3]

1 'Formed with the *pradeśa*' (probably 'indicator,' as a name of the forefinger; *cf.* *pradeśinī*, 'forefinger,' Āśvalāyana Śrauta Sūtra, i. 7; Śāṅkhāyana Śrauta Sūtra, i. 10, 1; ii. 9, 14).

2 Aitareya Brāhmaṇa, viii. 5; Śatapatha Brāhmaṇa, iii. 5, 4, 5; Chāndogya Upaniṣad, v. 18, 1, etc.

3 That is, between thumb and forefinger.

Prā-dhvaṃsana, 'descendant of Pradhvaṃsana,' is the patronymic, in the Bṛhadāraṇyaka Upaniṣad,[1] of the mythical **Mṛtyu**, who is there said to be the pupil of Pradhvaṃsana.

1 ii. 5, 22; iv. 5, 28, Mādhyaṃdina.

Prāyaś-citta[1] or **Prāyaś-citti**[2] denotes a 'penance' or 'expiation,' both words occurring frequently in the later Saṃhitās and the Brāhmaṇas. The penances are prescribed for every conceivable sort of ritual, social or moral; a complete list of them is included in the Sāmavidhāna Brāhmaṇa.[3]

1 Satapatha Brāhmaṇa, xii. 4, 1, 6; Kauṣītaki Brāhmaṇa, v. 9; vi. 12, etc.

2 Taittirīya Saṃhitā, ii. 1, 4, 1; iii. 1, 3, 2; v. 1, 9, 3; 3, 12, 1; Av. xiv. 1, 30; Vājasaneyi Saṃhitā, xxxix. 12; Aitareya Brāhmaṇa, iii. 11. 46; v. 27; vii. 2; Śatapatha Brāhmaṇa, i. 1, 4, 9; iv. 5, 7, 1; xi. 5, 3, 8, etc.

3 See Konow's Translation, p. 43 *et seq.*

Prā-vareya, 'descendant of Pravara,' is the patronymic of the **Gargas** in the Kāṭhaka Saṃhitā.[1]

1 xiii. 12 (*Indische Studien*, 3, 474).

Prā-vahi is the name of a teacher in the Kauṣītaki Brāhmaṇa (xxvi. 4), where, however, Lindner's edition has **Prāgahi**.

Prā-vāhaṇi, 'descendant of **Pravāhana,**' is the patronymic of a man called **Babara** in the Taittirīya Saṃhitā (vii. 1, 10, 2).

Prā-vṛṣ is the name of the 'rainy season' in the Rigveda[1] and later.[2]

[1] vii. 103. 3. 9.

[2] Av. xii. 1, 46; Kāṭhaka Saṃhitā, xxxvi. 2; Taittirīya Brāhmaṇa, i. 8, 4, 2; Śatapatha Brāhmaṇa, v. 5, 2, 3; vii. 2, 4, 26, etc.

Prā-vepa. See **Prākāśa.**

Prāś in the Atharvaveda[1] denotes a 'debater' or a 'debate,' while Pratiprāś[2] denotes an 'opponent in debate.'

[1] ii. 27, 1. 7.

[2] ii. 27, 1. *Cf.* Bloomfield, *American Journal of Philology*, 7, 479 *et seq.*; *Atharvaveda*, 73; *Hymns of the Atharvaveda*, 305, 306, who completely disproves the theory that Prāś meant 'means of life,' 'victuals' (*cf.* Böhtlingk, *s.v. pratiprāś*).

Prāśnī-putra ('son of Prāśnī') **Āsuri-vāsin** is mentioned in the last Vaṃśa (list of teachers) of the Bṛhadāraṇyaka Upaniṣad[1] as a pupil of **Āsurāyaṇa.**

[1] vi. 4, 33 (Mādhyaṃdina = vi. 5, 3 Kāṇva).

Prā-śravaṇa. See **Prāsravaṇa.**

Prā-saca, m., in the Taittirīya Saṃhitā[1] denotes a 'cloud-burst,' while in the Taittirīya Brāhmaṇa[2] the adjective *prāsacyaḥ* (*āpaḥ*) means '(waters) produced by torrential rain.'

[1] vii. 5, 11, 1; according to the commentator, 'congealing.'

[2] iii. 12, 7, 4; according to the commentator, 'congealed' (water).

Prā-sāda in the sense of 'palace' does not occur until the late Adbhuta Brāhmaṇa.[1] *Cf.* **Prākāra.**

[1] *Indische Studien*, 1, 40.

4—2

Prā-sravaṇa occurs as part of the local name **Plakṣa Prāsravaṇa.** It also appears as a patronymic 'descendant of Prasravaṇa,' applied to **Avatsāra** in the Kauṣītaki Brāhmaṇa.[1]

[1] xiii. 3. There is also a various reading, Prāśravaṇa.

Priyaṅgu denotes 'panic seed' (*Panicum italicum*) in the Yajurveda Saṃhitās[1] and the Brāhmaṇas.[2]

[1] Taittirīya Saṃhitā, ii. 2, 11, 4; Kāṭhaka Saṃhitā, x. 11; Maitrāyaṇī Saṃhitā ii. 1, 8; Vājasaneyi Saṃhitā, xviii. 12.

[2] Taittirīya Brāhmaṇa, iii. 8, 14, 6 Aitareya Brāhmaṇa, viii. 16; Bṛhad-āraṇyaka Upaniṣad, vi. 3, 22 (Mādhyaṃdina = vi. 3, 13 Kāṇva), with Śaṅkara's note.

Cf. Zimmer, *Altindisches Leben*, 241.

Priya-medha is the name of a seer in the Rigveda,[1] where his family, the Priyamedhas, are also repeatedly alluded to.[2] It is not probable that any hymns are really Priyamedha's own composition.[3] See also **Praiyamedha.**

[1] i. 139, 9; viii. 5, 25; *Priyamedhavat*, i. 45, 3; *Priyamedha-stuta*, viii. 6, 45.

[2] i. 45, 4; viii. 2, 37; 3, 16; 4, 20; 8, 18; 69, 8; 87, 3; x. 73, 11.

[3] Oldenberg, *Zeitschrift der Deutschen Morgenländischen Gesellschaft*, 42, 217.

Priya-ratha is the name of a patron of the **Pajras** in the Rigveda.[1]

[1] i. 122, 7. *Cf.* Ludwig, Translation of the Rigveda, 3, 150.

Priya-vrata Somāpi[1] or **Saumāpi** is the name of a teacher in the Aitareya Brāhmaṇa[1] and the Śāṅkhāyana Āraṇyaka,[2] in which he is said to be the son of **Somapa.** The name Priya-vrata is also found in the Śatapatha Brāhmaṇa,[3] where a **Rauhiṇāyana** of that name is mentioned as a teacher.

[1] vii. 34.

[2] xv. 1.

[3] x. 3, 5, 14.

Cf. Weber, *Indische Studien*, 8, 136, n.

Preṅkha, 'swing,' is mentioned in the description of the Mahāvrata rite, given in the Kāṭhaka Saṃhitā,[1] the Aitareya

[1] xxxiv. 5.

Āraṇyaka,[2] the Pañcaviṃśa Brāhmaṇa,[3] and elsewhere.[4] As far as can be judged from the notices available,[5] the swing was made just like a modern swing. See also **Plenkha.**

[2] i. 2, 3. 4; v. 1, 3, etc.
[3] v. 5, 7.
[4] Sāṅkhāyana Āraṇyaka, ii. 17, etc.
[5] Śāṅkhāyana Srauta Sūtra, xvii. 1, 11; 7, 2, etc.

Preta, 'departed,' is used to denote a 'dead man' in the Śatapatha Brāhmaṇa,[1] but not in the sense of 'ghost,' which only appears later, in post-Vedic literature.

[1] x. 5, 2, 13; Bṛhadāraṇyaka Upaniṣad, v. 11, 1, etc.

Predi. See **Proti.**

Preṣya ('to be sent' on an errand) denotes a menial servant or slave, being applied in the Aitareya Brāhmaṇa[1] to the **Śūdra.** In the Atharvaveda[2] the adjective *praiṣya*, 'menial,' occurs.

[1] vii. 29. See also Kauṣītaki Brāhmaṇa, xvii. 1.
[2] v. 22, 14.

Praiya-medha, 'descendant of **Priyamedha,**' is a patronymic of the priests who sacrificed for the **Ātreya Udamaya** in the Aitareya Brāhmaṇa.[1] They appear in the Yajurveda Saṃhitās[2] as priests who 'knew all' (sacrificial lore). Three Praiyamedhas are referred to in the Taittirīya Brāhmaṇa.[3] In the Gopatha Brāhmaṇa[4] they are called **Bharadvājas.**

[1] viii. 22.
[2] Kāṭhaka Saṃhitā, vi. 1 (*Indische Studien*, 3, 474); Maitrāyaṇī Saṃhitā, i. 8, 7; Lévi, *La doctrine du sacrifice*, 150.
[3] ii. 1, 9, 1 *et seq.*
[4] i. 3, 15. The name is also written Prayyamedha and, incorrectly, Praiyyamedha.

Praiṣa is a liturgical term meaning 'direction' or 'invitation, repeatedly found in the later Saṃhitās[1] and the Brāhmaṇas.[2]

[1] Av. v. 26, 4; xi. 7, 18; xvi. 7, 2; Taittirīya Saṃhitā, vii. 3, 11, 2; Vājasaneyi Saṃhitā, xix. 19, etc.
[2] Aitareya Brāhmaṇa, ii. 13; iii. 9; v. 9, etc.; Śatapatha Brāhmaṇa, iv. 1, 3, 15; xiii. 5, 2, 23; Kauṣītaki Brāhmaṇa, xxviii. 1, etc.

Proti Kauśāmbeya Kausuru-bindi ('descendant of **Kusuru-binda**') is mentioned in the Śatapatha Brāhmaṇa[1] as a pupil and contemporary of **Uddālaka.** In the Taittirīya Saṃhitā,[2] on the other hand, Kusurubinda is called **Auddālaki,** 'descendant of Uddālaka,' a fact which seems to indicate that little value is to be attached to these patronymics and allegations of contemporaneousness.

1 xii. 2, 2, 13. In the parallel passage, Gopatha Brāhmaṇa, i. 2, 24, Predi Kauśāmbeya Kausuravinda is the form of the name.

2 vii. 2, 2, 1. *Cf.* Bloomfield, *Atharvaveda*, p. 115.

Proṣṭha, denoting perhaps a 'bench,' is found in the Rigveda[1] in the adjective *proṣṭhaśaya*, 'lying on a bench,' used of women, and uncompounded in the Taittīriya Brāhmaṇa.[2] In the first passage it is distinguished from **Talpa** and **Vahya,** but what the exact difference was there is not sufficient evidence to show.

1 vii. 55, 8.

2 ii. 7, 17, 1.

Cf. Zimmer, *Altindisches Leben*, 154.

Proṣṭha-pada, m., **-padā,** f. ('foot of a bench'), is the name of a double **Nakṣatra.**

Proṣṭha-pāda Vārakya is mentioned in a Vaṃśa (list of teachers) of the Jaiminīya Upaniṣad Brāhmaṇa (iii. 41, 1) as a pupil of Kaṃsa Vāraki.

1. **Plakṣa** is the name of the waved leaf fig-tree (*Ficus infectoria*), a large and beautiful tree with small white fruit. It is mentioned in the Atharvaveda[1] and the Taittirīya Saṃhitā[2] along with the **Nyagrodha** and the **Parṇa.** Its name is altered in the latter Saṃhitā[3] to **Prakṣa** for the sake of an etymology. It is also mentioned in the Brāhmaṇas.[4]

1 v. 5, 5.

2 vii. 4, 12, 1. *Cf.* iii. 4, 8, 4; Maitrāyaṇī Saṃhitā, iii. 10, 2.

3 vi. 3, 10, 2.

4 Aitareya Brāhmaṇa, vii. 32; viii. 16; Taittirīya Brāhmaṇa, iii. 8, 19, 2; Śatapatha Brāhmaṇa, iii. 8, 3, 10. 12, etc.

Cf. Zimmer, *Altindisches Leben*, 58.

2. **Plakṣa Dayyāṃpāti** ('descendant of Dyāṃpati' or Dyāṃpāta) was a contemporary of **Atyaṃhas Āruṇi** in the Taittirīya Brāhmaṇa (iii. 10, 9, 3. 5).

3. **Plakṣa Prā-sravaṇa** is the name of a locality, forty-four days' journey from the spot where the **Sarasvatī** disappears. It is mentioned in the Pañcaviṃśa Brāhmaṇa[1] and the Jaiminīya Upaniṣad Brāhmaṇa.[2] In the latter text it is said that the middle of the earth is only a span (**Prādeśa**) to the north of it. In the Rigveda Sūtras[3] the locality is called Plākṣa Prasravaṇa, and is apparently meant to designate the source of the Sarasvatī rather than the place of its reappearance.

1 xxv. 10, 16. 22; Kātyāyana Srauta Sūtra, xxiv. 6, 7; Lāṭyāyana Śrauta Sūtra, x. 17, 12. 14.

2 iv. 26, 12.

3 Āśvalāyana Śrauta Sūtra, xii. 6, 1; Śāṅkhāyana Śrauta Sūtra, xiii. 29, 24.

Cf. Hopkins, *Transactions of the Connecticut Academy of Arts and Sciences*, 15, 31, n. 2.

Plati is the name of a man, the father of the seer of two hymns of the Rigveda.[1]

1 x. 63, 17; 64, 17. *Cf.* Ludwig, Translation of the Rigveda, 3, 133.

1. **Plava** ('float') denotes a 'boat' in the Rigveda[1] and later.[2]

1 i. 182, 5.

2 Av. xii. 2, 48; Taittirīya Saṃhitā, v. 3, 10, 2; vii. 3, 5, 2; Pañcaviṃśa Brāhmaṇa, xi. 10, 17, etc.

2. **Plava** is the name of an aquatic bird mentioned in the list of victims at the Aśvamedha ('horse sacrifice') in the Yajurveda Saṃhitās.[1] Perhaps the 'pelican' is meant.

1 Taittirīya Saṃhitā, v. 5, 20, 1; Maitrāyaṇī Saṃhitā, iii. 14, 15; Vājasaneyi Saṃhitā, xxiv. 34.
Cf. Zimmer, *Altindisches Leben*, 93.

Plākṣi, 'descendant of **Plakṣa**,' is the name of a man mentioned in the Taittirīya Āraṇyaka[1] and the Taittirīya

1 i. 7, 2.

Prātiśākhya.[2] In the same Prātiśākhya[3] a Plākṣāyana, or 'descendant of Plākṣa,' is mentioned.

[2] i. 5. 9; ii. 2. 6.
[3] i. 9; ii. 2. 6.
Cf. Weber, *Indische Studien*, 1, 35.

Plāta, 'descendant of **Plati**,' is the patronymic of **Gaya** in the Aitareya Brāhmaṇa (v. 2).

Plā-yogi, 'descendant of Playoga,' is the patronymic of **Āsaṅga** in the Rigveda.[1] According to the Śāṅkhāyana Śrauta Sūtra,[2] Āsaṅga was a woman, but became a man. This version, repeated by Sāyaṇa in his commentary on the Rigveda,[3] is a mere blunder based on the fact that an additional verse, tacked on to the hymn,[3] contains the expression *śaśvatī nārī*, which has been taken to mean 'his wife Śaśvatī,'[4] instead of merely 'every woman.'

[1] viii. 1, 33.
[2] xvi. 11, 17.
[3] viii. 1, 34. *Cf.* Hopkins, *Religions of India*, 150.
[4] So even Griffith, *Hymns of the Rigveda*, 2, 107. But see Oldenberg, *Ṛgveda-Noten*, 1, 354.

Plāśuka is found in the Śatapatha Brāhmaṇa (v. 3, 3, 2) as an epithet of **Vrīhi**, 'rice,' in the sense of 'shooting up rapidly.'

Plīhā-karṇa as an epithet of cattle in the Yajurveda Saṃhitās[1] probably denotes 'having a spleen-shaped mark branded on the ear,' not as Mahīdhara in his commentary on the Vājasaneyi Saṃhitā[2] takes it, 'having a disease called Plīhan in the ear.'

[1] Maitrāyaṇī Saṃhitā, iii. 13, 5 (*cf.* iv. 2, 9); Vājasaneyi Saṃhitā, xxiv. 24.
[2] *Loc. cit.*

Pluṣi is the name of some noxious insect in the Rigveda.[1] It is also included in the list of victims at the Aśvamedha

[1] i. 191, 1.

('horse sacrifice') in the Yajurveda Saṃhitās,[2] and is mentioned in the Bṛhadāraṇyaka Upaniṣad.[3] Possibly a species of ant may be meant.

[2] Maitrāyaṇī Saṃhitā, iii. 14, 8; Vājasaneyi Saṃhitā, xxiv. 29.

[3] i. 3, 24. *Cf.* Zimmer, *Altindisches Leben*, 98.

Pleṅkha is a variant form of **Preṅkha**, 'swing,' found in the Taittirīya Saṃhitā (vii. 5, 8, 5) and the Taittirīya Brāhmaṇa (i. 2, 6, 6).

PH.

Phaṇa occurs in some manuscripts of the Kauṣītaki Upaniṣad,[1] and is explained as meaning an 'ornament.' But it is merely a misreading of the correct word *phala* in the compound *phala-hastāḥ*, 'bearing fruits in their hands.'

[1] i. 4. *Cf.* Weber, *Indische Studien*, 1, 398; Keith, *Śāṅkhāyana Āraṇyaka*, 19, n. 1.

Pharvara, a word occurring only once in the Rigveda,[1] cannot be interpreted with certainty. It may mean a 'field in bloom.'[2] Sāyaṇa[3] explains it as 'filler,' and Grassmann as perhaps a 'sower.'[4]

[1] x. 106, 2.

[2] *Cf.* Weber, *Indische Studien*, 17, 260.

[3] In his commentary on Rv. x. 106, 2. He explains the intensive form *parpharat*, occurring in the same hymn (x. 106, 7), as from a verb meaning to 'fill.'

[4] *Wörterbuch*, *s.v.*

Phala, denoting 'fruit' generally, especially the fruit of a tree, occurs in the Rigveda[1] and later.[2]

[1] iii. 45, 4; x. 146, 5.

[2] Av. vi. 124, 2; Taittirīya Saṃhitā, vii. 3, 14, 1; Vājasaneyi Saṃhitā, x. 13; Śatapatha Brāhmaṇa, xiii. 4, 4, 8; Bṛhadāraṇyaka Upaniṣad, vi. 4, 1, etc., and see **Phaṇa**.

Phalaka denotes 'plank,' as applied in the construction of a cart or chariot,[1] or as used for pressing Soma (*adhi-ṣavaṇe phalake*),[2] or for any other purpose.[3]

[1] Pañcaviṃśa Brāhmaṇa, xvii. 1, 14 (*cf. Indische Studien*, 1, 33, 44).

[2] Aitareya Brāhmaṇa, vii. 30.

[3] Śatapatha Brāhmaṇa, iii. 3, 4, 9; xiii. 4, 3, 1; Aitareya Āraṇyaka, i. 2, 3 (of the swing), etc.

Phalavatī, 'fruitful,' is the name of a plant in the Ṣaḍviṃśa Brāhmaṇa,[1] identified by the scholiast with the **Priyaṅgu.**

[1] v. 2. *Cf.* Weber, *Omina and Portenta*, 315.

Phalgu. See **Nakṣatra.**

Phalgunī. See **Nakṣatra.**

Phāṇṭa in the Śatapatha Brāhmaṇa[1] is said to denote the first particles of butter produced by churning, 'creamy butter.'

[1] iii. 1, 3, 8. *Cf.* Eggeling, *Sacred Books of the East*, 26, 14, n. 1.

Phāla, 'ploughshare,' occurs in the Rigveda[1] and later.[2] *Cf.* **Lāṅgala.**

[1] iv. 57, 8; x. 117, 7.
[2] Kāṭhaka Saṃhitā, xix. 1. *Cf. su-phāla*, Av. iii. 17, 5; Maitrāyaṇī Saṃhitā, ii. 7, 12; *phāla-kṛṣṭa*, 'growing on ploughed land,' as opposed to *āraṇya*, 'wild,' Kāṭhaka Saṃhitā, xii. 7; Kauṣītaki Brāhmaṇa, xxv. 15.

B.

Baka Dālbhya ('descendant of Dalbha') is the name of a person mentioned in the Jaiminīya Upaniṣad Brāhmaṇa as constraining Indra for the **Ājakeśins** (i. 9, 2), and as a **Kuru-Pañcāla** (iv. 7, 2).

Bakura is mentioned in one passage of the Rigveda,[1] where it is said that the Aśvins made light for the Āryan by blowing their Bakura against the **Dasyus.** According to the Nirukta,[2] the thunderbolt[1] is meant; but much more probable is Roth's[3] view, that the object blown was a musical instrument. See also **Bākura.**

[1] i. 117, 21.
[2] vi. 25. *Cf.* Naighaṇṭuka, iv. 3.
[3] St. Petersburg Dictionary, *s.v.*

Cf. Zimmer, *Altindisches Leben*, 290; Muir, *Sanskrit Texts*, 5, 466.

Baja is the name in the Atharvaveda[1] of a plant used against a demon of disease. Some sort of mustard plant may be meant.[2]

[1] viii. 6, 3. 6. 7. 24. [2] Whitney, Translation of the Atharvaveda, 494.

Badara denoting, like **Karkandhu** and **Kuvala**, a kind of jujube, is mentioned in the Yajurveda Saṃhitās[1] and the Brāhmaṇas.[2]

[1] Kāṭhaka Saṃhitā, xii. 10; Maitrāyaṇī Saṃhitā, iii. 11, 2; Vājasaneyi Saṃhitā, xix. 22. 90; xxi. 30.
[2] Taittirīya Brāhmaṇa, i. 8, 5, 1; Satapatha Brāhmaṇa, v. 5. 4, 10; xii. 7, 1, 3; 2, 9; 9, 1, 8, etc.; Jaiminīya Brāhmaṇa, ii. 156, 5.

Badvan seems in one passage of the Pañcaviṃśa Brāhmaṇa[1] to denote a 'causeway.' It is said to be firmer than an ordinary road.

[1] i. 1, 4. *Cf.* Lāṭyāyana Srauta Sūtra, i. 1, 23.

Bandhana denotes a 'rope' or other fastening in the Atharvaveda[1] and later.[2]

[1] Av. iii. 6, 7 (of a boat, **Nau**); vi. 14, 2.
[2] Śatapatha Brāhmaṇa, xiii. 1, 6, 2 (of a horse); Taittirīya Brāhmaṇa, iii. 8, 9, 4; Chāndogya Upaniṣad, vi. 8, 2; Nirukta, xii. 38, etc.

Bandhu, denoting 'relationship'[1] in the abstract and 'relation'[2] in the concrete, occurs in the Rigveda and later.

[1] Rv. v. 73, 4; vii. 72, 2; viii. 73, 12, etc.; Av. v. 11, 10. 11; Vājasaneyi Saṃhitā, iv. 22; x. 6, etc.
[2] Rv. i. 164, 33; vii. 67, 9; Av. x. 10, 23; Taittirīya Brāhmaṇa, iii. 7, 5, 5, etc.; *bandhumant*, 'having relations,' Rv. viii. 21, 4; Taittirīya Saṃhitā, i. 5, 1, 4, etc.

Babara Prā-vāhaṇi ('descendant of **Pravāhaṇa**') is the name of a man who, according to the Taittirīya Saṃhitā,[1] wished to become an orator, and obtained rhetorical power by the use of the Pañcarātra sacrifice.

[1] vii. 1, 10, 2. *Cf.* Geldner, *Vedische Studien*, 2, 148.

1. **Babhru** is the name, in the Rigveda,[1] of a Ṛṣi who received gifts from King **Ṛṇaṃcaya.** The same Babhru may be meant in another passage,[2] where he is mentioned as a protégé of the Aśvins; but it is doubtful whether the word is a proper name at all in the Atharvaveda.[3]

[1] v. 30, 11. 14.

[2] viii. 22, 10.

[3] iv. 29, 2. It is here taken as a proper name by the St. Petersburg Dictionary, *s.v.*; Ludwig, Translation of the Rigveda, 3, 126. But Whitney, Translation of the Atharvaveda, 199, denies that a proper name is meant. *Cf.* Oldenberg, *Zeitschrift der Deutschen Morgenländischen Gesellschaft*, 42, 214.

2. **Babhru Kaumbhya** ('descendant of Kumbha') is the name of the seer of a Sāman or Chant in the Pañcaviṃśa Brāhmaṇa (xv. 3, 13).

3. **Babhru Daivā-vṛdha** is mentioned in the Aitareya Brāhmaṇa (vii. 34) as a pupil of **Parvata** and **Nārada.**

Bamba Āja-dviṣa ('descendant of Aja-dviṣ') is mentioned as a teacher in the Jaiminīya Upaniṣad Brāhmaṇa (ii. 7, 2). Bimba is a various reading.

Bambā-Viśvavayasau are the names, in the form of a compound, of two Ṛṣis who, according to the Yajurveda Saṃhitās,[1] invented a certain rite.

[1] Taittirīya Saṃhitā, vi. 6, 8, 4; Kāṭhaka Saṃhitā xxix. 7, where the reading adopted in the text is Bambhā, though the reading of the Berlin manuscript is Bambhār. The name is taken to be Bambā by the St. Petersburg Dictionary; but Bamba is possible, the Dvandva compound accounting for the form with *ā*. The Maitrāyaṇī Saṃhitā, iv. 7, 3, has Bamba-.

Barāsī is found in the Kāṭhaka Saṃhitā[1] and the Pañcaviṃśa Brāhmana[2] denoting a garment of some kind.

[1] xv. 4.

[2] xviii. 9, 16 (where the commentator explains it as made of bark); xxi. 3, 4.

Baru is the name of the author of a hymn of the Rigveda[1] according to the Brāhmaṇas[2] of that Veda.

[1] x. 96.

[2] Aitareya Brāhmaṇa, vi. 25; Kauṣītaki Brāhmaṇa, xxv. 8.

Barku Vārṣṇa ('descendant of **Vṛṣan**') is the name of a teacher in the Śatapatha Brāhmaṇa.[1]

[1] i. 1, 1, 10; Bṛhadāraṇyaka Upaniṣad, iv. 1, 8 (Mādhyaṃdina = iv. 1, 4 Kāṇva).

Barhis is found repeatedly in the Rigveda[1] and later[2] denoting the litter of grass strewn on the sacrificial ground on which the gods are summoned to seat themselves.

[1] i. 63, 7; 108, 4; iii. 4, 4, etc.

[2] Taittirīya Saṃhitā, vi. 2, 4, 5; Vājasaneyi Saṃhitā, ii. 1; xviii. 1, etc.

Balākā, 'crane,' is mentioned in the list of victims at the Aśvamedha ('horse sacrifice') in the Yajurveda Saṃhitās.[1]

[1] Taittirīya Saṃhitā, v. 5, 16, 1; Maitrāyaṇī Saṃhitā, iii. 14, 3. 14; Vājasaneyi Saṃhitā, xxiv. 22. 23. *Cf.* Zimmer, *Altindisches Leben*, 92.

Balāya is the name of an unknown animal mentioned in the list of victims at the Aśvamedha ('horse sacrifice') in the Yajurveda Saṃhitās.[1]

[1] Vājasaneyi Saṃhitā, xxiv. 38; Maitrāyaṇī Saṃhitā, iii. 14, 19.

Balāsa is the name of a disease mentioned several times in the Atharvaveda[1] and occasionally later.[2] Mahīdhara[3] and Sāyaṇa[4] interpret the term as 'consumption.' Zimmer[5] supports this view on the ground that it is mentioned[6] as a kind of **Yakṣma**, makes the bones and joints fall apart (*asthi-sraṃsa, paruḥ-sraṃsa*),[7] and is caused by love, aversion, and the heart,[8] characteristics which agree with the statements of the later Hindu medicine.[9] It is in keeping with a demon of the character of consumption that Balāsa should appear as an accompaniment of Takman.[10] Grohmann,[11] however, thought

[1] iv. 9, 8; v. 22, 11; vi. 14, 1; 127, 1; ix. 8, 8; xix. 34, 10.

[2] Vājasaneyi Saṃhitā, xii. 97.

[3] On Vājasaneyi Saṃhitā, *loc. cit.*

[4] On Av. xix. 34, 10.

[5] *Altindisches Leben*, 385-387.

[6] Av. ix. 8, 10.

[7] Av. vi. 14, 1.

[8] ix. 8, 8.

[9] Wise, *Hindu System of Medicine*, 321, 322.

[10] Av. iv. 9, 8; xix. 34, 10.

[11] *Indische Studien*, 9, 396 *et seq.*

that a 'sore' or 'swelling' (in the case of fever caused by dropsy) was meant. Bloomfield[12] considers that the question is still open. Ludwig[13] renders the word by 'dropsy.'

As remedies against the disease the salve (**Āñjasa**) from **Trikakud**[14] and the **Jaṅgiḍa**[15] plant are mentioned.

[12] *Hymns of the Atharvaveda*, 450.
[13] Translation of the Rigveda, 3, 510.
[14] Av. iv. 9, 8.
[15] Av. xix. 34, 10.

Bali occurs several times in the Rigveda[1] and often later[2] in the sense of tribute to a king or offering to a god. Zimmer[3] thinks that the offerings were in both cases voluntary. He compares the notices of the Germans in Tacitus,[4] where the kings of the tribes are said to receive gifts in kind as presents, but not a regular tribute. There seems to be no ground whatever for this view. No doubt in origin the prerogatives of monarchy were due to voluntary action on the part of the tribesmen,[5] but that the Vedic peoples, who were essentially a body of conquering invaders, were in this state is most improbable, and the attitude of the Vedic Indian to his gods was at least as compatible with tribute as with voluntary gifts. Zimmer admits that in the case of hostile tribes[6] tribute must be meant even in the Rigveda. See also **Rājan.**

[1] To a god, Rv. i. 70, 9; v. 1, 10; viii. 100, 9; to a king, in the compound *bali-hṛt*, 'paying tribute,' vii. 6, 5; x. 173, 6.

[2] Metaphorically: Av. vi. 117, 1; Taittirīya Brāhmaṇa, i. 2, 3, 2; Kāṭhaka Saṃhitā, xxix. 7; Taittirīya Upaniṣad, i. 5, 3, etc.; *bali-hṛt*, Av. xi. 4, 19; Kāṭhaka Saṃhitā, *loc. cit.*; *bali-hāra*, Av. xi. 1, 20; literally: Av. iii. 4, 3; Taittirīya Brāhmaṇa, ii. 7, 18, 3; iii. 12, 2, 7; Śatapatha Brāhmaṇa, i. 3, 2, 15; 5, 3, 18; 6, 3, 17; xi 2, 6, 14; Pañcaviṃśa Brāhmaṇa, xv. 7, 4; Aitareya Brāhmaṇa, vii. 29 (*cf.* vii. 34); *bali-hṛt*, Kāṭhaka Saṃhitā, xxix. 9; Taittirīya Saṃhitā, i. 6, 2, 1.

[3] *Altindisches Leben*, 166, 167.

[4] *Germania*, 15.

[5] Later, too, benevolences (*praṇayākriyā*) were known. See Fleet, *Journal of the Royal Asiatic Society*, 1909, 760-762.

[6] See Rv. vii. 6, 5; 18, 19.

Balkasa denotes impure matter given off in the process of fermentation in the Śatapatha Brāhmaṇa.[1] The exact sense

[1] xii. 8, 1, 16; 9, 1, 2.

may be either 'scum,' 'sediment,'[2] or perhaps more probably vegetable matter in the form of 'husks.'[3]

[2] St. Petersburg Dictionary, *s.v.*, *Flocken* ('flakes').

[3] Eggeling, *Sacred Books of the East*, 44, 236, n. 1.

Balbaja is the name of the grass called *Eleusine indica.* It is mentioned in the Atharvaveda,[1] and is said in the Yajurveda Saṃhitās[2] to be produced from the excrements of cattle. In the Kāṭhaka Saṃhitā[2] it is stated to be used for the sacrificial litter (**Barhis**) and for fuel. Baskets or other products made from this grass are referred to in a Dānastuti ('Praise of Gifts') in the Rigveda.[3]

[1] xiv. 2, 22. 23.

[2] Taittirīya Saṃhitā, ii. 2, 8, 2; Kāṭhaka Saṃhitā, x. 10; Maitrāyaṇī Saṃhitā, ii. 2, 5.

[3] viii. 55, 3.

Cf. St. Petersburg Dictionary, *s.v.*; Zimmer, *Altindisches Leben*, 69, 70.

1. **Balhika** is the name of a people in the Atharvaveda[1] where the fever (**Takman**) is called upon to go to the **Mūjavants**, the **Mahāvṛṣas**, and the Balhikas. The Mūjavants are quite certainly a northern tribe, and though, as Bloomfield[2] suggests, the passage may contain a pun on Balhika as suggesting 'outsider' (from *bahis*, 'without'), still no doubt the name was chosen from a northern tribe. But the view of Roth[3] and Weber,[4] which Zimmer[5] once accepted, that an Iranian tribe is referred to (*cf.* Balkh), is not at all probable. Zimmer[6] shows that there is no need whatever to assume Iranian influence. See also **Parśu.**

[1] v. 22, 5. 7. 9.

[2] *Hymns of the Atharvaveda*, 446.

[3] *Zur Litteratur und Geschichte des Weda*, 41.

[4] *Indische Studien*, 1, 205; *Proceedings of the Berlin Academy*, 1892, 985-995.

[5] *Altindisches Leben*, 130.

[6] *Op. cit.*, 431-433.

Cf. Whitney, Translation of the Atharvaveda, 260; Hopkins, *Great Epic of India*, 373.

2. **Balhika Prātipīya** is the name of a **Kuru** king in the Śatapatha Brāhmaṇa,[1] where he appears as having been opposed to the restoration of **Duṣṭarītu Paumsāyana** to his hereditary sovereignty over the **Sṛñjayas**, but as having failed to prevent

[1] xii. 9, 3, 3.

the restoration being carried out by **Revottaras Pāṭava Cākra Sthapati.** The epithet Prātipīya is curious: if it connects him with **Pratīpa** (whose son he is in the Epic), the form is remarkable, Zimmer[2] indeed tacitly altering it to Prātīpīya. In the Epic and the Purāṇas[3] he is in the form of Vāhlīka made a brother of **Devāpi** and **Śantanu**, and a son of Pratīpa. To base chronological conclusions on this[4] would be utterly misleading, for the facts are that Devāpi was son of Ṛṣṭiṣeṇa and a priest, while Śantanu was a Kuru prince of unknown parentage, but not probably a son of Pratīpa, who seems to be a late figure in the Vedic age, later than **Parikṣit**, being his great-grandson in the Epic. Very possibly Balhika was a descendant of Pratīpa. Why he bore the name Balhika must remain uncertain, for there is no evidence of any sort regarding it.

2 *Altindisches Leben*, 432.

3 See Muir, *Sanskrit Texts*, 1², 273 *et seq.*; Sieg, *Die Sagenstoffe des Ṛgveda*, 131-136.

4 Pargiter, *Journal of the Royal Asiatic Society*, 1910, 52.

Balbūtha is mentioned in one hymn of the Rigveda,[1] along with **Tarukṣa** and **Pṛthuśravas**, as a giver of gifts to the singer. He is called a **Dāsa**, but Roth[2] was inclined to amend the text so as to say that the singer received a hundred Dāsas from Balbūtha. Zimmer's[3] suggestion that he may have been the son of an aboriginal mother, or perhaps an aboriginal himself, seems probable.[4] If this was the case, it would be a clear piece of evidence for the establishment of friendly relations between the Āryans and the Dāsas.

1 viii. 46, 32.

2 St. Petersburg Dictionary, *s.v. dāsa*.

3 *Altindisches Leben*, 117.

4 Weber, *Episches im vedischen Ritual*, 30; Griffith, *Hymns of the Rigveda*, 2, 196.

1\. **Basta** denotes the 'goat' in the Rigveda[1] and the later literature.[2]

1 i. 161, 13. The passage is unintelligible; for a guess, see Tilak, *Orion*, 166 *et seq.*, and *cf.* Hillebrandt, *Vedische Mythologie*, 3, 145, n. 2.

2 Taittirīya Saṃhitā, ii. 3, 7, 4; v. 3, 1, 3; 7, 10, 1; Kāṭhaka Saṃhitā, xvii. 2; Vājasaneyi Saṃhitā, xiv. 9; Taittirīya Brāhmaṇa, i. 3, 7, 7; Bṛhadāraṇyaka Upaniṣad, i. 4, 9 (Mādhyaṃdina = i. 4, 4 Kāṇva), etc., and *cf.* Av. viii. 6, 12; xi. 9, 22.

2. **Basta Rāmakāyana** is the name of a teacher in the Maitrāyaṇī Saṃhitā (iv. 2, 10). The patronymic is variously read Samakāyana.

Bahu-vacana denotes in grammatical terminology the 'plural' in the Śatapatha Brāhmaṇa[1] and the Nirukta.[2] So *dvivat*, *bahuvat*, in the Nirukta[3] means 'in the dual and the plural.'

[1] xiii. 5, 1, 18.
[2] v. 23; xi. 16; xii. 7 (which recognises the plural *majestatis*).
[3] ii. 24. 27; xi. 16.

Bahv-ṛca denotes an adherent of the Rigveda. The term is found in the Brāhmaṇas[1] of the Rigveda, in the Śatapatha[2] and the Pañcaviṃśa Brāhmaṇas,[3] and in the Āraṇyakas of the Rigveda.[4]

[1] Aitareya Brāhmaṇa, ii. 36; v. 2; vi. 18; Kauṣītaki Brāhmaṇa, vi. 11; xvi. 9.
[2] x. 5, 2, 20; xi. 5, 1, 10.
[3] v. 6, 6.
[4] Aitareya Āraṇyaka, iii. 2, 3; Śāṅkhāyana Āraṇyaka, viii. 4.

Bākura in one passage of the Rigveda (ix. 1, 8) is used as an epithet of **Dṛti**, the combined words denoting a wind instrument of some kind. *Cf.* **Bakura.**

Bāḍeyī-putra ('son of Bāḍeyī') is mentioned in the last Vaṃśa (list of teachers) of the Mādhyaṃdina recension of the Bṛhadāraṇyaka Upaniṣad (vi. 4, 30) as a pupil of **Mauṣikī-putra.**

Bāṇa denotes 'arrow' in the Rigveda (vi. 75, 17) and later (Av. iii. 23, 2; vi. 105, 2, etc.).

Bāṇavant in the Bṛhadāraṇyaka Upaniṣad (iii. 8, 2) denotes an 'arrow' like **Bāṇa.** Its more normal sense is 'quiver' (lit., 'containing arrows'), which is its sense in the Vājasaneyi Saṃhitā (xvi. 10) and the Śatapatha Brāhmaṇa (v. 3, 1, 11).

Bādarāyaṇa ('descendant of Badara') is the name of a teacher in the Vaṃśa (list of teachers) at the end of the Sāmavidhāna Brāhmaṇa.[1]

[1] *Cf.* Weber, *Indische Studien*, 4, 377. Bādari is found in the Kātyāyana Śrauta Sūtra, iv. 3, 18; Weber, *Indische Studien*, 1, 34, n.

Bādhyoga ('descendant of Badhyoga') is the patronymic of **Jihvāvant**, a pupil of **Asita Vārṣagaṇa**, in the last Vaṃśa (list of teachers) in the Mādhyaṃdina recension of the Bṛhadāraṇyaka Upaniṣad (vi. 4, 33).

Bādhva is the name of a teacher in the Aitareya Āraṇyaka (iii. 2, 3). The reading in the Śāṅkhāyana Āraṇyaka (viii. 3) is **Vātsya.**[1]

[1] See Keith, *Aitareya Āraṇyaka*, 249, n. 1.

Bābhrava, 'descendant of **Babhru**,' is the patronymic of **Vatsanapāt** in the Bṛhadāraṇyaka Upaniṣad.[1] In the legend of **Śunaḥśepa**[2] the **Kāpileyas** and the Bābhravas are enumerated as the descendants of Śunaḥśepa under his adoptive name of **Devarāta Vaiśvāmitra.** A Sāman, or Chant, of Babhru is mentioned in the Pañcaviṃśa Brāhmaṇa.[3]

[1] ii. 5, 22; iv. 5, 28 (Mādhyaṃdina = ii. 6, 3; iv. 6, 3 Kāṇva).

[2] Aitareya Brāhmaṇa, vii. 17. The Śāṅkhāyana version omits the words.

[3] xv. 3, 12.

Bābhravya, 'descendant of **Babhru**,' is the patronymic of **Girija** in the Aitareya Brāhmaṇa (vii. 1), and of **Śaṅkha** in the Jaiminīya Upaniṣad Brāhmaṇa (iii. 41, 1; iv. 17, 1).

Bārhat-sāmā is an anomalously formed word meaning 'daughter of Bṛhatsāman' in the Atharvaveda,[1] where her name occurs in a hymn for easy conception.

[1] v. 25, 9. *Cf* Whitney, Translation of the Atharvaveda, 267.

Bārhas-patya, 'descendant of Bṛhaspati,' is the patronymic of the mythical **Śaṃyu.**[1]

[1] Taittirīya Saṃhitā, ii. 6, 10, 1; v. 2, 6, 4; Śatapatha Brāhmaṇa, i. 9, 1, 24; Nirukta, iv. 21, etc.

Bāla denotes 'boy,' 'young child,' in the Upaniṣads.[1] The later definition[2] makes childhood extend to the sixteenth year.

[1] Chāndogya Upaniṣad, v. 1, 11; 24, 5; Kāṭhaka Upaniṣad, ii. 6.
[2] St. Petersburg Dictionary, *s.v.*

Bālandana is a variant of **Bhālandana,** the patronymic of **Vatsaprī.**

[1] See Weber, *Indische Studien*, 3, 459, 478.

Bālāki, Bālākyā. See **Dṛpta-bālāki** and **Kāśyapī-bālākyā-māṭharī-putra.**

Bāleya is a patronymic ('descendant of Bali') of **Gandharvāyaṇa** in the Baudhāyana Śrauta Sūtra (xx. 25).

Bāṣkala. See **Vārkali.**

Bāṣkiha, 'descendant of Baṣkiha,' is the patronymic of **Śunaskarṇa** in the Pañcaviṃśa Brāhmaṇa.[1] In the Baudhāyana Śrauta Sūtra[2] he is a descendant of **Śibi.**

[1] xvii. 12, 6.
[2] xxi. 17. See Caland, *Über das rituelle Sūtra des Baudhāyana*, 28.

Bāhīka is applied in the Śatapatha Brāhmaṇa[1] to the people of the west, of the Panjab,[2] as opposed to the **Prācyas** or easterns. They are said to have called Agni by the name of Bhava.

[1] i. 7, 3, 8.
[2] *Cf.* Mahābhārata, viii. 2030 *et seq.*, where the Bāhīkas are defined as the people of the Panjab and the Indus. This coincides exactly with what seems to be meant by the Śatapatha Brāhmaṇa, which regards as the middle the land to the east of the **Sarasvatī.**

Cf. Weber, *Indische Studien*, 1, 189; 2, 37; Eggeling, *Sacred Books of the East*, 12, 201, n 2.

Bāhu, 'arm,' as a measure of length, is found in the Taittirīya Saṃhitā (vi. 2, 11, 1) and often in the Sūtras.

Bāhu-vṛkta is the name of a man, apparently a Ṛṣi, who overcame foes in battle, according to the Rigveda.[1]

[1] v. 44, 12. *Cf.* Ludwig, Translation of the Rigveda, 3, 138, 139. The Anukramaṇī (Index) attributes to him two hymns of the Rigveda, v. 71 and 72.

Bidala-kārī, 'female splitter of bamboos,' is the name of one of the victims at the Puruṣamedha ('human sacrifice') in the Yajurveda.[1] Eggeling[2] renders the word as 'basket-maker.'

[1] Vājasaneyi Saṃhitā, xxx. 8; *bidala-kāra*, Taittirīya Brāhmaṇa, iii. 4, 5, 1.

[2] *Sacred Books of the East*, 44, 414.

Bimba appears in one passage of the Jaiminīya Upaniṣad Brāhmaṇa (iii. 5, 6) to denote the plant *Momordica monadelpha.*

Bilva is the name of the wood-apple tree (*Aigle marmelos*). It is mentioned in the Brāhmaṇas[1] and in the Atharvaveda,[2] where a reference to its valuable fruit may be intended. According to the Taittirīya Saṃhitā,[3] the sacrificial post was made of Bilva wood in some cases. The Śāṅkhāyana Āraṇyaka[4] contains a hymn in praise of the virtues of an amulet of Bilva (*irā-maṇi bailva*).[5]

[1] Aitareya Brāhmaṇa, ii. 1; Śatapatha Brāhmaṇa, xiii. 4, 4, 8, etc. *Cf.* Maitrāyaṇī Saṃhitā, iii. 9, 3.

[2] xx. 136, 13.

[3] ii. 1, 8, 1. 2. *Cf.* Śatapatha Brāhmaṇa, i. 3, 3, 20 (*paridhayaḥ*); Aitareya Brāhmaṇa, *loc. cit.*

[4] xii. 20 *et seq.*

[5] At the present day the tree is called Bel, and its leaves are used in the ritual of Siva worship.

Bisa denotes the radical fibres of the lotus, which seem to have been eaten as a delicacy as early as the times of the Atharvaveda.[1] It is mentioned also in the Aitareya Brāhmaṇa[2] and the Aitareya Āraṇyaka.[3]

[1] iv. 34, 5.

[2] v. 30.

[3] iii. 2, 4; Śāṅkhāyana Āraṇyaka, xi. 4. *Cf.* Zimmer, *Altindisches Leben*, 70.

Bīja denotes 'seed,' the operation of sowing seed (*vap*) being several times referred to in the Rigveda[1] and later.[2] In a metaphorical sense the term is used in the Upaniṣads of the classes of beings according to origin, of which the Chāndogya Upaniṣad[3] enumerates three, the Aitareya[4] four. The former list includes *aṇḍa-ja*, 'egg-born,' *jīva-ja*, 'born alive,' and *udbhij-ja*, 'produced from sprouts,' 'germinating,' while the latter adds *sveda-ja*, 'sweat-born'—that is, 'generated by hot moisture,' an expression which is glossed to comprise flies, worms, etc. *Cf.* **Kṛṣi.**

1 x. 94, 13; 101, 3. *Cf.* metaphorically, x. 85, 37. In v. 53, 13, *dhānya bīja* means the 'seed which produces corn.'

2 Av. x. 6, 33; Śatapatha Brāhmaṇa, vii. 2, 2, 4, etc.

3 vi. 3, 1.

4 iii. 3. See Keith, *Aitareya Āraṇyaka*, 235.

Buḍila Āśvatarāśvi or **Āśvatara Āśvi** is mentioned several times in the Brāhmaṇa literature as a teacher. According to the Chāndogya[1] and the Bṛhadāraṇyaka[2] Upaniṣads, he was a contemporary of **Janaka** of **Videha**, and, according to the Śatapatha Brāhmaṇa,[3] of **Aśvapati**, the **Kekaya** king. He is also mentioned in the Aitareya Brāhmaṇa.[4]

1 v. 11, 1; 16, 1.

2 v. 15, 11 (Mādhyaṃdina = v. 14, 8 Kāṇva).

3 x. 6, 1, 1. *Cf.* iv. 6, 1, 9.

4 vi. 30.

Budha Saumāyana, 'descendant of **Soma,**' is the name of a teacher mentioned in a verse in the Pañcaviṃśa Brāhmaṇa.[1]

1 xxiv. 18, 6. *Cf.* Hopkins, *Transactions of the Connecticut Academy of Arts and Sciences*, 15, 55, n. 2.

Bunda means 'arrow' in a few passages of the Rigveda.[1]

1 viii. 45, 4; 77, 6. 11. *Cf.* Nirukta, vi. 32.

Bṛbu is mentioned in a hymn of the Rigveda,[1] where he is described as a most generous giver (*sahasra-dātama*), and as at the head of the **Paṇis.** According to the Śāṅkhāyana Śrauta Sūtra,[2] **Bharadvāja** received gifts from Bṛbu **Takṣan** and

1 vi. 45, 31. 33.

2 xvi. 11, 11.

Prastoka Sārñjaya, a fact alluded to in the Mānava Dharma Śāstra,[3] where *takṣan* is treated as a descriptive attribute, 'a carpenter.' Apparently Bṛbu was a Paṇi, though the words of the Rigveda[1] might be taken to mean that he was one who had overthrown them entirely. If so, Paṇi must here certainly mean a merchant in a good sense, Bṛbu being then a merchant prince.[4] According to Weber,[5] the name suggests connexion with Babylon, but this conjecture must be regarded as quite improbable. Hillebrandt[6] sensibly expresses no opinion as to Bṛbu, while Brunnhofer's[7] attempt to recognize a people named Τάσκοι, and to connect them with the Vedic word *takṣan*, is valueless, especially considering the fact that Takṣan is not found as an epithet of Bṛbu in the Rigveda.

[3] x. 107.

[4] *Cf.* Griffith, *Hymns of the Rigveda*, 1, 606, n.

[5] *Episches im vedischen Ritual*, 28 *et seq.*; *Proceedings of the Berlin Academy*, 1898, 563, n. 1; *Indische Studien*, 17, 198. The Bāveru Jātaka, on which stress is laid in connexion with the Indian knowledge of Babylon, being of quite unknown date, has no cogency as evidence for any early period. *Cf.* Bühler, *Indische Palæographie*, 17-19; *Indische Studien*, 3, 79 *et seq.*; Weber, *Indian Literature* 3; Rhys Davids, *Buddhist India*, 201 *et seq.*

[6] *Vedische Mythologie*, 1, 93, 104, 107.

[7] *Iran und Turan*, 127.

Cf. Ludwig, Translation of the Rigveda, 3, 275; Bṛhaddevatā, v. 108, 109, with Macdonell's notes; Max Müller, *Sacred Books of the East*, 32, 316.

Bṛsaya is mentioned twice in the Rigveda, being in the first passage[1] connected with the **Paṇis**, and in the second[2] with the **Pārāvatas** and the Paṇis. According to the St. Petersburg Dictionary, the word is the name of a demon,[3] but is in the second passage[2] used as an appellative, perhaps meaning 'sorcerer.'[4] Hillebrandt[5] thinks that a people is meant locating them in Arachosia or Drangiana with the Pārāvatas and the Paṇis, and comparing Βαρσαέντης, satrap of Arachosia and Drangiana in the time of Darius.[6] But this theory is not probable.

[1] i. 93, 4.

[2] vi. 61, 3.

[3] *Cf.* Sāyaṇa on Rv., *loc. cit.*

[4] Böhtlingk, Dictionary, *s.v.*, following Grassmann.

[5] *Vedische Mythologie*, 1, 97-104.

[6] Arrian, *Indica*, viii. 4; xxi. 1; xxv. 8.

Bṛsī, denoting a 'cushion' of grass, is mentioned in the Aitareya Āraṇyaka[1] and the Sūtras.[2] The incorrect forms Vṛśī and Vṛṣī also occur occasionally.

[1] i. 2, 4; v. 1, 3, with Keith's note; 3, 2.

[2] Śāṅkhāyana Srauta Sūtra, xvii. 4, 7; 6, 6; Kātyāyana Srauta Sūtra, xiii. 3, 1.

Bṛhac chandas is found in one passage of the Atharvaveda[1] as an epithet of **Śālā**, 'house.' It is apparently[2] an error for *bṛhad-chadis*, 'broad-roofed,' which in any case is the sense.[3]

[1] iii. 12, 3.

[2] *Cf.* Whitney, Translation of the Atharvaveda, 105.

[3] Bloomfield, *Hymns of the Atharvaveda*, 345.

Bṛhat-sāman is mentioned in the Atharvaveda (v. 19, 2) as an **Āṅgirasa** who was oppressed by Kṣatriyas. The latter are said to have been ruined in consequence. *Cf.* **Sṛñjaya** and **Bārhatsāmā.**

Bṛhad-uktha is mentioned in an obscure hymn of the Rigveda[1] as a priest; in two hymns of the tenth Maṇḍala[2] he is definitely a Ṛṣi. He is also mentioned in the Aitareya Brāhmaṇa[3] as having consecrated **Durmukha Pāñcāla**, and is called **Vāmadeva's** son in the Śatapatha Brāhmaṇa.[4] In the Pañcaviṃśa Brāhmaṇa[5] he appears as **Vāmneya**, 'descendant of Vāmnī.' Hopkins'[6] suggestion that he may have been there thought of as Vāmadevya also is quite probable,[7]

[1] v. 19, 3, where Roth, St. Petersburg Dictionary, *s.v.*, treats it as adjectival. *Cf.* Oldenberg, *Zeitschrift der Deutschen Morgenländischen Gesellschaft*, 42, 214; Ludwig, Translation of the Rigveda, 3, 126.

[2] x. 54, 6; 56, 7.

[3] viii. 23.

[4] xiii. 2, 2, 14.

[5] xiv. 9, 37. 38.

[6] *Transactions of the Connecticut Academy of Arts and Sciences*, 15, 55, n. 2.

[7] Pañcaviṃśa Brāhmaṇa, xiii. 9, 27, is parallel with xiv. 9, 38.

Bṛhad-giri is said in the Pañcaviṃśa Brāhmaṇa (viii. 1, 4) to have been one of the three **Yatis** who survived the slaughter of them by Indra. A Sāman, or Chant, of his is mentioned in the same Brāhmaṇa (xiii. 4, 15-17).

Bṛhad-diva appears in a hymn of the Rigveda[1] as its a ıthor, calling himself an Atharvan. He is mentioned in the Aitareya Brāhmaṇa,[2] and is named in the Vaṃśa (list of teachers) of the Śāṅkhāyana Āraṇyaka[3] as a pupil of **Sumnayu.**

[1] x. 120, 8. 9.
[2] iv. 14.
[3] xv. 1.

Cf. Ludwig, Translation of the Rigveda, 3, 133; Macdonell, *Vedic Mythology*, p. 141.

Bṛhad-ratha is mentioned twice in the Rigveda,[1] in both cases beside **Navavāstva.** The name may thus be an epithet of Navavāstva.

[1] i. 36, 18; x. 49, 6. *Cf.* Ludwig, Translation of the Rigveda, 3, 147, 148.

Bṛhad-vasu is the name of a teacher in the Vaṃśa Brāhmaṇa.[1]

[1] *Indische Studien*, 4, 374.

Bṛhaspati, 'lord of prayer,' is the name of a god in the Vedic texts. The view of Thibaut,[1] that the name designates the planet Jupiter, is certainly not supported by good evidence. Oldenberg[2] seems clearly right in rejecting it.

[1] *Astronomie, Astrologie und Mathematik*, 6.
[2] *Nachrichten der königlichen Gesellschaft der Wissenschaften zu Göttingen*, 1909, 568, n. 3; Whitney, *Journal of the American Oriental Society*, 16, xciv, correcting Tilak, *Orion*, 101. See also Fleet, *Journal of the Royal Asiatic Society*, 1911, 514-518; Keith, *ibid.*, 794-800.

Bṛhaspati-gupta Śāyasthi is mentioned in the Vaṃśa Brāhmaṇa[1] as a pupil of **Bhavatrāta Śāyasthi.**

[1] *Indische Studien*, 4, 372.

Bṛhaspati-sava is the name of a sacrifice by which, according to the Taittirīya Brāhmaṇa,[1] the priest who desired to become a **Purohita** obtained that office. According to the Āśvalāyana Śrauta Sūtra,[2] it was the sacrifice to be performed by a priest after the **Vājapeya**, while the king performed the **Rājasūya.** In

[1] ii. 7, 1, 2. *Cf.* Kāṭhaka Saṃhitā, xxxvii. 7; Pañcaviṃśa Brāhmaṇa, xvii. 11, 4; xxv. 1, 1. 7.
[2] ix. 9, 5.

the Śatapatha Brāhmaṇa,[3] on the other hand, the Bṛhaspatisava is identified with the Vājapeya; but such identity is clearly not primitive.[4]

[3] v. 2, 1, 19.

[4] Eggeling, *Sacred Books of the East*, 41, xxiv, xxv; Weber, *Indische Studien*, 10, 107, 108.

Bekanāṭa occurs only once in the Rigveda,[1] when Indra is said to overcome all the Bekanāṭas and the Paṇis. The natural sense, therefore, seems to be 'usurer,' the explanation given by Yāska.[2] The word has a foreign appearance, but its provenance can hardly be determined: it might just as well be aboriginal as Babylonian.[3] Hillebrandt[4] thinks Brunnhofer is right in identifying Bekanāṭa with Bikanir.

[1] viii. 16, 10.

[2] Nirukta, vi. 26.

[3] Hopkins, *Journal of the American Oriental Society*, 17, 44.

[4] *Vedische Mythologie*, 3, 268, n. 1. *Cf.* Zimmer, *Altindisches Leben*, 259.

Bekurā occurs in the Pañcaviṃśa Brāhmaṇa,[1] where it may mean 'voice' or 'sound,' the sense assigned to the word in the Naighaṇṭuka.[2] It is, however, possibly, like **Bakura**, the name of a musical instrument. In the Taittirīya[3] and the Kāṭhaka[4] Saṃhitās the words Bekuri and Vekuri occur as epithets of Apsarases, or celestial nymphs, meaning, perhaps, 'melodious'; in the Vājasaneyi Saṃhitā[5] and the Śatapatha Brāhmaṇa[6] the variations Bhakuri and Bhākuri are found.

[1] i. 3, 1; vi. 7, 6; Jaiminīya Brāhmaṇa, i. 82.

[2] i. 11.

[3] iii. 4, 7, 1.

[4] xviii. 14.

[5] xviii. 42.

[6] ix. 4, 1, 9.

Baija-vāpa, 'descendant of Bījavāpa,' is the name of a teacher in the first two Vaṃśas (lists of teachers) in the Mādhyaṃdina recension of the Bṛhadāraṇyaka Upaniṣad (ii. 5, 20; iv. 5, 26).

Baija-vāpāyana, 'descendant of **Baijavāpa,**' is the name of a teacher in the first two Vaṃśas (lists of teachers) in the Mādhyaṃdina recension of the Bṛhadāraṇyaka Upaniṣad (ii. 5, 20; iv. 5, 26). The name is also spelt Vaijavāpāyana.

Baija-vāpi, 'descendant of Bījavāpa, or Bījavāpin,' is the name of a teacher in the Maitrāyaṇī Saṃhitā (i. 4, 7).

Bainda is the name of one of the victims at the Puruṣamedha (' human sacrifice ') in the Yajurveda.[1] According to the commentator Mahīdhara, the word denotes a Niṣāda, but according to Sāyaṇa a catcher of fish. See **Mṛgayu**

[1] Vājasaneyi Saṃhitā, xxx. 16; Taittirīya Brāhmaṇa, iii. 4, 12, 1.

Bodha is the name of a Ṛṣi in the Mantra Pāṭha.[1] He is mentioned with **Pratibodha** in the Atharvaveda,[2] but Whitney[3] thinks that in the second passage, at least, the word is an ordinary noun meaning 'the wakeful one.'

[1] ii. 16, 14. *Cf.* Winternitz, *Mantra-pāṭha*, xlv.

[2] v. 30, 10; viii. 1, 13.

[3] Translation of the Atharvaveda, 474.

Baudhāyana, 'descendant of **Budha** or **Bodha,**' is the name of a teacher who is mentioned in the Baudhāyana Śrauta Sūtra,[1] and under whose name are current a Śrauta Sūtra described[2] and in part edited by Caland,[3] and a Dharma Sūtra which has been edited[4] and translated,[5] while the Gṛhya Sūtra is still unedited.

[1] iv. 11, etc.

[2] *Über das rituelle Sūtra des Baudhāyana,* 1903.

[3] *Bibliotheca Indica,* 1904, etc.

[4] By Hultzsch, Leipzig, 1884.

[5] Bühler, *Sacred Books of the East,* 14. See his Introduction, xxix *et seq.*, where, however, he tends to overestimate considerably the age of Baudhāyana.

Baudhī-putra, 'son of a female descendant of **Bodha,**' is the name of a pupil of **Śālaṅkāyanīputra** in the last Vaṃśa (list of teachers) of the Mādhyaṃdina recension of the Bṛhadāranyaka Upaniṣad (vi. 4, 31).

Brahma-carya denotes the condition of life of the **Brahmacārin**[1] or religious student. The technical sense is first found in

[1] Rv. x. 109, 5; Av. vi. 108, 2; 133, 3; xi. 5, 1 *et seq.*; Śatapatha Brāhmaṇa, xi. 3, 3, 1, etc.

the last Maṇḍala of the Rigveda.[2] The practice of studentship doubtless developed, and was more strictly regulated by custom as time went on, but it is regularly assumed and discussed in the later Vedic literature, being obviously a necessary part of Vedic society.

The Atharvaveda[3] has in honour of the Brahmacārin a hymn which already gives all the characteristic features of religious studentship. The youth is initiated (*upa-nī*) by the teacher[4] into a new life; he wears an antelope skin, and lets his hair grow long;[5] he collects fuel,[6] and begs,[7] learns, and practises penance. All these characteristics appear in the later literature. The student lives in the house of his teacher (*ācārya-kula-vāsin*;[8] *ante-vāsin*)[9]; he begs,[10] looks after the sacrificial fires,[11] and tends the house.[12] His term of studentship might be long extended: it was normally fixed at twelve years,[13] but much longer periods, such as thirty-two years, are mentioned.[14] The

[2] Rv., *loc. cit.*

[3] xi. 5. *Cf.* Gopatha Brāhmaṇa, i. 2, 1-8, which contains an independent account of the Brahmacārin (Bloomfield, *Atharvaveda*, 110); Śatapatha Brāhmaṇa, xi. 3, 3, 1 *et seq.*; Taittirīya Saṃhitā, vi. 3, 10, 5.

[4] Av. xi. 5, 3. It is used in the ritual of the Upanayana, according to the Kauśika Sūtra, lv. 18.

[5] Av. xi. 5, 6.

[6] Av. xi. 5, 4. 6.

[7] Av. xi. 5, 9.

[8] Chāndogya Upaniṣad, ii. 23, 2. So regularly *brahma-caryeṇa vas*, Av. vii. 109, 7; Aitareya Brāhmaṇa, v. 14, etc.; or *car*, Śatapatha Brāhmaṇa, xi. 3, 3, 7; Taittirīya Brāhmaṇa, iii. 7, 6, 3, etc.

[9] *Ibid.*, iii. 11, 5; iv. 10, 1; Bṛhadāraṇyaka Upaniṣad, vi. 3, 15 (Mādhyaṃdina = vi. 3, 7 Kāṇva); Taittirīya Upaniṣad, i. 3, 3; 11, 1.

[10] Chāndogya Upaniṣad, iv. 3, 5. *Cf.* Av. vi. 133, 3; Śatapatha Brāhmaṇa, xi. 3, 3, 5.

[11] Chāndogya Upaniṣad, iv. 10, 2 *et seq.*; Śatapatha Brāhmaṇa, xi. 3, 3, 4.

[12] Śatapatha Brāhmaṇa, iii. 6, 2, 15. A Mantra in the Āśvalāyana Gṛhya Sūtra, i. 22, 1. 2, and elsewhere, sums up the duties of the Brahmacārin as 'thou art a Brahmacārin: eat water; perform thy duty; sleep not in the daytime; obedient to thy teacher study the Veda (*brahmacāry asy; apo 'śāna; karma kuru; divā mā svāpsīr; ācāryāyādhīno vedam adhīṣva*).' One duty specially referred to in the Aitareya Āraṇyaka, iii. 1, 6; Śāṅkhāyana Āraṇyaka, vii. 19, and the Chāndogya Upaniṣad, iv. 5, 5, was the guarding of the teacher's cattle when they were grazing on their pasture grounds. From these grounds, too, the pupil would, no doubt, bring dried dung for fuel, as well as any available sticks. As regards obedience to the teacher, *cf.* Śatapatha Brāhmaṇa, xi. 3, 3, 6.

[13] Chāndogya Upaniṣad, iv. 10; vi. 1, 2.

[14] *Ibid.*, viii. 7, 3 (thirty-two years); 15 (for life), etc.

age at which studentship began varied:[15] **Śvetaketu** commenced at twelve and studied for twelve years.[16]

It is assumed in the Gṛhya Sūtras that the three Āryan castes were all required to pass through a period of studentship. But that this is much more than priestly schematism is uncertain. No doubt individuals of the **Kṣatriya** or **Vaiśya** caste might go through part of the period of studentship, just as Burmese boys of all classes now pass some time in a monastery as students. This is borne out by the reference in the Atharvaveda[17] to the king guarding his country by Brahmacarya—though that is susceptible of a different interpretation—and more clearly by the reference in the Kāṭhaka Saṃhitā[18] to a rite intended to benefit one who, although not a Brahmin, had studied (*vidyām anūcya*), but had not gained renown, and by references in the Upaniṣads to kings who like **Janaka** studied the Vedas and the Upaniṣads.[19] Normally, however, the Kṣatriya studied the art of war.[20]

One of the duties of the Brahmacārin was chastity. But reference is in several places[21] made to the possibility of misconduct between a student and the wife of his preceptor, nor is any very severe penance imposed in early times—later it is different—for such a sin. In certain cases the ritual required a breach of chastity, no doubt as a magic spell to secure fertility.[22]

Even an old man might on occasion become a pupil, as the story of **Āruṇi** shows.[23]

[15] See Weber, *Indische Studien*, 10, 21. The Sūtras allowed for a Brāhmaṇa the ages 8-16; for a Kṣatriya, 11-22; for a Vaiśya, 12-24. The difference between the Brāhmaṇa and the Kṣatriya, compared with that between the Kṣatriya and the Vaiśya, shows that the two latter castes were in a different position from the Brāhmaṇa.

[16] Chāndogya Upaniṣad, vi. 1, 2.

[17] xv. 5, 17. *Cf.* Lanman in Whitney's Translation of the Atharvaveda, 639.

[18] ix. 16 (reading *brāhmaṇa*).

[19] Bṛhadāraṇyaka Upaniṣad, iv. 2, 1.

[20] *Cf.* Hopkins, *Journal of the American Oriental Society*, 13, 106-113.

[21] Taittirīya Āraṇyaka, x. 65; Chāndogya Upaniṣad, v. 10, 9.

[22] Kāṭhaka Saṃhitā, xxxiv. 5; Taittirīya Saṃhitā, vii. 5, 9, 4; Weber, *Indische Studien*, 10, 125, n. 1; Keith, *Śāṅkhāyana Āraṇyaka*, 79.

[23] Bṛhadāraṇyaka Upaniṣad, vi. 1, 6 (Mādhyaṃdina = vi. 2, 4 Kāṇva).

Cf. von Schroeder, *Indiens Literatur und Cultur*, 202, 203; Jolly, *Recht und Sitte*, 151; Weber, *op. cit.*, 10, 121 *et seq.*; Deussen, *Philosophy of the Upanishads*, 370, 371, and see **Brāhmaṇa**.

Brahma-jya,[1] 'oppressor of a Brahmin,' and **Brahma-jyeya,**[2] 'oppression of a Brahmin,' are terms mentioned several times in the Atharvaveda as expressing a heinous crime which involves its perpetrator in ruin. See **Brāhmaṇa.**

[1] v. 19, 7. 12; xii. 5, 15 *et seq.*; xiii. 3, 1. *Cf.* Taittirīya Brāhmaṇa, iii. 7, 9, 2.
[2] Av. xii. 4, 11.

Brahma-datta Caikitāneya ('descendant of Cekitāna') is the name of a teacher in the Bṛhadāraṇyaka Upaniṣad (i. 3, 26). He is mentioned also in the Jaiminīya Upaniṣad (i. 38, 1; 59, 1) as patronized by **Abhipratārin,** the Kuru king.

1. **Brahman** (neut.) denotes the priestly class as opposed to the warrior class and the people (**Kṣatra** and **Viś**). The term is found in the Atharvaveda,[1] and repeatedly later on.[2] For the position, etc., of this class, see **Brāhmaṇa.**

[1] ii. 15, 4; ix. 7, 9; xii. 5, 8; xv. 10, 3. 4.
[2] Taittirīya Saṃhitā, iii. 3, 1, 1, etc.; Vājasaneyi Saṃhitā, vi. 3; vii. 21, etc. See also **Varṇa** and **Kṣatra.**

2. **Brahman** is found in many passages of the Rigveda and later in the sense of 'priest.' In many passages of the Rigveda[1] he is referred to as praising the gods; in others[2] the sense of 'priest' is adequate. In not a few cases[3] the priesthood as a profession is clearly alluded to, nor is there any reason to doubt[4] that in all cases the word has the technical sense of a member of the priesthood. There is, however, considerable doubt as to the number of cases in the Rigveda, where it has the technical

[1] i. 80, 1; 164, 34; ii. 2, 6; vi. 45, 7; vii. 33, 11; viii. 16, 7; x. 71, 11; 77, 1; 85, 3. 16. 34; 107, 6; 117, 7; 125, 5; Muir, *Sanskrit Texts*, 1², 244-246.
[2] i. 10, 1; 33, 9; 101, 5; 108, 7; 158, 6; ii. 39, 1; iv. 50, 8. 9; 58, 2; v. 29, 3; 31, 4; 32, 12; 40, 8; vii. 7, 5; 42, 1; viii. 7, 20; 17, 2; 31, 1; 32, 16; 33 19; 45, 39; 64, 7; 77, 5; 92, 30; 96, 5; ix. 96, 6; 112, 1; 113, 6; x. 28 11; 71, 11; 85, 29; 141, 3; Muir, *op. cit.*, 1², 246-251.
[3] i. 108, 7; iv. 50, 8. 9; viii. 7, 20; 45, 39; 64, 7; 92, 30; ix. 112, 1; x. 85, 29; Muir, 1², 258.
[4] *Loc. cit. Cf.* Zimmer, *Altindisches Leben*, 190 *et seq.*

sense of the priest who guides the sacrifice generally. It is undoubtedly found in that sense, both Muir[5] and Roth[6] recognizing instances of its being used thus. Geldner,[7] however, is anxious to find that sense in a large number of passages, and insists that the **Purohita** was normally a Brahman in the narrower sense. Oldenberg,[8] on the other hand, holds with greater probability that in most of the passages adduced Brahman means simply 'priest,' and that the Purohita, who was essentially not a member of the ordinary body of sacrificing priests (**Ṛtvij**), was, when he officiated at the sacrifice, more usually the Hotṛ priest, and only later became the Brahman. This change he regards as having taken place when the importance of the hymns declined, and most weight was laid on the functions of the priest who superintended the sacrifice as a whole, and by his magic repaired the flaws in the sacrifice.[9] In the later literature both senses of the word are quite common.[10]

[5] *Op. cit.*, 1², 251, citing ii. 1, 2 (=ix. 91, 10); iv. 9, 4; x. 52, 2.

[6] St, Petersburg Dictionary, *s.v.* 2, citing ii. 1, 2; ix. 96, 6; x. 71, 11; 107, 6. In none of the last three passages is the specific sense cogently required.

[7] *Vedische Studien*, 2, 145 *et seq.*; 3, 155. He thinks that the sense of 'superintending priest' is the older, and sees it in i. 158, 6; iv. 9, 4; 50, 7. 8; vii. 7, 5; 33, 11; x. 141, 3, etc.

[8] *Religion des Veda*, 396, 397, who thinks that the Brahman priest known to the Rigveda was the **Brāhmaṇācchaṃsin**, and who in most passages (*e.g.*, iv. 50, 7. 8) sees only the sense of 'priest.' *Cf.* Weber, *Indische Studien*, 9, 376, 377.

[9] *Cf.* Pischel, *Göttingische Gelehrte Anzeigen*, 1894, 420; Hillebrandt, *Rituallitteratur*, 13; Bloomfield, *Hymns of the Atharvaveda*, lxviii; *Atharvaveda*, 32; and see **Purohita**.

[10] As 'priest,' Av. ii. 7, 2; iv. 35, 1. 2; v. 8, 5; 17, 8; 18, 7; 19, 8; vi. 122, 5; viii. 9, 3; x. 1, 3; 4, 30. 33; 7, 24; xi. 1, 25; xii. 1, 38; xix. 32, 8; Taittirīya Saṃhitā, iv. 1, 7, 1; Vājasaneyi Saṃhitā, xxvi. 2; Aitareya Brāhmaṇa, v. 3, etc. As 'superintending priest,' Av. xviii. 4, 15; xx. 2, 3; Taittirīya Saṃhitā, i. 8, 9, 1; ii. 3, 11, 4; iii. 5, 2, 1, etc.; Kāṭhaka Saṃhitā, xxxvii. 17; and see Weber, *Indische Studien*, 10, 34, 35; 114; 135-138; 327; 330-337.

Brahma-putra in a few passages is used in the sense of a 'priest's son.'

[1] Rv. ii. 43, 2; Śatapatha Brāhmaṇa, xi. 4, 1, 2. 9. *Cf.* Weber, *Indische Studien*, 10, 43, 69; Muir, *Sanskrit Texts*, 1², 252.

Brahma-purohita is found in the Kāṭhaka Saṃhitā[1] and the Śatapatha Brāhmaṇa[2] where the St. Petersburg Dictionary gives the sense as 'having the priesthood as its Purohita.' This seems rather doubtful; more probably the sense should be 'having a Brahman priest as Purohita,' unless the word merely means 'having the priesthood superior to it,' as an epithet of **Kṣatra,** the 'warrior caste,' which seems to be Weber's view.[3]

[1] xix. 10; xxvii. 4. [2] xii. 8, 3, 29. [3] *Indische Studien*, 10, 30.

Brahma-bandhu ('priest fellow') denotes, in a deprecatory sense, an 'unworthy priest,' 'priest in name only,' in the Aitareya Brāhmaṇa[1] and the Chāndogya Upaniṣad.[2] *Cf.* **Rājanyabandhu.**

[1] vii. 27.
[2] vi. 1, 1. *Cf.* Lāṭyāyana Śrauta Sūtra, viii. 6, 28; Kātyāyana Śrauta Sūtra, xxii. 4, 22; Śāṅkhāyana Śrauta Sūtra, xvi. 29, 9; Weber, *Indische Studien*, 10, 99, 100.

Brahmarṣi-deśa. See **Madhyadeśa.**

Brahma-vadya. See **Brahmodya.**

Brahma-vādin ('expounder of the Veda') in the later Saṃhitās[1] and the Brāhmaṇas[2] denotes a 'theologian.' Brahma-vid ('knowing what is sacred') has the same sense.[3]

[1] Av. xi. 3, 26; xv. 1, 8; Taittirīya Saṃhitā, i. 7, 1, 4; ii. 6, 2, 3; 3, 1; v. 2, 7, 1; 5, 3, 2; vi. 1, 4, 5.
[2] Taittirīya Brāhmaṇa, i. 3, 10, 6; Pañcaviṃśa Brāhmaṇa, iv. 3, 13; vi. 4, 15; Taittirīya Āraṇyaka, i. 22, 9; v. 2, 2; 4, 6; Chāndogya Upaniṣad, ii. 24, 1, etc.
[3] Av. x. 7, 24. 27; 8, 43; xix. 43, 1; Taittirīya Brāhmaṇa, i. 4, 8, 6; Taittirīya Upaniṣad, ii. 1; Bṛhadāraṇyaka Upaniṣad, iii. 7, 4; iv. 4, 11. 12, etc.

Brahma-vidyā, 'knowledge of the Absolute,' is the name of one of the sciences enumerated in the Chāndogya Upaniṣad.[1] It is also mentioned elsewhere.[2]

[1] vii. 1, 2. 4; 2, 1; 7, 1. [2] Bṛhadāraṇyaka Upaniṣad, i. 4, 20, etc.

Brahma-vṛddhi is mentioned in the Vaṃśa Brāhmaṇa[1] as a pupil of **Mitravarcas.**

[1] *Indische Studien*, 4, 372, 382.

Brahma-hatyā, the 'murder of a Brahmin,' is mentioned in the Yajurveda Saṃhitās[1] and the Brāhmaṇas[2] as a heinous crime. The murderer is called Brahma-han.[3]

[1] Taittirīya Saṃhitā, ii. 5, 1, 2; v. 3, 12, 1; Vājasaneyi Saṃhitā, xxxix. 13, etc.

[2] Satapatha Brāhmaṇa, xiii. 3, 1, 1; 5, 3; 5, 4, 1; Taittirīya Āraṇyaka, x. 38; Nirukta, vi. 27, etc.

[3] Taittirīya Saṃhitā, ii. 5, 1, 2; vi. 5, 10, 3; Kāṭhaka Saṃhitā, xxxi. 7; Kapiṣṭhala Saṃhitā, xlvii. 7; Taittirīya Brāhmaṇa, iii. 2, 8, 12; Satapatha Brāhmaṇa, xiii. 3, 5, 4, etc. *Cf.* **Dharma.**

Brahmāvarta. See **Madhyadeśa.**

Brahmodya in the Brāhmaṇas[1] denotes a 'theological riddle,' such as formed an essential part of various ceremonies in the Vedic ritual, as at the Aśvamedha or the Daśarātra. Brahma-vadya is the form found in the Kauṣītaki Brāhmaṇa,[2] and Brahma-vādya in the Taittirīya Saṃhitā[3] probably has the same sense.

[1] Satapatha Brāhmaṇa, iv. 6, 9, 20; xi. 4, 1, 2; 5, 3, 1; 6, 2, 5; xiii. 2, 6, 9; 5, 2, 11; Bṛhadāraṇyaka Upaniṣad, iii. 8, 1; Aitareya Brāhmaṇa, v. 25

[2] xxvii. 4

[3] ii. 5, 8, 3.

Cf. Bloomfield, *Journal of the American Oriental Society*, 15, 172; *Religion of the Veda*, 216 *et seq.*; Weber, *Indische Studien*, 10, 118, 119; Ludwig, Translation of the Rigveda, 3, 390 *et seq.*; Eggeling, *Sacred Books of the East*, 26, 452, 453.

Brahmopaniṣad, a 'secret doctrine regarding the Absolute,' is the name of a discussion in the Chāndogya Upaniṣad (iii. 11, 3).

Brahmaudana denotes in the later Saṃhitās[1] and the Brāhmaṇas[2] the 'rice boiled (**Odana**) for the priests' officiating at the sacrifice.

[1] Av. iv. 35, 7; xi. 1, 1. 3. 20. 23 *et seq.*; Taittirīya Saṃhitā, iii. 4, 8, 7; v. 7, 3, 4; vi. 5, 6, 1, etc.

[2] Śatapatha Brāhmaṇa, xiii. 1, 1, 1. 4; 3, 6, 6; 4, 1, 5, etc.

1. **Brāhmaṇa**, 'descendant of a Brahman' (*i.e.*, of a priest), is found only a few times in the Rigveda,[1] and mostly in its latest

[1] i. 164, 45; vi. 75, 10; vii. 103, 1. 7. 8; x. 16, 6; 71, 8. 9; 88, 19; 90, 12; 97, 22; 109, 4. See Muir, *Sanskrit Texts*, 1², 251 - 257; Roth, *Nirukta, Erläuterungen*, 126; St. Petersburg Dictionary, *s.v.*, where Rv. viii. 58, 1, is added; Ludwig, Translation of the Rigveda, 3, 220-226.

parts. In the Atharvaveda[2] and later[3] it is a very common word denoting 'priest,' and it appears in the quadruple division of the castes in the Puruṣa-sūkta ('hymn of man') of the Rigveda.[4]

It seems certain that in the Rigveda this Brāhmaṇa, or Brahmin, is already a separate caste, differing from the warrior and agricultural castes.[5] The texts regularly claim for them a superiority to the **Kṣatriya** caste,[6] and the Brahmin is able by his spells or manipulation of the rite to embroil the people and the warriors[7] or the different sections of the warriors.[8] If it is necessary to recognize, as is sometimes done, that the Brahmin does pay homage to the king at the **Rājasūya**,[9] nevertheless the unusual fact is carefully explained away so as to leave the priority of the Brahmin unaffected. But it is expressly recognized that the union of the Kṣatriya and the Brāhmaṇa is essential for complete prosperity.[10] It is admitted[11] that the king or the nobles might at times oppress the Brahmins, but it is indicated that ruin is then certain swiftly to follow.

[2] ii. 6, 3; iv. 6, 1; v. 17, 9; 18, 1 *et seq.*; 19, 2 *et seq.*; xi. 1, 28; xix. 34, 6; 35, 2, etc.

[3] Taittirīya Saṃhitā, i. 6, 7, 2; ii. 1, 2, 8, etc.; Vājasaneyi Saṃhitā, vii. 46, etc.

[4] x. 90.

[5] *Cf.* Oldenberg, *Zeitschrift der Deutschen Morgenländischen Gesellschaft*, 42, 235; Geldner, *Vedische Studien*, 2, 146, n. 1; and see **Varṇa**.

[6] See Maitrāyaṇī Saṃhitā, iv. 3, 8; Kāṭhaka Saṃhitā, xxix. 10; Vājasaneyi Saṃhitā, xxi. 21; Śatapatha Brāhmaṇa, v. 4, 4, 15; xiii. 1, 9, 1; 3, 7, 8; Aitareya Brāhmaṇa, vii. 15; viii. 9 Pañcaviṃśa Brāhmaṇa, ii. 8, 2; xi. 11, 9; xv. 6, 3; and *cf.* **Brahmapurohita**; Weber, *Indische Studien*, 10, 27 *et seq.*

[7] See Maitrāyaṇī Saṃhitā, ii. 1, 7; iii. 3, 10; Taittirīya Saṃhitā, ii. 2, 11, 2, etc.

[8] Maitrāyaṇī Saṃhitā, iii. 3, 10.

[9] Bṛhadāraṇyaka Upaniṣad, i. 4, 23 (Mādhyaṃdina=i. 4, 11 Kāṇva). *Cf.* Kāṭhaka Saṃhitā, xxviii. 5; Śatapatha Brāhmaṇa, i. 2, 3, 2; v. 4, 2, 7. Contrast the claim that Soma alone is King of the Brahmins, Vājasaneyi Saṃhitā, x. 18; Śatapatha Brāhmaṇa, v. 4, 2, 3.

[10] See Taittirīya Saṃhitā, v. 1, 10, 3; Kāṭhaka Saṃhitā, xix. 10; xxvii. 4; xxix. 10; Maitrāyaṇī Saṃhitā, ii. 2, 3; 7, 7; iii. 1, 9; 2, 3; iv. 3, 9; Vājasaneyi Saṃhitā, xx. 25; Pañcaviṃśa Brāhmaṇa, xix. 17, 4; Śatapatha Brāhmaṇa, iv. 1, 4, 6; v. 4, 4, 15; Aitareya Brāhmaṇa, viii. 10. 17. 24. 25, etc. *Cf.* **Purohita**.

[11] Maitrāyaṇī Saṃhitā, i. 8, 7; Pañcaviṃśa Brāhmaṇa, xviii. 10, 8; Av. v. 17-19; Taittirīya Brāhmaṇa, i. 7, 2, 6; Śatapatha Brāhmaṇa, xiii. 1, 5, 4.

The Brahmins are gods on earth,[12] like the gods in heaven, but this claim is hardly found in the Rigveda.[13]

In the Aitareya Brāhmaṇa[14] the Brahmin is said to be the 'recipient of gifts' (*ādāyī*) and the 'drinker of the offering' (*āpāyī*). The other two epithets applied, *āvasāyī* and *yathā-kāma-prayāpya*, are more obscure; the former denotes either 'dwelling everywhere'[15] or 'seeking food';[16] the latter is usually taken as 'moving at pleasure,' but it must rather allude to the power of the king to assign a place of residence to the Brahmin.

In the Śatapatha Brāhmaṇa[17] the prerogatives of the Brahmin are summed up as (1) Arcā, 'honour'; (2) Dāna, 'gifts'; (3) Ajyeyatā, 'freedom from oppression'; and (4) Avadhyatā, 'freedom from being killed.' On the other hand, his duties are summed up as (5) Brāhmaṇya, 'purity of descent'; (6) Pratirūpa-caryā, 'devotion of the duties of his caste'; and (7) Loka-pakti, 'the perfecting of people' (by teaching).

1. *Respect paid to Brahmins.*—The texts are full[18] of references to the civilities to be paid to the Brahmin. He is styled *bhagavant*,[19] and is provided with good food[20] and entertainment wherever he goes. Indeed, his sanctity exempts him from any close inquiry into his real claim to Brahminhood according to the Pañcaviṃśa Brāhmaṇa.[21]

2. *Gifts to Brahmins.*—The Dānastuti ('Praise of gifts') is a recognized feature of the Rigveda, and the greed of the poets for **Dakṣiṇās**, or sacrificial fees, is notorious. Vedic texts[22] themselves recognize that the literature thence resulting (**Nārā-**

[12] Av. v. 3, 2; vi. 13, 1; 44, 2; xix. 62, 1 (compared with xix. 32, 8), and probably v. 11, 11; Taittirīya Saṃhitā, i. 7, 3, 1; ii. 5, 9, 6; Kāṭhaka Saṃhitā, viii. 13; Maitrāyaṇī Saṃhitā, i. 4, 6; Śatapatha Brāhmaṇa, ii. 2, 2, 6; 4, 3, 14; iii. 1, 1, 11; iv. 3, 4, 4. See Weber, *op. cit.*, 10, 35, 36; von Schroeder, *Indiens Literatur und Cultur*, 146, 147.

[13] Neither in i. 139, 7, nor ix. 99, 6 (see Roth, St. Petersburg Dictionary, *s.v. deva*), is this sense at all probable. Zimmer, *Altindisches Leben*, 206, quotes i. 128, 8, but that also is uncertain.

[14] vii. 29, 2. *Cf.* **Varṇa**, n. 71.

[15] Weber, *Indische Studien*, 9, 326.

[16] Muir, *Sanskrit Texts*, 5, 439.

[17] xi. 5, 7, 1 *et seq.* See Weber, *op. cit.*, 10, 41 *et seq.*

[18] *E.g.*, Kāṭhaka Saṃhitā, xxv. 3; Taittirīya Brāhmaṇa, i. 1, 10, 6; Śatapatha Brāhmaṇa, ii. 4, 1, 10; 3, 4, 6, etc.

[19] Śatapatha Brāhmaṇa, xiv. 6, 1, 2.

[20] Kāṭhaka Saṃhitā, xix. 12.

[21] vi. 5, 8; Kāṭhaka Saṃhitā, xxvii. 2.

[22] Kāṭhaka Saṃhitā, xiv. 5; Taittirīya Brāhmaṇa, i. 3, 2, 6. 7.

śaṃsī) was often false to please the donors. It was, however, a rule[23] that Brahmins should not accept what had been refused by others; this indicates a keen sense of the danger of cheapening their wares. So exclusively theirs was the right to receive gifts that the Pañcaviṃśa Brāhmaṇa[24] has to explain how **Taranta** and **Purumīḷha** became able to accept gifts by composing a Rigvedic hymn.[25] The exaggerations in the celebration of the gifts bestowed on the priests has the curious result of giving us a series of numerals of some interest (**Daśan**). In some passages[26] certain gifts—those of a horse or sheep—are forbidden, but this rule was not, it is clear, generally observed.

3. *Immunities of Brahmins.*—The Brahmin claimed to be exempt from the ordinary exercise of the royal power. When a king gives all his land and what is on it to the priests, the gift does not cover the property of the Brahmin according to the Śatapatha Brāhmaṇa.[27] The king censures all, but not the Brahmin,[28] nor can he safely oppress any Brahmin other than an ignorant priest.[29] An arbitrator (or a witness) must decide (or speak) for a Brahmin against a non-Brahmin in a legal dispute.[30]

The Brahmin's proper food is the **Soma**,[31] not **Surā**[32] or **Parisrut**,[33] and he is forbidden to eat certain forms of flesh.[34] On the other hand, he alone is allowed to eat the remains of the sacrifice,[35] for no one else is sufficiently holy to consume food which the gods have eaten. Moreover, though he cannot be a physician,[36] he helps the physician by being beside him

[23] Śatapatha Brāhmaṇa, iii. 5, 1, 25. *Cf.* also Bṛhadāraṇyaka Upaniṣad, iii. 15, 8; Śatapatha Brāhmaṇa, xiii. 4, 3, 14, etc.

[24] xiii. 7, 12.

[25] ix. 58, 3.

[26] Taittirīya Saṃhitā, ii. 3, 12, 1. 2; Kāṭhaka Saṃhitā, xii. 6, etc.

[27] xiii. 5, 4, 29; 6, 2, 18; 7, 1 13.

[28] *Ibid.*, v. 4, 2, 3.

[29] *Ibid.*, xiii. 4, 2, 17.

[30] Taittirīya Saṃhitā, ii. 5, 11, 9.

[31] Śatapatha Brāhmaṇa, xii. 7, 2, 2; Aitareya Brāhmaṇa, vii. 29. *Cf.* Kāṭhaka Saṃhitā, xi. 5; Vājasaneyi Saṃhitā, ix. 40; x. 18, etc.

[32] Śatapatha Brāhmaṇa, xii. 8, 1, 5.

[33] *Ibid.*, xii. 9, 1, 1.

[34] *Ibid.*, 1, 2, 3, 9; vii. 5, 2, 37; Aitareya Brāhmaṇa, ii. 8.

[35] Satapatha Brāhmaṇa, ii. 3, 1, 39; 5, 3, 16, etc. On the food of the Brahmins, *cf.* also Pañcaviṃśa Brāhmaṇa, x. 4, 5; xvii. 1, 9; Aitareya Brāhmaṇa, iv. 11.

[36] *Cf.* Śatapatha Brāhmaṇa, iv. 1, 5, 8-14, where the Aśvins, who are famous as physicians (viii. 2, 1, 3; xii. 7, 1, 11), are treated as impure.

while he exercises his art.[37] His wife[38] and his cow[39] are both sacred.

4. *Legal Position of Brahmins.*—The Taittirīya Saṃhitā[40] lays down a penalty of a hundred (the unit meant is unknown) for an insult to a Brahmin, and of a thousand for a blow; but if his blood is drawn, the penalty is a spiritual one. The only real murder is the slaying of a Brahmin according to the Śatapatha Brāhmaṇa.[41] The crime of slaying a Brahmin ranks above the sin of killing any other man, but below that of killing an embryo (*bhrūṇa*) in the Yajurveda;[42] the crime of slaying an embryo whose sex is uncertain is on a level with that of slaying a Brahmin.[43] The murder of a Brahmin can be expiated only by the horse sacrifice,[44] or by a lesser rite in the late Taittirīya Āraṇyaka.[45] The ritual slaying of a Brahmin is allowed in the later ceremonial,[46] and hinted at in the curious legend of **Śunaḥśepa**,[47] and a Purohita might be punished with death for treachery to his master.[48]

5. *Purity of Birth.*—The importance of pure descent is seen in the stress laid on being a descendant of a Ṛṣi (*ārṣeya*).[49] But, on the other hand, there are clear traces of another doctrine, which requires learning, and not physical descent, as the true criterion of Ṛṣihood.[50] In agreement with this is the fact that **Satyakāma Jābāla** was received as a pupil, though his parentage was unknown, his mother being a slave girl who had been connected with several men,[51] and that in the Śatapatha

[37] Taittirīya Saṃhitā, vi. 4, 9, 3. Contrast Rv. x. 97, 22, where no discredit attaches to the profession.

[38] Av. v. 17.

[39] *Ibid.*, v. 18.

[40] ii. 6, 10, 2.

[41] xiii. 3, 5, 3.

[42] Kāṭhaka Saṃhitā, xxxi. 7; Kapiṣṭhala Saṃhitā, xlvii. 7; Taittirīya Brāhmaṇa, iii. 2, 8, 12.

[43] Taittirīya Saṃhitā, vi. 5, 10, 2; Kāṭhaka Saṃhitā, xxvii. 9; Weber, *Indische Studien*, 9, 481; 10, 66.

[44] Śatapatha Brāhmaṇa, xiii. 3, 1, 1; 5, 4, 1 *et seq.*

[45] x. 38.

[46] Śāṅkhāyana Śrauta Sūtra, xvi. 10, 10; 12, 16-20; Weber, *Zeitschrift der Deutschen Morgenländischen Gesellschaft*, 18, 268, 269.

[47] Aitareya Brāhmaṇa, vii. 15; Śāṅkhāyana Śrauta Sūtra, xv. 20.

[48] Pañcaviṃśa Brāhmaṇa, xiv. 6, 8.

[49] See Taittirīya Saṃhitā, vi. 6, 1, 4; Vājasaneyi Saṃhitā, vii. 46; Taittirīya Brāhmaṇa, i. 4, 4, 2; Śatapatha Brāhmaṇa, iv. 3, 4, 19; xii. 4, 4, 6.

[50] Taittirīya Saṃhitā, vi. 6, 1, 4; Kāṭhaka Saṃhitā, xxx. 1; Maitrāyaṇī Saṃhitā, iv. 8, 1.

[51] Chāndogya Upaniṣad, vi. 4, 4.

Brāhmaṇa[52] the ceremony on acceptance as a pupil required merely the name of the pupil. So **Kavaṣa** is taunted in the Rigveda Brāhmaṇas[53] as being the son of a female slave (**Dāsī**), and **Vatsa** cleared himself of a similar imputation by a fire ordeal.[54] Moreover, a very simple rite was adequate to remove doubts as to origin.[55] In these circumstances it is doubtful whether much value attaches to the **Pravara** lists in which the ancestors of the priest were invoked at the beginning of the sacrifice by the Hotṛ and the Adhvaryu priests.[56] Still, in many parts of the ritual the knowledge of two or more generations was needed,[57] and in one ceremony[58] ten ancestors who have drunk the Soma are required, but a literal performance of the rite is excused. Moreover, there are clear traces of ritual variations in schools, like those of the **Vasiṣṭhas** and the **Viśvāmitras.**

6. *The Conduct of the Brahmin.*—The Brahmin was required to maintain a fair standard of excellence.[59] He was to be kind to all[60] and gentle,[61] offering sacrifice and receiving gifts.[62] Especial stress was laid on purity of speech;[63] thus **Viśvantara's** excuse for excluding the **Śyāparṇas** from his retinue was their impure (*apūtā*) speech.[64] Theirs was the craving for knowledge[65] and the life of begging.[66] False Brahmins are those who do not fulfil their duties[67] (*cf.* **Brahmabandhu**).

[52] xi. 5, 4, 1; and *cf.* a citation in the scholiast on Kātyāyana Śrauta Sūtra, i. 6, 14: 'Whoever studies the Stomabhāgas (a peculiarity of the Vasiṣṭhas) is a Vasiṣṭha'; Weber, *Indische Studien*, 10, 73.

[53] Aitareya Brāhmaṇa, ii. 19; Kauṣītaki Brāhmaṇa, xii. 3; Weber, *op. cit.*, 2, 311.

[54] Pañcaviṃśa Brāhmaṇa, xiv. 6, 6.

[55] Taittirīya Saṃhitā, vi. 2, 6, 4; Kāṭhaka Saṃhitā, xxv. 3; Pañcaviṃśa Brāhmaṇa, xxiii. 4, 2.

[56] See Weber, *op. cit.*, 9, 321; 10, 78-81; Max Müller, *Ancient Sanskrit Literature*, 380 *et seq.*

[57] *Cf.*, *e.g.*, Taittirīya Saṃhitā, ii. 1, 5, 5; Kāṭhaka Saṃhitā, xiii. 5.

[58] Śatapatha Brāhmaṇa, v. 4, 5, 4; Weber, *op. cit.*, 10, 85-88.

[59] Weber, 10, 88-96; Max Müller, *Ancient Sanskrit Literature*, 407 *et seq.*

[60] Śatapatha Brāhmaṇa, ii. 3, 2, 12.

[61] *Ibid.*, ii. 3, 4, 6.

[62] *Ibid.*, xiii. 1, 5, 6.

[63] *Ibid.*, iii. 2, 1, 24. *Cf.* iv. i, 3. 17; Nirukta, xiii. 9; Kāṭhaka Saṃhitā, xiv. 5; xxxvii. 2; Vājasaneyi Saṃhitā, xxiii. 62.

[64] Aitareya Brāhmaṇa, vii. 27; Muir, *Sanskrit Texts*, 1², 438.

[65] Bṛhadāraṇyaka Upaniṣad, iii. 8, 8; v. 1, 1.

[66] *Ibid.*, iii. 4, 1; iv. 4, 26.

[67] *Ibid.*, vi. 4, 4.

But the penances for breach of duty are, in the Sūtras, of a very light and unimportant character.[68]

7. *Brahminical Studies*.—The aim of the priest is to obtain pre-eminence in sacred knowledge (*brahma-varcasam*), as is stated in numerous passages of Vedic literature.[69] Such distinction is not indeed confined to the Brahmin: the king has it also, but it is not really in a special manner appropriate to the Kṣatriya.[70] Many ritual acts are specified as leading to Brahmavarcasa,[71] but more stress is laid on the study of the sacred texts: the importance of such study is repeatedly insisted upon.[72]

The technical name for study is Svādhyāya: the Śatapatha Brāhmaṇa is eloquent upon its advantages,[73] and it is asserted that the joy of the learned Śrotriya, or 'student,' is equal to the highest joy possible.[74] **Nāka Maudgalya** held that study and the teaching of others were the true penance (*tapas*).[75] The object was the 'threefold knowledge' (*trayī vidyā*), that of the Ṛc, Yajus, and Sāman,[76] a student of all three Vedas being called *tri-śukriya*[77] or *tri-śukra*,[78] 'thrice pure.' Other objects of study are enumerated in the Śatapatha Brāhmaṇa,[79] in the Taittirīya Āraṇyaka,[80] the Chāndogya Upaniṣad,[81] etc. (See **Itihāsa, Purāṇa; Gāthā, Nārāśaṃsī; Brahmodya; Anuśāsana, Anuvyākhyāna, Anvākhyāna, Kalpa,** 2. **Brāhmaṇa; Vidyā, Kṣatravidyā, Devajanavidyā, Nakṣatravidyā, Bhūtavidyā, Sarpavidyā; Atharvāṅgirasaḥ, Daiva, Nidhi, Pitrya, Rāśi; Sūtra,** etc.)

68 Taittirīya Āraṇyaka, ii. 18, etc.

69 Taittirīya Saṃhitā, iv. 1, 7, 1; vii. 5, 18, 1; Kāṭhaka Saṃhitā, Aśvamedha, v. 14; Vājasaneyi Saṃhitā, xxii. 22; xxvii. 2; Taittirīya Brāhmaṇa, iii. 8, 13, 1; Aitareya Brāhmaṇa, iv. 11, 6-9; Śatapatha Brāhmaṇa, xiii. 2, 6, 10; x. 3, 5, 16; xi. 4, 4, 1; Pañcaviṃśa Brāhmaṇa, vi. 3, 5.

70 Śatapatha Brāhmaṇa, ii. 1, 3, 6; xiii. 1, 5, 3. 5; 2, 6, 9.

71 Kāṭhaka Saṃhitā, xxxvii. 7; Taittirīya Brāhmaṇa, ii. 7, 1, 1; Pañcaviṃśa Brāhmaṇa, xxiii. 7, 3, etc.; Śatapatha Brāhmaṇa, ii. 3, 1, 31, etc.

72 Śatapatha Brāhmaṇa, i. 7, 2, 3; xi. 3, 3, 3-6; 5, 7, 10.

73 Śatapatha Brāhmaṇa, xi. 5, 6, 3. 9; 7, 1; Taittirīya Āraṇyaka, ii. 13.

74 Bṛhadāraṇyaka Upaniṣad, iv. 3, 35-39; Taittirīya Āraṇyaka, ix. 8.

75 *Ibid.*, vii. 8. 10.

76 Śatapatha Brāhmaṇa, i. 1, 4, 2. 3; ii. 6, 4, 2-7; iv. 6, 7, 1. 2; v. 5, 5, 9; vi. 3, 1, 10. 11. 20; x. 5, 2, 1. 2; xi. 5, 4, 18; xii. 3, 3, 2, etc.

77 Kāṭhaka Saṃhitā, xxxvii. 7.

78 Taittirīya Brāhmaṇa, ii. 7, 1, 2.

79 xi. 5, 7, 5-8.

80 ii. 9. 10.

81 vii. 1, 2. 4; 2, 1; 7, 1.

Directions as to the exact place and time of study are given in the Taittirīya Āraṇyaka[82] and in the Sūtras. If study is carried on in the village, it is to be done silently (*manasā*); if outside, aloud (*vācā*).

Learning is expected even from persons not normally competent as teachers, such as the **Carakas**, who are recognized in the Śatapatha Brāhmaṇa[83] as possible sources of information. Here, too, may be mentioned the cases of Brahmins learning from princes, though their absolute value is doubtful, for the priests would naturally represent their patrons as interested in their sacred science: it is thus not necessary to see in these notices any real and independent study on the part of the Kṣatriyas.[84] **Yājñavalkya** learnt from **Janaka**,[85] **Uddālaka Āruṇi** and two other Brahmins from **Pravāhaṇa Jaivali**,[86] **Dṛptabālāki Gārgya** from **Ajātaśatru**,[87] and five Brahmins under the lead of Aruṇa from **Aśvapati Kaikeya**.[88] A few notices show the real educators of thought: wandering scholars went through the country[89] and engaged in disputes and discussions in which a prize was staked by the disputants.[90] Moreover, kings like Janaka offered rewards to the most learned of the Brahmins;[91] Ajātaśatru was jealous of his renown, and imitated his generosity. Again, learned women are several times mentioned in the Brāhmaṇas.[92]

A special form of disputation was the **Brahmodya**, for which there was a regular place at the Aśvamedha ('horse sacrifice')[93] and at the Daśarātra ('ten-day festival').[94] The reward of learning was the gaining of the title of Kavi or Vipra, 'sage.'[95]

[82] ii. 11. 12-15.

[83] iv. 2, 4. 1.

[84] *Cf.* (1) **Kṣatriya** and (2) **Varṇa.**

[85] Satapatha Brāhmaṇa, xi. 6, 2, 5.

[86] Bṛhadāraṇyaka Upaniṣad, vi. 1, 11; Chāndogya Upaniṣad, v. 3, 1, and i. 8, 1. *Cf.* Muir, *Sanskrit Texts*, 5, 436, 514-516.

[87] Bṛhadāraṇyaka Upaniṣad, ii. 1, 1; Kauṣītaki Upaniṣad, iv. 1.

[88] Śatapatha Brāhmaṇa, x. 6, 1, 2.

[89] Bṛhadāraṇyaka Upaniṣad, iii. 3, 1. *Cf.* iii. 7, 1.

[90] Śatapatha Brāhmaṇa, xi. 4, 1, 1.

[91] *Ibid.*, xi. 6, 3, 1; Bṛhadāraṇyaka Upaniṣad, vi. 1, 1-9, 20. 29.

[92] Aitareya Brāhmaṇa, v. 29; Kauṣītaki Brāhmaṇa, ii. 9; Bṛhadāraṇyaka Upaniṣad, iii. 3, 1; 7, 1. *Cf.* Āśvalāyana Gṛhya Sūtra, iii. 4, 4; Sāṅkhāyana Gṛhya Sūtra, iv. 10.

[93] Śatapatha Brāhmaṇa, xiii. 5, 2, 11.

[94] *Ibid.*, iv. 6, 9, 20.

[95] Taittirīya Saṃhitā, ii. 5, 9, 1; Taittirīya Brāhmaṇa, iii. 5, 3, 1; Śatapatha Brāhmaṇa, i. 4, 2, 7; iii. 5, 3, 12. *Cf.* also Bṛhadāraṇyaka Upaniṣad, vi. 4, 29.

8. *The Functions of the Brahmin.*—The Brahmin was required not merely to practise individual culture, but also to give others the advantage of his skill, either as a teacher or as a sacrificial priest, or as a Purohita.

As a teacher the Brahmin has, of course, the special duty of instructing his own son in both study and sacrificial ritual.[96] The texts give examples of this, such as Āruṇi and **Śvetaketu,**[97] or mythically Varuṇa and Bhṛgu.[98] This fact also appears from some of the names in the Vaṃśa Brāhmaṇa[99] of the Sāmaveda and the Vaṃśa (list of teachers) of the Śāṅkhāyana Āraṇyaka.[100] On the other hand, these Vaṃśas and the Vaṃśas of the Śatapatha Brāhmaṇa show that a father often preferred to let his son study under a famous teacher. The relation of pupil and teacher is described under **Brahmacarya.** A teacher might take several pupils,[101] and he was bound to teach them with all his heart and soul.[102] He was bound to reveal everything to his pupil, at any rate to one who was staying with him for a year (*saṃvatsara-vāsin*),[103] an expression which shows, as was natural, that a pupil might easily change teachers. But, nevertheless, certain cases of learning kept secret and only revealed to special persons are enumerated.[104] The exact times and modes of teaching are elaborately laid down in the Sūtras,[105] but not in the earlier texts.

As priest the Brahmin operated in all the greater sacrifices; the simple domestic (*gṛhya*) rites could normally be performed without his help, but not the more important rites (*śrauta*).

[96] Śatapatha Brāhmaṇa, i. 6, 2, 4.

[97] Bṛhadāraṇyaka Upaniṣad, vi. 1, 1 (Mādhyaṃdina = vi. 2, 1 Kāṇva).

[98] Śatapatha Brāhmaṇa, xi. 6, 1, 1.

[99] *Indische Studien*, 4, 376.

[100] xv. 1.

[101] Taittirīya Āraṇyaka, vii. 3.

[102] See Taittirīya Āraṇyaka, vii. 4 (*Indische Studien*, 2, 211).

[103] Śatapatha Brāhmaṇa, xiv. 1, 1, 26. 27. *Cf.* Aitareya Āraṇyaka, v. 3, 3.

[104] So the Vasiṣṭhas and the Stomabhāgas, Pañcaviṃśa Brāhmaṇa, xv. 5, 24; Taittirīya Brāhmaṇa, iii. 5, 2. 1; Kāṭhaka Saṃhitā, xxxvii. 17; Pravāhaṇa Jaivali and his knowledge of Brahman, Bṛhadāraṇyaka Upaniṣad, vi. 1, 11; Chāndogya Upaniṣad, v. 3, where the claim is made that the *praśāsana* belongs to the Kṣatriyas. Śaṅkara, in his commentary, takes the word to mean the 'giving of instruction,' but this must be regarded as improbable, 'rule' being more probably the sense. *Cf.* Weber, *Indische Studien*, 10, 128; Böhtlingk, Translation of the Bṛhadāraṇyaka Upaniṣad, iii. 8, 9.

[105] Rigveda Prātiśākhya, xv. 1 *et seq.*; Aitareya Āraṇyaka, v. 3, 3; and see Weber, *op. cit.*, 10, 129-135.

The number varied : the ritual literature requires sixteen priests to be employed at the greatest sacrifices (see **Ṛtvij**), but other rites could be accomplished with four,[106] five,[107] six,[108] seven,[109] or ten[110] priests. Again, the Kauṣītakins[111] had a seventeenth priest beside the usual sixteen, the Sadasya, so called because he watched the performance from the Sadas, 'seat.' In one rite, the Sattra ('sacrificial session') of the serpents, the Pañcaviṃśa Brāhmaṇa,[112] adds three more to the sixteen, a second Unnetṛ, an Abhigara, and an Apagara. The later ritual places the Brahman at the head of all the priests, but this is probably not the early view (see **Brahman**).

The sacrifice ensured, if properly performed, primarily the advantages of the sacrificer (*yajamāna*),[113] but the priest shared in the profit, besides securing the **Dakṣiṇās.** Disputes between sacrificers and the priests were not rare, as in the case of **Viśvantara** and the **Śyāparṇas,**[114] or **Janamejaya** and the **Asitamṛgas**;[115] and the **Aiṣāvīras** are referred to as undesirable priests.[116] Moreover, **Viśvāmitra** once held the post of Purohita to **Sudās,** but gave place to **Vasiṣṭha.**

106 Taittirīya Brāhmaṇa, ii. 3, 6, 1-4; Pañcaviṃśa Brāhmaṇa, xxv. 4, 2. The four are the Hotṛ, Adhvaryu, Agnīdh, and Upavaktṛ: Weber, 10, 139, n. 4.

107 Kāṭhaka Saṃhitā, ix. 13; Pañcaviṃśa Brāhmaṇa, xxv. 4, 2, with a second Adhvaryu, as well as the four enumerated in the previous note.

108 Kāṭhaka Saṃhitā, ix. 13; Taittirīya Brāhmaṇa, ii. 2, 2, 3; Taittirīya Āraṇyaka, iii. 4, 6; Satapatha Brāhmaṇa, xi. 7, 2, 6, where the list has Adhvaryu, Hotṛ, Brahman, with the Pratiprasthātṛ, Maitrāvaruṇa, Āgnīdhra.

109 Kāṭhaka Saṃhitā, ix. 13; Taittirīya Brāhmaṇa, ii. 2, 2, 5; Taittirīya Āraṇyaka, iii. 5; Pañcaviṃśa Brāhmaṇa, xxv. 4, 2. The number seems to be made up of the five of note 107 and the Abhigarau—*i.e.*, probably the Abhigara and the Apagara.

110 Kāṭhaka Saṃhita, ix. 8. 13-16; Taittirīya Brāhmaṇa, ii. 2, 4, 1; 3, 6, 4; Taittirīya Āraṇyaka, iii. 1; Aitareya Brāhmaṇa, v. 25; Pañcaviṃśa Brāhmaṇa, xxv. 4, 2. What ten are meant is uncertain; the four of note 106 are enumerated.

111 *Cf.* Śatapatha Brāhmaṇa, x. 4, 2, 19; Keith, *Aitareya Āraṇyaka*, 37.

112 xxv. 14, 3.

113 Śatapatha Brāhmaṇa, i. 6, 1, 20; 9, 1, 12; ii. 2, 2, 7; iii. 4, 2, 15; iv. 2, 5, 9. 10; viii. 5, 3, 8; ix. 5, 2, 16; xii. 8, 1, 17, etc.

114 Aitareya Brāhmaṇa, vii. 27 *et seq.*; Muir, *Sanskrit Texts*, 5, 436 *et seq.*

115 Aitareya Brāhmaṇa, vii. 27.

116 *Cf.* Śatapatha Brāhmaṇa, xi. 2, 7, 32, where Weber, *Indische Studien*, 10, 153, n. 1, interprets Aiṣāvīra, not as a proper name, but as meaning 'contemptible'; but Sāyaṇa thinks a proper name is meant, a view accepted by Eggeling, *Sacred Books of the East*, 44, 45, n. 2.

The position of **Purohita** differed considerably from that of the ordinary priest, for the Purohita not merely might officiate at the sacrifice, but was the officiator in all the private sacrifices of his king. Hence he could, and undoubtedly sometimes did, obtain great influence over his master in matters of secular importance; and the power of the priesthood in political as opposed to domestic and religious matters, no doubt rested on the Purohita.

There is no recognition in Vedic literature of the rule later prevailing by which, after spending part of his life as a Brahmacārin, and part as a householder, the Brahmin became an ascetic[117] (later divided into the two stages of Vānaprastha, 'forest-dweller,' and Saṃnyāsin, 'mystic'). Yājñavalkya's case[118] shows that study of the Absolute might empty life of all its content for the sage, and drive him to abandon wife and family. In Buddhist times the same phenomenon is seen[119] applying to other than Brahmins. The Buddhist texts are here confirmed in some degree by the Greek authorities.[120] The practice bears a certain resemblance to the habit of kings, in the Epic tradition,[121] of retiring to the forest when active life is over.

From the Greek authorities[122] it also appears—what is certainly the case in the Buddhist literature[123]—that Brahmins practised the most diverse occupations. It is difficult to say how far this was true for the Vedic period. The analogy of the Druids[124]—in some respects very close—suggests that the Brahmins may have been mainly confined to their professional tasks, including all the learned professions such as astronomy[125]

[117] See Deussen, *Philosophy of the Upanishads*, 372 *et seq*.

[118] Bṛhadāraṇyaka Upaniṣad, ii. 4, 1; iv. 5, 1. See iii. 5, 1, for his teaching, of which his action is a logical consequence.

[119] Fick, *Die sociale Gliederung*, 40 *et seq*.; Oldenberg, *Buddha*,[5] 72 *et seq*.

[120] Arrian, *Indica*, xii. 8. 9; Strabo, xv. 1, 49. 60.

[121] Hopkins, *Journal of the American Oriental Society*, 13, 179 *et seq*.

[122] See Fick, *loc. cit*.

[123] Rhys Davids, *Buddhist India*, 57.

[124] Cæsar, *Bellum Gallicum*, vi. 14. The Druids did not fight, did not pay tribute, studied for many years, observed secrecy as to matters of ritual and learning, did not use writing, and had a certain belief in transmigration. *Cf*. Weber, *Indische Studien*, 5, 19.

[125] Hence the Brahman is the 28th **Nakṣatra**: Taittirīya Brāhmaṇa, i. 5, 3, 3; Weber, *Naxatra*, 2, 306, 311; *Indische Studien*, 10, 40.

and so forth. This is not contradicted by any Vedic evidence; for instance, the poet of a hymn of the Rigveda[126] says he is a poet, his father a physician (**Bhiṣaj**), and his mother a grinder of corn (**Upala-prakṣiṇī**). This would seem to show that a Brahmin could be a doctor, while his wife would perform the ordinary household duties. So a Purohita could perhaps take the field to assist the king by prayer, as Viśvāmitra,[127] and later on Vasiṣṭha[128] do, but this does not show that priests normally fought. Nor do they seem normally to have been agriculturists or merchants. On the other hand, they kept cattle: a Brahmacārin's duty was to watch his master's cattle.[129] It is therefore needless to suppose that they could not, and did not, on occasion turn to agricultural or mercantile pursuits, as they certainly did later. But it must be remembered that in all probability there was more purity of blood, and less pressure of life, among the Brahmins of the Vedic age than later in Buddhist times, when the Vedic sacrificial apparatus was falling into grave disrepute.

It is clear that the Brahmins, whatever their defects, represented the intellectual side of Vedic life, and that the Kṣatriyas, if they played a part in that life, did so only in a secondary degree, and to a minor extent. It is natural to suppose that the Brahmins also composed ballads, the precursors of the epic; for though none such have survived, a few stanzas of this character, celebrating the generosity of patrons, have been preserved by being embedded in priestly compositions. A legend in the Śatapatha Brāhmaṇa[130] shows clearly that the Brahmins regarded civilization as being spread by them only:

[126] ix. 112.

[127] Rv. iii. 33. 53.

[128] Rv. vii. 18.

[129] Chāndogya Upaniṣad, iv. 4, 5; Aitareya Āraṇyaka, iii. 1, 6.

[130] i. 4, 1, 14-17. *Cf.* Weber, *Indische Studien*, 9, 257, 277, 278, and Aitareya Brāhmaṇa, iii. 44.

Almost all that can be said of the Brahmins is collected in Weber's *Indische Studien*, 10, 40-158. *Cf.* also Ludwig, Translation of the Rigveda, 3, 220-226; Fick, *Die sociale Gliederung* (for Buddhist times; the evidence is, however, of uncertain, and much of it probably of late, date); Hopkins, *Journal of the American Oriental Society*, 13, 82, 182, etc. (for notices of the Brahmins in the Epic); *The Mutual Relations of the Four Castes according to the Mānavadharmaçāstram* (for the Dharma view). Muir, *Sanskrit Texts*, 1^2, 248 *et seq.*, discusses the priesthood in the Rigveda, and Zimmer, *Altindisches Leben*, 197-212, gives an excellent summary of the facts.

Kosala and **Videha,** no doubt settled by Āryan tribes, are only rendered civilized and habitable by the influence of pious Brahmins. We need not doubt that the non-Brahminical tribes (see **Vrātya**) had attained intellectual as well as material civilization, but it is reasonable to assume that their civilization was inferior to that of the Brahmins, for the history of Hinduism is the conquest by the Brahmins—not by arms, but by mind—of the tribes Āryan and non-Āryan originally beyond the pale.

2. **Brāhmaṇa,** 'religious explanation,'[1] is the title of a class of books which as such are only mentioned in the Nirukta[2] and the Taittirīya Āraṇyaka,[3] and then in the Sūtras, where the names of the Brāhmaṇas occur, showing that literary works were in existence.

[1] Aitareya Brāhmaṇa, i. 25, 15; iii. 45, 8; vi. 25, 1, etc.; Taittirīya Saṃhitā, iii. 1, 9, 5; 5, 2, 1; Śatapatha Brāhmaṇa, iii. 2, 4, 1, etc. In the Kauṣītaki Brāhmaṇa and the Śāṅkhāyana Āraṇyaka, i. and ii., the use is constant.

[2] ii. 16; xiii. 7.

[3] ii. 10.

3. **Brāhmaṇa** is taken by Roth in the St. Petersburg Dictionary[1] to mean the 'Soma cup of the Brahman' in two passages of the Rigveda[2] and one of the Atharvaveda.[3]

[1] *Cf.* Muir, *Sanskrit Texts*, 1[2], 253, n. 26.

[2] i. 15, 5; ii. 36, 5.

[3] xx. 2, 3.

Brāhmaṇāc-chaṃsin ('reciting after the Brāhmaṇa—*i.e.*, Brahman') is the name of a priest in the Brāhmaṇas.[1] In the technical division of the sacrificial priests (**Ṛtvij**) he is classed with the Brahman,[2] but it is clear that he was really a Hotraka or assistant of the Hotṛ.[3] According to Oldenberg,[4] he was known to the Rigveda as **Brahman.** This is denied by Geldner,[5] who sees in Brahman merely the 'superintending priest' or the 'priest.'

[1] Aitareya Brāhmaṇa, vi. 4, 2; 6, 3. 4; 10, 1; 18, 5; vii. 1, 2; Kauṣītaki Brāhmaṇa, xxviii. 3; Taittirīya Brāhmaṇa, i. 7, 6, 1; Śatapatha Brāhmaṇa, iv. 2, 3, 13, etc.

[2] Weber, *Indische Studien*, 10, 144.

[3] *E.g.*, Āśvalāyana Srauta Sūtra, v. 10, 10; Weber, *op. cit.*, 9, 374-376.

[4] *Religion des Veda*, 396.

[5] *Vedische Studien*, 2, 145 *et seq.* *Cf.* **Purohita.**

Bleṣka in the Kāṭhaka Saṃhitā[1] denotes a rope or noose for strangling. It is spelt Vleṣka in the Maitrāyaṇī Saṃhitā.[2]

[1] xxiii. 6; xxxvii. 13. 14.
[2] iii. 6, 10. In Āpastamba Śrauta Sūtra, x. 19, 1, *meṣka* is read.

BH.

Bhaga denotes a part of the chariot in one passage of the Rigveda[1] according to Hillebrandt.[2]

[1] ii. 34, 8.
[2] *Vedische Mythologie*, 3, 95.

Bhaginī, 'sister,' literally the 'fortunate one' in so far as she has a brother, occurs in the Nirukta (iii. 6).

Bhagī-ratha Aikṣvāka (' descendant of **Ikṣvāku**') is the name of a king in the Jaiminīya Upaniṣad Brāhmaṇa (iv. 6, 1. 2). It is important to note that he is regarded as being on friendly terms with the **Kuru-Pañcālas**, which points to the Ikṣvākus being allied to that people, and not belonging (as is the case in the Buddhist books) to the east of India.

Bhaṅga, 'hemp,' is mentioned in the Atharvaveda.[1] In the Rigveda[2] it is an epithet of Soma, presumably[3] in the sense of 'intoxicating,' which then came to designate hemp.[4]

[1] xi. 6, 15; conceivably in Śāṅkhāyana Āraṇyaka, xii. 14, but not probably.
[2] ix. 61, 13.
[3] Schrader, *Prehistoric Antiquities*, 299.
[4] Hence the modern 'Bang' or 'Bhang,' an intoxicant made from the dried leaves and small stalks of hemp, taken either by smoking or by eating when mixed up into a sweetmeat.

Cf. Zimmer, *Altindisches Leben*, 68; Grierson, *Indian Antiquary*, 23, 260; Yule and Burnell, *Hobson-Jobson*, *s.v.* *Bang*.

Bhaṅgāśvina is the name of the father of **Rtuparna** in the Baudhāyana Śrauta Sūtra.[1] In the Mahābhārata[2] he is called Bhāṅgāsuri. In the Āpastamba Śrauta Sūtra[3] mention is made of Ṛtuparṇa-Kayovadhī as the Bhaṅgyaśvinau.

[1] xx. 12.
[2] iii. 2745.
[3] xxi. 20; Caland, *Zeitschrift der Deutschen Morgenländischen Gesellschaft*, 57, 745.

Bhaṅgya-śravas is the name of a man in the Taittirīya Āraṇyaka.[1]

[1] Weber, *Indische Studien*, 1, 78.

Bhaje-ratha is mentioned in one passage of the Rigveda,[1] where Ludwig[2] thinks a place-name is meant. Griffith[3] is doubtful whether the word is the name of a place or a man. Roth[4] was inclined to see a corruption of the text.[5] *Cf.* **Bhagīratha.**

[1] x. 60, 2.

[2] Translation of the Rigveda, 3, 138, 165.

[3] *Hymns of the Rigveda*, 2, 463.

[4] St. Petersburg Dictionary, *s.v.*

[5] Grassmann, *Wörterbuch*, *s.v.*, thinks that the compound should be read as two words: *bhaje rathasya* (*satpatim*), 'to win (the lord) of the car.'

Bhadra-padā. See **Nakṣatra.**

Bhadra-sena Ājātaśatrava ('descendant of **Ajātaśatru**') is the name of a man, presumably a prince, whom **Uddālaka** is said in the Śatapatha Brāhmaṇa (v. 5, 5, 14) to have bewitched.

Bhaya-da Āsamātya ('descendant of **Asamāti**') is the name of a king in the Jaiminīya Upaniṣad Brāhmaṇa.[1] Oertel,[2] however, seems to take the name as Abhayada, but this is not probable, for Bhayada is a name in the Purāṇas.

[1] iv. 8, 7.

[2] *Journal of the American Oriental Society*, 16, 247.

Bhayamāna is, according to Sāyaṇa, the name of a man in one hymn of the Rigveda,[1] which is ascribed by the Anukramaṇī (Index) to his authorship. The interpretation is, however, uncertain.

[1] i. 100, 17. *Cf.* Muir, *Sanskrit Texts*, 1^2, 266.

Bharata is the name of a people of great importance in the Rigveda and the later literature. In the Rigveda they appear prominently in the third and seventh Maṇḍalas in connexion with **Sudās** and the **Tṛtsus,**[1] while in the sixth Maṇḍala they are associated with **Divodāsa.**[2] In one passage[3] the Bharatas are, like the Tṛtsus, enemies of the **Pūrus**: there can be little doubt that Ludwig's view of the identity of the Bharatas and and Tṛtsus is practically correct. More precisely Oldenberg[5] considers that the Tṛtsus are the **Vasiṣṭhas,** the family singers of the Bharatas; while Geldner[6] recognizes, with perhaps more probability, in the Tṛtsus the royal family of the Bharatas. That the Tṛtsus and Bharatas were enemies, as Zimmer[7] holds, is most improbable even on geographical grounds, for the Tṛtsus in Zimmer's view[8] occupied the country to the east of the **Paruṣṇī** (Ravi), and the Bharatas must therefore be regarded as coming against the Tṛtsus from the west, whereas the Rigveda[9] recognizes two Bharata chiefs on the **Sarasvatī, Āpayā,** and **Dṛṣadvatī**—that is, in the holy land of India, the **Madhyadeśa.** Hillebrandt[10] sees in the connexion of the Tṛtsus and the Bharatas a fusion of two tribes; but this is not supported by any evidence beyond the fact that in his opinion some such theory is needed to explain Divodāsa's appearing in connexion with the **Bharadvāja** family, while Sudās, his son,

iii. 53, 9. 12. 24; 33, 11. 12 (Viśvā mitra, who is accordingly hailed as *Bharata-ṛṣabha*, 'bull of the Bharatas,' in the Aitareya Brāhmaṇa, vii. 17, 7); vii. 8, 4; 33, 6, in which passage a defeat of the Bharatas, and their rescue by the aid of Vasiṣṭha, is clearly referred to; not, as was formerly thought (*e.g.*, Muir, *Sanskrit Texts*, 1², 354; Zimmer, *Altindisches Leben*, 127), a defeat of the Bharatas by the Tṛtsus.

[2] vi. 16, 4. 5. *Cf.* verse 19.

[3] vii. 8, 4.

[4] Translation of the Rigveda, 3, 172 *et seq.*

[5] *Zeitschrift der Deutschen Morgenländischen Gesellschaft*, 42, 207. In *Buddha*, 405 *et seq.*, he accepted the identification of Ludwig.

[6] *Vedische Studien*, 2, 136 *et seq.*

[7] *Altindisches Leben*, 127. This is also Bloomfield's view (see *Journal of the American Oriental Society*, 16, 41, 42).

[8] *Op. cit.*, 124.

[9] iii. 23, 4: in verse 2 **Devaśravas** and **Devavāta** are mentioned as Bhāratas. Oldenberg, *Buddha*, 410, n., mentions that in the Mahābhārata, iii. 6065, a tributary of the Sarasvatī is called Kauśikī, and the Kuśikas are, of course, the family of Viśvāmitra, whose connexion with the Bharatas is beyond question.

[10] *Vedische Mythologie*, 1, 111. His view is that Sudās and the Bharatas were later comers than the Tṛtsus, who joined them as one people, the Vasiṣṭhas becoming the priests of the Bharatas. He suggests that the Vasiṣṭhas were not originally adherents of the Indra-Soma cult, but were specially devoted to the Varuṇa cult; but there is no decisive evidence for either suggestion. *Cf.* Bloomfield, as cited in n. 7.

or perhaps grandson (*cf.* **Pijavana**), is connected with the Vasiṣṭhas and the **Viśvāmitras.**

In the later literature the Bharatas appear as especially famous. The Śatapatha Brāhmaṇa[11] mentions Bharata Dauḥṣanti as a king, sacrificer of the Aśvamedha ('horse sacrifice') and **Śatānīka Sātrājita,** as another Bharata who offered that sacrifice. The Aitareya Brāhmaṇa[12] mentions Bharata Dauḥṣanti as receiving the kingly coronation from **Dīrghatamas Māmateya,** and Śatānīka as being consecrated by **Somaśuṣman Vājaratnāyana,** a priest whose name is of quite late origin. The geographical position of the Bharata people is clearly shown by the fact that the Bharata kings win victories over the **Kāśis,** and make offerings on the **Yamunā** (Jumna) and **Gaṅgā** (Ganges).[13] Moreover, in the formula of the king's proclamation for the people, the variants recorded[14] include *Kuravaḥ, Pañcālāḥ, Kuru-Pañcālāḥ,* and *Bharatāḥ;* and the Mahābhārata consistently recognizes the royal family of the **Kurus** as a Bharata family.[15] It is therefore extremely probable that Oldenberg[16] is right in holding that the Bharatas in the times of the Brāhmaṇas were merging in the Kuru-Pañcāla people.

The ritual practices of the Bharatas are repeatedly mentioned in the Pañcaviṃśa Brāhmaṇa,[17] the Aitareya Brāhmaṇa,[18] the

11 xiii. 5, 4. 12 viii. 23 and 21.

13 Śatapatha Brāhmaṇa, xiii. 5, 4, 11. 21.

14 In the Taittirīya Saṃhitā, i. 8, 10, 2, and the Taittirīya Brāhmaṇa, i. 7, 4, 2, the phrase is *eṣa vo, Bharatā, rājā;* the Vājasaneyi Saṃhitā, in the Kāṇva recension, xi. 3, 3; 6, 3, has *Kuravaḥ, Pañcālāḥ* (evidently as a joint people); Āpastamba, xviii. 12, 7, gives *Bharatāḥ, Kuravaḥ, Pañcālāḥ, Kuru-Pañcālāḥ,* and *janatāḥ,* as alternatives, according to the people to whom the king belongs; the Kāṭhaka Saṃhitā, xv. 7, and the Maitrāyaṇī Saṃhitā, ii. 6, 7, read *esa te janate rājā*. See Weber, *Indian Literature,* 114, n.; von Schroeder, *Indiens Literatur und Cultur,* 465.

15 Oldenberg, *Buddha,* 409.

16 *Op. cit.,* 408. He points out (409, n.) that in the Satapatha Brāhmaṇa, xiii. 5, 4, only the Kuru king, **Janamejaya,** and the Bharata kings are mentioned without specification of the peoples over whom they ruled.

17 xiv. 3, 13; xv. 5, 24, and perhaps xviii. 10, 8, on which see Weber, *Indische Studien,* 10, 28, n. 2; below, p. 98.

18 ii. 25; iii. 18. The sense 'mercenary soldier,' here seen by the St. Petersburg Dictionary, *s.v.* 2 (no longer mentioned in the Dictionary of Böhtlingk), cannot be accepted. See Weber, *Indische Studien,* 9, 254; Oldenberg, *Buddha,* 407, n. On the other hand, there is no mention of the Bharatas in the geographical lists of the Aitareya Brāhmaṇa (viii. 14), in the Mānava Dharma Śāstra, or in the Buddhist texts. This means that the Bharatas were no longer a people, but a family or sub-tribe in a larger people.

Śatapatha Brāhmaṇa,[19] and the Taittirīya Āraṇyaka.[20] Already in the Rigveda[21] there is mention made of Agni Bhārata ('of the Bharatas'). In the Āprī hymns[22] occurs a goddess Bhāratī, the personified divine protective power of the Bharatas: her association in the hymns with Sarasvatī reflects the connexion of the Bharatas with the Sarasvatī in the Rigveda.[9] Again, in the Śatapatha Brāhmaṇa[23] Agni is referred to as *brāhmaṇa Bhārata*, 'priest of the Bharatas,' and is invited to dispose of the offering *Manuṣvat Bharatavat*, 'like Manu,' 'like Bharata.'[24]

In one or two passages[25] Sudās or Divodāsa and, on the other hand, Purukutsa or Trasadasyu appear in a friendly relation. Possibly this points, as Oldenberg[26] suggests, to the union of Bharatas and Pūrus with the Kurus.

A Bharata is referred to in the fifth Maṇḍala of the Rigveda:[27] who he was is uncertain.

19 v. 4, 4, 1.

20 i. 27, 2.

21 ii. 7, 1. 5; iv. 25, 4; vi. 16, 19; Taittirīya Saṃhitā, ii. 5, 9, 1; Śatapatha Brāhmaṇa, i. 4. 2, 2. Roth thinks this epithet of Agni perhaps means 'warlike,' but this is unlikely.

22 Rv. i. 22, 10; 142, 9; 188, 8; ii. 1, 11; 3, 8; iii. 4, 8, etc.

23 i. 4, 2, 2.

24 i. 5, 1, 7.

25 i. 112, 14; vii. 19, 8.

26 *Op. cit.*, 410.

27 v. 54, 14.

For a later legend of Bharata, *cf.* Leumann, *Zeitschrift der Deutschen Morgenländischen Gesellschaft*, 48, 80 *et seq.*; von Bradke, *ibid.*, 498-503; and see Muir, *Sanskrit Texts*, 1[2], 338, 340, etc.

Bharad-vāja is the name of the reputed[1] author of the sixth Maṇḍala of the Rigveda The attribution is so far correct that Bharadvāja[2] and the Bharadvājas[3] are repeatedly mentioned as singers in that Maṇḍala. Judging by the tone of the references to Bharadvāja, he can hardly be deemed to have been a contemporary of any of the hymns.[4] According to the Pañcaviṃśa

1 *Cf.* Āśvalāyana Gṛhya Sūtra, iii. 4, 2; Śāṅkhāyana Gṛhya Sūtra, iv. 10; Bṛhaddevatā, v. 102 *et seq.*, where he is said to be a son of Bṛhaspati, and a grandson of Aṅgiras (*cf.* Rv. vi. 2, 10; 11, 3, etc.); Arnold, *Vedic Metre*, 61, 62.

2 Rv. vi. 15, 3; 16, 5. 33; 17, 4; 31, 4; 48, 7, 13; 63, 10; 65, 6. See also Rv. i. 112, 13; 116, 18; x. 150, 5; 181, 2.

3 Rv. vi. 10, 6; 16, 33; 17, 14; 23, 10; 25, 9; 35, 4; 47, 25; 50, 15. See also Rv. i. 59, 7.

4 Oldenberg, *Zeitschrift der Deutschen Morgenländischen Gesellschaft*, 42, 210-212.

Brāhmaṇa,[5] he was the Purohita of **Divodāsa.** This interpretation is to be preferred to that of Roth,[6] who suggests that he and Divodāsa were identical. His connexion with the house of Divodāsa also appears from the statement of the Kāṭhaka Saṃhitā[7] that Bharadvāja gave **Pratardana** the kingdom. It is unnecessary to suppose that the same Bharadvāja was meant in both cases, and that Pratardana was a son of Divodāsa: the later Saṃhitās refer to Bharadvāja, like the other great sages, irrespective of chronology.

The Bharadvājas in their poems mention **Bṛbu, Bṛsaya,** and the **Pārāvatas.**[8] Hillebrandt[9] has pointed out that they are also connected with the **Sṛñjayas.** In particular, the Śāṅkhāyana Śrauta Sūtra[10] mentions that Bharadvāja gained largesse from **Prastoka Sārñjaya** and Bṛbu. But it is very doubtful if it is correct to place all these people and Divodāsa in Arachosia and Drangiana.

Bharadvāja as an author and a seer is frequently referred to in the later Saṃhitās[11] and the Brāhmaṇas.[12]

[5] xv. 3, 7.

[6] St. Petersburg Dictionary, *s.v.* See Rv. i. 116, 18; vi. 16, 5; 31, 4.

[7] xxi. 10 (*Indische Studien*, 3, 478).

[8] vi. 61, 1-3.

[9] *Vedische Mythologie*, 1, 104.

[10] xvi. 11, 11.

[11] Av. ii. 12, 2; iv. 29, 5; xviii. 3, 16; xix. 48, 6; Kāṭhaka Saṃhitā, xvi. 19; xx. 9; Maitrāyaṇī Saṃhitā, ii. 7, 19; iv. 8, 4; Vājasaneyi Saṃhitā, xiii. 55, etc.

[12] Aitareya Brāhmaṇa, vi. 18; viii. 3; Taittirīya Brāhmaṇa, iii. 10, 11, 13; Aitareya Āraṇyaka, i. 2, 2; 4, 2; ii. 2, 2. 4, etc.; Kauṣītaki Brāhmaṇa, xv. 1; xxix. 3; xxx. 9.

Cf. Ludwig, Translation of the Rigveda, 3, 128; Weber, *Episches im vedischen Ritual*, 31.

Bharant, 'bearing,' in the plural denotes in one passage of the Pañcaviṃśa Brāhmaṇa,[1] according to Böhtlingk,[2] following Sāyaṇa, 'the warrior caste,' but the sense is not certain. Weber[3] was inclined to see a reference to the Bharatas, though the form of the word is that of the present participle.[4]

[1] xviii. 10, 8.

[2] Dictionary, *s.v.*

[3] *Indische Studien*, 10, 28, n. 2. *Cf.* **Bharata**, n. 17.

[4] *Bharatām*, interpreted by Sāyaṇa as *bharaṇaṃ kurvatāṃ kṣatriyāṇām*.

Bharūjī in one passage of the Atharvaveda[1] may denote, according to Roth,[2] a noxious animal.

[1] ii. 24, 8.

[2] St. Petersburg Dictionary, *s.v.*

Bhartṛ, besides having the literal sense of 'bearer,' means 'supporter' or 'master' in the older literature[1]; but it is doubtful whether the sense of 'husband' is ever found there. In one passage of the Rigveda[2] 'husband' is certainly the most natural sense, but, as Delbrück[3] correctly remarks, even there 'father' may be meant, since 'mother' is here and there[4] called Bhartrī.

[1] Av. xi. 7, 15; xviii. 2, 30; Śatapatha Brāhmaṇa, ii. 3, 4, 7 (where 'husband' is possible); iv. 6, 7, 21, etc.

[2] v. 58, 7.

[3] *Die indogermanischen Verwandtschaftsnamen*, 415, n. 1.

[4] Av. v. 5, 2; Taittirīya Brāhmaṇa, iii. 1, 1, 4.

Bhalānas, plural, is the name in the Rigveda[1] of one of the five tribes, **Pakthas**, Bhalānases, **Alinas**, **Viṣāṇins**, and **Śivas**, who are mentioned as ranged on the side[2] of the enemies of **Sudās** in the battle of the ten kings (**Dāśarājña**), not opposed to them, as Roth,[3] and at one time Zimmer,[4] thought. Zimmer[5] suggests as their original home East Kabulistan, comparing the name of the Bolan pass. This seems a reasonably probable view.

[1] vii. 18, 7.

[2] Hopkins, *Journal of the American Oriental Society*, 15, 260, 261, who takes the form of the name to be Bhalāna (but the text of the Rv. has *bhalānásaḥ*), and who overlooks Zimmer's later view.

[3] *Zur Litteratur und Geschichte des Weda*, 95.

[4] Zimmer, *Altindisches Leben*, 126.

[5] *Op. cit.*, 431. *Cf.* Ludwig, Translation of the Rigveda, 3, 173, 207.

Bhava-trāta Śāyasthi is the name of a teacher in the Vaṃśa Brāhmaṇa.[1]

[1] *Indische Studien*, 4, 372; Max Müller, *Ancient Sanskrit Literature*, 443.

Bhastrā in the Śatapatha Brāhmaṇa (i. i, 2, 7; 6, 3, 16) denotes a leathern bottle or pouch.

Bhākuri. See **Bekurā**.

Bhāga-dugha, 'dealer out of portions,' 'distributor,' is the name of one of the king's 'jewels' (**Ratnin**) in the Yajurveda Saṃhitās[1] and Brāhmaṇas.[2] What his functions exactly were is uncertain. Sāyaṇa in some places[3] renders the word by 'tax-collector,' but in others[4] as 'carver,' thus making this functionary either a revenue officer or a mere court official.

[1] Taittirīya Saṃhitā, i. 8, 9 2; Kāṭhaka Saṃhitā, xv. 4; Maitrāyaṇī Saṃhitā, ii. 6, 5; iv. 3, 8; Vājasaneyi Saṃhitā, xxx. 13.

[2] Taittirīya Brāhmaṇa, i. 7, 3, 5; iii. 4, 8, 1; Satapatha Brāhmaṇa, i. 1, 2, 17; v. 3, 1, 9.

[3] On Taittirīya Saṃhitā and Taittirīya Brāhmaṇa, *loc. cit.*, and on Śatapatha Brāhmaṇa, v. 3, 1, 9.

[4] On Śatapatha Brāhmaṇa, i. 1, 2, 17.

Cf. Eggeling, *Sacred Books of the East*, 41, 63, n.

Bhāga-vitti ('descendant of Bhagavitta') is the patronymic of a teacher called Cūḍa[1] or Cūla[2] in the Bṛhadāraṇyaka Upaniṣad.

[1] Bṛhadāraṇyaka Upaniṣad, vi. 3, 17. 18 Mādhyaṃdina.

[2] *Ibid.*, vi. 3, 9 Kāṇva.

Bhāḍitāyana, 'descendant of Bhaḍita,' is the patronymic of **Śākadāsa** in the Vaṃśa Brāhmaṇa.[1]

[1] *Indische Studien*, 4, 373.

Bhānumant Aupamanyava ('descendant of **Upamanyu**') is the name of a teacher, a pupil of **Ānandaja**, in the Vaṃśa Brāhmaṇa.[1]

[1] *Indische Studien*, 4, 372.

Bhāya-jātya, 'descendant of Bhayajāta,' is the patronymic of **Nikothaka** in the Vaṃśa Brāhmaṇa.[1]

[1] *Indische Studien*, 4, 373; Max Müller, *Ancient Sanskrit Literature*, 444.

Bhārata. See **Bharata.**

Bhārad-vāja, 'descendant of **Bharadvāja**,' is the patronymic of many teachers. In the Vaṃśas (lists of teachers) of the Bṛhadāraṇyaka Upaniṣad, Bhāradvājas are mentioned as pupils of Bhāradvāja,[1] **Pārāśarya,**[2] **Balākākauśika,**[3] **Aitareya,**[4] **Āsurāyaṇa,**[5] and **Baijavāpāyana.**[6] A Bhāradvāja occurs in the Rigveda,[7] and **Śūṣa Vāhneya** is mentioned as a Bhāradvāja in the Vaṃśa Brāhmaṇa.[8]

1 ii. 5, 21; iv. 5, 27 (Mādhyaṃdina = ii. 6, 2 Kāṇva).

2 ii. 6, 2 Kāṇva.

3 iv. 5, 27 Mādhyaṃdina.

4 ii. 5, 21; iv. 5, 27 (Mādhyaṃdina = ii. 6, 3; iv. 6, 3 Kāṇva).

5 ii. 5, 21; iv. 5, 27 Mādhyaṃdina.

6 ii. 5, 21; iv. 5, 27 Mādhyaṃdina.

7 v. 61, 2.

8 *Indische Studien*, 4, 373.

Bhāradvājāyana, 'descendant of **Bharadvāja,**' is the patronymic of a teacher in the Pañcaviṃśa Brāhmaṇa.[1]

1 x. 12, 1; Nidāna Sūtra, ix. 9. *Cf.* Hopkins, *Transactions of the Connecticut Academy of Arts and Sciences*, 15, 61, n. 2.

Bhāradvājī-putra, 'son of a female descendant of **Bharadvāja,**' is the metronymic of several teachers in the Bṛhadāraṇyaka Upaniṣad, pupils of **Pārāśarīputra,**[1] **Paingīputra,**[2] and **Vātsīmāṇḍavīputra**[3] respectively.

1 vi. 4, 31 (Mādhyaṃdina = vi. 5, 2 Kāṇva).

2 vi. 4, 30 Mādhyaṃdina.

3 *Ibid.*

Bhārgava, 'descendant of **Bhṛgu,**' is the patronymic of several teachers, including **Cyavana**[1] and **Gṛtsamada.**[2] Other Bhārgavas are also mentioned without indication of their personal names.[3]

1 Śatapatha Brāhmaṇa, iv. 1, 5, 1; Aitareya Brāhmaṇa, viii. 21.

2 Kauṣītaki Brāhmaṇa, xxii. 4 (with a *varia lectio*, Bābhrava).

3 Taittirīya Saṃhitā, i. 8, 18, 1; Sāṅkhāyana Āraṇyaka, vii. 15; Aitareya Brāhmaṇa, viii. 2, 1. 5; Praśna Upaniṣad, i. 1 (Vaidarbhi), etc.; Pañcaviṃśa Brāhmaṇa, xii. 2, 23; 9, 19. 39, etc. *Cf.* Bloomfield, *Hymns of the Atharvaveda*, xxxv.

Bhārgāyaṇa, 'descendant of Bharga,' is the patronymic of **Sutvan** in the Aitareya Brāhmaṇa (viii. 28).

Bhārmy-aśva, 'descendant of Bhṛmyaśva,' is the patronymic of **Mudgala** in the Nirukta (ix. 23) and the Bṛhaddevatā (vi. 46; viii. 12).

Bhāryā, later a common expression for 'wife,' does not occur in that sense at all in the Saṃhitās. It first appears, according to the St. Petersburg Dictionary, in the Aitareya Brāhmaṇa,[1] where, however, Delbrück[2] suggests that merely a member of the household ('who is to be maintained') may be meant. In the Śatapatha Brāhmaṇa,[3] however, the two wives of Yājñavalkya are so designated.

[1] vii. 9. 8.
[2] *Die indogermanischen Verwandtschaftsnamen*, 415. *Cf.* Aitareya Brāhmaṇa, i. 29, 20.
[3] Bṛhadāraṇyaka Upaniṣad, iii. 4, 1; iv. 5, 1.

Bhālandana, 'descendant of Bhalandana,' is the patronymic of **Vatsaprī** in the Taittirīya Saṃhitā,[1] the Kāṭhaka Saṃhitā,[2] and the Pañcaviṃśa Brāhmaṇa.[3]

[1] v. 2, 1, 6.
[2] xix. 11.
[3] xii. 11, 25; Hopkins, *Transactions of the Connecticut Academy of Arts and Sciences*, 15, 59.

Bhālukī-putra, 'son of Bhālukī,' is the name of a teacher, a pupil of **Krauñcikīputra**[1] or of **Prācīnayogīputra**,[2] in the last Vaṃśa (list of teachers) in the Bṛhadāraṇyaka Upaniṣad.

[1] vi. 5, 2 Kāṇva.
[2] vi. 4, 32 Mādhyaṃdina.

Bhālla is the name or patronymic of a teacher who bears the patronymic Prātṛda in the Jaiminīya Upaniṣad Brāhmaṇa (iii. 31, 4).

Bhāllavi is the name of a school mentioned as authorities in the Pañcaviṃśa Brāhmaṇa (ii. 2, 4).

Bhāllavin, 'pupil of Bhallavin,' is the name of a school of teachers mentioned in the Jaiminīya Upaniṣad Brāhmaṇa.[1]

[1] ii. 4, 7 (spelt Bhāllabin). *Cf.* Weber, *Indische Studien*, 1, 44; 2, 100; 390; Nidāna Sūtra, v. 1; Anupada Sūtra, ii. 1; vii. 12; Bṛhaddevatā v. 23. 159.

Bhallaveya, 'descendant of **Bhāllavi,**'[1] is the patronymic of **Indradyumna** in the Śatapatha Brāhmaṇa[1] and the Chāndogya Upaniṣad.[2] Probably the same person is meant by the Bhāllaveya, who is cited frequently as an authority in the same Brāhmaṇa.[3]

1 x. 6, 1, 1.
2 v. 11, 1.
3 i. 7, 3, 19; ii. 1, 4, 6; xiii. 4, 2, 3; 5, 3, 4.

Bhāvayavya. See **Bhāvya.**

Bhāvya is the name of a patron, as it seems, in the Rigveda.[1] In the Śāṅkhāyana Śrauta Sūtra[2] the form given is Bhāvayavya, being a patronymic of **Svanaya,** who is the patron of **Kakṣīvant.** This combination is borne out by the Rigveda, where Kakṣīvant and Svanaya are mentioned in the same verse,[3] while Svanaya must be meant in the verse of the same hymn,[4] where Bhāvya is mentioned as 'living on the Sindhu' (Indus). Roth's[5] view that Bhāvya here is perhaps a gerundive meaning to be 'reverenced' is not probable. Ludwig[6] thinks Svanaya was connected with the **Nahuṣas.**

1 i. 126, 1; Nirukta, ix. 10.
2 xvi. 11, 5. *Cf.* Bṛhaddevatā, iii. 140.
3 i. 126, 3.
4 i. 126, 1.
5 St. Petersburg Dictionary, *s.v.* 1 f.
6 Translation of the Rigveda, 3, 151.
Cf. Weber, *Episches im Vedischen Ritual*, 22; Oldenberg, *Ṛgveda-Noten*, 1, 128.

Bhāṣā in the Nirukta[1] and Pāṇini[2] denotes the ordinary speech of the day as opposed to Vedic language. *Cf.* **Vāc.**

1 i. 4, 5. *Cf.* ii. 2.
2 iii. 2, 108; vi. 1, 181. *Cf.* Franke, Bezzenberger's *Beiträge*, 17, 54 *et seq.*, who distinguishes the Bhāṣā as the speech of conversational use from the language regulated by Pāṇini's rules. But see Wackernagel, *Altindische Grammatik*, 1, xliv; Keith, *Aitareya Āraṇyaka*, 179, 180.

Bhāsa is the name of a bird of prey in the Adbhuta Brāhmaṇa,[1] and often in the Epic.

1 vi. 8. See Weber, *Indische Studien*, 1, 40.

Bhikṣā, 'begging,' is one of the duties of the **Brahmacārin** according to the Śatapatha Brāhmaṇa.[1] The word has also the sense of 'alms,' as that which is obtained by begging, in the Atharvaveda.[2] According to the St. Petersburg Dictionary,[3] it has this sense in the Chāndogya Upaniṣad[4] also, but the correct reading there is probably **Āmikṣā.**

[1] xi. 3, 3, 7. *Cf.* a Mantra in Āśvalāyana Gṛhya Sūtra, i. 9, etc.; and *bhikṣācarya*, Bṛhadāraṇyaka Upaniṣad, iii. 4, 1; iv. 4, 26.

[2] xi. 5, 9.

[3] *s.v.* 2.

[4] viii. 8, 5, where the scholiast explains the word by 'perfumes, garlands, food,' etc. (*gandhamālyānnādi*).

Bhikṣu, 'beggar,' is a term not found in Vedic literature. The begging of the **Brahmacārin** is quite a different thing from the duties of the Bhikṣu in the later system of the Āśramas (religious stages of life), when the Brahmin in the last stage of his life, after leaving his home and family, lives on alms alone. See 1. **Brāhmaṇa.**

Bhitti in the Śatapatha Brāhmaṇa[1] denotes a mat made of split reeds.

[1] iii. 5, 3, 9. *Cf.* Sāṅkhāyana Srauta Sūtra, viii. 3, 24.

Bhiṣaj, 'physician,' is a word of common occurrence in the Rigveda[1] and later.[2] There is no trace whatever in the former text of the profession being held in disrepute: the Aśvins,[3] Varuṇa,[4] and Rudra[5] are all called physicians. On the other hand, in the Dharma literature[6] this profession is utterly

[1] ii. 33, 4; vi. 50, 7; ix. 112, 1; *bheṣaja*, adjective, ii. 33, 7; x. 137, 6; substantive, i. 23, 19. 20; ii. 33, 2. 4; vi. 74, 3; vii. 46, 3, etc.

[2] Av. v. 29, 1; vi. 24, 2; Taittirīya Saṃhitā, vi. 4, 9, 2; Vājasaneyi Saṃhitā, xvi. 5; xix. 12. 88; xxx. 10, etc.; *bheṣaja*, adjective, Av. vi. 109, 3; Vājasaneyi Saṃhitā, xvi. 45, etc.; substantive, Av. v. 29, 1; vi. 21, 2; xi. 1, 9, etc.

[3] Rv. i. 116, 16; 157, 6; viii. 18, 8; 86, 1; x. 39, 3. 5; Av. vii. 53, 1; Aitareya Brāhmaṇa, i. 18.

[4] See Rv. i. 24, 9.

[5] Rv. ii. 33, 4. 7.

[6] See Āpastamba Dharma Sūtra, i. 6, 18, 20; 19, 15; Gautama Dharma Sūtra, xvii. 17; Vasiṣṭha Dharma Sūtra, xiv. 2, 19; Viṣṇu, li. 10; lxxxii. 9; Bloomfield, *Hymns of the Atharvaveda*, l.

despised. This dislike is found as early as the Yajurveda Saṃhitās,[7] where the Aśvins are condemned because of their having to do with the practice of medicine (*bheṣaja*), on the ground that it brings them too much among men, an allusion to the caste dislike of promiscuous contact.

The Rigveda[8] contains a hymn in which a physician celebrates his plants and their healing powers. Moreover, wonderful cures are referred to as performed by the Aśvins: the healing of the lame[9] and of the blind;[10] the rejuvenation of the aged **Cyavana**[11] and of **Puramdhi's** husband;[12] the giving of an iron leg (*jaṅghā āyasī*) to **Viśpalā**,[13] a deed only more wonderful if we assume that Viśpalā was a mare, as has been suggested by Pischel.[14] It would in all probability be a mistake to assume[15] that the Vedic Indians had any surgical skill: they no doubt applied simples to wounds,[16] but both their medicine and their surgery must have been most primitive. All that the Atharvaveda shows in regard to medicine is the use of herbs combined with spells,[17] and of water (*cf.* **Jalāṣa**), remedies Indo-European in character, but not of much scientific value. On the other hand, the knowledge of anatomy shown (see **Śarīra**), though betraying grave inaccuracies, is not altogether insignificant; but that was due no doubt mainly to the practice of dissecting animals at the sacrifice.

There is some evidence in the Rigveda[18] that the practice of medicine was already a profession; this is supported by the inclusion of a physician in the list of victims at the Puruṣamedha ('human sacrifice') in the Yajurveda.[19] According to

[7] Taittirīya Saṃhitā, vi. 4, 9, 3. *Cf.* Maitrāyaṇī Saṃhitā, iv. 6, 2; Śatapatha Brāhmaṇa, iv. 1, 5, 14; Bloomfield, *op. cit.*, xxxix, xl.

[8] x. 97.

[9] Rv. i. 112, 8; x. 39, 3, etc.

[10] *Cf.* the case of **Ṛjrāśva**, Rv. i. 116, 17.

[11] Rv. x. 39, 4.

[12] i. 116, 13.

[13] Rv. i. 116, 15, etc.

[14] *Vedische Studien*, 1, 171 *et seq.*; 305.

[15] As Zimmer, *Altindisches Leben*, 398, is inclined to do.

[16] *Cf.* Rv. ix. 112, 1.

[17] So it is said in the Pañcaviṃśa Brāhmaṇa, xii. 9, 10: *bheṣajaṃ vā Ātharvaṇāni*, 'the Atharvan hymns are medicine'; xvi. 10, 10, and *cf. ibid.*, xxiii. 16, 7; Kāṭhaka Saṃhitā, xi. 5 and 2. **Bhiṣaj**.

[18] ix. 112, where a profession must be meant. *Ibid.*, 3, refers to the fees of the physician. *Cf.* also x. 97, 4. 8.

[19] Vājasaneyi Saṃhitā, xxx. 10; Taittirīya Brāhmaṇa, iii. 4, 4, 1.

Bloomfield,[20] a hymn of the Atharvaveda[21] contains a physician's deprecation of the use of home-made remedies instead of reliance on his professional training.

[20] *Hymns of the Atharvaveda*, 456.

[21] v. 30, 5. But this sense is doubtful. *Cf.* Whitney, Translation of the Atharvaveda, 277.

Cf. Zimmer, *op. cit.*, 397-399; Bloomfield, *op. cit.*, *passim* (see references on p. 697); *Atharvaveda*, 59 *et seq.*; Schrader, *Prehistoric Antiquities*, 420 *et seq.*; Jolly, *Medicin*, 16, 17; Winternitz, *Nature*, 1898, 233-235; Caland, *Altindisches Zauberritual*, *passim*.

2. **Bhiṣaj Ātharvaṇa** is the name of a mythic physician mentioned in the Kāṭhaka Saṃhitā.[1]

[1] xvi. 3 (*Indische Studien*, 3, 459). *Cf.* Bloomfield, *Hymns of the Atharvaveda*, xxi; *Journal of the American Oriental Society*, 17, 181.

Bhīma Vaidarbha ('prince of Vidarbha') is mentioned in the Aitareya Brāhmaṇa (vii. 34) as having received instruction regarding the substitute for the Soma juice, through a succession of teachers, from **Parvata** and **Nārada.**

Bhīma-sena is the name of one of the brothers of **Janamejaya,** the **Pārikṣitīyas,** in the Śatapatha Brāhmaṇa.[1]

[1] xiii. 5, 4, 3. *Cf.* Śāṅkhāyana Srauta Sūtra, xvi. 9, 3.

1. **Bhujyu** denotes, according to the St. Petersburg Dictionary, an 'adder' in two passages of the Rigveda,[1] and one of the Vājasaneyi Saṃhitā.[2] But the sense is uncertain in all these passages.

[1] iv. 27, 4; x. 95, 8.

[2] xviii. 42.

Cf. Geldner, *Rigveda*, *Glossar*, 126, who takes *bhujyu* in Rv. x. 95, 8, as meaning 'ardent,' 'rutting.'

2. **Bhujyu** is the name of a man, son of **Tugra,** who is repeatedly mentioned in the Rigveda[1] as saved from the deep by the Aśvins. According to Bühler,[2] the passages refer to

[1] i. 112, 6. 20; 116, 3; 117, 14; 119, 4; vi. 62, 6; vii. 68, 7; 69, 7; x. 40, 7; 65, 12; 143, 5.

[2] *Indische Palæographie*, 17.

Cf. Baunack, Kuhn's *Zeitschrift*, 35, 485; Oldenberg, *Religion des Veda*, 214; Hillebrandt, *Vedische Mythologie*, 3, 16, n. 5; Muir, *Sanskrit Texts*, 5, 244, 245; Macdonell, *Vedic Mythology*, p. 52.

Bhujyu being saved from shipwreck during a voyage in the Indian Ocean, but the evidence is inadequate to support this conclusion. *Cf.* **Samudra.**

Bhujyu Lāhyāyani ('descendant of Lahyāyana') is the name of a teacher, a contemporary of **Yājñavalkya,** in the Bṛhadāraṇyaka Upaniṣad (iii. 3, 1).

Bhurij (used in the dual only) is a word of somewhat doubtful sense. Roth[1] regarded it as meaning in some passages[2] 'scissors,' and in others[3] an apparatus consisting of two arms used by the chariot-maker for fixing the wood at which he worked, being of the nature of a carpenter's vice. See also **Kṣura.**

[1] St. Petersburg Dictionary, *s.v.* *Cf.* Muir, *Sanskrit Texts*, 5, 466.

[2] Rv. viii. 4, 16; Av. xx. 127, 4.

[3] Rv. iv. 2, 14; ix. 26, 4; 71, 5, where Pischel, *Vedische Studien*, 1, 239-243, considers that the shafts of the chariot are meant (*cf.* Gobhila Gṛhya Sūtra, iii. 4, 31, whence it appears that the chariot-pole, spoken of as having two arms, was forked). The same view regarding the passages cited in n. 2 gives the sense of a stropping apparatus, consisting of two pieces of wood, between which a grindstone moves.

Cf. Zimmer, *Altindisches Leben*, 252, 255.

Bhūta-vidyā is one of the sciences enumerated in the Chāndogya Upaniṣad.[1] It seems to mean the 'science of creatures' that trouble men, and of the means of warding them off, 'demonology.'

[1] vii. 1, 2. 4; 2, 1; 7, 1. *Cf.* Little, *Grammatical Index*, 115.

Bhūta-vīra is the name of a family of priests who, according to the Aitareya Brāhmaṇa,[1] were employed by **Janamejaya** to the exclusion of the **Kaśyapas.** A family of the latter, the **Asitamṛgas,** however, won back the favour of Janamejaya, and ousted the Bhūtavīras.

[1] vii. 27. *Cf.* Roth, *Zur Litteratur und Geschichte des Weda*, 118; Eggeling, *Sacred Books of the East*, 43, 344, n. 3; Muir, *Sanskrit Texts*, 1^2, 437 *et seq.*

Bhūtāṃśa is in the Rigveda[1] the name of a poet, a descendant of Kaśyapa.

[1] x. 106, 11. See Nirukta, xii, 41; Bṛhaddevatā. viii. 18. 19; Ludwig, Translation of the Rigveda, 3, 133.

Bhūti is the term used in the Rigveda[1] and later[2] for 'prosperity.'

[1] viii. 59, 7. *Cf.* i. 161, 1 (both late passages).

[2] Av. ix 6, 45; x. 3, 17; 6, 9; xi. 7, 22; 8, 21; Taittirīya Saṃhitā, ii. 1, 1, 1; 3, 5, etc.; *bhūti-kāma*, 'desiring prosperity,' Taittirīya Saṃhitā, ii. 1, 1, 1; 2, 3, 3; v. 1, 9, 1, etc.

Bhūmi or **Bhūmī** is a common word for 'earth' in the Rigveda[1] and later,[2] being practically a synonym of **Pṛthivī**. It is also used of the land given by the god to the Āryan,[3] and of grants of land.[4]

[1] i. 64, 5; 161, 14; ii. 14, 7, etc. So in x. 18, 10, 'mother earth' receives the remains of the dead.

[2] Av. vi. 2, 1, where it is said that the Bhūmi is the highest of the three earths (Pṛthivī); xi. 7, 14, where nine earths and seas are mentioned; ii. 9, 4; vi. 8, 2, etc.

[3] Rv. iv. 26, 2. *Cf.* vi. 47, 20.

[4] Śatapatha Brāhmaṇa, xiii. 5, 4, 24; 6, 2, 18.

Bhūmi-dundubhi, 'earth drum,' denotes a pit covered with a hide used at the Mahāvrata rite, and mentioned in the Saṃhitās[1] and the Brāhmaṇas.[2]

[1] Taittirīya Saṃhitā, vii. 5, 9, 3; Kāṭhaka Saṃhitā, xxxiv. 5.

[2] Pañcaviṃśa Brāhmaṇa, v. 5, 19; Aitareya Āraṇyaka, v. 1, 5.

Cf. Keith, *Aitareya Āraṇyaka*, 277, n. 14.

Bhūmi-pāśa, 'earth net,' is the name of a plant in the Śatapatha Brāhmaṇa, probably some sort of creeper.

[1] xiii. 8, 1, 16. *Cf.* Eggeling, *Sacred Books of the East*, 44, 427, n. 1.

Bhṛgavāṇa is found in one passage of the Rigveda[1] apparently[2] as a name of a man who is called **Śobha.** Ludwig,[3] however, thinks that his name was **Ghoṣa.** Elsewhere the word appears as an epithet of Agni, doubtless in allusion to his cult by the **Bhṛgus.**

[1] i. 120, 5.

[2] Pischel, *Vedische Studien*, i, 4; 2, 92.

[3] *Über Methode bei Interpretation*, 4.

Bhṛgu is a sage of almost entirely mythical character in the Rigveda and later. He counts as a son of Varuṇa,[1] bearing the patronymic Vāruṇi.[2] In the plural the Bhṛgus are repeatedly[3] alluded to as devoted to the fire cult. They are clearly[4] no more than a group of ancient priests and ancestors with an eponymous Bhṛgu[5] in the Rigveda, except in three passages,[6] where they are evidently regarded as an historic family. It is not clear, however, whether they were priests or warriors: in the battle of the ten kings the Bhṛgus appear with the **Druhyus**, perhaps as their priests, but this is not certain.[7]

In the later literature the Bhṛgus are a real family, with subdivisions like the **Aitaśāyana**, according to the Kauṣītaki Brāhmaṇa.[8] The Bhṛgus are mentioned as priests in connexion with various rites, such as the Agnisthāpana[9] and the Daśapeyakratu.[10] In many passages they are conjoined with the **Aṅgirases**:[11] the close association of the two families is shown

[1] Śatapatha Brāhmaṇa, xi. 6, 1, 1; Taittirīya Āraṇyaka, ix. 1. *Cf.* Pañcaviṃśa Brāhmaṇa, xviii. 9, 2; Nirukta, iii. 17.

[2] Aitareya Brāhmaṇa, iii. 34, and n. 14. For a different form of the legend, *cf.* Taittirīya Brāhmaṇa, i. 8, 2, 5.

[3] Rv. i. 58, 6; 127, 7; 143. 4; ii. 4, 2; iii. 2, 4; iv. 7, 1, etc. See Macdonell, *Vedic Mythology*, 51. The legend of their chariot-making (Rv. iv. 16, 20; x. 39, 14) may be due, as Roth, St. Petersburg Dictionary, *s.v.*, suggests, to a confusion with the Ṛbhus. It may, however, be an allusion to the historic Bhṛgus, whom we find in the battle of the ten kings.

[4] As shown by the legend of fire having been brought to them by Mātariśvan, Rv. iii. 5, 10.

[5] i. 60, 1, where, however, Roth, *loc. cit.*, takes the singular in a collective sense, an interpretation which may be correct, but is not necessary.

[6] Rv. vii. 18, 6; viii. 3, 9; 6, 18, to which list, given by Macdonell, *loc. cit.*, Roth adds viii. 102, 4, *Aurva-Bhṛgu-vat*, 'like Aurva and Bhṛgu.' *Cf.* the fact that the **Aurvas**, in the Aitareya Brāhmaṇa, vi. 33, take the place of the Bhṛgus of the Kauṣītaki Brāhmaṇa, xxx. 5.

[7] In viii. 3, 9; 6, 18; 102, 4, the reference to a priestly family is the more natural; in vii. 18, 6, warriors may be meant. *Cf.* Hopkins, *Journal of the American Oriental Society*, 15, 262, n., where he cites ix. 101, 13, as perhaps denoting the same thing.

[8] xxx. 5. See n. 6.

[9] Taittirīya Saṃhitā, iv. 6, 5, 2; v. 6, 8, 6; Av. iv. 14, 5; Maitrāyaṇī Saṃhitā, i. 4, 1 (p. 48).

[10] Taittirīya Saṃhitā, i. 8, 18; Taittirīya Brāhmaṇa, i. 8, 2, 5; Pañcaviṃśa Brāhmaṇa, xviii. 9, 2.

[11] Taittirīya Saṃhitā, i. 1, 7, 2; Maitrāyaṇī Saṃhitā, i. 1, 8; Vājasaneyi Saṃhitā, i. 18; Taittirīya Brāhmaṇa, i. 1, 4, 8; iii. 2, 7, 6; Śatapatha Brāhmaṇa, i. 2, 1, 13, etc. *Cf.* Rv. viii. 35, 3; 43, 13; x. 14, 6, in the first and last of which passages the Atharvans also occur. See Bloomfield, *Hymns of the Atharvaveda*, xxvii. n. 2. Hence, in the Atharvanic ritual texts, the term *Bhṛgvaṅgirasaḥ* is applied to the Atharvaveda (Bloomfield, *Atharvaveda*, 9, 10, 107 *et seq.*).

by the fact that Cyavana is called either a Bhargava or an Āṅgirasa in the Śatapatha Brāhmaṇa.[12] In the Atharvaveda[13] the name of Bhṛgu is selected to exemplify the dangers incurred by the oppressors of Brahmans: the **Sṛñjaya Vaitahavyas** perish in consequence of an attack on Bhṛgu. In the Aitareya Brāhmaṇa [14] also Bhṛgu has this representative character. *Cf.* **Bhṛgavāṇa** and **Bhārgava.**

12 iv. 1, 5, 1. 13 v. 19, 1.

14 ii. 20. In the Jaiminīya Brāhmaṇa, i. 42-44 (*Journal of the American Oriental Society*, 15, 204), Bhṛgu Vāruṇi appears as a student. *Cf.* Taittirīya Upaniṣad, iii. 1.

Cf. Hillebrandt, *Vedische Mythologie*, 2, 169-173; Ludwig, Translation of the Rigveda, 3, 140; Muir, *Sanskrit Texts*, 1², 443 *et seq.*

Bhṛṅgā is the name of a species of bee, later specified as large and black, in the Atharvaveda[1] and the Yajurveda Saṃhitās,[2] which include it in the list of victims at the Aśvamedha ('horse sacrifice').

1 ix. 2, 22.

2 Maitrāyaṇī Saṃhitā, iii. 14, 8; Vājasaneyi Saṃhitā, xxiv. 29. *Cf.* Zimmer, *Altindisches Leben*, 96.

Bhṛmy-aśva is the name of the father of **Mudgala** in the Nirukta (ix. 24).

Bhekuri. See **Bekurā.**

1. **Bheda,** one of the enemies of **Sudās** and the **Tṛtsu-Bharatas,** was defeated by the former in the **Yamunā** (Jumna),[1] apparently in a second conflict fought after the battle of the ten kings, in which Sudās successfully defended his western frontier against the confederate foes. The **Ajas, Śigrus,** and **Yakṣus,** who are mentioned as also defeated, may have been united under his leadership if he was a king; or the Bhedas may have been a separate people, as Roth[2] thinks. Hopkins'[3] opinion that the defeat was on the **Paruṣṇī,** Yamunā being another

1 Rv. vii. 18, 18. 19; 33, 3; 83, 4.

2 St. Petersburg Dictionary, *s.v.* 12 (the word is always used in the singular).

3 *India, Old and New*, 52.

name of that stream, is most improbable; nor is the view that Bheda was one of the ten kings essential.[4] *Cf.* **Turvaśa.**

[4] Hopkins, *Journal of the American Oriental Society*, 15, 260 *et seq.*
Cf. Griffith, *Hymns of the Rigveda*, 2, 20, n.; Zimmer, *Altindisches Leben*, 126; Muir, *Sanskrit Texts*, 1[2], 319, 327.

2. **Bheda** is mentioned in the Atharvaveda[1] as having come to a bad end because he refused a cow (*vaśā*) to Indra when asked for it. That he is different from the preceding Bheda, as Roth[2] assumes, is not certain. Indeed, it may very well be that his defeat led to his being chosen as the representative of the evil end of the wicked man. Moreover, the irreligious character of Bheda may be ascribed to his being a leader of non-Āryan folk, if the **Ajas** and **Śigrus**, with whom in the Rigveda he is connected or associated were, as is possible, though by no means certain, un-Āryan tribes of totemists.[3]

[1] xii. 4, 49. 50.
[2] St. Petersburg Dictionary, *s.v.* 13.
[3] *Cf.* Macdonell, *Vedic Mythology*, p. 153, who inclines to see in them totemistic tribes, but the names furnish the sole support of this conjecture. On this supposition they were probably non-Āryan. *Cf.* **Aja.**

1. **Bheṣaja,** denoting a 'remedial agent,' 'medicine,' is often mentioned in the Rigveda[1] and later,[2] being also used in a figurative sense.[3] Plants,[4] waters,[5] and spells[6] are repeatedly enumerated as medicines. Most of the medical practices of the Atharvaveda are merely examples of sympathetic magic. For example, in one hymn[7] the yellow of jaundice is entreated to pass into yellow birds. In another[8] fever is to be banished by means of a frog; for the frog, being a potent means of cooling fire[9] (because of its association with water), is regarded as analogously effective in banishing the fire of fever. See **Bhiṣaj.**

[1] i. 89, 4; ii. 33, 2, etc.
[2] Av. v. 29, 1; vi. 21, 2, etc.
[3] Śatapatha Brāhmaṇa, xiii. 3, 1, 1; 5, 4; Aitareya Brāhmaṇa, iii. 41.
[4] Rv. x. 97, and *passim* in the Atharvaveda.
[5] i. 23, 19. 20; 34, 6, etc.; Taittirīya Saṃhitā, vi. 4, 9, 2; Kauṣītaki Brāhmaṇa, xvi. 7, etc. Possibly there is some truth in Zimmer's view, *Altindisches Leben*, 399, that the reference is to the beneficial effects of bathing.
[6] Exemplified in the medical spells of the Atharvaveda and the Kauśika Sūtra.
[7] i. 22; Bloomfield, *Hymns of the Atharvaveda*, 264 *et seq.*
[8] vii. 116; Bloomfield, *op. cit.*, 565 *et seq.*
[9] *Cf.* Rv. x. 16, 14; Av. xviii. 3, 60.

2. **Bheṣaja** in the plural is found in the Atharvaveda[1] and in the Sūtras[2] denoting the hymns of the Atharvaveda in so far as they are regarded as having 'healing' powers.

[1] xi. 6, 14.

[2] Āśvalāyana Srauta Sūtra, x. 7, 3; Sāṅkhāyana Śrauta Sūtra, xvi. 2, 10; Pañcaviṃsa Brāhmaṇa, xii. 9, 10.

Cf. Bloomfield, *Hymns of the Atharvaveda*, xxxi, 628.

Bhaima-sena, 'descendant of **Bhīmasena,**' is the name of a man in the Maitrāyaṇī Saṃhitā (iv. 6, 6).

Bhaima-seni, 'descendant of **Bhīmasena,**' is the patronymic of **Divodāsa** in the Kāṭhaka Saṃhitā.[1]

[1] vii. 8 (*Indische Studien*, 3, 460, 472).

Bhaiṣajya in the Śatapatha Brāhmaṇa (xii, 7. 1, 12) and the Nirukta (x. 7. 25) denotes 'healing remedy' or 'medicine,' like **Bheṣaja.**

Bhoga in the Rigveda[1] and later[2] denotes the 'coil' of a serpent.

[1] v. 29, 6; vi. 75, 14 (where the **Hastaghna**, or 'hand-guard,' of the archer is compared to a snake).

[2] Av. xi. 9, 5; Taittirīya Saṃhitā, ii. 1, 4, 5. 6; v. 4, 5, 4; Kāṭhaka Saṃhitā, xiii. 4; xxi. 8, etc.

Bhoja in several passages of the Aitareya Brāhmaṇa (viii. 12. 14. 17) seems to be used as a king's title.

Bhaujya in the Aitareya Brāhmaṇa[1] denotes the rank of a prince bearing the title of **Bhoja.**

[1] vii. 32; viii. 6. 12. 14. 16.

Bhaumaka is the name of some animal in the late Adbhuta Brāhmaṇa.[1]

[1] *Indische Studien*, 1, 40.

Bhaumī is the name of an animal in the list of victims at the Aśvamedha ('horse sacrifice') in the Taittirīya Saṃhitā.[1]

[1] v. 5, 18, 1. *Cf.* Zimmer, *Altindisches Leben*, 99.

Bhauvana, 'descendant of Bhuvana,' is the patronymic of the mythical **Viśvakarman** in the Śatapatha (xiii. 7, 1, 15) and the Aitareya (viii. 21, 8. 10) Brāhmaṇas, and the Nirukta (x. 26).

Bhauvāyana, 'descendant of Bhuva,' is the patronymic of **Kapivana** in the Pañcaviṃśa Brāhmaṇa.[1] It is also found in the Yajurveda Saṃhitās.[2]

[1] xx. 13, 4.

[2] Kāṭhaka Saṃhitā, xxxii. 2 (*Indische Studien*, 3, 473); Maitrāyaṇī Saṃhitā, i. 4, 5; and Vājasaneyi Saṃhitā, xiii. 54, where Kapivana is not mentioned.

Cf. Hopkins, *Transactions of the Connecticut Academy of Arts and Sciences*, 15, 55, 69.

Bhrātṛ is the common designation of 'brother' from the Rigveda[1] onwards. The word is also applied to a relation or close friend generally,[2] but here the persons concerned are, it should be noted, in the Rigveda[3] deities, who are brothers of one another or of the worshipper. Thus in the early literature the word has not really lost its precise sense. The derivation from the root *bhṛ*, 'support,' is probably correct, designating the brother as the support of his sister. This harmonizes with the fact that in Vedic literature the brother plays the part of protector of his sister when bereft of her father, and that maidens deprived of their brothers (*abhrātṛ*) meet an evil fate.[4] The gradation of the relations in the home is shown by the order in the Chāndogya Upaniṣad,[5] where father, mother, brother, and sister are successively mentioned. Strife between brothers is occasionally referred to.[6]

[1] i. 164, 1; iv. 3, 13; v. 34, 4, etc.; Av. i. 14, 2; ii. 13, 5; Taittirīya Saṃhitā, vi. 2, 8, 4, etc.; *bhrātṛtva*, Rv. viii. 20, 22; 83, 8; x. 108, 10.

[2] Böhtlingk and Roth, St. Petersburg Dictionary, *s.v.*; Delbrück, *Die indogermanischen Verwandtschaftsnamen*, 462.

[3] i. 161, 1; 170, 2; iii. 53, 5; iv. 1, 2; vi. 51, 5; viii. 43, 16. *Cf.* Av. iv. 4, 5; v. 22, 12.

[4] Rv. i. 124, 7; iv. 5, 5; Av. i. 17, 1; Zimmer, *Altindisches Leben*, 328. *Cf.* **Ayogu**.

[5] vii. 15, 2.

[6] *Cf.* Av. iii. 30, 2; Śatapatha Brāhmaṇa, iv. 1, 5, 3, where it is a sign of serious confusion; *Journal of the American Oriental Society*, 11, cxlv; Bloomfield *Atharvaveda*, 72.

Bhrātṛvya is found in one passage of the Atharvaveda,[1] where, being named with brother and sister, it must be an expression of relationship. The sense appears to be '(father's) brother's son,' 'cousin,'[2] this meaning alone accounting for the sense of 'rival,' 'enemy,' found elsewhere in the Atharvaveda,[3] and repeatedly in the other Saṃhitās and the Brāhmaṇas.[4] In an undivided family the relations of cousins would easily develop into rivalry and enmity. The original meaning may, however, have been 'nephew,'[5] as the simple etymological sense would be 'brother's son'; but this seems not to account for the later meaning so well. The Kāṭhaka Saṃhitā[6] prescribes the telling of a falsehood to a Bhrātṛvya, who, further, is often given the epithets 'hating' (*dviṣan*) and 'evil' (*apriya*, *pāpman*) in the later Saṃhitās and the Brāhmaṇas.[7] The Atharvaveda[8] also contains various spells, which aim at destroying or expelling one's 'rivals.'

1 v. 22, 12, and perhaps x. 3, 9.

2 The word is rendered 'cousin' by Whitney in his Translation of the Atharvaveda (x. 6, 1; xv. 1, 8).

3 ii. 18, 1; viii. 10, 18. 33; x. 9, 1.

4 Taittirīya Saṃhitā, iii. 5, 9, 2, etc.; Kāṭhaka Saṃhitā, x. 7; xxvii. 8; Vājasaneyi Saṃhitā, i. 17; Aitareya Brāhmaṇa, iii. 7, etc.; Śatapatha Brāhmaṇa, i. 1, 1, 21, etc.; Pañcaviṃśa Brāhmaṇa, xii. 13, 2. *Cf.* Rv. viii. 21, 13.

5 Whitney, in his Translation of the Atharvaveda (ii. 18, 1), while rendering the word by 'adversary,' explains it in a note as meaning literally 'nephew,' or 'brother's son.'

6 xxvii. 8.

7 See several of the passages given in n. 4.

8 ii. 18, 1; x. 9, 1, etc. *Cf.* Taittirīya Saṃhitā, i. 3. 2. 1, etc.

Cf. Delbrück, *Die indogermanischen Verwandtschaftsnamen*, 501, 506, 507, who thinks it means a kind of brother, and through early family conditions was restricted to cousins; Böhtlingk and Roth, St. Petersburg Dictionary, *s.v.*; Weber, *Indische Studien*, 17, 307.

Bhrūṇa-han, 'slaying an embryo'; **Bhrūṇa-hatyā**, 'the slaying of an embryo,' are terms expressing a crime which is repeatedly and severely censured in the later Saṃhitās,[1] where it is said to be the greatest of all crimes, and one of which the

1 Maitrāyaṇī Saṃhitā, iv. 1, 9; Kāṭhaka Saṃhitā, xxxi. 7; Kapiṣṭhala Saṃhitā, xlvii. 7 (cited in Delbrück, *Die indogermanischen Verwandtschaftsnamen*, 579, 580); Av. vi. 112, 3; 113, 2. The Taittirīya Saṃhitā, vi. 5, 10, 3, and Taittirīya Brāhmaṇa, iii. 2, 8, 11, have *brahma-han* instead; but see *ibid.*, 12.

guilt cannot be removed. In many later passages[2] the same crime is referred to, always with reprobation: this fact alone shows the erroneousness of the theory[3] that daughters could be allowed, once born, to die if their fathers so desired.

[2] Taittirīya Brāhmaṇa, iii. 9, 15, 3; Taittirīya Āraṇyaka, ii. 8, 2; x. 1, 15; Bṛhadāraṇyaka Upaniṣad, iv. 3, 22. The substantive is found in Taittirīya Brāhmaṇa, iii. 8, 20, 1; Taittirīya Āraṇyaka, ii. 7, 3; 8, 3; Kauṣītaki Upaniṣad, iii. 1; Śāṅkhāyana Śrauta Sūtra, xvi. 18, 19; Nirukta, vi. 27. Bhrūṇa itself occurs in Rv. x. 155, 2.

[3] See **Pati**, p. 487, with n. 131.

Cf. Weber, *Indische Studien*, 9, 481; 10, 66; Bloomfield, *American Journal of Philology*, 17, 430; *Hymns of the Atharvaveda*, 521, 522.

M.

Makaka, a word occurring once in the Atharvaveda (viii. 6, 12), may be the name of some unknown animal; but it is possibly an adjective having some such sense as 'bleating.'

Makara is the name of an animal, probably the 'crocodile,'[1] which is included in the list of victims at the Aśvamedha ('horse sacrifice') in the Yajurveda Saṃhitās.[2]

[1] The Makara, as a Hindu sculptural ornament, originally represented a crocodile. *Cf.* Cousen's article in the *Annual Report of the Archæological Survey of India* for 1903-4, pp. 227-231 (where the Makara appears as the vehicle of Varuṇa and of Gaṅgā). *Cf.* also *op. cit.*, 1904-5, pp. 80, 83, 84.

[2] Taittirīya Saṃhitā, v. 5, 13, 1; Maitrāyaṇī Saṃhitā, iii. 14, 16; Vājasaneyi Saṃhitā, xxiv. 35. *Cf.* Zimmer, *Altindisches Leben*, 97.

Makṣa, 'fly,' is found in the Rigveda[1] and the Atharvaveda,[2] where its fondness for sweet things is alluded to. *Cf.* **Admasad.**

[1] iv. 45, 4; vii. 32, 2.

[2] ix. 1, 17.

Cf. Zimmer, *Altindisches Leben*, 97.

Makṣā, Makṣikā, denote both 'fly'[1] and 'bee'[2] in the Rigveda and later.

[1] Makṣikā, Rv. i. 162, 9; Av. xi. 1, 2; 9, 10; Bṛhadāraṇyaka Upaniṣad, iii. 3, 2.

[2] Makṣā, Rv. x. 40, 6; Makṣikā, i 119, 9; Praśna Upaniṣad, ii. 4, where a 'king bee' (*madhukara-rājan*) is referred to.

Cf. Zimmer, *Altindisches Leben*, 97; Hillebrandt, *Vedische Mythologie*, 1, 240, n. 1.

Makha appears to designate a person in two passages of the Rigveda,[1] but in neither passage does the context explain who he was. Probably a demon of some kind is meant. In the later Saṃhitās[2] mention is also made of the 'head of Makha,' an expression which has become unintelligible to the Brāhmaṇas.[3]

[1] ix. 101, 13, where the **Bhṛgus** are mentioned as opposed to Makha (*cf.* Macdonell, *Vedic Mythology*, p. 51); x. 171, 2.

[2] Vājasaneyi Saṃhitā, xi. 57; xxxvii. 7; Taittirīya Saṃhitā, i. 1, 8, 1; iii. 2, 4, 1.

[3] Śatapatha Brāhmaṇa, xiv. 1, 2, 17. *Cf.* St. Petersburg Dictionary, *s.v.*

Magadha is the name of a people who appear throughout Vedic literature as of little repute. Though the name is not actually found in the Rigveda,[1] it occurs in the Atharvaveda,[2] where fever is wished away to the **Gandhāris** and **Mūjavants**, northern peoples, and to the **Aṅgas** and Magadhas, peoples of the east. Again, in the list of victims at the Puruṣamedha ('human sacrifice') in the Yajurveda,[3] the Māgadha, or man of Magadha, is included as dedicated to *ati-kruṣṭa*, 'loud noise' (?), while in the **Vrātya** hymn of the Atharvaveda[4] the Māgadha is said to be connected with the Vrātya as his Mitra, his Mantra, his laughter, and his thunder in the four quarters. In the Srauta Sūtras[5] the equipment characteristic of the Vrātya is said to be given, when the latter is admitted into the Āryan Brahminical community, to a bad Brahmin living in Magadha (*brahma-bandhu Māgadha-deśīya*), but this point does not occur in the Pañcaviṃśa Brāhmaṇa.[6] On the other hand, respectable Brahmins sometimes lived there, for the Kauṣītaki Āraṇyaka[7] mentions **Madhyama, Prātībodhī-putra,** as *Magadha-vāsin*, 'living in Magadha.' Oldenberg,[8] however, seems clearly right in regarding this as unusual.

[1] See **Kīkaṭa**.

[2] v. 22, 14, where the Paippalāda recension has *mayebhiḥ*, which is a mere blunder, but substitutes the **Kāśis** for the Aṅgas.

[3] Vājasaneyi Saṃhitā, xxx. 5. 22; Taittirīya Brāhmaṇa, iii. 4, 1, 1.

[4] xv. 2, 1-4.

[5] Lāṭyāyana Śrauta Sūtra, viii. 6, 28; Kātyāyana Śrauta Sūtra, xxii. 4, 22. *Cf.* Sāyaṇa on Pañcaviṃśa Brāhmaṇa, xvii. 1, 16. 17.

[6] xvii. 1, 16.

[7] vii. 13; this is not mentioned in the earlier Aitareya Āraṇyaka.

[8] *Buddha*, 400, n.; Weber, *Indian Literature*, 112, n.

The Magadhas are evidently a people in the Baudhāyana and other Sūtras,[9] possibly also in the Aitareya Āraṇyaka.[10] It is therefore most improbable that Zimmer[11] can be right in thinking that in the Yajurveda[3] and the Atharvaveda[4] the Māgadha is not a man of Magadha, but a member of the mixed caste produced by a **Vaiśya** marrying a **Kṣatriya** woman.[12] But the theory of mixed castes, in any case open to some doubt, cannot be accepted when used to explain such obviously tribal names as Māgadha. The fact that the Māgadha is often in later times a minstrel is easily accounted for by the assumption that the country was the home of minstrelsy, and that wandering bards from Magadha were apt to visit the more western lands. This class the later texts recognize as a caste, inventing an origin by intermarriage of the old-established castes.

The dislike of the Magadhas, which may be Rigvedic, since the **Kīkaṭas** were perhaps the prototype of the Magadhas, was in all probability due, as Oldenberg[13] thinks, to the fact that the Magadhas were not really Brahminized. This is entirely in accord with the evidence of the Śatapatha Brāhmaṇa[14] that neither **Kosala** nor **Videha** were fully Brahminized at an early date, much less Magadha. Weber[15] suggests two other grounds that may have influenced the position—the persistence of aboriginal blood and the growth of Buddhism. The latter consideration is hardly applicable to the Yajurveda or the Atharvaveda; but the imperfect Brahminization of the land, if substituted for it in accordance with Oldenberg's suggestion,

[9] Baudhāyana Dharma Sūtra, i. 2, 13; Baudhāyana Śrauta Sūtra, xx. 13; Āpastamba Śrauta Sūtra, xxii. 6, 18; Hiraṇyakeśi Śrauta Sūtra, xvii. 6. See Caland, *Zeitschrift der Deutschen Morgenländischen Gesellschaft*, 56, 553.

[10] ii. 1, 1. See Keith, *Aitareya Āraṇyaka*, 200; *Śāṅkhāyana Āraṇyaka*, 46, n. 4.

[11] *Altindisches Leben*, 35. *Cf.* St. Petersburg Dictionary, *s.v.*, 2*c*.

[12] Manu, x. 11; Gautama Dharma Sūtra, iv. 17. So Sāyaṇa, on the Taittirīya Brāhmaṇa, *loc. cit.*, explains Māgadha, and Mahīdhara, on the Vājasaneyi Saṃhitā, offers this as one version.

[13] *Buddha*, 400, n.

[14] i. 4, 1, 10 *et seq.*; Weber, *Indische Studien*, 1, 170 *et seq.*; Oldenberg, *op. cit.*, 398. Kosala here appears as more Brahminical than Videha; it is interesting to note that, while Vaideha, like Māgadha, is used in the later theory as a name of a mixed caste, Kausalya is not so degraded (Oldenberg, 399, n.).

[15] See *Indische Studien*, 1, 52, 53; 185; 10, 99; *Indian Literature*, 79, n. 1; 111, 112.

would have some force. The former motive, despite Oldenberg's doubt, seems fully justified. Pargiter[16] has gone so far as to suggest that in Magadha the Āryans met and mingled with a body of invaders from the east by sea. Though there is no evidence for this view in the Vedic texts, it is reasonable to suppose that the farther east the Āryans penetrated, the less did they impress themselves upon the aborigines. Modern ethnology confirms this *a priori* supposition in so far as it shows Āryan types growing less and less marked as the eastern part of India is reached, although such evidence is not decisive in view of the great intermixture of peoples in India.

[16] *Journal of the Royal Asiatic Society*, 1908, pp. 851-853. *Cf.* Rhys Davids, *Buddhist India*, 6, 24, 260, 267.

Magundī is the name of some pest occurring in a verse of an Atharvaveda hymn[1] employed to exorcise evil influences. By that verse the 'daughters of the Magundī' are to be expelled from the cowstall, the wagon, and the house. It is uncertain whether an animal, insect, or demoness is meant.[2]

[1] ii. 14, 2.

[2] *Cf.* Whitney, Translation of the Atharvaveda, 58.

Magha in the Rigveda[1] denotes 'bounty,' and Maghavan[2] is the regular Vedic name for the 'generous giver' of bounties to priests. It is doubtful whether the Maghavans were more than this, or had any special rank as a class in Vedic society. See **Sabhā**.

[1] i. 11, 3; 104, 5; iii. 13, 3; 19, 1; iv. 17, 8; v. 30, 12; 32, 12, etc.; Nirukta, v. 16. Very rarely later, *e.g.*, Vājasaneyi Saṃhitā, xx. 67.

[2] Rv. i. 31, 12; ii. 6, 4; 27, 17; v. 39, 4; 42, 8; vi. 27, 8, etc. So Magha-tti, 'giving of gifts,' Rv. iv. 37, 8; v. 79, 5; viii. 24, 10, etc.; Magha-deya, 'giving of gifts,' vii. 67, 9; x. 156, 2; Maghavat-tva, 'liberality,' vi. 27, 3. The word Maghavan is the epithet *par excellence* of Indra in the Rv. (iii. 30, 3; iv. 16, 1; 31, 7; 42, 5, etc.), and survives in post-Vedic literature as a name of Indra; otherwise, even in the later Saṃhitās, it is very rare, occurring practically as a divine epithet only (of Indra, Taittirīya Saṃhitā, iv. 4, 8, 1; Bṛhadāraṇyaka Upaniṣad, i. 3, 13; Kauṣītaki Upaniṣad, ii. 11).

Maghā. See **Nakṣatra** and **Aghā**.

Maṅgala is the name of a teacher in the Baudhāyana Śrauta Sūtra (xxvi. 2).

Maṅgīra is found in an obscure verse in the Vaitāna[1] and other[2] Sūtras with reference to cows. It is quite uncertain whether a river or a man[3] is meant. The Gaṅgā (Ganges) and the Yamunā (Jumna) are mentioned in the same verse. The correct form of the word is doubtful.[4]

[1] xxxiv. 9.

[2] Mānava Srauta Sūtra, vii. 2, 7; *Mandīrasya*, Kātyāyana Śrauta Sūtra, xiii. 3, 21; *Maṅkīrasya*, Āpastamba Śrauta Sūtra, xxi. 20, 3.

[3] So apparently Garbe, Translation of the Vaitāna Sūtra, 97; Caland, *Das Vaitānasūtra*, 102; Böhtlingk, Dictionary, *s.v.*

[4] See the variants in n. 2.

Mañjiṣṭhā, 'madder,' is mentioned in the Aitareya (iii. 2, 4) and Śāṅkhāyana (viii. 7) Āraṇyakas.

Maṭacī occurs in a passage of the Chāndogya Upaniṣad,[1] where reference is made to the **Kurus** being overwhelmed by Maṭacīs.[2] Śaṅkara interprets the word by 'thunderbolts' (*aśanayaḥ*), while Ānandatīrtha in his commentary gives, as an alternative rendering, *pāṣāṇa-vṛṣṭayaḥ—i.e.*, 'hailstones,' which may be the sense. The Śabdakalpadruma,[3] agreeing with Ānandatīrtha,[4] says that Maṭacī means 'a kind of small red bird' (*rakta-varṇa-kṣudra-pakṣi-viśeṣa*, reading *-pakṣī-*), and Jacob[5] suggests that the 'locust' is meant.

[1] i. 10, 1.

[2] *Maṭacī-hata*.

[3] St. Petersburg Dictionary, *s.v.*

[4] On Brahmasūtra, iii. 4, 28.

[5] *Journal of the Royal Asiatic Society*, 1911, p. 510.

Maṇi is the name in the Rigveda[1] and later[2] of a 'jewel' used as an amulet against all kinds of evil. That either 'pearl'[3] or 'diamond'[4] is denoted is not clear.[5] It is evident that the

[1] i. 33, 8.

[2] Av. i. 29, 1; ii. 4, 1. 2; viii. 5, 1 *et seq.*; x. 6, 24; xii. 1, 44; Taittirīya Saṃhitā, vii. 3, 4, 1; Kāṭhaka Saṃhitā, xxxv. 15; Aitareya Brāhmaṇa, iv. 6; Nirukta, vii. 23, where Durga, in his commentary, takes Maṇi as *āditya-maṇi*, or 'sun-stone,' while the St. Petersburg Dictionary, *s.v.*, suggests that a crystal used as a burning glass may be meant.

[3] St. Petersburg Dictionary, *s.v.*

[4] *Cf.* Zimmer, *Altindisches Leben*, 53.

[5] The expression *hiraṇya maṇi* in Rv. i. 33, 8, might possibly mean 'gold as an ornament,' but 'gold (and) jewels' is more probable. *Cf.* Av. xii. 1, 44, where *maṇiṃ hiraṇyam* must mean 'a jewel (and) gold.'

Maṇi could be strung on a thread (*sūtra*), which is referred to in the Pañcaviṃśa Brāhmaṇa[6] and elsewhere;[7] the Maṇi was certainly also worn round the neck, for in the Rigveda[8] occurs the epithet *maṇi-grīva*, 'having a jewel on the neck.' An amulet of Bilva is celebrated in the Śāṅkhāyana Āraṇyaka,[9] and many varieties of amulet are there enumerated.[10] The 'jeweller' (*maṇi-kāra*) is mentioned in the list of victims at the Puruṣamedha ('human sacrifice') in the Yajurveda.[11]

6 xx. 16, 6.

7 Jaiminīya Upaniṣad Brāhmaṇa, i. 18, 8. *Cf.* iii. 4, 13; Jaiminīya Brāhmaṇa, ii. 248; Śatapatha Brāhmaṇa, xii. 3, 4, 2.

8 i. 122, 14.

9 xii. 18 *et seq.*

10 xii. 8.

11 Vājasaneyi Saṃhitā, xxx. 7; Taittirīya Brāhmaṇa, iii. 4, 3, 1.

Cf. Schrader, *Prehistoric Antiquities*, 337; Zimmer, *op. cit.*, 253; Weber, *Omina und Portenta*, 317, 374; *Indische Studien*, 2, 2, n. 4; 5, 386; 18, 37; *Proceedings of the Berlin Academy*, 1891, 796. Weber is inclined to detect a Babylonian origin of Maṇi (*cf.* **Manā**), but the evidence is not convincing.

Maṇika in the late Adbhuta Brāhmaṇa[1] and the Sūtras[2] denotes a large 'water bottle.'

1 Weber, *Omina und Portenta*, 316.

2 Āśvalāyana Gṛhya Sūtra, ii. 9, 3; iv. 6, 4; Gobhila Gṛhya Sūtra, i. 1, 26; iii. 9, 6. 7, etc.; Sāṅkhāyana Gṛhya Sūtra, ii. 14.

Maṇḍa, n., is found in the compound *nau-maṇḍa* (du.), denoting the two 'rudders' of a ship in the Śatapatha Brāhmaṇa.[1]

1 ii. 3, 3, 15. *Cf.* Eggeling, *Sacred Books of the East*, 12, 345, n. 3, who, following the commentary, accepts 'sides' as the meaning; Caland, *Über das rituelle Sūtra des Baudhāyana*, 60.

Maṇḍūka is the name of 'frog' in the Rigveda[1] and later,[2] the feminine Maṇḍūkī also occurring.[3] The famous frog hymn of the Rigveda[4] compares with Brahmins the frogs croaking

1 vii. 103, 1; x. 166, 5.

2 Av. vii. 112, 2; Taittirīya Saṃhitā, v. 4, 4, 3; 7, 11, 1; Kāṭhaka Saṃhitā, xiii. 1; xxi. 7; Maitrāyaṇī Saṃhitā, iii. 14, 2; Vājasaneyi Saṃhitā, xxiv. 36; Pañcaviṃśa Brāhmaṇa, xii. 4, 16; Śatapatha Brāhmaṇa, ix. 1, 2, 20 *et seq.*; Nirukta, ix. 5.

3 Rv. x. 16, 14; Av. xviii. 3, 60; Vājasaneyi Saṃhitā, xvii. 6; Taittirīya Saṃhitā, iv. 6, 1, 2; Kāṭhaka Saṃhitā, xvii. 17; Maitrāyaṇī Saṃhitā, ii. 10, 1; Taittirīya Āraṇyaka, vi. 4, 1.

4 vii. 103. *Cf.* Av. iv. 15, 12, as explained by Pischel, *Vedische Studien*, 2, 223, where reference is made to frogs in the clefts of the earth (**Iriṇa**).

as they awake to activity at the beginning of the rains. It has been explained by Max Müller[5] as a satire on the Brahmins. Geldner,[6] agreeing with this view, thinks that it is directed by its **Vasiṣṭha** composer against rival Brahmins, probably the **Viśvāmitras.**[7] The view, however, which interprets the hymn as a rain charm[8] seems on the whole more likely. The frog, from its connexion with water, was considered to have cooling properties. Thus after the burning of the dead body the frog is invited to come to the spot where the cremation has taken place in order to cool it down.[9] Similarly the frog is invoked in the Atharvaveda against the fire of fever.[10]

[5] *Ancient Sanskrit Literature*, 494, 495.

[6] *Rigveda, Kommentar*, 117.

[7] Geldner, *loc. cit.*, very plausibly points out that the last Pāda of this Vasiṣṭha hymn is borrowed from the most important Viśvāmitra hymn (Rv. iii. 53, 7).

[8] Yāska, *Nirukta*, ix. 5; Bloomfield, *Journal of the American Oriental Society*, 17, 173-179. *Cf.* Macdonell, *Vedic Mythology*, p. 151; *Sanskrit Literature*, 121, 122.

[9] Rv. x. 16, 14. See Bloomfield, *American Journal of Philology*, 11, 342-350; Lanman in Whitney's Translation of the Atharvaveda, 850.

[10] Av. vii. 116. See Bloomfield, *Hymns of the Atharvaveda*, 565.

Cf. Zimmer, *Altindisches Leben*, 95.

1. **Matsya,** 'fish,' is mentioned only once in the Rigveda,[1] but frequently later.[2]

[1] x. 68, 8.

[2] Av. xi. 2, 25; Maitrāyaṇī Saṃhitā, iii. 9, 5; 14, 2; Vājasaneyi Saṃhitā, xxiv. 21. 34; Taittirīya Saṃhitā, ii. 6, 6, 1; Satapatha Brāhmaṇa, i. 8, 1, 1 (the famous fish of the deluge legend); Chāndogya Upaniṣad, i. 4, 3; Kauṣītaki Upaniṣad, i. 2; *mahā-matsya*, 'great fish,' Bṛhadāraṇyaka Upaniṣad, iv. 3, 18. In the Śatapatha Brāhmaṇa, xiii. 4, 3, 12 (*cf.* Āśvalāyana Śrauta Sūtra, x. 7, 8; Sāṅkhāyana Śrauta Sūtra, xvi. 2, 23), a Matsya Sāṃmada is personified as the king of the fishes.

2. **Matsya** appears to be the name of a people in one passage of the Rigveda,[1] where they are ranged with the other enemies of **Sudās,** although it is possible to see merely the sense of 'fish' in that passage. In the list of Aśvamedhins, 'offerers of the horse sacrifice,' in the Śatapatha Brāhmaṇa,[2] **Dhvasan Dvaitavana** is mentioned as a Matsya king (**Mātsya**). The Matsyas as a people occur also in the Kauṣītaki Upaniṣad[3] in

[1] vii. 18, 6. [2] xiii. 5, 4, 9. [3] iv. 1.

connexion with the **Vaśas,**[4] and in the Gopatha Brāhmaṇa[5] in connexion with **Śālvas.** In Manu[6] the **Kurukṣetra,** the Matsyas, the **Pancālas,** and the **Śūrasenakas** comprise the land of the Brahmin Ṛṣis (*brahmarṣi-deśa*). There is no reason to doubt that the Matsyas occupied much the same territory as in Epic times, say Alwar, Jaipur, Bharatpur.[7]

[4] This is the most probable reading, which results from a comparison with Gopatha Brāhmaṇa, i. 2, 9, where *Śālva-Matsyeṣu* is followed by *savaśa-Uśīnareṣu* (misprinted *śavaśa-*). See Keith, *Journal of the Royal Asiatic Society*, 1908, 367. The older view was *Satvan-Matsyeṣu*, Max Müller, *Sacred Books of the East*, 1, lxxvii, following Cowell; St. Petersburg Dictionary, *s.v. Satvant.*

[5] i. 2, 9.

[6] ii. 19; vii. 193.

[7] See Vincent Smith, *Zeitschrift der Deutschen Morgenländischen Gesellschaft*, 56, 675.

Cf. von Schroeder, *Indiens Literatur und Cultur*, 166; Weber, *Indische Studien*, 1, 211; Zimmer, *Altindisches Leben*, 127.

Madā-vatī, 'intoxicating,' is the name of a plant in the Atharvaveda.[1]

[1] vi. 16, 2; *cf.* iv. 7, 4. *Cf.* Whitney, Translation of the Atharvaveda, 292; Bloomfield, *Hymns of the Atharvaveda*, 465; Zimmer, *Altindisches Leben*, 72.

Madugha, 'honey-plant,'[1] is the name of a sweet herb in the Atharvaveda.[2] The spelling is somewhat uncertain, since many manuscripts read Madhugha.[3]

[1] The literal meaning is probably 'yielding honey,' the word being, according to the commentator, derived from *madhu-dugha*, a word actually occurring in the Rigveda (vi. 70, 1. 5).

[2] i. 34, 4; vi. 102, 3. *Cf.* Weber, *Indische Studien*, 5, 386, n.; 404; Whitney, Translation of the Atharvaveda, 34, 35, 355; Bloomfield, *Hymns of the Atharvaveda*, 275; Zimmer, *Altindisches Leben*, 69.

[3] These two forms probably stand by haplology for *ma[dhu]-dugha* and *madhu-[du]gha*. *Cf.* Macdonell, *Vedic Grammar*, 64, 1a.

Madgu, 'diver' (from the root *majj*,[1] 'dive'), is the name of some aquatic bird which is included in the list of victims at the Aśvamedha ('horse sacrifice') in the Yajurveda Saṃhitās,[2] and is occasionally mentioned elsewhere.[3]

[1] See Macdonell, *Vedic Grammar*, 38c; 44a3a.

[2] Taittirīya Saṃhitā, v. 5, 20, 1; Maitrāyaṇī Saṃhitā, iii. 14, 3; Vājasaneyi Saṃhitā, xxiv. 22. 34.

[3] Chāndogya Upaniṣad, iv. 8, 1. 2.

Cf. Zimmer, *Altindisches Leben*, 93.

Madya, 'intoxicating liquor,' is not mentioned until the Chāndogya Upaniṣad,[1] where it occurs in the compound *madya-pā*, 'drinking intoxicating liquor.'

[1] v. 11, 5. The word is found in the Epic and often in the Dharmaśāstras, as well as in medical texts.

Madra denotes a people who are mentioned in the Bṛhadāraṇyaka Upaniṣad;[1] **Kāpya Patañcala** was then living among them. Their name appears elsewhere in Vedic literature, only in that of a branch, the **Uttara Madras**, the 'northern Madras,' who are referred to in the Aitareya Brāhmaṇa[2] as living beyond the Himālaya (*pareṇa Himavantam*) in the neighbourhood of the **Uttara Kurus**, probably, as Zimmer[3] conjectures, in the land of Kaśmīr. The Madras mentioned in the Upaniṣad were, like the **Kurus**, probably settled somewhere in **Kurukṣetra** in the **Madhyadeśa** or 'Middle Land.' *Cf.* **Madragāra**.

[1] iii. 3, 1; 7, 1. [2] viii. 14, 3. [3] *Altindisches Leben*, 102.

Madra-gāra Śauṅgāyani ('descendant of Śuṅga') is the name of a teacher, whose pupil was **Kāmboja Aupamanyava** in the Vaṃśa Brāhmaṇa.[1] Zimmer[2] concludes, with probability, that these names point to a connexion of the Kambojas and the Madras.

[1] *Indische Studien*, 4, 372. [2] *Altindisches Leben*, 102.

Madhu denotes anything sweet used as food, and especially drink, 'mead,'[1] a sense often found in the Rigveda.[2] More precisely it denotes either 'Soma'[3] or 'milk,'[4] or less often

[1] The word is etymologically identical with Greek *μέθυ*, 'intoxicating drink,' and Anglo-Saxon *medu*, 'mead.'

[2] Used as an adjective, 'sweet,' in Rv. i. 90, 6. 8; 187, 2; iii. 1, 8; iv. 34, 2; 42, 3; Vājasaneyi Saṃhitā, xxxviii. 10, etc.; as a substantive, Rv. i. 154, 4; ii. 37, 5; iii. 39, 6; iv. 38, 10, etc.; Av. vi. 69, 1; ix. 1, 22; Taittirīya Brāhmaṇa, iii. 1, 2, 4. 13, etc.

[3] Rv. i. 19, 9; ii. 19, 2; 34, 5; 36, 4; iii. 43, 3; iv. 18, 13, etc.

[4] Rv. i. 117, 6; 169, 4; 177, 3; iii. 8, 1; vii. 24, 2; Vājasaneyi Saṃhitā, vi. 2, etc.

'honey,'[5] which, however, is the most definite sense in the later literature. Taboos against the use of honey are recorded.[6]

[5] Rv. viii. 4, 8 (where the sense is made certain by the adjective *sāragha*, 'derived from the bee'); perhaps also iv. 45, 4; vii. 32, 2; viii. 24, 20, and, according to Hillebrandt, *Vedische Mythologie*, 1, 239 *et seq.*, in many other passages; Av. ix. 1, 17. 19; Taittirīya Saṃhitā, vii. 5, 10, 1; Maitrāyaṇī Saṃhitā, iv. 9, 7; Aitareya Brāhmaṇa, vii. 15; viii. 5. 20; Śatapatha Brāhmaṇa, i. 6, 2, 1. 2; xi. 5, 4, 18; Bṛhadāraṇyaka, ii. 5, 1; Chāndogya Upaniṣad, vi. 9, 1, etc.

[6] In the case of women, Jaiminīya Upaniṣad Brāhmaṇa, i. 55, 2; of students, Śatapatha Brāhmaṇa, xi. 5, 4, 18.

Cf. Schrader, *Prehistoric Antiquities*, 321; St. Petersburg Dictionary, *s.v.*

Madhuka Paiṅgya ('descendant of Piṅga') is the name of a teacher mentioned in the Śatapatha[1] and the Kauṣītaki[2] Brāhmaṇas.

[1] xi. 7, 2, 8; Bṛhadāraṇyaka Upaniṣad, vi. 3, 17. 18 (Mādhyaṃdina = vi. 3, 8 Kāṇva).

[2] xvi. 9.

Madhu-kaśā,[1] or **Madhoḥ Kaśā,**[2] is the name in the Rigveda of the Aśvins' 'honey-whip,' by which they impart sweetness to the sacrifice. Roth[3] ingeniously conjectures that the idea was derived from an instrument provided with thongs for whipping milk, a 'milk-whip.'

[1] Rv. i. 22, 3; 157, 4; Av. x. 7, 19; Pañcaviṃśa Brāhmaṇa, xxi. 10, 12.

[2] Av. ix. 1, 5.

[3] St. Petersburg Dictionary, *s.v.*

Madhu-kṛt, 'honey-maker,' denotes 'bee' in the later Saṃhitās[1] and the Brāhmaṇas.[2]

[1] Taittirīya Saṃhitā, i, 5, 6, 5; iv. 2, 9, 6, etc.

[2] Taittirīya Brāhmaṇa, iii. 10, 10, 1; Śatapatha Brāhmaṇa, i. 6, 2, 1. 2; Chāndogya Upaniṣad, iii. 1, 2; vi. 9, 1, etc.

Madhu-chandas, the reputed author of the first ten hymns of the first Maṇḍala of the Rigveda, is mentioned as a Ṛṣi in the Kauṣītaki Brāhmaṇa[1] and the Aitareya Āraṇyaka.[2] In the

[1] xxviii. 2.

[2] i. 1, 3.

Aitareya Brāhmaṇa[3] he counts as the fifty-first son of **Viśvāmitra**, and his Praüga (hymn at the morning service) is mentioned in the Śatapatha Brāhmaṇa.[4]

[3] vii. 17, 7; 18, 1; *cf.* Śāṅkhāyana Śrauta Sūtra, xv. 26, 1 *et seq.* *Cf.* Keith, *Aitareya Āraṇyaka*, 167.

[4] xiii. 5, 1, 8.

Madhu-brāhmaṇa, 'the Brāhmaṇa of the Honey,' is the designation of a certain mystical doctrine in the Satapatha Brāhmaṇa.[1]

[1] iv. 1, 5, 18; xiv. 1, 4, 13; Bṛhadāraṇyaka Upaniṣad, ii. 5, 16. *Cf.* Weber, *Indische Studien*, 1, 290.

Madhya-deśa, the 'Middle Country,' is, according to the Mānava Dharma Śāstra,[1] the land between the Himālaya in the north, the Vindhya in the south, **Vinaśana** in the west, and Prayāga (now Allahabad) in the east—that is, between the place where the **Sarasvatī** disappears in the desert, and the point of the confluence of the **Yamunā** (Jumna) and the **Gaṅgā** (Ganges). The same authority[2] defines Brahmarṣi-deśa as denoting the land of **Kurukṣetra**, the **Matsyas**, **Pañcālas**, and **Śūrasenakas**, and Brahmāvarta[3] as meaning the particularly holy land between the Sarasvatī and the **Dṛṣadvatī**. The Baudhāyana Dharma Sūtra[4] defines Āryāvarta as the land east of Vinaśana; west of the Kālaka-vana, 'Black Forest,' or rather Kanakhala, near Hardvār; south of the Himālaya; and north of the Pāriyātra or the Pāripātra Mountains; adding that, in the opinion of others,[5] it was confined to the country between the Yamunā and the Gaṅgā, while the **Bhāllavins**[6] took it as the country between the boundary-river (or perhaps the Saras-

[1] ii. 21.

[2] ii. 19.

[3] ii. 17. 19.

[4] i. 2, 9; Vasiṣṭha Dharma Sūtra, i. 8.

[5] Baudhāyana, i. 2, 10; Vasiṣṭha, i. 12. See on Kanakhala, Hultzsch, *Indian Antiquary*, 34, 179.

[6] Baudhāyana, i. 2, 11. 12; Vasiṣṭha, i. 14. 15, quoting in each case a verse of the Nidāna (what work is referred to is not certain; there is similar doubt as to the quotation in the Nidāna of the Bhāllavi Brāhmaṇa, according to the Bṛhaddevatā, v. 23, where see Macdonell's note, and *cf.* Bühler, *Sacred Books of the East*, 14, 3, n.).

vatī)[7] and the region where the sun rises. The Mānava Dharma Śāstra,[8] in accord with the Vasiṣṭha Dharma Sūtra,[9] defines Āryāvarta as the region between the Vindhya and the Himālaya, the two ranges which seem to be the boundaries of the Āryan world in the Kauṣītaki Upaniṣad also.[10]

The term Madhyadeśa is not Vedic, but it is represented in the Aitareya Brāhmaṇa[11] by the expression *madhyamā pratiṣṭhā diś*, 'the middle fixed region,' the inhabitants of which are stated to be the Kurus, the Pañcālas, the **Vaśas,** and the **Uśīnaras.** The latter two peoples practically disappear later on, the Madhyadeśa being the country of the Kuru-Pañcālas, the land where the Brāhmaṇas and the later Saṃhitās were produced, bounded on the east by the **Kosala-Videhas**, and on the west by the desert. The western tribes are mentioned with disapproval both in the Śatapatha Brāhmaṇa[12] and the Aitareya Brāhmaṇa,[13] while the tradition of the Brahminization of the Kosalas and the Videhas from the Kuru-Pancāla country is preserved in the former Brāhmaṇa.[14]

[7] The readings are doubtful, varying between *sindhur vidhāraṇī* or *vidharaṇī* and *sindhur vicaraṇī* or *visaraṇī.* The latter expression must refer to the Sarasvatī; the former may, but not necessarily. Conceivably the Sindhu (Indus) is meant; for it was a great boundary, with Āryan tribes to the east of it.

[8] ii. 22.

[9] i. 9.

[10] ii. 13. *Cf.* Keith, *Śāṅkhāyana Araṇyaka*, 28, n. 1.

[11] viii. 14, 3. The Uśīnaras may be recognized as in the north, for the Buddhist texts give Usīragiri as the northern boundary of the middle country. See Hultzsch, *Indian Antiquary*, 34, 179.

[12] ix. 3, 1, 8.

[13] iii. 44, 3; Ludwig, Translation of the Rigveda, 3, 245.

[14] i. 4, 1.

Cf. Bühler, *Sacred Books of the East*, 14, 2, 3; 146, 147, who points out that the Pāripātra Mountains are a part of the Vindhya range in Mālvā, and who suggests that the western boundary was originally the Ādarśa Mountains; for the reading of the manuscripts, and of the scholiast Kṛṣṇapaṇḍita, in the Vasiṣṭha Dharma Sūtra, i. 8, is *prāg ādarśanāt*, not *adarśanāt* (corresponding with the Vinaśana of Baudhāyana Dharma Sūtra, i. 2, 9), and the Mahābhāṣya on Pāṇini, ii. 4, 10, has *prāg ādarśāt.* See also for the Buddhist 'Middle Country' an article by Rhys Davids, *Journal of the Royal Asiatic Society*, 1904, 83 *et seq.*, with Fleet's corrections, *ibid.*, 1907, 657; and *cf.* Keith, *ibid.*, 1908, 1143; Max Müller, *Sacred Books of the East*, 32, 58, 59; *Indian Empire*, 1, 303, 304, where the extraordinary theory is adopted that the Madhyadeśa was peopled by a new race of immigrant Āryans, who, travelling viâ Chitral and Gilgit, and bringing no women with them, married Dravidian women, and produced the so-called Āryo-Dravidians. It is quite impossible to find any support for this theory in

Vedic literature. To say, as is there said, that the 'Vedic hymns contain no reference to the route by which the Āryans entered India or to their earlier settlements on the Indus,' and that this is explained by the theory of the entry of the Vedic Indians viâ Chitral, is to assert absurdities. The theory is based on the later dialects and their affinities (see Grierson, *Indian Empire*, 1, 357 *et seq.*); it can probably not be regarded as at all valid for any period—at any rate, it is not cogent for the eighth century, B.C.

Madhyaṃ-dina, 'mid-day,' is a frequent designation of time in the Rigveda,[1] the later Saṃhitās,[2] and the Brāhmaṇas.[3] *Cf.* **Ahan.**

[1] iv. 28, 3; viii. 1, 29; 13, 13; 27, 19; x. 151, 5, etc.

[2] Av. ix. 6, 46; Taittirīya Saṃhitā, vi. 2, 5, 4, etc.

[3] Pañcaviṃśa Brāhmaṇa, xv. 9, 16; Taittirīya Brāhmaṇa, i. 5, 3, 2; Śatapatha Brāhmaṇa, ii. 2 3, 9; Chāndogya Upaniṣad, ii. 9, 6; 14, 1, etc. The word is sometimes used as an abbreviation for the 'midday libation' (like *mittag* in German for 'midday meal') in Aitareya Brāhmaṇa, iii. 10, 2. 5; Kauṣītaki Brāhmaṇa, xxix. 8.

Madhyama-vah occurs in one passage of the Rigveda[1] as an epithet of the chariot. The exact interpretation is doubtful. Roth[2] assigns to it the expression the sense of 'driving with a single horse between the shafts.' According to Sāyana's explanation, it means 'driving with middling speed.' It might mean 'driving in the middle'—that is, 'only half-way.'[3]

[1] ii. 29, 4.

[2] St. Petersburg Dictionary, *s.v.*

Cf. Oldenberg, *Ṛgveda-Noten*, 1, 210.

The context seems to require the sense of 'keeping away' from the sacrifice.

Cf. **Pūrvavah.**

Madhyama-śi is found in one passage of the Rigveda,[1] where Roth[2] assigns to the word the meaning of *intercessor*, which Zimmer[3] accepts, in the sense of 'mediator' or 'arbiter,' as a legal term, but which Roth may, as Lanman[4] suggests, have intended to express 'adversary' or 'preventer' of the disease referred to in the hymn. Whitney[5] thinks that it means 'mid-

[1] x. 97, 12 = Av. iv. 9, 4 = Vājasaneyi Saṃhitā, xii. 86.

[2] St. Petersburg Dictionary, *s.v.*

[3] *Altindisches Leben*, 180. *Cf.* **Dharma.**

[4] In Whitney's Translation of the Atharvaveda, 159. But see Roth, *Siebenzig Lieder*, 174, which Lanman may have overlooked, since he does not refer to it.

[5] *Loc. cit.*

most man' or 'chief' as the one round whom his followers encamp.[6] Geldner,[7] however, thinks that a third king, who is 'neutral' between two enemies, is intended.

[6] *Madhyama-śīvan*, in the Jaiminīya Brāhmaṇa, ii. 408, is obscure.

[7] *Rigveda, Glossar*, 131; *Kommentar*, 196 (where he seems to decide in favour of derivation from *śī*, not *śṛ*).

Madhyama-stha,[1] **Madhyame-ṣṭha,**[2] in the later Saṃhitās denotes the chief in his relation to his followers (*sajāta*). *Cf.* **Madhyamaśī.**

[1] Vājasaneyi Saṃhitā, xxvii. 5.

[2] Av. iii. 8, 2, and *cf. Madhyama-stheya*, 'position of chief,' Taittirīya Saṃhitā, iv. 4, 5, 1.

Cf. Whitney, Translation of the Atharvaveda, 96.

Madhyā-varṣa, the 'middle of the rains,' is specially mentioned as a time of the year in the Kauṣītaki Brāhmaṇa[1] and in the Sūtras.[2]

[1] i. 3.

[2] Śāṅkhāyana Śrauta Sūtra, iii. 5, 5. 7, etc.

Manasa, occurring in one passage of the Rigveda,[1] seems clearly to be the name of a Ṛṣi, in accordance with Sāyaṇa's interpretation.

[1] v. 44, 10. *Cf.* Ludwig, Translation of the Rigveda, 3, 139.

Manā is found in one passage of the Rigveda[1] in an enumeration of gifts, where it is described as 'golden' (*sacā manā hiraṇyayā*). It therefore seems to designate some ornament, or possibly a weight, and has accordingly been compared[2] with the Greek μνᾶ (Herodotus has μνέα), the Latin *mina*. All three words have been considered Semitic in origin, as borrowed from the Phœnicians[3] in the case of Greece, from Carthage by way

[1] viii. 78, 2.

[2] As, *e.g.*, by Zimmer, *Altindisches Leben*, 50, 51; Weber, *Indische Studien*, 5, 386; 17, 202, 203; Wackernagel, *Altindische Grammatik*, 1, xxii; Hopkins, *Journal of the American Oriental Society*, 16, 278.

[3] Or perhaps from Babylon viâ Asia Minor. The part played by the Phœnicians in Greek life is now reduced within narrow limits; in the case of the *mina*, probably their commercial activities may be considered as likely to have caused the adoption of the term.

of Etruria or Sicily in the case of Rome, and from Babylon in the case of India. The identification as regards Manā is very conjectural, depending merely on the probabilities of Babylonian borrowing[4] seen—*e.g.*, in the legend of the flood, and in the system of the **Nakṣatras.** On the other hand, Manā may very well be identical with the word *manā* which occurs several times in the Rigveda[5] in the sense of 'desire' (from the root *man*, 'think'), and which may have in this one passage the concrete sense of 'desirable object.' It is to be noted that in Böhtlingk's Dictionary a single word Manā appears, to which the only senses assigned are 'wish,' 'desire,' 'jealousy.'

[4] See, *e.g.*, for borrowing, Oldenberg, *Religion des Veda*, 276; *Zeitschrift der Deutschen Morgenländischen Gesellschaft*, 50, 43 *et seq.*; Bühler, *Indian Studies*, 3, 16 *et seq.*; *Indische Palæographie*, 17; Vincent Smith, *Indian Antiquary*, 34, 230. On the other side, *cf.* Max Müller, *India*, 133-138; Hopkins, *Religions of India*, 160; Macdonell, *Vedic Mythology*, p. 139 (as regards the flood legend); Bloomfield, *Religions of India*, 133 *et seq.* (as regards the Ādityas).

[5] i. 173, 2; iv. 33, 2; x. 6, 3; Vājasaneyi Saṃhitā, iv. 19; 'jealousy. Rv. ii. 33, 5; Kauśika Sūtra, cvii. 2. There are also the derivatives *manā-ya*, 'think of,' 'be zealous': Rv. i. 133, 4; ii. 26, 2; *manā-yu*, 'desirous': Rv. i. 92, 9; iv. 24, 7; *manā-vasu*, 'rich in devotion': Rv. v. 74, 1.

Manāvī, 'wife of Manu,' is mentioned in the Kāṭhaka Saṃhitā[1] and the Śatapatha Brāhmaṇa.[2] See **Manu.**

[1] xxx. 1 (*Indische Studien*, 3, 462).

[2] i. 1, 4, 16.

Manu in the Rigveda[1] and later[2] has no claim to historical reality. He is simply the first man, father of the race, and its guide in all matters, sacrificial and other. Hence the views of the texts on inheritance are foisted on Manu and his youngest son, **Nābhānediṣṭha.**[3] He also plays the part of the hero in the Vedic legend of the flood.[4]

[1] i. 80, 16; ii. 33, 13; viii. 63, 1; x. 100, 5, etc. See Macdonell, *Vedic Mythology*, 50.

[2] Av. xiv. 2, 41; Taittirīya Saṃhitā, i. 5, 1, 3; vii. 5, 15, 3; ii. 5, 9, 1; 6, 7, 1; iii. 3, 2, 1; v. 4, 10, 5; vi. 6, 6, 1; Kāṭhaka Saṃhitā, viii. 15; Śatapatha Brāhmaṇa, i. 1, 4, 14, etc.; Jaiminīya Upaniṣad Brāhmaṇa, iii. 15, 2, etc.

[3] Taittirīya Saṃhitā, iii. 1, 9, 4; Aitareya Brāhmaṇa, v. 14, 1. 2.

[4] Śatapatha Brāhmaṇa, i. 8, 1, 1 *et seq.*; Kāṭhaka Saṃhitā, xi. 2.

Manu is called Vivasvan[5] or Vaivasvata,[6] 'son of Vivasvant' (the god); Sāvarṇi,[6] 'descendant of Savarṇā' (the substitute of Saraṇyū in the legend of her wedding); and Sāṃvaraṇi,[7] 'descendant of Saṃvaraṇa.' The first name is, of course, mythical. The other two have been regarded as historical, Sāvarṇi being taken by Ludwig[8] as a king of the **Turvaśas**, but this is very doubtful.

5 Rv. viii. 52, 1.

6 Av. viii. 10, 24; Śatapatha Brāhmaṇa, xiii. 4, 3, 3; Āśvalāyana Śrauta Sūtra, x. 7; Nirukta, xii. 10.

7 Rv. viii. 51, 1; Bloomfield, *Journal of the American Oriental Society*, 15, 180, n., conjectures Sāvarṇi instead. *Cf.* Scheftelowitz, *Die Apokryphen des Ṛgveda*, 38.

8 Translation of the Rigveda, 3, 166. *Cf.* Weber, *Indische Studien*, 1, 195; Hopkins, *Journal of the American Oriental Society*, 11, 240; Lévi, *La Doctrine du Sacrifice*, 114 *et seq.*; St. Petersburg Dictionary, *s.v.*; Muir, *Sanskrit texts*, 1², 161 *et seq.*; Bühler, *Sacred Books of the East*, 25, lvii *et seq.*; Lanman, *Sanskrit Reader*, 340 *et seq.*

Manor Avasarpaṇa is the name, in the Śatapatha Brāhmaṇa,[1] of the mountain on which the vessel of **Manu** rested. In the Epic the name is Naubandhana, but the view[2] that it is alluded to as **Nāvaprabhraṃśana** in the Atharvaveda[3] is now abandoned.[4]

1 i. 8, 1, 8.

2 See Macdonell, *Vedic Mythology*, p. 139; Whitney, *Indische Studien*, 1, 162; Zimmer, *Altindisches Leben*, 30; Bloomfield, *Hymns of the Atharvaveda*, 676.

3 xix. 39, 8.

4 Whitney, Translation of the Atharvaveda, 961; Macdonell, *Journal of the Royal Asiatic Society*, 1907, 1107.

Manuṣya-rāja[1] and **Manuṣya-rājan**[2] denote in the later Saṃhitās and the Brāhmaṇas a 'king of men.' *Cf.* **Rājan.**

1 Vājasaneyi Saṃhitā, xxiv. 30; Aitareya Brāhmaṇa, i. 15, 6; Kāṭhaka Saṃhitā, xxiv. 7.

2 Pañcaviṃśa Brāhmaṇa, xviii. 10, 5; Aitareya Brāhmaṇa, viii. 26, 4.

Manuṣya-viś,[1] **Manuṣya-viśa,**[2] and **Manuṣya-viśā**[3] denote 'mankind,' 'the human race,' in the later Saṃhitās and the Brāhmaṇas.

1 Aitareya Brāhmaṇa, i. 9. 1.

2 Taittirīya Saṃhitā, v. 4, 7, 7; vi. 1, 5, 3.

3 Kāṭhaka Saṃhitā, xi. 6; xxiii. 8.

Mantra (from the root *man*, 'think') denotes in the Rigveda[1] and later[2] the 'hymn' as the product of the singer's creative thought. In the Brāhmaṇas[3] the word is regularly used of the poetic and prose utterances of the Ṛṣis, including not merely the verse parts of the Saṃhitās, but also the prose formulæ that betray by their style their special and archaic character.[4]

[1] i. 31, 15; 40, 5; 67, 4; 74, 1; 152, 2; ii. 35, 2, etc.

[2] Av. xv. 2, 1; xix. 54, 3; Taittirīya Saṃhitā, i. 5, 4, 1; 5, 1, etc.

[3] Aitareya Brāhmaṇa, v. 14, 23; vi. 1; Kauṣītaki Brāhmaṇa, xxvi. 3, 5; Śatapatha Brāhmaṇa, i. 4, 4, 6; xi. 2, 1, 6; Nirukta, vii. 1, etc.; Chāndogya Upaniṣad, vii. 1, 3.

[4] Bloomfield, *Vedic Concordance*, viii; Keith, *Aitareya Āraṇyaka*, 298. Macdonell's *Vedic Grammar* covers the Mantra material of the Vedic Saṃhitās, prose as well as poetry.

Mantra-kṛt in the Rigveda[1] and the Brāhmaṇas[2] denotes a poet as a 'maker of Mantras.'

[1] ix. 114, 2.

[2] Aitareya Brāhmaṇa, vi. 1, 1; Pañcaviṃśa Brāhmaṇa, xiii. 3, 24; Taittirīya Āraṇyaka, iv. 1, 1.

Mantha in the Rigveda[1] and later[2] denotes a drink in which solid ingredients are mixed with a fluid by stirring, usually parched barley-meal (**Saktu**) with milk.[3] All sorts of mixed beverages of this type are mentioned in the Śāṅkhāyana Āraṇyaka.[4]

[1] x. 86, 15.

[2] Av. ii. 29, 6; v. 29, 7; x. 6, 2; xviii. 4, 42; xx. 127, 9; Taittirīya Saṃhitā, i. 8, 5, 1, etc.

[3] Śatapatha Brāhmaṇa, iv. 2, 1, 2; Suśruta, 1, 233, 12, in St. Petersburg Dictionary, *s.v.* 1*b ad fin*.

[4] xii. 8.

Cf. Zimmer, *Altindisches Leben*, 268, 269; Macdonell, *Vedic Mythology*, 108.

Manthā in one passage of the Rigveda[1] seems to mean a 'churn.' So the root *math* denotes to 'churn' in the Taittirīya Saṃhitā.[2] In one passage of the Atharvaveda[3] the word is used to denote a drink like **Mantha**.

[1] i. 28, 4.

[2] ii. 2, 10, 2; Śatapatha Brāhmaṇa, v. 3, 2, 6; Chāndogya Upaniṣad, vi. 6, 1. *Cf.* Hillebrandt, *Vedische Mythologie*, 1, 161.

[3] xx. 127, 9. Scheftelowitz in Khila, v. 10, 3, reads *manthām3* with Pluti, following the Kaśmīr MS., but misquoting the Atharvan text.

Manthāvala is the name of an animal in the Aitareya Brāhmaṇa,[1] a sort of snake according to the St. Petersburg Dictionary. Sāyaṇa[2] understands it to be a kind of animal which hangs head downwards from the branches of trees, meaning, presumably, the flying fox.[3] *Cf.* **Mānthāla, Mānthīlava.**

[1] iii. 26, 3.

[2] P. 291 (ed. Aufrecht). *Cf.* Zimmer, *Altindisches Leben*, 86.

[3] This is the probable meaning of the word according to Böhtlingk, Dictionary, *s.v.*

Manthin in the Rigveda[1] and later[2] denotes Soma juice mixed with meal (**Saktu**) by stirring.

iii. 32, 2; ix. 46, 4. Tilak's conjecture that the planets are referred to here is absurd. See *Orion*, 162; Whitney, *Journal of the American Oriental Society*, 16, xciv.

[2] Taittirīya Saṃhitā, iii. 1, 6, 3; vi. 4, 10, 1; vii. 2, 7, 3; Vājasaneyi Saṃhitā, vii. 18; viii. 57; xiii. 57; xviii. 19; Aitareya Brāhmaṇa, iii. 1, 6, etc.

Mandīra is perhaps the name of a man whose cattle, according to a Mantra in the Kātyāyana Śrauta Sūtra (xiii. 3, 21), did not drink the water of the **Gaṅgā** (Ganges). See **Maṅgīra.**

1. **Mandhātṛ** occurs in several passages of the Rigveda,[1] in all of which Roth[2] takes the word as merely an adjective used substantively, 'the pious man.' In one passage[3] the word, being applied to Agni, is thus used, but in another[4] *Mandhātṛvat* being parallel with *Aṅgirasvat*, 'like Aṅgiras,' is naturally to be understood as a proper name, which is probably also the sense of the word in the preceding hymn.[5] A different Mandhātṛ[6] may be meant in the first Maṇḍala,[6] where he is mentioned as a protégé of the Aśvins, and evidently as a king. To equate these persons, and make a Rājarṣi out of Mandhātṛ, as Ludwig[7] and Griffith do, is unnecessary and improbable.

[1] i. 112, 13; viii. 39, 8; 40, 12; x. 2, 2.

[2] St. Petersburg Dictionary, *s.v.*

[3] Rv. x. 2, 2.

[4] Rv. viii. 40, 12.

[5] Rv. viii. 39, 8.

[6] Rv. i. 112, 13.

[7] Translation of the Rigveda, 3, 107, where he attributes Rv. viii. 39-42 to him as a **Nābhāka**, 'descendant of **Nabhāka**.'

[8] *Hymns of the Rigveda*, 1, 147.

2. **Mandhātṛ Yauvanāśva** ('descendant of Yuvanāśva') is in the Gopatha Brāhmaṇa[1] the name of an emperor who was instructed by **Vicārin**, son of **Kabandha Ātharvaṇa**.

[1] i. 2, 10 *et seq.* *Cf.* Bloomfield, *Atharvaveda*, 111.

Manyā (plur.), 'nape of the neck,' occurs in a passage of the Atharvaveda[1] directed against a disease which Bloomfield[2] regards as scrofulous swellings on the neck. He compares the disease Manskunder, 'tumours of the neck' (which looks like a combination of the words *manyā* and *skandhyā*, 'pains of the neck and shoulders,' both occurring in verses 1 and 3 of the Atharvan hymn), mentioned by Wise.[3]

[1] vi. 25, 1.

[2] *Proceedings of the American Oriental Society*, October, 1887, xix; *American Journal of Philology*, 11, 327 *et seq.*; *Hymns of the Atharvaveda*, 472.

[3] *System of Hindu Medicine*, 316. *Cf.* Weber, *Indische Studien*, 17, 202; Whitney, Translation of the Atharvaveda, 298, 299.

Mamatā is, according to Sāyaṇa, in one passage of the Rigveda,[1] the wife of Ucathya and the mother of **Dīrghatamas**. But the word may be merely an abstract noun meaning 'self-interest,' a sense which it often has in the later language. Oldenberg[2] finds a mention of Mamata (masc.) in a verse of the Rigveda[3] as the name of a **Bharadvāja**.

[1] vi. 10, 2. *Cf.* Mahābhārata, i. 4179 *et seq.*

[2] *Zeitschrift der Deutschen Morgenländischen Gesellschaft*, 42, 212.

[3] vi. 50, 15, where the reading of the received text is *mama tasya*.

Maya is found once in the Vājasaneyi Saṃhitā (xxii. 19) in the sense of 'horse.'

Mayu occurs in the list of victims at the Aśvamedha ('horse sacrifice') in the Yajurveda Saṃhitās.[1] The commentator on the Taittirīya Saṃhitā[1] explains the word as meaning either an 'ape' (*kiṃpuruṣa*) or a 'forest peacock' (*āraṇya-mayūra*).

[1] Taittirīya Saṃhitā, v. 5, 12, 1; Vājasaneyi Saṃhitā, xxiv. 31.

The former sense is supported by another passage of the Vājasaneyi Saṃhitā,[2] where the Mayu, being a substitute for the man, must be an ape. This sense also suits the word in the other passage[3] where it occurs.

[2] viii. 47; *mayu āraṇya* in Taittirīya Saṃhitā, iv. 2, 10, 1.

[3] Śatapatha Brāhmaṇa, vii. 5, 2, 22.

Cf. Zimmer, *Altindisches Leben*, 85; Weber, *Indische Studien*, 9, 46.

Mayūkha denotes, from the Rigveda onwards,[1] a 'peg,' especially as used for keeping a web stretched.[2] *Cf.* **Otu.**

[1] Rv. vii. 99, 3; Taittirīya Saṃhitā, ii. 3, 1, 5; Kāṭhaka Saṃhitā, xi. 6; Aitareya Brāhmaṇa, v. 15, 9, etc.

[2] Rv. x. 130, 2 (in a metaphor); Av. x. 7, 42; Kāṭhaka Saṃhitā, xxvi. 6; Taittirīya Brāhmaṇa, ii. 5, 5, 3, etc.

Mayūra, 'peacock,' occurs in the Rigveda in the compounds describing Indra's horses, *mayūra-roman*,[1] 'with hair like peacocks' feathers,' and *mayūra-śepya*,[2] 'with tails like those of peacocks.' The peacock also appears in the list of victims at the Aśvamedha ('horse sacrifice') in the Yajurveda Saṃhitās.[3] The pea-hen, Mayūrī, is mentioned in the Rigveda[4] and the Atharvaveda,[5] in both cases with reference to the bird's efficacy against poison, a curious superstition to be compared with the modern dislike of peacocks' feathers.

[1] Rv. iii. 45, 1.

[2] Rv. viii. 1, 25.

[3] Maitrāyaṇī Saṃhitā, iii. 14, 4; Vājasaneyi Saṃhitā, xxiv. 23. 27.

[4] i. 191, 14 (a late hymn).

[5] vii. 56, 7.

Cf. Zimmer, *Altindisches Leben*, 90.

Marīci in the plural denotes, according to Weber,[1] the 'particles of light' or 'shining motes' that fill the air, as opposed to rays of light (*raśmi*). This meaning adequately suits the passages in the early Vedic literature[2] where the

[1] *Indische Studien*, 9, 9, accepted by the St. Petersburg Dictionary, *s.v.*

[2] Rv. x. 57, 12; 177, 1; Av. iv. 38, 5 (where *raśmi* and *marīci* are opposed); v. 21, 10; vi. 113, 2; Taittirīya Saṃhitā, vi. 4, 5, 5 (*marīci-pa*, 'drinking atoms of light,' said of the gods); Taittirīya Brāhmaṇa, ii. 2, 9, 2 (where Sāyaṇa's version, *sarvatra-prasṛta-prabhā-dravya*, refers to the light as everywhere diffused), etc.

word occurs; but the sense of 'ray' is quite clearly found in the Upaniṣads,[3] as well as the older sense.[4]

[3] Praśna Upaniṣad, iv. 2. *Cf.* Taittirīya Upaniṣad, i. 1, 2; 2, 1; Maitrāyaṇī Upaniṣad, vi. 31.
[4] Aitareya Upaniṣad, i. 2.

Maru, in the plural, is mentioned in the Taittirīya Āraṇyaka,[1] as the *utkara* ('mound of earth thrown up' from the excavation of the altar[2]) of **Kurukṣetra.** This seems to mean that the Maru deserts (the later Maru-sthala[3]) were so called because they stood to the 'altar,' Kurukṣetra, in the same relation as the waste earth of the *utkara* to the altar at the sacrifice.

[1] v. 1, 1.
[2] Eggeling, *Sacred Books of the East*, xii. 25. 54.
[3] *Cf.* Zimmer, *Altindisches Leben*, 48, and **Dhanvan.**
Cf. Weber, *Indische Studien*, 1, 78.

Marutta Āvi-kṣita ('descendant of Avikṣit') **Kāma-pri** ('descendant of Kāmapra') is the name of a king who was anointed by **Saṃvarta** according to the Aitareya Brāhmaṇa.[1] In the Śatapatha Brāhmaṇa[2] account of the same king he is called **Āyogava.**

[1] viii. 21, 12.
[2] xiii. 5, 4, 6. *Cf.* also Śāṅkhāyana Śrauta Sūtra, xvi. 9, 14. 16; Maitrāyaṇī Upaniṣad, i. 4.

Marud-vṛdhā[1] is the name of a stream mentioned in the Nadīstuti ('Praise of Rivers') in the Rigveda[2] along with the **Asiknī** (Akesines) and the **Vitastā** (Hydaspes). Roth[3] considers that the Marudvṛdhā denotes the stream formed by the combined waters of these two rivers down to its junction with the **Paruṣṇī** (Ravi), a view accepted by Zimmer.[4] On the other hand, Ludwig[5] thinks that the Marudvṛdhā designates

[1] Literally, 'rejoicing in the Maruts'—*i.e.*, 'swollen by the rainy winds.' The misspelling of the name as Marudvṛddhā in Macdonell, *Vedic Mythology*, pp. 80, 88, is corrected in the Index and the Addenda of that work. On the accentuation of the name, see Vārttika 2 on Pāṇini, vi. 2, 106.
[2] x. 75, 5.
[3] *Zur Litteratur und Geschichte des Weda*, 138 *et seq.*
[4] *Altindisches Leben*, 11, 12.
[5] Translation of the Rigveda, 3, 200.

the stream formed by the junction of the Paruṣṇī with the combined waters of the Asiknī and Vitastā, a view which seems less likely.

1. **Marka** is found in one passage of the Rigveda,[1] where Roth[2] sees in the expression *sūro markaḥ* the eclipse of the sun.' Sāyaṇa[3] thinks the meaning is 'purifying.'[4]

[1] x. 27, 20.

[2] St. Petersburg Dictionary, *s.v.* He thinks, however, that if the word means 'eclipse,' it cannot be derived from the root *mṛc*, 'injure.'

[3] As from the root *mṛj*, derivation from which is not phonetically justified.

[4] Ludwig cites this passage, in his essay on eclipses in the Rigveda (Proceedings of the Bohemian Academy, 1885), as a proof that the Vedic Ṛṣis knew of the moon as eclipsing the sun; but see Whitney s reply, *Journal of the American Oriental Society*, 13, lxi *et seq.*, and **Sūrya.**

2. **Marka** is mentioned in the Taittirīya Saṃhitā[1] and elsewhere[2] as the Purohita, along with **Śaṇḍa**, of the Asuras, while Bṛhaspati is, of course, the Purohita of the gods. Marka is mentioned elsewhere also.[3] The name may quite possibly have Iranian affinities, as believed by Hillebrandt[4] and by Hopkins.[5] Hillebrandt[6] also sees in a Gṛdhra mentioned in the Rigveda[7] and elsewhere[8] a prototype of Marka.

[1] vi. 4, 10, 1.

[2] Maitrāyaṇī Saṃhitā, iv. 6, 3; Taittirīya Brāhmaṇa, i. 1, 1, 5; Śatapatha Brāhmaṇa, iv. 2, 1, 4.

[3] Vājasaneyi Saṃhitā, vii. 16. 17.

[4] *Vedische Mythologie*, 3, 442 *et seq.*

[5] *Cf. Transactions of the Connecticut Academy of Arts and Sciences*, 15, 49, n. 1.

[6] *Op. cit.*, 1, 223 *et seq.*

[7] v. 77, 1.

[8] Taittirīya Āraṇyaka, iv. 29; Maitrāyaṇī Saṃhitā, iv. 9, 19.

Cf. Eggeling, *Sacred Books of the East*, 26, 279 *et seq.*

Markaṭa, 'ape,' is enumerated in the list of victims at the Aśvamedha ('horse sacrifice') in the Yajurveda Saṃhitās.[1] It is classified in the same Saṃhitās[2] with man and the elephant as 'taking hold by the hand' (*hastādāna*) instead of 'taking hold by the mouth' (*mukhādāna*). The animal is mentioned several times elsewhere also.[3] *Cf.* **Puruṣa Hastin, Mayu.**

[1] Taittirīya Saṃhitā, v. 5, 11, 1; Maitrāyaṇī Saṃhitā, iii. 14, 11; Vājasaneyi Saṃhitā, xxiv. 30.

[2] Taittirīya Saṃhitā, vi. 4, 5, 7; Maitrāyaṇī Saṃhitā, iv. 5, 7.

[3] Aitareya Āraṇyaka, iii. 2, 4; Jaiminīya Brāhmaṇa, i. 184; Taittirīya Āraṇyaka, iii. 11, 32, etc.

Cf. Zimmer, *Altindisches Leben*, 85.

1. **Marya** in the Rigveda[1] denotes a 'man' especially regarded as young and a lover, being constantly mentioned as in company with maidens (*yuvatī*).

[1] iii. 31, 7; 33, 10; iv. 20, 5; ix. 96, 20, etc.; *marya-śrī*, 'adorned as a lover,' ii. 10, 5. *Cf.* Nirukta, iii. 15; iv. 2.

2. **Marya**[1] in several passages of the Rigveda[1] denotes a 'stallion.'[2] It is once[3] described as *pastyāvant*, 'a stalled horse'—that is, one carefully tended, and not allowed out to graze.

[1] vii. 56, 16; viii. 43, 25.

[2] This is, of course, only a specialized sense of 1. Marya as meaning a 'male' (*cf.* Lat. *mas*, *maritus*). The specialized meaning is somewhat analogous to the use of 'sire' in English.

[3] Rv. ix. 97, 18. Roth, St. Petersburg Dictionary, *s.v.* 2, thinks Rv. i. 91, 13, may have the same sense.

Maryaka, occurring only once in the Rigveda,[1] seems to denote the bull which is described as separated from the cows.

[1] v. 2, 5. *Cf.* Oldenberg, *Ṛgveda-Noten*, 1, 313.

Maryādā, 'boundary,' is found in the Satapatha Brāhmaṇa[1] referring to the boundary between the **Kosalas** and the **Videhas**. Usually the word is metaphorically employed.[2]

[1] i. 4, 1, 17. *Cf.* xiii. 8, 4, 12.

[2] Rv. iv. 5, 13; x. 5, 6; Av. vi. 81, 2 (of an amulet). In the Atharvaveda passage Whitney, Translation of the Atharvaveda, 392, suggests, owing to the very curious use of the word, the emendation *marya-dā*, 'giver of a son.'

Mala in one passage of the Rigveda[1] is used of the garments of the Munis. The St. Petersburg Dictionary takes it to mean a 'leathern garment,'[2] but Ludwig and Zimmer[3] think it means only 'soiled' raiment, which, of course, suits the ordinary sense of the word ('dirt') in the Atharvaveda,[4] and the character of the long-haired (*keśin*) hermit (**Muni**). *Cf.* **Malaga.**

[1] x. 136, 2.

[2] If this were correct, the word might be derived from *mlā* in the sense of 'to tan.' *Cf.* **Carman**, especially notes 6 and 7.

[3] *Altindisches Leben*, 262.

[4] vi. 115, 3; vii. 89, 3; x. 5, 24, etc. *Cf.* Schrader, *Prehistoric Antiquities*, 333, n.

Mala-ga in one passage of the Atharvaveda[1] denotes a cleanser of clothes, a 'washerman,' but the origin of the word is somewhat uncertain.[2]

[1] xii. 3, 21.

[2] It may, perhaps, have primarily meant 'concerned with dirt.' See the St. Petersburg Dictionary, *s.v. ga* 1, on the use of *ga* as forming compounds; and *cf.* **Mala.**

Cf. Zimmer, *Altindisches Leben*, 262; Bloomfield, *Hymns of the Atharvaveda*, 188.

Malimlu in the Yajurveda Saṃhitā[1] denotes a 'robber,' specifically, according to the commentator Mahīdhara, a burglar or housebreaker. *Cf.* **Tāyu, Taskara, Stena,** and **Deva-malimluc.**

[1] Taittirīya Saṃhitā, vi. 3, 2, 6; Vājasaneyi Saṃhitā, xi. 78. 79; Av. xix. 49, 10.

Malimluca is the name of an intercalary month in the Kāṭhaka Saṃhitā.[1] See **Māsa.**

[1] xxxv. 10; xxxviii. 14. *Cf.* Weber, *Jyotiṣa*, 100, 102; *Naxatra*, 2, 350.

1. **Maśaka** denotes a 'biting fly' or 'mosquito,' being described in the Atharvaveda[1] as 'quickly (?) biting' (*tṛpra-daṃśin*), and as having a poisonous sting. The elephant is mentioned[2] as particularly subject to its stings. The insect is often referred to elsewhere.[3] *Cf.* **Daṃśa.**

[1] vii. 56, 3.

[2] Av. iv. 36, 9.

[3] Av. xi. 3, 5; at the Aśvamedha ('horse sacrifice'), Maitrāyaṇī Saṃhitā, iii. 14, 8; Vājasaneyi Saṃhitā, xxiv. 29; xxv. 3; Bṛhadāraṇyaka Upaniṣad, i. 3, 24 (Mādhyaṃdina = i. 3, 22 Kāṇva); Chāndogya Upaniṣad, vi. 9, 3; 10, 2.

Cf. Zimmer, *Altindisches Leben*, 97.

2. **Maśaka Gārgya** ('descendant of **Garga**') is the name of a teacher, a pupil of **Sthiraka Gārgya,** in the Vaṃśa Brāhmaṇa.[1] He is also mentioned in the Sūtras[2] of the Sāmaveda, and is the reputed author of an extant Kalpa Sūtra.

[1] *Indische Studien*, 4, 373. 382.

[2] Lāṭyāyana Śrauta Sūtra, vii. 9, 14; Anupada Sūtra, ix. 9.

Cf. Weber, *Indian Literature*, 75. 76; 83, 84.

Maśarśāra is the name of a king, according to Ludwig,[1] of the **Nahuṣas**, in the Rigveda.[2]

[1] Translation of the Rigveda, 3, 206.

[2] i. 122, 15.

Maṣṇāra is the name of a locality, the scene of the victory of a **Kuru** king, in the Aitareya Brāhmaṇa.[1]

[1] viii. 23, 3. *Cf.* Bhāgavata Purāṇa, v. 13, 26 *et seq.*; Leumann, *Zeitschrift der Deutschen Morgenländischen Gesellschaft*, 48, 80, n. 2.

Masūra is the name of a kind of lentil (*Ervum hirsutum*) in the Vājasaneyi Saṃhitā[1] and the Bṛhadāraṇyaka Upaniṣad.[2]

[1] xviii. 12.

[2] vi. 3, 22 (Mādhyaṃdina = vi. 3, 13 Kāṇva).

Cf. Weber, *Indische Studien*, 1, 355; Zimmer, *Altindisches Leben*, 241.

Masūsya, occurring in the Taittirīya Brāhmaṇa (iii. 8, 14, 6), is, according to the commentator, the name of a grain of the north country.

Mastu in the Yajurveda Saṃhitās[1] and the Brāhmaṇas[2] denotes 'sour curds.'

[1] Taittirīya Saṃhitā, vi. 1, 1, 4; Kāṭhaka Saṃhitā, xxxvi. 1.

[2] Satapatha Brāhmaṇa, i. 8, 1, 7; iii. 3, 3, 2, etc.

Maha-ṛtvij, 'great priest,' is the collective name of the four chief priests—Adhvaryu, Brahman, Hotṛ, and Udgātṛ—in the Brāhmaṇas.[1]

[1] Taittirīya Brāhmaṇa, iii. 8, 2, 4; Śatapatha Brāhmaṇa, xiii. 1, 1, 4; Śāṅkhāyana Srauta Sūtra, xvi. 1, 7, etc.

Maha-ṛṣabha, a 'great bull,' is mentioned in the Atharvaveda (iv. 15, 1).

Maha-ṛṣi, a 'great Ṛṣi,' is mentioned in the Taittirīya Āraṇyaka (i. 9, 6). *Cf.* **Mahābrāhmaṇa.**

Mahā-kula, 'sprung from a great family,' is the designation of a bowl or cup (**Camasa**) in the Rigveda (i. 161, 1). The metaphorical use of this word shows that the high position of certain families was already recognized in the times of the Rigveda.

Mahā-kauṣītaka, the 'Great Kauṣītaka (Brāhmaṇa),' is the name of a Vedic text in the Rigveda Gṛhya Sūtras.[1]

[1] Āśvalāyana Gṛhya Sūtra, iii. 4, 4; Mahākauṣītaki, the teacher, in Śāṅkhāyana Gṛhya Sūtra, iv. 10; vi. 1, etc. *Cf.* Oldenberg, *Sacred Books of the East*, 29, 3. 4.

Mahāja, a 'great goat' (**Aja**) is mentioned in the Śatapatha Brāhmaṇa (iii. 4, 1, 2).

Mahā-dhana in the Rigveda denotes either a 'great fight'[1] or a 'great prize'[2] as the result of a fight. In many cases the fight may mean merely the contest of the chariot race.

[1] Rv. i. 7, 5; 40, 8; 112, 17; vi. 59, 7, etc.

[2] ix. 86, 12.

Mahā-nagnī in the Atharvaveda[1] denotes a 'courtesan.' The masculine, Mahā-nagna,[2] 'paramour,' is probably secondarily derived from the feminine Mahānagnī.[3]

[1] xiv. 1, 36; xx. 136, 5 *et seq.*; Aitareya Brāhmaṇa, i. 27, 1.

[2] Av. xx. 136, 11; Śāṅkhāyana Śrauta Sūtra, xii. 24, 14. *Cf.* Whitney, Translation of the Atharvaveda, 747; Geldner, *Vedische Studien*, 1, 280, n. 1.

[3] As *sa-patna*, 'rival,' is unmistakably formed from *sa-patnī*, 'co-wife.'

Mahā-nāga, a 'great snake,' is mentioned in the Śatapatha Brāhmaṇa (xi. 2, 7, 12), where it is plainly mythical.

Mahā-niraṣṭa, a 'great castrated' ox, is mentioned as the **Dakṣiṇā,** or 'sacrificial fee,' in the house of the **Sūta** at the **Rājasūya** ('royal consecration') in the Yajurveda Saṃhitās.[1] *Cf.* **Anaḍvāh** and **Go.**

[1] Taittirīya Saṃhitā, i. 8, 9, 1; Kāṭhaka Saṃhitā, xv. 4. 9; Maitrāyaṇī Saṃhitā, ii. 6, 5.

Mahā-patha in the Brāhmaṇas[1] denotes the 'high road' between two villages.

[1] Aitareya Brāhmaṇa, iv. 17, 8; Chāndogya Upaniṣad, viii. 6, 2. *Cf.* Weber, *Indische Studien*, 1, 271, n.

Mahā-pura in the Yajurveda Saṃhitās[1] and the Brāhmaṇas[2] denotes a great fortress.[1] Probably the only difference between the **Pur** and the Mahāpura was size.

[1] Taittirīya Saṃhitā, vi. 2, 3, 1; Kāṭhaka Saṃhitā, xxiv. 10; Maitrāyaṇī Saṃhitā, iii. 8, 1.

[2] Aitareya Brāhmaṇa, i. 23, 2; Gopatha Brāhmaṇa, ii. 2, 7.

Mahā-brāhmaṇa, a 'great Brahmin,' is found in the Bṛhadāraṇyaka Upaniṣad (ii. 1, 19. 22) denoting a Brahmin of great consequence. *Cf.* **Maharṣi.**

Mahābhiṣeka, 'great consecration,' is mentioned in the Aitareya Brāhmaṇa,[1] and described as a ceremony performed for great kings, a list of whom is given. It is equivalent to the **Rājasūya.**

[1] viii. 14, 4; 19, 2. *Cf.* Weber, *Episches im vedischen Ritual*, 8. The list is **Janamejaya Pārikṣita**, whose friend was **Tura Kāvaṣeya**; **Śāryāta Mānava** and **Cyavana Bhārgava**; **Satānīka Sātrājita** and **Somaśuṣma Bhārgava**; **Ambarīṣa** and **Parvata** and **Nārada**; **Yudhāṃśrauṣṭi Augrasainya** and the same two Ṛṣis; **Viśvakarman Bhauvana** and **Kaśyapa**; **Sudās Paijavana** and **Vasiṣṭha**; **Marutta Āvikṣita** and **Saṃvarta**; **Aṅga Vairocana** and **Udamaya Ātreya**; **Bharata Dauḥṣanti** and **Dīrghatamas Māmateya**; **Durmukha Pāñcāla** and **Bṛhaduktha**; **Atyarāti Jānaṃtapi** and **Vāsiṣṭha Sātyahavya.**

Mahā-bhūta in the Nirukta (xiv. 5, 10) and the Aitareya Upaniṣad (iii. 2, 3) denotes the 'gross elements' (earth, water, fire, air, ether).

Mahā-matsya, a 'great fish,' is mentioned in the Bṛhadāraṇyaka Upaniṣad (iv. 3, 18).

Mahā-meru, 'great Meru,' is the name of a mountain in the Taittirīya Āraṇyaka.[1]

[1] i. 7, 1. 3. *Cf.* Weber, *Indische Studien*, 1, 78; 3, 123.

Mahā-ratha, 'having a great car'—*i.e.*, 'a great chariot fighter,' is an epithet of the hero who is prayed for in the ritual of the Aśvamedha (' horse sacrifice ') in the Yajurveda Saṃhitās.[1]

[1] Taittirīya Saṃhitā, vii. 5, 18, 1; Vājasaneyi Saṃhitā, xxii. 22.

Mahā-rāja, a 'great king,' is frequently referred to in the Brāhmaṇas.[1] It seems to mean no more than a king, or rather perhaps a reigning and powerful king, as opposed to a mere prince, who would also be called **Rājan.**

[1] Aitareya Brāhmaṇa, vii. 34, 9; Kauṣītaki Brāhmaṇa, v. 5; Śatapatha Brāhmaṇa, i. 6, 4, 21; ii. 5, 4, 9; Bṛhadāraṇyaka Upaniṣad, ii. 1, 19 *et seq.*; Maitrāyaṇī Upaniṣad, ii. 1, etc.

Mahā-rātra, 'advanced night,' is a phrase found in the Kauṣītaki Brāhmaṇa[1] and the Sūtras[2] to denote the latter part of the night, after midnight and before dawn.

[1] ii. 9; xi. 8.

[2] Śāṅkhāyana Śrauta Sūtra, vi 2, 1; xvii. 7, 1, etc.

Mahārṇava, a 'great ocean,' is a phrase not found before the late Maitrāyaṇī Upaniṣad (i. 4), where the drying up of 'great oceans' is one of the marvels enumerated. *Cf.* **Samudra.**

Mahā-vīra (' great hero ') is the name in the later Saṃhitās and the Brāhmaṇas[1] of a large earthenware pot which could be placed on the fire, and which was especially employed at the introductory Soma ceremony called Pravargya.

[1] Vājasaneyi Saṃhitā, xix. 14; Śatapatha Brāhmaṇa, xiv. 1, 2, 9. 17; 3, 1, 13; 4, 16; 2, 2, 13. 40; Pañcaviṃśa Brāhmaṇa, ix. 10, 1; Kauṣītaki Brāhmaṇa, viii. 3. 7, etc.

Mahā-vṛkṣa, a 'great tree,' is mentioned sometimes in the Pañcaviṃśa Brāhmaṇa (vii. 6, 15; xiv. 1, 12) and in the Sūtras.

Mahā-vṛṣa is the name of a tribe mentioned along with the **Mūjavants** in the Atharvaveda[1] as a locality to which fever is to be relegated. It is reasonable to suppose that they were

[1] v. 22, 4. 5. 8.

northerners, though Bloomfield[2] suggests that the name may be chosen more for its sound and sense (as 'of mighty strength' to resist the disease) than for its geographical position. In the Chāndogya Upaniṣad[3] the place **Raikvaparṇa** is said to be in the Mahāvṛṣa country. The king of the Mahāvṛṣas in the Jaiminīya Upaniṣad Brāhmaṇa[4] is said to be **Hṛtsvāśaya.** The Mahāvṛṣas are also known from a Mantra in the Baudhāyana Śrauta Sūtra.[5]

2 *Hymns of the Atharvaveda*, 446.
3 iv. 2, 5.
4 iii. 40, 2.
5 ii. 5.

Cf. Weber, *Indian Literature*, 70, 147; Zimmer, *Altindisches Leben*, 129; Whitney, Translation of the Atharvaveda, 259, 260.

1. **Mahā-śāla** (lit., 'having a great house'), a 'great householder,' is an expression applied in the Chāndogya Upaniṣad (v. 11, 1) to the Brahmins who were instructed by **Aśvapati,** no doubt to emphasize their importance. *Cf.* **Mahābrāhmaṇa.**

2. **Mahā-śāla Jābāla** is the name of a teacher twice mentioned in the Śatapatha Brāhmaṇa, once as instructing **Dhīra Śātaparṇeya,**[1] and once as one of the Brahmins who received instruction from **Aśvapati.**[2] In the parallel passage of the Chāndogya Upaniṣad[3] the name is **Prācīnaśāla Aupamanyava.**[4] The word must be considered a proper name rather than an adjective (1. **Mahāśāla**), as it is taken in the St. Petersburg Dictionary.[5]

1 x. 3, 3, 1.
2 x. 6, 1, 1.
3 v. 11, 1.
4 *Cf.* Eggeling, *Sacred Books of the East*, 43, 393, n. 1.

5 In Muṇḍaka Upaniṣad, i. 1, 3, the word is used of **Śaunaka**, perhaps merely as an epithet. *Cf.* Weber, *Indian Literature*, 161.

Mahā-suparṇa in the Śatapatha Brāhmaṇa (xii. 2, 3, 7) denotes a 'great bird' or 'great eagle.'

Mahā-suhaya, a 'great (*i.e.*, high-spirited) horse,' is the description in the Bṛhadāraṇyaka Upaniṣad[1] of the steed from

1 vi. 2, 13. *Cf.* Śāṅkhāyana Āraṇyaka, ix. 7; Chāndogya Upaniṣad, v. 1, 12; Pischel, *Vedische Studien*, 1, 234, 235; Keith, *Śāṅkhāyana Āraṇyaka*, 57, n. 3. *Cf.* **Paḍbīśa.**

the Indus (*saindhava*) which tears away the peg of its hobble (*paḍbīśa-śaṅkhu*).

Mahā-sūkta, m. plur., the 'composers of the long hymns' of the tenth Maṇḍala of the Rigveda[1] are mentioned in the Aitareya Āraṇyaka[2] and the Sūtras.[3] *Cf.* **Kṣudra-sūkta.**

[1] x. 1-128.
[2] ii. 2, 2.
[3] Aśvalāyana Gṛhya Sūtra, iii. 4, 2; Sāṅkhāyana Gṛhya Sūtra, iv. 10.

Cf. Weber, *Indische Studien*, 1, 115; 390; Roth, *Zur Litteratur und Geschichte des Weda*, 27.

Mahāhna in the Kauṣītaki Brāhmaṇa (ii. 9) denotes the 'advanced (time of the) day'—that is, 'afternoon.' *Cf.* **Mahārātra.**

Mahi-dāsa Aitareya ('descendant of Itara or Itarā') is the name of the sage from whom the Aitareya Brāhmaṇa and Āraṇyaka take their names. He is several times referred to in the Aitareya Āraṇyaka,[1] but not as its author. He is credited with a life of 116 years in the Chāndogya Upaniṣad[2] and the Jaiminīya Upaniṣad Brāhmaṇa.[3]

[1] ii. 1, 8; 3, 7.
[2] iii. 16, 7.
[3] iv. 2, 11 (*cf. Journal of the American Oriental Society*, 15, 246).

Cf. Keith, *Aitareya Āraṇyaka*, 16, 17.

Mahiṣa, the 'strong,' with[1] or without[2] **Mṛga**, 'wild beast,' denotes the 'buffalo' in the Rigveda and the later texts. The feminine, Mahiṣī, is found in the later Saṃhitās.[3]

[1] Rv. viii. 58, 15; ix. 92, 6; 96, 6; x. 123, 4.
[2] Rv. v. 29, 7; vi. 67, 11; viii. 12, 8; 66, 10; ix. 87, 7; x. 28, 10; 189, 2; Vājasaneyi Saṃhitā, xxiv. 28, etc.
[3] Kāṭhaka Saṃhitā, xxv. 6; Maitrāyaṇī Saṃhitā, iii. 8, 5; Ṣaḍviṃśa Brāhmaṇa, v. 7, 11.

1. **Mahiṣī.** See **Mahiṣa.**

2. **Mahiṣī**, 'the powerful one,' the name of the first of the four wives (see **Pati**) of the king, is mentioned frequently in

the later literature.[1] Perhaps even in the Rigveda[2] the technical sense of 'first wife' is present.

[1] Taittirīya Saṃhitā, i. 8, 9, 1; Kāṭhaka Saṃhitā, xv. 4; Maitrāyaṇī Saṃhitā, ii. 6, 5; Pañcaviṃśa Brāhmaṇa, xix. 1, 4; Śatapatha Brāhmaṇa, vi. 5, 3, 1; vii. 5, 1, 6, etc.

[2] v. 2, 2; 37, 3.

Mahaitareya is the title of a Vedic text according to the Gṛhya Sūtras of the Rgveda.[1]

[1] Āśvalāyana Gṛhya Sūtra, iii. 4, 4; of a teacher, in Śāṅkhāyana Gṛhya Sūtra, iv. 10; vi. 1. *Cf.* Keith, *Aitareya Āraṇyaka*, 39; Oldenberg, *Sacred Books of the East*, 29, 3, 4.

Mahokṣa, a 'great bull,' is mentioned in the Śatapatha Brāhmaṇa (iii. 4, 1, 2).

Māṃsa, 'flesh.' The eating of flesh appears as something quite regular in the Vedic texts, which show no trace of the doctrine of Ahiṃsā, or abstaining from injury to animals. For example, the ritual offerings of flesh contemplate that the gods will eat it, and again the Brahmins ate the offerings.[1] Again, the slaying of a 'great ox' (*mahokṣa*) or a 'great goat' (*mahāja*) for a guest was regularly prescribed;[2] and the name **Atithigva** probably means 'slaying cows for guests.'[3] The great sage **Yājñavalkya** was wont to eat the meat of milch cows and bullocks (*dhenv-anaḍuha*) if only it was *aṃsala* ('firm' or 'tender').[4] The slaughter of a hundred bulls (*ukṣan*) was credited to one sacrificer, **Agastya.**[5] The marriage ceremony was accompanied by the slaying of oxen, clearly for food.[6]

[1] So Agni is called 'eater of ox and cow' in Rv. viii. 43, 11 = Av. iii. 21, 6 = Taittirīya Saṃhitā, i. 3, 14, 7; Weber, *Indische Studien*, 17, 280, 281; Oldenberg, *Religion des Veda*, 355.

[2] Śatapatha Brāhmaṇa, iii. 4, 1, 2. *Cf.* Śāṅkhāyana Gṛhya Sūtra, ii. 15, 2.

[3] Bloomfield, *American Journal of Philology*, 17, 426; *Journal of the American Oriental Society*, 16, cxxiv. *Cf. atithinīr gāḥ*, 'cows fit for guests,' Rv. x. 68, 3.

[4] Śatapatha Brāhmaṇa, iii. 1, 2, 21. The sense of *aṃsala* is given as *sthūla*, 'firm,' in the scholiast. *Cf.* Kātyāyana Śrauta Sūtra, vii. 2, 23-25. Eggeling, *Sacred Books of the East*, 26, 11, has 'tender.' 'Off the shoulder' (*aṃsa*) is also a possible version.

[5] Taittirīya Brāhmaṇa, ii. 7, 11, 1; Pañcaviṃśa Brāhmaṇa, xxi. 14, 5.

[6] Rv. x. 85, 13. *Cf.* Winternitz, *Das altindische Hochzeitsrituell*, 33.

That there was any general objection to the eating of flesh is most improbable. Sometimes it is forbidden, as when a man is performing a vow,[7] or its use is disapproved, as in a passage of the Atharvaveda,[8] where meat is classed with **Surā**, or intoxicating liquor, as a bad thing. Again, in the Rigveda[9] the slaying of the cows is said to take place in the **Aghās**, a deliberate variation for **Maghās**; but this may be the outcome merely of a natural association of death with gloom, even when cows alone are the victims in question. The Brāhmaṇas also contain the doctrine of the eater in this world being eaten in the next,[10] but this is not to be regarded as a moral or religious disapproval of eating flesh, though it no doubt contains the germ of such a view, which is also in harmony with the persuasion of the unity of existence, which becomes marked in the Brāhmaṇas. But Ahiṃsā as a developed and articulate doctrine would seem to have arisen from the acceptance of the doctrine of transmigration, which in its fundamentals is later than the Brāhmaṇa period.[11]

On the other hand, it is to be noted that the cow was on the road to acquire special sanctity in the Rigveda,[12] as is shown by the name *aghnyā*,[13] 'not to be slain,' applied to it in several passages. But this fact cannot be regarded as showing that

[7] Kātyāyana Śrauta Sūtra, ii. 1, 8. So a **Brahmacārin** is not to eat flesh. See Oldenberg, *op. cit.*, 468, n. 3. The blood of an animal is always a somewhat mysterious and dangerous substance; hence taboos on meat-eating, which in another form arise from fear of the spirits of the dead (*cf.* Oldenberg, *op. cit.*, 414, n. 1). See also Śatapatha Brāhmaṇa, xiv. 1, 1, 29; Keith, *Journal of the Royal Asiatic Society*, 1909, 588, n. 4.

[8] vi. 70, 1. *Cf.* Bloomfield, *Hymns of the Atharvaveda*, 493.

[9] x. 85, 13. In the Atharvaveda, xiv. 1, 13, the ordinary word Maghās is found, and is, no doubt, really to be preferred. See Weber, Proceedings of the Berlin Academy, 1894, 807.

[10] *Cf.* the story of **Bhṛgu Vāruṇi** in the Śatapatha Brāhmaṇa, xi. 6, 1, 1 *et seq.*; Jaiminīya Brāhmaṇa, i. 42-44; Aitareya Āraṇyaka, ii. 1, 2, with Keith's notes (pp. 202, 203).

[11] *Cf.* Deussen, *Philosophy of the Upanishads*, 317 *et seq.*; Keith, *Journal of the Royal Asiatic Society*, 1909, 565.

[12] viii. 101, 15. 16; Vājasaneyi Saṃhitā, iv. 19, 20; Av. x. 10; xii. 4, 5; Macdonell, *Vedic Mythology*, p. 151.

[13] Found sixteen times in the Rigveda, as opposed to three instances of Aghnya (masculine); Macdonell, *loc. cit.* The sense of 'hard to overcome,' preferred by the St. Petersburg Dictionary, to that of 'not to be killed,' is, however, quite possible. Weber, *op. cit.*, 17, 281, tries to derive the word from *ahanya*, 'bright-coloured like day,' a derivation that must be regarded as illegitimate.

meat eating generally was condemned. Apart from mythical considerations, such as the identification of the cow with earth or Aditi (which are, of course, much more than an effort of priestly ingenuity), the value of the cow for other purposes than eating was so great as to account adequately for its sanctity, the beginnings of which can in fact be traced back to Indo-Iranian times.[14] Moreover, the ritual of the cremation of the dead required the slaughter of a cow as an essential part, the flesh being used to envelope the dead body.[15]

The usual food of the Vedic Indian, as far as flesh was concerned, can be gathered from the list of sacrificial victims: what man ate he presented to the gods—that is, the sheep, the goat, and the ox. The horse sacrifice was an infrequent exception: it is probably not to be regarded as a trace of the use of horseflesh as food, though the possibility of such being the case cannot be overlooked in view of the widespread use of horseflesh as food in different countries and times. It is, however, more likely that the aim of this sacrifice was to impart magic strength, the speed and vigour of the horse, to the god and his worshippers, as Oldenberg[16] argues.

[14] *Cf.* Macdonell, *Sanskrit Literature*, 68.

[15] Rv. x. 16, 7. See Oldenberg, *op. cit.*, 576.

[16] *Religion des Veda*, 356, n. 4. As to meat-eating in Buddhist times, *cf.* the death of the Buddha from a meal of pork, Fleet, *Journal of the Royal Asiatic Society*, 1906, 881, 882; Oldenberg, *Buddha*,[5] 231, n. 2 (*contra* Neumann, *Die Reden des Gotamo Buddho*, 1, xix). As to meat-eating in the Epic, see Hopkins, *Journal of the American Oriental Society*, 13, 119, 120; *Great Epic of India*, 377-379; and see for modern instances Jolly, *Deutsche Rundschau*, July, 1884. 118; Bühler, *Report*, 23.

Cf. Schrader, *Prehistoric Antiquities*, 316; Hopkins, *Religions of India*, 156, 189.

Maṃsaudana denotes in the Śatapatha Brāhmaṇa[1] a dish consisting of 'meat cooked with rice.'

[1] xi. 5, 7, 5; Bṛhadāraṇyaka Upaniṣad, vi. 4, 18; Śāṅkhāyana Āraṇyaka, xii. 8.

Mākṣavya, 'descendant of Makṣu,' is the patronymic of a teacher in the Aitareya Āraṇyaka.[1]

[1] iii. 1, 1, which is discussed in the preface to the Rigveda Prātiśākhya. *Cf.* Weber, *Indische Studien*, 1, 391, 2, 212.

Māgadha. See **Magadha.**

Māgadha-deśīya, 'belonging to the district of **Magadha,**' is the description in the Sūtras[1] of a Brahmin of Magadha.

[1] Kātyāyana Śrauta Sūtra, xxii. 4, 22; Lāṭyāyana Śrauta Sūtra, viii. 6, 28.

Mācala, mentioned in the Jaiminīya Brāhmaṇa,[1] apparently denotes some sort of dog found in **Vidarbha.**

[1] ii. 440. *Cf. Journal of the American Oriental Society*, 19, 103, n. 3.

Māṭharī, 'female descendant of Maṭhara,' occurs in the curious name, **Kāśyapī-bālākyā-māṭharī-putra,** of a teacher in the Bṛhadāraṇyaka Upaniṣad (vi. 4, 31 Mādhyaṃdina).

Māṇṭi is the name of a teacher, a pupil of **Gautama,** in the Bṛhadāraṇyaka Upaniṣad.[1]

[1] ii. 5, 22; iv. 5, 28 (Mādhyaṃdina = ii. 6, 3; iv. 6, 3 Kāṇva).

Māṇḍavī, 'female descendant of Maṇḍu,' occurs in the name of a teacher, **Vātsī-māṇḍavī-putra,** in the Bṛhadāraṇyaka Upaniṣad (vi. 4, 30 Mādhyaṃdina).

Māṇḍavya, 'descendant of Maṇḍu,' is mentioned as a teacher in the Śatapatha Brāhmaṇa,[1] in the Śāṅkhāyana Āraṇyaka,[2] and in the Sūtras.[3] He is also mentioned as a pupil of **Kautsa** in the last Vaṃśa (list of teachers) of the Bṛhadāranyaka Upaniṣad.[4]

[1] x. 6, 5, 9.
[2] vii. 2.
[3] Āśvalāyana Gṛhya Sūtra, iii. 4, 4; Śāṅkhāyana Gṛhya Sūtra, iv. 10; vi. 1. *Cf.* Weber, *Indische Studien* 1, 482 (in the Epic a friend of **Janaka** is so named).
[4] vi. 5, 4 Kāṇva.

Māṇḍūkāyani, 'descendant of Māṇḍūka,' is mentioned as a teacher in the Śatapatha Brāhmaṇa.[1]

[1] x. 6, 5, 9; Bṛhadāraṇyaka Upaniṣad, vi. 5, 4 Kāṇva.

Māṇḍūkāyanī-putra, 'son of a female descendant of Māṇḍūka,' is the name of a teacher, a pupil of **Māṇḍūkīputra** in the last Vaṃśa (list of teachers) of the Bṛhadāraṇyaka Upaniṣad.[1]

[1] vi. 4, 32 (Mādhyaṃdina = vi. 5, 2 Kāṇva).

Māṇḍūkī-putra, 'son of a female descendant of Maṇḍūka,' is mentioned as a teacher, a pupil of **Śāṇḍilīputra**, in the last Vaṃśa (list of teachers) in the Bṛhadāraṇyaka Upaniṣad.[1]

[1] vi. 4, 32 (Mādhyaṃdina = vi. 5, 2 Kāṇva).

Māṇḍūkeya, 'descendant of Māṇḍūka,' is the patronymic of several teachers in the Rigveda Āraṇyakas—viz., **Śūravīra**,[1] **Hrasva**,[2] **Dīrgha**,[3] **Madhyama Prātībodhīputra**.[4] The Māṇḍūkeyas also occur as a school in the Āraṇyakas[5]: a special form of the text of the Rigveda evidently appertained to them.[6]

[1] Aitareya Āraṇyaka, iii. 1, 1; Sāṅkhāyana Āraṇyaka, vii. 2. 8. 9. 10.
[2] Śāṅkhāyana Āraṇyaka, vii. 12; viii. 11.
[3] *Ibid.*, vii. 2.
[4] *Ibid.*, vii. 13.
[5] Aitareya Āraṇyaka, iii. 1, 1; Sāṅkhāyana Āraṇyaka, vii. 2.
[6] *Cf.* the *Māṇḍūkeyīya adhyāya* of the Aitareya Āraṇyaka, iii. 2, 6; Śāṅkhāyana Āraṇyaka, viii. 11; Scheftelowitz, *Die Apokryphen des Rigveda*, 12; Keith, *Journal of the Royal Asiatic Society*, 1907, 227; *Aitareya Āraṇyaka*, 239; Weber, *Indische Studien*, 1, 391.

Mātariśvan is mentioned in a Vālakhilya hymn of the Rigveda[1] as a sacrificer along with **Medhya** and **Pṛṣadhra**. He seems to be mentioned also in one other passage, possibly in two.[2] In the Śāṅkhāyana Śrauta Sūtra[3] a patron, **Pṛṣadhra Medhya Mātariśvan** or **Mātariśva** is created by a misunderstanding of the Rigvedic text.

[1] Rv. viii. 52, 2.
[2] Rv. x. 48, 2; 105, 6. The former reference is much more probable than the latter.
[3] xvi. 11, 26; Weber, *Episches im vedischen Ritual*, 39, 40. The manuscripts vary between Mātariśvan and Mātariśva.

Cf. Ludwig, Translation of the Rigveda, 3, 163.

Mātur-bhrātra is a curiously formed compound, occurring once in the Maitrāyaṇī Saṃhitā[1] as a designation of the 'maternal uncle,' who in the Sūtra period bears the name of **Mātula**. Thus little is heard of the maternal uncle in the Vedic period: it is not till the Epic[2] that traces appear of his prominence as compared with the paternal uncle (*pitṛvya*). This fact is significant for the 'patriarchal' character of the early Indian family organization.[3]

[1] i. 6, 12.

[2] Hopkins, *Journal of the American Oriental Society*, 13, 141.

[3] Delbrück, *Die indogermanischen Verwandtschaftsnamen*, 484, 586-588. *Cf.* also Rivers, *Journal of the Royal Asiatic Society*, 1907, 629 *et seq.*

Mātula,[1] 'maternal uncle,' is found only in the Sūtras[2] and later.

[1] This peculiarly formed word was presumably a dialectic form which made its way into the written speech.

[2] Āśvalāyana Gṛhya Sūtra, i. 24, 4, etc.

Mātṛ is the regular word for 'mother' from the Rigveda onwards,[1] being a formation probably developed under the influence of an onomatopœtic word *mā*,[2] used like Ambā[3] and **Nanā**.[4]

The relations of wife and husband, as well as of mother and children, are treated under **Pati**. It remains only to add that details are given in the Sūtras[5] of the respectful attention paid to a mother, and of the ceremonies in which she is concerned. The mother also appears interested in the fate of her children as in the story of the sale of **Śunaḥśepa** for adoption by **Viśvāmitra** in the Aitareya Brāhmaṇa.[6]

[1] i. 24, 1; vii. 101, 3, etc.; Vājasaneyi Saṃhitā, xiii. 21, etc.; Aitareya Brāhmaṇa, ii. 6, etc.

[2] Böhtlingk and Roth, St. Petersburg Dictionary, *s.v.*, note.

[3] *Cf. ambe ambike ambalike*, Vājasaneyi Saṃhitā, xxiii. 18, with variations in Taittirīya Saṃhitā, vii. 4, 19, 1; Maitrāyaṇī Saṃhitā, iii. 12, 20; Taittirīya Brāhmaṇa, iii. 9, 6, 3; also *ambā ambāyavī, ambayā*, in the Kauṣītaki Upaniṣad, i. 3.

[4] Rv. ix. 112, 3 (**Upalaprakṣiṇī**). See von Schroeder, *Mysterium und Mimus*, 412.

[5] *Cf.* Delbrück, *Die indogermanischen Verwandtschaftsnamen*, 460, 476, 477.

[6] vii. 18 *seq.* *Cf.* also Leist, *Altarisches Jus Gentium*, 104; Jolly, *Die Adoption in Indien*, 16, 17.

In the household the mother ranked after the father (see **Pitṛ**). Occasionally *mātarā* is used for 'parents,' as are also *pitarā* and *mātarā pitarā*[7] and *mātā-pitaraḥ*.[8]

[7] Rv. iii. 33, 3; vii. 2, 5, etc. For *mātarā pitarā*, see Rv. iv. 6, 7; Vājasaneyi Saṃhitā, ix. 19.

[8] Taittirīya Saṃhitā, i. 3, 10, 1; vi. 3, 11, 3.

Mātṛ-vadha, 'matricide,' is mentioned as a very grave crime in the Kauṣītaki Upaniṣad (iii. 1), but as one that can be expiated by the knowledge of the truth.

Mātṛ-han, 'mother-killer,' 'matricide,' occurs in a Vedic quotation mentioned by the commentator on Pāṇini.[1]

[1] Kāśikā Vṛtti on Pāṇini, iii. 2, 88: *mātṛhā saptamaṃ narakaṃ praviśet*.

Mātrā in the Upaniṣads[1] denotes a mora, the length of a short vowel.

[1] Taittirīya Upaniṣad, i. 2, 1; Aitareya Āraṇyaka, iii. 1, 5; Śāṅkhāyana Āraṇyaka, vii. 15.

1. **Mātsya**, 'prince of the Matsya people.' See **Matsya**.

2. **Mātsya** occurs in the Taittirīya Brāhmaṇa[1] as the name of a Ṛṣi skilled in sacrifice. Possibly,[2] but not probably, he may also be meant in the Atharvaveda.[3]

[1] i. 5, 2, 1, where he serves **Yajñeṣu** and **Śatadyumna**.

[2] Bloomfield, *Hymns of the Atharvaveda*, 681.

[3] xix. 39, 9.

Cf. Weber, *Naxatra*, 2, 306.

Māthava, 'descendant of Mathu,' is the patronymic of **Videgha**, perhaps 'king of Videha,' in the Śatapatha Brāhmaṇa.[1]

[1] i. 4, 1, 10. 17. *Cf.* Eggeling, *Sacred Books of the East*, 12, xli, 104, n. 1; 26, xxix.; Weber, *Indische Studien*, 1, 170.

Mādhuki, 'descendant of **Madhuka**, is the patronymic of a teacher mentioned with disapproval in the Śatapatha Brāhmaṇa.[1]

[1] ii. 1, 4, 27. *Cf.* Weber, *Indische Studien*, 1, 434.

Mādhyaṃdināyana, 'descendant of Madhyaṃdina,' is the patronymic of a teacher mentioned in the Kāṇva recension of the Bṛhadāraṇyaka Upaniṣad (iv. 6, 2).

Mādhyama ('relating to the middle') is a term applied in the Kauṣītaki Brāhmaṇa[1] and the Aitareya Āraṇyaka[2] to denote the 'authors of the middle books' (ii.-vii.) of the Rigveda.

[1] xii. 3.

[2] ii. 2, 2.

Cf. Weber, *Indische Studien*, 1, 115, 389; Āśvalāyana Gṛhya Sūtra, iii. 4, 2; Śāṅkhāyana Gṛhya Sūtra, iv. 10, etc.

1. **Māna** as a measure of weight is said to be the equivalent of the **Kṛṣṇala** or Raktikā—that is, the berry of the Guñjā (*Abrus precatorius*). It occurs in compounds in the later Saṃhitās and the Brāhmaṇas.[1]

[1] Taittirīya Saṃhitā, iii. 2, 6, 3; vi. 4, 10, 2; Taittirīya Brāhmaṇa, i. 3, 7, 7; 7, 6, 2; Śatapatha Brāhmaṇa, v. 4, 3, 24; 5, 5, 16, etc.

2. **Māna** is the name of a man occurring in several passages of the Rigveda. In one place[1] express mention is made of his son (*sūnu*), by whom, despite Bergaigne's view to the contrary,[2] **Agastya** must be meant. In another passage,[3] apparently the same meaning applies to Māna—that is, Agastya as 'a Māna.' In a third passage[4] the expression *sūnave Mānena* has been held by Sieg[5] to be an inversion of *Mānasya sūnunā*, 'by the son of Māna'—*i.e.*, Agastya; but it seems more likely[6] that either *sūnor Māna* is the fuller form of Agastya's name ('pride

[1] Rv. i. 189, 8.

[2] *Religion Védique*, 2, 394. *Cf.* Pischel, *Vedische Studien*, 1, 173; Oldenberg, *Zeitschrift der Deutschen Morgenländischen Gesellschaft*, 42, 221, n. 5; *Ṛgveda-Noten*, 1, 110; Sieg, *Die Sagenstoffe des Ṛgveda*, 107; Geldner, *Rigveda, Glossar*, 135.

[3] vii. 33, 13. *Cf.* verse 10.

[4] i. 117, 11.

[5] *Loc. cit.*

[6] Oldenberg, *Ṛgveda-Noten*, *loc. cit.*

of the son,' with reference to his high ancestry), or that the son[7] of Māna (= Agastya) is alluded to as interested in **Viśpalā.**

The Mānas—that is, the descendants of Māna, are in several passages alluded to as singers.[8] *Cf.* **Mānya, Māndārya.**

[7] Bergaigne, *loc. cit.*; Pischel, *loc. cit.* *Cf.* Roth, St. Petersburg Dictionary, *s.v.*, where *sūnoḥ* is taken as dependent on *vājam.*

[8] Rv. i. 169, 8; 171, 5; 182, 8; 184, 5. *Cf.* Ludwig, Translation of the Rigveda, 3, 116, 117, who thinks the Mānas were settled on the **Sindhu** (Indus). See Rv. i. 186, 5.

Mānava, 'descendant of **Manu,**'[1] is the patronymic of **Nābhānediṣṭha** and of **Śāryāta.**[2]

[1] Aitareya Brāhmaṇa, v. 14, 2.

[2] *Ibid.*, iv. 32, 7. *Cf.* Śatapatha Brāhmaṇa, iv. 1, 5, 2 (**Śaryāta**).

Mānavī, 'descendant of **Manu,**' is the patronymic of the mythical Iḍā ('oblation') in the Śatapatha Brāhmaṇa,[1] and of a woman named **Parśu** in the Rigveda.[2]

[1] i. 8, 1, 26; Taittirīya Saṃhitā, ii. 6, 7, 3.

[2] x. 86, 23.

Mānu-tantavya, 'descendant of Manutantu,' is the patronymic of **Aikādaśākṣa** in the Aitareya Brāhmaṇa (v. 30, 15). The Saumapau Mānutantavyau, 'two Saumāpas, descendants of Manutantu,' are mentioned in the Śatapatha Brāhmaṇa (xiii. 5, 3, 2).

Mānthāla is the form in the Taittirīya Brāhmaṇa (ii. 5, 8, 4) of the next name.

Mānthālava,[1] **Mānthīlava**[2] are the names in the Yajurveda Saṃhitās of a victim at the Aśvamedha ('horse sacrifice'). What it was is unknown: the commentator Mahīdhara[3] thinks it was a kind of mouse; Sāyaṇa explains it as a 'water-cock'

[1] Maitrāyaṇī Saṃhitā, iii. 14, 19, where there is a variant Mātālava; Vājasaneyi Saṃhitā, xxiv. 38.

[2] Taittirīya Saṃhitā, v. 5, 18, 1.

[3] On Vājasaneyi Saṃhitā, *loc. cit.*

(*jala-kukkuṭa*). Possiby, if Sāyaṇa's[4] version of the parallel word **Manthāvala** is to be trusted, the 'flying fox' may be meant.[5]

[4] On Taittirīya Saṃhitā, *loc. cit.* *Cf.* Zimmer, *Altindisches Leben*, 86.

[5] Böhtlingk, Dictionary, *s.v.*, and also *s.v. māndhāla*.

Māndārya Mānya, 'descendant of **Māna**,' is the name of a Ṛṣi in the Rigveda.[1] It seems most probable that **Agastya** himself is meant.[2]

[1] i. 165, 15 = i. 166, 15 = i. 167, 11 = i. 168, 10.

[2] *Cf.* Geldner, *Rigveda, Glossar*, 135; Bergaigne, *Religion Védique*, 2, 394; Oldenberg, *Zeitschrift der Deutschen Morgenländischen Gesellschaft*, 42, 221; Sieg, *Die Sagenstoffe des Ṛgveda*, 107; Max Müller, *Sacred Books of the East*, 32, 183 *et seq.*, 206.

Mānya, 'descendant of **Māna**,' is the patronymic of **Māndārya** in several passages of the Rigveda,[1] being also found alone in others.[2] It probably denotes **Agastya**.

[1] See **Māndārya**, n. 1.

[2] i. 165, 14; 177, 5; 184, 4. *Cf.* Sieg, *Die Sagenstoffe des Ṛgveda*, 107.

Mānyamāna occurs with the word **Devaka** in the Rigveda.[1] The word seems to be a patronymic from Manyamāna, meaning 'son of the proud one.'[2] Roth[3] renders the two words 'the godling, the proudling (hast thou smitten).'

[1] viii. 18, 20.

[2] Sāyaṇa takes Manyamāna as a proper name.

[3] St. Petersburg Dictionary, *s.v.* *Cf.* Hopkins, *Journal of the American Oriental Society*, 15, 264.

Māmateya, 'descendant of Mamatā,' is the metronymic of **Dīrghatamas** in the Rigveda[1] and the Aitareya Brāhmaṇa.[2]

[1] i. 147, 3; 152, 6; 158, 6.

[2] viii. 23, 1; Śāṅkhāyana Āraṇyaka, ii. 17. For Mamatā, *cf.* Bṛhaddevatā, iii. 56; iv. 11.

Māyava, 'descendant of Mayu or Māyu,' is the patronymic of a patron in the Rigveda,[1] perhaps of **Rāma**, as Ludwig[2] thinks.

[1] x. 93, 15.

[2] Translation of the Rigveda, 3, 166.

Māya in the Śatapatha Brāhmaṇa (xiii. 4, 3, 11) corresponds to **Asuravidyā**, 'magic.'

Māyu denotes the 'lowing' of a cow and the 'bleating' of a sheep or goat in the Rigveda,[1] as well as the 'chattering' of a monkey in the Atharvaveda.[2]

[1] i. 164, 28 (cow); vii. 103, 2 (cow); x. 95, 3 (ewe); Nirukta, ii. 9.

[2] vi. 38, 4; xix. 49, 4 (called *puruṣa*; *cf.* Zimmer, *Altindisches Leben*, 85, 86; St. Petersburg Dictionary, *s.v. Māyu*).

Māruta, 'descendant of Marut,' is the patronymic of **Dyutāna** and of **Nitāna**.

Mārutāśva, 'descendant of Marutāśva,' is, according to Ludwig,[1] the patronymic of a patron in the Rigveda.[2] The word may, however, be merely an adjective 'having wind-swift horses.'

[1] Translation of the Rigveda, 3, 155. It may be a patronymic of **Cyavatāna**.

[2] v. 33, 9.

Mārgaveya is the patronymic or metronymic of **Rāma** in the Aitareya Brāhmaṇa (vii. 27, 3. 4), where he is mentioned as a **Śyāparṇa**.

Mārgāra is the name of one of the victims at the Puruṣamedha ('human sacrifice') in the Yajurveda.[1] The sense of the word is apparently 'hunter, or possibly 'fisherman,'[2] as a patronymic from *mṛgāri*, 'enemy of wild beasts.'

[1] Vājasaneyi Saṃhitā, xxx. 16; Taittirīya Brāhmaṇa, iii. 4, 12, 1.

[2] *Cf.* Sāyaṇa on Taittirīya Brāhmaṇa, *loc. cit.*

1. **Mālya**, 'garland,' is found in the Upaniṣads.[1]

[1] Chāndogya Upaniṣad, viii. 2, 6; Kauṣītaki Upaniṣad, i. 4, etc.

2. **Mālya**, 'descendant of Māla,' is the patronymic of **Ārya** in the Pañcaviṃśa Brāhmaṇa (xiii. 4, 11).

Māṣa is the name of a kind of bean (*Phaseolus radiatus*) in the Atharvaveda[1] and later.[2] It is still one of the most valuable of similar plants in India. The seeds[3] were pounded (*piṣṭa*) according to the Atharvaveda.[4] These beans ripened in the winter (*hemanta*).[5] In the ritual the human head for the sacrifice is bought for twenty-one Māṣas[6]: it does not appear that the word here means a weight of metal, as it often does later.[7] A taboo on beans is found in the Yajurveda Saṃhitās.[8]

[1] vi. 140, 2; xii. 2, 53.

[2] Taittirīya Saṃhitā, v. 1, 8, 1; vii. 2, 10, 2; Kāṭhaka Saṃhitā, xii. 7; xxxii. 7; xxxvii. 1; Maitrāyaṇī Saṃhitā, iv. 3, 2; Vājasaneyi Saṃhitā, xviii. 12; Śatapatha Brāhmaṇa, i. 1, 1, 10; Bṛhadāraṇyaka Upaniṣad, vi. 3, 22 (Mādhyaṃdina=vi. 3, 13 (Kāṇva).

[3] Later described as marked with black and grey spots. *Cf.* St. Petersburg Dictionary, *s.v.*

[4] xii. 2, 53. *Ibid.*, xii. 2, 4, an offering of crushed beans (*māṣājya*) is mentioned.

[5] Taittirīya Saṃhitā, vii. 2, 10, 2.

[6] *Ibid.*, v. 1, 8, 1; Kāṭhaka Saṃhitā, xx. 8.

[7] Weber, *Zeitschrift der Deutschen Morgenländischen Gesellschaft*, 18, 267. According to Manu, viii. 134, one Māṣa is equivalent to five (erroneously stated as four above, vol. i., p. 185) **Kṛṣṇalas**. *Cf.* also St. Petersburg Dictionary, *s.v.* 2.

[8] Kāṭhaka Saṃhitā, xxxii. 7; Maitrāyaṇī Saṃhitā, i. 4, 10. *Cf.* von Schroeder, *Vienna Oriental Journal*, 15, 187-212; Keith, *Journal of the Royal Asiatic Society*, 1909, 587, 588. *Cf.* Zimmer, *Altindisches Leben*, 240.

Mās denotes rarely 'moon,'[1] and often 'month' in the Rigveda[2] and later.[3] See **Māsa.**

[1] Rv. x. 12, 7. *Cf.* also the compound *sūryā-māsā*, 'sun and moon,' viii. 94, 2; x. 64, 3; 68, 10; 92, 12; 93, 5, which may, however, be formed from *māsa*. *Cf.* Macdonell, *Vedic Grammar*, p. 220, n. 20.

[2] Rv. i. 25, 8; iv. 18, 4; v. 45, 7. 11; vii. 91, 2, etc.

[3] Av. viii. 10, 19; Taittirīya Saṃhitā, v. 5, 2, 2; Pañcaviṃśa Brāhmaṇa, iv. 4, 1; Taittirīya Brāhmaṇa, i. 4, 9, 1, etc.

Māsa denotes a 'month,' a period of time repeatedly mentioned in the Rigveda and later.

The characteristic days (or rather nights) of the month were those of the new moon, Amā-vasyā, 'home-staying (night),' and 'of the full moon,' Paurṇa-māsī. Two hymns of the Atharvaveda[1] celebrate these days respectively. A personification of the phases of the moon is seen in the four names Sinīvālī,[2]

[1] vii. 79 and 80. *Cf.* Taittirīya Saṃhitā, iii. 5, 1, 1; Taittirīya Brāhmaṇa, iii. 7, 5, 13, etc.

[2] Taittirīya Saṃhitā, i. 8, 8, 1; iii. 4, 9, 1; Rv. ii. 32, 6; Av. ii. 26, 2; vi. 11, 3; Vājasaneyi Saṃhitā, xi. 55. 56; xxxiv. 10; Kāṭhaka Saṃhitā, xii. 8; Ṣaḍviṃśa Brāhmaṇa, v. 6.

the day before new moon; Kuhū,[3] also called Guṅgū,[4] the new moon day; Anumati,[5] the day before full moon; and Rākā,[6] the day of new moon. The importance of the new and full moon days is seen in the Darśa-pūrṇamāsau, or festivals of the new and full moon days respectively.

One special day in the month, the **Ekāṣṭakā**, or eighth day after full moon, was important. In the Pañcaviṃśa Brāhmaṇa[7] there are stated to be in the year twelve such, mentioned between the twelve days of full moon and the twelve days of new moon. But one Ekāṣṭakā is referred to in the Yajurveda Saṃhitās and elsewhere[8] as of quite special importance. This was, in the accordant opinion of most commentators, the eighth day after the full moon of **Māgha.** It marked the end of the year, or the beginning of the new year. Though the Kauṣītaki Brāhmaṇa[9] places the winter solstice in the new moon of Māgha, the latter date probably means the new moon preceding full moon in Māgha,[10] not the new moon following

[3] Av. vii. 47; Taittirīya Saṃhitā, i. 8, 8, 1; iii. 4, 9, 1; Kāṭhaka Saṃhitā, xii. 8, etc.

[4] Rv. ii. 32, 8, where Sāyaṇa identifies it with Kuhū.

[5] Taittirīya Saṃhitā, i. 8, 8, 1; iii. 4, 9, 1; Kāṭhaka Saṃhitā, xii. 8; Vājasaneyi Saṃhitā, xxix. 60; xxxiv. 8. 9; Ṣaḍviṃśa Brāhmaṇa, v. 6.

[6] Rv. ii. 32, 4; v. 42, 12; Taittirīya Saṃhitā, i. 8, 8, 1; iii. 4, 9, 1. *Cf.* Nirukta, xi. 31; Weber, *Indische Studien*, 5, 228 *et seq.*; Ludwig, Translation of the Rigveda, 3, 189.

[7] x. 3, 11. *Cf.* Satapatha Brāhmaṇa, vi. 2, 2, 23; Av. xv. 16, 2.

[8] Taittirīya Saṃhitā, vii. 4, 8, 1; Pañcaviṃśa Brāhmaṇa, v. 9, 1. *Cf.* Taittirīya Saṃhitā, iii. 3, 8, 4; iv. 3, 11, 3; v. 7, 2, 2; Av. iii. 10; viii. 9, 10; Kāṭhaka Saṃhitā, xxxix. 10; Maitrāyaṇī Saṃhitā, ii. 13, 21, etc. See Kātyāyana Śrauta Sūtra, xiii. 1, 2, with the commentary; Pañcaviṃśa Brāhmaṇa, *loc. cit.*, with Sāyaṇa's notes; Weber, *Naxatra*, 2, 341, 342; *Indische Studien*, 17, 219 *et seq.*

[9] xix. 23.

[10] So Vināyaka on Kauṣītaki Brāhmaṇa, *loc. cit.*; Ānartīya on Śāṅkhāyana Śrauta Sūtra, xiii. 19, 1; Weber, *op. cit.*, 2, 345, 346, 353, 354. Weber accepts the scholiasts' view that Māgha is here regarded as beginning with the day after full moon in Taiṣa; but it is simpler to suppose the meaning to be that Māgha is regarded as commencing with, not after, the new moon and ending with the day before new moon. Several passages in the Baudhāyana Śrauta Sūtra (ii. 12; iii. 1; xxvi. 18; xxx. 3; see Caland, *Über das rituelle Sūtra des Baudhāyana*, 36, 37) and Kauṣītaki Brāhmaṇa, i. 3; Satapatha Brāhmaṇa, xi. 1, 1, 7, point to the full moon being the middle of the month, and the new moon being regarded as either the beginning or the end. Hopkins (n. 11) thinks Kauṣītaki Brāhmaṇa, v. 1; Śatapatha Brāhmaṇa, vi. 2, 2, 18, point to the commencement of the month with the full moon. If this could be accepted, then the Aṣṭakā would fall a week before the winter solstice in Māgha.

full moon; but it is perhaps possible to account adequately for the importance of the Ekāṣṭakā as being the first Aṣṭakā after the beginning of the new year.

It is not certain exactly how the month was reckoned, whether from the day after new moon to new moon—the system known as *amānta*, or from the day after full moon to full moon—the *pūrṇimānta* system, which later, at any rate, was followed in North India, while the other system prevailed in the south. Jacobi[11] argues that the year began in the full moon of Phālguna, and that only by the full moon's conjunction with the Nakṣatra could the month be known. Oldenberg[12] points to the fact that the new moon is far more distinctively an epoch than the full moon; that the Greek, Roman, and Jewish years began with the new moon; and that the Vedic evidence is the division of the month into the former (*pūrva*) and latter (*apara*) halves, the first being the bright (*śukla*), the second the dark (*kṛṣṇa*) period. Thibaut[13] considers that to assume the existence of the *pūrṇimānta* system for the Veda is unnecessary, though possible. Weber[10] assumes that it occurs in the Kauṣītaki Brāhmaṇa as held by the scholiasts. But it would probably be a mistake to press that passage, or to assume that the *amānta* system was rigidly accepted in the Veda: it seems at least as probable that the month was vaguely regarded as beginning with the new moon day, so that new moon preceded full moon, which was in the middle, not the end or the beginning of the month.

That a month regularly had 30 days is established by the conclusive evidence of numerous passages in which the year is given 12 months and 360 days. This month is known from the earliest records, being both referred to directly and alluded to[14]

[11] *Zeitschrift der Morgenländischen Gesellschaft*, 49, 229, n. 1; 50, 81. *Cf.* Hopkins, *Journal of the American Oriental Society*, 24, 20.

[12] *Ibid.*, 48, 633, n. 1; 49, 476, 477. This is the Epic rule, Hopkins, *loc. cit.*

[13] *Indian Antiquary*, 24, 87. None of the evidence is absolutely conclusive one way or the other. It is perfectly possible that the usage of families or districts differed. *Cf.* Thibaut, *Astronomie, Astrologie und Mathematik*, 12.

[14] Rv. i. 164, 11. 14. 48; x. 189, 3; 190, 2; Av. iv. 35, 4; x. 7, 6; 8, 23; xiii. 3, 8, etc.

It is the regular month of the Brāhmaṇas,[15] and must be regarded as the month which the Vedic Indian recognized. No other month is mentioned as such in the Brāhmaṇa literature; it is only in the Sūtras that months of different length occur. The Sāmaveda Sūtras[16] refer to (1) years with 324 days—*i.e.*, periodic years with 12 months of 27 days each; (2) years with 351 days—*i.e.*, periodic years with 12 months of 27 days each, plus another month of 27 days; (3) years with 354 days—*i.e.*; 6 months of 30 days, and 6 with 29 days, in other words, lunar synodic years; (4) years with 360 days, or ordinary civil (*sāvana*) years; (5) years with 378 days, which, as Thibaut[17] clearly shows, are third years, in which, after two years of 360 days each, 18 days were added to bring about correspondence between the civil year and the solar year of 366 days. But even the Sāmasūtras do not mention the year of 366 days, which is first known to the Jyotiṣa[18] and to Garga.[19]

That the Vedic period was acquainted with the year of 354 days cannot be affirmed with certainty. Zimmer,[20] indeed, thinks that it is proved by the fact that pregnancy is estimated at ten months, or sometimes a year.[21] But Weber[22] may be right in holding that the month is the periodic month of 27 days, for the period is otherwise too long if a year is taken. On the other hand, the period of ten months quite well suits the period of gestation, if birth takes place in the tenth month, so that in this sense the month of 30 days may well be meant.

15 Maitrāyaṇī Saṃhitā, i. 10, 8; Aitareya Brāhmaṇa, iv. 12; Kāṭhaka Saṃhitā, xxxvi. 2, 3; Kauṣītaki Brāhmaṇa, iii. 2; Aitareya Āraṇyaka, iii. 2, 1; Baudhāyana Śrauta Sūtra, xxvi. 10; Bṛhadāraṇyaka Upaniṣad, i. 5, 22. See also Weber, *Naxatra*, 2, 288; Thibaut, *Astronomie, Astrologie und Mathematik*, 8.

16 Lāṭyāyana Śrauta Sūtra, iv. 8, 1 *et seq.*; Nidāna Sūtra, v. 11. 12; Weber, *Naxatra*, 2, 281-288.

17 *Op. cit.*, 8, 9.

18 verse 28.

19 Cited in the commentary on the Jyotiṣa, 10.

20 *Altindisches Leben*, 365, 366.

21 Ten months is the period according to Rv. v. 78, 7-9; x. 184, 3; Av. i. 11, 6; iii. 23, 2; v. 25, 13; Kāṭhaka Saṃhitā, xxviii. 6; Śatapatha Brāhmaṇa, iv. 5, 2, 4. 5 (*ibid.*, ix. 5, 1, 63, a six months' embryo is alone able to live). A year is mentioned in Pañcaviṃśa Brāhmaṇa, x. 1, 9 (ten months in vi. 1, 3); Kāṭhaka Saṃhitā, xxxiii. 8; Śatapatha Brāhmaṇa, vi. 1, 3, 8; xi. 5, 4, 6-11; Aitareya Brāhmaṇa, iv. 22.

22 *Naxatra*, 2, 313, n. 1.

The year of 12 months of 30 days each being admittedly quite unscientific, Zimmer[23] is strongly of opinion that it was only used with a recognition of the fact that intercalation took place, and that the year formed part of a greater complex, normally the five year Yuga or cycle. This system is well known from the Jyotiṣa: it consists of 62 months of $29\frac{16}{31}$ days each = 1,830 days (two of these months being intercalary, one in the middle and one at the end), or 61 months of 30 days, or 60 months of $30\frac{1}{2}$ days, the unit being clearly a solar year of 366 days. It is not an ideal system, since the year is too long;[24] but it is one which cannot be claimed even for the Brāhmaṇa period, during which no decision as to the true length of the year seems to have been arrived at. The references to it seen by Zimmer in the Rigveda[25] are not even reasonably plausible, while the *pañcaka yuga*, cited by him from the Pañcaviṃśa Brāhmaṇa,[26] occurs only in a quotation in a commentary, and has no authority for the text itself.

On the other hand, there was undoubtedly some attempt to bring the year of 360 days—a synodic lunar year—roughly into connexion with reality. A Sāmasūtra[27] treats it as a solar year, stating that the sun perambulates each Naxatra in $13\frac{1}{3}$ days, while others again evidently interpolated 18 days every third year, in order to arrive at some equality. But Vedic literature, from the Rigveda[28] downwards,[29] teems with the assertion of the difficulty of ascertaining the month. The length is variously given as 30 days,[30] 35 days,[31] or

[23] *Op. cit.*, 369, 370.

[24] The Yuga is too long by nearly four days. The true year has 365 days, 5 hours, 48 minutes, 46 seconds. *Cf.* Thibaut, *op. cit.*, 24, 25.

[25] i. 164, 14; iii. 55, 18. These passages are, of course, obscure, but to interpret them as referring to the ten half years of the Yuga is particularly gratuitous.

[26] xvii. 13, 17. See also Thibaut, *op. cit.*, 7, 8; Weber, *Indische Streifen*, 1, 91, and references. The most that can be said is that a tendency to accept five years as a convenient period for intercalation was arising, which ultimately appears developed in the Jyotiṣa. But we cannot say that a year of 366 days is known until then.

[27] Lāṭyāyana Śrauta Sūtra, iv. 8, has nothing of this, but Nidāna Sūtra, v. 12, 2. 5, is quite clear.

[28] i. 25, 8; perhaps 165, 15.

[29] Śatapatha Brāhmaṇa, iv. 3, 1, 5; vi. 2, 2, 29; xii. 2, 1, 8; Aitareya Brāhmaṇa, i. 12; Kāṭhaka Saṃhitā, xxxiv. 13; Pañcaviṃśa Brāhmaṇa, x. 3, 2; xxiii. 2, 3; Taittirīya Āraṇyaka, v. 4, 29; Weber, *Naxatra*, 2, 336, n. 1.

[30] Av. xiii. 3, 8.

[31] Śatapatha Brāhmaṇa, x. 5, 4, 5.

36 days.[32] The last number possibly indicates an intercalation after six years (6×6=36, or for ritual purposes 35), but for this we have no special evidence. There are many references[33] to the year having 12 or 13 months.

The names of the months are, curiously enough, not at all ancient. The sacrificial texts of the Yajurveda give them in their clearest form where the Agnicayana, 'building of the fire-altar,' is described.[34] These names are the following: (1) Madhu, (2) Mādhava (spring months, *vāsantikāv ṛtū*); (3) Śukra, (4) Śuci (summer months, *graiṣmāv ṛtū*); (5) Nabha (or Nabhas),[35] (6) Nabhasya (rainy months, *vārṣikāv ṛtū*); (7) Iṣa, (8) Ūrja (autumn months, *śāradāv ṛtū*); (9) Saha (or Sahas),[35] (10) Sahasya (winter months, *haimantikāv ṛtū*); (11) Tapa (or Tapas),[35] (12) Tapasya (cool months, *śaiśirāv ṛtū*).

There are similar lists in the descriptions of the Soma sacrifice[36] and of the horse sacrifice,[37] all of them agreeing in essentials. There are other lists of still more fanciful names,[38] but these have no claim at all to represent actual divisions in popular use. It is doubtful if the list given above is more than a matter of priestly invention. Weber points out that Madhu and Mādhava later appear as names of spring, and that these two are mentioned in the Taittirīya Āraṇyaka[39] as if actually

[32] *Ibid.*, ix. 1, 1, 43; 3. 3. 18. *Cf.* Eggeling, *Sacred Books of the East*, 43, 167, n. 1. Shamasastry, *Gavām Ayana*, 122, interprets these passages in quite an impossible manner. There is no trace of a month of 35-36 days in the Epic: Hopkins, *Journal of the American Oriental Society*, 24, 42.

[33] Taittirīya Saṃhitā, v. 6, 7, 1; Kāṭhaka Saṃhitā, xxi. 5; xxxiv. 9; Maitrāyaṇī Saṃhitā, i. 10, 8; Kauṣītaki Brāhmaṇa, v. 8; Kauṣītaki Upaniṣad, i. 6; Śatapatha Brāhmaṇa, ii. 2, 3, 27; iii. 6, 4, 24; v. 4, 5, 23; vii. 2, 3, 9, etc.; Jaiminīya Upaniṣad Brāhmaṇa, i. 10, 6.

[34] Taittirīya Saṃhitā, iv. 4, 11, 1; Kāṭhaka Saṃhitā, xvii. 10; xxxv. 9; Maitrāyaṇī Saṃhitā, ii. 8, 12: Vājasaneyi Saṃhitā, xiii. 25; xiv. 6. 15. 16 27; xv. 57.

[35] In Maitrāyaṇī, Kāṭhaka, and Vājasaneyi Saṃhitās. See notes 34, 36.

[36] Taittirīya Saṃhitā, i. 4, 14, 1; Maitrāyaṇī Saṃhitā, i. 3, 16; iv. 6, 7; Kāṭhaka Saṃhitā, iv. 7; Vājasaneyi Saṃhitā, vii. 30 (where Iṣ and Ūrj appear as the names of the months).

[37] Maitrāyaṇī Saṃhitā, iii, 12, 13; Vājasaneyi Saṃhitā, xxii. 31.

[38] See, *e.g.*, Taittirīya Saṃhitā, i. 7, 9, 1; iv. 7, 11, 2; Vājasaneyi Saṃhitā, ix. 20; xviii. 28; xxii. 32; Kāṭhaka Saṃhitā, xxxv. 10. Weber, 2, 349, 350.

[39] iv. 7, 2; v. 6, 16.

employed; but the evidence is very inadequate to show that the other names of the months given in the list were in ordinary use.[40]

In some of these lists the intercalary month is mentioned. The name given to it in the Vājasaneyi Saṃhitā[41] is Aṃhasaspati, while that given in the Taittirīya[42] and Maitrāyaṇī Saṃhitās[43] is Saṃsarpa. The Kāṭhaka Saṃhitā[44] gives it the name of Malimluca, which also occurs elsewhere, along with Saṃsarpa, in one of the lists of fanciful names.[45] The Atharvaveda[46] describes it as *sanisrasa*, 'slipping,' owing no doubt to its unstable condition.

The other method of naming the months is from the **Nakṣatras**. It is only beginning to be used in the Brāhmaṇas, but is found regularly in the Epic and later. The Jyotiṣa[47] mentions that Māgha and Tapa were identical: this is the fair interpretation of the passage, which also involves the identification of Madhu with Caitra, a result corresponding with the view frequently found in the Brāhmaṇas, that the full moon in Citrā, and not that in Phalgunī, is the beginning of the year.[48]

In the Śatapatha Brāhmaṇa[49] are found two curious expressions, *yava* and *ayava*, for the light and dark halves of the month, which is clearly considered to begin with the light half. Possibly the words are derived, as Eggling[50] thinks, from *yu*, 'ward off,' with reference to evil spirits. The word **Parvan**

[40] Cases like that of *nabhas*, used by Mallinātha on Meghadūta, i. 4, are merely scholastic.

[41] vii. 30; xxii. 31.

[42] i. 4, 14, 1.

[43] iii. 12, 13.

[44] xxxviii. 4.

[45] *Ibid.*, xxxv. 10; Vājasaneyi Saṃitā, xxii. 30.

[46] v. 6, 4.

[47] Verse 6 Yajus recension = verse 5 Ṛc recension: Weber, 2, 354 *et seq.*

[48] Weber's theory (359) that Caitra was as the first spring month secondary to Phālguna is, of course, an error; for, owing to the precession of the equinoxes, Phālguna became the first month of spring *de facto*, while Caitra became virtually the last month of the preceding season. The truth is that the six seasons are an arbitrary division of the year, and that either Phālguna or Caitra could be regarded as the beginning of spring without much impropriety. See Weber, *Indische Studien*, 9, 457; 10, 231, 232; Whitney, *Journal of the American Oriental Society*, 8, 71, 397, 398.

[49] viii. 4, 2, 12; 3, 18. See Vājasaneyi Saṃhitā, xiv. 26. 31. The Taittirīya Saṃhitā, iv. 3, 10, 3, has the words in the form of *yāva* and *ayāva*, which are explained in v. 3, 4, 5.

[50] *Sacred Books of the East*, 43, 69, n.

('joint' = division of time) probably[51] denotes a half of the month, perhaps already in the Rigveda.[52] More precisely the first half, the time of the waxing light, is called *pūrva-pakṣa*,[53] the second, that of the waning light, *apara-pakṣa*.[54] Either of these might be called a half-month (*ardha-māsa*).[55]

[51] The months and the half months are the *parvāṇi* of the sacrificial horse in the Bṛhadāraṇyaka Upaniṣad, i. 1, 1. *Cf.* Śatapatha Brāhmaṇa, i. 6, 3, 35; vi. 2, 2, 24; Vājasaneyi Saṃhitā, xiii. 43; St. Petersburg Dictionary, *s.v.* 4, where the sense is left vague.

[52] i. 94, 4. *Cf.* Ludwig, Translation of the Rigveda, 3, 189.

[53] Taittirīya Saṃhitā, iii. 4, 9, 6; Aitareya Brāhmaṇa, iv. 25, 3; Śatapatha Brāhmaṇa, vi. 7, 4, 7; viii. 4, 2, 11; Nirukta, v. 11, ; xi. 5. 6.

[54] Śatapatha Brāhmaṇa, vi. 7, 4, 7; viii. 4, 2, 11; xi. 1, 5, 3; Bṛhadāraṇyaka Upaniṣad, iii. 1, 5; Nirukta, v. 11; xi. 6, etc.

[55] Śatapatha Brāhmaṇa, v. 4, 5, 21; Bṛhadāraṇyaka Upaniṣad, i. 1, 1; ii. 8, 9, etc.; Taittirīya Saṃhitā, vii. 1, 15, 1; Taittirīya Saṃhitā, iii. 12, 7; Vājasaneyi Saṃhitā, xxii. 28.

Cf. Zimmer, *Altindisches Leben*, 364 *et seq.*; Thibaut, *Astronomie, Astrologie und Mathematik*, 7-9; Weber, Proceedings of the Berlin Academy, 1894, 37 *et seq.*; *Naxatra*, 2, *passim*.

Māsara is mentioned as a beverage in the Yajurveda Saṃhitās.[1] Its composition is described fully in the Kātyāyana Śrauta Sūtra.[2] It seems to have been a mixture of rice and **Śyāmāka** with grass, parched barley, etc.

[1] Maitrāyaṇī Saṃhitā, iii. 11, 2. 9; Vājasaneyi Saṃhitā, xix. 14. 82; xx. 68; Taittirīya Brāhmaṇa, ii. 6, 11, 4, etc.

[2] xix. 1, 20. 21; Mahīdhara on Vājasaneyi Saṃhitā, xix. 1. 14.

Cf. Griffith, Vājasaneyi Saṃhitā, 172, n.

Māhaki, 'descendant of Mahaka,' is the patronymic of a teacher in the Vaṃśa Brāhmaṇa.[1]

[1] *Indische Studien*, 4, 382.

Māhā-camasya, 'descendant of Mahācamasa,' is the patronymic of a teacher to whom the Taittirīya Āraṇyaka[1] ascribes the addition of Mahas to the triad Bhūr Bhuvas Svar.[2]

[1] i. 5, 1.

[2] *Cf.* Keith, *Aitareya Āraṇyaka*, 180.

Māhā-rajana, 'dyed with saffron' (*mahā-rajana*), is applied to a garment (**Vāsas**) in the Bṛhadāraṇyaka Upaniṣad (ii. 3, 10).

Mahā-rājya, 'the dignity of a great king' (*mahā-rāja*), is mentioned in the Aitareya Brāhmaṇa (viii. 6, 5; 12, 4; 15, 3).

Māhitthi, 'descendant of Mahittha,' is the patronymic of a teacher mentioned several times in the Śatapatha Brāhmaṇa.[1] He is said to be a pupil of **Vāmakakṣāyaṇa** in the Bṛhadāraṇyaka Upaniṣad.[2]

[1] vi. 2, 2, 10; viii. 6, 1, 16 *et seq.*; ix. 5, 1, 57; x. 6, 5, 9.
[2] vi. 5, 4 Kāṇva.

Māhīna occurs in one passage of the Rigveda,[1] which celebrates **Asamāti** as a king. The word, used in the plural, may be a patronymic referring to the priests who praised Asamāti, or it may be an adjective of uncertain meaning.

[1] x. 60, 1. *Cf.* Ludwig, Translation of the Rigveda, 3, 138.

Mitra denotes 'friend' in the Rigveda[1] and later.[2] According to the Taittirīya Saṃhitā[3] a wife is a man's friend, and in the Śatapatha Brāhmaṇa[4] the value of a friend is insisted upon. Treachery to a friend is reprobated.[5]

[1] Masculine: i. 58, 1; 67, 1; 75, 4; 156, 1; 170, 5; ii. 4, 1. 3, etc. The neuter does not with certainty occur in the sense of 'friend' in the Rv.

[2] Masculine: Av. v. 19, 15; xi. 9, 2; Kāṭhaka Saṃhitā, xxvii. 4; Taittirīya Āraṇyaka, x. 80. Neuter: Taittirīya Saṃhitā, vi. 4, 8, 1; Taittirīya Brāhmaṇa, i. 7, 8, 7; Aitareya Brāhmaṇa, vi. 20, 17; viii. 27, 2; Śatapatha Brāhmaṇa, iv. 1, 4, 8; v. 3, 5, 13; xi. 4, 3, 20, etc.

[3] vi. 2, 9, 2.

[4] i. 5, 3, 17.

[5] *Cf.* Taittirīya Brāhmaṇa, i. 7, 1, 7.

Mitra-bhū Kāśyapa ('descendant of Kaśyapa') is the name of a teacher, a pupil of **Vibhaṇḍaka Kāśyapa,** in the Vaṃśa Brāhmaṇa.[1]

[1] *Indische Studien*, 4, 374.

Mitra-bhūti Lauhitya ('descendant of Lohita') is mentioned in the Vaṃśa (list of teachers) in the Jaiminīya Upaniṣad Brāhmaṇa (iii. 42, 1) as a pupil of **Kṛṣṇadatta Lauhitya.**

Mitra-varcas Sthairakāyaṇa ('descendant of Sthiraka') is the name of a teacher, a pupil of **Supratīta Auluṇḍya**, in the Vaṃśa Brāhmaṇa.[1]

[1] *Indische Studien*, 4, 372.

Mitra-vinda Kāśyapa ('descendant of Kaśyapa') is the name of a teacher, a pupil of **Sunītha**, in the Vaṃśa Brāhmaṇa.[1]

[1] *Indische Studien*, 4, 372.

Mitrātithi is mentioned in one hymn of the Rigveda[1] as the father of **Kuruśravaṇa** and the grandfather of **Upamaśravas**, all being evidently kings.

[1] x. 33, 7. *Cf.* Ludwig, Translation of the Rigveda, 3, 165; Geldner, *Vedische Studien*, 2, 150, 184; Keith, *Journal of the Royal Asiatic Society*, 1910, 922, 923; Lanman, *Sanskrit Reader*, 384; Bṛhaddevatā, vii. 35. 36, with Macdonell's notes.

Mukṣījā is found in one passage of the Rigveda,[1] where the sense seems clearly to be 'net' for catching animals. *Cf.* **Padi.**

[1] i. 125, 2; Nirukta, v. 19. *Cf.* Zimmer, *Altindisches Leben*, 244.

1. **Muñja** denotes a grass, the *Saccharum Muñja*, which is of luxuriant growth, attaining to a height of ten feet. It is mentioned in the Rigveda[1] along with other kinds of grasses as the lurking-place of venomous creatures. In the same text[2] the Muñja grass is spoken of as purifying, apparently being used as the material of a filter for Soma. The grass is often mentioned in the later Saṃhitās[3] and the Brāhmaṇas.[4] It is in the Śatapatha Brāhmaṇa[5] said to be 'hollow' (*suṣira*) and to be used for the plaited part of the throne (**Āsandī**).[6]

[1] i. 191, 3.

[2] i. 161, 8 (*muñja-nejana*, which Sāyaṇa explains as *apagata-tṛṇa*, 'with the grass removed').

[3] Av. i. 2, 4; Taittirīya Saṃhitā, v. 1, 9, 5; 10, 5, etc.

[4] Kauṣītaki Brāhmaṇa, xviii. 7; Śatapatha Brāhmaṇa, iv. 3, 3. 16; vi. 6, 1, 23; 2, 15. 16, etc. *Cf.* St. Petersburg Dictionary, *s.v. mauñja.*

[5] vi. 3, 1, 26.

[6] Śatapatha Brāhmaṇa, xii. 8, 3, 6. *Cf.* Zimmer, *Altindisches Leben*, 72.

2. **Muñja Sāma-śravasa** ('descendant of Sāmaśravas') is the name of a man, possibly a king, mentioned in the Jaiminīya Upaniṣad Brāhmaṇa[1] and the Ṣaḍviṃśa Brāhmaṇa.[2]

[1] iii. 5, 2.

[2] iv. 1 (*Indische Studien*, 1, 39).

Muṇḍibha Audanya[1] or **Audanyava**[2] is the name of a man in the Śatapatha Brāhmaṇa[1] and the Taittirīya Brāhmaṇa.[2]

[1] Śatapatha Brāhmaṇa, xiii. 3, 5, 4. Apparently the word is a patronymic, 'son of Udanya' (so Eggeling, *Sacred Books of the East*, 44, 341, n. 1), or 'son of Odana' (so St. Petersburg Dictionary, *s.v.*).

[2] Taittirīya Brāhmaṇa, iii. 9, 15, 3 ('descendant of Udanyu').

Mudga, denoting a kind of bean (*Phaseolus Mungo*), occurs in a list of vegetables in the Vājasaneyi Saṃhitā.[1] A 'soup of rice with beans' (*mudgaudana*) is mentioned in the Śāṅkhāyana Āraṇyaka[2] and the Sūtras. *Cf.* perhaps **Mudgala.**

[1] xviii. 12.

[2] xii. 8.

Cf. Zimmer, *Altindisches Leben*, 240.

Mudgala and **Mudgalānī**, 'Mudgala's wife,' both figure in a hopelessly obscure hymn of the Rigveda,[1] variously interpreted by Pischel[2] and Geldner[3] and von Bradke[4] as telling of a real chariot race in which, despite difficulties, Mudgala won by his wife's aid. The Indian tradition is as variant as the interpretations of modern authorities. Ṣaḍguruśiṣya[5] explains that Mudgala's oxen were stolen, that he pursued the thieves with the one old ox he had left, and that hurling his hammer (*dru-ghaṇa*) he caught the marauders. Yāska,[6] on the other hand, says that Mudgala won a race with a *drughaṇa* and an ox instead of with two oxen. It is pretty clear that, as Roth[7] observed, the tradition is merely a guess, and a bad one, at the meaning of an obscure hymn, and this view is

[1] x. 102.

[2] *Vedische Studien*, 1, 124.

[3] *Ibid.*, 1, 138; 2, 1-22.

[4] *Zeitschrift der Deutschen Morgenländischen Gesellschaft*, 46, 445 *et seq.*

[5] Macdonell's edition of the Sarvānukramaṇī, p. 158.

[6] Nirukta, ix. 23. 24.

[7] *Nirukta, Erläuterungen*, 129.

accepted by Oldenberg.[8] Bloomfield[9] has interpreted the legend as one of heavenly, not of human, events. Mudgala, probably a variant form of Mudgara,[10] which in the later language means a hammer or a similar weapon, may be meant as a personification of the thunderbolt of Indra, rather than a real man.[11] Later[12] Mudgala is a mythical sage.

[8] *Zeitschrift der Deutschen Morgenländischen Gesellschaft*, 39, 78.

[9] *Ibid.*, 48, 547.

[10] According to Geldner, *Vedische Studien*, 2, 1, Indrasenā in x. 102, 2, is the name of Mudgalānī; but its sense, 'Indra's bolt,' rather indicates the mythical character of the passage.

[11] If the name means a real man, it may be connected with **Mudga**, 'bean.' See Zimmer, *Altindisches Leben*, 240.

[12] Av. iv. 29, 6; Āśvalāyana Śrauta Sūtra, xii. 12; Bṛhaddevatā, vi. 46; viii. 12. 90.

Cf. Ludwig, Translation of the Rigveda, 3, 166, 167; Oldenberg, *Religion des Veda*, 280; Keith, *Journal of the Royal Asiatic Society* 1911, 1005, n. 1.

Muni occurs in one hymn of the Rigveda[1] where it seems to denote an ascetic of magic powers with divine afflatus (*deveṣita*), the precursor of the strange ascetics of later India. This agrees with the fact that **Aitaśa**, the Muni, is in the Aitareya Brāhmaṇa[2] regarded by his son as deranged, a view not unjustified if the nonsense which passes as the Aitaśapralāpa,[3] 'Chatter of Aitaśa,' was really his. The Rigveda[4] calls Indra the 'friend of Munis,' and the Atharvaveda[5] refers to a 'divine Muni' (*deva muni*), by whom a similar ascetic may be meant.

In the Upaniṣads[6] the Muni is of a more restrained type: he is one who learns the nature of the Brahman, the Absolute, by study, or sacrifice, or penance, or fasting, or faith (*śraddhā*). It must not of course be thought that there is any absolute distinction between the older Muni and the later: in both cases the man is in a peculiar ecstatic condition, but the ideal of the Upaniṣads is less material than the earlier picture of the Muni, who is more of a 'medicine man' than a sage. Nor would it be wise to conclude from the comparative rareness

[1] x. 136, 2. 4. 5. In verse 1 he is described as 'long-haired.'

[2] vi. 33, 3.

[3] See Bloomfield, *Atharvaveda*, 98 *et seq.*

[4] viii. 17, 14. *Cf.* vii. 56, 8; Max Müller, *Sacred Books of the East*, 32, 376.

[5] vii. 74, 1. *Cf.* Whitney, Translation of the Atharvaveda, 440; Śatapatha Brāhmaṇa, ix. 5, 2, 15, and **Munimaraṇa**.

[6] Bṛhadāraṇyaka Upaniṣad, iii. 4, 1; iv. 4, 25; Taittirīya Āraṇyaka, ii. 20.

of the mention of the Muni in the Vedic texts that he was an infrequent figure in Vedic times: he was probably not approved by the priests who followed the ritual, and whose views were essentially different from the ideals of a Muni, which were superior to earthly considerations, such as the desire for children and **Dakṣiṇās**.[7]

[7] *Cf.* Bṛhadāraṇyaka Upaniṣad, iii. 4, 1.
Cf. Oldenberg, *Religion des Veda*, 406; *Zeitschrift der Deutschen Morgenländischen Gesellschaft*, 49, 480; *Buddha*,[5] 36.

Muni-maraṇa, 'Saints' Death,' is the name of the place where, according to the Pañcaviṃśa Brāhmaṇa (xiv. 4, 7), the **Vaikhānasas** were slain.

Mulālin (masc.) or **Mulālī** (fem.) is the name of some part of an edible lotus (perhaps the *Nymphaea esculenta*) in the Atharvaveda.[1]

[1] iv. 34, 5. *Cf.* Kauśika Sūtra, lxvi. 10; Weber, *Indische Studien*, 18, 138; Zimmer, *Altindisches Leben*, 70; Whitney, Translation of the Atharvaveda, 207.

Muṣīvan denotes 'robber' in one passage of the Rigveda (i. 42, 3).

Muṣkara occurs in one passage of the Atharvaveda,[1] possibly in the sense of a small animal or insect, as suggested by Roth,[2] who, however, thought the passage corrupt. Bloomfield[3] suggests that the reading of the Paippalāda text *puṣkaram*, ('blue lotus') is the correct form.

[1] vi. 14, 2.
[2] St. Petersburg Dictionary, *s.v.*
[3] *Hymns of the Atharvaveda*, 463, 464.
Cf. Whitney, Translation of the Atharvaveda, 297.

Muṣṭi-han,[1] **Muṣṭi-hatyā**,[2] in the Rigveda and the Atharvaveda denote, respectively, the 'hand to hand fighter'—that is, the ordinary warrior as opposed to the charioteer, and the

[1] Rv. v. 58, 4; vi. 26, 2; viii. 20, 20; Av. v. 22, 4.
[2] Rv. i. 8, 2.

'fight' itself. So also in the Atharvaveda[3] the charioteer (*rathin*) is opposed to the foot-soldier (*patti*), and in the Rigveda[4] the chariots are opposed to the troops (*grāma*) of the infantry. The parallel of the Greek and other Āryan races shows that the Kṣatriyas were the fighters from chariots, while the ordinary host fought on foot.

[3] vii. 62, 1.

[4] i. 100, 10.

Cf. Zimmer, *Altindisches Leben*, 297.

Musala denotes a 'pestle' in the later Saṃhitās[1] and in the Brāhmaṇas.[2]

[1] Av. x. 9, 26; xi. 3, 3; xii. 3, 13; Taittirīya Saṃhitā, i. 6, 8, 3, etc.

[2] Śāṅkhāyana Āraṇyaka, xii. 8; Śatapatha Brāhmaṇa, xii. 5, 2, 7; in the Jaiminīya Brāhmaṇa, i. 42. 44 (*Journal of the American Oriental Society*, 15, 235, 237), *musalin* means a 'man armed with a club.'

Muhūrta denotes a division of time, one-thirtieth of a day, or an hour of forty-eight minutes, in the Brāhmaṇas.[1] In the Rigveda[2] the sense of 'moment' only is found. *Cf.* **Ahan.**

[1] Taittirīya Brāhmaṇa, iii. 10, 1, 1 (for the names); 9, 7; 12, 9, 6; Śatapatha Brāhmaṇa, x. 4, 2, 18. 25. 27; 3, 20; xii. 3, 2, 5; x. 4, 4, 4, etc.

[2] iii. 33, 5; 53, 8. The sense of 'moment' is also common in the Brāhmaṇas.

Cf. Zeitschrift der Deutschen Morgenländischen Gesellschaft, 9, 139 *et seq.*; *Indische Streifen*, 1, 92 *et seq.*

Mūcīpa or **Mūvīpa** is the variant in the Śāṅkhāyana Śrauta Sūtra (xv. 26, 6) of the **Mūtiba** of the Aitareya Brāhmaṇa as the name of a barbarian tribe.

Cf. Weber, *Indische Studien*, 10, 67, n. 1.

Mūjavant is the name of a people who, along with the **Mahāvṛṣas**, the **Gandhāris**, and the **Balhikas**, are mentioned in the Atharvaveda[1] as dwelling far away, and to whom fever is to be banished. Similarly in the Yajurveda Saṃhitās[2] the Mūjavants are chosen as a type of distant folk, beyond

[1] v. 22, 5. 7. 8. 14. *Cf.* Baudhāyana Śrauta Sūtra, ii. 5.

[2] Taittirīya Saṃhitā, i. 8. 6, 2; Kāṭhaka Saṃhitā, ix. 7; xxxvi. 14; Maitrāyaṇī Saṃhitā, i. 4, 10. 20; Vājasaneyi Saṃhitā, iii. 61; Śatapatha Brāhmaṇa, ii. 6, 2, 17.

which Rudra with his bow is entreated to depart. In the Rigveda[3] Soma is described as Maujavata, 'coming from the Mūjavants,' or, as Yāska[4] takes it, 'from Mount Mūjavant.' The Indian commentators[5] agree with Yāska in taking Mūjavant as the name of a mountain, and though Hillebrandt[6] is justified in saying that the identification of Mūjavant by Zimmer[7] with one of the lower hills on the south-west of Kaśmīr lacks evidence, it is not reasonable to deny that Mūjavant was a hill from which the people took their name. Yāska[8] suggests that Mūjavant is equivalent to Muñjavant, which actually occurs later, in the Epic,[9] as the name of a mountain in the Himālaya.

[3] x. 34, 1.
[4] Nirukta, ix. 8.
[5] Mahīdhara on Vājasaneyi Saṃhitā, *loc. cit.*; Sāyaṇa on Rv. i. 161, 8; Baudhāyana Śrauta Sūtra and Prayoga, cited by Hillebrandt, *Vedische Mythologie*, 1, 63.
[6] *Op. cit.*, 1, 65.
[7] *Altindisches Leben*, 29.
[8] *Loc. cit.* *Cf.* Siddhānta Kaumudī on Pāṇini, iv. 4, 110, where instead of Maujavata in Rv. x. 34, 1, Mauñjavata is read.
[9] Mahābhārata, x. 785; xiv. 180.

Cf. Ludwig, Translation of the Rigveda, 3, 198.

Mūta in the later Saṃhitās and the Brāhmaṇas[1] denotes a 'woven basket.' Mūtaka means a 'small basket.'[2]

[1] Kāṭhaka Saṃhitā, xxxvi. 14; Taittirīya Brāhmaṇa, i. 6, 10, 5; Lāṭyāyana Śrauta Sūtra, viii. 3, 8.
[2] Śatapatha Brāhmaṇa, ii. 6, 2, 17.

Mūtiba appears in the Aitareya Brāhmaṇa[1] as the name of one of the barbarous peoples enumerated as nominally **Viśvāmitra's** outcast offspring. The Śāṅkhāyana Śrauta Sūtra[2] gives the name as **Mūcīpa** or **Mūvīpa.**

[1] vii. 18, 2.
[2] xv. 26, 6.

Cf. Muir, *Sanskrit Texts*, 1^2, 358, 483.

Mūla, Mūlabarhaṇa. See **Nakṣatra.**

Mūs,[1] **Mūṣikā,**[2] are the names of 'mouse' occurring in the Rigveda[1] and the Yajurveda Saṃhitās.[2]

[1] Rv. i. 105, 8 = x. 33, 3; Nirukta, iv. 5.
[2] Maitrāyaṇī Saṃhitā, iii. 14, 17; Vājasaneyi Saṃhitā, xxiv. 36.

Cf. Zimmer, *Altindisches Leben*, 85; Schrader, *Prehistoric Antiquities*, 248.

1. **Mṛga** has the generic sense of 'wild beast' in the Rigveda[1] and later.[2] Sometimes it is qualified by the epithet 'terrible' (*bhīma*),[3] which indicates that a savage wild beast is meant. Elsewhere the buffalo is shown to be denoted by the epithet *mahiṣa*,[4] 'powerful,' which later becomes the name of the buffalo. More particularly the word has the sense of an animal of the gazelle type.[5] In some passages[6] Roth[7] sees the sense of 'bird.' See also **Mṛga Hastin, Puruṣa Hastin.**

[1] i. 173, 2; 191, 4; viii. 1, 20; 5, 36; x. 146, 6, etc.

[2] Av. iv. 3, 6; x. 1, 26; xii. 1, 48 (*sūkara*, 'boar'); xix. 38, 2; Pañcaviṃśa Brāhmaṇa, vi. 7, 10; xxiv. 11, 2; Aitareya Brāhmaṇa, iii. 31, 2; viii. 23, 3, etc.

[3] Rv. i. 154, 2; 190, 3; ii. 33, 11; 34, 1; x. 180, 2, etc.

[4] Rv. viii. 69, 15; ix. 92, 6; x. 123, 4.

[5] Rv. i. 38, 5; 105, 7; vi. 75, 11; ix. 32, 4; Av. v. 21, 4 (not a certain instance); Taittirīya Saṃhitā, vi. 1, 3, 7; Taittirīya Brāhmaṇa, iii. 2, 5 6; Śatapatha Brāhmaṇa, xi. 8, 4, 3, etc.

[6] Rv. i. 182, 7; x. 136, 6, and perhaps i. 145, 5; vii. 87, 6.

[7] St. Petersburg Dictionary, *s.v.*, 1e. *Cf.* Pischel, *Vedische Studien*, i. 99; 2, 122.

2. **Mṛga** in the Aitareya Brāhmaṇa[1] denotes, according to Sāyaṇa's commentary, the constellation **Mṛgaśiras.** But it seems more probable[2] that Mṛga there really covers the whole of Orion, not merely the inconspicuous group of stars in the head of Orion that make up the Nakṣatra Mṛgaśiras, but also the star α in his shoulder, which is reckoned as Ārdrā, and γ in his left shoulder. Tilak,[3] however, makes Mṛga or Mṛgaśiras into a different group, consisting of the belt of Orion, with two stars in the knees and one in the left shoulder, which he deems to resemble a deer's head with an arrow through it, an implausible and unlikely theory. *Cf.* **Mṛgavyādha.**

[1] iii. 33, 5.

[2] See Whitney, *Journal of the American Oriental Society*, 16, xcii.

[3] *Orion*, 99 *et seq.*

3. **Mṛga Hastin**, the 'animal with a hand,' is mentioned in two passages of the Rigveda,[1] in which Roth[2] recognizes that the elephant is meant, but concludes that the compound name

[1] i. 64, 7; iv. 16, 14.

[2] St. Petersburg Dictionary, *s.v.*; *Nirukta, Erläuterungen*, 79.

is a proof of the newness of the elephant to the Vedic Indians.[3] Later the adjective **Hastin** alone became the regular name of the animal (like **Mahiṣa** of the 'buffalo'). The elephant is also denoted in the Rigveda by the descriptive term Mṛga Vāraṇa,[4] the 'wild or dangerous animal,' the adjective *vāraṇa* similarly becoming one of the names for 'elephant' in the later language. Pischel's view[5] that the catching of elephants by the use of tame female elephants is already alluded to in the Rigveda[6] seems very doubtful. In the Aitareya Brāhmaṇa[7] elephants are described as 'black, white-toothed, adorned with gold.'

[3] Pischel, *Vedische Studien*, 1, 99, 100, combats the view that the elephant was new to the Vedic Indian, because of the similar use of *mṛga mahiṣa* and *mṛga sūkara* (Av. xii. 1, 48) to denote the 'buffalo' and the 'boar' respectively. But **Mahiṣa** seems rather to bear out Roth's conclusion; while **Sūkara** appears alone in the Rigveda, and *mṛga sūkara*, 'wild hog,' seems to be used in one passage of the Av. (xii. 1, 48) to distinguish it from **Varāha**, boar,' in the same verse.

[4] Rv. viii. 33, 8; x. 40, 8.

[5] *Vedische Studien*, 2, 121-123; 317-319. *Cf.* Strabo, pp. 704, 705; Arrian, *Indica*, 13. 14 (from Megasthenes).

[6] viii. 2, 6; x. 40, 8.

[7] viii. 23, 3 (*hiraṇyena parīvṛtān kṛṣṇāñ chukladato mṛgān*). See Pischel, *op. cit.*, 2, 122.

Cf. Zimmer, *Altindisches Leben*, 80.

Mṛgaya occurs in several passages of the Rigveda[1] as defeated by Indra. That he was a human foe, as Ludwig[2] thinks, seems unlikely: more probably he was a demon, as Mṛga unquestionably is.[3]

[1] iv. 16, 13; viii. 3, 19; x. 49, 5.

[2] Translation of the Rigveda, 3, 166.

[3] Rv. i. 80, 7; v. 29, 4, etc.

Mṛgayu, 'hunter,' occurs in the later Saṃhitās[1] and the Brāhmaṇas,[2] but not very often. The Vājasaneyi Saṃhitā[3] and the Taittirīya Brāhmaṇa,[4] however, in the list of victims at the Puruṣamedha ('human sacrifice') include a number of names which seem to be those of persons who make a livelihood by fishing or by hunting, such as the **Mārgāra**, 'hunter,'

[1] Av. x. 1, 26; Vājasaneyi Saṃhitā, xvi. 27; xxx. 7, etc. *Cf. mṛgaṇyu*, Rv. x. 40, 4.

[2] Taittirīya Brāhmaṇa, i. 5, 1, 1; iii. 4, 3, 1; Pañcaviṃśa Brāhmaṇa, xiv. 9, 12, etc.

[3] xxx.

[4] iii. 4.

the **Kaivarta** or **Kevarta, Pauñjiṣṭha, Dāśa, Maināla,** 'fisherman,' and perhaps the **Bainda** and the Ānda,[5] who seem to have been some sort of fishermen.

It is not probable that even in the earliest Vedic period hunting formed the main source of livelihood for any of the Vedic tribes: pastoral pursuits and agriculture (**Kṛṣi**) were, no doubt, the mainstay of their existence. But it would be unreasonable to suppose that not much hunting was done, both for recreation and for purposes of food, as well as for protection of flocks from wild beasts. The Rigveda is naturally our chief source of information in regard to hunting. The arrow was sometimes employed,[6] but, as is usual with primitive man, the normal instruments of capture were nets and pitfalls. Birds were regularly caught in nets (**Pāśa,**[7] **Nidhā,**[8] **Jāla**[9]), the bird-catcher being called *nidhā-pati*,[10] 'master of snares.' The net was fastened on pegs[11] (as is done with modern nets for catching birds). Another name of net is apparently **Mukṣījā.**

Pits were used for catching antelopes (**Ṛśya**), and so were called *ṛśya-da*,[12] 'antelope-catching.' Elephants were captured as in Greek times, perhaps through the instrumentality of tame females (see **Mṛga Hastin**). Apparently the boar was captured in the chase, dogs being used,[13] but the passage from which this view is deduced is of uncertain mythological content. There is also an obscure reference[14] to the capture of the buffalo (**Gaura**), but it is not clear whether the reference is to shooting with an arrow or capturing by means of ropes, perhaps a lasso, or a net. The lion was captured in pitfalls,[15] or was surrounded by the hunters and slain;[16] one very obscure passage refers to the lion being caught by ambuscade, which perhaps merely alludes to the use of the hidden pit.[17]

The modes of catching fish are little known, for the only evidence available are the explanations of the various names

[5] Vājasaneyi Saṃhitā, xxx. 16; Taittirīya Saṃhitā, iii. 4, 12, 1.

[6] Rv. ii. 42, 2.

[7] **Pāśin,** 'hunter,' Rv. iii. 45, 1.

[8] Rv. ix. 83, 4; x. 73, 11.

[9] Av. x. 1, 30.

[10] Rv. ix. 83, 4.

[11] Av. viii. 8, 5.

[12] Rv. x. 39, 8.

[13] Rv. x. 86, 4.

[14] Rv. x. 51, 6.

[15] Rv. x. 28, 10.

[16] Rv. v. 15, 3.

[17] Rv. v. 74, 4. *Cf.* Griffith, *Hymns of the Rigveda*, 1, 542, n.

mentioned in the Yajurveda. Sāyaṇa[18] says that **Dhaivara** is one who takes fish by netting a tank on either side; Dāśa and **Śauṣkala** do so by means of a fish-hook (*baḍiśa*); Bainda, Kaivarta, and Maināla by means of a net (*jāla*); Mārgāra catches fish in the water with his hands; Ānda by putting in pegs at a ford (apparently by building a sort of dam); **Parṇaka** by putting a poisoned leaf on the water. But none of these explanations can claim much authority.

18 On Taittirīya Brāhmaṇa, iii. 4, 12, 1. *Cf.* Weber, *Zeitschrift der Deutschen Morgenländischen Gesellschaft*, 18, 281. *Cf.* Zimmer, *Altindisches Leben*, 243-245.

Mṛga-vyādha, 'the hunter,' is the name of Sirius in the legend of Prajāpati's daughter in the Aitareya Brāhmaṇa.[1] Prajāpati (Orion) pursues his daughter (Rohiṇī), and is shot by the archer Sirius. The transference of the legend of Prajāpati to the sky is no doubt secondary, caused by the obvious similarity of the constellation in question to the idea of an archer.

1 iii. 33, 5. *Cf.* Hillebrandt, *Vedische Mythologie*, 2, 205, n. 1, 208, n. 3; Tilak, *Orion*, 98 *et seq.*; Sūrya Siddhānta, viii. 10; ix. 12, preserves the name.

Mṛga-śiras, Mṛga-śīrṣa. See **Nakṣatra,** 1. and 2. **Mṛga.**

Mṛgākhara in the Taittirīya Saṃhitā (vii. 5, 21, 1) and Brāhmaṇa (iii. 9, 17, 3) denotes the 'lair of wild beasts.'

Mṛḍa is found only in compounds in the Yajurveda Saṃhitās,[1] where it seems to denote a small weight of gold. It is uncertain whether the reading should not be Pṛda, as in the grammatical tradition.[2]

1 *Upacāya-mṛḍaṃ hiraṇyam*, Kāṭhaka Saṃhitā, xi. 1; *aṣṭā-mṛḍaṃ hiraṇyam*, *ibid.*, xiii. 10; *aṣṭā-pruḍ-ḍhiraṇyam*, Taittirīya Saṃhitā, iii. 4, 1, 4, etc.

2 See Pāṇini, iii. 1, 123, with the Vārttika; von Schroeder, *Zeitschrift der Deutschen Morgenländischen Gesellschaft*, 49, 164.

Mṛttikā, 'clay,' is mentioned in the later Saṃhitās and the Brāhmaṇas.[1] *Cf.* **Mṛd.**

1 Vājasaneyi Saṃhitā, xviii. 13; Aitareya Brāhmaṇa, iii. 34, 2; Chāndogya Upaniṣad, vi. 1, 4; Taittirīya Āraṇyaka, x. 1, 8. 9.

Mṛtyu, 'death,' is repeatedly mentioned in the Rigveda[1] and later[2] as a thing of terror. There are a hundred and one forms of death, the natural one by old age[3] (*jarā*), and a hundred others, all to be avoided.[4] To die before old age (*purā jarasaḥ*)[5] is to die before the allotted span (*purā āyuṣaḥ*),[6] the normal length of life being throughout Vedic literature spoken of as a hundred years.[7] On the other hand, the evils of old age in the loss of physical strength were clearly realized:[8] one of the feats of the Aśvins was to restore old **Cyavāna** to his former youth and powers, and another was the rejuvenation of **Kali**.[9] The Atharvaveda[10] is full of charms of all sorts to avert death and secure length of years (*āyuṣya*).

The modes of disposing of the dead were burial and cremation (see **Agnidagdha**). Both existed in the early Vedic period,[11] as in Greece;[12] but the former method was on the whole less favoured, and tended to be regarded with disapproval. The bones of the dead, whether burned or not, were marked by the erection of a tumulus (**Śmaśāna**): the Śatapatha Brāhmaṇa[13] preserves traces of strong differences of opinion as to the mode in which these tumuli should be constructed. There is little or no trace[14] of the custom common in northern lands of sending the dead man to sea in a burning ship: the reference

1 vii. 59, 12; x. 13, 4; 18, 1. 2; x. 48, 5; 60, 5. So *mṛtyu-bandhu*, 'akin to death,' Rv. viii. 18, 22; x. 95, 18.

2 Taittirīya Saṃhitā, i. 5, 9, 4, where the world is said to be 'yoked with death' (*mṛtyu-saṃyuta*); Taittirīya Brāhmaṇa, i. 5, 9, 6; Aitareya Brāhmaṇa, iii. 8, 2; 14, 1. 2. 3; Śatapatha Brāhmaṇa, x. 6, 5, 1, etc. So often the 'bonds of death' (*mṛtyu-pāśa*), Av. viii. 2, 2; 8, 10. 16; xvii. 1, 30; Taittirīya Brāhmaṇa, iii. 10, 8, 2; Kāṭhaka Upaniṣad, i. 18, etc.

3 Av. ii. 13, 2; 28, 2.

4 Av. i. 30, 3; ii. 28, 1; iii. 11, 5; viii. 2, 27; xi. 6, 16, etc.

5 Rv. viii. 67, 20; Av. v. 30, 17; x. 2, 30; xiii. 3, 56.

6 Śatapatha Brāhmaṇa, ii. 1, 4, 1.

7 Rv. i. 64, 14; 89, 9; ii. 33, 2, etc. *Cf.* Lanman, *Sanskrit Reader*, 384; Weber, *Indische Studien*, 17, 193; *Festgruss an Roth*, 137.

8 Rv. i. 71, 10; 179, 1.

9 x. 39, 8. *Cf.* Muir, *Sanskrit Texts*, 5, 243.

10 See Bloomfield, *Atharvaveda*, 62 *et seq.*

11 See Hopkins, *Journal of the American Oriental Society*, 16, clii; Winternitz, *Geschichte der indischen Literatur*, 1, 84, 85.

12 See Lang, *Homer and his Age*, 82 *et seq.*; *cf.* Burrows, *Discoveries in Crete*, 209-213.

13 xiii. 8, 2, 1.

14 *Cf.* Zimmer, *Altindisches Leben*, 410; Weinhold, *Altnordisches Leben*, 483 *et seq.*

to a ship[15] seems to point to mythical perils after death, not to the mode of burial.

The life after death was to the Vedic Indian a repetition of the life in this world. He passed into the next world *sarva-tanuḥ sāṅgaḥ*, 'with whole body and all his members,'[16] enjoying there the same pleasures as he had enjoyed on earth. Even in the Rigveda[17] there are hints of evil awaiting evil-doers, but it is not until the Atharvaveda[18] and the Brāhmaṇas[19] that a hell of punishment is set out, and it is in the Brāhmaṇas[20] that good and evil deeds are said to produce happiness or hell hereafter. But there is no hint of extinction[21] in the Rigveda as the fate of the wicked, as Roth[22] inclined to think. The Vedic poet not being deeply moral, his verses do not convey, as would those of a man convinced of sin, warnings of future judgment.

15 Rv. x. 63. 10; 135, 4; Av. vii. 6, 3, and *cf.* Weber, Proceedings of the Berlin Academy, 1895, 856.

16 Av. v. 6, 11; xviii. 4, 64; Śatapatha Brāhmaṇa, v. 6, 1, 1; xi. 1, 8, 6; xii. 8, 3, 31, and *cf.* Taittirīya Saṃhitā, v. 3, 5, 2; 6, 3; 6, 6, 3; Taittirīya Brāhmaṇa, iii. 8, 20, 5; 10, 11, 1.

17 Rv. ii. 29, 6; iii. 26, 8; iv. 5, 5; 25, 6; vii. 104, 3. 11. 17; x. 152, 4.

18 ii. 14, 3; v. 19, 3; 30, 11; viii. 2, 24; xii. 4, 36; xviii. 3, 3. *Cf.* also v. 19; Vājasaneyi Saṃhitā, xxx. 5.

19 Śatapatha Brāhmaṇa, xi. 6, 1, 1 *et seq.*; Weber, *Zeitschrift der Deutschen Morgenländischen Gesellschaft*, 9, 240 *et seq.*; Jaiminīya Brāhmaṇa, i. 42-44 (*Journal of the American Oriental Society*, 15, 236 *et seq.*).

20 Śatapatha Brāhmaṇa, vi. 2, 2, 27; x. 6, 3, 1; Kauṣītaki Brāhmaṇa, xii. 3, etc.

21 *Cf.* Macdonell, *Vedic Mythology*, p. 169.

22 *Journal of the American Oriental Society*, 3, 329-347; Weber, *op. cit.*, 238 *et seq.*

Mṛd denotes 'clay' in the later Saṃhitās[1] and the Brāhmaṇas[2] (*cf.* **Mṛttikā**). A 'lump of clay' also occurs in the Brāhmaṇas,[3] and a Mṛt-paca, 'potter,' in the Maitrāyaṇī Upaniṣad.[4] A 'clay vessel,' Mṛtpātra,[5] and vessels (*pātra*) made of clay (*mṛn-maya*),[6] are mentioned, and the grave is called the 'house of clay.'[7]

1 Taittirīya Saṃhitā, v. 7, 9, 2; Vājasaneyi Saṃhitā, xi. 55.

2 Śatapatha Brāhmaṇa, vi. 1, 1, 13; 2, 34; 3, 3; 3, 1, 22. 32; 3, 1; Maitrāyaṇī Upaniṣad vi. 27, etc.

3 Śatapatha Brāhmaṇa, vi. 4, 2, 1; 5, 2, 1; xiv. 2, 1, 8; Chāndogya Upaniṣad, vi. 1, 4.

4 ii. 6; iii. 3.

5 Kāṭhaka Saṃhitā, xxxi. 2.

6 Taittirīya Brāhmaṇa, i. 4, 1, 3. 4, etc.

7 Rv. vii. 89, 1 (*mṛnmaya gṛha*).

Mṛdh in the Rigveda[1] and later[2] denotes 'enemy.'

[1] i. 131, 6; 138, 2; 182, 4; ii. 22, 3; 23, 13; 28, 7; iii. 47, 2; v. 30, 7, etc.

[2] Av. v. 20, 12; vi. 2, 2; viii. 5, 8; xiii. 1, 5. 27; xviii. 2, 59; Taittirīya Saṃhitā, ii. 2, 7, 4; 5, 3, 1; Vājasaneyi Saṃhitā, v. 37; xi. 18. 72, etc.

Mṛdhra-vāc. See **Dasyu** and **Dāsa**.

Mekṣaṇa is the name in the Brāhmaṇas[1] of a wooden ladle used for stirring up the oblation (**Caru**).

[1] Taittirīya Brāhmaṇa, i. 3, 10, 4; iii. 7, 4, 9; Śatapatha Brāhmaṇa, ii. 4, 2, 13, etc.

Mekhalā denotes 'girdle' in the later Saṃhitās[1] and the Brāhmaṇas.[2] The **Brahmacārin** wore a girdle.[3]

[1] Av. vi. 133, 1; Taittirīya Saṃhitā, i. 3, 3, 5; vi. 2, 2, 7; Kāṭhaka Saṃhitā, xxiii. 4; xxiv. 9; Maitrāyaṇī Saṃhitā, iii. 6, 7, etc.

[2] Śatapatha Brāhmaṇa, iii. 2, 1, 10; iv. 4, 5, 2; vi. 2, 2, 39, etc.

[3] In the Gṛhya Sūtras the girdle of the Brahmin is of Muñja, that of the Kṣatriya of a bowstring, and that of the Vaiśya of wool or hemp. See Āśvalāyana Gṛhya Sūtra, i. 19, 12, etc.

Megha denotes 'cloud' in the Rigveda[1] and later.[2]

[1] i. 181, 8.

[2] Av. iv. 15, 7; Śatapatha Brāhmaṇa, iii. 2, 2, 5; xii. 3, 2, 6; *mahā-megha*, Aitareya Āraṇyaka, iii. 2, 4; Śāṅkhāyana Āraṇyaka, vii. 3; viii. 7. The verb *meghay*, 'to make cloudy weather,' is found in the Taittirīya Saṃhitā, iv. 4, 5, 1, and *meghayantī* is the name of one of the seven **Kṛttikās**, Taittirīya Brāhmaṇa, iii. 1, 4, 1; Weber, *Naxatra*, 2, 301, 368.

Methi is found in the Atharvaveda[1] denoting 'post.' The word is also found in the marriage ritual,[2] when the sense is, according to the St. Petersburg Dictionary, a post to support the pole of a chariot. In one passage of the Rigveda it is perhaps used of posts forming a palisade.[3] In the Pañcaviṃśa

[1] viii. 5, 20.

[2] Av. xiv. 1, 40. *Cf.* Taittirīya Saṃhitā, vi. 2, 9, 4; Kāṭhaka Saṃhitā, xxv. 8; Aitareya Brāhmaṇa, i. 29, 22; Śatapatha Brāhmaṇa, iii. 5, 3, 21.

[3] viii. 53, 5 (*mita-methībhiḥ* for *-medhābhiḥ*, conjectured by Roth, *Zeitschrift der Deutschen Morgenländischen Gesellschaft*, 48, 109).

Brāhmaṇa[4] it appears in the form of Methī to denote the post to which the sacrificial cow is tied. The word is very variously spelt, Medhi and Meṭhī also being found.

[4] xiii. 9, 17. *Cf.* Jaiminīya Brāhmaṇa, i. 19, 1 (*Journal of the American Oriental Society*, 23, 329).

Medha is a word of uncertain sense occurring in a Vālakhilya hymn of the Rigveda.[1] According to the St. Petersburg Dictionary, the proper name of a sacrificer may be meant.

[1] viii. 50, 10 (*cf.* viii. 49, 10), where, as a rule, the sense of 'sacrifice' is accepted as adequate.

Medhātithi,[1] **Medhyātithi**[2] ('having a guest at the sacrifice') appear to be the names of one and the same man, a descendant of **Kaṇva** and a famous Vedic Ṛṣi, to whom the authorship of various hymns[3] is attributed in the Anukramaṇī (Index). To him Indra is said in the Rigveda[4] to have come in the form of a ram: this myth is perpetuated in the Subrahmaṇyā formula[5] recited by the priest while the Soma is being carried within the sacrificial enclosure, when Indra is hailed as 'ram of Medhātithi.' He appears also as a rival of **Vatsa**, whom he accused of low birth, but who convinced him of his error by undergoing a fire ordeal (*cf.* **Divya**).[6] In the Atharvaveda[7] he is mentioned with many other sages, and occurs elsewhere[8] also as a sage.

[1] This is the form of the later texts and of Rv. viii. 8, 20, where he occurs with **Kaṇva**.

[2] This is the usual form in the Rv.: i. 36, 10. 11. 17; viii. 1, 30; 2, 40; 33, 4; 49, 9; 51, 1; ix. 43, 3.

[3] i. 12-23; viii. 1-3; 22. 23; ix. 41-43. In the ascriptions Medhātithi and Medhyātithi are confused.

[4] viii. 2, 40. *Cf.* i. 51, 1, where, however, there is no mention of Medhāithi.

[5] Jaiminīya Brāhmaṇa, ii. 79; Ṣaḍviṃśa Brāhmaṇa, i. 1; Śatapatha Brāhmaṇa, iii. 3, 4, 18; Taittirīya Āraṇyaka, i. 12, 3. Moreover, the legend is alluded to in the Śāṭyāyanaka. See Sāyaṇa on Rv. i. 51, 1; viii. 2, 40, and Oertel, *Journal of the American Oriental Society*, 16, ccxl. On the explanation of the legend, *cf.* Weber, *Indische Studien*, 9, 38 *et seq.*

[6] Pañcaviṃśa Brāhmaṇa, xiv. 6, 6.

[7] iv. 29, 6.

[8] As a Gṛhapati at the sacrifice of the **Vibhindukīyas**, Jaiminīya Brāhmaṇa, iii. 233 (*Journal of the American Oriental Society*, 18, 38); Pañcaviṃśa Brāhmaṇa, xv. 10, 1; Kauṣītaki Brāhmaṇa, xxviii. 2.

Cf. Ludwig, Translation of the Rigveda, 3, 102, 105; Macdonell, *Vedic Mythology*, p. 146.

Medhya is the name of a man, an ancient sacrificer, in a hymn of the Rigveda.[1] In the Śāṅkhāyana Śrauta Sūtra[2] he is erroneously transmuted into **Pṛṣadhra Medhya Mātariśvan,** the patron of **Praskaṇva Kāṇva.**

[1] viii. 52, 2.
[2] xvi. 11, 26.
Cf. Weber, *Episches im vedischen Ritual,* 39; Ludwig, Translation of the Rigveda, 3, 163.

Medhyātithi. See **Medhātithi.**

Menakā. See 2. **Menā.**

1. **Menā** in a few passages of the Rigveda denotes 'woman.'[1] The word is also used in the sense of the 'female' of an animal, either mare[2] or cow.[3]

[1] Rv. i. 62, 7; 95, 6; ii. 39, 2.
[2] Rv. i. 121, 2.
[3] x. 111, 3.
Cf. Pischel, *Indische Studien,* 2, 316, 317.

2. **Menā**[1] or **Menakā**[2] is mentioned in the Rigveda[3] and in the Brāhmaṇas[4] as the daughter, or perhaps wife, of **Vṛṣaṇaśva.** The meaning of the legend connected with her is quite unknown. *Cf.* **Maināka** or **Maināga.**

[1] This is the ordinary form of the name.
[2] So Ṣaḍviṃśa Brāhmaṇa, i. 1, where the masculine form Mena is the epithet of Vṛṣaṇaśva.
[3] Rv. i. 51, 13, where Sāyaṇa tells the legend from the Śāṭyāyanaka. *Cf.* Oertel, *Journal of the American Oriental Society,* 16, ccxl.
[4] Ṣaḍviṃśa Brāhmaṇa, i. 1; Śatapatha Brāhmaṇa, iii. 3, 4, 18; Taittirīya Āraṇyaka, i. 12, 3; Lāṭyāyana Śrauta Sūtra, i. 3, 17.
Cf. Eggeling, *Sacred Books of the East,* 26, 81, n.

Meṣa denotes 'ram' in the Rigveda[1] and later,[2] while Meṣī means 'sheep.'[3] Both words are also used to denote the

[1] i. 43, 6; 116, 16; viii 2, 40; x. 27, 17, etc.
[2] Av. vi. 49, 2; Vājasaneyi Saṃhitā, iii. 59; xix. 90; xxiv. 30; Taittirīya Saṃhitā, vii. 4, 12, 1; Ṣaḍviṃśa Brāhmaṇa, i. 1; Śatapatha Brāhmaṇa, iii. 3, 4, 18, etc.
[3] Rv. i. 43, 6; Vājasaneyi Saṃhitā, iii. 59; xxiv. 1; Taittirīya Brāhmaṇa, i. 6, 4, 4, etc.

'wool'[4] of the sheep, especially as employed for the Soma filter. A wild (*āraṇya*) ram is mentioned in the Vājasaneyi Saṃhitā.[5]

[4] *Meṣa*, Rv. viii. 86, 11; *Meṣī*. ix. 8, 5; 86, 47; 107, 11.
[5] xxiv. 30.

Cf. Hopkins, *Journal of the American Oriental Society*, 17, 66, 67.

Mehatnū is the name of a stream in the Nadīstuti ('Praise of Rivers') in the Rigveda.[1] It must apparently have been a tributary of the **Sindhu** (Indus), entering that river before the **Krumu** (Kurum) and **Gomatī** (Gomal). It may conceivably have been a tributary of the **Krumu.**

[1] x. 75, 6. *Cf.* Zimmer, *Altindisches Leben*, 14; Muir, *Sanskrit Texts*, 5, 344.

Maitrāyaṇīya Brāhmaṇa is the name of a text mentioned in the Śulba Sūtra of Baudhāyana.[1]

[1] Baudhāyana Śrauta Sūtra, xxxii. 8. *Cf.* Caland, *Über das rituelle Sūtra des Baudhāyana*, 41, who cannot trace the citation in the Maitrāyaṇī Saṃhitā.

Maitreya is the patronymic or metronymic[1] of **Kauṣārava** in the Aitareya Brāhmaṇa.[2] It is also applied to **Glāva** in the Chāndogya Upaniṣad.[3]

[1] Patronymic from Mitrayu, according to Pāṇini, vi. 4, 174; vii. 3, 2; metronymic from Mitrā, according to the commentator on Chāndogya Upaniṣad, i. 12, 1.
[2] viii. 28, 18.
[3] i. 12, 1; Gopatha Brāhmaṇa, i. 1, 31 *et seq.*; Bloomfield, *Atharvaveda*, 110.

Maitreyī is the name of one of the wives of **Yājñavalkya** according to the Bṛhadāraṇyaka Upaniṣad (ii. 4, 1 *et seq.*; iv. 5, 2 *et seq.*).

Maināka, 'descendant of **Menakā,**' is the name of a mountain among the Himālayas in the Taittirīya Āraṇyaka.[1] There is a various reading Maināga.

[1] i. 31, 2. *Cf.* Weber, *Indische Studien*, 1, 78; *Indian Literature*, 93.

Maināla occurs in the list of victims at the Puruṣamedha ('human sacrifice') in the Yajurveda.[1] It seems clearly to mean 'fisherman' from Mīna, 'fish,' as Sāyaṇa[2] and Mahīdhara[3] explain it.

[1] Vājasaneyi Saṃhitā, xxx. 16; Taittirīya Brāhmaṇa, iii. 4, 12, 1.

[2] On Taittirīya Brāhmaṇa, *loc. cit.*

[3] On Vājasaneyi Saṃhitā, *loc. cit.*

Maujavata. See **Mūjavant.**

Maudgalya, 'descendant of **Mudgala,**' is the patronymic of several persons, **Nāka,**[1] **Śatabalākṣa,**[2] and **Lāṅgalāyana.**[3] A **Brahmacārin** of the name is mentioned in the Gopatha Brāhmaṇa[4] as disputing with **Glāva Maitreya.**

[1] Śatapatha Brāhmaṇa, xii. 5, 2, 1; Bṛhadāraṇyaka Upaniṣad, vi. 4, 4; Taittirīya Upaniṣad, i. 9, 1.

[2] Nirukta, xi. 6.

[3] Aitareya Brāhmaṇa, v. 3, 8.

[4] i. 1, 31; Bloomfield, *Atharvaveda*, 110. *Cf.* also Caland, *Über das rituelle Sūtra des Baudhāyana*, 35.

Mauna, 'descendant of Muni,' is the patronymic of **Aṇīcin** in the Kauṣītaki Brāhmaṇa (xxiii. 5).

Mauṣikī-putra, 'son of a female descendant of Mūṣikā,' is the name of a teacher, a pupil of **Hārikarṇīputra** in the last Vaṃśa (list of teachers) in the Mādhyaṃdina recension of the Bṛhadāraṇyaka Upaniṣad (vi. 4, 30).

Mleccha occurs in the Śatapatha Brāhmaṇa[1] in the sense of a barbarian in speech. The Brahmin is there forbidden to use barbarian speech. The example[2] given of such speech is *he 'lavo*, explained by Sāyaṇa as *he 'rayaḥ*, 'ho, foes.' If this is correct—the Kāṇva recension has a different reading[3]—the barbarians referred to were Āryan speakers, though not speakers of Sanskrit, but of a Prākṛta form of speech.[4] *Cf.* **Vāc.**

[1] iii. 2, 1, 24.

[2] iii. 2, 1, 23.

[3] See Eggeling, *Sacred Books of the East*, 26, 31, n. 3

[4] Weber, *Indian Literature*, 180; *cf.* Keith, *Aitareya Āraṇyaka*, 179, 180, 196.

Y.

Yakṣa is found several times in the Rigveda[1] and the Atharvaveda[2] in passages in which Ludwig[3] sees the meaning of a feast or holy practice in accordance with the native commentators. It is, however, very doubtful whether this sense ever occurs.[4]

[1] i. 190, 4; iv. 3, 13; v. 70, 4; vii. 56, 16; 61, 5; x. 88, 13.

[2] viii. 9, 25; x. 2, 32; 7, 38; 8, 43; xi. 2, 24, etc.

[3] Translation of the Rigveda, 3, 262.

[4] *Cf.* St. Petersburg Dictionary, *s.v.*, and Geldner's full discussion, *Vedische Studien*, 3, 126-143.

Yakṣu is mentioned, once in the singular and once in the plural, in the hymn of the Rigveda[1] which celebrates **Sudās'** battle with the ten kings. Who they were and what part they played in that conflict is quite uncertain. They seem, from the wording of the text, to have taken part in two conflicts, as Zimmer[2] says—one on the **Paruṣṇī** (Ravi), and one on the **Yamunā** (Jumna)—with the aid of the **Ajas** and **Śigrus**, under the leadership of **Bheda.** It is, however, at least possible that in the former passage **Yadu** should be read for Yakṣu, or, at any rate, Yakṣu be deemed a contemptuous substitute of the name of a possibly un-Āryan or unimportant tribe (as their allies, the Ajas and Śigrus, clearly were) for the name of the certainly famous Yadus, as is suggested by Hopkins.[3] *Cf.* **Turvaśa.**

[1] vii. 18, 6. 19.

[2] *Altindisches Leben*, 126, 127.

[3] *Journal of the American Oriental Society*, 15, 259 *et seq.* It is not clear, however, whether Hopkins thinks that the Yadus are alluded to, but it seems probable.

Yakṣma in the Rigveda[1] and the Atharvaveda[2] frequently denotes 'illness,' in general, perhaps as rendering the body emaciated. A hundred kinds of Yakṣma are referred to in the Vājasaneyi Saṃhitā,[3] and *a-yakṣma* in the Kāṭhaka Saṃhitā,[4]

[1] i. 122, 9; x. 85, 31; 97, 11. 12; 137, 4; 163, 1-6.

[2] ii. 10, 5. 6; iii. 31, 1; v. 4, 9; 30, 6; viii. 7, 2; ix. 8, 3. 7. 10; xii. 2, 1. 2; 4, 8; xix. 36, 1; 38, 1.

[3] xii. 97.

[4] xvii. 11.

denotes 'free from disease.' In the Yajurveda Saṃhitās[5] an account is given of the origin of Yakṣma, which is distinguished as of three kinds—**Rāja-yakṣma,** 'royal Yakṣma,' Pāpa-yakṣma, 'evil Yakṣma,' and **Jāyenya,** most probably 'syphilis.' The second of the series is elsewhere unknown, and can hardly be defined, for it merely means 'serious or deadly disease.' *Cf.* also **Ajñātayakṣma.**

[5] Taittirīya Saṃhitā, ii. 3, 5, 2; 5, 6, 5; Kāṭhaka Saṃhitā, xi. 3; Maitrāyaṇī Saṃhitā, ii. 2, 7; Śatapatha Brāhmaṇa, iv. 1, 3, 9. *Cf.* Zimmer, *Altindisches Leben*, 375 *et seq.*; Grohmann, *Indische Studien*, 9, 400; Bloomfield, *Atharvaveda*, 60; Jolly, *Medicin*, 89.

Yajata occurs in a hymn of the Rigveda,[1] where he is apparently a Ṛṣi or a sacrificer.

[1] v. 44, 10. 11. *Cf.* Ludwig, Translation of the Rigveda, 3, 138.

Yajur-veda, the 'Veda of the sacrificial utterance' (**Yajus**), is mentioned frequently in the Brāhmaṇas[1] and Upaniṣads.[2]

[1] Taittirīya Brāhmaṇa, iii. 12, 9, 1; Aitareya Brāhmaṇa, v. 32, 1; Śatapatha Brāhmaṇa, xi. 5, 8, 3; xii. 3, 4, 9.

[2] Aitareya Āraṇyaka, iii. 2, 3. 5; Sāṅkhāyana Āraṇyaka, viii. 3. 8; Bṛhadāraṇyaka Upaniṣad, i. 5, 5; ii. 4, 10; iv. 1, 2; 5, 11; Chāndogya Upaniṣad, i. 3, 7; iii. 2, 1. 2; 15, 7; vii. 1, 2. 4; 2, 1; 7, 1; Āśvalāyana Srauta Sūtra, x. 7, 2; Sāṅkhāyana Srauta Sūtra, xvi. 2, 6, etc.

Yajus is repeatedly distinguished from the Ṛc and the **Sāman** in Vedic literature.[1] The Yajus is the utterance accompanying the sacrifice, and may have the form of verse or prose, the term covering both.

[1] Rv. x. 90, 9; Av. v. 26, 1; ix. 6, 2; Taittirīya Saṃhitā, v. 5, 3, 1; 9, 4; Vājasaneyi Saṃhitā, i. 30; iv. 1; xix. 28; Aitareya Brāhmaṇa, i. 29, 21; viii. 13, 2; Śatapatha Brāhmaṇa, i. 2, 1, 7; vi. 5, 1, 2; 3, 4, etc. In the Bṛhadāraṇyaka Upaniṣad, vi. 4, 33, there is a reference to the *śuklāni Yajūṃṣi*, 'white or pure Yajus,' as promulgated by **Vājasaneya Yājñavalkya,** whence the Vājasaneyi Saṃhitā is popularly known as the 'White Yajurveda.' The theory that this is due to the fact that in the Vājasaneyi the Mantra parts of the text are not accompanied by Brāhmaṇa passages is, though accepted by Weber, *Indian Literature*, 103, 104; Eggeling, *Sacred Books of the East*, 12. xxvii, and others, now to be abandoned. In the Taittirīya Āraṇyaka, v. 10, the expression *śukrayajūṃṣi* seems to refer to books iv. and v. of that text. *Cf.* also Winternitz, *Geschichte der indischen Literatur*, 1, 149, n.

Yajña-gāthā denotes a verse (**Gāthā**) containing a maxim as to the sacrifice of any kind or sort,[1] or, as it is expressed in the Mahābhārata,[2] a 'verse sung regarding the sacrifice' (*gāthā yajña-gītā*).

[1] Aitareya Brāhmaṇa, iii. 43, 5; Āśvalāyana Śrauta Sūtra, ii. 12, 6; Śāṅkhāyana Śrauta Sūtra, xvi. 8, 26; 9, 6, etc.

[2] xii. 791. 2316.

Yajña-vacas Rājastambāyana, 'descendant of Rājastamba,' is the name of a teacher, a pupil of **Tura Kāvaṣeya**, according to the Śatapatha Brāhmaṇa.[1] He is also mentioned in the Maitrāyaṇī Saṃhitā.[2]

[1] x. 4, 2, 1; 6, 5, 9; Bṛhadāraṇyaka Upaniṣad, vi. 5, 4 Kāṇva.

[2] iii. 10, 3; iv. 8, 2.

Yajña-sena is the name of a teacher with the patronymic **Caitra** or **Caitriyāyaṇa** mentioned in the Yajurveda Saṃhitās.[1]

[1] Taittirīya Saṃhitā. v. 3, 8, 1 (Caitriyāyaṇa); Kāṭhaka Saṃhitā, xxi. 4 (Caitra).

Yajñeṣu is the name of a man in the Taittirīya Brāhmaṇa.[1] He was made to prosper by his priest **Mātsya**, who knew the exact moment of sacrificing.

[1] i. 5, 2, 1. *Cf.* Weber, *Naxatra*, 2, 306.

Yajñopavīta denotes the 'wearing of the Brahminical thread over the left shoulder at the sacrifice,' and is mentioned as early as the Taittirīya Brāhmaṇa.[1] Tilak,[2] however, urges that it was not originally a thread that was worn, but a garment of cloth (**Vāsas**) or of deerskin (**Ajina**). This seems quite probable.

[1] iii. 10, 9, 12. *Cf.* Taittirīya Saṃhitā, ii. 5, 11, 1; Satapatha Brāhmaṇa, ii. 4, 2, 1; 6, 1, 12; and **Prācīnāvīta**.

[2] *Orion*, 145 *et seq.*, quoting Taittirīya Āraṇyaka, ii. 1, and the view of the Mīmāmsists, Jaiminīyanyāyamālāvistara, iii. 4, 1. This view is not prejudiced by the quite implausible conjectures as to Orion's belt with which it is combined. *Cf.* Eggeling, *Sacred Books o the East*, 12, 361, 424.

Yati is the name of an ancient clan which is connected with the **Bhṛgus** in two passages of the Rigveda,[1] where the Yatis certainly seem to be real persons. In another hymn,[2] however, they already appear as almost mythical. In the Yajurveda Saṃhitās,[3] and elsewhere,[4] the Yatis are a race whom Indra, in an evil moment, gave over to the hyænas (**Sālāvṛka**): exactly what is referred to is uncertain. Yati is mentioned with Bhṛgu in a verse of the Sāmaveda.[4]

[1] viii. 3, 9; 6, 18; Weber, *Indische Studien*, 3, 465, n.

[2] x. 72, 7.

[3] Taittirīya Saṃhitā, ii. 4, 9, 2; vi. 2, 7, 5; Kāṭhaka Saṃhitā, viii. 5; xi. 10; xxv. 6; xxxvi. 7; Pañcaviṃśa Brāhmaṇa, viii. 1, 4; xiii. 4, 16; Aitareya Brāhmaṇa, vii. 28, 1; Kauṣītaki Upaniṣad, i. 3, etc.; Muir, *Sanskrit Texts*, 1², 437 *et seq.*

[4] ii. 304. In the parallel passage, Av. ii. 5, 3, the reading *Yatīr* is found, possibly an error for *Yatīn*, or merely a blunder. *Cf.* Muir, *op. cit.*, 5, 49, n. 92; Whitney, Translation of the Atharvaveda, 44; Āśvalāyana Śrauta Sūtra, vi. 3, 1.

Cf. Macdonell, *Vedic Mythology*, p. 146.

Yadu is the name of a tribe and of the king of the tribe. They are mentioned repeatedly in the Rigveda,[1] normally in conjunction with **Turvaśa.** They seem to have taken part in the great battle against **Sudās**:[2] the Yadu and the Turvaśa kings seem to have escaped with their lives, while the **Anu** and the **Druhyu** kings perished. This is at least the most natural explanation of several passages,[3] though these passages possibly refer to a successful raid across the **Sarayu**, and a defeat of two princes, Arṇa and Citraratha.[4] That Turvaśa was the Yadu king, as Hopkins[5] holds, is most improbable.

[1] i. 36, 18; 54, 6; 174, 9; iv. 30, 17; v. 31, 8; vi 45, 1; viii. 4, 7; 7, 18; 9, 14; 10, 5; 45, 27; ix. 61, 2; x. 49, 8; plural, i. 108, 8. See **Turvaśa**, and Hopkins, *Journal of the American Oriental Society*, 15, 258 *et seq.*

[2] Whether Yadu should be read in Rv. vii. 18, 6, or not, the Yadus seem to be meant. *Cf.* **Yakṣu.**

[3] Rv. i. 174, 9; iv. 30, 17; v. 31, 8; vi. 20, 12.

[4] Rv. iv. 30, 18.

[5] *Loc. cit.*

Cf. Zimmer, *Altindisches Leben*, 122, 124; Ludwig, Translation of the Rigveda, 3, 205; 5, 142; Weber, *Episches im vedischen Ritual*, 37.

Yantṛ in the Rigveda[1] and in the Sūtras[2] denotes a 'driver' of horses or 'charioteer.'

[1] i. 162, 19; x. 22, 5.

[2] Kātyāyana Śrauta Sūtra, xv. 6, 29, etc.

Yama denotes 'twins,' the birth of which is frequently alluded to in Vedic literature.[1] Twins of different sex seem to be indicated by the expression *yamau mithunau*.[2] There are traces of the belief—widely spread among negro and other races—that twins are uncanny and of evil omen,[3] but there are also vestiges of the opposite opinion, that twins are lucky.[4]

[1] Rv. i. 66, 4; 164, 15; ii. 39, 2; iii. 39, 3; v. 57, 4; vi. 59, 2; x. 13, 2; 117, 9; Pañcaviṃśa Brāhmaṇa, xvi. 4, 10, etc.

[2] Kāṭhaka Saṃhitā, xiii. 4; Nirukta, xii. 10.

[3] Av. iii. 28; Aitareya Brāhmaṇa, vii. 9, 8; Kātyāyana Śrauta Sūtra, xxv. 4, 35; Śāṅkhāyana Śrauta Sūtra, iii. 4, 14, etc. *Cf.* **Yamasū**; **Yuktāśva.**

[4] Taittirīya Saṃhitā, vii. 1, 1, 3; Pañcaviṃśa Brāhmaṇa, xxiv. 12, 3; Śatapatha Brāhmaṇa, v. 3, 1, 8, and *cf.* Rv. iii. 39, 3.

Cf. Weber, *Indische Studien*, 17, 298-300; *Naxatra*, 2, 314, n.

Yama-nakṣatra. See **Nakṣatra.**

Yama-sū, a 'bearer of twins,' is one of the victims at the Puruṣamedha ('human sacrifice') in the Yajurveda.[1]

[1] Vājasaneyi Saṃhitā, xxx. 15; Taittirīya Brāhmaṇa, iii. 4, 11, 1.

Yamunā, 'twin,' the name of a river, so called as running parallel with the Ganges, is mentioned thrice in the Rigveda,[1] and not rarely later. According to the Rigveda,[2] the **Tṛtsus** and **Sudās** won a great victory against their foes on the Yamunā; there is no reason[3] whatever to accept Hopkins'[4] view that the Yamunā here was another name of the **Paruṣṇī** (Ravi). In the Atharvaveda[5] the salve (**Āñjana**) of the Yamunā (*Yāmuna*) is mentioned along with that of **Trikakud** (*Traikakuda*) as of value. In the Aitareya[6] and the Śatapatha[7] Brāhmaṇas the **Bharatas** are famed as victorious on the Yamunā. Other Brāhmaṇas[8]

[1] v. 52, 17; vii. 18, 19; x. 75, 5.

[2] vii. 18, 19. See **Bharata** and **Kuru**.

[3] The Tṛtsus' territory lay between the Yamunā and the **Sarasvatī** on the east and the west respectively.

[4] *India, Old and New*, 52.

[5] iv. 9, 10.

[6] viii. 23.

[7] xiii. 5, 4, 11.

[8] Pañcaviṃśa Brāhmaṇa, ix. 4, 11 (*cf.* **Pārāvata**); xxv. 10, 24; 13, 4; Śāṅkhāyana Śrauta Sūtra, xiii. 29, 25. 33; Kātyāyana Śrauta Sūtra, xxiv. 6, 10. 39; Lāṭyāyana Śrauta Sūtra, x. 19, 9. 10; Āśvalāyana Śrauta Sūtra, xii. 6, 28, etc.

also mention this river. In the Mantrapāṭha[9] the **Sālvas** are spoken of as dwelling on its banks.

[9] ii. 11, 12.

Cf. Zimmer, *Altindisches Leben*, 5; Max Müller, *Sacred Books of the East*, 32, 323.

Yayāti is mentioned twice in the Rigveda,[1] once as an ancient sacrificer, and once as Nahuṣya, 'descendant of **Nahuṣa**,' apparently a king. There is no trace whatever of his connexion with **Pūru**, as in the Epic,[2] the tradition of which must be deemed to be inaccurate.

[1] i. 31, 17; x. 63, 1.

[2] *Cf.* Ludwig, Translation of the Rigveda, 3, 147; Muir, *Sanskrit Texts* 1^2, 232.

1. **Yava** in the Rigveda[1] appears to be a generic term for any sort of 'grain,' and not merely 'barley.' The latter sense is probably found in the Atharvaveda,[2] and is regular later. The barley harvest came after spring,[3] in the summer.[4] That barley was cultivated in the period of the Rigveda[5] is not certain, but on the whole very probable.[6]

[1] i. 23, 15; 66, 3; 117, 21; 135, 8; 176, 2; ii. 5, 6; 14, 11; v. 85, 3; vii. 3, 4; viii. 2, 3; 22, 6; 63, 9; 78, 10, etc.

[2] ii. 8, 3; vi. 30, 1; 50, 1. 2; 91, 1; 141, 2; 142 1. 2; viii. 7, 20; ix. 1, 22; 6, 14; xii. 1, 42; Taittirīya Saṃhitā, vi. 2, 10, 3; 4, 10, 5; vii. 2, 10, 2; Kāṭhaka Saṃhitā, xxv. 10; xxvi. 5; Maitrāyaṇī Saṃhitā, iv. 3, 2; Vājasaneyi Saṃhitā, v. 26; xviii. 12; xxiii. 30; Taittirīya Brāhmaṇa, i. 8, 4, 1; Śatapatha Brāhmaṇa, i. 1, 4, 20; ii. 5, 2, 1; iii. 6, 1, 9. 10; iv. 2, 1, 11; xii. 7, 2, 9; Chāndogya Upaniṣad, iii. 14, 3, etc.; Kauṣītaki Brāhmaṇa, iv. 12.

[3] Kauṣītaki Brāhmaṇa, iv. 13.

[4] Taittirīya Saṃhitā, vii. 2, 10, 2.

[5] Hopkins, *Journal of the American Oriental Society*, 17, 86, n.

[6] Sowing (*vap*) grain is referred to in Rv. i. 117, 21; ripening of grain in 135, 8; ploughing (*kṛṣ*) in i. 176, 2. Grain rejoicing in rain is alluded to in ii. 5, 6. See **Kṛṣi**.

Cf. Schrader, *Prehistoric Antiquities*, 282; Kuhn, *Indische Studien*, 1, 355, 356; Zimmer, *Altindisches Leben*, 238, 239.

2. **Yava.** See **Māsa**.

Yavasa in the Rigveda[1] and later[2] denotes the 'grass' on which animals feed, and which is burned by the forest fire.[3]

[1] i. 38, 5; 91, 13; iii. 45, 3; iv. 41, 10; 42, 5; vii. 18, 10; 87, 2; 93, 2; 102, 1, etc.

[2] Vājasaneyi Saṃhitā, xxi. 43, etc.

[3] *Cf.* Agni, *yavasād*, in Rv. i. 94, 11.

Cf. Zimmer, *Altindisches Leben*, 47; Max Müller, *Sacred Books of the East*, 32, 87.

Yavāgū means 'barley-gruel,'[1] but is also used of weak decoctions of other kinds of grain.[2]

[1] Taittirīya Saṃhitā, vi. 2, 5, 2; Kāṭhaka Saṃhitā, xi. 2; Taittirīya Āraṇyaka, ii. 8, 8; Kauṣītaki Brāhmaṇa, iv. 13, etc.

[2] Of **Jartila** and **Gavīdhuka**, Taittirīya Saṃhitā, v. 4, 3, 2.

Yavāśir is used in the Rigveda[1] as an epithet of **Soma**, meaning 'mixed with grain.'

[1] i. 187, 9; ii. 22, 1; iii. 42, 7; viii. 94, 4. *Cf.* Hillebrandt, *Vedische Mythologie*, 1, 227; Zimmer, *Altindisches Leben*, 279.

Yavāṣa. See **Yevāṣa.**

Yavya in the Śatapatha Brāhmaṇa (i. 7, 2, 46) denotes 'month' (lit., 'containing a first half,' see **2. Yava**).

Yavyāvatī is the name of a river in the Rigveda[1] and in the Pañcaviṃśa Brāhmaṇa.[2] Hillebrandt[3] thinks that the river is one in Iran, the Djob (Zhobe), near the Iryāb (Haliāb), but there is no reason to accept this identification.

[1] vi. 27, 6.

[2] xxv. 7, 2.

[3] *Vedische Mythologie*, 3, 268, n. 1. *Cf.* Zimmer, *Altindisches Leben*, 18, 19; Ludwig, Translation of the Rigveda, 3, 204; Kaegi, *Rigveda*, n. 338; Oldenberg, *Ṛgveda-Noten*, 1, 168, n. 1.

Yaśasvin Jayanta Lauhitya ('descendant of Lohita') is the name of a teacher, a pupil of **Kṛṣṇarāta Triveda Lauhitya** in the Vaṃśa (list of teachers) in the Jaiminīya Upaniṣad Brāhmaṇa (iii. 42, 1).

Yaṣṭi, 'staff,' is mentioned in the latest parts of the Brāhmaṇas.[1]

[1] Śatapatha Brāhmaṇa, ii. 6, 2, 17 of *veṇu*, 'bamboo'); Bṛhadāraṇyaka Upaniṣad, vi. 4, 7; Kauṣītaki Upaniṣad iv. 19, etc.

Yaska is the name of a man. The Yaskas, descendants of Girikṣit (*Gairikṣitāḥ*) are mentioned in the Kāṭhaka Saṃhitā.[1] *Cf.* **Yāska.**

[1] xiii. 12. *Cf.* Weber, *Indische Studien*, 3, 475 *et seq.*; 8, 245 *et seq.*; *Indian Literature*, 41, n. 30.

Yājña-tura, 'descendant of Yajñatura,' is the patronymic of 2. **Ṛṣabha** in the Śatapatha Brāhmaṇa.[1]

[1] xii. 8, 3, 7; xiii. 5, 4, 15; Śāṅkhāyana Śrauta Sūtra, xvi. 9, 8. 10.

Yājña-valkya, 'descendant of Yajñavalkya,' is repeatedly mentioned in the Śatapatha Brāhmaṇa[1] as an authority on questions of ritual. He is, however, also given as an authority on questions of philosophy in the Bṛhadāraṇyaka Upaniṣad,[2] but Oldenberg[3] is, no doubt, right in thinking that no possible importance can be attached to the mention of Yājñavalkya in the latter capacity. He is said to have been a pupil of **Uddālaka Āruṇi,**[4] whom he opposed successfully in a dispute.[5] His two wives, **Maitreyī** and **Kātyāyanī,** are mentioned in the Bṛhadāraṇyaka Upaniṣad,[6] which concludes[7] with a passage ascribing to Yājñavalkya Vājasaneya the 'white Yajus' (*śuklāni yajūṃṣi*). It is remarkable that Yājñavalkya is never mentioned in any other Vedic text outside the Śatapatha Brāhmaṇa except the Śāṅkhāyana Āraṇyaka,[8] where, however, both references are merely transcripts from the Śatapatha.[9] It has

[1] i. 1, 1, 9; 3, 1, 21. 26; 9, 3, 16; ii. 3, 1, 21; 4, 3, 2; 5, 1, 2 (where he is said to be in contradiction with the Rigveda); iii. 1, 1, 4; 2, 21; 3, 10; 8, 2, 24 (cursed by a **Caraka** teacher); iv. 2, 1, 7; 6, 1, 10; 8, 7, etc. There are no references to Yājñavalkya in books v-ix, which, on the contrary, owe their doctrine to **Tura Kāvaṣeya** and **Śāṇḍilya**; but the fame of Yājñavalkya revives in books x-xiv—*e.g.*, xi. 3, 1, 2; 4, 2, 17; 3, 20; 6, 2, 1; 3, 1; xii. 4, 1, 10, etc.

[2] iii. 1, 2 *et seq.*; 2, 10 *et seq.*; 3, 1; 4, 1; 5, 1; 6, 1; 7, 1, etc.

[3] *Buddha*,[5] 34, n. 1.

[4] vi. 4, 33 (Mādhyaṃdina = vi. 5, 4 Kāṇva).

[5] iii. 7, 1.

[6] ii. 4, 1; iv. 5, 1 *et seq.*

[7] vi. 4, 33 (Mādhyaṃdina = vi. 5, 4 Kāṇva).

[8] ix. 7; xiii. 1.

[9] Weber, *Indian Literature*, 132, n *; Keith, *Journal of the Royal Asiatic Society*, 1908, 374.

been supposed by Oldenberg[10] and others that Yājñavalkya belonged to **Videha**, but despite the legend of Janaka's patronage of him, his association with **Uddālaka**, the **Kuru-Pañcāla**, renders this doubtful.

10 *Buddha*,[5] 34, n. 1.
Cf. Weber, *Indian Literature*, 120 *et seq.*; *Indische Studien*, 1, 173; 13, 265-269; Eggeling, *Sacred Books of the East*, 12, xxx *et seq.*; von Schroeder, *Indiens Literatur und Cultur*, 188.

Yājyā (scil. ṛc, 'verse') denotes the words uttered at the moment of offering the sacrifice, 'consecrating sacrificial formula,' in the later Saṃhitās[1] and the Brāhmaṇas.[2]

1 Taittirīya Saṃhitā, i. 5, 2, 1; 6, 10, 5; Vājasaneyi Saṃhitā, xix. 20; xx. 12, etc.
2 Aitareya Brāhmaṇa, i. 4, 8; 11, 10; ii. 13, 2; 26, 3. 5. 6; 40, 8; iii. 32, 1; Śatapatha Brāhmaṇa, i. 4, 2, 19; iii. 4, 4, 2; vii. 2, 7, 11, etc.

Yātu-dhāna in the Rigveda[1] and later[2] denotes a 'sorcerer,' 'wizard,' or 'magician.' The sense of the Rigveda[3] is clearly unfavourable to sorcery. The feminine, Yātudhānī, is also found in the Rigveda and later.[4]

1 i. 35, 10; x. 87, 2. 3. 7. 10; 120, 4.
2 Av. i. 7, 1; iv. 3, 4; vi. 13, 3; 32, 2; vii. 70, 2; xix. 46, 2; Kāṭhaka Saṃhitā, xxxvii. 14; Vājasaneyi Saṃhitā, xiii. 7; Śatapatha Brāhmaṇa, vii. 4, 1, 29, etc
3 vii. 104, 15.
4 Rv. i. 191, 8; x. 118, 8; Av. i. 28, 24; ii. 14, 3; iv. 9, 9; 18, 17; xix. 37, 8, etc.
Cf. Bloomfield, *Atharvaveda*, 26, 65 *et seq.*

Yātu-vid, denoting in the plural 'those who know sorcery,' designates the Atharvaveda in the Śatapatha Brāhmaṇa.[1]

1 x. 5, 2, 20. *Cf.* Bloomfield, *Hymns of the Atharvaveda*, xxii.; *Atharvaveda*, 1. 8, 9, 23.

Yādva, '**descendant of Yadu**,' is used of the Yadu prince in one passage of the Rigveda,[1] while the largesse of the Yādvas[2] is alluded to elsewhere. In another passage a beast (*paśu*) of the Yadus or Yādvas is mentioned.[3] *Cf.* **Yadu.**

1 vii. 19, 8.
2 Rv. viii. 6, 46. *Cf.* Ludwig, Translation of the Rigveda, 5, 142.
3 Rv. viii. 1, 31.
Cf. Weber, *Indian Literature*, 3; *Episches im vedischen Ritual*, 37.

Yāna denotes 'vehicle' in the Rigveda[1] and later.[2]

[1] iv. 43, 6.

[2] Śatapatha Brāhmaṇa, v. 5, 3, 7; Ṣaḍviṃśa Brāhmaṇa, vi. 3, 10; Chāndogya Upaniṣad, viii. 12, 3, etc.

Yāma, used in the plural, denotes in one passage of the Atharvaveda,[1] according to Roth,[2] the planets among which the sun (*bhaga*) wanders. But both Bloomfield[3] and Whitney[4] accept the sense—the regular one in the later language—of 'night watches.'

[1] vi. 21, 2.

[2] St. Petersburg Dictionary, *s.v.* 1*d*.

[3] *Hymns of the Atharvaveda*, 30.

[4] Translation of the Atharvaveda, 396.

Yāman denotes in the Rigveda[1] a 'march' or 'expedition' in war.

[1] iv. 24, 2; vii. 66, 5; 85, 1; ix. 64, 10; x. 78, 6; 80, 5.

Yāyāvara[1] denotes a person of no fixed abode in the Yajurveda Saṃhitās.[2]

[1] Literally, 'wandering about,' from the intensive of *yā*, 'to go.'

[2] Taittirīya Saṃhitā, v. 2, 1, 7; Kāṭhaka Saṃhitā, xix. 12.

Yāva. See **Māsa.**

Yāska (' descendant of Yaska ') is mentioned in the first two Vaṃśas (lists of teachers) of the Bṛhadāraṇyaka Upaniṣad[1] as a contemporary of **Āsurāyaṇa** and a teacher of **Bhāradvāja.** Whether Yāska, author of the Nirukta,[2] was the same person, it is, of course, impossible to say.

[1] ii. 5, 21; iv. 5, 27 (Mādhyaṃdina = ii. 6, 3; iv. 6, 3 Kāṇva). *Cf.* Weber, *Indian Literature*, 128.

[2] Ṛgveda Prātiśākhya, xvii. 25; Weber, *op. cit.*, 25, 26, etc.; *Indische Studien*, 1, 17, 103; 3, 396; 8, 243, etc.; *Indian Literature*, 41, n. 30.

Yu, appearing in the dual in the Śatapatha Brāhmaṇa (iii. 7, 4, 10), seems to mean 'yoke animals.'

Yukta in the Śatapatha Brāhmaṇa (vi. 7, 4, 8; xii. 4, 1, 2) denotes a 'yoke' of oxen. *Cf.* 1. **Yuga.**

Yuktāśva is the name of a man who is mentioned in the Pañcaviṃśa Brāhmaṇa[1] as the seer of a Sāman, or chant. He is said to have exposed a pair of twins,[2] but Hopkins[3] thinks that the reference is only to an exchange of children.

[1] xi. 8, 8.

[2] *Cf.* Weber, *Naxatra*, 2, 314, n., whose view is that of Sāyaṇa on the passage. *Cf.* **Yama**.

[3] *Transactions of the Connecticut Academy of Arts and Sciences*, 15, 61, 62.

Cf. Hillebrandt, *Vedische Mythologie*, 2, 160.

1. **Yuga** in the Rigveda[1] and later[2] denotes 'yoke.' *Cf.* **Ratha.**

[1] i. 115, 2; 184, 3; ii. 39, 4; iii. 53, 17; viii. 80, 7; x. 60, 8; 101, 3, etc.

[2] Av. iv. 1, 40; Śatapatha Brāhmaṇa, iii. 5, 1, 24. 34; Taittirīya Brāhmaṇa, i. 5, 1, 3, etc.

2. **Yuga** in the Rigveda[1] frequently denotes a 'generation'; but the expression *daśame yuge* applied to **Dīrghatamas** in one passage[2] must mean 'tenth decade' of life.

There is no reference in the older Vedic texts to the five-year cycle (see **Saṃvatsara**). The quotation from the Pañcaviṃśa Brāhmaṇa[3] given in the St. Petersburg Dictionary, and by Zimmer[4] and others, is merely a citation from a modern text in the commentary on that work.

Nor do the older Vedic texts know of any series of Yugas or ages such as are usual later. In the Atharvaveda[5] there are mentioned in order a hundred years, an *ayuta* (10,000?), and then two, three, or four Yugas: the inference from this seems to be that a Yuga means more than an *ayuta*, but is not very

[1] *Yuge-yuge*, 'in every age,' i. 139, 8; iii. 26, 3; vi. 8, 5; 15, 8; 36, 5; ix. 94, 12; *uttarā yugāni*, 'future ages,' iii. 33, 8; x. 10, 10; *pūrvāṇi yugāni*, vii. 70, 4; *uttare yuge*, x. 72, 1, etc. In i. 92, 11; 103, 4; 115, 2; 124, 2: 144, 4, etc., the phrase 'generations of men' (*manuṣyā*, *mānuṣā*, *manuṣaḥ*, *janānām*) are referred to. See Muir, *Sanskrit Texts*, 1², 45, 46.

[2] i. 158, 6. Wilson, Translation, 2, 104, n., suggests that *yuga* here means a lustrum of five years; but the tenth decade is far more likely, as Dīrghatamas is said to be 'aged' (*jujurvān*).

[3] xvii. 13, 17.

[4] *Altindisches Leben*, 368.

[5] viii. 2, 21.

certain. Zimmer[6] adduces a passage from the Rigveda,[7] but the reference there, whatever it may be,[8] is certainly not to the four ages (*cf.* also **Triyuga**).[9] The Taittirīya Brāhmaṇa[10] recognizes long periods of time—*e.g.*, one of 100,000 years.

To the four ages, Kali, Dvāpara, Tretā, and Kṛta, there is no certain reference in Vedic literature, though the names occur as the designations of throws at dice (see **Akṣa**). In the Aitareya Brāhmaṇa[11] the names occur, but it is not clear that the ages are really meant. Haug[12] thought that the dice were meant: this view is at least as probable as the alternative explanation, which is accepted by Weber,[13] Roth,[14] Wilson,[15] Max Müller,[16] and Muir.[17] Roth, indeed, believes that the verse is an interpolation; but in any case it must be remembered that the passage is from a late book of the Aitareya Brāhmaṇa. Four ages—Puṣya, Dvāpara, Khārvā, and Kṛta—are mentioned in the late Ṣaḍviṃśa Brāhmaṇa,[18] and the Dvāpara in the Gopatha Brāhmaṇa.[19]

[6] *Op. cit.*, 371.

[7] viii. 101, 4=Av. x. 8, 3.

[8] *Cf.* Aitareya Āraṇyaka, ii. 1, 1, with Keith's note; Griffith, *Hymns of the Rigveda*, 2, 253.

[9] In Rv. x. 72, 2, *devānāṃ pūrvye yuge*, 'in the earlier age of the gods,' occurs.

[10] iii. 12, 9, 2. *Cf.* Muir, 1^2, 42, n. 66.

[11] vii. 15, 4 (in the description of the merits of exertion): 'A man while lying is the Kali; moving himself, he is the Dvāpara; rising, he is the Tretā; walking, he becomes the Kṛta' (*Kaliḥ śayāno bhavati saṃjihānas tu Dvāparaḥ | uttiṣṭhaṃs Tretā bhavati, Kṛtaṃ sampadyate caran ||*).

[12] Aitareya Brāhmaṇa, 2, 464, criticized by Weber, *Indische Studien*, 9, 319.

[13] *Indische Studien*, 1, 286; 9, 315 *et seq.*

[14] *Indische Studien*, 1, 460.

[15] *Journal of the Royal Asiatic Society*, 1851, 99.

[16] *Ancient Sanskrit Literature*, 412.

[17] *Sanskrit Texts*, 1^2, 48, n. 86.

[18] v. 6.

[19] i. 1, 28; Weber, *Indian Literature*, 151, n. 166; Windisch, *Buddha und Māra*, 151.

Cf. Zimmer, *Altindisches Leben*, 367-371; Weber, *Indische Streifen*, 1, 91. A quite different theory of the Yugas is given by Shamasastry, *Gavām Ayana*, 141 *et seq.*, but his whole theory is quite impossible. Weber once (*Indian Literature*, 113, n. 127) found the mention of the quinquennial Yuga in Rv. iii. 55, 18, but that passage refers to the five or six seasons (see Griffith, *Hymns of the Rigveda*, 1, 382, n.), while i. 25, 8, merely alludes to the intercalary month. Weber also (*op. cit.*, 70, 247) considers that the Yugas are derived from the phases of the moon, but this idea was long since disposed of by Roth, *Die Lehre von den vier Weltaltern* (Tübingen, 1860).

Yuddha in the Rigveda[1] and later[2] denotes 'battle.' The more usual word earlier[3] is Yudh.

[1] x. 54, 2.

[2] Taittirīya Brāhmaṇa, i. 5, 9, 1; Aitareya Brāhmaṇa, iii. 39, 1. 2; vi. 36, 2; Śatapatha Brāhmaṇa, xiii. 1, 5, 6; Kauṣītaki Upaniṣad, iii. 1, etc.

[3] Rv. i. 53, 7; 59, 1; v. 25, 6; vi. 46, 11, etc.; Av. i. 24, 1; iv. 24, 7; vi. 66, 1; 103, 3, etc.; Śatapatha Brāhmaṇa, v. 2, 4, 16, etc.

Yudhāṃ-śrauṣṭi Augra-sainya ('descendant of **Ugrasena**') is the name, in the Aitareya Brāhmaṇa,[1] of a king who was anointed by **Parvata** and **Nārada**.

[1] viii. 21, 7. *Cf.* Weber, *Episches im vedischen Ritual*, 8. The Paurāṇic form is Yuddha-muṣṭi.

Yudhyāmadhi is apparently the name of a king who was defeated by **Sudās**. The mention of him occurring only in the verses added at the end of the hymn celebrating the victory of Sudās over the ten kings[1] can claim little authenticity as a notice of Sudās.

[1] Rv. vii. 18, 24. *Cf.* Ludwig, Translation of the Rigveda, 3, 173.

Yuvati is the ordinary expression for a 'young woman' or 'maiden' in the Rigveda[1] and later.[2]

[1] i. 118, 5; ii. 35, 4; iii. 54, 14; iv. 18, 8; v. 2, 1. 2; ix. 86, 16; x. 30, 5.

[2] Av. xiv. 2, 61; Taittirīya Brāhmaṇa, iii. 1, 1, 9; 2, 4; Śatapatha Brāhmaṇa, xiii. 1, 9, 6; 4, 3, 8, etc.

Yūtha is the word for 'herd' of cows in the Rigveda[1] and later.[2]

[1] i. 10, 2; 81, 7; iii. 55, 17; iv. 2, 18; 38, 5; v. 41, 19; ix. 71, 9, etc. *Cf.* *yūthya*, 'of the herd,' viii. 56, 4; ix. 15, 4; x. 23, 4.

[2] Av. v. 20, 3; Taittirīya Saṃhitā, v. 7, 2, 1, etc.

Yūpa in the Rigveda[1] and later[2] means a 'post,' usually that to which the sacrificial victim was tied. It also designates the post to which the door of the house was attached (**Durya**).[3]

[1] v. 2, 7 (of **Sunaḥśepa**).

[2] Av. ix. 6, 22; xii. 1, 38; xiii. 1, 47; Taittirīya Saṃhitā, vi. 3, 4, 1; vii. 2, 1, 3; Vājasaneyi Saṃhitā, xix. 17; Pañcaviṃśa Brāhmaṇa, ix. 10, 2, etc.

[3] Rv. i. 51, 14. *Cf.* Zimmer, *Altindisches Leben*, 153.

Yūṣan, occurring in the description of the horse-sacrifice in the Rigveda[1] and the Yajurveda Saṃhitās,[2] denotes the 'broth' which was made from the flesh of the sacrificial animal, and was no doubt used as food. Vessels employed for holding it, **Pātra** and **Āsecana**, are mentioned. Another form of the word, found in the Taittirīya Saṃhitā,[3] is Yūs, which corresponds to the Latin *jus*.

[1] i. 162, 13.

[2] Taittirīya Saṃhitā, vi. 3, 11, 1. 4; Vājasaneyi Saṃhitā, xxv. 9

[3] vi. 3, 11, 1. 4.

Cf. Zimmer, *Altindisches Leben*, 271: Schrader, *Prehistoric Antiquities*, 316.

Yevāṣa is the name of a destructive insect in the Atharvaveda.[1] The form Yavāṣa is found in the Kāṭhaka Saṃhitā.[2] *Cf.* **Vṛṣa.**

[1] v. 23, 7. 8.

[2] xxx. 1 (*Indische Studien*, 3, 462). The same form occurs in the Gaṇas, *kumudādi* and *prekṣādi* (Pāṇini, iv. 2, 80). *Cf.* Maitrāyaṇī Saṃhitā, iv. 8, 1, where Yavāṣa should be read; Kapiṣṭhala Saṃhitā, xlvi. 4.

Cf. Zimmer, *Altindisches Leben*, 98; St. Petersburg Dictionary, *s.v.*

Yoktra in the Rigveda[1] and later[2] denotes the 'thongs' used for yoking the chariot or cart.

[1] iii. 33, 13; v. 33, 2.

[2] Av. iii. 30, 6; vii. 78, 1; Taittirīya Saṃhitā, i. 6, 4, 3, Taittirīya Brāhmaṇa, iii. 3, 3, 3; Śatapatha Brāhmaṇa, i. 3, 1, 13; vi. 4, 3, 7, etc.

Yoga denotes the yoke of oxen or horses drawing a car in the Atharvaveda[1] and the Bṛhadāraṇyaka Upaniṣad.[2]

[1] vi. 91, 1 (yokes of six or eight); Kāṭhaka Saṃhitā, xv. 2, etc. *Cf.* **Sīra.**

[2] iv. 3, 11 (*ratha-yogāḥ*, 'chariot teams').

Yojana occurs frequently in the Rigveda[1] and later[2] as a measure of distance,[3] but there is no reference defining its real

[1] i. 123, 8; ii. 16, 3; x. 78, 7; 86, 20, etc.

[2] Av. iv. 26, 1; Maitrāyaṇī Saṃhitā, ii. 9, 9; iii. 8, 4; Taittirīya Brāhmaṇa, ii. 4, 2, 7, etc. *Cf.* Zimmer, *Altindisches Leben*, 363, who finds in Rv. i. 123, 8, *yojana* as a division of time equivalent to the **Muhūrta**. But this is most improbable.

[3] That is, the distance driven in one 'harnessing' (without unyoking), a 'stage.'

length. Later it is reckoned at four **Krośas**, or about nine miles.[4]

[4] Sometimes calculated at 8 krośas, or 18 miles. The estimate of 2½ miles is also found.

Yodha in the Rigveda[1] means 'fighter,' 'warrior,' 'soldier.'

[1] i. 143, 5; iii. 39, 4; vi. 25, 5; x. 78, 3.

Yoṣan, Yoṣaṇā, Yoṣā, Yoṣit, all denote 'young woman,' 'maiden,' as an object of affection, and as meet for wedlock.[1] So these terms are often opposed in the Brāhmaṇas to **Vṛṣan,** 'male,' in the general sense of 'female,'[2] but they also occur in the sense of 'wife,'[3] or 'daughter,'[4] or merely 'girl.'[5] See **Strī.**

[1] *Yoṣan*, Rv. iv. 5, 5; *Yoṣaṇā*, iii. 52, 3; 56, 5; 62, 8; vii. 95, 3, etc.; *Yoṣā*, i. 48, 5; 92, 11; iii. 33, 10; 38, 8, etc.; Av. xii. 3, 29; xiv. 1, 56, etc.; *Yoṣit*, Rv. ix. 28, 4; Av. vi. 101, 1, etc. *Cf.* Delbrück, *Die indogermanischen Verwandtschaftsnamen*, 418.

[2] Śatapatha Brāhmaṇa, i. 2, 5, 15 (*yoṣā*), and often in the Brāhmaṇas.

[3] Av. xii. 3, 29 (*yoṣā*).

[4] So *yoṣā* in Rv. i. 117, 20. *Cf.* Zimmer, *Altindisches Leben*, 310.

[5] Śatapatha Brāhmaṇa, i. 8, 1, 7.

Yaugaṃ-dhari, 'descendant of Yugaṃdhara,' is the name of a king of the **Sālvas** in the Mantrapāṭha (ii. 11, 12).

Yauvana, 'youth,' is found in the Atharvaveda (xviii. 4, 50), where it is opposed to 'old age.'

R.

Rakṣitṛ, 'protector,' 'guardian,' occurs in the Rigveda[1] and later,[2] usually in a metaphorical sense.

[1] i. 89, 1. 5; ii. 39, 6; guardian of Soma, vi. 7, 7; of the dogs of Yama, x. 14, 11, etc.

[2] Av. iii. 27, 1; xii. 3, 55; xix. 15, 3; Śatapatha Brāhmaṇa, xiii. 4, 2, 5, etc.

Raghaṭ occurs once in the plural in the Atharvaveda,[1] where the Paippalāda recension reads *vaghaṭaḥ*. Roth[2] once con-

[1] viii. 7, 24.

[2] St. Petersburg Dictionary, *s.v.*, 1*a*.

jectured *raghavaḥ*, 'swift,' as the correct reading. Bloomfield,[3] who in his translation explains the word as 'falcons,' in his notes inclines to think Roth's conjecture likely. Ludwig[4] suggests 'bees' as the meaning. Possibly some kind of bird may be intended.[5]

[3] *Hymns of the Atharvaveda*, 580.
[4] Translation of the Rigveda, 3, 504.
[5] Böhtlingk, Dictionary, *s.v.* *Cf.* Whitney, Translation of the Atharvaveda, 501.

Rajata as an adjective with **Hiraṇya**[1] designates 'silver,' and ornaments (**Rukma**),[2] dishes (**Pātra**),[3] and coins (**Niṣka**)[4] 'made of silver' are mentioned. The word is also used alone as a substantive to denote 'silver.'[5]

[1] Taittirīya Saṃhitā, i. 5, 1, 2; Kāṭhaka Saṃhitā, x. 4; Śatapatha Brāhmaṇa, xii. 4, 4, 7; xiii. 4, 2, 10; xiv. 1, 3, 4, etc.
[2] Śatapatha Brāhmaṇa, xii. 8, 3, 11.
[3] Taittirīya Brāhmaṇa, ii. 2, 9, 7; iii. 9, 6, 5.
[4] Pañcaviṃśa Brāhmaṇa, xvii. 1, 14.
[5] Av. v. 28, 1; xiii. 4, 51; Aitareya Brāhmaṇa, vii. 12, 2; Chāndogya Upaniṣad, iv. 17, 7; Jaiminīya Upaniṣad Brāhmaṇa, iii. 17, 3; Ṣaḍviṃśa Brāhmaṇa, vi. 6.

Cf. Schrader, *Prehistoric Antiquities*, 180; Zimmer, *Altindisches Leben*, 56; Macdonell, *Sanskrit Literature*, 151, 152; Vincent Smith, *Indian Antiquary*, 34, 230.

Rajana Koṇeya, or **Kauṇeya**, is the name of a teacher mentioned in the Yajurveda Saṃhitās.[1] It is said in the Kāṭhaka Saṃhitā[2] that **Kratujit Jānaki** successfully sacrificed for him when he desired to obtain eyesight. He is also mentioned in the Pañcaviṃśa Brāhmaṇa,[3] where the name of his son, **Ugradeva Rājani**, also occurs.[4]

[1] Taittirīya Saṃhitā, ii. 3, 8, 1; Kāṭhaka Saṃhitā, xxvii. 2 (*Indische Studien*, 3, 474).
[2] xi. 1 (*Indische Studien*, 3, 474).
[3] xiii. 4, 11. *Cf.* Hopkins, *Transactions of the Connecticut Academy of Arts and Sciences*, 15, 58, n. 2.
[4] He was a leper, and the **Rajanī** is used against leprosy, Bloomfield, *Hymns of the Atharvaveda*, 266.

Rajanī is found in one passage of the Atharvaveda,[1] where it denotes some sort of plant, probably so called because of its

[1] i. 23, 1. *Cf.* Roth in Whitney's Translation of the Atharvaveda, 24; Bloomfield, *Hymns of the Atharvaveda*, 267.

power of 'colouring' (from *rañj*, 'to colour'). The species cannot be identified owing to the untrustworthiness of the later authorities who attempt its identification.

Rajayitrī, a 'female dyer,' is included in the list of victims at the Puruṣamedha ('human sacrifice') in the Yajurveda.[1]

[1] Vājasaneyi Saṃhitā, xxx. 12; Taittirīya Brāhmaṇa, iii. 4, 7, 1.

1. **Rajas** denotes the region of the atmosphere between heaven and earth in the Rigveda[1] and later.[2] The atmosphere, like the sky (**Div**), is divided into three regions,[3] but more normally into two, the 'earthly' (*pārthiva*)[4] and the 'heavenly' (*divya* or *divaḥ*).[5] In some passages[6] the word refers in the plural to the dusty fields on earth.

[1] i. 56, 5; 62, 5; 84, 1; 124, 5; 168, 6; 187, 4; ii. 40, 3; vi. 62, 9, etc.

[2] Av. iv. 25, 2; vii. 25, 1; 41, 1; x. 3, 9; xiii. 2, 8. 43; Taittirīya Saṃhitā, iii. 5, 4, 2; Vājasaneyi Saṃhitā, xiii. 44, etc.

[3] Rv. iv. 53, 5; v. 69, 1; ix. 74, 6; x. 45, 3; 123, 8; Av. xiii. 1, 11, etc. In Rv. i. 164, 6, six 'regions' are mentioned.

[4] Rv. i. 81, 5; 90, 7; 154, 1; vi. 49, 3; viii. 88, 5; ix. 72, 8, etc.

[5] Rv. iv. 53, 3; i. 110, 6. *Cf.* Macdonell, *Vedic Mythology*, p. 10; St. Petersburg Dictionary, *s.v.*

[6] Rv. i. 166, 3; iii. 62, 16; x. 75, 7.

2. **Rajas** in one passage of the Yajurveda Saṃhitās[1] clearly means 'silver,' like **Rajata**. It is also taken in this sense in one passage of the Rigveda[2] by Zimmer,[3] but this interpretation is doubtful.

[1] *Rajaḥ-śaya*, Vājasaneyi Saṃhitā, v. 8; *rajāśaya*, Taittirīya Saṃhitā, i. 2, 11, 2 (Sāyaṇa on Aitareya Brāhmaṇa, i. 23, 2); Maitrāyaṇī Saṃhitā, i. 2, 7; Kāṭhaka Saṃhitā, ii. 8.

[2] x. 105, 7.

[3] *Altindisches Leben*, 55, 56.

Rajasa occurs once in the Atharvaveda,[1] apparently as the name of a kind of 'fish.' Roth,[2] however, understood it as an adjective meaning 'impure.'

[1] x. 2, 25.

[2] St. Petersburg Dictionary, *s.v.* *Cf.* Bloomfield, *Hymns of the Atharvaveda*, 621; Whitney, Translation of the Atharvaveda, 624.

Raji occurs in the Rigveda[1] seemingly as the name of a king, or perhaps demon, slain by Indra for **Piṭhīnas.**

[1] vi. 26, 6. *Cf.* Ludwig, Translation of the Rigveda, 3, 156; St. Petersburg Dictionary, *s.v.*, where Roth compares a conjecture in Av. xx. 128, 13.

Rajjavya in the Śatapatha Brāhmaṇa (vi. 7, 1, 28) denotes a 'cord' or 'rope.'

Rajju in the Rigveda[1] and later[2] denotes 'rope.' In the Atharvaveda[3] the serpent is called the 'toothed rope' (*rajju datvatī*).

[1] i. 162, 8 (*śīrṣaṇyā raśanā rajjuḥ*, referring to the horse presumably means the head harness).

[2] Av. iii. 11, 8; vi. 121, 2; Taittirīya Saṃhitā, ii. 5, 1, 7; Śatapatha Brāhmaṇa, i. 3, 1, 14; x. 2, 3, 8; xi. 3, 1, 1, etc.

[3] iv. 3, 2; xix. 47, 7. 8; Bloomfield, *Hymns of the Atharvaveda*, 368.

Rajju-dāla is the name of a tree (*Cordia myxa* or *latifolia*) in the Śatapatha Brāhmaṇa.[1]

[1] xiii. 4, 4, 6. *Cf.* Eggeling, *Sacred Books of the East*, 44, 373, n. 2.

Rajju-sarja, 'rope-maker,' is one of the victims at the Puruṣamedha ('human sacrifice') in the Yajurveda.[1]

[1] Vājasaneyi Saṃhitā, xxx. 7; Taittirīya Brāhmaṇa, iii. 4, 3, 1.

Raṇa denotes properly the 'joy' of battle, then 'battle,' 'combat' itself in the Rigveda[1] and later.[2]

[1] i. 61, 1. 9; 74, 3; 119, 3; vi. 16, 15, etc.

[2] Av. v. 2, 4, etc.

Ratna in the Rigveda[1] and later[2] denotes a precious object, not specifically a 'jewel,' as in post-Vedic literature.

[1] i. 20, 7; 35, 8; 41, 6; 125, 1; 140, 11; 141, 10; ii. 38, 1, etc.

[2] Av. v. 1, 7; vii. 14, 4; Śatapatha Brāhmaṇa, v. 3, 1, 1.

Ratni, 'ell,' occurring in the Ṣaḍviṃśa Brāhmaṇa (iv. 4) is a corruption of **Aratni.**

Ratnin, 'receiving gifts,' is the term applied to those people of the royal entourage in whose houses the Ratna-havis, a special rite, was performed in the course of the **Rājasūya** or 'royal consecration.' The list given in the Taittirīya Saṃhitā[1] and the Taittirīya Brāhmaṇa[2] consists of the Brahman (*i.e.*, the Purohita), the Rājanya, the Mahiṣī (the first wife of the king), the **Vāvāta** (the favourite wife of the king), the Parivṛktī (the discarded wife), the Senānī, 'commander of the army'; the Sūta, 'charioteer'; the Grāmaṇī, 'village headman'; the Kṣattṛ, 'chamberlain'; the Saṃgrahītṛ, 'charioteer' or 'treasurer'; the Bhāgadugha, 'collector of taxes' or 'divider of food'; and the Akṣāvāpa, 'superintender of dicing' or 'thrower of dice.' In the Śatapatha Brāhmaṇa[3] the order is Senānī; Purohita; Mahiṣī; Sūta; Grāmaṇī; Kṣattṛ; Saṃgrahitṛ; Bhāgadugha; Akṣāvāpa; Go-nikartana, 'slayer of cows' or 'huntsman'; and Pālāgala, 'courier'; the 'discarded wife' being mentioned as forbidden to stay at home[4] on the day of the ceremony of offering a pap for Nirṛti in her house. In the Maitrāyaṇī Saṃhitā[5] the list is Brahman (*i.e.*, Purohita); Rājan; Mahiṣī; Parivṛktī; Senānī; Saṃgrahītṛ; Kṣattṛ; Sūta; Vaiśyagrāmaṇī; Bhāgadugha; Takṣa-Rathakārau, 'carpenter and chariot-maker'; Akṣāvāpa; and Go-vikarta. The Kāṭhaka Saṃhitā[6] substitutes Go-vyacha for Govikarta, and omits Takṣa-Rathakārau.

It will be seen that the list is essentially that of the royal household, and of the king's servants in the administration of the country, though the exact sense of **Saṃgrahītṛ, Bhāgadugha, Sūta, Grāmaṇī, Kṣattṛ,** is open to reasonable doubt, mainly as to whether public officers or private servants[7] are meant, for the names are of uncertain significance. A briefer list of eight **Vīras**, 'heroes,' as among the friends of the king,

[1] i. 8, 9, 1 *et seq.*

[2] i. 7, 3, 1 *et seq.*

[3] v. 3, 1, 1 *et seq.*

[4] According to Kātyāyana Śrauta Sūtra, xv. 3, 35, she goes to a Brahmin's house, where she shares his inviolability and exemption from jurisdiction.

[5] ii. 6, 5; iv. 3, 8.

[6] xv. 4.

[7] Similarly Akṣāvāpa is either the man who dices for the king—*i.e.*, a professional dicer who plays with the king or watches his play—or a public officer who superintends the gambling halls of the state and collects the revenue, as was regularly done later on. Early English history shows similar evolution of household officers into ministers of state.

is given in the Pañcaviṃśa Brāhmaṇa:[8] brother, son, Purohita, Mahiṣī, Sūta, Grāmaṇī, Kṣattṛ, and Saṃgrahītṛ.

[8] xix. 1, 4.

Cf. Weber, *Indische Studien*, 17, 200; *Über den Rājasūya*, 4; Hopkins, *Journal of the American Oriental Society*, 13, 128; Eggeling, *Sacred Books of the East*, 41, 58-65; Hopkins, *Transactions of the Connecticut Academy of Arts and Sciences*, 15, 30, n. 2.

Ratha in the Rigveda[1] and later[2] denotes 'chariot' as opposed to **Anas,** 'cart,' though the distinction is not absolute. Of differences in the structure of the two we have no information, except that the **Kha,** or nave hole, in the wheel of the chariot was greater than in that of the cart.[3]

The chariot has, as a rule, two wheels (**Cakra**), to which reference is frequently made.[4] The wheel consisted of a rim (**Pavi**), a felly (**Pradhi**), spokes (**Ara**),[5] and a nave (**Nabhya**). The rim and the felly together constitute the **Nemi.** The hole in the nave is called **Kha:** into it the end of the axle was inserted; but there is some uncertainty whether **Āṇi** denotes the extremity of the axle that was inserted in the nave, or the lynch-pin used to keep that extremity in the wheel. Sometimes a solid wheel was used.[6]

The axle (**Akṣa**) was, in some cases, made of **Araṭu** wood;[7] round its ends the wheels revolved. To the axle was attached the body of the chariot (**Kośa**). This part is also denoted by the word **Vandhura,** which more precisely means the 'seat' of the chariot. The epithet *tri-vandhura* is used of the chariot of the Aśvins, seemingly to correspond with another of its epithets, *tri-cakra:* perhaps, as Weber[8] thinks, a chariot with three seats and three wheels was a real form of vehicle; but Zimmer[9] considers that the vehicle was purely mythical. **Garta** also denotes the seat of the warrior.

[1] i. 20, 3; iii. 15, 5; iv. 4, 10; 16, 20; 36, 2; 43, 25, etc.

[2] Av. v. 14, 5; x. 1, 8: Aitareya Brāhmaṇa, vii. 12, 3, etc.

[3] viii. 91, 7, with Sāyaṇa's note; *Vedische Studien*, 2, 333.

[4] *Cf.* Chāndogya Upaniṣad, iv. 16, 5; Jaiminīya Upaniṣad Brāhmaṇa, iii. 16, 7; Kauṣītaki Upaniṣad, i. 4.

[5] *Cf.* Rv. i. 32, 15; 141, 9; v. 13, 6; 58, 5; viii. 20, 14; 77, 3; x. 78, 4; Kāṭhaka Saṃhitā, x. 4, etc.

[6] *Cf.* **Pradhi.**

[7] Rv. viii. 46, 27; Zimmer, *Altindisches Leben*, 247, n.

[8] *Proceedings of the Berlin Academy*, 1898, 564; Virchow, *Zeitschrift für Ethnologie*, 5, 200. *Cf.* note 21.

[9] *Op. cit.*, viii.

At right angles to the axle was the pole of the chariot (**Īṣā**, **Prauga**). Normally there was, it seems, one pole, on either side of which the horses were harnessed, a yoke (**Yuga**) being laid across their necks; the pole was passed through the hole in the yoke (called Kha[10] or Tardman[11]), the yoke and the pole then being tied together.[12]

The horses were tied by the neck (*grīvā*), where the yoke was placed, and also at the shoulder, presumably by traces fastened to a bar of wood at right angles to the pole, or fastened to the ends of the pole, if that is to be regarded, as it probably should, as of triangular shape, wide at the foot and coming to a point at the tip.[13] The traces seem to be denoted by **Raśmi** and **Raśanā.** These words also denote the 'reins,' which were fastened to the bit (perhaps *śiprā*) in the horse's mouth. The driver controlled the horses by reins, and urged them on with a whip (*Kaśā*).[14] The girths of the horse were called Kakṣyā.[15]

The normal number of horses seems to have been two, but three or four[16] were often used. It is uncertain whether, in these cases, the extra horse was attached in front or at the side; possibly both modes were in use. Even five steeds could be employed.[17] Horses were normally used for chariots, but the ass (*gardabha*)[18] or mule (*aśvatarī*)[19] are also mentioned. The ox was employed for drawing carts, and in fact derived its

[10] This seems to be the sense of Rv. viii. 91, 7; but it has also been taken as the opening in the yoke through which the ox's head passed (the Homeric ζεύγλη). See Cowell's note on Wilson's translation; Griffith, *Hymns of the Rigveda*, 2, 237, n.

[11] Av. xiv. 1, 40.

[12] Rv. iii. 6, 6; v. 56, 4; x. 60, 8.

[13] Zimmer, *op. cit.*, 249, thinks that *vāṇī* in Rv. i. 119, 5, denotes the two bars of wood to which the traces were fastened. This is also the view of Roth, St. Petersburg Dictionary, *s.v.*, Böhtlingk's Lexicon, and Grassmann. The word may mean 'two voices' (Griffith, *Hymns of the Rigveda*, 1,162).

[14] Rv. v. 83, 3; vi. 75, 6.

[15] Rv. x. 10, 13; *kakṣya-prā*, 'filling out the girths' (*i.e.*, 'well fed'), is an epithet of Indra's horses, i. 10, 3.

[16] Three horses are mentioned in Rv. x. 33, 5, and **Praṣṭi** in Rv. i. 39, 6; viii. 7, 28, etc., may have the sense of 'third horse.' See also Śatapatha Brāhmaṇa, v. 1, 4, 11; 2, 4, 9, etc.; Pañcaviṃśa Brāhmaṇa, xvi. 13, 12. For four horses, *cf.* Rv. ii. 18, 1; Śatapatha Brāhmaṇa, v. 4, 3, 17; 1, 4, 11; Eggeling, *Sacred Books of the East*, 41, 21, n. 1.

[17] *Rathaḥ pañcavāhī*, Kāṭhaka Saṃhitā, xv. 2; Maitrāyaṇī Saṃhitā, ii. 6, 3. In the parallel passage the Taittirīya Saṃhitā, i. 8, 7, 2, has *praṣṭivāhī*.

[18] Aitareya Brāhmaṇa, iv. 9, 4.

[19] Chāndogya Upaniṣad, iv. 2, 1; v. 13, 2; Aitareya Brāhmaṇa, iv. 9, 1.

name, **Anaḍvāh**, from this use. Sometimes a poor man had to be content with a single steed, which then ran between two shafts.[20]

In the chariot the driver stood on the right, while the warrior was on the left, as indicated by his name, **Savyeṣṭha** or **Savyaṣṭhā.**[21] He could also sit when he wanted, for the chariot had seats, and an archer would naturally prefer to sit while shooting his arrows.

The dimensions of the chariot are given in the Śulba Sūtra[22] of Āpastamba at 188 Aṅgulis (finger-breadths) for the pole, 104 for the axle, and 86 for the yoke. The material used in its construction was wood, except for the rim of the wheel.[23]

Many other parts of the chariot are mentioned, their names being often obscure in meaning: see **Aṅka, Nyaṅka, Uddhi, Pakṣas, Pātalya, Bhurij, Rathopastha, Rathavāhana.**

[20] Rv. x. 101, 11; 131, 3, and vi. 15, 19; Pañcaviṃśa Brāhmaṇa, xvi. 13, 12; xxi. 13, 8, etc.

[21] This is the case in Av. viii. 8, 23, with Savyaṣṭhā, and in the Taittirīya Saṃhitā, i. 7, 9, 1, *savyeṣṭha-sārathi* occurs as a compound where the sense is certainly 'the warrior and the charioteer.' See also Śatapatha Brāhmaṇa, v. 3, 1, 8, and Eggeling, *Sacred Books of the East*, 41, 62, n. 1. The Greek notices speak of two warriors and a charioteer. *Cf.* the Aśvins' car with its three seats. See von Schroeder, *Indiens Literatur und Cultur*, 435.

[22] vi. 5 (Bürk, *Zeitschrift der Deutschen Morgenländischen Gesellschaft*, 56, 344, 345).

[23] Śatapatha Brāhmaṇa, v. 4, 3, 16. The chariot used at the bridal procession was made of Śalmali wood, Rv. x. 85, 20.

For the chariot in the Epic, see Hopkins, *Journal of the American Oriental Society*, 13, 235-262; and *cf.* Schrader, *Prehistoric Antiquities*, 338, 339; Zimmer, *Altindisches Leben*, 245-252; Hopkins, *Transactions of the Connecticut Academy of Arts and Sciences*, 15, 38, n. 1.

Ratha-kāra, 'chariot-maker,' is mentioned in the Atharvaveda[1] as one of those who are to be subject to the king, seeming to stand generally as an example of the industrial population. He is also referred to in the Yajurveda Saṃhitās[2] and in the Brāhmaṇas:[3] in all these passages, as well as probably in the Atharvaveda also, the Rathakāra already forms a caste. The

[1] iii. 5, 6.

[2] Kāṭhaka Saṃhitā, xvii. 13; Maitrāyaṇī Saṃhitā, ii. 9, 5; Vājasaneyi Saṃhitā, xvi. 17; xxx. 6.

[3] Taittirīya Brāhmaṇa, i. 1, 4, 8; iii. 4, 2, 1; Śatapatha Brāhmaṇa, xiii. 4, 2, 17.

later system[4] regards the Rathakāra as the offspring of a Māhiṣya (the son of a Kṣatriya husband and a Vaiśya wife) and a Karaṇī (the daughter of a Vaiśya husband and a Śūdra wife), but it is unreasonable to suppose that such an origin is historically accurate. The Rathakāras must rather be deemed to have been a functional caste. Hillebrandt[5] suggests that the **Anu** tribe formed the basis of the Rathakāra caste, referring to their worship of the Ṛbhus, who are, of course, the chariot-makers *par excellence*. But there is little ground for this view.

[4] Yājñavalkya, i. 95. On the special position, in the later ritual, of the Rathakāra as a caste below the Vaiśya, but superior to the Śūdra, *cf.* Weber, *Indische Studien*, 10, 12, 13, and *cf.* **Varṇa**; see also Fick, *Die sociale Gliederung*, 209, 210.

[5] *Vedische Mythologie*, 3, 152, 153. *Cf.* Weber, *Indische Studien*, 17, 196 *et seq.*

Ratha-gṛtsa in the Vājasaneyi Saṃhitā (xv. 15) and the Aitareya Brāhmaṇa (iii. 48, 9) denotes a 'skilled charioteer.'[1]

[1] *Cf.* Taittirīya Saṃhitā, iv. 4, 3, 1; °kṛtsna, Maitrāyaṇī Saṃhitā, ii. 8, 10; °kṛtsa, Kāṭhaka Saṃhitā, xvii. 9.

Ratha-cakra, 'chariot wheel,' is often mentioned in the Brāhmaṇas.[1] See **Ratha** and **Cakra**.

[1] Aitareya Brāhmaṇa, iii. 43, 4; Taittirīya Brāhmaṇa, i. 1, 6, 8; Śatapatha Brāhmaṇa, ii. 3, 3, 12; v. 1, 5, 2; xi. 8, 1, 11, etc.

Ratha-carṣaṇa occurs once in the Rigveda,[1] where the sense is doubtful. Roth[2] thought that some part of the chariot was meant, but the sense is perhaps only the 'pathway of the chariot.'[3]

[1] viii. 5, 19.

[2] St. Petersburg Dictionary, *s.v.*

[3] *Cf.* also the citation and explanation in Durga's commentary on the Nirukta, v. 12.

Ratha-jūti in the Atharvaveda (xix. 44, 3) is either an adjective meaning 'driving swiftly in a chariot,'[1] or a proper name, as Roth in the St. Petersburg Dictionary suggests.

[1] 'Of chariot-swiftness' according to Whitney, Translation of the Atharvaveda, 967. *Cf.* his note on the passage.

Ratha-nābhi, the 'nave of the chariot-wheel,' is mentioned in the Vājasaneyi Saṃhitā[1] and in the Upaniṣads.[2]

[1] xxxiv. 5.

[2] Bṛhadāraṇyaka Upaniṣad, ii. 5 5; Aitareya Āraṇyaka, iii. 2, 4; Kauṣītaki Upaniṣad, iii. 8; Chāndogya Upaniṣad, vii. 15, 1, etc.

Ratha-prota Dārbhya ('descendant of Darbha') is mentioned in the Maitrāyaṇī Saṃhitā (ii. 1, 3) perhaps as a king, but possibly as a priest.

Ratha-proṣṭha occurs as the name of a princely family in the Rigveda (x. 60, 5). See **Subandhu**.

Ratha-mukha in the later Saṃhitās[1] denotes the fore-part of a chariot. *Cf.* **Rathaśīrṣa.**

[1] Av. viii. 8, 23; Taittirīya Saṃhitā, iii. 4, 8, 2; v. 4, 9, 3, etc.

Ratharvī is the name of a snake in the Atharvaveda (x. 4, 5).

Ratha-vāhana is the name in the Rigveda[1] and later[2] for a movable stand to hold the chariot. According to Roth,[3] it corresponds to the Greek βωμός, on which the chariot rested when out of use. The word Rathavāhana-vāha is employed in the sense of the two horses that draw the stand.[4] Weber[5] thinks it was used to convey the war chariot to the scene of action.

[1] vi. 75, 8.

[2] Av. iii. 17, 3 = Taittirīya Saṃhitā, iv. 2, 5, 5 = Kāṭhaka Saṃhitā, xvi. 11 = Maitrāyaṇī Saṃhitā, ii. 7, 12 = Vāsiṣṭha Dharma Sūtra, ii. 34. 35. See also Kāṭhaka Saṃhitā, xxi. 10; Taittirīya Brāhmaṇa, i. 7, 9, 6; Śatapatha Brāhmaṇa, v. 4, 3, 23 *et seq.*

[3] *Festgruss an Böhtlingk*, 95 *et seq.*; Whitney, Translation of the Atharvaveda, 116.

[4] Taittirīya Saṃhitā, i. 8, 20, 1; Taittirīya Brāhmaṇa, i. 8, 4, 3; Kāṭhaka Saṃhitā, xv. 9; Maitrāyaṇī Saṃhitā, ii. 2, 1.

[5] *Über den Vājapeya*, 27, n. 2, followed by Geldner, *Vedische Studien*, 2, 275. Weber, however, admits that the Rathavāhana may at times have served as a mere stand, like the Homeric βωμός, while Geldner expresses the opinion that it never has that sense. The use of the term Rathavāhanavāha shows that the stand was movable.

Rathavīti Dārbhya ('descendant of Darbha') is mentioned once in the Rigveda[1] as residing in places abounding in kine (*gomatīr anu*) far away among the hills, possibly the Himālayas, and as the patron of the singer of the hymn. Later the tradition[2] makes him the king, whose daughter **Śyāsvāśva** won for his wife by his father's and the Maruts' aid.

[1] v. 61, 17. 19.

[2] See Sieg, *Die Sagenstoffe des Ṛgveda*, 50 *et seq.*, 62, n. 2, and the criticism in Oldenberg, *Ṛgveda-Noten*, 1, 353, 354; Max Müller, *Sacred Books of the East*, 32, 359, 362.

Ratha-śīrṣa, the 'head of the chariot'—that is, its fore-part—is mentioned in the Śatapatha Brāhmaṇa (ix. 4. 1, 13).

Ratha-saṅga in the Rigveda (ix. 53, 2) denotes the hostile encounter of chariots.

Rathākṣa in the Yajurveda Saṃhitās[1] denotes the 'axle of the chariot.' Its length is given by the scholiast on the Kātyāyana Śrauta Sūtra[2] as 104 Aṅgulas ('finger-breadths'), which agrees with the statement in the Āpastamba Śulba Sūtra.[3] See **Ratha.**

[1] Taittirīya Saṃhitā, vi. 6, 4, 1; Kāṭhaka Saṃhitā, xxix. 8.

[2] viii. 8, 6.

[3] vi. 5 (Bürk, *Zeitschrift der Deutschen Morgenländischen Gesellschaft*, 56, 344, 345).

Rathāhnya in the Śatapatha Brāhmana (xii. 2, 3, 12) denotes a 'day's journey by chariot.'

Rathin and **Rathī** in the Rigveda[1] and later[2] denote 'one who goes in a chariot,' an expression which includes both the driver and the warrior who accompanied him.

[1] Rathin, i. 122, 8; v. 83, 3; vi. 47, 31; viii. 4, 9; x. 40, 5; 51, 6; Rathī, i. 25, 3; ii. 39, 2; iii. 3, 6; v. 87, 8; vii. 39, 1, etc.

[2] Rathin, Av. iv. 34, 4; vii. 62, 1; 73, 1; xi. 10, 24; Taittirīya Saṃhitā, v. 2, 2, 3; Vājasaneyi Saṃhitā, xvi. 26; Śatapatha Brāhmaṇa, viii. 7, 3, 7, etc.; Rathī, Taittirīya Saṃhitā, iv. 7, 15, 3. *Cf.* Zimmer, *Altindisches Leben*, 296.

Rathītara ('good charioteer') is the name of a teacher mentioned in the Baudhāyana Śrauta Sūtra[1] and the Bṛhad-devatā.[2]

[1] xxii. 11.

[2] i. 26; iii. 40; vii. 145 (ed. Macdonell).

Rathe-ṣṭhā, 'standing on the chariot,' denotes in the Rig-veda[1] the warrior who fights from the chariot, 'car-fighter.'

[1] i. 173, 4. 5; ii. 17, 3; vi. 21, 1; 22, 5; 29, 1; viii. 4, 13; 33, 14; ix. 97, 49; Vājasaneyi Saṃhitā, xxii. 32. *Cf.* Zimmer, *Altindisches Leben*, 296.

Rathopastha, 'lap of the chariot,' in the Atharvaveda[1] and the Brāhmaṇas[2] seems to denote the 'bottom' or lower part on which the driver and the fighter stand.

[1] viii. 8, 23.

[2] Aitareya Brāhmaṇa, viii. 10, 2; Śatapatha Brāhmaṇa, ii. 3, 3, 12, etc. *Cf.* Hopkins, *Journal of the American Oriental Society*, 13, 238, n.

Randhra seems, in the phrase Ukṣṇo Randhra occurring in one passage of the Rigveda (viii. 7, 26), to be the name of a place, but the sense is very doubtful. In the Pañcaviṃśa Brāhmaṇa (xiii. 9, 13) Ukṣṇo randhra is the name of a man.

Rabhi, occurring once in the Rigveda (viii. 5, 29), designates some part of the chariot. The term perhaps means 'supporting shaft.'

Rambha seems to mean a 'staff' or 'support' in one passage of the Rigveda (viii. 45, 20). In another place (ii. 15, 9) a man is described as Rambhin, apparently as carrying a staff to support himself in old age; Sāyaṇa explains this word as 'door-keeper' (like one of the senses of *daṇḍin*, 'staff-bearer,' in later Sanskrit).

Rambhiṇī occurs in one passage of the Rigveda[1] as being on the shoulders of the Maruts. A 'spear' seems to be meant, perhaps conceived as clinging (*rambh* = *rabh*, 'clasp') to the shoulders of a man.

[1] i. 168, 3. *Cf.* i. 167, 3, and see Max Müller, *Sacred Books of the East*, 32, 283.

Rayi is the common word for 'wealth' in the Rigveda[1] and later.[2] Special mention is often made of wealth in 'heroes' (*vīra*)—*i.e.*, in 'good sons,'[3] in horses,[4] in cattle,[5] etc.

[1] i. 73, 1; 159, 4; ii. 21, 6; iii. 1, 19; iv. 2, 7; 34, 10; 36, 9; vi. 6, 7; 31, 1, etc.

[2] Av. iii. 14, 1; vi. 33, 3; vii. 80, 2; Taittirīya Saṃhitā, vii. 1, 72; Vājasaneyi Saṃhitā, ix. 22; xiv. 22; xxvii. 6, etc.

[3] Rv. ii. 11, 13; 30, 11; iv. 51, 10, etc.

[4] Rv. v. 41, 5; viii. 6, 9, etc.

[5] Rv. v. 4, 11, etc.

Raśanā means generally 'cord' or 'rope.' In the Rigveda the word ofter refers to various fastenings of a horse. In one passage[1] the expression *śīrṣaṇyā raśanā*, 'head rope,' perhaps means not so much 'reins' as 'headstall.' In others[2] the sense of 'traces' seems certain, though sometimes[3] 'reins' or 'traces' may equally well be intended. Elsewhere the more general sense of 'rope' for stening is meant.[4]

[1] i. 162, 8. *Cf.* **Rajju.**

[2] Rv. i. 163, 2. 5; x. 79, 7.

[3] Rv. iv. 1, 9; ix. 87, 1; x. 18, 14. *Cf.* Taittirīya Saṃhitā, i. 6, 4, 3.

[4] Rv. ii. 28, 5; Av. viii. 78, 1; x. 9, 2; Vājasaneyi Saṃhitā, xxi. 46; xxii. 2; xxviii. 33; Taittirīya Saṃhitā, vi. 6, 4, 3; Śatapatha Brāhmaṇa, iii. 6, 3, 10, etc. *Cf.* the use of Raśanā as equivalent to 'finger' in Rv. x. 4, 6.

Cf. Zimmer, *Altindisches Leben*, 249.

1. **Raśmi** is not rarely found in the sense of 'rope'[1] generally; but more usually it denotes either the 'reins' or the 'traces'[2] of a chariot, either sense being equally good in most passages.

[1] Rv. i. 28, 4; iv. 22, 8; viii. 25, 18, etc.; Aitareya Brāhmaṇa, iv. 19, 3, etc.

[2] Rv. viii. 7, 8; x. 130, 7, etc.; Taittirīya Saṃhitā, i. 6, 4, 3; Vājasaneyi Saṃhitā, xxiii. 14; Taittirīya Brāhmaṇa, i. 2, 4, 2, etc. In Aitareya Brāhmaṇa, ii. 37, 1, the two inner (*antarau*) reins or traces of the chariot are mentioned.

Cf. Zimmer, *Altindisches Leben*, 249.

2. **Raśmi** in the Rigveda[1] and later[2] regularly denotes a 'ray' of the sun.

[1] i. 35, 7; iv. 52, 7; vii. 36, 1; 77, 3, etc.

[2] Av. ii. 32, 1; xii. 1, 15; Taittirīya Brāhmaṇa, iii. 1, 1, 1; Śatapatha Brāhmaṇa, ix. 2, 3, 14, etc.

Rasā is found in three passages of the Rigveda,[1] clearly as the name of a real stream in the extreme north-west of the Vedic territory. Elsewhere[2] it is the name of a mythic stream at the ends of the earth, which as well as the atmosphere it encompasses. It is reasonable to assume that, as in the case of the **Sarasvatī**, the literal is the older sense, and to see in the river a genuine stream, perhaps originally the Araxes or Jaxartes, because the Vendidad mentions the Raṅhā, the Avestan form of Rasā. But the word seems originally to allude merely to the 'sap' or 'flavour' of the waters,[3] and so could be applied to every river, like Sarasvatī.

[1] i. 112, 12; v. 53, 9; x. 75, 6. In v. 53, 9, the phrase *rasānitabhā* is found. Ludwig, Translation of the Rigveda, 3, 202, is inclined to regard *anitabhā* as an epithet of Rasā, perhaps for *amitabhā*, 'of unmeasured splendour,' but this is hardly probable. It seems better to take **Anitabhā** as the name of an otherwise unknown river. *Cf.* Max Müller, *India*, 166, 173, n.

[2] Rv. v. 41, 15; ix. 41, 6; x. 108, 1. 2 (*cf.* Jaiminīya Brāhmaṇa, ii. 348; *Journal of the American Oriental Society*, 19, 100 *et seq.*); 121, 4.

[3] Rv. iv. 43, 6; viii. 72, 13.

Cf. Zimmer, *Altindisches Leben*, 15, 16; Max Müller, *Sacred Books of the East*, 32, 323; Brunnhofer, *Iran und Turan*, 86; Weber, Proceedings of the Berlin Academy, 1898, 567-569.

Rasāśir as an epithet of Soma in the Rigveda[1] means 'mixed with juice'—*i.e.*, with milk.

[1] iii. 48, 1, where Sāyaṇa explains *rasa* as 'milk.' *Cf.* Hillebrandt, *Vedische Mythologie*, 1, 211, n. 5.

Raha-sū, 'bearing in secret,' is a term applied in one passage of the Rigveda (ii. 29, 1) to an unmarried mother. *Cf.* **Pati** and **Dharma.**

Rahasyu Deva-malimluc is the name, in the Pañcaviṃśa Brāhmaṇa (xiv. 4, 7), of a mythical person who at **Munimaraṇa** slew the saintly **Vaikhānases.**

Rahū-gaṇa is the name of a family mentioned in the plural in one passage of the Rigveda.[1] According to Ludwig,[2] they were connected with the **Gotamas,** as is shown by the name **Gotama Rāhūgaṇa.**

[1] i. 78, 5.

[2] Translation of the Rigveda, 3, 110.

Cf. Oldenberg, *Zeitschrift der Deutschen Morgenländischen Gesellschaft*, 42, 236, n. 1.

Rākā in the Rigveda[1] and later[2] denotes the full moon day as a personification. *Cf.* **Candramās.**

[1] ii. 32, 4; v. 42, 12.

[2] Taittirīya Saṃhitā, i. 8, 8, 1; iii. 4, 9, 1. 6; Kāṭhaka Saṃhitā, xii. 8; Aitareya Brāhmaṇa, iii. 37, 2. 6; 47, 4, etc.; Pañcaviṃśa Brāhmaṇa, xvi. 13, 1, etc.

Rāja-kartṛ,[1] or **Rāja-kṛt,**[2] 'king-maker,' is the term applied in the Atharvaveda and the Brāhmaṇas to those who, 'not themselves kings,'[3] aid in the consecration of the king. In the Śatapatha[2] the persons meant and specified are the **Sūta,** 'charioteer,' and the **Grāmaṇī,** 'village chief,' probably a representative chief from the village nearest to the place of consecration, as Eggeling[4] suggests. In the Aitareya Brāhmaṇa,[1] according to the commentator's explanation, the father, brother, etc., are meant; in the Atharvaveda,[2] also, the meaning of the expression is not stated in the text.

[1] Aitareya Brāhmaṇa, viii. 17, 5.

[2] Av. iii. 5, 7; Śatapatha Brāhmaṇa, iii. 4, 1, 7; xiii. 2, 2, 18.

[3] *Loc. cit.*

[4] *Sacred Books of the East*, 41, 60, n. *Cf.* Weber, *Indische Studien*, 17, 199 *et seq.*

Rāja kula, a 'kingly family,' is mentioned in the Jaiminīya Upaniṣad Brāhmaṇa (iii. 28, 4), where, it is to be noted, such a family is ranked after, not before, a Brāhmaṇa Kula, a 'Brahmin family.'

1. **Rājan,** 'king,' is a term repeatedly occurring in the Rigveda[1] and the later literature.[2] It is quite clear that the normal, though not universal form of government, in early India was that by kings, as might be expected in view of the fact that the Āryan Indians were invaders in a hostile territory: a situation which, as in the case of the Āryan invaders of Greece and of the German invaders of England, resulted almost necessarily in strengthening the monarchic element of the constitution.[3] The mere patriarchal organization of society is not sufficient, as Zimmer[4] assumes, to explain the Vedic kingship.

[1] iii. 43, 5; v. 54, 7, etc.

[2] Av. iv. 22, 3. 5; viii. 7, 16, etc.

[3] *Cf.* Stubbs, *Constitutional History of England*, 59 *et seq.*

[4] *Altindisches Leben*, 162.

Tenure of Monarchy.—Zimmer[5] is of opinion that while the Vedic monarchy was sometimes hereditary, as is indeed shown by several cases where the descent can be traced,[6] yet in others the monarchy was elective, though it is not clear whether the selection by the people was between the members of the royal family only or extended to members of all the noble clans. It must, however, be admitted that the evidence for the elective monarchy is not strong. As Geldner[7] argues, all the passages cited[8] can be regarded not as choice by the cantons (**Viś**), but as acceptance by the subjects (*viś*): this seems the more probable sense. Of course this is no proof that the monarchy was not sometimes elective: the practice of selecting one member of the family to the exclusion of another less well qualified is exemplified by the legend in Yāska[9] of the Kuru brothers, **Devāpi** and **Śantanu**, the value of which, as evidence of contemporary views, is not seriously affected by the legend itself being of dubious character and validity.

Royal power was clearly insecure: there are several references to kings being expelled from their realms, and their efforts to recover their sovereignty,[10] and the Atharvaveda contains spells in the interest of royalty.[11]

The King in War.—Naturally the Vedic texts, after the Rigveda, contain few notices of the warlike adventures that no doubt formed a very considerable proportion of the royal functions. But the Taittirīya Brāhmaṇa[12] contains the statement that the **Kuru-Pañcāla** kings, who, like the Brahmins of

[5] *Op. cit.*, 162 *et seq.* So Weber, *Indische Studien*, 17, 188; Bloomfield, *Hymns of the Atharvaveda*, 336.

[6] *E.g.*, **Vadhryaśva**, **Divodāsa**, **Pijavana**, **Sudās**; or **Purukutsa**, **Trasadasyu**, **Mitrātithi**, **Kuruśravaṇa**, **Upamaśravas**, etc.; Lanman, *Sanskrit Reader*, 386. So a 'kingdom of ten generations' (**Daśapuruṣaṃrājya**) is mentioned in the Śatapatha Brāhmaṇa, xii. 9, 3, 3; and *cf.* v. 4, 2, 8; Aitareya Brāhmaṇa, viii. 12. 17.

[7] *Vedische Studien*, 2, 303.

[8] Rv. x. 124, 8; 173; Av. i. 9; iii. 4; iv. 22.

[9] Nirukta, ii. 10.

[10] The technical term is *apa-ruddha*. *Cf.* Av. iii. 3, 4; Kāṭhaka Saṃhitā, xxviii. 1; Taittirīya Saṃhitā, ii. 3, 1; Maitrāyaṇī Saṃhitā, ii. 2, 1; Pañcaviṃśa Brāhmaṇa, xii. 12, 6; Śatapatha Brāhmaṇa, xii. 9, 3, 3, etc.; Kauśika Sūtra, xvi. 30; Caland, *Altindisches Zauberritual*, 37 *et seq.*

[11] Especially iii. 3. *Cf.* Bloomfield, *Hymns of the Atharvaveda*, 111 *et seq.*

[12] i. 8, 4, 1.

those tribes, stand as representatives of good form, used to make their raids in the dewy season. The word **Udāja,** too, with its variant Nirāja, records that kings took a share of the booty of war. The Rigveda[13] has many references to Vedic wars: it is clear that the Kṣatriyas were at least as intent on fulfilling their duty of war as the Brahmins on sacrificing and their other functions. Moreover, beside offensive war, defence was a chief duty of the king: he is emphatically the 'protector of the tribe' (*gopā janasya*), or, as is said in the **Rājasūya** ('royal consecration'), 'protector of the Brahmin.'[14] His **Purohita** was expected to use his spells and charms to secure the success of his king's arms. The king no doubt fought in person: so **Pratardana** met death in war according to the Kauṣītaki Upaniṣad;[15] and in the Rājasūya the king is invoked as 'sacker of cities' (*purāṃ bhettā*).

The King in Peace.—In return for his warlike services the king received the obedience[16]—sometimes forced[17]—of the people, and in particular their contributions for the maintenance of royalty. The king is regularly[18] regarded as 'devouring

[13] *E.g.*, the **Dāśarājña,** Rv. vii. 18. 33. 83, and *cf.* Rv. iii. 33. 53.

[14] Rv. iii. 43, 5. References to attacks on aborigines are common in the Rigveda—*e.g.*, ii. 12, 11; iv. 26, 3; vi. 26, 5; 33, 4, etc. For later references to war, *cf.* Kāṭhaka Saṃhitā, ix. 17; x. 3; xxviii. 2; Taittirīya Saṃhitā, vi. 4, 8, 3; Kauṣītaki Brāhmaṇa, v. 5; Śatapatha Brāhmaṇa, ii. 6, 4, 2 *et seq.*; and Hopkins, *Journal of the American Oriental Society*, 13, 187, 215. In the Rājasūya the protection of the Brahmin is compensated with the 'eating' of the Viś, the latter interesting the king more than the older duty of protection. See Aitareya Brāhmaṇa, viii. 12. 17.

[15] iii. 1.

[16] See, *e.g.*, **Janaka's** offer of the **Videhas** as slaves to **Yājñavalkya,** Bṛhadāraṇyaka Upaniṣad, iv. 4, 30, and see *ibid.*, ii. 1, 20; Maitrāyaṇī Saṃhitā, i. 6, 10, etc.; Rv. i. 67, 1; iv. 50, 8.

[17] Rv. ix. 7, 5. *Cf.* vii. 6, 5, etc.; Taittirīya Brāhmaṇa, ii. 7, 18, 2.

[18] See **Bali**, and *cf.* Rv. i. 65, 4; Av. iv. 22, 7; Aitareya Brāhmaṇa, vii. 29; viii. 12. 17; Kauṣītaki Brāhmaṇa, iv. 12; Śatapatha Brāhmaṇa, i. 8, 2, 17; iv. 2, 1, 3. 17; v. 3, 3, 12; 4, 2, 3; x. 6, 2, 1; xiii. 2, 9, 6. 8, etc.; Weber, *Indische Studien*, 18, 93, n.; Ludwig, Translation of the Rigveda, 3, 246; Pischel and Geldner, *Vedische Studien*, 1, xvi; Winternitz, *Geschichte der indischen Litteratur*, 1, 173, 174; Keith, *Aitareya Āraṇyaka*, 161. It is to this form of taxation that the share of village (*grāme*), horses (*aśveṣu*), and kine (*goṣu*) of Av. iv. 22, 2, is to be referred. It is significant that the village and cattle are put on the same footing, as tending to refute the argument that the king was supreme landowner. See n. 31 below. For the rate of taxation, which later was one-sixth, *cf.* Hopkins, *Journal of the American Oriental Society*, 13, 85, 86; *India, Old and New*, 238 *et seq.*; 333; Mrs. Rhys Davids, *Journal of the Royal Asiatic Society*, 1901, 860.

the people,' but this phrase must not be explained as meaning that he necessarily oppressed them. It obviously has its origin in a custom by which the king and his retinue were fed by the people's contributions, a plan with many parallels. It is also probable that the king could assign the royal right of maintenance to a Kṣatriya, thus developing a nobility supported by the people. Taxation would not normally fall on Kṣatriya or Brahmin; the texts contain emphatic assertions of the exemption of the goods of the latter from the royal bounty.[19] In the people, however, lay the strength of the king.[20] See also **Bali.**

In return the king performed the duties of judge. Himself immune from punishment (*a-daṇḍya*), he wields the rod of punishment (**Daṇḍa**).[21] It is probable that criminal justice remained largely in his actual administration, for the Sūtras[22] preserve clear traces of the personal exercise of royal criminal jurisdiction. Possibly the jurisdiction could be exercised by a royal officer, or even by a delegate, for a Rājanya is mentioned as an overseer (*adhyakṣa*) of the punishment of a Śūdra in the Kāṭhaka Saṃhitā.[23] In civil justice it may be that the king played a much less prominent part, save as a court of final appeal, but evidence is lacking on this head. The **Madhyamaśī** of the Rigveda was probably not a royal, but a private judge or arbitrator. A wide criminal jurisdiction is, however, to some extent supported[24] by the frequent mention of Varuṇa's spies, for Varuṇa is the divine counterpart of the human king.[25] Possibly such spies could be used in war also.[26]

There is no reference in early Vedic literature to the exercise of legislative activity by the king, though later it is an essential

19 Śatapatha Brāhmaṇa, xiii. 6, 2, 18; 7, 1, 13. See also **Brāhmaṇa** (above, 2, 83) for the claim of the Brahmins to serve only king Soma, not the temporal king.

20 *Cf.*, *e.g.*, Maitrāyaṇī Saṃhitā, ii. 1, 8; iii. 11, 8; iv. 4, 3; Śatapatha Brāhmaṇa, v. 4, 4, 11; Taittirīya Brāhmaṇa, ii. 6, 5.

21 Śatapatha Brāhmaṇa, v. 4, 4, 7.

22 *E.g.*, Gautama Dharma Sūtra, xii. 43 *et seq.*

23 xxvii. 4. *Cf.* **Kṣatriya**, n. 18.

24 *Cf.* Rv. i. 25, 13; iv. 4, 3; vi. 67, 5; vii. 61, 3; 87, 3; x. 10, 8 (= Av. xviii. 1, 9); Av. iv. 16, 4.

25 See Foy, *Die königliche Gewalt*, 80 *et seq.*

26 *Cf.* Rv. viii. 47, 11; Foy, *op. cit.*, 84. The reference is not certain.

part of his duties.[27] Nor can we say exactly what executive functions devolved on the king.

In all his acts the king was regularly advised by his **Purohita**; he also had the advantage of the advice of the royal ministers and attendants (see **Ratnin**). The local administration was entrusted to the **Grāmaṇī**, or village chief, who may have been selected or appointed by the king. The outward signs of the king's rank were his palace[28] and his brilliant dress.[29]

The King as Landowner.—The position of the king with regard to the land is somewhat obscure. The Greek notices,[30] in which, unhappily, it would be dangerous to put much trust, since they were collected by observers who were probably little used to accurate investigations of such matters, and whose statements were based on inadequate information, vary in their statements. In part they speak of rent being paid, and declare that only the king and no private person could own land, while in part they refer to the taxation of land. Hopkins[31] is strongly of opinion that the payments made were paid for protection —*i.e.*, in modern terminology as a tax, but that the king was recognized as the owner of all the land, while yet the individual or the joint family also owned the land. As against Baden-Powell,[32] who asserted that the idea of the king as a landowner was later, he urges for the Vedic period that the king, as we have seen, is described as devouring the people, and that, according to the Aitareya Brāhmaṇa,[33] the **Vaiśya** can be devoured at will and maltreated (but, unlike the **Śūdra**, not killed); and for the period of the legal Sūtras and Śāstras he cites Bṛhaspati and Nārada as clearly recognizing the king's overlordship, besides a passage of the Mānava Dharma Śāstra[34] which describes the king as 'lord of all,' a phrase which

[27] See Foy, *op. cit.*, chap. iii.

[28] *Cf.* Varuṇa's palace, Rv. ii. 41, 5; vii. 88, 5. The throne, **Āsandī**, is used to form the name of **Janamejaya's** royal city, Āsandīvant. *Cf.* also Śatapatha Brāhmaṇa, v. 4, 4, 1 *et seq.*; Aitareya Brāhmaṇa, viii. 12, 3-5.

[29] See, *e.g.*, Rv. i. 85, 8; viii. 5, 38; x. 78, 1, etc. So the king is the great lord of riches (*dhana-patir dhanānām*), Av. iv. 22, 3, and in the Aitareya Brāhmaṇa, vii. 31, he is likened to the **Nyagrodha** tree.

[30] See Diodorus, ii. 40; Arrian, *Indica*, 11; Strabo, p. 703, and Hopkins, *Journal of the American Oriental Society*, 13, 87 *et seq.*

[31] *India, Old and New*, 221 *et seq.*

[32] *Village Communities in India*, 145; *Indian Village Community*, 207 *et seq.*

[33] vii. 29, 3.

[34] viii. 39.

Bühler[35] was inclined to interpret as a proof of landowning. The evidence is, however, inadequate to prove what is sought. It is not denied that gradually the king came to be vaguely conceived—as the English king still is—as lord of all the land in a proprietorial sense, but it is far more probable that such an idea was only a gradual development than that it was primitive. The power of devouring the people is a political power, not a right of ownership; precisely the same feature can be traced in South Africa,[36] where the chief can deprive a man arbitrarily of his land, though the land is really owned by the native. The matter is ultimately to some extent one of terminology, but the parallel cases are in favour of distinguishing between the political rights of the crown, which can be transferred by way of a grant, and the rights of ownership. Hopkins[37] thinks that the gifts of land to priests, which seems to be the first sign of land transactions in the Brāhmaṇas, was an actual gift of land; it may have been so in many cases, but it may easily also have been the grant of a superiority: the Epic grants are hardly decisive one way or the other.

For the relations of the king with the assembly, see **Sabhā**; for his consecration, see **Rājasūya**. A-rāja-tā, 'lack of a king,' means 'anarchy.'[38]

35 In his note on Manu, *loc. cit.*, *Sacred Books of the East*, 25, 259.

36 See Keith, *Journal of the African Society*, 6, 202 *et seq.* The evidence, so far as it goes, of other Āryan peoples does not support the theory of original kingly ownership. Such ownership did not exist, as far as can be seen, in Anglo-Saxon times (*English Historical Review*, viii. 1-7), nor in Homeric Greece (Lang, *Homer and His Age*, 236 *et seq.*), nor at Rome.

37 *Loc. cit.*

38 Taittirīya Brāhmaṇa, i. 5, 9, 1; Aitareya Brāhmaṇa, i. 14, 6; Lévi, *La Doctrine du Sacrifice*, 74.

Cf. Zimmer, *Altindisches Leben*, 162 *et seq.*; Hopkins, *Journal of the American Oriental Society*, 13, 84 *et seq.*; Foy, *Die königliche Gewalt nach den Dharmasūtren* (Leipzig, 1895); Rhys Davids, *Buddhist India*, 46 *et seq.*; *Journal of the Royal Asiatic Society*, 1901, 860, 861.

2. **Rājan** in several passages[1] means no more than a 'noble of the ruling house,' or perhaps even merely a 'noble,' there being

1 *Cf.* Rv. i. 40, 8; 108, 7; x. 42, 10; 97, 6; Taittirīya Saṃhitā, iv. 6, 8, 3; v. 7, 6, 4; Kāṭhaka Saṃhitā, xl. 13; Vājasaneyi Saṃhitā, xviii. 48; xxvi. 2; Av. xix. 62, 1, and possibly ii. 6, 4, etc.; Ludwig, Translation of the Rigveda, 3. 236, 237. Possibly *rājñaḥ* in Jaiminīya Upaniṣad Brāhmaṇa, i. 4, 5, may be taken in this sense. The king there is said to be a non-Āryan, but the reading is corrupt, and Oertel's conjecture is not probable. *Cf.* **Rājya**, n. 2.

no decisive passage. Zimmer[2] sees traces in one passage of the Rigveda[3] that in times of peace there was no king in some states, the members of the royal family holding equal rights. He compares this with the state of affairs in early Germany.[4] But the passage merely shows that the nobles could be called Rājan, and is not decisive for the sense ascribed to it by Zimmer. Of course this state of affairs is perfectly possible, and is exemplified later in Buddhist times.[5]

[2] *Altindisches Leben*, 176, 177.

[3] x. 97, 6. He also compares Av. i. 9; iii. 4; iv. 22, where the king is referred to as superior to the other royal personages.

[4] The case of the Cherusci and Arminius' attempt to make himself king, which his relatives, the royal family, foiled (see Tacitus, *Annals*, ii. 88).

[5] *Cf.* Rhys Davids, *Buddhist India*, 19.

Rājani, 'descendant of **Rajana**,' is the patronymic of **Ugradeva** in the Pañcaviṃśa Brāhmaṇa (xiv. 3, 17; xxiii. 16, 11) and the Taittirīya Āraṇyaka (v. 4, 12).

Rājanya is the regular term in Vedic literature[1] for a man of the royal family, probably including also those who were not actually members of that family, but were nobles, though it may have been originally restricted to members of the royal family. This, however, does not appear clearly from any passage; the term may originally have applied to all the nobles irrespective of kingly power. In the Śatapatha Brāhmaṇa[2] the Rājanya is different from the Rājaputra, who is literally a son of the king. The functions and place of the Rājanya are described under **Kṣatriya**, which expression later normally takes the place of Rājanya as a designation for the ruling class. His high place is shown by the fact that in the Taittirīya Saṃhitā[3] he is ranked with the learned Brahmin and the

[1] Only once in the Rv. in the late Puruṣa-sūkta, x. 90, 12; but often in the Av.: v. 17, 9; 18, 2; vi. 38, 4; x. 10, 18; xii. 4, 32 *et seq.*; xv. 8, 1; xix. 32, 8; Taittirīya Saṃhitā, ii. 4, 13, 1; 5. 4, 4; 10, 1; v. 1, 10, 3, etc. Even in the Śatapatha Brāhmaṇa, where, on the whole, the later use of Kṣatriya prevails, the Rājanya is often mentioned. See Eggeling's index, *Sacred Books of the East*, 44, 561.

[2] *Cf.* xiii. 4, 2, 17, with xiii. 1, 6, 2.

[3] ii. 5, 4, 4.

Grāmaṇī (who was a **Vaiśya**) as having reached the height of prosperity (*gata-śrī*).

Cf. Muir, *Sanskrit Texts*, 1², 258 *et seq.*; Zimmer, *Altindisches Leben*, 191. It is quite likely that the noble families not related to the royal family were families of minor princes whose rule was merged in that of the king on the formation of a powerful tribe, as was the case in Germany.

Rājanya-bandhu denotes a Rājanya, but usually with a depreciating sense. Thus in the Śatapatha Brāhmaṇa[1] **Janaka** is called by the Brahmins, whom he defeated in disputation, 'a fellow of a Rājanya'; the same description is applied to **Pravāhaṇa Jaivali** in the Bṛhadāraṇyaka Upaniṣad[2] for a similar reason. On the other hand, in one passage[3] where reference is made to men eating apart from women, princes are said to do so most of all: the term Rājanyabandhu cannot here be deemed to be contemptuous, unless, indeed, it is the expression of Brahmin contempt for princes, such as clearly appears in the treatment of **Nagnajit** in another passage.[4] Again, in a passage[5] in which the four castes are mentioned, the **Vaiśya** precedes the Rājanyabandhu, a curious inversion of the order of the second and third castes.[6]

[1] xi. 6, 2, 5.
[2] vi. 1, 5.
[3] Śatapatha Brāhmaṇa, x. 5, 2. 10, where *cf.* Eggeling's note, *Sacred Books of the East*, 43, 370, n. 1. A similar case is apparently i. 2, 4, 2, where any special contempt cannot be meant.
[4] viii. 1, 4, 10. *Cf.* Muir, *Sanskrit Texts*, 1², 515.
[5] i. 1, 4, 12.
[6] Eggeling, *op. cit.*, 12, 28.

Rājanya-ṛṣi, 'royal sage,' is a term applied to **Sindhukṣit** in the Pañcaviṃśa Brāhmaṇa.[1] The story about him is, however, purely mythical.

[1] xii. 12, 6. *Cf.* Oldenberg, *Zeitschrift der Deutschen Morgenländischen Gesellschaft*, 42, 235, n. 3, and see **Varṇa** (p. 261).

Rāja-pati, 'lord of kings,' is found in the Śatapatha Brāhmaṇa (xi. 4, 3, 9) as an epithet of Soma. It is not used elsewhere as a title of imperial temporal supremacy: see **Rājya.**

Rāja-pitṛ is one of the titles given to the king in the rite of the **Rājasūya** ('royal consecration') according to the Aitareya Brāhmaṇa (viii. 12, 5; 17, 5). It probably designates the king as 'father of a king,' and indicates the hereditary character of the monarchy. Possibly the later plan[1] of associating the king's son in the monarchy prevailed in earlier times also.

[1] Hopkins, *Journal of the American Oriental Society*, 13, 139. The sense of 'having a king as father' is also possible.

Rāja-putra, 'king's son,' 'prince,' seems to be capable of being interpreted literally in every passage of the older literature[1] in which it is found, though it may also be capable of a wider interpretation.[2] Later the Rājaputra degenerates into a mere 'landowner.'[3]

[1] Rv. x. 40, 3; Aitareya Brāhmaṇa, vii. 17, 6 (of **Viśvāmitra**, but probably in a mythical sense); Pañcaviṃśa Brāhmaṇa, xix. 1, 4; Kāṭhaka Saṃhitā, xiv. 8; Taittirīya Brāhmaṇa, iii. 8, 5, 1; Śatapatha Brāhmaṇa, xiii. 4, 2, 5; 5, 2, 5, etc.

[2] Kāṭhaka Saṃhitā, xxviii. 1, may be cited as identifying the **Rājanya** and the Rājaputra.

[3] Jolly, *Zeitschrift der Deutschen Morgenländischen Gesellschaft*, 50, 514, who points out that in the Rājataraṅgiṇī, vii. 360, traces of the older position of the Rājaputra are seen.

Rāja-puruṣa denotes a 'royal servant' in the Nirukta (ii. 3). *Cf.* **Pūruṣa.**

Rāja-bhrātṛ, the 'brother of the king,' is mentioned as one of the eight **Vīras**, or supporters of the monarchy, in the Pañcaviṃśa Brāhmaṇa.[1] He is also alluded to elsewhere.[2]

[1] xix. 1, 4. *Cf.* Hopkins, *Transactions of the Connecticut Academy of Arts and Sciences*, 15, 30, n. 2.

[2] Aitareya Brāhmaṇa, i. 13, 18, etc.

Rāja-mātra is found in the Kauṣītaki Brāhmaṇa (xxvii. 6) and the Śāṅkhāyana Śrauta Sūtra (xvii. 5, 3. 4; 15, 3), where it seems to include 'the whole class of persons (who could be called) Rājan'—*i.e.*, the **Rājaputras** and the **Rājanyas.**

Rāja-yakṣma, 'royal sickness,' is mentioned in the Rigveda[1] and several times later on.[2] Zimmer[3] identifies it with consumption: this identification seems certain, being supported by the later view of the disease.[4] Bloomfield[5] suggests 'king's evil,' or syphilis, as the sense, but this is not probable.

[1] i. 161, 1.

[2] Av. xi. 3, 39; xii. 5; Taittirīya Saṃhitā, ii. 3, 5, 2; Kāṭhaka Saṃhitā, xi. 3; xxvii. 3; Maitrāyaṇī Saṃhitā, ii. 2, 7.

[3] *Altindisches Leben*, 375 *et seq.*

[4] *Cf.* Wise, *System of Hindu Medicine*, 321 *et seq.*; Jolly, *Medicin*, 88, 89, n. 2, who takes Rājayakṣma as denoting the worst of diseases, not the disease cured by the king. *Cf.* **Rājāśva.**

[5] *Hymns of the Atharvaveda*, 697. But contrast *ibid.*, 415.

Rāja-sūya is the name in the Atharvaveda[1] and the later literature[2] of the ceremony of the 'royal consecration.' The rite is described at great length in the Sūtras,[3] but its main features are clearly outlined in the Brāhmaṇas,[4] while the verses used in the ceremony are preserved in the Saṃhitās of the Yajurveda.[5] Besides much mere priestly elaboration, the ritual contains traces of popular ceremonial. For example, the king is clothed in the ceremonial garments of his rank, and provided with bow and arrow as emblems of sovereignty. He is formally anointed; he performs a mimic cow raid against a relative of his;[6] or engages in a sham fight with a **Rājanya.**[7] A game of dice is played in which he is made to be the victim;[8] he symbolically ascends the quarters of the sky as an indication of his universal rule; and steps on a tiger skin, thus gaining the strength and the pre-eminence of the tiger.

[1] iv. 8, 1; xi. 7, 7.

[2] Taittirīya Saṃhitā, v. 6, 2, 1; Aitareya Brāhmaṇa, vii. 15, 8; Śatapatha Brāhmaṇa, v. 1, 1, 12, etc.

[3] See Weber, *Über die Königsweihe, den Rājasūya*; Hillebrandt, *Rituallitteratur*, 144-147; Oldenberg, *Religion des Veda*, 472, 491. The relation of the **Śunaḥśepa** episode formed part of the ritual. That this points to human sacrifice having once formed part of the ritual of the Rājasūya as supposed by Hillebrandt, *loc. cit.*; Weber, 47; and Oldenberg, 366, n. 1, seems very doubtful. *Cf.* Keith, *Journal of the Royal Asiatic Society*, 1907, 844, 845.

[4] Especially Śatapatha Brāhmaṇa, v. 2, 3, 1 *et seq.* See also Maitrāyaṇī Saṃhitā, iv. 3, 1 *et seq.*; Taittirīya Saṃhitā, i. 8, 1, 1 *et seq.*

[5] See Taittirīya Saṃhitā, i. 8; Kāṭhaka Saṃhitā, xv; Maitrāyaṇī Saṃhitā, ii. 6; Vājasaneyi Saṃhitā, x.

[6] Śatapatha Brāhmaṇa, v. 4, 3, 1 *et seq.*

[7] *Cf.* Taittirīya Saṃhitā, i. 8, 15 with commentary; Eggeling, *Sacred Books of the East*, 41, 100, n. 1.

[8] See 2. **Akṣa** (p. 3).

A list of the consecrated kings is given in the Aitareya Brāhmaṇa,[9] where the royal inauguration is called the 'great unction' (*mahābhiṣeka*) connected with Indra. It corresponds generally with a list of Aśvamedhins, 'performers of the horse sacrifice,' given in the Śatapatha Brāhmaṇa[10] and the Śāṅkhāyana Śrauta Sūtra.[11]

[9] viii. 21-23. *Cf.* Weber, *Episches im vedischen Ritual*, 8.
[10] xiii. 5, 4.
[11] xvi. 9.
Cf. Eggeling, *Sacred Books of the East*, 41, xxiv, xxv.

Rāja-stambāyana, 'descendant of Rājastamba,' is the patronymic of **Yajñavacas** in the Śatapatha Brāhmaṇa.[1]

[1] x. 4, 2, 1 (oxytone), 6, 5, 9 (proparoxytone). No stress need be laid on the accents of the Satapatha Brāhmaṇa.

Rājādhirāja, 'king of kings,' later a title of paramount sovereignty, is only found in Vedic literature in the late Taittirīya Āraṇyaka (i. 31, 6) as a divine epithet.

Rājāśva ('king's horse') in the Atharvaveda (vi. 102, 2) seems merely to denote a powerful horse.

Rājñī, 'queen,' is found in the Yajurveda Saṃhitās[1] and in the Brāhmaṇas.[2]

[1] Taittirīya Saṃhitā, iv. 3, 6, 2; 4, 2, 1; Maitrāyaṇī Saṃhitā, ii. 8, 3. 9; Kāṭhaka Saṃhitā, xvii. 3, 8; Vājasaneyi Saṃhitā, xiv. 13; xv. 10.
[2] Taittirīya Brāhmaṇa, ii. 2, 6, 2; iii. 11, 3, 1; Aitareya Brāhmaṇa, v. 23, 2, etc.

Rājya in the Atharvaveda[1] and later[2] regularly denotes 'sovereign power,' from which, as the Śatapatha Brāhmaṇa[3] notes, the Brahmin is excluded.

In addition to Rājya, the texts give other expressions of sovereign power. Thus the Śatapatha Brāhmaṇa[4] contends

[1] iii. 4, 2; iv. 8, 1; xi. 6, 15; xii. 3, 31; xviii. 4, 31.
[2] Taittirīya Saṃhitā, ii. 1, 3, 4; 6, 6, 5; vii. 5, 8, 3, etc.; Aitareya Brāhmaṇa, vii. 23, etc.; Jaiminīya Upaniṣad Brāhmaṇa, i. 4, 5, as emended by Roth, *Journal of the American Oriental Society*, 16, ccxliii.
[3] v. 1, 1, 12.
[4] v. 1, 1, 3.

that the Rājasūya sacrifice is that of a king, the **Vājapeya** that of a Samrāj or emperor, the status of the latter (Sāmrājya) being superior to that of the former (Rājya). The sitting on a throne (**Āsandī**) is given in the same text[5] as one of the characteristics of the Samrāj. Elsewhere[6] Svārājya, 'uncontrolled dominion,' is opposed to Rājya. In the ritual of the **Rājasūya** the Aitareya Brāhmaṇa[7] gives a whole series of terms: Rājya, Sāmrājya, Bhaujya, Svārājya, Vairājya, Pārameṣṭhya, and Māhārājya, while Ādhipatya, 'supreme power,' is found elsewhere.[8] But there is no reason to believe that these terms refer to essentially different forms of authority. A king might be called a **Mahārāja** or a **Samrāj**, without really being an overlord of kings; he would be so termed if he were an important sovereign, or by his own entourage out of compliment, as was **Janaka** of **Videha.**[9] That a really great monarchy of the Aśoka or Gupta type ever existed in the Vedic period seems highly improbable.[10]

[5] xii. 8, 3, 4.

[6] Kāṭhaka Saṃhitā, xiv. 5; Maitrāyaṇī Saṃhitā, i. 11, 5. *Cf.* Taittirīya Brāhmaṇa, i. 3, 2, 2.

[7] viii. 12, 4. 5. *Cf.* Śāṅkhāyana Srauta Sūtra, xvii. 16, 3.

[8] Pañcaviṃśa Brāhmaṇa, xv. 3, 35; Chāndogya Upaniṣad, v. 2, 6.

[9] Satapatha Brāhmaṇa, xi. 3, 1, 2. 6; 2, 2, 3, etc.

[10] *Cf.* Hopkins, *Transactions of the Connecticut Academy of Arts and Sciences*, 15, 30.

Rātrī is the most usual word in the Rigveda[1] and later[2] for night.' *Cf.* **Māsa.**

[1] i. 35, 1; 94. 7; 113, 1, etc.

[2] Av. i. 16, 1; v. 5, 1, etc.

Rāthītara, 'descendant of Rathītara,' is the patronymic of **Satyavacas** in the Taittirīya Upaniṣad (i. 9, 1), and occurs several times as the name of a teacher in the Baudhāyana Śrauta Sūtra (vii. 4, etc.).

Rāthītarī-putra, 'son of a female descendant of Rathītara,' is the name of a teacher in the last Vaṃśa (list of teachers) of the Bṛhadāraṇyaka Upaniṣad, the pupil of **Bhālukī-putra,** according to the Kāṇva recension (vi. 5, 1), of the **Krauñcikīputras** according to the Mādhyaṃdina (vi. 4, 32).

Rādha Gautama ('descendant of **Gotama**') is the name of two teachers in the Vaṃśa Brāhmaṇa.[1]

[1] *Indische Studien*, 4, 373, 384.

Rādheya, 'descendant of Rādhā,' is the metronymic of a teacher in the Śāṅkhāyana Āraṇyaka (vii. 6).

Cf. Keith, *Journal of the Royal Asiatic Society*, 1908, 372.

1. **Rāma** is the name of a man in the Rigveda.[1] Ludwig[2] thinks that he bore the patronymic **Māyava**,[3] but this is doubtful.

[1] x. 93, 14. [2] Translation of the Rigveda, 3, 166. [3] Rv. x. 93, 15.

2. **Rāma Aupa-tasvini** ('descendant of Upatasvina') is the name of a teacher in the Śatapatha Brāhmaṇa (iv. 6, 1, 7).

3. **Rāma Krātu-jāteya** ('descendant of Kratu-jāta') **Vaiyāghra-padya** ('descendant of Vyāghrapad') is the name of a teacher, a pupil of **Śaṅga Śāṭyāyani Ātreya**, who is mentioned in two Vaṃśas (lists of teachers) in the Jaiminīya Upaniṣad Brāhmaṇa (iii. 40, 1; iv. 16, 1).

4. **Rāma Mārga-veya** is the name of a man of the priestly family of the **Śyāparṇas** in the Aitareya Brāhmaṇa.[1]

[1] vii. 27, 3. *Cf.* Eggeling, *Sacred Books of the East*, 43, 345, n.; Muir *Sanskrit Texts*, 1^2, 438.

Rāmakāyana. See **Basta.**

Rāmā in a few passages[1] seems to have the sense of a 'hetaera.'

[1] Taittirīya Saṃhitā, v. 6, 8, 3; Taittirīya Āraṇyaka, v. 8, 13; Kāṭhaka Saṃhitā, xxii. 7. *Cf.* Weber, *Indische Studien*, 10, 74, 84.

Rāyo-vāja is the name of a seer of Sāmans or chants in the Pañcaviṃśa Brāhmaṇa (viii. 1, 4; xiii. 4, 17; *cf.* xxiv. 1, 7).

Rāṣṭra in the Rigveda[1] and later[2] denotes 'kingdom' or 'royal territory.'

[1] iv. 42, 1; vii. 34, 11; 84, 2; x. 109, 3; 124, 4, etc.

[2] Av. x. 3, 12; xii. 1, 8; xiii. 1, 35; Vājasaneyi Saṃhitā, ix. 23; xx. 8; Taittirīya Saṃhitā, i. 6, 10, 3; iii. 5, 7, 3; v. 7, 4, 4; Taittirīya Brāhmaṇa, i. 2, 1, 13, etc.; Maitrāyaṇī Saṃhitā, iii. 3, 7; 7, 4; 8, 6; iv. 6, 3.

Rāṣṭra-gopa, 'protector of the realm,' is the epithet applied, in the Aitareya Brāhmaṇa (viii. 25), to the **Purohita**, whose special charge it was to preserve the king and realm from harm by his spells and rites.

Rāsabha in the Rigveda[1] and later[2] denotes an 'ass.'

[1] i. 34, 9; 116, 2; 162, 21; iii. 53, 5; viii. 85, 7.

[2] Taittirīya Brāhmaṇa, v. 1, 5, 7; Kauṣītaki Brāhmaṇa, xviii. 1; Śatapatha Brāhmaṇa, vi. 1, 1 11; 3, 1, 23; 2, 3; 4, 4, 3, etc.

Cf. Zimmer, *Altindisches Leben*, 233; Geldner, *Rigveda*, *Glossar*, 149, who suggests 'mule' as a possible sense in Rv. iii. 53, 5.

Rāsnā in the Yajurveda Saṃhitās[1] and the Śatapatha Brāhmaṇa denotes 'girdle' or 'band,' like **Raśanā** and **Raśmi**.

[1] Vājasaneyi Saṃhitā, i. 30; xi. 59; xxxviii. 1; Taittirīya Saṃhitā, i. 1, 2, 2; iv. 1, 5, 4; Kāṭhaka Saṃhitā, i. 2; xvi. 5; xix. 6, etc.

[2] vi. 2, 2, 25; 5, 2, 11. 13. *Cf.* *rāsnāva*, 'girdled,' iv. 1, 5, 19.

Rāhu, the demon that eclipses the sun, seems to be referred to in one passage of the Atharvaveda.[1] The reading here is somewhat uncertain, but Rāhu is probably meant.

[1] xix. 9, 10. *Cf.* Kauśika Sūtra, 100; *Indische Studien*, 1, 87; Whitney, Translation of the Atharvaveda, 914.

Rāhū-gaṇa, 'descendant of **Rahū-gaṇa**,' is the patronymic of **Gotama** in the Śatapatha Brāhmaṇa.[1]

[1] i. 4, 1, 10. 18; xi. 4, 3, 20. *Cf.* also Sāyaṇa on Rv. i. 81, 3; Geldner, *Vedische Studien*, 3, 151, 152; Weber, *Indische Studien*, 2, 8.

Riktha is found in the Rigveda[1] and later[2] denoting 'inheritance.'[1]

[1] iii. 31, 2, on which *cf.* Nirukta, iii. 5; Geldner, *Rigveda, Kommentar*, 49, 50; Oldenberg, *Ṛgveda-Noten*, 1, 239 *et seq.*

[2] Aitareya Brāhmaṇa, vii. 18, 9 (of **Śunaḥśepa's** double inheritance, which, according to that text, is the learning of the **Gāthins** and the sovereignty of the **Jahnus**; but see Weber, *Episches im vedischen Ritual*, 16, who thinks the real succession was to the two houses, the **Āṅgirasa** and the **Kuśika**).

Ripu is a common word for 'foe,' 'enemy,' in the Rigveda.[1] It occurs in the Atharvaveda[2] also.

[1] i. 36, 16; 147, 3; 148, 5; ii. 23, 16; 27, 16; 34, 9, etc.

[2] xix. 49, 9.

Rukma in the Rigveda[1] denotes an ornament, probably of gold, usually worn on the breast. Being in several passages used of the sun, it probably had the form of a disk. In the Brāhmaṇas[2] it designates a gold plate. See also **Rajata.**

[1] i. 166, 10; iv. 10, 5; v. 53, 4; 56, 1, etc. So *rukma-vakṣas*, 'wearing golden ornaments on the breast,' ii. 34, 2. 8; v. 55, 1; 57, 5, etc; *rukmin*, i. 66, 6; ix. 15, 5. *Cf.* Taittirīya Saṃhitā, ii. 3, 2, 3; v. 1, 10, 3; Vājasaneyi Saṃhitā, xiii. 40, etc.

[2] Śatapatha Brāhmaṇa, iii. 5, 1, 20; v. 2, 1, 21; 4, 1, 13; Taittirīya Brāhmaṇa, i. 8, 2, 3; 9, 1, etc. So *rukmin* in Śatapatha Brāhmaṇa, xiii. 5, 4, 2; Aitareya Brāhmaṇa, viii. 21, 3.

Cf. Zimmer, *Altindisches Leben*, 260, 263; Geldner, *Rigveda, Glossar*, 160, who suggests as a possible sense 'gold coin'; Max Müller, *Sacred Books of the East*, 32, 112, 299.

Rukma-pāśa[1] denotes the 'cord' on which 'the gold plate' is hung.

[1] Śatapatha Brāhmaṇa, vi. 7, 1, 7. 27; 3, 8; vii. 2, 1, 15, etc.

Rudra-bhūti Drāhyāyaṇa is the name of a teacher, a pupil of **Trāta** in the Vaṃśa Brāhmaṇa.[1]

[1] *Indische Studien*, 4, 372.

Ruma is mentioned in one hymn of the Rigveda (viii. 4, 2) with **Ruśama, Śyāvaka,** and **Kṛpa** as a favourite of Indra.

Ruru is one of the victims at the Aśvamedha ('horse sacrifice') in the Yajurveda.[1] A kind of deer is meant. The Rigveda[2] mentions 'deer-headed' (*ruru-śīrṣan*) arrows, meaning such as have points made of deer's horn.

[1] Taittirīya Saṃhitā, v. 5, 19, 1; Vājasaneyi Saṃhitā, xxiv. 27. 39; Maitrāyaṇī Saṃhitā, iii. 14, 9.

[2] vi. 75, 15.

Cf. Zimmer, *Altindisches Leben*, 83.

Ruśama is mentioned three times in the Rigveda[1] as a protégé of Indra. The Ruśamas occur in another passage of the Rigveda[2] with their generous king **Ṛṇaṃcaya**; they are also referred to, with their king **Kaurama**, in a passage of the Atharvaveda.[3]

[1] viii. 3, 13; 4, 2; 51, 9.

[2] v. 30, 12-15.

[3] xx. 127, 1.

Cf. Zimmer, *Altindisches Leben*, 129; Ludwig, Translation of the Rigveda, 3, 154; Oldenberg, *Buddha*, 409; *Zeitschrift der Deutschen Morgenländischen Gesellschaft*, 42, 214; Bloomfield, *Hymns of the Atharvaveda*, 690.

Ruśamā is mentioned in the Pañcaviṃśa Brāhmaṇa (xxv. 13, 3), where she is said to have run round **Kurukṣetra**, and so to have defeated Indra, who understood her challenge to refer to the earth proper. The story indicates the connexion of the Ruśamas with the **Kurus**.

Ruṣatī in one passage of the Rigveda[1] denotes, according to Ludwig,[2] a maiden who was married to **Śyāva**. On the other hand, Roth[3] treats the word as *ruśatī*, 'white,' and *ruśatīm* seems clearly to be the reading of the text. It is doubtful what the meaning is, and whether Śyāva is a proper name at all.[4]

[1] i. 117, 8.

[2] Translation of the Rigveda, 3, 150.

[3] St. Petersburg Dictionary, *s.v.* *ruśant.*

[4] *Cf.* Oldenberg, *Ṛgveda-Noten*, 1, 110, who suggests that Kṣoṇa may be a man's name.

Rekṇas in the Rigveda[1] denotes 'inherited property,' and then 'property' in general.

[1] i. 31, 14; 121, 5; 158, 1; 162, 2; vi. 20, 7; vii. 4, 7; 40, 2, etc.

Reṇu is the name of a son of **Viśvāmitra** in the Aitareya Brāhmaṇa (vii. 17, 7) and the Śāṅkhāyana Śrauta Sūtra (xv. 26, 1).

1. **Rebha** in the Rigveda[1] denotes a 'singer' of praise, a 'panegyrist.'

[1] i. 127, 10; vi. 3, 6; 11, 3; vii. 63, 3; viii. 97, 11; ix. 7, 6, etc. *Cf.* Av. xx. 127, 4.

2. **Rebha** occurs in the Rigveda[1] as the name of a protégé of the Aśvins, who saved him from the waters and from imprisonment.[1]

[1] i. 112, 5; 116, 24; 117, 4; 118, 6; 119, 6; x. 39, 9.

Revā, a name of the Narmadā (Nerbudda) river, otherwise occurring only in post-Vedic literature, is seen by Weber[1] in the word **Revottaras**, which is found in the Śatapatha Brāhmaṇa,[2] and is certainly a man's name.

[1] *Indian Literature*, 123 ('a native of the country south of the Revā'). *Cf.* *Indian Antiquary*, 30, 273, n. 17.

[2] xii. 8, 1, 17; 9, 3, 1.

Revatī. See **Nakṣatra.**

Revottaras is the name of **Pāṭava Cākra Sthapati**,[1] who was expelled, with **Duṣṭarītu Pauṃsāyana**, by the **Sṛñjayas**, and who was in part instrumental in the restoration of his master to power, despite the opposition of **Balhika Prātipīya**, the **Kuru** king.

[1] Śatapatha Brāhmaṇa, xii. 9, 3, 1 *et seq.* *Cf.* xii. 8, 1, 17.

Reṣman in the Atharvaveda (vi. 102, 2; xv. 2, 1), the Maitrāyaṇī Saṃhitā (iii. 15, 2), and the Vājasaneyi Saṃhitā (xxv. 2) denotes a 'whirlwind.'

Raikva is the name of a man who is mentioned several times in the Chāndogya Upaniṣad (iv. 1, 3. 5. 8; 2, 2. 4).

Raikva-parṇa, masc. plur., is the name of a locality in the **Mahāvṛṣa** country according to the Chāndogya Upaniṣad.[1]

[1] iv. 2, 5. *Cf.* Zimmer, *Altindisches Leben*, 130.

Raibhī, fem. plur., occurs in the Rigveda[1] and the Taittirīya Saṃhitā,[2] together with **Gāthā** and **Nārāśaṃsī**, as a form of literature. Later on[3] the Raibhī verses are identified with certain verses of the Atharvaveda,[4] but that this identification holds[5] in the Rigveda and the Taittirīya Saṃhitā seems very doubtful.[6]

[1] x. 85, 6.
[2] vii. 5, 11, 2; Kāṭhaka, Aśvamedha, v. 2.
[3] Aitareya Brāhmaṇa, vi. 32, 1; Kauṣītaki Brāhmaṇa, xxx. 5, etc.
[4] xx. 127, 4-6 = Khila, v. 9.
[5] Bloomfield, *Hymns of the Atharvaveda*, 689.
[6] Oldenberg, *Zeitschrift der Deutschen Morgenländischen Gesellschaft*, 42, 238.

Raibhya, 'descendant of **Rebha**,' is the name of a teacher in the first two Vaṃśas (lists of teachers) in the Mādhyaṃdina recension of the Bṛhadāraṇyaka Upaniṣad (ii. 5, 20; iv. 5, 26), where he is said to be a pupil of **Pautimāṣyāyaṇa** and **Kauṇḍinyāyana**.

Roga in the Atharvaveda[1] and later[2] denotes 'disease' generally.

[1] i. 2, 4; ii. 3, 3; iii. 28, 5; vi. 44, 1; 120, 3; of the head (*śīrṣaṇya*), ix. 8, 1. 21 *et seq.*
[2] Chāndogya Upaniṣad, vii. 26, 2.

Ropaṇākā is the name of a bird mentioned in the Rigveda[1] and the Atharvaveda.[2] The 'thrush' seems to be meant;[3] but Keśava, the commentator on the Kauśika Sūtra,[4] is inclined to understand the word to mean a sort of wood.

[1] i. 50, 12.
[2] i. 22, 4. *Cf.* Taittirīya Brāhmaṇa, iii. 7, 6, 22.
[3] *Śārikā*, Sāyaṇa on Rv., *loc. cit.* On Av. i. 22, 4, he explains it as *kāṣṭhaśuka*, perhaps a kind of parrot.
[4] xxvi. 20.

Cf. Zimmer, *Altindisches Leben*, 92; Bloomfield, *Hymns of the Atharvaveda*, 266; Caland, *Altindisches Zauberritual*, 76, n. 13; Whitney, Translation of the Atharvaveda, 23.

Romaśā is mentioned in the Bṛhaddevatā[1] as the wife of king **Bhāvayavya**, and is credited with the authorship of a Rigvedic verse.[2] But in reality the word *romaśā* in that verse, which is the source of the legend, is merely an adjective meaning 'hairy.'

[1] iii. 156 *et seq.*, with Macdonell's notes.

[2] i. 126, 7. *Cf.* Oldenberg, *Ṛgveda-Noten*, 1, 128.

1. **Rohiṇī** in the Rigveda[1] and later[2] denotes a 'red cow.'

[1] viii. 93, 13; 101, 13 (reading *rohiṇyāḥ* with Roth, St. Petersburg Dictionary, *s.v.*).

[2] Av. xiii. 1, 22; Taittirīya Saṃhitā, vi. 1, 6, 2; Satapatha Brāhmaṇa, ii. 1, 2, 6; iv. 5, 8, 2, etc.

2. **Rohiṇī**. See **Nakṣatra.**

Rohit in some passages of the Rigveda[1] denotes, according to the St. Petersburg Dictionary, a 'red mare,' while later[2] it denotes a 'red doe.'

[1] i. 14, 12; 100, 16; v. 56, 5; vii. 42, 2.

[2] Taittirīya Saṃhitā, vi. 1, 6, 5; Maitrāyaṇī Saṃhitā, iii. 14, 11, 18; Vājasaneyi Saṃhitā, xxiv. 30. 37; Av. iv. 4, 7; Aitareya Brāhmaṇa, ii. 33, 1 (*cf.* Bloomfield, *Journal of the American Oriental Society*, 15, 178, n.).

Cf. Zimmer, *Altindisches Leben*, 82.

1. **Rohita** denotes a 'red horse' in the Rigveda[1] and later.[2]

[1] i. 94, 10; 134, 9; ii. 10, 2; iii. 6, 6, etc.

[2] Taittirīya Saṃhitā, i. 6, 4, 3; Pañcaviṃśa Brāhmaṇa, xiv. 3, 12, etc. So Rohita in Av. xiii. 1, 1 *et seq.*, represents the sun as a 'red horse.'

2. **Rohita** is a son of **Hariścandra** in the famous tale of **Śunaḥśepa** in the Aitareya Brāhmaṇa (vii. 14) and the Śāṅkhāyana Śrauta Sūtra (xv. 18, 8).

Rohitaka occurs in the Maitrāyaṇī Saṃhitā (iii. 9, 3) with a variant Rohītaka,[1] as the name of the tree *Andersonia Rohitaka.*

[1] So Āpastamba Śrauta Sūtra, i. 5, 8.

Rohitaka-kūla is in the Pañcaviṃśa Brāhmaṇa[1] the name of a locality after which a Sāman or chant was called.

[1] xiv. 3, 12. *Cf.* xv. 11,.6; Lāṭyāyana Śrauta Sūtra, vi. 11, 4.

Rohītaka. See **Rohitaka.**

1. **Rauhiṇa** is mentioned in the Rigveda[1] and the Atharvaveda[2] as a demon foe of Indra's. Hillebrandt[3] is inclined to see in the word the name of a planet (*cf.* **Rohiṇī**), but without any clear reason.

[1] i. 103, 2; ii. 12, 12. [2] xx. 128, 13. [3] *Vedische Mythologie*, 3, 207.

2. **Rauhiṇa** ('born under the Nakṣatra Rohiṇī') **Vāsiṣṭha** ('descendant of **Vasiṣṭha**'), is the name of a man in the Taittirīya Āraṇyaka (i. 12, 5).

Rauhiṇāyana ('descendant of **Rauhiṇa**') is the patronymic of **Priyavrata** in the Śatapatha Brāhmaṇa (x. 3, 5, 14). It is also in the first two Vaṃśas (lists of teachers) in the Mādhyaṃdina recension of the Bṛhadāraṇyaka Upaniṣad (ii. 5, 20; iv. 5, 26) the name of a teacher, a pupil of **Śaunaka** and others.

L.

Lakṣa in the Rigveda[1] denotes the 'prize' at dicing.

[1] ii. 12, 4. *Cf.* Lüders, *Das Würfelspiel im alten Indien*, 4, n. 1; Zimmer, *Altindisches Leben*, 287.

Lakṣaṇa[1] or **Lakṣman**[2] denotes the 'mark' made on cattle by branding to distinguish ownership. According to the Maitrāyaṇī Saṃhitā,[3] it was to be made under the **Nakṣatra Revatī**, clearly because of the property indicated in the name ('wealthy') of that Nakṣatra. See **Aṣṭakarṇī.**

[1] Gobhila Gṛhya Sūtra, iii. 6, 5. *Cf.* Śāṅkhāyana Gṛhya Sūtra, iii. 10; Weber, *Indische Studien*, 5, 35; 13, 466.

[2] Av. vi. 141, 2; Maitrāyaṇī Saṃhitā, iv. 2, 9.

[3] *Loc. cit.*

Lakṣmaṇya in one verse of the Rigveda[1] seems to be a patronymic of **Dhvanya**, 'son of Lakṣmaṇa.'

[1] v. 33, 10. *Cf.* Ludwig, Translation of the Rigveda, 3, 155.

Lakṣman. See **Lakṣaṇa.**

Laba, 'quail' (*Perdix chinensis*) is one of the victims at the Aśvamedha ('horse sacrifice') in the Yajurveda.[1]

[1] Maitrāyaṇī Saṃhitā, iii. 14, 5; Vājasaneyi Saṃhitā, xxiv. 24. *Cf.* Nirukta, vii. 2, where Rv. x. 119 is called the Labasūkta; the Anukramaṇī (Index), too, gives Aindra Laba as the author of that hymn. *Cf.* Bṛhaddevatā, viii. 40, with Macdonell's note. *Cf.* Zimmer, *Altindisches Leben*, 90.

Lambana is the reading in the Kāṇva recension (v. 10, 1) of the Bṛhadāraṇyaka Upaniṣad for **Āḍambara,** 'drum,' in the Mādhyaṃdina recension (v. 12, 1).

Lavaṇa, 'salt,' is never mentioned in the Rigveda, only once in the Atharvaveda,[1] and not after that until the latest part of the Brāhmaṇas,[2] where it is regarded as of extremely high value.[3] This silence in the early period is somewhat surprising if the regions then occupied by the Indians were the Panjab and the Indus valley, where salt abounds; it would at first sight seem less curious if the home of the early Vedic Indian is taken to be **Kurukṣetra.**[4] It is, however, quite conceivable that a necessary commodity might happen to be passed over without literary mention in a region where it is very common, but to be referred to in a locality where it is not found, and consequently becomes highly prized.

[1] vii. 76, 1.

[2] Chāndogya Upaniṣad, iv. 17, 7= Jaiminīya Upaniṣad, iii. 17, 3. *Cf.* also Chāndogya Upaniṣad, vi. 13, 1; Bṛhadāraṇyaka Upaniṣad, ii. 4, 12; Śatapatha Brāhmaṇa, v. 2, 1, 16; and see Strabo, xv. 1, 30.

[3] It seems to be placed above gold in value in Chāndogya Upaniṣad, iv. 17, 7.

[4] *Cf.* Map 19 in the Atlas of the *Imperial Gazetteer of India*, vol. 26, and see Hopkins, *Journal of the American Oriental Society*, 19, 21 *et seq.*; *India, Old and New*, 30 *et seq.*

Cf. Zimmer, *Altindisches Leben*, 54, 55; Schrader, *Prehistoric Antiquities*, 318; Geiger, *Ostiranische Kultur*, 419; Macdonell, *Sanskrit Literature*, 150.

Lavana in the Nirukta (ii. 2) denotes the 'mowing' or 'reaping' of corn.

Lākṣā occurs once in the Atharvaveda[1] as the name of a plant.

[1] v. 5, 7. *Cf.* Whitney, Translation of the Atharvaveda, 229; Bloomfield, *Hymns of the Atharvaveda*, 387, 421.

Lāṅgala is the regular word for 'plough' in the Rigveda[1] and later.[2] It is described in a series of passages[3] as 'lance-pointed' (*pavīravat* or *pavīravam*), 'well-lying' (*suśīmam*),[4] and 'having a well-smoothed handle' (see **Tsaru**). See also **Sīra.**

[1] iv. 57, 4.
[2] Av. ii. 8, 4; Taittirīya Saṃhitā, vi. 6, 7, 4; Nirukta, vi. 26, etc.; *lāṅgaleṣā*, Āpastamba Śrauta Sūtra, xxii. 4, 7.
[3] Av. iii. 17, 3 = Taittirīya Saṃhitā, iv. 2, 5, 6 = Kāṭhaka Saṃhitā, xvi. 11 = Maitrāyaṇī Saṃhitā, ii. 7, 12 = Vājasaneyi Saṃhitā, xii. 71 = Vāsiṣṭha Dharma Sūtra, ii. 34. 35.
[4] The texts have *suśevam;* Roth conjectures *susīmam*. See Whitney, Translation of the Atharvaveda, 116.

Cf. Zimmer, *Altindisches Leben*, 236.

Lāṅgalāyana, 'descendant of Lāṅgala,' is the patronymic of **Brahman Maudgalya** ('descendant of **Mudgala**') in the Aitareya Brāhmaṇa (v. 3, 8).

Lāja, masc. plur., in the later Saṃhitās[1] and the Brāhmaṇas[2] denotes 'fried or parched grain.'

[1] Maitrāyaṇī Saṃhitā, iii. 11, 2, etc.; Vājasaneyi Saṃhitā, xix. 13. 81; xxi. 42, etc.
[2] Śatapatha Brāhmaṇa, xii. 8, 2, 7. 10; 9, 1, 2; xiii. 2, 1, 5; Taittirīya Brāhmaṇa, ii. 6, 4.

Cf. Zimmer, *Altindisches Leben*, 269.

Lāji in the Vājasaneyi Saṃhitā (xxiii. 8) and the Taittirīya Brāhmaṇa (iii. 9, 4, 8) is a word of uncertain meaning: according to Sāyaṇa, it is a vocative of Lājin, 'having parched grain'; according to Mahīdhara, it denotes a 'quantity of parched grain.'

Lātavya, 'descendant of Latu,' is the patronymic of **Kūśāmba Svāyava** in the Pañcaviṃśa Brāhmaṇa.[1]

[1] viii. 6, 8. *Cf.* Ṣaḍviṃśa Brāhmaṇa, iv. 7; Gopatha Brāhmaṇa; i. 1, 25 (a Gotra is there mentioned).

Lāmakāyana, 'descendant of Lamaka,' is often mentioned as an authority in the Lāṭyāyana Śrauta Sūtra,[1] the Nidāna Sūtra,[2] and the Drāhyāyaṇa Śrauta Sūtra;[3] also with the name **Saṃvargajit** in the Vaṃśa Brāhmaṇa.[4]

[1] iv. 9, 22; vi. 9, 18, etc.; Weber, *Indische Studien*, 1, 49.
[2] iii. 12. 13; vii. 4, 8, etc.; Weber, *op. cit.*, 1, 45.
[3] Weber, *op. cit.*, 4, 384.
[4] *Indische Studien*, 4, 373.

Lāhyāyana, 'descendant of Lahya,' is the patronymic of **Bhujyu** in the Bṛhadāraṇyaka Upaniṣad (iv. 5, 1. 2).

Libujā in the Rigveda[1] and later[2] denotes a creeping plant that climbs trees.

[1] x. 10, 13.
[2] vi. 8, 1; Pañcaviṃśa Brāhmaṇa, xii. 13, 11; Nirukta, vi. 28; xi. 34. *Cf.* Zimmer, *Altindisches Leben*, 70.

Luśa is represented in a series of passages in the Brāhmaṇas[1] as a rival of **Kutsa** for the favour of Indra. To Luśa Dhānāka the authorship of certain hymns[2] is ascribed by the Anukramaṇī (Index) of the Rigveda.

[1] Pañcaviṃśa Brāhmaṇa, ix. 2, 22; Jaiminīya Brāhmaṇa, i. 128; Śāṭyāyanaka in Oertel, *Journal of the American Oriental Society*, 18, 31 *et seq.*
[2] x. 35. 36. *Cf.* Bṛhaddevatā, ii. 129; iii. 55, with Macdonell's notes. *Cf.* Hillebrandt, *Vedische Mythologie*, 3, 291, n. 3; Lévi, *La Doctrine du Sacrifice*, 37, 38.

Luśākapi Khārgali ('descendant of Khṛgala') is mentioned in the Pañcaviṃśa Brāhmaṇa[1] as having cursed **Kuṣītaka** and the **Kauṣītakins.** He was a contemporary of **Keśin Dālbhya** according to the Kāṭhaka Saṃhitā.[2]

[1] xvii. 4, 3. *Cf.* Weber, *Indische Studien*, 10, 145, n. 3.
[2] xxx. 2 (*Indische Studien*, 3, 471); Kapiṣṭhala Saṃhitā, xlvi. 5.

Loka denotes 'world' in the Rigveda[1] and later.[2] Mention is often made of the three worlds,[3] and *ayaṃ lokaḥ*, 'this world,'[4] is constantly opposed to *asau lokaḥ*,[5] 'yonder world' —*i.e.*, 'heaven.' Loka itself sometimes means 'heaven,'[6] while in other passages several different sorts of world are mentioned.[7]

[1] Roth, St. Petersburg Dictionary, *s.v.* 2, quotes no example of this meaning for the Rigveda, where he sees the word used only in the sense of 'place,' 'room,' 'free or open space.' But Rv. x. 14, 9, is a fairly certain example of the wider sense.

[2] Av. viii. 9, 1. 15; iv. 38, 5; xi. 5, 7; 8, 10, etc.; in ix. 5, 14, the worlds of heaven (*divya*) and of earth (*pārthiva*) are distinguished; Vājasaneyi Saṃhitā, xxxii. 11 *et seq.*, etc.

[3] Av. x. 6, 31; xii. 3, 20; Aitareya Brāhmaṇa, i. 5, 8; Satapatha Brāhmaṇa, xiii. 1, 7, 3, etc.

[4] Av. v. 30, 17; viii. 8, 8; xii. 5, 38; xix. 54, 5; Vājasaneyi Saṃhitā, xix. 46, etc.

[5] Av. xii. 5, 38. 57; Taittirīya Saṃhitā, i. 5, 9, 4; Aitareya Brāhmaṇa, v. 28, 2; viii. 2, 3, etc.

[6] Śatapatha Brāhmaṇa, ii. 6, 1, 7; x. 5, 4, 16; xi. 2, 7, 19; and so probably Aitareya Brāhmaṇa, vii. 13, 12.

[7] Kāṭhaka Saṃhitā, xxvi. 4; Kauṣītaki Brāhmaṇa, xx. 1; Bṛhadāraṇyaka Upaniṣad, iii. 6, 1; iv. 3, 36 *et seq.*; vi. 1, 18, etc.

Lodha occurs in a very obscure verse of the Rigveda,[1] where Roth[2] conjectures that some sort of 'red' animal is meant, and Oldenberg[3] shows some reason for thinking that a 'red goat' is intended.

[1] iii. 53, 23.

[2] St. Petersburg Dictionary, *s.v.*

[3] *Ṛgveda-Noten*, 1, 255.

Cf. the obscure *adhī-lodha-karṇa* in the Taittirīya Saṃhitā, v. 6, 16, 1, perhaps meaning 'having quite red ears.' Yāska, Nirukta, iv. 12, equates the word with *lubdha*, 'confused,' but this does not suit the context. So also Zimmer, *Altindisches Leben*, 84; Geldner, *Vedische Studien*, 2, 160; *Ṛgveda, Glossar*, 151, who sees in the word the designation of a noble steed.

Lopā is mentioned in the list of victims at the Aśvamedha ('horse sacrifice') in the Taittirīya Saṃhitā,[1] where Sāyaṇa explains it as a kind of bird, perhaps the carrion crow (*śmaśāna-śakuni*).

[1] v. 5, 18, 1. *Cf.* Zimmer, *Altindisches Leben*, 93.

Lopā-mudrā appears in one hymn of the Rigveda,[1] where she is seemingly the wife of **Agastya,** whose embraces she solicits.[2]

[1] i. 179, 4.

[2] The story is differently told in the Bṛhaddevatā, iv. 57 *et seq.*, with Macdonell's notes. See also Oldenberg, *Zeitschrift der Deutschen Morgenländischen Gesellschaft*, 39, 68; *Göttingische Gelehrte Anzeigen*, 1909, 76 *et seq.*; Sieg, *Die Sagenstoffe des Ṛgveda*, 120 *et seq.*; Winternitz, *Vienna Oriental Journal*, 20, 2 *et seq.*; von Schroeder, *Mysterium und Mimus*, 156 *et seq.*; Keith, *Journal of the Royal Asiatic Society*, 1909, 204; 1911, 997, n. 3.

Lopāśa is the name of an animal, probably the 'jackal' or 'fox,' which is mentioned in the Rigveda[1] and is included in the list of victims at the Aśvamedha ('horse sacrifice') in the Yajurveda Saṃhitās.[2]

[1] x. 28, 4.

[2] Taittirīya Saṃhitā, v. 5, 21, 1; Maitrāyaṇī Saṃhitā, iii. 14, 17; Vājasaneyi Saṃhitā, xxiv. 36.

Cf. Zimmer, *Altindisches Leben*, 84.

Loha, primarily an adjective meaning 'red,' is used as a neuter substantive to designate a metal, probably 'copper,' but possibly 'bronze.' It is mentioned in the Vājasaneyi Saṃhitā[1] and the Taittirīya Saṃhitā[2] as distinguished from **Śyāma.** It also occurs several times in the Brāhmaṇas.[3] See **Ayas.**

[1] xviii. 13.

[2] iv. 7, 5, 1.

[3] Śatapatha Brāhmaṇa, xiii. 2, 2, 18; Chāndogya Upaniṣad, iv. 17, 7; vi. 1, 5; Jaiminīya Upaniṣad Brāhmaṇa, iv. 1, 4, where Oertel takes 'copper' to be meant in contrast with **Ayas**, which he renders 'brass.' The sense of 'iron' is nowhere needed.

Cf. Vincent Smith, *Indian Antiquary*, 34, 230; and on the early history of metals; Mosso, *Mediterranean Civilization*, 57-62.

Loha-maṇi in the Chāndogya Upaniṣad (vi. 2, 5) denotes a 'copper amulet,' as Böhtlingk[1] renders it, rather than a 'lump of gold,' as translated by Max Müller following the scholiast.

[1] *Cf.* Little, *Grammatical Index*, 134.

Lohāyasa, 'red metal,' is mentioned in the Śatapatha Brāhmaṇa,[1] where it is distinguished from **Ayas** and gold. In the Jaiminīya Upaniṣad Brāhmaṇa[2] the contrast is with Kārṣṇā-

[1] v. 4, 1, 1. 2.

[2] iii. 17, 3.

yasa, 'iron,' and in the Taittirīya Brāhmaṇa[3] with Kṛṣṇāyasa, 'iron.' 'Copper' seems to be meant.

[3] iii. 62, 6, 5.
Cf. Eggeling, *Sacred Books of the East*, 41, 90, n.; Schrader, *Prehistoric Antiquities*, 189.

Lohita, often occurring as an adjective meaning 'red,' is used as a neuter substantive in the Atharvaveda (xi. 3, 7) to denote a metal, presumably 'copper.' As a proper name it is found in Āpastamba Śrauta Sūtra, xxiv. 9, 7.

Lohitāyasa, 'red metal,' 'copper,' is the variant of **Loha** in the Maitrāyaṇī (ii. 11, 5; iv. 4, 4) and Kāṭhaka (xviii. 10) Saṃhitās.

Lohitāhi, 'red snake,' is the name of a variety of serpent mentioned in the list of victims at the Aśvamedha ('horse sacrifice') in the Yajurveda Saṃhitās.[1]

[1] Taittirīya Saṃhitā, v. 5, 14, 1; Maitrāyaṇī Saṃhitā, iii. 14, 12; Vājasaneyi Saṃhitā, xxiv. 31. *Cf.* Zimmer, *Altindisches Leben*, 95.

Lauhitya, 'descendant of Lohita,' is the patronymic of a large number of teachers in the Jaiminīya Upaniṣad Brāhmaṇa, which clearly must have been the special object of study of the Lauhitya family. See **Kṛṣṇadatta, Kṛṣṇarāta, Jayaka, Triveda Kṛṣṇarāta, Dakṣa Jayanta, Palligupta, Mitrabhūti, Yaśasvin Jayanta, Vipaścit Dṛḍhajayanta, Vaipaścita Dārḍhajayanti, Vaipaścita Dārḍhajayanti Dṛḍhajayanta, Śyāmajayanta, Śyāmasujayanta, Satyaśravas.** A Lauhitya or Lauhikya is also mentioned as a teacher in the Śāṅkhāyana Āraṇyaka.[1] The form of name (Jayanta) affected by the family, and the silence of the older texts, proves that they were modern.

[1] vii. 22; Keith, *Śāṅkhāyana Āraṇyaka*, 50, n. 1.

V.

1. **Vaṃśa**, denoting the 'rafters' or 'beams' of the house as made of bamboo cane, is found in this sense from the Rigveda[1] onwards.[2] *Cf.* **Tiraścīnavaṃśa, Prācīnavaṃśa,** and see **Gṛha.**

[1] i. 10, 1.

[2] Av. iii. 12, 6; ix. 3, 4; Maitrāyaṇī Saṃhitā, iv. 8, 10; Taittirīya Brāhmaṇa, i. 2, 3, 1; Śatapatha Brāhmaṇa, ix. 1, 2, 25; *śālā-vaṃśa*, Aitareya Āraṇyaka, iii. 2, 1; Śāṅkhāyana Āraṇyaka, viii. 1, where perhaps the main beam of the house is meant. *Cf.* Zimmer, *Altindisches Leben*, 71, 153; Bloomfield, *Hymns of the Atharvaveda*, 346.

2. **Vaṃśa** (lit. 'bamboo') in the sense of 'spiritual genealogy,'[1] 'list of teachers,' is found in the Śatapatha Brāhmaṇa,[2] the Vaṃśa Brāhmaṇa,[3] and the Śāṅkhāyana Āraṇyaka.[4]

[1] From the analogy of the successive joints of the bamboo. *Cf.* 'family-tree.'

[2] x. 6, 5, 9; Bṛhadāraṇyaka Upaniṣad, vi. 3, 14.

[3] *Indische Studien*, 4, 374.

[4] xv. 1.

Vaṃśa-nartin is mentioned as one of the victims at the Puruṣamedha ('human sacrifice') in the Yajurveda.[1] A 'pole-dancer' or 'acrobat' seems to be meant.

[1] Vājasaneyi Saṃhitā, xxx. 21; Taittirīya Brāhmaṇa, iii. 4, 17, 1. *Cf.* Zimmer, *Altindisches Leben*, 290.

Vaṃsaga is in the Rigveda[1] a common name of the 'bull' that leads the herds.

[1] i. 7, 8; 55, 1; 58, 4; v. 36, 1, etc.; Av. xviii. 3, 36.

Vaka Dālbhya ('descendant of Dalbha') is the name of a teacher in the Chāndogya Upaniṣad.[1] According to the Kāṭhaka Saṃhitā,[2] he was engaged in a ritual dispute with **Dhṛtarāṣṭra.**

[1] i. 2, 13; 12, 1.

[2] xxx. 2 (*Indische Studien*, 3, 471).

Vakala denotes in the Brāhmaṇas[1] the 'inner bark' of a tree, 'bast.'

[1] Taittirīya Brāhmaṇa, iii. 7, 4, 2; Kauṣītaki Brāhmaṇa, x. 2.

Vakṣaṇā, fem. plur., denotes in one passage of the Rigveda[1] the bed of a stream.

[1] iii. 33, 12. *Cf.* Pischel, *Vedische Studien*, 1, 175-181.

Vaghā is the name of a noxious animal in the Atharvaveda.[1]

[1] vi. 50, 3; ix. 2, 22. *Cf.* Zimmer, *Altindisches Leben*, 98.

Vaṅga, the designation of Bengal proper, is not found in the earlier Vedic literature unless it is to be recognized in the curious word *Vaṅgāvagadhāḥ*, which occurs in the Aitareya Āraṇyaka,[1] and which suggests amendment to *Vaṅga-Magadhāḥ*, 'the Vaṅgas and the Magadhas,' two neighbouring peoples. The name is certainly found in the Baudhāyana Dharma Sūtra.[2]

[1] ii. 1, 1. *Cf.* Keith, *Aitareya Āraṇyaka*, 200; *Magadha-Vaṅga-Matsyāḥ* occurs in the Atharvaveda Pariśiṣṭas (i. 7, 7), but that is very late.

[2] i. 1, 14. *Cf.* Oldenberg, *Buddha*, 394, n.; Caland, *Zeitschrift der Deutschen Morgenländischen Gesellschaft*, 56, 553.

Vaṅgṛda is the name of a demon or a human foe in the Rigveda.[1]

[1] i. 53, 8. *Cf.* Ludwig, Translation of the Rigveda, 3, 149.

Vajra in the Aitareya Brāhmaṇa[1] denotes, according to Geldner,[2] the 'handle,' while **Kūṭa** means the 'head' of the hammer.

[1] vi. 24, 1.

[2] *Vedische Studien*, 1, 138.

Vaḍavā is a common name for a 'mare' in the later Saṃhitās and the Brāhmaṇas.[1]

[1] Taittirīya Saṃhitā, vii. 1, 1, 2; Taittirīya Brāhmaṇa, i. 8, 6, 3; iii. 8, 22, 3; Śatapatha Brāhmaṇa, vi. 5, 2, 19, etc. A derivative of this word is the masculine Vaḍava, Taittirīya Saṃhitā, ii. 1, 8, 3.

Vaṇij denotes 'merchant' in the Rigveda[1] and later.[2] See **Paṇi** and **Kraya**; *cf.* also **Vāṇija**.

[1] i. 112, 11; v. 45, 6.

[2] Av. iii. 15, 1, etc.

Cf. Zimmer, *Altindisches Leben*, 257.

Vaṇijyā in the Brāhmaṇas[1] denotes the business of a merchant (**Vaṇij**) 'trade.'

[1] Śatapatha Brāhmaṇa, i. 6, 4, 21; Pañcaviṃśa Brāhmaṇa, xvii. 1, 2.

1. **Vatsa** is often found in the Rigveda[1] and later[2] in the sense of 'calf.' Reference is made to the use of a calf to induce the cow to give milk,[3] and to the separation of the cows from the calves at certain times.[4]

[1] iii. 33, 3; iv. 18, 10, etc.

[2] Av. iv. 18, 2; xii. 4, 7 (wolves kill them); Taittirīya Saṃhitā, vi. 4, 11, 4 (the cow caresses the calf on birth), etc.

[3] Taittirīya Saṃhitā, ii. 3, 6, 2; Jaiminīya Upaniṣad Brāhmaṇa, ii. 13, 2.

[4] Rv. v. 30, 10; viii. 88, 1. See Geldner, *Vedische Studien*, 3, 114.

2. **Vatsa** occurs several times in the Rigveda[1] as the name of a singer, a son or descendant of **Kaṇva**. In the Pañcaviṃśa Brāhmaṇa[2] he is said to have passed successfully through a fire ordeal to which he resorted for the purpose of proving to his rival, **Medhātithi**, the purity of his descent. He is also mentioned in the Śāṅkhāyana Śrauta Sūtra[3] as the recipient of bounty from **Tirindara Pāraśavya**.

[1] viii. 6, 1; 8, 8; 9, 1; 11, 7.

[2] xiv. 6, 6.

[3] xvi. 11, 20. He also occurs in Āpastamba Śrauta Sūtra, xxiv. 5, 11.

Cf. Ludwig, Translation of the Rigveda, 3, 105; Weber, *Episches im vedischen Ritual*, 36-38.

Vatsatara, Vatsatarī, denotes a 'young calf' in the later Saṃhitās and the Brāhmaṇas.[1]

[1] Taittirīya Saṃhitā, i. 8, 17, 1; 18, 1; Vājasaneyi Saṃhitā, xxiv. 5; Kāṭhaka Saṃhitā, xxiv. 2; Aitareya Brāhmaṇa, i. 27, 2, etc.

Vatsa-napāt Bābhrava ('descendant of Babhru') is the name of a teacher, a pupil of **Pathin Saubhara**, in the first two Vaṃśas (lists of teachers) of the Bṛhadāraṇyaka Upaniṣad.[1]

[1] ii. 5, 22; iv. 5, 28 (Mādhyaṃdina = ii. 6, 3; iv. 6, 3 Kāṇva).

Vatsa-prī Bhālandana ('descendant of Bhalandana') is the name of a sage who 'saw' the Vātsapra Sāman (chant). He is mentioned in the later Saṃhitās[1] and the Pañcaviṃśa Brāhmaṇa.[2]

[1] Taittirīya Saṃhitā, v. 2, 1, 6; Kāṭhaka Saṃhitā, xix. 12 (*Indische Studien*, 3, 470); Maitrāyaṇī Saṃhitā, iii. 2, 2.

[2] xii. 11, 25. *Cf.* Śatapatha Brāhmaṇa, vi. 7, 4, 1.

Vadhaka is the name of some sort of 'reed' in the Atharvaveda[1] and the Śatapatha Brāhmaṇa.[2]

[1] viii. 8, 3.

[2] v. 4, 5, 14.

Cf. Zimmer, *Altindisches Leben*, 72; St. Petersburg Dictionary, *s.v.*

Vadhar means a 'weapon' generally; it is used not merely of a divine,[1] but also of a human[2] weapon in the Rigveda.

[1] i. 32, 9, etc.

[2] Rv. iv. 22, 9; viii. 22, 8; 24, 27.

Cf. Schrader, *Prehistoric Antiquities*, 221.

1. **Vadhū** is a frequent word for 'woman' in the Rigveda[1] and later.[2] It denotes, according to Delbrück,[3] the woman as either married or as seeking a husband, or as a bride in the wedding ceremony. The word appears to be derived from a form of the root *vah*, 'to carry,' as is *vahatu*, 'the bridal procession,' thus meaning 'she who is to be or has been conducted home.' Zimmer,[4] however, objects to this explanation, regarding *vadhū* as a derivative from a different root meaning 'to marry.'

[1] v. 37, 3; 47, 6; vii. 69, 3; viii. 26, 13; x. 27, 12; 85, 30; 107, 9.

[2] Av. i. 14, 2; iv. 20, 3; x. 1, 1; xiv. 2, 9. 41, etc.

[3] *Die indogermanischen Verwandtschaftsnamen*, 414, 439.

[4] *Altindisches Leben*, 108.

2. **Vadhū** is in one passage of the Rigveda[1] taken by Roth[2] to denote a 'female animal,' while Zimmer[3] urges that it means a 'female slave.' As far as the use of Vadhū goes, either meaning is abnormal, for if Vadhū never elsewhere

[1] viii. 19, 36. *Cf.* also v. 47, 6, as taken by Pischel, *Vedische Studien*, 2, 319.

[2] St. Petersburg Dictionary, *s.v.* 3.

[3] *Altindisches Leben*, 108, 109.

means a female animal (from *vah*, to 'draw' a cart), neither does it denote a slave: as the passage refers to a gift of fifty Vadhūs by **Trasadasyu Paurukutsya** to the singer, the latter must have been a polygamist of an advanced type to require fifty wives. The same doubt arises in the case of *vadhūmant*, which is used in the Rigveda and Atharvaveda as an epithet of the chariot (**Ratha**),[4] of horses (**Aśva**),[5] and of buffaloes (**Uṣṭra**).[6] Zimmer sees in all cases a reference to slaves in the chariots or with the horses: this interpretation has the support of the Bṛhaddevatā.[7] Roth's version of the references to horses or buffaloes as 'suitable for draught' is not very happy; if *vadhū* is really a female animal *vadhūmant* means rather 'together with mares,' or 'together with female buffaloes,' which makes reasonable sense.[8]

4 i. 126, 3; vii. 18, 22.

5 viii. 68, 17. *Cf.* vi. 27, 8.

6 Av. xx. 127, 2.

7 iii. 147 *et seq.*, with Macdonell's notes.

8 *Cf.* Bloomfield, *Hymns of the Atharvaveda*, 197; Pischel, *Zeitschrift der Deutschen Morgenländischen Gesellschaft*, 35. 712 *et seq.*; Böhtlingk, Dictionary, *s.v.*

Vadhrimatī, 'having an impotent man as a husband,' seems in the Rigveda[1] to be the name of a woman who owed the restoration of her husband's virility to the Aśvins, and obtained a son, **Hiraṇyahasta**. The word is, however, possibly only descriptive.

1 i. 116, 13; 117, 24; vi. 62, 7; x. 39, 7; 65, 12.

1. **Vadhry-aśva**, 'having castrated horses,' is the name in the Rigveda[1] of a prince, the father of **Divodāsa**, and an energetic supporter of the fire cult, as was his son after him. He is mentioned in a long list of names in the Atharvaveda.[2]

1 vi. 61, 1; x. 69, 1 *et seq.* **Sumitra**, in the latter hymn, can hardly be a name of his.

2 iv. 29, 4. *Cf.* Āpastamba Śrauta Sūtra, xxiv. 6, 6.

Cf. Hillebrandt, *Vedische Mythologie*, 1, 97.

2. **Vadhry-aśva Ānūpa** ('descendant of Anūpa') is the name of the seer of a Sāman, or chant, in the Pañcaviṃśa Brāhmaṇa (xiii. 3, 17).

Vana in the Rigveda[1] and later[2] denotes the 'forest,' not necessarily of trees only, but, like Araṇya, the wild uninhabited land.[3] It also means 'wooden cup' used in the Soma ritual,[4] and in one passage perhaps a part of the chariot.[5]

[1] i. 54, 1; 65, 8; iii. 51, 5; v. 41, 11, etc.

[2] Kauśika Sūtra, lxxvi. 3, etc.

[3] Rv. vii. 1, 19 (opposed to *dama*, 'home').

[4] Rv. i. 55, 4; ii. 14, 9, etc. See Hillebrandt, *Vedische Mythologie*, 1, 163, 166, 193.

[5] viii. 34, 18.

Vana-pa, 'forest-guardian,' is included in the list of victims at the Puruṣamedha ('human sacrifice') in the Yajurveda.[1] *Cf.* **Dāvapa.**

[1] Vājasaneyi Saṃhitā, xxx. 19; Taittirīya Brāhmaṇa, iii. 4, 11, 1.

Vanar-gu, 'forest-goer,' is used in the Rigveda[1] and the Atharvaveda[2] to designate robbers who haunt the forests. In the Sāmaveda[3] the term is more generally opposed to civilized men (*kavayaḥ*, 'sages'; *vanargavaḥ*, 'savages').

[1] x. 4, 6.

[2] iv. 36, 7.

[3] Āraṇya Saṃhitā, iv. 9.

Cf. St. Petersburg Dictionary, *s.v.*

Vanas-pati, 'lord of the forest,' primarily denotes 'tree,'[1] and then 'post' or 'pole.'[2] In some passages it is applied either to a part of the chariot or to the chariot as a whole.[3] It also means a 'wooden drum'[4] and a 'wooden amulet,'[5] while in some passages[6] it denotes the plant *par excellence*, Soma.

[1] Rv. i. 166, 5; iii. 34, 10; v. 7, 4; 41, 8, etc.; Av. xi. 6, 1 (distinguished from **Vīrudh** and **Oṣadhi**); 9, 24, etc.

[2] Taittirīya Saṃhitā, vi. 2, 8, 4; Av. ix. 3, 11, etc.

[3] Rv. ii. 37, 3; iii. 53, 20; vi. 47, 26; Nirukta, ix. 11. See Zimmer, *Altindisches Leben*, 251.

[4] Vājasaneyi Saṃhitā, ix. 12. *Cf.* Av. xii. 3, 15.

[5] Av. vi. 85, 1; x. 3, 8. 11.

[6] Rv. i. 91, 6; Vājasaneyi Saṃhitā, x. 23, etc.

1. **Vandana** is mentioned in the Rigveda[1] as the name of a disease, apparently some sort of eruption spreading over the body.

[1] vii. 50, 2. *Cf.* 21, 5; Av. vii. 115, 2; *tṛṣṭa-vandanā*, 'having a rough eruption,' vii. 113, 1; Zimmer, *Altindisches Leben*, 391; Bloomfield, *Hymns of the Atharvaveda*, 564, 565; Whitney, Translation of the Atharvaveda, 469.

2. **Vandana** is the name of a protégé of the Aśvins in the Rigveda.[1]

[1] i. 112, 5; 116, 11; 117, 5; 118, 8; x. 39, 8. *Cf.* Baunack, *Zeitschrift der Deutschen Morgenländischen Gesellschaft*, 50, 263 *et seq.*; Oldenberg, *Ṛgveda-Noten*, 1, 109.

Vandhura denotes in the Rigveda[1] and later[2] the 'seat' of the chariot. See **Ratha.**

[1] i. 139, 4; iii. 14, 3; vi. 47, 9, etc.

[2] Av. x. 4, 2. The Aśvins' car is *trivandhura*, 'having three seats,' because the Aśvins are a pair, and the charioteer makes a third. *Cf.* Rv. i. 47, 2; 118, 1. 2; 157, 3; 183, 1; vii. 69, 2; 71, 4; viii. 22, 5; and *cf.* ix. 62, 17. See Zimmer, *Altindisches Leben*, viii, 247; Weber, Proceedings of the Berlin Academy, 1898, 564; Muir, *Sanskrit Texts*, 5, 241, n. 371.

Vapa, 'sower,' is mentioned in the list of victims at the Puruṣamedha ('human sacrifice') in the Yajurveda.[1]

[1] Vājasaneyi Saṃhitā, xxx. 7; Taittirīya Brāhmaṇa, iii. 4, 3, 1.

Vapana in the Brāhmaṇas[1] denotes the process of 'shaving.' *Cf.* **Kṣura** and **Keśa.**

[1] Taittirīya Saṃhitā, ii. 7, 17, 1; Śatapatha Brāhmaṇa, iii. 1, 2, 1.

Vapā in the later Saṃhitās and the Brāhmaṇas[1] denotes an ant-hill.

[1] Taittirīya Saṃhitā, v. 1, 2, 5; Taittirīya Brāhmaṇa, i. 1, 3, 4; Satapatha Brāhmaṇa, vi. 3, 3, 5.

Vaptṛ in the Rigveda[1] and later[2] denotes a 'shaver,' 'barber.'

[1] x. 142, 4.

[2] Av. viii. 2, 17; Taittirīya Brāhmaṇa, i. 5, 6, 3.

Cf. Zimmer, *Altindisches Leben*, 266; Max Müller, *Sacred Books of the East*, 32, 235, n. 4.

Vapra, 'rampart,' is a conjectural reading in the Atharvaveda.[1]

[1] vii. 71, 1. See Whitney, Translation of the Atharvaveda, 435, 436.

1. **Vamra,**[1] **Vamrī,**[2] are the names of the male and female 'ant' in the Rigveda and later. *Cf.* **Vapā.**

[1] Rv. i. 51, 9; viii. 102, 21.

[2] Rv. iv. 19, 9 (where the son of an unmarried maiden is exposed to be eaten by ants); Vājasaneyi Saṃhitā, xxxvii. 4; Taittirīya Brāhmaṇa, i. 2, 1, 3; Śatapatha Brāhmaṇa, xiv. 1, 1, 8. 14, etc. *Cf.* Zimmer, *Altindisches Leben*, 97.

2. **Vamra** is the name of a Ṛṣi in the Rigveda.[1] *Cf.* **Vamraka.**

[1] i. 51, 9; 112, 15; x. 99, 5.

Vamraka is mentioned in one passage of the Rigveda,[1] where Roth[2] thinks that an 'ant' is meant. But Pischel,[3] with more probability, thinks that it is a proper name, perhaps equivalent to **Vamra**, and denoting the child of a maiden who was saved from being devoured by ants.[4]

[1] x. 99, 12.

[2] St. Petersburg Dictionary, *s.v.*

[3] *Vedische Studien*, 1, 238, 239.

[4] Rv. iv. 19, 9; 30, 16.

1. **Vayas** is a common name for 'bird' in the Atharvaveda[1] and later.[2]

[1] iii. 21, 2; vi. 59, 1; vii. 96, 1; viii. 7, 24, etc.

[2] Taittirīya Saṃhitā, iii. 1, 1, 1; v. 2, 5, 1; 5, 3, 2, etc.

2. **Vayas** denotes in the Atharvaveda[1] and later[2] the 'age' of animals or men.

[1] xii. 3, 1.

[2] Kāṭhaka Saṃhitā, xi. 2; Taittirīya Brāhmaṇa, iii. 12, 5, 9; Śatapatha Brāhmaṇa, iii. 1, 2, 21; 3, 3, 3, etc.

Vayā in the Rigveda[1] denotes the 'branch' of a tree.

[1] ii. 5, 4; v. 1, 1; vi. 7, 6; 13, 1; viii. 13, 6. 17, etc.

Vayitrī in the Pañcaviṃśa Brāhmaṇa (i. 8, 9) denotes a female weaver.'

Vayya occurs in several passages of the Rigveda[1] in connexion with **Turvīti**, of whom the word is, according to Sāyaṇa,[2] a patronymic in one passage. Roth[3] is inclined to think that the sense of 'companion' would suit all passages.

[1] i. 54, 6; 112, 6 (where Turvīti does not occur); ii. 13, 12; iv. 19, 6.
[2] On Rv. i. 54, 6.
[3] St. Petersburg Dictionary, *s.v.*, quoting ix. 68, 8, as a clear case.

Vara in the Rigveda[1] and later[2] regularly denotes a 'wooer.'

[1] i. 83, 2; v. 60, 4; ix. 101, 14; x. 85, 8. 9.
[2] Av. ii. 36, 1. 5. 6; xi. 8, 1; Aitareya Brāhmaṇa, iv. 7, 1, etc.

Varaṇa is the name of a tree (*Crataeva Roxburghii*) in the Atharvaveda[1] and the Brāhmaṇas.[2]

[1] vi. 85, 1; x. 3, 1, etc.; xix. 32, 9.
[2] Pañcaviṃśa Brāhmaṇa, v. 3, 9. 10; Śatapatha Brāhmaṇa, xiii. 8, 4, 1.

Cf. Zimmer, *Altindisches Leben*, 60, 61; Bloomfield, *Hymns of the Atharvaveda*, 505.

Varaṇāvatī is found in one passage of the Atharvaveda.[1] It seems to be, as Roth[2] thought, the name of a stream, and is regarded by Ludwig[3] as the Ganges. Bloomfield,[4] while considering that a plant may, as Sāyaṇa thinks, be meant, yet regards a reference to a river as probable. *Cf.* **Kāśi.**

[1] iv. 7, 1.
[2] St. Petersburg Dictionary, *s.v.*
[3] Translation of the Rigveda, 3, 201. *Cf.* Zimmer, *Altindisches Leben*, 20.
[4] *Hymns of the Atharvaveda*, 376. *Cf.* Weber, *Indische Studien*, 18, 26. 27; Whitney, Translation of the Atharvaveda, 154.

Varatrā in the Rigveda[1] and later[2] denotes a 'thong' or 'strap.' It was used to fasten the oxen to the yoke,[3] or perhaps to fasten the yoke to the pole.[4] Or, again, it denotes[5] the strap which was used in drawing up water from the well (**Avata**).

[1] iv. 57, 4 (of the plough), etc.
[2] Av. xi. 3, 10; xx. 135, 13.
[3] Rv. x. 60, 8; 102, 8; Geldner, *Vedische Studien*, 2, 13.
[4] This suits x. 60, 8, rather more naturally, and is so taken by Zimmer, *Altindisches Leben*, 248, 249.
[5] Rv. x. 106, 5; Zimmer, *op. cit.*, 156.

Varaśikha is the name of a leader whose tribe is mentioned in the Rigveda[1] as being defeated by **Abhyāvartin Cāyamāna.**

[1] vi. 27, 4. 5. *Cf.* Ludwig, Translation of the Rigveda, 3, 156; Hillebrandt, *Vedische Mythologie*, 1, 105; Zimmer, *Altindisches Leben*, 133, who thinks that Varaśikha was the leader of the **Turvaśa-Vṛcīvants**, but this is conjectural, and not very probable. *Cf.* **Pārthava.** In the Bṛhaddevatā, v. 124 *et seq.*, the form of the name is Vāraśikha ('descendant of Varaśikha'), occurring in the plural only.

Varāha, 'boar,' is found in the Rigveda[1] and later.[2] The god Rudra is described as the 'boar of heaven.'[3] The use of dogs to hunt the boar is once alluded to.[4] The variant form of the word, Varāhu, is not used except metaphorically of divinities.[5]

[1] i. 61, 7; viii. 77, 10; ix. 97, 7; x. 28, 4 (*cf.* **Kroṣṭṛ**), etc.

[2] Av. viii. 7, 23; xii. 1, 48; Kāṭhaka Saṃhitā, viii. 2; xxv. 2, etc.; Maitrāyaṇī Saṃhitā, iii. 14. 19, etc.

[3] Rv. i. 114, 5. *Cf.* Taittirīya Saṃhitā, vi. 2, 4, 2; vii. 1, 5, 1, etc.

[4] Rv. x. 86, 4, an obscure passage.

[5] Rv. i. 88, 5; 121, 11; Taittirīya Āraṇyaka, i. 9, 4.

Cf. Zimmer, *Altindisches Leben*, 81, 82; Hopkins, *Journal of the American Oriental Society*, 17, 67, who points out that, even in the Rigveda, its use is predominantly metaphorical, x. 28, 4, and x. 86, 4, being the only clear instances of the real sense, and of these x. 86, 4, is doubtful. See also Geldner, *Vedische Studien*, 3, 66 *et seq.*

Varu is held by Sāyaṇa to be a proper name in several passages of the Rigveda,[1] where it is accented as a vocative followed by *suṣāmṇe*. Roth[2] considers that the name must be Varosuṣāman, despite its doubtful formation.

[1] viii. 23, 28; 24, 28; 26, 2.

[2] St. Petersburg Dictionary, *s.v.*

Cf. Oldenberg, *Zeitschrift der Deutschen Morgenländischen Gesellschaft*, 39, 84, 85.

Varuṇa-gṛhīta, 'seized by Varuṇa,' is found in several passages[1] as a description of a man afflicted with dropsy, which is the disease sent by Varuṇa as a punishment for sin.[2]

[1] Taittirīya Saṃhitā, ii. 1, 2, 1; vi. 4, 2, 3; Kāṭhaka Saṃhitā, xii. 4; Śatapatha Brāhmaṇa, iv. 4, 5, 11; Taittirīya Brāhmaṇa, i. 6, 4, 1, etc.

[2] Rv. vi. 74, 4; vii. 88, 7; Av. ii. 10, 1; iv. 16, 6. 7; xiv. 1, 57; 2, 49, etc.

Cf. Oldenberg, *Religion des Veda*, 203; Macdonell, *Vedic Mythology*, p. 29, n. 16.

Varcin is the name of a foe of Indra in the Rigveda.[1] Being called a **Dāsa**,[2] and coupled with Śambara, he is probably to be regarded as a terrestrial foe, though he is also spoken of as an Asura.[3] He may possibly have been connected with the **Vṛcīvants**.

[1] ii. 14, 6; iv. 30, 14. 15; vi. 47, 21; vii. 99, 5.
[2] Rv. iv. 30, 15; vi. 47, 21.
[3] Rv. vii. 99, 5.

Cf. Ludwig, Translation of the Rigveda, 3, 152; Hillebrandt, *Vedische Mythologie*, 1, 103, n. 3; 3, 273; Macdonell, *Vedic Mythology*, p. 162 (F).

1. **Varṇa**, 'colour,' is a common word in the Rigveda[1] and later.[2] A large number of colours are enumerated in Vedic literature, but it is not possible to deduce any clear information as to the accuracy with which the Vedic Indian distinguished colours, or as to the principle on which his distinctions were based. The Rigveda seems to show that red or yellow colours were the most noticed, but this may be accidental.[3] 'Black' or 'dark' is denoted by *kṛṣṇa*, 'white' or 'light-coloured' by *śukla* or *śveta*. 'Black' seems to be meant in one passage of the Rigveda[4] by *śyenī* also. 'Dark-grey' or 'dusky' is expressed by *śyāma*.[5] The sense of *nīla*[6] is doubtful, perhaps 'dark-blue,' 'bluish-black.' The series of words *hari*, *hariṇa*, *harit*, *harita*, seems, on the whole, to denote 'yellow,' but 'green' is also a possible rendering, since the epithet is used of the frog.[7] 'Brown' is certainly the meaning of *babhru*, which is used of the **Vibhītaka** nut (see **Akṣa**). 'Reddish-brown' seems to be the tinge implied by *kapila*[8] ('monkey-coloured'), while *piṅgala* appears to denote a shade of brown in which yellow pre-

[1] i. 73, 7; 96, 5; 113, 2; iv. 5, 13; ix. 97, 15; 104, 4; 105, 1; x. 3, 3, etc.
[2] Av. i. 22, 1. 2; 23, 2; xi. 8, 16; Vājasaneyi Saṃhitā, iv. 2, 26, etc.
[3] *Cf.* Hopkins, *Journal of the American Oriental Society*, 11, cxxi *et seq.*
[4] i. 140, 9. *Cf.* Maitrāyaṇī Saṃhitā, iv. 3, 8; Geldner, *Vedische Studien*, 2, 250, 251.
[5] Śatapatha Brāhmaṇa, v. 1, 3, 7.
[6] The *nīla* of the Chāndogya Upaniṣad, viii. 6, 1, is replaced by *kṛṣṇa* in the Kauṣītaki Upaniṣad, iv. 19. *Cf.* Rv. viii. 19, 31. In the post-Vedic language *nīla* describes the colour of dark blue objects, such as indigo, sapphire, etc. That the word already had some such sense in the Rigveda is suggested by its use in allusions to the smoke of Agni.
[7] Rv. vii. 103, 6, and *cf.* iii. 44, 3; Griffith, *Hymns of the Rigveda*, 1, 365, n.
[8] Rv. x. 27, 16; Bṛhadāraṇyaka Upaniṣad, vi. 4, 14.

dominates, 'tawny.'[9] 'Yellow' is expressed by *pīta* as well as *pāṇḍu*.[10] A garment of saffron (*māhārajana*) is mentioned in the Bṛhadāraṇyaka Upaniṣad.[11] *Rudhira* and *lohita* are red, while *aruṇa* is 'ruddy.' *Kalmāṣa* means 'spotted,'[12] and *śilpa* 'dappled,'[13] while mingled shades like *aruṇa-piśaṅga*, 'reddish brown,' also occur.[14]

9 Av. xi. 5, 26; Kāṭhaka Saṃhitā, xv. 1; Taittirīya Saṃhitā, vii. 1, 6, 2; Bṛhadāraṇyaka Upaniṣad, vi. 4, 14.

10 Bṛhadāraṇyaka Upaniṣad, ii. 3, 6.

11 *Loc. cit.*

12 Vājasaneyi Saṃhitā, xxix. 58.

13 Vājasaneyi Saṃhitā, xxiv. 5; xxix. 58; Taittirīya Saṃhitā, v. 5, 22, 1; 6, 13, 1; 20, 1.

14 Taittirīya Saṃhitā vi. 6, 11, 6. *Cf.* Schrader, *Prehistoric Antiquities*, 119 *et seq.*

2. **Varṇa** (lit. 'colour') in the Rigveda[1] is applied to denote classes of men, the **Dāsa** and the Āryan Varṇa being contrasted, as other passages[2] show, on account of colour. But this use is confined to distinguishing two colours: in this respect the Rigveda differs fundamentally from the later Saṃhitās and Brāhmaṇas,[3] where the four castes (*varṇāḥ*) are already fully recognized.

(*a*) *Caste in the Rigveda.*—The use of the term Varṇa is not, of course, conclusive for the question whether caste existed in the Rigveda. In one sense it must be admitted to have existed: the Puruṣa-sūkta, 'hymn of man,' in the tenth

1 *Dāsa*, Rv. ii. 12, 4; *ārya varṇa* as against *dasyu*, iii. 34, 9; *varṇa* itself opposed to *dāsa*, i. 104, 2. *Cf.* ii. 3, 5. *Cf.* a verse in Śāṅkhāyana Śrauta Sūtra, viii. 25, 2; Pañcaviṃśa Brāhmaṇa, v. 5, 14. Roth, *Zeitschrift der Deutschen Morgenländischen Gesellschaft*, 48, 113, reads *varṇaśeṣas* in Rv. v. 65, 5.

2 See **Dasyu, Dāsa**; Zimmer, *Altindisches Leben*, 113, 114. There is no trace in Vedic literature of any real distinction of colour save this main one. In the Gopatha Brāhmaṇa, i. 1, 23, the Brahman's colour is white (*śukla*); the Kāṭhaka Saṃhitā, xi. 6, calls the Vaiśya 'white' (*śukla*), the Rājanya 'swarthy' (*dhūmra*); and the later view makes the four castes black, yellow (*pīta*), red (*rakta*), and white respectively. See Weber, *Indische Studien*, 10, 10, 11; Muir, *Sanskrit Texts*, 1², 153, etc., 176. *Cf.* also Av. iii. 4, 6, where Whitney, Translation of the Atharvaveda, 90, with hesitation suggests the reading *varṇaiḥ*, 'castes.'

3 *Catvāro varṇāḥ*, 'four castes,' Śatapatha Brāhmaṇa, v. 5, 4, 9; vi. 4, 4, 13; *śaudra varṇa*, 'Śūdra caste,' *ibid.*, vi. 4, 4, 9; Bṛhadāraṇyaka Upaniṣad, i. 2, 25; Aitareya Brāhmaṇa, viii. 4. *Cf.* also *ārya varṇa* opposed to Śūdra, Kāṭhaka Saṃhitā, xxxiv. 5; Pañcaviṃśa Brāhmaṇa, v. 5, 17, and see Taittirīya Brāhmaṇa, i. 2, 6, 7. *Vaṇṇa* appears in this sense sometimes in Pāli. See Fick, *Die sociale Gliederung*, 22, n. 4; Rhys Davids, *Buddhist India*, 53.

Maṇḍala[4] clearly contemplates the division of mankind into four classes—the Brāhmaṇa, Rājanya, Vaiśya, and Śūdra. But the hymn being admittedly late,[5] its evidence is not cogent for the bulk of the Rigveda. Zimmer[6] has with great force combatted the view that the Rigveda was produced in a society that knew the caste system. He points out that the Brāhmaṇas[7] show us the Vedic Indians on the Indus as unbrahminized, and not under the caste system; he argues that the Rigveda was the product of tribes living in the Indus region and the Panjab; later on a part of this people, who had wandered farther east, developed the peculiar civilization of the caste system. He adopts the arguments of Muir,[8] derived from the study of the data of the Rigveda, viz.: that (*a*) the four castes appear only in the late Puruṣasūkta; (*b*) the term Varṇa, as shown above, covers the three highest castes of later times, and is only contrasted with Dāsa; (*c*) that Brāhmaṇa is rare in the Rigveda, Kṣatriya occurs seldom,[9] Rājanya only in the Puruṣasūkta, where too, alone, Vaiśya and Śūdra are found; (*d*) that Brahman denotes at first 'poet,' 'sage,' and then 'officiating priest,' or still later a special class of priest; (*e*) that in some only of the passages[10] where it occurs does Brahman denote a 'priest by profession,' while in others it denotes something peculiar to the individual, designating a person distinguished for genius or virtue, or specially chosen to receive divine inspiration.[11] Brāhmaṇa, on the other hand, as Muir admits,[12] already denotes a hereditary professional priesthood.

Zimmer connects the change from the casteless system of the Rigveda to the elaborate system of the Yajurveda with the

[4] Rv. x. 90, 12=Av. xix. 6, 6=Vājasaneyi Saṃhitā, xxxi. 11=Taittirīya Āraṇyaka, iii. 12, 5. *Cf*. Muir, 1², 7-15, and references.

[5] Max Müller, *Sanskrit Literature*, 570 *et seq.*; Muir, *loc. cit.*; Weber, *Indische Studien*, 9, 3 *et seq.*; Colebrooke, *Essays*, 1, 309; Arnold, *Vedic Metre*, p. 167.

[6] *Altindisches Leben*, 185-203.

[7] Pañcaviṃśa Brāhmaṇa, xvii. 1. *Cf*. Av. xv., and see **Vrātya**.

[8] *Sanskrit Texts*, 1², 239 *et seq.*, especially 258.

[9] Rv. viii. 104, 13; x. 109, 3, and *cf*. **Kṣatriya**.

[10] Rv. i. 108, 7; iv. 50, 8 *et seq.*; viii. 7, 20; 45, 39; 53, 7; 81, 30; ix. 112, 1; x. 85, 29.

[11] Rv. x. 107, 6; 125, 5.

[12] *Op. cit.*, 2, 259.

advance of the Vedic Indians to the east, comparing the Germanic invasions that transformed the German tribes into monarchies closely allied with the church. The needs of a conquering people evoke the monarch; the lesser princes sink to the position of nobles; for repelling the attacks of aborigines or of other Āryan tribes, and for quelling the revolts of the subdued population, the state requires a standing army in the shape of the armed retainers of the king, and beside the nobility of the lesser princes arises that of the king's chief retainers, as the Thegns supplemented the Gesiths of the Anglo-Saxon monarchies.[13] At the same time the people ceased to take part in military matters, and under climatic influences left the conduct of war to the nobility and their retainers, devoting themselves to agriculture, pastoral pursuits, and trade. But the advantage won by the nobles over the people was shared by them with the priesthood, the origin of whose power lies in the Purohitaship, as Roth first saw.[14]

Originally the prince could sacrifice for himself and the people, but the Rigveda[15] itself shows cases, like those of **Viśvāmitra** and **Vasiṣṭha** illustrating forcibly the power of the Purohita, though at the same time the right of the noble to act as Purohita is seen in the case of **Devāpi Ārṣṭiṣeṇa.**[16] The Brahmins saw their opportunity, through the Purohitaship, of gaining practical power during the confusion and difficulties of the wars of invasion, and secured it, though only after many struggles, the traces of which are seen in the Epic tradition.[17] The Atharvaveda[18] also preserves relics of these conflicts in its narration of the ruin of the **Sṛñjayas** because of oppressing Brahmins, and besides other hymns of the Atharvaveda (viii-xii), the Śatarudriya litany of the Yajurveda[19] reflects the period of storm and stress when the aboriginal population was

13 Maitland, *Domesday Book*, 164 *et seq.*

14 *Zur Litteratur und Geschichte des Weda*, 117 *et seq.*

15 Rv. iii. 33. 8; vii. 18; 83.

16 Yāska, Nirukta, ii. 10, explaining Rv. x. 98.

17 Lassen, *Indische Alterthumskunde*, 1^2, 705 *et seq.*; Muir, *op. cit.*, 2^2, 296-479.

18 v. 17-19; Muir, 2^2, 280-289.

19 Vājasaneyi Saṃhitā, xvi = Taittirīya Saṃhitā, iv. 5, 1-11 = Kāṭhaka Saṃhitā, xvii. 11-16 = Maitrāyaṇī Saṃhitā, ii. 9. 1-10.

still seething with discontent, and Rudra was worshipped as the patron god of all sorts of evil doers.[20]

This version of the development of caste has received a good deal of acceptance in its main outlines, and it may almost be regarded as the recognized version.[21] It has, however, always been opposed by some scholars, such as Haug,[22] Kern,[23] Ludwig,[24] and more recently by Oldenberg[25] and by Geldner.[26] The matter may be to some extent simplified by recognizing at once that the caste system is one that has progressively developed, and that it is not legitimate to see in the Rigveda the full caste system even of the Yajurveda; but at the same time it is difficult to doubt that the system was already well on its way to general acceptance. The argument from the non-brahminical character of the **Vrātyas** of the Indus and Panjab loses its force when it is remembered that there is much evidence in favour of placing the composition of the bulk of the Rigveda, especially the books[27] in which **Sudās** appears with Vasiṣṭha and Viśvāmitra, in the east, the later **Madhyadeśa**, a view supported by Pischel,[28] Geldner,[29] Hopkins,[30] and Macdonell.[31] Nor is it possible to maintain that Brahman in the Rigveda merely means a 'poet' or 'sage.' It is admitted by Muir that in some passages it must mean a hereditary profession; in fact, there is not a single passage in which it occurs where the sense of 'priest' is not allowable, since the priest was of course the singer. Moreover, there are traces in the Rigveda of the threefold[32] or fourfold[33] division of the people

[20] Weber, *Indische Studien*, 2, 22 *et seq.*; *Indian Literature*, 110, 111.

[21] See, *e.g.*, von Schroeder, *Indiens Literatur und Cultur*, 152 *et seq.*; Macdonell, *Sanskrit Literature*, 159 *et seq.*; Weber, *Indische Studien*, 10, 1 *et seq.*; Kaegi, *Rigveda*, n. 58.

[22] *Brahma und die Brahmanen*, 1871.

[23] *Indische Theorien over de Standenverdeeling*, 1871. *Cf.* for this, and the preceding work, Muir, *op. cit.*, 2^2, 454 *et seq.*

[24] *Die Nachrichten des Rig und Atharvaveda über Geographie, Geschichte und Verfassung des alten Indien*, 36 *et seq.*; Translation of the Rigveda, 3, 237-243, etc.

[25] *Religion des Veda*, 373 *et seq.*, and *cf. Zeitschrift der Deutschen Morgenländischen Gesellschaft*, 51, 267 *et seq.*

[26] *Vedische Studien*, 2, 146, n.

[27] iii. and vii.

[28] *Vedische Studien*, 2, 218.

[29] *Ibid.*, 3, 152.

[30] *Journal of the American Oriental Society*, 19, 18.

[31] *Sanskrit Literature*, 145.

[32] Rv. viii. 35, 16-18.

[33] Rv. i. 113, 6. More doubtful are the references seen by Ludwig to the three castes in ii. 27, 8; vi. 51, 2; vii. 66, 10

into *brahma*, *kṣatram*, and *viśaḥ*, or into the three classes and the servile population. Nor even in respect to the later period, any more than to the Rigveda, is the view correct that regards the Vaiśyas as not taking part in war. The Rigveda evidently[34] knows of no restriction of war to a nobility and its retainers, but the late Atharvaveda[35] equally classes the folk with the *bala*, 'power,' representing the Viś as associated with the **Sabhā**, **Samiti**, and **Senā**, the assemblies of the people and the armed host. Zimmer[36] explains these references as due to tradition only; but this is hardly a legitimate argument, resting, as it does, on the false assumption that only a Kṣatriya can fight. But it is (see **Kṣatriya**) very doubtful whether Kṣatriya means anything more than a member of the nobility, though later, in the Epic, it included the retainers of the nobility, who increased in numbers with the growth of military monarchies, and though later the ordinary people did not necessarily take part in wars, an abstention that is, however, much exaggerated if it is treated as an absolute one. The Kṣatriyas were no doubt a hereditary body; monarchy was already hereditary (see **Rājan**), and it is admitted that the Śūdras were a separate body: thus all the elements of the caste system were already in existence. The Purohita, indeed, was a person of great importance, but it is clear, as Oldenberg[37] urges, that he was not the creator of the power of the priesthood, but owed his position, and the influence he could in consequence exert, to the fact that the sacrifice required for its proper performance the aid of a hereditary priest in whose possession was the traditional sacred knowledge.

Nor can any argument for the non-existence of the caste system be derived from cases like that of **Devāpi**. For, in the first place, the Upaniṣads show kings in the exercise of the priestly functions of learning and teaching, and the Upaniṣads are certainly contemporaneous with an elaborated caste system. In the second place the Rigvedic evidence is very weak, for Devāpi, who certainly acts as Purohita, is not stated in the

[34] See Ludwig, *op. cit.*, 3, 231 *et seq.*, Hopkins, *Journal of the American Oriental Society*, 13, 94, 95, and see **Viś**, **Vaiśya**.

[35] iii. 19, 1; ix. 7, 9; xv. 9, 2. 3.

[36] *Op. cit.*, 194.

[37] *Religion des Veda*, 382, 383.

Rigveda to be a prince at all, though Yāska[38] calls him a Kauravya; the hymns attributed to kings and others cannot be vindicated for them by certain evidence, though here, again, the Brāhmaṇas do not scruple to recognize Rājanyarṣis, or 'royal sages'; and the famous Viśvāmitra shows in the Rigveda no sign of the royal character which the Brāhmaṇas insist on fastening on him in the shape of royal descent in the line of **Jahnu.**[39]

(*b*) *Caste in the later Saṃhitās and Brāhmaṇas.*—The relation between the later and the earlier periods of the Vedic history of caste must probably be regarded in the main as the hardening of a system already formed by the time of the Rigveda.

1. *The Names of the Castes.*—The most regular names are Brāhmaṇa, Rājanya, Vaiśya, and Śūdra,[40] or later Brāhmaṇa, Kṣatriya, Vaiśya, and Śūdra.[41] There are many other variants: Brahman, Kṣatra, Śūdrāryau;[42] Brahman, Rājanya, Śūdra, Ārya;[43] Brahman, Rājanya, Vaiśya, Śūdra;[44] Brāhmaṇa, Rājan, Viśya, Śūdra;[45] Deva, Rājan, Śūdra, Ārya;[46] and Brahman, Kṣatra, Viś, and Śūdra.[47] In other cases the fourth class is represented by a special member: Brāhmaṇa, Kṣatriya, Vaiśya, and Cāṇḍāla.[48] Often only the three upper classes are mentioned, as Brāhmaṇa, Rājanya, Vaiśya;[49] Brahman, Kṣatram, Viś,[50]

[38] ii. 10.

[39] See **Viśvāmitra** and **Jahnu.**

[40] Rv. x. 90; Taittirīya Saṃhitā, vii. 1, 1, 4. 5; Aitareya Brāhmaṇa, vii. 19, 1; Śatapatha Brāhmaṇa, i. 1, 4, 12; iii. 1, 1, 10; v. 5, 4, 9; Pañcaviṃśa Brāhmaṇa, vi. 1, 6-11.

[41] Bṛhadāraṇyaka Upaniṣad, i. 2, 27 (Mādhyaṃdina = i. 4, 15 Kāṇva); Śatapatha Brāhmaṇa, vi. 4, 4, 13; xiii. 6, 2, 10; Vājasaneyi Saṃhitā, xxx. 5.

[42] Taittirīya Saṃhitā, iv. 3, 10, 1-3; Kāṭhaka Saṃhitā, xvii. 5; Vājasaneyi Saṃhitā, xiv. 28-30.

[43] Av. xix. 32, 8. *Cf.* 62, 1. *Cf.* Whitney, Translation of the Atharvaveda, 949, 1003.

[44] Kāṭhaka Saṃhitā, xxxvii. 1.

[45] Taittirīya Saṃhitā, v. 7, 6, 4; Kāṭhaka Saṃhitā, xl. 13; Maitrāyaṇī Saṃhitā, iii. 4, 8; Vājasaneyi Saṃhitā, xviii. 48; Śatapatha Brāhmaṇa, v. 6, 4, 9, etc.

[46] Av. xix. 62, 1; Vājasaneyi Saṃhitā, xxvi. 2. *Cf.* **Arya, Ārya.**

[47] Bṛhadāraṇyaka Upaniṣad, i. 2, 13 (Mādhyaṃdina = i. 4, 15 Kāṇva).

[48] Chāndogya Upaniṣad, v. 10, 7.

[49] Av. v. 17, 9; Maitrāyaṇī Saṃhitā, iii. 1, 5; 2, 2; iv. 4, 9 (with Vaiśya before Rājanya); Taittirīya Brāhmaṇa, iii. 12, 9, 2; Taittirīya Saṃhitā, vi. 2, 5, 2. 3; Taittirīya Āraṇyaka, ii. 8, 8.

[50] Vājasaneyi Saṃhitā, x. 10-12; xxxviii. 14; Śatapatha Brāhmaṇa, ii. 1, 4, 11; xi. 2, 7, 15 *et seq.*; xiv. 2, 2, 30; Taittirīya Āraṇyaka, iv. 10, 10-12.

etc.[51] Three castes—Brāhmaṇa, Rājan, Śūdra—are mentioned in the Atharvaveda,[52] and two castes are repeatedly mentioned together, either Brahman and Kṣatra, or Kṣatra and Viś.[53]

2. *The Relation of the Castes.*—The ritual literature is full of minute differences respecting the castes. Thus, for example, the Śatapatha prescribes different sizes of funeral mounds for the four castes.[54] Different modes of address are laid down for the four castes,[55] as *ehi*, 'approach'; *āgaccha*, 'come'; *ādrava*, 'run up'; *ādhāva*, 'hasten up,' which differ in degrees of politeness. The representatives of the four castes are dedicated at the Puruṣamedha ('human sacrifice') to different deities.[56] The Sūtras have many similar rules.[57]

But the three upper castes in some respects differ markedly from the fourth, the Śūdras. The latter are in the Śatapatha Brāhmaṇa[58] declared not fit to be addressed by a Dīkṣita, 'consecrated person,' and no Śūdra is to milk the cow whose milk is to be used for the Agnihotra[59] ('fire-oblation'). On the other hand, in certain passages, the Śūdra is given a place in the Soma sacrifice,[60] and in the Taittirīya Brāhmaṇa[61] there are given formulæ for the placing of the sacrificial fire not only for the three upper castes, but also for the **Rathakāra**,

[51] *Cf.* Av. v. 18, 15, where the two lower castes are addressed (Kṣatriya and Vaiśya) respectively as *nṛ-pati* and *paśu-pati*, Whitney, Translation of the Atharvaveda, 252; Kāṭhaka Saṃhitā, xii. 1; xxix. 10; Vājasaneyi Saṃhitā, xxxviii. 19.

[52] x. 1, 13.

[53] See **Kṣatriya**, **Vaiśya**, **Viś**.

[54] xiii. 8, 3, 11.

[55] Śatapatha Brāhmaṇa, i. 1, 4, 12.

[56] Vājasaneyi Saṃhitā, xxx. 5; Taittirīya Brāhmaṇa, iii. 4, 1, 1; Śatapatha Brāhmaṇa, xiii. 6, 2, 10. For other similar differences in the Brāhmaṇas, see Taittirīya Saṃhitā, ii. 5, 10, 1. 2; vii. 1, 1, 4. 5; Kāṭhaka Saṃhitā, xvii. 4; xxxvii. 1; xxxix. 7; Vājasaneyi Saṃhitā, x. 10; xiv. 24; Aitareya Brāhmaṇa, vii. 23. 24; viii. 4, etc.

[57] Āśvalāyana Gṛhya Sūtra, i. 24, 11. 12, and see Weber, *Indische Studien*, 10, 20 *et seq.*

[58] iii. 1, 1, 10. *Cf.* Āpastamba, cited in scholia on Kātyāyana Śrauta Sūtra, vii. 5, 7; Āśvalāyana Śrauta Sūtra, xii. 8, 7; Weber, *Indische Studien*, 10, 12 *et seq.* Generally Śūdras are impure, and cannot be allowed at the place of sacrifice (*deva-yajana*), Śatapatha Brāhmaṇa, iii. 1, 1, 9. *Cf.* v. 3, 3, 2; Taittirīya Saṃhitā, vii. 1, 1, 6; Kāṭhaka Saṃhitā, xi. 10 (Maitrāyaṇī Saṃhitā, ii. 4, 8, does not contain this notice).

[59] Kāṭhaka Saṃhitā, xxxi. 2; Maitrāyaṇī Saṃhitā, iv. 1, 3.

[60] Śatapatha Brāhmaṇa, v. 5, 4, 9. *Cf.* also *ibid.*, i. 1, 4, 12. The scholiast on Kātyāyana Śrauta Sūtra, i. 1, 6, refers these notices to the Rathakāra alone, but this is obviously secondary.

[61] i. 1, 4, 8.

'chariot-maker.' Again, in the Aitareya Brāhmaṇa,[62] the Brāhmaṇa is opposed as 'eater of the oblation' to the members of the other three castes.

The characteristics of the several castes are given under **Brāhmaṇa, Kṣatriya** and **Rājan, Vaiśya, Śūdra**: they may be briefly summed up as follows: The Viś forms the basis of the state on which the Brahman and Kṣatra rest;[63] the Brahman and Kṣatra are superior to the Viś;[64] while all three classes are superior to the Śūdras. The real power of the state rested with the king and his nobles, with their retainers, who may be deemed the Kṣatriya element. Engaged in the business of the protection of the country, its administration, the decision of legal cases, and in war, the nobles subsisted, no doubt, on the revenues in kind levied from the people, the king granting to them villages (see **Grāma**) for their maintenance, while some of them, no doubt, had lands of their own cultivated for them by slaves or by tenants. The states were seemingly small:[65] there are no clear signs of any really large kingdoms, despite the mention of **Mahārājas**. The people, engaged in agriculture, pastoral pursuits, and trade (**Vaṇij**), paid tribute to the king and nobles for the protection afforded them. That, as Baden-Powell suggests,[66] they were not themselves agriculturists is probably erroneous; some might be landowners on a large scale, and draw their revenues from Śūdra tenants, or even Āryan tenants, but that the people as a whole were in this

[62] vii. 19, 1; Maitrāyaṇī Saṃhitā, i. 4, 6; Gopatha Brāhmaṇa, ii. 1, 6; Lévi, *La Doctrine du Sacrifice*, 81.

[63] Śatapatha Brāhmaṇa, xi. 2, 7, 16; Kauṣītaki Brāhmaṇa, xvi. 4.

[64] Pañcaviṃśa Brāhmaṇa, ii. 8, 2; xi. 11, 9; xv. 6, 3; Aitareya Brāhmaṇa, ii. 33, 1; Kāṭhaka Saṃhitā, xxix. 10; Taittirīya Saṃhitā, ii. 5, 10, 1; Śatapatha Brāhmaṇa, vi. 4, 4, 13, etc.

[65] *Cf.* Hopkins, *Transactions of the Connecticut Academy of Arts and Sciences*, 15, 32, for the Pañcaviṃśa Brāhmaṇa. The Śatapatha Brāhmaṇa and the later parts of the Aitareya Brāhmaṇa, with their traditions of Aśvamedhas, 'horse sacrifices,' and their recollections of the glories of the **Bharatas**, represent a more advanced stage of social relations and of city life, but even they hardly know really great kingdoms.

[66] *Indian Village Community* and *Village Communities in India*, where much stress is laid on the idea of a settlement of Āryans on lands already occupied by Dravidian clans, much as Anglo-Saxon invaders on one theory occupied lands already held by Britons who became serfs, while the invaders were a land-holding aristocracy, a theory supported by the fact that the normal holding of a hide is estimated at 120 acres.

position is extremely unlikely.[67] In war the people shared the conflicts of the nobles, for there was not yet any absolute separation of the functions of the several classes. The priests may be divided into two classes—the Purohitas of the kings, who guided their employers by their counsel, and were in a position to acquire great influence in the state, as it is evident they actually did, and the ordinary priests who led quiet lives, except when they were engaged on some great festival of a king or a wealthy noble.[68]

The relations and functions of the castes are well summed up in a passage of the Aitareya Brāhmaṇa,[69] which treats of them as opposed to the Kṣatriya. The Brāhmaṇa is a receiver of gifts (*ā-dāyī*), a drinker of Soma (*ā-pāyī*), a seeker of food (*āvasāyī*),[70] and liable to removal at will (*yathākāma-prayāpyaḥ*).[71] The Vaiśya is tributary to another (*anyasya balikṛt*), to be lived on by another (*anyasyādyaḥ*), and to be oppressed at will (*yathākāma-jyeyaḥ*).[72] The Śūdra is the servant of another (*anyasya preṣyaḥ*), to be expelled at will (*kāmotthāpyaḥ*), and to be slain

[67] *Cf.* Hopkins, *India, Old and New*, 222. The point is much the same as that at issue between the different schools of opinion as to early English history. Did the Āryans in India occupy the land as a people, driving out or exterminating or enslaving the Dāsas, and themselves carrying on the occupations of a people, or did they merely form a small aristocracy of superior military force, and were the Kṣatriyas the true Āryans? The evidence of the Rigveda is really fatal to the latter alternative hypothesis.

[68] For the superiority of the Brāhmaṇa to the Kṣatriya or Rājanya, see Pañcaviṃśa Brāhmaṇa, xi. 11, 3; Vājasaneyi Saṃhitā, xxi. 21; Śatapatha Brāhmaṇa, v. 1, 1, 12; 4, 4, 15; xiii. 1, 9, 1; 3, 7, 8; Aitareya Brāhmaṇa, vii. 15, 8; viii. 9, 6; Śāṅkhāyana Śrauta Sūtra, xv. 20, 12. The Brāhmaṇa is, in his turn, dependent on the king (Śatapatha Brāhmaṇa, i. 2, 3, 3; v. 4, 2, 7), and at the Rājasūya sits beside him, but is none the less superior (Bṛhadāraṇyaka Upaniṣad, i. 2, 23). The Kāṭhaka Saṃhitā, xxviii. 5, says the Kṣatra is over the Brahman, but this is not a usual view. *Cf.* xxvii. 4. A Brāhmaṇa can get along without a Kṣatriya, but not *vice versa* (Śatapatha Brāhmaṇa, iv. 1, 4, 6), and a Rājanya with a Brāhmaṇa surpasses all other Rājanyas (Taittirīya Saṃhitā, v. 1, 10, 3; Kāṭhaka Saṃhitā, xix. 10; xxvii. 4, etc.).

[69] vii. 29. See Muir, *op. cit.*, 1², 436 *et seq.*; Weber, *Indische Studien*, 10, 14.

[70] Weber, *op. cit.*, 9, 326; 10, 14, prefers 'moving' or 'dwelling' everywhere.

[71] Muir, Haug, and Weber take the word as active in sense, 'moving at will.' But both the parallelism of the passage and the formation of the word require a passive causative sense. The reference is perhaps to the general political control of the king over the priest, whom he can 'move on' from place to place.

[72] Aitareya Brāhmaṇa, vii. 29, 3.

at pleasure (*yathākāma-vadhyaḥ*).[73] The descriptions seem calculated to show the relation of each of the castes to the Rājanya. Even the Brāhmaṇa he can control, whilst the Vaiśya is his inferior and tributary, whom he can remove without cause from his land,[74] but who is still free, and whom he cannot maim or slay without due process. The Śūdra has no rights of property or life against the noble, especially the king.

The passage is a late one, and the high place of the Kṣatriya is to some extent accounted for by this fact. It is clear that in the course of time the Vaiśya fell more and more in position with the hardening of the divisions of caste. Weber[75] shows reason for believing that the Vājapeya sacrifice, a festival of which a chariot race forms an integral part,[76] was, as the Sāṅkhāyana Śrauta Sūtra[77] says, once a sacrifice for a Vaiśya, as well as for a priest or king. But the king, too, had to suffer diminution of his influence at the hands of the priest: the Taittirīya texts[78] show that the Vājapeya was originally a lesser sacrifice which, in the case of a king, was followed by the Rājasūya, or consecration of him as an overlord of lesser kings, and in that of the Brahmin by the Bṛhaspatisava, a festival celebrated on his appointment as a royal Purohita. But the Śatapatha Brāhmaṇa[79] exalts the Vājapeya, in which a priest could be the sacrificer, over the Rājasūya, from which he was excluded, and identifies it with the Bṛhaspatisava, a clear piece of juggling in the interests of the priestly pretentions. But we must not overestimate the value of such passages, or the exaltation of the Purohita in the later books of the Śatapatha

73 Aitareya Brāhmaṇa, vii. 29, 4.

74 This seems to be the most probable reference of *yathākāmajyeyaḥ*. The expulsion of the Vaiśya is here not in allusion to quasi-ownership of land by the King or Kṣatriya; it is an act of royal authority, not an incident of tenure. See Keith, *Journal of the African Society*, 6, 202 *et seq.*, and *cf.* Hopkins, *India, Old and New*, 222, 223.

75 *Ueber den Vājapeya*, 10 *et seq.*

76 *Ibid.* *Cf.* Hillebrandt, *Vedische Mythologie*, 1, 247; *Festgruss an Böhtlingk*, 40 *et seq.*; *Rituallitteratur*, 141.

77 xvi. 17, 4. *Cf.* xv. 1, 1.

78 Taittirīya Saṃhitā, v. 6, 2, 1; Taittirīya Brāhmaṇa, ii. 7, 6, 1. *Cf.* Lāṭyāyana Śrauta Sūtra, viii. 11, 1; Āśvalāyana Śrauta Sūtra, ix. 9, 19; Eggeling, *Sacred Books of the East*, 41, xxiv, xxv.

79 v. 1, 1, 1 *et seq.*; 2, 1, 19; Kātyāyana Śrauta Sūtra, xv. 1, 1-2. Weber, *op. cit.*, 8, 9, interprets the situation differently from Eggeling.

and Aitareya Brāhmaṇas as evidence of a real growth in the priestly power: these books represent the views of the priests of what their own powers should be, and to some extent were in the Madhyadeśa. Another side of the picture is presented in the Pāli literature,[80] which, belonging to a later period than the Vedic, undoubtedly underestimates the position of the priests; while the Epic,[81] more nearly contemporaneous with the later Vedic period, displays, despite all priestly redaction, the temporal superiority of the nobility in clear light.

Although clear distinctions were made between the different castes, there is little trace in Vedic literature of one of the leading characteristics of the later system, the impurity communicated by the touch or contact of the inferior castes,[82] which is seen both directly in the purification rendered necessary in case of contact with a Śūdra, and indirectly in the prohibition of eating in company with men of lower caste.[83] It is true that prohibition of eating in company with others does appear,[84] but not in connexion with caste: its purpose is to preserve the peculiar sanctity of those who perform a certain rite or believe in a certain doctrine; for persons who eat of the same food together, according to primitive thought, acquire the same characteristics and enter into a sacramental communion. But Vedic literature does not yet show that to take food from an inferior caste was forbidden as destroying

80 Fick, *Die sociale Gliederung*, 107 *et seq.*; Rhys Davids, *Buddhist India*, 53 *et seq.*; 158.

81 Hopkins, *Journal of the American Oriental Society*, 13, 984 *et seq.*

82 See, *e.g.*, Manu, iii. 239; v. 85; Fick, *op. cit.*, 26 *et seq.*

83 Vāsiṣṭha Dharma Sūtra, xiv. 1 *et seq.*; Gautama Dharma Sūtra, xvii. 17; Āpastamba Dharma Sūtra, i. 6, 18, 16 *et seq.*; ii. 4, 9, 7, with Bühler's note; Manu, iv. 210 *et seq.*; Viṣṇu, 41, 7 *et seq.*; Fick, *op. cit.*, 30-33, who points out that the Jātakas contain little evidence on the practice. Senart, *Les Castes dans l'Inde*, 48 *et seq.*, 212 *et seq.*, attributes great importance to the question of eating together, and compares the sacrificial meals of the *gens* at Rome, where strangers were excluded (Fustel de Coulanges, *La Cité Antique*, 117). But this is not conclusive; a caste is not a *gens*, and the *gens* excluded strangers only at a solemn festival, when the whole *gens* renewed its blood kinship. If we have no evidence exactly establishing this for the Gotra in early Vedic literature, we need not hesitate to believe that in the earliest Vedic period the Gotra had solemn festivals of union, and of communication with the dead, but that again does not explain or amount to the caste prohibition of taking food from an inferior.

84 *E.g.*, Aitareya Āraṇyaka, v. 3, 3, with Keith's note.

purity.[85] Nor, of course, has the caste system developed the constitution with a head, a council, and common festivals which the modern caste has; for such an organization is not found even in the Epic or in the Pāli literature.[86] The Vedic characteristics of caste are heredity, pursuit of a common occupation, and restriction on intermarriage.

3. *Restrictions on Intermarriage.*—Arrian, in his *Indica*,[87] probably on the authority of Megasthenes, makes the prohibition of marriage between γένη, no doubt 'castes,' a characteristic of Indian life. The evidence of Pāli literature[88] is in favour of this view, though it shows that a king could marry whom he wished, and could make his son by that wife the heir apparent. But it equally shows that there were others who held that not the father's but the mother's rank determined the social standing of the son. Though Manu[89] recognizes the possibility of marriage with the next lower caste as producing legitimate children, still he condemns the marriage of an Āryan with a woman of lower caste. The Pāraskara Gṛhya Sūtra[90] allows the marriage of a Kṣatriya with a wife of his own caste or of the lower caste, of a Brahmin with a wife of his own caste or of the two lower classes, and of a Vaiśya with a Vaiśya wife only. But it quotes the opinion of others that all of them can marry a Śūdra wife, while other authorities condemn the marriage with a Śūdra wife in certain circumstances, which implies that in other cases it might be justified.[91] The earlier

85 For a case of objection to eating food after another, see Chāndogya Upaniṣad, i. 10, 1. Possibly the idea there is that eating the food of a chief is dangerous, since the eater thus enters into possession of part of his substance, and consequently at once becomes an object of anger to the chief, as well as of danger to himself; for the chief may be so full of divine force that it would be unsafe for an ordinary man to be assimilated to him—a common idea in primitive societies. See also Taittirīya Āraṇyaka, v. 8, 13.

86 Fick, *op. cit.*, 24. Senart, *op. cit.*, 219, 220, compares the family councils of Greece, Rome, and Germany (Leist, *Altarisches Jus Civile*, 273 *et seq.*; Kovalevsky, *Famille et Propriété Primitives*, 119; Fustel de Coulanges, *op. cit.*, 118, 119). But here again the system may have applied to the Gotra without its really explaining the later appearance of the practice in the caste, and the absence of the mention of a council in the early and late literature alike is conclusive against its existence.

87 xii. 8. 9.

88 Fick, *op. cit.*, 34-40.

89 x. 5; iii. 15.

90 i. 4. *Cf.* Weber, *Indische Studien*, 10, 21, 74.

91 Gobhila Gṛhya Sūtra, iii. 2, 42.

literature bears out this impression: much stress is laid on descent from a Ṛṣi, and on purity of descent;[92] but there is other evidence for the view that even a Brāhmaṇa need not be of pure lineage. **Kavaṣa** Ailūṣa is taunted with being the son of a Dāsī, 'slave woman,'[93] and **Vatsa** was accused of being a Śūdrā's son, but established his purity by walking unhurt through the flames of a fire ordeal.[94] He who is learned (*śuśruvān*) is said to be a Brāhmaṇa, descended from a Ṛṣi (*ārṣeya*), in the Taittirīya Saṃhitā;[95] and **Satyakāma**, son of **Jabālā**, was accepted as a pupil by **Hāridrumata** Gautama, though he could not name his father.[96] The Kāṭhaka Saṃhitā[97] says that knowledge is all-important, not descent. But all this merely goes to show that there was a measure of laxity in the hereditary character of caste, not that it was not based on heredity. The Yajurveda Saṃhitās[98] recognize the illicit union of Ārya and Śūdrā, and *vice versa*: it is not unlikely that if illicit unions took place, legal marriage was quite possible. The Pañcaviṃśa Brāhmaṇa,[99] indeed, recognizes such a case in that of **Dīrghatamas**, son of the slave girl Uśij, if we may adopt the description of Uśij given in the Bṛhaddevatā.[100]

In a hymn of the Atharvaveda[101] extreme claims are put

[92] See Taittirīya Saṃhitā, vi. 6, 1, 4; Vājasaneyi Saṃhitā, vii. 46; Taittirīya Brāhmaṇa, i. 4, 4, 2; Śatapatha Brāhmaṇa, iv. 3, 4, 19; xii. 4, 4, 6; Kātyāyana Śrauta Sūtra, xxv. 3, 17; Lāṭyāyana Śrauta Sūtra, i. 1, 7; Kauśika Sūtra, 67, etc. So one of the characteristics of a Brāhmaṇa given in the Śatapatha Brāhmaṇa, xi. 5, 7, 1, is *brāhmaṇya*, which Weber, *op. cit.*, 10, 69, takes as referring to descent. *Brahma-putra* is a title of honour, Śatapatha Brāhmaṇa, xi. 4, 1, 2. 9; Āśvalāyana Śrauta Sūtra, ii. 18, 12; Śāṅkhāyana Śrauta Sūtra, xii. 21, 1. 2; and to be born the son of a wise Brāhmaṇa is the highest fortune, Bṛhadāraṇyaka Upaniṣad, vi. 4, 29.

[93] Aitareya Brāhmaṇa, ii. 19, 1; Kauṣītaki Brāhmaṇa, xii. 3. *Cf.* Weber, *op. cit.*, 2, 311; 9, 42, 44, 46.

[94] Pañcaviṃśa Brāhmaṇa, xiv. 6. 6.

[95] vi. 6, 1, 4.

[96] Chāndogya Upaniṣad, vi. 4, 4; Weber, *op. cit.*, 1, 263. *Cf.* Śatapatha Brāhmaṇa, xi. 5, 4, 1.

[97] xxx. 1. *Cf.* Weber, *op. cit.*, 3, 462.

[98] Taittirīya Saṃhitā, vii. 4, 19, 3. 4; Kāṭhaka Saṃhitā, Aśvamedha, iv. 7; Vājasaneyi Saṃhitā, xxiv. 30. 31. The word Arya here must refer in all probability to any Āryan, not merely to a Vaiśya, Weber, *op. cit.*, 10, 6.

[99] xiv. 11, 17; Hopkins, *Transactions of the Connecticut Academy of Arts and Sciences*, 15, 56, n. But there is no mention here of Uśij being a slave.

[100] iv. 24. 25.

[101] v. 17, 8. 9. See Muir, 1², 282, n. 76; Whitney, Translation of the Atharvaveda, 249. The exact sense is not clear, but the passage is intended to show in the strongest light the high position of the Brāhmaṇa.

forward for the Brāhmaṇa, who alone is a true husband and the real husband, even if the woman has had others, a Rājanya or a Vaiśya: a Śūdra husband is not mentioned, probably on purpose.[102] The marriage of Brāhmaṇas with Rājanya women is illustrated by the cases of **Sukanyā**, daughter of king **Śaryāta**, who married **Cyavana**,[103] and of **Rathavīti's** daughter, who married **Śyāvāśva**.[104]

4. *Occupation and Caste.*—The Greek authorities[105] and the evidence of the Jātakas[106] concur in showing it to have been the general rule that each caste was confined to its own occupations, but that the Brāhmaṇas did engage in many professions beside that of simple priest, while all castes gave members to the Śramaṇas, or homeless ascetics. The Jātakas[107] recognize the Brahmins as engaged in all sorts of occupations, as merchants, traders, agriculturists, and so forth. Matters are somewhat simpler in Vedic literature, where the Brāhmaṇas and Kṣatriyas appear as practically confined to their own professions of sacrifice and military or administrative functions. Ludwig[108] sees in **Dīrghaśravas** in the Rigveda[109] a Brahmin reduced by indigence to acting as a merchant, as allowed even later by the Sūtra literature; but this is not certain, though it is perfectly possible. More interesting is the question how far the Kṣatriyas practised the duties of priests; the evidence here is conflicting. The best known case is, of course, that of **Viśvāmitra.** In the Rigveda he appears merely as a priest who is attached to the court of **Sudās**, king of the **Tṛtsus**; but in the Pañcaviṃśa Brāhmaṇa[110] he is called a king, a descendant of **Jahnu**, and the Aitareya Brāhmaṇa[111] refers to **Śunaḥśepa's**

[102] The sense of v. 17, 18, is obscure; it can be interpreted to mean that the Brāhmaṇa should be provided with a temporary wife on each occasion when he pays a visit (*cf.* Whitney, 250). But this is hardly likely. Muir takes it as referring to his own wife.

[103] Śatapatha Brāhmaṇa, iv. 1, 5, 7. *Cf.* Ludwig, Translation of the Rigveda, 3, 244, 245; Weber, *op. cit.*, 10, 73 *et seq.*; Hopkins, *Journal of the American Oriental Society*, 13, 352, 353.

[104] *Cf.* Bṛhaddevatā, v. 50 *et seq.*

[105] Arrian, *Indica*, xii. 8. 9; Strabo, xv. 4, 49.

[106] Fick, *op. cit.*, 40 *et seq.*

[107] Rhys Davids, *op. cit.*, 54 *et seq.*

[108] *Op. cit.*, 3, 237 *et seq.*

[109] i. 112, 11.

[110] xxi. 12, 2. See Hopkins, *Transactions of the Connecticut Academy of Arts and Sciences*, 15, 54.

[111] vii. 18, 9. *Cf.* Śāṅkhāyana Śrauta Sūtra, xv. 21, where the reading is different, but worse. But see Weber, *Episches im vedischen Ritual*, 16.

succeeding, through his adoption by Viśvāmitra, to the divine lore (*daiva veda*) of the **Gāthins** and the lordship of the Jahnus. That in fact this tradition is correct seems most improbable, but it serves at least to illustrate the existence of seers of royal origin. Such figures appear more than once in the Pañcaviṃśa Brāhmaṇa,[112] which knows the technical terms **Rājanyarṣi** and **Devarājan** corresponding to the later Rājarṣi, 'royal sage.' The Jaiminīya Brāhmaṇa[113] says of one who knows a certain doctrine, 'being a king he becomes a seer' (*rājā sann ṛṣir bhavati*), and the Jaiminīya Upaniṣad Brāhmana[114] applies the term Rājanya to a Brāhmaṇa. Again, it is argued that **Devāpi Ārṣṭiṣeṇa**, who acted as Purohita, according to the Rigveda,[115] for **Śantanu**, was a prince, as Yāska[116] says or implies he was.[117] But this assumption seems to be only an error of Yāska's. Since nothing in the Rigveda alludes to any relationship, it is impossible to accept Sieg's view[118] that the Rigveda recognizes the two as brothers, but presents the fact of a prince acting the part of Purohita as unusual and requiring explanation. The principle, however, thus accepted by Sieg as to princes in the Rigveda seems sound enough. Again, Muir[119] has argued that Hindu tradition, as shown in Sāyaṇa,[120] regards many hymns of the Rigveda as composed by royal personages, but he admits that in many cases the ascription is wrong; it may be added that in the case of **Pṛthī Vainya**, where the hymn[121] ascribed to him seems to be his, it is not shown in the hymn itself that he is other than a seer; the Śatapatha Brāhmaṇa[122] calls him a king, but that is probably of no more value than the later tradition as to Viśvāmitra. The case of **Viśvantara**

[112] xii. 12, 6; xviii. 10, 5. *Cf.* Oldenberg, *Zeitschrift der Deutschen Morgenländischen Gesellschaft*, 42, 235, n. 3.

[113] P. 562 of the manuscript, cited by Hopkins, *Journal of the American Oriental Society*, 13, 154, n.

[114] i. 4, 2. *Cf.* Aitareya Brāhmaṇa, vii. 17, 6, where Viśvāmitra is addressed as Rājaputra.

[115] x. 98. See Zimmer, *Altindisches Leben*, 196; Senart, *Les Castes dans l'Inde*, 165; Muir, 1², 269 *et seq.*

[116] Nirukta, ii. 10.

[117] It may be added that a family of Ārṣṭiṣeṇas appear as ritual authorities in a scholium on Kātyāyana Śrauta Sūtra, i. 9, 3; Weber, *op. cit.*, 10, 95.

[118] *Die Sagenstoffe des Ṛgveda*, 142.

[119] *Op. cit.*, 1², 265 *et seq.*

[120] On Rv. i. 100; iv. 42. 43. 44; v. 27; vi. 15; x. 9. 75. 133. 134. 148. 179, etc.

[121] x. 148, 5.

[122] v. 3, 5, 4.

and the **Śyāparṇas** mentioned in the Aitareya Brāhmaṇa[123] has been cited[124] as that of a king sacrificing without priestly aid, but the interpretation is quite uncertain, while the parallel of the **Kaśyapas, Asitamṛgas,** and **Bhūtavīras** mentioned in the course of the narrative renders it highly probable that the king had other priests to carry out the sacrifice.

Somewhat different are a series of other cases found in the Upaniṣads, where the Brahma doctrine is ascribed to royal persons. Thus **Janaka** is said in the Śatapatha Brāhmaṇa[125] to have become a Brahman; **Ajātaśatru** taught **Gārgya Bālāki**;[126] **Pravāhaṇa Jaivali** instructed **Śvetaketu Āruṇeya**,[127] as well as **Śilaka Śālāvatya**[128] and **Caikitāyana Dālbhya**;[128] and **Aśvapati Kaikeya** taught Brahmins.[129] It has been deduced[130] from such passages that the Brahma doctrine was a product of the Kṣatriyas. This conclusion is, however, entirely doubtful,[131] for kings were naturally willing to be flattered by the ascription to them of philosophic activity, and elsewhere[132] the opinion of a Rājanya is treated with contempt.

It is probably a fair deduction that the royal caste did not much concern itself with the sacred lore of the priests, though it is not unlikely that individual exceptions occurred. But that warriors became priests, that an actual change of caste took place, is quite unproved by a single genuine example. That it was impossible we cannot say, but it seems not to have taken place. To be distinguished from a caste change, as Fick[133] points out, is the fact that a member of any caste could, in the later period at least, become a Śramaṇa, as is recorded in effect

[123] vii. 27 *et seq.*

[124] Zimmer, *op. cit.*, 196.

[125] xi. 6, 2, 10; Muir, 1^2, 426-430.

[126] Bṛhadāraṇyaka Upaniṣad, ii. 1, 1; Kauṣītaki Upaniṣad, iv. 1.

[127] Bṛhadāraṇyaka Upaniṣad, vi. 1, 1 (Mādhyaṃdina = vi. 2, 1 Kāṇva); Chāndogya Upaniṣad, v. 3, 1.

[128] Chāndogya Upaniṣad, i. 8, 1.

[129] Śatapatha Brāhmaṇa, x. 6, 1, 2.

[130] Deussen, *Allgemeine Geschichte der Philosophie*, 1, 2, 354; *Philosophy of the Upanishads*, 17 *et seq.*; Garbe, *Beiträge zur indischen Kulturgeschichte*, 1 *et seq.*; *Philosophy of Ancient India*, 73 *et seq.*; Grierson, *Journal of the Royal Asiatic Society*, 1908, 602 *et seq.*; Winternitz, *Geschichte der indischen Litteratur*, 1, 256 *et seq.*

[131] Bloomfield, *Religion of the Veda*, 218 *et seq.*; Keith, *Journal of the Royal Asiatic Society*, 1908, 838, 868, 1142; *Aitareya Āraṇyaka*, 50, 51, 257; Oldenberg, *Buddha*,[5] 73, n. 1.

[132] Śatapatha Brāhmaṇa, viii. 1, 4, 10.

[133] *Op. cit.*, 44, n. 1.

of many kings in the Epic.[134] Whether the practice is Vedic is not clear: Yāska[135] records it of Devāpi, but this is not evidence for times much anterior to the rise of Buddhism.

On the other hand, the Brahmins, or at least the Purohitas, accompanied the princes in battle, and probably, like the mediæval clergy, were not unprepared to fight,[136] as Vasiṣṭha and Viśvāmitra seem to have done, and as priests do even in the Epic from time to time.[137] But a priest cannot be said to change caste by acting in this way.

More generally the possibility of the occurrence of change of caste may be seen in the Śatapatha Brāhmaṇa,[138] where **Śyāparṇa Sāyakāyana** is represented as speaking of his offspring as if they could have become the nobles, priests, and commons of the Śalvas; and in the Aitareya Brāhmaṇa,[139] where Viśvantara is told that if the wrong offering were made his children would be of the three other castes. A drunken Ṛṣi of the Rigveda[140] talks as if he could be converted into a king. On the other hand, certain kings, such as **Para Āṭṇāra**, are spoken of as performers of Sattras, 'sacrificial sessions.'[141] As evidence for caste exchange all this amounts to little; later a Brahmin might become a king, while the Ṛṣi in the Rigveda is represented as speaking in a state of intoxication; the great kings could be called sacrificers if, for the nonce, they were consecrated (*dīkṣita*), and so temporarily became Brahmins.[142] The hypothetical passages, too, do not help much. It would be unwise to deny the possibility of caste exchange, but it is not clearly indicated by any record. Even cases like that of Satyakāma Jābāla do not go far; for *ex hypothesi* that teacher

134 Hopkins, *Journal of the American Oriental Society*, 13, 179 *et seq.*, who treats this as a change of caste.

135 Nirukta, ii. 10. He went to the forest and practised asceticism, which is not necessarily a change of caste.

136 See Rv. iii. 53, 12. 13; i. 129, 4; 152, 7; 157, 2; vii. 83, 4; x. 38; 103, etc; Ludwig, Translation of the Rigveda, 3, 220-226; Geldner, *Vedische Studien*, 2, 135, n. 3.

137 Hopkins, *op. cit.*, 13, 184.

138 x. 4, 1, 10.

139 vii. 29.

140 iii. 43, 5.

141 Pañcaviṃśa Brāhmaṇa, xxv. 16, 3. *Cf.* for their share in the piling of the sacrificial altar, Taittirīya Saṃhitā, v. 6, 5, 3; Kāṭhaka Saṃhitā, xxii. 3 (*Indische Studien*, 3, 473); Weber, *op. cit.*, 10, 25.

142 Śatapatha Brāhmaṇa, xiii. 4, 1, 13; Weber, *op. cit.*, 10, 17, and *cf.* the case of Janaka, Śatapatha Brāhmaṇa, xi. 6, 2, 1 *et seq.*

did not know who his father was, and the latter could quite well have been a Brahmin.

It may therefore be held that the priests and the nobles practised hereditary occupations, and that either class was a closed body into which a man must be born. These two Varṇas may thus be fairly regarded as castes. The Vaiśyas offer more difficulty, for they practised a great variety of occupations (see **Vaiśya**). Fick[143] concludes that there is no exact sense in which they can be called a caste, since, in the Buddhist literature, they were divided into various groups, which themselves practised endogamy such as the *gahapatis*, or smaller landowners, the *setthis*, or large merchants and members of the various guilds, while there are clear traces[144] in the legal textbooks of a view that Brāhmaṇa and Kṣatriya stand opposed to all the other members of the community. But we need hardly accept this view for Vedic times, when the Vaiśya, the ordinary freeman of the tribe, formed a class or caste in all probability, which was severed by its free status from the Śūdras, and which was severed by its lack of priestly or noble blood from the two higher classes in the state. It is probably legitimate to hold that any Vaiśya could marry any member of the caste, and that the later divisions within the category of Vaiśyas are growths of divisions parallel with the original process by which priest and noble had grown into separate entities. The process can be seen to-day when new tribes fall under the caste system: each class tries to elevate itself in the social scale by refusing to intermarry with inferior classes on equal terms—hypergamy is often allowed—and so those Vaiśyas who acquired wealth in trade (**Śreṣṭhin**) or agriculture (the Pāli Gahapatis) would become distinct, as sub-castes, from the ordinary Vaiśyas. But it is not legitimate to regard Vaiśya as a theoretic caste; rather it is an old caste which is in process of dividing into innumerable sub-castes under influences of occupation, religion, or geographical situation.

Fick[145] denies also that the Śūdras ever formed a single

[143] *Op. cit.*, 19 *et seq.*; 162 *et seq.*

[144] Hopkins, *The Mutual Relations of the Four Castes according to the Mānavadharmaśāstram*, 78, 82 *et seq.*

[145] *Op. cit.*, 202 *et seq.*

caste: he regards the term as covering the numerous inferior races and tribes defeated by the Āryan invaders, but originally as denoting only one special tribe. It is reasonable to suppose that Śūdra was the name given by the Vedic Indians to the nations opposing them, and that these ranked as slaves beside the three castes—nobles, priests, and people—just as in the Anglo-Saxon and early German constitution beside the priests, the *nobiles* or eorls, and the *ingenui*, ordinary freemen or ceorls, there was a distinct class of slaves proper; the use of a generic expression to cover them seems natural, whatever its origin (see **Śūdra**). In the Āryan view a marriage of Śūdras could hardly be regulated by rules; any Śūdra could wed another, if such a marriage could be called a marriage at all, for a slave cannot in early law be deemed to be capable of marriage proper. But what applied in the early Vedic period became no doubt less and less applicable later when many aboriginal tribes and princes must have come into the Āryan community by peaceful means, or by conquest, without loss of personal liberty, and when the term Śūdra would cover many sorts of people who were not really slaves, but were freemen of a humble character occupied in such functions as supplying the numerous needs of the village, like the **Caṇḍālas**, or tribes living under Āryan control, or independent, such as the **Niṣādas.**

But it is also probable that the Śūdras came to include men of Āryan race, and that the Vedic period saw the degradation of Āryans to a lower social status. This seems, at any rate, to have been the case with the **Rathakāras.** In the Taittirīya Brāhmaṇa[146] the Rathakāra is placed as a special class along with the Brāhmaṇas, Rājanyas, and Vaiśyas: this can hardly be interpreted except to mean that the Rathakāras were not included in the Āryan classes, though it is just possible that only a subdivision of the Vaiśyas is meant. There is other evidence[147] that the Rathakāras were regarded as Śūdras. But in the Atharvaveda[148] the Rathakāras and the **Karmāras** appear in a position of importance in connexion with the

146 i. 1, 4, 8.

147 *Cf.* Kātyāyana Śrauta Sūtra, i. 1, 9, with the scholiast; iv. 7, 7; 9, 5; Weber, *op. cit.*, 10, 12, 13.

148 Av. iv. 5, 6. That the words *karmāra* and *rathakāra* are here appellatives, as Weber, *op. cit.*, 17, 198, suggests, is quite impossible.

selection of the king; these two classes are also referred to in an honourable way in the Vājasaneyi Saṃhitā;[149] in the Śatapatha Brāhmaṇa,[150] too, the Rathakāra is mentioned as a a person of high standing. It is impossible to accept the view suggested by Fick[151] that these classes were originally non-Āryan; we must recognize that the Rathakāras, in early Vedic times esteemed for their skill, later became degraded because of the growth of the feeling that manual labour was not dignified. The development of this idea was a departure from the Āryan conception; it is not unnatural, however undesirable, and has a faint parallel in the class distinctions of modern Europe. Similarly, the Karmāra, the **Takṣan,**[152] the Carmamna, or 'tanner,' the weaver and others, quite dignified occupations in the Rigveda, are reckoned as Śūdras in the Pāli texts.[153]

The later theory, which appears fully developed in the Dharma Sūtras,[154] deduces the several castes other than the original four from the intermarriage of the several castes. This theory has no justification in the early Vedic literature. In some cases it is obviously wrong; for example, the **Sūta** is said to be a caste of this kind, whereas it is perfectly clear that if the Sūtas did form a caste, it was one ultimately due to occupation. But there is no evidence at all that the Sūtas, Grāmaṇīs, and other members of occupations were real castes in the sense that they were endogamic in the early Vedic period. All that we can say is that there was a steady progress by which caste after caste was formed, occupation being an important determining feature, just as in modern times there are castes bearing names like Gopāla ('cowherd') Kaivarta or Dhīvara ('fisherman'), and Vaṇij ('merchant').[155]

[149] xxx. 6. 7. *Cf.* xiv. 27; Taittirīya Brāhmaṇa, iii. 4, 2, 1 (Rathakāra); 3, 1 (Karmāra).

[150] xiii. 4, 2, 17.

[151] *Op. cit.*, 209, 210.

[152] The name is applied to Bṛbu (Rv. vi. 45, 31) in the Śāṅkhāyana Śrauta Sūtra, xvi. 11, 11. According to Brunnhofer, *Iran und Turan*, 127, the name is a people's name, but this is very unlikely. See Hillebrandt, *Vedische Mythologie*, 1, 107.

[153] Fick, *op. cit.*, 160, 210.

[154] Gautama Dharma Sūtra, iv; Vāsiṣṭha Dharma Sūtra, xviii; Baudhāyana Dharma Sūtra, i. 16. 17.

[155] *Cf.* Jolly, *Zeitschrift der Deutschen Morgenländischen Gesellschaft*, 50, 507 *et seq.*; Bühler, *Sacred Books of the East*, 14, xxxviii, xxxix.

Fick[156] finds in the Jātakas mention of a number of occupations whose members did not form part of any caste at all, such as the attendants on the court, the actors and dancers who went from village to village, and the wild tribes that lived in the mountains, fishermen, hunters, and so on. In Vedic times these people presumably fell under the conception of Śūdra, and may have included the **Parṇaka, Paulkasa, Bainda,** who are mentioned with many others in the Vājasaneyi Saṃhitā and the Taittirīya Brāhmaṇa in the list of victims at the Puruṣamedha ('human sacrifice'). The slaves also, whom Fick[157] includes in the same category, were certainly included in the term Śūdra.

5. *Origin of the Castes.*—The question of the origin of the castes presents some difficulty. The ultimate cause of the extreme rigidity of the caste system, as compared with the features of any other Āryan society, must probably be sought in the sharp distinction drawn from the beginning between the Āryan and the Śūdra. The contrast which the Vedic Indians felt as existing between themselves and the conquered population, and which probably rested originally on the difference of colour between the upper and the lower classes, tended to accentuate the natural distinctions of birth, occupation, and locality which normally existed among the Āryan Indians, but which among other Āryan peoples never developed into a caste system like that of India. The doctrine of hypergamy which marks the practical working of the caste system, seems clearly to point to the feeling that the Āryan could marry the Śūdrā, but not the Śūdra the Āryā. This distinction probably lies at the back of all other divisions: its force may be illustrated by the peculiar state of feeling as to mixed marriages, for example, in the Southern States of America and in South Africa, or even in India itself, between the new invaders from Europe and the mingled population which now peoples the country. Marriages between persons of the white and the dark race are disapproved in principle, but varying degrees of condemnation attach to (1) the marriage of a man of the white race with a woman of the dark race;

[156] *Op. cit.*, 184 *et seq.*

[157] *Ibid.*, 197 *et seq.*

(2) an informal connexion between these two; (3) a marriage between a woman of the white race and a man of the dark race; and (4) an informal connexion between these two. Each category, on the whole, is subject to more severe reprobation than the preceding one. This race element, it would seem, is what has converted social divisions into castes. There appears, then, to be a large element of truth in the theory, best represented by Risley,[158] which explains caste in the main as a matter of blood, and which holds that the higher the caste is, the greater is the proportion of Āryan blood.

The chief rival theory is undoubtedly that of Senart,[159] which places the greatest stress on the Āryan constitution of the family. According to Senart the Āryan people practised in affairs of marriage both a rule of exogamy, and one of endogamy. A man must marry a woman of equal birth, but not one of the same *gens*, according to Roman law as interpreted by Senart and Kovalevsky;[160] and an Athenian must marry an Athenian woman, but not one of the same *γένος*. In India these rules are reproduced in the form that one must not marry within the **Gotra**, but not without the caste. The theory, though attractively developed, is not convincing; the Latin and Greek parallels are not even probably accurate;[161] and in India the rule forbidding marriage within the Gotra is one which grows in strictness as the evidence grows later in date.[162]

On the other hand, it is not necessary to deny that the development of caste may have been helped by the family traditions of some *gentes*, or *γένη*, or Gotras. The Patricians of Rome for a long time declined intermarriage with the plebeians; the Athenian Eupatridai seem to have kept their *γένη* pure from contamination by union with lower blood; and there may well have been noble families among the Vedic Indians who intermarried only among themselves. The

158 Best stated and summed up in *The Peoples of India*. See also the summary in *The Indian Empire*, 1, chap. 6.

159 *Les Castes dans l'Inde*.

160 *Famille et Propriété Primitives*, 19, *et seq*. *Cf*. L. de la Vallée Poussin, *Le Védisme*, 15 *et seq*., with *Le Brahmanisme*, 7.

161 Keith, *Journal of the Royal Asiatic Society*, 1909, 472.

162 Weber, *Indische Studien*, 10, 74 *et seq*.

Germans known to Tacitus[163] were divided into *nobiles* and *ingenui*, and the Anglo-Saxons into eorls and ceorls, noble and non-noble freemen.[164] The origin of nobility need not be sought in the Vedic period proper, for it may already have existed. It may have been due to the fact that the king, whom we must regard as originally elected by the people, was as king often in close relation with, or regarded as an incarnation of, the deity;[165] and that hereditary kingship would tend to increase the tradition of especially sacred blood: thus the royal family and its offshoots would be anxious to maintain the purity of their blood. In India, beside the sanctity of the king, there was the sanctity of the priest. Here we have in the family exclusiveness of king and nobles, and the similar exclusiveness of a priesthood which was not celibate, influences that make for caste, especially when accompanying the deep opposition between the general folk and the servile aborigines.

Caste, once created, naturally developed in different directions. Nesfield[166] was inclined to see in occupation the one ground of caste. It is hardly necessary seriously to criticize this view considered as an ultimate explanation of caste, but it is perfectly certain that gilds of workers tend to become castes. The carpenters (**Takṣan**), the chariot-makers (**Rathakāra**), the fishermen (**Dhaivara**) and others are clearly of the type of caste, and the number extends itself as time goes on. But this is not to say that caste is founded on occupation pure and simple in its first origin, or that mere difference of occupation would have produced the system of caste without the interposition of the fundamental difference between Āryan and Dāsa or Śūdra blood and colour. This difference rendered increasingly important what the history of the Āryan peoples shows us to be declining, the distinction between the noble and the non-noble

163 *Germania*, 7. 13, etc.

164 Medley, *English Constitutional History*,[2] 21 *et seq.*, and authorities there cited. In the formation of a kingdom minor chiefs, once petty kings, would become nobles.

165 *E.g.*, Frazer, *Early History of the Kingship* and *The Golden Bough* (ed. 3), Part I., *The Magic Art and the Evolution of Kings*. The traces of this conception in Āryan peoples are clear—*e.g.*, the *rex sacrificulus* in Rome, the sacred functions of the Archon Basileus in Athens; *cf.* Ridgway, *Origin of Tragedy*, p. 29.

166 *Brief View of the Caste System of the North-Western Provinces and Oudh*, Allahabad, 1885

freemen, a distinction not of course ultimate, but one which seems to have been developed in the Āryan people before the separation of its various branches.

It is well known that the Iranian polity presents a division of classes comparable in some respects[167] with the Indian polity. The priests (Athravas) and warriors (Rathaesthas) are unmistakably parallel, and the two lower classes seem to correspond closely to the Pāli Gahapatis, and perhaps to the Śūdras.[168] But they are certainly not castes in the Indian sense of the word. There is no probability in the view of Senart[169] or of Risley[170] that the names of the old classes were later superimposed artificially on a system of castes that were different from them in origin. We cannot say that the castes existed before the classes, and that the classes were borrowed by India from Iran, as Risley maintains, ignoring the early Brāhmaṇa evidence for the four Varṇas, and treating the transfer as late. Nor can we say with Senart that the castes and classes are of independent origin. If there had been no Varṇa, caste might never have arisen; both colour and class occupation are needed for a plausible account of the rise of caste.[171]

[167] Ludwig, Translation of the Rigveda, 3, 243. 244.

[168] Senart, *op. cit.*, 141.

[169] *Ibid.* 140.

[170] *Indian Empire*, 1, 336-348.

[171] The Indian theories of the origin of caste are merely religious or philosophical, and have no value. See for them, Rv. x. 90 (which is repeated in other Saṃhitās); Taittirīya Saṃhitā, vii. 1, 1, 4 *et seq.*; *ibid.*, iv. 3, 10, 1-3 = Kāṭhaka Saṃhitā, xvii. 5 = Vājasaneyi Saṃhitā, xiv. 28-30; Śatapatha Brāhmaṇa, viii. 4, 3, 1 *et seq.* For the origin of the Brahmins, see Av. iv. 6, 1; xv. 9, 1; of the Rājanya, Av. xv. 8, 1; Taittirīya Saṃhitā, ii. 4, 13, 1 *et seq.*; Muir, 1², 8 *et seq.*; Zimmer, *op. cit.*, 217-220.

The most important collection of texts on caste are those of Muir, *Sanskrit Texts*, 1², and of Weber, *Indische Studien*, 10, where practically all the data of the Brāhmaṇas are extracted; there have to be added only the data of the Maitrāyaṇī Saṃhitā, which are merely confirmatory of those of the Taittirīya and Kāṭhaka Saṃhitās. The Epic materials concerning caste are given by Hopkins, *Journal of the American Oriental Society*, 13, who has also analyzed the caste relations of the Mānavadharmaśāstra in *The Mutual Relation of the Four Castes according to the Mānavadharmaśāstram*. *Cf.* also Ludwig, Translation of the Rigveda, 3, 212 *et seq.*; Zimmer, *Altindisches Leben*, 185 *et seq.*; Senart, *Les Castes dans l'Inde;* Barth, *Revue de l'Histoire des Religions*, 1894, 75 *et seq.*; Jolly, *Zeitschrift der Deutschen Morgenländischen Gesellschaft*, 50, 507 *et seq.*; Oldenberg, *ibid.*, 51, 267-290, a valuable criticism of Senart's views; von Schroeder, *Indiens Literatur und Cultur*, 152 *et seq.*; 425 *et seq.*; Schlagintweit, *Zeitschrift der Deutschen Morgenländischen Gesellschaft*,

33, 549; Shridhar V. Katkar, *History of Caste in India.* The Jātaka evidence is all collected by Fick, *Die sociale Gliederung im nordöstlichen Indien zu Buddha's Zeit* (1897); its value is considerable, but its date is extremely doubtful, and it certainly cannot be regarded as really contemporary with Buddha (fifth century B.C.). The Dharma Sūtras also give full details, but their date likewise is uncertain.

Varta. See **Vartra.**

Vartani as a part of a chariot seems to denote the 'felly' in the Rigveda[1] and later.[2]

[1] i. 53, 8; vii. 69, 3; viii. 63, 8.
[2] Aitareya Brāhmaṇa, v. 33, 2; as part of the sacrificial Soma vehicle, Taittirīya Saṃhitā, vi. 4, 9, 5; Ṣaḍviṃśa Brāhmaṇa, i. 5, etc.

Vartikā, a 'quail,' is mentioned in the Rigveda[1] as having been saved by the Aśvins from a wolf's jaws. It is also included in the list of victims at the Aśvamedha ('horse sacrifice') in the Yajurvedas.[2]

[1] i. 112, 18; 116, 4; 117, 16; 118, 8; x. 39, 13.
[2] Taittirīya Saṃhitā, v. 5, 11, 1; Vājasaneyi Saṃhitā, xxiv. 20. 30; Maitrāyaṇī Saṃhitā, iii. 14, 1.
As to the form of the word, *cf.* Vārttika on Pāṇini, vii. 3, 45 where it is said to be 'northern,' as opposed to the eastern Vartakā. *Cf.* also Weber, *Indische Studien*, 5, 45, n.; Zimmer, *Altindisches Leben*, 90.

Vartra in the Atharvaveda[1] and the Taittirīya Brāhmaṇa[2] denote the 'dam' of a tank. In the former passage the commentator and some manuscripts have Varta.[3]

[1] i. 3, 7.
[2] i. 6, 8, 1.
[3] Whitney, Translation of the Atharvaveda, 4.

Vardhra denotes a 'thong' or 'strap' with which a woven couch is fastened. It is mentioned in the Atharvaveda[1] and the Śatapatha Brāhmaṇa.[2]

[1] xiv. 1, 60, where the Paippalāda recension has *varadhrā*.
[2] v. 4, 4, 1.

Varman denotes 'body armour,' 'coat of mail,' 'corselet,' in the Rigveda[1] and later.[2] Of what material it was made is

[1] i. 31, 15; 140, 10; vi. 75, 1. 8. 18. 19; viii. 47, 8; x. 107, 7, etc.
[2] Atharvaveda, viii. 5, 7 *et seq.*; ix. 5, 26; xvii. 1, 27, etc.

uncertain; there are references to sewing (*syūta*)[3] which may be reckoned in favour of the use of linen corselets such as those recorded by Herodotus,[4] but there is a later reference[5] to corselets of **Ayas, Loha, or Rajata**, on which it is doubtful whether much stress can be laid. They may, however, have been either of metal or of leather covered with metal.

[3] Rv. i. 31, 15; x. 101, 8.
[4] *Cf.* Hehn, *Kulturpflanzen*,[6] 167 *et seq.*; Lang, *Homer and his Age*, 150 *et seq.*
[5] Jaiminīya Upaniṣad Brāhmaṇa, iv. 1, 3.
Cf. Zimmer, *Altindisches Leben*, 298; Schrader, *Prehistoric Antiquities*, 222; von Schroeder, *Indiens Literatur und Cultur*, 34.

Varṣa denotes primarily 'rain,'[1] then 'rainy season'[2] and 'year.'[3]

[1] Neuter: Rv. v. 58, 7; 83, 10; Av. iii. 27, 6; iv. 15, 2, etc.
[2] Feminine plural: Av. vi. 55, 2; Taittirīya Saṃhitā, i. 6, 2, 3; ii. 6, 1, 1; v. 6, 10, 1; Vājasaneyi Saṃhitā, x. 12, etc.
[3] Aitareya Brāhmaṇa, iv. 17, 5; Śatapatha Brāhmaṇa, i. 9, 3, 19, etc.

Valaga in the Atharvaveda[1] and later[2] seems to denote a 'secret spell.'

[1] v. 31, 4; x. 1, 18; xix. 9, 9.
[2] Taittirīya Saṃhitā, i. 3, 2, 1 (where see Sāyaṇa's note); vi. 2, 11, 1. 2; Kāṭhaka Saṃhitā, ii. 11; xxv. 9; Vājasaneyi Saṃhitā, v. 23; Śatapatha Brāhmaṇa, iii. 5, 4, 2.

Valka in the later Saṃhitās and the Brāhmaṇas[1] denotes 'bark' of a tree.

[1] Taittirīya Saṃhitā, ii. 5, 3, 5; iii. 7, 4, 2; Taittirīya Brāhmaṇa, i. 4, 7. 6.

Valmīka denotes an 'ant-hill' in the later Saṃhitās[1] and the Brāhmaṇas.[2]

[1] Taittirīya Saṃhitā, i. 1, 3, 4; Kāṭhaka Saṃhitā, xix. 2; xxxi. 12; xxxv. 19; Vājasaneyi Saṃhitā, xxv. 8.
[2] Śatapatha Brāhmaṇa, ii. 6, 2, 17; Bṛhadāraṇyaka Upaniṣad, iv. 4, 10; Taittirīya Brāhmaṇa, i. 1, 3, 4.

Valśa denotes 'twig,'[1] usually in the compounds *śata-valśa*, 'having a hundred twigs,'[2] or *sahasra-valśa*, 'having a thousand twigs,'[3] which is applied metaphorically of 'offspring.'[4]

[1] Taittirīya Saṃhitā, vii. 3, 9, 1.
[2] Rv. iii. 8, 11; Av. vi. 30, 2, etc.
[3] Rv. iii. 8, 11; vii. 33, 9, etc.
[4] Taittirīya Saṃhitā, i. 3, 5, 1; Kāṭhaka Saṃhitā, iii. 2, etc.

1. **Vaśa Aśvya** is the name in the Rigveda[1] of a protégé of the Aśvins. He is also mentioned in the Śāṅkhāyana Śrauta Sūtra[2] as having received bounty from **Pṛthuśravas Kānīta.** He is the reputed author of a Rigvedic hymn,[3] which is repeatedly referred to by his name Vaśa.[4] *Cf.* also **Vyaśva.**

[1] i. 112, 10; 116, 21; viii. 8, 20; 24, 14; 46, 21. 23; 50, 9; x. 40, 7.
[2] xvi. 11, 13.
[3] viii. 46.
[4] Śatapatha Brāhmaṇa, viii. 6, 2, 3; ix. 3, 3, 19; Aitareya Āraṇyaka, i. 5, 1. 2; Śāṅkhāyana Āraṇyaka, ii. 10. 11.

Cf. Weber, *Episches im vedischen Ritual*, 38, 39.

2. **Vaśa,** plur., is the name of a tribe mentioned in the Aitareya Brāhmaṇa[1] as being in **Madhyadeśa** along with the **Kurus,** the **Pañcālas,** and the **Uśīnaras.** They are also connected with the **Matsyas** according to the Kauṣītaki Upaniṣad.[2] The Vaśas and Uśīnaras are spoken of as united in the Gopatha Brāhmaṇa:[3] the names[4] seem to indicate that the Vaśas and Uśīnaras were connected.

[1] viii. 14, 3.
[2] iv. 1 (reading *sa-Vaśa-Matsyeṣu* for the *savasan-Matsyeṣu* of the manuscripts, which is otherwise emended to *Satvan-Matsyeṣu*, Keith, *Śāṅkhāyana Āraṇyaka*, 36, n. 2; *Journal of the Royal Asiatic Society*, 1908, 367).
[3] i. 2, 9, where the text has *Śava-sa-Uśīnareṣu*, which is nonsense. *Cf.* *Sa-Vaśa-Uśīnarāṇām* in Aitareya Brāhmaṇa, viii. 14, 3, and n. 2.
[4] As both derived from the root *vaś*, 'desire.'

Cf. Oldenberg, *Buddha*, 393, n.; 407, n.

Vaśā denotes 'cow' in the Rigveda[1] and later.[2] According to the commentators, the word means a 'barren cow,' but this is not a necessary sense except in a few passages.[3]

[1] ii. 7, 5; vi. 63, 9; x. 91, 14, etc.
[2] Av. iv. 24, 4; x. 10, 2; xii. 4, 1, etc.; Taittirīya Saṃhitā, ii. 1, 4, 4. 5; iii. 4, 2, 2; Kāṭhaka Saṃhitā, xiii. 4, etc.
[3] Av. vii. 113, 2, where the **Parivṛktā**, 'rejected wife,' is compared with a Vaśā. In xii. 4 (where *vaśā* alternates with *go*) there is no indication that Vaśā means a barren cow, except perhaps in verse 16, on which *cf.* Bloomfield, *Hymns of the Atharvaveda*, 656, 658. The Brahmins there claim as their own a barren cow. A *sūta-vaśā—i.e.*, a cow barren after once calving—is mentioned in the Taittirīya Saṃhitā, ii. 1, 5, 4, etc. In the Taittirīya Saṃhitā, ii. 1, 2, 2, and the Taittirīya Brāhmaṇa, i. 2, 5, 2, used with **Avi**, Sūtā denotes a 'mother sheep,' 'ewe.'

Vasati denotes in the Rigveda[1] and later[2] 'abode,' 'house.'

[1] i. 31, 15; v. 2, 6.
[2] Vājasaneyi Saṃhitā, xviii. 15; Taittirīya Brāhmaṇa, ii. 3, 5, 4; iii. 7, 3, 3, etc.

Vasana in the Rigveda[1] and later[2] denotes 'dress.'

[1] i. 95, 7.
[2] Chāndogya Upaniṣad, viii. 8, 5; Kauṣītaki Upaniṣad, ii. 15; Nirukta, viii. 9, etc.

Vasanta, 'spring,' is mentioned in the Rigveda[1] and later.[2] It is regularly identified with the first of the months. See **Ṛtu.**

[1] x. 90, 6; 161, 4.
[2] Av. vi. 55, 2; viii. 2, 22; xii. 1, 36, etc.

Vasāvi in one passage of the Rigveda[1] denotes, according to Roth,[2] a 'treasure house.'

[1] x. 73, 4.
[2] St. Petersburg Dictionary, *s.v.*

Vasiṣṭha is the name of one of the most prominent priestly figures of Vedic tradition. The seventh Maṇḍala of the Rigveda is ascribed to him; this ascription is borne out by the fact that the Vasiṣṭhas[1] and Vasiṣṭha[2] are frequently mentioned in that Maṇḍala, besides being sometimes referred to elsewhere. That by the name Vasiṣṭha a definite individual is always meant is most improbable, as Oldenberg[3] shows; Vasiṣṭha must normally mean simply 'a Vasiṣṭha.' But it is not necessary to deny that a real Vasiṣṭha existed, for one hymn[4] seems to show clear traces of his authorship, and of his assistance to **Sudās** against the ten kings.

The most important feature of Vasiṣṭha's life was apparently

[1] Rv. vii. 7, 7; 12, 3; 23, 6; 33, 1 *et seq.*; 37, 4; 39, 7; 40, 7; 76, 6. 7; 77, 6; 80, 1; 90, 7; 91, 7; x. 15, 8; 66, 14; 122, 8.

[2] Rv. vii. 9, 6; 13, 4. 21; 22, 3; 23, 1; 26, 5; 33, 11 *et seq.*; 42, 6; 59, 3; 70, 6; 73, 3; 86, 5; 88, 1; 95, 6; 96, 1; x. 65, 15; 150, 5; i. 112, 9.

[3] *Zeitschrift der Deutschen Morgenländischen Gesellschaft*, 42, 204 *et seq.* *Cf.* vii. 23, 1 (singular) with verse 6 (plural).

[4] Rv. vii. 18. As to vii. 33, Oldenberg and Geldner differ. See *Vedische Studien*, 2, 130. But it is rather doubtful whether it can possibly be said to be as early as vii. 18, or to have any claim to be really an utterance of Vasiṣṭha.

his hostility to **Viśvāmitra.** The latter was certainly[5] at one time the **Purohita** ("domestic priest") of Sudās, but he seems to have been deposed from that post, to have joined Sudās' enemies, and to have taken part in the onslaught of the kings against him, for the hymn of Sudās' triumph[4] has clear references to the ruin Viśvāmitra brought on his allies.[6] Oldenberg,[7] however, holds that the strife of Viśvāmitra and Vasiṣṭha is not to be found in the Rigveda. On the other hand, Geldner[8] is hardly right in finding in the Rigveda[9] a compressed account indicating the rivalry of **Śakti,** Vasiṣṭha's son, with Viśvāmitra, the acquisition by Viśvāmitra of special skill in speech, and the revenge of Viśvāmitra, who secured the death of Śakti by Sudās' servants, an account which is more fully related by Ṣaḍguruśiṣya,[10] which appeared in the Śāṭyāyanaka,[11] and to which reference seems to be made in the brief notices of the Taittirīya Saṃhitā[12] and the Pañcaviṃśa Brāhmaṇa[13] regarding Vasiṣṭha's sons having been slain, and his overcoming the Saudāsas. But it is important to note that no mention is made in these authorities of Sudās himself being actually opposed to Vasiṣṭha, while in the Aitareya Brāhmaṇa[14] Vasiṣṭha appears as the Purohita and consecrator of Sudās Paijavana. Yāska[15] recognizes Viśvāmitra as the Purohita of Sudās; this accords with what seems to have been the fact

[5] See Rv. iii. 33. 53; Muir, *Sanskrit Texts*, 1², 328 *et seq.*

[6] Hopkins, *Journal of the American Oriental Society*, 15, 260 *et seq.*

[7] *Op. cit.*, 204, n. 3.

[8] *Op. cit.*, 2, 158 *et seq.*

[9] iii. 53. 15. 16. 21-24, the last four verses being the famous *Vasiṣṭha-dveṣiṇyaḥ*, which Durga, the commentator on the Nirukta, declines to explain, because he was a Kāpiṣṭhala Vāsiṣṭha (see Muir, *op. cit.*, 1², 344; Bṛhaddevatā, iv. 117 *et seq.*, with Macdonell's notes). What the verses really mean is not at all certain. See Oldenberg, *Ṛgveda-Noten*, 1, 254 *et seq.*

[10] *Cf.* Sāyaṇa on Rv. vii. 32, and Macdonell's edition of the Sarvānukramaṇī, 107; Weber, *Indische Studien*, 1, 119.

[11] See the note in the Anukramaṇī on vii. 32, where both the Tāṇḍaka and the Śāṭyāyanaka are quoted (Muir, *op. cit.*, 1², 328).

[12] vii. 4, 7. 1. In iii. 1, 7. 3; v. 4, 11, 3, also Vasiṣṭha is a foe of Viśvāmitra.

[13] iv. 7, 3; viii. 2, 3; xix. 3, 8; xxi. 11, 2. The story is alluded to in the Kauṣītaki Brāhmaṇa, iv. 8, and in the Jaiminīya Brāhmaṇa, i. 150; iii. 26. 83. 149. 204. In ii. 390 it is definitely stated, as in the Śāṭyāyanaka (n. 10), that Śakti was cast into the fire by the Saudāsas.

[14] vii. 34. 9; viii. 21, 11. *Cf.* Śāṅkhāyana Śrauta Sūtra, xvi. 11, 14.

[15] Nirukta, ii. 24; Śāṅkhāyana Śrauta Sūtra, xxvi. 12, 13.

that Viśvāmitra originally held the post. Probably, however, with the disappearance of Sudās, Viśvāmitra recovered his position, whereupon Vasiṣṭha in revenge for the murder of his sons secured in some way unspecified the defeat of the Saudāsas.[16]

At any rate it is hardly necessary to suppose that the enmity of the Saudāsas and Vasiṣṭhas was permanent. There is evidence[17] that the Bharatas had the Vasiṣṭhas as Purohitas, while other versions[18] regard them as Purohitas for people (*prajāḥ*) generally. It seems that the Vasiṣṭhas were pioneers in adopting the rule that Purohitas should act as Brahman priest[19] at the sacrifice: the Śatapatha Brāhmaṇa[20] states that the Vasiṣṭhas were once the only priests to act as Brahmans, but that later any priest could serve as such.[21] A rivalry with Jamadgni and Viśvāmitra is reported in the Taittirīya Saṃhitā.[22] Parāśara and Śatayātu are associated with Vasiṣṭha in the Rigveda,[23] being apparently, as Geldner[24] thinks, the grandson and a son of Vasiṣṭha. According to Pischel,[25] in another hymn,[26] Vasiṣṭha appears as attempting to steal the goods of his father Varuṇa; Geldner[27] also shows that the Rigveda[28] contains a clear reference to Vasiṣṭha's being a son of Varuṇa and the nymph Urvaśī. Perhaps this explains the fact that the Vasiṣṭhas are called the **Tṛtsus** in one passage

[16] Roth, *Zur Litteratur und Geschichte des Weda*, 121 *et seq.*, considered that the Vasiṣṭhas were finally successful in the effort to remove the Viśvāmitras from favour. Weber, *Indische Studien*, 1, 120; *Episches im vedischen Ritual*, 34, doubted this, and Muir, *op. cit.*, 1², 371-375, held the problem to be insoluble. Roth and Muir, however, both complicated the question by regarding the Bharatas as enemies of the Tṛtsus, which (see **Tṛtsu**) is not at all probable, though it is still the view of Bloomfield, *Journal of the American Oriental Society*, 16, 41, 42.

[17] Pañcaviṃśa Brāhmaṇa, xv. 4, 24; Weber, *Indische Studien*, 10, 34.

[18] Taittirīya Saṃhitā, iii. 5, 2, 1; Kāṭhaka Saṃhitā, xxxvii. 17.

[19] Vasiṣṭha was Brahman at the sacrifice of **Śunaḥśepa**, Aitareya Brāhmaṇa, vii. 16; Śāṅkhāyana Srauta Sūtra, xv. 21, 4.

[20] xii. 6, 1, 41. *Cf.* iv. 6, 6, 5.

[21] Ṣaḍviṃśa Brāhmaṇa, i. 5; Weber, *Indische Studien*, 10, 35.

[22] iii. 1, 7, 3. *Cf.* n. 11.

[23] vii. 18, 21.

[24] *Vedische Studien*, 2, 132.

[25] *Vedische Studien*, 2, 55 *et seq.*

[26] vii. 55. Aufrecht, *Indische Studien*, 4, 337, took the hymn to refer to a lover's visit to a maiden. *Cf.* Lanman, *Sanskrit Reader*, 370; Bṛhaddevatā, vi. 11, with Macdonell's notes.

[27] *Vedische Studien*, 2, 138. So also Nirukta, v. 13; Muir, *Sanskrit Texts*, 1², 231, n. 97; Bṛhaddevatā, v. 150. 151.

[28] vii. 33, 11.

of the Rigveda;[29] for being of miraculous parentage, Vasiṣṭha would need adoption into a Gotra, that of the princes whom he served, and to whom Agastya seems to have introduced him.

There are numerous other references to Vasiṣṭha as a Ṛṣi in Vedic literature,[30] in the Sūtras,[31] and in the Epic, where he and Viśvāmitra fight out their rivalry.[32]

[29] vii. 83, 8.

[30] Rv. i. 112, 9; vii. 88, 4; 96, 3; x. 95, 17; 181, 1; Kāṭhaka Saṃhitā, xvi. 19; xx. 9; xxxii. 2 (*Indische Studien*, 3, 478); Maitrāyaṇī Saṃhitā, i. 4, 12; ii. 7, 9; iv. 2, 9; Taittirīya Saṃhitā, v. 2, 10, 5; Av. iv. 29, 4; Aitareya Brāhmaṇa, vi. 18, 3; Kauṣītaki Brāhmaṇa, xxvi. 14; xxix. 2. 3; xxx. 3; Jaiminīya Upaniṣad Brāhmaṇa, iii. 3, 13; 15, 2; 18, 6; Aitareya Āraṇyaka, ii. 2, 2; Bṛhadāraṇyaka Upaniṣad, ii. 2, 4, etc.

[31] See Weber, *Indische Studien*, 10, 89-92; *Episches im vedischen Ritual*, 35.

[32] Muir, *Sanskrit Texts*, 1², 375-414. *Cf.* Ludwig, Translation of the Rigveda, 3, 131 *et seq.*; Weber, *Episches im vedischen Ritual*, 31-34; *Indian Literature*, 31, 37, 53, 79, 123, 162; Oldenberg, *Zeitschrift der Deutschen Morgenländischen Gesellschaft*, 42, 204-207.

Vasu in the Rigveda[1] and later[2] denotes 'wealth,' 'property.'

[1] iv. 17, 11. 13; 20, 8; vi. 55, 3; viii. 13, 22, etc.

[2] Av. vii. 115, 2; ix. 4, 3; x. 8, 20; xiv. 2, 8, etc.

Vasukra and his wife are the reputed composers of certain hymns of the Rigveda.[1] The ascription goes back to the Rigveda Āraṇyakas.[2]

[1] x. 27-29.

[2] Aitareya Āraṇyaka, i. 2, 2; Śāṅkhāyana Āraṇyaka, i. 3.

Vasu-rocis is a name occurring only once in the Rigveda[1] in a form which may be interpreted as either plural or singular. In the former alternative it denotes a family of singers;[2] in the latter a patron.[3]

[1] viii. 34, 16.

[2] Ludwig, Translation of the Rigveda, 3, 162.

[3] Griffith, *Hymns of the Rigveda*, 2, 175, n.

Vastu as a designation of time is the 'early morning' in the Rigveda.[1]

[1] i. 79, 6; 104, 1; 179, 1, etc. So Vājasaneyi Saṃhitā, xxviii. 12. *Cf.* Zimmer, *Altindisches Leben*, 361.

Vastra in the Rigveda[1] and later[2] denotes 'dress,' 'clothing.' See **Vāsas.**

[1] i. 26, 1; 134, 4; iii. 39, 2; v. 29, 15, etc.

[2] Av. v. 1, 3; ix. 5, 25; xii. 3, 21, etc.

Vasna in the Rigveda[1] and later[2] denotes the 'price' paid for anything or its 'value,' or the thing itself as an object of purchase, 'ware.'

[1] iv. 24, 9, where the phrase *bhūyasā vasnam acarat kanīyaḥ* must mean 'with a greater price he obtained a lesser value.' For the exact sense, *cf.* Oldenberg, *Ṛgveda-Noten*, 1, 419, 420.

[2] Av. xii. 2, 36 ('price') = Vājasaneyi Saṃhitā, iii. 49 = Taittirīya Saṃhitā, i. 8, 4, 1; Kāṭhaka Saṃhitā, ix. 5; Maitrāyaṇī Saṃhitā, i. 10, 2, where the sense seems to be 'let us barter food and drink like wares.' *Cf.* also *vasnikā*, 'worth a price,' in Pañcaviṃśa Brāhmaṇa, xiv. 3, 13.

Cf. Zimmer, *Altindisches Leben*, 247; Schrader, *Prehistoric Antiquities*, 382.

Vahatu is the regular name in the Rigveda[1] and later[2] for the ceremonial conducting of the bride from the house of her parents to that of her husband.

[1] i. 184, 3; iv. 58, 9; x. 17, 1 (= Av. iii. 31, 5); 32, 3; 85, 13 *et seq.*

[2] Av. x. 1, 1; xiv. 2, 9. 12. 66. 73; Aitareya Brāhmaṇa, iv. 7, 1; Taittirīya Brāhmaṇa, i. 5, 1, 2.

Vahni, 'carrier,' denotes any draught animal—*e.g.*, a 'horse,'[1] a 'goat,'[2] or an 'ox.'[3]

[1] Rv. ii. 24, 13; 37, 3; iii. 6, 2, etc.

[2] Rv. vi. 57, 3.

[3] Taittirīya Brāhmaṇa, i. 8, 2, 5, etc.

Vahya denotes in the Rigveda[1] and the Atharvaveda[2] a 'couch' or 'bed' of a comfortable kind used by women.

[1] vii. 55, 8.

[2] iv. 5, 3; 20, 3; xiv. 2, 30.

Cf. Zimmer, *Altindisches Leben*, 154.

Vāko-vākya, 'dialogue,' is the name given in the Brāhmaṇas[1] to certain portions of the Vedic texts. In one place[2] the **Brahmodya** is said to be a dialogue; very probably in all the passages the Brahmodya is meant by this term. Geldner's

[1] Śatapatha Brāhmaṇa, iv. 6, 9, 20; xi. 5, 6, 8; 7, 5; Chāndogya Upaniṣad, vii. 1, 2, 4; 2, 1; 7, 1.

[2] Śatapatha Brāhmaṇa, iv. 6, 9, 20.

view[3] is different: he sees in the Vākovākya an essential part of the **Itihāsa-Purāṇa**, the dialogue or dramatic element as opposed to the narrative portion.

[3] *Vedische Studien*, 1, 291.

Cf. Weber, *Indische Studien*, 1, 267; Eggeling, *Sacred Books of the East*, 44, 98, n. 3. It is certain that 'logic' is not meant, though Max Müller so renders it in his translation of the Chāndogya Upaniṣad.

Vāc, 'speech,' plays a great part in Vedic speculation, but only a few points are of other than mythological significance. Speech is in the Śatapatha Brāhmaṇa[1] divided into four kinds—that of men, of animals, of birds (*vayāṃsi*), and of small creeping things (*kṣudraṃ sarīsṛpam*). The discrimination or making articulate of speech is ascribed to Indra by the Saṃhitās.[2] The 'speech' of the following musical instruments—**Tūṇava, Vīṇā, Dundubhi**[3]—is mentioned, and in one Saṃhitā[4] also that of the axle of a chariot. The speech of the **Kuru-Pañcālas** was especially renowned,[5] as well as that of the northern country, according to the Kauṣītaki Brāhmaṇa,[6] so that men went there to study the language. On the other hand, barbarisms in speech were known, and were to be avoided.[7]

[1] iv. 1, 3, 16. There are quite different accounts in the Kāṭhaka Saṃhitā, xiv. 5; Maitrāyaṇī Saṃhitā, i. 11, 5. Oldenberg finds traces of the origin of the legend in Rv. viii. 100; but see v. Schroeder, *Mysterium und Mimus*, 339 *et seq.*; Keith, *Journal of the Royal Asiatic Society*, 1911, 993 *et seq.*

[2] Taittirīya Saṃhitā, vi. 4, 7, 3; Maitrāyaṇī Saṃhitā, iv. 5, 8.

[3] Pañcaviṃśa Brāhmaṇa, vi. 5, 10-13; Taittirīya Saṃhitā, vi. 1, 4, 1; Maitrāyaṇī Saṃhitā, iii. 6, 8; Kāṭhaka Saṃhitā, xxiii. 4.

[4] Pañcaviṃśa Brāhmaṇa, *loc. cit.*

[5] Śatapatha Brāhmaṇa, iii. 2, 3, 15. The difficult phrase has caused some doubt as to the sense, for *uttarāhi vāg vadati Kurupañcālatrā* seems to mean 'speech in the north among the Kuru-Pañcālas,' this version being slightly supported by the Kāṇva recension of the passage quoted by Eggeling, *Sacred Books of the East*, 12, xlii, n. 1. That recension, however, is not merely obscure, but it seems to couple the Kurus with the northern **Mahāvṛṣas** (so we must emend *Mahāviṣeṣu*), and it cannot be relied on. Eggeling's attempt to remove the difficulty by taking *uttarāhi* as 'higher' in tone is not satisfactory. The most probable solution is that of Weber, *Indische Studien*, 1, 191, who takes *Kurupañcālatrā* to be 'as among the Kuru-Pañcālas,' which gives a good sense, especially when it is remembered that the northerners were probably the **Uttara-Kurus** in Kaśmīr, which seems to have been a home of Sanskrit (*cf.* Franke, *Pāli und Sanskrit*, 89).

[6] vii. 6.

[7] Śatapatha Brāhmaṇa, iii. 2, 1, 23. 24, where the Asuras are described as saying *he 'lavaḥ*, perhaps for *he 'rayaḥ*. But the Kāṇva version is different. See Eggeling, *Sacred Books of the East*, 26, 31, n. 3.

One division of speech referred to[8] is that of the divine (*daivī*) and the human (*mānuṣī*), of which some specimens are given, such as *om*, the divine counterpart of *tathā*, and so forth. The Brahmin is said to know both;[9] it seems best to regard the distinction not as between Sanskrit and Apabhraṃśa, as Sāyaṇa[10] suggests, but as between the Sanskrit of the ritual and the hymns and that of ordinary life.

Reference is also made to Āryan[11] and to Brahmin[12] speech, by which Sanskrit, as opposed to non-Āryan tongues, seems to be meant. The **Vrātyas** are described as speaking the language of the initiated (*dīkṣita-vāc*), though not themselves initiated (*a-dīkṣita*), but as calling that which is easy to utter (*a-durukta*), difficult to utter.[13] This may mean that the non-Brahminical Indians were advancing more rapidly than the Brahminical tribes to Prākrit speech, especially if it is legitimate to connect the Vrātyas with the barbarians in speech alluded to in the Śatapatha Brāhmaṇa.[7]

[8] See Kāṭhaka Saṃhitā, xiv. 5; Maitrāyaṇī Saṃhitā, i. 11, 5 (where the words *yaś ca veda vaś ca na* replace the ordinary distinction of *daivī* and *mānuṣī*: perhaps *vedo* should be read); Śatapatha Brāhmaṇa, vi. 2, 1, 34; Aitareya Brāhmaṇa, vii. 18, 13; Aitareya Āraṇyaka, i. 3, 1; a Brāhmaṇa in Nirukta, xiii. 9, etc.

[9] Kāṭhaka Saṃhitā, *loc. cit.*; Maitrāyaṇī Saṃhitā, *loc. cit.*, etc.

[10] See Eggeling, *Sacred Books of the East*, 41, 200, n.

[11] Aitareya Āraṇyaka, iii. 2, 5; Śāṅkhāyana Āraṇyaka, viii. 9.

[12] Aitareya Āraṇyaka, i. 5, 2.

[13] Pañcaviṃśa Brāhmaṇa, xvii. 1, 9. *Cf.* Lévi, *La Doctrine du Sacrifice*, 34, 35; Weber, *Indian Literature*, 175-180; Keith, *Aitareya Āraṇyaka*, 179, 180; 196.

Vācaknavī, 'descendant of Vacaknu,' is the patronymic of a woman with the further patronymic of **Gārgī**, who appears as a student of Brahman in the Bṛhadāraṇyaka Upaniṣad.[1]

[1] iii. 6, 1; 8, 1. *Cf.* Āśvalāyana Gṛhya Sūtra, iii. 4, 4; Śāṅkhāyana Gṛhya Sūtra, iv. 10; Atharvaveda Pariśiṣṭa, xliii. 4, 23.

Vāja from the meaning of 'strength,' 'speed,' in its application to horses derives the sense of 'race'[1] and 'prize,'[2] or

[1] Rv. ii. 23, 13; iii. 11, 9; 37, 6; 42, 6; v. 35, 1; 86, 2, etc.

[2] Rv. i. 64, 13; ii. 26, 3; 31, 7; iii. 2, 3; viii. 103, 5, etc.

merely 'prosperity.'[3] That it ever means 'horse' is most improbable, that sense being given by **Vājin.**[4]

[3] Rv. i. 27, 5; 92, 7; vi. 45, 21. 23, etc.; Av. xiii. 1, 22; Pañcaviṃśa Brāhmaṇa, xviii. 7, 1. 12.

[4] See Pischel, *Vedische Studien*, 1, 10 *et seq.*, where he explains otherwise all the passages cited for the sense by the St. Petersburg Dictionary, *s.v.* 8.

Vājapeya is the name of a ceremony which, according to the Śatapatha Brāhmaṇa[1] and later authorities,[2] is only performed by a Brahmin or a Kṣatriya. The same Brāhmaṇa[3] insists that this sacrifice is superior to the **Rājasūya**, but the consensus of other authorities[4] assigns to it merely the place of a preliminary to the **Bṛhaspatisava** in the case of a priest, and to the Rājasūya in the case of a king, while the Śatapatha[5] is compelled to identify the Bṛhaspatisava with the Vājapeya. The essential ceremony is a chariot race in which the sacrificer is victorious. There is evidence in the Śāṅkhāyana Śrauta Sūtra[6] showing that once the festival was one which any Āryan could perform. Hillebrandt,[7] indeed, goes so far as to compare it with the Olympic games; but there is hardly much real ground for this: the rite seems to have been developed round a primitive habit of chariot racing, transformed into a ceremony which by sympathetic magic secures the success of the sacrificer. In fact[8] Eggeling seems correct in holding that the Vājapeya was a preliminary rite performed by a Brahmin prior to his formal installation as a Purohita, or by a king prior to his consecration. The Kuru Vājapeya was specially well known.[9]

[1] v. 1, 5, 2. 3.

[2] See Weber, *Über den Rājasūya;* Hillebrandt, *Rituallitteratur*, 147 *et seq.*

[3] v. 1, 1, 13; Kātyāyana Śrauta Sūtra, xv. 1, 1. 2.

[4] Taittirīya Saṃhitā, v. 6, 2, 1; Taittirīya Brāhmaṇa, i. 7, 6, 1; Āśvalāyana Śrauta Sūtra, ix. 9, 19; Lāṭyāyana Srauta Sūtra, viii. 11, 1, etc.

[5] v. 2, 1, 2. *Cf.* Kātyāyana Srauta Sūtra, xiv. 1, 2.

[6] xv. 1. See Weber, *op. cit.*, 41 *et seq.*

[7] *Vedische Mythologie*, 1, 247.

[8] *Sacred Books of the East*, 41, xxiv, xxv.

[9] Sāṅkhāyana Srauta Sūtra, xv. 3, 14 *et seq.*; Āpastamba Śrauta Sūtra, xviii. 3, 7.

Vāja-bandhu in one verse of the Rigveda (viii. 68, 19) may be a proper name. It may, however, merely be an adjective meaning 'ally in conflict.'

Vāja-ratnāyana, 'descendant of Vājaratna,' is the patronymic of **Somaśuṣman** in the Aitareya Brāhmaṇa (viii. 21, 5).

Vāja-śravas is mentioned in the last Vaṃśa (list of teachers) of the Bṛhadāraṇyaka Upaniṣad[1] as a pupil of **Jihvāvant Bādhyoga.**

[1] vi. 4, 33 (Mādhyaṃdina = vi. 5, 3 Kāṇva).

Vāja-śravasa, 'descendant of **Vājaśravas,**' is the patronymic of **Kuśri** in the Śatapatha Brāhmaṇa.[1] It is also the patronymic of the father of **Naciketas** in the Taittirīya Brāhmaṇa,[2] where the name is apparently Uśant, though it is understood by Sāyaṇa as a participle in the sense of 'desiring.' The Vājaśravases are in the Taittirīya Brāhmaṇa said to have been sages.[3] They were **Gotamas.**[4]

[1] x. 5, 5, 1.

[2] iii. 11, 8, 1. *Cf.* Kāṭhaka Upaniṣad, i. 1, with different names, on which see Weber, *Indian Literature*, 157, n.

[3] i. 3, 10, 3.

[4] *Cf.* Taittirīya Brāhmaṇa, iii. 11, 8.

Vājasaneya is the patronymic of **Yājñavalkya** in the Bṛhadāraṇyaka Upaniṣad[1] and the Jaiminīya Brāhmaṇa.[2] His school, the Vājasaneyins, are mentioned in the Sūtras.[3]

[1] vi. 3, 15; 4, 33 (Mādhyaṃdina = vi. 3, 7; 5, 3 Kāṇva).

[2] ii. 76 (*Journal of the American Oriental Society*, 15, 238).

[3] Anupada Sūtra, vii. 12; viii. 1. *Cf.* Weber, *Indische Studien*, 1, 44, 53, 83, 283; 2, 9; 4, 140, 257, 309; 10, 37, 76, 393, etc.

Vājin in several passages of the Rigveda[1] denotes 'steed' with reference to its swiftness and strength. In one passage[2] it is perhaps, as Ludwig[3] thinks, a proper name, that of a son of **Bṛhaduktha,** but this view seems forced.

[1] ii. 5, 1; 10, 1; 34, 7; iii. 53, 23; vi. 75, 6; x. 103, 10, etc.

[2] x. 56, 2.

[3] Translation of the Rigveda, 3, 133.

Vājina in the later Saṃhitās[1] and the Brāhmaṇas[2] denotes a mixture of hot fresh milk with sour milk.

[1] Taittirīya Saṃhitā, i. 6, 3, 10; Vājasaneyi Saṃhitā, xix. 21. 23.

[2] Śatapatha Brāhmaṇa, ii. 4, 4, 21; iii. 3, 3, 2; ix. 5, 1, 57, etc.

Cf. Eggeling, *Sacred Books of the East*, 12, 381, n. 2; Garbe, Āpastamba Śrauta Sūtra, 3, 445, calls it 'whey.'

Vājya, 'descendant of Vāja,' is the patronymic of **Ketu** in the Vaṃśa Brāhmaṇa.[1]

[1] *Indische Studien*, 4, 372, 383.

Vāḍeyī-putra. See **Bāḍeyīputra.**

Vāṇa in the Rigveda[1] and the Atharvaveda[2] denotes 'instrumental music' according to the St. Petersburg Dictionary; but in the later Saṃhitās[3] and the Brāhmaṇas[4] a 'harp' or 'lyre' with a hundred strings (*śata-tantu*), used at the Mahāvrata ceremony. The Rigveda[5] clearly refers to the seven 'notes' (*dhātu*) of the instrument, which are called elsewhere[6] the seven Vāṇīs, unless the latter expression be taken as referring to the metres.[7]

[1] i. 85, 10; viii. 20, 8; ix. 97, 8; x. 32, 4. *Cf.* Hopkins, *Journal of the American Oriental Society*, 17, 67.

[2] x. 2, 17.

[3] Taittirīya Saṃhitā, vii. 5, 9, 2; Kāṭhaka Saṃhitā, xxxiv. 5.

[4] Pañcaviṃśa Brāhmaṇa, v. 6, 12; xiv. 7, 8; Aitareya Āraṇyaka, v. 1, 4, etc.

[5] x. 32, 4.

[6] i. 164, 24; iii. 1, 6; 7, 1; ix. 103, 3, etc.

[7] Macdonell, *Vedic Grammar*, 64.

Cf. Zimmer, *Altindisches Leben*, 289, who thinks the meaning is 'flute' in Rv. i. 85, 10, but not necessarily. Max Müller, *Sacred Books of the East*, 32, 138, render it 'voice' in i. 85, 10; ix. 97, 8, and 'arrow' in viii. 20, 8; ix. 50, 1, and this sense is accepted in Böhtlingk's Dictionary, *s.v.* 1 *vāṇa* for ix. 50, 1.

Vāṇija denotes a 'merchant' as a hereditary profession ('son of a **Vaṇij**') in the list of victims at the Puruṣamedha ('human sacrifice') in the Yajurveda.[1].

[1] Vājasaneyi Saṃhitā, xxx. 17; Taittirīya Brāhmaṇa, iii. 4, 14, 1.

Vāṇī. See **Vāṇa.**

Vāṇīcī occurs in a verse of the Rigveda (v. 75, 4), where the St. Petersburg Dictionary ascribes to it the sense of 'musical instrument.'

Vāta is the regular word for 'wind' in the Rigveda[1] and later.[2] Five winds are mentioned.[3] In one passage[4] Zimmer[5] sees a reference to the north-east monsoon. *Cf.* **Salilavāta.**

[1] i. 28, 6; ii. 1, 6; 38, 3; iii. 14, 3, etc.

[2] Av. iv. 5, 2; v. 5, 7; xii. 1, 51, etc.

[3] Taittirīya Saṃhitā, i. 6, 1, 2; Kāṭhaka Saṃhitā, xxxii. 6.

[4] Rv. v. 53, 8.

[5] *Altindisches Leben*, 45, who compares also Rv. x. 137, 2, which refers to two winds.

Vāta-pāna ('wind guard') apparently means some sort of garment as protecting against wind in the Taittirīya Saṃhitā (vi. 1, 1, 3).

Vāta-raśana, 'wind-girt,' is applied to the **Munis** in the Rigveda[1] and to the Ṛṣis in the Taittirīya Āraṇyaka.[2] Naked ascetics, such as are known throughout later Indian religious history, are evidently meant.

[1] x. 136, 2.

[2] i. 23, 2; 24, 4; ii. 7, 1. Weber, *Indische Studien*, 1, 78, was inclined, though without sufficient reason, to take the word as a proper name.

Vātavant is the name of a Ṛṣi in the Pañcaviṃśa Brāhmaṇa (xxv. 3, 6). He and **Dṛti** performed a certain Sattra or sacrificial session, but by stopping at a particular time he came to grief, and his descendants, the Vātavatas, were less prosperous than the **Dārteyas.**

Vātavata, 'descendant of **Vātavant**,' is the patronymic of **Vṛṣaśuṣma** in the Aitareya Brāhmaṇa.[1] The Kauṣītaki Brāhmaṇa[2] has the same form with a variant Vādhāvata.

[1] v. 29. *Cf. Indische Studien*, 4, 373.

[2] ii. 9.

Vātsi, 'descendant of **Vatsa**,' is the patronymic of **Sarpi** in the Aitareya Brāhmaṇa (vi. 24, 16).

Vātsī-putra, 'son of a female descendant of **Vatsa**,' as the name of a teacher mentioned in the last Vaṃśa (list of teachers) of the Bṛhadāraṇyaka Upaniṣad as a pupil of **Pārāśarīputra** according to the Kāṇva recension (vi, 5, 2), as a pupil of **Bhāradvājīputra** according to the Mādhyaṃdina (vi. 4, 31).

Vātsī-Māṇḍavī-putra is the name of a teacher, a pupil of **Pārāśarīputra**, according to the last Vaṃśa (list of teachers) in the Mādhyaṃdina recension of the Bṛhadāraṇyaka Upaniṣad (vi. 4, 30).

Vātsya, 'descendant of **Vatsa**,' is the name of one or more teachers. One is mentioned in the Śāṅkhāyana Āraṇyaka,[1] where the Aitareya Āraṇyaka[2] in the parallel passage has **Bādhva.** Others occur in the Vaṃśas (lists of teachers) of the Bṛhadāraṇyaka Upaniṣad as pupils of **Kuśri,**[3] **Śāṇḍilya,**[4] or another Vātsya,[5] while a Vātsya is mentioned in the Śatapatha Brāhmaṇa.[6]

1 viii. 3.
2 iii. 2, 3.
3 vi. 5, 4 Kāṇva.
4 ii. 5, 22; iv. 5, 28 (Mādhyaṃdina =ii. 6, 3; iv. 6, 3 Kāṇva); Śatapatha Brāhmaṇa, x. 6, 5, 9.
5 ii. 5, 20; iv. 5, 26 Kāṇva.
6 ix. 5, 1, 62.

Vātsyāyana, 'descendant of **Vātsya**,' is the name of a teacher in the Taittirīya Āraṇyaka (i. 7, 2).

Vādana denotes the plectrum of a harp in the Āraṇyakas of the Rigveda.[1]

1 Aitareya Āraṇyaka, iii. 2, 5; Śāṅkhāyana Āraṇyaka, viii. 9; Śāṅkhāyana Śrauta Sūtra, xvii. 3, 14, etc.

Vādita is found denoting 'music' in the compound *gīta-vādita*, 'song and music,' in the Chāndogya Upaniṣad (viii. 2, 8), and uncompounded in the Kauṣītaki Brāhmaṇa (xxix. 5) along with **Nṛtya**, 'dance,' and Gīta, 'song.' See **Śilpa.**

Vādhāvata is a various reading in the Kauṣītaki Brāhmaṇa[1] for **Vātāvata.**

1 ii. 9. *Cf.* Weber, *Indische Studien*, 1, 215, n.; 2, 293, n.

Vādhūya denotes the garment of the bride worn at the marriage ceremony and afterwards given to a Brahmin.[1]

[1] Rv. x. 85, 34; Av. xiv. 2, 41. *Cf.* Kauśika Sūtra, lxxix. 21; Āśvalāyana Gṛhya Sūtra, i. 8, 12, etc.

Vādhryaśva, 'connected with **Vadhryaśva**,' is apparently the epithet of Agni in a hymn of the Rigveda (x. 69, 5).

Vānaspatya (as a masculine) in one or two passages of the Atharvaveda[1] seems to denote a 'small tree.' Elsewhere[2] (as a neuter) it has the sense of the 'fruit of a tree' (**Vanaspati**).

[1] viii. 8, 14; xi. 9, 24. *Cf.* xii. 1, 27.

[2] Śatapatha Brāhmaṇa, xi. 1, 7, 2; 3, 1, 3; Aitareya Brāhmaṇa, viii. 16, 1.

Vāma-kakṣāyaṇa is the name of a teacher, a pupil of **Vātsya**[1] or **Śāṇḍilya**[2] in the Śatapatha Brāhmaṇa.

[1] x. 6, 5, 9. *Cf.* vii. 2, 1, 11.

[2] Bṛhadāraṇyaka Upaniṣad, vi. 5, 4 Kāṇva. *Cf.* Satapatha Brāhmaṇa, x. 4, 1, 11.

Vāma-deva is credited[1] by tradition with the authorship of the fourth Maṇḍala of the Rigveda, and he is once mentioned in that Maṇḍala.[2] He is, moreover, credited with the authorship of the fourth hymn of the Maṇḍala by the Yajurveda Saṃhitās.[3] He there appears as a son of **Gotama**, while in one hymn of the fourth Maṇḍala of the Rigveda[4] Gotama is mentioned as the father of the singer, and in another[5] the Gotamas occur as praising Indra. In the Bṛhaddevatā[6] two absurd legends are narrated of Vāmadeva. One describes Indra as revealing himself in the form of an eagle to the seer as he cooked the entrails of a dog; the other tells of his successful conflict with Indra, whom he sold among the seers. Sieg[7] has endeavoured to trace these tales in the

[1] Aitareya Āraṇyaka, ii. 2, 1, etc.

[2] iv. 16, 18.

[3] Kāṭhaka Saṃhitā, x. 5; Maitrāyaṇī Saṃhitā, ii. 1, 11; iii. 2, 6.

[4] iv. 4, 11.

[5] iv. 32, 9. 12.

[6] iv. 126 131 *et seq.*, with Macdonell' notes.

[7] *Die Sagenstoffe des Ṛgveda*, 76 *et seq.*

Rigveda,[8] but without any success. Moreover, though Vāmadeva is mentioned in the Atharvaveda[9] and often in the Brāhmaṇas,[10] he never figures there as a hero of these legends.

[8] Rv iv. 27 and iv. 24 respectively. On the former hymn, see Oldenberg, *Ṛigveda-Noten*, 1, 291 *et seq.*; on the latter, *ibid.*, 419 *et seq.*

[9] See Av. xviii. 3, 15. 16.

[10] Aitareya Brāhmaṇa, iv. 30, 2; vi. 18, 1. 2; Aitareya Āraṇyaka, ii. 5, 1 (= Aitareya Upaniṣad, ii. 5, where Vāmadeva is credited with knowledge before birth); Bṛhadāraṇyaka Upaniṣad, i. 4, 22 (Mādhyaṃdina = i. 4, 10 Kāṇva); Pañcaviṃśa Brāhmaṇa, xiii. 9, 27.

Cf. Ludwig, Translation of the Rigveda, 3, 123, 124; Weber, Proceedings of the Berlin Academy, 1894, 789 *et seq.*; Oldenberg, *Zeitschrift der Deutschen Morgenländischen Gesellschaft*, 42, 215.

Vāyata, 'descendant of Vayant,' is the patronymic of **Pāśadyumna** in the Rigveda (vii. 33, 2). *Cf.* **Vyant.**

Vāyasa in the Rigveda[1] and later[2] denotes a 'large bird.' The sense of 'crow'[3] occurs in the Ṣaḍviṃśa Brāhmaṇa only.[4]

[1] i. 164, 32.

[2] In a Vedic citation in Nirukta, iv. 17; and in verse 1 of Khila after Rv. v. 51.

[3] The only sense of the word in the post-Vedic language.

[4] vi. 8.

Vāyo-vidyika, 'bird-catcher,' is found in the Śatapatha Brāhmaṇa.[1]

[1] xiii. 4, 3, 13. *Cf.* Eggeling, *Sacred Books of the East*, 44, 369, n. 5.

Vāyya, 'descendant of **Vayya**,' is the patronymic of **Satyaśravas** in the Rigveda (v. 79, 1. 2).

Vār is found in the Rigveda[1] and later[2] denoting 'water.' In some passages[3] 'stagnant water,' 'pond,' is meant.

[1] i. 116, 22; ii. 4, 6; x. 12, 3; 99, 4; 105, 1, etc.

[2] Av. iii. 13, 8; Śatapatha Brāhmaṇa, vi. 1, 1, 9, etc.

[3] Rv. iv. 19, 4; viii. 98, 8; ix. 112, 4.

Vāraki, 'descendant of Varaka,' is the patronymic of **Kaṃsa** in the Jaiminīya Upaniṣad Brāhmaṇa (iii. 41, 1).

Vārakya, 'descendant of Varaka,' is the patronymic, in the Jaiminīya Upaniṣad Brāhmaṇa, of **Kaṃsa, Kubera, Janaśruta, Jayanta**, and **Proṣṭhapad.**

Vāraṇa in two passages of the Rigveda[1] is taken by Roth[2] as an adjective with **Mṛga**, meaning 'wild beast.' But the sense intended must have been 'elephant,' the usual sense of Vāraṇa in the classical literature. Probably the feminine Vāraṇī in the Atharvaveda[3] likewise denotes a 'female elephant.'

[1] viii. 33, 8; x. 40, 4.
[2] St. Petersburg Dictionary, *s.v.*, 1c.
[3] v. 14, 11.
Cf. Pischel and Geldner, *Vedische Studien*, 1, xv, 100-102; Whitney, Translation of the Atharvaveda, 296; Muir, *Sanskrit Texts*, 5, 467; Zimmer, *Altindisches Leben*, 80.

Vāruṇi, 'descendant of Varuṇa,' is the patronymic of **Bhṛgu.**[1]

[1] Aitareya Brāhmaṇa, iii. 34, 1; Satapatha Brāhmaṇa, xi. 6, 1, 1; Taittirīya Upaniṣad, iii. 1, etc.

Vārkali, 'descendant of Vṛkalā,' is the metronymic of a teacher in the Śatapatha Brāhmaṇa.[1] The name in the form of Vārkalin has been seen in the Aitareya Āraṇyaka,[2] but wrongly.

[1] xii. 3, 2, 6.
[2] iii. 2, 2, and Keith's note; Śāṅkhāyana Āraṇyaka, viii. 2. *Cf.* Weber, *Indian Literature*, 33, 123, who thinks Vārkali is equivalent to Vāṣkali.

Vārkāruṇī-putra is the name of a teacher, a pupil of **Ārtabhāgīputra**, in the last Vaṃśa (list of teachers) of the Bṛhadāraṇyaka Upaniṣad.[1]

[1] vi. 4, 31 (Mādhyaṃdina = vi. 5, 2 Kāṇva, where also Vārkāruṇīputra is duplicated, one being the pupil of the other).

Vārdhrā-ṇasa,[1] **Vārdhrī-nasa**[2] is the name of an animal in the list of victims at the Aśvamedha ('horse sacrifice') in the

[1] Taittirīya Saṃhitā, v. 5, 20, 1; Maitrāyaṇī Saṃhitā, iii. 14, 20.
[2] Vājasaneyi Saṃhitā, xxiv. 39 (Prātiśākhya, iii. 89; vi. 28).

Yajurveda Saṃhitās. The meaning seems to be, as taken by Sāyaṇa,[3] 'rhinoceros.' Böhtlingk[4] quotes as other interpretations 'an old white he-goat' or 'a kind of crane.'

[3] On Taittirīya Saṃhitā, *loc. cit.*

[4] Dictionary, *s.v.*

Cf. Zimmer, *Altindisches Leben*, 80.

Vārṣa-gaṇa, 'descendant of Vṛṣagaṇa,' is the patronymic of **Asita** in the Bṛhadāraṇyaka Upaniṣad.[1]

[1] vi. 4, 33 (Mādhyaṃdina = vi. 5, 3 Kāṇva).

Vārṣagaṇī-putra, 'son of a female descendant of Vṛṣagaṇa,' is the name of a teacher, a pupil of **Gautamī-putra** in the last Vaṃśa (list of teachers) in the Mādhyaṃdina recension of the Bṛhadāraṇyaka Upaniṣad (vi. 4, 31).

Vārṣa-gaṇya, 'descendant of Vṛṣagaṇa,' is the name of a teacher in the Vaṃśa Brāhmaṇa.[1]

[1] *Indische Studien*, 4, 372; Nidāna Sūtra, ii. 9; vi. 7, etc. *Cf.* Garbe, *Sāṃkhya Philosophie*, 36.

Vārṣā-gira, 'descendant of Vṛṣāgir,' is the patronymic of **Ambarīṣa**, **Ṛjrāśva**, **Bhayamāna**, **Sahadeva**, and **Surādhas**, in the Rigveda (i. 100, 17).

Cf. Ludwig, Translation of the Rigveda, 3, 113.

Vārṣṇa, 'descendant of Vṛṣan or Vṛṣṇi or Vṛṣṇa,' is the patronymic of **Gobala**[1] and **Barku**,[2] and of **Aikṣvāka**.[3]

[1] Taittirīya Brāhmaṇa, iii. 11, 9, 3; Jaiminīya Upaniṣad Brāhmaṇa, i. 6, 1.

[2] Śatapatha Brāhmaṇa, i. 1, 1, 10; Bṛhadāraṇyaka Upaniṣad, iv. 1, 8, where the Kāṇva recension (iv. 1, 4) has a *varia lectio* **Vārṣṇa**.

[3] Jaiminīya Upaniṣad Brāhmaṇa, i. 5, 4.

Vārṣṇi-vṛddha, 'descendant of Vṛṣṇivṛddha,' is the patronymic of **Ula** in the Kauṣītaki Brāhmaṇa (vii. 4).

Vārṣṇeya, 'descendant of Vṛṣṇi,' is the patronymic of **Śūṣa** in the Taittirīya Brāhmaṇa (iii. 10, 9, 15).

Vārṣṇya, 'descendant of Vṛṣṇi,' is the patronymic of a man in the Śatapatha Brāhmaṇa.[1]

[1] iii. 1, 1, 4. The Kāṇva recension omits the name. See Eggeling *Sacred Books of the East*, 26, 2, n. 2.

Vārṣma. See **Vārṣṇa.**

Vāla denotes a 'hair sieve' in the later Saṃhitās and he Brāhmaṇas.[1]

[1] Vājasaneyi Saṃhitā, xix. 88; Śatapatha Brāhmaṇa, xii. 7, 3, 11; 8, 1, 14, etc.

Vāla-khilya is the term applied in the Brāhmaṇas[1] to the supplementary hymns inserted after Rigveda viii. 48. The Ṛṣis of these hymns are so named in the Taittirīya Āraṇyaka.[2] *Cf.* 2. **Khila.**

[1] Aitareya Brāhmaṇa, v. 15, 1. 3. 4; vi. 24, 1. 4. 5. 10. 11; Kauṣītaki Brāhmaṇa, xxx. 4. 8; Pañcaviṃśa Brāhmaṇa, xiii. 11, 3; xiv. 5, 4; Aitareya Āraṇyaka, v. 2, 4, etc.; Gopatha Brāhmaṇa, ii. 6, 9.

[2] i. 23.

Cf. Max Müller, *Ancient Sanskrit Literature*, 220; *Sacred Books of the East*, 32, xlvi *et seq.*; Bṛhaddevatā, vi. 84 *et seq.*, with Macdonell's notes; Scheftelowitz, *Die Apokryphen des Ṛgveda*, 35 *et seq.*

Vāla-dāman denotes a 'horse-hair strap' in the Śatapatha Brāhmaṇa (v. 3, 1, 10).

Vāliśikhāyani is the name of a teacher in the Śāṅkhāyana Āraṇyaka.[1]

[1] vii. 21. *Cf.* Keith, *Śāṅkhāyana Āraṇyaka*, 49, n. 5.

Vāvātā is in the Brāhmaṇas[1] the name of the king's 'favourite' wife, inferior to the **Mahiṣī** only.

[1] Aitareya Brāhmaṇa, iii. 22, 1. 7; Taittirīya Brāhmaṇa, i. 7, 3, 3; Śatapatha Brāhmaṇa, xiii. 2, [illegible] 5 4, 1 8; 5, 2, 6, etc.

Vāśitā in the Atharvaveda[1] and later[2] denotes a cow desiring the bull.

[1] v. 20, 2.
[2] Kāṭhaka Saṃhitā, xiii. 4; Taittirīya Brāhmaṇa, i. 1, 9, 9; Aitareya Brāhmaṇa, vi. 18, 10; 21, 14, etc.

Vāśī is mentioned in the Rigveda both as a weapon of the Maruts[1] and as held by the god Tvaṣṭṛ,[2] as well as in other mythical surroundings.[3] It is used, however, in the Atharvaveda[4] of the carpenter's knife; here it may mean 'awl,' in accordance with Sāyaṇa's view.

[1] i. 37, 2; 88, 3; v. 53, 4.
[2] viii. 29, 3.
[3] viii. 12, 12; x. 53, 10; 101, 10 (of the stones with which the Soma plant is manipulated), all doubtful passages.
[4] x. 6, 3 (where the manuscripts all have *vāsyā*: perhaps this is really a different word).
[5] Zimmer, *Altindisches Leben*, 301.

Vāsaḥ-palpūlī, 'washer of clothes,' is the name of one of the victims at the Puruṣamedha ('human sacrifice') in the Yajurveda.[1]

[1] Vājasaneyi Saṃhitā, xxx. 12; Taittirīya Brāhmaṇa, iii. 4, 7, 1.

Vāsas is the most usual word in the Rigveda[1] and later[2] for 'clothing.' Clothes were often woven of sheep's wool (*cf.* **Ūrṇā**); the god Pūṣan is called a 'weaver of garments' (*vāso-vāya*)[3] because of his connexion with the fashioning of forms. The garments worn were often embroidered (*cf.* **Peśas**), and the Maruts are described as wearing mantles adorned with gold.[4] When the "giver of garments' (*vāso-dā*)[5] is mentioned along with the giver of horses and gold, ornamental garments are probably meant. There are several references in the Rigveda[6] to the Indians' love of ornament, which is attested by Megas-

[1] i. 34, 1; 115, 4; 162, 16; viii. 3, 24; x. 26, 6; 102, 2, etc.
[2] Taittirīya Saṃhitā, vi. 1, 9, 7; 11, 2; Vājasaneyi Saṃhitā, ii. 32; xi. 40; Aitareya Brāhmaṇa, i. 3, etc. A garment of Kuśa grass is mentioned in Śatapatha Brāhmaṇa, v. 2, 1, 8, as worn by the wife of the sacrificer at the consecration, but it is doubtful whether such dresses were normally worn. *Cf.* also *kausumbha-paridhāna*, 'a silken garment,' Śāṅkhāyana Āraṇyaka, xi. 4.
[3] Rv. x. 26, 6.
[4] Rv. v. 55, 6 (*hiraṇyayān atkān*).
[5] Rv. x. 107, 2. *Cf. vastra-dā*, v. 24, 8.
[6] Rv. i. 85, 1; 92, 4; ix. 96, 1; x. 1, 6.

thenes for his day.[7] The Rigveda also presents epithets like *su-vasana*[8] and *su-rabhi*,[9] implying that garments were becoming or well-fitting.

The Vedic Indian seems often to have worn three garments —an undergarment (*cf.* **Nīvi**),[10] a garment,[11] and an over-garment (*cf.* **Adhīvāsa**),[12] which was presumably a mantle, and for which the names **Atka** and **Drāpi** also seem to be used. This accords with the description of the sacrificial garments given in the Śatapatha Brāhmaṇa,[13] which comprise a **Tārpya**, perhaps a 'silken undergarment'; secondly, a garment of undyed wool, and then a mantle, while the ends of the turban, after being tied behind the neck, are brought forward and tucked away in front. The last point would hardly accord with the usual practice in ordinary life, but seems to be a special sacrificial ritual act. A similar sort of garments in the case of women appears to be alluded to in the Atharvaveda[14] and the Śatapatha Brāhmaṇa.[15] There is nothing to show exactly what differences there were between male and female costume, nor what was exactly the nature of the clothes in either case.

It is important to note that the Vedic Indian evidently assumed that all civilized persons other than inspired Munis would wear clothing of some sort.[16]

See also **Vasana, Vastra, Otu, Tantu.** For the use of skin garments, see **Mala.**

[7] See Strabo, p. 709; Arrian, *Indica*, v. 9.

[8] Rv. ix. 97, 50.

[9] With *atka*, vi. 29, 3; x. 123, 7, this word may possibly indicate that early Vedic dress was fitted like the Minoan style of dress, and unlike the later Achæan style as seen in Homer (*cf.* Lang, *The World of Homer*, 60 *et seq.*).

[10] Av. viii. 2, 16; xiv. 2, 50. *Cf.* Taittirīya Saṃhitā, vi. 1, 1, 3; Vājasaneyi Saṃhitā, iv. 10, etc.

[11] Vāsas in the narrower sense, Av. viii. 2, 16.

[12] Rv. i. 140, 9; 162, 16; x. 5, 4.

[13] v. 3, 5, 20 *et seq.* See Eggeling, *Sacred Books of the East*, 41, 85 *et seq.*

[14] viii. 2, 16; xiv. 2, 50.

[15] v. 2, 1, 8.

[16] *Cf.* Śatapatha Brāhmaṇa, xi. 5, 1, 1; and iii. 1, 2, 13-17, where the fact that man alone wears clothes is accounted for by a silly legend.

Cf. Zimmer, *Altindisches Leben*, 261, 262.

Vāsiṣṭha, 'descendant of **Vasiṣṭha**,' is the patronymic of **Sātyahavya**, a teacher mentioned several times in the later

Saṃhitās,[1] of **Rauhiṇa** in the Taittirīya Āraṇyaka,[2] and of **Caikitāneya.**[3] Moreover, reference is made to the claim of the Vāsiṣṭhas to be Brahman priest at the sacrifice.[4] A Vāsiṣṭha is mentioned as a teacher in the Vaṃśa Brāhmaṇa[5] and the Jaiminīya Upaniṣad Brāhmaṇa.[6]

1 Taittirīya Saṃhitā, vi. 6, 2, 2; Kāṭhaka Saṃhitā, xxxiv. 17 (*Indische Studien*, 3, 474); Maitrāyaṇī Saṃhitā, iii. 3, 9; iv. 8, 7. For his enmity to **Atyarāti**, see Aitareya Brāhmaṇa, viii. 23, 9. 10.

2 i. 12, 7.

3 Jaiminīya Upaniṣad Brāhmaṇa, i. 42, 1; Ṣaḍviṃśa Brāhmaṇa, iv. 1; *Indische Studien*, 4, 384. *Cf.* Gopatha Brāhmaṇa, ii. 2, 10.

4 Taittirīya Saṃhitā, iii. 5, 2, 1; Kāṭhaka Saṃhitā, xxxvii. 17; Śatapatha Brāhmaṇa, xii. 6, 1, 41. See Weber, *Indische Studien*, 10, 34; Eggeling, *Sacred Books of the East*, 44, 212, n. (correcting the rendering of Delbrück, *Altindische Syntax*, 570).

5 *Indische Studien*, 4, 373.

6 iii. 15, 2.

Vāstu-paśya, according to Böhtlingk[1] a name of a Brāhmaṇa, is a mere error for *Vāstupasya*[2] in the Jaiminiya Brāhmaṇa.[3]

1 Dictionary, *s.v.*, supplement 6.

2 Hopkins, *Journal of the American Oriental Society*, 26, 61.

3 iii. 120.

Vāha is found in the Rigveda (iv. 57, 4. 8) and the Atharvaveda (vi. 102, 1) apparently denoting an ox for 'drawing' the plough. See also **Rathavāhana.**

Vāhana (neut.) in the Brāhmaṇas[1] denotes a 'beast of burden,' or occasionally[2] a 'cart.' *Cf.* **Rathavāhana.**

1 Aitareya Brāhmaṇa, iv. 9, 4; Śatapatha Brāhmaṇa, i. 8, 2, 9; ii. 1, 4, 4; iv. 4, 4, 10.

2 Śatapatha Brāhmaṇa, ix. 4, 2, 11.

Vāhasa, 'boa constrictor,' is included in the list of victims at the Aśvamedha ('horse sacrifice') in the Yajurveda Saṃhitās.[1]

1 Taittirīya Saṃhitā, v. 5, 13, 1; 14, 1; Maitrāyaṇī Saṃhitā, iii. 14, 15; Vājasaneyi Saṃhitā, xxiv. 34. *Cf.* Zimmer, *Altindisches Leben*, 94.

Vi in the Rigveda,[1] and sometimes later,[2] denotes 'bird.'

[1] ii. 29, 5; 38, 7; vi. 64, 6, etc.

[2] Pañcaviṃśa Brāhmaṇa, v. 6, 15, etc. *Cf.* Zimmer, *Altindisches Leben*, 87.

Vi-kakara is the name of some bird, a victim at the Aśvamedha ('horse sacrifice') according to the Vājasaneyi Saṃhitā.[1]

[1] xxiv. 20. *Cf.* Zimmer, *Altindisches Leben*, 94; in Āpastamba Śrauta Sūtra, xx. 14, 5, *vikira* (with variants *vikikira*, *vikakara*) is read.

Vi-kaṅkata is the name of a tree (*Flacourtia sapida*), often mentioned in the later Saṃhitās[1] and the Brāhmaṇas.[2]

[1] Taittirīya Saṃhitā, iii. 5, 7, 3; vi. 4, 10, 5; Kāṭhaka Saṃhitā, xix. 10; Maitrāyaṇī Saṃhitā, iii. 1, 9. *Cf.* Av. xi. 10, 3.

[2] Śatapatha Brāhmaṇa, ii. 2, 4, 10; v. 2, 4, 18, etc. *Cf.* Zimmer, *Altindisches Leben*, 59.

Vi-kraya is found in the Atharvaveda (iii. 15, 4) and the Nirukta (iii. 4) denoting 'sale.' See **Kraya.**

Vi-klindu is the name of a disease in the Atharvaveda.[1] Bloomfield[2] suggests 'catarrh.'

[1] xii. 4, 5.

[2] *Hymns of the Atharvaveda*, 658.

Vi-ghana in the Taittirīya Saṃhitā[1] seems to denote 'club.'

[1] iii. 2, 4, 1. The Av., vii. 28, 1, has *drughaṇa*.

Vi-cakṣaṇa Tāṇḍya is the name of a teacher, a pupil of **Gardabhīmukha** in the Vaṃśa Brāhmaṇa.[1]

[1] *Indische Studien*, 4, 373.

Vi-cārin Kābandhi ('descendant of **Kabandha**') is the name of a mythical teacher in the Gopatha Brāhmaṇa.[1]

[1] i. 2, 9. 18. *Cf.* Hillebrandt, *Vedische Mythologie*, 2, 176, n. 4; Bloomfield, *Atharvaveda*, 111, 112.

Vi-cṛt in the dual is found in three passages of the Atharvaveda,[1] where Roth[2] sees in the term the name of two stars, while in the Taittirīya Saṃhitā[3] he thinks they mean the **Nakṣatra** called Mūla. There can, however, be no doubt that the asterism is intended in all the passages.[4]

[1] ii. 8, 1; vi. 110, 2; 121, 3. See also iii. 7, 4.
[2] St. Petersburg Dictionary, *s.v.*
[3] iv. 4, 10, 2.
[4] Zimmer, *Altindisches Leben*, 356; Whitney, Translation of the Atharvaveda, 361, points out that Vicṛtau are λ and υ Scorpionis, while Mūla includes the tail as a whole.

Vij. See 2. **Akṣa.**

Vi-jāmātṛ. See **Jāmātṛ.**

Vitastā, the most westerly of the five rivers of the Panjab, is only mentioned in the Rigveda[1] in the Nadīstuti ('Praise of Rivers').[2] It is the Hydaspes of Alexander's historians, more correctly reproduced by Ptolemy as Bidaspes. The name appears in the Mohammedan historians corrupted to Bihat or Wihat, and survives in the modern Kashmīrī form of Veth.

[1] x. 75, 5; Nirukta, ix. 26; *cf.* Kāśikā Vṛtti on Pāṇini, i. 4, 31. *Cf.* Zimmer, *Altindisches Leben*, 12; *Imperial Gazetteer of India*, 14, 160.
[2] The rareness of the name in the Rigveda points to the Panjab not having been the seat of the activity of the greater part of the Vedic Indians.

Vitta in the Rigveda[1] and later[2] denotes 'wealth,' 'possessions.' The earth is referred to in the Taittirīya Upaniṣad[3] as full of riches (*vittasya pūrṇā*). The doctrine that a man's greatness depends on his wealth is found as early as the Taittirīya Brāhmaṇa.[4] The striving after wealth (*vittaiṣaṇā*) is mentioned in the Bṛhadāraṇyaka Upaniṣad[5] as one of the things abandoned by the sage.

[1] v. 42, 9; x. 34, 13.
[2] Av. xii. 3, 52; Taittirīya Saṃhitā, i. 5, 9, 2; vi. 2, 4, 3; Vājasaneyi Saṃhitā, xviii. 11. 14, etc.
[3] ii. 8. *Cf.* the name *vasumatī* found in the Śāṅkhāyana Āraṇyaka, xiii. 1.
[4] i. 4, 7, 7.
[5] iii. 4, 1; iv. 4 26.

Vidagdha Śākalya is the name of a teacher, a contemporary and rival of **Yājñavalkya** at the court of **Janaka** of **Videha** in the Bṛhadāraṇyaka Upaniṣad,[1] the Jaiminīya Upaniṣad Brāhmaṇa,[2] and the Śatapatha Brāhmaṇa.[3]

[1] iii. 9, 1; iv. 1, 17 (Mādhyaṃdina = 7 Kāṇva).

[2] ii. 76 (*Journal of the American Oriental Society*, 15, 239).

[3] xi. 6, 3, 3.

Vidatha is a word of obscure sense, confined mainly to the Rigveda. According to Roth,[1] the sense is primarily 'order,' then the concrete body which gives orders, then 'assembly' for secular[2] or religious ends,[3] or for war.[4] Oldenberg[5] once thought that the main idea is 'ordinance' (from *vi-dhā*, 'dispose,' 'ordain'), and thence 'sacrifice.' Ludwig[6] thinks that the root idea is an 'assembly,' especially of the **Maghavans** and the Brahmins. Geldner[7] considers that the word primarily means 'knowledge,' 'wisdom,' 'priestly lore,' then 'sacrifice' and 'spiritual authority.' Bloomfield,[8] on the other hand, insists that Vidatha refers to the 'house'[9] in the first place (from *vid*, 'acquire'), and then to the 'sacrifice,' as connected with the house; this interpretation, at any rate, appears to suit all the passages. The term *vidathya*, once[10] applied to the king (*samrāṭ*), might seem to be against this view, but it may refer to his being 'rich in homesteads'; and the connexion of the woman with the Vidatha, as opposed to

[1] Rv. i. 31, 6; 117, 25; iii. 1, 18; 27, 7; iv. 38, 4; vi. 8, 1; x. 85, 26; 92, 2; Av. iv. 25, 1; v. 20, 12; xviii. 3, 70, etc.

[2] ii. 1, 4; 27, 12. 17; iii. 38, 5. 6; v. 63, 2; vii. 66, 10; viii. 39, 1; x. 12, 7; Av. xvii. 1, 15. So Whitney renders the word in Av. i. 13, 4, as 'council,' Translation of the Atharvaveda, 15.

[3] Rv. i. 60, 1; ii. 4, 8; 39, 1; iii. 1, 1; 56, 8, etc.

[4] Rv. i. 166, 2; 167, 6; v. 59, 2, etc.

[5] *Sacred Books of the East*, 46, 26 *et seq.* But in *Zeitschrift der Deutschen Morgenländischen Gesellschaft*, 54, 609-611, he falls back on the derivation from *vidh*, 'worship.' *Cf.* Macdonell, *Vedic Grammar*, p. 23, n. 10.

[6] Translation of the Rigveda, 3, 259 *et seq.*

[7] *Vedische Studien*, 1, 147; *Zeitschrift der Deutschen Morgenländischen Gesellschaft*, 52, 757; *Rigveda, Glossar*, 161.

[8] *Journal of the American Oriental Society*, 19, 12 *et seq.*

[9] See Rigveda, x. 85, 26. 27 (of the wife in the marriage ritual); i. 117, 25; ii. 1, 6; Av. xviii. 3, 70.

[10] iv. 27, 2. In i. 91, 20; 167, 3; Av. xx. 128, 1, *vidathya*, 'having an establishment,' seems adequate.

the **Sabhā**, tells in favour[11] of Bloomfield's explanation. That the word ever denotes an asylum, like the house of the Brahmin,[12] as Ludwig[13] suggests, is doubtful.[14]

11 *Cf.* Av. vii. 38, 4; Maitrāyaṇī Saṃhitā, iv. 7, 4.

12 Śatapatha Brāhmaṇa, v. 3, 1, 13, with Kātyāyana Śrauta Sūtra, xv. 3, 35.

13 *Op. cit.*, 3, 261.

14 Rv. i. 31, 6; v. 62, 6; Aitareya Brāhmaṇa, i. 30, 27. 28, certainly does not show this clearly. *Cf.* Zimmer, *Altindisches Leben*, 177, who suggests that Vidatha sometimes means (*e.g.*, in *vidatheṣu praśastaḥ*, Rv. ii. 27, 12) a smaller assembly than the Samiti. But we have no ground to be certain that such smaller assemblies ever existed at an early date either in India or elsewhere among Āryan peoples.

Vidanvant Bhārgava ('descendant of **Bhṛgu**') is mentioned as the seer of a Sāman or chant in the Pañcaviṃśa Brāhmaṇa[1] and in the Jaiminīya Upaniṣad Brāhmaṇa.[2]

1 xiii. 11, 10.

2 iii. 159 *et seq.* (*Journal of the American Oriental Society*, 26, 64).

Vidarbha occurs in the earlier Vedic literature as the name of a place only in the Jaiminīya Upaniṣad Brāhmaṇa,[1] where its **Mācalas** (perhaps a species of dog) are said to kill tigers.

1 ii. 440 (*Journal of the American Oriental Society*, 19, 103, n. 3).

Vidarbhī-Kauṇḍineya is the name of a teacher, a pupil of **Vatsanapāt** in the first two Vaṃśas (lists of teachers) of the Bṛhadāraṇyaka Upaniṣad.[1]

1 ii. 5, 22; iv. 5, 28 (Mādhyaṃdina = ii. 6, 3; iv. 6, 3 Kāṇva).

Vi-diś denotes[1] an 'intermediate quarter.' See **Diś**.

1 Vājasaneyi Saṃhitā, vi. 19; Ṣaḍviṃśa Brāhmaṇa, iv. 4.

Vidīgaya is the name of an animal in the Taittirīya Saṃhitā[1] and the Taittirīya Brāhmaṇa.[2] The commentary on the former takes it as a kind of cock (*kukkuṭa-viśeṣa*), that on the latter as a white heron (*śveta-baka*).

1 v. 6, 22, 1.

2 iii. 9, 9, 3; Āpastamba Śrauta Sūtra, xx. 22, 13. *Cf.* Zimmer, *Altindisches Leben*, 94.

Videgha is the name of a man, **Māthava,** in the Śatapatha Brāhmaṇa.[1] It is legitimate to assume[2] that it is a name given to him as king of the Videghas who are the later **Videhas.**

[1] i. 4, 1, 10 *et seq.*

[2] *Cf.* Eggeling, *Sacred Books of the East*, 12, xli, n. 4; 104, n.; Weber, *Indische Studien*, 1, 170; *Indische Streifen*, 1, 13; *Indian Literature*, 134.

Videha is the name of a people who are not mentioned before the Brāhmaṇa period. In the Śatapatha Brāhmaṇa[1] the legend of **Videgha Māthava** preserves clearly a tradition that in Videha culture came from the Brahmins of the West, and that **Kosala** was brahminized before Videha. The Videhas, however, derived some fame later from the culture of their king **Janaka,** who figures in the Bṛhadāraṇyaka Upaniṣad[2] as one of the leading patrons of the Brahman doctrine. In the Kauṣītaki Upaniṣad[3] the Videhas are joined with the **Kāśis**; in the list of peoples in the Aitareya Brāhmaṇa[4] the Videhas are passed over, probably because, with Kosala and Kāśi, they are included in the term **Prācyas,** 'easterners.' Again, in the Śāṅkhāyana Śrauta Sūtra[5] it is recorded that the Kāśi, Kosala, and Videha kingdoms had each the one Purohita, **Jala Jātūkarṇya**; and in another passage of the same text[6] the connexion between the Videha king, **Para Āṭṇāra**, and the Kosala king, **Hiraṇyanābha,** is explained, while the Śatapatha Brāhmaṇa[7] speaks of Para Āṭṇāra as the Kosala king, descendant of Hiraṇyanābha.

Another king of Videha was **Namī Sāpya,** mentioned in the Pañcaviṃśa Brāhmaṇa.[8] In the Saṃhitās of the Yajurveda[9] 'cows of Videha' seem to be alluded to, though the commentator on the Taittirīya Saṃhitā merely takes the adjective *vaidehī* as 'having a splendid body' (*viśiṣṭa-deha-sambandhinī*), and the point of a place name in the expression is not very obvious. The Videhas also occur in the Baudhāyana Śrauta Sūtra[10] in Brāhmana-like passages.

The boundary of Kosala and Videha was the **Sadānīrā,**

[1] i. 4, 1, 10 *et seq.*

[2] iii. 8, 2. *Cf.* iv. 2, 6; 9, 30; Śatapatha Brāhmaṇa, xi. 3, 1, 2; 6, 2, 1; 3, 1; Taittirīya Brāhmaṇa, iii. 10, 9, 9.

[3] iv. 1.

[4] viii. 14.

[5] xvi. 29, 5.

[6] xvi. 9, 11. 13.

[7] xiii. 5, 4, 4.

[8] xxv. 10, 17.

[9] Taittirīya Saṃhitā, ii. 1, 4, 5; Kāṭhaka Saṃhitā, xiv. 5.

[10] ii. 5; xxi. 13.

probably the modern Gandak[11] (the Kondochates of the Greek geographers), which, rising in Nepal, flows into the Ganges opposite Patna. Videha itself corresponds roughly to the modern Tirhut.

[11] *Cf*. *Imperial Gazetteer of India*, 12, 125.
Cf. Weber, *Indische Studien*, 1, 170; *Indian Literature*, 10, 33, 53, 127, 129, etc.; Eggeling, *Sacred Books of the East*, 12, xli; Oldenberg, *Buddha*, 398, 399; Rhys Davids, *Buddhist India*, 26, 37; Pargiter, *Journal of the Royal Asiatic Society*, 1910, 19 *et seq*.

Vidyā in the Atharvaveda[1] and later[2] denotes 'knowledge,' especially that of the three Vedas, which are called the *trayī vidyā*, 'the threefold knowledge,' as early as the Taittirīya Brāhmaṇa.[3] In a more special sense Vidyā occurs in lists of objects of study in the Śatapatha Brāhmaṇa.[4] What exactly the expression here means is uncertain: Sāyaṇa[5] suggests the philosophic systems; Geldner[6] the first Brāhmaṇas; and Eggeling,[7] more probably, special sciences like the **Sarpavidyā** or the **Viṣavidyā.**

[1] vi. 116, 1; xi. 7, 10; 8, 3.
[2] Taittirīya Saṃhitā, ii. 1, 2, 8; v. 1, 7, 2; Aitareya Brāhmaṇa, viii. 23, 8. 9, etc.
[3] iii. 10, 11, 5. *Cf*. Śatapatha Brāhmaṇa, v. 5, 5, 6, etc.
[4] xi. 5, 6, 8; Bṛhadāraṇyaka Upaniṣad, ii. 4, 10; iv. 5, 11.
[5] On Śatapatha Brāhmaṇa, xi. 5, 6, 8.
[6] *Vedische Studien*, 1, 290, n. 4.
[7] *Sacred Books of the East*, 44, 98, n. 2.

Vidradha denotes a disease, 'abscesses,' in the Atharvaveda.[1] According to Zimmer,[2] it was a symptom accompanying **Yakṣma.** Later it is called Vidradhi. Ludwig[3] compares the obscure Vidradha of the Rigveda,[4] where, however, the sense of the word is very uncertain.[5]

[1] vi. 127, 1; ix. 8, 20.
[2] *Altindisches Leben*, 386.
[3] Translation of the Rigveda, 5, 93. *Cf*. Roth, *Nirukta*, *Erläuterungen*, 42, 43.
[4] iv. 32, 23.
[5] Oldenberg, *Ṛgveda-Noten*, 1, 295.
Cf. Wise, *System of Hindu Medicine*, 210; Bloomfield, *Hymns of the Atharvaveda*, 531, 602; *Atharvaveda*, 60; Grohmann, *Indische Studien*, 9, 397; Whitney, Translation of the Atharvaveda, 376.

Vidhavā denotes 'widow' as the 'desolate one,' from the root *vidh*, 'be bereft.' The masculine *vidhava* is conjectured by Roth[1] in a difficult passage of the Rigveda,[2] where the received text presents the apparent false concord *vidhantaṃ vidhavām*, in which he sees a metrical lengthening for *vidhavam*, 'the sacrificing widower.' Ludwig in his version takes *vidhantam* as equivalent to a feminine, while Delbrück[3] prefers 'the worshipper and the widow.' Possibly 'the widower and the widow' may be meant; but we know nothing of the mythological allusion in question, the feat being one of those attributed to the Aśvins, and the natural reference to **Ghoṣā** as 'husbandless' being rendered unlikely because their feat in regard to her has already been mentioned a few verses before in the same hymn.[4] The word Vidhavā is not of common occurrence.[5]

[1] St. Petersburg Dictionary, *s.v.*; so also Grassmann.

[2] x. 40, 8.

[3] *Die indogermanischen Verwandtschaftsnamen*, 443.

[4] x. 40. 5.

[5] Rv. iv. 18, 12; x. 40, 2; Ṣaḍviṃśa Brāhmaṇa, iii. 7; Nirukta, iii. 15.

Vidhu seems clearly to mean (as it does in the post-Vedic language) the 'moon' in a passage of the Rigveda,[1] where it is alluded to as 'wandering solitary in the midst of many' (*vidhuṃ dadrāṇaṃ samane bahūnām*).

[1] x. 55, 5; Nirukta, xiv. 18. *Cf.* Hillebrandt, *Vedische Mythologie*, 1, 465. That the 'many' are the **Nakṣatras** is neither certain nor even probable. The stars are an adequate explanation.

Vi-naśana, 'disappearance,' is the name of the place where the **Sarasvatī** is lost in the sands of the desert. It is mentioned in the Pañcaviṃśa Brāhmaṇa[1] and the Jaiminīya Upaniṣad Brāhmaṇa.[2] The locality is the Patiala district of the Panjab.[3] *Cf.* **Plakṣa Prāsravaṇa.**

[1] xxv. 10, 6; Kātyāyana Śrauta Sūtra, xxiv. 5, 30; Lāṭyāyana Śrauta Sūtra, x. 15, 1; Baudhāyana Dharma Sūtra, i. 1, 2, 12. *Cf.* Bühler, *Sacred Books of the East*, 14, 2, 147.

[2] iv. 26.

[3] *Cf. Imperial Gazetteer of India*, 22, 97.

Vip in several passages of the Rigveda[1] refers, according to Roth,[2] to the rods which form the bottom of the Soma filter,

[1] ix. 3, 2; 65, 12; 99, 1.

[2] St. Petersburg Dictionary, *s.v.*

and on which the straining cloth is stretched. But this explanation is very doubtful.[3]

[3] Hillebrandt, *Vedische Mythologie*, 1, 203; Bergaigne, *Religion Védique*, 1, v; Oldenberg, *Zeitschrift der Deutschen Morgenländischen Gesellschaft*, 54, 171; Geldner, *Vedische Studien*, 3, 97-110.

Vi-patha, in the description of the **Vrātya,**[1] denotes a vehicle suited for rough roads. *Cf.* **Anas.**

[1] Av. xv. 2, 1; Pañcaviṃśa Brāhmaṇa, xvii. 1, 14; Lāṭyāyana Śrauta Sūtra, viii. 6, 9; Anupada Sūtra, v. 4; Kātyāyana Śrauta Sūtra, xxii. 4, 11; Āpastamba Srauta Sūtra, xxii. 5, 5; *cf.* vii. 3, 8. *Cf.* Weber, *Indische Studien*, 1, 44.

1. **Vipaścit Dṛḍha-jayanta Lauhitya** ('descendant of Lohita') is mentioned in the Jaiminīya Upaniṣad Brāhmaṇa (iii. 42, 1) as the pupil of **Dakṣa Jayanta Lauhitya.**

2. **Vipaścit Śakuni-mitra Pārāśarya** ('descendant of **Parāśara**') is the name of a teacher, pupil of **Aṣāḍha Uttara Pārāśarya,** in a Vaṃśa (list of teachers) of the Jaiminīya Upaniṣad Brāhmaṇa (iii. 41, 1).

Vi-pāś ('fetterless') is the name of a river mentioned twice in the Rigveda.[1] It is the modern Beās in the Panjab, the Hyphasis, Hypanis or Bipasis of the Greeks. Its small importance for the Vedic Indians is indicated by the fact that it is never mentioned in the earlier Vedic literature except in two hymns of the Rigveda. The Nirukta[2] preserves the notice that its earlier name was **Uruñjirā,** while the Gopatha Brāhmaṇa[3] places in the middle of it the *Vasiṣṭha-śilāḥ*. Pāṇini[4] mentions the name, which otherwise in post-Vedic literature appears as Vipāśā. This river has changed its course considerably since ancient times.[5]

[1] iii. 33, 1. 3; iv. 30, 11. Yāska, Nirukta, xi. 48, sees in the latter passage an adjective *vi-pāśin*, but this is very improbable. See Oldenberg, *Ṛgveda-Noten*, 1, 294.

[2] ix. 26. The Vipāś is also mentioned in connexion with the **Śutudrī** in ii. 24; ix. 36.

[3] i. 2, 7.

[4] iv. 2, 74.

[5] See *Imperial Gazetteer of India*, 7, 138 (Beās).

Cf. Zimmer, *Altindisches Leben*, 11.

Vi-pūjana Śaurāki[1] or Saurāki[2] is the name of a teacher in the Yajurveda Saṃhitās.

[1] Maitrāyaṇī Saṃhitā, iii. 1, 3.

[2] Kāṭhaka Saṃhitā, xxvii. 5.

Vipṛthu in the Śāṅkhāyana Śrauta Sūtra (xiv. 72, 3) is apparently equivalent to the **Vipatha**, 'rough cart,' of other texts. It is probably a mere blunder.

Vipra seems to mean 'inspired singer' (from *vip*, 'quiver') in the Rigveda[1] and later.[2] More especially in the later texts[3] it denotes a 'learned Brahmin.' In the epic style it comes to mean no more than 'Brahmin.'

[1] i. 129, 2. 11; 162, 7; iv. 26, 1, etc. Seven are spoken of in iii. 7, 7; 31, 5; iv. 2, 15, etc.

[2] Taittirīya Saṃhitā, ii. 5, 9, 1; Vājasaneyi Saṃhitā, ix. 4; Śatapatha Brāhmaṇa, i. 4, 2, 7, etc.

[3] Śatapatha Brāhmaṇa, iii. 5, 3, 12, etc.

Vipra-citti[1] or **Vipra-jitti**[2] is the name of a teacher in the first two Vaṃśas (lists of teachers) in the Bṛhadāraṇyaka Upaniṣad.

[1] ii. 6, 3; iv. 6, 3 Kāṇva.

[2] ii. 5, 22; iv. 5, 28 Mādhyaṃdina.

Vipra-jana Saurāki is the form of the name of **Vipūjana** given by the St. Petersburg Dictionaries for the Kāṭhaka Saṃhitā.[1]

[1] xxvii. 5; Weber, *Indische Studien*, 3, 477, gives this form, which is due to a misreading of the ligature for *ū*.

Vibālī is found once in the Rigveda,[1] apparently as the name of an unknown stream.

[1] iv. 30, 12. *Cf.* Zimmer, *Altindisches Leben*, 12, 18.

Vibhaṇḍaka Kāśyapa ('descendant of **Kaśyapa**') is the name of a teacher, a pupil of **Ṛṣyaśṛṅga** in the Vaṃśa Brāhmaṇa.[1]

[1] *Indische Studien*, 4, 374. *Cf.* St. Petersburg Dictionary, *s.v. Vibhāṇḍaka*, which is the more correct spelling (Böhtlingk, Dictionary, *s.v.*).

Vi-bhindu is the name of a sacrificer in the Rigveda (viii. 2, 91).

Cf. Hopkins, *Journal of the American Oriental Society*, 17, 59.

Vibhinduka occurs in the Pañcaviṃśa Brāhmaṇa[1] as the name of a man or a demon[2] from whom **Medhātithi** drove away the cows. Hopkins[3] is inclined to read Vaibhinduka as a patronymic of Medhātithi. *Cf.* **Vibhindukīya**.

[1] xv. 10, 11.
[2] *Cf.* Sāyaṇa, *a.l.*
[3] *Transactions of the Connecticut Academy of Arts and Sciences*, 15, 60, n. 1.

Vibhindukīya is the name of a group of priests whose Sattra is mentioned in the Jaiminīya Upaniṣad Brāhmaṇa.[1]

[1] iii. 233 (*Journal of the American Oriental Society*, 18, 38).

Vibhītaka[1] and **Vibhīdaka**,[2] the latter being the old form, denote a large tree, the *Terminalia bellerica*, the nut of which was used in dicing.[3] The wood was also used for making the sacrificial fire burn.[4]

[1] This form is the regular one after the Rigveda.
[2] Rv. vii. 86, 6; x. 34, 1.
[3] Rv., *loc. cit.* See 2. **Akṣa.**
[4] Taittirīya Saṃhitā, ii. 1, 5, 8; 7, 3. *Cf.* Śatapatha Brāhmaṇa, xiii. 8, 1, 16, etc.

Cf. Zimmer, *Altindisches Leben*, 62; Roth, *Gurupūjākaumudī*, 1-4; Lüders, *Das Würfelspiel im alten Indien*, 17-19.

1. **Vi-mada** is credited by the Anukramaṇī (Index) with the authorship of a number of hymns of the Rigveda.[1] This attribution is supported by the occurrence in this group of the name of the seer,[2] and once of his family, the Vimadas,[3] besides the repeated refrain[4] *vi vo made*, 'in your carouses.' Vimada is occasionally alluded to later.[5]

[1] Rv. x. 20-26.
[2] Rv. x. 20, 10; 23, 7.
[3] Rv. x. 23, 6.
[4] Rv. x. 21, 1-8; 24, 1-3.
[5] Av. iv. 29, 4; Aitareya Brāhmaṇa, v. 5, 1.

2. **Vimada** is mentioned in several passages of the Rigveda[1] as a protégé of the Aśvins, who gave him a wife, **Kamadyū.** His identity with the preceding is improbable.

[1] i. 51, 3; 112, 19; 116, 1; 117, 20; x. 39, 7; 65, 12. From viii. 9, 15, Ludwig, Translation of the Rigveda, 3, 105, has inferred that Vimada and Vatsa were identical.

Vi-muktā (lit., 'secreted'), 'pearl,' is found in the late Ṣaḍviṃśa Brāhmaṇa (v. 6).

Vi-moktṛ in the list of victims at the Puruṣamedha[1] ('human sacrifice') denotes one who unharnesses horses from the chariot, as opposed to Yoktṛ, 'one who yokes.' The corresponding verbal noun Vimocana, 'unyoking,' is often found.[2]

[1] Vājasaneyi Saṃhitā, xxx. 14; Taittirīya Brāhmaṇa, iii. 4, 10, 1 (*cf. vimoktrī*, used metaphorically, *ibid.*, iii. 7, 14, 1).

[2] Rv. iii. 53, 5, 20; iv. 46, 7, etc.; Taittirīya Saṃhitā, vii. 5, 1, 5, etc.

Vi-rāj as a title of royalty is mentioned several times in the Rigveda,[1] but only in a metaphorical sense. As an actual title, it is asserted in the Aitareya Brāhmaṇa[2] to be used by the **Uttara Kurus** and the **Uttara Madras.**

[1] i. 188, 5; ix. 96, 18; x. 166, 1, etc.; Av. xii. 3, 11; xiv. 2, 15, etc.

[2] viii. 14, 3.

Vi-rūpa is the name of an **Aṅgirasa** who is twice mentioned in the Rigveda,[1] and to whom certain hymns are attributed by the Anukramaṇī (Index).

[1] i. 45, 3; viii. 75, 6.

[2] viii. 43 *et seq.*; 64.

Viligī denotes a kind of snake in the Atharvaveda (v. 13, 7).

Viliṣṭa-bheṣaja in the Atharvaveda (Paippalāda, xx. 5, 2) denotes a remedy for a dislocation or a sprain.

Vi-lohita is the name of a disease mentioned in the Atharvaveda.[1] Bloomfield[2] thinks that 'flow of blood from the nose' is meant; Henry[3] renders it 'decomposition of the blood'; and Whitney[4] has 'anæmia.'

[1] ix. 8, 1; xii. 4, 4

[2] *Hymns of the Atharvaveda*, 657.

[3] *Les livres viii. et ix. de l'Atharvaveda*, 105, 142.

[4] Translation of the Atharvaveda, 549.

Vi-vadha or **Vī-vadha** seems to denote a yoke borne on the shoulders to enable one to carry a weight. But it is found in the Brāhmaṇas used only metaphorically in such phrases as *vi-vivadha*,[1] 'with the weight unequally distributed,' and *sa-vīvadhatā*,[2] 'equality of burden.'

[1] Taittirīya Saṃhitā, vii. 2, 5, 2; 7, 3; *vivīvadha*, Pañcaviṃśa Brāhmaṇa, iv. 5, 19; *ubhayato-vīvadha*, Kāṭhaka Saṃhitā, xxvii. 10.

[2] Aitareya Brāhmaṇa, viii. 1, 4; Pañcaviṃśa Brāhmaṇa, xiv. 1, 10; *sa-vivadha-tva*, v. 1, 11; xxii. 5, 7, etc.

Vi-vayana denotes in the Brāhmaṇas 'plaited work,' such as that used in a couch (**Asandī**).

[1] Aitareya Brāhmaṇa, viii. 5, 3; Śatapatha Brāhmaṇa, xii. 8, 3, 6. In the Sūtras *vivāna* has the same sense: Lāṭyāyana Srauta Sūtra, iii. 12, 1, etc.

Vi-vāha, 'marriage,' is mentioned in the Atharvaveda[1] and later.[2] See **Pati.**

[1] xii. 1, 24; xiv. 2, 65. The Rigvedic term is **Vahatu.**

[2] Taittirīya Saṃhitā, vii. 2, 8, 7; Kāṭhaka Saṃhitā, xxv. 3; Pañcaviṃśa Brāhmaṇa, vii. 10, 4; Aitareya Brāhmaṇa, iv. 27, 5, and often in the Sūtras.

Viś is an expression of somewhat doubtful significance. In many passages of the Rigveda[1] the sense of 'settlement' or 'dwelling' is adequate and probable, since the root *viś* means to 'enter' or 'settle.' In other passages, where the Viśaḥ

[1] iv. 4, 3; 37, 1; v. 3, 5; vi. 21, 4; 48, 8; vii. 56, 22; 61, 3; 70, 3; 104, 18; x. 91, 2, etc.

stand in relation to a prince, the term must mean 'subject';[2] so, for example, when the people of **Tṛṇaskanda**[3] or of the **Tṛtsus** are mentioned.[4] Again, in some passages[5] the general sense of 'people' is adequate; as when the Rigveda speaks of the 'Āryan people,'[6] or the 'divine people,'[7] or the 'Dāsa people,' and so on.[8]

Sometimes,[9] however, the Viś appear in a more special sense as a subdivision of the **Jana** or whole people. This is, however, not common, for in most passages one or other of the senses given above is quite possible. Moreover, it is very difficult to decide whether the Viś as a subdivision of the Jana is to be considered as being a local subdivision (canton) or a blood kinship equivalent to a clan in the large sense of the word, while the relation of the Viś to the **Grāma** or to the **Gotra** is quite uncertain. In one passage of the Atharvaveda[10] the Viśaḥ are mentioned along with the *sabandhavaḥ* or relatives, but no definite conclusion can be drawn from that fact. Nor does the analogy of the Roman *curia* or the Greek *φρήτρη* throw much light, as these institutions are themselves of obscure character, and the parallelism need not be cogent. It is, at any rate, possible that the Viś may in some cases have been no more than a Gotra or clan, or different clans may sometimes

[2] Rv. iv. 50, 8; vi. 8, 4; x. 124, 8; 173, 6; Av. iii. 4, 1; iv. 8, 4; 22, 1. 3; Taittirīya Saṃhitā, iii. 2, 8, 6; Vājasaneyi Saṃhitā, viii. 46; Śatapatha Brāhmaṇa, i. 8, 2, 17; iv. 2, 1, 3; v. 3, 3, 12; 4, 2, 3; x. 6, 2, 1; xiii. 6, 2, 8; Kauṣītaki Upaniṣad, iv. 12, etc. Many of the passages cited under note 11 may also belong here, while in Av. iii. 4, 1, etc., reference to the cantons as electing a king has been seen; but see **Rājan** and *cf.* Pischel, *Vedische Studien*, 1, 179; Geldner, *Vedische Studien*, 2, 303; Hopkins, *Journal of the American Oriental Society*, 13, 113.

[3] Rv. i. 172, 3.

[4] Rv. vii. 33, 6; Geldner, *op. cit.*, 136.

[5] *E.g.*, Rv. vi. 1, 8; 26, 1; viii. 71, 11; *manuṣo viśaḥ*, vi. 14, 2; viii. 23, 13; *mānuṣīḥ*, x. 80, 6, etc.

[6] Rv. x. 11, 4.

[7] Rv. iii. 34, 2; Av. vi. 98, 2; Vājasaneyi Saṃhitā, xvii. 86.

[8] Rv. iv. 28, 4; vi. 25, 2; *adevīḥ*, viii. 96, 15; *asiknīḥ*, vii. 5, 3, etc.

[9] Rv. ii. 26, 3, where it is opposed to *jana*, *janman*, and *putrāḥ*; x. 84, 4, where in battle *viśam-viśam* apparently refers to divisions of the host (*cf.* also iv. 24, 4, *viśo yudhmāḥ*); x. 91, 2, where it is opposed to *gṛha* and *jana*; Av. xiv. 2, 27, where *gṛhebhyaḥ* is followed by *asyai sarvasyai viśe*, which must mean a division less than a whole people. Zimmer, *Altindisches Leben*, 159, reckons here Rv. i. 172, 3; vii. 33, 6; ix. 7, 5; x. 124, 8; 173, 1; but these cases and many others are rather instances of 'subjects' than of a division of the tribe such as 'canton.'

[10] xv. 8, 2. 3. *Cf.* xiv. 2, 27, and Rv. x. 91, 2, in n. 9.

have made up a Viś, while Grāma is more definitely, perhaps, a local designation. But the Vedic evidence is quite inconclusive.[11] *Cf.* **Viśpati.**

In the later period the sense of Viś is definitely restricted in some cases[12] to denote the third of the classes of the Vedic polity, the people or clansmen as opposed to the nobles (**Kṣatra, Kṣatriya**) and the priests (**Brahman, Brāhmaṇa**). For the position of this class, see **Vaiśya.**

[11] The Viś may have been originally a clan settled in one place: there is no passage where 'Gotra' would not probably make sense; Rv. ii. 26, 3, cannot be pressed unduly to distinguish *janman* and Viś. Compare the phrase used of the Maruts *śardhaṃ śardham, vrātaṃ vrātam, gaṇaṃ gaṇam*, in Rv. v. 53, 11, where no precise sense can fairly be attributed to the words, though Zimmer sees in them a threefold division of the host corresponding to Jana, Viś, and Grāma. The rendering 'Gau' has therefore little foundation.

[12] Perhaps to this sense belong the numerous passages in the Brāhmaṇas and later Saṃhitās referring to strife between the Viś and the Kṣatra, the clansmen and the chiefs, or the peasantry and the nobles—*e.g.*, Taittirīya Saṃhitā, ii. 2, 11, 2; Maitrāyaṇī Saṃhitā, ii. 1, 9; iii. 3, 10; Kāṭhaka Saṃhita, xix. 9 and often. • See also Pañcaviṃśa Brāhmaṇa, xviii. 10, 9; Śatapatha Brāhmaṇa, ii. 1, 3, 5; viii. 7, 2, 3; xiii. 2, 2, 17. 19; 9, 6; xiv. 1, 3, 27, etc.; Chāndogya Upaniṣad, viii. 14. *Cf.* Zimmer, *Altindisches Leben*, 15 *et seq.*; Schrader, *Prehistoric Antiquities*, 800 *et seq.*; Macdonell, *Sanskrit Literature*, 158; von Schroeder, *Indiens Literatur und Cultur*, 32, 33; St. Petersburg Dictionary, *s.v.* For the Roman *curia*, which was apparently a collection of *gentes*, perhaps local, *cf.* Mommsen, *History of Rome*, 1, 72 *et seq.*; *Römische Forschungen*, 1, 140-150; *Rōmisches Staatsrecht*, 3, 9; Taylor, *History of Rome*, 11, 12; Smith, *Dictionary of Antiquities*, 1, 576; Cuq, *Les institutions juridiques des Romains*, 30-36. For the Greek Phratria, which was probably similar in character, consisting of a union of γένη, see *Dictionary of Antiquities*, 2, 876 *et seq.*; Greenidge, *Greek Constitutional History*, 128 *et seq.*; Bury, *History of Greece*, 69, 70; Gilbert, *Greek Constitutional Antiquities*, 1, 104 *et seq.*, 210. For the English hundreds, and the supposed analogy of the *pagi* of Tacitus, see the references in Medley, *English Constitutional History*,[2] 318 *et seq.*

Vi-śara is found as the name of a disease, perhaps 'tearing pains,' in the Atharvaveda.[1] Zimmer[2] thinks that the pains in the limbs attendant on fever (**Takman**) are alluded to. Roth[3] sees in the word the name of a demon. The view of Zimmer is supported by the use of *viśarīka*, 'rending,' beside **Balāsa** in another passage.[4]

[1] ii. 4, 2.

[2] *Altindisches Leben*, 391.

[3] St. Petersburg Dictionary, *s.v.*

[4] xix. 34, 10. *Cf.* Bloomfield, *Hymns of the Atharvaveda*, 284.

Vi-śākhe. See **Nakṣatra.**

Viś-pati is a word of somewhat uncertain signification, reflecting in this respect the nature of **Viś**. Zimmer holds that in its strict sense it denotes the head of a canton, but he admits that there is no passage requiring this sense, the only one quoted by him[2] being certainly indecisive. In the great majority of passages the word simply means the 'lord of the dwelling,' whether used of a man or of the god Agni as the householder *par excellence*, or possibly as the fire of the **Sabhā** or assembly house of the people. This sense suits even the passage of the Rigveda[4] in which the Viśpati, as well as the father and the mother of a maiden,[5] are to be lulled to sleep in order to allow her lover to approach her, for the household may well be deemed to have been a joint family, in which the Viśpati could easily be different from the father of the girl—*e.g.*, a grandfather or uncle. In other passages[6] the Viśpati is the king as 'lord of the subject-people' (*viśām*), though here Zimmer[7] thinks reference is made to the election of a king.[8] Or again,[7] the Viśpati is the chief of the Viś, probably in the sense of 'subjects.'

[1] *Altindisches Leben*, 171.

[2] Rv. i. 37. 8.

[3] Rv. i. 12, 2; 26, 7; 164, 1; ii. 1, 8; iii. 2, 10; 40, 3; vii. 39, 2; ix. 108, 10; x. 4, 4; 135, 1, etc. So Viśpatnī of the lady of the house, Taittirīya Saṃhitā, iii. 1, 11, 4.

[4] vii. 55, 5 = Av. iv. 5, 6.

[5] So Aufrecht, *Indische Studien*, 4, 337 *et seq.*; Zimmer, *op. cit.*, 308. *Cf.* Lanman, *Sanskrit Reader*, 370. Geldner, *Vedische Studien*, 2, 55 *et seq.*, accepts the view of the Bṛhaddevatā, vi. 11 *et seq.* (where see Macdonell's note), that the hymn refers to Vasiṣṭha's approaching a house as a thief! The interpretation does not affect the sense of Viśpati, which here is clearly not the title of a cantonal chief. Viś is sometimes equivalent to **Sajāta**; *cf.* Taittirīya Saṃhitā, ii. 1, 3, 2. 3.

[6] Av. iii. 4, 1; iv. 22, 3. Perhaps Rv. iii. 13, 5, is so to be taken; *cf.* vii. 39, 2. *Cf.* Weber, *Indische Studien*, 18, 22.

[7] *Op. cit.*, 164, 165.

[8] But see **Rājan.**

[9] *E.g.*, Taittirīya Saṃhitā, ii. 3, 1, 3, where Viś must clearly be the people or subject class, and the Viśpati their chief representative; we cannot from such a passage infer a formal office of Viśpati even as head of the Viś.

Viśpalā is, according to the tradition in the Rigveda,[1] the name of a woman to whom the Aśvins gave an iron (*āyasī*)

[1] i. 112, 10; 116 15; 11, 11; 118, 8; x. 39, 8.

limb to replace one lost by her in a contest. Pischel[2] considers that a racing horse miraculously cured of a broken limb by the Aśvins is meant, but this is no more than an improbable conjecture.

[2] *Vedische Studien*, 1, 171-173. *Cf.* Macdonell, *Vedic Mythology*, 52; Muir, *Sanskrit Texts*, 5, 245; Bloomfield, *Religion of the Veda*, 113; Oldenberg, *Ṛgveda-Noten*, 1, 110, 111.

Viśvaka, in the Rigveda[1] called Kṛṣṇiya (possibly 'son of **Kṛṣṇa**') is a protégé of the Aśvins, who restored to him his lost son, **Viṣṇāpu.** See 2. **Kṛṣṇa.**

[1] i. 116, 23; 117, 7; viii. 86, 1; x. 65, 12. *Cf.* Macdonell, *Vedic Mythology*, 52.

Viśva-karman Bhauvana ('descendant of Bhuvana') is the name of a quite mythical king. He is said in the Aitareya Brāhmaṇa to have been consecrated by **Kaśyapa**, to whom he offered the earth (*i.e.*, presumably a piece of land) as a sacrificial fee; in the Śatapatha Brāhmaṇa[2] he performed the Sarvamedha ('universal sacrifice'), and made a similar offer; in both cases the earth refused to be given. The story seems to contain a reference to the early dislike of gifts of land,[3] but it cannot be stated with certainty that this is the meaning.

[1] viii. 21, 8.
[2] xiii. 7, 1, 15.
[3] Rhys Davids, *Buddhist India*, 47.

Cf. Eggeling, *Sacred Books of the East*, 44, 421, n. 1; Muir, *Sanskrit Texts*, 1[2], 456, 457.

Viśvan-tara Sau-ṣadmana ('descendant of Suṣadman') is the name in the Aitareya Brāhmaṇa[1] of a prince who set aside the **Śyāparṇas**, his priests, and performed a sacrifice without their help, presumably with the aid of others. **Rāma Mārgaveya**, one of the Śyāparṇas, however, succeeded in inducing the king to reinstate the Śyāparṇas, and to give him a thousand cows.

[1] vii. 27, 3. 4; 34, 7. 8. *Cf.* Muir, *Sanskrit Texts*, 1[2], 431-440; Eggeling, *Sacred Books of the East*, 43, 344, n.

Viśva-manas is the name of a Ṛṣi mentioned in two passages of the Rigveda,[1] and as a friend of Indra in the Pañcaviṃśa

[1] viii. 23, 2; 24, 7.

Brāhmaṇa.[2] According to the Anukramaṇī (Index), he was a descendant of **Vyaśva,** and the author of certain hymns.[3]

[2] xv. 5, 20.

[3] Rv. viii. 23-26. *Cf.* Ludwig, Translation of the Rigveda, 3, 106.

Viśva-mānuṣa in one passage of the Rigveda[1] may be a proper name, but more probably merely means 'all mankind.'

[1] viii. 45, 22. *Cf.* Ludwig, Translation of the Rigveda, 3, 187.

Viśva-vāra occurs in one passage of the Rigveda[1] apparently as the name of a sacrificer.

[1] v. 44, 11. *Cf.* Ludwig, Translation of the Rigveda, 3, 138.

Viśvā-sāman is the name of a Ṛṣi, an **Atreya,** in the Rigveda.[1]

[1] v. 22, 1. *Cf.* Oldenberg, *Zeitschrift der Deutschen Morgenländischen Gesellschaft*, 42, 215.

Viśva-sṛj is the name of certain mythical beings to whom, however, a Sattra, or sacrificial session, is ascribed in the Pañcaviṃśa Brāhmaṇa (xxv. 18, 1 *et seq.*).

Viśvā-mitra ('friend of all') is the name of a Ṛṣi who is mentioned in the Rigveda,[1] and to whom the third Maṇḍala is attributed by tradition. In one hymn[2] which appears to be his own composition, he praises the rivers **Vipāś** (Beas) and **Śutudrī** (Sutlej). There he calls himself the son of **Kuśika,** and seems unquestionably to be the helper of the **Bharatas,** whom he mentions. The tribe, engaged in a raid, apparently came to the rivers from the east.[4] Anxious to cross them, they

[1] As son of Kuśika in Rv. iii. 33, 5; as Viśvāmitra in iii. 53, 7. 12.

[2] iii. 33. Ludwig, Translation of the Rigveda, 3, 121, thinks the hymn too poetical to be a re l composition of the reputed author.

[3] Rv. iii. 33, 5.

[4] So Geldner, *Vedische Studien*, 3, 152. Zimmer, *Altindisches Leben*, 127, 128, takes a different view: with Roth, *Zur Litteratur und Geschichte des Weda*, 90, he assumes that the Bharatas were different from the **Tṛtsus,** and that they came under Viśvāmitra from the West, but were defeated (see Rv. vii. 33, 6). But see Weber, *Episches im vedischen Ritual*, 34, n. 1; Pischel, *Vedische Studien*, 2, 136. Bloomfield, *Journal of the American Oriental Society*, 16, 41, 42, still defends Roth's view.

found them in high flood, but Viśvāmitra by prayer induced the waters to subside. The same feat appears to be referred to in another passage of the same book of the Rigveda.[5] Curiously enough, Sāyaṇa[6] quite misunderstands the situation: according to him, Viśvāmitra having obtained wealth by the exercise of his office, went off with it to the rivers, pursued by others. Yāska's[7] version of the tale merely seems to mean that the king paid Viśvāmitra to act as his **Purohita,** or domestic priest. For the relations of Viśvāmitra to Vasiṣṭha connected with their service of **Sudās,** see **Vasiṣṭha.**

The Viśvāmitras are mentioned in several other passages of the Rigveda,[8] and are also designated as a family by the term **Kuśikas.**[9]

In the later literature Viśvāmitra becomes, like Vasiṣṭha, a mythical sage, usually[10] mentioned in connection with **Jamadagni**; he was Hotṛ priest at the sacrifice of **Śunaḥśepa,** whom he adopted, and to whom he gave the name of **Devarāta.**[11] He was a protégé of Indra, with whom he had an interview according to the Rigveda Āraṇyakas.[12] He is also often mentioned as a Ṛṣi.[13]

In the Epic[14] Viśvāmitra is represented as a king, who becomes a Brahmin. There is no trace of his kingship in the Rigveda, but the Nirukta[15] calls his father, Kuśika, a king; the

5 iii. 53, 9-11. This hymn is probably later.

6 Sāyaṇa on Rv. iii. 33.

7 Nirukta, ii. 24.

8 iii. 1, 21; 18, 4; 53, 13; x. 89, 17; Av. xviii. 3, 6; 4, 54; Jaiminīya Upaniṣad Brāhmaṇa, iii. 15, 1.

9 Rv. iii. 26, 1. 3; 29, 15; 30, 20; 42, 9; 53, 9. 10.

10 *Cf.* Rv. iii. 53, 15. 16; Ṣaḍguruśiṣya in Macdonell's edition of the Sarvānukramaṇī, p. 107; Weber, *Indische Studien*, 1, 117; Muir, *Sanskrit Texts*, 1², 343; Geldner, *Vedische Studien*, 3, 158 *et seq.*

11 Aitareya Brāhmaṇa, vii. 16 *et seq.*; Śāṅkhāyana Śrauta Sūtra, xv. 17 *et seq.*

12 Aitareya Āraṇyaka. ii. 2, 3; Śāṅkhāyana Āraṇyaka, i. 5.

13 Aitareya Āraṇyaka, ii. 2, 1; Aitareya Brāhmaṇa, vi. 18, 1; 20, 3; Taittirīya Saṃhitā, ii. 2, 1, 2; iii. 1, 7, 3; v. 2, 3, 4, etc.; Kāṭhaka Saṃhitā, xvi. 19; xx. 9; Maitrāyaṇī Saṃhitā, ii. 7, 19; Kauṣītaki Brāhmaṇa, xv. 1; xxvi. 14; xxviii. 1. 2; xxix. 3; Pañcaviṃśa Brāhmaṇa, xiv. 3, 12; Bṛhadāraṇyaka Upaniṣad, ii. 2, 4; Jaiminīya Upaniṣad Brāhmaṇa, iii. 3, 13; 15, 1, etc. Jamadagni is often associated with him, Av. iv. 29, 5, etc.

14 Muir, *Sanskrit Texts*, 1², 388 *et seq.*

15 ii. 24.

Aitareya Brāhmaṇa[16] refers to Śunaḥśepa as succeeding to the lordship of the **Jahnus**, as well as the 'divine lore' (*daiva veda*) of the **Gāthins**; and the Pañcaviṃśa Brāhmaṇa[17] mentions Viśvāmitra as a king. But there is no real trace of this kingship of Viśvāmitra: it may probably be dismissed as a mere legend, with no more foundation at most than that Viśvāmitra was of a family which once had been royal. But even this is doubtful.

[16] vii. 18, 9. But the Śāṅkhāyana Śrauta Sūtra, xv. 27, has a completely different version, which Weber, *Episches im vedischen Ritual*, 16, n. 3, prefers, and which omits all allusion to the 'lordship' of the Jahnus. This shows how little stress can be laid on this late tradition.

[17] xxi. 12, 2.

Cf. Ludwig, Translation of the Rigveda, 3, 121; Oldenberg, *Zeitschrift der Deutschen Morgenländischen Gesellschaft*, 42, 209, 210; Muir, *Sanskrit Texts*, 1², 337 *et seq.*; Weber, *op. cit.*, 16 *et seq.*; *Indian Literature*, 31, 37, 38, 53, etc.

Viṣa in the Rigveda[1] and later[2] regularly denotes 'poison' as an antidote, for which the Atharvaveda supplies spells.[3]

[1] i. 117, 16; 191, 11; vi. 61, 3; x. 87, 18, etc.

[2] Av. iv. 6, 2; v. 19, 10; vi. 90, 2, etc.

[3] Bloomfield, *Atharvaveda*, 61.

Viṣa-vidyā, the 'science of poison,' is enumerated with other sciences in the Āśvalāyana Śrauta Sūtra (x. 75). *Cf.* **Vidyā**.

Viṣāṇā in the Atharvaveda[1] and later[2] denotes an animal's 'horn.'

[1] iii. 7, 1. 2; vi. 121, 1; Aitareya Brāhmaṇa, ii. 11, 10; Śatapatha Brāhmaṇa, vii. 3, 2, 17. Primarily a deciduous horn is meant. See Whitney, Translation of the Atharvaveda, 94.

Viṣāṇakā is the name of a plant in the Atharvaveda.[1] Bloomfield,[2] however, thinks that the word may merely mean 'horn.' It is used as a remedy against the disease Vātīkāra.[3] That

[1] vi. 44, 3. *Cf.* Viṣāṇikā in Wise, *Hindu System of Medicine*, 146, perhaps the *Asclepias geminata*; Bloomfield, *American Journal of Philology*, 12, 426; Zimmer, *Altindisches Leben*, 68. But *cf.* Whitney, Translation of the Atharvaveda, 313.

[2] *Hymns of the Atharvaveda*, 482.

[3] Av. ix. 8, 20; Vātī-kṛta, vi. 44, 3; 109, 3.

disease is of doubtful character: Zimmer[4] thinks that it is one 'caused by wounds,' comparing the adjective *a-vāta*, 'uninjured,' in the Rigveda,[5] but Bloomfield[6] shows that 'wind' in the body is meant as causing the disease.

[4] *Op. cit.*, 389, 390.
[5] vi. 16, 20; ix. 96, 8.
[6] *Op. cit.*, 481 *et seq.*, 516.

Viṣāṇin occurs once in the Rigveda[1] as the name of a tribe in the list of the enemies of the **Tṛtsus,** not as Roth[2] thought, of their allies. The word seems to mean 'having horns,' but in what sense is unknown; perhaps their helmets were horn-shaped or ornamented with horns. They may, like their allies, the **Alinas, Bhalānas, Śivas,** and **Pakthas,** be reckoned as belonging to the tribes of the north-west.

[1] vii. 18, 7.
[2] *Zur Litteratur und Geschichte des Weda*, 95; Zimmer, *Altindisches Leben*, 126. But Zimmer, *op. cit.*, 430, 431, altered his view, and Hopkins' criticism, overlooking this retractation, in the *Journal of the American Oriental Society*, 15, 260, 261, is so far unjustified.
Cf. Ludwig, Translation of the Rigveda, 3, 173.

1. **Viṣuvant** denotes in the Atharvaveda[1] and later[2] the middle day in the Sattra or sacrificial session of a year's duration. Tilak[3] argues that the Viṣūvant literally means the day when night and daylight are equal—*i.e.*, the equinoctial day—and that this is the true sense of the word. But the theory is without probability.

[1] xi. 7, 15.
[2] Pañcaviṃśa Brāhmaṇa, iv. 5, 2; 7, 1; v. 9, 10; Aitareya Brāhmaṇa, iii. 41, 4; iv. 18, 1; 22, 1. 2; vi. 18, 8; Kauṣītaki Brāhmaṇa, xxv. 1; xxvi. 1; Taittirīya Brāhmaṇa, i. 2, 3, 2; Satapatha Brāhmaṇa, x. 1, 2, 2; 3, 14. 23; 4, 2; 2, 1, 8, etc.
[3] *Orion*, 21, 22.
[4] *Cf.* Whitney, *Journal of the American Oriental Society*, 16, lxxxiii. *et seq.*

2. **Viṣūvant** occurs in the description of the house in the Atharvaveda.[1] The meaning seems to be the 'ridge of the roof.'[2]

[1] ix. 3, 8.
[2] *Cf.* Zimmer, *Altindisches Leben*, 151 (who thinks it is a metaphor from the parting of the hair); Bloomfield, *Hymns of the Atharvaveda*, 598; Whitney, Translation of the Atharvaveda, 526.

Viṣūcikā is the name of a disease mentioned in the Vājasaneyi Saṃhitā[1] as a result of over-indulgence in **Soma** drinking. It seems clearly to be 'dysentery,' or, as Wise calls it, 'sporadic cholera.' The term apparently means 'causing evacuations in both directions.'

[1] xix. 10 = Maitrāyaṇī Saṃhitā, iii. 11, 7 = Kāṭhaka Saṃhitā, xxxvii. 18 = Taittirīya Brāhmaṇa, ii. 6, 1, 5 = Śatapatha Brāhmaṇa, xii. 7, 3, 2.

[2] *Hindu System of Medicine*, 330. *Cf.* Zimmer, *Altindisches Leben*, 275, 392.

Vi-ṣkandha occurs several times in the Atharvaveda[1] as the name of a disease. As remedies against it a lead amulet,[2] or hemp,[3] or a salve,[4] or the **Jaṅgiḍa** plant are recommended for use.[5] Weber[6] suggests that the disease meant is 'rheumatism,' because it draws the shoulders apart (*vi-skandha*), but Bloomfield[7] thinks that it is rather the name of a demon, like the Rigvedic Vyaṃśa[8] and Vigrīva,[9] both of which are similarly formed and are names of demons. Possibly Karśapha and Viśapha mentioned in one hymn[10] are plants used to cure the disease.

[1] i. 16, 3; ii. 4, 1 *et seq.*; iii. 9, 2. 6; iv. 9, 5; xix. 34, 5. It is also found in the Taittirīya Saṃhitā, vii. 3, 11, 1.

[2] Av. i. 16, 3. *Cf.* ii. 4; iii. 9, 6.

[3] Av. ii. 4, 5.

[4] Av. iv. 9, 5.

[5] Av. ii. 4, 1. 5; xix. 34, 5; 35, 1.

[6] *Indische Studien*, 4, 410; 13, 141; 17, 215. See Zimmer, *Altindisches Leben*, 390, 391; Grill, *Hundert Lieder*,[2] 75.

[7] *Hymns of the Atharvaveda*, 282, 283.

[8] Rv. i. 32, 5, etc.

[9] Rv. viii. 4, 24.

[10] Av. iii. 9, 1. *Cf.* Bloomfield, *op. cit.*, 340. Roth, St. Petersburg Dictionary, *s.v.*, thinks demons are meant: this seems the more probable view.

Vi-ṣṭārin in the Atharvaveda[1] denotes a special sort of **Odana** or porridge.

[1] iv. 34, 1 *et seq.* According to Whitney, Translation of the Atharvaveda, 206, the designation 'outspread' is due to the fact that the rice mess was kneaded into furrows and juices (*rasa*) were poured into them. See Kauśika Sūtra, lxvi. 6.

Viṣṭhā-vrājin is a word of doubtful significance in the Śatapatha Brāhmaṇa.[1] According to Sāyaṇa, it means 'remaining in one and the same place'; if this is right, the rendering of the

[1] v. 1, 12.

St. Petersburg Dictionary and of Böhtlingk's Dictionary, 'one whose herd is stationary,' seems legitimate. But, as Eggeling[2] points out, the Kāṇva recension of the Śatapatha Brāhmaṇa in another passage[3] seems to treat the word as denoting a disease: thus Viṣṭhāvrājin may mean 'one afflicted by dysentery.'

[2] *Sacred Books of the East*, 41, 123, n. 1.

[3] *Ibid.*, 50, n. 1.

Viṣṇāpu is the son of **Viśvaka** in the Rigveda.[1] When lost he was restored to his father by the Aśvins.

[1] i. 116, 23; 117, 7; viii. 86, 3; x. 65, 12.

Viṣphuliṅga denotes a 'spark' of fire in the Upaniṣads.[1]

[1] Bṛhadāraṇyaka Upaniṣad, ii. 1, 23; vi. 1, 12; Kauṣītaki Upaniṣad, iii. 3; iv. 20, etc. *Cf. viṣpuliṅgaka*, 'scattering sparks of fire,' in Rv. i. 191, 12 (Sāyaṇa, 'a tongue of fire,' or 'sparrow').

Viṣvak-sena is the name of a teacher, a pupil of **Nārada**, mentioned in the Vaṃśa (list of teachers) at the end of the Sāmavidhāna Brāhmaṇa.

Visalya[1] and **Visalyaka**[2] are names of a disease in the Atharvaveda. Since Shaṅkar Paṇḍit's reciters[3] pronounced the word as Visalpaka in all the passages, that should probably be adopted as the right reading.[4] Some sort of pain is meant, perhaps 'neuralgia,' in connexion with fever.

[1] ix. 8, 20.

[2] vi. 127, 1 *et seq.*; ix. 8, 2. 5; xix. 44, 2.

[3] See Bloomfield, *Hymns of the Atharvaveda*, 601; Whitney, Translation of the Atharvaveda, 376. *Cf.* Zimmer, *Altindisches Leben*, 378, 384.

[4] The commentator Sāyaṇa on vi. 127 reads *visalpakaḥ*, and on xix. 44, 2, *visarpakaḥ*.

Vi-sras denotes the 'decay' of old age, 'decrepitude,' 'senility.'[1]

[1] Av. xix. 34, 3, where Böhtlingk, Dictionary, *s.v.*, suggests for *visrasas* the emendation *visruhas* (*cf.* Rv. vi. 7, 6); Taittirīya Brāhmaṇa, iii. 8, 20, 5; Aitareya Āraṇyaka, ii. 3, 7; Aitareya Brāhmaṇa, viii. 20, 7; Kāthaka Upaniṣad, vi. 4.

Vihalha is found in the Atharvaveda[1] apparently as the name of a plant. The forms Vihaṃla and Vihahla occur as variants.

[1] vi. 16, 2. *Cf.* Zimmer, *Altindisches Leben*, 72.

Vīṇā in the later Saṃhitās[1] and the Brāhmaṇas[2] denotes a 'lute.' A Vīṇā-vāda, 'lute-player,' is included in the list of victims at the Puruṣamedha ('human sacrifice') in the Yajurveda,[3] and is also mentioned elsewhere.[4] The Aitareya Āraṇyaka,[5] which states that the instrument was once covered with a hairy skin, enumerates its parts as Śiras, 'head' (*i.e.*, neck); Udara, 'cavity'; Ambhaṇa, 'sounding board'; Tantra, 'string'; and Vādana, 'plectrum.' In the Śatapatha Brāhmaṇa[6] the Uttaramandrā is either a tune or a kind of lute. *Cf.* **Vāṇa.**

[1] Taittirīya Saṃhitā, vi. 1, 4, 1; Kāṭhaka Saṃhitā, xxxiv. 5; Maitrāyaṇī Saṃhitā, iii. 6, 8.

[2] Śatapatha Brāhmaṇa, iii. 2, 4, 6; xiii. 1, 5, 1; *śata-tantrī*, 'hundred-stringed' (like the **Vāṇa**), at the Mahāvrata rite, Śāṅkhāyana Śrauta Sūtra, xvii. 3, 1, etc.; Jaiminīya Brāhmaṇa, i. 42 (*Journal of the American Oriental Society*, 15, 235).

[3] Vājasaneyi Saṃhitā, xxx. 20; Taittirīya Brāhmaṇa, iii. 4, 15, 1.

[4] Bṛhadāraṇyaka Upaniṣad, ii. 4, 8; iv. 5, 9.

[5] iii. 2, 5; *cf.* Śāṅkhāyana Āraṇyaka, viii. 9.

[6] xiii. 4, 2, 8. *Cf.* Eggeling, *Sacred Books of the East*, 44, 356, n. 3.

Cf. Zimmer, *Altindisches Leben*, 289; Hopkins, *Journal of the American Oriental Society*, 13, 328; von Schroeder, *Indiens Literatur und Cultur*, 755.

Vīṇā-gāthin denotes 'lute-player' in the Brāhmaṇas.[1] In the Śatapatha Brāhmaṇa Vīṇāgaṇagin denotes the 'leader of a band.'

[1] Taittirīya Brāhmaṇa, iii. 9, 14, 1; Śatapatha Brāhmaṇa, xiii. 1, 5, 1; 4, 2, 8. 11. 14; 3, 5.

[2] xiii. 4, 3, 3; 4, 2; Śāṅkhāyana Śrauta Sūtra, xvi. 1, 29.

Vīṇā-vāda. See **Vīṇā.**

Vīta-havya is the name of a prince who is mentioned in the Rigveda[1] along with **Bharadvāja**, and as a contemporary of **Sudās**,[2] though in both passages it is possible to understand the

[1] vi. 15, 2. 3.

[2] vii. 19, 3.

word as a mere adjective. In the Atharvaveda[3] Vītahavya appears as connected with **Jamadagni** and **Asita**, but it is clear that the legend there has no value. It is possible, though not certain, that he was a king of the **Sṛñjayas**.[4] In the Yajurveda Saṃhitās[5] a Vītahavya **Śrāyasa** appears as a king: he may be identical with the Vītahavya of the Rigveda, or belong to the same line. *Cf.* **Vaitahavya.**

[3] vi. 137, 1.

[4] Hillebrandt, *Vedische Mythologie*, 1, 105.

[5] Taittirīya Saṃhitā, v. 6, 5, 3; Kāṭhaka Saṃhitā, xxii. 3; Pañcaviṃśa Brāhmaṇa, xxv. 16, 3. *Ibid.*, ix. 1, 9, he is represented as being *niruddha*, apparently in 'banishment'; but the scholiast explains him as not a king, but a Ṛṣi, which is quite possible.

Cf. Oldenberg, *Zeitschrift der Deutschen Morgenländischen Gesellschaft*, 42, 212; *Buddha*, 405.

Vīra in the Rigveda[1] and later[2] denotes 'man' as the strong and heroic. Collectively in the singular[3] the word denotes 'male offspring,' an object of great desire (*cf.* **Putra**) to the Vedic Indian. The Pancaviṃśa Brāhmaṇa[4] gives a list of eight Vīras of the king, constituting his supporters and entourage.

[1] i. 18, 4; 114, 8; iv. 29, 2; v. 20, 4; 61, 5, etc.

[2] Av. ii. 26, 4; iii. 5, 8, etc.

[3] Rv. ii. 32, 4; iii. 4, 9; 36, 10; vii. 34, 20, etc.; Taittirīya Saṃhitā, vii. 1, 8, 1, etc.

[4] xix. 1, 4. Viz., the king's brother, his son, **Purohita, Mahiṣī, Sūta, Grāmaṇī, Kṣattṛ**, and **Saṃgrahītṛ**. See **Ratnin.**

Vīraṇa is the form in the late Ṣaḍviṃśa Brāhmaṇa (v. 2) of the name of the plant **Vīriṇa.**

Vīra-hatyā, 'murder of a man,' is one of the crimes referred to in the Taittirīya Āraṇyaka.[1] The Vīra-han, 'man-slayer,' is often mentioned in the older texts.[2] *Cf.* **Vaira.**

[1] x. 40.

[2] Taittirīya Saṃhitā, i. 5, 2, 1; ii. 2, 5, 5; Kāṭhaka Saṃhitā, xxxi. 7; Kapiṣṭhala Saṃhitā, xxxvii. 7; Maitrāyaṇī Saṃhitā, iv. 1, 9; Taittirīya Brāhmaṇa, iii. 2, 8, 12; Vājasaneyi Saṃhitā, xxx. 5; Pañcaviṃśa Brāhmaṇa, xii. 6, 8; xvi. 1, 12, etc.

Vīriṇa in the Śatapatha Brāhmaṇa[1] denotes a kind of grass (*Andropogon muricatus*). See **Vairiṇa.**

[1] xiii. 8, 1, 15. *Cf.* Zimmer, *Altindisches Leben*, 70.

Vīrudh means 'plant' in the Rigveda[1] and later.[2] As contrasted with **Oṣadhi,** it denotes the inferior order of plants, but it often has practically the same sense as Oṣadhi.

[1] i. 67, 9; 141, 4; ii. 1, 14; 35, 8, etc.

[2] Av. i. 32, 3; 34, 1; ii. 7, 1; v. 4, 1; xix. 35, 4, etc.

Cf. Zimmer, *Altindisches Leben*, 57.

1. **Vṛka,** 'wolf,' is mentioned frequently in the Rigveda,[1] and also later.[2] It was an enemy of sheep[3] and of calves,[4] being dangerous even to men.[5] Its colour is stated to be reddish (*aruṇa*).[6] The 'she-wolf,' Vṛkī, is also mentioned several times in the Rigveda.[7]

[1] i. 42, 2; 105, 7; 116, 14; ii. 29, 6; vi. 51, 14; vii. 38, 7, etc.

[2] Av. vii. 95, 2; xii. 1, 49; Kāṭhaka Saṃhitā, xii. 10; Maitrāyaṇī Saṃhitā, iii. 14, 4; Vājasaneyi Saṃhitā, iv. 34; xix. 10. 92, etc.

[3] Rv. viii. 34, 3; **urā-mathi,** 'worrying sheep,' x. 66, 8.

[4] Av. xii. 4, 7.

[5] Rv. i. 105, 11. 18; ii. 29, 6. In Nirukta, v. 21, Roth, St. Petersburg Dictionary, *s.v.* 16, sees the sense of 'dog,' which seems needless. *Cf. Nirukta, Erläuterungen*, 67.

[6] Rv. i. 105, 18.

[7] i. 116, 16; 117, 17; 183, 4; vi. 51, 6; x. 127, 6.

Cf. Zimmer, *Altindisches Leben*, 81; Weber, *Indische Studien*, 18, 14.

2. **Vṛka** in two passages of the Rigveda[1] denotes 'plough.'

[1] i. 117, 21; viii. 22, 6; Nirukta, v. 26.

Vṛka-dvaras is found in one passage of the Rigveda,[1] which Ludwig[2] interprets as referring to a battle against Vṛkadvaras, king of the **Śaṇḍikas.** But this is quite uncertain. Roth[3] and Oldenberg[4] incline to read *vṛkadhvaras*. Hillebrandt[5] suggests Iranian connections, but without any clear reason.

[1] ii. 30, 4.

[2] Translation of the Rigveda, 3, 153; Griffith, *Hymns of the Rigveda*, 1, 297, n.

[3] St. Petersburg Dictionary, *s.v.*; *Zeitschrift der Deutschen Morgenländischen Gesellschaft*, 48, 110.

[4] *Ṛgveda-Noten*, 1, 211.

[5] *Vedische Mythologie*, 3, 442.

Vṛkṣa is the ordinary term for 'tree' in the Rigveda[1] and later.[2] In the Atharvaveda[3] it denotes the coffin made from a tree, no doubt by hollowing it out. The Ṣaḍviṃśa Brāhmaṇa[4] refers to the portent of a tree secreting blood.

[1] i. 164, 20. 22; ii. 14, 2; 39, 1; iv. 20, 5; v. 78, 6, etc.

[2] Av. i. 14, 1; ii. 12, 3; vi. 45, 1; xii. 1, 27. 51, etc.

[3] Av. xviii. 2, 25. *Cf.* Bṛhaddevatā, v. 83, with Macdonell's note (*d*).

[4] *Indische Studien*, 1, 40, and *cf. Journal of the American Oriental Society*, 15, 214.

Vṛkṣa-sarpī, 'tree-creeper,' is the name of a species of worm or female serpent in the Atharvaveda.[1]

[1] ix. 2, 22. *Cf.* Zimmer, *Altindisches Leben*, 98.

Vṛkṣya in the Śatapatha Brāhmaṇa (i. 1, 1, 10) denotes the 'fruit of a tree.'

Vṛcayā is referred to once in the Rigveda[1] as the spouse given by the Aśvins to **Kakṣīvant.**

[1] i. 51, 3. *Cf.* Pischel, *Vedische Studien*, 1, 3, 203, who distinguishes two Kakṣīvants, but without sufficient reason, since i. 116, 17, must clearly refer to Vṛcayā.

Vṛcīvant is the name of a tribe referred to once in the Rigveda,[1] where it is clearly stated that the **Sṛñjaya** king, **Daivavāta**, conquered the **Turvaśa** king and the Vṛcīvants. Zimmer[2] thinks that the Vṛcīvants and the Turvaśa people should be identified, but this is both unnecessary and improbable; it is adequate to assume that they were allied against[3] the Sṛñjayas. The Vṛcīvants appear again only in the strange legend in the Pañcaviṃśa Brāhmaṇa,[4] according to which the **Jahnus** and the Vṛcīvants contended for sovereignty, **Viśvāmitra**, the Jahnu king, winning it by his knowledge of a certain rite. See also **Hariyūpīyā.**

[1] vi. 27, 5 *et seq.*

[2] *Altindisches Leben*, 124.

[3] Oldenberg, *Buddha*, 404; Ludwig, Translation of the Rigveda, 3, 153; Hillebrandt, *Vedische Mythologie*, 1, 105.

[4] xxi. 12, 2.

Vṛjana, according to Roth,[1] denotes in several passages of the Rigveda[2] the 'settlement' or 'village,' the German 'Mark' and its inhabitants. Zimmer,[3] accepting this view, sees in Vṛjana the 'secure abode' (*kṣiti dhruvā*) where the clan lives,[4] the clan itself as a village community (like **Grāma**), and the clan in war.[5] Geldner,[6] on the other hand, takes the literal sense of Vṛjana to be 'net,' developing all the other senses from that idea, but the traditional view seems more natural.

[1] St. Petersburg Dictionary, *s.v.* 2.
[2] i. 51, 15; 73, 2; 91, 21; 105, 19; 128, 7; 165, 15; 166, 14, etc.
[3] *Altindisches Leben*, 142, 159, 161.
[4] Rv. i. 51, 15; 73, 2 (*cf.* i. 73, 4).
[5] Rv. vii. 32, 27; x. 42, 10.
[6] *Vedische Studien*, 1, 139 *et seq.*

Vṛtra-ghna occurs in a passage of the Aitareya Brāhmaṇa,[1] where in a **Gāthā** reciting the prowess of **Bharata** it is said that he bound horses on the **Yamunā** (Jumna) and **Gaṅgā** (Ganges) *Vṛtraghne*, which Sāyaṇa renders 'at Vṛtraghna,' as the name of a place. Roth,[2] however, seems right in interpreting the form as a dative, 'for the slayer of Vṛtra'—*i.e.*, Indra.

[1] viii. 23, 5.
[2] St. Petersburg Dictionary, *s.v.* *Cf.* Aufrecht, *Aitareya Brāhmaṇa*, 425.

Vṛtra-śaṅku, literally 'Vṛtra-peg,' found in one passage of the Śatapatha Brāhmaṇa,[1] is said by the scholiast on the Kātyāyana Śrauta Sūtra[2] to denote a stone pillar. This improbable interpretation is based on another passage in the same Brāhmaṇa.[3]

[1] xiii. 8, 4, 1.
[2] xxi. 3, 31.
[3] iv. 2, 5, 15. *Cf.* Eggeling, *Sacred Books of the East*, 44, 437, n. 1.

Vṛddha-dyumna Ābhipratāriṇa ('descendant of Abhipratārin') is the name of a prince (*rājanya*) in the Aitareya Brāhmaṇa (iii. 48, 9), where his priest, **Śucivṛkṣa Gaupalāyana**, is praised. In the Śāṅkhāyana Śrauta Sūtra (xv, 16, 10-13), on the contrary, he is said to have erred in the sacrifice, when a Brahmin prophesied that the result would be the expulsion of the **Kurus** from **Kurukṣetra**, an event which actually came to pass.

Vṛddha-vāśinī in the Nirukta (v. 21) denotes the 'female jackal.'

1. **Vṛśa.** See **Vṛṣa.**

2. **Vṛśa Jāna** ('descendant of Jana') is the name of a famous Purohita, who was unfortunate enough, while with his royal master, **Tryaruṇa**, to see a boy killed by the chariot which the king drove too fast. He thereupon recalled the boy to life. The story is told briefly in the Pañcaviṃśa Brāhmaṇa,[1] the Śāṭyāyanaka,[2] the Tāṇḍaka,[3] was also narrated in the Bhāllavi Brāhmaṇa,[4] and is preserved in the Bṛhaddevatā.[5] Sieg[6] has endeavoured to trace the story in part in the Rigveda,[7] but there is a consensus of opinion[8] against the correctness of such a view.

[1] xiii. 3, 12.
[2] See Sāyaṇa on Rv. v. 2, and the Jaiminīya version in the *Journal of the American Oriental Society*, 18, 20.
[3] See Sāyaṇa, *loc. cit.*
[4] Referred to in the Bṛhaddevatā, v. 23, apparently as cited in the Nidāna. The passage is not in the extant text of the Nidāna Sūtra. See Sieg, *Die Sagenstoffe des Ṛgveda* 65, n. 5.
[5] v. 14 *et seq.*, where see Macdonell's notes.
[6] *Op. cit.*, 64-76.
[7] v. 2.
[8] Ludwig, Translation of the Rigveda, 4, 324; Hillebrandt, *Zeitschrift der Deutschen Morgenländischen Gesellschaft*, 33, 248 *et seq.*; Oldenberg, *Sacred Books of the East*, 46, 366 *et seq.*; *Ṛgveda-Noten*, 1, 312. On the other hand, Geldner, *Festgruss an Roth*, 192, supports the tradition. *Cf.* Weber, *Indische Studien*, 10, 32.

Vṛścika in the Rigveda[1] and the Atharvaveda[2] denote 'scorpion.' Its poison was feared[3] like that of serpents. It is described as lying torpid in the earth during winter.[4]

[1] i. 191, 16.
[2] x. 4, 9. 15; xii. 1, 46; Śāṅkhāyana Āraṇyaka, xii. 27.
[3] Rv., *loc. cit.*; Av. x. 4, 9. 15.
[4] Av. xii. 1, 46.
Cf. Zimmer, *Altindisches Leben*, 98.

Vṛṣa is the name of a plant of some kind in the Kāṭhaka Saṃhitā.[1] Later the *Gendarussa vulgaris* is so styled. Maitrāyaṇī Saṃhitā[2] has Vṛśa, which Böhtlingk[3] takes to mean a small animal, a quite possible sense. *Cf.* **Yevāṣa.**

[1] xxx. 1.
[2] iv. 8, 1.
[3] Dictionary, General Index to Supplements, 376.

Vṛṣa-khādi is used as an epithet of the Maruts in the Rigveda.[1] The sense is doubtful: Bollensen[2] thought the expression referred to the wearing of rings in the ears; Max Müller[3] renders it 'strong rings,' comparing the later Cakra or discus.

[1] i. 64, 10.
[2] *Orient und Occident*, 2, 461, n.
[3] *Sacred Books of the East*, 32, 107, 120. *Cf.* Zimmer, *Altindisches Leben*, 263.

Vṛṣa-gaṇa is the name of a family of singers mentioned in one passage of the Rigveda.[1]

[1] ix. 97, 8. *Cf.* Ludwig, Translation of the Rigveda, 3, 132.

Vṛṣaṇ-aśva is the name of a man referred to in the Rigveda,[1] where Indra is called **Menā**, perhaps his 'wife' or 'daughter.' The same legend is alluded to in the Jaiminīya Brāhmaṇa,[2] the Śatapatha Brāhmaṇa,[3] the Ṣaḍviṃśa Brāhmaṇa,[4] and the Taittirīya Āraṇyaka,[5] but it is clear that all of these texts had no real tradition of what was referred to.

[1] i. 51, 13.
[2] ii. 79 (*Journal of the American Oriental Society*, 18, 37).
[3] iii. 3, 4, 18.
[4] i. 1, 16.
[5] i. 12, 3.
Cf. Eggeling, *Sacred Books of the East*, 26, 81, n. 2.

Vṛṣa-daṃśa, 'strong-toothed,' is the name of the cat in the Yajurveda Saṃhitās,[1] where it figures as a victim at the Aśvamedha ('horse sacrifice'). It also appears in the Pañcaviṃśa Brāhmaṇa;[2] the fact that the sneeze of the cat is here referred to renders it likely that the animal was already tamed. Geldner[3] sees a house cat in the animal alluded to in a hymn of the Atharvaveda[4] by a set of curious epithets, including *vṛṣadatī*, 'strong-toothed,' but Whitney[5] decisively rejects the idea that the hymn refers to the domestic cat.

[1] Taittirīya Saṃhitā, v. 5, 21, 1; Maitrāyaṇī Saṃhitā, iii. 14, 12; Vājasaneyi Saṃhitā, xxiv. 31.
[2] viii. 2, 2.
[3] *Vedische Studien*, 1, 313-315.
[4] i. 18.
[5] Translation of the Atharvaveda, 19, 20; Bloomfield, *Journal of the American Oriental Society*, 15, 153, n.; *Hymns of the Atharvaveda*, 261.
Cf. Zimmer, *Altindisches Leben*, 86.

Vṛṣan in two passages of the Rigveda[1] seems to denote a man, with the patronymic **Pāthya** in one of them.

[1] i. 36, 10; vi. 16, 14. 15. *Cf.* Max Müller, *Sacred Books of the East*, 32, 152, 153; Ludwig, Translation of the Rigveda, 3, 104.

Vṛṣabha regularly denotes a 'bull' in the Rigveda,[1] but usually in a metaphorical sense.

[1] i. 94, 10; 160, 3; vi. 46, 4; of Parjanya, vii. 101, 1. 6, etc. Roth renders *vṛṣabhānna*, ii. 16, 5, 'eating strong food'; but the literal sense, 'whose food is bulls,' will answer. *Cf.* **Māṃsa.**

Vṛṣala in the dicing hymn of the Rigveda[1] denotes an 'outcast'; the same sense appears in the Bṛhadāraṇyaka Upaniṣad,[2] where the touch of either a Vṛṣala or a Vṛṣalī is to be avoided.

[1] x. 34, 11. *Cf.* Nirukta, iii. 16.

[2] vi. 4, 12 Mādhyaṃdina.

Vṛṣa-śuṣma Vātāvata ('descendant of Vātāvant') **Jātūkarṇya** is the name of a priest in the Brāhmaṇas of the Rigveda.[1] Vṛṣaśuṣma in the Vaṃśa Brāhmaṇa[2] is probably intended for the same name.

[1] Aitareya Brāhmaṇa, v. 29, 1; Kauṣītaki Brāhmaṇa, ii. 9 (with a *varia lectio* Vādhāvata: *Indische Studien*, 1, 215, n. 1).

[2] *Indische Studien*, 4, 373.

Vṛṣā-rava, 'roaring like a bull,' is the name of some animal in the Rigveda.[1] In the Śatapatha Brāhmaṇa[2] the word occurs in the dual, meaning perhaps 'mallet' or 'drumstick.'

[1] x. 146, 2 = Taittirīya Brāhmaṇa, ii. 5, 5, 6.

[2] xii. 5, 2, 7.

Cf. Bloomfield, *Hymns of the Atharvaveda*, 426; Zimmer, *Altindisches Leben*, 90.

Vṛṣṭi is the regular word for 'rain' in the Rigveda[1] and later.[2]

[1] i. 116, 12; ii. 5, 6, etc.

[2] Av. iii. 31, 11; vi. 22, 3, etc.

Vṛṣṭi-havya is in the Rigveda[1] the name of a Ṛṣi, whose sons were the **Upastutas.**

[1] x. 115, 9. *Cf.* Max Müller, *Sacred Books of the East*, 32, 152, 153; Ludwig, Translation of the Rigveda, 3, 108, 109.

Veṇu in the Atharvaveda[1] and later[2] denotes a 'reed' of bamboo. It is described in the Taittirīya Saṃhitā[3] as 'hollow' (*su-ṣira*). In the Rigveda[4] it occurs only in a Vālakhilya hymn in a Dānastuti ('praise of gifts'), where Roth[5] thinks that 'flutes of reed' are meant, a sense which Veṇu has in the later texts. The Kauṣītaki Brāhmaṇa[6] couples Veṇu with **Sasya,** stating that they ripen in Vasanta, 'spring.' Apparently bamboo reeds are meant.[7]

[1] i. 27, 3.

[2] Taittirīya Saṃhitā, v. 2, 5, 2; vii. 4, 19, 2; Kāṭhaka Saṃhitā, xiii. 12; Satapatha Brāhmaṇa, i. 1, 4, 19; ii. 6, 2, 17, etc.

[3] v. 1, 1, 4.

[4] viii. 55, 3.

[5] St. Petersburg Dictionary, *s.v.* 2.

[6] iv. 12.

[7] *Cf.* Kātyāyana Śrauta Sūtra, iv. 6, 17, with the scholiast; Weber, *Indische Studien*, 10, 343.

Cf. Zimmer, *Altindisches Leben*, 71.

Vetasa is the name of the water plant *Calamus Rotang*, or a similar reed, in the Rigveda[1] and later.[2] It is called 'golden' (*hiraṇyaya*) and 'water-born' (*apsuja*).[4]

[1] iv. 58, 5.

[2] Av. x. 7, 41; xviii. 3, 5; Taittirīya Saṃhitā, v. 3, 12, 2; 4, 4, 2; Vājasaneyi Saṃhitā, xvii. 6; Taittirīya Brāhmaṇa, iii. 8, 4, 3, etc.

[3] Rv., *loc. cit.*; Av. x. 7, 41.

[4] Taittirīya Saṃhitā, v. 3, 12, 2, etc.

Cf. Zimmer, *Altindisches Leben*, 71.

Vetasu is a name occurring in the singular in two passages of the Rigveda[1] and once in the plural.[2] It seems that he was defeated by Indra, but there is no reason to assume that he was a demon. Zimmer[3] thinks that the Vetasus were probably the tribe of which **Daśadyu** was a member, and that they defeated the **Tugras.** The passages are too obscure to render any version probable.

[1] vi. 20, 8; 26, 4.

[2] x. 49, 4.

[3] *Altindisches Leben*, 128. *Cf.* Kaegi, *Der Rigveda*, n. 337.

Cf. Oldenberg, *Zeitschrift der Deutschen Morgenländischen Gesellschaft*, 55, 328.

Vetasvant, 'abounding in reeds,' is the name of a place in the Pañcaviṃśa Brāhmaṇa,[1] not, as Weber[2] once took it, a part of the name of **Ekayāvan Gāṃdama.**

[1] xxi. 14, 20.

[2] *Indische Studien*, 1, 32. *Cf.* Hopkins, *Transactions of the Connecticut Academy of Arts and Sciences*, 15, 69.

Veda in the Atharvaveda[1] and later[2] denotes 'sacred lore.' In the plural[3] it more definitely refers to the Vedas of the Ṛc, Yajus, and Sāman. *Cf.* **Vidyā.**

[1] Av. vii. 54, 2; x. 8, 17; xv. 3, 7.

[2] *Traya*, 'threefold,' Śatapatha Brāhmaṇa, v. 5, 5, 10; xiii. 4, 3, 3; Nirukta, i. 2. 18. 20, etc.

[3] Av. iv. 35, 6; xix. 2, 12; Taittirīya Saṃhitā, vii. 5, 11, 2; Aitareya Brāhmaṇa, v. 32, 1; vi. 15, 11; Taittirīya Brāhmaṇa, iii. 10, 11, 4; Śatapatha Brāhmaṇa, xi. 3, 3, 7; xii. 3, 4, 11, etc. In the Brāhmaṇas the word, no doubt, has normally the sense of the extant collections, which appear under their accepted titles, **Ṛgveda, Yajurveda, Sāmaveda,** in the Āraṇyakas.

Vedāṅga, as the name of a text subsidiary to the study of the Rigveda, is first found in the Nirukta[1] and the Rigveda Prātiśākhya.[2]

[1] i. 20.

[2] xii. 40.

Cf. Roth, *Nirukta*, xv. *et seq.*; Weber, *Indische Studien*, 9, 42.

1. **Vena** occurs in one passage of the Rigveda[1] as a generous patron. **Pṛthavāna,** found in the same passage, may or may not be another name of his, and **Pārthya** in the following stanza of the hymn is perhaps his patronymic.

[1] x. 93, 14. *Cf.* Ludwig, Translation of the Rigveda, 3, 166.

2. **Vena** in the Rigveda[1] is thought by Tilak[2] to be the planet Venus. But this is certainly impossible.

[1] x. 123.

[2] *Orion*, 163 *et seq.*

Cf. Whitney, *Journal of the American Oriental Society*, 16, xciv.

1. **Veśa** is a term of somewhat doubtful sense, apparently denoting 'vassal,' 'tenant,' in a few passages,[1] and, according to Roth,[2] 'dependent neighbour.'

[1] Rv. iv. 3, 13; v. 85, 7; possibly x. 49, 5; but *cf.* 2. **Veśa**; Kāṭhaka Saṃhitā, xii. 5 (*veśatva*); xxxi. 12; xxxii. 4; Vājasaneyi Saṃhitā, Kāṇva, ii. 5, 7; Maitrāyaṇī Saṃhitā, i. 4, 8; ii. 3, 7; iv. 1, 13. *Cf.* Weber, *Indische Studien*, 13, 204, who takes *veśas* in Av. ii. 32, 5, where *pari-veśas* also occurs in the same sense, and compares *vaiśya* in Taittirīya Saṃhitā, ii. 3, 7, 1, as meaning 'servitude'

[2] St. Petersburg Dictionary, *s.v.* 1, *veśa*, and *veśatva*. *Cf.* Whitney, Translation of the Atharvaveda, 75, who seems inclined to read *veṣas* in Av. ii. 32, 5; but Weber's explanation of the origin of the sense of 'servant' is adequate. Geldner, *Vedische Studien*, 3, 135, n. 4, sees in Veśa either a neighbour or a member of the same village community. *Cf.* **Sajāta**.

2. **Veśa** may be a proper name in two passages of the Rigveda;[1] if so, it is quite uncertain whether a demon is meant or not.

[1] ii. 13, 8; x. 49, 5. *Cf.* Ludwig, Translation of the Rigveda, 3, 152, 164.

Veśantā,[1] **Veśantī,**[2] **Veśāntā,**[3] all denote a 'pond' or 'tank.' *Cf.* **Vaiśanta.**

[1] Av. xi. 6, 10; xx. 128, 8. 9; Taittirīya Brāhmaṇa, iii. 4, 12, 1.

[2] Av. i. 3, 7.

[3] Bṛhadāraṇyaka Upaniṣad, iv. 3, 11.

Veśas. See 1. **Veśa.**

Veśāntā. See **Veśantā.**

Veśī in one passage of the Rigveda[1] seems to denote a 'needle.'

[1] vii. 18, 17. *Cf.* Hopkins, *Journal of the American Oriental Society*, 15, 264, n.

Veśman, 'house,' occurs in the Rigveda[1] and later.[2] It denotes the house as the place where a man is 'settled' (*viś*).

[1] x. 107, 10; 146, 3.

[2] Av. v. 17, 13; ix. 6, 30; Aitareya Brāhmaṇa, viii. 24, 6, etc. In Śatapatha Brāhmaṇa, i. 3, 2, 14, the single house (*eka-veśman*) of the king is contrasted with the numerous dwellings of the people.

Veśya in two passages of the Rigveda (iv. 26, 3; vi. 61, 14) seems to denote the relation of 'dependence' rather than 'neighbourhood.' *Cf.* 1. **Veśa.**

Veṣka in the Śatapatha Brāhmaṇa (iii. 8, 1, 15) denotes the 'noose' for strangling the sacrificial animal. See **Bleṣka.**

Vehat seems to mean a 'cow that miscarries.' It is mentioned in the Atharvaveda[1] and later.[2]

[1] xii. 4, 37 *et seq.* In iii. 23, 1, a woman is called *vehat.*

[2] Vājasaneyi Saṃhitā, xviii. 27; xxiv. 1, etc.; Taittirīya Saṃhitā, ii. 1, 5, 3, etc. In Śatapatha Brāhmaṇa, xii. 4, 4, 6, Eggeling, *Sacred Books of the East*, 44, 195, adopts the sense 'a cow desiring the bull.' But *cf.* Whitney, Translation of the Atharvaveda, 127.

Vaikarṇa occurs but once in the Rigveda[1] in the description of the **Dāśarājña,** where **Sudās** is stated to have overthrown the twenty-one tribes (*janān*) of the kings or folk of the two Vaikarṇas. Zimmer[2] conjectures that they were a joint people, the **Kuru-Krivis:** this is quite possible, and even probable. Vikarṇa as the name of a people is found in the Mahābhārata,[3] and a lexicographer[4] places the Vikarṇas in Kaśmīr, a reminiscence probably of a real settlement of the Kurus in that country. *Cf.* **Uttara Kuru.**

[1] vii. 18, 11.

[2] *Altindisches Leben*, 103.

[3] vi. 2105.

[4] St. Petersburg Dictionary, *s.v.* *Cf.* Hopkins, *Journal of the American Oriental Society*, 15, 261 *et seq.*, who sees in Vaikarṇau the two Vaikarṇa kings.

Vaikhānasa is the name of a mythical group of Ṛṣis who are said in the Pañcaviṃśa Brāhmaṇa[1] to have been slain at **Munimaraṇa** by **Rahasyu Devamalimluc,** and who are mentioned in the Taittirīya Āraṇyaka also.[2] An individual Vaikhānasa is **Puruhanman.**[3]

[1] xiv. 4, 7.

[2] i. 23, 3 (*Indische Studien*, 1, 78).

[3] xiv. 9, 29.

Vaijāna, 'descendant of Vijāna,' is Sāyaṇa's version of the patronymic of **Vṛśa** in the Pañcaviṃśa Brāhmaṇa.[1] The real reading is *vai Jānaḥ*, as pointed out by Weber.[2]

[1] xiii. 3, 12.

[2] *Indische Studien*, 10, 32.

Vaiṭṭabhaṭī-putra is the name in the Kāṇva recension of the Bṛhadāraṇyaka Upaniṣad (vi. 5, 2) of a teacher, a pupil of **Kārśakeyīputra**, *Cf.* **Vaidabhṛtīputra.**

Vaiḍava, 'descendant of **Vīḍu**,' is the patronymic of a **Vasiṣṭha** in the Pañcaviṃśa Brāhmaṇa (xi. 8, 14), where he is said to have been the seer of a Sāman or Chant.

Vaidūrya, 'beryl,' is first found in the late Adbhuta Brāhmaṇa.[1]

[1] Weber, *Indische Studien*, 1, 40; *Omina und Portenta*, 325 *et seq.*

Vaitaraṇa occurs once in the Rigveda.[1] Roth[2] thinks the word is a patronymic, but it seems rather[3] to be an adjective in the sense of 'belonging to Vitaraṇa' used of Agni, like Agni of **Bharata** or of **Vadhryaśva.**

[1] x. 61, 17.

[2] St. Petersburg Dictionary, *s.v.* 2.

[3] Ludwig, Translation of the Rigveda, 3, 165; Griffith, *Hymns of the Rigveda*, 2, 457, n.

Vaitahavya, 'descendant of **Vītahavya**,' is the name of a family who are said in the Atharvaveda[1] to have come to ruin because they devoured a Brahmin's cow. They are said to be **Sṛñjayas**, but as the exact form of the legend here referred to does not occur elsewhere, its authenticity is open to some doubt.[2] According to Zimmer,[3] Vaitahavya is a mere epithet of the Sṛñjayas, but this is not probable[4] in view of the existence of a Vītahavya.

[1] v. 18, 10. 11; 19, 1.

[2] Bloomfield, *Hymns of the Atharvaveda*, 434.

[3] *Altindisches Leben*, 132.

[4] *Cf.* Oldenberg, *Buddha*, 405; Weber *Indische Studien*, 18, 233.

Vaida, 'descendant of Vida,' is the patronymic of **Hiraṇyadant** in the Aitareya Brāhmaṇa[1] and the Aitareya Āraṇyaka.[2] The word is also written Baida.

[1] iii. 6, 4; Āśvalāyana Śrauta Sūtra, xii. 10, 9.

[2] ii. 1. 5.

Vaidathina, 'descendant of Vidathin,' is the patronymic of **Ṛjiśvan** in the Rigveda (iv. 16, 11; v. 29, 13).

Vaidad-aśvi, 'descendant of Vidadaśva,' is the patronymic of **Taranta** in the Rigveda.[1] In the Pañcaviṃśa Brāhmaṇa[2] and the Jaiminīya Brāhmaṇa[3] the Vaidadaśvis are Taranta and **Purumīḷha.** The latter is not a Vaidadaśvi in the Rigveda, a clear sign of the worthlessness of the legends relative to these two men in the Brāhmaṇas.

[1] v. 61, 10.

[2] xiii. 7, 12. *Cf.* Śāṭyāyanaka in Sāyaṇa on Rv. ix. 58, 3.

[3] i. 151; iii. 139, where Vaitadaśvi is the form. *Cf.* Ārṣeya Brāhmaṇa, p. 54 (ed. Burnell).

Cf. Max Müller, *Sacred Books of the East*, 32, 360; Oldenberg, *Zeitschrift der Deutschen Morgenländischen Gesellschaft*, 42, 232, n.; *Ṛgveda-Noten*, 1, 354; Sieg, *Die Sagenstoffe des Ṛgveda*, 62 *et seq.*

Vaidabhṛtī-putra, 'son of a female descendant of Vedabhṛt,' is the name of a teacher in the last Vaṃśa (list of teachers) of the Mādhyaṃdina recension of the Bṛhadāraṇyaka Upaniṣad (vi. 4, 32). *Cf.* **Vaiṭṭabhaṭīputra.**

Vaidarbha, 'prince of Vidarbha,' is applied to **Bhīma** in the Aitareya Brāhmaṇa (vii. 34, 9).

Vaidarbhi, 'descendant of **Vidarbha,**' is the patronymic of a **Bhārgava** in the Praśna Upaniṣad (i. 1; ii. 1).

Vaideha, 'prince of Videha,' is the title of **Janaka** and of **Namī Sāpya.**

Vaidhasa, 'descendant of Vedhas,' is the patronymic of **Hariścandra** in the Aitareya Brāhmana (vii. 13, 1) and the Śāṅkhāyana Śrauta Sūtra (xv. 17, 1).

Vainya, 'descendant of **Vena**,' is the patronymic of the mythic **Pṛthi, Pṛthī**, or **Pṛthu**.[1]

[1] Rv. viii. 9, 10; Pañcaviṃśa Brāhmaṇa, xiii. 5, 20; Śatapatha Brāhmaṇa, v. 3. 5, 4, etc.

Vaipaścita ('descendant of **Vipaścit**') **Dārḍha-jayanti** ('descendant of **Dṛḍhajayanta**') **Gupta Lauhitya** ('descendant of **Lohita**') is the name of a teacher, a pupil of **Vaipaścita Dārḍhajayanti Dṛḍhajayanta Lauhitya**, in a Vaṃśa (list of teachers) of the Jaiminīya Upaniṣad Brāhmaṇa (iii. 42, 1).

Vaipaścita ('descendant of **Vipaścit**') **Dārḍhajayanti** ('descendant of **Dṛdhajayanta**') **Dṛḍhajayanta Lauhitya** ('descendant of Lohita') is the name of a teacher, a pupil of **Vipaścit Dṛḍha'ayanta Lauhitya**, in a Vaṃśa (list of teachers) of the Jaiminīya Upaniṣad Brāhmaṇa (iii. 42, 1).

Vaiyaśva, 'descendant of **Vyaśva**,' is the patronymic of **Viśvamanas** in the Rigveda (viii. 23, 24; 24, 23; 26, 11).

Vaiyāghrapadī-putra, 'son of a female descendant of Vyāghrapad,' is the name of a teacher, a pupil of **Kāṇvī-putra**, in the Kāṇva recension of the last Vaṃśa (list of teachers) in the Bṛhadāraṇyaka Upaniṣad (vi. 5, 1).

Vaiyāghra-padya, 'descendant of Vyāghrapad,' is the patronymic of **Indradyumna Bhāllaveya** in the Śatapatha Brāhmaṇa[1] and the Chāndogya Upaniṣad,[2] of **Buḍila Āśvatarāśvi** in the Chāndogya Upaniṣad,[3] and of **Gośruti** in that Upaniṣad[4] and in the Śāṅkhāyana Āraṇyaka.[5] In the Jaiminīya Upaniṣad Brāhmaṇa[6] the patronymic is applied to **Rāma Krātujāteya**.

[1] x. 6, 1, 8.
[2] v. 14, 1.
[3] v. 16, 1.
[4] v. 2, 3.
[5] ix. 7 (Gośruta-vaiyāghrapadya as a compound).
[6] iii. 40, 1; iv. 16, 1.

Vaiyāska is read in one passage of the Rigveda Prātiśākhya,[1] as the name of an authority on the metres of the Rigveda. Roth[2] is clearly right in thinking that **Yāska** is meant.[3]

[1] xvii. 25.

[2] St. Petersburg Dictionary, *s.v.*

[3] The name not being a patronymic from Viyāska, but standing for *vai Yāskaḥ*. *Cf.* **Vaijāna.**

Vaira[1] and **Vaira-deya**[2] seem to have in the later Saṃhitās and the Brāhmaṇas the definite and technical sense of 'wergeld,' the money to be paid for killing a man as a compensation to his relatives. This view is borne out by the Sūtras of Āpastamba[3] and Baudhāyana.[4] Both prescribe the scale of 1,000 cows for a **Kṣatriya,**[5] 100 for a **Vaiśya,** 10 for a **Śūdra,** and a bull over and above in each case. Āpastamba leaves the destination of the payment vague, but Baudhāyana assigns it to the king. It is reasonable to suppose that the cows were intended for the relations, and the bull was a present to the king for his intervention to induce the injured relatives to abandon the demand for the life of the offender. The Āpastamba Sūtra[6] allows the same scale of wergeld for women, but the Gautama Sūtra[7] puts them on a level with men of the Śūdra caste only, except in one special case. The payment is made for the purpose of *vaira-yātana* or *vaira-niryātana*, 'requital of enmity,' 'expiation.'

The Rigveda[8] preserves, also, the important notice that a man's wergeld was a hundred (cows), for it contains the epithet *śata-dāya*, 'one whose wergeld is a hundred.' No doubt the values varied, but in the case of **Śunaḥśepa** the amount is a hundred (cows) in the Aitareya Brāhmaṇa.[9] In the Yajurveda Saṃhitās[10] *śata-dāya* again appears.

[1] Pañcaviṃśa Brāhmaṇa, xvi. 1, 12. *Cf.* Taittirīya Saṃhitā, i. 5, 2, 1; Kāṭhaka Saṃhitā, ix. 2; Kapiṣṭhala Saṃhitā, viii. 5; Maitrāyaṇī Saṃhitā, i. 7, 5, all of which have *vīram* for *vairam*, perhaps wrongly.

[2] Rv. v. 61, 8 (on the exact sense of which, *cf.* Max Müller, *Sacred Books of the East*, 32, 361; Hillebrandt, *Vedische Mythologie*, 1, 92; Oldenberg, *Ṛgveda-Noten*, 1, 354); Kāṭhaka Saṃhitā, xxiii. 8; xxviii 2. 3. 6.

[3] i. 9, 24, 1-4.

[4] i. 10, 19, 1. 2.

[5] The crime of slaying a Brahmin is too heinous for a wergeld. See Āpastamba, i. 9. 24, 7 *et seq.*; Baudhāyana, i. 10, 18, 18.

[6] i. 9, 24, 5.

[7] i. 10, 19, 3.

[8] ii. 32, 4.

[9] vii. 15, 7.

[10] See n. 1. The word is not found in the Taittirīya.

The fixing of the price shows that already public opinion, and perhaps the royal authority, was in Rigvedic times diminishing the sphere of private revenge; on the other hand, the existence of the system shows how weak was the criminal authority of the king (*cf.* **Dharma**).

Cf. Roth, *Zeitschrift der Deutschen Morgenländischen Gesellschaft*, 41, 672-676; Bühler and von Schroeder, *Festgruss an Roth*, 44-52; Bühler, *Sacred Books of the East*, 2, 78, 79; 14, 201 Schrader, *Prehistoric Antiquities*, 402 Jolly, *Recht und Sitte*, 131, 132; Delbrück in Leist, *Altarisches Jus Gentium*, 297.

Vaira-hatya, 'manslaughter,' is mentioned in the Vājasaneyi Saṃhitā (xxx. 13) and the Taittirīya Brāhmaṇa (i. 5, 9, 5). *Cf.* **Vīrahan.**

Vai-rājya. See **Rājya.**

Vairūpa, 'descendant of Virūpa,' is the patronymic of **Aṣṭādaṃṣṭra** in the Pañcaviṃśa Brāhmaṇa (viii. 9, 21).

Vaiśanta is the name in the Rigveda[1] of a prince whose offering Indra is said to have deserted for that of **Sudās** through the aid of the **Vasiṣṭhas.** Ludwig[2] thinks that the name is Veśanta, and that he was a priest of the **Pṛthu-Parśus**; Griffith[3] says that probably a river is meant, but neither of these views is plausible.

[1] vii. 33, 2.

[2] Translation of the Rigveda, 3, 173.

[3] *Hymns of the Rigveda*, 2, 24, n. *Cf.* Geldner, *Vedische Studien*, 2, 130.

Vaiśaṃpāyana, 'descendant of Viśaṃpa,' is the name of a teacher, famous later, but in the earlier Vedic literature known only to the Taittirīya Āraṇyaka (i. 7, 5) and the Gṛhya Sūtras.

Vai-śāleya, 'descendant of Viśāla,' is the patronymic of the mythic **Takṣaka** in the Atharvaveda (viii. 10, 29).

Vaiśī-putra, 'the son of a Vaiśya wife,' is mentioned in the Brāhmaṇas.[1]

[1] Taittirīya Brāhmaṇa, iii. 9, 7, 3; Satapatha Brāhmaṇa, xiii. 2

Vaiśya denotes a man, not so much of the people, as of the subject class, distinct from the ruling noble (**Kṣatriya**) and the **Brāhmaṇa**, the higher strata of the Āryan community on the one side, and from the aboriginal **Śūdra** on the other. The name is first found in the Puruṣa-sūkta ('hymn of man') in the Rigveda,[1] and then frequently from the Atharvaveda[2] onwards,[3] sometimes in the form of Viśya.[4]

The Vaiśya plays singularly little part in Vedic literature, which has much to say of Kṣatriya and Brahmin. His characteristics are admirably summed up in the Aitareya Brāhmaṇa[5] in the adjectives *anyasya bali-kṛt*, 'tributary to another'; *anyasyādya*, 'to be lived upon by another'; and *yathākāma-jyeyaḥ*, 'to be oppressed at will.' He was unquestionably taxed by the king (**Rājan**), who no doubt assigned to his retinue the right of support by the people, so that the Kṣatriyas grew more and more to depend on the services rendered to them by the Vaiśyas. But the Vaiśya was not a slave: he could not be killed by the king or anyone else without the slayer incurring risk and the payment of a wergeld (**Vaira**), which even in the Brahmin books extends to 100 cows for a Vaisya. Moreover, though the Vaiśya could be expelled by the king at pleasure, he cannot be said to have been without property in his land. Hopkins[6] thinks it is absurd to suppose that he could really be a landowner when he was subject to removal at will, but this is to ignore the fact that normally the king could not remove the landowner, and that kings were ultimately dependent on the people, as the tales of exiled kings show.

On the other hand, Hopkins[7] is clearly right in holding that the Vaiśya was really an agriculturist, and that Vedic society was not merely a landholding aristocracy, superimposed upon an agricultural aboriginal stock, as Baden Powell[8] urged. Without ignoring the possibility that the Dravidians were agriculturists, there is no reason to deny that the Āryans were

[1] x. 90, 12.

[2] v. 17, 9.

[3] Vājasaneyi Saṃhitā, xxx. 5, etc. See **Varṇa**.

[4] Av. vi. 13, 1; Vājasaneyi Saṃhitā, xviii. 48, etc.

[5] vii. 29. *Cf.* Muir, *Sanskrit Texts*, 1[2], 439.

[6] *India, Old and New*, 222 *et seq.*

[7] *Op. cit.*, 210 *et seq.*

[8] *Indian Village Community*, 190 *et seq.*

so likewise, and the goad of the plougher was the mark of a Vaiśya in life[9] and in death.[10] It would be absurd to suppose that the Āryan Vaiśyas did not engage in industry and commerce (*cf.* **Paṇi, Vaṇij**), but pastoral pursuits and agriculture must have been their normal occupations.

In war the Vaiśyas must have formed the bulk of the force under the Kṣatriya leaders (see **Kṣatriya**). But like the Homeric commoners, the Vaiśyas may well have done little of the serious fighting, being probably ill-provided with either body armour or offensive weapons.

That the Vaiśyas were engaged in the intellectual life of the day is unlikely; nor is there any tradition, corresponding to that regarding the Kṣatriyas, of their having taken part in the evolution of the doctrine of Brahman, the great philosophic achievement of the age. The aim of the Vaiśya's ambition was, according to the Taittirīya Saṃhitā,[11] to become a **Grāmaṇī**, or village headman, a post probably conferred by the king on wealthy Vaiśyas, of whom no doubt there were many. It is impossible to say if in Vedic times a Vaiśya could attain to nobility or become a Brahmin. No instance can safely be quoted in support of such a view,[12] though such changes of status may have taken place (see **Kṣatriya** and **Varṇa**).

It is denied by Fick[13] that the Vaiśyas were ever a caste, and the denial is certainly based on good grounds if it is held that a caste means a body within which marriage is essential, and which follows a hereditary occupation (*cf.* **Varṇa**). But it would be wrong[14] to suppose that the term Vaiśya was merely applied by theorists to the people who were not nobles or priests. It must have been an early appellation of a definite class which was separate from the other classes, and properly to be compared with them. Moreover, though there were differences among Vaiśyas, there were equally differences among Kṣatriyas and Brāhmaṇas, and it is impossible to deny

[9] Kāṭhaka Saṃhitā, xxxvii. 1.

[10] Kauśika Sūtra, lxxx.

[11] ii. 5, 4, 4.

[12] Rhys Davids, *Buddhist India*, 55 *et seq.*, argues to the contrary from Buddhist evidence; but this has no cogency for the Vedic period, and much, if not all, of it is hardly in point as concerns this issue.

[13] *Die sociale Gliederung*, 163 *et seq.*

[14] *Cf. Indian Empire*, 1, 347.

the Vaiśyas' claim to be reckoned a class or caste if the other two are such, though at the present day things are different.

Cf. Zimmer, *Altindisches Leben*, 213 *et seq.*; Weber, *Indische Studien*, 10, 1 *et seq.*; Muir, *Sanskrit Texts*, 1², 7 *et seq.*; Ludwig, Translation of the Rigveda, 3, 242, 243; Hopkins, *Journal of the American Oriental Society*, 13, 76 *et seq.* (for the Epic Vaiśya).

Vaiśvā-mitra, 'descendant of **Viśvāmitra,**' is the term by which that famous priest's line is referred to in the Aitareya Brāhmaṇa (vii. 17 *et seq.*).

Vaiṣṭha-pureya, 'descendant of Viṣṭhapura,' is the name of a teacher in the first two Vaṃśas (lists of teachers) of the Bṛhadāraṇyaka Upaniṣad in the Mādhyaṃdina recension (ii. 5, 20; iv. 5, 25). He was a pupil of **Śāṇḍilya** and **Rauhiṇāyana.**

Vyacha in *go-vyacha*, the name of one of the victims at the Puruṣamedha ('human sacrifice') in the Yajurveda,[1] is of uncertain signification. According to Sāyaṇa,[2] the compound denotes a 'driver out of cows.' Perhaps it means a 'tormentor of cows,' as the St. Petersburg Dictionary takes it. Weber[3] renders it as 'knacker of cows,' Eggeling as 'one who approaches cows.'

1 Vājasaneyi Saṃhitā, xxx. 18; Taittirīya Brāhmaṇa, iii. 4, 16, 1. *Cf.* Kāṭhaka Saṃhitā, xv. 4.

2 On Taittirīya Brāhmaṇa, *loc. cit.*

3 *Indische Streifen*, 1, 82, n. 11. This interpretation is supported by the use of the word in the Kāṭhaka, where it replaces the **Govikartana** of other texts. See **Ratnin** (p. 200).

4 *Sacred Books of the East*, 44, 416.

Vy-advara,[1] **Vy-advarī,**[2] are the names of a 'gnawing' (*ad*, 'eat') animal in the Atharvaveda and the Śatapatha Brāhmaṇa. *Cf.* also **Vyadhvara**, which the St. Petersburg Dictionary would read throughout.

1 Śatapatha Brāhmaṇa, vii. 4, 1, 27. *Cf.* Av. vi. 50, 2.

2 Av. iii. 28, 2, where a worm is certainly not meant.

Vyadhvara, 'perforating,' designates a worm in one passage of the Atharvaveda,[1] where there seems to be no good reason to alter the reading to Vyadvara, though Whitney[2] thinks that it may rather be connected with *vi-adhvan*[3] than with the root *vyadh*, 'pierce.'[4] The term occurs with **Maśaka,** 'fly,' in the Hiraṇyakeśi Gṛhya Sūtra,[5] and perhaps also in another passage of the Atharvaveda,[6] where, however, both Whitney[7] and Shaṅkar Paṇḍit read **Vyadvara.**

1 ii. 31, 4.

2 Translation of the Atharvaveda, 74.

3 This would mean 'diverging from the road,' 'devious.'

4 The Padapāṭha analyzes the word as *vi-adhvara.*

5 ii. 16, 3.

6 vi. 50, 3.

7 *Op. cit.*, 318. *Cf.* 135.

Cf. also Bloomfield, *Hymns of the Atharvaveda*, 316, 361, 487; Lanman in Whitney, *op. cit.*, 318.

Vyalkaśā is the name of a plant in the Rigveda.[1]

1 x. 16, 13. *Cf.* Zimmer *Altindisches Leben*, 70.

Vy-aśva is the name of a Ṛṣi, a protégé of the Aśvins,[1] mentioned in several hymns of the eighth Maṇḍala,[2] which may have been the composition of a descendant of his, **Viśvamanas.** In two other passages[3] he is referred to only as a Ṛṣi of the past, and Oldenberg[4] points out that none of his own work appears in the Saṃhitā. The Rigveda also mentions[5] the Vyaśvas, with whom Ludwig[6] is inclined to connect **Vaśa Aśvya.** An **Āṅgirasa** Vyaśva occurs as a seer of Sāmans or Chants in the Pañcaviṃśa Brāhmaṇa.[7]

1 Rv. i. 112, 15.

2 viii. 23, 16. 23; 24, 22; 26, 9.

3 Rv. viii. 9, 10; ix. 65, 7.

4 *Zeitschrift der Deutschen Morgenländischen Gesellschaft* 42, 217.

5 Rv. viii. 24, 28

6 Translation of the Rigveda, 3. 106.

7 xiv. 10, 9.

Vy-aṣṭi is the name of a mythical teacher in the first two Vaṃśas (lists of teachers) in the Bṛhadāraṇyaka Upaniṣad.[1]

1 iv. 5, 22; iv. 5, 28 Mādhyaṃdina.

Vyā-khyāna in one passage of the Satapatha Brāhmaṇa[1] clearly denotes a 'narrative' merely—*viz.*, that of the dispute of Kadrū and Suparnī. In other passages[2] the word means simply 'commentary.' In the Bṛhadāraṇyaka Upaniṣad,[3] used in the plural, it signifies a species of writing, apparently 'commentaries,' though its exact relation to **Anuvyākhyāna** must remain obscure. Sieg[4] thinks that the Vyākhyānas were forms of narrative like **Anvākhyāna** and Anuvyākhyāna.

[1] iii. 6, 2, 7.

[2] vi. 1, 27. 33; vii. 2, 4, 28.

[3] ii. 4, 10; iv. 1, 6 (Mādhyaṃdina = 2 Kāṇva); 5, 11.

[4] *Die Sagenstoffe des Ṛgveda*, 21, 34.

Vyāghra, 'tiger,' is never found in the Rigveda, but frequently occurs in the Atharvaveda,[1] as well as the lion. This fact is legitimately regarded as an indication that the Atharvaveda belongs to a period when the Vedic Indian had approached and entered the territory of Bengal. Later,[2] also, mention of the tiger is quite common. The Taittirīya Saṃhitā[3] preserves a reference to the danger of waking a sleeping tiger. The destructive character of the animal is often alluded to, the man-eater (*puruṣād*)[5] being also mentioned. Like the lion, the tiger passes as a symbol of strength.[6] This idea is illustrated by the fact that the king at the **Rājasūya** ('royal consecration') steps[7] on a tiger's skin to win himself the strength of the animal. *Cf.* also **Śārdūla, Petva.**

[1] iv. 3, 1; 36, 6; vi. 38, 1; 103, 3; 140, 1; xii. 1, 49; 2, 43; xix. 46, 5; 49, 4.

[2] Taittirīya Saṃhitā, vi. 2, 5, 5; Kāṭhaka Saṃhitā, xvii. 2; Maitrāyaṇī Saṃhitā, ii. 1, 9; Vājasaneyi Saṃhitā, xiv. 9; xix. 10; Aitareya Brāhmaṇa, vii. 5, 3 Śatapatha Brāhmaṇa, xii. 7, 1, 8; Chāndogya Upaniṣad, vi. 9, 3; 10, 2, etc.

[3] v. 4, 10, 5.

[4] *Cf.* Av. iv. 36, 6; viii. 5, 11, and see **Śaśayu.**

[5] Av. xii. 1, 49.

[6] Av. iv. 8, 4. 7. *Cf.* Yāska, Nirukta, iii. 18.

[7] Av. iv. 8, 4. *Cf.* Eggeling, *Sacred Books of the East*, 41, 92. He does not wear the skin, as Zimmer, *Altindisches Leben*, 79, says.

Cf. Schrader, *Prehistoric Antiquities* 249, 250.

Vyāghra-padya is a false reading in the Chāndogya Upaniṣad (v. 16, 1) for **Vaiyāghrapadya.**

Vyādhi, 'disease,' occurs several times in Vedic literature.[1] The specific diseases are dealt with under the separate names, but the Vedic texts also mention innumerable bodily defects. The list of victims[2] at the Puruṣamedha ('human sacrifice') includes a 'dwarf' (*vāmana, kubja*), a 'bald' person (*khalati*),[3] a 'blind' man (*andha*),[4] a 'deaf' man (*badhira*),[5] a 'dumb' man (*mūka*),[6] a 'fat' man (*pīvan*), a 'leper' (*sidhmala, kilāsa*),[7] a 'yellow-eyed' man (*hary-akṣa*), a 'tawny-eyed' man (*piṅg-ākṣa*), a 'cripple' (*pīṭha-sarpin*), a 'lame' man (*srāma*), a 'sleepless' man (*jāgaraṇa*), a 'sleepy' man (*svapana*), one[8] 'too tall' (*ati-dīrgha*), one 'too short' (*ati-hrasva*), one 'too stout' (*ati-sthūla* or *aty-aṃsala*), one 'too thin' (*ati-kṛśa*), one 'too white' (*ati-śukla*), one 'too dark' (*ati-kṛṣṇa*), one 'too bald' (*ati-kulva*), and one 'too hairy' (*ati-lomaśa*).

In the Maitrāyaṇī Saṃhitā[9] the man with bad nails and the man with brown teeth are mentioned along with sinners like the **Didhiṣūpati.** The Śatapatha Brāhmaṇa[10] mentions a 'white-spotted (*śukla*), bald-headed man, with projecting teeth (*viklidha*) and reddish-brown eyes.' Interesting is Zimmer's[11] suggestion that *kirmira* found in the Vājasaneyi Saṃhitā[12] means 'spotty' as an intermixture of races, but it is only a conjecture, apparently based on a supposed connexion of the word with *kṛ*, 'mix.' In the Vājasaneyi Saṃhitā[13] and the

1 Chāndogya Upaniṣad, iv. 10, 3; Ṣaḍviṃśa Brāhmaṇa, v. 4; Śāṅkhāyana Śrauta Sūtra, iii. 4, 8.

2 Vājasaneyi Saṃhitā, xxx. 10. 17. 21; Taittirīya Brāhmaṇa, iii. 4, 6, 1; 14, 1; 17, 1.

3 *Cf.* Śatapatha Brāhmaṇa, xiii. 3, 6, 5.

4 *Cf.* Bṛhadāraṇyaka Upaniṣad, vi. 2, 9; Chāndogya Upaniṣad, v. 1, 9; 13, 2; viii. 4, 2; 9, 1; 10, 1; Kauṣītaki Upaniṣad, iii. 3.

5 Bṛhadāraṇyaka Upaniṣad, vi. 2, 10; Chāndogya Upaniṣad, v. 1, 10; Kauṣītaki Upaniṣad, *loc. cit.*

6 Kauṣītaki Upaniṣad, *loc. cit.*

7 *Kilāsa* also in Pañcaviṃśa Brāhmaṇa, xiv. 3, 17; xxiii. 16, 11, etc.

8 Vājasaneyi Saṃhitā, xxx. 22; Taittirīya Brāhmaṇa, iii. 4, 19, 1, where are added the man who winks too much (*ati-mirmira*), has too prominent teeth (*ati-dantura*) or too small teeth (*ati-kiriṭa*), and who stares excessively (*ati-memiṣa*). *Cf.* Weber, *Indische Streifen*, 1, 84, n. 4.

9 iv. 1, 9; Taittirīya Brāhmaṇa, iii. 2, 8, 9. *Cf.* Av. vii. 65, 3.

10 xiii. 3, 6, 5. See Eggeling, *Sacred Books of the East*, 44, 323, n.

11 *Altindisches Leben*, 428.

12 xxx. 21.

13 xxx. 15, especially *avijātā* and *vijarjarā*, beside *avatokā* and *paryāyiṇī*; *atītvarī* and *atiṣkadvarī* are also possibly so to be understood. *Cf.* Weber, *Indische Streifen*, 1, 80.

Taittirīya Brāhmaṇa[14] various epithets are applied to women, some of which seem to denote disease, and in the Atharvaveda[15] the feminine adjectives, 'antelope-footed' (*ṛśya-padī*) and 'bull-toothed' (*vṛṣa-datī*), probably refer to bodily defects.

[14] iii. 4, 11, 1, where *apaskadvarī* and *paryāriṇī* are read.

[15] i. 18, 4. Geldner, *Vedische Studien*, 1, 314, understands the hymn as referring to the domestic cat, but this lacks plausibility. The sense of the other epithets there occurring is quite obscure.

Vy-āna is the name of one of tbe vital airs. See **Prāṇa.**

Vyāma in the Saṃhitās[1] and the Brāhmaṇas[2] denotes the 'span' of the outstretched arms as a measure of length. It may be estimated at six feet or equivalent to a fathom.[3]

[1] Av. vi. 137, 2; Taittirīya Saṃhitā, v. 1, 1, 4; 2, 5, 1, etc.

[2] Śatapatha Brāhmaṇa, x. 2, 3, 1. 2; i. 2, 5, 14; vii. 1, 1, 37, where the scholiast equates it to 4 Aratnis or cubits (while the scholiast on Āśvalāyana Gṛhya Sūtra, ix. 1, 9, regards it as equal to 5 Aratnis). According to the Śulva Sūtra of Baudhāyana, the **Aratni** equals 24 *aṅgula* (=$\frac{3}{4}$ inch). See Fleet, *Journal of the Royal Asiatic Society*, 1912, 231, 233, 234.

[3] See Eggeling, *Sacred Books of the East*, 41, 309, n. 5.

Vyāsa Pārāśarya ('descendant of **Parāśara**') is the name of a mythical sage who in the Vedic period is found only as a pupil of **Viṣvaksena** in the Vaṃśa (list of teachers) at the end of the Sāmavidhāna Brāhmaṇa and in the late Taittirīya Āraṇyaka.[1]

[1] i. 9, 2. *Cf.* Weber, *Indische Studien*, 1, 156; 4, 377; *Indian Literature*, 184, n. 199.

Vra, according to Roth,[1] means 'troop' in the Rigveda[2] and the Atharvaveda.[3] Zimmer[4] sees in the word (in the feminine form of *vrā*) a designation in one passage of the village host which formed part of the **Viś,** and was composed of relations (*su-bandhu*). On the other hand, Pischel[5] thinks that in all the passages Vrā means 'female,' used either of animals[6] or of

[1] St. Petersburg Dictionary, *s.v.* *Cf.* Bechtel, *Nachrichten der königlichen Gesellschaft der Wissenschaften zu Göttingen*, 1894, 393.

[2] i. 124, 8; 126, 5; iv. 1, 16; viii. 2, 6; x. 123, 2. He omits i. 121, 2, where Böhtlingk, Dictionary, *s.v.*, treats the word as a feminine (*vrā*).

[3] ii. 1, 1, a confused passage, on which see Whitney, Translation of the Atharvaveda, 37, 38.

[4] *Altindisches Leben*, 162.

[5] *Vedische Studien*, 2, 121, 313 *et seq.*

[6] Rv. i. 121, 2; viii. 2, 6 (female elephants).

women who go to the feast (**Samana**),[7] or courtezans (*viśyā*, 'of the people'),[8] or, metaphorically,[9] the hymns compared with courtezans: these senses are perhaps adequate.

7 Rv. i. 124, 8.

8 Rv. i. 126, 5.

9 Rv. iv. 1, 16; x. 123, 2; Av., *loc. cit.*

Vraja denotes in the first instance, in the Rigveda,[1] the place to which the cattle resort (from *vraj*, 'go'), the 'feeding ground' to which the milk-giving animals go out[2] in the morning from the village (**Grāma**), while the others stay in it all day and night.[3] Secondarily it denotes the 'herd'[4] itself. This is Geldner's view,[5] which seems clearly better than that of Roth[6] who regards Vraja as primarily the 'enclosure' (from *vṛj*), and only thence the 'herd'; for the Vraja does not normally mean an 'enclosure' at all: the Vedic cattle were not stall-fed as a general rule. In some passages, however, 'pen,'[7] in others 'stall,'[8] is certainly meant. The word is often used in the myth of the robbing of the kine.[9] It occasionally denotes a 'cistern.'[10]

1 Rv. ii. 38, 8; x. 26, 3, and perhaps 97, 10; 101, 8. *Cf.* Medhātithi on Manu, iv. 45, and Mahābhārata, i. 41, 15, where *go-vraja* is equal to *gavāṃ pracārāḥ*, 'the pastures of the kine,' in i. 40, 17.

2 Rv. ii. 38, 8.

3 *Cf.* Sāyaṇa on Aitareya Brāhmaṇa, ii. 18, 14.

4 Rv. v. 35, 4; vii. 27, 1; 32, 10; viii. 46, 9; 51, 5.

5 *Vedische Studien*, 2, 282 *et seq.*; *Rigveda, Glossar*, 174. *Cf.* Hopkins, *Journal of the American Oriental Society*, 13, 77.

6 St. Petersburg Dictionary, *s.v.* But *cf.* Böhtlingk, Dictionary, *s.v.*

7 Av. iii. 11, 5; iv. 38, 7; Śāṅkhāyana Āraṇyaka, ii. 16. Metaphorically, in the Bṛhadāraṇyaka Upaniṣad, vi. 4, 22, Mādhyaṃdina, it is a pen with a bolt (*sārgala*) and with a palisade (*sa-pari-śraya*). The sense of 'pen' is also possible in Rv. x. 97, 10; 101, 8, and is not radically opposed to it, for Vraja denotes the place where the cattle are fed, and can therefore be applied to the stall where they are during the night. *Cf.* **Goṣṭha.**

8 Rv. x. 4, 2, where the 'warm Vraja' to which the cows resort is alluded to, and iv. 51, 2, where the Dawns open wide the doors of the Vraja of darkness; Taittirīya Brāhmaṇa, iii. 8, 12, 2, where the Vraja is said to be made of Aśvattha wood. The sense of 'stall' is probable in Vājasaneyi Saṃhitā, i. 25.

9 See Geldner, *op. cit.*, 2, 283 *et seq.*

10 Vājasaneyi Saṃhitā, x. 4 = Taittirīya Brāhmaṇa, i. 8, 11, 1 = Maitrāyaṇī Saṃhitā, ii. 6.

Vrata ('vow') in the later Saṃhitās[1] and the Brāhmaṇas[2] has the peculiar sense of the 'milk' used by one who is living on that beverage alone as a vow or penance.

[1] Av. vi. 133, 2; Taittirīya Saṃhitā, vi. 2, 5, 3. 4; Vājasaneyi Saṃhitā, iv. 11, etc.

[2] Śatapatha Brāhmaṇa, iii. 2, 2, 10. 14. 17; 4, 2, 15; ix. 2, 1, 18. *Cf. ghṛta-vrata*, Pañcaviṃśa Brāhmaṇa, xviii. 2, 5. 6, and *vrata-dughā*, the 'cow that gives the Vrata milk,' Śatapatha Brāhmaṇa, iii. 2, 2, 14; xiv. 3, 1, 34, etc.

Vratati in the Rigveda[1] and later[2] denotes a 'creeping plant.'

[1] viii. 40, 6; Nirukta, i. 14; vi. 28.

[2] Taittirīya Brāhmaṇa, i. 5, 1, 3, etc.

Vrāja-pati is found in one passage of the Rigveda,[1] where it is said that comrades attend Indra, as the **Kulapas** the Vrāja-pati, when he goes about. Zimmer[2] thinks that this refers to the heads of families being subordinate in war to the village headman (**Grāmaṇī**), but Whitney[3] seems to be right in seeing merely the chieftain surrounded by the leading men, the family heads, not necessarily merely a village headman. Vrāja alone occurs in one passage of the Atharvaveda,[4] adverbially in the sense of 'in troops.'

[1] x. 179, 2 = Av. vii. 72, 2.

[2] *Altindisches Leben*, 171.

[3] Translation of the Atharvaveda, 436.

[4] i. 16, 1. *Cf.* Whitney, *op. cit.*, 17.

Vrāja-bāhu is used in the Kauṣītaki Brāhmaṇa (ii. 9) of the 'encompassing arms' of death, Vrāja here apparently meaning a 'pen,' like **Vraja.** *Cf.* **Viṣṭhā-vrājin.**

Vrāta is found in several passages of the Rigveda[1] and later[2] in the sense of 'troop.' In one passage of the Rigveda[3] the troops of the Maruts are referred to by three different terms—*śardha*, *vrāta*, and *gaṇa*. From this fact Zimmer[4] has

[1] i. 163, 8; iii. 26, 2; v. 53, 11; ix. 14, 2 (perhaps an allusion to the five tribes); x. 34, 8. 12 (of dice). In x. 57, 5, the host of the living (*jīva vrāta*) is referred to.

[2] Av. ii. 9, 2 ('host of the living'); Taittirīya Saṃhitā, i. 8, 10, 2; Vājasaneyi Saṃhitā, xvi. 25; Pañcaviṃśa Brāhmaṇa, vi. 9, 24; xvii. 1, 5. 12, etc.

[3] v. 53, 11. *Cf.* iii. 26, 2, where *śardha* is not mentioned.

[4] *Altindisches Leben*, 162.

deduced that a Vedic host fought according to clan (**Viś**), village (**Grāma**), and family, but this conclusion is hardly warranted, there being nothing to show that there is any intention to present a distinct series of divisions. It is not probable that the word ever has the technical sense of 'guild,' as Roth[5] thinks. *Cf.* **Vrātapati.**

[5] In the St. Petersburg Dictionary, where this is taken to be the sense; Pañcaviṃśa Brāhmaṇa, vi. 9, 25; xvii. 1, 5. 12; Vājasaneyi Saṃhitā, xvi. 25; Taittirīya Saṃhitā, i. 8, 10, 2.

Vrāta-pati, 'lord of troops,' is an epithet included in the names of Rudra in the Yajurveda Saṃhitās,[1] along with the epithet Gaṇa-pati, 'lord of groups.' The exact sense is quite uncertain, but the term may allude to the chief of a band of robbers, as Zimmer[2] thinks.

[1] Taittirīya Saṃhitā, iv. 5, 4, 1; Kāthaka Saṃhitā, xvii. 13; Maitrāyaṇī Saṃhitā, ii. 9, 4; Vājasaneyi Saṃhitā, xvi. 25.

[2] *Altindisches Leben*, 179.

Vrātya is included in the list of victims at the Puruṣamedha ('human sacrifice') in the Yajurveda,[1] where, however, no further explanation of the name is given. Fuller information is furnished by the Atharvaveda,[2] the Pañcaviṃśa Brāhmaṇa,[3] and the Sūtras,[4] which describe at length a certain rite intended for the use of Vrātyas. According to the Pañcaviṃśa Brāhmaṇa, there are four different kinds of 'outcasts'—viz., the *hīna*, who are merely described as 'depressed'; those who have become outcasts for some sin (*nindita*); those who become outcasts at an early age, apparently by living among outcasts; and those old men who, being impotent (*śama-nīcameḍhra*), have gone to live with outcasts. The last three categories are by no means of the same importance as the first. The motive of the fourth is hard to understand: according to Rājārām Rām-

[1] Vājasaneyi Saṃhitā, xxx. 8; Taittirīya Brāhmaṇa, iii. 4, 5, 1.

[2] xv. 1, 1 *et seq.*

[3] xvii. 1-4.

[4] Kātyāyana Srauta Sūtra, xii. 1; xxii. 4; Lāṭyāyana Śrauta Sūtra, viii. 6; Āpastamba Śrauta Sūtra, xxii. 5, 4-14. See Hillebrandt, *Ritualliteratur*, 139, 140.

krishṇa Bhāgavat,[5] they were men who had enfeebled their constitutions by undue intercourse with women in the lands of the outcasts, and returned home in a debilitated state. But this is not stated in the text.

It seems probable that the really important Vrātyas were those referred to as *hīna*, and that the other classes were only subsidiary. According to Rājārām,[6] there were two categories of the first class: (*a*) The depressed (*hīna*), who were non-Āryan; and (*b*) degraded Āryans (*gara-gir*). This, however, is a mere guess, and devoid of probability. There seems to have been but one class of Vrātyas. That they were non-Āryan is not probable, for it is expressly said[7] that, though unconsecrated, they spoke the tongue of the consecrated: they were thus apparently Āryans. This view is confirmed by the statement that 'they call what is easy of utterance, difficult to utter': probable they had already a somewhat Prakritic form of speech (*cf.* **Vāc**). The Sūtras mention their Arhants ('saints') and Yaudhas ('warriors'), corresponding to the Brahminical **Brāhmaṇa** and Kṣatriya.

Other particulars accord with the view that they were Āryans outside the sphere of Brahmin culture. Thus they are said[8] not to practise agriculture or commerce (an allusion to a nomadic life), nor to observe the rules of **Brahmacarya**—*i.e.*, the principle regulating the Brahminic order of life. They were also allowed to become members of the Brahminical community by performance of the ritual prescribed, which would hardly be so natural in the case of non-Āryans.

Some details are given of the life and dress of the Vrātyas. Their principles were opposed to those of the Brahmins: they beat those unworthy of correction.[9] Their leader (Gṛhapati) or householder wore a turban (**Uṣṇīṣa**), carried a whip (**Pratoda**), a kind of bow (**Jyāhroḍa**), was clothed in a black (*kṛṣṇaśa*) garment and two skins (**Ajina**), black and white (*kṛṣṇa-valakṣa*), and owned a rough wagon (**Vipatha**) covered with planks

[5] *Journal of the Bombay Branch of the Royal Asiatic Society*, 19, 360.

[6] *Ibid.*, 359.

[7] Pañcaviṃśa Brāhmaṇa, xvii. 1, 9.

[8] *Ibid.*, xvii. 1, 2.

[9] *Ibid.*, xvii. 1, 14.

(*phalakāstīrṇa*). The others,[10] subordinate to the leader, had garments with fringes of red (*valūkāntāni dāmatūṣāṇi*), two fringes on each, skins folded double (*dviṣaṃhitāny ajināni*), and sandals (**Upānah**). The leader wore also an ornament (**Niṣka**) of silver, which Rājārām[11] converts into a silver coinage. The Vrātyas, on becoming consecrated, were expected to hand over their goods to the priest. Many other details are given in the Sūtras (*e.g.*, that the shoes or sandals were of variegated black hue and pointed), but these are not authenticated by the Pañcaviṃśa Brāhmaṇa.

The locality in which the Vrātyas lived cannot be stated with certainty, but their nomad life[12] suggests the western tribes beyond the Sarasvatī. But they may equally well have been in the east: this possibility is so far supported by the fact that the Sūtras make the Brahmin receiving the gift of the Vrātya's outfit an inhabitant of **Magadha.** The Atharvaveda[13] does not help, for it treats the Vrātya in so mystical a way that he is represented as being in all the quarters. Indeed, Roth[14] believed that it was here not a case of the Vrātya of the Pañcaviṃśa Brāhmaṇa at all, but of a glorification of the Vrātya as the type of the pious vagrant or wandering religious mendicant (**Parivrājaka**). This view is clearly wrong, as the occurrence of the words *uṣṇīsa*, *vipatha*, and *pratoda* shows. It is probable that the 15th Book of the Atharvaveda, which deals with the Vrātya, and is of a mystical character, exalts the converted Vrātya as a type of the perfect **Brahmacārin,** and, in so far, of the divinity.[15]

[10] *Ibid.*, xvii. 1, 15. The exact sense of the passages is obscure, and was, as Lāṭyāyana shows, already obscure in his time and earlier; the translations given are all vague. *Cf.* Weber, *Indische Studien*, 1, 32 *et seq.*; *Indian Literature*, 67, 68; Hopkins, *Transactions of the Connecticut Academy of Arts and Sciences*, 15, 31, 32; Rājārām, *loc. cit.*

[11] *Op. cit.*, 361.

[12] Which is indicated by their name, 'belonging to a roving band' (*vrāta*), 'vagrant.'

[13] See Whitney, Translation of the Atharvaveda, 770 *et seq.*, with Lanman's additions.

[14] St. Petersburg Dictionary, *s.v.*

[15] Bloomfield, *Atharvaveda*, 94.

Cf. Weber, *Indische Studien*, i. 33, 52, 445, n.; *Indian Literature*, 67, 78, 110-112, 141, 146; Aufrecht, *Indische Studien*, 1, 130 *et seq.*; Ludwig, Translation of the Rigveda, 3, xxvi *et seq.*; Zimmer, *Altindisches Leben*, 216.

Vrīhi, 'rice,' is never mentioned in the Rigveda,[1] but is frequently alluded to in the Atharvaveda[2] and later.[3] Rice seems to be indigenous in the south-east of India:[4] this fact accounts well for the absence of any mention of it in the Rigveda. Black and white rice is contrasted in the Taittirīya Saṃhitā,[5] where also[6] the distinctions of dark, swift-growing (*āśu*), and large rice (*mahā-vrīhi*) are found. Probably the swift-growing variety is that later known as *ṣaṣṭika*, 'ripening in sixty days.' Vrīhi and **Yava,** 'barley,' are normally conjoined in the texts.[7] *Cf.* **Plāśuka.**

[1] To take *dhānya bīja* in Rv. v. 53, 13, as 'rice seeds' is unnecessary and very improbable, nor is there better reason to see in *dhānya rasa* in Av. ii. 26, 5, a 'rice drink.'

[2] vi. 140, 2; viii. 7, 20; ix. 6, 14, etc.

[3] Taittirīya Saṃhitā, vii. 2, 10, 3, where it is said to ripen in autumn; Kāṭhaka Saṃhitā, x. 6; xi. 5; Maitrāyaṇī Saṃhitā, iii. 10, 2; iv. 3, 2; Vājasaneyi Saṃhitā, xviii. 12; Aitareya Brāhmaṇa, ii. 8, 7; 11, 12; viii. 16, 3. 4; Śatapatha Brāhmaṇa, v. 5, 5, 9; Bṛhadāraṇyaka Upaniṣad, vi. 3, 22 (Mādhyaṃdina = vi. 3, 13 Kāṇva); Chāndogya Upaniṣad, iii. 14, 3.

[4] ii. 3, 1, 3. *Cf.* Taittirīya Brāhmaṇa, 1. 7, 3, 4; Kāṭhaka Saṃhitā, xii. 4. 5. 6, etc.

[5] i. 8, 10, 1.

[6] Av. xi. 4, 13; Jaiminīya Brāhmaṇa, i. 43; Chāndogya Upaniṣad, v. 10, 6, etc.

Cf. Zimmer, *Altindisches Leben*, 239.

Vleṣka. See **Bleṣka.**

S.

Śaṃyu is the name of a mythical son of Bṛhaspati. He is quoted as a teacher in the texts of the Yajurveda.[1]

[1] Taittirīya Saṃhitā, ii. 6, 10, 1; v. 2, 6, 4; Taittirīya Brāhmaṇa, iii. 3, 8, 11; Śatapatha Brāhmaṇa, i. 9, 1, 24; Taittirīya Āraṇyaka, i. 5, 2.

Cf. Lévi, *La Doctrine du Sacrifice*, 113.

Śakaṭa,[1] **Śakaṭī,**[2] are rare words in the older literature for a 'cart.' The creaking of a cart is referred to in the Rigveda[2] as like the sound heard by night in the forest.

[1] Nirukta, vi. 22; xi. 47; Chāndogya Upaniṣad, iv. 1, 8.

[2] Rv. x. 146, 3; Saḍviṃśa Brāhmaṇa, iv. 7.

Śaka-dhūma is found in one hymn of the Atharvaveda,[1] where it is celebrated as the king of the asterisms. The word seems to mean the 'smoke of (burning) cow-dung,' or else the 'smoke (rising) from (fresh) cow-dung': it may well be, as Weber[2] thinks, that this was deemed to be significant of the weather. Bloomfield,[3] however, considers that the word is to be rendered as 'weather prophet,' that is, one who foretells the weather by means of the smoke of a fire. Whitney[4] objects to this view with reason. It is not at all improbable that, as Roth[5] believed, an asterism of some sort is meant, probably the 'milky way.'

[1] vi. 128, 1. 3. 4, and in the Nakṣatra Kalpa.

[2] *Omina und Portenta*, 363; *Indische Studien*, 5, 257; 10, 65; *Naxatra*, 2, 272, n.; 293.

[3] *American Journal of Philology*, 7, 484 *et seq.*; *Journal of the American Oriental Society*, 13, cxxxiii; *Hymns of the Atharvaveda*, 532, 533.

[4] Translation of the Atharvaveda, 377, 378.

[5] St. Petersburg Dictionary, *s.v.*

Cf. Zimmer, *Altindisches Leben*, 353; Caland, *Altindisches Zauberritual*, 175, n. 3.

Śakan. See **Śakṛt.**

Śaka-pūta ('purified by cow-dung') is the name, apparently, of a prince, in one hymn of the Rigveda (x. 132, 5).

Śakaṃ-bhara, 'bearer of dung,' is found in one passage of the Atharvaveda,[1] where the sense is doubtful. Ludwig[2] and Grill[3] see in it a tribal name, Bloomfield[4] the personification of excessive evacuation (diarrhœa), while Whitney[5] considers that it may refer to the **Mahāvṛṣas,** despised as having to collect dung for fuel in the absence of wood in their country.

[1] v. 22, 4.

[2] Translation of the Rigveda, 3, 510.

[3] *Hundert Lieder*,[2] 154.

[4] *Hymns of the Atharvaveda*, 445, 446.

[5] Translation of the Atharvaveda, 259.

Cf. Weber, *Indische Studien*, 18, 253.

Śakā is the name of one of the victims at the Aśvamedha ('horse sacrifice') in the Yajurveda Saṃhitās.[1] It is uncer-

[1] Taittirīya Saṃhitā, v. 5, 12, 1; 18, 1; Maitrāyaṇī Saṃhitā, iii. 14, 13; Vājasaneyi Saṃhitā, xxiv. 32.

tain whether a kind of bird[2] or fly,[3] or long-eared beast[4] is intended.

[2] Mahīdhara on Vājasaneyi Saṃhitā, *loc. cit.*

[3] Sāyaṇa on Taittirīya Saṃhitā, v. 5, 12, 1; 18, 1.

[4] Sāyaṇa on Taittirīya Saṃhitā, v. 5, 12, 1.

Cf. Zimmer, *Altindisches Leben*, 99.

Śakuna, 'bird,' is mentioned frequently in the Rigveda[1] and later.[2] It usually denotes a large bird,[3] or a bird which gives omens.[4] Zimmer[5] compares κύκνος, which also is a bird of omen.

[1] iv. 26, 6; ix. 85, 11; 86, 13; 107, 20; 112, 2; x. 68, 7; 106, 3; 123, 6; 165, 2.

[2] Av. xii. 1, 51; 3, 13; xx. 127, 4; Taittirīya Saṃhitā, iii. 2, 6, 2; Vājasaneyi Saṃhitā, xviii. 53, etc.

[3] *Cf.* Av. xi. 2, 24, as compared with **Vayas**; Nirukta, iii. 18.

[4] *Cf.* Kauṣītaki Brāhmaṇa, vii. 4; Maitrāyaṇī Upaniṣad, vi. 34, etc.

[5] *Altindisches Leben*, 430.

Śakuni, 'bird,' is used practically like **Śakuna**, but with a much clearer reference to divination. It was smaller than the **Śyena** or **Suparṇa**,[1] gave signs,[2] and foretold ill-luck.[3] When it is mentioned[4] in the list of sacrificial victims at the Aśvamedha ('horse sacrifice'), a special species must be meant: later the falcon is so called, but the 'raven' may be intended; the commentator on the Taittirīya Saṃhitā thinks that it is the 'crow.' It is mentioned several times elsewhere.[5]

[1] Rv. ii. 42, 2.

[2] Rv. ii. 42, 1; 43, 3.

[3] Av. x. 3, 6.

[4] Taittirīya Saṃhitā, v. 5, 19, 1; Vājasaneyi Saṃhitā, xxiv. 40; Maitrāyaṇī Saṃhitā, iii. 14, 21.

[5] Av. ii. 25, 2; vii. 64, 1; xi. 9, 9; Kāṭhaka Saṃhitā, xxv. 7; Aitareya Brāhmaṇa, ii. 15, 12; iv. 7, 3; Śatapatha Brāhmaṇa, xiv. 1, 1, 31; Chāndogya Upaniṣad, vi. 8, 2, etc.

Cf. Zimmer, *Altindisches Leben*, 88, 430.

Śakuni-mitra is one of the names of **Vipaścit Pārāśarya** in the Jaiminīya Upaniṣad Brāhmaṇa (iii. 41, 1).

Śakunta is a name for 'bird' in the Atharvaveda (xi. 6, 8).

Śakuntaka,[1] **Śakuntikā**,[2] are diminutives, meaning 'little bird' in the Saṃhitās.

[1] Khila after Rv. ii. 43; Vājasaneyi Saṃhitā, xxiii. 23.

[2] Rv. i. 191, 1; Vājasaneyi Saṃhitā, xxiii. 22.

Śakuntalā is the name of an Apsaras who bore **Bharata**, according to the Śatapatha Brāhmaṇa,[1] at **Nāḍapit**. Weber[2] doubtfully reads the latter word as Nāḍapitī, an epithet of Śakuntalā.

[1] xiii. 5, 4, 13.

[2] *Episches im vedischen Ritual*, 6.

Śakunti is found in the Rigveda (ii. 42, 3; 43, 1) denoting a 'bird' of omen.

Śakula in the later Saṃhitās[1] denotes an unknown species of fish.

[1] Av. xx. 136, 1; Vājasaneyi Saṃhitā, xxiii. 28. *Cf.* Zimmer, *Altindisches Leben*, 97.

Śakṛt,[1] **Śakan**,[2] denotes 'dung' in the Rigveda and later. It is clear that the value of manure was early appreciated (see **Karīṣa**). For the use of the smoke of dung or of a dung fire for prognosticating the weather, see **Śakadhūma**.

[1] Used only in nominative and accusative: Rv. i. 161, 10; Av. xii. 4, 9; Taittirīya Saṃhitā, vii. 1, 19, 3, etc.

[2] In the oblique cases Śakan is the base, Av. xii. 4, 4; Taittirīya Saṃhitā, v. 7, 23, 1; Vājasaneyi Saṃhitā, xxxvii. 9.

Cf. Zimmer, *Altindisches Leben*, 236.

1. **Śakti** is said in the Jaiminīya Brāhmaṇa[1] to have been the son of **Vasiṣṭha**, and to have been cast into the fire by the **Viśvāmitras**. According to Ṣaḍguruśiṣya,[2] who appears to follow the Śāṭyāyanaka,[3] the story of Śakti is as follows: Viśvāmitra, being defeated in a contest by Śakti, had recourse

[1] ii. 390 (*Journal of the American Oriental Society*, 18, 47).

[2] Sarvānukramaṇī, ed. Macdonell, p. 107, and on Rv. vii. 32.

[3] Geldner, *Vedische Studien*, 2, 159, n. 3.

to **Jamadagni**, who taught him the **Sasarparī**; later he revenged himself on Śakti by having him burnt in the forest. The Bṛhaddevatā[4] relates the first part of the tale only. Geldner[5] sees in the Rigveda[6] a description of the death struggle of Śakti, but this interpretation is more than doubtful.[7]

[4] iv. 112 *et seq.*, with Macdonell's notes.

[5] *Op. cit.*, 2, 159 *et seq.*; more doubtfully, *Rigveda, Kommentar*, 89.

[6] iii. 53, 22.

[7] Oldenberg, *Ṛgveda-Noten*, 1, 254.

2. **Śakti Āṅgirasa** ('descendant of **Aṅgiras**') is the name of a seer of a Sāman or Chant in the Pañcaviṃśa Brāhmaṇa.[1]

[1] xii. 5, 16. *Cf.* Hillebrandt, *Vedische Mythologie*, 2, 160.

Śakvarī, fem. plur., denotes the Śakvarī verses, known also as the Mahānāmnī verses, to which the Śākvara Sāman (chant) is sung. This sense seems to occur in the Rigveda,[1] and is certain later.[2]

[1] vii. 33, 4; x. 71, 14; Nirukta, i. 8.

[2] Av. xiii. 1, 5; Taittirīya Saṃhitā, ii. 2, 8, 5; 6, 2, 3; iii. 4, 4, 1; v. 4, 12, 2; Kāṭhaka Saṃhitā, xxvi. 4; Pañcaviṃśa Brāhmaṇa, x. 6, 5; xii. 13, 12; Taittirīya Brāhmaṇa, ii. 1, 5, 11; Śatapatha Brāhmaṇa, iii. 3, 1, 1; 9, 2, 17, etc.

Cf. Keith, *Aitareya Āraṇyaka*, 258 *et seq.*

Śaṅku in the Rigveda[1] and later[2] denotes a 'wooden peg.' Thus the term is used of the pegs by which a skin is stretched out in the Śatapatha Brāhmaṇa,[3] and of the pin of hobbles (**Paḍbīśa**).[4] In the Chāndogya Upaniṣad[5] it may mean 'stalk'[6] or 'fibre of a leaf.'[7]

[1] i. 164, 48.

[2] Śatapatha Brāhmaṇa, iii. 5, 1, 1; 2, 2; 6, 1, 3; xiii. 8, 4, 1; Aitareya Brāhmaṇa, iii. 18, 6, etc.

[3] ii. 1, 1, 10.

[4] Bṛhadāraṇyaka, vi. 2, 13 (Mādhyaṃdina = vi. 1, 13 Kāṇva), etc.

[5] ii. 23, 4.

[6] Max Müller, *Sacred Books of the East*, 1, 35.

[7] Little, *Grammatical Index*, 149. But *cf.* Oertel, *Journal of the American Oriental Society*, 16, 228, who compares *śūci* in Jaiminīya Brāhmaṇa, ii. 10; Jaiminīya Upaniṣad Brāhmaṇa, i. 10, 3.

1. **Śaṅkha** in the Atharvaveda,[1] with the epithet **Kṛśana,** denotes a pearl-shell used as an amulet. In the later literature[2] it denotes a 'shell' or 'conch' used for blowing as a wind instrument.

[1] iv. 10, 1. See Lanman in Whitney, Translation of the Atharvaveda, 161.

[2] Bṛhadāraṇyaka Upaniṣad, ii. 4, 9; iv. 5, 10.

2. **Śaṅkha Kauṣya** is mentioned as a teacher whom **Jāta Śākāyanya** criticized in the Kāṭhaka Saṃhitā (xxii. 7; *cf.* 6).

3. **Śaṅkha Bābhravya** ('descendant of **Babhru**') is the name of a teacher, a pupil of **Rāma,** in the Jaiminīya Upaniṣad Brāhmaṇa (iii. 41, 1; iv. 17, 1).

Śaṅkha-dhma, a 'conch-blower,' is enumerated among the victims at the Puruṣamedha ('human sacrifice') in the Yajurveda,[1] and is mentioned in the Bṛhadāraṇyaka Upaniṣad.[2]

[1] Vājasaneyi Saṃhitā, xxx. 19; Taittirīya Brāhmaṇa, iii. 4, 13, 1.

[2] ii. 4, 9; iv. 5, 10.

Śaṅga Śāṭyāyani ('descendant of Śāṭyāyana') **Ātreya** ('descendant of **Atri**') is the name of a teacher, a pupil of **Nagarin,** in the Jaiminīya Upaniṣad Brāhmaṇa (iii. 40, 1).

Śacīvant is apparently the name of a man in one passage of the Rigveda,[1] where the vocative *Śacīvaḥ* occurs. But Roth[2] prefers to read *Śacī ca* instead.

[1] x. 74, 5.

[2] St. Petersburg Dictionary, *s.v.* *Cf.* Ludwig, Translation of the Rigveda, 3, 108; Griffith, *Hymns of the Rigveda*, 2, 489, n.

Śaṇa denotes a kind of 'hemp' (*Cannabis sativa* or *Crotolaria juncea*). It is mentioned in the Atharvaveda[1] as growing in the forest, and as used like the **Jaṅgiḍa** as a remedy against **Viṣkandha.** It also occurs in the Śatapatha Brāhmaṇa.[2]

[1] ii. 4, 5.

[2] iii. 2, 1, 11 vi. 6, 1, 24; 2, 15.

Cf. Zimmer, *Altindisches Leben*, 68.

Śaṇḍa is joined with **Marka** as a Purohita of the Asuras in the Yajurveda Saṃhitās[1] and Brāhmaṇas.[2]

[1] Taittirīya Saṃhitā, vi. 4, 10, 1; Maitrāyaṇī Saṃhitā, iv. 6, 3; Vājasaneyi Saṃhitā, vii. 12. 13 (Marka in 16. 17).

[2] Śatapatha Brāhmaṇa, iv. 2, 1, 4; Taittirīya Brāhmaṇa, i. 1, i, 5. *Cf.* Hillebrandt, *Vedische Mythologie*, 1, 223.

Śaṇḍika is found in one passage of the Rigveda[1] in the plural. According to Ludwig,[2] the hymn is a prayer for victory over the Śaṇḍikas and their king.

[1] iii. 30, 8.

[2] Translation of the Rigveda, 3, 153.

Śata-dyumna ('possessing a hundred glories') is the name of a man who, along with **Yajñeṣu,** was made prosperous by the priest **Mātsya** through his knowledge of the exact moment for sacrifice, according to the Taittirīya Brāhmaṇa (i. 5, 2, 1).

Śata-pati occurs in a verse of the Maitrāyaṇī Saṃhitā[1] and the Taittirīya Brāhmaṇa[2] as an epithet of Indra, who is described as alone the 'lord of a hundred' among men. To interpret the expression as 'lord of a hundred gods,' as does the commentary on the Taittirīya Brāhmaṇa, is obviously impossible. It seems clear that there is a reference to an analogous human functionary—viz., the lord of a hundred villages, known in the later law[3]—who was probably at once a judicial deputy of the sovereign and a revenue collector, an ancient magistrate and collector.

[1] iv. 14, 12.

[2] ii. 8, 4, 2.

[3] See Foy, *Die königliche Gewalt*, 74.

Śata-balākṣa Maudgalya ('descendant of **Mudgala**') is the name of a grammarian in the Nirukta (xi. 6).

Śata-māna. See **Māna** and **Kṛṣṇala.**

Śata-yātu ('having a hundred magic powers') is the name of a Ṛṣi in the Rigveda.[1] He is enumerated after **Parāśara** and before **Vasiṣṭha.** Geldner[2] thinks he may have been a son of Vasiṣṭha.

[1] vii. 18, 21.
[2] *Vedische Studien*, 2, 132.

Cf. Ludwig, Translation of the Atharvaveda, 3, 139.

Śata-rudriya,[1] **Śata-rudrīya**[2] (hymn 'relating to the hundred Rudras'), is the name of a section of the Yajurveda,[3] which celebrates the god Rudra in his hundred aspects, enumerating his many epithets.

[1] Kāṭhaka Saṃhitā, xxi. 6; Śatapatha Brāhmaṇa, ix. 1, 1, 1; 2, 1; x. 1, 5, 3. 15.
[2] Taittirīya Saṃhitā, v. 4, 3, 1; 5, 9, 4; 7 3, 3; Taittirīya Brāhmaṇa, iii. 11, 9, 9, etc.
[3] Taittirīya Saṃhitā, iv. 5, 1-11; Kāṭhaka Saṃhitā, xvii. 11-16; Maitrāyaṇī Saṃhitā, ii. 9, 1 *et seq.*; Vājasaneyi Saṃhitā, xvi. 1 *et seq.*

Cf. Zimmer, *Altindisches Leben*, 202; Weber, *Indian Literature*, 108, 111, 159, 169, 170; Eggeling, *Sacred Books of the East*, 43, 150 *et seq.*

Śata-śārada in the Rigveda[1] and the Atharvaveda[2] denotes a 'period of a hundred autumns' or years.

[1] vii. 101, 6; x. 161, 2.
[2] i. 35, 1; viii. 2, 2; 5, 21.

Śatānīka Sātrājita is mentioned in the Aitareya Brāhmana[1] and the Śatapatha Brāhmaṇa[2] as a great king who defeated **Dhṛtarāṣṭra,** the prince of **Kāśi,** and took away his sacrificial horse. He was clearly a **Bharata.** He is also alluded to in the Atharvaveda.[3]

[1] viii. 21, 5.
[2] xiii. 5, 4, 9-13.
[3] i. 35, 1 = Vājasaneyi Saṃhitā, xxxiv. 52, in connexion with the **Dākṣāyaṇas.**

Śatri Āgni-veśi ('descendant of Agniveśa') is the name of a generous patron in the Rigveda.[1]

[1] v. 34, 9. *Cf.* Ludwig, Translation of the Rigveda, 3, 155.

Śatru denotes 'enemy' in the Rigveda[1] and later.[2]

[1] i. 33, 13; 61, 13; ii. 23, 11; 30, 3 *et seq.*; iii. 16, 2; iv. 28, 4, etc.
[2] Av. iv. 3, 1; vi. 4, 2; x. 3, 1, etc.

Śaṃ-tanu is the hero of a tale told by Yāska,[1] and often found later.[2] He supersedes his elder brother **Devāpi** as king of the **Kurus.** When his improper deed brings on a prolonged drought in his realm, he is compelled to ask his brother to assume the kingship; Devāpi, however, refuses, but instead performs a sacrifice which produces rain. Sieg[3] endeavours to trace this story in the Rigveda,[4] but all that is there stated is that Devāpi **Ārṣṭiṣeṇa** obtained (no doubt as priest) rain for Śaṃtanu (no doubt a king). There is no hint of relationship at all.

[1] Nirukta, ii. 10.

[2] Bṛhaddevatā, vii. 155 *et seq.*, with Macdonell's notes; Sieg, *Die Sagenstoffe des Ṛgveda*, 129 *et seq.*

[3] *Loc. cit.*

[4] x. 98.

Śapatha in the Rigveda[1] and later[2] denotes a 'curse,' not an 'oath,' as a judicial process. But that an oath of such a kind was possible as it was later,[2] is shown by at least one passage of the Rigveda,[3] where the speaker, possibly **Vasiṣṭha**, imprecates death on himself if he is a wizard, and death on his foes if he is not.

[1] x. 87, 15; Nirukta, vii. 3.

[2] Av. iii. 9, 5; iv. 9, 5; 18, 7; 19, 7, etc.

[3] vii. 104, 15.

Cf. Muir, *Sanskrit Texts*, 1², 326, 327.

1. **Śapha**, 'hoof,' comes to be used to denote the fraction 'one-eighth,' because of the divided hoofs of the cow, just as **Pāda,** the 'foot' of a quadruped, also means a 'quarter.' This sense in found as early as the Rigveda,[1] and is not rare later.[2]

[1] viii. 47, 17.

[2] Av. vi. 46, 3; xix. 57, 1; Taittirīya Saṃhitā, vi. 1, 10, 1; Śatapatha Brāhmaṇa, iii. 3, 3, 3, etc.

Cf. Hopkins, *Journal of the American Oriental Society*, 16, 278; 17, 47; Zimmer, *Altindisches Leben*, 259.

2. **Śapha** in the Brāhmaṇa[1] is the name (used in the dual) of a wooden implement, acting like a pair of tongs, for lifting an iron pot from the fire. It is probably so called because it resembled a hoof in being divided.

[1] Aitareya Brāhmaṇa, i. 22, 14; Śatapatha Brāhmaṇa, xiv. 2, 1, 16. *Cf.* Eggeling, *Sacred Books of the East*, 44, 458, n. 4; 476.

Śaphaka is the name of some plant in the Atharvaveda.[1] It is also mentioned in the Āpastamba Śrauta Sūtra,[2] where it seems to denote an edible water plant or fruit, perhaps a water nut. It may be so called from its leaves being shaped like hoofs (**Śapha**).

[1] iv. 34, 5.
[2] ix. 14, 14.
Cf. Weber, *Indische Studien*, 18, 138; Zimmer, *Altindisches Leben*, 70; Whitney, Translation of the Atharvaveda 207.

Śaphāla is the name of **Ṛtuparṇa's** kingdom in the Baudhāyana Śrauta Sātra.[1]

[1] xx. 12. *Cf.* Caland, *Über das rituelle Sūtra des Baudhāyana*, 21, 36.

Sabara is the name of a wild tribe who in the Aitareya Brāhmaṇa[1] are classed as **Dasyus**, with the **Andhras, Pulindas, Mūtibas**, and **Puṇḍras**.

[1] vii. 18, 2; Śāṅkhāyana Śrauta Sūtra, xv. 26, 6. *Cf.* Muir, *Sanskrit Texts*, 1², 483.

Śamitṛ denotes the 'man who cuts up' the slaughtered animal in the Rigveda[1] and later,[2] sometimes having merely the sense of 'cook.'

[1] i. 162, 9 *et seq.*; ii. 3, 10; iii. 4, 10; v. 43, 4, etc.
[2] Av. x. 9, 7 ('cook' of the Śataudanā, or offering of a cow and a hundred rice-dishes); Vājasaneyi Saṃhitā, xvii. 57; xxi. 21; xxiii. 39; Aitareya Brāhmaṇa, ii. 6, 2; 7, 10-12; vii. 1, 2; Pañcaviṃśa Brāhmaṇa, xxv. 18, 4, etc.

Śamī is the name of a tree in the Atharvaveda[1] and later.[2] It is described in the Atharvaveda[3] as destructive to the hair,[4] as producing intoxication, and as broad-leaved. These characteristics are totally wanting in the two trees, *Prosopis spicigera* or *Mimosa suma*, with which the Śamī is usually identified.[5]

[1] Av. vi. 11, 1; 30, 2. 3.
[2] Taittirīya Saṃhitā, v. 1, 9, 6; 4, 7, 4 (for the lower *araṇī*); Kāṭhaka Saṃhitā, xxxvi. 6; Taittirīya Brāhmaṇa, i. 1, 3, 11 *et seq.*; 6, 4, 5; Śatapatha Brāhmaṇa, ii. 5, 2, 12; ix. , 3, 37, etc.
[3] Av. vi. 30, 2. 3.
[4] In the Dhanvantarīya Nighaṇṭu, p. 188 (ed. Poona), the Śamī and its fruit are said to destroy the hair.
[5] See Roth in Whitney, Translation of the Atharvaveda, 302.

From the soft wood of the Śamī was formed the lower of the two sticks (*araṇī*) used for kindling the sacred fire,[6] the upper one (the drill) being of **Aśvattha.** The fruit of the tree is called Śamīdhānya.[7]

[6] Av. vi. 11, 1; Śatapatha Brāhmaṇa, xi. 5, 1, 15; *cf.* 13; iii. 4, 1, 22; Taittirīya Saṃhitā, v. 1, 9, 6; 4, 7, 4.

[7] Śatapatha Brāhmaṇa, i. 1, 1, 10. *Cf.* Zimmer, *Altindisches Leben*, 59 60.

Śambara is the name of an enemy of Indra in the Rigveda.[1] He is mentioned along with **Śuṣṇa, Pipru,** and **Varcin,** being in one passage called a **Dāsa,** son of Kulitara.[2] In another passage[3] he is said to have deemed himself a godling (*devaka*). His forts, ninety,[4] ninety-nine,[5] or a hundred[6] in number, are alluded to, the word itself in the neuter plural once[7] meaning the 'forts of Śambara.' His great foe was **Divodāsa Atithigva,** who won victories over him by Indra's aid.[8]

It is impossible to say with certainty whether Śambara was a real person or not. Hillebrandt[9] is strongly in favour of the theory that he was a real chief as enemy of Divodāsa: he relies on the statistics[10] of the mention of the name to show that, whereas he was conceived as a real foe in the hymns of the time of Divodāsa, later texts, like those of the seventh Maṇḍala, make him into a demon, as a result of the change of scene from Arachosia to India. As a matter of fact, apart from this theory, Śambara was quite possibly an aboriginal enemy in India, living in the mountains.[11]

[1] i. 51, 6; 54, 4; 59, 6; 101, 2; 103, 8; 112, 14; 130, 7; ii. 12, 11; 14, 6; 19, 6; iv. 26, 3; 30, 14; vi. 18, 8; 26, 5; 31, 4; 43, 1; 47, 2. 21; vii. 18, 20; 99, 5.

[2] Rv. vi. 26, 5.

[3] Rv. vii. 18, 20.

[4] Rv. i. 130, 7.

[5] Rv. ii. 19, 6.

[6] Rv. ii. 14, 6.

[7] Rv. ii. 24, 2.

[8] Rv. i. 51, 6; 130, 7; ii. 19, 6; iv. 26, 3, etc.

[9] *Vedische Mythologie*, 1, 103, 108; 3, 273.

[10] Seven times in Maṇḍala i; four in ii; two in iv; six in vi; two in vii. These references show *primâ facie* greater reality in Maṇḍala vi than elsewhere. The references in ii are certainly all of the mythical kind, and those in vii are of much the same sort.

[11] Rv. i. 130, 7; iv. 30, 14; vi. 26, 5. *Cf.* Ludwig, Translation of the Rigveda, 3, 177; Macdonell, *Vedic Mythology*, p. 161; Oldenberg, *Zeitschrift der Deutschen Morgenländischen Gesellschaft*, 42, 210; Geldner, *Rigveda, Glossar*, 178.

Śambin, a word occurring only once, appears to mean 'ferryman' in the Atharvaveda (ix. 2, 6). The literal sense is probably 'pole-man' (from *śamba*, a word of doubtful signification found in the Rigveda, x. 42, 7).

Śaṃmad Āṅgirasa ('descendant of **Aṅgiras**') is the name of the seer of a Sāman or Chant in the Pañcaviṃśa Brāhmaṇa (xv. 5, 11).

Cf. Hillebrandt, *Vedische Mythologie*, 2, 160.

Śamyā denotes in the Rigveda[1] and later[2] a 'peg,' more particularly one on the millstone;[3] and on the yoke,[4] where it seems to mean the pin of wood attached to either end so as to keep the yoke in place on the ox's neck.[5] The Śamyā was also used as a measure of length.[6]

[1] x. 31, 10.

[2] Av. vi. 138, 4; xx. 136, 9; Taittirīya Saṃhitā, vi. 2, 7, 1; Pañcaviṃśa Brāhmaṇa, xxv. 10, 4; Śatapatha Brāhmaṇa, xii. 5, 2, 7, etc.

[3] Taittirīya Brāhmaṇa, i. 6, 1, 1; Śatapatha Brāhmaṇa, i. 1, 1, 22; 2, 1, 16 *et seq.*; v. 2, 3, 2, etc.

[4] Rv. iii. 33, 13; Śatapatha Brāhmaṇa, iii. 3, 4, 25; Taittirīya Saṃhitā, i. 6, 8, 3.

[5] Pañcaviṃśa Brāhmaṇa, vi. 5, 20. *Cf.* xi. 1, 6; xv. 7, 6; Grierson, *Bihar Peasant Life*, 194, and illustration, p. 33; Cunningham, *The Stûpa of Bharhut*, Plate xxviii.; Caland and Henry, *L'Agniṣṭoma*, 49.

[6] Taittirīya Brāhmaṇa, iii. 2, 6, 2. According to the commentary on Kātyāyana Śrauta Sūtra, v. 3, 20, the length was 32 Aṅgulas, or finger-breadths This would be equivalent to 2 feet: *cf.* Fleet, *Journal of the Royal Asiatic Society*, 1912, 232.

Śayaṇḍaka. See **Śayāṇḍaka.**

Śayana in the Atharvaveda[1] and later[2] denotes a 'couch.' *Cf.* **Talpa, Vahya.**

[1] iii. 25, 1; v. 29, 8.

[2] Śatapatha Brāhmaṇa, xi. 5, 1, 2; 7, 4.

Śayāṇḍaka is the form in the Taittirīya Saṃhitā[1] of the name of an animal which in the Maitrāyaṇī[2] and Vājasaneyi Saṃhitās[3] is written as Śayaṇḍaka. Some sort of bird is meant according to Roth,[4] but the commentator on the Taittirīya Saṃhitā equates the word with **Kṛkalāsa,** 'chameleon.'

[1] v. 5, 14, 1.

[2] iii. 14, 14.

[3] xxiv. 33.

[4] St. Petersburg Dictionary, *s.v.* *Cf.* Zimmer, *Altindisches Leben*, 95.

Śayu is the name in the Rigveda[1] of a protégé of the Aśvins, who made his cow to give milk.

[1] i. 112, 16; 116, 22; 117, 20; 118, 8; 119, 6; vi. 62, 7; vii. 68, 8; x. 39, 13; 40, 8.

1. **Śara** in the Rigveda[1] and later[2] denotes a kind of 'reed' (*Saccharum Sara*). Its use for arrow shafts,[3] and its brittleness,[4] are expressly referred to in the Atharvaveda. *Cf.* **Śarya.**

[1] i. 191, 3.
[2] Av. iv. 7, 4; Taittirīya Saṃhitā, v. 2, 6, 2; vi. 1, 3, 3; Kāṭhaka Saṃhitā, xi. 5; xxiii. 4; Śatapatha Brāhmaṇa, i. 2, 4, 1; iii. 1, 3, 13; Bṛhadāraṇyaka Upaniṣad, vi. 4, 11, etc.; Nirukta, v. 4, etc.
[3] Av. i. 2, 1; 3, 1.
[4] Av. viii. 8, 4.
Cf. Zimmer, *Altindisches Leben*, 71.

2. **Śara Arcatka** ('descendant of Ṛcatka') is the name of a Ṛṣi in the Rigveda.[1] It is very doubtful, however, whether Ārcatka is really a patronymic.

[1] i. 116, 22; *cf.* perhaps i. 112, 16; Oldenberg, *Ṛgveda-Noten*, 1, 103. *Cf.* Ludwig, Translation of the Rigveda, 3, 150.

3. **Śara Śaura-devya** ('descendant of Śūradeva') is the name of a generous prince in the Rigveda,[1] who gave one calf to three singers. That this Dānastuti ('praise of gifts') is ironical seems certain.[2]

[1] viii. 70, 13-15.
[2] Pischel, *Vedische Studien*, 1, 5-7; Ludwig, Translation of the Rigveda, 3, 163; 5, 175.

Śarad. See **Ṛtu.**

1. **Śarabha** is the name of some wild animal in the Atharvaveda[1] and later.[2] In the classical literature it is a fabulous, eight-legged beast, dwelling in the snowy mountains, a foe of lions and elephants: the commentator Mahīdhara sees this sense, but without reason, in the Vājasaneyi Saṃhitā. The

[1] ix. 5, 9. *Cf.* **Śalabha.**
[2] Taittirīya Saṃhitā, iv. 2, 10, 4; Vājasaneyi Saṃhitā, xiii. 51; Aitareya Brāhmaṇa, ii. 8, 5; Śatapatha Brāhmaṇa, i. 2, 3, 9, etc

animal is spoken of as akin to the goat;[3] it was probably a kind of deer.

[3] Av., *loc. cit.*; Satapatha Brāhmaṇa, *loc. cit.* Eggeling, *Sacred Books of the East*, 12, 52, n. 1, accepts the traditional rendering.

Cf. Zimmer, *Altindisches Leben*, 89.

2. **Śarabha** is the name of a Ṛṣi in the Rigveda.[1]

[1] viii. 100, 6. *Cf.* Ludwig, Translation of the Rigveda, 3, 163.

Śaravyā, 'arrow-shot,' is an expression found in the Rigveda[1] and later.[2]

[1] vi. 75, 16; x. 87, 13.
[2] Av. i. 19, 1. 3; v. 18, 9; xi. 10, 6; xii. 5, 25. 29; Taittirīya Saṃhitā, iv. 5, 1, 1, etc.

Śarāva is a measure of corn in the Brāhmaṇas.[1]

[1] *Saptadaśa-śarāva*, Taittirīya Brāhmaṇa, i. 3, 4, 5; 6, 8; Śatapatha Brāhmaṇa, v. 1, 4, 12.

Śarīra, 'body,' is a word of frequent occurrence in Vedic literature.[1] The interest of the Vedic Indians seems early to have been attracted to the consideration of questions connected with the anatomy of the body. Thus a hymn of the Atharvaveda[2] enumerates many parts of the body with some approach to accuracy and orderly arrangement.[3] It mentions the heels (*pārṣṇī*), the flesh (*māṃsa*), the ankle-bones (*gulphau*), the fingers (*aṅgulīḥ*), the apertures (*kha*), the two metatarsi (*uchlakau*), the tarsus (*pratiṣṭhā*), the two knee-caps (*aṣṭhīvantau*), the two legs (*jaṅghe*), the two knee-joints (*jānunoḥ sandhī*). Then comes above the two knees (*jānū*) the four-sided (*catuṣṭaya*), pliant (*śithira*) trunk (*kabandha*). The two hips (*śroṇī*) and the two thighs (*ūrū*) are the props of the frame

[1] Rv. i. 32, 10; x. 16, 1, etc.; Av. v. 9, 7; xviii. 3, 9, etc.; Vājasaneyi Saṃhitā, xxxiv. 55; Taittirīya Saṃhitā, i. 7, 2, 1; Aitareya Brāhmaṇa, ii. 6, 13; 14, 2; Śatapatha Brāhmaṇa, x. 1, 4, 1; Taittirīya Brāhmaṇa, i. 2, 1, 8.

[2] x. 2.

[3] *Cf.* Hoernle, *Journal of the Royal Asiatic Society*, 1907, 10-12; *Osteology*, 109-111, 242.

(*kusindha*). Next come the breast-bone (*uras*), the cervical cartilages (*grīvāḥ*), the two breast pieces (*stanau*), the two shoulder-blades (*kaphoḍau*), the neck-bones (*skandhau*), and the backbones (*pṛṣṭīḥ*), the collar-bones (*aṃsau*), the arms (*bāhū*), the seven apertures in the head (*sapta khāni śīrṣaṇi*), the ears (*karṇau*), the nostrils (*nāsike*), the eyes (*cakṣaṇī*), the mouth (*mukha*), the jaws (*hanū*), the tongue (*jihvā*), the brain (*mastiṣka*), the forehead (*lalāṭa*), the facial bone (*kakāṭikā*), the cranium (*kapāla*), and the structure of the jaws (*cityā hanvoḥ*).

This system presents marked similarities with the later system of Caraka and Suśruta,[4] which render certain the names ascribed to the several terms by Hoernle. *Kaphoḍau*, which is variously read in the manuscripts,[5] is rendered 'collar-bone' by Whitney, but 'elbow' in the St. Petersburg Dictionary. *Skandha* in the plural regularly[6] denotes 'neck-bones,' or, more precisely, 'cervical vertebræ,' a part denoted also by *uṣṇihā* in the plural.[7] *Pṛṣṭī*[8] denotes not 'rib,' which is *parśu*,[9] but a transverse process of a vertebra, and so the vertebra itself, there being in the truncal portion of the spinal column seventeen vertebræ and thirty-four transverse processes. The vertebræ are also denoted by *kīkasā* in the plural,[10] which sometimes[11] is limited to the upper portion of the vertebral column, sometimes[12] to the thoracic portion of the spine. *Anūka* also denotes the vertebral column,[13] or more specially the lumbar[14] or thoracic[15] portion of the spine; it is said in the Śatapatha Brāhmaṇa[15]

[4] *Osteology*, 112.

[5] Whitney, Translation of the Atharvaveda, 568.

[6] Av. x. 7, 3 (where the Skandhas are compared with the Kṛttikās, probably because both were seven in number, but this is not certain); 9, 20; vi. 135, 1; xii. 5, 67; Hoernle, *Journal*, 1906, 918; 1907, 1, 2.

[7] Av. vi. 134, 1; Rv. vi. 163, 2 = Av. ii. 33, 2; Av. ix. 8, 21; x. 10, 20.

[8] Rv. x. 87, 10 = Av. viii. 3, 10; Av. ix. 7, 5. 6; x. 9, 20; xii. 1, 34; xviii. 4, 10; Śatapatha Brāhmaṇa, vii. 6, 2, 7. See Hoernle, *Journal*, 1907, 2 *et seq.*; Whitney, *op. cit.*, 548; Eggeling, *Sacred Books of the East*, 44, 164, n. 2.

[9] Av. ix. 7, 6, etc.

[10] Av. ix. 7, 5; 8, 14.

[11] Av. xi. 8, 15.

[12] Av. ii. 33, 2; Śatapatha Brāhmaṇa, vii. 6, 2, 10.

[13] Av. iv. 14, 8. *Cf.* ix. 8, 21 (the spine of the trunk).

[14] Av. ii. 33, 2.

[15] Śatapatha Brāhmaṇa, xii. 2, 4, 12. 14. *Cf.* the phrase *iṣe anūkye*, Av. xi. 3, 9, where the two shafts of a cart are compared with the transverse processes of a vertebra.

that there are twenty transverse processes in the lumbar spine (*udara*) and thirty-two in the thoracic, which gives twenty-six vertebræ, the true number (but the modern division is seven cervical, twelve thoracic, five lumbar, and two false—the sacrum and the coccyx). The vertebral column is also denoted by *karūkara*,[16] which, however, is usually found in the plural[17] denoting the transverse processes of the vertebræ, a sense expressed also by *kuntāpa*.[18]

Grīvā, in the plural, denotes cervical vertebræ, the number seven being given by the Śatapatha Brāhmaṇa,[19] but usually[20] the word simply means windpipe, or, more accurately, the cartilaginous rings under the skin. **Jatru**, also in the plural, denotes the cervical cartilages,[21] or possibly the costal cartilages, which are certainly so called in the Śatapatha Brāhmaṇa,[22] where their number is given as eight.

Bhaṃsas, which occurs thrice in the Atharvaveda,[23] seems to denote the pubic bone or arch rather than the 'buttocks' or 'fundament,' as Whitney[24] takes it.

In the Satapatha Brāhmaṇa[25] the number of bones in the the human body is given as 360. The number of the bones of the head and trunk are given in another passage[26] as follows: The head is threefold, consisting of skin (*tvac*), bone (*asthi*), brain (*matiṣka*); the neck has 15 bones: 14 transverse processes (*karūkara*) and the strength (*vīrya*)—*i.e.*, the bone of the centre regarded as one—as the 15th; the breast has 17: 16 cervical cartilages (*jatru*), and the sternum (*uras*) as the 17th; the abdominal portion of the spine has 21: 20 trans-

16 Av. xi. 9, 8; Bloomfield, *Hymns of the Atharvaveda*, 124.

17 Satapatha Brāhmaṇa, xii. 2, 4, 10. 14.

18 *Ibid.*, xii. 2, 4, 12.

19 *Ibid.*, xii. 2, 4, 10.

20 Rv. vi. 163, 2 = Av. ii. 33, 2; Av. vi. 134, 1; ix. 7, 3; x. 9, 20; xi. 8, 15; Hoernle, *Journal*, 1906, 916 *et seq.*

21 Rv. vii. 1, 12 = Av. xiv. 2, 12.

22 xii. 2, 4, 11. *Cf.* vii. 6, 2, 10; Hoernle, *Journal*, 1906, 922 *et seq.*

23 Av. ii. 33, 5; ix. 8, 21, with a fuller version in the Paippalāda recension (Whitney, Translation of the Atharvaveda, 77, 551). In viii. 6, 5, it denotes vulva: Hoernle, 16-18.

24 *Loc. cit.*

25 x. 5, 4, 12; xii. 3, 2, 3. 4; Hoernle, *Osteology*, 238, 239, and the criticism in 106-109, which shows how far removed the Satapatha Brāhmaṇa is from a scientific system. *Cf.* Keith, *Zeitschrift der Deutschen Morgenländischen Gesellschaft*, 62, 135 *et seq.*

26 xii. 2, 4, 9-14; Hoernle, *Osteology*, 240.

verse processes (*kuntāpa*), and the abdominal portion (*udara*) as the 21st; the two sides have 27: 26 ribs (*parśu*), and the two sides as the 27th; the thoracic portion of the spine (*anūka*) has 33: 32 transverse processes, and the thoracic portion as 33rd.

There are several enumerations of the parts of the body, not merely of the skeleton, in the Yajurveda Saṃhitās.[27] They include the hair (*lomāni*), skin (*tvac*), flesh (*māṃsa*), bone (*asthi*), marrow (*majjan*), liver (*yakṛt*), lungs (*kloman*), kidneys (*matasne*), gall (*pitta*), entrails (*āntrāṇi*), bowels (*gudāḥ*), spleen (*plīhan*), navel (*nābhi*), belly (*udara*), rectum (*vaniṣṭhu*), womb (*yoni*), penis (*plāśi* and *śepa*), face (*mukha*), head (*śiras*), tongue (*jihvā*), mouth (*āsan*), rump (*pāyu*), leech (*vāla*), eye (*cakṣus*), eyelashes (*pakṣmāṇi*), eyebrows (*utāni*), nose (*nas*), breath (*vyāna*), nose-hairs (*nasyāni*), ears (*karṇau*), brows (*bhrū*), body or trunk (*ātman*), waist (*upastha*), hair on the face (*śmaśrūṇi*), and on the head (*keśāḥ*). Another enumeration[28] gives *śiras*, *mukha*, *keśāḥ*, *śmaśrūṇi*, *prāṇa* (breath), *cakṣus*, *śrotra* (ear), *jihvā*, *vāc* (speech), *manas* (mind), *aṅgulīḥ*, *aṅgāni* (limbs), *bāhū*, *hastau* (hands), *karṇau*, *ātmā*, *uras* (sternum), *pṛṣṭīḥ* (vertebræ), *udara*, *aṃsau*, *grīvāḥ*, *śroṇī*, *ūrū*, *aratnī* (elbows), *jānūni*, *nābhi*, *pāyu*, *bhasat* (fundament), *āṇḍau* (testicles), *pasas* (membrum virile), *jaṅghā*, *pad* (foot), *lomāni*, *tvac*, *māṃsa*, *asthi*, *majjan*. Another set of names[29] includes *vaniṣṭhu*, *purītat* (pericardium), *lomāni*, *tvac*, *lohita* (blood), *medas* (fat), *māṃsāni*, *snāvāni* (sinews), *asthīni*, *majjānaḥ*, *retas* (semen), *pāyu*, *kośya* (flesh near the heart), *pārśvya* (intercostal flesh), etc.

The bones of the skeleton of the horse are enumerated in the Yajurveda Saṃhitās.[30]

In the Aitareya Āraṇyaka[31] the human body is regarded as made up of one hundred and one items; there are four parts,

[27] Vājasaneyi Saṃhitā, xix. 81-93; Maitrāyaṇī Saṃhitā, iii. 11, 9; Kāṭhaka Saṃhitā, xxxviii. 3; Taittirīya Brāhmaṇa, ii. 6, 4.

[28] Vājasaneyi Saṃhitā, xx. 5-13; Maitrāyaṇī Saṃhitā, iii. 11, 8; Kāṭhaka Saṃhitā, xxxviii. 4; Taittirīya Brāhmaṇa, ii. 6, 5.

[29] Vājasaneyi Saṃhitā, xxxix. 8. 9. 10.

[30] Vājasaneyi Saṃhitā, xxv. 1-9; Maitrāyaṇī Saṃhitā, iii. 15. *Cf.* Aitareya Brāhmaṇa, vii. 1.

[31] i. 2, 2.

each of twenty-five members, with the trunk as one hundred and first. In the two upper parts there are five four-jointed[32] fingers, two *kakṣasī* (of uncertain meaning),[33] the arm (*dos*), the collar-bone (*akṣa*), and the shoulder-blade (*aṃsa-phalaka*). In the two lower portions there are five four-jointed toes, the thigh, the leg, and three articulations, according to Sāyaṇa's commentary.

The Śāṅkhāyana Āraṇyaka[34] enumerates three bones in the head,[35] three joints (*parvāṇi*) in the neck,[36] the collar-bone (*akṣa*),[37] three joints in the fingers,[38] and twenty-one transverse processes in the spine (*anūka*).[39] The Maitrāyaṇī Saṃhitā[40] enumerates four constituents in the head (*prāṇa*, *cakṣus*, *śrotra*, *vāc*), but there are many variations, the number going up to twelve on one calculation.[41] In the Taittirīya Upaniṣad[42] an enumeration is given consisting of *carma* (skin), *māṃsa*, *snāvan*, *asthi*, and *majjan*; the Aitareya Brāhmaṇa[43] has *lomāni*, *māṃsa*, *tvac*, *asthi*, *majjan*, and the Aitareya Āraṇyaka[44] couples *majjānaḥ*, *snāvāni*, and *asthīni*. Other terms relating to the body are *kankūṣa*,[45] perhaps a part of the ear,[46] *yoni* (female organ), *kakṣa*[47] (armpit), **Danta** (tooth), *nakha* (nail), *prapada*[48] (forepart of the foot), *halīkṣṇa*[49] (gall).

32 This is contrary to fact: Hoernle, *Osteology*, 122, 123.

33 Perhaps the armpit regarded as in some way double; Keith, *Aitareya Āraṇyaka*, 175.

34 ii. 2.

35 *Cf.* Hoernle, *Osteology*, 172 *et seq.*; Satapatha Brāhmaṇa, xii. 2, 4, 9.

36 ii. 3. See Keith, *Śāṅkhāyana Āraṇyaka*, 9, n. 4.

37 ii. 4; Hoernle, *Osteology*, 202 *et seq.*; Keith, *op. cit.*, 9, n. 5.

38 ii. 5. *Cf.* n. 32. The later Śāṅkhāyana here improves on the Aitareya osteology.

39 ii. 6. See Keith, *op. cit.*, 10, n. 4.

40 iii. 2, 9.

41 See references in Keith, *Aitareya Āraṇyaka*, 185, 192, 195. The numbers vary and are fanciful, being of no scientific importance.

42 i. 7, 1.

43 vi. 29, 4.

44 iii. 2, 1. 2; Śāṅkhāyana Āraṇyaka, viii. 1. 2.

45 Av. ix. 8, 2, where the Paippalāda recension has *kaṅkukha*.

46 Zimmer, *Altindisches Leben*, 378.

47 Av. vi. 127, 2. *Cf. kakṣī*, Maitrāyaṇī Saṃhitā, iv. 5, 9.

48 Av. ii. 33, 5, with Lanman's note in Whitney's Translation, p. 77; Keith, *Aitareya Āraṇyaka*, 204. In that Āraṇyaka the passage ii. 1, 4 makes the sense 'toe' improbable.

49 Av. ii. 33, 3; Whitney, *op. cit.*, 76. *Cf.* Hoernle, *Journal of the Royal Asiatic Society*, 1906, 916 *et seq.*; 1907, 1 *et seq.*; *Osteology*, *passim*.

Śaru denotes in the Rigveda[1] and Atharvaveda[2] a missile weapon, often certainly an 'arrow,'[3] but perhaps sometimes a 'dart' or 'spear.'[4]

[1] i. 100, 18; 172, 2; 186, 9; ii. 12, 10; iv. 3, 7; 28, 3, etc.
[2] i. 2, 3; 19, 2; vi. 65, 2; xii. 2, 47.
[3] *E.g.*, Rv. x. 125, 6; and x. 87, 6.
[4] Perhaps Rv. iv. 3, 7, where *bṛhatī* is applied to it, and where 'lance' seems the best sense, the use being metaphorical.

Cf. Schrader, *Prehistoric Antiquities* 223; Zimmer, *Altindisches Leben*, 301.

Śarkarā, fem. plur., denotes in the later Saṃhitās[1] and the Brāhmaṇas[2] 'grit' or 'gravel.'

[1] Av. xi. 7, 21; Taittirīya Saṃhitā, v. 1, 6, 2; 2, 6, 2; 6, 4, 4, etc.
[2] Taittirīya Brāhmaṇa, i. 1, 3, 7; 2, 1, 4; iii. 12, 6, 2; Śatapatha Brāhmaṇa, ii. 1, 1, 8, etc.

Śarkarākhya. See **Śārkarākṣa.**

Śarkoṭa is the name of an animal in the Atharvaveda,[1] either a 'serpent,' as Roth[2] and Zimmer[3] held, or a 'scorpion,' as Grill,[4] Henry,[5] and Bloomfield[6] think.

[1] vii. 56, 5.
[2] St. Petersburg Dictionary, *s.v.*, comparing the later Karkoṭaka.
[3] *Altindisches Leben*, 95.
[4] *Hundert Lieder*,[2] 183.
[5] *Le livre vii de l'Atharvavéda*, 82.
[6] *Hymns of the Atharvaveda*, 554, 555.

Śardha. See **Vrāta.**

Śardhya in one passage of the Rigveda[1] is taken by Roth[2] as perhaps denoting a part of the chariot. The sense is, however, quite uncertain.

[1] i. 119, 5.
[2] St. Petersburg Dictionary, *s.v.*

Śarya,[1] **Śaryā,**[2] seem in the Rigveda to denote an 'arrow.'[3] Perhaps, also, Śaryā[4] and Śarya[5] (neut.) mean the 'wicker-

[1] i. 119, 10, where the sense is not certain.
[2] i. 148, 4; x. 178, 3. *Cf.* Nirukta v. 4; x. 29.
[3] As derived from 1. **Śara**, and meaning literally 'made from a reed.'
[4] Rv .ix. 110, 5; x. 61, 3.
[5] Rv. ix. 14, 4; 68, 2.

work' in the Soma sieve, but the exact sense of the passages is doubtful.[6]

[6] Hillebrandt, *Vedische Mythologie*, 1, 52, takes *śaryāṇi* in Rv. ix. 68, 2, as denoting the outer husk of the Soma plant. See also Geldner, *Vedische Studien*, 2, 255, n. 1.

Śaryaṇāvant occurs in several passages of the Rigveda,[1] in all of which Sāyaṇa sees a local name. According to his account, Śaryaṇāḥ (masc. plur.) is a district in **Kurukṣetra**, Śaryaṇāvant being a lake not far from it in the back part (*jaghanārdhe*) of Kurukṣetra. The unusual consistency of his statements on this point is in favour of the word being a place name; it is also to be noted that Kurukṣetra contained the lake **Anyataḥplakṣā.** Roth,[2] however, thought that in two passages[3] the word denoted merely a 'lake,' literally '(water) covered with a thicket of reeds' (*śaryaṇa*), and in the others a Soma vessel. Zimmer[4] inclines to this rendering. On the other hand, Pischel[5] accepts Sāyaṇa's view. Hillebrandt[6] also sees in the word a place name, but he is inclined to locate it among the 'five tribes,'[7] which is not quite inconsistent with its being in Kurukṣetra, for the connexion of the **Pūrus** with the later **Kurus** is known;[8] or perhaps, he suggests, Śaryaṇāvant is an old name for the Wular sea of Kaśmīr, which was only a reminiscence in Vedic times. This is not probable; still less so is Ludwig's hypothesis[9] that the Śaryaṇāvant is the later eastern **Sarasvatī.** Bergaigne[10] regards the name as that of a celestial preparer of Soma.

[1] i. 84, 14; viii. 6, 39; 7, 29; 64, 11; ix. 65, 22; 113, 1; x. 35, 2. See Jaiminīya Brāhmaṇa, iii. 64 (*Journal of the American Oriental Society*, 18, 17); Śāṭyāyanaka in Sāyaṇa on Rv. i. 84, 13.

[2] St. Petersburg Dictionary, *s.v.*

[3] i. 84, 14; x. 35, 2.

[4] *Altindisches Leben*, 19, 20.

[5] *Vedische Studien*, 2, 217. So Max Müller, *Sacred Books of the East*, 32, 398, 399.

[6] *Vedische Mythologie*, 1, 126 *et seq.*

[7] This is deduced, not with any certainty, from Rv. ix. 65, 22.

[8] Hillebrandt, *op. cit.*, 1, 142, n. 4; Ludwig, Translation of the Rigveda, 3, 205.

[9] *Op. cit.*, 3, 201.

[10] *Religion Védique*, 1, 206.

Śaryāta is mentioned once in the Rigveda[1] as a protégé of the Aśvins. Of him in the Śatapatha Brāhmaṇa[2] and the

[1] i. 112, 17.

[2] iv. 1, 5, 2.

Jaiminīya Brāhmaṇa[3] is told a story how **Cyavana** was annoyed by the **Śāryātas**, and appeased by the gift of **Sukanyā**, Śaryāta's daughter, as a wife, and how Cyavana was then restored to youth by the Aśvins. He is there called **Mānava** ('descendant of Manu'). He appears also as Śaryāta Mānava, a sacrificer, in the Jaiminīya Upaniṣad Brāhmaṇa.[4]

[3] iii. 120-122 (*Journal of the American Oriental Society*, 11, cxlv).

[4] iv. 7, 1; 8, 3. 5.

Cf. Muir, *Sanskrit Texts*, 5, 250 *et seq.*; Eggeling, *Sacred Books of the East*, 26, 272 *et seq.*; Oertel, *Journal of the American Oriental Society*, 16, 236, 237.

Śarva-datta ('given by the god Śarva') **Gārgya** ('descendant of **Garga**') is the name of a teacher in the Vaṃśa Brāhmaṇa.[1]

[1] *Indische Studien*, 4, 372.

Śala is explained by the St. Petersburg Dictionary as a measure of length in the Atharvaveda,[1] Kāṭhaka Saṃhitā,[2] and Taittirīya Brāhmaṇa.[3] Whitney[4] objects that the sense in all[5] these passages is not suited by this meaning.

[1] viii. 7, 28.

[2] xii. 10 (*Indische Studien*, 3, 464).

[3] i. 5, 10, 1 (where this is the interpretation of the commentator).

[4] Translation of the Atharvaveda, 501.

[5] He does not notice the Kāṭhaka. Against his criticism it must be noted that in every one of the passages a numeral is compounded with Śala, as *tri-śala*, etc.

Śalabha, 'locust,' appears in the Paippalāda recension of the Atharvaveda[1] for **Śarabha**, the reading of the received text, and is regarded by Whitney[2] as making better sense.

[1] ix. 5, 9.

[2] Translation of the Atharvaveda, 534. But the mention of the goat in the passage strongly supports Śarabha. See Śatapatha Brāhmaṇa, i. 2, 3, 9.

Śalalī denotes the 'quill' of the porcupine, used for parting the hair and anointing the eyes.[1]

[1] Kāṭhaka Saṃhitā, xxiii. 1; Taittirīya Brāhmaṇa, i. 5, 6, 6; Śatapatha Brāhmaṇa, ii. 6, 4, 5.

Śaluna is found in the Atharvaveda[1] denoting a 'worm.' The Paippalāda recension reads Śalūla, and Sāyaṇa Śalga.

[1] ii. 31, 2. *Cf.* Whitney, Translation of the Atharvaveda, 73; Bloomfield, *Hymns of the Atharvaveda*, 315; Zimmer, *Altindisches Leben*, 98 (Śalunna).

Śalka denotes in the later Saṃhitās[1] and the Brāhmaṇas[2] chip' or 'shaving' used for kindling a fire, etc.

[1] Taittirīya Saṃhitā, v. 2, 9, 3; 4, 2, 3; Kāṭhaka Saṃhitā, xx. 8; xxvii. 7, etc.

[2] Aitareya Brāhmaṇa, ii. 14, 4; Taittirīya Brāhmaṇa, i. 1, 9, 9; 2, 1, 15.

Śalmali is the name of the 'silk cotton tree' (*Salmalia Malabarica*). Its fruit is regarded as poisonous in the Rigveda,[1] but the car of the bridal procession is made of its wood.[2] It is described as the tallest of trees.[3]

[1] vii. 50, 3.

[2] x. 85, 20.

[3] Taittirīya Saṃhitā, vii. 4, 12, 1; Vājasaneyi Saṃhitā, xxiii. 13; Śatapatha Brāhmaṇa, xiii. 2, 7, 4; Pañcaviṃśa Brāhmaṇa, ix. 4, 11, etc.

Cf. Eggeling, *Sacred Books of the East*, 44, 317, n. 2.

Śalya. See **Iṣu.**

Śalyaka denotes in the Vājasaneyi Saṃhitā[1] and later[2] the 'porcupine.'

[1] xxiv. 35.

[2] Aitareya Brāhmaṇa, iii. 26, 3.

Cf. Zimmer, *Altindisches Leben*, 82.

Śavarta is the name of a species of 'worm' in the Atharvaveda[1] and the Taittirīya Saṃhitā.[2]

[1] ix. 4, 16, with the various reading Svavarta, Whitney, Translation of the Atharvaveda, 531.

[2] v. 7, 23, 1.

Cf. Zimmer, *Altindisches Leben*, 98. Possibly Roth is right in holding that the word = *śava-varta*, a worm living on carrion.'

Śavas is the name of a teacher, a pupil of **Agnibhū Kāśyapa** in the Vaṃśa Brāhmaṇa.[1]

[1] *Indische Studien*, 4, 373.

Śavasa occurs only in the false reading *Savasa-Uśinareṣu* in the Gopatha Brāhmaṇa (i, 2, 9) for *sa-Vaśośīnareṣu.* See **Vaśa.**

Śaviṣṭha is, according to Ludwig,[1] the name of a generous patron in the Rigveda.[2]

[1] Translation of the Rigveda, 3, 163.

[2] viii. 74, 14. 15.

Śaśa, 'hare,' is found once in the Rigveda,[1] where it is said to have swallowed a razor. The animal is occasionally mentioned later also.[2]

[1] x. 28, 2. Later, a goat supplants the hare in this curious story; see Böthling, Proceedings of the Saxon Academy, 1894, *et seq.*

[2] Vājasaneyi Saṃhitā, xxiii. 56; xxiv. 38; Maitrāyaṇī Saṃhitā, iii. 14, 15; the hare in the moon, Śatapatha Brāhmaṇa, xi. 1, 5, 3.

Cf. Zimmer, *Altindisches Leben*, 84.

Śaśayu, 'pursuing the hare,' is the epithet of some animal (**Mṛga**) in the Atharvaveda.[1] Zimmer[2] thinks the tiger is meant, but this is not likely. Roth[3] considers that a bird of prey is intended, while Whitney,[4] following the commentator, renders the word by 'lurking.'

[1] iv. 3, 6.

[2] *Altindisches Leben*, 79, 84.

[3] In Whitney, Translation of the Atharvaveda, 149

[4] *Loc. cit.*

Cf. Bloomfield, *Hymns of the Atharvaveda*, 368.

Śaśvatī. See **Āsaṅga.**

Śaṣpa in the later Saṃhitās and the Brāhmaṇas[1] denotes 'young or sprouting grass.'

[1] Vājasaneyi Saṃhitā, xix. 13, 81; xxi. 29; Aitareya Brāhmaṇa, viii. 5, 3; 8, 4; Śatapatha Brāhmaṇa, xii. 7, 2, 8; 9, 1, 2, etc.

Śastṛ in the Rigveda (i. 162, 5) and the Atharvaveda (ix. 3, 3) denotes the slaughterer of an animal.

Śastra is the technical term[1] for the 'recitation' of the Hotṛ priest, as opposed to the **Stotra** of the Udgātṛ. The recitations at the morning offering of Soma are called the Ājya and Praüga; at the midday offering, the Marutvatīya and the Niṣkevalya; at the evening offering, the Vaiśvadeva and the Āgnimāruta.

[1] Taittirīya Saṃhitā, iii. 2, 7, 2, etc.; Kāṭhaka Saṃhitā, xxix. 2, etc.; Vājasaneyi Saṃhitā, xix. 25. 28, etc.; Śatapatha Brāhmaṇa, iv. 2, 4. 20, etc. *Cf.* Weber, *Indische Studien*, 10, 353, and Caland and Henry, *L'Agniṣṭoma*, *passim*, where the Śastras are set out at length.

Śākaṭāyana, 'descendant of Śakaṭa,' is the patronymic of a grammarian referred to by Yāska[1] and in the Prātiśākhyas,[2] as well as often later.

[1] Nirukta, i. 3. 12 *et seq.*

[2] Rigveda Prātiśākhya, i. 3; xiii. 16; Vājasaneyi Prātiśākhya, iii. 8, etc. *Cf.* Weber, *Indian Literature*, 143, 151, 152, 217.

Śāka-dāsa Bhāḍitāyana ('descendant of Bhaḍita') is mentioned in the Vaṃśa Brāhmaṇa[1] as the pupil of **Vicakṣaṇa Tāṇḍya.**

[1] *Indische Studien*, 4, 373

Śāka-pūṇi, 'descendant of Śakapūṇa,' is the name of a grammarian often mentioned in the Nirukta.[1]

[1] iii. 11; viii. 5. 6. 14; xii. 19; xiii. 10. 11. *Cf.* Weber, *Indian Literature*, 85.

Śākala in the Aitareya Brāhmaṇa[1] denotes the 'teaching of **Śākalya**' according to the St. Petersburg Dictionary. But Böhtlingk[2] seems right in taking it as a kind of snake in that passage.

[1] iii 43. 5 (Weber, *Indische Studien*, 9, 277). *Cf.* Weber, *Indian Literature*, 33, n.

[2] Dictionary, *s.v.*

Śākalya, 'descendant of Śakala,' is the patronymic of **Vidagdha** in the Śatapatha Brāhmaṇa,[1] and of **Sthavira** in the Aitareya[2] and Śāṅkhāyana Āraṇyakas.[3] An undefined Śākalya

[1] xi. 6, 3, 3; Bṛhadāraṇyaka Upaniṣad, iii. 9, 1; iv. 1, 7, etc.

[2] iii. 2, 1. 6.

[3] vii. 16; viii. 1. 11.

is mentioned in the same Āraṇyakas,[4] in the Nirukta,[5] and often later, as a teacher dealing with the text of the Rigveda. Weber[6] is inclined to identify Vidagdha with the Śākalya who is known as the maker of the Pada Pāṭha of the Rigveda, but Oldenberg[7] thinks that the latter was later than the Brāhmaṇa period. Geldner[8] identifies the two; this view, however, is not very probable.[9]

[4] Aitareya, iii. 1, 1; Śāṅkhāyana, vii. 1.
[5] vi. 28.
[6] *Indian Literature*, 32, 33.
[7] *Prolegomena*, 380, n.
[8] *Vedische Studien*, 3, 144-146.
[9] Keith, *Aitareya Āraṇyaka*, 239, 240.

Śākāyanin, in the plural, denotes the followers of **Śākāyanya** in the Śatapatha Brāhmaṇa (x. 4, 5, 1).

Śākāyanya, 'descendant of Śāka,' is the patronymic of **Jāta** in the Kāṭhaka Saṃhitā.[1]

[1] xxii. 7 (*Indische Studien*, 3, 472). *Cf.* Maitrāyaṇī Upaniṣad, i. 2; vi. 29.

Śākin, plur., is believed by Ludwig[1] to designate a group of generous donors in the Rigveda.[2]

[1] Translation of the Rigveda, 3, 155; Griffith, *Hymns of the Rigveda*, 1, 521, n.
[2] v. 52, 17.

Śāktya, 'descendant of **Śakti**,' is the patronymic of **Gaurivīti**.[1]

[1] Aitareya Brāhmaṇa, iii. 19, 4; Śatapatha Brāhmaṇa, xii. 8, 3, 7; Pañcaviṃśa Brāhmaṇa, xi. 5, 14; xii. 13, 10; xxv. 7, 2; Āpastamba Śrauta Sūtra, xxiii. 11, 14; xxiv. 10, 6. 8.

Śākvara. See **Śakvarī**.

Śākhā in the Rigveda[1] and later[2] denotes the 'branch' of a tree. **Vayā** is more often used in this sense in the Rigveda.

[1] i. 8, 8; vii. 43, 1; x. 94, 3.
[2] Av. iii. 6, 8; x. 7, 21; xi. 2, 19, etc.

Śāṅkhāyana as the name of a teacher is not mentioned in the Kauṣītaki Brāhmaṇa, but it occurs in the Vaṃśa (list of teachers) at the end of the Śāṅkhāyana Āraṇyaka,[1] where Guṇākhya is given as the authority for that work. In the Śrauta Sūtras[2] the name of Śāṅkhāyana never occurs, but the Gṛhya Sūtras[3] seem to recognize as a teacher **Suyajña Śāṅkhāyana.** In later times[4] the school flourished in Northern Gujarat. Śāṅkhāyana appears in the Taittirīya Prātiśākhya[5] along with Kāṇḍamāyana.

[1] xv. 1. Oldenberg's suggestion (*Sacred Books of the East*, xxix. 4, 5) that Guṇākhya is intended as the author of the Sūtras is quite unnecessary; Keith, *Aitareya Āraṇyaka*, 328.

[2] Hillebrandt, Śāṅkhāyana Śrauta Sūtra, 1, viii *et seq.*

[3] Śāṅkhāyana Gṛhya Sūtra, iv. 10; vi. 10; Śāmbavya Gṛhya Sūtra in *Indische Studien*, 15, 154; Āśvalāyana Gṛhya Sūtra, iii. 4, 4. *Cf.* Kārikā in Nārāyaṇa on Śāṅkhāyana Gṛhya Sūtra, i. 1, 10; Ānartīya on Śāṅkhāyana Śrauta Sūtra, i. 2, 18.

[4] Bühler, *Sacred Books of the East*, 2, xxxi.

[5] xv. 7.

Cf. Weber, *Indian Literature*, 32, 44, 50 *et seq.*; 80, 313, 314; Macdonell, *Sanskrit Literature*, 45, 191, 205, 245, 249.

Śāṭyāyana, 'descendant of Śāṭya,' is the patronymic of a teacher mentioned twice in the Śatapatha Brāhmaṇa[1] and often in the Jaiminīya Upaniṣad Brāhmaṇa.[2] In a Vaṃśa (list of teachers) in the latter work[3] he is called a pupil of **Jvālāyana,** while in the Vaṃśa at the end of the Sāmavidhāna Brāhmaṇa he appears as a pupil of **Bādarāyaṇa.** The Śāṭyāyanins, his followers, are frequently mentioned in the Sūtras,[4] the Śāṭyāyani Brāhmaṇa[5] and the Śāṭyāyanaka[6] being also referred to in them. It has been shown by Oertel[7] that this Brāhmaṇa bore a close resemblance to, and probably belonged to the same period as, the Jaiminīya Brāhmaṇa.

[1] viii. 1, 4, 9; x. 4, 5, 2.

[2] i. 6, 2; 30, 1; ii. 2, 8; 4, 3; 9, 10; iii. 13, 6; 28, 5.

[3] iv. 16, 1.

[4] Lāṭyāyana Śrauta Sūtra, iv. 5, 18; Anupada Sūtra, i. 8; ii. 9; iii. 2. 11; iv. 8, etc.; Weber, *Indische Studien*, 1, 44.

[5] Āpastamba Śrauta Sūtra, v. 23, 3.

[6] *Ibid.*, x. 12, 13. 14; Lāṭyāyana Śrauta Sūtra, i. 2, 24; Āśvalāyana Śrauta Sūtra, i. 4, 13.

[7] *Journal of the American Oriental Society*, 16, ccxli; 18, 20 *et seq.*

Cf. Macdonell, *Sanskrit Literature*, 203; Aufrecht, *Zeitschrift der Deutschen Morgenländischen Gesellschaft*, 42, 151, 152.

Śāṇḍa, 'descendant of **Śaṇḍa**,' is the name of a man in the Rigveda[1] who is praised for his generosity. It is not likely that he is identical with **Purupanthā** mentioned in the next verse.

[1] vi. 63, 9. *Cf.* Ludwig, Translation of the Rigveda, 3, 158.

Śāṇḍila, masc. plur.. is the term applied to the 'descendants of **Śāṇḍilya**' in the Taittirīya Āraṇyaka (i. 22, 10).

Śāṇḍilī-putra, 'pupil of a female descendant of Śaṇḍila,' is the name of a teacher, a pupil of **Rāthītarīputra**, in the last Vaṃśa (list of teachers) of the Bṛhadāraṇyaka Upaniṣad.[1]

[1] vi. 4, 32 (Mādhyaṃdina = vi. 5, 2 Kāṇva).

Śāṇḍilya, 'descendant of Śaṇḍila,' is the patronymic of several teachers (see **Udara** and **Suyajña**). The most important Śāṇḍilya is the one cited several times as an authority in the Śatapatha Brāhmaṇa,[1] where his Agni, or 'sacrificial fire,' is called Śāṇḍila.[2] From this it appears clearly that he was one of the great teachers of the fire ritual which occupies the fifth and following books of the Śatapatha Brāhmaṇa. In the Vaṃśa (list of teachers) at the end of the tenth book[3] he is given as a pupil of **Kuśri** and a teacher of **Vātsya**; another list at the end of the last book in the Kāṇva recension[4] gives him as a pupil of Vātsya, and the latter as a pupil of Kuśri. In the confused and worthless[5] lists of teachers at the end of the second and fourth books of the Bṛhadāraṇyaka Upaniṣad he is said to be the pupil of various persons—**Kaiśorya Kāpya**,[6] **Vaiṣṭapureya**,[7] **Kauśika**,[8] **Gautama**,[9] **Baijavāpa**,[10] and **Āna-**

[1] ix. 4, 4, 17; 5, 2, 15; x. 1, 4, 10; 4, 1, 11; 6, 3, 5; 5, 9. *Cf.* Chāndogya Upaniṣad, iii. 11, 4.

[2] ix. 1, 1, 43; 3, 3, 18; 5, 1, 61, 68, etc.

[3] x. 6, 5, 9.

[4] vi. 5, 4.

[5] Eggeling, *Sacred Books of the East*, 12, xxxiv, n. 2.

[6] ii. 5, 22; iv. 5, 28 (Mādhyaṃdina = ii. 6, 3; iv. 6, 3 Kāṇva).

[7] ii. 5, 20; iv. 5, 26 Mādhyaṃdina.

[8] ii. 6, 1; iv. 6, 1 Kāṇva.

[9] ii. 5, 20; iv. 5, 26 (Mādhyaṃdina = ii. 6, 1; iv. 6, 1 Kāṇva).

[10] ii. 5, 20; iv. 5, 26 Mādhyaṃdina.

bhimlāta.[11] No doubt different Śāṇḍilyas may be meant, but the lists are too confused to claim serious consideration.

[11] ii. 6, 2 Kāṇva.
Cf. Eggeling, *Sacred Books of the East*, 12, xxxi *et seq.*; 43, xviii *et seq.*; Weber, *Indian Literature*, 71, 76 *et seq.*; 120, 131, 132; Macdonell, *Sanskrit Literature*, 213.

Śāṇḍilyāyana, 'descendant of **Śāṇḍilya,**' is the patronymic of a teacher in the Śatapatha Brāhmaṇa.[1] Apparently he is identical with **Celaka,** also mentioned in that text;[2] it is thus reasonable to suppose that **Cailaki Jīvala**[3] was his son. It is much more doubtful whether he was[4] the grandfather of **Pravāhaṇa Jaivala,** who was a prince rather than a Brahmin.

[1] ix. 5, 1, 64.
[2] x. 4, 5, 3. The name Śāṇḍilyāyana, like that of Sāṇḍilya, is common in the Sūtras. See Weber, *Indische Studien*, 1, 45 *et seq.*
[3] Śatapatha Brāhmaṇa, ii. 3, 1, 34.
[4] Weber, *op. cit.*, 1, 259.
Cf. Weber, *Indian Literature*, 53, 76, 120.

Śāta-parṇeya 'descendant of Śataparṇa,' is the patronymic of **Dhīra** in the Śatapatha Brāhmaṇa (x. 3, 3, 1).

Śāda denotes 'grass' in the Rigveda[1] and later.[2]

[1] ix. 15, 6.
[2] Vājasaneyi Saṃhitā, xxv. 1, etc.

Śāpa in the Rigveda[1] and later[2] denotes the 'drift' brought down by streams, possibly conceived as the 'curse' of the waters.[3]

[1] vii. 18, 5; x. 28, 4.
[2] Av. iii. 24, 3; Śāṅkhāyana Āraṇyaka, xii. 11.
[3] *Cf.* Geldner, *Rigveda, Glossar*, 178; *Vedische Studien*, 3, 184, 185.

Śāmulya in the marriage hymn of the Rigveda[1] denotes a 'woollen garment' worn at night.

[1] x. 85, 29. *Cf.* Zimmer, *Altindisches Leben*, 262.

Śāmūla in the Jaiminīya Upaniṣad Brāhmaṇa[1] seems to have much the same sense as **Śāmulya**, 'a woollen shirt,' generally. Roth[2] emends to *śamīla*, 'pieces of Śamī wood.'

[1] i. 38, 4. *Cf.* Oertel, *Journal of the American Oriental Society*, 16, 116, 233; Lāṭyāyana Śrauta Sūtra, ix. 4, 7; Kauśika Sūtra, lxix. 3.

[2] *Journal of the American Oriental Society*, 16, ccxliii.

Śāmba. See **Śārkarākṣa.**

Śāmbara, properly an adjective in the sense of 'relating to **Śambara**,' appears in one passage of the Rigveda (iii. 47, 4) to be used as a substantive denoting 'the contest with Śambara.'

Śāmbu occurs in the plural with the **Aṅgirases** in a passage of the Atharvaveda,[1] no doubt as the name of a family of ancient teachers. There is extant in manuscript a Gṛhya Sūtra of the Śāmbavyas.[2]

[1] xix. 39, 5, where Whitney, Translation of the Atharvaveda, 960, retracts the emendation *Bhṛgubhyaḥ* for *Śāmbubhyaḥ* in the text.

[2] Oldenberg, *Indische Studien*, 15, 4, 154. *Cf.* Bloomfield, *Hymns of the Atharvaveda*, 678.

Śāyasthi is the name of a teacher in the Vaṃśa Brāhmaṇa.[1]

[1] *Indische Studien*, 4, 372.

Śārada. See **Pur.**

1. **Śāri** occurs in the list of victims at the Aśvamedha ('horse sacrifice') in the Yajurveda Saṃhitās.[1] It seems clear, since it is described as 'of human speech' (*puruṣa-vāc*), that it was some kind of bird, possibly the later Sārikā ('starling'), as Zimmer[2] suggests. See also **Śāriśākā.**

[1] Taittirīya Saṃhitā, v. 5, 12, 1; Maitrāyaṇī Saṃhitā, iii. 14, 14; Vājasaneyi Saṃhitā, xxiv. 33.

[2] *Altindisches Leben*, 90, 91.

2. **Śāri**, occurring in one passage of the Rigveda,[1] is said by Sāyaṇa to mean 'arrow.' This is uncertain, but connexion with **Śara** or 1. **Śāri** is quite possible.[2]

[1] i. 112, 16.

[2] Oldenberg, *Ṛgveda-Noten*, 1, 103.

Śāriśākā is an utterly obscure expression found in one passage of the Atharvaveda.[1] Weber[2] thinks it means 'dung (*śakan*) of the Śāri bird'; Grill[3] sees in the word the *śārikā*, 'the hooded crow'; Roth[4] suggests the emendation (*śāriḥ* (=*śāliḥ*) *śaka iva*, 'like rice in manure'; and Bloomfield[5] emends *śāri-śukeva*, 'like starlings and parrots.'

[1] iii. 14, 5.

[2] *Indische Studien*, 17, 246.

[3] *Hundert Lieder*,[2] 112.

[4] In Whitney, Translation of the Atharvaveda, 110.

[5] *Hymns of the Atharvaveda*, 351. But see Lanman's note in Whitney, *loc. cit*.

Śārkarākṣa is found in the Vaṃśa Brāhmaṇa[1] as the patronymic of a teacher, **Śāmba**, perhaps by a blunder for **Śārkarākṣya**, 'descendant of Śarkarākṣa.' In the Kāṭhaka Saṃhitā[2] a teacher, Śarkarākhya, occurs, again probably a blunder, in this case for Śarkarākṣa himself. The patronymic Śārkarākṣi is found in the Āśvalāyana Śrauta Sūtra.[3]

[1] *Indische Studien*, 4, 372.

[2] xxii. 8.

[3] xii. 10, 10.

Śārkarākṣya, 'descendant of Śarkarākṣa,' is the patronymic of **Jana** in the Śatapatha Brāhmaṇa[1] and the Chāndogya Upaniṣad.[2] In the plural they occur in the Aitareya Āraṇyaka[3] and the Taittirīya Āraṇyaka.[4] It is not necessary to assume that the form is incorrect for Śārkarākṣa.

[1] x. 6, 1, 1.

[2] v. 11, 1; 15, 1.

[3] ii. 1, 4.

[4] *Indische Studien*, 4, 382. *Cf.* Keith, *Aitareya Āraṇyaka*, 204; Weber, *Indische Studien*, 1, 388; 3, 259.

Śārga is the name of a bird in the list of victims at the Aśvamedha ('horse sacrifice') in the Yajurveda Saṃhitās.[1] Sāyaṇa on the Taittirīya Saṃhitā calls it the 'wild Caṭaka.'

[1] Taittirīya Saṃhitā, v. 5, 19, 1; Maitrāyaṇī Saṃhitā, iii. 14, 14; Vājasaneyi Saṃhitā, xxiv. 33. *Cf.* Zimmer, *Altindisches Leben*, 93.

Śārṅga.—The Anukramaṇī[1] (Index) of the Rigveda ascribes a hymn of that text[2] to the Śārṅgas, Jaritṛ, Droṇa, Sārisṛkva, and Stambamitra. The Mahābhārata[3] contains a tale describing how the four Śārṅgas, sons of the Ṛṣi Mandapāla, were saved from the great fire in the Khāṇḍava forest by means of prayers. Sieg[4] has attempted to use this tale for the elucidation of the hymn in question, but without substantial success. As Oldenberg[5] says, the tale is based on the hymn rather than *vice versa.*

1 See also Sāyaṇa on Rv. x. 142; Ṣaḍguruśiṣya on the Sarvānukramaṇī (ed. Macdonell), p. 163.
2 x. 142.
3 i. 8334 *et seq.*
4 *Die Sagenstoffe des Ṛgveda*, 44-50.
5 *Zeitschrift der Deutschen Morgenländischen Gesellschaft*, 39, 79.

Śārdūla, 'tiger,' is mentioned in the later Saṃhitās[1] and the Brāhmaṇas.[2] *Cf.* **Vyāghra.**

1 Taittirīya Saṃhitā, v. 5, 11, 1; Kāṭhaka Saṃhitā, xii. 10; Maitrāyaṇī Saṃhitā, iii. 14, 11; Vājasaneyi Saṃhitā, xxiv. 30.
2 Satapatha Brāhmaṇa, v. 3, 5, 3; iv. 1, 9, 11; 5, 4, 10; xi. 8, 4, 1; Taittirīya Brāhmaṇa, i. 7, 8, 1; 8, 5, 2; Kauṣītaki Upaniṣad, i. 2, etc.
Cf. Zimmer, *Altindisches Leben*, 79.

Śāryāta, perhaps 'descendant of **Śaryāta**,' is the name of a singer in the Rigveda.[1] A Śāryāta appears also in the Aitareya Brāhmaṇa[2] with the patronymic **Mānava** as the seer of a Rigvedic hymn,[3] and as having been anointed by **Cyavana.**[4] The same man is evidently meant by Śaryāta in the story of Cyavana in the Śatapatha Brāhmaṇa[5] and the Jaiminīya Brāhmaṇa.[6] In both these passages the Śāryātas are mentioned as his descendants, and his daughter is called Śāryātī.

1 i. 51, 12; iii. 51, 7.
2 iv. 32, 7.
3 x. 92.
4 viii. 21, 4.
5 iv. 1, 5, 1 *et seq.*
6 iii. 121 *et seq.* (Whitney, *Journal of the American Oriental Society*, 11, cxlv.; Hopkins, *ibid.*, 26, 58.

Śālaṅkāyana, 'descendant of Śalaṅku,' is the patronymic of a teacher in the Vaṃśa Brāhmaṇa.[1]

1 *Indische Studien*, 4, 383; Āśvalāyana Śrauta Sūtra, xii. 10, 10; Āpastamba Śrauta Sūtra, xxiv. 9, 1. *Cf.* Weber, *Indian Literature*, 75; *Indische Studien*, 1, 49.

Śālaṅkāyanī-putra, 'son of a female descendant of Śalaṅku,' is the name of a teacher, a pupil of **Vārṣagaṇīputra** in the last Vaṃśa (list of teachers) of the Mādhyaṃdina recension of the Bṛhadāraṇyaka Upaniṣad (vi. 4, 31).

Śālā in the Atharvaveda[1] and later[2] denotes a 'house' in the wide sense of the word, including such meanings as 'stall' for cattle, 'shed' for corn, etc.[3] See **Gṛha.** The householder is called Śālā-pati, 'lord of the house,' in the Atharvaveda.[4]

[1] v. 31, 5; vi. 106, 3; viii. 6, 10; ix. 3, 1 *et seq.*; xiv. 1, 63.

[2] Taittirīya Brāhmaṇa, i. 2, 3, 1; Satapatha Brāhmaṇa, iii. 1, 1, 6, etc.

[3] Av. iii. 12, 1 *et seq.*, and *cf.* ix. 3, 1 *et seq.*

[4] ix. 3, 12.

Śālāvatya, 'descendant of Śalāvant,' is the patronymic of **Śilaka** in the Chāndogya Upaniṣad (i. 8, 1), and of **Galūnasa Ārkṣākāyaṇa** in the Jaiminīya Upaniṣad Brāhmaṇa (i. 38, 4).

Śāli, a later word for 'rice,' is conjectured by Roth to be the equivalent of Śāri in the word **Śāriśākā** in the Atharvaveda.

Śālūka in the Atharvaveda[1] denotes the edible roots of the lotus.

[1] iv. 34, 5. *Cf.* Zimmer, *Altindisches Leben*, 70; Whitney, Translation of the Atharvaveda, 207.

Śālva as the name of a people is found in the Gopatha Brāhmaṇa[1] coupled with that of the **Matsyas.**

[1] i. 2, 9. *Cf.* **Salva.**

Śāvasāyana, 'descendant of Śavas,' is the patronymic of **Devataras** in the Vaṃśa Brāhmaṇa.[1]

[1] *Indische Studien*, 4, 373.

Śāsa denotes in the Brāhmaṇas[1] a 'sword' or 'knife.'

[1] Aitareya Brāhmaṇa, vii. 17, 5; Śāṅkhāyana Śrauta Sūtra, xv. 25, 1 (of the knife to be used in slaying **Śunaḥśepa**); Śatapatha Brāhmaṇa, iii. 8, 1, 4. 5; xiii. 2, 3, 16.

Śiṃśapā is the name of a tree (*Dalbergia Sisu*) in the Rigveda[1] and later.[2] It is a stately and beautiful tree.

[1] iii. 53, 19 (with the **Khadira**).

[2] Av. xx. 129, 7. *Cf.* *śāṃśapa* in vi. 129, 1; Whitney, Translation of the Atharvaveda, 378.

Cf. Zimmer, *Altindisches Leben*, 61.

Śiṃśu-māra,[1] or **Śiśu-māra,**[2] is the name of an aquatic creature in the Rigveda and the later Saṃhitās. It is either the 'crocodile,' the 'alligator,'[3] or the 'porpoise'[4] (*Delphinus Gangeticus*).

[1] Rv. i. 116, 18; Taittirīya Saṃhitā, v. 5, 11; Av. xi. 2, 25. In Śāṅkhāyana Āraṇyaka, xii. 28, the reading is doubtful.

[2] Maitrāyaṇī Saṃhitā, iii. 14, 2; Vājasaneyi Saṃhitā, xxiv. 30, and the Paippalāda recension of the Av., *loc. cit.*; Taittirīya Āraṇyaka, ii. 19.

[3] Weber, *Indische Studien*, 5, 325, and Sāyaṇa on Rv., *loc. cit.*; Av., *loc. cit.*; Taittirīya Saṃhitā, *loc. cit.*

[4] St. Petersburg Dictionary, *s.v.* *śiśumāra;* Bloomfield, *Hymns of the Atharvaveda*, 157; Whitney, Translation of the Atharvaveda, 624.

Cf. Zimmer, *Altindisches Leben*, 96; Geldner, *Rigveda, Glossar*, 179.

Śikya in the Atharvaveda[1] and later[2] seems to mean a carrying 'sling' of rope.[3]

[1] ix. 3, 6, where Whitney suggests that it may be an ornamental hanging appendage. See Lanman in Whitney, Translation of the Atharvaveda, 526. Whitney's alternative rendering 'slings' is better. See Bloomfield, *Hymns of the Atharvaveda*, 597. *Cf.* perhaps Av. xiii. 4, 8.

[2] Taittirīya Saṃhitā, v. 2, 4, 2. 3; 6, 9, 1, etc.

[3] This is pretty clearly the meaning in Śatapatha Brāhmaṇa, v. 5, 4, 28; vi. 7, 1, 16. *Cf.* Eggeling, *Sacred Books of the East*, 41, 268, n. 3.

Śikha and **Anuśikha** are the names of two priests who served as **Neṣṭṛ** and **Potṛ** at the snake festival in the Pañcaviṃśa Brāhmaṇa.[1]

[1] xxv. 15, 3. *Cf.* Weber, *Indische Studien*, 1, 35.

Śikhaṇḍa denotes a 'tuft' or 'lock,' as a mode of wearing the hair, in the later Saṃhitās and the Brāhmaṇas.[1]

[1] Taittirīya Saṃhitā, vii. 3, 16, 2 (in the plural); *catuḥ-śikhaṇḍa*, Taittirīya Brāhmaṇa, i. 2, 1, 27; iii. 7, 6, 4 (corresponding to *catuḥ-kaparda*, Rv. x. 114, 3). So *śikhaṇḍin* means 'wearing a tuft of hair,' and is found in Av. iv. 37, 7; xi. 2, 12, etc.

Śikhaṇḍin Yājñasena ('descendant of Yajñasena') is mentioned in the Kauṣītaki Brāhmaṇa (vii. 4) as a priest of **Keśin Dālbhya.**

Śikhara as a 'peak' of a mountain is found in the Kauṣītaki Brāhmaṇa (xxvi. 1), and often in the Epic.

Śikhā denotes in the Śatapatha Brāhmaṇa[1] the 'knot of hair' worn on the top of the head. Wearing the top-knot unloosened was the sign of mourning in the case of women and men alike.[2]

[1] i. 3, 3, 5.
[2] Āśvalāyana Gṛhya Sūtra, iv. 2, 9. *Cf.* Bloomfield, *American Journal of Philology*, 11, 340; *Hymns of the Atharvaveda*, 534, on Av. ix. 9, 7.

Śigru is the name of a tribe occurring in the passage of the Rigveda,[1] in which they are mentioned with the **Ajas** and the **Yakṣus** as having been defeated by the **Tṛtsus** and King **Sudās.** It is impossible to say whether they were or were not under the leadership of **Bheda**, as Ludwig[2] plausibly suggests. If Śigru is connected with the later *śigru*, 'horse-radish' (*Moringa pterygosperma*), which is quite probable, it is possible that the tribe was totemistic and non-Āryan, but this is a mere matter of conjecture.[3] The **Matsyas** ('Fishes') were probably Āryan.

[1] vii. 18, 19.
[2] Translation of the Rigveda, 3, 173.
[3] *Cf.* Oldenberg, *Religion des Veda*, 85; Macdonell, *Vedic Mythology*, 153; Hopkins, *Journal of the American Oriental Society*, 16, cliv; Keith, *Journal of the Royal Asiatic Society*, 1907, 929 *et seq.*; *Aitareya Āraṇyaka*, 200, n.
Cf. Zimmer, *Altindisches Leben*, 127.

Śiñjāra is the name of a Ṛṣi twice mentioned in the Rigveda[1] along with **Kaṇva, Priyamedha, Upastuta,** and **Atri.** Geldner[2] takes the word either as a name of Atri or an adjective.

[1] viii. 5, 25; x. 40, 7. *Cf.* Ludwig, Translation of the Atharvaveda, 3, 139.
[2] *Rigveda, Glossar*, 179.

Śiti-kakṣī in the Taittirīya Saṃhitā[1] is explained by Sāyaṇa as a 'white-breasted' (*pāṇḍarodara*) vulture. The word may, however, well be only an adjective.[2]

[1] v. 5, 20, 1. *Cf.* Vājasaneyi Saṃhitā, xxiv. 4; Av. v. 23, 5. *Cf.* Zimmer, *Altindisches Leben*, 93.

Śiti-pṛṣṭha ('white-backed') is the name of the Maitrāvaruṇa priest at the snake festival in the Pañcaviṃśa Brāhmaṇa.[1]

[1] xxv. 15, 3. *Cf.* Weber, *Indische Studien*, 1, 35.

Śiti-bāhu Aiṣakṛta Naimiśi is mentioned as a sacrificer in the Jaiminīya Brāhmaṇa,[1] where it is recorded that a monkey ran off with his sacrificial cake.

[1] i. 363 (*Journal of the American Oriental Society*, 26, 192).

Śitpuṭa in the Taittirīya Saṃhitā[1] denotes, according to the commentator, a kind of cat.

[1] v. 5, 17, 1. *Cf.* Zimmer, *Altindisches Leben*, 86.

Śipada occurs only in the Rigveda[1] in the negative form *a-śipada*, together with *a-śimida*. Both Śipada and Śimida are perhaps names of unknown diseases.[2]

[1] vii. 50, 4.

[2] Zimmer, *Altindisches Leben*, 394.

Śipavitnuka in the Atharvaveda[1] seems to denote a species of worm.

[1] v. 20, 7. *Cf.* Zimmer, *Altindisches Leben*, 98; Whitney, Translation of the Atharvaveda, 262.

Śiprā is a word of somewhat uncertain sense: it seems to mean 'cheeks' in several passages;[1] in others[2] it appears to

[1] Rv. iii. 32, 1; v. 36, 2; viii. 76, 10; x. 96, 9; 105, 5, all according to Roth, St. Petersburg Dictionary, *s.v.* Geldner, *Rigveda, Glossar*, 179, who treats the word as a neuter (*śipra*), takes it in i. 101, 10, as 'lip' (*cf.* Zimmer, *Altindisches Leben*, 249, n.), and sees in iii. 32, 1; viii. 76, 10; x. 96, 9, the sense of 'moustache.' Yāska, Nirukta, vi. 17, gives the alternative senses of 'jaw' and 'nose.'

[2] Rv. v. 54, 11; viii. 7, 25. Geldner, *loc. cit.*, here accepts *śiprā* as 'helmet.'

designate the 'cheek-pieces' of a helmet, or of the 'bit'[3] of a horse. In *ayaḥ-śipra*, used of the Aśvins,[4] and the other compounds, *hiraṇya-śipra*,[5] *hari-śipra*,[6] and *hiri-śipra*,[7] the word probably has the extended sense of 'helmet,' described as 'of iron,' 'of gold,' or 'yellow.' Similarly *śiprin*[8] would mean 'wearing a helmet.'

[3] Rv. i. 101, 10; Zimmer, *loc. cit.*
[4] Rv. iv. 37, 4.
[5] Rv. ii. 34, 3.
[6] Rv. x. 96, 4.
[7] Rv. ii. 2, 3; vi. 25, 9.
[8] Rv. i. 29, 2; 81, 4; vi, 44, 14, etc.
Cf. Max Müller, *Sacred Books of the East*, 32, 301; Geldner, *Vedische Studien*, 2, 39, n. 2.

Śiphā is found in one passage of the Rigveda,[1] where Sāyaṇa explains the word as the name of a river, quite a possible interpretation.

[1] i. 104, 3. *Cf.* Zimmer, *Altindisches Leben*, 18; Perry, *Journal of the American Oriental Society*, 11, 201.

Śibi, son of **Uśīnara**, is mentioned in the Baudhāyana Śrauta Sūtra[1] as a protégé of Indra, who sacrificed for him on the Varṣiṣṭhīya plain, and saved him from fear of foreign invasion.

[1] xxi. 18. *Cf.* Caland, *Über das rituelle Sūtra des Baudhāyana*, 28.

Śimida, occurring in the Rigveda[1] in the compound *a-śimida*, perhaps denotes a disease. The feminine form, Śimidā, is found as the name of a demoness in the Atharvaveda[2] and the Śatapatha Brāhmaṇa.[3] *Cf.* **Śipada.**

[1] vii. 50, 4. *Cf.* Zimmer, *Altindisches Leben*, 394.
[2] iv. 25, 4.
[3] vii. 4, 1, 27.

Śimbala in the Rigveda[1] denotes, according to Sāyaṇa, the flower of the Śālmali (=**Śalmali**), 'silk-cotton tree.'

[1] iii. 53, 22. *Cf.* Geldner, *Rigveda, Glossar*, 179; Oldenberg, *Ṛgveda-Noten*, 1, 254.

Śimyu occurs in the Rigveda[1] as the name of one of the peoples or kings who were defeated by **Sudās** in the **Dāśarājña** ('battle of the ten kings'). Since in another passage[2] the Śimyus are coupled with the **Dasyus**, Zimmer[3] plausibly concludes that they were non-Āryans.

[1] vii. 18, 5.
[2] i. 100, 18, where Roth, St. Petersburg Dictionary, *s.v.*, thinks that the word simply means 'enemy.'
[3] *Altindisches Leben*, 118, 119. *Cf.* Hopkins, *Journal of the American Oriental Society*, 15, 261.

Śirimbiṭha occurs in one passage of the Rigveda,[1] where the name of a man may possibly be meant, the Anukramaṇī (Index) ascribing the hymn in which the word occurs to his authorship. Yāska,[2] however, renders the term by 'cloud.'

[1] x. 155, 1.
[2] Nirukta, vi. 30. *Cf.* Ludwig, Translation of the Rigveda, 3. 167.

Śilaka Śālāvatya ('descendant of Śalāvant') is the name of a teacher, a contemporary of **Caikitāyana Dālbhya** and **Pravāhaṇa Jaivala**, in the Chāndogya Upaniṣad (i. 8, 1).

1. **Śilpa** means 'art,' of which three kinds—*nṛtya*, 'dance'; *gīta*, 'song'; and *vādita*, 'instrumental music,' are enumerated in the Kauṣītaki Brāhmaṇa (xxix. 5).

2. **Śilpa Kaśyapa** is named in the last Vaṃśa (list of teachers) in the Bṛhadāraṇyaka Upaniṣad[1] as a teacher, a pupil of **Kaśyapa Naidhruvi.**

[1] vi. 4, 33 (Mādhyaṃdina = vi. 5, 3 Kāṇva).

Śiva as the name of a people occurs once in the Rigveda,[1] where they share with the **Alinas, Pakthas, Bhalānases,** and **Viṣāṇins** the honour of being defeated by **Sudās,** not of being, as Roth[2] thought, his allies. There can hardly be any doubt

[1] vii. 18, 7.
[2] *Zur Litteratur und Geschichte des Veda*, 95 *et seq.*; once accepted by Zimmer, *Altindisches Leben*, 126.

of their identity with the Σίβαι[3] or Σίβοι[4] of the Greeks, who dwelt between the Indus and the Akesines (**Asiknī**) in Alexander's time. The village of Śiva-pura, mentioned by the scholiast on Pānini[5] as situated in the northern country, may also preserve the name. *Cf.* **Śibi.**

[3] Arrian, *Indica*, v. 12.

[4] Diodorus, xvii. 96.

[5] iv. 2, 109. Connected with Śiva by Weber, *Indische Studien*, 13, 376. *Cf.* St. Petersburg Dictionary, *s.v.* *Cf.* Zimmer, *op. cit.*, 431; Ludwig, Translation of the Rigveda, 3, 173; Hopkins, *Journal of the American Oriental Society*, 15, 260 *et seq.*

Śiśira. See **Ṛtu.**

Siśu Āṅgirasa ('descendant of **Aṅgiras**') is the name of the seer of a Sāman or Chant in the Pañcaviṃśa Brāhmaṇa.[1]

[1] xiii. 3, 24. *Cf.* Hillebrandt, *Vedische Mythologie*, 2, 160.

Śiśuka in the Atharvaveda[1] seems to be an adjective meaning 'young,' but according to Bloomfield[2] it has the sense of 'foal.' The commentator, Sāyaṇa, reads Śuśuka, which he explains as a 'wild animal so called.' *Cf.* **Āśuṃga.**

[1] vi. 14, 3. *Cf.* Whitney, Translation of the Atharva eda, 291.

[2] *Hymns of the Atharvaveda*, 464.

1. **Śiśumara.** See **Śiṃśumāra.**

2. **Śiśumāra** is a term applied to **Śarkara** in the Pañcaviṃśa Brāhmaṇa (xiv. 5, 15), where he is called a Siśumārarṣi, explained by the commentator to mean a Ṛṣi in the form of a Siśumāra.

Śiśna-deva, occurring twice in the Rigveda[1] in the plural, means 'those who have the phallus for a deity.' The term most probably refers to the phallus worship of the aborigines.

[1] vii. 21, 5; x. 99, 3. *Cf.* Zimmer, *Altindisches Leben*, 118; Hopkins, *Religions of India*, 150; von Schroeder, *Vienna Oriental Journal*, 9, 237; Macdonell, *Vedic Mythology*, 155; Keith, *Journal of the Royal Asiatic Society*, 1911, 1002, n. 5.

Śīpāla is the name of a water plant (*Blyxa Octandra*) mentioned in the Rigveda.[1] Its later name is Śaivala.

[1] x. 68, 5. *Cf.* the derivative adjective *śīpalya*, 'overgrown with Śīpāla plants,' Ṣaḍviṃśa Brāhmaṇa, iii. 1. *Cf.* Zimmer, *Altindisches Leben*, 71.

Śīpālā is found once in the Atharvaveda,[1] where it may mean either a 'pool abounding in **Śīpāla** plants' or the proper name of a river or lake.

[1] vi. 12, 3. *Cf.* Zimmer, *Altindisches Leben*, 71; Whitney, Translation of the Atharvaveda, 289, 290; Bloomfield, *Hymns of the Atharvaveda*, 462.

Śīpudru is merely an incorrect reading in the text of the Atharvaveda[1] for **Cīpudru.**

[1] vi. 127, 1. See Whitney, Translation of the Atharvaveda, 376.

Śīrṣakti is a common word for 'headache' in the Atharvaveda.[1]

[1] i. 12, 3; ix. 8, 1; xii. 2, 19; 5, 23. *Cf.* Bloomfield, *Journal of the American Oriental Society*, 16, xxxv; *Hymns of the Atharvaveda*, 252; *American Journal of Philology*, 17, 416, who sees in it *śīrṣa-sakti* (*cf.* Macdonell, *Vedic Grammar*, 64, 2). Böhtlingk, Proceedings of the Saxon Academy, 1897, 50, thinks the word means 'a stiff neck, with head awry.' See Lanman in Whitney, Translation of the Atharvaveda, 14. In Av. xix. 39, 10, *śīrṣa-śoka* is used for 'headache.'

Śīrṣaṇya in the Brāhmaṇas[1] denotes the 'head' of a couch (**Asandī**).

[1] Aitareya Brāhmaṇa, viii. 5, 3; 12, 3; 17, 2; Kauṣītaki Upaniṣad, i. 5 Sāṅkhāyana Śrauta Sūtra, xvii. 2, 8.

Śīrṣāmaya, 'disease of the head,' is mentioned in the Atharvaveda (v. 4, 10; ix. 8, 1).

Śīṣṭa occurs only in a Vālakhilya hymn of the Rigveda,[1] where the word seems to be the name of an unimportant clan.

[1] viii. 53, 4. *Cf.* Ludwig, Translation of the Rigveda, 3, 163.

Śuka, 'parrot,' is mentioned in the Rigveda,[1] where a desire is expressed to transfer to the Śuka and the **Ropaṇākā** the yellowness of jaundice. The bird is included in the list of sacrificial victims at the Aśvamedha ('horse sacrifice') in the Yajurveda Saṃhitās.[2] It is described as yellow and as 'of human speech' (*puruṣa-vāc*).[3] According to Bloomfield,[4] this word is the correct reading for the second half of the obscure **Śāriśākā** of the Atharvaveda.[5]

[1] i. 50, 12.

[2] Taittirīya Saṃhitā, v. 5, 12, 1; Maitrāyaṇī Saṃhitā, iii. 14, 14; Vājasaneyi Saṃhitā, xxiv. 33; and *cf. śuka-babhru*, 'reddish, like a parrot,' *ibid.*, xxiv. 2.

[3] Taittirīya and Maitrāyaṇī Saṃhitās, *loc. cit.*

[4] *Hymns of the Atharvaveda*, 352.

[5] iii. 14, 5.

Cf. Zimmer, *Altindisches Leben*, 90.

Śukti Āṅgirasa ('descendant of **Aṅgiras**') is the name of the seer of a Sāman or Chant in the Pañcaviṃśa Brāhmaṇa (xii. 5, 16).

1. **Śukra,** according to Tilak,[1] has in two passages of the Rigveda[2] the sense of a planet. This is most improbable. *Cf.* **Manthin.**

[1] *Orion*, 162.

[2] iii. 32, 2; ix. 46, 4.

2. **Śukra Jābāla** ('descendant of Jabālā') is the name of a teacher in the Jaiminīya Upaniṣad Brāhmaṇa (iii. 7, 7).

Śukla. See **Yajus.**

Śukla-dant, 'white-tusked,' is applied as an epithet to **Mṛga,** 'wild beast,' in the Aitareya Brāhmaṇa (viii. 23, 3). 'Elephants' must be meant.

Śuca and **Śucā** occur in an obscure verse of the Rigveda (x. 26, 6), where a man and a woman may be meant.

Śucanti is the name of a protégé of the Aśvins in the Rigveda.[1]

[1] i. 112, 7. *Cf.* Ludwig, Translation of the Rigveda, 3, 165.

Śuci-vṛkṣa Gaupālāyana ('descendant of Gopāla') is the name of the priest of **Vṛddhadyumna Abhipratāriṇa** in the Aitareya Brāhmaṇa.[1] He is also mentioned in the Maitrāyaṇī Saṃhitā.[2]

[1] iii. 48, 9 (Gaupalāyana in Aufrecht's edition).

[2] iii. 10, 4.

Śutudrī, twice mentioned in the Rigveda,[1] is the name of the most easterly river of the Panjab, the modern Sutlej, the Zaradros of Ptolemy and Arrian.[2] In the post-Vedic period the name of this river appears transformed to Śatadru ('flowing in a hundred channels'). The Sutlej has changed its course very considerably within historical times.[3]

[1] iii. 33, 1; x. 75, 5; Nirukta, ix, 26.

[2] In Arrian's time the Sutlej flowed independently into the Rann of Cutch: *Imperial Gazetteer of India*, 23, 179.

[3] *Ibid.*

Cf. Zimmer, *Altindisches Leben*, 10, 11.

Śunaḥ-puccha, 'Dog's tail,' is the name of a brother of **Śunaḥśepa**.[1]

[1] Aitareya Brāhmaṇa, vii. 15, 7; Śāṅkhāyana Śrauta Sūtra, v. 20, 1.

Śunaḥ-śepa, 'Dog's tail,' is the name of a man with the patronymic **Ājīgarti**. According to a tale told in the Aitareya Brāhmaṇa[1] and the Śāṅkhāyana Śrauta Sūtra,[2] he was purchased as a victim by **Rohita**, King **Hariścandra's** son, who had been promised by his father to Varuṇa as a sacrifice. He was actually bound to the stake, but was released in time through his supplications, supposed to be preserved in certain hymns of the Rigveda.[3] He was adopted by **Viśvāmitra**, to whose advice he owed the inspiration to ask the gods to release him, and became his son as **Devarāta**, much to the annoyance

[1] vii. 13-18.

[2] xv. 20, 1 *et seq.* *Cf.* xvi. 11, 2.

[3] i. 24 *et seq.* *Cf.* v. 2, 7.

of some of Viśvāmitra's sons, who in consequence were cursed by their father. The Rigveda, however, contains merely the statement of Śunaḥśepa's deliverance from peril of death by the divine help, and the Yajurvedas[4] simply say that he was seized by Varuṇa (perhaps with dropsy),[5] but saved himself from Varuṇa's bonds.

[4] Taittirīya Saṃhitā, v. 2, 1, 3; Kāṭhaka Saṃhitā, xix. 11. The story is not found in Maitrāyaṇī Saṃhitā, iii 2, 1.

[5] *Cf.* **Varuṇa gṛhīta.**

Cf. Max Müller, *Ancient Sanskrit Literature*, 408 *et seq.*; 573 *et seq.*; Roth, *Indische Studien*, 1, 457; ii. 112 *et seq.*; Weber, *Indian Literature*, 47, 48; *Episches im vedischen Ritual*, 10-16; Muir, *Sanskrit Texts*, 1[2], 355 *et seq.*; Macdonell, *Sanskrit Literature*, 207; Ludwig, Translation of the Rigveda, 3, 146; Keith, *Journal of the Royal Asiatic Society*, 1911, 988, 989.

Śunas-karṇa, 'Dog-ear,' is the name of a king,[1] son of **Śibi** or of Baṣkiha,[2] who performed a certain rite, the Sarvasvāra, and so died without disease.

[1] Baudhāyana Śrauta Sūtra, xxi. 17; Caland, *Über das rituelle Sūtra des Baudhāyana*, 28.

[2] Pañcaviṃśa Brāhmaṇa, xvii. 12, 6.

Śuna-hotra, in the plural, denotes a family of seers in the Rigveda (ii. 18, 6; 41, 14. 17).

Śunā-sīra, in the dual, occurs in the Rigveda[1] and later[2] as the names of two agricultural deities, the personifications, probably, of 'the share and the plough,' as Roth[3] thinks.

[1] iv. 57, 5. 8.

[2] Av. iii. 17. 5; Maitrāyaṇī Saṃhitā, i. 7, 12; Vājasaneyi Saṃhitā, xii. 69, etc.

[3] St. Petersburg Dictionary, *s.v.* For the native explanations, see Bṛhaddevatā, v. 8 *et seq.*, with Macdonell's notes. Whitney, Translation of the Atharvaveda, 116, 117, renders *śunam* adverbially as 'successfully.'

Śuno-lāṅgūla, 'Dog's tail,' is the name of a brother of **Śunaḥ-śepa.**[1]

[1] Aitareya Brāhmaṇa, vii. 15, 7; Sāṅkhāyana Srauta Sūtra, xv. 20, 1.

Śumbala is found in the Śatapatha Brāhmaṇa.[1] The meaning of the word is uncertain: Harisvāmi in his commentary takes it to be 'straw'; Eggeling[2] suggests that dried cotton fibre or pods may be meant. In any case, some substance that easily catches fire is intended.[3]

[1] xii. 5, 2. 3.

[2] *Sacred Books of the East*, 44, 202, n. 3; comparing Kātyāyana Śrauta Sūtra, xxv. 7, 12.

[3] Roth, St. Petersburg Dictionary, *s.v.*

Śulka in the Rigveda[1] clearly means 'price.' In the Dharma Sūtras[2] it denotes a 'tax,' a sense which is found by Muir[3] in a passage of the Atharvaveda,[4] where *śukla* is read in the edition with great detriment to the sense. This correction is accepted by Bloomfield[5] and by Whitney.[6] In another passage the same change made by Weber[7] is not accepted by Whitney,[8] and doubtfully by Bloomfield.[9]

[1] vii. 82, 6; viii. 1, 5.

[2] See Foy, *Die königliche Gewalt*, 39 *et seq.*

[3] *Sanskrit Texts*, 5, 310.

[4] iii. 29, 3.

[5] *Hymns of the Atharvaveda*, 434.

[6] Translation of the Atharvaveda, 136.

[7] *Indische Studien*, 17, 304.

[8] *Op. cit.*, 253.

[9] *Loc. cit.*

Cf. Zimmer, *Altindisches Leben*, 413.

Śuśuka. See **Aśuṃga** and **Śiśuka.**

Śuśulūka is found in the Rigveda[1] in the compound *śuśulūka-yātu*, the name of a demon. According to Sāyaṇa, the word means a 'small owl.' It appears in the feminine form, Śuśulūkā, in the list of victims at the Aśvamedha ('horse sacrifice') in the Maitrāyaṇī Saṃhitā.[2]

[1] vii. 104, 22.

[2] iii. 14, 17. *Cf.* Zimmer, *Altindisches Leben*, 93.

Śuṣka-bhṛṅgāra is the name of a teacher in the Kauṣītaki Upaniṣad.[1]

[1] ii. 6. *Cf.* Śāṅkhāyana Śrauta Sūtra, xvii. 7, 13.

Suśmiṇa is a name of **Amitratapana,** a king of the **Śibis,** in the Aitareya Brāhmaṇa (viii. 23, 10).

Śūdra is the designation of the fourth caste in the Vedic state (see **Varṇa**). It is quite unknown in the Rigveda except in the Puruṣasūkta[1] ('hymn of man') in the tenth Maṇḍala, where in the earliest version of the origin of the castes the Śūdra for the first time appears. The Rigveda, on the other hand, knows **Dasyu** and **Dāsa**, both as aborigines independent of Āryan control and as subjugated slaves: it is reasonable to reckon the Śūdra of the later texts as belonging to the aborigines who had been reduced to subjection by the Āryans. Strictly speaking, the defeated aborigines must have been regarded as slaves, but it is obvious that, except on occasions when most of the men were slain, which may have occurred quite often, there must have remained too many of them to be used as slaves of individual owners. The villages of the aborigines must have continued to subsist, but under Āryan lordship and control: there may be this amount of truth in Baden Powell's theory, which practically traced all the early cultivating villages in India to Dravidian origin. On the other hand, the term Śūdra would also cover the wild hill tribes which lived by hunting and fishing, and many of which would acknowledge the superiority of their Āryan neighbours: it could, in fact, be applied to all beyond the pale of the Āryan state.

This view of the Śūdra suits adequately the Vedic references to his condition, which would not apply adequately to domestic slaves only. The Śūdra is continually opposed to the Āryan,[2] and the colour of the Śūdra is compared with that of the Āryan,[3] just as his ways are so contrasted.[4] The Aitareya Brāhmaṇa,[5] in its account of the castes, declares that the

[1] x. 90, 12. See Muir, *Sanskrit Texts*, 1[2], 8 *et seq.*

[2] Av. iv. 20, 4; xix. 32, 8; 62, 1; Vājasaneyi Saṃhitā, xiv. 30; xxiii. 30. 31; Taittirīya Saṃhitā, iv. 2, 10, 2; vii. 4, 19, 3; Kāṭhaka Saṃhitā, Aśvamedha, iv. 7; xvii. 5; Maitrāyaṇī Saṃhitā, ii. 8, 6; iii. 13, 1, etc. See also **Ārya** and **Arya**. In Taittirīya Saṃhitā, i. 8, 3, 1; Vājasaneyi Saṃhitā, xx. 17; Kāṭhaka Saṃhitā, xxxviii. 5, Śūdra is opposed to Arya.

[3] Kāṭhaka Saṃhitā, xxxiv. 5; Pañcaviṃśa Brāhmaṇa, v. 5, 17. *Cf.* Śatapatha Brāhmaṇa, vi. 4, 4, 9; Bṛhadāraṇyaka Upaniṣad, i. 4, 25; Aitareya Brāhmaṇa, viii. 4, 5; Taittirīya Brāhmaṇa, i. 2, 6, 7; Weber, *Indische Studien*, 10, 4; Muir, *op. cit.*, 1[2], 140; Mahābhārata, xii. 188, 5.

[4] Aitareya Brāhmaṇa, vii. 17, 3. 4; Śāṅkhāyana Śrauta Sūtra, xv. 24.

[5] vii. 29, 4; Muir, *Sanskrit Texts*, 1[2], 439.

Śūdra is *anyasya preṣya,* 'the servant of another'; *kāmotthāpya,* 'to be expelled at will'; and *yathākāmavadhya,* 'to be slain at will.' All these terms well enough describe the position of the serf as the result of a conquest: the epithets might have been applied to the English serf after the Norman Conquest with but slight inaccuracy, especially if his master had received a grant of jurisdiction from the Crown. The Pañcaviṃśa Brāhmaṇa[6] explains that even if prosperous (*bahu-paśu,* 'having many cows') a Śūdra could not be other than a servant: his business was *pādāvanejya,* 'the washing of the feet' of his superiors. The Mahābhārata[7] says out and out that a Śūdra has no property (*na hi svam asti śūdrasya,* 'the Śūdra has nothing he can call his own'). On the other hand, just as in England the royal justice would protect the serf in life and limb,[8] so it appears that the slaying of a Śūdra involved a wergeld of ten cows according to both Baudhāyana[9] and Āpastamba.[10] It may, indeed, be held that this wergeld was only due in case of murder by another than the master, but such limitation is nowhere stated.

In sacred matters the distinction between Āryan and Śūdra was, of course, specially marked. The texts[11] do not hesitate to declare that the upper castes were 'all,' ignoring the Śūdras; the Śūdra is prohibited[12] from milking the cow for the milk required at the Agnihotra ('oblation to Agni'); and the Śatapatha Brāhmaṇa[13] forbids a man who has been consecrated (*dīkṣita*) for a sacrifice to speak to a Śūdra at all for the time, though the Śāṭyāyanaka[14] seems to have relaxed this rule by confining it to cases in which the Śūdra was guilty of some sin.

[6] vi. 1, 11.

[7] xii. 30, 7 (Hopkins, *Journal of the American Oriental Society,* 13, 73). The same text, xii. 294, 21 (*ibid.*, 74, n.), insists on his duty of service.

[8] Pollock and Maitland, *History of English Law,* 1, 350, 355, etc.

[9] Dharma Sūtra, i. 10, 19, 1.

[10] Dharma Sūtra, i. 9, 24, 3.

[11] Śatapatha Brāhmaṇa, ii. 1, 4, 2; iv. 2, 2, 14, etc. *Cf.* Eggeling, *Sacred Books of the East,* 12, xvi *et seq.*; 26, 292. *Cf.* Hopkins, *op. cit.*, 13, 73, 75, n.

[12] Kāṭhaka Saṃhitā, xxxi. 2; Maitrāyaṇī Saṃhitā, iv. 1, 3. So the *sthālī,* 'cooking vessel,' is to be prepared by an Āryan, Maitrāyaṇī Saṃhitā, i. 8, 3.

[13] iii. 1, 1, 10. *Cf.* v. 3, 2, 2.

[14] Quoted by Āpastamba, cited in the scholiast on Kātyāyana Śrauta Sūtra, vii. 5, 7. The sense is not quite certain, but that given in the text seems reasonable. *Cf.* Weber, *op. cit.*, 10, 11.

At the sacrifice itself the Śūdra could not be present in the *śālā*, 'hall'; he is definitely classed in the Śatapatha Brāhmaṇa[15] and the Pañcaviṃśa Brāhmaṇa[16] as unfit for 'sacrifice' (*ayajñiya*); and declared in the Kāṭhaka Saṃhitā[17] not to be admitted to drink Soma. At the Pravargya (introductory Soma) rite the performer is not allowed to come in contact with a Śūdra,[18] who here, as in the Kāṭhaka Saṃhitā,[17] is reckoned as excluded from a share in the Soma-draught. On the other hand, the Śūdra is one of the victims at the Puruṣamedha ('human sacrifice') in the Yajurveda,[19] and a fight between an Āryan and a Śūdra, in which, of course, the former wins, forms a part of the Mahāvrata rite, being perhaps a precursor of the Indian drama.[20]

Other indications, however, exist, showing that it would be undesirable to ignore the real importance of the Śūdra, which again reminds us of the condition of the serf, who, though legally restrained, still gradually won his way to the rank of a free man. Rich Śūdras are mentioned in the early texts,[21] just as Śūdra *gahapatis*, 'householders,' occur in the Buddhist texts, and Śūdra kings in the legal literature.[22] Sin against Śūdra and Āryan is mentioned;[23] prayers for glory on behalf of Śūdras, as well as of the other castes[24] occur; and the desire to be dear to Śūdra as well as to Āryan is expressed.[25]

[15] iii. 1, 1, 10. See also Maitrāyaṇī Saṃhitā, vii. 1, 1, 6; Lévi, *La Doctrine du Sacrifice*, 82.

[16] vi. 1, 11.

[17] xi. 10, where he therefore does not receive **Karīras**.

[18] Śatapatha Brāhmaṇa, xiv. 1, 1, 31.

[19] Vājasaneyi Saṃhitā, xxx. 5; Taittirīya Brāhmaṇa, iii. 4, 1, 1; Śatapatha Brāhmaṇa, xiii. 6, 2, 10. He is also present at the **Rājasūya**, Kāṭhaka Saṃhitā, xxxvii. 1.

[20] Keith, *Zeitschrift der Deutschen Morgenländischen Gesellschaft*, 64, 534.

[21] Maitrāyaṇī Saṃhitā, iv. 2, 7, 10; Pañcaviṃśa Brāhmaṇa, vi. 1, 11. Some of the kings' ministers were Śūdras: Śatapatha Brāhmaṇa, v. 3, 2, 2, with Sāyaṇa's note.

[22] Foy, *Die königliche Gewalt*, 8; Fick, *Die sociale Gliederung*, 83, 84. See Manu, iv. 61; Viṣṇu, lxxi. 64; perhaps Jaiminīya Upaniṣad Brāhmaṇa, i. 4, 5. But see Roth's emendation, *Journal of the American Oriental Society*, 16, ccxliii.

[23] Kāṭhaka Saṃhitā, xxxviii. 5; Taittirīya Saṃhitā, i. 8, 3, 1; Vājasaneyi Saṃhitā, xx. 17.

[24] Taittirīya Saṃhitā, v. 7, 6, 4; Kāṭhaka Saṃhitā, xl. 13; Maitrāyaṇī Saṃhitā, iii. 4, 8; Vājasaneyi Saṃhitā, xviii. 48. On the other hand, the Śūdra uses magic just as an Ārya does, Av. x. 1, 3.

[25] Av. xix. 32, 8; 62, 1; Vājasaneyi Saṃhitā, xxvi. 2, etc.

The Sūtras also, while they emphasize as general rules points earlier not insisted on, such as their inferiority in sitting, etc.,[26] their exclusion from the study of the Vedas,[27] the danger of contact with them[28] or their food,[29] still recognize that Śūdras can be merchants,[30] or even exercise any trade.[31]

Moreover, the Sūtras[32] permit the marriage of a Śūdrā woman with members of all castes. Though it was a reproach to **Vatṣa**[33] and to **Kavaṣa**[34] that they were the sons of a Śūdrā and a Dāsī respectively, still the possibility of such a reproach shows that marriages of this kind did take place. Moreover, illicit unions of Ārya and Śūdrā, or Śūdra and Āryā, are referred to in the Saṃhitās of the Yajurveda.[35]

The origin of the term Śūdra is quite obscure, but Zimmer[36] points out that Ptolemy[37] mentions Σύδροι as a people, and he thinks that the Brāhui may be meant. Without laying any stress on this identification,[38] it is reasonable to accept the

[26] Gautama Dharma Sūtra, xii. 7; Āpastamba Dharma Sūtra, ii. 10, 27, 15. So he can be insulted with impunity, Gautama, xii. 13, and is punished for insult by mutilation, *ibid.*, xii. 1; Āpastamba, ii. 10, 27, 14.

[27] Gautama, xii. 4-6.

[28] Āpastamba, i. 5, 17, 1; ii. 2, 3, 4, etc.

[29] Āpastamba, i. 5, 16, 2, etc.

[30] Gautama, x. 60. *Cf.* x. 50-67 for an exhaustive account of the Śūdra's duties in theory. His relations to his master are those of mutual support.

[31] Viṣṇu, ii. 14.

[32] Pāraskara Gṛhya Sūtra, i. 4, 11. Rules to the contrary (*e.g.*, Gobhila Gṛhya Sūtra, iii. 2, 52) are for special occasions. See Weber, *op. cit.*, 10, 74. On the other hand, criminal intercourse of a Śūdra and an Āryan woman is severely punished in the Sūtras. See Āpastamba, i. 10, 26, 20; 27, 9; Gautama, xii. 2. 3.

[33] Pañcaviṃśa Brāhmaṇa, xiv. 6, 6.

[34] Aitareya Brāhmaṇa, ii. 19, 1.

[35] Ārya and Śūdrā: Vājasaneyi Saṃhitā, xxiii. 30; Taittirīya Saṃhitā, vii. 4, 19, 3; Maitrāyaṇī Saṃhitā, iii. 13, 1; Kāṭhaka Saṃhitā, Aśvamedha, iv. 8; Śūdra and Āryā: Vājasaneyi Saṃhitā, xxiii. 31. This verse the Śatapatha Brāhmaṇa no doubt deliberately ignores.

[36] *Altindisches Leben*, 216, 435.

[37] vi. 20.

[38] The Brāhui are now held not to be Dravidian ethnologically, but Turco-Iranian (*Indian Empire*, 1, 292, 310). It is suggested (*ibid.*, 1, 382) that they represent the original Dravidian type, which in India has been merged in the Muṇḍā type; but this suggestion is invalidated by the fact that the Rigveda speaks of the Dasyus as *anās*, 'noseless' (*cf.* **Dasyu**, 1, 347, n. 7), a term admirably applicable to Dravidians, but ludicrous as applied to the Turco-Iranian type. It is much more plausible to assume that the Brāhuis are a mixed race, which in course of time has lost most of its Dravidian features. On the relation of Dravidians and speakers of Muṇḍā tongues, the Vedic texts throw no light.

view[39] that the term was originally the name of a large tribe opposed to the Āryan invasion. See also **Niṣāda.**

[39] See Weber, *Indische Studien*, 18, 85, 255; Ludwig, Translation of the Rigveda, 3, 212; Fick, *Die sociale Gliederung*, 201, 202.

Cf. von Schroeder, *Indiens Literatur und Cultur*, 154, 155; Jolly, *Zeitschrift der Deutschen Morgenländischen Gesellschaft*, 50, 515; Fick, *Die sociale Gliederung*, 201 *et seq.*; Rhys Davids, *Buddhist India*, 54; Hopkins, *Journal of the American Oriental Society*, 13, 73 *et seq.* (for the Śūdra in the Epic); Zimmer, *Altindisches Leben*, 191 *et seq.*; Weber, *Indian Literature*, 18, 77, 111, 112, 276; *Indische Studien*, 10, 4 *et seq.*; Muir, *Sanskrit Texts*, 1[2], 8 *et seq.*

Śūdrā denoted a Śūdra woman in the Atharvaveda[1] and later.[2]

[1] v. 22, 7 (= Dāsī, v. 22, 6).

[2] Taittirīya Saṃhitā, vii. 4, 19, 3; Kāṭhaka Saṃhitā, Aśvamedha, iv. 8; Maitrāyaṇī Saṃhitā, iii. 13, 1; Vājasaneyi Saṃhitā, xxiii. 30, etc.; *śūdrā-putra*, 'son of a Śūdra woman,' Pañcaviṃśa Brāhmaṇa, xiv. 6, 6.

Śūra is the regular word in the Rigveda,[1] and occasionally later,[2] to denote a 'hero' or 'brave warrior.'

[1] i. 70, 11; 101, 6; 141, 8; 158, 3; ii. 17, 2; 30, 10, etc.

[2] Av. viii. 8, 1; Vājasaneyi Saṃhitā, xvi. 34; xx. 37, etc. (of gods, Indra and Agni); *śūra-vīra*, Av. viii. 5, 1.

Śūra-vīra Māṇḍūkya ('descendant of Maṇḍūka') is the name of a teacher in the Āraṇyakas of the Rigveda.[1]

[1] Aitareya Āraṇyaka, iii. 1, 1. 3. 4; Śāṅkhāyana Āraṇyaka, vii. 2. 8. 9. 10 (where the name is read Śaura-vīra).

Śūrpa in the Atharvaveda[1] and later[2] denotes a wickerwork basket for winnowing grain. It is called *varṣa-vṛddha*, 'swollen by rain, in the Atharvaveda,[3] which shows, as Zimmer[4] says, that it was sometimes made of reeds, not of dry wood.

[1] ix. 6, 16; x. 9, 26; xi. 3, 4; xii. 3, 19 *et seq.*; xx. 136, 8.

[2] Taittirīya Saṃhitā, i. 6, 8, 3; Taittirīya Brāhmaṇa, i. 6, 5, 4; iii. 2, 5, 11, etc.

[3] xii. 3, 19.

[4] *Altindisches Leben*, 238.

Cf. Lanman in Whitney's Translation of the Atharvaveda, 685; Bloomfield, *Hymns of the Atharvaveda*, 649.

Śūla, denoting the 'spit,' used for roasting flesh on, is found in the Rigveda[1] and the later Brāhmaṇas.[2]

[1] i. 162, 11.

[2] Śatapatha Brāhmaṇa, xi. 4, 2, 4; 7, 3, 2; 4, 3; Chāndogya Upaniṣad, vii. 15, 3 (used at cremation and suggestive of roasting). The Śūla, as the weapon of Rudra, is not mentioned till the late Ṣaḍviṃśa Brāhmaṇa, v. 11. In the post-Vedic language the *tri-śūla*, or 'trident,' is the regular emblem of Śiva.

Cf. Zimmer, *Altindisches Leben*, 271.

1. **Śūṣa Vārṣṇa** ('descendant of Vṛṣṇi') is mentioned in the Taittirīya Brāhmaṇa (iii. 10, 9, 15) as having been honoured by a consecration with Āditya.

2. **Śūṣa Vāhneya** ('descendant of Vahni') **Bhāradvāja** ('descendant of **Bharadvāja**') is the name of a teacher, a pupil of **Arāḍa Dātreya Śaunaka**, in the Vaṃśa Brāhmaṇa.[1] *Cf.* **Śruṣa.**

[1] *Indische Studien*, 4, 373.

Śṛṅga in the Rigveda[1] and later[2] denotes the 'horn' of any sort of animal. Hence the 'barb' of the arrow is called its horn in the Atharvaveda.[3]

[1] i. 140, 6; 163, 11; ii. 39, 3; iii. 8, 10, etc.

[2] Av. ii. 32, 6; viii. 6, 14; ix. 4, 17, etc.

[3] iv. 6, 5. *Cf.* Whitney, Translation of the Atharvaveda, 154.

Śṛṅga-vṛṣ is the name of a man in one hymn of the Rigveda.[1] According to Ludwig,[2] he is father of **Pṛdākusānu.**

[1] viii. 17, 13.

[2] Translation of the Rigveda, 3, 161.

Cf. Griffith, *Hymns of the Rigveda*, 2, 142, n.

Śerabha and **Śerabhaka** are names of snakes or demons in the Atharvaveda.[1]

[1] ii. 24, 1. *Cf.* Whitney, Translation of the Atharvaveda, 64.

Śeva-dhi denotes 'treasure' in the Rigveda[1] and later.[2]

[1] ii. 13, 6; vii. 53, 5; ix. 3, 15 (metaphorically). *Cf.* viii. 52, 9.

[2] Av. v. 22, 14; Vājasaneyi Saṃhitā, xviii. 59, etc.

Śevṛdha and **Śevṛdhaka** are the names of snakes or demons in the Atharvaveda.[1]

[1] ii. 24, 1. *Cf.* Whitney, Translation of the Atharvaveda, 64.

Śeṣaṇa in the Atharvaveda (vii. 109, 5), means the 'leaving' of the dice as opposed to Glahana (*grahaṇa*), the 'taking up' of them for the throw. *Cf.* **Glaha.**

Śeṣas denotes 'offspring' in the Rigveda.[1]

[1] i. 93, 4; v. 12, 6; 70, 4; vi. 27, 4. 5; vii. 1, 12; 4, 7; x. 16, 5.

Śaibya, 'belonging to the **Śibis,**' is a designation of king **Amitratapana Śuṣmiṇa** in the Aitareya Brāhmaṇa (viii. 23, 10). In the Praśna Upaniṣad (i. 1; v. 1) Śaibya is the patronymic of a teacher, **Satyakāma.**

Śailana, in the plural, is the name of a school of teachers in the Jaiminīya Upaniṣad Brāhmaṇa (i. 2, 3; ii. 4, 6).

Sailāli, 'descendant of Śilālin,' is the name of a ritual teacher in the Śatapatha Brāhmaṇa.[1] A Śailāli Brāhmaṇa is mentioned in the Āpastamba Śrauta Sūtra,[2] and the school of the Śailālins often occurs in the Sūtras.[3]

[1] xiii. 5, 3, 3.
[2] vi. 4, 7.
[3] Anupada Sūtra, iv. 5, etc. *Cf.* Weber, *Indische Studien*, 1, 156; *Indian Literature*, 197, who compares the Naṭa Sūtra attributed to Śilālin by Pāṇini, iv. 2, 110, 111.

Śailina or **Śailini,** 'descendant of Śilina,' is the patronymic of **Jitvan** in the Śatapatha Brāhmaṇa.[1] Perhaps **Śailana** should be compared.

[1] Śailina in Bṛhadāraṇyaka Upaniṣad, iv. 1, 5 Mādhyaṃdina; Śailini, iv. 1, 2 Kāṇva. *Cf.* Max Müller, *Sacred Books of the East*, 15, 152, n. 2.

Śailūṣa is included in the list of victims at the Puruṣamedha ('human sacrifice') in the Yajurveda.[1] An 'actor' or 'dancer' may be meant. Sāyaṇa says it is a man who lives on the prostitution of his wife.

[1] Vājasaneyi Saṃhitā, xxx. 6; Taittirīya Brāhmaṇa, iii. 4, 2, 1. *Cf.* Zimmer, *Altindisches Leben*, 290; Weber, *Indian Literature*, 111, 196, 197. The exact sense of Śailūṣa depends on the question of how old the drama is in India. As to this, *cf.* **Itihāsa**; Keith, *Journal of the Royal Asiatic Society*, 1911, 995 *et seq.*

Śoṇa Sātrāsāha, king of **Pañcāla** and father of **Koka**, is mentioned in the Śatapatha Brāhmaṇa[1] as having offered the horse sacrifice, which was attended by the **Turvaśas** also.

[1] xiii. 5, 4, 16-18. *Cf.* Eggeling, *Sacred Books of the East*, 44, 400.

Śauṅgāyani, 'descendant of Śauṅga,' is the name of a teacher in the Vaṃśa Brāhmaṇa.[1]

[1] *Indische Studien*, 4, 372, 383. The Śuṅgas are known as teachers in the Āśvalāyana Śrauta Sūtra, xii. 13, 5, etc.

Śauṅgī-putra, 'son of a female descendant of Śuṅga,' is the name of a teacher, a pupil of **Sāṃkṛtī-putra** in the last Vaṃśa (list of teachers) in the Bṛhadāraṇyaka Upaniṣad.[1]

[1] vi. 4, 31 (Mādhyaṃdina = vi. 5, 2 Kāṇva).

Śauca ('descendant of Śuci') is the patronymic of a man, called also **Āhneya**, who is mentioned as a teacher in the Taittirīya Āraṇyaka (ii. 12).

Śaucad-ratha ('descendant of Śucad-ratha') is the patronymic of **Sunītha** in the Rigveda (v. 79, 2).

Śauceya ('descendant of Śuci') **Prācīnayogya** ('descendant of Prācīnayoga') is the name of a teacher in the Śatapatha Brāhmaṇa (xi. 5, 3, 1. 8). Śauceya is also the patronymic of **Sārvaseni** in the Taittirīya Saṃhitā (vii. 1, 10, 2).

Śaunaka, 'descendant of Śunaka,' is a common patronymic. It is applied to **Indrota**[1] and **Svaidāyana.**[2] A Śaunaka appears as a teacher of **Rauhiṇāyana** in the Bṛhadāraṇyaka Upaniṣad.[3] A Śaunaka-yajña, or Śaunaka sacrifice, occurs in the Kauṣītaki Brāhmaṇa.[4] In the Chāndogya Upaniṣad[5] **Atidhanvan** Śaunaka appears as a teacher. That Upaniṣad[6] and the Jaiminīya Upaniṣad Brāhmaṇa[7] mention a Śaunaka Kāpeya who was a contemporary of **Abhipratārin Kākṣaseni,** whose Purohita Śaunaka was according to another passage[8] of the latter Upaniṣad. In the Sūtras, the Bṛhaddevatā, etc., a Śaunaka appears as a great authority on grammatical, ritual, and other matters.[9]

[1] Śatapatha Brāhmaṇa, xiii. 5, 3, 5; 4, 1.
[2] *Ibid.*, xi. 4, 1, 2.
[3] ii. 5, 20; iv. 5, 26 Mādhyaṃdina.
[4] iv. 7.
[5] i. 9, 3.
[6] iv. 3, 5. 7.
[7] iii. 1, 21.
[8] i. 59, 2.
[9] *Cf.* Weber, *Indian Literature*, 24, 32-34, 49, 54, 56, 59, 62, 85, 143; Macdonell, *Bṛhaddevatā*, 1, xxiii; Keith, *Aitareya Āraṇyaka*, 18, 19, 297.

Śaunakī-putra, 'son of a female descendant of Śunaka,' is the name of a teacher, a pupil of **Kāśyapībālākyāmāṭharīputra** in the last Vaṃśa (list of teachers) in the Mādhyaṃdina recension of the Bṛhadāraṇyaka Upaniṣad (vi. 4, 30. 31).

Śaurpa-ṇāyya, 'descendant of Śūrpaṇāya,' is the patronymic of a teacher, a pupil of **Gautama**, in the first two Vaṃśas (lists of teachers) in the Mādhyaṃdina recension of the Bṛhadāraṇyaka Upaniṣad (ii. 5, 20; iv. 5, 26).

Śaulbāyana or **Śaulvāyana**, 'descendant of Śulba,' is the patronymic of a teacher, **Udaṅka.**[1] According to the Śatapatha Brāhmaṇa,[2] a Śaulbāyana was the Adhvaryu, or sacrificing priest, of those who had **Ayasthūṇa** as Gṛhapati ('householder,' the title of the sacrificer who has precedence at a *sattra*, or sacrificial session).

[1] Taittirīya Saṃhitā, vii. 4, 5, 4; 5, 4. 2; Bṛhadāraṇyaka Upaniṣad, iv. 1, 2 Mādhyaṃdina.
[2] xi. 4, 2, 17 *et seq.*

Śauṣkala is the name of one of the sacrificial victims at the Puruṣamedha ('horse sacrifice') in the Yajurveda.[1] It means, according to the St. Petersburg Dictionary, 'living on dried fish or flesh,'[2] or, according to the native lexicographers, 'selling dried fish,' while Sāyaṇa's commentary on the Taittirīya Brāhmaṇa explains the meaning to be one who catches fish with a hook, 'angler.'

[1] Vājasaneyi Saṃhitā, xxx. 16; Taittirīya Brāhmaṇa, iii. 4, 12, 1. *Cf.* Weber, *Indische Streifen*, 1, 81, n. 7; Eggeling, *Sacred Books of the East*, 44, 415.

[2] The literal meaning is, 'relating to what is dried' (*śuṣkala*).

Śruṣṭi Āṅgirasa ('descendant of **Aṅgiras**') is the name of the seer of a Sāman or Chant in the Pañcaviṃśa Brāhmaṇa.[1]

[1] xiii. 11, 21. *Cf.* Hillebrandt, *Vedische Mythologie*, 2, 160; Hopkins, *Transactions of the Connecticut Academy of Arts and Sciences*, 15, 68.

Śmaśāna is the name of the 'burial mound' in which the bones of the dead man were laid to rest (*cf.* **Anagnidagdha**). It is mentioned in the Atharvaveda,[1] and often later.[2] The Śatapatha Brāhmaṇa[3] prescribes a four-cornered mound facing the south-east, on ground inclined to the north, out of sight of the village, in a peaceful spot amid beautiful surroundings, or on barren ground. For an Agni-cit ('builder of a fire-altar') a funeral mound like a fire-altar is prescribed. The Easterners (*Prācyāḥ*) made their mounds round.

[1] v. 31, 8; x. 1, 18.

[2] Taittirīya Saṃhitā, v. 2, 8, 5; 4, 11, 3; Kāṭhaka Saṃhitā, xxi. 4; Maitrāyaṇī Saṃhitā, iii. 4, 7; Śatapatha Brāhmaṇa, iv. 5, 2, 15, etc.

[3] xiii. 8, 1, 1 *et seq.* *Cf.* Eggeling, *Sacred Books of the East*, 44, 424 *et seq.*

Cf. Zimmer, *Altindisches Leben*, 407; Hopkins, *Journal of the American Oriental Society*, 16, cliii.

Śmaśru in the Rigveda[1] and later[2] means 'beard' and 'moustache,' being sometimes contrasted with **Keśa**,[3] 'hair of the head.' Shaving was known (see **Vaptṛ** and **Kṣura**). The

[1] ii. 11, 17; viii. 33, 6; x. 23, 1. 4; 26, 7; 142, 4.

[2] Av. v. 19, 14; vi. 68, 2; Vājasaneyi Saṃhitā, xix. 92; xx. 5, etc. Applied to animals, *ibid.*, xxv. 1; Śatapatha Brāhmaṇa, xii. 9, 1, 6, etc.

[3] Śatapatha Brāhmaṇa, ii. 5, 2, 48, etc.

wearing of a beard was a sign of manhood according to the Taittirīya Saṃhitā,[4] with which agrees the notice of Megasthenes[5] that the Indians carefully tended their beards up to the day of their death.

[4] v. 5, 1, 1.
[5] In Diodorus, iii. 63. *Cf.* Zimmer, *Altindisches Leben*, 265-267.

Śyāparṇa Sāyakāyana is the name of a man, the last for whom five victims were slain at the building of the sacrificial altar according to the Śatapatha Brāhmaṇa.[1] The same text[2] again mentions him as a builder of the fire-altar. He must have been connected in some way with the **Salvas.**[3] His family, the Śyāparṇas, appear in the Aitareya Brāhmaṇa[4] as a self-assertive family of priests whom king **Viśvantara** excluded from his sacrifice, but whose leader, **Rāma Mārgaveya,** induced him to take them back. In some way Śyāparṇa was connected with the defeat of the **Pañcālas** by the **Kuntis.**[5]

[1] vi. 2, 1, 39.
[2] ix. 5, 2, 1.
[3] x. 4, 1, 10.
[4] vii. 27. *Cf.* Eggeling, *Sacred Books of the East*, 43, 344, 345; Muir, *Sanskrit Texts*, 1², 437 *et seq.*; Weber, *Indische Studien*, 1, 215, 216.
[5] Weber, *Indische Studien*, 3, 471.

Śyāma ('swarthy') with **Ayas** ('metal') in all probability denotes 'iron' in the Atharvaveda.[1] Śyāma alone has the same sense in the Atharvaveda[2] and later.[3]

[1] xi. 3, 7.
[2] ix. 5, 4.
[3] Taittirīya Saṃhitā, iv. 7, 5, 1; Kāṭhaka Saṃhitā, xviii. 10; Maitrāyaṇī Saṃhitā, ii. 11, 5; Vājasaneyi Saṃhitā, xviii. 13.
Cf. Zimmer, *Altindisches Leben*, 52, 54; Schrader, *Prehistoric Antiquities*, 189.

Śyāma-jayanta Lauhitya ('descendant of Lohita') is the name of a teacher, a pupil of **Jayanta Pārāśarya,** in a Vaṃśa (list of teachers) in the Jaiminīya Upaniṣad Brāhmaṇa (iii. 42, 1). Another man of the same name occurs in the same place as a pupil of **Mitrabhūti Lauhitya.**

Śyāma-parṇa is, in the Kāṭhaka[1] and Maitrāyaṇī[2] Saṃhitās, the name of a man who was instructed by **Somadakṣa Kauśreya.**

[1] xx. 8 (*Indische Studien*, 3, 472).
[2] iii. 2, 7.

Śyāma-sujayanta Lauhitya ('descendant of Lohita') is the name of a teacher, a pupil of **Kṛṣṇadhṛti Sātyaki,** in a Vaṃśa (list of teachers) of the Jaiminīya Upaniṣad Brāhmaṇa (iii. 42, 1).

Śyāmāka is the name of a cultivated millet (*Panicum frumentaceum*) in the later Saṃhitās[1] and the Brāhmaṇas.[2] The lightness of its seed is alluded to in the Atharvaveda,[3] where it is spoken of as blown away by the wind. There it is also mentioned as the food of pigeons.[4] The Śyāmāka and its seed (**Taṇḍula**) are referred to as very small in the Chāndogya Upaniṣad,[5] where Max Müller[6] renders it as 'canary seed.'

[1] Taittirīya Saṃhitā, i. 8, 1, 2; ii. 3, 2, 6; iv. 7, 4, 2; Maitrāyaṇī Saṃhitā, ii. 11, 4; Vājasaneyi Saṃhitā, xviii. 12; Kāṭhaka Saṃhitā, x. 2.

[2] Śatapatha Brāhmaṇa, x. 6, 3, 2; xii. 7, 1, 9, etc.; Kauṣītaki Brāhmaṇa, iv. 12.

[3] xix. 50, 4.

[4] xx. 135, 12.

[5] iii. 14, 3.

[6] *Sacred Books of the East*, 1, 48. *Cf.* Zimmer, *Altindisches Leben*, 241, 275.

1. **Śyāva** is the name of a protégé of the Aśvins in the Rigveda.[1] He may be identical with **Hiraṇyahasta.**

[1] i. 117, 24; x. 65, 2. *Cf.* Ludwig, Translation of the Rigveda, 3, 150; Macdonell, *Vedic Mythology*, p. 32.

2. **Śyāva** is mentioned in the Rigveda[1] as a generous donor on the **Suvāstu** river.

[1] viii. 19, 37. *Cf.* Ludwig, Translation of the Rigveda, 3, 161.

3. **Śyāva** in one passage of the Rigveda (v. 61, 9) seems clearly, as Sāyaṇa thinks, to denote **Śyāvāśva.**

Śyāvaka is mentioned as a sacrificer and friend of Indra in the Rigveda (viii. 3, 12; 4, 2). He may be identical with 2. **Śyāva.**

Śyāvasāyana is the patronymic of **Devataras** in the Jaiminīya Upaniṣad Brāhmaṇa (iii. 40, 2). The form is perhaps an error for **Śāvasāyana.**

Śyāvāśva is the name of a man mentioned several times in the Rigveda.[1] The Anukramaṇī (Index) assigns to him a series of hymns in the fifth, eight, and ninth books.[2] In one of the hymns[3] Śyāvāśva mentions, apparently as his patrons, **Taranta** (a son of **Vidadaśva**) and **Purumīḷha,** as well as **Rathavīti.** On this hymn is based a legend found in the Bṛhaddevatā,[4] that he was the son of **Arcanānas,** who was sacrificing for Rathavīti Dālbhya. The father was anxious to obtain the king's daughter for his son in marriage; but though the father was willing, his wife insisted on her son-in-law being a Ṛṣi. The father and son, repulsed, were returning home, when they met on the way Taranta and Purumīḍha, former patrons of the father. These showed him respect, while Taranta's wife, Śaśīyasī, presented Śyāvāśva with much wealth. The son was then fortunate enough to meet the Maruts in the forest, and praised them, thus becoming a seer. As a result the king himself ultimately offered his daughter to Śyāvāśva. Sieg[5] seeks to show that this legend is presupposed in the Rigveda; but it is difficult to accept this view, since the references in the Rigveda are very obscure, and Śaśīyasī is probably no more than an epithet.[6] That there is some Itihāsa at the back of the hymn is clear: what it is can hardly now be determined.

Śyāvāśva's obtaining gifts from Vaidadaśvi is referred to also in the Śāṅkhāyana Śrauta Sūtra.[7] His name occurs in the Atharvaveda[8] in two lists of persons, of which the former includes Purumīḍha, the latter also Arcanānas and Atri. A Sāman is ascribed to him in the Pañcaviṃśa Brāhmaṇa,[9] and he is perhaps referred to in the Taittirīya Āraṇyaka.[10] In the

[1] v. 52, 1; 61, 5. 9 (Syāva, a short form of the name, is here used); 81, 5; viii. 35, 19; 36, 7; 37, 7; 38, 8.

[2] v. 52-61; 81; 82; viii. 35-38; ix. 32.

[3] v. 61.

[4] v. 49 *et seq.* See also Ṣaḍguruśiṣya on Anukramaṇī to Rv. v. 61 (ed. Macdonell, p. 117 *et seq.*); Sāyaṇa on Rv. v. 61, 17-19; Nītimañjarī in Sieg, *Die Sagenstoffe des Ṛgveda*, 50 *et seq.*

[5] *Op. cit.*; 50-60. *Cf.* Geldner, *Vedische Studien*, 3, 148.

[6] v. 61, 6. The word is taken as an epithet by Roth, St. Petersburg Dictionary, *s.v.*, and by Weber, *Episches im vedischen Ritual*, 27.

[7] xvi. 11, 7-9.

[8] iv. 29, 4; xviii. 3, 15.

[9] viii. 5, 9. Weber, *Episches im vedischen Ritual*, 27, n. 4, bases on this an improbable conjecture that he was a Kṣatriya.

[10] i 11, 2. But *cf.* Sieg, *op. cit.*, 61, n. 4, who takes the word adjectivally, as in Av. xi. 2, 18; Śāṅkhāyana Śrauta Sūtra, xiv. 33, 26.

Śāṅkhāyana Śrauta Sūtra and the Pañcaviṃśa Brāhmaṇa[11] he is styled Ārcanānasa, 'son of Arcanānas,' and later[12] he is called Ātreya, 'descendant of Atri.'

[11] viii. 5, 9.

[12] The Anukramaṇī calls him and his father Ātreya. In the passages from book viii. of the Rv., cited in n. 1, Atri is mentioned with him.

Cf. Ludwig, Translation of the Rigveda, 3, 126, 127; Oldenberg, *Zeitschrift der Deutschen Morgenländischen Gesellschaft*, 42, 214; *Ṛgveda-Noten*, 1, 354; Max Müller, *Sacred Books of the East*, 32, 359 *et seq.*; Lévi, *La Doctrine du Sacrifice*, 122.

Śyena is the name in the Rigveda[1] of a strong bird of prey, most probably the 'eagle'; later[2] (as in post-Vedic Sanskrit) it seems to mean the 'falcon' or 'hawk.' It is the swiftest of birds,[3] and a source of terror to smaller birds.[4] It is the strongest of birds,[5] and even attacks herds.[6] It watches over men (*nṛ-cakṣas*),[7] a reference, no doubt, to its lofty flight in air. It brings the Soma from heaven.[8]

[1] i. 32, 14; 33, 2; 118, 11; 163, 1; 165, 2, etc.

[2] Av. iii. 3, 4; vii. 41, 2; xi. 9, 9, etc.

[3] Taittirīya Saṃhitā, ii. 4, 7, 1; v. 4, 11, 1; Ṣaḍviṃśa Brāhmaṇa, iii. 8.

[4] Rv. ii. 42, 2; Av. v. 21, 6.

[5] Kāṭhaka Saṃhitā, xxxvii. 14.

[6] Rv. iv. 38, 5. This corresponds well enough with the eagle's known habit of carrying off young lambs.

[7] Av. vii. 41, 2.

[8] See Bloomfield, *Journal of the American Oriental Society*, 16, 1-24, who cites all relevant passages.

Cf. Zimmer, *Altindisches Leben*, 87, 88, who points out that the epithet *ṛjipya*, 'flying upwards,' applied to the eagle, appears as an actual name of the eagle in Iranian.

Śrapayitṛ, 'cook,' is a term mentioned in the Śatapatha Brāhmaṇa (i. 2, 2, 14).

Śramaṇa 'mendicant monk,' is first found in the Upaniṣads.[1] According to Fick,[2] anyone could become a Śramaṇa. For the time of Megasthenes this seems indicated by his evidence, which, however, refers only to the east of India, beyond the **Madhyadeśa** proper.[3] The Vedic evidence is merely the name and the fact that **Tāpasa**, 'ascetic,' follows it in the Bṛhadāraṇyaka Upaniṣad and the Taittirīya Āraṇyaka.

[1] Bṛhadāraṇyaka Upaniṣad, iv. 3, 22; Taittirīya Āraṇyaka, ii. 7, in *Indische Studien*, 1, 78.

[2] *Die sociale Gliederung*, 39 *et seq.*

[3] Strabo, xv. 1, 49, 60; Arrian, *Indica*, xii. 8. 9.

Cf. Weber, *Indian Literature*, 27, 28, 129, 138.

Śravaṇa. See **Nakṣatra.**

Śravaṇa-datta ('given by **Śravaṇa**') **Kauhala** ('descendant of Kohala') is the name of a teacher, a pupil of **Suśārada Śālaṅkāyana** in the Vaṃśa Brāhmaṇa.[1]

[1] *Indische Studien*, 4, 372.

Śraviṣṭha. See **Nakṣatra.**

Śrāyasa is the patronymic of **Kaṇva** in the Taittirīya Saṃhitā[1] and the Kāṭhaka Saṃhitā,[2] where he appears as a teacher, and of **Vītahavya** in the Taittirīya Saṃhitā[3] and the Pañcaviṃśa Brāhmaṇa.[4]

[1] v. 4, 7, 5.
[2] xxi. 8.
[3] v. 6, 5, 3.
[4] ix. 1, 9; xxv. 16, 3.

Śrī is the regular word for 'prosperity,' found once in the Rigveda[1] and often later.[2] **Śreṣṭhin.**

[1] viii. 2, 19, seems to have this sense.
[2] Av. vi. 54, 1; 73, 1; ix. 5, 31; x. 6, 26; xi. 1, 12. 21; xii. 1, 63; 5, 7; Taittirīya Saṃhitā, ii. 2, 8, 6; v. 1, 8, 6; vi. 1, 10, 3; vii. 2, 7, 3, etc. Already in the Śatapatha Brāhmaṇa (xi. 4, 3) she is regarded as a goddess. See Rhys Davids, *Buddhist India*, 217 *et seq*. She already appears in the earliest Buddhist sculptures seated on a lotus between two elephants that pour water over her. This type of the goddess has survived down to the present day in India.

Śruta-kakṣa is mentioned once in the Rigveda[1] as the Ṛṣi of a hymn, the authorship of which the Anukramaṇī (Index) ascribes to him. A Sāman or chant of his is mentioned in the Pañcaviṃśa Brāhmaṇa.[2]

[1] viii. 92, 25. *Cf.* Ludwig, Translation of the Rigveda, 3, 108.
[2] ix. 2, 7 (*śrauta-kakṣa*).

Śruta-ratha is the name of a young king in the Rigveda.[1] He is also the patron of the **Pajra** family, including **Kakṣīvant.**[2]

[1] i. 122, 7.
[2] Rv. v. 36, 6. *Cf.* Ludwig, Translation of the Rigveda, 3, 155; Pischel, *Vedische Studien*, 1. 97.

Śrutarya occurs once in the Rigveda (i. 112, 9) as the name of a protégé of the Aśvins.

Śrutarvan Ārkṣa ('descendant of Ṛkṣa') is the name of a prince whose liberality is celebrated in one hymn of the Rigveda (viii. 74, 4. 13), and whose victory over **Mṛgaya** is mentioned in another (x. 49, 5).

Śrutar-vid is the name of a man in the Rigveda.[1]

[1] v. 44, 12. *Cf.* Ludwig, Translation of the Rigveda, 3, 138, 139.

Śruta-sena is mentioned in the Śatapatha Brāhmaṇa (xiii. 5, 4, 3) and the Śāṅkhāyana Śrauta Sūtra (xvi. 9, 4) as one of the brothers of **Janamejaya.**

Śruṣa Vāhneya ('descendant of Vahni') **Kāśyapa** ('descendant of **Kaśyapa**') is the name of a teacher, a pupil of **Devataras,** in the Jaiminīya Upaniṣad Brāhmaṇa (iii. 40, 1). It is much more likely that Śruṣa is a mere misreading for **Śūṣa.**

Śruṣṭi-gu ('possessing obedient oxen') is the name of a man in a Vālakhilya hymn of the Rigveda.[1]

[1] viii. 51, 1. *Cf.* Ludwig, Translation of the Rigveda, 3, 140, 141; Hopkins, *Journal of the American Oriental Society,* 17, 90.

Śreṇi means a 'row' or 'line' of birds,[1] or horses,[2] or chariots,[3] and so forth.

[1] Rv. v. 59, 7.
[2] Rv. i. 126, 4.
[3] Rv. iv. 38, 6; Chāndogya Upaniṣad, v. 14, 1.

Śreṣṭhin occurs in several passages of the Brāhmaṇas,[1] where the St. Petersburg Dictionary assigns to the word the sense of 'a man of consequence.' It is, however, possible that

[1] Aitareya Brāhmaṇa, iii. 30, 3; Kauṣītaki Brāhmaṇa, xxviii. 6; Kauṣītaki Upaniṣad, iv. 20. Bhaga is the Śreṣṭhin of the gods, Taittirīya Brāhmaṇa, iii. 1, 4, 10.

the word may already have the sense of the 'headman of a guild,' the modern Seth.[2] There is a similar doubt in the use of *śraiṣṭhya*,[3] which is perhaps not merely 'the foremost place,' as usually assumed, but definitely 'the presidency of a guild.'

Guilds are referred to in the Dharma Sūtras,[4] and they play a considerable part in the Buddhist texts[5] and the Epic.[6] But the Vedic evidence is inadequate to afford ground for positive assertion or denial of their existence or organization in Vedic times.

[2] *Cf.* Hopkins, *India, Old and New*, 168 *et seq.*

[3] Av. i. 9, 3 = Taittirīya Saṃhitā, iii. 5, 4, 2 = Kāṭhaka Saṃhitā, v. 6 = Maitrāyaṇī Saṃhitā, i. 4, 3. See also for the word, Av. x. 6, 31; Aitareya Brāhmaṇa, iv. 25, 8; vii. 18, 8; Taittirīya Brāhmaṇa, iii. 8, 9, 1; Śatapatha Brāhmaṇa, xiii. 7, 1, 1; Chāndogya Upaniṣad, v. 2, 6; Kauṣītaki Upaniṣad, ii. 6; iv. 15. 20, etc. The use of *śraiṣṭhya* is, on the whole, not in favour of the theory that it is a technical term.

[4] Gautama Dharma Sūtra, xi. 20. 21, etc.; Foy, *Die königliche Gewalt*, 14, n. 2, etc.

[5] Rhys Davids, *Buddhist India*, 88 *et seq.*

[6] Hopkins, *Journal of the American Oriental Society*, 13, 81 *et seq.*

Śrotriya in the Atharvaveda[1] and later[2] denotes a 'Brahmin learned in holy lore,' 'theologian.'

[1] ix. 6, 37; x. 2, 20 *et seq.*

[2] Kāṭhaka Saṃhitā, xxiii. 4; xxviii. 4; Aitareya Brāhmaṇa, i. 25, 15; Śatapatha Brāhmaṇa, v. 4, 4, 5; xiii. 4, 3, 14; Taittirīya Upaniṣad, ii. 8, etc. *Cf.* *mahā-śrotriya*, 'a great theologian,' in Chāndogya Upaniṣad, v. 11, 1.

Śrauta-ṛṣi[1] or **Śrautarṣi**,[2] 'descendant of Śrutarṣi or Śrutarṣi,' is the patronymic of **Devabhāga.**

[1] Aitareya Brāhmaṇa, vii. 1, 6.

[2] Śatapatha Brāhmaṇa, ii. 4, 4, 5; Taittirīya Brāhmaṇa, iii. 10, 9, 11.

Śraumatya, 'descendant of Śrumant,' is the name of a teacher in the Śatapatha Brāhmaṇa (x. 4, 5, 1).

Śleṣman means generally that with which parts of a thing are joined together (from *śliṣ*, 'join'): with reference to a hide,[1]

[1] Aitareya Brāhmaṇa, v. 32, 6; Jaiminīya Upaniṣad Brāhmaṇa, iii. 17, 3; Chāndogya Upaniṣad, iv. 17, 4.

'laces' of some sort may be intended; to a chariot,[2] 'bonds' or 'cords' are probably meant; and to wood,[3] 'glue' is perhaps the sense.

[2] Kāṭhaka Saṃhitā, xxxiv. 9. *Cf.* Pañcaviṃśa Brāhmaṇa, xvi. 1, 13, where a chariot (**Ratha**) is called *śleṣmavant*, 'tied with ropes.'

[3] Kauṣītaki Brāhmaṇa, vi. 12. *Cf.* the Upaniṣads, cited in n. 1, and Śāṅkhāyana Āraṇyaka, ii. 1, which looks like a bad secondary version of the passage in the Jaiminīya.

Śloka, in the plural, is found enumerated after the **Upaniṣads,** and before the **Sūtras,** in the list of literary types given in the Bṛhadāraṇyaka Upaniṣad.[1] In the Taittirīya Upaniṣad[2] the Śloka-kṛt appears: he is rather the 'poet,' as Max Müller[3] renders it, than merely one who 'calls aloud,' as the St. Petersburg Dictionary explains the term.[4] Exactly what is meant cannot be said: 'verses' generally may be intended, several kinds being preserved in the Brāhmaṇas and called Ślokas.[5]

[1] ii. 4, 10; iv. 1, 6 (Mādhyaṃdina = iv. 1, 2 Kāṇva); 5, 11.

[2] iii. 10, 6.

[3] *Sacred Books of the East*, 15, 69

[4] In Av. v. 20, 7, the word has the sense assigned to it by the Dictionary.

[5] *E.g.*, Satapatha Brāhmaṇa, xi. 3, 1, 5; 5, 4, 12; xiii. 7, 1, 15; Aitareya Brāhmaṇa, viii. 22, 3; Aitareya Āraṇyaka, ii. 3, 8; Pañcaviṃśa Brāhmaṇa, xxiv. 18, 4; Taittirīya Āraṇyaka, viii. 1; Kauṣītaki Upaniṣad, i. 6, etc.

Śloṇya in the Taittirīya Brāhmaṇa[1] denotes 'lameness,' not 'skin disease' (*tvag-doṣa*), as explained by the commentator.

[1] iii. 9, 17, 2. *Cf.* *śloṇa*, 'lame,' Av. xii. 4, 3; Taittirīya Saṃhitā, vi. 1, 6, 7, etc.

Śva-ghnin in the Rigveda[1] and the Atharvaveda[2] clearly means a 'gamester' or 'professional gambler.' It may originally have denoted a 'hunter.'[3]

[1] i. 92, 10; ii. 12, 4; iv. 20, 3; viii. 45, 38.

[2] iv. 16, 5.

[3] Weber, *Indische Studien*, 18, 71.

Śvan in the Rigveda[1] and later[2] is the word for 'dog,' the feminine being Śunī.[3] The dog was a tame animal,[4] and used

[1] i. 161, 13 (where the sense is quite obscure); 182, 4; ii. 39, 4, etc.

[2] Av. vi. 37, 3; xi. 2, 2; Pañcaviṃśa Brāhmaṇa, viii. 8, 22, etc.

[3] Av. iv. 20, 7 (*catur-akṣī*); Śatapatha Brāhmaṇa, vi. 5, 2, 19.

[4] Rv. ii. 39, 4.

to guard the house from thieves or other intruders.[5] He was also employed in hunting the boar (*varāha-yu*),[6] but was no match for the lion.[7] A hundred dogs are mentioned as a gift in a Dānastuti ('Praise of Gifts') in a Vālakhilya hymn.[8] Elsewhere the dog is regarded as unfit for sacrifice, as being unclean,[9] and is driven away from the sacrifice.[10] To eat dog's flesh was a last resort of despair and hunger.[11] The bones of the feast were given to the dog.[12] Saramā figures in legend as Indra's faithful dog[13] searching for the cows. Rudra is lord of dogs (*śva-pati*) in the Yajurveda;[14] the 'dog-keeper' (*śvanin*) is mentioned in the list of sacrificial victims at the Puruṣamedha ('human sacrifice') in the same Saṃhitā.[15] The four-eyed (*catur-akṣa*) dogs of certain texts[16] are, of course, mythological.[17] *Cf.* **Kurkura.**

[5] Rv. vii. 55, 5.

[6] Rv. x. 86, 4.

[7] Av. iv. 36, 6.

[8] Rv. viii. 55, 3.

[9] Jaiminīya Brāhmaṇa, i. 51, 4; Satapatha Brāhmaṇa, xii. 4, 1, 4.

[10] Rv. ix. 101, 1.

[11] Rv. iv. 18, 3. Later, *śva-paca* ('dog-cooking') denotes a degraded caste.

[12] Av. vi. 37, 3. *Cf.* ix. 4, 16.

[13] i. 62, 3; 72, 8, etc. See Macdonell, *Vedic Mythology*, p. 151.

[14] Vājasaneyi Saṃhitā, xvi. 28; Kāṭhaka Saṃhitā, xvii. 13; Maitrāyaṇī Saṃhitā, ii. 9, 5.

[15] Vājasaneyi Saṃhitā, xvi. 27; xxx. 7; Taittirīya Brāhmaṇa, iii. 4, 3, 1, etc. *Cf. śva-nī* ('dog-leader'), Maitrāyaṇī Saṃhitā, ii. 9, 5.

[16] *Cf.* Rv. x. 14, 10. 11; Av. xviii. 2, 11. 12; Taittirīya Āraṇyaka, vi. 3, 1; Taittirīya Brāhmaṇa, iii. 8, 4, 1; Śatapatha Brāhmaṇa, xiii. 1, 2, 9, etc.

[17] Bloomfield, *Journal of the American Oriental Society*, 15, 163 *et seq.*; *Hymns of the Atharvaveda*, 500, thinks that Yama's two dogs are the sun and the moon (*cf.* **Divya Śvan**).

Cf. Zimmer, *Altindisches Leben*, 233; Hopkins, *American Journal of Philology*, 15, 154-163.

Śva-pad denotes a 'savage animal,' 'beast of prey,' in the Atharvaveda (viii. 5, 11; xix. 39, 4).

Śvayatha in the Śatapatha Brāhmaṇa[1] means 'swelling.' Possibly *śīyathu*, the disease prevalent in **Videha** according to the Baudhāyana Śrauta Sūtra,[2] was a kind of 'swelling' (? goitre).

[1] iv. 2, 1, 11 (of the eye, in a myth).

[2] ii. 5; Caland, *Über das rituelle Sūtra des Baudhāyana*, 35, 36.

Śva-varta, 'found in dogs,' is, according to some manuscripts, the name of a species of worm in the Atharvaveda (ix. 4, 16). See **Śavarta.**

Śvaśura from the Rigveda onwards[1] denotes the 'father-in-law' of the wife; not till the Sūtra period does it include the 'father-in-law' of the husband.[2] The daughter-in-law (**Snuṣā**), in the normal case when the father-in-law was the head of the family to which her husband belonged in fact as well as in age, was bound to pay him all respect.[3] When the old man had ceased to exercise control, she became mistress (*samrājñī*) over him and his wife.[4] In the plural[5] the word denotes the 'parents-in-law.'

[1] x. 28, 1; 85, 46; 95, 4; Av. viii. 6, 24; xiv. 2, 26, etc.

[2] Pāraskara Gṛhya Sūtra, iii. 10, 46.

[3] See Rv. x. 95, 4; Av. viii. 6, 24; Maitrāyaṇī Saṃhitā, ii. 4, 2; Kāṭhaka Saṃhitā, xii. 12 (*Indische Studien*, 5, 260); Aitareya Brāhmaṇa, iii. 22, 7. So in Av. xiv. 2, 26, the daughter-in-law is to be 'helpful' to the father-in-law.

[4] Rv. x. 85, 46. See **Pati.**

[5] Rv. x. 95, 12; Av. xiv. 2, 27; Kāṭhaka Saṃhitā, *loc. cit.* Or it may be a plural *majestatis*, but not a sign of polyandry.

Cf. Delbrück, *Die indogermanischen Verwandtschaftsnamen*, 515, 516.

Śvaśrū denotes 'mother-in-law' of the husband[1] as well as of the wife.[2] She, together with her husband, if he became unable to manage the family,[3] fell under the daughter-in-law's sway, but otherwise was entitled to regard.[4] The gambler in the Rigveda[5] complains of his having lost the favour of his wife's mother as one of the misfortunes brought upon him by dicing.

[1] Rv. x. 85, 46; Av. xiv. 2, 26.

[2] Rv. x. 34, 3.

[3] Rv. x. 85, 46.

[4] Av. xiv. 2, 26.

[5] Rv. x. 34, 3.

Cf. Delbrück, *Die indogermanischen Verwandtschaftsnamen*, 516.

Śvājani is the name of a Vaiśya in the Jaiminīya Upaniṣad Brāhmaṇa (iii. 5, 2).

Śvāpada, like **Śvapad,** denotes a 'savage animal' or 'beast of prey.' It is mentioned in the Rigveda,[1] in the Atharvaveda,[2] and occasionally later.[3]

[1] x. 16, 6.
[2] xi. 10, 8.
[3] Śatapatha Brāhmaṇa, v. 5, 4, 10 (where the tiger, **Śārdūla**, is mentioned as the chief of them); xii. 2, 4, 16; Bṛhadāraṇyaka Upaniṣad, i. 4, 29; Śāṅkhāyana Āraṇyaka, xii. 16, etc.

Śvā-vidh ('dog-piercing') is the name of the 'porcupine' in the Atharvaveda[1] and later.[2] It is called 'long-eared' (*karṇa*).[3] See also **Śalyaka.**

[1] v. 13, 9.
[2] Taittirīya Saṃhitā, v. 5, 20, 1; Maitrāyaṇī Saṃhitā, iii. 14, 14; Vājasaneyi Saṃhitā, xxiii. 56; xxiv. 33, etc.
[3] Av., *loc. cit.*
Cf. Zimmer, *Altindisches Leben*, 82.

Śvikna is the name of a people twice mentioned in the Śatapatha Brāhmaṇa[1] in connexion with their king, **Ṛṣabha Yājñatura.** *Cf.* **Śvaikna.**

[1] xii. 8, 3, 7; xiii. 5, 4, 15. *Cf.* Weber, *Indische Studien*, 1, 209, 210.

1. **Śvitra** ('white') is the name of a species of serpent in the Atharvaveda[1] and the later Saṃhitās.[2]

[1] iii. 27, 6 (where there is a variant *citra*); x. 4, 5. 13.
[2] Taittirīya Saṃhitā, v. 5, 10, 2; Maitrāyaṇī Saṃhitā, ii. 13, 21, has in the parallel passage *citra*, probably by error.
Cf. Zimmer, *Altindisches Leben*, 95; Whitney, Translation of the Atharvaveda, 134. Perhaps Śvitra, in the list of victims at the Aśvamedha ('horse sacrifice') in the Vājasaneyi Saṃhitā, xxiv. 39, has this sense; but the St. Petersburg Dictionary explains it as 'a certain domestic animal,' or, generally, 'a white animal.'

2. **Śvitra** is found as an adjective in the Pañcaviṃśa Brāhmaṇa (xii. 11, 11) in the sense of 'afflicted with white leprosy.'

Śvitrya. See **Śvaitreya.**

Śveta-ketu Āruṇeya[1] ('descendant of **Aruṇa**') or **Auddālaki**[2] ('son of **Uddālaka**') is mentioned repeatedly in the Śatapatha Brāhmaṇa and the Chāndogya Upaniṣad. In the Kauṣītaki Upaniṣad[3] he appears as Śvetaketu, son of **Āruṇi**, and as a **Gautama.** In the Kauṣītaki Brāhmaṇa[4] he is quoted as an authority on the vexed question of the duty of the **Sadasya,** or the seventeenth priest, at the ritual of the Kauṣītakins, to notify errors in the sacrifice; Āruṇi, his father, is also cited. He was a person of some originality, for he insisted on eating honey despite the general prohibition of the use of that delicacy by Brahmacārins or religious students.[5] He was a contemporary of, and was instructed by the **Pañcāla** king **Pravāhaṇa Jaivala.**[6] He was also a contemporary of **Janaka,** of **Videha**, and figured among the Brahmin disputants at his court.[7] A story is told of him in the Śāṅkhāyana Śrauta Sūtra:[8] **Jala Jātūkarṇya** was lucky enough to become the Purohita of three peoples or kings, of **Kāśi**, **Kosala**, and **Videha.** Seeing this, Śvetaketu felt annoyed and reproached his father with his excessive devotion to sacrifice, which merely enriched and glorified others, not himself. His father replied, forbidding him to speak thus: he had learned the true method of sacrificing, and his ambition in life had been to discuss it with every Brahmin.

All the references to Śvetaketu belong to the latest period of Vedic literature. It is, therefore, not surprising that the Āpastamba Dharma Sūtra[9] should refer to him as an Avara, or

[1] Śatapatha Brāhmaṇa, xi. 2, 7, 12; 5, 4, 18; 6, 2, 1; xii. 2, 1, 9; Bṛhadāraṇyaka Upaniṣad, iii. 7, 1; vi. 1, 1 (Mādhyaṃdina = vi. 2, 1 Kāṇva); Chāndogya Upaniṣad, v. 3, 1; vi. 1, 1; 8, 1.

[2] Śatapatha Brāhmaṇa, iii. 4, 3, 13; iv. 2, 5, 14.

[3] i. 1.

[4] xxvi. 4.

[5] Śatapatha Brāhmaṇa, xi. 5, 4, 18.

[6] Bṛhadāraṇyaka Upaniṣad, vi. 1, 1 (Mādhyaṃdina = vi. 2, 1 Kāṇva); Chāndogya Upaniṣad, v. 3, 1.

[7] Śatapatha Brāhmaṇa, xi. 6, 2, 1 (it is to be noted that he came upon Janaka when travelling about with some other Brahmins: he was never settled in the Videha country, but was clearly a **Kuru-Pañcāla**, like his father); Bṛhadāraṇyaka Upaniṣad, iii. 7, 1, where he shares the usual fate of defeat in argument by Yājñavalkya.

[8] xvi. 27, 6 *et seq*. The exact sense of *kṛtsnake brahmabandhau vyajijñāsiṣi* is not quite certain. But Āruṇi seems to assert the love of knowledge, not of material advantages accruing to the Purohita, to have been his concern in life.

[9] i. 2, 5, 4-6.

person of later days, who still became a Ṛṣi by special merit. His date, however, must not be fixed too low, because the Śatapatha Brāhmaṇa in which he plays so marked a part is certainly earlier than Pāṇini, and was apparently even in that grammarian's time believed to be an ancient work; hence 500 B.C. is probably rather too late than too early a period for Śvetaketu as a rough approximation to a date.[10]

[10] See on this, Bühler, *Sacred Books of the East*, 2, xxxvii *et seq.*; Eggeling, *Sacred Books of the East*, 12, xxxv *et seq.*; Max Müller, *Ancient Sanskrit Literature*, 360 *et seq.*; Weber, *Indische Studien*, 5, 65; 13, 443; Keith, *Aitareya Āraṇyaka*, 22 *et seq.*
Cf. Muir, *Sanskrit Texts*, 1[2], 433; Max Müller, *Ancient Sanskrit Literature*, 421 *et seq.*; Oldenberg, *Buddha*, 397, n.

Śvetyā appears in the Nadī-stuti[1] ('praise of rivers') to be a stream, probably a tributary of the Indus.[2]

[1] x. 75, 6.
[2] Zimmer, *Altindisches Leben*, 14, 15; udwig, Translation of the Rigveda, 3, 200, gives the form as Śvetī; Geldner, *Rigveda, Glossar*, 184, gives both forms.

Śvaikna, 'king of the **Śviknas**,' is the title of **Pratīdarśa**, who was, according to the Śatapatha Brāhmaṇa,[1] one of those who offered the Dākṣāyaṇa sacrifice. He also taught **Suplan Sārñjaya** the sacrifice: hence Weber[2] has inferred a connexion of the Śviknas and the **Sṛñjayas.**

[1] ii. 4, 4, 3.
[2] *Indische Studien*, 1, 209, 210.

Śvaitreya occurs in two passages of the Rigveda,[1] where Sāyaṇa sees in the word the name of a man, a 'descendant of Śvitrā.' The first passage is almost identical with one in the sixth Maṇḍala of the Rigveda,[2] where, however, **Daśadyu** appears alone without Śvaitreya. Ludwig[3] identifies Daśadyu with Śvaitreya ('son of Śvitrī'), and considers him a son of **Kutsa.**[4] Bergaigne[5] and Baunack[6] think he is really **Bhujyu.** Geldner[7] considers that he was a bull used for fighting, the son

[1] i. 33, 14; v. 19, 3.
[2] vi. 26, 4.
[3] Translation of the Rigveda, 3, 147.
[4] *Cf.* Rv. i. 51, 6; vi. 26, 3. 4.
[5] *Religion Védique*, 3, 11.
[6] Kuhn's *Zeitschrift*, 35, 527.
[7] *Rigveda, Glossar*, 7, 8.

of a Śvitrā cow,[8] but this is very doubtful, though the term *śvaitreya* is elsewhere applied to a bull.[9] Śvitrya[10] seems to have the same sense as Śvaitreya.

[8] *Cf. śvaitarī*, Rv. iv. 33, 1.
[9] Keith, *Journal of the Royal Asiatic Society*, 1910, 935.
[10] Rv. i. 33, 15, where Roth, St. Petersburg Dictionary, *s.v.*, takes *śvitryam* as the accusative of *śvitrī*.

Ṣ.

Ṣaṇḍa is the name of a priest at the snake festival described in the Pañcaviṃśa Brāhmaṇa.[1] *Cf.* **Kuṣaṇḍa.**

[1] xxv. 15, 3. *Cf.* Weber, *Indische Studien*, 1, 35.

Ṣaṇḍika is mentioned in the Maitrāyaṇī Saṃhitā[1] as a contemporary of **Keśin.** Probably **Khaṇḍika** should be read as usual elsewhere.

[1] i. 4, 12, where von Schroeder gives no variant. But *ṣ* and *kh* are constantly interchanged in manuscripts.

S.

Saṃ-rudh and **Saṃ-likhita** occur in the Atharvaveda (vii. 50, 5) as two technical terms, of unknown sense, used in dicing.

Saṃ-vatsara, 'year,' is repeatedly mentioned from the Rigveda onwards.[1]

Its duration was, according to the concurrent evidence of the Saṃhitās and Brāhmaṇas, 360 days, divided into 12 months, being, no doubt, roughly a lunar synodic year, which, however, it exceeded in length by 6 days.[2] As a solar year it appears only in the Nidāna Sūtra[3] of the Sāmaveda, where the sun is stated to spend $13\frac{1}{3}$ days in each of the 27 Nakṣatras.

[1] Rv. i. 110, 4; 140, 2; 161, 13; vii. 103, 1. 7, etc.; Av. i. 35, 4; ii. 6, 1; iii. 10, 2; iv. 35, 4; vi. 53, 3, etc.
[2] See **Māsa.**
[3] v. 12, 2. 5. *Cf.* Weber, *Naxatra*, 2, 284.

The year being obviously out of harmony with the solar year (whether sidereal or tropical), efforts were certainly made to effect an assimilation of the natural and the accepted year. As has been seen (see **Māsa**), the evidence goes strongly to show that the intercalation was not an easy matter in the Brāhmaṇa period, though there are traces of what may be regarded as a five-yearly or six-yearly intercalation. But there is no conclusive evidence that these periods were really observed.

*Z*immer,[4] indeed, considers that the evidence required is afforded by the lists of the years, which are sometimes enumerated as five: Saṃvatsara, Parivatsara, Idāvatsara, Idvatsara, and Vatsara;[5] or Saṃvatsara, Parivatsara, Idāvatsara, Iduvatsara, Vatsara;[6] or Saṃvatsara, Idāvatsara, Iduvatsara, Idvatsara, Vatsara;[7] or Saṃvatsara, Parivatsara, Idāvatsara, Anuvatsara, Udvatsara;[8] or Saṃvatsara, Parivatsara, Idāvatsara, Anuvatsara, Idvatsara.[9] But it must be noted not merely that the names vary considerably, but that four only are mentioned in some places,[10] in others[11] three, in others[12] two, and in yet others[13] six. Moreover, in none of these enumerations is there any reference to the names being connected with a system of intercalation. It is most probable that here we have no more that a mere series of priestly variations of Vatsara, based on the older and more genuine Saṃvatsara and Parivatsara as variants of the simple Vatsara, 'year.' The key to the invention of the series is probably to be found in passages like that of the Pañcaviṃśa Brāhmaṇa,[14] where the several **Cāturmāsya** ('four-monthly') sacrifices are equated

[4] *Altindisches Leben*, 369, 370, and *cf.* St. Petersburg Dictionary, *s.v. saṃvatsara*, 2.

[5] Vājasaneyi Saṃhitā, xxvii. 45.

[6] Taittirīya Saṃhitā, v. 5, 7, 3. 4.

[7] Taittirīya Brāhmaṇa, iii. 10, 4, 1.

[8] Kāṭhaka Saṃhitā, xiii. 15; xxxix. 6; xl. 6.

[9] Garga, quoted in the commentary on Jyotiṣa, 10.

[10] Saṃ-, Pari-, Idā-, Anu-vatsara, Pañcaviṃśa Brāhmaṇa, xvii. 13, 17; Taittirīya Brāhmaṇa, i. 4, 10, 1.

[11] Idā-, Pari-, Saṃ-vatsara, Av. vi. 55, 3; Idu-, Pari-, Saṃ-vatsara, Taittirīya Saṃhitā, v. 7, 2, 4.

[12] Saṃ-, Pari-vatsara, Av. viii. 8, 23; Taittirīya Āraṇyaka, x. 80.

[13] Saṃ-, Pari-, Idā-, Anu-, Vatsara, Saṃ-vatsara, Vājasaneyi Saṃhitā, xxx. 15; Saṃ-, Pari-, Idā-, Idu-, Id-, Vatsara, Taittirīya Āraṇyaka, iv. 19, 1. *Cf.* Weber, *Naxatra*, 2, 298, n. 1; Max Müller, *Rigveda*, 4[2], xxv., n. 1.

[14] xvii. 13, 17.

with the different years.[15] Particularly unjustifiable is the attempt of Zimmer to see in the two-year series a series of two years of 354 days each, with an intercalary month in the second; for the year of 354 days, as such, is not known to have existed before the Sūtra period.

Zimmer[16] also finds an attempt at intercalation in the famous 12 days in which the Ṛbhus are said to have slept in the house of Agohya.[17] He thinks that they represent twelve days added at the winter solstice to equate the lunar year of 354 days and the solar year of 366 days; and from the reverence paid in German antiquity to the '12 nights,' he infers that this mode of intercalation is Indo-Germanic.[18] There can be little doubt that this view is wrong, and that the 12 days are merely the 'reflexion of the year' (*saṃvatsarasya pratimā*)[19] in the sense that they represent the twelve months, and have no relation to chronology at all.

A reference to the use of Saṃvatsara alone as the fifth year of the cycle is seen by Shamasastry[20] in the peculiar dating of certain notices in the Baudhāyana Śrauta Sūtra,[21] but this view is improbable.[22]

[15] *Cf.* Weber, *Indische Streifen*, 1, 91; Thibaut, *Astronomie, Astrologie und Mathematik*, 12; Hopkins, *Journal of the American Oriental Society*, 24, 42.

[16] *Op. cit.*, 366, 367; Tilak, *Orion*, 16 *et seq.*; Hillebrandt, *Vedische Mythologie*, 3, 145.

[17] Rv. iv. 33, 7. *Cf.* i. 110, 2; 161, 13. See on this legend, Macdonell, *Vedic Mythology*, p. 133; Oldenberg, *Religion des Veda*, 236.

[18] See Weber, *Indische Studien*, 10, 242 *et seq.*; 17, 223, 224; 18, 45, 46; *Proceedings of the Berlin Academy*, 1894, 809; Thibaut, *op. cit.*, 10; Schrader, *Prehistoric Antiquities*, 308, 310; Whitney, *Journal of the American Oriental Society*, 16, xciv.

[19] Kāṭhaka Saṃhitā, vii. 15; Taittirīya Brāhmaṇa, i. 1, 9, 10; Kauṣītaki Brāhmaṇa, xxv. 15. See also Atharvaveda, iv. 11, 11; Weber, *Omina und Portenta*, 388.

[20] *Gavām Ayana*, 137, 138.

[21] ii. 12; iii. 1; xxvi. 18; xxx. 3. See also Kauṣītaki Brāhmaṇa, i. 3; Śatapatha Brāhmaṇa, xi. 1, 1, 7.

[22] Caland, *Über das rituelle Sūtra des Baudhāyana*, 36, 37, gives a much more reasonable explanation of the anomaly.

Saṃvaraṇa is the name of a Ṛṣi mentioned in one passage of the Rigveda.[1]

[1] v. 33, 10. *Cf.* Oldenberg, *Zeitschrift der Deutschen Morgenländischen Gesellschaft*, 42, 215.

Saṃvarga-jit Lāmakāyana is the name of a teacher, a pupil of **Śākadāsa** in the Vaṃśa Brāhmaṇa.[1]

[1] *Indische Studien*, 4, 373.

1. **Saṃ-varta** occurs once in the Rigveda[1] with **Kṛśa** as an ancient sacrificer. He may be identical with the next.

[1] viii. 54, 2. *Cf.* Ludwig, Translation of the Rigveda, 3, 141, 164.

2. **Saṃ-varta Āṅgirasa** ('descendant of **Aṅgiras**') is said in the Aitareya Brāhmaṇa[1] to have consecrated **Marutta.**

[1] viii. 21, 12. *Cf.* Leumann, *Zeitschrift der Deutschen Morgenländischen Gesellschaft*, 48, 67 *et seq.*

Saṃ-śravas Sauvarcanasa is the name of a teacher who, according to the Taittirīya Saṃhitā (i. 7, 2, 1), discussed a point of ritual with **Tumiñja.**

Saṃ-śrāvayitṛ in the Kauṣītaki Upaniṣad (ii. 1) denotes the attendant who announces visitors, the 'doorkeeper.'

Saṃ-śliṣṭakā[1] or **Saṃśviṣṭikā**[2] is the name of an animal mentioned in the Jaiminīya Brāhmaṇa and the Śāṭyāyanaka along with the **Godhā.**

[1] Śāṭyāyanaka in Sāyaṇa on Rv. viii. 91.

[2] Jaiminīya Brāhmaṇa, i. 221 (*Journal of the American Oriental Society*, 18, 29).

Saṃ-sarpa. See **Māsa.**

Saṃ-skandha ('having the shoulders together') is the name of a disease mentioned with **Viṣkandha** in the Atharvaveda.[1] Whitney,[2] however, thinks it is intended as an adjective implying the sense of 'counteracting the disease Viṣkandha.'

[1] xix. 34, 5, with Sāyaṇa's note.

[2] Translation of the Atharvaveda, 952.

Cf. Zimmer, *Altindisches Leben*, 65, 391; Bloomfield, *Hymns of the Atharvaveda*, 283.

Saṃ-hotra occurs once in the Rigveda,[1] where Geldner[2] thinks the sense of 'school,' referring to a school of pupils of the ritual, is most appropriate.

[1] x. 86, 10.

[2] *Vedische Studien*, 2, 38.

Saktu in the later Saṃhitās and the Brāhmanas[1] denotes 'coarsely ground meal,' 'groats,' especially 'barley meal.' In the Rigveda,[2] where the word occurs only once, it seems rather to mean grain before it is winnowed by the **Titaü**. If the latter word, however, designates a 'sieve,' Saktu might still mean 'groats,' as opposed to fine meal.

[1] Taittirīya Saṃhitā, vi. 4, 10, 6; Vājasaneyi Saṃhitā, xix. 21 *et seq.*; Śatapatha Brāhmaṇa, i. 6, 3, 16; ix. 1, 1, 8 (*cf.* **Gavedhukā**), etc.; Kāṭhaka Saṃhitā, xv. 2 (*cf.* **Apāmārga**). *Cf.* **Kuvala**, **Karkandhu**, **Badara**: Śatapatha Brāhmaṇa, v. 5, 4, 22, etc.

[2] x. 71, 2.

Cf. Zimmer, *Altindisches Leben*, 238.

Sakhi, 'friend,' is common from the Rigveda[1] onwards,[2] both literally and metaphorically.

[1] i. 164, 20 (of birds); iii. 43, 4 (of steeds); ii. 1, 9; v. 12, 5; vi. 75, 3, etc.

[2] Av. v. 4, 7; 11, 9; 13, 5, etc. So *sakhitva* and *sakhya*, 'friendship,' are also common—*e.g.*, Rv. i. 10, 6; iii. 1, 15; iv. 25, 2, etc., and Rv. 1. 178, 2; ii. 18, 8; vii. 22, 9, etc.

Saghan is the name of a bird, perhaps 'eagle' or 'vulture,' in the Taittirīya Saṃhitā[1] and the Taittirīya Brāhmaṇa.[2]

[1] iii. 2, 1, 1.

[2] ii. 8, 6. 1; Böhtlingk, Dictionary, *s.v.* ('vulture'). *Cf.* Zimmer, *Altindisches Leben*, 88.

Saṅga Prayogi seems to be mentioned as a teacher in the Maitrāyaṇī Saṃhitā (iii. 1, 9).

Saṃ-gati in one passage of the Rigveda (x. 141, 4) seems to have the sense of **Samiti**, 'assembly of the people.'

Saṃ-gava denotes the time when the grazing cows are driven together for milking. In the division of the day the word denotes the period before midday, 'forenoon.' It is found in the Rigveda[1] and often later.[2] *Cf.* **Go** and **Ahan**.

[1] v. 76, 3.

[2] Av. ix. 6, 46; Maitrāyaṇī Saṃhitā, iv. 2, 11; Taittirīya Brāhmaṇa, i. 4, 9, 2; 5, 3, 1; ii. 1, 1, 3; Śatapatha Brāhmaṇa, ii. 2, 3, 9; Chāndogya Upaniṣad, ii. 9, 4; Jaiminīya Upaniṣad Brāhmaṇa, i. 12, 4.

Cf. St. Petersburg Dictionary, *s.v.*; Geldner, *Vedische Studien*, 3, 112 *et seq.*

Saṃ-gavinī is found in the Aitareya Brāhmaṇa,[1] where it is said that the animals of the **Bharatas** in the evening were at the **Goṣṭha**, 'pasture,' but at midday came to the Saṃgavinī, apparently a shed or an enclosure in which during the heat of the day they were milked.

[1] iii. 18, 14. *Cf.* Geldner, *Vedische Studien*, 3, 112, 113; Zimmer, *Altindisches Leben*, 362.

Saṃ-grahītṛ is found in the later Saṃhitās[1] and the Brāhmaṇas.[2] He is an official who figures among the **Ratnins** of the king. The sense of 'charioteer' seems adequate for every passage, but Sāyaṇa[3] in some passages inclines to think that the meaning is 'treasurer' of the king.

[1] Taittirīya Saṃhitā, i. 8, 9, 2; Kāṭhaka Saṃhitā, xv. 4; Maitrāyaṇī Saṃhitā, ii. 6, 5; iv. 3, 8 (as a Ratnin); in the Śatarudriya in the plural: Taittirīya Saṃhitā, iv. 5, 4, 2; Kāṭhaka Saṃhitā, xvii. 13; Maitrāyaṇī Saṃhitā, ii. 9, 4; Vājasaneyi Saṃhitā, xvi. 26.

[2] Taittirīya Brāhmaṇa, i. 7, 3, 5; 9, 6; iii. 8, 5, 3; Aitareya Brāhmaṇa, ii. 25, 6; Śatapatha Brāhmaṇa, v. 3, 1, 8; 4, 3, 23.

[3] On Taittirīya Saṃhitā, i. 8, 9, 2, and optionally on i. 8, 16; but as 'charioteer' on i. 8, 15; Taittirīya Brāhmaṇa, i. 7, 10, 6.

Cf. Eggeling, *Sacred Books of the East*, 41, 63, n. 1.

Saṃ-grāma denotes primarily, it seems, 'assembly' either in peace[1] or in war,[2] when it means an 'armed band.' Its normal sense in the Atharvaveda[3] and later[4] is 'war,' 'battle.'

[1] Av. xii. 1, 56, where it is joined with **Samiti**. We might see in this passage, and that cited in n. 2, the technical name of the village assembly as opposed to the larger assemblies of the people, but there is no good warrant for so doing.

[2] Av. iv. 24, 7, where *saṃgrāmān* is read; but the parallel passages (Taittirīya Saṃhitā, iv. 7, 15, 2; Maitrāyaṇī Saṃhitā, iii. 16, 5) have *saṃgrāmam*.

[3] v. 21, 7; xi. 9, 26.

[4] Taittirīya Saṃhitā, ii. 1, 3, 1; 8, 4, etc.

Little is known of Vedic warfare, but it seems to have been simple. A body of foot soldiers with charioteers composed every army, the two going together,[5] and the foot soldiers being often overthrown by the charioteers,[6] who were doubtless the Kṣatriyas and their foremost retainers. Probably the foot soldiers bore little armour, and used only the bow for offence, as is suggested by the account that Herodotus gives of the Indian contingent of the army with which Xerxes invaded Greece.[7] The nobles, on the other hand, may have had cuirass (**Varman**), helmet (**Śiprā**), and hand-guard (**Hastaghna**) as a protection from the friction of the bowstring. On the car was the charioteer, and on his left the warrior (**Sārathi, Savyaṣṭhā**). Riding is never mentioned in war,[8] and would hardly have been suited to Vedic ideas, for the warrior mainly depended on his bow, which he could not have used effectively from horseback. The offensive weapon (**Āyudha**) was practically the bow; spear and sword and axe were very seldom used.

Whether there was a strict tribal organization of the host, such as is once alluded to in the Homeric poems,[9] and is also recognized in Germany by Tacitus,[10] is uncertain (*cf.* **Vrāta**), but in the Epic relations (**Jñāti**) fight together,[11] and this rule, no doubt, applied more or less in Vedic times also.

Cities were besieged and invested (*upa-sad, pra-bhid*),[12] probably as a rule by blockade, since the ineffective means of assault of the time would have rendered storming difficult and expensive. Hillebrandt[13] thinks that the *pur cariṣṇū* of the Rigveda[14] was a kind of chariot; it may—like the Trojan horse—have been an Indian anticipation of the Roman means of assaulting a town.

Besides ordinary wars of defence and conquest, raids into

[5] Rv. ii. 12, 8.

[6] Av. vii. 62, 1. *Cf.* **Muṣṭihan**.

[7] Herodotus, vii. 65.

[8] Zimmer, *Altindisches Leben*, 296, where he admits riding to be mentioned elsewhere; Whitney, *Journal of the American Oriental Society*, 3, 312.

[9] *Iliad*, ii. 362.

[10] *Germania*, 7.

[11] Hopkins, *Journal of the American Oriental Society*, 13, 193.

[12] *Cf.* Taittirīya Saṃhitā, vi. 2, 3, 1; Śatapatha Brāhmaṇa, iii. 4, 4, 3-5; Aitareya Brāhmaṇa, i. 23, 2, etc.; Gopatha Brāhmaṇa, ii. 2, 7; Hillebrandt, *Vedische Mythologie*, 1, 300, n.

[13] *Op. cit.* 3, 289, n.

[14] viii. 1, 2-8, where it is attributed to the demon Śuṣṇa.

neighbouring territory seem to have been frequent and normal,[15] no doubt because of the booty (**Udāja, Nirāja**) which was to be won, and which the king had to share with the people.

Banners (**Dhvaja**) were borne in war, and musical instruments (**Dundubhi, Bakura**)[16] were used by the combatants.

[15] *Cf.* Rv. x. 142, 4, as interpreted by Sāyaṇa and by Hillebrandt, *op. cit.*, 2, 64, n. 5; Taittirīya Brāhmaṇa, i. 8, 4, 1 (of the model Kuru kings).

[16] So, later, Arrian, *Indica*, vii. 9. The shouts of either side are shown in the word *krandas* (Rv. ii. 12, 8; *cf.* vi. 25, 6; x. 121, 6), which came to mean the 'shouting host.' *Cf.* also Tacitus, *Germania*, 2. *Cf.* Muir, *Sanskrit Texts*, 5, 469-472; Weber, Proceedings of the Berlin Academy, 1898, 564; Zimmer, *Altindisches Leben*, 293-301. See also **Iṣu, Dhanvan, Ratha**. Hopkins, *Journal of the American Oriental Society*, 13, 281 *et seq.*, gives a full account of the later Epic armour and warfare. See also his note, *ibid.*, 15, 265, 266. For sacrifice in battle, *cf.* **Purohita.**

Saṃ-ghāta seems in a few passages[1] to have the sense of 'battle.'

[1] Kāṭhaka Saṃhitā, xxix. 1; Vājasaneyi Saṃhitā, i. 16; Śatapatha Brāhmaṇa, i. 1, 4, 18.

Saciva 'companion,' 'attendant' (from *sac*, 'follow'), later a common word for the comrade of a king, his minister, is found in Vedic literature in the Aitareya Brāhmaṇa (iii. 20, 1), where it is used by Indra of the Maruts. It seems to correspond in sense to the German *comes* or the English *gesith*.[1]

[1] Stubbs, *Select Charters*, 57.

Sa-jāta ('born together') is found once in the Rigveda,[1] and very often later.[2] The word must clearly mean a 'relative,' and then more widely a man of the same position or rank, but the senses cannot be distinguished, so much do they merge into each other. The Sajātas of a king are of course princes;[3] of an

[1] i. 109, 1.

[2] Av. i. 9, 3; 19, 3; ii. 6, 4; iii. 3, 6; vi. 5, 2; 73, 1; xi. 1, 6. 7; Taittirīya Saṃhitā, ii. 1, 3, 2; 2, 1, 2; 6, 9, 7; Maitrāyaṇī Saṃhitā, ii. 1, 8; Kāṭhaka Saṃhitā, xi. 12. 13; xii. 1; Vājasaneyi Saṃhitā, v. 23; x. 29; xxvii. 5, and often in the Brāhmaṇas.

[3] Av. iii. 3, 4. 6; Weber, *Indische Studien*, 17, 188.

ordinary man, Vaiśyas;[4] of a military man, Kṣatriyas. But there is no clear reference to caste as in the later Sajāti[5] ('man of the same caste'). The disputes of Sajātas were notorious.[6]

[4] Śatapatha Brāhmaṇa, v. 4, 4, 19 (the Sajātas of a **Grāmaṇī**).

[5] Manu, ix. 87; x. 41, etc. The abstract *sajātya* ('kinship') is found in Rv. ii. 1, 5; iii. 54, 16; viii. 18, 19; 20, 21; 27, 10; x. 64, 13; but even it has no definite caste reference.

[6] *Cf.* Taittirīya Brāhmaṇa, iii. 7, 12, 2.

Saṃ-cara in the Taittirīya Saṃhitā[1] has the sense of the 'path' of animals. Normally it is the term designating the 'passage' or 'space' on the sacrificial ground used or occupied by the several persons taking part in the rite.[2]

[1] v. 4, 3, 5.

[2] Śatapatha Brāhmaṇa, i. 9, 2, 4; iii. 1, 3, 28; Lāṭyāyana Śrauta Sūtra, iii. 7, 11; Kātyāyana Śrauta Sūtra, i. 3, 42, etc.

Saṃ-jñāna, 'concord,' 'harmony,' is mentioned from the Rigveda[1] onwards[2] as a matter of great consequence; the Atharvaveda contains many spells to bring it about. The lack of peace in the Vedic village was almost inevitable in view of its small size ana the economic interdependence of its inhabitants. *Cf.* **Bhrātṛvya.**

[1] x. 19, 6.

[2] Av. iii. 30, 4; vii. 52, 1; xi. 1, 26, etc.; Taittirīya Saṃhitā, v. 2, 3, 2; 3, 1, 14; Vājasaneyi Saṃhitā, xxvi. 1; xxx. 9; Nirukta, iv. 21, etc.

Sata is the name of a vessel of some kind mentioned in the ritual.[1]

[1] Vājasaneyi Saṃhitā, xix. 27. 88; Śatapatha Brāhmaṇa, xii. 7, 2, 13; 8, 3, 14.

Satīna-kaṅkata[1] is, in the Rigveda,[2] the name of some animal, according to Sāyaṇa an 'aquatic snake.'[3]

[1] The literal meaning seems to be 'having a real comb.'

[2] i. 191, 1.

[3] *Cf.* Zimmer, *Altindisches Leben*, 98.

Satya-kāma ('lover of truth') **Jābāla** ('descendant of **Jabālā**') is the name of a teacher, the son of a slave girl by an unknown father. He was initiated as a **Brahmacārin**, or religious student, by **Gautama Hāridrumata** according to the Chāndogya Upaniṣad.[1] He is often cited as an authority in that Upaniṣad[2] and in the Bṛhadāraṇyaka Upaniṣad,[3] where he learns a certain doctrine from **Jānaki Āyasthūṇa.**[4] He is also mentioned in the Aitareya[5] and the Śatapatha Brāhmaṇas.[6]

[1] iv. 4, 1 *et seq.*
[2] iv. 5, 1; 6, 2; 7, 2; 8, 2; 9, 10; 10, 1; v. 2, 3.
[3] iv. 1, 14 (Mādhyaṃdina = iv. 1, 6 Kāṇva).
[4] vi. 3, 19 (=vi. 3, 12).
[5] viii. 7, 8.
[6] xiii. 5, 3, 1.

Satya-yajña ('true sacrificer') **Pauluṣi** ('descendant of **Puluṣa**') **Prācīnayogya** ('descendant of Prācīnayoga') is the name of a teacher in the Śatapatha Brāhmaṇa,[1] the Chāndogya Upaniṣad,[2] and the Jaiminīya Upaniṣad Brāhmaṇa.[3] In the latter text he is said to have been the pupil of **Puluṣa Prācīnayogya.**

[1] x. 6, 1, 1.
[2] v. 11, 1.
[3] iii. 40, 2 (in a Vaṃśa, 'list of teachers').

Satya-vacas ('true-speaking') **Rāthītara** ('descendant of **Rathītara**') is, in the Taittirīya Upaniṣad (i. 9, 1), the name of a teacher who insisted on the importance of truth.

Satya-śravas ('of true renown') **Vāyya** ('descendant of Vayya') is the name of a Ṛṣi in the Rigveda.[1] Ludwig[2] thinks that he was the son of **Sunītha Śaucadratha.**

[1] v. 79, 1 *et seq.*
[2] Translation of the Rigveda, 3, 156.

Satya-havis is the name of a mythical Adhvaryu, or sacrificial priest, in the Maitrāyaṇī Saṃhitā (i. 9, 1, 5).

Satyādhivāka Caitrarathi ('descendant of **Citraratha**') is the name of a man in the Jaiminīya Upaniṣad Brāhmaṇa (i. 39, 1).

Satvan in the Rigveda,[1] and occasionally later,[2] has the sense of 'warrior.'

[1] i. 133, 6; 173, 5; ii. 25, 4; 30, 10; iii. 49, 2, etc.

[2] v. 20, 8; vi. 65, 3; Vājasaneyi Saṃhitā, xvi. 8. 20, etc.

Satvant is the name of a people who are stated in the Aitareya Brāhmaṇa[1] to belong to the south. In the Śatapatha Brāhmaṇa[2] the defeat by **Bharata** of the Satvants, and his taking away the horse which they had prepared for an Aśvamedha ('horse sacrifice'), are referred to: this reference clearly shows that in another passage of the Aitareya Brāhmaṇa[3] the text must be altered from *satvanām* to *Satvatām*, 'of the Satvants,' against whom it seems the Bharatas made regular raids. The name has also been found by the St. Petersburg Dictionary, Cowell, and Max Müller in the Kauṣītaki Upaniṣad,[4] but it is certain[5] that the reading there is not *Satvan-Matsyeṣu*, but *sa-Vaśa-Matsyeṣu*.

[1] viii. 14, 3.

[2] xiii. 5, 4, 21.

[3] ii. 25, 6.

[4] iv. 1.

[5] Oldenberg, *Buddha*, 393, n., correcting Max Müller, *Sacred Books of the East*, 1, lxxvii.

Cf. Weber, *Indische Studien*, 1. 211. 212, 419; 9, 254; Keith, *Journal of the Royal Asiatic Society*, 1908, 367.

Sadana. See **Gṛha.**

Sadaṃdi. See **Takman.**

Sadas. See **Gṛha.**

Sadasya. See **Ṛtvij.**

Sadā-nīrā, 'having water always' ('perennial'), is the name of a stream which, according to the Śatapatha Brāhmaṇa,[1] was the boundary between the **Kosalas** and the **Videhas**. The river is identified by the native lexicographers with the Karatoyā,[2] but this seems to be too far east. Weber's[3] identification

[1] i. 4, 1, 14 *et seq.*

[2] See *Imperial Gazetteer of India*, 15, 24.

[3] *Indische Studien*, 1, 172, 181.

of it with the Gaṇḍakī[4] is probably correct; for though the Mahābhārata[5] distinguishes the two rivers, there is nothing to show that this is due to any good tradition.

[4] See *s.v.* Great Gandak, *Imperial Gazetteer of India*, 12, 125.

[5] ii. 794. *Cf.* Oldenberg, *Buddha*, 398, n.

Sadā-pṛṇa is the name of a Ṛṣi in the Rigveda.[1]

[1] v. 44, 12. *Cf.* Ludwig, Translation of the Rigveda, 3, 139.

Sadyan in the Taittirīya Brāhmaṇa (ii. 8, 6, 1) is a misreading of **Saghan.**

Sadhri is the name of a Ṛṣi in the Rigveda.[1]

[1] v. 44, 10. *Cf.* Ludwig, Translation of the Rigveda, 3, 138.

Sanaka occurs as the name of one of the two **Kāpyas** (the other being **Navaka**) who took part in the sacrifice of the **Vibhindukīyas**, which is mentioned in the Jaiminīya Brāhmaṇa.[1] Ludwig[2] thinks that the Sanakas are referred to as non-sacrificers in one passage of the Rigveda,[3] but this is very doubtful.[4]

[1] iii. 233 (*Journal of the American Oriental Society*, 18, 38).

[2] Translation of the Rigveda, 3, 147.

[3] i. 33, 4.

[4] Geldner, *Rigveda*, *Glossar*, 189.

Sànaga. See **Sanātana.**

Sanat-kumāra is the name of a mythical sage in the Chāndogya Upaniṣad (vii. 1, 1; 26, 2).

Sana-śruta ('famed of old') **Ariṃdama** ('tamer of foes') is mentioned as a Mahārāja in the Aitareya Brāhmaṇa (vii. 34, 9).

Sanāc-chava is perhaps the proper name of a teacher in the Kāṭhaka Saṃhitā.[1] The Kapiṣṭhala Saṃhitā[2] has *Śahanāśchiva*. Very probably the reading of both texts is bad.

[1] xx. 1.

[2] xxxi. 3 (von Schroeder, Kāṭhaka Saṃhitā, 2, 18, n. 5).

Sanātana is the name of a mythical Ṛṣi in the Taittirīya Saṃhitā.[1] In the Bṛhadāraṇyaka Upaniṣad[2] he appears in the first two Vaṃśas (lists of teachers) as the pupil of **Sanaga** and the teacher of **Sanāru**, both equally mythical persons.

[1] iv. 3, 3 1.
[2] ii. 5, 22; iv. 5, 28 (Mādhyaṃdina = ii. 6, 3; iv. 6, 3 Kāṇva).

Sanāru. See **Sanātana.**

Sanisrasa. See **Māsa.**

Saṃ-daṃśa. See **Gṛha.**

Saṃ-dāna in the Rigveda[1] and later[2] denotes a 'bond,' 'halter,' or 'fetter.'

[1] i. 162, 8. 16.
[2] Av. vi. 103, 1; 104, 1; xi. 9, 3; Taittirīya Saṃhitā, ii. 4, 7, 2; Śatapatha Brāhmaṇa, xiv. 3, 1, 22, etc.

Saṃ-dhā denotes in the later Saṃhitās and the Brāhmaṇas[1] an 'agreement' or 'compact.'

[1] Av. xi. 10, 9, 15; Taittirīya Saṃhitā, i. 7, 8, 4; Taittirīya Brāhmaṇa, i. 7, 1, 6; ii. 1, 1, 3; Kauṣītaki Upaniṣad, iii. 1.

Saṃ-dhi denotes the 'juncture' of heaven and earth, the 'horizon,' in the Śatapatha Brāhmaṇa.[1] It also has the sense of 'twilight'[2] as the juncture of light and dark.

[1] iii. 2, 1, 5; x. 5, 4, 2.
[2] Vājasaneyi Saṃhitā, xxiv. 25; Taittirīya Brāhmaṇa, i. 4, 5, 1; ii. 2, 9, 8; dual: Śatapatha Brāhmaṇa, i. 6, 3, 55; ix. 4, 4, 13, etc. The later term is Saṃdhyā.

Saṃ-nahana in the later Saṃhitās and the Brāhmaṇas[1] denotes a 'band' or 'rope.'

[1] Taittirīya Saṃhitā, i. 1, 2, 2; Śatapatha Brāhmaṇa, i. 3, 3, 6; ii. 6, 1, 15, etc.

Sa-patna, 'rival,' is a common word in the later Saṃhitās,[1] being also found in the tenth Maṇḍala of the Rigveda.[2] It is a curious masculine formed by analogy from **Sa-patnī,** 'co-wife,' and so 'female rival.'

[1] Av. i. 19, 4; x. 6, 30; xii. 2, 46; Taittirīya Saṃhitā, i. 6, 2, 2; iii. 2, 8, 5, etc.

[2] x. 166, 1, etc.; also in the compound *sapatna-han*, 'slaying rivals,' x. 159, 5, etc.; Av. i. 29, 5, etc.

Sa-patnī occurs in the Rigveda in the sense of 'co-wife';[1] in the first and the last Maṇḍalas it means co-wife as a 'rival.'[2] In post-Vedic Sanskrit the word becomes a synonym for 'rival.'

[1] iii. 1, 10; 6, 4.

[2] i. 105, 8; x. 145, 1-5 (*cf.* in verse 2, *patim me kevalam kuru*, 'make my husband exclusively mine').

Sapta-gu is the reputed author of a Rigvedic hymn in a verse of which he is mentioned.[1]

[1] x. 47, 6. *Cf.* Bloomfield, *American Journal of Philology*, 17, 423.

Sapta Sindhavaḥ, 'the seven rivers,' occur only once in the Rigveda as the designation of a definite country,[1] while elsewhere[2] the seven rivers themselves are meant. Max Müller[3] thinks that the five streams of the Panjab, with the Indus and the **Sarasvatī,** are intended; others[4] hold that the **Kubhā** should be substituted for the Sarasvatī, or that perhaps the Oxus[5] must originally have been one of the seven. Zimmer[6] is probably right in laying no stress at all on any identifications; 'seven' being one of the favourite numbers in the Rigveda and later.

[1] viii. 24, 27.

[2] Rv. i. 32, 12; 34, 8; 35, 8; 71, 7; 102, 2; iv. 28, 1; viii. 96, 1, etc.; Vājasaneyi Saṃhitā, xxxviii. 26; Atharvaveda, iv. 6, 2; Taittirīya Saṃhitā, iv. 3, 6, 1, etc.

[3] *Chips*, 1, 63. *Cf.* Muir, *Sanskrit Texts*, 1², 490, n.

[4] Ludwig, Translation of the Rigveda, 3, 200; Lassen, *Indische Alterthumskunde*, 1², 3; Whitney, *Journal of the American Oriental Society*, 3, 311.

[5] *Cf.* Thomas, *Journal of the Royal Asiatic Society*, 1883, 371 *et seq.*

[6] *Altindisches Leben*, 21.

Cf. Hopkins, *Journal of the American Oriental Society*, 16, 278; *India, Old and New*, 33.

Sapta Sūryāḥ, the 'seven suns' referred to in the Saṃhitās,[1] are named in the Taittirīya Āraṇyaka[2] as Āroga, Bhrāja, Paṭara, Pataṅga, Svarṇara, Jyotiṣīmant, and Vibhāsa, but these occur very rarely even later.[3] Weber at one time[4] thought that the seven planets (see **Graha**) were meant by the phrase, but later he abandoned the idea.[5] Probably the 'seven rays' of the Rigveda[6] are meant.

[1] Av. xiii. 3, 10; Kāṭhaka Saṃhitā, xxxvii. 9.

[2] i. 7. *Cf.* the 'seven tongues' of Agni which are mentioned in the Rigveda, and each of which later receives an individual name: Macdonell, *Vedic Mythology*, p. 89.

[3] Keith, *Aitareya Āraṇyaka*, 266; Hopkins, *Great Epic of India*, 475.

[4] *Indische Studien*, 1, 170; 2, 238.

[5] *Ibid.*, 10, 271, n., where he compares the *sapta diśo nānā-sūryāḥ*, 'seven regions with various suns,' of Rv. ix. 114, 3.

[6] Rv. i. 105, 9; viii. 72, 16; Hopkins, *Journal of the American Oriental Society*, 16, 277.

Sapta-mānuṣa is found in one passage of the Rigveda[1] as an epithet of Agni, 'belonging to the seven tribes.' Hopkins[2] thinks that this is a reference to the seven 'family' books of the Rigveda (ii.-viii.), but this seems less likely than the view of Roth,[3] that *saptamānuṣa* is equivalent to *vaiśvānara*.

[1] viii. 39, 8.

[2] *Journal of the American Oriental Society*, 16, 278.

[3] St. Petersburg Dictionary, *s.v.*

Sapta-vadhri is the name of a protégé of the Aśvins, who appear from several passages of the Rigveda[1] to have rescued him from a tree in which he had got fastened. He is mentioned in the Atharvaveda.[2] According to Geldner,[3] he is identical with **Atri**.

[1] v. 78, 5; viii. 73, 9; x. 39, 9.

[2] iv. 29, 4.

[3] *Rigveda, Glossar*, 190. *Cf.* Ludwig, Translation of the Rigveda, 3, 156; Baunack, *Zeitschrift der Deutschen Morgenländischen Gesellschaft*, 50, 268.

Sapti in the Rigveda[1] and later[2] denotes a 'swift steed.'

[1] i. 85, 1. 6; 162, 1; ii. 34, 7; iii. 22, 1, etc.

[2] Vājasaneyi Saṃhitā, xxii. 19. 22.

Saptya in one passage of the Rigveda (viii. 41, 4) seems to denote a 'racecourse.'

Sa-bandhu ('of the same kin') in the Rigveda[1] and later[2] denotes 'related.'

[1] iii. 1, 10; v. 47, 5; viii. 20, 21, etc.

[2] Av. vi. 15, 2; viii. 2, 26; xv. 8, 2. 3, etc.

Sabhā is the name of an 'assembly' of the Vedic Indians as well as of the 'hall' where they met in assembly. It is often mentioned in the Rigveda[1] and later,[2] but its exact character is not certain. The hall was clearly used for dicing,[3] presumably when the assembly was not transacting public business: a dicer is called *sabhā-sthāṇu*, 'pillar of the assembly hall,' doubtless because of his constant presence there.[4] The hall also served, like the Homeric λέσχη, as a meeting-place for social intercourse and general conversation about cows and so forth,[5] possibly for debates and verbal contests.[6]

According to Ludwig,[7] the Sabhā was an assembly not of all the people, but of the Brahmins and **Maghavans** ('rich patrons'). This view can be supported by the expressions

[1] vi. 28, 6; viii. 4, 9; x. 34, 6. *Cf.* *sabhā-saha*, 'eminent in the assembly,' x. 71, 10.

[2] Av. v. 31, 6; vii. 12, 1. 2; viii. 10, 5; xii. 1, 56; xix. 55, 6; Taittirīya Saṃhitā, i. 7, 6, 7; Maitrāyaṇī Saṃhitā, iv. 7, 4; Vājasaneyi Saṃhitā, iii. 45; xvi. 24; xx. 17; Taittirīya Brāhmaṇa, i. 1, 10, 6; Śatapatha Brāhmaṇa, ii. 3, 2, 3; v. 3, 1, 10; Kauṣītaki Brāhmaṇa, vii. 9, etc.

[3] Rv. x. 34, 6; Av. v. 31, 6; xii. 3, 46 (here *dyūta* is used in place of Sabhā).

[4] Vājasaneyi Saṃhitā, xxx. 18; Taittirīya Brāhmaṇa, iii. 4, 16, 1, with Sāyaṇa's note. Zimmer, *Altindisches Leben*, 172, inclines to see in the formula (Vājasaneyi Saṃhitā, iii. 45; xx. 17; Taittirīya Saṃhitā, i. 8, 3, 1; Kāṭhaka Saṃhitā, ix. 4; Maitrāyaṇī Saṃhitā, i. 10, 2) 'what sin we have committed in the village, the jungle, the Sabhā' a reference to attacks on the great (Mahīdhara on Vājasaneyi Saṃhitā, iii. 45), or partiality in deciding disputes (Mahīdhara, *ibid.*, xx. 17). But it may refer to gambling or other non-political activity, as Eggeling, *Sacred Books of the East*, 12, 398, takes it, though he renders it differently, *ibid.*, 44, 265.

[5] Rv. vi. 28, 6. *Cf.* viii. 4, 9. So in Av. vii. 12, 2, the assembly is hailed as *nariṣṭā*, 'merriment.' But the same hymn (vii. 12, 3) contains a clear reference to serious speech in the Sabhā. For the blending of serious political work and amusement, *cf.* Tacitus, *Germania*, 22.

[6] So Zimmer, *op. cit.*, 174, takes *sabheya* in Rv. ii. 24, 13.

[7] Translation of the Rigveda, 3, 253-256. He quotes for this view Rv. viii. 4, 9; x. 71, 10 (passages which are quite vague). *Cf.* also Rv. vii. 1, 4; Av. xix. 57, 2.

sabheya, 'worthy of the assembly,' applied to a Brahmin,[8] *rayiḥ sabhāvān*, 'wealth fitting for the assembly,'[9] and so on. But Bloomfield[10] plausibly sees in these passages a domestic use of Sabhā, which is recognized by the St. Petersburg Dictionary in several passages[11] as relating to a house, not to the assembly at all. Zimmer[12] is satisfied that the Sabhā was the meeting-place of the village council, presided over by the **Grāmaṇī.** But of this there is no trace whatever. Hillebrandt[13] seems right in maintaining that the Sabhā and the **Samiti** cannot be distinguished, and that the reference to well-born (*su-jāta*)[14] men being there in session is to the Āryan as opposed to the Dāsa or Śūdra, not to one class of Āryan as opposed to the other. Hillebrandt also sees in Agni 'of the hall' (*sabhya*) a trace of the fire used in sacrifice on behalf of the assembly when it met.[15]

Women did not go to the Sabhā,[16] for they were, of course, excluded from political activity. For the Sabhā as a court-house, *cf.* **Grāmyavādin.** There is not a single notice of the work done by the Sabhā.

[8] Rv. ii. 24, 13. *Cf.* i. 91, 20; Av. xx. 128, 1; Vājasaneyi Saṃhitā, xxii. 22, etc. Max Müller, *Sacred Books of the East*, 32, 276, sees in *sabheya* the implication of 'courtly manners,' but this is rather doubtful; manner is not conspicuous in Vedic society as in Homeric.

[9] Rv. iv. 2, 5; in i. 167, 3, *sabhāvatī* is applied to 'speech,' or perhaps to *yoṣā*, 'woman.'

[10] *Journal of the American Oriental Society*, 19, 13.

[11] Av. viii. 10, 5 (where the sense is, however, clearly 'assembly'; see viii. 10, 6); Taittirīya Saṃhitā, iii. 4, 8, 6; Taittirīya Brāhmaṇa, i. 1, 10, 3; Chāndogya Upaniṣad, viii. 14 (but here the sense is certainly 'assembly hall'; see v. 3, 6, where the king is described as going to the assembly hall: *sabhā-ga*) The exact sense given by the St. Petersburg Dictionary is the 'society room' in a dwelling-house.

[12] *Altindisches Leben*, 174. But he ignores Śatapatha Brāhmaṇa, iii. 3, 4, 14; Chāndogya Upaniṣad, v. 3, 6, which show that the king went to the Sabhā just as much as to the Samiti, and he cannot adduce any passage to show that the Grāmaṇī presided.

[13] *Vedische Mythologie*, 2, 123-125.

[14] Rv. vii. 1, 4.

[15] Agni is *sabhya*, Av. viii. 10, 5; xix. 55, 6. For the Rv., see iii. 23, 4; v. 3, 11; vii. 7, 5.

[16] Maitrāyaṇī Saṃhitā, iv. 7, 4.

Cf. Zimmer, *Altindisches Leben*, 172-174.

Sabhā-cara is one of the victims at the **Puruṣamedha** ('human sacrifice') in the Yajurveda.[1] The St. Petersburg

[1] Vājasaneyi Saṃhitā, xxx. 6; Taittirīya Brāhmaṇa, iii. 4, 2, 1, with Sāyaṇa's note. *Cf.* Weber, *Indische Streifen*, 1, 77, n. 1.

Dictionary thinks it is an adjective equivalent in sense to *sabhā-ga*,' 'going to the assembly.' As he is dedicated to Dharma, 'Justice,' it is difficult not to see in him a member of the Sabhā as a law court, perhaps as one of those who sit to decide cases: there is nothing to show whether the whole assembly did so, or only a chosen body. The special use of Sabhācara suggests the latter alternative. See also **Sabhāsad.**

Sabhā-pati, 'lord of the assembly,' is an epithet in the Śatarudriya.[1]

[1] Vājasaneyi Saṃhitā, xvi. 24; Taittirīya Saṃhitā, iv. 5, 3, 2; Kāṭhaka Saṃhitā, xvii. 13, etc.

Sabhā-pāla is found in the Taittirīya Brāhmaṇa (iii. 7, 4, 6), where the sense may be 'guardian of an assembly hall.'

Sabhāvin in the Taittirīya Brāhmaṇa (iii. 4, 16, 1) denotes, according to the commentator Sāyaṇa, the 'keeper of a gambling hall.'

Sabhā-sad, 'sitter in the assembly,' is probably a technical description of the assessors who decided legal cases in the assembly (*cf.* **Sabhācara**). The term, which is found in the Atharvaveda[1] and later,[2] cannot well merely denote any member of the assembly. It is also possible that the Sabhāsads, perhaps the heads of families, were expected to be present at the Sabhā oftener than the ordinary man: the meetings of the assembly for justice may have been more frequent than for general discussion and decision.

[1] iii. 29, 1 (of Yama); vii. 12, 2; xix. 55, 6.

[2] Kāṭhaka Saṃhitā, viii. 7; Maitrāyaṇī Saṃhitā, i. 6, 11; Taittirīya Brāhmaṇa, i. 2, 1, 26; Aitareya Brāhmaṇa, viii. 21, 14.

Sabhā-sthāṇu. See **Sabhā.**

Sabheya. See **Sabhā.**

Sam-aṅka is a word of obscure sense occurring in two passages of the Atharvaveda.[1] Bloomfield[2] renders it 'hook' in the first, and takes it to mean an insect destructive of grain in the other.

[1] i. 12, 2; vi. 50, 1.

[2] *Hymns of the Atharvaveda*, 7, 142. *Cf.* St. Petersburg Dictionary, *s.v.*

Samana is a word of somewhat doubtful sense in the Rigveda. Roth[1] renders it either 'battle'[2] or 'festival.'[3] Pischel[4] thinks that it was a general popular festivity to which women went to enjoy themselves,[5] poets to win fame,[6] bowmen to gain prizes at archery,[7] horses to run races;[8] and which lasted until morning[9] or until a conflagration, caused by the fires kept burning all night, scattered the celebrators.[10] Young women,[11] elderly women,[12] sought there to find a husband, and courtezans to make profit of the occasion.[13]

[1] St. Petersburg Dictionary, *s.v.*

[2] Rv. vi. 75, 3. 5; ix. 96, 9; x. 143, 4; Av. vi. 92, 2; Vājasaneyi Saṃhitā, ix. 9.

[3] Rv. ii. 16, 7; vi. 60, 2; vii. 2, 5; viii. 12, 9; ix. 97, 47; x. 55, 5; 86, 10; Av. ii. 36, 1.

[4] *Vedische Studien*, 2, 314.

[5] Rv. i. 124, 8 (*cf.* **Vrā**); iv. 58, 8; vi. 75, 4; vii. 2, 5; x. 86, 10; 168, 2.

[6] Rv. ii. 16, 7; ix. 97, 47. *Cf.* Geldner, *Vedische Studien*, 2, 38.

[7] Rv. vi. 75, 3. 5.

[8] Rv. ix. 96, 9; Av. vi. 92, 2.

[9] Rv. i. 48, 6, which Roth takes as referring to men going to business.

[10] Rv. x. 69, 11. *Cf.* vii. 9, 4.

[11] Av. ii. 36, 1.

[12] Rv. vii. 2, 5.

[13] Rv. iv. 58, 8, where, as in vi. 75, 4; x. 168, 2, Roth sees the sense of 'embrace.' The parallel with the festivals of Greece, where only young girls were able freely to mix with strangers, and which afforded the basis of so many of the comedies of the later school, is striking (*cf.* Mahaffy, *Greek Literature*, 1, 2, 259 *et seq.*).

Cf. Geldner, *Rigveda, Glossar*, 190.

Samara in the sense of 'battle' is found in the Kauṣītaki Brāhmaṇa,[1] and, according to Geldner,[2] in the Rigveda.[3]

[1] vii. 9; Sāṅkhāyana Śrauta Sūtra, xv. 15, 12.

[2] *Rigveda, Glossar*, 190.

[3] vi. 9, 2 (at the sacrifice; *cf. samarya*, iv. 24, 8, etc.).

Samā appears originally to have denoted 'summer,' a sense which may be seen in a few passages of the Atharvaveda.[1]

[1] i. 35, 4; ii. 6, 1; iii. 10, 9. *Cf.* Whitney, Translation of the Atharvaveda, 36.

Hence it also denotes more generally 'season,' a rare use.[2] More commonly it is simply 'year';[3] but in one place the Śatapatha Brāhmaṇa[4] interprets it in the Vājasaneyi Saṃhitā[5] as meaning 'month,' a doubtful sense.

[2] Aitareya Brāhmaṇa, iv. 25, 7; Nirukta, ix. 41.

[3] Rv. iv. 57, 7; x. 85, 5; 124, 4; Av. v. 8, 8; vi. 75, 2, etc.

[4] vi. 2, 1, 25.

[5] xxvii. 1, with Mahīdhara's note. See Eggeling, *Sacred Books of the East*, 41, 168, n. 1.

Cf. Zimmer, *Altindisches Leben*, 372; Schrader, *Prehistoric Antiquities*, 301.

Samāna. See **Prāṇa.**

Samāna-gotra[1] and **Samāna-jana**[2] mean 'belonging to the same family' and 'class' respectively in the Brāhmaṇas. **Samāna-bandhu**, 'having the same kin,' is found in the Rigveda.[3]

[1] Kauṣītaki Brāhmaṇa, xxv. 15.

[2] Pañcaviṃśa Brāhmaṇa, xvi. 6, 9; Lāṭyāyana Śrauta Sūtra, viii. 2, 10.

[3] i. 113, 2; Śatapatha Brāhmaṇa, iii. 5, 1, 25.

Samānta ('having the same boundary'), 'neighbour,' and therefore 'foe,' occurs in the Maitrāyaṇī Saṃhitā (ii. 1, 24).

Sam-iti denotes an 'assembly' of the Vedic tribe. It is alreadv mentioned in the Rigveda,[1] and often later,[2] sometimes in connexion with **Sabhā**.[3] Ludwig[4] considers that the Samiti included all the people, primarily the *viśaḥ*, 'subjects,' but also the **Maghavans** and Brahmins if they desired, though the Sabhā was their special assembly. This view is not probable, nor is that of Zimmer,[5] that the Sabhā was the village assembly. Hillebrandt appears to be right in holding that Samiti and Sabhā are much the same, the one being the assembly, the other primarily the place of assembly.

[1] i. 95, 8; ix. 92, 6; x. 97, 6; 166, 4; 191, 3.

[2] Av. v. 19, 15; vi. 88, 3; vii. 12, 1; xii. 1, 56, etc.

[3] Av. vii. 12, 1; xii. 1, 56; xv. 9, 2. 3; viii. 10, 5. 6.

[4] Translation of the Rigveda, 3, 253 *et seq.*

[5] *Altindisches Leben*, 172 *et seq.*

[6] *Vedische Mythologie*, 2, 124, n. 6.

The king went to the assembly[7] just as he went to the Sabhā. That he was elected there, as Zimmer[8] thinks, is as uncertain as whether he was elected at all (see **Rājan**). But there are clear signs that concord between king and assembly were essential for his prosperity.[9]

It is reasonable to assume that the business of the assembly was general deliberation on policy of all kinds, legislation so far as the Vedic Indian cared to legislate, and judicial work (*cf.* **Sabhāsad**). But of all these occupations there is, perhaps as a result of the nature of the texts, little or no evidence directly available.

The gods had a Samiti, hence called *daivī*, 'divine,'[10] just as they had a Sabhā.[11]

The assembly disappears as an effective part of government in the Buddhist texts,[12] the Epic,[13] and the law-books.[14]

[7] Rv. ix. 92, 6; x. 97, 6 (where the reference is hardly to an oligarchy, as Zimmer, 176, 177, holds, but merely to the princes of the blood going to the assembly with the rest).

[8] *Op. cit.*, 175, quoting Av. vi. 87. 88, with Rv. x. 173, and Av. v. 19, 15, with Av. iii. 4, 6.

[9] Av. vi. 88, 3. Roth, St. Petersburg Dictionary, *s.v.* 2, takes Samiti here and in v. 19, 15; Rv. x. 166, 4; 191, 3, to mean 'union,' but this is neither necessary nor probable

[10] Rv. x. 11, 8.

[11] Jaiminīya Upaniṣad Brāhmaṇa, ii. 11, 13. 14.

[12] *Cf.* Bühler, *Zeitschrift der Deutschen Morgenländischen Gesellschaft*, 48, 55, on the Parīsa.

[13] Hopkins, *Journal of the American Oriental Society*, 13, 148-152, who traces the decay of the old assembly through the aristocratic war council and the secret priestly conclave. It is, of course, very probable that at no time was the Samiti a place where any or much attention was paid to the views of the common man. Princes and great men spoke; the rest approved or disapproved, as in Homeric times and in Germany (*cf.* Lang, *Anthropology and the Classics*, 51 *et seq.*; Tacitus, *Germania*, 11. 12, where their general duty of discussion and their criminal jurisdiction are mentioned).

[14] Foy, *Die königliche Gewalt*, 6, 7, 10.

Sam-idh in the Rigveda[1] and later[2] denotes the 'fuel' for kindling fire. Geldner[3] inclines to see in one passage[4] the name of a priest, the later Agnidh.

[1] iv. 4, 15; vi. 15, 7; 16, 11; vii. 14, 1; x. 12, 2, etc.

[2] Vājasaneyi Saṃhitā, iii. 4; xx. 25, etc.

[3] *Rigveda, Glossar*, 191.

[4] Rv. x. 52, 2.

Sam-udra (literally 'gathering of waters'), 'ocean,' is a frequent word in the Rigveda and later. It is of importance in

so far as it indicates that the Vedic Indians knew the sea. This is, indeed, denied by Vivien de Saint Martin,[1] but not only do Max Müller[2] and Lassen[3] assert it, but even Zimmer,[4] who is inclined to restrict their knowledge of the sea as far as possible, admits it in one passage of the Rigveda,[5] and of course later.[6] He points out that the ebb and flow of the sea are unknown, that the mouths of the Indus are never mentioned, that fish is not a known diet in the Rigveda (*cf.* **Matsya**), and that in many places Samudra is metaphorically used, as of the two oceans,[7] the lower and the upper oceans,[8] etc. In other passages he thinks that Samudra denotes the river Indus when it receives all its Panjab tributaries.[9] It is probable that this is to circumscribe too narrowly the Vedic knowledge of the ocean, which was almost inevitable to people who knew the Indus. There are references to the treasures of the ocean,[10] perhaps pearls or the gains of trade,[11] and the story of **Bhujyu** seems to allude to marine navigation.

That there was any sea trade with Babylon in Vedic times cannot be proved: the stress laid[12] on the occurrence in the Hebrew Book of Kings[13] of *qof* and *tukhiīm*, 'monkey' (*kapi*) and 'peacock,' is invalidated by the doubtful date of the Book of Kings. There is, besides, little reason to assume an early date for the trade that no doubt developed later, perhaps about 700 B.C.[14]

[1] *Étude sur la géographie du Véda*, 62 *et seq.* *Cf.* Wilson, *Rigveda*, 1, xli.

[2] *Sacred Books of the East*, 32, 61 *et seq.*, quoting Rv. i. 71, 7; 190, 7; v. 78, 8; vii. 49, 2; 95. 2; x. 58.

[3] *Indische Alterthumskunde*, 1^2, 883.

[4] *Altindisches Leben*, 22 *et seq.* *Cf.* Macdonell, *Sanskrit Literature*, 143, 144.

[5] vii. 95, 2.

[6] Av. iv. 10, 4 (pearl shell); vi. 105, 3 (the outflow, *vi-kṣara*, of the ocean); xix. 38, 2; Taittirīya Saṃhitā, vii. 4, 13, 1, etc.

[7] Rv. x. 136, 5. *Cf.* Av. xi. 5, 6.

[8] Rv. vii. 6, 7; x. 98, 5.

[9] See, *e.g.*, Rv. i. 71, 7; iii. 36, 7; 46, 4; v. 85, 6; vi. 36, 3; vii. 95, 2; viii. 16, 2; 44, 25; ix. 88, 6; 107, 9; 108, 16 (where reference is made to streams); or Rv. i. 163, 1; iv. 21, 3; v. 55, 5; viii. 6, 29, where land and Samudra are contrasted.

[10] *Cf.* Rv. i. 47, 6; vii. 6, 7; ix. 97, 44.

[11] *Cf.* Rv. i. 48, 3; 56, 2; iv. 55, 6; and the general parallelism of the Dioscuri and the Aśvins.

[12] *E.g.*, by Weber, *Indian Literature*, 3.

[13] 1 Kings x. 22.

[14] See Kennedy, *Journal of the Royal Asiatic Society*, 1898, 241-288; Bühler, *Indische Studien*, 3, 79 *et seq.*; *Indische Palæographie*, 17-19, who much exaggerates the antiquity of the traffic; Vincent Smith, *Early History of India*, 25, n.

In the later texts Samudra repeatedly means the sea.[15]

15 Taittirīya Saṃhitā, ii. 4, 8, 2; vii. 5, 1, 2. It is described as unfailing in the Aitareya Brāhmaṇa, v. 16, 7 (*cf.* iii. 39, 7); it encircles the earth, *ibid.*, viii. 25, 1. The eastern and western oceans in Śatapatha Brāhmaṇa, i. 6, 3, 11 (*cf.* x. 6, 4, 1), though metaphorical, probably indicate an acquaintance with both seas, the Indian Ocean and the Arabian Sea.

Cf. Hillebrandt, *Vedische Mythologie*, 3, 14-19; Pischel and Geldner, *Vedische Studien*, 1, xxiii.

Samrāj in the Rigveda[1] and later[2] means 'superior ruler,' 'sovereign,' as expressing a greater degree of power than 'king' (**Rājan**). In the Śatapatha Brāhmaṇa,[3] in accordance with its curious theory of the **Vājapeya** and **Rājasūya**, the Samrāj is asserted to be a higher authority than a king, and to have become one by the sacrifice of the Vājapeya. There is, however, no trace of the use of the word as 'emperor' in the sense of an 'overlord of kings,' probably because political conditions furnished no example of such a status, as for instance was attained in the third century B.C. by Aśoka. At the same time Samrāj denotes an important king like **Janaka** of **Videha**.[4] It is applied in the Aitareya Brāhmaṇa[5] as the title of the eastern kings. *Cf.* **Rājya**.

1 iii. 55, 7; 56, 5; iv. 21, 1; vi. 27, 8; viii. 19, 32.

2 Vājasaneyi Saṃhitā, v. 32; xiii. 35; xx. 5, etc.

3 v. 1, 1, 13. *Cf.* xii. 8, 3, 4; xiv. 1, 3, 8.

4 Śatapatha Brāhmaṇa, xi. 3, 2, 1. 6; 2, 2, 3; Bṛhadāraṇyaka Upaniṣad, iv. 1, 1; 3, 1. *Cf.* Weber, *Über den Vājapeya*, 8.

5 viii. 14, 2. 3. The other names are given as follows: For the northerners it is Virāj; for the southerners, Svarāj; for the **Satvants**, Bhoja; for the middle people (**Kuru-Pañcāla**, **Vaśa**, and **Uśīnara**), Rājan simply. This is probably a sound tradition.

Saragh,[1] **Saraghā**,[2] both denote 'bee' in the Brāhmaṇas. See also **Sarah**.

1 Satapatha Brāhmaṇa, iii. 4, 3, 14.

2 Pañcaviṃśa Brāhmaṇa, xxi. 4, 4; Taittirīya Brāhmaṇa, iii. 10, 10, 1.

Sarayu is mentioned thrice in the Rigveda as the name of a river. **Citraratha** and Arṇa are said to have been defeated apparently by the **Turvaśas** and **Yadus** who crossed the

Sarayu.[1] Sarayu appears in one passage with **Sarasvatī** and **Sindhu**,[2] and in another with **Rasā**, **Anitabhā**, and **Kubhā**.[3] Later, in the post-Vedic period, Sarayū, rarely Sarayu, is the name of a river in Oudh, the modern Sarjū.[4] Zimmer[5] regards this as the river meant in all the Vedic passages, seeing in the last,[3] which may be used as an argument for locating the Sarayu in the Panjab, a reference to the north-east monsoon as well as to the usual monsoon from the west. Hopkins[6] thinks that the Sarayu is to be found in the west, and Ludwig[7] identifies it with the Kurum (**Krumu**). Vivien de St. Martin considered it to be probably identical with the united course of the **Śutudrī** (Sutlej) and **Vipāś** (Beas).

[1] iv. 30, 18. This passage gives no help, because the possibility is open either to suppose that the Turvaśa-Yadu are not mentioned as defeating the Āryans Citraratha and Arṇa; or, if they are, to suppose that they may have come east against the two.

[2] x. 64, 9.

[3] v. 53, 9.

[4] This is a tributary joining the Gogrā, the great river of Oudh, on the left of its upper course. The name Sarjū is also applied to the Gogrā itself below Bahrāmghāt. A branch of the Lower Gogrā, given off on the right, flowing in an old bed of the Gogrā, and falling into the Ganges after passing Balliā, is called the Chhotī (Lesser) Sarjū. *Cf. Imperial Gazetteer of India*, 22, 109; 12, 302 (Gogrā); 23, 418 (Eastern Tons); 26, Plate 31.

[5] *Altindisches Leben*, 17, 45. *Cf.* Muir, *Sanskrit Texts*, 2^2, xxv; Max Müller, *Sacred Books of the East*, 32, 323.

[6] *Religions of India*, 34.

[7] Translation of the Rigveda, 3, 280.

Saras denotes 'lake' in the later Saṃhitās[1] and the Brāhmaṇas.[2]

[1] Vājasaneyi Saṃhitā, xxiii. 47. 48; xxx. 16.

[2] Aitareya Brāhmaṇa, iii. 33, 6; Śatapatha Brāhmaṇa, xiii. 5, 4, 9; Chāndogya Upaniṣad, viii. 5, 3.

Sarasvatī[1] is the name of a river frequently mentioned in the Rigveda and later. In many passages[2] of the later texts it is certain the river meant is the modern Sarasvatī, which loses

[1] Literally, 'abounding in pools,' perhaps with reference to its condition when the water was low. The name corresponds phonetically to the Iranian Haraqaiti (the modern Helmand).

[2] Taittirīya Saṃhitā, vii. 2, 1, 4; Pañcaviṃśa Brāhmaṇa, xxv. 10, 1; Kauṣītaki Brāhmaṇa, xii. 2. 3; Śatapatha Brāhmaṇa, i. 4, 1, 14; Aitareya Brāhmaṇa, ii. 19, 1. 2; probably Av. vi. 30, 1. This list is according to Roth's view, St. Petersburg Dictionary, *s.v.* 3*c*.

itself in the sands of Patiala (see **Vinaśana**). Even Roth[3] admits that this river is intended in some passages of the Rigveda. With the **Dṛṣadvatī**[4] it formed the western boundary of Brahmāvarta (see **Madhyadeśa**). It is the holy stream of early Vedic India. The Sūtras[5] mention sacrifices held on its banks as of great importance and sanctity.

In many other passages of the Rigveda,[6] and even later,[7] Roth held that another river, the **Sindhu** (Indus), was really meant: only thus could it be explained why the Sarasvatī is called the 'foremost of rivers' (*nadītamā*),[8] is said to go to the ocean,[9] and is referred to as a large river, on the banks of which many kings,[10] and, indeed, the five tribes, were located.[11] This view is accepted by Zimmer[12] and others.[13]

On the other hand, Lassen[14] and Max Müller[15] maintain the identity of the Vedic Sarasvatī with the later Sarasvatī.[16] The latter is of opinion that in Vedic times the Sarasvatī was as large a stream as the Sutlej, and that it actually reached the

[3] Rv. iii. 23, 4 (where the Dṛṣadvatī appears); x. 64, 9; 75, 5 (where the Sindhu also is mentioned).

[4] Probably the modern Chautang, which flows to the east of Thanesar. *Cf.* Oldham, *Journal of the Royal Asiatic Society*, 25, 58; *Imperial Gazetteer of India*, 26, Plate 32.

[5] Kātyāyana Śrauta Sūtra, xii. 3, 20; xxiv. 6, 22; Lāṭyāyana Śrauta Sūtra, x. 15, 1; 18, 13; 19, 4; Āśvalāyana Śrauta Sūtra, xii. 6, 2. 3; Śāṅkhāyana Śrauta Sūtra, xiii. 29.

[6] i. 89, 3; 164, 19; ii. 41, 16 *et seq.*; 30, 8; 32, 8; iii. 54, 13; v. 42, 12; 43, 11; 46, 2; vi. 49, 7; 50, 12; 52, 6; vii. 9, 5; 36, 6; 39, 5; 40, 3; viii. 21, 17; 54, 4; x. 17, 7; 30, 12; 131, 5; 184, 2.

[7] Av. iv. 4, 6; v. 23, 1; vi. 3, 2; 89, 3; vii. 68, 1; xiv. 2, 15. 20; xvi. 4, 4; xix. 32, 9; Taittirīya Saṃhitā, i. 8, 13, 3; Vājasaneyi Saṃhitā, xix. 93; xxxiv. 11; Śatapatha Brāhmaṇa, i. 6, 2, 4; xi. 4, 3, 3; xii. 7, 1, 12; 2, 5; Bṛhadāraṇyaka Upaniṣad, vi. 3, 8. These passages should all be classed in n. 2.

[8] Rv. ii. 41, 16.

[9] Rv. vi. 61, 2. 8; vii. 96, 2.

[10] Rv. viii. 21, 18.

[11] Rv. vi. 61, 12.

[12] *Altindisches Leben*, 5-10.

[13] *E.g.*, Griffith, *Hymns of the Rigveda*, 1, 60; 2, 90, etc.; Ludwig, Translation of the Rigveda, 3, 201, 202.

[14] *Indische Alterthumskunde*, 1^2, 118.

[15] *Sacred Books of the East*, 32, 60.

[16] In the enumeration of rivers (evidently from east to west) in Rv. x. 75, 5, Gaṅgā, Yamunā, Sarasvatī, Śutudrī, the Sarasvatī comes between the Jumna and the Sutlej, the position of the modern Sarsūti (Saraswatī), which, flowing to the west of Thanesar, is joined in Patiala territory by a more westerly stream, the Ghaggar, and, passing Sirsa, is lost in the desert at Bhatnair; but a dry river bed (Hakra or Ghaggar) can be traced from that point to the Indus. See *Imperial Gazetteer of India*, 26, Plate 32. *Cf.* also Oldham, *Journal of the Royal Asiatic Society*, 25, 49-76.

sea either after union with the Indus or not, being the 'iron citadel,' as the last boundary on the west, a frontier of the Panjab against the rest of India. There is no conclusive evidence of there having been any great change in the size or course of the Sarasvatī, though it would be impossible to deny that the river may easily have diminished in size. But there are strong reasons to accept the identification of the later and the earlier Sarasvatī throughout. The insistence on the divine character of the river is seen in the very hymn[17] which refers to it as the support of the five tribes, and corresponds well with its later sacredness. Moreover, that hymn alludes to the **Pārāvatas,** a people shown by the later evidence of the Pañcaviṃśa Brāhmaṇa[18] to have been in the east, a very long way from their original home, if Sarasvatī means the Indus. Again, the **Pūrus,** who were settled on the Sarasvatī,[19] could with great difficulty be located in the far west. Moreover, the five tribes might easily be held to be on the Sarasvatī, when they were, as they seem to have been, the western neighbours of the **Bharatas** in **Kurukṣetra,** and the Sarasvatī could easily be regarded as the boundary of the Panjab in that sense. Again, the 'seven rivers' in one passage[20] clearly designate a district: it is most probable that they are not the five rivers with the Indus and the **Kubhā** (Cabul river), but the five rivers, the Indus and the Sarasvatī. Nor is it difficult to see why the river is said to flow to the sea: either the Vedic poet had never followed the course of the river to its end, or the river did actually penetrate the desert either completely or for a long distance, and only in the Brāhmaṇa period was its disappear-

17 Rv. ii. 41, 16 (*devitame*).

18 See **Pārāvata.** and *cf.* **Bṛsaya.**

19 Rv. vii. 95. 96. Ludwig, *op. cit.*, 3, 175, admits that the Indus cannot be meant here. See Hillebrandt, *Vedische Mythologie*, 1, 115.

20 Rv. viii. 24, 27. The connexion of Sarasvatī and the seven rivers is rather vague. In Rv. viii. 54, 4, Sarasvatī and the seven rivers are separately invoked, and in vi. 61, 10. 12, she is referred to as 'seven-sistered' (*saptasvasā*). In vii. 36, 6, she is called the 'seventh,' which makes the Sarasvatī one of the rivers. If the former passages are to be treated as precise, then *saptasvasā* may be considered to show that the Sarasvatī was outside the river system (which would then be Indus, Kubhā, and the five rivers of the Panjab; see **Sapta Sindhavaḥ**); but the expression may be loosely meant for one of seven sisters.

ance in the desert found out. It is said, indeed, in the Vājasaneyi Saṃhitā[21] that the five rivers go to the Sarasvatī, but this passage is not only late (as the use of the word **Deśa** shows), but it does not say that the five rivers meant are those of the Panjab. Moreover, the passage has neither a parallel in the other Saṃhitās, nor can it possibly be regarded as an early production; if it is late it must refer to the later Sarasvatī.

Hillebrandt,[22] on the whole, adopts this view of the Sarasvatī,[23] but he also sees in it, besides the designation of a mythical stream, the later Vaitaraṇī,[24] as well as the name of the Arghandab in Arachosia.[25] This opinion depends essentially on his theory that the sixth Maṇḍala of the Rigveda places the scene of its action in Iranian lands, as opposed to the seventh Maṇḍala: it is as untenable as that theory itself.[26] Brunnhofer[27] at one time accepted the Iranian identification, but later[28] decided for the Oxus, which is quite out of the question. See also **Plakṣa Prāsravaṇa.**

[21] xxxiv. 11.

[22] *Vedische Mythologie*, 1, 99 *et seq.*; 3, 372-378.

[23] He sees this sense in the Rigveda everywhere, except in the passages indicated in notes 24 and 25.

[24] vii. 95, 6; x. 17, 7; Av. vii. 68, 2; xiv. 2, 20; Pañcaviṃśa Brāhmaṇa, xxxv. 10, 11.

[25] Rv. vi. 49, 7; 61; possibly Vājasaneyi Saṃhitā, xxxiv. 11.

[26] See **Divodāsa.**

[27] Bezzenberger's *Beiträge*, 10, 261, n. 2.

[28] *Iran und Turan*, 127.

Cf. Muir, *Sanskrit Texts*, 5, 337 *et seq.*; Macdonell, *Sanskrit Literature*, 141, 142; *Vedic Mythology*, pp. 86-88; von Schroeder, *Indiens Literatur und Cultur*, 84, 164.

Sarah in the Rigveda[1] and later[2] denotes 'bee.' *Cf.* **Saragha.**

[1] i. 112, 21.

[2] Taittirīya Saṃhitā, v. 3 12, 12; Śatapatha Brāhmaṇa, xiii. 3, 1, 4. The stem is given as Saraṭ in the Uṇādi-sūtra, 1, 133; but **Saragh** shows that Sarah must be meant (*cf.* Macdonell, *Vedic Grammar*, p. 238, n. 2).

Cf. Zimmer, *Altindisches Leben*, 97.

Sarit denotes 'stream' in the Rigveda[1] and later.[2]

[1] iv. 58, 6; vii. 70, 2; Av. xii. 2, 41; Vājasaneyi Saṃhitā, xxxiv. 11; Taittirīya Brāhmaṇa, i. 2, 1, 11, etc.

Sarīsṛpa denotes in the Rigveda,[1] and often later,[2] any 'creeping animal' or 'reptile.'

[1] x. 162, 3.

[2] Av. iii. 10, 6; xix. 7, 1; 48, 3, etc.

Sarpa, 'serpent,' occurs once in the Rigveda,[1] where **Ahi** is the usual word, but often later.[2]

[1] x. 16, 6.

[2] Av. x. 4, 23; xi. 3, 47; Taittirīya Saṃhitā, i. 5, 4, 1; iii. 1, 1, 1, etc.

Sarpa-rājñī, 'serpent-queen,' is the alleged authoress of a hymn of the Rigveda[1] according to the Taittirīya Saṃhitā.[2]

[1] x. 189.

[2] i. 5, 4, 1; vii. 3, 1, 3; Taittirīya Brāhmaṇa, i. 4, 6, 6; ii. 2, 6, 1; Aitareya Brāhmaṇa, v. 23, 1. 2.

Sarpa-vidyā, the 'science of snakes,' is enumerated in the Śatapatha Brāhmaṇa among branches of learning. It must have been reduced to fixed rules, since a section (*parvan*) of it is referred to as studied. The Gopatha Brāhmaṇa[2] has the form Sarpa-veda.

[1] xiii. 4, 3, 9. *Cf.* Sāṅkhāyana Śrauta Sūtra, xvi. 2, 25. The Āśvalāyana Srauta Sūtra, x. 7, 5, has **Viṣa-vidyā,** and the Chāndogya Upaniṣad (vii. 1. 2. 4; 2, 1; 4, 1; 7, 1) has *sarpa-devajana-vidyā*.

[2] i. 1, 10. *Cf.* Eggeling, *Sacred Books of the East*, 44, 367, n. 3.

Sarpi Vātsi ('descendant of **Vatsa**') is the name of a teacher in the Aitareya Brāhmaṇa.[1]

[1] vi. 24, 15. Aufrecht, *Aitareya Brāhmaṇa*, 424, takes the name to be Sarpir. The point is, of course, doubtful, since the word occurs in the nominative only.

Sarpis denotes 'melted butter,' whether in a liquid or solidified condition, and not differing from **Ghṛta** according to the St. Petersburg Dictionary. Roth there rejects the definition cited by Sāyaṇa in his commentary on the Aitareya Brāhmaṇa,[1] which discriminates Sarpis as the liquid and Ghṛta as the solid condition of the butter. The word is repeatedly mentioned in the Rigveda[2] and later.[3]

[1] i. 3, 5.

[2] i. 127, 1; v. 6, 9; x. 18, 7.

[3] Av. i. 15, 4; ix. 6, 41; x. 9, 12; xii. 3, 45; Taittirīya Saṃhitā, ii. 3, 10, 1, etc.

Sarva-caru is found in a passage of the Aitareya Brāhmaṇa[1] and of the Kauṣītaki Brāhmaṇa,[2] where the gods are referred to as holding a sacrifice *sarvacarau.* The word is the name of a man according to the St. Petersburg Dictionary; the name of a place[3] seems possible, or even a mere adjective may be meant.[4]

[1] vi. 1, 1.

[2] xxix. 1.

[3] Sāyaṇa on Aitareya Brāhmaṇa, *loc. cit.*

[4] Aufrecht, *Aitareya Brāhmaṇa,* 425, n. 1, who suggests that *yajñe* is to be supplied.

Sarva-vedasa denotes in the later Saṃhitās and the Brāhmaṇas either a sacrifice in which the sacrificer gives his all to the priests,[1] or the whole property of a man.[2]

[1] Taittirīya Brāhmaṇa, i. 4, 7, 7; Kauṣītaki Brāhmaṇa, xxv. 14; Pañcaviṃśa Brāhmaṇa, ix. 3, 1.

[2] Taittirīya Saṃhitā, vii. 1, 1, 3; Taittirīya Brāhmaṇa, iii. 2, 8, 1; Pañcaviṃśa Brāhmaṇa, vi. 7, 15; Śatapatha Brāhmaṇa, iv. 6, 1, 15, etc.

Sarṣapa, denoting 'mustard' or 'mustard seed,' occurs only a few times in later Vedic texts.[1]

[1] Chāndogya Upaniṣad, iii. 14, 3. *Cf.* Ṣaḍviṃśa Brāhmaṇa, v. 2; Śāṅkhāyana Srauta Sūtra, iv. 15, 8, etc. It is common in the later language.

Salā-vṛkī. See **Sālāvṛka.**

Salila-vāta occurs in the Yajurveda Saṃhitās[1] as an adjective meaning 'favoured with a wind from the water.'[2] It probably refers to the wind from the ocean, the south-west monsoon.[3]

[1] Taittirīya Saṃhitā, iv. 4, 12, 3; Kāṭhaka Saṃhitā, xxiv. 4; Maitrāyaṇī Saṃhitā, iii. 16, 4.

[2] Or, according to the commentator, *salilākhyena vāta-viśeṣeṇa anugṛhītaḥ,* 'favoured by a kind of wind called Salila.'

[3] *Indian Empire,* 1, 110. The monsoon is little noted in the Vedic texts, except in so far as the Marut hymns may be deemed to be a description of the monsoon. See Rv. i. 19, 7; 37, 6 *et seq.*; 38, 8; 64, 8; 88, 5; v. 83, 1 *et seq.*; 85, 4; Zimmer, *Altindisches Leben,* 42-44.

Salva is the name of a people mentioned in a passage of the Śatapatha Brāhmaṇa,[1] which records a boast by **Śyāparṇa Sāyakāyana** that if a certain rite of his had been completed, his race would have been the nobles, Brahmins, and peasants of the Salvas, and even as it was his race would surpass the Salvas. This people appears also to be alluded to as *Sālvīḥ* (*prajāḥ*) in the Mantra Pāṭha,[2] where they are said to have declared that their king was **Yaugandhari** when they stayed their chariots[3] on the banks of the **Yamunā**. There is later evidence[4] indicating that the Sālvas or Śālvas were closely connected with the **Kuru-Pañcālas**, and that apparently some of them, at least, were victorious near the banks of the Yamunā. There is no good evidence to place them in the north-west in Vedic times.[5]

1 x. 4, 1, 10.

2 ii. 11, 12.

3 Winternitz, *Mantra-pāṭha*, xlv-xlvii, sees in the verse an allusion to the Sālva women turning round the wheel (? spinning-wheel). But a reference to a warlike raid seems more plausible.

4 Mahābhārata, iv. 1, 12; viii. 44 (45), 14. The Yugandharas are also referred to in a Kārikā quoted in the Kāśikā Vṛtti on Pāṇini, iv. 1, 173.

5 *Cf.* Weber, *Indische Studien*, 1, 215. Later, they may have been found in Rājasthān, Lassen, *Indische Alterthumskunde*, 1², 760.

Savya-ṣṭhā,[1] **Savya-ṣṭhṛ**,[2] **Savye-ṣṭha**,[3] and **Savya-stha**[4] are all various forms of the word for 'car-fighter,' as opposed to **Sārathi**, 'charioteer,' showing that, as was natural, the fighter stood on the left of the driver. The commentators[5] are inclined to see in the Savyaṣṭhā merely another 'charioteer,' but this is quite unjustifiable,[6] and is perhaps due to later caste prejudice against a Śūdra charioteer.

1 Av. viii. 8, 23.

2 Satapatha Brāhmaṇa, v. 2, 4, 9; 3, 1, 8; 4, 3, 17. 18.

3 Taittirīya Brāhmaṇa, i. 7, 9, 1.

4 Kāṇva recension of the Śatapatha Brāhmaṇa, Eggeling, *Sacred Books of the East*, 41, 62, n. 1; Maitrāyaṇī Saṃhitā, iv. 3, 8.

5 On Śatapatha Brāhmaṇa, v. 3, 1, 8; Taittirīya Brāhmaṇa, *loc. cit.*

6 Eggeling, *loc. cit.*; Hopkins, *Journal of the American Oriental Society*, 13, 235.

Cf. Zimmer, *Altindisches Leben*, 296.

Sasa in the Rigveda[1] denotes 'herb' or 'grass.'[1] The word is also applied to the Soma plant[2] and the sacrificial straw.[3]

1 i. 51, 3; x. 79, 3.

2 iii. 5, 6; iv. 5, 7, etc.

3 v. 21, 4.

Sasarparī is a word occurring in two curious verses of the Rigveda.[1] According to a later interpretation,[2] it designates a particular kind of skill in speech which **Viśvāmitra** obtained from **Jamadagni.** What it was is quite uncertain.

[1] iii. 53, 15. 16.

[2] Bṛhaddevatā, iii. 113, with Macdonell's notes. *Cf.* Geldner, *Vedische Studien*, 2, 159.

Sasya in the Atharvaveda[1] and later[2] regularly denotes 'corn' generally. It corresponds to the Avestan *hahya*. See **Kṛṣi.**

[1] vii. 11, 1; viii. 10, 24.

[2] Taittirīya Saṃhitā, iii. 4, 3, 3; v. 1, 7, 3; vii. 5, 20, 1; Maitrāyaṇī Saṃhitā, iv. 2, 2, etc.

Cf. Schrader, *Prehistoric Antiquities*, 284.

Saha in the Atharvaveda[1] is, according to Roth,[2] the name of a plant, but Bloomfield[3] thinks the word is only an adjective meaning 'mighty.'

[1] xi. 6, 15. *Cf.* Sāmavidhāna Brāhmaṇa, ii. 6, 10.

[2] St. Petersburg Dictionary, *s.v.* 2*b*.

[3] *Hymns of the Atharvaveda*, 648.

Cf. Whitney, Translation of the Atharvaveda, 642; Zimmer, *Altindisches Leben*, 72.

Saha-deva is the name of a prince in the Rigveda,[1] where he is victorious over the **Śimyus** and **Dasyus**. It is quite probable that he is identical with King Sahadeva Sārñjaya, who is mentioned in the Śatapatha Brāhmaṇa[2] as having once been called **Suplan Sārñjaya**, and as having changed his name because of his success in performing the Dākṣāyaṇa sacrifice. In the Aitareya Brāhmaṇa[3] he is mentioned with **Somaka Sāhadevya**, who also appears in the Rigveda.[4]

[1] i. 100, 17.

[2] ii. 4, 4, 3. 4. *Cf.* xii. 8, 2, 3.

[3] vii. 34, 9.

[4] iv. 15, 7 *et seq.*

Cf. Zimmer, *Altindisches Leben*, 132; Hillebrandt, *Vedische Mythologie*, 1, 105, 106.

Saha-devī is the name of a plant in the Atharvaveda[1] according to the reading of the commentary.

[1] vi. 59, 2. *Cf.* Grill, *Hundert Lieder*,[2] 163; Whitney, Translation of the Atharvaveda, 325; Bloomfield, *Hymns of the Atharvaveda*, 490, who does not accept this reading. A plant called Sahadeva occurs in the Sāmavidhāna Brāhmaṇa, ii. 6, 10.

Sahamāna is the name of a plant in the Atharvaveda (ii. 25, 2; iv. 17, 2; viii. 2, 6; 7, 5).

Saho-jit. See **Jaitrāyaṇa.**

Sāṃvaraṇi is found in the Rigveda[1] in one passage, where it naturally seems to be a patronymic ('descendant of Saṃvaraṇa') of Manu. According to Bloomfield,[2] it is a corruption for **Sāvarṇi,** a reference to Manu's birth from the *savarṇā*, 'similar' female who was substituted for Saraṇyū according to the legend (see **Manu**). This is possible, but not certain. Scheftelowitz[3] thinks that the reading of the Kaśmir manuscript of the Rigveda, which has *sāṃvaraṇam*, 'found on the sacrificial ground,' as an epithet of Soma, is to be preferred. But this seems quite improbable.[4] We must either recognize a real man called Manu Sāṃvaraṇi; or take Manu as one name, Sāṃvaraṇi as another; or admit that Manu Sāṃvaraṇi is simply Manu with a patronymic derived from an unknown legend.

[1] viii. 51, 1.

[2] *Journal of the American Oriental Society*, 15, 180, n.

[3] *Die Apokryphen des Ṛgveda*, 38.

[4] See Oldenberg, *Göttingische Gelehrte Anzeigen*, 1907, 237.

Sākam-aśva Devarāta is the name of a teacher, a pupil of **Viśvāmitra,** in the Vaṃśa (list of teachers) which concludes the Śāṅkhāyana Āraṇyaka (xv. 1).

Sāṃkṛtī-putra ('son of a female descendant of Saṃkṛta') is the name of a teacher, a pupil of **Ālambāyanīputra**[1] or **Ālambīputra,**[2] in the last Vaṃśa (list of teachers) of the Bṛhadāraṇyaka Upaniṣad.

[1] Bṛhadāraṇyaka Upaniṣad, vi. 5, 2 Kāṇva.

[2] *Ibid.*, vi. 4, 32 Mādhyaṃdina.

Sāṃkṛtya, 'descendant of Saṃkṛti,' is the name of a teacher whose pupil was **Pārāśarya** in the first two Vaṃśas (lists of teachers) in the Mādhyaṃdina recension of the Bṛhadāraṇyaka Upaniṣad.[1]

[1] ii. 5, 20; iv. 5, 26. A Sāṃkṛtya occurs also in the Taittirīya Prātiśākhya, viii. 21; x. 21; xvi. 16.

Sācī-guṇa is mentioned, apparently as a place in the territory of the **Bharatas**, in a verse occurring in the Aitareya Brāhmaṇa.[1] Leumann,[2] however, thinks an epithet of Indra, Śācīgu, may be meant.

[1] viii. 23, 4.

[2] *Zeitschrift der Deutschen Morgenländischen Gesellschaft*, 48, 80, n. 5. This conjecture seems improbable.

Sāṃjīvī-putra, 'son of Sāṃjīvī,' is the name of a teacher who appears in the Vaṃśa (list of teachers) at the end of the tenth Kāṇḍa of the Śatapatha Brāhmaṇa,[1] and at the end of the fourteenth Kāṇḍa in the Kāṇva recension,[2] as a pupil of **Māṇḍūkāyani.** In the Vaṃśas at the end of the Bṛhadāraṇyaka Upaniṣad in both recensions[3] he is given as a pupil of **Prāśnīputra Āsurivāsin.** It seems clear that he united in himself two lines of teachers—that of the tradition of the fire-cult from **Śāṇḍilya,** and that of the tradition of **Yājñavalkya.**

[1] x. 6, 5, 9.

[2] Bṛhadāraṇyaka Upaniṣad, vi. 5, 4 Kāṇva.

[3] *Ibid.*, vi. 4, 32 (Mādhyaṃdina = vi. 5, 2 Kāṇva).

Cf. Eggeling, *Sacred Books of the East*, 12, xxxiv *et seq.*; Weber, *Indian Literature*, 131.

Sāti Auṣṭrākṣi ('descendant of Uṣṭrākṣa') is the name of a teacher in the Vaṃśa Brāhmaṇa.[1]

[1] *Indische Studien*, 4, 372.

Sātya-kāmi ('descendant of **Satyakāma**') is the patronymic of **Keśin** in the Taittirīya Saṃhitā (ii. 6, 2, 3).

Sātya-kīrta is the name of a school of teachers mentioned in the Jaiminīya Upaniṣad Brāhmaṇa (iii. 32, 1).

Sātya-yajña ('descendant of Saryayajña') is the name of a teacher in the Śatapatha Brāhmaṇa (iii. 1, 1, 4).

1. **Sātya-yajñi** ('descendant of Satyayajña') is the patronymic of **Somaśuṣma** in the Śatapatha Brāhmaṇa (xi. 6, 2, 1. 3; xiii. 4, 2, 4; 5, 3, 9).

2. **Sātya-yajñi** is the name of a school of teachers mentioned in the Jaiminīya Upaniṣad Brāhmaṇa (ii. 4, 5) with the **Śailanas** and the **Kārīradis.**

Sātya-havya ('descendant of Satyahavya') is the patronymic of a **Vāsiṣṭha** who is mentioned as a contemporary of **Atyarāti Jānaṃtapi** in the Aitareya Brāhmaṇa (viii. 23, 9), and of **Devabhāga** in the Taittirīya Saṃhitā (vi. 6, 2, 2).

Sātrājita ('descendant of Satrājit') is the patronymic of **Śatānīka.**[1]

[1] Aitareya Brāhmaṇa, viii. 21, 5; Śatapatha Brāhmaṇa, xiii. 5, 4, 19. 21.

Sātrā-sāha ('descendant of Satrāsāha') is the patronymic of **Śoṇa.**

[1] Śatapatha Brāhmaṇa, xiii. 5, 4, 16. 18.

Sādin in the Atharvaveda[1] denotes the 'rider' of a horse as opposed to *a-sāda*, 'pedestrian.' An *aśva-sādin*, 'horse-rider,' is known to the Vājasaneyi Saṃhitā.[2] The Taittirīya Brāhmaṇa[3] and the Rigveda[4] itself contain clear references to horse-riding, while the Aitareya Āraṇyaka[5] refers to mounting a horse sideways. Āśvalāyana[6] knows *sādya* as a 'riding horse' opposed to *vahya*, a 'draught animal.'

[1] xi. 10, 24.
[2] xxx. 13.
[3] iii. 4, 7, 1.
[4] i. 162, 17; v. 61, 3. *Cf.* i. 163, 9.
[5] i. 2. 4; Śatapatha Brāhmaṇa, vii. 3, 2, 17.
[6] Sūtra, ix. 9, 14.

Cf. Zimmer, *Altindisches Leben*, 230, 295. 296; Max Müller, *Sacred Books of the East*, 32, 358; Keith, *Aitareya Āraṇyaka*, 177; Weber, Proceedings of the Berlin Academy, 1898, 564.

Sādhāraṇī in one passage of the Rigveda[1] seems to refer not so much to an *uxor communis*, like Draupadī in the Epic, as Max Müller[2] suggests, but to a courtezan.

[1] i. 167, 4.
[2] *Sacred Books of the East*, 32, 277.

Cf. Zimmer, *Altindisches Leben*, 332; Muir, *Sanskrit Texts*, 5, 461; Pischel and Geldner, *Vedische Studien*, 1, xxv.

Sāpta in the Rigveda[1] may be a proper name, but the sense is quite uncertain.

[1] viii. 55, 5. *Cf.* Ludwig, Translation of the Rigveda, 5, 552; Griffith, *Hymns of the Rigveda*, 2, 266.

Sāptaratha vāhani ('descendant of Saptarathavāhana') is the patronymic of a teacher, a pupil of **Śāṇḍilya**, in the Śatapatha Brāhmaṇa.[1]

[1] x. 1, 4, 10. 11. *Cf.* Weber, *Indische Studien*, 1, 259, n.

Sāpya or **Sāyya** is the patronymic of **Namī** in the Rigveda (vi. 20, 6).

Sāma-veda, 'the Veda of the Sāman chants,' is the name of a collection of verses for chanting, often mentioned in the Brāhmaṇas.[1] The Sāman itself is repeatedly referred to in the Rigveda,[2] and the triad Ṛc, Yajus, and Sāman is common from the Atharvaveda onwards.[3] These texts know also the Sāma-ga, the 'Sāman-chanter,'[4] who occurs later.[5]

[1] Taittirīya Brāhmaṇa, iii. 12, 9, 1; Aitareya Brāhmaṇa, v. 32, 1; Śatapatha Brāhmaṇa, xi. 5, 8, 3; xii. 3, 4, 9; Aitareya Āraṇyaka, iii. 2, 3; Bṛhadāraṇyaka Upaniṣad, i. 5, 13 (Mādhyaṃdina = i. 5, 5 Kāṇva); ii. 4, 10; iv. 1, 6 (= iv. 1, 2); 5, 11; Chāndogya Upaniṣad, i. 3, 7; iii. 3, 1. 2; 15, 7; vii. 1, 2. 4; 2, 1; 7, 1, etc.

[2] i. 62, 2; 107, 2; 164, 24, etc. *Cf.* Oldenberg, *Zeitschrift der Deutschen Morgenländischen Gesellschaft*, 38, 439 *et seq.*

[3] x. 7, 14; xi. 7, 5; Vājasaneyi Saṃhitā, xxxiv. 5, etc.

[4] Rv. ii. 43, 1; x. 107, 6; Av. ii. 12, 4.

[5] Aitareya Brāhmaṇa, ii. 22, 3; 37, 4; iii. 4, 1.

Sāma-śravas ('famed for chants') occurs in the Bṛhadāraṇyaka Upaniṣad.[1] According to Max Müller,[2] the word is an epithet of **Yājñavalkya**, but Böhtlingk[3] takes it as the name of a pupil of that teacher.

[1] iii. 1, 3. [2] *Sacred Books of the East*, 15, 121. [3] Translation, 36.

Sāma-śravasa ('descendant of **Sāmaśravas**') is the patronymic of **Kuṣītaka** in the Pañcaviṃśa Brāhmaṇa (xvii. 4, 3).

Sāmudri ('descendant of **Samudra**') is the name of a mythical sage, Aśva, in the Śatapatha Brāhmaṇa (xiii. 2, 2, 14).

Sāṃmada ('descendant of Saṃmada') is the patronymic of the mythical Matsya in the Śatapatha Brāhmaṇa (xiii. 4, 3, 12).

Sāmrājya. See **Samrāj** and **Rājya.**

Sāya[1] denotes 'evening' in the Rigveda and later, usually appearing in the adverbial form Sāyam,[2] 'in the evening.' *Cf.* **Ahar.**

[1] Taittirīya Brāhmaṇa, i. 5, 3, 3; Kauṣītaki Brāhmaṇa, ii. 8; Śatapatha Brāhmaṇa, vii. 3, 2, 18.

[2] Rv. v. 77, 2; x. 146, 4; Av. iii. 12, 3; iv. 11, 12; viii. 6, 10, etc. *Cf. Sāyaṃ-prātar*, 'morning and evening,' Av. iii. 30, 7; xix. 39, 2, etc.

1. **Sāyaka** denotes 'arrow' in the Rigveda (ii. 33, 10; iii. 53, 23; x. 48, 4).

2. **Sāyaka Jāna-śruteya** ('descendant of Janaśruta') **Kāṇḍviya** is the name of a teacher, a pupil of **Janaśruta Kāṇḍviya**, in the Jaiminīya Upaniṣad Brāhmaṇa (iii. 40, 2).

Sāyakāyana ('descendant of **Sāyaka**') is the patronymic of **Śyāparṇa** in the Śatapatha Brāhmaṇa,[1] and also of a teacher, a pupil of **Kauśikāyani** in the second Vaṃśa (list of teachers) in the Bṛhadāraṇyaka Upaniṣad.[2]

[1] x. 3, 6, 10; 5, 2, 1.

[2] iv. 5, 27 (Mādhyaṃdina = iv. 6, 3 Kāṇva).

Sāyya. See **Sāpya.**

Sārathi denotes the 'charioteer' as opposed to the 'warrior' (**Savyaṣṭhā**) in the Rigveda[1] and later.[2]

[1] i. 55, 7; 144, 3; ii. 19, 6; vi. 20, 5; 57, 6; x. 102, 6.

[2] Av. xv. 2, 1; Taittirīya Brāhmaṇa, i. 7, 9, 1; Maitrāyaṇī Saṃhitā, iv. 3, 8, etc.

Cf. Zimmer, *Altindisches Leben*, 296.

Sārameya, 'descendant of Saramā,' Indra's mythical dog, is applied to a dog on earth in the Rigveda,[1] as also to the dogs of Yama.[2]

[1] vii. 55, 2 (unless that passage be deemed to refer to the souls of the departed).
[2] x. 14, 10.

Sārñjaya is found in the Rigveda[1] in a Dānastuti ('praise of gifts') where the word probably denotes the '**Sṛñjaya** king' rather than a 'descendant of Sṛñjaya.' According to the Śāṅkhāyana Śrauta Sūtra,[2] he was **Prastoka**, mentioned in the same hymn, but this conclusion is not very cogent. He was clearly a patron of the **Bharadvājas.** The same epithet belongs to **Sahadeva,** *alias* **Suplan.**

[1] vi. 47, 25.
[2] xvi. 11, 11.
[3] Satapatha Brāhmaṇa, ii. 4, 4, 4; xii. 8, 2, 3.

Cf. Hillebrandt, *Vedische Mythologie,* 1, 104, 105.

Sārpa-rājñī in the Pañcaviṃśa (iv. 9, 4) and the Kauṣītaki (xxvii. 4) Brāhmaṇas is identical with **Sarparājñī.**

Sārva-seni ('descendant of Sarvasena') is the patronymic of **Śauceya** in the Taittirīya Saṃhitā (vii. 1, 10, 3).

Sālā-vṛka is found twice in the Rigveda[1] apparently denoting the 'hyæna' or 'wild dog.' This sense also seems appropriate in the later narrative of the destruction of the **Yatis** by Indra,[2] who is said to have handed them over to the Sālāvṛkas. Sālāvṛkeya[3] is a variant form of the same word, meaning literally 'descendant of a Sālāvṛka.' The feminine is Sālāvṛkī,[4] but in the Taittirīya Saṃhitā[5] it appears as Salāvṛkī. *Cf.* **Tarakṣu.**

[1] x. 73, 2; 95, 15.
[2] Taittirīya Saṃhitā, vi. 2, 7, 5; Aitareya Brāhmaṇa, vii. 28, 1; Kauṣītaki Upaniṣad, iii. 1 (*varia lectio*).
[3] Pañcaviṃśa Brāhmaṇa, viii. 1, 4; xiii. 4, 16; xiv. 11, 28; xviii. 1, 9; xix. 4, 7; Jaiminīya Brāhmaṇa, i. 185 (*Journal of the American Oriental Society,* 19, 123); Kāṭhaka Saṃhitā, viii. 5; xi. 10; xxv. 6; xxxvi. 7 (*Indische Studien,* 3, 465, 466); Kauṣītaki Upaniṣad, iii. 1 (according to Śaṅkarānanda's recension). In Av. ii. 27, 5, Indra is alluded to as an enemy of the Sālāvṛkas.
[4] Kāṭhaka Saṃhitā, xxviii. 4.
[5] vi. 2, 7, 5; also in Maitrāyaṇī Saṃhitā, iii. 8, 3; Āpastamba Dharma Sūtra, i. 10, 17; 11, 33.

Cf. Zimmer, *Altindisches Leben,* 81; Weber, *Indische Studien,* 13, 192; Whitney, Translation of the Atharvaveda, 68; Bloomfield, *Hymns of the Atharvaveda,* 306, who decides in favour of 'jackal.'

Sāvayasa ('descendant of Savayasa') is the patronymic of Aṣāḍha, or Āṣāḍha, in the Śatapatha Brāhmaṇa (i. 1, 1, 7).

Sā-varṇi is found as a patronymic in the Rigveda[1] together with Sāvarṇya.[2] It is clear that no man called Savarṇa ever existed, though Roth[3] accepted that view, and that the reference is to the mythical **Manu** Sāvarṇi, the descendant of the *sa-varṇā* female, who, according to the legend,[4] took the place of Saraṇyū.

[1] x. 62, 11.

[2] x. 62, 9.

[3] St. Petersburg Dictionary, *s.v.* *Cf.* Muir, *Sanskrit Texts*, 1², 17.

[4] Bloomfield, *Journal of the American Oriental Society* 15, 179 *et seq.*

Siṃha denotes the 'lion' in the Rigveda[1] and later.[2] The roaring (*nad*) of the lion is often alluded to,[2] and is called thundering (*stanatha*).[4] He wanders about (*ku-cara*) and lives in the hills (*giri-ṣṭha*),[5] and is clearly the 'dread wild beast that slays' (*mṛgo bhīma upahatnuḥ*)[6] to which Rudra is compared. When Agni, who has entered the waters, is compared to a lion,[7] the reference may be to the lion's habit of springing on animals at drinking places. That a jackal should defeat the lion is spoken of as a marvel.[8] The lion, being dangerous to men,[9] was trapped,[10] lain in wait for in ambush,[11] or chased by hunting bands.[12] But dogs were terrified of lions.[13] The lioness (*siṃhī*) was also famous for her courage: the aid given by Indra to **Sudās** against the vast host of his enemies is compared to the defeat of a lioness by a ram (**Petva**).[14] The gaping jaws of the lioness when attacking men are alluded to in

[1] i. 64, 8; 95, 5; iii. 2, 11; 9, 4; 26, 5; iv. 16, 14, etc.

[2] Av. iv. 36, 6; v. 20, 1. 2; 21, 6; viii. 7, 15; Taittirīya Saṃhitā, v. 5, 21, 1; Kāṭhaka Saṃhitā, xii. 10, etc.; Maitrāyaṇī Saṃhitā, ii. 1, 9; Kauṣītaki Upaniṣad, 1. 2.

[3] See Rv. i. 64, 8; iii. 26, 5. The sound of the drum is compared with it, Av. v. 20, 1.

[4] Rv. v. 83, 3; Av. v. 21, 6; viii. 7, 15.

[5] Rv. i. 154, 2; x. 160, 2.

[6] Rv. ii. 33, 11.

[7] Rv. iii. 9, 4.

[8] Rv. x. 28, 4.

[9] Rv. i. 174, 3.

[10] Rv. x. 28, 10.

[11] Rv. v. 74, 4.

[12] Rv. v. 15, 3. *Cf.* Strabo, xv. 1, 31.

[13] Av. v. 36, 6.

[14] Rv. vii. 18, 17.

the Aitareya Brāhmaṇa.[15] The lioness is also mentioned in the Yajurveda Saṃhitās and the Brāhmaṇas.[16] See also **Halīkṣṇa.**

[15] vi. 35, 1.

[16] Taittirīya Saṃhitā, i. 2, 12, 2; vi. 2, 7, 1; Vājasaneyi Saṃhitā, v. 10; Śatapatha Brāhmaṇa, iii. 5, 1, 21; Maitrāyaṇī Saṃhitā, iii. 8, 5.

Cf. Zimmer, *Altindisches Leben*, 78, 79.

1. **Sic** denotes the 'border' of a garment. The Rigveda refers to a son clutching the hem of his father's robe to attract his attention,[1] and to a mother's covering her son with the edge of her garment.[2] The word also occurs later.[3]

[1] iii. 53, 2.

[2] x. 18, 11.

[3] Av. xiv. 2, 51; Śatapatha Brāhmaṇa, iii. 2, 1, 18.

2. **Sic** denotes, in the dual, the 'wings' of an army,[1] or, in the plural, the 'lines.'

[1] Rv. x. 75, 4.

[2] Av. xi. 9, 18; 10, 20.

Cf. Pischel, *Vedische Studien*, 2, 65; Geldner, *ibid.*, 3, 31.

3. **Sic** seems in one passage of the Rigveda (i. 95, 7), where it is used in the dual, to denote the 'horizon' (meaning literally the 'two borders'; *i.e.*, of heaven and of earth).

Sidhmala, 'leprous,' is found in the Vājasaneyi Saṃhitā (xxx. 17) and the Taittirīya Brāhmaṇa (iii. 4, 14, 1) as a designation of one of the victims at the Puruṣamedha ('human sacrifice'). *Cf.* **Kilāsa.**

Sinīvālī denotes the day of new moon and its presiding spirit, which, in accordance with widespread ideas concerning the connexion of the moon and vegetation, is one of fertility and growth. It occurs very frequently from the Rigveda[1] onwards.[2]

[1] ii. 32, 7. 8; x. 184, 2.

[2] Av. ii. 26, 2; vi. 11, 3; ix. 4, 14; xiv. 2, 15; xix. 31, 10; Taittirīya Saṃhitā, ii. 4, 6, 2; iii. 4, 9, 1. 6; v. 5, 17, 1; 6, 18, 1; Kāṭhaka Saṃhitā, xxxv. 2, etc.

Cf. Zimmer, *Altindisches Leben*, 352; Macdonell, *Vedic Mythology*, p. 125.

Sindhu in the Rigveda[1] and the Atharvaveda[2] often means 'stream' merely (*cf.* **Sapta Sindhavaḥ**), but it has also[3] the more exact sense of 'the stream' *par excellence*, 'the Indus.' The name is, however, rarely mentioned after the period of the Saṃhitās,[4] always then occurring in such a way as to suggest distance. The horses from the Indus (*saindhava*) were famous.[5] See **Saindhava.** *Cf.* also **Sarasvatī.**

[1] i. 97, 8; 125, 5; ii. 11, 9; 25, 3. 5; iii. 53, 9, etc.

[2] iii. 13, 1; iv. 24, 2; x. 4, 15; xiii. 3, 50, etc.

[3] Rv. i. 122, 6; 126, 1; iv. 54, 6; 55, 3; v. 53, 9; vii. 95, 1; viii. 12, 3; 25, 14; 20, 25; 26, 18; x. 64, 9; Av. xii. 1, 3; xiv. 1, 43; perhaps also vi. 24, 1; vii. 45, 1; xix. 38, 2; Vājasaneyi Saṃhitā, viii. 59.

[4] The Sindhu-Sauvīras occur in the Baudhāyana Dharma Sūtra, i. 2, 14. *Cf.* Bühler, *Sacred Books of the East*, 14, 148; Oldenberg, *Buddha*, 394, n.

[5] Bṛhadāraṇyaka Upaniṣad, vi. 2, 15 (Mādhyaṃdina = vi. 1, 13 Kāṇva).

Cf. Zimmer, *Altindisches Leben*, 16, 17, 27.

Sindhu-kṣit is the name of a long-banished but finally restored **Rājanyarṣi** in the Pañcaviṃśa Brāhmaṇa,[1] probably quite a mythical personage.[2]

[1] xii. 12, 6.

[2] Oldenberg, *Zeitschrift der Deutschen Morgenländischen Gesellschaft*, 42, 235, n. 3.

Sirī in the Rigveda (x. 71, 9) seems to denote a 'female weaver.'

Silācī is, in the Atharvaveda,[1] the name of a healing plant, also called **Lākṣā.**

[1] v. 5, 1. 8. *Cf.* Bloomfield, *Hymns of the Atharvaveda*, 419; Whitney, Translation of the Atharvaveda, 228.

Silāñjālā, which the commentator reads as Śalāñjālā, is the name of a plant, perhaps a 'grain creeper,' in the Atharvaveda.[1] The Kauśika Sūtra[2] reads the word as Śilāñjālā. *Cf.* **Silācī.**

[1] vi. 16, 4.

[2] li. 16. *Cf.* Bloomfield, *Hymns of the Atharvaveda*, 466; Whitney, Translation of the Atharvaveda, 292, 293.

Sīcāpū in the list of victims at the Aśvamedha ('horse sacrifice') in the Yajurveda[1] seems to denote a kind of bird.

1 Maitrāyaṇī Saṃhitā, iii. 19, 6; Vājasaneyi Saṃhitā, xxiv. 25. *Cf.* Zimmer, *Altindisches Leben*, 94.

Sītā, 'furrow,' occurs in the Rigveda,[1] and often later.[2]

1 iv. 57, 6. 7 (the most agricultural of Rigvedic hymns, and probably late).

2 Av. xi. 3, 12; Taittirīya Saṃhitā, v. 2, 5, 4. 5; 6, 2, 5; Kāṭhaka Saṃhitā, xx. 3, etc.

Cf. Hopkins, *Journal of the American Oriental Society*, 17, 86, n.

Sīman denotes the 'parting' of the hair in the Atharvaveda[1] and later.[2]

1 ix. 8, 13.

2 Aitareya Brāhmaṇa, v. 7, 4; Pañcaviṃśa Brāhmaṇa, xiii. 4, 1; xv. 5, 20; Śatapatha Brāhmaṇa, vii. 4, 1, 14. *Cf. sīmanta* in Av. vi. 134, 3; Taittirīya Brāhmaṇa, ii. 7, 17, 3.

Sīra, 'plough,' is mentioned in the Rigveda,[1] and often later.[2] It was large and heavy, as is shown by the fact that six oxen,[3] or eight,[4] or twelve,[5] or even twenty-four,[6] were used to drag it. The animals which drew the plough were oxen, which were, no doubt, yoked and harnessed with traces.[7] The ox was guided by the **Aṣṭrā**, or 'goad,' of the ploughman (*cf.* **Vaiśya**).[8] Little is known of the parts of the plough. See **Lāṅgala** and **Phāla.**

1 iv. 57, 8; x. 101, 3. 4.

2 Av. vi. 30, 1; 91, 1; viii. 9, 16, etc.; Taittirīya Brāhmaṇa, i. 7, 1, 2; ii. 5, 8, 12; Vājasaneyi Saṃhitā, xviii. 7; Maitrāyaṇī Saṃhitā, ii. 11, 4.

3 Av. vi. 91, 1; viii. 9, 16; Taittirīya Saṃhitā, v. 2, 5, 2; Kāṭhaka Saṃhitā, xv. 2; xx. 3; Śatapatha Brāhmaṇa, vii. 2, 2, 6; xiii. 8, 2, 6.

4 Av. vi. 91, 1.

5 Taittirīya Saṃhitā, i. 8, 7, 1; v. 2, 5, 2; Kāṭhaka Saṃhitā, xv. 2; Maitrāyaṇī Saṃhitā, ii. 6, 2, etc.

6 Kāṭhaka Saṃhitā, xv. 2. *Cf.* Weber, *Indische Studien*, 13, 244, n. 1.

7 **Varatrā** is found in Rv. iv. 57, 4, and (of the ox in the **Mudgala** story) in x. 102, 8. It may denote the fastening of the ox to the yoke rather than to the plough by traces.

8 *Cf.* Rv. iv. 57, 4; x. 102, 8.

Cf. Zimmer, *Altindisches Leben*, 236, 237.

Sīla, 'plough,' is found in the Kapiṣṭhala Saṃhitā (xxviii. 8).

Sīlamāvatī in the Rigveda[1] is, according to Ludwig,[2] the name of a river; but this is most improbable.[3] Sāyaṇa thinks the word means 'rich in hemp.'

[1] x. 75, 8.
[2] Translation of the Rigveda, 3, 200.
[3] Zimmer, *Altindisches Leben*, 429; Böhtlingk, Dictionary, *s.v.*; Geldner, *Rigveda, Glossar*, 195.

Sīsa, 'lead,' occurs first in the Atharvaveda,[1] where it is mentioned as used for amulets.[2] The word is then quite common.[3] The use of lead by the weaver as a weight is perhaps also referred to.[4]

[1] xii. 2, 1. 19 *et seq.*, 53.
[2] i. 16. 2. 4.
[3] Maitrāyaṇī Saṃhitā, ii. 4, 2; Vājasaneyi Saṃhitā, xviii. 13; Taittirīya Brāhmaṇa, iii. 12, 6, 5; Śatapatha Brāhmaṇa, v. 1, 2, 14; 4, 1, 9; xii. 7, 1, 7; 2, 10; Chāndogya Upaniṣad, iv. 17, 7, etc.
[4] Vājasaneyi Saṃhitā, xix. 80; Maitrāyaṇī Saṃhitā, iii. 11, 9; Taittirīya Brāhmaṇa, ii. 6, 4. This is the view of Roth, St. Petersburg Dictionary, *s.v.*, and of Zimmer, *Altindisches Leben*, 53. But Griffith, Translation of the Vājasaneyi Saṃhitā, 183, n., thinks that in xix. 80 lead is referred to not as a weight, but as a charm against demons and sorcery.
Cf. Bloomfield, *Journal of the American Oriental Society*, 15, 157, 158.

Su-kanyā is the name of **Śaryāta's** daughter, who married **Cyavana** according to the Śatapatha Brāhmaṇa.[1]

[1] iv. 1, 5, 6; 10, 13; Jaiminīya Brāhmaṇa, iii. 121 *et seq.*

Su-kaparda. See **Kaparda.**

Su-karīra in the Maitrāyaṇī Saṃhitā (ii. 7, 5) is a misreading of *su-kurīra*. See **Kurīra.**

Su-kīrti Kākṣīvata ('descendant of **Kakṣīvant**') is the name of a Ṛṣi to whom the Brāhmaṇas of the Rigveda[1] ascribe the authorship of a Vedic hymn.[2]

[1] Aitareya Brāhmaṇa, v. 15, 4; vi. 29, 1; Kauṣītaki Brāhmaṇa, xxx. 5.
[2] x. 131.

Su-keśin Bhāradvāja ('descendant of **Bharadvāja**') is the name of a teacher in the Praśna Upaniṣad (i. 1).

Su-kurīra. See **Kurīra.**

Su-kha. See **Kha.**

Sugandhi-tejana in the later Saṃhitās[1] and the Brāhmaṇas[2] denotes a kind of fragrant grass.

[1] Taittirīya Saṃhitā, vi. 2, 8, 4; Kāṭhaka Saṃhitā, xxv. 6.

[2] Aitareya Brāhmaṇa, i. 28, 28; Satapatha Brāhmaṇa, iii. 5, 2, 17; Pañcaviṃśa Brāhmaṇa, xxiv. 13, 5.

Su-citta Śailana is the name of a teacher in the Jaiminīya Upaniṣad Brāhmaṇa (i. 14, 4).

Su-jāta, 'well-born,' is an epithet found applied to men in a few passages of the Rigveda. It would probably be a mistake to press the sense so as to denote 'nobles' as compared with the people. See **Sabhā.**

[1] ii. 2, 11; v. 6, 2; vii. 1, 4. 15; viii. 20, 8.

Sutaṃ-bhara is credited by the Anukramaṇī (Index) with the authorship of certain hymns of the Rigveda.[1] The word does not occur in those hymns, but it appears as an adjective ('carrying away Soma') elsewhere,[2] and may, in a second passage,[3] by a conjecture[4] be taken as a man's name.

[1] v. 11-14.

[2] v. 44, 13.

[3] ix. 6, 6.

[4] If *sutaṃ-bharāya* be read for *sutáṃ bhárāya*, as Roth suggests in the St. Petersburg Dictionary, *s.v.*

Sutvan Kairiśi Bhārgāyaṇa is, in the Aitareya Brāhmaṇa (viii. 28, 18), the name of a king who, being taught a spell by **Maitreya Kauṣārava,** slew five kings and became great.

Su-dakṣiṇa Kṣaimi ('descendant of Kṣema') is the name of a teacher in the Jaiminīya Upaniṣad Brāhmaṇa (iii. 6, 3; 7, 1 *et seq.*; 8, 6).

Su-datta Pārāśarya ('descendant of **Parāśara**') is in the Jaiminīya Upaniṣad Brāhmaṇa (iii. 41, 1; iv. 17, 1) the name of a teacher who was a pupil of **Janaśruta Vārakya.**

Su-dāman is the name of a river in the Pañcaviṃśa Brāhmaṇa (xxii. 18, 1).

Su-dās is the name of the **Tṛtsu** king who won a famous victory over the ten kings, as described in a hymn of the Rigveda.[1] At one time **Viśvāmitra** was his **Purohita,** and accompanied him in his victorious raids over the **Vipāś** (Beās) and **Śutudrī** (Sutlej).[2] The Aśvins gave him a queen, **Sudevī,**[3] and also helped him on another occasion.[4] He appears with **Trasadasyu** in a late hymn without hint of rivalry,[5] but elsewhere he seems to be referred to as defeated by **Purukutsa,** Trasadasyu's father.[6] In the Aitareya Brāhmaṇa[7] he is recognized as a great king, with **Vasiṣṭha** as his Purohita, and similarly in the Śāṅkhāyana Śrauta Sūtra,[8] where his generosity to his priest is related.

His exact ancestry is a little uncertain, because he is called **Paijavana,** 'son of Pijavana,' as Yāska explains the patronymic. If this explanation is correct, **Divodāsa** must have been his grandfather. If he was the son of Divodāsa, Pijavana must be understood as a more remote ancestor. The former alternative seems the more probable. *Cf.* **Turvaśa, Dāśarājña. Paijavana, Bharata, Saudāsa.**

[1] vii. 18. See also Rv. vii. 20, 2; 25, 3; 32, 10; 33, 3; 64, 3; 83, 1 *et seq.*

[2] Rv. iii. 53, 9. 11. See also **Viśvāmitra** and **Vasiṣṭha.**

[3] Rv. i. 112, 19.

[4] Rv. i. 47, 9, where, however, Roth, St. Petersburg Dictionary, *s.v.* 1, takes *su-dās* as an adjective ('worshipping well').

[5] Rv. vii. 19, 3.

[6] Rv. i. 63, 7, reading *Sudāsam* for *Sudāse* with Ludwig, Translation of the Rigveda, 3, 174. *Cf.* Hillebrandt, *Vedische Mythologie*, 1, 112, n. 1; Geldner, *Vedische Studien*, 1, 153; Oldenberg, *Ṛgveda-Noten*, 1, 63.

[7] vii. 34, 9.

[8] xvi. 11, 14.

Cf. Hillebrandt, *Vedische Mythologie*, 1, 107 *et seq.*; Weber, *Episches im vedischen Ritual*, 31 *et seq.*

1. **Su-deva** is, according to Ludwig,[1] the proper name of a sacrificer in one hymn of the Rigveda.[2]

[1] Translation of the Rigveda, 3, 160.

[2] viii. 5, 6.

2. **Su-deva Kāśyapa** ('descendant of **Kaśyapa**') is the name of a teacher in the Taittirīya Āraṇyaka[1] who set forth the expiation for lack of chastity.

[1] ii. 18. *Cf.* x. 1, 8; Weber, *Indische Studien*, 1, 188, n.; 10, 103.

Su-devalā was the name of **Ṛtuparṇa** as a woman according to the Baudhāyana Śrauta Sūtra (xx. 12).

Su-devī. See **Sudās.**

Su-dhanvan Āṅgirasa ('descendant of **Aṅgiras**') is the name of a teacher in the Bṛhadāraṇyaka Upaniṣad (iii. 3, 1).

1. **Su-nītha Śaucad-ratha** ('descendant of Śucadratha') is the name of a man in the Rigveda (v. 79, 2). *Cf.* **Satya-śravas.**

2. **Su-nītha Kāpaṭava** is the name of a teacher in the Vaṃśa Brāhmaṇa.[1]

[1] *Indische Studien*, 4, 372.

1. **Su-parṇa,** 'well-winged,' designates a large bird of prey, the 'eagle' or the 'vulture,' in the Rigveda[1] and later.[2] In the passages in which it appears as an eater of carrion[3] it must be the vulture. The Jaiminīya Brāhmaṇa[4] mentions an eagle which separates milk from water like the **Kruñc.** In the Rigveda[5] the Suparṇa is said to be the child of the **Śyena,** and is distinguished from the latter in another passage:[6] this led Zimmer[7] to think that the falcon is probably meant.[8] The Atharvaveda alludes to its cry,[9] and describes it as living in the hills.[10]

[1] i. 164, 20; ii. 42, 2; iv. 26, 4; viii. 100, 8; ix. 48, 3, etc.

[2] Av. i. 24, 1; ii. 27, 2; 30, 3; iv. 6, 3, etc.; Taittirīya Saṃhitā, vii. 5, 8, 5, etc.

[3] Maitrāyaṇī Saṃhitā, iv. 9, 19; Taittirīya Āraṇyaka, iv. 29.

[4] ii. 438 (*Journal of the American Oriental Society*, 19, 101).

[5] x. 144, 4.

[6] ii. 42, 2.

[7] *Altindisches Leben*, 88.

[8] In the post-Vedic period Suparṇa became a mythical bird, identified with Viṣṇu's vehicle, Garuḍa, who, however, is also regarded as king of the Suparṇas.

[9] ii. 30, 3.

[10] v. 4, 2.

2. **Suparṇa** is personified in the Yajurveda Saṃhitās[1] as a Ṛṣi.

[1] Taittirīya Saṃhitā, iv. 3, 3, 2; Kāṭhaka Saṃhitā, xxxix. 7.

Su-pitrya, a word occurring once in the Rigveda,[1] is probably an adjective ('maintaining his paternal character well'). Ludwig,[2] however, regards it, but without any great probability, as a proper name.

[1] x. 115, 6.

[2] Translation of the Rigveda, 3, 169.

Su-pratīta Auluṇḍya is the name of a teacher, a pupil of **Bṛhaspatigupta,** in the Vaṃśa Brāhmaṇa.[1]

[1] *Indische Studien*, 4, 372.

Suplan Sārñjaya is the name of a prince of the **Sṛñjayas** who was taught the Dākṣāyaṇa sacrifice by **Pratīdarśa,** and took the name of **Sahadeva** as a token of his success.[1]

[1] Śatapatha Brāhmaṇa, ii. 4, 4, 4; xii. 8, 2, 3. *Cf.* Lévi, *La Doctrine du Sacrifice*, 139; Hillebrandt, *Vedische Mythologie*, 1, 105, 106.

Su-bandhu in the hymns of the Rigveda[1] is taken by Sāyaṇa to be a proper name; but this is not certain, Roth[2] seeing in the passages only an ordinary noun meaning 'a good friend.' The later tradition[3] explains that Subandhu and his brothers, called **Gaupāyanas,** were priests of **Asamāti,** who cast them off and took two others, **Kirāta** and **Ākuli.** By these two in pigeon form Subandhu was caused to swoon, but was revived by his three brothers, who recited certain hymns.[4]

[1] x. 59, 8; 60, 7. 10.

[2] St. Petersburg Dictionary, *s.v.* 1.

[3] Bṛhaddevatā, vii. 83 *et seq.*, with Macdonell's notes. See also **Asamāti,** n. 1.

[4] Rv. x. 57-60.

Cf. Max Müller, *Journal of the Royal Asiatic Society*, 2, 420-455; Oldenberg, *Zeitschrift der Deutschen Morgenländischen Gesellschaft*, 39, 90.

Su-brahmaṇya in the Brāhmaṇas[1] denotes a priest who officiates as one of the three assistants of the Udgātṛ (see **Ṛtvij**). His office is Subrahmaṇyā.[2]

[1] Pañcaviṃśa Brāhmaṇa, xxv. 4, 6; 18, 4; Śatapatha Brāhmaṇa, iii. 3, 4, 9. *Cf.* Weber, *Indische Studien*, 10, 362, 374.

[2] Aitareya Brāhmaṇa, vi. 3, 1-7. 11. 12; Kauṣītaki Brāhmaṇa, xxvii. 6, etc. The priest himself is so styled, Aitareya Brāhmaṇa, vii. 1, 2; Pañcaviṃśa Brāhmaṇa, xviii. 9, 19, etc.

Su-bhagā, in the vocative *subhage*, is a frequent form of courteous address to women from the Rigveda onwards.[1]

[1] Rv. x. 10, 10. 12; 108, 5; Av. v. 5, 6; vi. 30, 3, etc.

Su-bhadrikā occurs in the Aśvamedha ('horse sacrifice') section of the Yajurveda[1] as in some way connected with the rite. Weber[2] thinks that a proper name, that of the wife of the king of **Kāmpīla**, is intended, but Mahīdhara[3] explains the word merely as a lady with many lovers or a courtezan, a view followed by Roth.[4] Since the Taittirīya[5] and Kāṭhaka[6] Saṃhitās have no Subhadrikā, but a vocative *subhage* (see **Subhagā**), the sense remains very doubtful.

[1] Vājasaneyi Saṃhitā, xxiii. 18 (*cf.* Satapatha Brāhmaṇa, xiii. 2, 8, 3); Maitrāyaṇī Saṃhitā, iii. 12, 20.

[2] *Indische Studien*, 1, 183, 184; *Indian Literature*, 114, 115. *Cf.* Griffith, Translation of the Vājasaneyi Saṃhitā, 212, n.

[3] On Vājasaneyi Saṃhitā, *loc. cit.*

[4] St. Petersburg Dictionary, *s.v. subhadraka*, 2*b*; Böhtlingk's Dictionary, *s.v.* 2*a*.

[5] vii. 4, 19, 1; Taittirīya Brāhmaṇa, iii. 9, 6.

[6] *Aśvamedha*, iv. 8.

Cf. Zimmer, *Altindisches Leben*, 36, 37; Eggeling, *Sacred Books of the East*, 44, 321, 322.

Sumati-tsaru. See **Tsaru.**

Su-mantra Bābhrava ('descendant of Babhru') **Gautama** ('descendant of **Gotama**') is the name of a teacher, a pupil of **Śūṣa Vāhneya Bhāradvāja**, in the Vaṃśa Brāhmaṇa.[1]

[1] *Indische Studien*, 4, 373.

Su-mitra Vādhryaśva ('descendant of **Vadhryaśva**') is the name of a Ṛṣi in the Rigveda,[1] where also[2] the **Sumitras**, his family, are mentioned.

[1] x. 69, 3. 5.

[2] x. 69, 1. 7. 8. *Cf.* Ludwig, Translation of the Rigveda, 3, 133.

Su-mīḷha is the name of a patron in the Rigveda.[1]

[1] vi. 63, 9. *Cf.* Ludwig, Translation of the Rigveda, 3, 158.

Su-medha occurs in an obscure hymn of the Rigveda[1] either as an adjective ('of good understanding') or a proper name, perhaps identical with **Nṛmedha** or his brother.

[1] x. 132, 7. *Cf.* Ludwig, Translation of the Rigveda, 3, 133; Griffith, *Hymns of the Rigveda*, 2, 579, n.

Sumna-yu is mentioned in the Vaṃśa (list of teachers) at the end of the Śāṅkhāyana Āraṇyaka (xv. 1) as a pupil of **Uddālaka.**

Su-yajña Śāṇḍilya is the name of a pupil of **Kaṃsa Vārakya** in the Jaiminīya Upaniṣad Brāhmaṇa (iv. 17, 1). Another Suyajña is a **Śāṅkhāyana**, author of the Gṛhya Sūtra.

Su-yavasa denotes a 'good pasture' in the Rigveda[1] and later.[2]

[1] i. 42, 8; vi. 28, 7; vii. 18, 4, etc.

[2] Taittirīya Saṃhitā, i. 7, 5, 2, etc.

Surā is the name of an intoxicating 'spirituous liquor,' often mentioned in Vedic literature. In some passages[1] it is referred to favourably, in others with decided disapproval.[2] It is classed with the use of meat and with dicing as an evil in the Atharvaveda,[3] and often with dicing.[4] It was, as opposed to **Soma,** essentially a drink of ordinary life.[5] It was the drink of men in the **Sabhā,**[6] and gave rise to broils.[7]

Its exact nature is not certain. It may have been a strong spirit prepared from fermented grains and plants, as Eggeling[8]

[1] Rv. i. 116, 7; x. 131, 4. 5. *Cf.* Av. iv. 34, 6; x. 6, 5; Taittirīya Saṃhitā, i. 3, 3, 2; Śatapatha Brāhmaṇa, xii. 7, 3, 8.

[2] Rv. vii. 86, 6; viii. 2, 12; 21, 14; Maitrāyaṇī Saṃhitā, i. 11, 6; ii. 4, 2; iv. 2, 1, etc.

[3] vi. 70, 1. *Cf.* Bloomfield, *Hymns of the Atharvaveda*, 493.

[4] Rv. vii. 86, 6; Av. xiv. 1, 35. 36; xv. 9, 1. 2.

[5] Taittirīya Brāhmaṇa, i. 3, 3, 2.

[6] See n. 4.

[7] Rv. viii. 2, 12; 21, 14. *Cf.* Kāṭhaka Saṃhitā, xiv 6; Śatapatha Brāhmaṇa, i. 6, 3, 4; Maitrāyaṇī Saṃhitā, ii. 4, 2, etc.

[8] *Sacred Books of the East*, 44, 223, n. 2; Caland, *Altindisches Zauberritual*, 21, n. 1; Zimmer, *Altindisches Leben*, 280, 281. *Cf.* Kātyāyana Śrauta Sūtra, xix. 1, 20-27; Mahīdhara on Vājasaneyi Saṃhitā, xix. 1.

holds, or, as Whitney[9] thought, a kind of beer or ale. Geldner[10] renders it 'brandy.' It is sometimes mentioned in connexion with **Madhu.**[11] It was kept in skins.[12]

[9] Translation of the Atharvaveda, 207. *Cf.* Schrader, *Prehistoric Antiquities*, 326.

[10] *Rigveda, Glossar*, 198.

[11] Av. vi. 69, 1; ix. 1, 18. 19; Vājasaneyi Saṃhitā, xix. 95. See Hillebrandt, *Vedische Mythologie*, 1, 251, who attempts to show that Surā and Soma were rival priestly drinks at one time, belonging to different sections of the people.

[12] Pañcaviṃśa Brāhmaṇa, xiv. 11, 26. *Cf.* Rv. i. 191, 10.

Cf. Hopkins, *Journal of the American Oriental Society*, 13, 121.

Surā-kāra, 'maker of **Surā,**' is included in the list of victims at the Puruṣamedha ('human sacrifice') in the Yajurveda.[1]

[1] Vājasaneyi Saṃhitā, xxx. 11; Taittirīya Brāhmaṇa, iii. 4, 7, 1. *Cf.* Zimmer, *Altindisches Leben*, 281, who compares Rv. i. 191, 10, which may refer to such a person.

Su-rādhas is the name of a man in the Rigveda (i. 100, 17), where he is mentioned with **Ambarīṣa** and others.

Surāma in the Rigveda[1] refers to the illness caused by drinking **Surā** to excess. Indra is described as suffering from it in the Namuci legend.[2] Later Surāma[3] was treated as an epithet of **Soma,** meaning 'delightful.'

[1] x. 131, 5.

[2] Bloomfield, *Journal of the American Oriental Society*, 15, 148 *et seq.*

[3] Or Surāman. *Cf.* Vājasaneyi Saṃhitā, xxi. 42; Maitrāyaṇī Saṃhitā, iii. 11, 4; iv. 12, 5. Hillebrandt, *Vedische Mythologie*, 1, 245 *et seq.*, renders it 'Surā mixed,' which is doubtful.

Su-varṇa, 'beautiful coloured,' is an epithet of gold (**Hiraṇya**), and then comes to be used as a substantive denoting 'gold.'

[1] Taittirīya Brāhmaṇa, i. 4, 7, 4; 8, 9, 1, etc.

[2] Av. xv. 1, 2; Taittirīya Brāhmaṇa, iii. 12, 6, 6; Satapatha Brāhmaṇa, xi. 4, 1, 8, etc.; Chāndogya Upaniṣad, i. 6, 6; iii. 19, 1; iv. 17, 7, etc.

Su-vasana in the Rigveda denotes a 'splendid garment,'[1] and is also used adjectivally, 'clothing well.'[2] Su-vāsas, 'well-dressed,' is a common adjective.[3] See **Vāsas.**

[1] vi. 51, 4.

[2] ix. 97, 50.

[3] Rv. i. 124, 7; iii. 8, 4; x. 71, 4, etc. *Cf.* Zimmer, *Altindisches Leben*, 262.

Su-vāstu ('having fair dwellings') is the name of a river in the Rigveda.[1] It is clearly the Soastos of Arrian[2] and the modern Swāt, a tributary of the **Kubhā** (Kabul river) which is itself an affluent of the Indus.

[1] viii. 19, 37; Nirukta, iv. 15.
[2] *Indica*, iv. 11.
Cf. Roth, *Nirukta, Erläuterungen*, 43; Zimmer, *Altindisches Leben*, 18; Ludwig, Translation of the Rigveda, 3. 200; *Imperial Gazetteer of India*, 23, 187.

Su-śārada Śālaṅkāyana is the name of a teacher, a pupil of **Urjayant Aupamanyava**, in the Vaṃśa Brāhmaṇa.[1]

[1] *Indische Studien*, 4, 372.

1. **Su-śravas** is the name of a man in the Rigveda (i. 53, 9) according to Sāyaṇa.

2. **Su-śravas** is the name of the father of **Upagu Sauśravasa** in the Pañcaviṃśa Brāhmaṇa (xiv. 6, 8).

3. **Su-śravas Kauṣya** is the name of a teacher, a contemporary of **Kuśri Vājaśravasa**, in the Śatapatha Brāhmaṇa (x. 5, 5, 1 *et seq.*).

4. **Su-śravas Vārṣa-gaṇya** ('descendant of Vṛṣagaṇa') is the name of a teacher, a pupil of **Prātarahna Kauhala**, in the Vaṃśa Brāhmaṇa.[1]

[1] *Indische Studien*, 4, 372.

Su-ṣāman is the name of a man in one verse of the Rigveda,[1] and probably forms part of the strange name, Varo Suṣāman, in other passages.[2] *Cf.* **Varu.**

[1] viii. 25, 22; possibly 60, 18.
[2] viii. 23, 28; 24, 28; 26, 2.
Cf. Ludwig, Translation of the Rigveda, 3, 162.

Su-ṣomā occurs certainly as the name of a river in the Nadīstuti ('praise of rivers') in the Rigveda.[1] In two other passages it would seem to be a proper name, once masculine,[2] perhaps

[1] x. 75, 5; Nirukta, ix. 26, where it is absurdly identified with the **Sindhu** (Indus).
[2] viii. 7, 29.

the people, and once feminine,[3] though Roth[4] sees in the word the designation of a Soma vessel. Its identification is quite uncertain, though it has been thought to be the Σόανος of Megasthenes,[5] the modern Suwan.

[3] viii. 64, 11.
[4] St. Petersburg Dictionary, *s.v.* 2.
[5] See Arrian, *Indica*, iv. 12; Schwanbeck, *Megasthenes*, 31, where there is a various reading Σόαμος.

Cf. Hillebrandt, *Vedische Mythologie*, 1, 126 *et seq.*; Max Müller, *Sacred Books of the East*, 32, 398, 399; Zimmer, *Altindisches Leben*, 12-14.

Su-sartu is the name of a river in the Nadī-stuti ('praise of rivers') in the Rigveda.[1] That it was a tributary of the Indus is certain, but which one is unknown.

[1] x. 75, 6. *Cf.* Zimmer, *Altindisches Leben*, 14; Ludwig, Translation of the Rigveda, 3, 200.

Su-havis Āṅgirasa ('descendant of **Aṅgiras**') is the name of the seer of a Sāman or chant in the Pañcaviṃśa Brāhmaṇa (xiv. 3, 25).

Sū-kara 'wild boar,' has the appearance of being an onomatopoetic word ('making the sound *sū*'); it is more probably a very old word going back to the Indo-European period, and cognate with the Latin *su-culus* ('little pig'), being transformed in sense by popular etymology.[1] It occurs in the Rigveda[2] and later.[3] It appears once in the Atharvaveda accompanied by *mṛga*,[4] the combined words apparently meaning 'wild hog,' as opposed to **Varāha**, 'boar.'

[1] The *sū-* corresponding to Lat. *sū-s*, Gk. ὗ-ς, Old High German, *sū*. *Cf.* Brugmann, *Grundriss*, 2², 483.
[2] vii. 55, 4.
[3] Av. ii. 27, 2; v. 14, 1; Maitrāyaṇī Saṃhitā, iii. 14, 21; Vājasaneyi Saṃhitā, xxiv. 40; Chāndogya Upaniṣad, v. 10, 2, etc. None of the passages refer to the flesh as eaten: Buddha's death was due to a meal of *sūkara-maddava*, which may well mean 'tender parts of pork' (see Fleet, *Journal of the Royal Asiatic Society*, 1906, 881, n.), though the Rājanighaṇṭu, vii. 85, gives *sūkara* as meaning the *Batatas edulis*.
[4] xii. 1, 48. The use of *mṛga* here does not indicate that *sūkara* is a new name, because the latter word elsewhere always occurs alone both in the Rigveda and later (n. 3). *Cf.* **Mṛga** above, 2, 172, n. 3.

Cf. Zimmer, *Altindisches Leben*, 82; Pischel, *Vedische Studien*, 1, 100.

Sūktà, 'well uttered,' is the regular term for a 'hymn' as part of the Śastra in the later Saṃhitās[1] and the Brāhmaṇas.[2] The sense of 'hymn' must also be recognized in several passages of the Rigveda.[3]

[1] Taittirīya Saṃhitā, v. 4, 5, 5; vii. 1, 5, 4, etc.

[2] Aitareya Brāhmaṇa, ii. 33; iii. 11, 9. 12-15; iv. 21, 5; vi. 8, 10; Kauṣītaki Brāhmaṇa, xiv. 1; xv. 3; Satapatha Brāhmaṇa, xiii. 5, 1, 18; Nirukta, iv. 6; xi. 16.

[3] i. 42, 20; 171, 1; ii. 6, 2; vii. 29, 3, etc.

Sūcī, 'needle,' is found in the Rigveda[1] and later.[2]

[1] ii. 32, 4.

[2] Av. xi. 10, 3; Vājasaneyi Saṃhitā, xxiii. 33; Taittirīya Brāhmaṇa, iii. 9, 6, 4; Aitareya Brāhmaṇa, iii. 18, 6; Śatapatha Brāhmaṇa, xiii. 2, 10, 2. 3; Jaiminīya Brāhmaṇa, ii. 10; Jaiminīya Upaniṣad Brāhmaṇa, i. 10, 3 (Oertel, *Journal of the American Oriental Society*, 16, 228).

Sūcīka is the name of a stinging insect in the Rigveda.[1]

[1] i. 191, 7. *Cf.* Zimmer, *Altindisches Leben*, 98.

Sūta is the name of a court official who is often mentioned with the **Grāmaṇī**. He is one of the eight **Vīras** in the Pañcaviṃśa Brāhmaṇa,[1] and of the eleven **Ratnins** in other texts.[2] He also appears in the Atharvaveda[3] among the kingmakers (**Rājakṛt**) and in the Śatrarudriya[4] ('section dealing with the hundred Rudras') of the Yajurveda. The commentators are agreed in seeing in him the 'charioteer' (**Sārathi**) or 'master of the horse,' of the king; this sense is accepted by Roth,[5] by Whitney,[6] and by Bloomfield.[7] But the fact that the **Saṃ-**

[1] ix. 1, 4, where he follows the chief queen (**Mahiṣī**), and precedes the Grāmaṇī in the list.

[2] Kāṭhaka Saṃhitā, xv. 4; Maitrāyaṇī Saṃhitā, ii. 6, 5; iv. 3, 8; Taittirīya Brāhmaṇa, i. 7, 3, 1; Taittirīya Saṃhitā, i. 8, 9, 1; Śatapatha Brāhmaṇa, v. 3, 1, 5.

[3] iii. 5, 7.

[4] Taittirīya Brāhmaṇa, iv. 5, 2, 1; Kāṭhaka Saṃhitā, xvii. 2; Maitrāyaṇī Saṃhitā, ii. 9, 3; Vājasaneyi Saṃhitā, xvi. 18. So also in the list of victims at the Puruṣamedha ('human sacrifice'), Vājasaneyi Saṃhitā, xxx. 6; Taittirīya Brāhmaṇa, iii. 4, 2, 1. For other references to the Sūta, see Taittirīya Brāhmaṇa, ii. 7, 18, 4; Śatapatha Brāhmaṇa, v. 4, 4, 7; xiii. 4, 2, 5; 7, 1, 43; Kāṭhaka Saṃhitā, xxviii. 3; Bṛhadāraṇyaka Upaniṣad, iv. 3, 37. 38.

[5] St. Petersburg Dictionary, *s.v.*

[6] Translation of the Atharvaveda, 62.

[7] *Hymns of the Atharvaveda*, 114.

grahītṛ, who occurs in several passages beside the Sūta, is the 'charioteer,' renders this version improbable. Eggeling[8] thinks that he was, in the Brāhmaṇas at least, a minstrel and court poet, while Weber[9] considers that his name denotes him as 'consecrated'—that is, one who has constant access to the king. In the Epic the Sūta serves as a royal herald and bard:[10] it may be that the curious words *ahanti*,[11] *ahantya*,[12] or *ahantva*[13] applied to him[14] in the Śatarudriya denote his sacred character at once as minstrel and as herald—a combination of functions not unknown elsewhere.

[8] *Sacred Books of the East*, 41, 62, n. 1.
[9] *Indische Studien*, 17, 200.
[10] Hopkins, *Journal of the American Oriental Society*, 13, 254, 255.
[11] Vājasaneyi Saṃhitā, xvi. 18. This word means 'non-fighter' according to Weber, *Indische Studien*, 17, 200.
[12] Taittirīya Saṃhitā, iv. 5, 2, 1.
[13] Kāṭhaka Saṃhitā, xvii. 2; Maitrāyaṇī Saṃhitā, ii. 9, 3.
[14] The last two forms appear to be equivalent in sense to *ahanya*, 'not to be slain,' 'inviolable.'

Sūta-vaśā denotes in the Yajurveda[1] a cow barren after having one calf.

[1] Taittirīya Saṃhitā, ii. 1, 5, 4; vi. 1, 3, 6; Kāṭhaka Saṃhitā, xxxvii. 5; Taittirīya Brāhmaṇa, ii. 7, 4, 1, etc.

Sūtra has the sense of 'thread' in the Atharvaveda[1] and later.[2] In the sense of a 'book of rules' for the guidance of sacrificers and so forth, the word occurs in the Bṛhadāraṇyaka Upaniṣad.[3]

[1] iii. 9, 3; xviii. 8, 37.
[2] Śatapatha Brāhmaṇa, iii. 2, 4, 14; vii. 3, 2, 13; xii. 3, 4, 2; 7, 2, 10; Chāndogya Upaniṣad, vi. 8, 2; Nirukta, iv. 6.
[3] ii. 4, 10; iv. 1, 6 (Mādhyaṃdina= iv. 1, 2 Kāṇva); 5, 11.
Cf. Weber, *Indische Studien*, 5, 24, 25; Sieg, *Die Sagenstoffe des Ṛgveda*, 21.

Sūda, according to the St. Petersburg Dictionary, means 'well'[1] and the 'mud of a dried-up pool.'[2] Pischel,[3] however, shows clearly that Sūda denotes what is added to Soma to

[1] Rv. vii. 36, 3; ix. 97, 4.
[2] Rv. x. 61, 2; Kāṭhaka Saṃhitā, xvi. 13; Taittirīya Brāhmaṇa, i. 1, 3, 5; 2, 1, 3; Śatapatha Brāhmaṇa, viii. 7, 3, 21.
[3] *Vedische Studien*, 1, 72, 73.

make it fit for use, especially the warm milk, and this sense suits all the passages. Eggeling[4] renders it 'well,' and Grassmann 'sweet drink.'

[4] *Sacred Books of the East*, 43, 144.
Cf. Hillebrandt, *Vedische Mythologie*, 1, 211.

Sūda-dohas in the Rigveda[1] denotes 'milking **Sūda**'—*i.e.*, what is requisite to mix with Soma, according to Pischel.[2] According to Roth,[3] it means 'yielding milk like a well.'

[1] viii. 69, 3.
[2] *Vedische Studien*, 1, 72. *Sūdayitnu* in Rv. x. 64, 9, may be taken in the same way, and *sūdin* in Kāṭhaka Saṃhitā, xxvii. 2; *sūdya* in Taittirīya Saṃhitā, vii. 4, 13, 1; Vājasaneyi Saṃhitā, xxii. 25, etc.
[3] St. Petersburg Dictionary, *s.v.*

Sūnā means, in the Rigveda[1] and the Atharvaveda,[2] apparently a 'woven (from *sīv*, 'sew') wickerwork basket' for holding flesh.

[1] i. 161, 10; 162, 13; x. 86, 18.
[2] Av. v. 17, 14. Crates of **Palāśa** wood are mentioned in the Śāṅkhāyana Śrauta Sūtra, xvii. 3, 2. 3.
Cf. Zimmer, *Altindisches Leben*, 271.

Sūnu is a common word for 'son' from the Rigveda onwards.[1] The etymological sense seems to be 'he who is borne,' and then 'the begotten.'[2] But the use of Sūnu in the Rigveda[3] is predominantly in relation to the father, and only rarely in its connexion with words for mother.[4] Thus a father is 'easy of access' (*sūpāyana*) to his son (*sūnu*);[5] but in another passage,[6] where the same term is applied to earth as a mother, the word used for son is **Putra**. No conclusion as to matriarchy can of course be drawn from the etymology. On the relation of son and father, see **Pitṛ**.

[1] Rv. i. 26, 3; ii. 38, 5; vi. 52, 9, etc.; Av. vi. 1, 2; vii. 2, 2; xii. 3, 23, etc.
[2] Delbrück, *Die indogermanischen Verwandtschaftsnamen*, 453.
[3] Usually in a figurative sense—*e.g.*, *sahasaḥ, adreḥ sūnuḥ*.
[4] v. 42, 2.
[5] Rv. i. 1, 9.
[6] Rv. x. 18, 11.

Sūri is the regular word in the Rigveda[1] for the sacrificer, the later Yajamāna—that is, the man who pays the priests for performing the rite, and reaps the benefit of that service. The Sūris are often coupled with the **Maghavans**,[1] described as heroes or warriors,[2] and as related to the priests by their patronage[3] or as companions.[4]

[1] i. 31, 7. 12; 48, 24; 54, 11; 73, 5. 8. 9; iii. 31, 14; v. 42, 4; 79, 6; vi. 4, 8; 23, 10; vii. 32, 15; viii. 70, 15; x. 61, 22; 115, 5. 7. 8.

[2] i. 69, 3; 73, 9; 119, 3; 122, 12; 180, 9; vii. 32, 15.

[3] i. 97, 3. 4; v. 10, 6; vi. 8, 7; 25, 7; vii. 3, 8; 44, 18; viii. 60, 6; x. 66, 2.

[4] v. 64, 5; vii. 32, 25; viii. 45, 36; ix. 96, 4; x. 115, 7.

Cf. Ludwig, Translation of the Rigveda, 3, 236.

Sūrmi denotes in the Rigveda[1] and later,[2] according to the St. Petersburg Dictionary, a kind of 'tube' serving as a lamp. In one passage of the Rigveda[3] it means a 'pipe' for conveying water. *Cf.* **Avata**.

[1] vii. 1, 3.

[2] Taittirīya Saṃhitā, i. 5, 7, 6; v. 4, 7, 3; Kāṭhaka Saṃhitā, xxi. 9, where it is described as *karṇakāvatī*, rendered by Roth as 'provided with a handle.'

[3] viii. 69, 12. **Sūrmya** in Taittirīya Saṃhitā, iv. 5, 9, 2, may mean 'being in pipes or channels.'

Sūrya, the 'sun,' plays a great part in Vedic mythology and religion,[1] corresponding with the importance of the sun as a factor in the physical life of the peninsula. In the Rigveda[2] the sun is normally regarded as a beneficent power, a not unnatural view in a people which must apparently have issued from the cold regions of the Himālaya mountains. Its heat is, however, alluded to in some passages of the Rigveda,[3] as well as referred to in the Atharvaveda and the literature of the Brāhmaṇas.[4]

In one myth Indra is said to have vanquished Sūrya and to have stolen his wheel:[5] this is possibly a reference to the

[1] See Macdonell, *Vedic Mythology*, p. 30 *et seq.*

[2] *E.g.*, i. 50, 6; 115, 1. 3; 164, 11. 13; 191, 8. 9; vii. 63, 1; x. 37, 4, 85, 9; 88, 11; 139, 3, etc.

[3] Rv. vii. 34, 19; ix. 107, 20.

[4] Ehni, *Yama*, 134; Macdonell *op. cit.*, p. 31.

[5] i. 175, 4; iv. 30, 4; x. 43, 5.

obscuration of the sun by a thunderstorm.[6] The Aitareya Brāhmaṇa[7] presents a naive conception of the course of the sun, which it regards as bright on one side only, and as returning from west to east by the same road, but with the reverse side turned towards the earth, thus at night illumining the stars in heaven.[8] In the Rigveda[9] wonder is expressed that the sun does not fall.

There are several references to eclipses in the Rigveda. In one passage[10] Svarbhānu, a demon, is said to have eclipsed the sun with darkness, while **Atri** restores the light of the sun, a similar feat being elsewhere attributed to his family, the Atris.[11] In the Atharvaveda[12] **Rāhu** appears for the first time in connexion with the sun. Indra's defeat of Sūrya[6] may also be explained as alluding to an eclipse; in two other passages[13] such an interpretation seems at least probable. Ludwig[14] not only argues that the Rigveda knows the theory of eclipses caused by an occultation of the sun by the moon, and regards the sun as going round the earth,[15] but even endeavours to identify an eclipse referred to in the Rigveda with one that occurred in 1029 B.C. These views are completely refuted by Whitney.[16]

The sun as a maker of time[17] determines the year of 360 days, which is the civil year and the usual year (**Saṃvatsara**) of

[6] Macdonell, *loc. cit.*

[7] iii. 44, 4.

[8] Macdonell, p. 10, who compares Rv. i. 115. 5; x. 37, 3. See also Speyer, *Journal of the Royal Asiatic Society*, 1906, 723; Thibaut, *Astronomie, Astrologie und Mathematik*, 6.

[9] Rv. iv. 13, 5.

[10] Rv. v. 40, 5-9. *Cf.* Macdonell, p. 160; Pañcaviṃśa Brāhmaṇa, iv. 5, 2; 6, 14; Kauṣītaki Brāhmaṇa, xxiv. 3; Tilak, *Orion*, 159.

[11] Av. xiii. 2, 4. 12. 36; Śatapatha Brāhmaṇa, iv. 3, 4, 21.

[12] Av. xix. 9, 10; Zimmer, *Altindisches Leben*, 351.

[13] Rv. iv. 28, 2. 3; v. 33, 4. In x. 27, 20, *sūro markaḥ* means, according to Roth, St. Petersburg Dictionary, *s.v.*, and Zimmer, *loc. cit.*, a demon of eclipse; but it may also mean the 'cleansing' sun. Av. ii. 10, 8, clearly refers to an eclipse. See Lanman, *Festgruss an Roth*, 187-190.

[14] Proceedings of the Bohemian Academy of Sciences, May, 1885; Translation of the Rigveda, 6, x.

[15] See Rv. iv. 28, 23; v. 33, 4; x. 37, 3; 138, 4.

[16] *Proceedings of the American Oriental Society*, October, 1885, xvii (*Journal of the American Oriental Society*, 13, lxi-lxvi); *Journal of the American Oriental Society*, 16, lxxxii, lxxxiii; Eggeling, *Sacred Books of the East*, 41, 65, 66; Thibaut, *Astronomie, Astrologie und Mathematik*, 6.

[17] Rv. v. 81, 1.

Vedic literature. This solar year is divided into two halves—the Uttarāyaṇa,[18] when the sun goes north, and the Dakṣiṇāyana,[19] when it goes south. There can be no doubt that these periods denote the time when the sun turns north from the winter solstice, and when it turns south from the summer solstice, for the Kauṣītaki Brāhmaṇa[20] says so in perfectly clear language. The alternative theory is to regard the periods as those when the sun is in the north—*i.e.*, when it is north of the equator, and when it is in the south, taking as points of departure the equinoxes, not the solstices; but this view has no support in Vedic literature, and is opposed to the fact that the equinoxes play no part in Vedic astronomical theory.[21] There are only doubtful references to the solstices in the Rigveda.[22]

The Brāhmaṇas,[23] and perhaps the Rigveda,[24] regard the moon as entering the sun at new moon. According to Hillebrandt,[25] the Rigveda[26] recognizes that the moon shines by the borrowed light of the sun, but this seems very doubt-

[18] The form Uttarāyaṇa is later (Manu, vi. 10, etc.). Udagayana occurs in the Bṛhadāraṇyaka Upaniṣad, vi. 3, 1; Kauśika Sūtra, lxvii. 4; Lāṭyāyana Śrauta Sūtra, viii. 1, 1; Gobhila Gṛhya Sūtra, i. 1, 3; Āśvalāyana Gṛhya Sūtra, i. 4, etc.; Weber, *Naxatra*, 2, 201, 212; *Jyotiṣa*, 107 *et seq.*; Yāska, *Nirukta*, xiv. 10.

[19] The form is late (Manu, i. 67, etc.). In the Śatapatha Brāhmaṇa, ii. 1, 3, the two Ayanas are equated each with three seasons—the northern course with spring, summer, and rains; the southern with autumn, winter, and cool season. But this is merely an inevitable inaccuracy, since no real season begins with the winter solstice.

[20] xix. 3. *Cf.* Taittirīya Saṃhitā, vi. 5, 3; Bṛhadāraṇyaka Upaniṣad, vi. 1, 18 (Mādhyaṃdina = vi. 2, 18 Kāṇva); Weber, *Naxatra*, 2, 345 *et seq.*

[21] Thibaut, *Indian Antiquary*, 24, 96; *Astronomie, Astrologie und Mathematik*, 10; Oldenberg, *Zeitschrift der Deutschen Morgenländischen Gesellschaft*, 48, 631 *et seq.*; 49, 473 *et seq.*; *Nachrichten der königlichen Gesellschaft der Wissenschaften zu Göttingen*, 1909, 564, n. 1; Keith, *Journal of the Royal Asiatic Society*, 1909, 1103. On the other side, see Tilak, *Orion*, 22-31.

[22] See Hillebrandt, *Vedische Mythologie*, 3, 279-283, who cites Rv. i. 61, 15; v. 29, 5; x. 171, 4; 179, 2. But none of these passages are conclusive. *Cf.* Thibaut, *op. cit.*, 6.

[23] Śatapatha Brāhmaṇa, i. 6, 4, 18; iv. 6, 7, 12; x. 6, 2, 3; xi. 1, 6, 19; Bṛhadāraṇyaka Upaniṣad, i. 2, 13; Aitareya Brāhmaṇa, viii. 28, 8.

[24] v. 47, 3; ix. 25, 6; 71, 2; x. 55, 5; 138, 4. *Cf.* Hillebrandt, *op. cit.*, 1, 463-466.

[25] *Ibid.*, 3, 467, 468.

[26] ix. 71, 9; 76, 4; 86, 32; perhaps i. 190, 3; Sāmaveda, ii. 9, 2, 12, 1. Thibaut, *op. cit.*, 6, considers that the meaning of the passages is merely that the moon is filled up during the bright half of the month by light emanating from the sun.

ful. See also **Aryamṇaḥ Panthā**,[27] **Nakṣatra**, and **Sapta Sūryāḥ**.

[27] Ludwig, Translation of the Rigveda, 3, 188, finds in the Rigveda, i. 110, 2, a mention of the inclination of the ecliptic to the equator, and in x. 86, 4, a reference to the axis of the earth. *Cf.* Tilak, *Orion*, 158 *et seq.*; Oldenberg, *Ṛgveda-Noten*, 1, 102, 105. These views are clearly quite wrong. The notions of the sun given in the Brāhmaṇas are all very naive and simple: the distance of heaven and the sun from the earth is the height of a thousand cows one on the top of the other (Pañcaviṃśa Brāhmaṇa, xvi. 8, 6), or forty-four days' journey for a horse (*ibid.*, xxv. 10, 16), or a thousand days' journey for a horse (Aitareya Brāhmaṇa, ii. 17, 8), or a hundred leagues (Kauṣītaki Brāhmaṇa, viii. 3). They record also such facts as that the sun rises from and sets in the waters (Aitareya Brāhmaṇa, iv. 20, 13; *cf.* Nirukta, vi. 17; Kauṣītaki Brāhmaṇa, xxiv. 4. 5; xxvi. 1), and that it sets in the west (*ibid.*, xviii. 9). The Śatapatha Brāhmaṇa calls the sun circular (vii. 4, 1, 17), and also four-cornered (*catuḥ-śrakti*) in xiv. 3, 1, 17, and so on. See Weber, *Indische Studien*, 9, 358 *et seq.*

Sūrya-nakṣatra is found in the Śatapatha Brāhmaṇa[1] in a passage where Sāyaṇa takes it as denoting a **Nakṣatra**, which gives out rays of light like the sun. But the real sense (as the Kāṇva text helps to show) is that the sacrificer may take the sun for his Nakṣatra—*i.e.*, he may neglect the Nakṣatras altogether and rely on the sun.

[1] ii. 1, 2, 19. *Cf.* Eggeling, *Sacred Books of the East*, 12, 288.

Sūrya-candramasā or **Sūrya-candramasau** denotes 'sun and moon' as a pair of luminaries in the Rigveda[1] and later.[2]

[1] i. 102, 2; v. 51, 15; x. 190, 3.

[2] Bṛhadāraṇyaka Upaniṣad, iii. 8, 9; Chāndogya Upaniṣad, vii. 12, 1. *Cf.* Weber, *Naxatra*, 2, 293; *Jyotiṣa* 28, 50; *Indische Studien*, 9, 112.

Sṛka in a couple of passages of the Rigveda[1] denotes a weapon of Indra, perhaps a 'lance.'

[1] i. 32, 12; x. 180, 2. *Cf. sṛkāyin*, *sṛkā-hasta*, 'bearing a lance in his hand,' in the Śatarudriya, Vājasaneyi Saṃhitā, xvi. 21. 61, etc.

Sṛgāla, 'jackal,' is not found until the Śatapatha Brāhmaṇa (xii. 5, 2, 5), but is common in the Epic.

Sṛjaya is the name of one of the victims at the Aśvamedha ('horse sacrifice') in the Yajurveda.[1] What it was is unknown: Mahīdhara on the Vājasaneyi passage calls it a kind of bird; Sāyaṇa on the Taittirīya Saṃhitā gives the alternatives 'black fly' (when *sṛjayā* must be read), 'white serpent,' and 'black buffalo.'

[1] Taittirīya Saṃhitā, v. 5, 14, 1; Maitrāyaṇī Saṃhitā, iii. 14, 14; Vājasaneyi Saṃhitā, xxiv. 23. *Cf.* Zimmer, *Altindisches Leben*, 99.

Sṛñjaya is the name of a people mentioned as early as the Rigveda. Sṛñjaya (that is, the king of this people) **Daivavāta** is celebrated as victorious over the **Turvaśas** and the **Vṛcīvants**,[1] and his sacrificial fire is referred to.[2] In connexion with Daivavāta is also mentioned **Sāhadevya Somaka**,[3] no doubt another prince; for in the Aitareya Brāhmaṇa[4] we find Somaka Sāhadevya and his father, Sahadeva (originally **Suplan**) Sārñjaya, as kings who were anointed by **Parvata** and **Nārada**. The Rigveda[5] has also a Dānastuti ('praise of gifts') of **Prastoka**,[6] a Sṛñjaya, who is lauded along with **Divodāsa**. Moreover, **Vītahavya**[7] seems to have been a Sṛñjaya, though Zimmer[8] prefers to take the derivative word, **Vaitahavya**, not as a patronymic, but as an epithet.

It seems probable that the Sṛñjayas and the **Tṛtsus** were closely allied, for Divodāsa and a Sṛñjaya prince are celebrated together,[9] and the Turvaśas were enemies of both.[10] This view is borne out by the Śatapatha Brāhmaṇa,[11] which recognizes **Devabhāga Śrautarṣa** as Purohita of the **Kurus** and the Sṛñjayas.

[1] Rv. vi. 27, 7.

[2] Rv. iv. 15, 4.

[3] Rv. iv. 15, 7.

[4] vii. 34, 9.

[5] Rv. vi. 47, 22. 25.

[6] *Cf.* Śāṅkhāyana Śrauta Sūtra, xvi. 11, 11.

[7] Oldenberg, *Zeitschrift der Deutschen Morgenländischen Gesellschaft*, 42, 212; Hillebrandt, *Vedische Mythologie*, 1, 105.

[8] *Altindisches Leben*, 132 (on *vaitahavya*).

[9] *Cf.* also the connexion of the **Bharadvājas** and Divodāsa (Rv. vi. 16, 5; 31, 4; Hillebrandt, *op. cit.*, 1, 104), and their connexion with the Sṛñjayas (Vītahavya in Rv. vi. 15, 2. 3, and see vi. 27, 7, both passages that can safely be accepted as derived from the Bharadvāja family).

[10] See, on the one hand, Rv. vii. 18 (Turvaśas and Tṛtsus), and, on the other, vi. 27, 7.

[11] ii. 4, 4, 5.

On the other hand, some disaster certainly befel the Sṛñjayas, at least the Vaitahavyas, for they are said in the Atharvaveda[12] to have offended the **Bhṛgus** and to have ended miserably. There is, it is true, no precise confirmation of this notice, but both the Kāṭhaka Saṃhitā[13] and the Taittirīya Saṃhitā,[14] in independent passages, refer to the Sṛñjayas having sustained some serious loss, though the notice is in each case coupled with a ritual error, much as in the Old Testament the fate of kings depends on their devotion to Jahve or their disobedience. It is justifiable to recognize some disaster in this allusion.

The geographical position of the Sṛñjayas is uncertain. Hillebrandt[15] suggests that in early times they must be looked for west of the Indus with Divodāsa; he also mentions, though he does not definitely adopt, the suggestion of Brunnhofer that the Sṛñjayas are to be compared with the Σαράγγαι[16] of the Greeks, and to be located in Drangiana. Zimmer[17] is inclined to locate them on the upper Indus; but it is difficult to decide definitely in favour of any particular location. They may well have been a good deal farther east than the Indus, since their allies, the Tṛtsus, were in the **Madhyadeśa,** and were certainly absorbed in the Kurus.

Of the history of this clan we have one notice.[18] They expelled **Duṣṭarītu Pauṃsāyana,** one of their kings, from the hereditary monarchy—of ten generations—and also drove out **Revottaras Pāṭava Cākra Sthapati,** probably his minister, who, however, succeeded in effecting the restoration of the king, despite the opposition of the Kuru prince, **Balhika Prātīpya**. Very probably this Kuru prince may have been at the bottom of the movement which led to the expulsion of the king and his minister. But the restoration of the king can

[12] v. 19, 1. *Cf.* v. 18, 10. 11.

[13] xii. 3.

[14] vi. 6, 2, 2. 3.

[15] *Op. cit.*, 1, 106.

[16] Herodotus has the form Σαράγγαι and Σαράγγεες, Strabo and Arrian Δράγγαι. The Avestic is *zrayaṅh*, Old Persian *daraya*. The Indian *s* is curious if the words are parallel (see, however, Bloomfield, *American Journal of Philology*, 25, 11; Oldenberg, *Journal of the Royal Asiatic Society*, 1909, 1098).

[17] *Altindisches Leben*, 132, 133; Weber, *Indische Studien*, 1, 232. This is a guess from Rv. i. 100, where Sahadeva occurs and the **Sindhu** is mentioned.

[18] Śatapatha Brāhmaṇa, xii. 9, 3, 1 *et seq.*

hardly be regarded, in accordance with Bloomfield's view,[19] as a defeat of the Sṛñjayas.

[19] *Hymns of the Atharvaveda*, 433. So also Zimmer, *op. cit.*, 132.

Cf. Weber, *Indische Studien*, 1, 208; 3, 472; 18, 237; *Episches im vedischen Ritual*, 31; Ludwig, Translation of the Rigveda, 3, 153; Oldenberg, *Buddha*, 405.

Sṛṇī is found certainly in one,[1] and probably also in two other[2] passages of the Rigveda. The sense appears to be 'sickle.' In one other passage Sṛṇya is coupled with *jetā*:[3] the sense is doubtful, Roth[4] conjecturing *cetā*, and Oldenberg[5] pointing out that *chettā* is also possible. Hopkins[6] thinks that a 'hook' is here meant.

[1] i. 58, 4, where *sṛṇyā*, according to Geldner, *Vedische Studien*, 1, 116, n. 1, and to Pischel, *ibid.*, 2, 111, stands for *sṛṇyābhiḥ*, and, as an adjective agreeing with *juhūbhiḥ*, means 'sickle-shaped sacrificial ladles.' But this is very doubtful.

[2] x. 101, 3 (Nirukta, v. 28); 106, 6 (*ibid.*, xiii. 5). It is certain in Śatapatha Brāhmaṇa, vii. 2, 2, 5.

[3] iv. 20, 5.

[4] *Zeitschrift der Deutschen Morgenländischen Gesellschaft*, 48, 111.

[5] *Ṛgveda-Noten*, 1, 284.

[6] *Journal of the American Oriental Society*, 17, 86, n.

Cf. Zimmer, *Altindisches Leben*, 238; Oldenberg, *op. cit.*, 1, 58.

Sṛṇya. See **Sṛṇī.**

Sṛbinda is the name of a foe of Indra[1] in the Rigveda.[2] The word may denote a real foe, since it has no obvious Āryan derivation.

[1] *Cf.* Macdonell, *Vedic Mythology*, p. 162.

[2] viii. 32, 2.

Sṛmara is the name of an unknown animal at the Aśvamedha ('horse sacrifice') in the Yajurveda Saṃhitās.[1]

[1] Taittirīya Saṃhitā, v. 5, 16, 1 (according to Sāyaṇa = *camara*); Maitrāyaṇī Saṃhitā, iii. 14, 20; Vājasaneyi Saṃhitā, xxiv. 39 (where Mahīdhara identifies it with the **Gavaya**).

Setu appears in the Rigveda[1] and later[2] to denote merely a raised bank for crossing inundated land,[3] a 'causeway,' such as are common all the world over. This sense explains best the later meaning of 'boundary.' The word in Vedic literature is probably always metaphorical.

[1] ix. 41, 2.

[2] Taittirīya Saṃhitā, iii. 2, 2, 1; vi. 1, 4, 9; 5, 3, 3; vii. 5, 8, 5; Kāṭhaka Saṃhitā, xxviii. 4; Aitareya Brāhmaṇa, iii. 35; Taittirīya Brāhmaṇa, ii. 4, 2, 6; Śatapatha Brāhmaṇa, xiii. 2, 10, 1; Bṛhadāraṇyaka Upaniṣad, iv. 4, 24; Chāndogya Upaniṣad, viii. 4, 1. 2, etc.

[3] Max Müller, *Sacred Books of the East*, 1, 130, n. 2.

Cf. Zimmer, *Altindisches Leben*, 257.

Senā denotes primarily a 'missile,' a sense found in the Rigveda[1] and the Atharvaveda,[2] and then a 'host' or 'army,' which is its normal meaning.[3] See **Saṃgrāma**.

[1] Rv. i. 66, 7; 116, 1 (*senā-jū*, 'swift as an arrow'); 143, 5; 186, 9; ii. 33, 11; v. 30, 9; vii. 3, 4; viii. 75, 7; x. 23, 1.

[2] viii. 8, 7; xi. 10, 4.

[3] Rv. i. 33, 6; vii. 25, 1; ix. 96, 1; x. 103, 1. 4. 7; 142, 4; 156, 2; Av. iii. 1, 1; 19, 6; iv. 19, 2; v. 21, 9, etc.

Cf. von Bradke, *Zeitschrift der Deutschen Morgenländischen Gesellschaft*, 46, 456; Bloomfield, *ibid.*, 48, 549. 550; Pischel, *Vedische Studien*, 1, 231, n. 2, denies that Senā ever means 'missile,' and compares *exercitus effusus*, *agmen effusum*.

Senā-nī, 'leader of an army,' is the title of the royal 'general.' He is mentioned in the Rigveda,[1] where also[2] the word is used metaphorically. He is also referred to in the Śatarudriya,[3] as well as elsewhere in the Yajurveda Saṃhitās and Brāhmaṇas.[4] He is one of the **Ratnins** of the king.[5] Presumably he was appointed by the king, not by the people, to command in war when the king became too important to lead every little fray in person. In the Aitareya Brāhmaṇa[6] this official is called Senā-pati.

[1] vii. 20, 5; ix. 96, 1; x. 84, 2.

[2] x. 34, 12 (the gambling hymn).

[3] Vājasaneyi Saṃhitā, xvi. 17; Kāṭhaka Saṃhitā, xvii. 11; Maitrāyaṇī Saṃhitā, ii. 9, 4; Taittirīya Saṃhitā, iv. 5, 2, 1.

[4] Vājasaneyi Saṃhitā, xv. 15; Kāṭhaka Saṃhitā, xvii. 9; Maitrāyaṇī Saṃhitā, ii. 8, 10; Śatapatha Brāhmaṇa, viii. 6, 1, 21.

[5] Taittirīya Saṃhitā, i. 8, 9, 1; Taittirīya Brāhmaṇa, i. 7, 3, 4; Maitrayaṇī Saṃhitā, ii. 6, 5; iv. 3, 8; Kāṭhaka Saṃhitā, xv. 4; Satapatha Brāhmaṇa, v. 3, 1, 1.

[6] viii. 23, 10.

Selaga in the Brāhmaṇas[1] appears to denote 'robber.' See **Sailaga**.

[1] Aitareya Brāhmaṇa, vii. 1, 5; viii. 11, 8; Śatapatha Brāhmaṇa, xiii. 4, 3, 10.

Sehu occurs in a comparison in the Atharvaveda,[1] where it must denote a very sapless (*arasa*) substance.

[1] vii. 76, 1. *Cf.* Zimmer, *Altindisches Leben*, 54; Whitney, Translation of the Atharvaveda, 441.

Saitava, 'descendant of Setu,' is the name of a teacher in the first two Vaṃśas (list of teachers) in the Bṛhadāraṇyaka Upaniṣad.[1] He is described as a pupil of **Pārāśarya** or of **Pārāśaryāyaṇa**.[2]

[1] ii. 5, 21; iv. 5, 27 Mādhyaṃdina; ii. 6, 2 Kāṇva.

[2] iv. 6, 2 Kāṇva

Saindhava, 'coming from the Indus,' is a term applied to water in the Taittirīya Saṃhitā,[1] to **Guggulu** in the Atharvaveda,[2] to a horse in the Śatapatha Brāhmaṇa,[3] and to salt in the same text.[4]

[1] vii. 4, 13, 1.

[2] xix. 38, 2.

[3] xi. 5, 5, 12; Bṛhadāraṇyaka Upaniṣad, vi. 2, 13 (Mādhyaṃdina = vi. 1, 13 Kāṇva).

[4] Bṛhadāraṇyaka Upaniṣad, ii. 4, 12 (°*khilya*); iv. 5, 13 (°*ghana*).

Sairya is the name in the Rigveda[1] of some species of grass infested by insects.

[1] i. 191, 3. *Cf.* Zimmer, *Altindisches Leben*, 72.

Sailaga is found in the Vājasaneyi Saṃhitā[1] and the Taittirīya Brāhmaṇa[2] as the name of one of the victims at the Puruṣamedha ('human sacrifice'). 'Robber' seems to be the sense of this word, as of **Selaga**.

[1] xxx. 18.

[2] iii. 4, 16, 1; Sāṅkhāyana Āraṇyaka, xii. 23 (also spelt Śailaga).

Cf. Eggeling, *Sacred Books of the East*, 44, 367, n. 4.

Sobhari is the name of a Ṛṣi frequently mentioned in the Rigveda.[1] The family is also referred to,[2] and a father, Sobharī.[3]

[1] viii. 5, 26; 19, 2; 20, 19; 22, 2.
[2] Rv. viii. 19, 32; 20, 8.
[3] Rv. viii. 22, 15. *Cf.* viii. 103, 14; Av. xviii. 3, 15.

Cf. Ludwig, Translation of the Rigveda, 3, 105; Oldenberg, *Zeitschrift der Deutschen Morgenländischen Gesellschaft*, 42, 217.

Soma was the famous plant which was used for the preparation of the libation of Soma made at the Vedic sacrifice. Its importance is sufficiently shown by the fact that the whole of the ninth Maṇḍala of the Rigveda, and six hymns in other Maṇḍalas, are devoted to its praise.

Nevertheless, little is actually known of the plant. Its twigs or shoots are described as brown (*babhru*),[1] ruddy (*aruṇa*),[2] or tawny (*hari*).[3] Possibly its twigs hang down if the epithet **Naicāśākha**[4] refers to the plant as Hillebrandt[5] thinks. The shoot is called *aṃśu*,[6] while the plant as a whole is called *andhas*,[7] which also denotes the juice.[8] *Parvan*[9] is the stem. *Kṣip*,[10] 'finger,' is used as a designation of the shoots, which may therefore have resembled fingers in shape; *vakṣaṇā*[11] and *vāṇa*[12] also seem to have the sense of the shoot. There is some slight evidence to suggest that the stem was not round, but angular.[13]

[1] The word is not actually found applied to the plant itself; but the Pañcaviṃśa Brāhmaṇa, ix. 5, 3, prescribes *arjunāni*, plants of this indefinite colour, as a substitute for Soma, if **Pūtīkas** cannot be obtained.

[2] Rv. vii. 98, 1; x. 94, 3; 144, 5. *Cf.* Śatapatha Brāhmaṇa, iv. 5, 10, 1 *et seq.*

[3] Rv. ix. 92, 1. The Soma cow, with which Soma was purchased, is called *babhru* or *aruṇā*, Śatapatha Brāhmaṇa, iii. 3, 1, 15; Maitrāyaṇī Saṃhitā, iii. 7, 5, etc.

[4] Rv. iii. 53, 14. *Cf.* **Naicāśākha**.

[5] *Vedische Mythologie*, 1, 14-18; 2, 241-245.

[6] Rv. i. 168, 3 iii. 48, 2, etc.

[7] Rv. i. 28, 7; iii. 48, 1; iv. 16, 1, etc.

[8] ii. 14, 1; 19, 1; 35, 1, etc.

[9] Rv. i. 9, 1. *Cf. parus*, Taittirīya Brāhmaṇa, iii. 7, 13; Vaitāna Sūtra, 24.

[10] Rv. ix. 79, 4. *Cf.*, however, Pischel, *Vedische Studien*, 1, 70.

[11] Rv. viii. 1, 17.

[12] Rv. iv. 24, 9; ix. 50, 1. But these passages are both very doubtful. *Cf.* **Vāna**. The husk left after the pressing is called *andhas* (ix. 86, 44), *vavri* (ix. 69, 9), *tvac* (ix. 86, 44; Taittirīya Brāhmaṇa, iii. 7, 13, 1), *śarīra* (*ibid.*, 2), *śarya* (ix. 68, 2), *tānva* (ix. 78, 1).

[13] *Cf. pṛṣṭhya* in Rv. iv. 20, 4; Hillebrandt, 1, 54, 55.

The plant grew on the mountains,[14] that of **Mūjavant** being specially renowned.

These notices are inadequate to identify the plant. It has been held[15] to be the *Sarcostemma viminale* or the *Asclepias acida* (= *Sarcostemma brevistigma*). Roth[16] held that the *Sarcostemma acidum* more nearly met the requirements of the case. Watt[17] suggested the Afghan grape as the real Soma, and Rice[18] thought a sugar-cane might be meant, while Max Müller and Rājendralāla Mitra suggested that the juice was used as an ingredient in a kind of beer—*i.e.*, that the Soma plant was a species of hop. Hillebrandt[19] considers that neither hops nor the grape can explain the references to Soma. It is very probable that the plant cannot now be identified.[20]

In the Yajurveda[21] the plant is purchased ere it is pressed. Hillebrandt[22] considers that the sale must be assumed for the Rigveda. It grew on a mountain, and could not be obtained by ordinary people: perhaps some special tribe or prince owned it, like the **Kīkaṭas.**[23] As it stands, the ritual performance is clearly an acquisition of the Soma from the Gandharvas (represented by a Śūdra), a ritual imitation of the action which may have been one of the sources of the drama. Owing to the difficulty of obtaining the real plant from a great

[14] Rv. i. 93, 6; iii. 48, 2; v. 36, 2; 43, 4; 85, 2; ix. 18, 1; 46, 1; 71, 4; 82, 3; Av. iii. 21, 10. So in the Avesta, Yasna, x. 4, etc.

[15] Lassen, *Indische Alterthumskunde*, 1², 931; Muir, *Sanskrit Texts*, 5, 261 *et seq*. *Cf*. Haug, *Aitareya Brahmaṇa*, 2, 489; Max Müller, *Zeitschrift der Deutschen Morgenländischen Gesellschaft*, 9, liv.

[16] *Zeitschrift der Deutschen Morgenländischen Gesellschaft*, 35, 680 *et seq*. *Cf*. also 38, 134 *et seq*.

[17] See Hillebrandt, 1, 7 *et seq*.

[18] *Ibid*., 10.

[19] *Ibid*., 12. The dispute between Max Müller, Roth, J. G. Baker, W. T. Thiselton Dyer, Charles G. Leland, and A. Houtum-Schindler, as to the identity of the plant, is reprinted in Max Müller's *Biographies of Words*, 222 *et seq*., and reviewed by Hillebrandt. See also Eggeling, *Sacred Books of the East*, 26, xxiv *et seq*., who thinks that the traditional identification is not far wrong. Caland, *Altindisches Zauberritual*, 188, gives it as *Sarcostemma acidum*.

[20] The original Soma plant was, doubtless, identical with the Haoma of the Avesta. On the plant from which the present Parsis of Kermān and Yezd obtain their Hūm juice, and which they regard as identical with the Avestic Haoma, see Eggeling, *Sacred Books of the East*, 26, xxiv *et seq*.

[21] Śatapatha Brāhmaṇa, iii. 3, 1, 1 *et seq*.; Hillebrandt, 1, 89 *et seq*.

[22] *Ibid*., 70.

[23] Rv. iii. 53, 14.

distance, several substitutes were allowed in the Brāhmaṇa period.[24]

The plant was prepared for use by being pounded with stones or in a mortar. The former was the normal method of procedure, appearing in the Rigveda as the usual one. The stones are called *grāvan*[25] or *adri*,[26] and were, of course, held in the hands.[27] The plant was laid on boards one beside the other (**Adhiṣavana**), and, according at least to the later ritual,[28] a hole was dug below, so that the pounding of the plant by means of the stones resulted in a loud noise, doubtless a prophylactic against demoniac influences.

The plant was placed on a skin and on the Vedi[29]—which was no longer done in the later ritual—**Dhiṣaṇā** in some passages denoting the Vedi.[30]

Sometimes the mortar and pestle were used in place of the stones.[31] This use, though Iranian, was apparently not common in Vedic times.

Camū denotes the vessel used for the offering to the god,[32] **Kalaśa** and **Camasa** those used for the priests to drink from. Sometimes[33] the Camū denotes the mortar and pestle. Perhaps the vessel was so called because of its mortar-like shape.

The skin on which the shoots were placed was called **Tvac**,[34] or twice *go* ('cow-hide').[35] **Kośa**,[36] Sadhastha,[37] **Dru**,[38]

[24] See Śatapatha Brāhmaṇa, iv. 5, 10, 1-6, and *cf.* Eggeling, *Sacred Books of the East*, 26, xxvii; Pañcaviṃśa Brāhmaṇa, ix. 5, 3.

[25] i. 83, 6; 135, 7, etc.

[26] i. 130, 2; 135, 5; 137, 1, etc. *Adri* is used oftener with the verb *su*, 'press,' than *grāvan*, which is more personally conceived, and so appears with *vad*, 'speak,' and so forth; Hillebrandt, 1, 153, n. 1.

[27] Rv. v. 45, 7; ix. 11, 5; x. 76, 2, etc.

[28] Kātyāyana Śrauta Sūtra, iv. 4, 28; that *ākhara*, Rv. x. 94, 5, denotes this is uncertain.

[29] Rv. v. 31, 12.

[30] Rv. i. 109, 3; iii. 2, 1; vi. 11, 3, etc.

[31] Rv. i. 28. The pestle is *manthā*, the mortar *ulūkhala;* in x. 101, 11, *vanaspati* and *vana* may have the same senses respectively.

[32] Not the pressing boards, which are unknown in the Rigveda. *Cf.* Rv. ix. 99, 8; x. 91, 15, etc.

[33] Rv. i. 28, 9; iv. 18, 3; vi. 57, 2, etc.; Hillebrandt, 1, 170, 173.

[34] Rv. ix. 65, 25; 66, 29; 70, 7; 79, 4, etc.

[35] Rv. x. 94, 9; 116, 4.

[36] Rv. vii. 101, 4; viii. 20, 8, etc. It denotes the larger vessel from which the Soma is poured into the Kalaśas, or cups.

[37] Rv. iii. 62, 15; ix. 1, 2; 17, 8, etc.

[38] Rv. ix. 1, 2; 65, 6; 98, 2; in x. 101, 10, *dru*=mortar.

Vana,[39] **Droṇa**,[40] are all terms used for Soma vessels, while **Sruva**[41] denotes the 'ladle.'

Apparently the plant was sometimes steeped in water to increase its yield of juice.[42]

It is not possible to describe exactly the details of the process of pressing the Soma as practised in the Rigveda. It was certainly purified by being pressed through a sieve[43] (**Pavitra**). The Soma was then used unmixed (*śukra*,[44] *śuci*)[45] for Indra and Vāyu, but the **Kaṇvas** seem to have dropped this usage.[46] The juice is described as brown (*babhru*),[47] tawny (*hari*),[48] or ruddy (*aruṇa*),[49] and as having a fragrant smell,[50] at least as a rule.[51]

Soma was mixed with milk (**Gavāśir**),[52] curd or sour milk (**Dadhyāśir**),[53] or grain (**Yavāśir**).[54] The admixtures are

[39] Rv. ii. 14, 9; ix. 66, 9, etc. The word can mean both the vessel into which the Soma was poured after preparation, and the vessel from which it was offered to the gods.

[40] Rv. ix. 15, 7; 33, 2, etc. The word, having no definite sense, can denote any of the vessels. The *camū*, on the other hand, was the cup for the gods, the *kalaśa* that for the priests (later it was also used as = *kośa*, when *camasa* had replaced *kalaśa* as cup for the priests; Hillebrandt, 1, 187).

[41] Rv. i. 116, 24. *Cf.* also **Amatra** and **Khārī**.

[42] This process is technically called *āpyāyana*, 'causing to swell.' *Cf.* Rv. ix. 74, 9; Maitrāyaṇī Saṃhitā, iv. 5, 5. The exact nature and extent of this process is quite uncertain; Hillebrandt, 1, 193-195; Eggeling, *Sacred Books of the East*, 26, xxvi.

[43] Whether the later practice of purification by means of shoots held in the hands was known to the Rigveda is uncertain, since ii. 14, 8; ix. 71, 3, are quite indecisive. For the various terms used to designate the sieve, see **Pavitra**.

[44] Rv. i. 137, 1; iii. 32, 2; viii. 2, 10, etc.

[45] Rv. i. 5, 5; 30, 2; viii. 2, 9, etc.

[46] *Cf.* Rv. viii. 2, 5. 9. 10. 28, etc. The Maitrāyaṇī Saṃhitā, iv. 7, 4, disapproves of the unmixed Soma. Possibly Hillebrandt, 1, 207, 208, may be right in thinking that the Kāṇvas had to lay special stress on the use of the mixtures, because they used a plant which was deficient in the true Soma character.

[47] Rv. ix. 33, 2; 63, 4. 6.

[48] Rv. ix. 3, 9; 7, 6; 65, 8. 12. 25, etc.

[49] Rv. ix. 40, 2; 45, 3; *aruṣa*, ix. 61, 21; *śoṇa*, ix. 97, 13.

[50] ix. 97, 19; 107, 2.

[51] Śatapatha Brāhmaṇa, iv. 1, 3, 6. This passage has been relied on by Eggeling, *op. cit.*, 26, xxv, as a confirmation of the later description, in a medical work, of the plant as ill-smelling. But this plant may have been a different one from that used in Vedic times. The smell may have been due to a substitute being used, or to the genuine plant, brought from a distance, being old and withered.

[52] Hillebrandt, 1, 219-222.

[53] *Ibid.*, 221.

[54] *Ibid.*, 222 *et seq.*

alluded to with various figurative expressions, as **Atka**, 'armour';[55] **Vastra**[56] or **Vāsas**,[57] 'garment'; **Abhiśrī**,[58] 'admixture'; *rūpa*,[59] 'beauty'; *śrī*,[60] 'splendour'; *rasa*,[61] 'flavour'; *prayas*,[62] 'dainty'; and perhaps *nabhas*,[63] 'fragrance.' The adjective *tīvra*[64] denotes the 'pungent' flavour of Soma when so mixed. The Soma shoots, after the juice has been pressed out, are denoted by *ṛjīṣa*, 'residue.'[65]

It seems probable that in some cases honey was mixed with Soma: perhaps the *kośa madhu-ścut*, 'the pail distilling sweetness,' was used for the mixing.[66] It seems doubtful if Surā was ever so mixed.[67]

There were three pressings a day of Soma, as opposed to the two of the Avesta.[68] The evening pressing was specially connected with the Ṛbhus, the midday with Indra, the morning with Agni, but the ritual shows that many other gods also had their share.[69] The drinker of Soma and the non-drinker are sharply discriminated in the texts.[70] Localities where Soma was consumed were **Ārjīka, Pastyāvant, Śaryaṇāvant, Suṣomā,** the territory of the **Pañcajanāḥ** or 'five

[55] Rv. ix. 69, 4.

[56] ix. 8, 6.

[57] ix. 69, 5.

[58] ix. 79, 5; 86, 27.

[59] Av. ix. 25, 4.

[60] Rv. iv. 41, 8; ix. 16, 6.

[61] Rv. iii. 48, 1; vi. 47, 1; ix. 97, 14. See also **Sūda**.

[62] Rv. iii. 30, 1; ix. 46, 3; 66, 23.

[63] Rv. ix. 83, 5; 97, 21, etc.

[64] Rv. i. 23, 1; ii. 41, 14; v. 37, 4; vi. 47, 1, etc.

[65] Maitrāyaṇī Saṃhitā, iv. 8, 5; Av. ix. 6, 16, etc.; Vājasaneyi Saṃhitā, xix. 72; citation in Nirukta, v. 12, etc. *Ṛjīṣa* as an adjective occurs in Rv. i. 32, 6, and *ṛjīṣin* in the Rigveda means, according to Hillebrandt, 1, 236, 237, generally 'one to whom the Soma shoots belong.' *Soma tiroahnya* is 'Soma pressed the day before yesterday.'

[66] Rv. ix. 103, 3. *Cf.* ix. 17, 8; ix. 86, 48; 97, 11; 109, 20.

[67] See **Surāma**. *Cf.* Maitrāyaṇī Saṃhitā, iv. 12, 5; Vājasaneyi Saṃhitā, xxi. 42, and *surā-somā*, *ibid.*, xxi. 60.

[68] Yasna, x. 2.

[69] Hillebrandt, 1, 257 *et seq.*

[70] Rv. i. 110, 7; ii. 30, 7; v. 34, 3. 5; iv. 17, 17; 25, 6. 7; v. 37, 3; vi. 41, 4; vii. 26, 1, etc. There were also rivalries with other Soma sacrifices, Rv. ii. 18, 3; viii. 33, 14; 66, 12, and especially vii. 33, 2, where the Vasiṣṭhas take away Indra from **Pāśadyumna Vāyata's** Soma sacrifice to **Sudās**'. Many famous Soma offerers are mentioned: **Atri**, v. 51, 8; 72, 1; viii. 42, 5; **Śāryāta**, i. 51, 12; iii. 51, 7; Vājasaneyi Saṃhitā, vii. 35; **Śiṣtas**, viii. 53, 4, etc.; **Turvaśa Yadu**, viii. 45, 27; **Saṃvarta Kṛśa**, viii. 54, 2; **Nīpātithi, Medhyātithi, Puṣṭigu, Śruṣṭigu**, viii. 51, 1, etc. The ritual lays stress on the need of continuity in Soma-drinking in a family: Taittirīya Saṃhitā, ii. 1, 5, 5 *et seq.*; Maitrāyaṇī Saṃhitā, ii. 5, 5, etc.

peoples,' and so on.[71] The effects of Soma in exhilarating and exciting the drinkers are often alluded to.[72]

It is difficult to decide if Soma was ever a popular, as opposed to a hieratic drink. The evidence for its actual popularity is very slight,[73] and not decisive.

[71] See *s.v.*; Hillebrandt, 1, 125-143. It is possible that Soma may have grown on the mountains to the north of **Madhyadeśa**, whatever may have been its original home, on which *cf.* Roth, *Zeitschrift der Deutschen Morgenländischen Gesellschaft*, 38, 134 *et seq.*

[72] See Rv. viii. 48. It was equally prized in Avestic times. It is, however, seldom spoken of as giving the priests pleasure: Rv. i. 91, 13; viii. 2, 12; x. 167, 3. There are many references to sickness caused by it (Maitrāyaṇī Saṃhitā, ii. 2, 13 etc.). The Sautrāmaṇī was a rite designed to expiate the ill caused by vomiting Soma as Indra had done: Taittirīya Saṃhitā, ii. 3, 2, 5. 6; Śatapatha Brāhmaṇa, v. 5, 4, 9; xii. 7, 1, 11. The name of the rite is already found in Av. vii. 3, 2, and the rite itself is no doubt older (see also **Viṣūcikā**). This fact tells in favour of the traditional identification of the plant, for the medical passage quoted by Max Müller refers to its producing vomiting. See also Zimmer, *Altindisches Leben*, 275; Rv. i. 91, 13; 118, 3; viii. 2, 12; 17, 6; 48, 12. Perhaps **Vamra** in i. 112, 15, got his name thence.

[73] Rv. viii. 69, 8-10. *Cf.* viii. 31, 5; i. 28, 5; Hillebrandt, 1, 143-147. The evidence is not decisive; the ordinary Soma sacrifice was clearly a sacrifice of rich patrons.

Cf. Zimmer, *Altindisches Leben*, 272-280; Hillebrandt, *Vedische Mythologie*, 1, 1-266; 2, 209 *et seq.*; Macdonell, *Vedic Mythology*, p. 104 *et seq.*

2. **Soma Prāti-veśya** ('descendant of Prativeśya') is the name of a teacher, a pupil of Prativeśya, in the Vaṃśa (list of teachers) at the end of the Śāṅkhāyana Āraṇyaka (xv. 1).

Somaka Sāha-devya ('descendant of Sahadeva') is the name of a king of the **Sṛñjayas** in the Rigveda.[1] He is mentioned in the Aitareya Brāhmaṇa[2] as having **Parvata** and **Nārada** as his priests.

[1] iv. 15, 7-10.

[2] vii. 34, 9.

Cf. Ludwig, Translation of the Rigveda, 3, 154; Hillebrandt, *Vedische Mythologie*, 1, 105.

Soma-dakṣa Kauśreya ('descendant of **Kuśri**') is the name of a teacher in the Kāṭhaka[1] and the Maitrāyaṇī[2] Saṃhitās.

[1] xx. 8; xxi. 9, where Somarakṣa Kośreya is read by the Chambers MS. in xx. 8, and Kośreya in xxi. 9.

[2] iii. 2, 7.

Cf. Weber, *Indische Studien*, 3, 472, 473.

Somapi-tsaru. See **Tsaru.**

Soma-śuṣma Sātya-yajñi (' descendant of **Satyayajña** ') is the name in the Śatapatha Brāhmaṇa (xi. 6, 2, 1. 3) of a travelling Brahmin who met **Janaka** of **Videha.** He may be identical with the man of the same name with the additional patronymic **Prācīnayogya** (' descendant of Prācīnayoga '), who is mentioned as a pupil of Satyayajña in the Jaiminīya Upaniṣad Brāhmaṇa (iii. 40, 2).

Soma-śuṣman Vāja-ratnāyana (' descendant of Vājaratna ') is the name in the Aitareya Brāhmaṇa (viii. 21, 5) of the priest who consecrated **Śatānīka.**

Saukarāyaṇa is the name of a teacher, a pupil of **Kāṣāyaṇa**[1] or **Traivaṇi**,[2] in the second Vaṃśa (list of teachers) of the Bṛhadāraṇyaka Upaniṣad.

[1] iv. 6, 2 (Kāṇva).

[2] iv. 5, 27 (Mādhyaṃdina)

Sau-jāta Ārāḍhi is the name of a teacher in the Aitareya Brāhmaṇa (vii. 22, 1).

Sautrāmaṇī. See **Soma.**

Sau-danti (' descendant of Sudanta ') occurs in the plural in the Pañcaviṃśa Brāhmaṇa (xiv. 3, 13), apparently as the name of priests who were contemporaries of **Viśvāmitra.**

Saudāsa in the plural designates the ' descendants of **Sudās,**' who are referred to in the Jaiminīya Brāhmaṇa[1] as having cast **Śakti,** the son of **Vasiṣṭha,** into the fire. Other texts[2] relate

[1] ii. 390 (*Journal of the American Oriental Society*, 18, 47). The story must have appeared in the Śāṭyāyanaka also. *Cf.* Geldner, *Vedische Studien*, 2, 159, n. 3

[2] Taittirīya Saṃhitā, vii. 4, 7, 1; Kauṣītaki Brāhmaṇa, iv. 8; Pañcaviṃśa Brāhmaṇa, iv. 7, 3. See also Caland, *Über das rituelle Sūtra des Baudhāyana*, 20.

that Vasiṣṭha, his son being slain, desired to avenge himself on the Saudāsas, and eventually succeeded. Geldner[3] sees a reference to the story in the Rigveda,[4] but without cause.

[3] *Loc. cit.*

[4] iii. 53, 22.

Sau-dyumni ('descendant of Sudyumna') is the patronymic of king **Bharata Dauḥṣanti** in the Śatapatha Brāhmaṇa (xiii. 5, 4, 12).

Sau-bala, 'descendant of Subala,' is the name of a pupil of **Sarpi Vātsi** in the Aitareya Brāhmaṇa (vi. 24, 16).

Saubhara, 'descendant of Sobhari,' is the patronymic of **Pathin** in the Bṛhadāraṇyaka Upaniṣad.[1]

[1] ii. 5, 22 (Mādhyaṃdina = ii. 6, 3 Kāṇva); iv. 5, 28 (Mādhyaṃdina = iv. 6, 3 Kāṇva).

Saumāpa 'descendant of Somāpa,' is the patronymic of the two **Mānutantavyas,** teachers in the Śatapatha Brāhmaṇa.[1]

[1] xiii. 5, 3, 2, where Eggeling, *Sacred Books of the East*, 44, 392, has Saumapa.

Saumāpi, 'descendant of Somāpa,' is the patronymic of a teacher called **Priyavrata** in the Śāṅkhāyana Āraṇyaka (xv. 1).

Saumāyana, 'descendant of Soma,' is the patronymic of **Budha** in the Pañcaviṃśa Brāhmaṇa (xxiv. 18, 6).

Saumya is a term of affectionate address ('my dear') in the Upaniṣads.[1]

[1] Bṛhadāraṇyaka Upaniṣad, iii. 1, 3; 2, 13 (*varia lectio*, *somya*); Chāndogya Upaniṣad, iv. 4, 4 *et seq.*

Sau-yavasi, 'descendant of Suyavasa,' is the patronymic of **Ajīgarta.**[1]

[1] Aitareya Brāhmaṇa, vii. 15, 6; Śāṅkhāyana Śrauta Sūtra, xv. 19, 29.

Saurī is given by Zimmer[1] as the name of an unknown animal at the Aśvamedha ('horse sacrifice') in the Taittirīya Saṃhitā.[2] But this is an error: *saurī* means 'dedicated to the sun.'

[1] *Altindisches Leben*, 99.
[2] v. 5, 16, 1 = Vājasaneyi Saṃhitā, xxiv. 33 = Maitrāyaṇī Saṃhitā, iii. 14, 14.

Sau-varcanasa is the patronymic of **Saṃśravas** in the Taittirīya Saṃhitā (i. 7, 2, 1).

Sau-śravasa, 'descendant of **Suśravas,**' is the patronymic of **Upagu** in the Pañcaviṃśa Brāhmaṇa,[1] and the **Kaṇva** Sauśravasas are mentioned in the Kāṭhaka Saṃhitā.[2]

[1] xiv. 6, 8.
[2] xiii. 12 (*Indische Studien*, 3, 474).

Sau-śromateya, 'descendant of Suśromatā,' is the metronymic of **Aṣāḍhi** in the Śatapatha Brāhmaṇa.[1] *Cf.* **Āṣāḍhi.**

[1] vi. 2, 1, 37. *Cf.* Eggeling, *Sacred Books of the East*, 41, 171, n. 1.

Sau-ṣadmana, 'descendant of Suṣadman,' is the patronymic of **Viśvantara** in the Aitareya Brāhmaṇa (vii. 27, 1; 34, 7).

Skandhhyā, fem. plur., is used in the Atharvaveda[1] of a disease 'of the shoulders,' probably tumours of some kind.

[1] vi. 25, 3. *Cf.* Bloomfield, *Hymns of the Atharvaveda*, 472, 473.

Stanayitnu, sing. and plur., denotes 'thunder' from the Rigveda[1] onwards.[2]

[1] v. 83, 6.
[2] Av. i. 13, 1; iv. 15, 11; vii. 11, 1, etc.

Stamba in the Atharvaveda[1] and later[2] denotes a 'tuft of grass,' or more generally a 'bunch' or 'cluster.'

[1] viii. 6, 14.
[2] Taittirīya Saṃhitā, v. 6, 4, 1 (of **Darbha**); Taittirīya Brāhmaṇa, ii. 7, 17, 3; iii. 2, 2, 4; 3, 3, 4; Aitareya Brāhmaṇa, v. 23, 9, etc.

Stambha, 'pillar,' is found in the Kāṭhaka Saṃhitā,[1] and often in the Sūtras. Earlier Skambha[2] is used, but only metaphorically.

[1] xxx. 9; xxxi. 1.

[2] Rv. i. 34, 2; iv. 13, 5, etc.

Starī denotes a 'barren cow' in the Rigveda (i. 101, 3; 116, 22; 117, 20, etc.).

Sti. See **Upasti.**

Sti-pā. See **Upasti.**

Stukā denotes a 'tuft' of hair or wool in the Rigveda[1] and later.[2]

[1] ix. 97, 17.

[2] Kāṭhaka Saṃhitā, xxv. 6; Av. vii. 74, 2; Śatapatha Brāhmaṇa, iii. 2, 1, 13, etc.

Stuti in the Rigveda[1] and later[2] denotes a 'song of praise.'

[1] i. 84, 2; vi. 34, 1; x. 31, 5.

[2] Śatapatha Brāhmaṇa, vii. 5, 2, 39.

Stupa means 'tuft of hair' in the Vājasaneyi Saṃhitā (ii. 2; xxv. 2) and the Śatapatha Brāhmaṇa (i. 3, 3, 5; iii. 5, 3, 4). See **Stukā.**

Stūpa in the Rigveda[1] and later[2] denotes the 'top-knot' of hair as designating the upper part of the head.

[1] vii. 2, 1. *Cf.* i. 24, 7.

[2] Taittirīya Saṃhitā, iii. 3, 6, 5; Pañcaviṃśa Brāhmaṇa, xiii. 4, 4.

Stṛ (used in the instrumental plural only) denotes the 'stars' of heaven.[1]

[1] i. 68, 5; 166, 11; ii. 2, 5; 34, 2; iv. 7, 3; vi. 49, 3. 12. In i. 87, 1, it seems to denote a 'star-like spot' on the forehead of a cow or bull, but this is uncertain. *Cf.* Grassmann, *Wörterbuch, s.v.*; above, 1, 233.

Stega in the Yajurveda Saṃhitās[1] seems to denote a species of 'worm.' The word occurs in the Rigveda[2] also, where its sense is unknown, but may possibly be 'ploughshare.'[3]

[1] Taittirīya Saṃhitā, v. 7, 11, 1; Vājasaneyi Saṃhitā, xxv. 1.

[2] x. 31, 9 = Av. xviii. 1, 39. *Cf.* Zimmer, *Altindisches Leben*, 98.

[3] Weber, Proceedings of the Berlin Academy, 1895, 833. *Cf.* Whitney, Translation of the Atharvaveda, 824.

Stena is a common word for 'thief' from the Rigveda[1] onwards.[2] See **Taskara.**

[1] ii. 23, 16; 28, 10; 42, 3, etc.

[2] Av. iv. 3, 4. 5; 36, 7; xix. 47, 6; Aitareya Brāhmaṇa; v. 30, 11, etc.

Cf. Zimmer, *Altindisches Leben*, 178 *et seq.*

Steya denotes 'theft' in the Atharvaveda[1] and later.[2] *Cf.* **Dharma.**

[1] xi. 8, 20; xiv. 1, 57.

[2] Nirukta, vi. 27; Kauṣītaki Upaniṣad, iii. 1. *Cf. steya-kṛt*, 'thief,' in Rv. vii. 104, 10.

Stotṛ denotes 'praiser' or 'panegyrist' in the Rigveda[1] and later.[2] The word often[3] occurs in connexion with patrons, the **Maghavan** or **Sūri.**

[1] i. 11, 3; 38, 4; iii. 18, 5; vi. 34, 3, etc.

[2] Av. vi. 2, 1; xix. 48, 4.

[3] Rv. i. 124, 10; ii. 1, 16; v. 64, 1; vii. 7, 7; Nirukta, vii. 2.

Stotra denotes the 'song' of the Udgātṛ and his assistant priests (see **Ṛtvij**), just as **Śastra** denotes the 'recitation' of the **Hotṛ** and his assistants. The word has this technical sense quite frequently in the later Saṃhitās and the Brāhmaṇas.[1]

[1] Taittirīya Saṃhitā, iii. 1, 2, 4; Kāṭhaka Saṃhitā, xxix. 2; Aitareya Brāhmaṇa, ii. 37, 4; iii. 46, 8; iv. 12, 6; Kauṣītaki Brāhmaṇa, xvii. 7; Śatapatha Brāhmaṇa, iv. 1, 1, 7; viii. 1, 3, 4, etc. *Cf.* Weber, *Indische Studien*, 10, 353, and Caland and Henry, *L'Agniṣṭoma*, where the Stotras for that sacrifice are given at length.

Stoma denotes 'song of praise' in the Rigveda.[1] Later[2] the term has the technical sense of the typical forms in which the **Stotras** are chanted.

[1] i. 114, 9; iii. 5, 2; 58, 1, etc.

[2] Taittirīya Saṃhitā, iii. 1, 2, 4; Vājasaneyi Saṃhitā, ix. 33; x. 10, etc. *Cf.* Weber, *Indische Studien*, 9, 229, 276; 10, 355; Hillebrandt, Rituallitteratur, 101.

Strī is the ordinary word in poetry and prose for 'woman,' without special reference to her as a wife or as a maiden. **Nārī** has the same sense, but disappears in later prose, while **Gnā** refers only to the wives of the gods, and **Yoṣit**, with its cognate words, denotes the young woman as ripe for marriage.[1] In the Rigveda[2] Strī stands opposed to **Pumāṃs**, 'man,' and once to *vṛṣan*, 'male person'; not until the Atharvaveda[3] does it mean 'wife' as opposed to **Pati**, 'husband,' and even in the Sūtras it is sharply opposed to **Jāyā**.

In Vedic India by far the greater part of a woman's life was taken up in her marriage and marital relations (see Pati and Mātṛ). There is no trace in the Rigveda of the seclusion of women, which was practically complete in all but the earliest Epic:[4] the maiden may be assumed to have grown up in her father's house, enjoying free intercourse with the youth of the village, and sharing in the work of the house. Education[5] was not denied to them, at any rate in certain cases, for we hear in the Upaniṣads of women who could take no unimportant part in disputations on philosophical topics. Moreover, women were taught to dance and sing, which were unmanly accomplishments.[6]

Of the exact legal position of daughters the notices are few and meagre. The Rigveda,[7] however, shows that in the place

[1] *Cf.* Delbrück, *Die indogermanischen Verwandtschaftsnamen*, 417.

[2] Rv. i. 164, 16; v. 61, 8, etc. So also often later—*e.g.*, Maitrāyaṇī Saṃhitā, iv. 7, 4; Taittirīya Saṃhitā, vi. 5, 8, 2.

[3] xii. 2, 39. *Cf.* Aitareya Brāhmaṇa, iii. 22, 1.

[4] Hopkins, *Journal of the American Oriental Society*, 13, 349, 350.

[5] *Cf.* Hopkins, *op. cit.*, 351, 352. See **Gārgī Vācaknavī** and others enumerated in the Āśvalāyana Gṛhya Sūtra, iii. 4, 4; Weber, *Indische Studien*, 10, 118, 119.

[6] Taittirīya Saṃhitā, vi. 1, 6, 5; Maitrāyaṇī Saṃhitā, iii. 7, 3; Śatapatha Brāhmaṇa, iii. 2, 4, 3-6.

[7] i. 124, 7. *Cf.* Av. i. 14, 2; 17, 1; Zimmer, *Altindisches Leben*, 328; Hopkins, *op. cit.*, 341, and see **Syāla**, **Putrikā**.

of a father the brother was looked to for aid, and that brotherless maidens were apt to be ruined, though religious terrors were believed to await the man who took advantage of their defencelessness.[8] Moreover, women could not take an inheritance,[9] and were not independent persons in the eyes of the law, whether married or not. Presumably before marriage they lived on their parents or brothers, and after that on their husbands, while in the event of their husbands predeceasing them, their relatives took the property, burdened with the necessity of maintaining the wife.[10] Their earnings would be appropriated by their nearest relative—usually father or brother—in the few cases in which unmarried women could earn anything, as in the case of courtezans.

[8] Rv. iv. 5, 5.

[9] Taittirīya Saṃhitā, vi. 5, 8, 2; Maitrāyaṇī Saṃhitā, iv. 6, 4; Śatapatha Brāhmaṇa, iv. 4, 2, 13; Nirukta, iii. 4.

[10] *Cf.* the Attic ἐπίκληρος. Keith, *Journal of the Royal Asiatic Society*, 1912, 427.

Stha-pati is the name of a royal official mentioned in the Atharvaveda,[1] and often later.[2] **Revottaras Cākra** was the Sthapati of the exiled **Duṣṭarītu Pauṃsāyana,** a king of the **Sṛñjayas,** and succeeded in restoring him to his royal dignity.[3] The exact sense of the term is not certain: 'governor'[4] is possible, but perhaps 'chief judge'[5] is more likely; as in the case of the early English judges, his functions may have been both executive and judicial. He is inferior in position to the king's brother.[6]

[1] ii. 32, 4; v. 23, 11 (of the chief of the worms in both cases).

[2] Taittirīya Saṃhitā, iv. 5, 2, 2; Kāṭhaka Saṃhitā, xvii. 12; Maitrāyaṇī Saṃhitā, ii. 9, 3; Vājasaneyi Saṃhitā, xvi. 19; Pañcaviṃśa Brāhmaṇa, xvii. 11, 6. 7; xxiv. 18, 2; Śatapatha Brāhmaṇa, v. 4, 4, 17, etc.

[3] Śatapatha Brāhmaṇa, xii. 8, 1, 17; 9, 3, 1 *et seq.* Sthapati here is part, as it were, of the name of the man.

[4] In the Kātyāyana Śrauta Sūtra, i. 1, 12; Āpastamba Śrauta Sūtra, ix. 14, 12, is found Niṣāda-sthapati; perhaps 'governor of **Niṣādas**.' But it may also mean (*cf.* Weber, *Indische Studien*, 1, 207, n.) a Niṣāda as a Sthapati; thus, little can be deduced from this passage in particular. Eggeling, *Sacred Books of the East*, 41, 111, renders it 'governor.' *Cf.* also St. Petersburg Dictionary, *s.v.*, and **Aupoditi**.

[5] Weber, *Indische Studien*, 10, 13, n. 3; 13, 203; 17, 200; 18, 260; *Über den Rājasūya*, 15, n. 6; *Über den Vājapeya*, 9, 10. *Cf.* Kātyāyana Śrauta Sūtra, xxii. 5, 28; 11, 11; Lāṭyāyana Śrauta Sūtra, viii. 7, 11; Āpastamba Śrauta Sūtra, xxii. 7, 6.

[6] Śatapatha Brāhmaṇa, v. 4, 4, 17.

Sthavira, literally 'elder,' is used as a sort of epithet of several men; Sthavira **Śākalya** occurs in the Aitareya Āraṇyaka[1] and the Śāṅkhāyana Āraṇyaka,[2] and Sthavira **Jātūkarṇya** in the Kauṣītaki Brāhmaṇa.[3] *Cf.* the names **Hrasva** and **Dīrgha.**

[1] iii. 2, 1. 6.
[2] vii. 16; viii. 1. 11.
[3] xxvi. 5.

Sthāgara in the Taittirīya Brāhmaṇa[1] is applied to an ornament (*alaṃkāra*) meaning 'made of the fragrant substance Sthagara,' which elsewhere[2] appears as Sthakara.

[1] ii. 3, 10, 2; Āpastamba Śrauta Sūtra, xiv. 15, 2.
[2] See Weber, *Indische Studien*, 13, 198; Bloomfield, *Hymns of the Atharvaveda*, 311, n. 2; Muir, *Sanskrit Texts*, 5, 265.

Sthāṇu in the Rigveda[1] and later[2] denotes a 'stump' or 'post' of wood.

[1] x. 40, 13.
[2] Av. x. 4, 1; xiv. 2, 48; xix. 49, 10, etc.

Sthātṛ ('he who stands') in the Rigveda[1] denotes the 'driver' of horses or a car.

[1] i. 33, 5; 181, 3; iii. 45, 2, etc.

Sthā-patya denotes in the Pañcaviṃśa Brāhmaṇa (xvii. 11, 6. 7) the 'rank or status of a **Sthapati.**'

Sthālī denotes a 'cooking pot,' usually of earthenware, in the Atharvaveda[1] and later.[2]

[1] viii. 6, 17.
[2] Taittirīya Saṃhitā, vi. 5, 10, 5; Vājasaneyi Saṃhitā, xix. 27. 86; Aitareya Brāhmaṇa, i. 11, 8, etc. *Sthālī-pāka*, a dish of rice or barley boiled in milk, is mentioned in the Bṛhadāraṇyaka Upaniṣad, vi. 4, 18; Aitareya Āraṇyaka, iii. 2, 4; Śāṅkhāyana Āraṇyaka, xi. 6, etc.

Sthiraka Gārgya ('descendant of **Garga**') is the name of a teacher in the Vaṃśa Brāhmaṇa.[1]

[1] *Indische Studien*, 4, 373.

Sthivi occurs once (used in the plural) in the Rigveda,[1] probably meaning 'bushel.' The word is also found once in the adjective *sthivimant*,[2] 'provided with bushels.'

[1] x. 68, 3.
[2] Rv. x. 27, 15. *Cf.* Zimmer, *Altindisches Leben*, 238.

Sthūṇā in the Rigveda[1] and later[2] denotes the 'pillar' or 'post' of a house.

[1] i. 59, 1; v. 45, 2; 62, 7; viii 17, 14; x. 18, 13 (of the grave).
[2] Av. iii. 12, 6 (of the **Vaṃśa**, 'beam,' being placed on the pillar); xiv. 1, 63; Śatapatha Brāhmaṇa, xiv. 1, 3, 7; 3, 1, 22, etc.; *sthūṇā-rāja*, 'main pillar,' iii. 1, 1, 11; 5, 1, 1.
Cf. Zimmer, *Altindisches Leben*, 153.

Sthūri has in the Rigveda[1] and later[2] the sense of 'drawn by one animal' instead of the usual two (see **Ratha**), and always with an implication of inferiority.

[1] x. 131, 3.
[2] Taittirīya Brāhmaṇa, i. 8, 2, 4; iii. 8, 21, 3; Pañcaviṃśa Brāhmaṇa, xvi. 13, 12; xviii. 9, 7; Aitareya Brāhmaṇa, v. 30, 6; Śatapatha Brāhmaṇa, xiii. 3, 3, 9, etc.

Sthairakāyaṇa, 'descendant of **Sthiraka**,' is the patronymic of **Mitravarcas** in the Vaṃśa Brāhmaṇa.[1]

[1] *Indische Studien*, 4, 372 (where the word is spelt with *n*).

Sthaulāṣṭhīvi, 'descendant of Sthūlāṣṭhīva,' is the patronymic of a grammarian in the Nirukta (vii. 14; x. 1).

Snātaka, the designation of the student 'who has taken the bath,' marking the termination of his studentship under a religious teacher, occurs in the Śatapatha Brāhmaṇa (xii. 1, 1, 10), and repeatedly in the Sūtras. *Cf.* **Brahmacārin.**

1. **Snāvanya**, used in the plural, denotes particular parts of the body of a horse in the Taittirīya Saṃhitā (v. 7, 23, 1).

2. **Snāvanya** appears to be the name of a people in the Baudhāyana Śrauta Sūtra.[1]

[1] ii. 5 (in a Mantra). *Cf.* Caland, *Über das rituelle Sūtra des Baudhāyana*, 35.

Snuṣā denotes the 'daughter-in-law' in relation primarily to her father-in-law, but also to her mother-in-law. In the latter sense the word appears in the Rigveda[1] in the epithet *su-snuṣā*,

[1] x. 86, 13.

'having a good daughter-in-law,' used of Vṛṣākapāyī, while in the former it occurs in several passages, where the daughter-in-law's respect for her father-in-law is mentioned,[2] a respect which spirituous liquor alone causes to be violated.[3] See also **Śvaśura** and **Pati.**

[2] Av. viii. 6, 24; Aitareya Brāhmaṇa, iii. 22, 7; Taittirīya Brāhmaṇa, ii. 4, 6, 12.

[3] Maitrāyaṇī Saṃhitā, ii. 4, 2; Kāṭhaka Saṃhitā, xii. 12 (*Indische Studien*, 5, 260).

Cf. Delbrück, *Die indogermanischen Verwandtschaftsnamen*, 414, 415.

Spandana in one passage of the Rigveda[1] denotes a certain tree. Roth,[2] however, reads *syandana*, 'chariot.'

[1] iii. 53, 19.

[2] St. Petersburg Dictionary, *s.v.*

Cf. Aufrecht, *Rigveda*, 2, vi; Zimmer, *Altindisches Leben*, 63.

Sparśu is apparently the name of a western people in the Baudhāyana Śrauta Sūtra (xxi. 13).

Spaś. See **Rājan.**

Sphūrjaka denotes a tree (*Diospyros embryopteris*) mentioned in the Śatapatha Brāhmaṇa (xiii. 8, 1, 16).

Smad-ibha is found once in the Rigveda,[1] where Roth[2] takes the word as perhaps the name of an enemy of **Kutsa.** *Cf.* **Ibha.**

[1] x. 49, 4.

[2] St. Petersburg Dictionary, *s.v.*

Cf. Oldenberg, *Ṛgveda-Noten*, 1, 380; Hillebrandt, *Vedische Mythologie*, 3, 291, n. 5.

Syandana, 'chariot,' is found in the earlier literature only, if at all, in one passage of the Rigveda,[1] where **Spandana** is the received reading.

[1] iii. 53, 19, according to Roth. A wood called Syandana seems to be meant in the Kauśika Sūtra, viii. 15.

Syāla, a word occurring in only one passage of the Rigveda,[1] appears to denote the brother of a man's wife, who is regarded as willing to protect her, and so secure a marriage for her.[2]

[1] i. 109, 2.

[2] So Sāyaṇa on Rv., *loc. cit.* *Cf.* Delbrück, *Die indogermanischen Verwandtschaftsnamen*, 517; Pischel, *Vedische Studien*, 2, 79.

Syūma-gabhasti. See **Gabhasti.**

Syūma-gṛbh, used of a horse in the Rigveda (vi. 36, 2) seems to mean 'grasping the bit between his teeth,' as a horse does when anxious to break away from control.

Syūman in one passage of the Rigveda[1] denotes, according to Roth,[2] the strap fastening the door of a house, the Homeric *ἱμάς, δεσμός*.

[1] iii. 61, 4.

[2] St. Petersburg Dictionary, *s.v.*

Syūma-raśmi is the name of a protégé of the Aśvins in the Rigveda.[1]

[1] i. 112 16; viii. 52, 2. *Cf.* Ludwig, Translation of the Rigveda, 3, 150, 163.

Srakti is found in the description of the **Dāśarājña** in the Rigveda,[1] where Hopkins[2] thinks the sense of 'spears' essential.

[1] vii. 18, 17.

[2] *Journal of the American Oriental Society*, 15, 264, n.

Sraj, 'garland,' is mentioned in the Rigveda[1] and later[2] as often worn by men when anxious to appear handsome, as at a wedding and so on. The Aśvins are described as 'lotus-wreathed' (*puṣkara-sraj*).[3]

[1] iv. 38, 6; v. 53, 4; viii. 47, 15; 56, 3.

[2] Av. i. 14, 1 (where it means a 'cluster of flowers' from a tree); Pañcaviṃśa Brāhmaṇa, xvi. 4, 1; xviii. 3, 2; 7, 6; Śatapatha Brāhmaṇa, xiii. 5, 4, 2, etc.

[3] Rv. x. 184, 3. *Cf.* Zimmer, *Altindisches Leben*, 265.

Srāktya is an adjective describing an amulet (**Maṇi**) in the Atharvaveda.[1] According to Weber,[2] it designates a crystal (literally 'many-cornered'). The commentators,[3] however, agree in explaining the word to mean 'derived from the Sraktya'—*i.e.*, from the Tilaka tree (*Clerodendrum phlomoides*).

[1] viii. 5, 4. 7. 8. *Cf.* ii. 11.
[2] *Indische Studien*, 13. 164.
[3] See Bloomfield, *American Journal of Philology*, 7, 477; *Hymns of the Atharvaveda*, 577.

Sruc denotes a 'large wooden sacrificial ladle' (used for pouring clarified butter on the fire) in the Rigveda[1] and later.[2] It is of the length of an arm, with a bowl of the size of a hand and a beaklike spout.

[1] i. 84, 18; 110, 6; 144, 1, etc.
[2] Av. v. 27, 5; vi. 114, 3; ix. 6, 17, etc.
Cf. for its shape, etc., Max Müller, *Zeitschrift der Deutschen Morgenländischen Gesellschaft*, 9, xli, lxxx; Eggeling, *Sacred Books of the East*, 12, 67; 26, 20, 23.

Sruva, as opposed to **Sruc**, denotes in the ritual literature[1] a small ladle used to convey the offering (**Ājya**) from the cooking-pot (**Sthālī**) to the large ladle (**Juhū**). In the Rigveda,[2] however, it was clearly used for the actual Soma libation.

[1] Āśvalāyana Śrauta Sūtra, i. 11, 10, etc.
[2] i. 116, 24; 121, 6, etc.
Cf. Max Müller, *Zeitschrift der Deutschen Morgenländischen Gesellschaft*, 9, viii; Caland and Henry, *L'Agniṣṭoma* xliv; Plate I., No. 9; Plate II., No. 11 Eggeling, *Sacred Books of the East*, 12, 68; 26, 20.

Sreka-parṇa in the Brāhmaṇas[1] seems to mean 'like the oleander leaf.'

[1] Taittirīya Brāhmaṇa, iii. 6, 6, 3; Aitareya Brāhmaṇa, ii. 6, 15.

Svaja in the Atharvaveda[1] and later[2] denotes the 'viper.' The word is explained by the commentators as *sva-ja*, 'self-

[1] iii. 27, 4; v. 14, 10; vi. 56, 2; x. 4, 10. 15. 17; xii. 3, 58.
[2] Taittirīya Saṃhitā, v. 5, 10, 2; 14, 1; Aitareya Brāhmaṇa, iii. 26, 3.

born,' but Roth,[3] Weber,[4] and Zimmer[5] prefer to derive it from the root *svaj*, 'clasp,' 'encircle.' In the Maitrāyaṇī Saṃhitā[6] the **Hariṇa** is said to kill the viper.

[3] St. Petersburg Dictionary, *s.v.*, gives the alternative *vivipara*.

[4] Taittirīya Saṃhitā, 2, 89, n.

[5] *Altindisches Leben*, 95.

[6] iii. 9, 3.

1. **Svadhiti** in the Rigveda[1] denotes the 'axe' or 'knife' used for dissecting the sacrificial horse. In all the other passages in that Saṃhitā[2] the sense of 'axe' for cutting wood is adequate; reference is made in one place[3] to sharpening the axe on the whetstone (*kṣṇotra*). In the Atharvaveda[4] the term seems once to denote the copper (*lohita*)[5] knife used to mark the ears of cattle; the carpenter's knife or axe is also twice referred to there.[6] Later the word means 'axe' generally.[7] As a weapon it does not appear at all.[8]

[1] i. 162, 9. 18. 20.

[2] ii. 39, 7; iii. 2, 10; 8, 6. 11; v. 7, 8; vii. 3, 9; viii. 102, 19; x. 89, 7. *Cf.* n. 8.

[3] ii. 39, 7.

[4] vi. 141, 2. *Cf.* Mantra Brāhmaṇa, i. 8, 7; Whitney, Translation of the Atharvaveda, 386, 387; Geldner, *Vedische Studien*, 2, 159, who is inclined to compare **Paraśu** in Rv. iii. 53, 22.

[5] Geldner, *loc. cit.*, understands this word to mean 'red-hot.'

[6] ix. 4, 6 (probably so to be taken); xii. 3, 33. In xviii. 2, 35, the sense is quite different. See Whitney, *op. cit.*, 845.

[7] Taittirīya Saṃhitā, vi. 3, 3, 2; Vājasaneyi Saṃhitā, ii. 15 (the slaughtering-knife); v. 43 (the axe to fell the tree), etc.

[8] In Rv. x. 92, 15, Svadhiti may refer to the thunderbolt of Indra.

2. **Svadhiti** in certain passages of the Rigveda[1] denotes, according to the St. Petersburg Dictionary, a great tree with hard wood. This interpretation seems probable.

[1] v. 32, 10; ix. 96, 6. *Cf.* i. 88, 2.

Svanad-ratha ('having a rattling car') is taken by Ludwig[1] as a proper name of **Āsaṅga** in the Rigveda.[2] But the word is most probably only an epithet.

[1] Translation of the Rigveda, 3, 159.

[2] viii. 1, 32.

Svanaya Bhāvya is the name of a prince on the **Sindhu** (Indus) who bestowed gifts on **Kakṣīvant**, according to the Rigveda (i. 126, 1. 3). He is called Svanaya Bhāvayavya in the Śāṅkhāyana Śrauta Sūtra (xvi. 11, 5).

Svapna, 'dream,' is referred to in the Rigveda[1] and later.[2] Evil dreams[3] are often mentioned. The Āraṇyakas of the Rigveda[4] contain a list of dreams with their signification, as well as of *pratyakṣa-darśanāni*, 'sights seen with one's own eyes.'

[1] ii. 28, 10; x. 162. 6.
[2] Av. vii. 101, 1; x. 3, 6; Vājasaneyi Saṃhitā, xx. 16; Śatapatha Brāhmaṇa, iii. 2, 2, 23, etc.
[3] Rv. ii. 28, 10; Av. x. 3, 6.
[4] Aitareya Āraṇyaka, iii. 2, 4; Śāṅkhāyana Āraṇyaka, xi. 3. *Cf.* Kauśika Sūtra, xlvi. 9 *et seq.*; Atharvaveda Pariśiṣṭa, lxviii.

Svar denotes the 'sun'[1] and the 'heaven of light' in the Rigveda[1] and later.[2]

[1] i. 71, 2; 105, 3; 148, 1, etc.; Nirukta, ii. 14.
[2] Rv. iii. 2, 7; v. 83, 4; x. 66, 4. 9, etc.; Av. iv. 11, 6; 14, 2, etc.

Svara denotes in the Upaniṣads[1] the sound of a vowel: these are described[2] as being *ghoṣavant*, 'sonant,' and also as *balavant*, 'uttered with force.' The precise word for a mute is *sparśa*,[3] 'contact,' while *ūṣman* denotes a 'sibilant,' and *svara* a 'vowel,' in the Aitareya[3] and Śāṅkhāyana Āraṇyakas.[4] The semivowels are there denoted by *anta-sthā* ('intermediate')[5] or *akṣara*.[6] Another division in the Aitareya Āraṇyaka[7] is into *ghoṣa*, *ūṣman*, and *vyañjana*, apparently 'vowels,' 'sibilants,' and 'consonants' respectively. *Ghoṣa* elsewhere in that Āraṇyaka[8] seems to have the general sense of 'sounds.' The Taittirīya Upaniṣad[9] refers to *mātrā*, a 'mora';[10] *bala*, 'force' of utterance, and *varṇa*, 'letter,' an expression found elsewhere[11] in the explanation of *om*, as compacted of *a* + *u* + *m*.

[1] Chāndogya Upaniṣad, ii. 22, 5; Taittirīya Upaniṣad, i. 2, 1.
[2] Chāndogya Upaniṣad, *loc. cit.*
[3] iii. 2, 1, etc.
[4] viii. 1, etc.
[5] Aitareya Āraṇyaka, iii. 2, 1.
[6] Śāṅkhāyana Āraṇyaka, viii. 1.
[7] ii. 2, 4.
[8] ii. 2, 2. *Cf.* Keith's edition, p. 213.
[9] *Loc. cit.*
[10] Also Aitareya Āraṇyaka, iii. 1, 5; Sāṅkhāyana Āraṇyaka, vii. 13.
[11] Aitareya Brāhmaṇa, v. 32, 2; Kauṣītaki Brāhmaṇa, xxvi. 5; Āśvalāyana Śrauta Sūtra, x. 4; Weber, *Indische Studien*, v. 32.

The Aitareya Āraṇyaka[12] and the Śāṅkhāyana Āraṇyaka[13] recognize the three forms of the Rigveda text as *pratṛṇṇa*, *nirbhuja*, and *ubhayam-antareṇa*, denoting respectively the Saṃhitā, Pada, and Krama Pāṭhas of the Rigveda.[14] The same authorities[15] recognize the importance of the distinction of the cerebral and dental *n* and *s*, and refer[16] to the **Māṇḍūkeyas'** mode of recitation. They also discuss[17] Sandhi, the euphonic 'combination' of letters.

The Prātiśākhyas of the several Saṃhitās develop in detail the grammatical terminology, and Yāska's Nirukta[18] contains a good deal of grammatical material. The Śatapatha Brāhmaṇa[19] distinguishes the genders, and the Pañcaviṃśa Brāhmaṇa[20] the division of words in the Sāman recitation.

12 iii. 1, 3. 5.

13 vii. 10, 12.

14 Max Müller, *Ṛgveda Prātiśākhya*, ii *et seq.*; *Nachträge*, ii; Oldenberg, *Prolegomena*, 380 *et seq.*; *Sacred Books of the East*, 30, 146 *et seq.*; Macdonell, *Sanskrit Literature*, 51.

15 Aitareya, iii. 2, 6; Śāṅkhāyana, viii. 11.

16 Aitareya, iii. 1, 1; 2, 6; Sāṅkhāyana, vii. 2; viii. 11.

17 Aitareya, iii. 1, 2. 3. 5; 2, 2; Śāṅkhāyana, vii. 13; viii. 1. 2.

18 See Roth's edition (1852), p. 222, for a list of teachers cited by Yāska, especially **Kautsa** and **Śākaṭāyana**.

19 x. 5, 1, 2. 3.

20 x. 9, 1. 2.

Cf. von Schroeder, *Indiens Literatur und Cultur*, 701 *et seq.*

Sva-rāj, 'self-ruler,' 'king,' is found frequently in the Rigveda[1] and later.[2] It is the technical term for the kings of the west according to the Aitareya Brāhmaṇa.[3]

1 i. 36, 7; 51, 15; 61, 9, etc. (of gods).

2 Av. xvii. 1, 22; Taittirīya Saṃhitā, ii. 3, 6, 2; iv. 4, 8, 1; v. 5, 4, 1, etc.

3 viii. 14. *Cf.* perhaps the republican form of government of which traces are seen in the Buddhist literature by Rhys Davids, *Buddhist India*, 19.

Svaru in the Rigveda[1] or later[2] denotes a 'post,' or more precisely in the ritual a splinter of the Yūpa, or sacrificial post.[3]

1 i. 92, 5; 162, 9; iii. 8, 6, etc.

2 Av. iv. 24, 4; xii. 1, 13, etc.

3 Aitareya Brāhmaṇa, ii. 3, 8; Taittirīya Saṃhitā, v. 5, 7, 1; vi. 3, 4 9. etc.; Śatapatha Brāhmaṇa, iii. 7, 1, 22; 8, 1, 5, etc.

Svar-jit Nāgna-jita ('descendant of **Nagna-jit**') is the name of a royal personage in the Śatapatha Brāhmaṇa,[1] a **Gandhāra** prince, whose views on the ritual are referred to with contempt.

[1] viii. 1, 4, 10. *Cf.* Muir, *Sanskrit Texts*, 1², 515.

Svar-ṇara appears to be the proper name of a sacrificer in two verses of the Rigveda.[1] According to Geldner,[2] it everywhere[3] means a specially sacred lake and the Soma-producing district around it.

[1] viii. 3, 12; 12, 2. *Cf.* Ludwig, Translation of the Rigveda, 3, 160; Hopkins, *Journal of the American Oriental Society*, 17, 89.

[2] *Rigveda, Glossar*, 209.

[3] Rv. iv. 21, 3; v. 18, 4; 14, 1; viii. 6, 39; 65, 2; 103, 14; ix. 70, 6; x. 65, 4. Perhaps in viii. 12, 2, it means 'coming from Svarṇara.'

Svar-bhānu Asura is the name, in the Rigveda[1] and later,[2] of a demon supposed to have eclipsed the sun. See **Sūrya.**

[1] v. 40, 5. 6. 8. 9.

[2] Taittirīya Saṃhitā, ii. 1, 2, 2; Pañcaviṃśa Brāhmaṇa, iv. 5, 2; 6, 13; vi. 6, 8; Śatapatha Brāhmaṇa, v. 3, 2, 2; Kauṣītaki Brāhmaṇa, xxiv. 3.

Sva-sara, according to the St. Petersburg Dictionary, denotes 'cattle stall,'[1] and more generally 'dwelling-place,' 'house,'[2] and then 'nest of birds.'[3] Geldner,[4] however, shows that the real sense is the 'wandering at will' of cattle, more precisely their 'grazing in the morning,'[5] and in the case of birds their 'early flight' from the nest,[6] while metaphorically it is applied first to the morning pressing of Soma and then to all three pressings.[7]

[1] Rv. i. 3, 8; ii. 2, 2; 34, 8; v. 62, 2; viii. 88, 1; Sāmaveda, i. 5, 2, 3, 2.

[2] Rv. i. 34, 7; iii. 60, 6; 61, 4; vi. 68, 10; viii. 99, 1; Śatapatha Brāhmaṇa, iv. 3, 5, 20.

[3] Rv. ii. 19, 2; 34, 5.

[4] *Vedische Studien*, 2, 110-115.

[5] Rv. i. 3, 8; ii. 2, 2; 34, 8; v. 62, 2; viii. 88, 1.

[6] Rv. ii. 19, 2; 34, 5.

[7] Rv. i. 34, 7; iii. 60, 6; vi. 68, 10; viii. 99, 1. In Śatapatha Brāhmaṇa, *loc. cit.*, it is equivalent to 'libation.'

Svasṛ is the regular word from the Rigveda onwards[1] for 'sister.' Like the word **Bhrātṛ,** the term sister can be applied

[1] Rv. ii. 32, 6; vi. 55, 4. 5; viii. 101, 15; x. 108, 9, etc.

to things not precisely so related. For example, in the Rigveda the fingers and the seasons are 'sisters,' and night is the sister of dawn, for whom, as the elder, she makes way.[2] The **Paṇis** offer to adopt Saramā as their sister;[3] but this use is not applied—any more than in the case of Bhrātṛ—to ordinary human beings.

The sister stood in a close relation to her brother. If the father was dead or feeble, the sister was dependent on her brother and on his wife, as appears from the Rigveda[4] and the Aitareya Brāhmaṇa.[5] Moreover, maidens without brothers were apt to find marriage difficult, and to degenerate into Hetairai;[6] but it is not certain whether this was due, as Zimmer[7] thinks, to brothers being required to arrange marriages for orphan girls, or because sonless fathers were anxious to make their daughters **Putrikās**, in order that they themselves, instead of the husbands, should count the daughters' sons as their own.[8] See also **Jāmi.**

[2] Rv. i. 124, 8. See Delbrück, *Die indogermanischen Verwandtschaftsnamen*, 463; Rv. i. 62, 10; 64, 7; 71, 1, etc.

[3] Rv. x. 108, 9.

[4] x. 85, 46. *Cf.* ix. 96, 22.

[5] iii. 37, 5.

[6] Av. i. 17, 1; Rv. i. 124, 7; iv. 5, 5; Nirukta, iii. 5.

[7] *Altindisches Leben*, 328.

[8] *Cf.* Geldner, *Rigveda, Kommentar*, 22, 48, 49 (on Rv. iii. 31, 1 *et seq.*).

Svasrīya occurs in the sense of 'sister's son' in the description of Viśvarūpa's ancestry in the Yajurveda Saṃhitās.[1]

[1] Taittirīya Saṃhitā, ii. 5, 1, 1; Maitrāyaṇī Saṃhitā, ii, 4, 1. *Cf.* Delbrück, *Die indogermanischen Verwandtschaftsnamen*, 485.

Svātī. See **Nakṣatra.**

Svādhyāya ('reciting to oneself') in the Brāhmaṇas[1] denotes the study or repetition of the Vedic texts. The Sūtras give rules for it in great detail. *Cf.* **Brāhmaṇa.**

[1] Śatapatha Brāhmaṇa, iii. 4, 3, 6; iv. 6, 9, 6; xi. 5, 6, 3; 7, 1. 4. 7; Chāndogya Upaniṣad, i. 12, 1; 8, 15; Kauṣītaki Upaniṣad, i. 1.

Svāyava, 'descendant of Svāyu,' is the patronymic of **Kūśāmba Lātavya** in the Pañcaviṃśa Brāhmaṇa (viii. 6, 8).

Svā-rājya. See **Rājya.**

Sveda-ja, 'born of sweat'—that is, 'engendered by hot moisture'—is used in the Aitareya Upaniṣad (iii. 3, 3) as a term designating a class of creatures comprising vermin of all sorts. The Mānava Dharma Śāstra (i. 45) explains it as 'flies, mosquitos, lice, bugs, and so forth.'

Cf. Keith, *Aitareya Āraṇyaka*, 235.

Svaidāyana, 'descendant of Sveda,' is the patronymic of a **Śaunaka** in the Brāhmaṇas.[1]

1 Śatapatha Brāhmaṇa, xi. 4, 1, 2. 3; Gopatha Brāhmaṇa, i. 3, 6.

Svaupaśa. See **Opaśa.**

H.

Haṃsa in the Rigveda[1] and later[2] denotes the 'gander.' These birds are described as dark in colour on the back (*nīla-pṛṣṭha*);[3] they fly in troops,[4] swim in the water (*uda-prut*),[5] make loud noises,[6] and are wakeful at night.[7] The Haṃsa is credited with the power of separating Soma from water (as later milk from water) in the Yajurveda.[8] It is also mentioned as one of the victims at the Aśvamedha ('horse sacrifice').[9]

1 i. 65, 5; 163, 10; ii. 34, 5; iii. 8, 9, etc.

2 Av. vi. 12, 1, etc.

3 Rv. vii. 59, 7.

4 Rv. iii. 8, 9.

5 Rv. i. 65, 5; iii. 45, 4.

6 Rv. iii. 53, 10.

7 Av. vi. 12, 1.

8 Kāṭhaka Saṃhitā, xxxviii. 1; Maitrāyaṇī Saṃhitā, iii. 11, 6; Vājasaneyi Saṃhitā, xix. 74; Taittirīya Brāhmaṇa, ii. 6, 2, 1.

9 Taittirīya Saṃhitā, v. 5, 21, 1; Maitrāyaṇī Saṃhitā, iii. 14, 3; Vājasaneyi Saṃhitā, xxiv. 22. 35.

Cf. Zimmer, *Altindisches Leben*, 89, 90; Lanman, *Journal of the American Oriental Society*, 19, 151; Macdonell, *Sanskrit Literature*, 150.

Haṃsa-sāci is the name of an unknown bird mentioned in the Taittirīya Saṃhitā[1] as one of the victims at the Aśvamedha ('horse sacrifice').

[1] v. 5, 20, 1. *Cf.* Zimmer, *Altindisches Leben*, 93.

Haya denotes 'horse' in the Rigveda[1] and later.[2]

[1] v. 46, 1; vii. 74, 4; ix. 107, 25.
[2] Vājasaneyi Saṃhitā, vii. 47; xxii. 19, etc.
Cf. Zimmer, *Altindisches Leben*, 231

Hara-yāṇa in the Rigveda[1] is clearly the name of a man mentioned along with **Ukṣaṇyāyana** and **Suṣāman.**

[1] viii. 28, 22; Nirukta, v. 15. *Cf.* Ludwig, Translation of the Rigveda, 3, 162.

Hariṇa in the Rigveda[1] and later[2] denotes a 'gazelle.' It is at once a type of speed[3] and terror.[4] Its horns are used as amulets.[5] It is fond of eating barley (**Yava**).[6] In the Maitrāyaṇī Saṃhitā[7] it is said to kill vipers (**Svaja**). *Cf.* **Kuluṅga, Nyaṅku.** The feminine is Hariṇī.[8]

[1] i. 163, 1; v. 78, 2.
[2] Av. vi. 67, 3, etc.
[3] Av. iii. 7, 1.
[4] Av. vi. 67, 3.
[5] Av. iii. 7, 1. 2.
[6] Taittirīya Saṃhitā, vii. 4, 19, 2 (*hariṇī*); Vājasaneyi Saṃhitā, xxiii. 30; Maitrāyaṇī Saṃhitā, iii. 13, 1; Kāṭhaka Saṃhitā, Aśvamedha, iv. 8 (also *hariṇī*); Taittirīya Brāhmaṇa, iii. 9, 7, 2 (*hariṇī*).
[7] iii. 9, 3.
[8] Taittirīya Saṃhitā, vii. 4, 19, 2, and see n. 6.
Cf. Zimmer, *Altindisches Leben*, 83; Bloomfield, *Hymns of the Atharvaveda*, 336, 337.

1. **Harita** seems to mean 'gold' in a few passages of the Saṃhitās.[1]

[1] Av. v. 28, 5. 9; xi. 3, 8; Kāṭhaka Saṃhitā, viii. 5.

2. **Harita Kaśyapa** is mentioned as a teacher, a pupil of **Śilpa Kaśyapa,** in the last Vaṃśa (list of teachers) of the Bṛhadāraṇyaka Upaniṣad.[1]

[1] vi. 4, 33 (Mādhyaṃdina = vi. 5, 3 Kāṇva).

Hari-dru in the Śatapatha Brāhmaṇa (xiii. 8, 1, 16) is the name of a tree (*Pinus deodora*).

Hariman in the Rigveda[1] and the Atharvaveda[2] denotes 'yellowness' as a disease, 'jaundice.'

[1] i. 50, 11 *et seq.*
[2] i. 22, 1; ix. 8, 9; xix. 44, 2.

Cf. Zimmer, *Altindisches Leben*, 378, 388.

Hari-yūpīyā is mentioned in a hymn of the Rigveda[1] as the scene of the defeat of the **Vṛcīvants** by **Abhyāvartin Cāyamana.** It may denote either a place or a river, since many battles seem to have been fought on the banks of rivers. Ludwig[2] took it as the name of a town on the river **Yavyāvatī,** which is identified with it in Sāyaṇa's commentary on the passage. Hillebrandt[3] thinks that it is the river Iryāb (Haliāb), a tributary of the Kurum (**Krumu**), but this is not at all probable.

[1] vi. 27, 5.
[2] Translation of the Rigveda, 3, 158.
[3] *Vedische Mythologie*, 3, 268, n. 1.

Cf. Zimmer, *Altindisches Leben*, 18, 19; Kaegi, *Rigveda*, n. 328.

Hari-varṇa Āṅgirasa ('descendant of **Aṅgiras**') is the name of the seer of a Sāman or chant in the Pañcaviṃśa Brāhmaṇa.[1]

[1] viii. 9, 4. 5. *Cf.* Hopkins, *Transactions of the Connecticut Academy of Arts and Sciences*, 15, 63.

Hari-ścandra Vaidhasa ('descendant of Vedhas') **Aikṣvāka** ('descendant of **Ikṣvāku**') is the name of a probably mythical king whose rash vow to offer up his son **Rohita** to Varuṇa is the source of the tale of **Śunaḥśepa** in the Aitareya Brāhmaṇa (vii. 14, 2) and the Śāṅkhāyana Śrauta Sūtra (xv. 17).

Harmya denotes the Vedic 'house' as a unity including the stabling[1] and so forth, and surrounded by a fence or wall of

[1] Rv. vii. 56, 16. *Cf.* x. 106, 5.

some sort.[2] It is several times referred to in the Rigveda[3] and later.[4] *Cf.* **Gṛha.**

[2] Rv. vii. 55, 6. Geldner, *Vedische Studien*, 2, 278, n. 2, takes *harmyeṣṭhāḥ*, 'standing on a house' (Rv. vii. 56, 16), to refer to princes on the roof of a palace.

[3] i. 121, 1 (the people, *viśaḥ*, of the house); 166, 4; ix. 71, 4; 78, 3; x. 43, 3; 73, 10, etc.

[4] Av. xviii. 4, 55 (a palace of Yama); Taittirīya Brāhmaṇa, iii. 7, 6, 3, etc.

Cf. Zimmer, *Altindisches Leben*, 149.

Halikṣṇa[1] or **Halīkṣṇa**[2] is mentioned as one of the victims at the Aśvamedha ('horse sacrifice') in the Yajurveda Saṃhitās. The commentator Mahīdhara[3] thinks that it is a kind of lion, Sāyaṇa[4] that a green Caṭaka bird or a lion (*tṛṇa-hiṃsa*)[5] is meant. In the Atharvaveda[6] Halīkṣṇa seems to be some particular intestine, but Weber[7] thinks it may mean 'gall.'

[1] Maitrāyaṇī Saṃhitā, iii. 14, 12; Vājasaneyi Saṃhitā, xxiv. 31.

[2] Taittirīya Saṃhitā, v. 5, 12, 1; 7, 23, 1.

[3] On Vājasaneyi Saṃhitā, *loc. cit.*

[4] On Taittirīya Saṃhitā, *loc. cit.*

[5] *Tṛṇa-siṃha* is not much more intelligible.

[6] ii. 33, 3.

[7] *Indische Studien*, 13, 206.

Cf. Zimmer, *Altindisches Leben*, 79.

Havir-dhāna ('oblation receptacle') denotes primarily the cart on which the Soma plants are conveyed to be pressed,[1] then the shed in which these Soma vehicles were kept.[2]

[1] Taittirīya Saṃhitā, iii. 1, 3, 1; vi. 2, 9, 1. 4, etc.

[2] Taittirīya Saṃhitā, vi. 2, 11, 1. 4, etc.

See **Gṛha**; Zimmer, *Altindisches Leben*, 154.

Haviṣ-kṛt Āṅgirasa ('descendant of **Aṅgiras**') is the name of the seer of a Sāman or chant according to the Pañcaviṃśa Brāhmaṇa[1] and the Taittirīya Saṃhitā.[2] See the following.

[1] xi. 10, 9. 10; xx. 11, 3.

[2] vii. 1, 4, 1.

Cf. Hillebrandt, *Vedische Mythologie*, 2, 160; Hopkins, *Transactions of the Connecticut Academy of Arts and Sciences*, 15, 62.

Haviṣmant Āṅgirasa is mentioned along with **Haviṣkṛt**, in the Taittirīya Saṃhitā and the Pañcaviṃśa Brāhmaṇa,[2] as the seer of a Sāman or chant.

[1] vii. 1, 4, 1.

[2] xi. 10, 9. 10; xx. 11, 3.

Havis is the general term for an offering to the gods, 'oblation,' whether of grain, or Soma, or milk, or clarified butter, etc. It is common from the Rigveda[1] onwards.[2]

[1] i. 24, 11; 26, 6; 170, 5, etc.

[2] Av. iii. 10, 5; vi. 5, 3, etc.

Hasta. See **Nakṣatra.**

Hasta-ghna denotes in the Rigveda[1] a 'hand-guard,' a covering used as a protection of the hand and arm from the impact of the bowstring. The word is of remarkable and still unexplained formation.[2] Lāṭyāyana[3] has *hasta-tra* and the Epic *hastāvāpa*[4] as its equivalent in sense.

[1] vi. 75, 14; Nirukta, ix. 14. The reading is assured by the parallels in the Saṃhitās: Taittirīya Saṃhitā, iv. 6, 6, 5; Maitrāyaṇī Saṃhitā, iii. 16, 3; Vājasaneyi Saṃhitā, xxix. 51.

[2] Pischel, *Vedische Studien*, 1, 296; Oldenberg, *Ṛgveda-Noten*, 1, 416.

[3] Śrauta Sūtra, iii. 10, 7.

[4] Hopkins, *Journal of the American Oriental Society*, 13, 308.

Hastādāna. See **Paśu.**

Hastin, 'having a hand,' with **Mṛga,** 'beast,' denotes in the Rigveda[1] and the Atharvaveda[2] the 'elephant.' Later the adjective alone comes to mean 'elephant.'[3] The animal was famed for its strength[4] as well as its virility.[5] It is mentioned with man and monkey as one of the beasts that take hold by the hand (*hastādāna*), as opposed to those that take hold by the mouth (*mukhādāna*).[6] It was tamed, as the expression **Hastipa,** 'elephant-keeper,' shows, and tame elephants were used to catch others (see **Vāraṇa**). But there is no trace of its use in war, though Ktesias and Megasthenes both record such use for

[1] i. 64, 7; iv. 16, 14.

[2] xii. 1, 25. Elsewhere Hastin is used alone: iii. 22, 3; iv. 36, 9; vi. 38, 2; 70, 2; xix. 1, 32.

[3] Taittirīya Saṃhitā, v. 5, 11, 1; Maitrāyaṇī Saṃhitā, iii. 14, 8; Vājasaneyi Saṃhitā, xxiv. 29; Pañcaviṃśa Brāhmaṇa, vi. 8, 8; xxiii. 13, 2; Aitareya Brāhmaṇa, iv. 1, 14; v. 31, 2; vi. 27, 2; Śatapatha Brāhmaṇa, iii. 1, 3, 4, etc.; Chāndogya Upaniṣad, vii. 24, 2 (coupled with gold), etc.; Jaiminīya Upaniṣad Brāhmaṇa, iii. 22. 1.

[4] Rv. *loc. cit.*; Av. ii. 22, 1. 3.

[5] Av. iii. 22, 6; vi. 70, 2.

[6] Taiittirīya Saṃhitā, vi. 4, 5, 7; Maitrāyaṇī Saṃhitā, iv, 5, 7.

their times.[7] The Atharvaveda[8] alludes to its being pestered by mosquitoes.

[7] Von Schroeder, *Indiens Literatur und Cultur*, 434.

[8] Av. iv. 36, 9.

Cf. Zimmer, *Altindisches Leben*, 80.

Hasti-pa, 'elephant-keeper,' is mentioned as one of the victims at the Puruṣamedha ('human sacrifice') in the Yajurveda.[1]

[1] Vājasaneyi Saṃhitā, xxx. 11; Taittirīya Saṃhitā, iii. 4, 9, 1.

Hasrā ('laughing woman') in the Rigveda[1] denotes a courtesan according to Pischel.[2]

[1] i. 124, 7.

[2] *Vedische Studien*, 1, 196, 308.

Hāyana denotes a 'year,' usually in compounds.[1] In the Kāṭhaka Saṃhitā[2] and the Śatapatha Brāhmaṇa[3] the term appears as a designation of a species of red rice. As an adjective in the sense of 'lasting a year' or 'recurring every year,' it is applied to fever in the Atharvaveda.[4]

[1] Av. viii. 2, 21; *śata-hāyana*, 'a hundred years old,' viii. 2, 8; 7, 22; *hāyanī*, xii. 1, 36 (probably corrupt).

[2] xv. 5.

[3] v. 3, 3, 6 (the Taittirīya Saṃhitā, i. 8, 10, 1, has instead *mahā-vrīhi*, 'great rice').

[4] xix. 39, 10.

Cf. Schrader, *Prehistoric Antiquities*, 301.

Hārikarṇī-putra, 'son of a female descendant of Harikarṇa,' is the name of a teacher, a pupil of **Bhāradvājī-putra**, in the last Vaṃśa (list of teachers) in the Mādhyaṃdina recension of the Bṛhadāraṇyaka Upaniṣad (vi. 4, 30).

Hāridrava is the name of a yellow bird in the Rigveda,[1] perhaps the 'yellow water-wagtail.'[2] Geldner[3] compares the Greek χαραδριός.

[1] i. 50, 12; viii. 35, 7.

[2] Sāyaṇa on Rv. i. 50, 12; Taittirīya Brāhmaṇa, iii. 7, 6, 2, treats it as the name of a plant (*cf.* Zimmer, *Altindisches Leben*, 62). But on Av. i. 22, 4, he takes it as *gopītanaka*, 'wagtail.'

[3] *Rigveda, Glossar*, 213.

Cf. Bloomfield, *Hymns of the Atharvaveda*, 264, n. 1; 266; Whitney, Translation of the Atharvaveda, 23.

Hāridravika is the title of a work by Hāridravin mentioned in the Nirukta.[1]

[1] ix. 5. See Roth, *Nirukta*, xxiii; von Schroeder, Maitrāyaṇī Saṃhitā, 1, xiii.

Hāri-drumata, 'descendant of Haridrumant,' is the patronymic of a **Gautama** in the Chāndogya Upaniṣad (iv. 4, 3).

Hāliṅgava, 'descendant of Haliṅgu,' is the name of a teacher in the Śatapatha Brāhmaṇa (x. 4, 5, 1).

Hitā in the Brāhmaṇas[1] is the name of certain 'veins.' *Cf.* **Hirā.**

[1] Bṛhadāraṇyaka Upaniṣad, ii. 1, 21; iv. 2, 4; 3, 20; Kauṣītaki Upaniṣad, iv. 19.

Hima, denoting 'cold,' 'cold weather,' is quite common in the Rigveda,[1] but less frequent later.[2] As 'snow' the word appears as a masculine in the Taittirīya Brāhmaṇa,[3] and often later as a neuter.[4] *Cf.* **Hemanta.**

[1] i. 116, 8; 119, 6; viii. 32, 26, etc.
[2] Av. vii. 18, 2; xiii. 1, 46; xix. 49, 5 (night as mother of coolness), etc.
[3] iii. 12, 7, 2.
[4] Ṣaḍviṃśa Brāhmaṇa, vi. 9, etc.
Cf. Hillebrandt, *Vedische Mythologie*, 3, 192-195.

Himavant, 'snowy,' appears as an epithet of mountains in the Atharvaveda.[1] It is also used both there[2] and in the Rigveda,[3] as well as later,[4] as a noun. There seems no reasen to deny that in all the passages the word refers vaguely to the mountains now called Himālaya, though it is possible that the name may include mountains not strictly in that system, like the Suleiman hills.[5] See also **Mūjavant** and **Trikakubh.**

[1] xii. 1, 11.
[2] vi. 95, 3. See also iv. 9, 9; v. 4, 2. 8; 25, 7; vi. 24, 1 (where reference is made to the rivers of the Himālayas); xix. 39, 1.
[3] x. 121, 4.
[4] Taittirīya Saṃhitā, v. 5, 11, 1; Vājasaneyi Saṃhitā, xxiv. 30; xxv. 12; Aitareya Brāhmaṇa, viii. 14, 3 (the **Uttara Kurus** and **Uttara Madras** live beyond it; perhaps in Kaśmīr), etc.
[5] Ludwig, Translation of the Rigveda, 3, 198.
Cf. Zimmer, *Altindisches Leben*, 29; Weber, *Indische Studien*, 18, 12, who inclines to see a reminiscence of the Caucasus.

Himā denotes 'winter' in the combination a 'hundred winters' in the Rigveda[1] and elsewhere.[2]

[1] i. 64, 14; ii. 33, 2; v. 54, 15; vi. 48, 8.

[2] Av. ii. 28, 4; xii. 2, 28; Taittirīya Saṃhitā, i. 6, 6, 3; Vājasaneyi Saṃhitā, ii. 27.

Hiraṇin, 'rich in gold,' is apparently an epithet of **Trasadasyu** in one verse of the Rigveda,[1] referring to the golden raiment or possessions of the king. Ludwig,[2] however, thinks the word is a proper name, possibly of **Trasadasyu's son.**

[1] v. 53, 8.

[2] Translation of the Rigveda, 3, 155.

Hiraṇina is found in one passage of the Rigveda,[1] where Ludwig[2] takes the word as a name of **Śāṇḍa.** But it seems to be an adjectival form of *hiraṇin*, 'golden.'

[1] vi. 63, 9.

[2] Translation of the Rigveda, 3, 158.

Hiraṇya in the Rigveda[1] and later[2] denotes 'gold.' It is hardly possible to exaggerate the value attached to gold by the Vedic Indians. The metal was, it is clear, won from the bed of rivers. Hence the Indus is called 'golden'[3] and 'of golden stream.'[4] Apparently the extraction of gold from the earth was known,[5] and washing for gold is also recorded.[6]

Gold is the object of the wishes of the Vedic singer,[7] and golden treasures (*hiraṇyāni*) are mentioned as given by patrons[8] along with cows and horses. Gold was used for ornaments for neck and breast (**Niṣka**), for ear-rings (**Karṇa-śobhana**), and even for cups.[9] Gold is always associated with the gods.[10]

[1] i. 43, 5; iii. 34, 9; iv. 10, 6; 17, 11, etc.

[2] Av. i. 9, 2; ii. 36, 7; v. 28, 6; vi. 38, 2, etc.

[3] Rv. x. 75, 8.

[4] Rv. vi. 61, 7; viii. 26, 18.

[5] Rv. i. 117, 5; Av. xii. 1, 6. 26. 44.

[6] Taittirīya Saṃhitā, vi. 1, 7, 1; Śatapatha Brāhmaṇa, ii. 1, 1, 5.

[7] Rv. vi. 47, 23; viii. 78, 9; Pischel and Geldner, *Vedische Studien*, 1, xxiv.

[8] *Cf.* also **Hiraṇyastūpa** as a proper name.

[9] Taittirīya Saṃhitā, v. 7, 1, 3; Taittirīya Brāhmaṇa, i. 3, 3, 7; Śatapatha Brāhmaṇa, v. 1, 2, 19; 5, 28.

[10] All that is connected with them is of gold; the horses of the sun are *hiraṇya-tvacas*, 'gold-skinned' (Av. xiii. 2, 8), and so on.

In the plural Hiraṇya denotes 'ornaments of gold.'[11]

A gold currency was evidently beginning to be known in so far as definite weights of gold are mentioned: thus a weight, *aṣṭā-prūḍ*, occurs in the Saṃhitās,[12] and the golden *śatamāna*, 'weight of a hundred (**Kṛṣṇalas**)' is found in the same texts.[13] In several passages,[14] moreover, *hiraṇya* or *hiraṇyāni* may mean 'pieces of gold.'

Gold is described sometimes as *harita*,[15] 'yellowish,' sometimes as *rajata*,[16] 'whitish,' when probably 'silver' is alluded to. It was obtained from the ore by smelting.[17] Megasthenes[18] bears testimony to the richness in gold of India in his time.

[11] Rv. i. 122, 2; 162, 16; ii. 33, 9; v. 60, 4; Av. iv. 10, 6; Vājasaneyi Saṃhitā, xv. 50; xx. 37; also in the singular, Av. i. 35, 1; xviii. 4, 56.

[12] Taittirīya Saṃhitā, iii. 4, 1, 4; Kāṭhaka Saṃhitā, xi. 1; xiii. 10; von Schroeder, *Zeitschrift der Deutschen Morgenländischen Gesellschaft*, 49, 164.

[13] Śatapatha Brāhmaṇa, v. 5, 5, 16; xii. 7, 2, 13; 9, 1, 4. *Cf.* xiii. 1, 1, 4; 2, 3, 2; 4, 1, 13; 2, 7, 13; xiv. 3, 1, 32; Taittirīya Saṃhitā, ii. 3, 11, 5; Kāṭhaka Saṃhitā, viii. 5; xxii. 8; Weber, *Indische Streifen*, 1, 101. Geldner, *Vedische Studien*, 1, 268, is inclined to think that a gold unit is alluded to in the vague phrases 'thousands,' etc., of the Rigveda. See viii. 1, 13; 65, 12; x. 95, 3, etc.

[14] Taittirīya Brāhmaṇa, i. 4, 7, 4; iii. 8, 2, 2; Śatapatha Brāhmaṇa, xii 7, 1, 7; xiii. 4, 1, 6, etc.

[15] Kāṭhaka Saṃhitā, x. 4; Śatapatha Brāhmaṇa, xii. 4, 4, 6; Ṣaḍviṃśa Brāhmaṇa, ii. 9.

[16] Taittirīya Saṃhitā, i. 5, 1, 2; Śatapatha Brāhmaṇa, xii. 4, 4, 7; xiii. 4, 2, 10, etc.

[17] Śatapatha Brāhmaṇa, vi. 1, 3, 5. *Cf.* ii. 2, 3, 28; xii. 4, 3, 1; Pañcaviṃśa Brāhmaṇa, xvii. 6, 4 (*niṣ-ṭap*, 'heat'); Jaiminīya Brāhmaṇa, i. 10 (*Journal of the American Oriental Society*, 16, 234, ccxliii); Lāṭyāyana Śrauta Sūtra, iii. 1, 9, etc.; Jaiminīya Upaniṣad Brāhmaṇa, iii. 34, 6.

[18] See Diodorus Siculus, ii. 36; Strabo, pp. 703, 711.

Cf. Zimmer, *Altindisches Leben*, 49-51; Macdonell, *Sanskrit Literature*, 151.

Hiraṇya-kaśipu in the Brāhmaṇas[1] denotes a 'golden seat,' probably one covered with cloth of gold.

[1] Taittirīya Brāhmaṇa, iii. 9, 20, 1; Aitareya Brāhmaṇa, vii. 18, 12. *Cf.* the word as an adjective with the sense of 'having a golden cloth,' Av. v. 7, 10.

Hiraṇya-kāra denotes a 'worker in gold' mentioned in the list of victims at the Puruṣamedha ('human sacrifice') in the Yajurveda.[1]

[1] Vājasaneyi Saṃhitā, xxx. 17; Taittirīya Brāhmaṇa, iii. 4, 14, 1.

Hiraṇya-dant ('gold-toothed') **Vaida** ('descendant of Veda') is the name of a teacher in the Aitareya Brāhmaṇa (iii. 6, 3) and the Aitareya Āraṇyaka (ii. 1, 5). The name presumably refers to the use of gold to stop the teeth; see **Dant.**

Hiraṇya-nābha is the name of a **Kausalya** or Kosala prince, whose horse sacrifice appears to be alluded to in the Śāṅkhāyana Śrauta Sūtra (xvi. 9, 13). He is also referred to in the Praśna Upaniṣad (vi. 1), and may have been connected with **Para Āṭṇāra.** *Cf.* **Hairaṇya-nābha.**

Hiraṇya-stūpa is the name of a man in the Rigveda[1] and in the Śatapatha Brāhmaṇa.[2] He is called an **Āṅgirasa** in the Aitareya Brāhmaṇa,[3] which credits him with the authorship of a Rigvedic hymn.[4] The Anukramaṇī (Index) ascribes to him several other hymns.[5]

[1] x. 149, 5.
[2] i. 6, 4, 2.
[3] iii. 24, 11.
[4] i. 32.
[5] i. 31-35; ix. 4. 69. *Cf.* Ludwig, Translation of the Rigveda, 3, 104, 141.

Hiraṇya-hasta is in the Rigveda[1] the name of a son given by the Aśvins to **Vadhrimatī** (who, as her name denotes, was the wife of a eunuch).

[1] i. 116, 13; 117, 24; vi. 62, 7; x. 39, 7. He appears to be called **Śyāva** in x. 65, 12. *Cf.* Macdonell, *Vedic Mythology*, p. 52.

Hirā in the Atharvaveda[1] denotes 'vein,' like **Hitā.**

[1] i. 17, 1; vii. 35, 2; Vājasaneyi Saṃhitā, xxv. 8. *Cf.* Weber, *Omina und Portenta*, 346.

Hṛtsv-āśaya Āllakeya is mentioned in the Jaiminīya Upaniṣad Brāhmaṇa (iii. 40, 2) in the Vaṃśa (list of teachers) as a pupil of **Somaśuṣma Sātyayajñi Prācīnayogya.**

Hṛdayāmaya, 'disease of the heart,' is mentioned in the Atharvaveda in connexion with **Yakṣma**[1] and with **Balāsa.**[2]

[1] v. 30, 9.
[2] vi. 14, 1; 127, 3.

Zimmer,[3] who thinks that **Balāsa** is consumption, connects the name with the later view of the medical Saṃhitās,[4] that love is one of the causes of the disease. But it would be more natural to see in it a disease affecting the heart.

[3] *Altindisches Leben*, 387.

[4] Wise, *Hindu System of Medicine*, 321, 322.

Hṛd-yota[1] (for **Hṛd-dyota**) and **Hṛd-roga,**[2] 'heart disease,' are mentioned in the Atharvaveda and the Rigveda respectively. Zimmer[3] identifies the disease in the Atharvaveda with **Hṛdayāmaya,** 'consumption caused by love.' In the Rigveda this is not at all likely: later in the medical Saṃhitās the word probably denotes *angina pectoris*.[4]

[1] Av. i. 22, 1. *Cf.* vi. 24, 1.

[2] Rv. i. 50, 11.

[3] *Altindisches Leben*, 388.

[4] Wise, *Hindu System of Medicine*, 321.

Heman (used only in the locative singular) denotes 'winter' in the later Saṃhitās and the Brāhmaṇas.[1]

[1] Taittirīya Saṃhitā, ii. 6, 1, 1; Kāṭhaka Saṃhitā, xxxvi. 6; Taittirīya Brāhmaṇa, i. 4, 10, 10; Śatapatha Brāhmaṇa, i. 5, 4, 5; xi. 2, 7, 32.

Hemanta, 'winter,' occurs only once in the Rigveda,[1] but often in the later texts.[2] Zimmer[3] is inclined to trace differences of climate in the Rigveda: he thinks that certain hymns,[4] which ignore winter and insist on the rains, indicate a different place and time of origin from those which refer to the snowy mountains.[5] It is, however, quite impossible to separate parts of the Rigveda on this basis. It is probable that that text owes its composition in the main to residents in the later **Madhyadeśa**; hence the references to cold and snow are rather a sign of local than of temporal differences. It is otherwise with the later expansion of the three into four seasons,

[1] x. 161, 4.

[2] Av. vi. 55, 2; viii. 2, 22; xii. 1, 36; Taittirīya Saṃhitā, v. 7 2, 4; Vājasaneyi Saṃhitā, xiii. 58; Pañcaviṃśa Brāhmaṇa, xxi. 15, 2; Taittirīya Brāhmaṇa, i. 4, 10, 10; Śatapatha Brāhmaṇa, x. 4, 5, 2 etc.

[3] *Altindisches Leben*, 40.

[4] Rv. vii. 103; x. 90.

[5] Rv. x. 68, 10; 121, 4 (both these are not early hymns).

which represents clearly the earlier advance of the Indians (see **Ṛtu**).

The Śatapatha Brāhmaṇa[6] describes winter as the time when the plants wither, the leaves fall from the trees, the birds fly low and retire more and more.

[6] i. 5, 4, 5.

Haita-nāmana, 'descendant of Hitanāman,' is the patronymic of a teacher apparently called Āhṛta in the Maitrāyaṇī Saṃhitā,[1] though the verse is a strange one.

[1] iii. 4, 6. See Pāṇini, vi. 4, 170, Vārttika, and von Schroeder, Maitrāyaṇī Saṃhitā, 2, ix.

Hairaṇya-nābha, 'descendant of **Hiraṇyanābha,**' is the patronymic of **Para Āṭṇāra,** the **Kosala** king, in a **Gāthā** occurring in the Śatapatha Brāhmaṇa (xiii. 5, 4, 4).

Hotṛ is the name of one of the oldest and most important priests of the Vedic ritual, the counterpart of the *Z*aotar of the Avestan priesthood.[1] The word must be derived from *hu*, 'sacrifice,' as was held by **Aurṇavābha**;[2] this indicates a time when the Hotṛ was at once sacrificer (the later Adhvaryu) and singer. But the functions were already clearly divided in the Rigveda, where the Hotṛ's chief duty was the recitation of the **Śastras.** He was also in the older period often the **Purohita** of the king, an office later filled by the **Brahman** priest.

[1] Rv. i. 1, 1; 14, 11; 139, 10, etc.; **Hotra,** the 'Hotṛ's office,' Rv. ii. 1, 2; 36, 1; 37, 1, etc.

[2] Nirukta, iv. 26. *Cf.* Oldenberg, *Religion des Veda,* 380 *et seq.*

Hotraka in the Aitareya Brāhmaṇa[1] denotes 'assistant of the Hotṛ' priest.

[1] ii. 36, 5; vi. 6, 2. In the Sūtras it is variously used—sometimes in this sense, sometimes more widely—so as to include all the priests except the four chief priests (*cf.* Āśvalāyana Śrauta Sūtra, v. 6, 17).

Hyas in the Rigveda[1] and later[2] denotes 'yesterday.'

[1] viii. 66, 7; 99, 1; x. 55, 5.

[2] Pañcaviṃśa Brāhmaṇa, xi. 9, 3.

Hrada in the Rigveda[1] and later[2] denotes a 'lake' or 'pond.'

[1] i. 52, 7; iii. 36, 8; 45, 3; x. 43, 7; 71, 7; 102, 4; 142, 8, etc.

[2] Av. iv. 15, 4; vi. 37, 2; Pañcaviṃśa Brāhmaṇa, xxv. 10, 18; Śatapatha Brāhmaṇa, iv. 1, 5, 12; 4, 5, 10; xi. 5, 5, 8, etc.

Hrade-cakṣus in one passage of the Rigveda[1] is thought by Jackson[2] to mean 'will of the wisp.'

[1] x. 95, 6.

[2] *Proceedings of the American Oriental Society*, May, 1890, iv.

Hrasva Māṇḍūkeya (' descendant of Maṇḍūka ') is the name of a teacher in the Aitareya Āraṇyaka.[1]

[1] iii. 1, 5; 2, 1. 6. *Cf.* Weber, *ndische Studien*, 1, 391. The word must be regarded as a proper name, given from a personal characteristic, much as **Sthavira** is used.

Hrāduni denotes 'hail' in the Rigveda[1] and later.[2]

[1] i. 32, 13; v. 54, 3.

[2] Taittirīya Saṃhitā, vii. 4, 13, 1; Vājasaneyi Saṃhitā, xxii. 26; xxvi. 9, etc.

Hrūḍu is a word of unknown meaning applied to **Takman** in the Atharvaveda.[1] It is variously spelled in the manuscript as *hruḍa, hūḍu, rūḍu,* and so forth; the Paippalāda recension reads *huḍu*, 'ram.' Henry[2] has conjectured that the word is the equivalent of a proto-Semitic *ḥarūḍu*, 'gold' (Assyrian *huraçu* and Hebrew *ḥarūç*), while Halévy[3] suggests that it may be the Greek χλωρός, 'greenish-yellow'; but both conjectures are highly improbable.[4] Weber[5] thinks 'cramp' is meant.

[1] i. 25, 2. 3.

[2] *Journal Asiatique*, 9th series, 10, 513.

[3] *Ibid.*, 11, 320 *et seq.*

[4] Macdonell, *Journal of the Royal Asiatic Society*, 1907, 1106.

[5] *Indische Studien*, 4, 420.

Cf. Lanman on Whitney, Translation of the Atharvaveda, 26; Bloomfield, *Hymns of the Atharvaveda*, 273.

Hvaras in three passages of the Rigveda[1] denotes, according to Roth,[2] a part of the Soma sieve, perhaps the part through which the Soma juice flowed. But Geldner[3] thinks that in all these cases the sense is merely 'hindrance.'

[1] ix. 3, 2; 63, 4; 106, 13.

[2] St. Petersburg Dictionary, *s.v.* 1; Zimmer, *Altindisches Leben*, 278, n.; Hillebrandt, *Vedische Mythologie*, 1. 203.

[3] *Vedische Studien*, 2, 20

ADDENDA AND CORRIGENDA

Aṅguli, 'finger-breadth,' is mentioned as the 'lowest measure' in the Śatapatha Brāhmaṇa.[1]

[1] x. 2, 1, 2. See Fleet, *Journal of the Royal Asiatic Society*, 1912, 231.

Anas.—In the Sūtras[1] mention is made of a part of the cart called Gadhā, which in Garbe's[2] opinion means 'roof.'

[1] Baudhāyana Śrauta Sūtra, xiii. 38; Āpastamba Śrauta Sūtra, xix. 26, 4. *Cf. tri-gadha, ibid.*, xix. 26, 2.
[2] Edition of Āpastamba, 3, 356.

Araṇī is the designation, in the Rigveda[1] and later,[2] of the two pieces of wood used in producing the sacrificial fire by friction. The upper (*uttarā*) and the lower (*adharā*) are distinguished.[3] The upper, in the form of a drill, is made of the hard wood of the **Aśvattha**,[4] the lower, in the form of a slab, of the soft wood of the **Śamī**.[5] The drill is twirled forcibly (*sahasā*)[6] backwards and forwards with the arms (*bāhubhyām*)[7] by means of cords (*raśanābhiḥ*).[8] The action doubtless resembled that by which butter is separated from milk in India

[1] i. 127, 4; 129, 5; iii. 29, 2; v. 9, 3; vii. 1, 1; x. 184, 3.
[2] Av. x. 8, 20; Śatapatha Brāhmaṇa, iii. 1, 1, 11; iv. 6, 8, 3; xii. 4, 3, 3. 10; Kaṭha Upaniṣad, iv. 7; Śvetāśvatara Upaniṣad, i. 14. 15; Āśvalāyana Gṛhya Sūtra, iv. 6.
[3] Śatapatha Brāhmaṇa, iii. 4, 1, 22; xi. 5, 1, 15; Kātyāyana Śrauta Sūtra, v. 1, 30, etc.
[4] Av. vi. 11, 1; Śatapatha Brāhmaṇa, xi. 5, 1, 13; Kātyāyana Śrauta Sūtra, iv. 7, 22.
[5] Av. vi. 11, 1; 30, 2. 3; Taittirīya Brāhmaṇa, i. 1, 3, 11 *et seq.*
[6] Rv. vi. 48, 5.
[7] Aitareya Brāhmaṇa, iii. 4, 7. *Cf.* Rv. x. 7, 5.
[8] *Cf.* Rv. x. 4, 6. See Macdonell, *Vedic Mythology*, p. 91.

at the present day, the same verb (*math*, 'twirl,' 'churn')[9] being used for both processes. This method of producing the sacrificial fire still survives in India. Specimens of the modern apparatus may be seen in the Indian Institute and in the Pitt-Rivers Museum at Oxford.

[9] Fire: Rv. vi. 15, 17; 48, 5, etc. Butter: *dugdhaṃ mathitam ājyaṃ bhavati*, Taittirīya Saṃhitā, ii. 2, 10, 2; Śatapatha Brāhmaṇa, v. 3, 2, 6; Kātyāyana Śrauta Sūtra, v. 8, 18.

Aratni, 'cubit.' According to the Śulvasūtra of Baudhāyana,[1] this measure is equal to 24 Aṅgulas or 'finger-breadths.' The Śatapatha Brāhmaṇa[2] also mentions 24 Aṅgulis or 'finger-breadths' as a measure, but without reference to the Aratni.[3]

[1] Fleet, *Journal of the Royal Asiatic Society*, 1912, 231, n. 2.
[2] x. 2, 1, 3.
[3] *Cf.* Eggeling, *Sacred Books of the East*, 43, 300, n. 3.

Arka (*Calotropis gigantea*) is often referred to in the Śatapatha Brāhmaṇa (ix. 1, 1, 4. 9; its leaf: *arka-parṇa*, 42; *arka-palāśa*, i. 2, 3, 12. 13).

Ādhāna denotes 'bridle,' and especially the 'bit' of the bridle in the Yajurveda Saṃhitās.[1]

[1] Taittirīya Saṃhitā, vi. 5, 9, 2. 3; Kāṭhaka Saṃhitā, xxviii. 9; Maitrāyaṇī Saṃhitā, iv. 7, 4; Taittirīya Brāhmaṇa, i. 6, 3, 10.

Itihāsa.—The question of the nature of the Vedic Itihāsa has been further considered by Keith, *Journal of the Royal Asiatic Society*, 1911, 979-995; 1912, 429-438; and by Oldenberg, *Nachrichten der königlichen Gesellschaft der Wissenschaften zu Göttingen*, 1911, 441-468.

Aikṣvāka. For 'Vārṣṇi' read 'Vārṣṇa.'

Kakṣa, 1, 131, should be 2. **Kaṃsa**, coming before **Kakara**, 1, 130, and after **Kaṃsa**, 'pot or vessel of metal,' which should be 1. **Kaṃsa.**

Kamboja.—For these Iranian connexions, see Kuhn, *Avesta, Pehlvi and Ancient Persian Studies in Honour of the late Shams-ul-ulema Dastur Peshotanji Behramji Sanjana* (Strassburg und Leipzig, 1904), 213 *et seq.*; Grierson, *Journal of the Royal*

Asiatic Society, 1911, 801, 802; 1912, 255; G. K. Nariman, *ibid*, 255-257; Muir, *Sanskrit Texts*, 2[2], 355, 356.

Kāṇḍā-viṣa, 1, 148, should be **Kāndā-viṣa.**

Kāṇvī-putra, 1, 147, should come after **Kāṇvāyana.**

Kumāra-hārita, 1, 172, should come after **Kubhra**, 1, 162.

Kumala barhis, 1, 172, should be **Kulmala-barhis**.

Kuṣumbhaka, according to Egerton (*Journal of the American Oriental Society*, 31, 134), denotes 'poison-bag' in both passages of the Rigveda.

Kṛṣṇala, line 1 and note [4], read 'seed' for 'berry.'

Kraivya,—For 'on the **Parivakrā**' read 'at **Parivakrā**.'

Krośa.—In note [1], for 'about two miles' read '1⅛ miles.' See Fleet, *Journal of the Royal Asiatic Society*, 1912, 237.

Grāma.—The phrase Grāmin, 'possessing a village,' occurs often in the Taittirīya Saṃhitā (ii. 1, 3, 2; 6, 7; 2, 8, 1; 11, 1; 3, 3, 5; 9, 2), usually in connexion with various rites for acquiring a village. Since in these cases repeated mention is made of obtaining pre-eminence over **Sajātas** and Samānas, 'equals,' it is probable that allowance must also be made for the control over his fellow-villagers which an ambitious man could obtain (*e.g.*, by loans), and which might end by giving him the position of a great landlord, even without the intervention of the king.

Caṇḍātaka in the Śatapatha Brāhmaṇa (v. 2, 1, 8) and the Kātyāyana Śrauta Sūtra (xiv. 5, 3) denotes an undergarment worn by women.

Camū.—Oldenberg[1] considers that even in the dual the word denotes two vessels into which the Soma, often mixed with water in the **Kośa** and purified with the sieve, was poured, and that, in the plural, reference is made to these and other vessels into which the Soma was put at the various stages of the

[1] *Zeitschrift der Deutschen Morgenländischen Gesellschaft*, 62, 459-470.

process. **Kalaśa** similarly denoted either one (sing.) or several (plur.) of the vessels, the dual not being used, since the dual of **Camū** was reserved for the two vessels *par excellence*. In the later ritual the Camūs are replaced by the Droṇa-Kalaśa and the Pūtabhṛt, which was, however, assimilated in form and material (being made of clay, not of wood) to the Ādhāvanīya, the later name of the Kośa. The main difficulty of this theory is that it is hard to explain why Kalaśa never occurs in the dual. Geldner[2] falls back on the older view that in Camū (dual) the two boards of the Soma press are meant.

[2] *Ṛgveda, Glossar*, 60.

Cāṇḍāla, 1, 258, should come after **Cākṣuṣa.**

Jābāla.—For 'descendant of **Jabāla**' read 'descendant of **Jabālā.**'

Talava, 1, 302, should come after **Tarya**, 1, 301.

Dṛṣadvatī.—The identification of this river with the Ghaggar (Macdonell, *History of Sanskrit Literature*, 142) seems to be wrong. It is almost certainly the modern Chitang (which is the correct spelling according to Raverty, *Journal of the Asiatic Society of Bengal*, 61, 422), or Chitrung (Oldham, *Journal of the Royal Asiatic Society*, 25, 58; *cf.* the sketch map opposite p. 49). See **Sarasvatī**, 2, 435, note [4].

Devabhāga, is also mentioned in the Taittirīya Saṃhitā (vi. 6, 2, 2) as having ruined the **Sṛñjayas** by an error in the sacrifice, and as a contemporary of **Vāsiṣṭha Sātahavya.**

Nakṣatra.—In note [137], 1, 424, supply 'of' before 'the criticisms made,' and in the following lines read '*Journal*' and '466.'

Niṣāda.—The Niṣādas, according to the Mahābhārata (iii. 10, 538), are situated beyond **Vinaśana**, the 'place of disappearance' of the **Sarasvatī.**

Nṛmedha.—For **Sumedhas** read **Sumedha.**

Pati, 1, 489, note 145, line 7, after 'ritual' delete 'of.'

Parāvṛj, 1, 493, headline, for '49,' read '493.'

Paṣṭhavāh in the later literature appears sometimes as Praṣṭhavāh: if Bloomfield's view[1] that **Praṣṭi** is from *pra* and *as*, 'be,' is correct, this may be the older form. Against this, however, is to be set the constant earlier tradition.[2] Macdonell[3] connects the word with *pṛṣṭhavāh*, 'carrying on the back.'

[1] *Journal of the American Oriental Society*, 29, 78 *et seq.*

[2] Wackernagel, *Altindische Grammatik*, 1, 235.

[3] *Vedic Grammar*, p. 48.

Pratiṣṭhā.—For the succour of a fugitive offender may be compared the phrase in the Taittirīya Saṃhitā (vi. 5, 6, 3; 8, 4. 5), 'men do not deliver up even one deserving death (*vadhya*) who has come to them for protection (*prapanna*).' *Cf.* **Paridā.**

Pravarta.—The sense of 'ear-ornament' is justified by Āpastamba Śrauta Sūtra, xix. 23, 11; 24, 10. *Cf.* Baudhāyana Śrauta Sūtra, xiii. 31.

Praṣṭi is considered by Bloomfield[1] to refer to a horse yoked in front to guide the team, a sense clearly occurring in some places, and to be derived from *pra* and *as*, 'be,' as in **Upasti.** The word is usually[2] considered to be connected with *parśu*, 'rib.'

[1] *Journal of the American Oriental Society*, 29, 78 *et seq.*

[2] Wackernagel, *Altindische Grammatik*, 1, 230, 235; Macdonell, *Vedic Grammar*, p. 43.

Balbūtha, 2, 64, should come after **Balbaja**, 2, 63.

Bāhīka.—For the later traditions, see Muir, *Sanskrit Texts*, 2[2], 482 *et seq.*; Grierson, *Zeitschrift der Deutschen Morgenländischen Gesellschaft*, 66, 68, 73.

Brahmacarya.—The later rules are exhaustively given by Glaser, *Zeitschrift der Deutschen Morgenländischen Gesellschaft*, 66, 1 *et seq.*

Bhaṅga-śravas is the form of a man's name found in the Kāṭhaka Saṃhitā (xxxviii. 12) in the parallel to the passage of the Taittirīya Āraṇyaka (vi. 5, 2), which has **Bhaṅgyaśravas.**

Bhiṣaj, 2, 104, should be 1. **Bhiṣaj.**

Matya, 'harrow' or 'roller,' is found in the Brāhmaṇa portions of the Saṃhitās.[1] Sāyaṇa[2] takes it as 'manure.'

[1] Taittirīya Saṃhitā, vi. 6, 7, 4; Kāṭhaka Saṃhitā, xxix. 4; Pañcaviṃśa Brāhmaṇa, ii. 9, 2. *Cf.* *sumatitsaru* above, i. 334.

[2] On Taittirīya Saṃhitā, *loc. cit.*

Māya, 2, 155, should be **Māyā.**

Māsa, 2, 157, note [10], add: according to Taittirīya Saṃhitā, iii. 5, 1, 3, the new moon begins the month.

Yuga.—Tilak[1] has pressed this word into his theory of the reminiscence in the Vedas of an arctic home. He finds in it the sense of 'month,' interpreting the legend of **Dīrghatamas** (=the sun) as an allusion to the arctic summer of ten months, followed by a night of two, traces of which he thinks exist in the notices of the seasons. This theory is, however, most improbable, as is his explanation[2] of the Aitareya Brāhmaṇa[3] reference by the theory that it portrays the various stages of the life of the Āryans.

[1] *The Arctic Home in the Vedas*, 172-187. *Cf.* Bloomfield, *Journal of the American Oriental Society*, 30, 60.

[2] *Op. cit.*, 455.

[3] vii. 15.

Yojana.—From the attribution of thirty Yojanas to the dawn in the Rigveda,[1] Tilak[2] has argued that the dawns of the arctic regions in the interglacial period must be meant. But the reference is apparently to the thirty dawns of the thirty days which constitute the Vedic month. See **Māsa.**

[1] i. 123, 8. *Cf.* vi. 59, 6, and the thirty dawns of Taittirīya Saṃhitā, iv. 3, 11, 1.

[2] *The Arctic Home in the Vedas*, 103-107.

Rakṣas in the early Vedic literature normally refers to demons, and is only metaphorically[1] applied to human foes. No definite tribe is meant.[2]

[1] Rv. iii. 30, 15-17; vii. 104, 1. 2; Muir, *Sanskrit Texts*, 2[2], 389 *et seq.*

[2] *Cf.* Grierson, *Zeitschrift der Deutschen Morgenländischen Gesellschaft*, 66, 68. Similarly **Piśācas** are not a tribe in Vedic literature, whatever they may be later.

Rājasūya.—Read 'victor' for 'victim' in line 12.

Lāhyāyana, 2, 232, should be **Lāhyāyani,** and the reference, iii. 3, 1, 2.

1. **Varṣā-hū**, 'frog' ('calling in the rains'), is one of the victims at the Aśvamedha ('horse sacrifice') in the Vājasaneyi Saṃhitā (xxiv. 38).

2. **Varṣā-hū** ('produced in the rains') is the name[1] of a plant (*Boerhavia procumbens*) in the Taittirīya Saṃhitā (iii. 4, 10, 3).

[1] The form seems to show *h* for *bh*, as in other cases given by Wackernagel, *Altindische Grammatik*, 1, 217*b*; *varṣā-bhū* actually occurs in the same sense in post-Vedic Sanskrit.

Vaśā is frequently qualified by *anūbandhyā*[1] ('to be bound for slaughtering'); the economy of killing a barren cow probably tended to produce the sense of 'barren' in the word.

[1] *E.g.*, Taittirīya Saṃhitā, ii. 2, 9, 7; Kāṭhaka Saṃhitā, x. 1.

Vāc.—Grierson, in his discussion[1] of the Paiśācī speech, holds that the passage cited as the speech of the Asuras in the Śatapatha Brāhmaṇa, *he 'lavo* (=*he 'rayaḥ*),[2] can be regarded as in Paiśācī just as much as in Māgadhī, since the change of *r* to *l*, and of *y* to *v*, is found in Paiśācī also. Sten Konow,[2] however, considers that Paiśācī was the speech used in the Vindhya region. It would be unwise, as a matter of fact, to lay stress on the phrase *he 'lavo*, because both the reading and the sense are by no means certain.[3] But it should be noted that the easterners and the Asuras are elsewhere in the Śatapatha Brāhmaṇa[4] connected: this tells against Dr. Grierson's view.

[1] *Zeitschrift der Deutschen Morgenländischen Gesellschaft*, 66, 66, n. 1.

[2] *Op. cit.*, 64, 104 *et seq.*

[3] It should be noted that the phrase cannot be genuine Prākrit as it stands, for that would not give us *he 'lavo he 'lavaḥ*.

[4] xiii. 8, 1, 5. Probably the view of the earlier part of the Śatapatha Brāhmaṇa (iii. 2, 1, 23) would be the same, since its reputed author, **Yājñavalkya**, is connected in tradition with the East. Dr. Grierson's argument would have been stronger had the reference occurred in one of the **Śāṇḍilya** books

Vātāvata and **Vātāvant**, 2, 284, should be read for **Vātavata** and **Vātavant**.

Vāsas.—In the Taittirīya Saṃhitā (ii. 2, 11, 4) *upādhāyyapūrvaya*, as an epithet of Vāsas, appears to denote 'fringed (*citrānta*) according to Āpastamba Śrauta Sūtra, xix. 20, 2.

Viṣāṇakā, 2, 313, headline, for '31,' read '313.'

Vehat occurs in conjunction with **Vaśā** in the Kāṭhaka Saṃhitā (xxxviii. 10), the Maitrāyaṇī Saṃhitā (iii. 11, 11), the Vājasaneyī Saṃhitā (xxi. 21), and the Taittirīya Brāhmaṇa (ii. 6, 18, 4).

Vairiṇa, 2, 318, should be **Vīraṇa**.

Vyat, 1, 523, should be Vyant.

Śamyā in the Brāhmaṇas[1] frequently denotes the wooden support on which the lower of the two millstones (**Dṛṣad**) is placed.

[1] Taittirīya Brāhmaṇa, i. 6, 1, 1; Satapatha Brāhmaṇa, i. 1, 1, 22; 2, 1, 16; v. 2, 3, 2; Baudhāyana Śrauta Sūtra, i. 7; Āpastamba Śrauta Sūtra, xviii. 8, 12, etc.

Śyāmaiajayanta, 1, 185, should be **Śyāmasujayanta**.

Śruṣṭi (more correctly **Śnuṣṭi**) **Āṅgirasa**, 2, 397, should come on p. 403, before **Śruṣṭigu ; and Sukurīra** before **Sukeśin**, 2, 453.

Saṃvatsara.—Tilak[1] argues that the Rigveda[2] and the Atharvaveda[3] contain signs of a dating by season and day, but neither of the passages adduced by him is at all probably so taken.

[1] *The Arctic Home in the Vedas*, 280-288.

[2] ii. 12, 11 (*catvāriṃśyāṃ śaradi*).

[3] xii. 3, 34 (*ṣaṣṭyāṃ śaratsu*; the plural, Tilak thinks, denotes 'every year').

Sāyakāyana, 1, 155, **Sobhari**, 1, 261, **Saukarāyaṇa**, 1, 155, should be read for Sāyakāyana, Sobhari, and Saukarāyaṇa respectively.

Several misprints are due to the loss of diacritical marks: thus for Ajya read Ājya, 2, 20; for Arcatka, Ārcatka, 2, 357; for Artava, Ārtava, 1, 63; for Apayā, Āpayā, 1, 218; for Amikṣā, Āmikṣā, 1, 250; for Aśuṃga, Āśuṃga, 2, 387; for Asandī, Āsandī, 2, 383; for Dirghatamas, Dīrghatamas, 1, 366; for Satapatha, Śatapatha, 1, 18, 34, 55, 67, 111, 119, 157, 242, 291, 371, 463, 516, 523; 2, 24, 80, 220, 221, 358, 362, 433; for Srauta, Śrauta, 1, 18, 55, 281, 282, 373; 2, 34, 71, 281, 301; for Sāṅkhāyana, Śāṅkhāyana, 1, 257, 281, 400, 469; 2, 34, 87, 281, 383; for Sāṭyāyanaka, Śāṭyāyanaka, i. 407; for Sāvasāyana, Śāvasāyana, 2, 376.

I. SANSKRIT INDEX

When a word is given without a meaning, it is either clearly a patronymic or of doubtful signification.

II. ENGLISH INDEX